PRIVACY, INFORMATION, AND TECHNOLOGY

ASPEN PUBLISHERS

PRIVACY, INFORMATION, AND TECHNOLOGY

Second Edition

Daniel J. Solove
Professor of Law
George Washington University Law School

Paul M. Schwartz
Professor of Law
U.C. Berkeley Law School

™ Wolters Kluwer
Law & Business

AUSTIN   BOSTON   CHICAGO   NEW YORK   THE NETHERLANDS

Aspen Publishers
Attn: Permissions Department
76 Ninth Avenue, 7th Floor
New York, NY   10011-5201

To contact Customer Care, e-mail customer.care@aspenpublishers.com,
call 1-800-234-1660, fax 1-800-901-9075, or mail correspondence to:

Aspen Publishers
Attn: Order Department
PO Box 990
Frederick, MD 21705

Printed in the United States of America.

1 2 3 4 5 6 7 8 9 0

ISBN 978-0-7355-7910-1

Library of Congress Cataloging-in-Publication Data

Solove, Daniel J., 1972-
  Privacy, information, and technology / Daniel J. Solove, Paul M. Schwartz. — 2nd ed.
    p. cm.
  ISBN 978-0-7355-7910-1
  1. Privacy, Right of — United States. 2. Data protection — Law and legislation —
United States. I. Schwartz, Paul M., 1959- II. Title.

  KF1262.S664 2008
  342.7308'58 — dc22

                    2008044313

About Wolters Kluwer Law & Business

Wolters Kluwer Law & Business is a leading provider of research information and workflow solutions in key specialty areas. The strengths of the individual brands of Aspen Publishers, CCH, Kluwer Law International and Loislaw are aligned within Wolters Kluwer Law & Business to provide comprehensive, in-depth solutions and expert-authored content for the legal, professional and education markets.

CCH was founded in 1913 and has served more than four generations of business professionals and their clients. The CCH products in the Wolters Kluwer Law & Business group are highly regarded electronic and print resources for legal, securities, antitrust and trade regulation, government contracting, banking, pension, payroll, employment and labor, and healthcare reimbursement and compliance professionals.

Aspen Publishers is a leading information provider for attorneys, business professionals and law students. Written by preeminent authorities, Aspen products offer analytical and practical information in a range of specialty practice areas from securities law and intellectual property to mergers and acquisitions and pension/benefits. Aspen's trusted legal education resources provide professors and students with high-quality, up-to-date and effective resources for successful instruction and study in all areas of the law.

Kluwer Law International supplies the global business community with comprehensive English-language international legal information. Legal practitioners, corporate counsel and business executives around the world rely on the Kluwer Law International journals, loose-leafs, books and electronic products for authoritative information in many areas of international legal practice.

Loislaw is a premier provider of digitized legal content to small law firm practitioners of various specializations. Loislaw provides attorneys with the ability to quickly and efficiently find the necessary legal information they need, when and where they need it, by facilitating access to primary law as well as state-specific law, records, forms and treatises.

Wolters Kluwer Law & Business, a unit of Wolters Kluwer, is headquartered in New York and Riverwoods, Illinois. Wolters Kluwer is a leading multinational publisher and information services company.

To my parents and grandparents—DJS

To Steffie, Clara, and Leo—PMS

SUMMARY OF CONTENTS

CONTENTS

2 PRIVACY AND LAW ENFORCEMENT

3 PRIVACY AND GOVERNMENT RECORDS AND DATABASES   243

PREFACE

The rapid growth of the Internet, coupled with new business practices and new efforts by government to deploy technology for law enforcement and the administration of programs, has raised far-reaching questions about the future of privacy.

Central to many of these debates is the role of law. To what extent can the law safeguard the right of privacy in an era of rapidly evolving technology? What competing interests must be considered? What is the appropriate role of the courts and the legislatures? These questions are not new, but they have acquired greater urgency as the law is asked to evaluate an increasingly complex array of privacy matters.

For lawyers, this rapid growth has raised both new challenges and new opportunities. In the private sector, attorneys now routinely advise business clients about the development of privacy policies, compliance with privacy statutes, and privacy regulations in new markets. Attorneys litigate on behalf of clients who believe that their privacy has been violated, while others defend against these allegations. State attorneys general have become leading champions of privacy rights. Policymakers in government evaluate new legislative proposals both to expand and to limit privacy claims. Legal advisors on trade policy, technology development, consumer protection, and national security all consider privacy issues in the course of their work. Clearly, information privacy has emerged as one of the critical legal subjects in the modern era.

This text aims to provide a comprehensive and accessible introduction to the legal, social, and political issues involving information privacy. The text begins with a broad introduction to the conceptual underpinnings of information privacy. It sets forth clearly and concisely the range of laws that address information privacy, and it discusses the basic policy issues that inhabit the field. The text then examines the legal and policy implications of the growing accumulation and use of personal information by the government and by businesses. We have included extensive notes and commentary, and have integrated cases and statutes with theoretical and policy perspectives. To facilitate discussion and debate, we have included excerpts from commentators with a wide range of viewpoints. Technical terms are clearly explained.

When selecting cases, we have included the leading cases as well as endeavoured to provide a solid historical background and a timely and fresh perspective on the major privacy issues facing lawyers in the twenty-first century. Important majority opinions are followed by equally important dissents. The text includes extensive notes and commentary, and it integrates cases and statutes with theoretical and policy perspectives. To facilitate discussion and debate, we have included excerpts from commentators with a wide range of viewpoints. Technical terms are clearly explained.

A Note on the Casebook Website. We strive to keep the book up to date between editions, and we maintain a web page for the book with downloadable updates and other useful information. We invite you to visit the website:

http://informationprivacylaw.com

A Note on New Changes to the Book. We made many changes and updates to the book but have retained its basic organizational structure and pedagogical style. Specific changes and additions to the book are documented in the Teacher's Manual.

A Note on the Editing. We have deleted many citations and footnotes from the cases to facilitate readability. The footnotes that have been retained in the cases have been renumbered. When discussing books, articles, and other materials in the notes and commentary, we have included full citations in footnotes in order to make the text easier to read. We have also included many citations to additional works in the footnotes that may be of interest to the reader.

Daniel J. Solove
Paul M. Schwartz

November 2008

ACKNOWLEDGMENTS

Daniel J. Solove: I would like to thank Carl Coleman, Scott Forbes, Susan Freiwald, Tomás Gómez-Arostegui, Stephen Gottlieb, Marcia Hofmann, Chris Hoofnagle, John Jacobi, Orin Kerr, Raymond Ku, Peter Raven-Hansen, Joel Reidenberg, Neil Richards, Michael Risinger, Lior Strahilevitz, Peter Swire, William Thompson, and Peter Winn for helpful comments and suggestions. Charlie Sullivan and Jake Barnes provided indispensable advice about how to bring this project to fruition. Special thanks to Richard Mixter at Aspen Publishers for his encouragement and faith in this project. Thanks as well to the other folks at Aspen who have contributed greatly to the editing and development of this book: John Devins, Christine Hannan, Carmen Reid, Jessica Barmack, John Burdeaux, and Sandra Doherty. I would like to thank my research assistants Peter Choy, Monica Contreras, Carly Grey, Maeve Miller, James Murphy, Poornima Ravishankar, Sheerin Shahinpoor, John Spaccarotella, Tiffany Stedman, Eli Weiss, and Kate Yannitte. I would also like to thank Dean Fred Lawrence for providing the resources I needed.

Paul M. Schwartz: For their suggestions, encouragement, and insights into information privacy law, I would like to thank Ken Bamberger, Fred Cate, Malcolm Crompton, Chris Gulotta, Andrew Guzman, Chris Hoofnagle, Ted Janger, Ronald D. Lee, Lance Liebman, Steven McDonald, Deirdre Mulligan, Joel Reidenberg, Ira Rubinstein, Pam Samuelson, Lior Strahilevitz, Viktor Mayer-Schönberger, Peter Swire, Peter Winn, and William M. Treanor. I benefited as well from the help of my talented research assistants: Cesar Alvarez, Kai-Dieter Classen, Alpa Patel, Karl Saddlemire, and Laura Sullivan. Many thanks to my co-author, Daniel Solove. Many thanks as well to my mother, Nancy Schwartz, and to Laura Schwartz and Ed Holden; David Schwartz and Kathy Smith; and Daniel Schwartz.

A profound debt is owed Spiros Simitis. My interest in the subject of information privacy began in 1985 with his suggestion that I visit his office of the Hessian Data Protection Commissioner in Wiesbaden and sit in on meetings there. Through his scholarship, example, and friendship, Professor Simitis has provided essential guidance during the decades since that initial trip to Wiesbaden. My portion of the book is dedicated to Steffie, Clara, and Leo, with my gratitude and love.

Finally, both of us would like to thank Marc Rotenberg, who helped us shape the book in its first two editions and provided invaluable input.

We are grateful to the following sources for their permission to reprint excerpts of their scholarship:

Anita L. Allen, *Coercing Privacy*, 40 William & Mary L. Rev. 723 (1999). Used by permission. © 1999 by William & Mary Law Review and Anita L. Allen.

William C. Banks & M.E. Bowman, *Executive Authority For National Security Surveillance,* 50 Am. U. L. Rev. 1 (2000). Reprinted with permission.

Fred H. Cate, *The Privacy Problem: A Broader View of Information Privacy and the Costs and Consequences of Protecting It*, 4 First Reports 1 (March 2003). Reprinted with permission.

Julie E. Cohen, *Examined Lives: Informational Privacy*, 52 Stan. L. Rev. 1371 (2000). © 2000. Reprinted by permission of the Stanford Law Review in the format textbook via Copyright Clearance Center and Julie Cohen.

Julie E. Cohen, *A Right to Read Anonymously: A Closer Look at "Copyright Management"* in *Cyberspace,* 28 Conn. L. Rev. 981 (1996). © 1996 by Connecticut Law Review and Julie E. Cohen. Reprinted with permission.

Mary DeRosa, *Data Mining and Data Analysis for Counterterrorism,* Center for Strategic and International Studies 6-8 (CSIS) (2004). Reprinted with permission.

Amitai Etzioni, The Limits of Privacy 2-3, 213-214 (1999). © 1999 by Amitai Etzioni. Reprinted by permission of Basic Books, a member of Perseus Books, LLC and Amitai Etzioni.

Eric Goldman, *The Privacy Hoax,* Forbes (Oct. 14, 2002) available at http://www.ericgoldman.org/Articles/privacyhoax.htm. Reprinted with permission. Lawrence O. Gostin, Health Information Privacy, 80 Cornell L. Rev. 451 (1995). Reprinted with permission.

Steven Hetcher, *The FTC as Internet Privacy Norm Entrepreneur*, 53 Vand. L. Rev. 2041 (2000). Reprinted with the permission of Steven Hetcher.

Edward Janger & Paul M. Schwartz, *The Gramm-Leach-Bliley Act, Information Privacy, and the Limits of Default Rules*, 86 Minn. L. Rev. 1219 (2002). Reprinted with permission.

Orin S. Kerr, *A User's Guide to the Stored Communications Act — and a Legislator's Guide to Amending It*, 72 Geo. Wash. L. Rev. 1208 (2004). Reprinted with permission.

Orin S. Kerr, *Internet Surveillance Law After the USA PATRIOT Act: The Big Brother That Isn't,* 97 Nw. U. L. Rev. 607 (2003). Reprinted with permission.

Catharine A. MacKinnon, Toward a Feminist Theory of the State 190-193 (1989). © 1989 by Harvard University Press. Reprinted with permission.

Richard A. Posner, *The Right of Privacy,* 12 Ga. L. Rev. 393 (1978). Reprinted with permission.

Marc Rotenberg, *Fair Information Practices and the Architecture of Privacy (What Larry Doesn't Get)*, 2001 Stan. Tech. L. Rev. 1, 43 (2001). Reprinted with permission.

Paul M. Schwartz, *Privacy and Democracy in Cyberspace*, 52 Vand. L. Rev. 1609 (1999). Reprinted with the permission of Paul Schwartz.

Reva B. Seigel, *The Rule of Love: Wife Beating as Prerogative of Privacy*, 105 Yale L.J. 2117 (1996). Reprinted by permission of the *Yale Law Journal* Company and the William S. Hein Company, from the *Yale Law Journal,* vol. 105, pages 2117-2207.

Spiros Simitis, *Reviewing Privacy in an Informational Society*, 135 U. Pa. L. Rev. 707, 709-710, 724-726, 732-738, 746 (1987). © 1987 by the University of Pennsylvania Law Review. Reprinted by permission of the University of Pennsylvania Law Review and Spiros Simitis.

Daniel J. Solove, *Conceptualizing Privacy,* 90 California Law Review 1087 (2002). © 2002 by the California Law Review.

Daniel J. Solove, *Reconstructing Electronic Surveillance Law*, 72 George Washington Law Review 1264 (2004). © 2004 by Daniel J. Solove.

Daniel J. Solove, *The Virtues of Knowing Less: Justifying Privacy Protections Against Disclosure*, 53 Duke Law Journal 967 (2003). © 2003 by Daniel J. Solove.

Jeff Sovern, *Opting In, Opting Out, or No Options at All: The Fight for Control of Personal Information*, 74 Wash. L. Rev. 1033 (1999). Reprinted with permission.

Michael E. Staten & Fred H. Cate, *The Impact of Opt-In Privacy Rules on Retail Markets: A Case Study of MBNA*, 52 Duke L.J. 745 (2003). Reprinted with permission.

Alan Westin, Privacy and Freedom 7, 31-38 (1967). A study sponsored by the Association of the Bar of the City of New York. Reprinted with permission.

Peter A. Winn, *Online Court Records: Balancing Judicial Accountability and Privacy in an Age of Electronic Information*, 79 Wash. L. Rev. 307 (2004). Reprinted with permission.

PRIVACY, INFORMATION, AND TECHNOLOGY

CHAPTER **1**

INTRODUCTION

A. INFORMATION PRIVACY, TECHNOLOGY, AND THE LAW

We live in a world shaped by technology and fueled by information. Technological devices — such as telephones, video and audio recording devices, computers, and the Internet — have revolutionized our ability to capture information about the world and to communicate with each other. Information is the lifeblood of today's society. Increasingly, our everyday activities involve the transfer and recording of information. The government collects vast quantities of personal information in records pertaining to an individual's birth, marriage, divorce, property, court proceedings, motor vehicles, voting activities, criminal transgressions, professional licensing, and other activities. Private sector entities also amass gigantic databases of personal information for marketing purposes or to prepare credit histories. Wherever we go, whatever we do, we could easily leave behind a trail of data that is recorded and gathered together.

These new technologies, coupled with the increasing use of personal information by business and government, pose new challenges for the protection of privacy. This book is about the law's response to new challenges to privacy. A significant amount of law regulates information privacy in the United States and around the world. Is this law responsive to the present and future dangers to privacy? Can information privacy itself endanger other important values? What duties and responsibilities must corporations, government agencies, and other private and public sector entities have with regard to personal data? What rights do individuals have to prevent and redress invasions to their privacy? When and how should privacy rights be limited? Does the war on terrorism require less privacy and more sharing of information? These are some of the questions that this text will address.

This book's topic is information privacy law. Information privacy concerns the collection, use, and disclosure of personal information. Information privacy is often contrasted with "decisional privacy," which concerns the freedom to make decisions about one's body and family. Decisional privacy involves matters such as contraception, procreation, abortion, and child rearing, and is at the center of a series of Supreme Court cases often referred to as "substantive due process" or "the constitutional right to privacy." But information privacy increasingly incorporates elements of decisional privacy as the use of data both expands and limits individual autonomy.

Information privacy law is an interrelated web of tort law, federal and state constitutional law, federal and state statutory law, evidentiary privileges, property law, contract law, and criminal law. Information privacy law is relatively new, although its roots reach far back. It is developing coherence as privacy doctrines in one area are being used to inform and structure legal responses in other areas. Information privacy law raises a related set of political, policy, and philosophical questions: What is privacy? Why is privacy important? What is the impact of technology on privacy? How does privacy affect the efforts of law enforcement and national security agencies to protect the public? What is the role of the courts, the legislatures, and the law in safeguarding, or in placing limits on, privacy?

Furthermore, one might wonder: Why study information privacy law? There are a number of answers to this question. First, in today's Information Age, privacy is an issue of paramount significance for freedom, democracy, and security. One of the central issues of information privacy concerns the power of commercial and government entities over individual autonomy and decision making. Privacy also concerns the drawing of rules that may limit this autonomy and decision making by necessarily permitting commercial and government entities access to personal information. Understood broadly, information privacy plays an important role in the society we are constructing in today's Information Age.

Second, information privacy is an issue of growing public concern. Information privacy has become a priority on the legislative agenda of Congress and many state legislatures. Information privacy problems are also timely, frequently in the news, and often the subject of litigation.

Third, there are many new laws and legal developments regarding information privacy. It is a growth area in the law. Increased litigation, legislation, regulation, as well as public concern over privacy are spurring corporations in a variety of businesses to address privacy. Lawyers are drafting privacy policies, litigating privacy issues, and developing ways for dot-com companies, corporations, hospitals, insurers, and banks to conform to privacy regulations. A new position, the Chief Privacy Officer, is a mainstay at most corporations. The leading organization of these officers, the International Association of Privacy Professionals (IAPP), boasts thousands of members. Attorneys increasingly are grappling with privacy issues — either through litigation of privacy violations or through measures to comply with privacy regulations and to prevent litigation. All of these developments demand lawyers who are well-versed in the grand scheme and subtle nuances of information privacy law.

Fourth, information privacy law is an engaging and fascinating topic. The issues are controversial, complex, relevant, and current. Few areas of law are more closely intertwined with our world of rapid technological innovation. Moreover, concerns regarding information privacy play an important role in debates regarding security in post 9-11 America. The study of privacy law also helps us understand how our legal institutions respond to change and may help prepare us for other challenges ahead.

SIDIS V. F-R PUBLISHING CORP.

113 F.2d 806 (2d Cir. 1940)

[William James Sidis (1898–1944) was perhaps the most famous child prodigy of his day. According to Amy Wallace's biography of Sidis, *The Prodigy*, he was able to read the *New York Times* at the age of 18 months.[1] By the time he was three, William had learned to operate a typewriter and used it to compose a letter to Macy's to order toys. At that age, he also learned Latin "as a birthday present for his father." That year, after his father taught him the Greek alphabet, he taught himself to read Homer with the aid of a Greek primer. By the time he started elementary school, at the age of six, he could speak and read at least eight languages. At the age of five, he had already devised a method for calculating the day of the week on which any given date occurred, and when he was seven years old, he wrote a book about calendars. At that time, he had already prepared manuscripts about anatomy, astronomy, grammar, linguistics, and mathematics. At the age of eight, he created a new table of logarithms, which used a base of twelve instead of the conventional ten. From early childhood on, Sidis was also passionately interested in politics and world events. According to Wallace, Sidis was one of the few child prodigies in world history whose talents were not limited to a single field.

In 1909, Harvard University permitted Sidis to enroll in it; he was 11 years old and the youngest student in the history of Harvard. Sidis also made the front pages of newspapers around the nation when on January 5, 1910, he delivered a two-hour lecture to the Harvard Mathematics Club. The *New York Times* featured Sidis on its front page of October 11, 1909, as "Harvard's Child Prodigy."[2]

Boris Sidis, William's father, was a distinguished physician, early pioneer of American psychology (and opponent of Sigmund Freud), and prolific author. In 1911, Boris published a book about his educational theories and his virulent opposition to the educational institutions of the day. At the time of the publication of this book, *Philistine and Genius*, William was 13, and in Wallace's description, "teetering on the edge of his endurance to public exposure." Although the book did not mention his son by name, it did discuss him and his accomplishments, which brought William additional publicity. Sarah Sidis, William's mother and herself a physician, had a domineering and deeply troubled relationship with her son. Neither she nor Boris did anything to shelter William from the great publicity that followed him from an early age and the tremendous stress that it created in his life.

When he graduated from Harvard at age 16, William told reporters: "I want to live the perfect life. The only way to live the perfect life is to live it in seclusion. I have always hated crowds." After graduating from college, Sidis accepted a teaching position at the Rice University in Houston. After a difficult eight months as a professor of mathematics there, William returned to Boston

---

[1] Amy Wallace, *The Prodigy* (1986).

[2] *Harvard's Child Prodigy: All Amazed at Mathematical Grasp of Youngest Matriculate, Aged 13 Years*, N.Y. Times (Oct. 10, 1909), at A1.

and enrolled in Harvard Law School in 1916. He left the law school in his last semester there without taking a degree.

From 1918 until a *New Yorker* article about him in 1937, Sidis engaged in socialist and other radical politics, published numerous newsletters, lived an active social life, addressed a monthly study group, wrote a treatise about the classification of streetcar transfers, and financed his life through a series of modest clerical jobs and sales of his patented "perpetual calendar." During this period, in 1925, Sidis also published *The Animate and the Inanimate*. In Wallace's view, this book is the first work on the subject of "black holes" in space as well as an extraordinary work in the field of cosmogony, or the study of the origins of the universe. The book did not receive a single review at the time and was ignored by academia.

Before 1937, Sidis had done an excellent job of avoiding publicity for a decade. In that year, however, a local paper, the *Boston Sunday Advertiser*, published an article about him. This was followed by the August 14, 1937, issue of the *New Yorker*, which contained a brief biographical sketch about Sidis, his life following his graduation from Harvard, and the subsequent decades during which he lived in obscurity.[3] The article was part of a regular feature of the magazine called "Where Are They Now?," which provided brief updates on the lives of famous figures of the past. The article was printed under the subtitle *April Fool*, a reference to the fact that Sidis was born on April Fool's Day. The article recounted the history of Sidis's life and his current whereabouts: "William James Sidis lives today, at the age of thirty-nine, in a hall bedroom of Boston's shabby south end." The article also contained numerous errors about Sidis's life.

A mystery still exists regarding the interview at the basis of this article. According to Wallace, Sidis's contemporary biographer, a member of the monthly study group, whom she refers to only as "John," had brought along a friend to one meeting. Several members of this group suspected that this woman, who was the daughter of a publisher at a large company, served as the basis for the *New Yorker*'s report. Yet, the mystery remains as this individual did not interview Sidis at the time of the monthly meeting. Wallace writes: "William always maintained that the entire article was a combination of imagination and old stories about him, and no strangers had gained access to his room." Another possibility is that Sidis spoke to someone without knowing that she was a reporter, which seems unlikely due to his aversion to publicity.

The *New Yorker* article described Sidis's famous childhood and then recounted his subsequent career as an insignificant clerk: "He seems to get a great and ironic enjoyment out of leading a life of wandering irresponsibility after a childhood of scrupulous regimentation." Sidis never remained at one job for too long because "his employers or fellow-workers [would] soon find out that he is the famous boy wonder, and he can't tolerate a position after that." According to Sidis: "The every sight of a mathematical formula makes me physically ill. . . . All I want to do is run an adding machine, but they won't let me alone." The article also described Sidis's dwelling, a small bedroom in a poor part of Boston and his personal activities, interests, and habits.

---

[3] J.L. Manley, *Where Are They Now?: April Fool!*, New Yorker 22 (Aug. 14, 1937).

In his legal action against the *Boston Sunday Advertiser*, Sidis won a settlement of $375. Sidis also sued F-R Publishing Corporation, the publisher of the *New Yorker*. Among his claims were a violation of his privacy rights under §§ 50-51 of the N.Y. Civil Rights Law.]

CLARK, C. J. . . . It is not contended that any of the matter printed is untrue. Nor is the manner of the author unfriendly; Sidis today is described as having "a certain childlike charm." But the article is merciless in its dissection of intimate details of its subject's personal life, and this in company with elaborate accounts of Sidis' passion for privacy and the pitiable lengths to which he has gone in order to avoid public scrutiny. The work possesses great reader interest, for it is both amusing and instructive; but it may be fairly described as a ruthless exposure of a once public character, who has since sought and has now been deprived of the seclusion of private life.

The article of December 25, 1937, was a biographical sketch of another former child prodigy, in the course of which William James Sidis and the recent account of him were mentioned. The advertisement published in the New York World-Telegram of August 13, 1937, read: "Out Today. Harvard Prodigy. Biography of the man who astonished Harvard at age 11. Where are they now? by J.L. Manley. Page 22. The New Yorker."

The complaint contains a general allegation, repeated for all the claims, of publication by the defendant of *The New Yorker*, "a weekly magazine of wide circulation throughout the United States." Then each separate "cause" contains an allegation that the defendant publicly circulated the articles or caused them to be circulated in the particular states upon whose law that cause is assumed to be founded. Circulation of the New York World-Telegram advertisement is, however, alleged only with respect to the second "cause," for asserted violation of New York law.

Under the first "cause of action" we are asked to declare that this exposure transgresses upon plaintiff's right of privacy, as recognized in California, Georgia, Kansas, Kentucky, and Missouri. Each of these states except California grants to the individual a common law right, and California a constitutional right, to be let alone to a certain extent. The decisions have been carefully analyzed by the court below, and we need not examine them further. None of the cited rulings goes so far as to prevent a newspaper or magazine from publishing the truth about a person, however intimate, revealing, or harmful the truth may be. Nor are there any decided cases that confer such a privilege upon the press. . . .

It must be conceded that under the strict standards suggested by [Warren and Brandeis in their article, *The Right to Privacy*] plaintiff's right of privacy has been invaded. Sidis today is neither politician, public administrator, nor statesman. Even if he were, some of the personal details revealed were of the sort that Warren and Brandeis believed "all men alike are entitled to keep from popular curiosity."

But despite eminent opinion to the contrary, we are not yet disposed to afford to all of the intimate details of private life an absolute immunity from the prying of the press. Everyone will agree that at some point the public interest in obtaining information becomes dominant over the individual's desire for privacy. Warren and Brandeis were willing to lift the veil somewhat in the case of public officers. We would go further, though we are not yet prepared to say how far. At least we would permit limited scrutiny of the "private" life of any person who has achieved, or has had thrust upon him, the questionable and indefinable status of a "public figure."

William James Sidis was once a public figure. As a child prodigy, he excited both admiration and curiosity. Of him great deeds were expected. In 1910, he was a person about whom the newspapers might display a legitimate intellectual interest, in the sense meant by Warren and Brandeis, as distinguished from a trivial and unseemly curiosity. But the precise motives of the press we regard as unimportant. And even if Sidis had loathed public attention at that time, we think his uncommon achievements and personality would have made the attention permissible. Since then Sidis has cloaked himself in obscurity, but his subsequent history, containing as it did the answer to the question of whether or not he had fulfilled his early promise, was still a matter of public concern. The article in *The New Yorker* sketched the life of an unusual personality, and it possessed considerable popular news interest.

We express no comment on whether or not the newsworthiness of the matter printed will always constitute a complete defense. Revelations may be so intimate and so unwarranted in view of the victim's position as to outrage the community's notions of decency. But when focused upon public characters, truthful comments upon dress, speech, habits, and the ordinary aspects of personality will usually not transgress this line. Regrettably or not, the misfortunes and frailties of neighbors and "public figures" are subjects of considerable interest and discussion to the rest of the population. And when such are the mores of the community, it would be unwise for a court to bar their expression in the newspapers, books, and magazines of the day.

Plaintiff in his first "cause of action" charged actual malice in the publication, and now claims that an order of dismissal was improper in the face of such an allegation. We cannot agree. If plaintiff's right of privacy was not invaded by the article, the existence of actual malice in its publication would not change that result. Unless made so by statute, a truthful and therefore non-libelous statement will not become libelous when uttered maliciously. A similar rule should prevail on invasions of the right of privacy. "Personal ill-will is not an ingredient of the offence, any more than in an ordinary case of trespass to person or to property." Warren and Brandeis, supra at page 218. Nor does the malice give rise to an independent wrong based on an intentional invasion of the plaintiff's interest in mental and emotional tranquility.

If the article appearing in the issue of August 14, 1937, does not furnish grounds for action, then it is clear that the brief and incidental reference to it contained in the article of December 25, 1937, is not actionable. . . .

[The court concluded that the second cause of action under N.Y. Civil Rights Law was properly dismissed as well. The second cause of action charged invasion of the rights conferred on plaintiff by §§ 50 and 51 of the N.Y. Civil Rights Law. Section 50 states: "A person, firm or corporation that uses for advertising purposes, or for the purposes of trade, the name, portrait or picture of any living person without having first obtained the written consent of such person, or if a minor of his or her parent or guardian, is guilty of a misdemeanor." Section 51 gives the injured person an injunction remedy and damages. The court found: "Though a publisher sells a commodity, and expects to profit from the sale of his product, he is immune from the interdict of Secs. 50 and 51 so long as he confines himself to the unembroidered dissemination of facts. . . . *The New Yorker* articles limit themselves to the unvarnished, unfictionalized truth."]

NOTES & QUESTIONS

1. ***Involuntary Public Figures.*** After losing his privacy suit against the *New Yorker,* Sidis sued it for libel for the false information in the story. Among his charges, he claimed that a reader of the article would think that he was a reprehensible character, disloyal to his country, a loathsome and filthy person in personal habits, suffered a mental breakdown, and was a fool, who lived in misery and poverty. The *New Yorker* settled this case out of court for a small amount of money, which Wallace estimates in her biography of Sidis at between $500 and $600.

   Sidis suffered from high blood pressure, and, approximately three months after receiving the settlement from the *New Yorker*, on July 17, 1944, he died from a cerebral hemorrhage and pneumonia. He was 46 years old and had $652.81 in his bank account.

   The life of William Sidis illustrates a man profoundly disturbed by being thrust by his parents into the limelight as a child and by the media hounding him. He tried to spend his adult life fleeing from being the focus of any public attention. If he had been an involuntary public figure in the past, should this affect whether he should be able to retreat from the public eye in the future? Does it matter that he became a public figure as a child, that is, that he did not voluntarily choose this status as an adult?

   The *Sidis* case suggests the principle that once one is a public figure, one is always a public figure. Can people who were once famous ever retreat into obscurity?

2. ***Who Was J.L. Manley? What Did He Try to Convey in His Article?*** The Sidis article was written by a "J.L. Manley." In a biography of James Thurber, the famous American humorist, Burton Bernstein reveals that Thurber used Jared L. Manley as a pseudonym.[4] Under this signature, Thurber wrote 24 profiles of onetime celebrities, including the Sidis piece. All pieces were based on the research of other reporters at the *New Yorker*, including the unnamed reporter who actually interviewed Sidis.

---

[4] *See* Burton Bernstein, *Thurber* 261 (1975). Bernstein writes:

> For all the distractions of city life and his sleepless schedule, Thurber was getting a lot of good work done. In early 1936, he began to write (really rewrite, since some of the New Yorker's best reporters, like Eugene Kinkead, were doing the research) a number of short, retrospective Profiles. His nonfiction craft rose to a new high in these excellent pieces, which lent themselves to his human approach.

> *Id.* Bernstein also reveals that Jared L. Manley was a name that Thurber cobbled together when writing his first piece about an old boxer based on the initials of the boxer John L. Sullivan and "Manley" based on "the manly art of self-defense."

In Thurber's own account of his time at the *New Yorker*, he faulted the *Sidis* court on one matter: "[N]owhere was there any indication of what I thought had stood out all through my story, implicit though it was — my feeling that the piece would help to curb the great American thrusting of talented children into the glare of fame or notoriety, a procedure in so many cases disastrous to the later career and happiness of the exploited youngsters."[5]

3. ***J.D. Salinger's Letters.*** In 1998, Joyce Maynard wrote an autobiography, *At Home in the World*, that describes her romance with J.D. Salinger in the 1970s. J.D. Salinger, an acclaimed author who wrote *The Catcher in the Rye*, had long ago completely retreated from public life and adopted a highly secluded existence in New Hampshire. In 1999, Maynard auctioned the letters J.D. Salinger wrote to her. She received $156,500 for the letters from the auction at Sotheby's. CNN reported at that time, "California philanthropist Peter Norton, who bought the letters, said he plans to return them to Salinger." Should Salinger have a right to privacy in the disclosure of the letters? Copyright law does create a copyright interest in unpublished letters — which prevents not only the publication of the entire contents of the letters, but a paraphrase of the letters that is too close to the actual text of the letters. *See Salinger v. Random House, Inc.*, 811 F.2d 90 (2d Cir. 1987). Should privacy law provide Salinger with the right to sue over the writing of Maynard's book?

4. ***Girls Gone Wild.*** A company markets videotapes of young college women at spring break or Mardi Gras flashing and undressing. The women, often intoxicated, reveal their nudity in public and give their permission to use the video footage on the company's videotapes, which are called "Girls Gone Wild." Later on, when sober, some of the women regret their decision to be in the video. Have they waived all privacy rights to their nude images on the video if they sign a consent form? Or should they be entitled to have some time to reconsider? Should they not be able to sign away these rights even when sober? Others have sued claiming that they were just filmed in public without signing a consent form. Do they have a valid privacy claim even when they exposed themselves in public?

5. ***Privacy Inalienability.*** Do we care whether or not Sidis knew he was talking to a reporter as opposed to a new neighbor? Can we assume that anyone who talks to a reporter has abandoned a privacy interest in the information that she shares with the journalist? More broadly, to what extent should privacy interests be tradable, waiveable, or otherwise alienable?[6]

6. ***Googleization.*** The Internet makes the preservation and dissemination of information much easier. Information about a person can be easily discovered by "Googling" them — running a search on their name with the Internet search engine Google. Google will pull up dozens, sometimes hundreds of

---

[5] James Thurber, *My Years with Ross* (1959).
[6] Paul M. Schwartz, *Property, Privacy, and Personal Data*, 117 Harv. L. Rev. 2055, 2074 (2004).

thousands, of information fragments about a person. It is becoming increasingly difficult for people to hide their personal information, which used to fade into obscurity but is now preserved forever on the Internet. Youthful indiscretions become permanent baggage. Consider the plight of one Michael, who was briefly imprisoned as a minor. The information comes up on a Google search, and Michael finds that it is inhibiting his ability to date, since many of the women he dates inquire about his time in prison. They have obviously Googled him:

> "When you meet someone," Michael says, "you don't say, 'I had an affair one time,' or 'I was arrested for DUI once,' or 'I cheated on my taxes in 1984.'"... [W]hat Michael finds most disturbing are the sudden silences. "Instead of thinking, 'Was I curt last week?' or 'Did I insult this political party or that belief?' I have to think about what happened when I was 17."[7]

Is Sidis's claim to privacy quaint by today's standards? How do we protect privacy in a post-Google world?

7. ***The* Star Wars *Kid and the Numa Numa Dance.*** An overweight, awkward 15-year-old kid videotaped himself pretending to be a character from a *Star Wars* movie.[8] He swung around a golf ball retriever pretending that it was a light saber and made his own sound effects. Somebody found the video, digitized it, and posted it on the Internet. The video created a buzz on the Internet, and it was downloaded millions of times around the world. Versions of the video with music and special effects were soon posted. People made fun of the kid in various discussions throughout the Internet.

In December 2005, Gary Brolsma placed on the Internet a clip of himself lip-synching and dancing in a chair to a Romanian pop song.[9] He called his performance the "Numa Numa Dance." The video was featured on newsgrounds.com, a web site devoted to animation and videos, as well as elsewhere on the Internet. Newsgrounds.com alone soon received almost two million hits for the "Numa Numa Dance." Brolsma appeared on Good Morning America, and CNN and VH1 showed his clip.

Suddenly, however, he decided that he disliked the attention. The *New York Times* reported that Brolsma "has now sought refuge from his fame in his family's small house on a gritty street in Saddle Brook." The article added: "According to his relatives, he mopes around the house. . . . He is distraught, embarrassed." His grandmother quoted him as saying: "I just want this to end."

Is this simply life in the Internet Age? Does it matter that the parents of the "*Star Wars* kid" alleged that the clip of their son was placed online without his permission? In contrast, Brolsma posted the video of his dance himself. Is

---

[7] Neil Swidey, *A Nation of Voyeurs: How the Internet Search Engine Google Is Changing What We Can Find Out About Each Other and Raising Questions About Whether We Should,* Boston Globe Mag., Feb. 2, 2003, at 10.

[8] Amy Harmon, *Fame Is No Laughing Matter for the "Star Wars" Kid,* N.Y. Times, May 19, 2003, at C3.

[9] Alan Feuer & Jason George, *Internet Fame Is Cruel Mistress for Dancer of the Numa Numa,* N.Y. Times, Feb. 26, 2005, at A1.

there something that the law can do to protect people like the *Star Wars* kid or Numa Numa dancer? If so, what?

As an update to the story of the Numa Numa Dance, Brolsma had gotten over his anguish at his fame. In September 2006, he released a second video, "New Numa" with corporate sponsorship at newnuma.com. The new video features Brolsma and members of a rock band, the Nowadays, and a new song. The video was released along a promotion that allowed the public to submit their own videos and win a share of $45,000 in prizes. Brolsma also offered a selection of t-shirts and a coffee mug for sale to the public.

B. INFORMATION PRIVACY LAW: ORIGINS AND TYPES

Information privacy law is a wide-ranging body of law, encompassing common law, constitutional law, statutory law, and international law. This section will provide a brief introduction to the various strands of information privacy law that will be covered throughout this book. It begins by looking in detail at the most important article ever written about privacy.

1. COMMON LAW

(a) The Warren and Brandeis Article

The common law's development of tort remedies to protect privacy is one of the most significant chapters in the history of privacy law. In the late nineteenth century, considerable concerns about privacy captured the public's attention, ultimately resulting in the 1890 publication of Samuel Warren and Louis Brandeis's pathbreaking article, *The Right to Privacy*.[10] According to Roscoe Pound, the article did "nothing less than add a chapter to our law."[11] Harry Kalven even hailed it as the "most influential law review article of all."[12] The clearest indication of the article's ongoing vitality can be found in the Supreme Court's decision *Kyllo v. United States*, 533 U.S. 27 (2001). The Brandeis and Warren article is cited by the majority, those in concurrence, and even those in dissent.

Several developments in the late nineteenth century created a growing interest in privacy. First, the press became increasingly sensationalistic. Prior to the Civil War, wide-circulation newspapers were rare. However, the development of a new form of sensationalistic journalism, known as "yellow journalism," made newspapers wildly successful. In 1833, Benjamin Day began publishing a newspaper called the *Sun* patterned after the "penny presses" in London (so named because they sold for a penny). The *Sun* contained news of scandals, such as family squabbles, public drunkenness, and petty crimes. In about four months,

---

[10] Samuel Warren & Louis Brandeis, *The Right to Privacy*, 4 Harv. L. Rev. 193 (1890).

[11] Quoted in Alpheus Mason, *Brandeis: A Free Man's Life* 70 (1946).

[12] Harry Kalven, Jr., *Privacy in Tort Law — Were Warren and Brandeis Wrong?*, 31 L. & Contemp. Probs. 326, 327 (1966).

the *Sun* had a circulation of 4,000, almost the same as the existing New York daily papers. Just two months later, the *Sun* was reaching 8,000 in circulation. Other penny press papers soon followed. In reporting on his travels in America, Charles Dickens observed that New York newspapers were "pulling off the roofs of private houses."[13] In his great novel of 1844, *The Life and Adventures of Martin Chuzzlewit*, he listed (imaginary) New York newspapers called *The Sewer, The Stabber, The Family Spy, The Private Listener, The Peeper, The Plunderer,* and *The Keyhole Reporter*.[14]

Between 1850 and 1890, newspaper circulation increased about 1,000 percent — from 100 papers with 800,000 readers to 900 papers with more than 8 million readers. Joseph Pulitzer and William Randolph Hearst became the leading rivals in the newspaper business, each amassing newspaper empires. Their highly sensationalistic journalism became the paradigm for yellow journalism.[15]

Second, technological developments caused great alarm for privacy. In their article, Warren and Brandeis pointed to the invention of "instantaneous photography" as a new challenge to privacy. Photography had been around for many years before Warren and Brandeis penned their article. However, the equipment was expensive, cumbersome, and complicated to use. In 1884, the Eastman Kodak Company introduced the "snap camera," a handheld camera that was small and cheap enough for use by the general public. The snap camera allowed people to take candid photographs in public places for the first time. In the late nineteenth century, few daily newspapers even printed drawings, let alone photographs. Warren and Brandeis, however, astutely recognized the potential for the new technology of cameras to be used by the sensationalistic press.

The question of the origin of Warren and Brandeis's article has led to considerable debate. Some scholars suggest that Warren and Brandeis were strongly influenced by an article written in 1890 by E.L. Godkin, a famous social commentator in his day.[16] In the article, Godkin observed:

> . . . Privacy is a distinctly modern product, one of the luxuries of civilization, which is not only unsought for but unknown in primitive or barbarous societies. . . .
>
> The chief enemy of privacy in modern life is that interest in other people and their affairs known as curiosity, which in the days before newspapers created personal gossip. . . . [A]s long as gossip was oral, it spread, as regarded any one individual, over a very small area, and was confined to the immediate circle of his acquaintances. It did not reach, or but rarely reached, those who knew nothing of him. It did not make his name, or his walk, or his

---

[13] Charles Dickens, *American Notes* (1842).

[14] Charles Dickens, *The Life and Adventures of Martin Chuzzlewit* (1844).

[15] For more information about yellow journalism, *see generally* Gini Graham Scott, *Mind Your Own Business: The Battle for Personal Privacy* 37-38 (1995); Robert Ellis Smith, *Ben Franklin's Web Site: Privacy and Curiosity from Plymouth Rock to the Internet* 102-20 (2000).

[16] *See* Elbridge L. Adams, *The Right to Privacy and Its Relation to the Law of Libel*, 39 Am. L. Rev. 37 (1905); Dorothy J. Glancy, *The Invention of the Right to Privacy*, 21 Ariz. L. Rev. 1 (1979).

conversation familiar to strangers. . . . [G]ossip about private individuals is now printed, and makes its victim, with all his imperfections on his head, known to hundreds or thousands miles away from his place of abode; and, what is worst of all, brings to his knowledge exactly what is said about him, with all its details. It thus inflicts what is, to many men, the great pain of believing that everybody he meets in the street is perfectly familiar with some folly, or misfortune, or indiscretion, or weakness, which he had previously supposed had never got beyond his domestic circle. . . .

In truth, there is only one remedy for the violations of the right to privacy within the reach of the American public, and that is but an imperfect one. It is to be found in attaching social discredit to invasions of it on the part of conductors of the press. At present this check can hardly be said to exist. It is to a large extent nullified by the fact that the offence is often pecuniarily profitable.[17]

Warren and Brandeis referred to Godkin's essay, and their article does bear some similarities to his work. One difference is that Godkin, although recognizing the growing threats to privacy, remained cynical about the possibility of a solution, expressing only the hope that attitudes would change to be more respectful of privacy. Warren and Brandeis had a different view. In their judgment, the law could and should provide protection for privacy.

Another theory suggests that incursions by journalists into the privacy of Samuel Warren inspired the article. Warren, a wealthy and powerful attorney in Boston, practiced law with Louis Brandeis, who later went on to become a U.S. Supreme Court Justice. In 1883, Samuel Warren married Mabel Bayard, the daughter of a prominent senator from Delaware, and set up house in Boston's Back Bay. The Warrens were among the Boston elite and were frequently reported on in the *Saturday Evening Gazette*, "which specialized in 'blue blood items,'" and "reported their activities in lurid detail."[18]

According to William Prosser, Warren was motivated to write the article because reporters intruded upon his daughter's wedding. However, this certainly could not have been the reason because in 1890, Warren's oldest daughter was not even ten years old![19] Most likely, the impetus for writing the article was Warren's displeasure about a number of stories in the *Gazette* about his dinner parties.[20]

Whatever inspired them to write, Warren and Brandeis published an article that profoundly shaped the development of the law of privacy.

---

[17] E.L. Godkin, *The Rights of the Citizen: To His Own Reputation*, Scribner's Mag. (1890); *see also* E.L. Godkin, *The Right to Privacy*, The Nation (Dec. 25, 1890).

[18] Mason, *Brandeis, supra*, at 46.

[19] *See* James H. Barron, *Warren and Brandeis*, The Right to Privacy, 4 Harv. L. Rev. 193 (1890): *Demystifying a Landmark Citation*, 13 Suffolk L. Rev. 875 (1979).

[20] *See* Smith, *Ben Franklin's Web Site, supra*, at 118-19. For further discussion of the circumstances surrounding the publication of the article, see Martin Burgess Green, *The Mount Vernon Street Warrens: A Boston Story, 1860–1910* (1989); Morris L. Ernst & Alan U. Schwartz, *Privacy: The Right to Be Let Alone* 45-46 (1962); Philippa Strum, *Brandeis: Beyond Progressivism* (1993); Lewis J. Paper, *Brandeis* (1983); Irwin R. Kramer, *The Birth of Privacy Law: A Century Since Warren and Brandeis*, 39 Cath. U. L. Rev. 703 (1990); Dorothy Glancy, *The Invention of the Right to Privacy*, 21 Ariz. L. Rev. 1, 25-27 (1979); Symposium, *The Right to Privacy One Hundred Years Later*, 41 Case W. Res. L. Rev. 643-928 (1991).

SAMUEL D. WARREN AND LOUIS D. BRANDEIS, *THE RIGHT TO PRIVACY*
4 Harv. L. Rev. 193 (1890)

It could be done only on principles of private justice, moral fitness, and public convenience, which, when applied to a new subject, make common law without a precedent; much more when received and approved by usage.

— Willes, J., in *Millar v. Taylor,* 4 Burr. 2303, 2312

That the individual shall have full protection in person and in property is a principle as old as the common law; but it has been found necessary from time to time to define anew the exact nature and extent of such protection. Political, social, and economic changes entail the recognition of new rights, and the common law, in its eternal youth, grows to meet the demands of society. Thus, in very early times, the law gave a remedy only for physical interference with life and property, for trespasses *vi et armis.*[21] Then the "right to life" served only to protect the subject from battery in its various forms; liberty meant freedom from actual restraint; and the right to property secured to the individual his lands and his cattle. Later, there came a recognition of man's spiritual nature, of his feelings and his intellect. Gradually the scope of these legal rights broadened; and now the right to life has come to mean the right to enjoy life, — the right to be let alone; the right to liberty secures the exercise of extensive civil privileges; and the term "property" has grown to comprise every form of possession — intangible, as well as tangible.

Thus, with the recognition of the legal value of sensations, the protection against actual bodily injury was extended to prohibit mere attempts to do such injury; that is, the putting another in fear of such injury. From the action of battery grew that of assault. Much later there came a qualified protection of the individual against offensive noises and odors, against dust and smoke, and excessive vibration. The law of nuisance was developed. So regard for human emotions soon extended the scope of personal immunity beyond the body of the individual. His reputation, the standing among his fellow-men, was considered, and the law of slander and libel arose. Man's family relations became a part of the legal conception of his life, and the alienation of a wife's affections was held remediable. Occasionally the law halted, — as in its refusal to recognize the intrusion by seduction upon the honor of the family. But even here the demands of society were met. A mean fiction, the action *per quod servitium amisit,*[22] was resorted to, and by allowing damages for injury to the parents' feelings, an adequate remedy was ordinarily afforded. Similar to the expansion of the right to life was the growth of the legal conception of property. From corporeal property arose the incorporeal rights issuing out of it; and then there opened the wide realm of intangible property, in the products and processes of the mind, as works of literature and art, goodwill, trade secrets, and trademarks.

This development of the law was inevitable. The intense intellectual and emotional life, and the heightening of sensations which came with the advance of

---

[21] Editors' Note: Latin — By or with force and arms.

[22] Editors' Note: Latin — Whereby he lost the services (of his servant).

civilization, made it clear to men that only a part of the pain, pleasure, and profit of life lay in physical things. Thoughts, emotions, and sensations demanded legal recognition, and the beautiful capacity for growth which characterizes the common law enabled the judges to afford the requisite protection, without the interposition of the legislature.

Recent inventions and business methods call attention to the next step which must be taken for the protection of the person, and for securing to the individual what Judge Cooley calls the right "to be let alone."[23] Instantaneous photographs and newspaper enterprise have invaded the sacred precincts of private and domestic life; and numerous mechanical devices threaten to make good the prediction that "what is whispered in the closet shall be proclaimed from the house-tops." For years there has been a feeling that the law must afford some remedy for the unauthorized circulation of portraits of private persons; and the evil of invasion of privacy by the newspapers, long keenly felt, has been but recently discussed by an able writer. The alleged facts of a somewhat notorious case brought before an inferior tribunal in New York a few months ago, directly involved the consideration of the right of circulating portraits; and the question whether our law will recognize and protect the right to privacy in this and in other respects must soon come before our courts for consideration.

Of the desirability — indeed of the necessity — of some such protection, there can, it is believed, be no doubt. The press is overstepping in every direction the obvious bounds of propriety and of decency. Gossip is no longer the resource of the idle and of the vicious, but has become a trade, which is pursued with industry as well as effrontery. To satisfy a prurient taste the details of sexual relations are spread broadcast in the columns of the daily papers. To occupy the indolent, column upon column is filled with idle gossip, which can only be procured by intrusion upon the domestic circle. The intensity and complexity of life, attendant upon advancing civilization, have rendered necessary some retreat from the world, and man, under the refining influence of culture, has become more sensitive to publicity, so that solitude and privacy have become more essential to the individual; but modern enterprise and invention have, through invasions upon his privacy, subjected him to mental pain and distress, far greater than could be inflicted by mere bodily injury. Nor is the harm wrought by such invasions confined to the suffering of those who may be made the subjects of journalistic or other enterprise. In this, as in other branches of commerce, the supply creates the demand. Each crop of unseemly gossip, thus harvested, becomes the seed of more, and, in direct proportion to its circulation, results in a lowering of social standards and of morality. Even gossip apparently harmless, when widely and persistently circulated, is potent for evil. It both belittles and perverts. It belittles by inverting the relative importance of things, thus dwarfing the thoughts and aspirations of a people. When personal gossip attains the dignity of print, and crowds the space available for matters of real interest to the community, what wonder that the ignorant and thoughtless mistake its relative importance. Easy of comprehension, appealing to that weak side of human nature which is never wholly cast down by the misfortunes and frailties of our neighbors, no one can be surprised that it usurps the place of interest in brains

---

[23] Cooley on Torts, 2d ed., p. 29.

capable of other things. Triviality destroys at once robustness of thought and delicacy of feeling. No enthusiasm can flourish, no generous impulse can survive under its blighting influence.

It is our purpose to consider whether the existing law affords a principle which can properly be invoked to protect the privacy of the individual; and, if it does, what the nature and extent of such protection is.

Owing to the nature of the instruments by which privacy is invaded, the injury inflicted bears a superficial resemblance to the wrongs dealt with by the law of slander and of libel, while a legal remedy for such injury seems to involve the treatment of mere wounded feelings, as a substantive cause of action. The principle on which the law of defamation rests, covers, however, a radically different class of effects from those for which attention is now asked. It deals only with damage to reputation, with the injury done to the individual in his external relations to the community, by lowering him in the estimation of his fellows. The matter published of him, however widely circulated, and however unsuited to publicity, must, in order to be actionable, have a direct tendency to injure him in his intercourse with others, and even if in writing or in print, must subject him to the hatred, ridicule, or contempt of his fellow-men, — the effect of the publication upon his estimate of himself and upon his own feelings not forming an essential element in the cause of action. In short, the wrongs and correlative rights recognized by the law of slander and libel are in their nature material rather than spiritual. That branch of the law simply extends the protection surrounding physical property to certain of the conditions necessary or helpful to worldly prosperity. On the other hand, our law recognizes no principle upon which compensation can be granted for mere injury to the feelings. However painful the mental effects upon another of an act, though purely wanton or even malicious, yet if the act itself is otherwise lawful, the suffering inflicted is *damnum absque injuria*.[24] Injury of feelings may indeed be taken account of in ascertaining the amount of damages when attending what is recognized as a legal injury; but our system, unlike the Roman law, does not afford a remedy even for mental suffering which results from mere contumely and insult, from an intentional and unwarranted violation of the "honor" of another.

It is not however necessary, in order to sustain the view that the common law recognizes and upholds a principle applicable to cases of invasion of privacy, to invoke the analogy, which is but superficial, to injuries sustained, either by an attack upon reputation or by what the civilians called a violation of honor; for the legal doctrines relating to infractions of what is ordinarily termed the common-law right to intellectual and artistic property are, it is believed, but instances and applications of a general right to privacy, which properly understood afford a remedy for the evils under consideration.

The common law secures to each individual the right of determining, ordinarily, to what extent his thoughts, sentiments, and emotions shall be communicated to others. Under our system of government, he can never be compelled to express them (except when upon the witness-stand); and even if he has chosen to give them expression, he generally retains the power to fix the

---

[24] Editors' Note: Latin — Loss or harm from something other than a wrongful act and which occasions no legal remedy.

limits of the publicity which shall be given them. The existence of this right does not depend upon the particular method of expression adopted. It is immaterial whether it be by word or by signs, in painting, by sculpture, or in music. Neither does the existence of the right depend upon the nature or value of the thought or emotion, nor upon the excellence of the means of expression. The same protection is accorded to a casual letter or an entry in a diary and to the most valuable poem or essay, to a botch or daub and to a masterpiece. In every such case the individual is entitled to decide whether that which is his shall be given to the public. No other has the right to publish his productions in any form, without his consent. This right is wholly independent of the material on which, or the means by which, the thought, sentiment, or emotion is expressed. It may exist independently of any corporeal being, as in words spoken, a song sung, a drama acted. Or if expressed on any material, as in a poem in writing, the author may have parted with the paper, without forfeiting any proprietary right in the composition itself. The right is lost only when the author himself communicates his production to the public, — in other words, publishes it. It is entirely independent of the copyright laws, and their extension into the domain of art. The aim of those statutes is to secure to the author, composer, or artist the entire profits arising from publication; but the common-law protection enables him to control absolutely the act of publication, and in the exercise of his own discretion, to decide whether there shall be any publication at all. The statutory right is of no value, *unless* there is a publication; the common-law right is lost *as soon as* there is a publication.

What is the nature, the basis, of this right to prevent the publication of manuscripts or works of art? It is stated to be the enforcement of a right of property; and no difficulty arises in accepting this view, so long as we have only to deal with the reproduction of literary and artistic compositions. They certainly possess many of the attributes of ordinary property: they are transferable; they have a value; and publication or reproduction is a use by which that value is realized. But where the value of the production is found not in the right to take the profits arising from publication, but in the peace of mind or the relief afforded by the ability to prevent any publication at all, it is difficult to regard the right as one of property, in the common acceptation of that term. A man records in a letter to his son, or in his diary, that he did not dine with his wife on a certain day. No one into whose hands those papers fall could publish them to the world, even if possession of the documents had been obtained rightfully; and the prohibition would not be confined to the publication of a copy of the letter itself, or of the diary entry; the restraint extends also to a publication of the contents. What is the thing which is protected? Surely, not the intellectual act of recording the fact that the husband did not dine with his wife, but that fact itself. It is not the intellectual product, but the domestic occurrence. A man writes a dozen letters to different people. No person would be permitted to publish a list of the letters written. If the letters or the contents of the diary were protected as literary compositions, the scope of the protection afforded should be the same secured to a published writing under the copyright law. But the copyright law would not prevent an enumeration of the letters, or the publication of some of the facts contained therein. The copyright of a series of paintings or etchings would prevent a reproduction of the paintings as pictures; but it would not prevent a publication of list or even a description of them. Yet in the famous case of *Prince Albert v. Strange*, the court held that the common-law rule prohibited not merely the reproduction of the etchings which the plaintiff and Queen Victoria had made for their own pleasure, but also "the publishing (at least by printing or writing), though not by copy or resemblance, a description of them, whether more or less limited or summary, whether in the form of a catalogue or otherwise." Likewise, an unpublished collection of news possessing no element of a literary nature is protected from piracy.

That this protection cannot rest upon the right to literary or artistic property in any exact sense, appears the more clearly when the subject-matter for which protection is invoked is not even in the form of intellectual property, but has the attributes of ordinary tangible property. Suppose a man has a collection of gems or curiosities which he keeps private: it would hardly be contended that any person could publish a catalogue of them, and yet the articles enumerated are certainly not intellectual property in the legal sense, any more than a collection of stoves or of chairs.

The belief that the idea of property in its narrow sense was the basis of the protection of unpublished manuscripts led an able court to refuse, in several cases, injunctions against the publication of private letters, on the ground that "letters not possessing the attributes of literary compositions are not property entitled to protection;" and that it was "evident the plaintiff could not have considered the letters as of any value whatever as literary productions, for a letter cannot be considered of value to the author which he never would consent to have published." But those decisions have not been followed, and it may now be considered settled that the protection afforded by the common law to the author of any writing is entirely independent of its pecuniary value, its intrinsic merits, or of any intention to publish the same and, of course, also, wholly independent of the material, if any, upon which, or the mode in which, the thought or sentiment was expressed.

Although the courts have asserted that they rested their decisions on the narrow grounds of protection to property, yet there are recognitions of a more liberal doctrine. Thus in the case of *Prince Albert v. Strange*, already referred to, the opinions both of the Vice-Chancellor and of the Lord Chancellor, on appeal, show a more or less clearly defined perception of a principle broader than those which were mainly discussed, and on which they both placed their chief reliance. Vice-Chancellor Knight Bruce referred to publishing of a man that he had "written to particular persons or on particular subjects" as an instance of possibly injurious disclosures as to private matters, that the courts would in a proper case prevent; yet it is difficult to perceive how, in such a case, any right of privacy, in the narrow sense, would be drawn in question, or why, if such a publication would be restrained when it threatened to expose the victim not merely to sarcasm, but to ruin, it should not equally be enjoined, if it threatened to embitter his life. To deprive a man of the potential profits to be realized by publishing a catalogue of his gems cannot *per se* be a wrong to him. The possibility of future profits is not a right of property which the law ordinarily recognizes; it must, therefore, be an infraction of other rights which constitutes the wrongful act, and that infraction is equally wrongful, whether its results are to forestall the profits that the individual himself might secure by giving the matter a publicity obnoxious to him, or to gain an advantage at the expense of his mental pain and suffering. . . .

These considerations lead to the conclusion that the protection afforded to thoughts, sentiments, and emotions, expressed through the medium of writing or of the arts, so far as it consists in preventing publication, is merely an instance of the enforcement of the more general right of the individual to be let alone. It is like the right not be assaulted or beaten, the right not be imprisoned, the right not to be maliciously prosecuted, the right not to be defamed. In each of these rights, as indeed in all other rights recognized by the law, there inheres the quality of being owned or possessed — and (as that is the distinguishing attribute of property) there may be some propriety in speaking of those rights as property. But, obviously, they bear little resemblance to what is ordinarily comprehended under that term. The principle which protects personal writings and all other personal productions, not against theft and physical appropriation, but against publication in any form, is in reality not the principle of private property, but that of an inviolate personality.

If we are correct in this conclusion, the existing law affords a principle which may be invoked to protect the privacy of the individual from invasion either by the too enterprising press, the photographer, or the possessor of any other modern device for recording or reproducing scenes or sounds. For the protection afforded is not confined by the authorities to those cases where any particular medium or form of expression has been adopted, not to products of the intellect. The same protection is afforded to emotions and sensations expressed in a musical composition or other work of art as to a literary composition; and words spoken, a pantomime acted, a sonata performed, is no less entitled to protection than if each had been reduced to writing. The circumstance that a thought or emotion has been recorded in a permanent form renders its identification easier, and hence may be important from the point of view of evidence, but it has no significance as a matter of substantive right. If, then, the decisions indicate a general right to privacy for thoughts, emotions, and sensations, these should receive the same protection, whether expressed in writing, or in conduct, in conversation, in attitudes, or in facial expression.

It may be urged that a distinction should be taken between the deliberate expression of thoughts and emotions in literary or artistic compositions and the casual and often involuntary expression given to them in the ordinary conduct of life. In other words, it may be contended that the protection afforded is granted to the conscious products of labor, perhaps as an encouragement to effort. This contention, however plausible, has, in fact, little to recommend it. If the amount of labor involved be adopted as the test, we might well find that the effort to conduct one's self properly in business and in domestic relations had been far greater than that involved in painting a picture or writing a book; one would find that it was far easier to express lofty sentiments in a diary than in the conduct of a noble life. If the test of deliberateness of the act be adopted, much casual correspondence which is now accorded full protection would be excluded from the beneficent operation of existing rules. After the decisions denying the distinction attempted to be made between those literary productions which it was intended to publish and those which it was not, all considerations of the amount of labor involved, the degree of deliberation, the value of the product, and the intention of publishing must be abandoned, and no basis is discerned upon which the right to restrain publication and reproduction of such so-called literary and artistic works can be rested, except the right to privacy, as a part of the more general right to the immunity of the person, — the right to one's personality.

It should be stated that, in some instances where protection has been afforded against wrongful publication, the jurisdiction has been asserted, not on the ground of property, or at least not wholly on that ground, but upon the ground of an alleged breach of an implied contract or of a trust or confidence. . . .

This process of implying a term in a contract, or of implying a trust (particularly where the contract is written, and where there is no established usage or custom), is nothing more nor less than a judicial declaration that public morality, private justice, and general convenience demand the recognition of such a rule, and that the publication under similar circumstances would be considered an intolerable abuse. So long as these circumstances happen to present a contract upon which such a term can be engrafted by the judicial mind, or to supply relations upon which a trust or confidence can be erected, there may be no objection to working out the desired protection through the doctrines of contract or of trust. But the court can hardly stop there. The narrower doctrine may have satisfied the demands of society at a time when the abuse to be guarded against could rarely have arisen without violating a contract or a special confidence; but now that modern devices afford abundant opportunities for the perpetration of such wrongs without any participation by the injured party, the protection granted by the law must be placed upon a broader foundation. While, for instance, the state of the photographic art was such that one's picture could seldom be taken without his consciously "sitting" for the purpose, the law of contract or of trust might afford the prudent man sufficient safeguards against the improper circulation of his portrait; but since the latest advances in photographic art have rendered it possible to take pictures surreptitiously, the doctrines of contract and of trust are inadequate to support the required protection, and the law of tort must be resorted to. The right of property in its widest sense, including all possession, including all rights and privileges, and hence embracing the right to an inviolate personality, affords alone that broad basis upon which the protection which the individual demands can be rested.

Thus, the courts, in searching for some principle upon which the publication of private letters could be enjoined, naturally came upon the ideas of a breach of confidence, and of an implied contract; but it required little consideration to discern that this doctrine could not afford all the protection required, since it would not support the court in granting a remedy against a stranger; and so the theory of property in the contents of letters was adopted. Indeed, it is difficult to conceive on what theory of the law the casual recipient of a letter, who proceeds to publish it, is guilty of a breach of contract, express or implied, or of any breach of trust, in the ordinary acceptation of that term. Suppose a letter has been addressed to him without his solicitation. He opens it, and reads. Surely, he has not made any contract; he has not accepted any trust. He cannot, by opening and reading the letter, have come under any obligation save what the law declares; and, however expressed, that obligation is simply to observe the legal right of the sender, whatever it may be, and whether it be called his right or property in the contents of the letter, or his right to privacy. . . .

We must therefore conclude that the rights, so protected, whatever their exact nature, are not rights arising from contract or from special trust, but are rights as against the world; and, as above stated, the principle which has been applied to protect these rights is in reality not the principle of private property, unless that word be used in an extended and unusual sense. The principle which protects personal writings and any other productions of the intellect of or the emotions, is the right to privacy, and the law has no new principle to formulate when it extends this protection to the personal appearance, sayings, acts, and to personal relation, domestic or otherwise.

If the invasion of privacy constitutes a legal *injuria*, the elements for demanding redress exist, since already the value of mental suffering, caused by an act wrongful in itself, is recognized as a basis for compensation.

The right of one who has remained a private individual, to prevent his public portraiture, presents the simplest case for such extension; the right to protect one's self from pen portraiture, from a discussion by the press of one's private affairs, would be a more important and far-reaching one. If casual and unimportant statements in a letter, if handiwork, however inartistic and valueless, if possessions of all sorts are protected not only against reproduction, but against description and enumeration, how much more should the acts and sayings of a man in his social and domestic relations be guarded from ruthless publicity. If you may not reproduce a woman's face photographically without her consent, how much less should be tolerated the reproduction of her face, her form, and her actions, by graphic descriptions colored to suit a gross and depraved imagination.

The right to privacy, limited as such right must necessarily be, has already found expression in the law of France.

It remains to consider what are the limitations of this right to privacy, and what remedies may be granted for the enforcement of the right. To determine in advance of experience the exact line at which the dignity and convenience of the individual must yield to the demands of the public welfare or of private justice would be a difficult task; but the more general rules are furnished by the legal analogies already developed in the law of slander and libel, and in the law of literary and artistic property.

1. The right to privacy does not prohibit any publication of matter which is of public or general interest.

In determining the scope of this rule, aid would be afforded by the analogy, in the law of libel and slander, of cases which deal with the qualified privilege of comment and criticism on matters of public and general interest. There are of course difficulties in applying such a rule; but they are inherent in the subject-matter, and are certainly no greater than those which exist in many other branches of the law, — for instance, in that large class of cases in which the reasonableness or unreasonableness of an act is made the test of liability. The design of the law must be to protect those persons with whose affairs the community has no legitimate concern, from being dragged into an undesirable and undesired publicity and to protect all persons, whatsoever; their position or station, from having matters which they may properly prefer to keep private, made public against their will. It is the unwarranted invasion of individual privacy which is reprehended, and to be, so far as possible, prevented. The distinction, however, noted in the above statement is obvious and fundamental.

There are persons who may reasonably claim as a right, protection from the notoriety entailed by being made the victims of journalistic enterprise. There are others who, in varying degrees, have renounced the right to live their lives screened from public observation. Matters which men of the first class may justly contend, concern themselves alone, may in those of the second be the subject of legitimate interest to their fellow-citizens. Peculiarities of manner and person, which in the ordinary individual should be free from comment, may acquire a public importance, if found in a candidate for public office. Some further discrimination is necessary, therefore, than to class facts or deeds as public or private according to a standard to be applied to the fact or deed *per se*. To publish of a modest and retiring individual that he suffers from an impediment in his speech or that he cannot spell correctly, is an unwarranted, if not an unexampled, infringement of his rights, while to state and comment on the same characteristics found in a would-be congressman could not be regarded as beyond the pale of propriety.

The general object in view is to protect the privacy of private life, and to whatever degree and in whatever connection a man's life has ceased to be private, before the publication under consideration has been made, to that extent the protection is to be withdrawn. Since, then, the propriety of publishing the very same facts may depend wholly upon the person concerning whom they are published, no fixed formula can be used to prohibit obnoxious publications. Any rule of liability adopted must have in it an elasticity which shall take account of the varying circumstances of each case, — a necessity which unfortunately renders such a doctrine not only more difficult of application, but also to a certain extent uncertain in its operation and easily rendered abortive. Besides, it is only the more flagrant breaches of decency and propriety that could in practice be reached, and it is not perhaps desirable even to attempt to repress everything which the nicest taste and keenest sense of the respect due to private life would condemn.

In general, then, the matters of which the publication should be repressed may be described as those which concern the private life, habits, acts, and relations of an individual, and have no legitimate connection with his fitness for a public office which he seeks or for which he is suggested, or for any public or quasi public position which he seeks or for which he is suggested, and have no legitimate relation to or bearing upon any act done by him in a public or quasi public capacity. The foregoing is not designed as a wholly accurate or exhaustive definition, since that which must ultimately in a vast number of cases become a question of individual judgment and opinion is incapable of such definition; but it is an attempt to indicate broadly the class of matters referred to. Some things all men alike are entitled to keep from popular curiosity, whether in public life or not, while others are only private because the persons concerned have not assumed a position which makes their doings legitimate matters of public investigation.

2. The right to privacy does not prohibit the communication of any matter, though in its nature private, when the publication is made under circumstances which would render it a privileged communication according to the law of slander and libel.

Under this rule, the right to privacy is not invaded by any publication made in a court of justice, in legislative bodies, or the committees of those bodies; in municipal assemblies, or the committees of such assemblies, or practically by any communication made in any other public body, municipal or parochial, or in any body quasi public, like the large voluntary associations formed for almost every purpose of benevolence, business, or other general interest; and (at least in many jurisdictions) reports of any such proceedings would in some measure be accorded a like privilege. Nor would the rule prohibit any publication made by one in the discharge of some public or private duty, whether legal or moral, or in conduct of one's own affairs, in matters where his own interest is concerned.

3. The law would probably not grant any redress for the invasion of privacy by oral publication in the absence of special damage.

The same reasons exist for distinguishing between oral and written publications of private matters, as is afforded in the law of defamation by the restricted liability for slander as compared with the liability for libel. The injury resulting from such oral communications would ordinarily be so trifling that the law might well, in the interest of free speech, disregard it altogether.

4. The right to privacy ceases upon the publication of the facts by the individual, or with his consent.

This is but another application of the rule which has become familiar in the law of literary and artistic property. The cases there decided establish also what should be deemed a publication, — the important principle in this connection being that a private communication of circulation for a restricted purpose is not a publication within the meaning of the law.

5. The truth of the matter published does not afford a defence. Obviously this branch of the law should have no concern with the truth or falsehood of the matters published. It is not for injury to the individual's character that redress or prevention is sought, but for injury to the right of privacy. For the former, the law of slander and libel provides perhaps a sufficient safeguard. The latter implies the right not merely to prevent inaccurate portrayal of private life, but to prevent its being depicted at all.

6. The absence of "malice" in the publisher does not afford a defence.

Personal ill-will is not an ingredient of the offence, any more than in an ordinary case of trespass to person or to property. Such malice is never necessary to be shown in an action for libel or slander at common law, except in rebuttal of some defence, *e.g.*, that the occasion rendered the communication privileged, or, under the statutes in this State and elsewhere, that the statement complained of was true. The invasion of the privacy that is to be protected is equally complete and equally injurious, whether the motives by which the speaker or writer was actuated are, taken by themselves, culpable or not; just as the damage to character, and to some extent the tendency to provoke a breach of the peace, is equally the result of defamation without regard to the motives leading to its publication. Viewed as a wrong to the individual, this rule is the same pervading the whole law of torts, by which one is held responsible for his intentional acts, even though they are committed with no sinister intent; and viewed as a wrong to society, it is the same principle adopted in a large category of statutory offences.

The remedies for an invasion of the right of privacy are also suggested by those administered in the law of defamation, and in the law of literary and artistic property, namely: —

1. An action of tort for damages in all cases. Even in the absence of special damages, substantial compensation could be allowed for injury to feelings as in the action of slander and libel.

2. An injunction, in perhaps a very limited class of cases.

It would doubtless be desirable that the privacy of the individual should receive the added protection of the criminal law, but for this, legislation would be required. Perhaps it would be deemed proper to bring the criminal liability for such publication within narrower limits; but that the community has an interest in preventing such invasions of privacy, sufficiently strong to justify the introduction of such a remedy, cannot be doubted. Still, the protection of society must come mainly through a recognition of the rights of the individual. Each man is responsible for his own acts and omissions only. If he condones what he reprobates, with a weapon at hand equal to his defence, he is responsible for the results. If he resists, public opinion will rally to his support. Has he then such a weapon? It is believed that the common law provides him with one, forged in the slow fire of the centuries, and to-day fitly tempered to his hand. The common law has always recognized a man's house as his castle, impregnable, often, even to its own officers engaged in the execution of its command. Shall the courts thus close the front entrance to constituted authority, and open wide the back door to idle or prurient curiosity?

NOTES & QUESTIONS

1. *The Need for a New Right.* The article argued for the creation of a new right — the right to privacy. Why did the authors believe that other legal claims were inadequate? For example, why does the law of defamation or the law of contracts not provide a sufficient remedy for the harm described by the authors? Why do Warren and Brandeis reject property rights and copyright as tools to protect privacy?

2. *Deriving a Right to Privacy in the Common Law.* How do Warren and Brandeis derive a right to privacy from the common law? Under what principle do they locate this right? In a footnote in the article, Warren and Brandeis observe:

> The application of an existing principle to a new state of facts is not judicial legislation. To call it such is to assert that the existing body of law consists practically of the statutes and decided cases, and to deny that the principles (of which these cases are ordinarily said to be evidence) exist at all. It is not the application of an existing principle to new cases, but the introduction of a new principle, which is properly termed judicial legislation.
>
> But even the fact that a certain decision would involve judicial legislation should not be taken against the property of making it. This power has been commonly exercised by our judges, when applying to a new subject principles of private justice, moral fitness, and public convenience. Indeed, the elasticity of our law, its adaptability to new conditions, the capacity for

growth, which has enabled it to meet the wants of an ever changing society and to apply immediate relief for every recognized wrong, have been its greatest boast. . . .

Why do they include this footnote? Do you agree with their argument?

3. *Inviolate Personality.* The authors describe privacy as not "the principle of private property but that of inviolate personality." What does that mean? James Whitman traces the idea of the personality right from Warren and Brandeis back to nineteenth-century German legal philosophy:

> . . . [N]ineteenth-century Germans often thought of "freedom" as opposed primarily to determinism. To be free was, in the first instance, not to be free from government control, nor to be free to engage in market transactions. Instead, to be free was to exercise free will, and the defining characteristic of creatures with free will was that they were unpredictably individual, creatures whom no science of mechanics or biology could ever capture in their full richness. For Germans who thought of things in this way, the purpose of "freedom" was to allow each individual fully to realize his potential as an individual: to give full expression to his peculiar capacities and powers.[25]

What interests are protected by this right? Is this a unified view of privacy, or are there differing interests?

4. *"The Right to Be Let Alone."* Warren and Brandeis refer to privacy as "the right to be let alone." This phrase was coined by Judge Thomas Cooley earlier in his famous treatise on torts.[26] Do Warren and Brandeis define what privacy is or elaborate upon what being "let alone" consists of? If so, what do they say privacy is? Is this a good account of what constitutes privacy?

5. *The Scope of the Right to Privacy.* Brandeis and Warren were careful not to describe privacy as an absolute right. They set out six limitations on the right to privacy. Consider the first limitation and the relationship between the right to privacy and the need for publication on matters of public concern. What conclusions do the authors reach about these competing claims? According to Warren and Brandeis, would the reporting that a public official engaged in illegal business practices be protected by a right to privacy? What about illicit sexual activity? Consider the holding of the *Sidis* court regarding a person who was once of public interest due to his great achievements. Do you think that Warren and Brandeis would agree with the conclusion of *Sidis*?

6. *The Nature of the Injury Caused by Privacy Invasions.* Warren and Brandeis argue that privacy invasions are more harmful than bodily injuries. Do you agree? Warren and Brandeis characterize the injury caused by the violation of privacy as an injury to the feelings. Do you agree? Or do you think that the injury extends beyond an injury to the feelings?

7. *Remedies.* Brandeis and Warren suggest two remedies for an invasion of privacy — an action in tort and injunction. These remedies are similar to

---

[25] James Q. Whitman, *The Two Western Cultures of Privacy: Dignity Versus Liberty*, 113 Yale L.J. 1151, 1181 (2004).

[26] Thomas C. Cooley, *Law of Torts* 29 (2d ed. 1888).

those in defamation and copyright. What do the authors say about a criminal remedy?

8. *Criticisms.* Some have argued that the article is a defense of bourgeois values, i.e., the freedom of an elite group to avoid public scrutiny.[27] Which aspects of the article support this view? Do parts of the article suggest otherwise? Is privacy, as described in the Warren and Brandeis article, a class-based right?

(b) The Recognition of Warren and Brandeis's Privacy Torts

Warren and Brandeis's 1890 article suggested that the existing causes of action under the common law did not adequately protect privacy but that the legal concepts in the common law could be modified to achieve the task. As early as 1903, courts and legislatures responded to the Warren and Brandeis article by creating a number of privacy torts to redress the harms that Warren and Brandeis had noted. In *Roberson v. Rochester Folding Box Co.*, 64 N.E. 442 (N.Y. 1902), the New York Court of Appeals refused to recognize a common law tort action for privacy invasions. Franklin Mills Flour displayed a lithograph of Abigail Roberson (a teenager) on 25,000 advertisement flyers without her consent. The lithograph printed her photograph with the advertising pun: "Flour of the Family." Roberson claimed that the use of her image on the flyer caused her great humiliation and resulted in illness requiring medical help. The court, however, concluded:

> . . . There is no precedent for such an action to be found in the decisions of this court. . . . Mention of such a right is not to be found in Blackstone, Kent, or any other of the great commentators upon the law; nor, so far as the learning of counsel or the courts in this case have been able to discover, does its existence seem to have been asserted prior to about the year 1890. . . .
>
> The legislative body could very well interfere and arbitrarily provide that no one should be permitted for his own selfish purpose to use the picture or the name of another for advertising purposes without his general consent. In such event no embarrassment would result to the general body of law, for the law would be applicable only to cases provided for by statute. The courts, however, being without authority to legislate, are required to decide cases upon principle, and so are necessarily embarrassed by precedents created by an extreme, and therefore unjustifiable, application of an old principle. . . . [W]hile justice in a given case may be worked out by a decision of the court according to the notions of right which govern the individual judge or body of judges comprising the court, the mischief which will finally result may be almost incalculable under our system, which makes a decision in one case a precedent for decisions in all future cases which are akin to it in the essential facts. . . .

Shortly after the decision, a note in the *Yale Law Journal* criticized the *Roberson* decision because it enabled the press "to pry into and grossly display

---

[27] *See* Donald R. Pember, *Privacy and the Press* (1972).

before the public matters of the most private and personal concern."[28] One of the judges in the majority defended the opinion in the *Columbia Law Review.*[29]

In 1903, the New York legislature responded to the explicit invitation in *Roberson* to legislate by creating a privacy tort action by statute. *See* N.Y. Civ. Rights Act § 51. This statute is still in use today. As you will see again later on in this text, courts are frequently engaged in a dialogue with legislatures about the scope of privacy rights.

In the 1905 case *Pavesich v. New England Life Insurance Co.*, 50 S.E. 68 (Ga. 1905), Georgia became the first state to recognize a common law tort action for privacy invasions. There, a newspaper published a life insurance advertisement with a photograph of the plaintiff without the plaintiff's consent. The court held:

> . . . The right of privacy has its foundation in the instincts of nature. It is recognized intuitively, consciousness being the witness that can be called to establish its existence. Any person whose intellect is in a normal condition recognizes at once that as to each individual member of society there are matters private, and there are matters public so far as the individual is concerned. Each individual as instinctively resents any encroachment by the public upon his rights which are of a private nature as he does the withdrawal of those of his rights which are of a public nature. A right of privacy in matters purely private is therefore derived from natural law. . . .
>
> One who desires to live a life of partial seclusion has a right to choose the times, places, and manner in which and at which he will submit himself to the public gaze. Subject to the limitation above referred to, the body of a person cannot be put on exhibition at any time or at any place without his consent. . . .
>
> It therefore follows from what has been said that a violation of the right of privacy is a direct invasion of a legal right of the individual. . . .

In 1960, Dean William Prosser wrote his famous article, *Privacy*, examining the over 300 privacy tort cases decided in the 70 years since the Warren and Brandeis article.

WILLIAM PROSSER, *PRIVACY*
48 Cal. L. Rev. 383 (1960)

. . . The law of privacy comprises four distinct kinds of invasion of four different interests of the plaintiff, which are tied together by the common name, but otherwise have almost nothing in common except that each represents an interference with the right of the plaintiff, in the phrase coined by Judge Cooley, "to be let alone." Without any attempt at exact definition, these four torts may be described as follows:

1. Intrusion upon the plaintiff's seclusion or solitude, or into his private affairs.
2. Public disclosure of embarrassing private facts about the plaintiff.

---

[28] *An Actionable Right to Privacy?*, 12 Yale L.J. 34 (1902).
[29] Denis O'Brien, *The Right to Privacy*, 2 Colum. L. Rev. 486 (1902).

3. Publicity which places the plaintiff in a false light in the public eye.
4. Appropriation, for the defendant's advantage, of the plaintiff's name or likeness. . . .

Judge Briggs has described the present state of the law of privacy as "still that of a haystack in a hurricane." Disarray there certainly is; but almost all of the confusion is due to a failure to separate and distinguish these four forms of invasion and to realize that they call for different things. . . .

Taking them in order — intrusion, disclosure, false light, and appropriation — the first and second require the invasion of something secret, secluded or private pertaining to the plaintiff; the third and fourth do not. The second and third depend upon publicity, while the first does not, nor does the fourth, although it usually involves it. The third requires falsity or fiction; the other three do not. The fourth involves a use for the defendant's advantage, which is not true of the rest. Obviously this is an area in which one must tread warily and be on the lookout for bogs. Nor is the difficulty decreased by the fact that quite often two or more of these forms of invasion may be found in the same case, and quite conceivably in all four.

NOTES & QUESTIONS

1. *The Restatement of Torts.* Prosser's analytical framework imposed order and clarity on the jumbled line of cases that followed the Warren and Brandeis article. The Restatement of Torts recognizes the four torts Prosser described in his article. These torts are known collectively as "invasion of privacy." The torts include (1) intrusion upon seclusion, (2) public disclosure of private facts, (3) false light, and (4) appropriation.

2. *The Interests Protected by the Privacy Torts.* In response to Prosser's assertion that the privacy torts have almost "nothing in common," Edward Bloustein replied that "what provoked Warren and Brandeis to write their article was a fear that a rampant press feeding on the stuff of private life would destroy individual dignity and integrity and emasculate individual freedom and independence." This underlying principle is a protection of "human dignity" and "personality."[30]

   In contrast to Bloustein, Robert Post contends that the privacy torts do "not simply uphold the interests of individuals against the demands of the community, but instead safeguard[ ] rules of civility that in some significant measure constitute both individuals and community." Post argues that the torts establish boundaries between people, which when violated create strife. The privacy torts promote "forms of respect [for other people] by which we maintain a community."[31]

---

[30] Edward J. Bloustein, *Privacy as an Aspect of Human Dignity: An Answer to Dean Prosser*, 39 N.Y.U. L. Rev. 962, 974, 1000-01 (1964).

[31] Robert C. Post, *The Social Foundations of Privacy: Community and Self in the Common Law Tort*, 77 Cal. L. Rev. 957 (1989).

LAKE V. WAL-MART STORES, INC.

582 N.W.2d 231 (Minn. 1998)

BLATZ, C. J. . . . Elli Lake and Melissa Weber appeal from a dismissal of their complaint for failure to state a claim upon which relief may be granted. The district court and court of appeals held that Lake and Weber's complaint alleging intrusion upon seclusion, appropriation, publication of private facts, and false light publicity could not proceed because Minnesota does not recognize a common law tort action for invasion of privacy. We reverse as to the claims of intrusion upon seclusion, appropriation, and publication of private facts, but affirm as to false light publicity.

Nineteen-year-old Elli Lake and 20-year-old Melissa Weber vacationed in Mexico in March 1995 with Weber's sister. During the vacation, Weber's sister took a photograph of Lake and Weber naked in the shower together. After their vacation, Lake and Weber brought five rolls of film to the Dilworth, Minnesota Wal-Mart store and photo lab. When they received their developed photographs along with the negatives, an enclosed written notice stated that one or more of the photographs had not been printed because of their "nature."

In July 1995, an acquaintance of Lake and Weber alluded to the photograph and questioned their sexual orientation. Again, in December 1995, another friend told Lake and Weber that a Wal-Mart employee had shown her a copy of the photograph. By February 1996, Lake was informed that one or more copies of the photograph were circulating in the community.

Lake and Weber filed a complaint against Wal-Mart Stores, Inc. and one or more as-yet unidentified Wal-Mart employees on February 23, 1996, alleging the four traditional invasion of privacy torts — intrusion upon seclusion, appropriation, publication of private facts, and false light publicity. . . . The district court granted Wal-Mart's motion to dismiss, explaining that Minnesota has not recognized any of the four invasion of privacy torts. The court of appeals affirmed.

Whether Minnesota should recognize any or all of the invasion of privacy causes of action is a question of first impression in Minnesota. . . .

This court has the power to recognize and abolish common law doctrines. The common law is not composed of firmly fixed rules. Rather, as we have long recognized, the common law:

> is the embodiment of broad and comprehensive unwritten principles, inspired by natural reason, an innate sense of justice, adopted by common consent for the regulation and government of the affairs of men. It is the growth of ages, and an examination of many of its principles, as enunciated and discussed in the books, discloses a constant improvement and development in keeping with advancing civilization and new conditions of society. Its guiding star has always been the rule of right and wrong, and in this country its principles demonstrate that there is in fact, as well as in theory, a remedy for all wrongs.

As society changes over time, the common law must also evolve:

> It must be remembered that the common law is the result of growth, and that its development has been determined by the social needs of the community which it governs. It is the resultant of conflicting social forces, and those forces which

are for the time dominant leave their impress upon the law. It is of judicial origin, and seeks to establish doctrines and rules for the determination, protection, and enforcement of legal rights. Manifestly it must change as society changes and new rights are recognized. To be an efficient instrument, and not a mere abstraction, it must gradually adapt itself to changed conditions.

To determine the common law, we look to other states as well as to England.

The tort of invasion of privacy is rooted in a common law right to privacy first described in an 1890 law review article by Samuel Warren and Louis Brandeis. The article posited that the common law has always protected an individual's person and property, with the extent and nature of that protection changing over time. The fundamental right to privacy is both reflected in those protections and grows out of them:

> Thus, in the very early times, the law gave a remedy only for physical interference with life and property, for trespass vi et armis. Then the "right to life" served only to protect the subject from battery in its various forms; liberty meant freedom from actual restraint; and the right to property secured to the individual his lands and his cattle. Later, there came a recognition of a man's spiritual nature, of his feelings and his intellect. Gradually the scope of these legal rights broadened; and now the right to life has come to mean the right to enjoy life, — the right to be let alone; the right to liberty secures the exercise of extensive civil privileges; and the term "property" has grown to comprise every form of possession — intangible, as well as tangible.

Although no English cases explicitly articulated a "right to privacy," several cases decided under theories of property, contract, or breach of confidence also included invasion of privacy as a basis for protecting personal violations. The article encouraged recognition of the common law right to privacy, as the strength of our legal system lies in its elasticity, adaptability, capacity for growth, and ability "to meet the wants of an ever changing society and to apply immediate relief for every recognized wrong.". . .

Today, the vast majority of jurisdictions now recognize some form of the right to privacy. Only Minnesota, North Dakota, and Wyoming have not yet recognized any of the four privacy torts. Although New York and Nebraska courts have declined to recognize a common law basis for the right to privacy and instead provide statutory protection, we reject the proposition that only the legislature may establish new causes of action. The right to privacy is inherent in the English protections of individual property and contract rights and the "right to be let alone" is recognized as part of the common law across this country. Thus, it is within the province of the judiciary to establish privacy torts in this jurisdiction.

Today we join the majority of jurisdictions and recognize the tort of invasion of privacy. The right to privacy is an integral part of our humanity; one has a public persona, exposed and active, and a private persona, guarded and preserved. The heart of our liberty is choosing which parts of our lives shall become public and which parts we shall hold close. . . .

We decline to recognize the tort of false light publicity at this time. We are concerned that claims under false light are similar to claims of defamation, and to the extent that false light is more expansive than defamation, tension between this tort and the First Amendment is increased.

False light is the most widely criticized of the four privacy torts and has been rejected by several jurisdictions. . . .

Thus we recognize a right to privacy present in the common law of Minnesota, including causes of action in tort for intrusion upon seclusion, appropriation, and publication of private facts, but we decline to recognize the tort of false light publicity. . . .

TOMLJANOVICH, J. dissenting. I would not recognize a cause of action for intrusion upon seclusion, appropriation or publication of private facts. . . .

An action for an invasion of the right to privacy is not rooted in the Constitution. "[T]he Fourth Amendment cannot be translated into a general constitutional 'right to privacy.'" *Katz v. United States*, 389 U.S. 347, 350 (1967). Those privacy rights that have their origin in the Constitution are much more fundamental rights of privacy — marriage and reproduction. *See Griswold v. Connecticut*, 381 U.S. 479, 485 (1965) (penumbral rights of privacy and repose protect notions of privacy surrounding the marriage relationship and reproduction).

We have become a much more litigious society since 1975 when we acknowledged that we have never recognized a cause of action for invasion of privacy. We should be even more reluctant now to recognize a new tort.

In the absence of a constitutional basis, I would leave to the legislature the decision to create a new tort for invasion of privacy.

NOTES & QUESTIONS

1. ***Other Remedies?*** If the Minnesota Supreme Court had rejected the privacy tort, what other legal remedies might be available to Elli Lake?
2. ***Postscript.*** What happened in *Lake* after the Minnesota Supreme Court's decision? In response to a query from the casebook authors, the lead attorney for the *Lake* plaintiff, Keith L. Miller of Miller, Norman & Associates, Ltd., explained that his client lost at the trial that followed the remand. He writes: "The jury found that an invasion of Ms. Lake's privacy had occurred, but that it did not happen 'in the course and scope' of a Wal-Mart worker's employment." In other words, tort notions of agency were found to apply, and a privacy tort violation could be attributed to Wal-Mart only if the employee had carried out the tort in the course and scope of employment. Miller added: "Our proof was problematic because, expectedly, no employee could specifically be identified as the culprit. It was all circumstantial." Finally, he summarized his experience litigating this case: "Gratifying? Certainly. Remunerative? Not so much."
3. ***Legislatures vs. Courts.*** The dissent in *Lake* contends, in a similar way as *Roberson*, that it should be the legislature, not the courts, that recognize new tort actions to protect privacy. In New York, the statute passed in response to *Roberson* remains the state's source for privacy tort remedies. Like New York, some states have recognized the privacy torts legislatively; other states,

like Georgia in *Pavesich* and Minnesota in *Lake*, have recognized them judicially. Which means of recognizing the torts do you believe to be most justifiable? Why? Does the legislature have expertise that courts lack? Are courts more or less sensitive to civil rights issues, such as privacy?

(c) Privacy Protection in Tort Law

The Privacy Torts. Prosser's classification of these torts survives to this day. The Restatement (Second) of Torts recognizes four privacy torts:

(1) *Public Disclosure of Private Facts.* This tort creates a cause of action for one who publicly discloses a private matter that is "highly offensive to a reasonable person" and "is not of legitimate concern to the public." Restatement (Second) of Torts § 652D (1977).

(2) *Intrusion upon Seclusion.* This tort provides a remedy when one intrudes "upon the solitude or seclusion of another or his private affairs or concerns" if the intrusion is "highly offensive to a reasonable person." Restatement (Second) of Torts § 652B (1977).

(3) *False Light.* This tort creates a cause of action when one publicly discloses a matter that places a person "in a false light" that is "highly offensive to a reasonable person." Restatement (Second) of Torts § 652E (1977).

(4) *Appropriation.* Under this tort, a plaintiff has a remedy against one "who appropriates to his own use or benefit the name or likeness" of the plaintiff. Restatement (Second) of Torts § 652C (1977).

Today, most states recognize some or all of these torts.

Breach of Confidentiality. The tort of breach of confidentiality provides a remedy when a professional (i.e., doctor, lawyer, banker) divulges a patient or client's confidential information.

Defamation. The law of defamation existed long before Warren and Brandeis's article. Defamation law, consisting of the torts of libel and slander, creates liability when one makes a false statement about a person that harms the person's reputation. The Supreme Court has held that the First Amendment places certain limits on defamation law.

Infliction of Emotional Distress. The tort of intentional infliction of emotional distress can also serve as a remedy for certain privacy invasions. This tort provides a remedy when one "by extreme and outrageous conduct intentionally or recklessly causes severe emotional distress to another." Restatement (Second) of Torts § 46 (1977). Since privacy invasions can often result in severe emotional distress, this tort may provide a remedy. However, it is limited by the requirement of "extreme and outrageous conduct."

(d) Privacy Protection in Evidence Law

The law of evidence has long recognized privacy as an important goal that can override the truth-seeking function of the trial. Under the common law, certain communications are privileged, and hence cannot be inquired into during a legal proceeding. The law of evidence has recognized the importance of protecting the privacy of communications between attorney and client, priest and penitent, husband and wife, physician and patient, and psychotherapist and patient.

(e) Privacy Protection via Property Rights

Property Rights. Although there are few property laws specifically governing privacy, these laws often implicate privacy. The appropriation tort is akin to a property right, and some commentators suggest that personal information should be viewed as a form of property.[32] If personal information is understood as a form of property, the tort of conversion might apply to those who collect and use a person's private data. Recall, however, that Warren and Brandeis rejected property as an adequate protection for privacy. What kind of market structures might be needed if personal data is to be traded or sold?

Trespass. The law of trespass, which provides tort remedies and criminal penalties for the unauthorized entry onto another's land, can protect privacy. There is some overlap between the torts of intrusion and trespass, as many forms of intrusion involve a trespass as well.

(f) Privacy Protection in Contract Law

Sometimes specific contractual provisions protect against the collection, use, or disclosure of personal information. In certain contexts, courts have entertained actions for breach of implied contract or tort actions based on implicit duties once certain relationships are established, such as physician-patient relationships, which have been analogized to fiduciary relationships. Privacy policies as well as terms of service containing privacy provisions can sometimes be analogized to a contract.

Contract often functions as a way of sidestepping state and federal privacy laws. Many employers make employees consent to drug testing as well as e-mail and workplace surveillance in their employment contracts.

Some commentators advocate a contractual approach to privacy, such as Jerry Kang, who suggests a contractual default rule that limits the way personal information can be used but that can be contracted around by parties who do not desire to be governed by the rule.[33]

(g) Privacy Protection in Criminal Law

Warren and Brandeis noted that under certain circumstances, criminal law would be appropriate to protect privacy. The criminal law protects bodily invasions, such as assault, battery, and rape. The privacy of one's home is also

---

[32] *See, e.g.,* Alan Westin, *Privacy and Freedom* 324 (1967); *see also* Richard S. Murphy, *Property Rights in Personal Information: An Economic Defense of Privacy*, 84 Geo. L.J. 2381 (1996); Richard A. Posner, *The Economics of Justice* (1981); Lawrence Lessig, *Code and Other Laws of Cyberspace* 154-62 (1999).

[33] *See* Jerry Kang, *Information Privacy in Cyberspace Transactions*, 50 Stan. L. Rev. 1193 (1998).

protected by criminal sanctions for trespass. Stalking and harassing can give rise to criminal culpability. The crime of blackmail prohibits coercing an individual by threatening to expose her personal secrets. Many of the statutes protecting privacy also contain criminal penalties, such as the statutes pertaining to wiretapping and identity theft.

2. CONSTITUTIONAL LAW

Federal Constitutional Law. Although the United States Constitution does not specifically mention privacy, it has a number of provisions that protect privacy, and it has been interpreted as providing a right to privacy. In some instances the First Amendment serves to safeguard privacy. For example, the First Amendment protects the right to speak anonymously. *See McIntyre v. Ohio Election Comm'n*, 514 U.S. 334 (1995). The First Amendment's freedom of association clause protects individuals from being compelled to disclose the groups to which they belong or contribute. Under the First Amendment "Congress shall make no law . . . abridging . . . the right of the people peaceably to assemble. . . ." For example, the Court has struck down the compulsory disclosure of the names and addresses of an organization's members, *see NAACP v. Alabama*, 357 U.S. 449 (1958), as well as a law requiring public teachers to list all organizations to which they belong or contribute. *See Shelton v. Tucker*, 364 U.S. 479 (1960).

The Third Amendment protects the privacy of the home by preventing the government from requiring soldiers to reside in people's homes: "No Soldier shall, in time of peace be quartered in any house, without the consent of the Owner, nor in time of war, but in a manner to be prescribed by law."

The Fourth Amendment provides that people have the right "to be secure in their persons, houses, papers, and effects, against unreasonable searches and seizures. . . ." Almost 40 years after writing *The Right to Privacy*, Brandeis, then a Supreme Court Justice, wrote a dissent that has had a significant influence on Fourth Amendment law. The case was *Olmstead v. United States*, 277 U.S. 438 (1928), where the Court held that wiretapping was not an invasion of privacy under the Fourth Amendment because it was not a physical trespass into the home. Justice Brandeis dissented, contending that the central interest protected by the Fourth Amendment was not property but the "right to be let alone":

> The protection guaranteed by the amendments is much broader in scope. The makers of our Constitution undertook to secure conditions favorable to the pursuit of happiness. They recognized the significance of man's spiritual nature, of his feelings and of his intellect. They knew that only a part of the pain, pleasure and satisfactions of life are to be found in material things. They sought to protect Americans in their beliefs, their thoughts, their emotions and their sensations. They conferred, as against the government, the right to be let alone — the most comprehensive of rights and the right most valued by civilized men. To protect that right, every unjustifiable intrusion by the government upon the privacy of the individual, whatever the means employed, must be deemed a violation of the Fourth Amendment.

Brandeis's dissent demonstrated that the "right to be let alone" did not merely have common law roots (as he had argued in *The Right to Privacy*) but also had constitutional roots as well in the Fourth Amendment.

Modern Fourth Amendment law incorporates much of Brandeis's view. In *Katz v. United States*, 389 U.S. 347 (1967), the Court held that the Fourth Amendment "protects people, not places" and said that the police must obtain a warrant when a search takes place in a public pay phone on a public street. The Court currently determines a person's right to privacy by the "reasonable expectations of privacy" test, a standard articulated in Justice Harlan's concurrence to *Katz*. First, a person must "have exhibited an actual (subjective) expectation of privacy" and, second, "the expectation [must] be one that society is prepared to recognize as 'reasonable.' "

The Fifth Amendment guarantees that: "No person . . . shall be compelled in any criminal case to be a witness against himself. . . ." This right, commonly referred to as the "privilege against self-incrimination," protects privacy by restricting the ability of the government to force individuals to divulge certain information about themselves.

In the landmark 1965 case *Griswold v. Connecticut*, 318 U.S. 479 (1965), the Court declared that an individual has a constitutional right to privacy. The Court located this right within the "penumbras" or "zones" of freedom created by an expansive interpretation of the Bill of Rights. Subsequently, the Court has handed down a line of cases protecting certain fundamental life choices such as abortion and aspects of one's intimate sexual life.

In *Whalen v. Roe*, 433 U.S. 425 (1977), the Court extended its substantive due process privacy protection to information privacy, holding that the "zone of privacy" protected by the Constitution encompasses the "individual interest in avoiding disclosure of personal matters." This offshoot of the right to privacy has become known as the "constitutional right to information privacy."

State Constitutional Law. A number of states have directly provided for the protection of privacy in their constitutions. For example, the Alaska Constitution provides: "The right of the people to privacy is recognized and shall not be infringed." Alaska Const. art. I, § 22. According to the California Constitution: "All people are by their nature free and independent and have inalienable rights. Among these are enjoying and defending life and liberty, acquiring, possessing, and protecting property, and pursuing and obtaining safety, happiness, and privacy." Cal. Const. art. I, § 1. Unlike most state constitutional provisions, the California constitutional right to privacy applies not only to state actors but also to private parties. *See, e.g., Hill v. NCAA*, 865 P.2d 638 (Cal. 1994). The Florida Constitution provides: "Every natural person has the right to be let alone and free from governmental intrusion into his private life except as otherwise provided herein." Fla. Const. art. I, § 23.[34]

---

[34] For more examples, see Ariz. Const. art. II, § 8; Mont. Const. art. II, § 10; Haw. Const. art. I, § 6; Ill. Const. art. I, §§ 6, 12; La. Const. art. I, § 5; S.C. Const. art. I, § 10; Wash. Const. art. I, § 7. For a further discussion of state constitutional protections of privacy, see Timothy O. Lenz, *"Rights Talk" about Privacy in State Courts*, 60 Alb. L. Rev. 1613 (1997); Mark Silverstein, Note, *Privacy Rights in State Constitutions: Models for Illinois?*, 1989 U. Ill. L. Rev. 215.

3. STATUTORY LAW

Federal Statutory Law. From the mid-1960s to the mid-1970s, privacy emerged as a central political and social concern. In tune with the heightened attention to privacy, philosophers, legal scholars, and others turned their focus on privacy, raising public awareness about the growing threats to privacy from technology.[35]

In the mid-1960s electronic eavesdropping erupted into a substantial public issue, spawning numerous television news documentaries as well as receiving significant attention in major newspapers. A proposal for a National Data Center in 1965 triggered public protest and congressional hearings. At this time, the computer was a new and unexplored technological tool that raised risks of unprecedented data collection about individuals, with potentially devastating effects on privacy. Indeed, toward the end of the 1960s, the issue of the collection of personal information in databases had become one of the defining social issues of American society.

During this time the Supreme Court announced landmark decisions regarding the right to privacy, including *Griswold v. Connecticut* in 1965 and *Roe v. Wade* in 1973, which were landmark decisions regarding the right to decisional/reproductive privacy and autonomy. The famous reasonable expectations of privacy test in Fourth Amendment jurisprudence emerged in 1967 with *Katz v. United States.*

Due to growing fears about the ability of computers to store and search personal information, Congress devoted increasing attention to the issue of privacy. As Priscilla Regan observes:

> In 1965, a new problem was placed on the congressional agenda by subcommittee chairs in both the House and the Senate. The problem was defined as the invasion of privacy by computers and evoked images of *1984*, the "Computerized Man," and a dossier society. Press interest was high, public concern was generated and resulted in numerous letters being sent to members of Congress, and almost thirty days of congressional hearings were held in the late 1960s and early 1970s.[36]

In 1973, in a highly influential report, the United States Department of Health, Education, and Welfare (HEW) undertook an extensive review of data processing in the United States. Among many recommendations, the HEW report proposed that a Code of Fair Information Practices be established. The Fair Information Practices consist of a number of basic information privacy principles that allocate rights and responsibilities in the collection and use of personal information:

---

[35] *See, e.g.,* Vance Packard, *The Naked Society* (1964); Myron Brenton, *The Privacy Invaders* (1964); Alan Westin, *Privacy and Freedom* (1967); Arthur Miller, *The Assault on Privacy* (1971); *Nomos XII: Privacy* (J. Ronald Pennock & J.W. Chapman eds., 1971); Alan Westin & Michael A. Baker, *Databanks in a Free Society: Computers, Record-Keeping and Privacy* (1972); Aryeh Neier, *The Secret Files They Keep on You* (1975); Kenneth L. Karst, *"The Files": Legal Controls over the Accuracy and Accessibility of Stored Personal Data*, 31 L. & Contemp. Probs. 342 (1966); Symposium, *Computers, Data Banks, and Individual Privacy*, 53 Minn. L. Rev. 211-45 (1968); Symposium, *Privacy*, 31 L. & Contemp. Probs. 251-435 (1966).

[36] Priscilla M. Regan, *Legislating Privacy: Technology, Social Values, and Public Policy* 82 (1995).

- There must be no personal-data record-keeping systems whose very existence is secret.

- There must be a way for an individual to find out what information about him is in a record and how it is used.

- There must be a way for an individual to prevent information about him obtained for one purpose from being used or made available for other purposes without his consent.

- There must be a way for an individual to correct or amend a record of identifiable information about him.

- Any organization creating, maintaining, using, or disseminating records of identifiable personal data must ensure the reliability of the data for their intended use and must take reasonable precautions to prevent misuse of the data.[37]

As Marc Rotenberg observes, the Fair Information Practices have "played a significant role in framing privacy laws in the United States."[38]

Beginning in the 1970s, Congress has passed a number of laws protecting privacy in various sectors of the information economy:

- Fair Credit Reporting Act of 1970, Pub. L. No. 90-32, 15 U.S.C. §§ 1681 et seq. — provides citizens with rights regarding the use and disclosure of their personal information by credit reporting agencies.

- Privacy Act of 1974, Pub. L. No. 93-579, 5 U.S.C. § 552a — provides individuals with a number of rights concerning their personal information maintained in government record systems, such as the right to see one's records and to ensure that the information in them is accurate.

- Family Educational Rights and Privacy Act of 1974, Pub. L. No. 93-380, 20 U.S.C. §§ 1221 note, 1232g — protects the privacy of school records.

- Right to Financial Privacy Act of 1978, Pub. L. No. 95-630, 12 U.S.C. §§ 3401–3422 — requires a subpoena or search warrant for law enforcement officials to obtain financial records.

- Foreign Intelligence Surveillance Act of 1978, Pub. L. No. 95-511, 15 U.S.C. §§ 1801-1811 — regulates foreign intelligence gathering within the U.S.

- Privacy Protection Act of 1980, Pub. L. No. 96-440, 42 U.S.C. § 2000aa — restricts the government's ability to search and seize the work product of the press and the media.

- Cable Communications Policy Act of 1984, Pub. L. No. 98-549, 47 U.S.C. § 551 — mandates privacy protection for records maintained by cable companies.

---

[37] *See* U.S. Dep't of Health, Education, and Welfare, *Secretary's Advisory Committee on Automated Personal Data Systems, Records, Computers, and Rights of Citizens* viii (1973).

[38] Marc Rotenberg, *Fair Information Practices and the Architecture of Privacy (What Larry Doesn't Get)*, Stan. Tech. L. Rev. 1, 44 (2001).

- Electronic Communications Privacy Act of 1986, Pub. L. No. 99-508 and Pub. L. No. 103-414, 18 U.S.C §§ 2510–2522, 2701–2709 — updates federal electronic surveillance law to respond to the new developments in technology.

- Computer Matching and Privacy Protection Act of 1988, Pub. L. No. 100-503, 5 U.S.C. §§ 552a — regulates automated investigations conducted by government agencies comparing computer files.

- Employee Polygraph Protection Act of 1988, Pub. L. No. 100-347, 29 U.S.C. §§ 2001–2009 — governs the use of polygraphs by employers.

- Video Privacy Protection Act of 1988, Pub. L. No. 100-618, 18 U.S.C. §§ 2710–2711 — protects the privacy of videotape rental information.

- Telephone Consumer Protection Act of 1991, Pub. L. No. 102-243, 47 U.S.C. § 227 — provides certain remedies from repeat telephone calls by telemarketers.

- Driver's Privacy Protection Act of 1994, Pub. L. No. 103-322, 18 U.S.C. §§ 2721–2725 — restricts the states from disclosing or selling personal information in their motor vehicle records.

- Health Insurance Portability and Accountability Act of 1996, Pub. L. No. 104-191 — gives the Department of Health and Human Services (HHS) the authority to promulgate regulations governing the privacy of medical records.

- Identity Theft and Assumption Deterrence Act of 1998, Pub. L. No. 105-318, 18 U.S.C. § 1028 — criminalizes the transfer or use of fraudulent identification with the intent to commit unlawful activity.

- Children's Online Privacy Protection Act of 1998, Pub. L. No. 106-170, 15 U.S.C. §§ 6501–6506 — restricts the use of information gathered from children under age 13 by Internet websites.

- Gramm-Leach-Bliley Act of 1999, Pub. L. No. 106-102, 15 U.S.C. §§ 6801–6809 — requires privacy notices and provides opt-out rights when financial institutions seek to disclose personal data to other companies.

- CAN-SPAM Act of 2003, Pub. L. No. 108-187 — provides penalties for the transmission of unsolicited e-mail.

- Fair and Accurate Credit Transactions Act of 2003, Pub. L. No. 108-159 — amends and updates the Fair Credit Reporting Act, providing (among other things) additional protections against identity theft.

- Video Voyeurism Prevention Act of 2004, Pub. L. No. 108-495, 18 U.S.C. § 1801 — criminalizes the capturing of nude images of people (when on federal property) under circumstances where they have a reasonable expectation of privacy.

Not all of Congress's legislation regarding privacy has been protective of privacy. A number of statutes have mandated the government collection of sensitive personal data or facilitated government investigation techniques:

- Bank Secrecy Act of 1970, Pub. L. No. 91-508 — requires banks to maintain reports of people's financial transactions to assist in government white collar investigations.

- Communications Assistance for Law Enforcement Act of 1994, Pub. L. No. 103-414 — requires telecommunication providers to help facilitate government interceptions of communications and surveillance.

- Personal Responsibility and Work Opportunity Reconciliation Act of 1996, Pub. L. No. 104-193 — requires the collection of personal information (including Social Security numbers, addresses, and wages) of all people who obtain a new job anywhere in the nation, which will be placed into a national database to help track down deadbeat parents.

- USA-PATRIOT Act of 2001, Pub. L. No. 107-56 — amends a number of electronic surveillance statutes and other statutes to facilitate law enforcement investigations and access to information.

State Statutory Law. The states have passed statutes protecting privacy in many contexts, regulating both the public and private sectors. These laws cover a wide range of subjects, from employment records and medical records to library records and student records. However, fewer than a third have enacted a general privacy law akin to the Privacy Act.[39] As Paul Schwartz observes, most states lack "omnibus data protection laws."[40]

4. INTERNATIONAL LAW

Privacy is a global concern. International law, and more precisely, the privacy laws of other countries and international privacy norms, implicate privacy interests in the United States. For example, commercial firms in the United States must comply with the various standards for global commerce. The Organization of Economic Cooperation and Development (OECD) developed an extensive series of privacy guidelines in 1980 that formed the basis for privacy laws in North America, Europe, and East Asia. In 1995, the European Union issued the *European Community Directive on Data Protection*, which outlines the basic principles for privacy legislation for European Union member countries.[41] The Directive became effective on October 25, 1998. In November 2004, an Asian-Pacific Economic Cooperative (APEC) Privacy Framework was endorsed by the ministers of the APEC countries. The APEC countries are more than 20 nations, mostly in Asia, but also including the United States.

---

[39] *See* Smith, *Ben Franklin's Web Site, supra,* at 333. For a compilation of state privacy laws, see Robert Ellis Smith, *Compilation of State and Federal Privacy Laws* (2002).

[40] Paul M. Schwartz, *Privacy and Participation: Personal Information and Public Sector Regulation in the United States,* 80 Iowa L. Rev. 553, 605 (1995).

[41] *See* Directive of the European Parliament and the Council of Europe on the Protection of Individuals with Regard to the Processing of Personal Data and on the Free Movement of Such Data (1996). For more information about the EU Data Directive, see Paul M. Schwartz & Joel R. Reidenberg, *Data Privacy Law* (1996); Peter P. Swire & Robert E. Litan, *None of Your Business: World Data Flows, Electronic Commerce, and the European Privacy Directive* (1998); Colin J. Bennett, *Regulating Privacy: Data Protection of Public Policy in Europe and the United States* (1992); David H. Flaherty, *Protecting Privacy in Surveillance Societies* (1989).

C. PERSPECTIVES ON PRIVACY

1. THE PHILOSOPHICAL DISCOURSE ABOUT PRIVACY

(a) The Concept of Privacy and the Right to Privacy

At the outset, it is important to distinguish between the concept of privacy and the right of privacy. As Hyman Gross observed, "[t]he law does not determine what privacy is, but only what situations of privacy will be afforded legal protection."[42] Privacy as a concept involves what privacy entails and how it is to be valued. Privacy as a right involves the extent to which privacy is (and should be) legally protected.

While instructive and illuminative, law cannot be the exclusive material for constructing a concept of privacy. Law is the product of the weighing of competing values, and it sometimes embodies difficult trade-offs. In order to determine what the law *should* protect, we cannot merely look to what the law *does* protect.

(b) The Public and Private Spheres

A long-standing distinction in philosophical discourse is between the public and private spheres. Some form of boundary between public and private has been maintained throughout the history of Western civilization.[43]

Generally, the public sphere is the realm of life experienced in the open, in the community, and in the world of politics. The private sphere is the realm of life where one retreats to isolation or to one's family. At its core is the world of the home. The private sphere, observes Edward Shils, is a realm where the individual "is not bound by the rules that govern public life. . . . The 'private life' is a secluded life, a life separated from the compelling burdens of public authority."[44]

According to Hannah Arendt, both spheres are essential dimensions of human life:

> . . . In ancient feeling, the privative trait of privacy, indicated in the word itself, was all-important; it meant literally a state of being deprived of something, and even of the highest and most human of man's capacities. A man who lived only a private life, who like the slave was not permitted to enter the public realm, or like the barbarian had chosen not to establish such a realm, was not fully human. We no longer think primarily of deprivation when we use the word "privacy," and this is partly due to the enormous enrichment of the private sphere through modern individualism. . . .
>
> To live an entirely private life means above all to be deprived of things essential to a truly human life: to be deprived of the reality that comes from being seen and heard by others, to be deprived of an "objective" relationship

---

[42] Hyman Gross, *The Concept of Privacy*, 42 N.Y.U. L. Rev. 34, 36 (1967).

[43] *See* Georges Duby, *Foreword*, in *A History of the Private Life I: From Pagan Rome to Byzantium* viii (Paul Veyne ed. & Arthur Goldhammer trans., 1987); *see also* Jürgen Habermas, *The Structural Transformation of the Public Sphere* (Thomas Burger trans., 1991).

[44] Edward Shils, *Privacy: Its Constitution and Vicissitudes*, 31 L. & Contemp. Probs. 281, 283 (1966).

with them that comes from being related to and separated from them through the intermediary of a common world of things, to be deprived of the possibility of achieving something more permanent than life itself. . . .

. . . [T]he four walls of one's private property offer the only reliable hiding place from the common public world, not only from everything that goes on in it but also from its very publicity, from being seen and being heard. A life spent entirely in public, in the presence of others, becomes, as we would say, shallow. While it retains visibility, it loses the quality of rising into sight from some darker ground which must remain hidden if it is not to lose its depth in a very real, non-subjective sense. . . . [45]

John Stuart Mill relied upon a notion of the public/private dichotomy to determine when society should regulate individual conduct. Mill contended that there was a realm where people had social responsibilities and where society could properly restrain people from acting or punish them for their deeds. This realm consisted in acts that were hurtful to others or to which people "may rightfully be compelled to perform; such as to give evidence in a court of justice; to bear his fair share in the common defence, or in any other joint work necessary to the interest of the society of which he enjoys the protection." However, "there is a sphere of action in which society, as distinguished from the individual, has, if any, only an indirect interest; comprehending all that portion of a person's life and conduct which affects only himself, or if it also affects others, only with their free, voluntary, and undeceived consent and participation." Conduct within this sphere consists of "self-regarding" acts, and society should not interfere with such acts. As Mill further elaborated:

. . . I fully admit that the mischief which a person does to himself may seriously affect, both through their sympathies and their interests, those nearly connected with him and, in a minor degree, society at large. When, by conduct of this sort, a person is led to violate a distinct and assignable obligation to any other person or persons, the case is taken out of the self-regarding class, and becomes amenable to moral disapprobation in the proper sense of the term. . . . Whenever, in short, there is a definite damage, or a definite risk of damage, either to an individual or to the public, the case is taken out of the province of liberty, and placed in that of morality or law.

But with regard to the merely contingent, or, as it may be called, constructive injury which a person causes to society, by conduct which neither violates any specific duty to the public, nor occasions perceptible hurt to any assignable individual except himself; the inconvenience is one which society can afford to bear, for the sake of the greater good of human freedom. . . . [46]

2. THE DEFINITION AND THE VALUE OF PRIVACY

The following excerpts explore the definition and value of privacy. Those who attempt to define privacy seek to describe what privacy constitutes. Over the past four decades, academics have defined privacy as a right of personhood, intimacy, secrecy, limited access to the self, and control over information. However, defining privacy has proven to be quite complicated, and many commenta-

---

[45] Hannah Arendt, *The Human Condition* (1958).
[46] John Stuart Mill, *On Liberty* 12, 13, 74-75 (1859).

tors have expressed great difficulty in defining precisely what privacy is. In the words of one commentator, "even the most strenuous advocate of a right to privacy must confess that there are serious problems of defining the essence and scope of this right."[47] According to Robert Post, "[p]rivacy is a value so complex, so entangled in competing and contradictory dimensions, so engorged with various and distinct meanings, that I sometimes despair whether it can be usefully addressed at all."[48]

Conceptualizing privacy not only involves defining privacy but articulating the value of privacy. The value of privacy concerns its importance — how privacy is to be weighed relative to other interests and values. The excerpts that follow attempt to grapple with the complicated task of defining privacy and explaining why privacy is worth protecting.

ALAN WESTIN, *PRIVACY AND FREEDOM*

(1967)

. . . Privacy is the claim of individuals, groups, or institutions to determine for themselves when, how, and to what extent information about them is communicated to others. Viewed in terms of the relation of the individual to social participation, privacy is the voluntary and temporary withdrawal of a person from the general society through physical or psychological means, either in a state of solitude or small-group intimacy or, when among larger groups, in a condition of anonymity or reserve. The individual's desire for privacy is never absolute, since participation in society is an equally powerful desire. Thus each individual is continually engaged in a personal adjustment process in which he balances the desire for privacy with the desire for disclosure and communication of himself to others, in light of the environmental conditions and social norms set by the society in which he lives. The individual does so in the face of pressures from the curiosity of others and from the processes of surveillance that every society sets in order to enforce its social norms. . . .

Recognizing the differences that political and sensory cultures make in setting norms of privacy among modern societies, it is still possible to describe the general functions that privacy performs for individuals and groups in Western democratic nations. Before describing these, it is helpful to explain in somewhat greater detail the four basic states of individual privacy [which are solitude, intimacy, anonymity, and reserve.] . . .

The first state of privacy is solitude; here the individual is separated from the group and freed from the observation of other persons. He may be subjected to jarring physical stimuli, such as noise, odors, and vibrations. His peace of mind may continue to be disturbed by physical sensations of heat, cold, itching, and pain. He may believe that he is being observed by God or some supernatural force, or fear that some authority is secretly watching him. Finally, in solitude he will be especially subject to that familiar dialogue with the mind or conscience.

---

[47] William M. Beaney, *The Right to Privacy and American Law*, 31 L. & Contemp. Probs. 253, 255 (1966).

[48] Robert C. Post, *Three Concepts of Privacy*, 89 Geo. L.J. 2087, 2087 (2001).

But, despite all these physical or psychological intrusions, solitude is the most complete state of privacy that individuals can achieve.

In the second state of privacy, the individual is acting as part of a small unit that claims and is allowed to exercise corporate seclusion so that it may achieve a close, relaxed, and frank relationship between two or more individuals. Typical units of intimacy are husband and wife, the family, a friendship circle, or a work clique. Whether close contact brings relaxed relations or abrasive hostility depends on the personal interaction of the members, but without intimacy a basic need of human contact would not be met.

The third state of privacy, anonymity, occurs when the individual is in public places or performing public acts but still seeks, and finds, freedom from identification and surveillance. He may be riding a subway, attending a ball game, or walking the streets; he is among people and knows that he is being observed; but unless he is a well-known celebrity, he does not expect to be personally identified and held to the full rules of behavior and role that would operate if he were known to those observing him. In this state the individual is able to merge into the "situational landscape." Knowledge or fear that one is under systematic observation in public places destroys the sense of relaxation and freedom that men seek in open spaces and public arenas. . . .

Still another kind of anonymity is the publication of ideas anonymously. Here the individual wants to present some idea publicly to the community or to a segment of it, but does not want to be universally identified at once as the author — especially not by the authorities, who may be forced to take action if they "know" the perpetrator. The core of each of these types of anonymous action is the desire of individuals for times of "public privacy."

Reserve, the fourth and most subtle state of privacy, is the creation of a psychological barrier against unwanted intrusion; this occurs when the individual's need to limit communication about himself is protected by the willing discretion of those surrounding him. Most of our lives are spent not in solitude or anonymity but in situations of intimacy and in group settings where we are known to others. Even in the most intimate relations, communication of self to others is always incomplete and is based on the need to hold back some parts of one's self as either too personal and sacred or too shameful and profane to express. This circumstance gives rise to what Simmel called "reciprocal reserve and indifference," the relation that creates "mental distance" to protect the personality. This creation of mental distance—a variant of the concept of "social distance" — takes place in every sort of relationship under rules of social etiquette; it expresses the individual's choice to withhold or disclose information — the choice that is the dynamic aspect of privacy in daily interpersonal relations. . . .

This analysis of the various states of privacy is useful in discussing the basic question of the functions privacy performs for individuals in democratic societies. These can also be grouped conveniently under four headings — personal autonomy, emotional release, self-evaluation, and limited and protected communication. . . .

Personal Autonomy. . . . Each person is aware of the gap between what he wants to be and what he actually is, between what the world sees of him and what he knows to be his much more complex reality. In addition, there are aspects of himself that the individual does not fully understand but is slowly exploring and shaping as he develops. Every individual lives behind a mask in this manner; indeed, the first etymological meaning of the word "person" was "mask," indicating both the conscious and expressive presentation of the self to a social audience. If this mask is torn off and the individual's real self bared to a world in which everyone else still wears his mask and believes in masked performances, the individual can be seared by the hot light of selective, forced exposure. . . .

The autonomy that privacy protects is also vital to the development of individuality and consciousness of individual choice in life. . . . This development of individuality is particularly important in democratic societies, since qualities of independent thought, diversity of views, and non-conformity are considered desirable traits for individuals. Such independence requires time for sheltered experimentation and testing of ideas, for preparation and practice in thought and conduct, without fear of ridicule or penalty, and for the opportunity to alter opinions before making them public. The individual's sense that it is he who decides when to "go public" is a crucial aspect of his feeling of autonomy. Without such time for incubation and growth, through privacy, many ideas and positions would be launched into the world with dangerous prematurity. . . .

Emotional Release. Life in society generates such tensions for the individual that both physical and psychological health demand periods of privacy for various types of emotional release. At one level, such relaxation is required from the pressure of playing social roles. Social scientists agree that each person constantly plays a series of varied and multiple roles, depending on his audience and behavioral situation. On any given day a man may move through the roles of stern father, loving husband, car-pool comedian, skilled lathe operator, union steward, water-cooler flirt, and American Legion committee chairman — all psychologically different roles that he adopts as he moves from scene to scene on the social stage. Like actors on the dramatic stage, Goffman has noted, individuals can sustain roles only for reasonable periods of time, and no individual can play indefinitely, without relief, the variety of roles that life demands. There have to be moments "off stage" when the individual can be "himself": tender, angry, irritable, lustful, or dream-filled. . . .

Another form of emotional release is provided by the protection privacy gives to minor non-compliance with social norms. Some norms are formally adopted — perhaps as law — which society really expects many persons to break. This ambivalence produces a situation in which almost everyone does break some social or institutional norms — for example, violating traffic laws, breaking sexual mores, cheating on expense accounts, overstating income-tax deductions, or smoking in rest rooms when this is prohibited. Although society will usually punish the most flagrant abuses, it tolerates the great bulk of the violations as "permissible" deviations. If there were no privacy to permit society to ignore these deviations — if all transgressions were known — most persons in society would be under organizational discipline or in jail, or could be manipulated by threats of such action. The firm expectation of having privacy for permissible deviations is a distinguishing characteristic of life in a free society. At a lesser but still important level, privacy also allows individuals to deviate temporarily from social etiquette when alone or among intimates, as by putting feet on desks, cursing, letting one's face go slack, or scratching wherever one itches.

Another aspect of release is the "safety-valve" function afforded by privacy. Most persons need to give vent to their anger at "the system," "city hall," "the boss," and various others who exercise authority over them, and to do this in the intimacy of family or friendship circles, or in private papers, without fear of being held responsible for such comments. . . . Without the aid of such release in accommodating the daily abrasions with authorities, most people would experience serious emotional pressure. . . .

Limited and Protected Communication. The greatest threat to civilized social life would be a situation in which each individual was utterly candid in his communications with others, saying exactly what he knew or felt at all times. The havoc done to interpersonal relations by children, saints, mental patients, and adult "innocents" is legendary. . . .

Privacy for limited and protected communication has two general aspects. First, it provides the individual with the opportunities he needs for sharing confidences and intimacies with those he trusts — spouse, "the family," personal friends, and close associates at work. The individual discloses because he knows that his confidences will be held, and because he knows that breach of confidence violates social norms in a civilized society. "A friend," said Emerson, "is someone before . . . [whom] I can think aloud." In addition, the individual often wants to secure counsel from persons with whom he does not have to live daily after disclosing his confidences. He seeks professionally objective advice from persons whose status in society promises that they will not later use his distress to take advantage of him. To protect freedom of limited communication, such relationships — with doctors, lawyers, ministers, psychiatrists, psychologists, and others — are given varying but important degrees of legal privilege against forced disclosure. . . .

NOTES & QUESTIONS

1. ***Privacy as Control over Information.*** A number of theorists, including Westin, conceive of privacy as a form of control over personal information.[49] Consider Charles Fried's definition of privacy:

> At first approximation, privacy seems to be related to secrecy, to limiting the knowledge of others about oneself. This notion must be refined. It is not true, for instance, that the less that is known about us the more privacy we have. Privacy is not simply an absence of information about what is in the minds of others; rather it is the *control* we have over information about ourselves.
>
> To refer for instance to the privacy of a lonely man on a desert island would be to engage in irony. The person who enjoys privacy is able to grant or deny access to others. . . .

---

[49] *See* Adam Carlyle Breckenridge, *The Right to Privacy* 1 (1970); Randall P. Bezanson, *The Right to Privacy Revisited: Privacy, News, and Social Change, 1810–1990*, 80 Cal. L. Rev. 1133 (1992). For a critique of privacy as control, see Anita L. Allen, *Privacy as Data Control: Conceptual, Practical, and Moral Limits of the Paradigm*, 32 Conn. L. Rev. 861 (2000).

Privacy, thus, is control over knowledge about oneself. But it is not simply control over the quantity of information abroad; there are modulations in the quality of the knowledge as well. We may not mind that a person knows a general fact about us, and yet feel our privacy invaded if he knows the details.[50]

Is this a compelling definition of privacy?

2. *Privacy as Limited Access to the Self.* Another group of theorists view privacy as a form of limited access to the self. Consider Ruth Gavison:

> . . . Our interest in privacy . . . is related to our concern over our accessibility to others: the extent to which we are known to others, the extent to which others have physical access to us, and the extent to which we are the subject of others' attention. This concept of privacy as concern for limited accessibility enables us to identify when losses of privacy occur. Furthermore, the reasons for which we claim privacy in different situations are similar. They are related to the functions privacy has in our lives: the promotion of liberty, autonomy, selfhood, and human relations, and furthering the existence of a free society. . . .
>
> The concept of privacy suggested here is a complex of these three independent and irreducible elements: secrecy, anonymity, and solitude. Each is independent in the sense that a loss of privacy may occur through a change in any one of the three, without a necessary loss in either of the other two. The concept is nevertheless coherent because the three elements are all part of the same notion of accessibility, and are related in many important ways.[51]

How does this theory of privacy differ from the notion of privacy as "the right to be let alone"? How does it differ from privacy as control over information? How much control should individuals have over access to themselves? Should the decision depend upon each particular person's desires? Or should there be an objective standard — a reasonable degree of control over access?

3. *Privacy as Intimacy.* A number of theorists argue that "intimacy" appropriately defines what information or matters are private. For example, Julie Inness argues that "intimacy" is the common denominator in all the matters that people claim to be private. Privacy is "the state of the agent having control over decisions concerning matters that draw their meaning and value from the agent's love, caring, or liking. These decisions cover choices on the agent's part about access to herself, the dissemination of information about herself, and her actions."[52]

---

[50] Charles Fried, *Privacy*, 77 Yale L.J. 475 (1968).

[51] Ruth Gavison, *Privacy and the Limits of Law*, 89 Yale L.J. 421 (1980); *see also* Edward Shils, *Privacy: Its Constitution and Vicissitudes*, 31 L. & Contemp. Probs. 281, 281 (1996); Sissela Bok, *Secrets: On the Ethics of Concealment and Revelation* 10-11 (1982); Ernest Van Den Haag, *On Privacy*, in *Nomos XII: Privacy* 149 (J. Ronald Pennock & J.W. Chapman eds., 1971); Sidney M. Jourard, *Some Psychological Aspects of Privacy*, 31 L. & Contemp. Probs. 307, 307 (1966); David O'Brien, *Privacy, Law, and Public Policy* 16 (1979); Hyman Gross, *The Concept of Privacy*, 42 N.Y.U. L. Rev. 34 (1967).

[52] Julie C. Inness, *Privacy, Intimacy, and Isolation* 56, 58, 63, 64, 67 (1992). For other proponents of privacy as intimacy, see Robert S. Gerstein, *Intimacy and Privacy*, in *Philosophical Dimensions of Privacy: An Anthology* 265, 265 (Ferdinand David Schoeman ed., 1984); James Rachels, *Why Privacy Is Important*, in *Philosophical Dimensions of Privacy: An Anthology* 290,

Jeffrey Rosen adopts a similar view when he writes:

. . . Privacy protects us from being misdefined and judged out of context in a world of short attention spans, a world in which information can easily be confused with knowledge. True knowledge of another person is the culmination of a slow process of mutual revelation. It requires the gradual setting aside of social masks, the incremental building of trust, which leads to the exchange of personal disclosures. It cannot be rushed; this is why, after intemperate self-revelation in the heat of passion, one may feel something close to self-betrayal. True knowledge of another person, in all of his or her complexity, can be achieved only with a handful of friends, lovers, or family members. In order to flourish, the intimate relationships on which true knowledge of another person depends need space as well as time: sanctuaries from the gaze of the crowd in which slow mutual self-disclosure is possible.

When intimate personal information circulates among a small group of people who know us well, its significance can be weighed against other aspects of our personality and character. By contrast, when intimate information is removed from its original context and revealed to strangers, we are vulnerable to being misjudged on the basis of our most embarrassing, and therefore most memorable, tastes and preferences. . . . In a world in which citizens are bombarded with information, people form impressions quickly, based on sound bites, and these impressions are likely to oversimplify and misrepresent our complicated and often contradictory characters.[53]

Does "intimacy" adequately separate private matters from public ones? Can something be private but not intimate? Can something be intimate but not private?

In reaction to Rosen's views on privacy, Lawrence Lessig restates the problem of short attention spans in this fashion: "Privacy, the argument goes, would remedy such a problem by concealing those things that would not be understood with the given attention span. Privacy's function . . . is not to protect the presumptively innocent from true but damaging information, but rather to protect the actually innocent from damaging conclusions drawn from misunderstood information."[54] Lessig notes his skepticism regarding this approach: privacy will not alone solve the problem with the information market. Moreover, there "are possible solutions to this problem of attention span. But what should be clear is that there is no guarantee that a particular problem of attention span will have any solution at all."

JULIE E. COHEN, *EXAMINED LIVES: INFORMATIONAL PRIVACY AND THE SUBJECT AS OBJECT*

52 Stan. L. Rev. 1373 (2000)

Prevailing market-based approaches to data privacy policy — including "solutions" in the form of tradable privacy rights or heightened disclosure require-

---

292 (Ferdinand David Schoeman ed., 1984); Tom Gerety, *Redefining Privacy*, 12 Harv. C.R.-C.L. L. Rev. 233 (1977).

[53] Jeffrey Rosen, *The Unwanted Gaze: The Destruction of Privacy in America* 8-9 (2000).

[54] Lawrence Lessig, *Privacy and Attention Span*, 89 Geo. L. J. 2063, 2065 (2001).

ments before consent — treat preferences for informational privacy as a matter of individual taste, entitled to no more (and often much less) weight than preferences for black shoes over brown or red wine over white. But the values of informational privacy are far more fundamental. A degree of freedom from scrutiny and categorization by others promotes important noninstrumental values, and serves vital individual and collective ends.

First, informational autonomy comports with important values concerning the fair and just treatment of individuals within society. From Kant to Rawls, a central strand of Western philosophical tradition emphasizes respect for the fundamental dignity of persons, and a concomitant commitment to egalitarianism in both principle and practice. Advocates of strong data privacy protection argue that these principles have clear and very specific implications for the treatment of personally-identified data: They require that we forbid data-processing practices that treat individuals as mere conglomerations of transactional data, or that rank people as prospective customers, tenants, neighbors, employees, or insureds based on their financial or genetic desirability. . . .

Autonomous individuals do not spring full-blown from the womb. We must learn to process information and to draw our own conclusions about the world around us. We must learn to choose, and must learn something before we can choose anything. Here, though, information theory suggests a paradox: "Autonomy" connotes an essential independence of critical faculty and an imperviousness to influence. But to the extent that information shapes behavior, autonomy is radically contingent upon environment and circumstance. . . . Autonomy in a contingent world requires a zone of relative insulation from outside scrutiny and interference — a field of operation within which to engage in the conscious construction of self. The solution to the paradox of contingent autonomy, in other words, lies in a second paradox: To exist in fact as well as in theory, autonomy must be nurtured.

A realm of autonomous, unmonitored choice, in turn, promotes a vital diversity of speech and behavior. The recognition that anonymity shelters constitutionally-protected decisions about speech, belief, and political and intellectual association — decisions that otherwise might be chilled by unpopularity or simple difference — is part of our constitutional tradition. . . .

The benefits of informational privacy are related to, but distinct from, those afforded by seclusion from visual monitoring. It is well-recognized that respite from visual scrutiny affords individuals an important measure of psychological repose. Within our society, at least, we are accustomed to physical spaces within which we can be unobserved, and intrusion into those spaces is experienced as violating the boundaries of self. But the scrutiny, and the repose, can be informational as well as visual, and this does not depend entirely on whether the behavior takes place "in private." The injury, here, does not lie in the exposure of formerly private behaviors to public view, but in the dissolution of the boundaries that insulate different spheres of behavior from one another. The universe of all information about all record-generating behaviors generates a "picture" that, in some respects, is more detailed and intimate than that produced by visual observation, and that picture is accessible, in theory and often in reality, to just about anyone who wants to see it. In such a world, we all may be more cautious.

The point is not that people will not learn under conditions of no-privacy, but that they will learn differently, and that the experience of being watched will constrain, ex ante, the acceptable spectrum of belief and behavior. Pervasive monitoring of every first move or false start will, at the margin, incline choices toward the bland and the mainstream. The result will be a subtle yet fundamental shift in the content of our character, a blunting and blurring of rough edges and sharp lines. . . . The condition of no-privacy threatens not only to chill the expression of eccentric individuality, but also, gradually, to dampen the force of our aspirations to it. . . .

. . . [T]he insulation provided by informational privacy also plays a subtler, more conservative role in reinforcing the existing social fabric. Sociologist Erving Goffman demonstrated that the construction of social facades to mediate between self and community is both instinctive and expected. Alan Westin describes this social dimension of privacy as "reserve." This characterization, though, seems incomplete. On Goffman's account, the construction of social personae isn't just about withholding information that we don't want others to have. It is about defining the parameters of social interaction in ways that maximize social ease, and thus is about collective as well as individual comfort. We do not need, or even want, to know each other that well. Less information makes routine interactions easier; we are then free to choose, consensually and without embarrassment, the interactions that we wish to treat as less routine. Informational privacy, in short, is a constitutive element of a civil society in the broadest sense of that term. . . .

NOTES & QUESTIONS

1. ***Privacy and Respect for Persons.*** Julie Cohen's theory locates the purpose of privacy as promoting the development of autonomous individuals and, more broadly, civil society. Compare her theory to the following theory by Stanley Benn:

   > Finding oneself an object of scrutiny, as the focus of another's attention, brings one to a new consciousness of oneself, as something seen through another's eyes. According to [Jean-Paul] Sartre, indeed, it is a necessary condition for knowing oneself as anything at all that one should conceive oneself as an object of scrutiny. It is only through the regard of the other that the observed becomes aware of himself as an object, knowable, having a determinate character, in principle predictable. His consciousness of pure freedom as subject, as originator and chooser, is at once assailed by it; he is fixed as *something* — with limited probabilities rather than infinite, indeterminate possibilities. . . .
   >
   > The underpinning of a claim not to be watched without leave will be more general if it can be grounded in this way on the principle of respect for persons than on a utilitarian duty to avoid inflicting suffering. . . . But respect for persons will sustain an objection even to secret watching, which may do no actual harm at all. Covert observation — spying — is objectionable because it deliberately deceives a person about his world, thwarting, for reasons that *cannot* be his reasons, his attempts to make a rational choice. One cannot be said to respect a man as engaged on an enterprise worthy of consideration if

one knowingly and deliberately alters his conditions of action, concealing the fact from him. . . .[55]

How is Cohen's theory similar to and/or different from Benn's?

Benn argues that privacy is a form of respect for persons. By being watched, Benn contends, the observed becomes "fixed as *something* — with limited probabilities rather than infinite indeterminate possibilities." Does Benn adequately capture why surveillance is harmful? Is Benn really concerned about the negative consequences of surveillance on a person's behavior? Or is Benn more concerned about the violation of respect for another?

DANIEL J. SOLOVE, *CONCEPTUALIZING PRIVACY*

90 Cal. L. Rev. 1087 (2002)

Despite what appears to be a welter of different conceptions of privacy, I argue that they can be dealt with under six general headings, which capture the recurrent ideas in the discourse. These headings include: (1) the right to be let alone — Samuel Warren and Louis Brandeis's famous formulation for the right to privacy; (2) limited access to the self — the ability to shield oneself from unwanted access by others; (3) secrecy — the concealment of certain matters from others; (4) control over personal information — the ability to exercise control over information about oneself; (5) personhood — the protection of one's personality, individuality, and dignity; and (6) intimacy — control over, or limited access to, one's intimate relationships or aspects of life. Some of the conceptions concentrate on means to achieve privacy; others focus on the ends or goals of privacy. Further, there is overlap between conceptions, and the conceptions discussed under different headings are by no means independent from each other. For example, control over personal information can be seen as a subset of limited access to the self, which in turn bears significant similarities to the right to be let alone. . . .

The most prevalent problem with the conceptions is that they are either too narrow or too broad. The conceptions are often too narrow because they fail to include the aspects of life that we typically view as private, and are often too broad because they fail to exclude matters that we do not deem private. Often, the same conceptions can suffer from being both too narrow and too broad. I contend that these problems stem from the way that the discourse goes about the task of conceptualizing privacy. . . .

Most attempts to conceptualize privacy thus far have followed the traditional method of conceptualizing. The majority of theorists conceptualize privacy by defining it *per genus et differentiam*. In other words, theorists look for a common set of necessary and sufficient elements that single out privacy as unique from other conceptions. . . .

[Philosopher Ludwig] Wittgenstein suggests that certain concepts might not share one common characteristic; rather they draw from a common pool of simi-

---

[55] Stanley I. Benn, *Privacy, Freedom, and Respect for Persons*, from *Nomos XIII: Privacy* (J. Ronald Pennock & J.W. Chapman eds., 1971).

lar characteristics, "a complicated network of similarities overlapping and criss-crossing: sometimes overall similarities, sometimes similarities of detail." . . . Wittgenstein uses the term "family resemblances," analogizing to the overlapping and crisscrossing characteristics that exist between members of a family, such as "build, features, colour of eyes, gait, temperament, etc." For example, in a family, each child has certain features similar to each parent; and the children share similar features with each other; but they may not all resemble each other in the same way. Nevertheless, they all bear a resemblance to each other. . . .

When we state that we are protecting "privacy," we are claiming to guard against disruptions to certain practices. Privacy invasions disrupt and sometimes completely annihilate certain practices. Practices can be disrupted in certain ways, such as interference with peace of mind and tranquility, invasion of solitude, breach of confidentiality, loss of control over facts about oneself, searches of one's person and property, threats to or violations of personal security, destruction of reputation, surveillance, and so on.

There are certain similarities in particular types of disruptions as well as in the practices that they disrupt; but there are differences as well. We should conceptualize privacy by focusing on the specific types of disruption and the specific practices disrupted rather than looking for the common denominator that links all of them. If privacy is conceptualized as a web of interconnected types of disruption of specific practices, then the act of conceptualizing privacy should consist of mapping the typography of the web. . . .

It is reductive to carve the world of social practices into two spheres, public and private, and then attempt to determine what matters belong in each sphere. First, the matters we consider private change over time. While some form of dichotomy between public and private has been maintained throughout the history of Western civilization, the matters that have been considered public and private have metamorphosed throughout history due to changing attitudes, institutions, living conditions, and technology. The matters we consider to be private are shaped by culture and history, and have differed across cultures and historical epochs.

Second, although certain matters have moved from being public to being private and vice versa, the change often has been more subtle than a complete transformation from public to private. Particular matters have long remained private but in different ways; they have been understood as private but because of different attributes; or they have been regarded as private for some people or groups but not for others. In other words, to say simply that something is public or private is to make a rather general claim; what it means for something to be private is the central question. We consider our Social Security number, our sexual behavior, our diary, and our home private, but we do not consider them private in the same way. A number of aspects of life have commonly been viewed as private: the family, body, and home to name a few. To say simply that these things are private is imprecise because what it means for them to be private is different today than it was in the past. . . .

. . . [P]rivacy is not simply an empirical and historical question that measures the collective sense in any given society of what is and has long been considered to be private. Without a normative component, a conception of privacy can only provide a status report on existing privacy norms rather than guide us toward shaping privacy law and policy in the future. If we focus simply on people's current expectations of privacy, our conception of privacy would continually shrink given the increasing surveillance in the modern world. Similarly, the government could gradually condition people to accept wiretapping or other privacy incursions, thus altering society's expectations of privacy. On the other hand, if we merely seek to preserve those activities and matters that have historically been considered private, then we fail to adapt to the changing realities of the modern world. . . .

NOTES & QUESTIONS

1. ***Core Characteristics vs. Family Resemblances.*** Is there a core characteristic common in all the things we understand as being "private"? If so, what do you think it is? Can privacy be more adequately conceptualized by shifting away from the quest to find the common core characteristics of privacy?

2. ***Context.*** Solove contends that the meaning of privacy depends upon context, that there is no common denominator to all things we refer to as "privacy." Does this make privacy too amorphous a concept?

   Consider Helen Nissenbaum:

   > Specifically, whether a particular action is determined a violation of privacy is a function of several variables, including the nature of the situation, or context; the nature of the information in relation to that context; the roles of agents receiving information; their relationships to information subjects; on what terms the information is shared by the subject; and the terms of further dissemination. . . .
   >
   > [N]orms of privacy in fact vary considerably from place to place, culture to culture, period to period; this theory not only incorporates this reality but systematically pinpoints the sources of variation. A second consequence is that, because questions about whether particular restrictions on flow are acceptable call for investigation into the relevant contextual details, protecting privacy will be a messy task, requiring a grasp of concepts and social institutions as well as knowledge of facts of the matter.[56]

3. ***Revising the Prosser Taxonomy.*** Daniel Solove contends that the taxonomy of four privacy interests identified by William Prosser, *supra,* must be revised as well as expanded beyond tort law. Solove identifies 16 different kinds of activity that create privacy harms or problems:

   > The first group of activities that affect privacy involve information collection. *Surveillance* is the watching, listening to, or recording of an individual's activities. *Interrogation* consists of various forms of questioning or probing for information.
   >
   > A second group of activities involves the way information is stored, manipulated, and used — what I refer to collectively as "information processing." *Aggregation* involves the combination of various pieces of data about a person. *Identification* is linking information to particular individuals. *Insecurity* involves carelessness in protecting stored information from being leaked or

---

[56] Helen Nissenbaum, *Privacy as Contextual Integrity,* 79 Wash. L. Rev. 119, 155-56 (2004).

improperly accessed. *Secondary use* is the use of information collected for one purpose for a different purpose without a person's consent. *Exclusion* concerns the failure to allow people to know about the data that others have about them and participate in its handling and use. These activities do not involve the gathering of data, since it has already been collected. Instead, these activities involve the way data is maintained and used.

The third group of activities involves the dissemination of information. *Breach of confidentiality* is breaking the promise to keep a person's information confidential. *Disclosure* involves the revelation of truthful information about a person which impacts the way others judge that person's character. *Exposure* involves revealing another's nudity, grief, or bodily functions. *Increased accessibility* is amplifying the accessibility of information. *Blackmail* is the threat to disclose personal information. *Appropriation* involves the use of another's identity to serve the aims and interests of another. *Distortion* consists of the dissemination of false or misleading information about individuals. Information dissemination activities all involve the spreading or transfer of personal data — or the threat to do so.

The fourth and final group of activities involves invasions into people's private affairs. Invasion, unlike the other groupings, need not involve personal information (although in numerous instances, it does). *Intrusion* concerns invasive acts that disturb one's tranquility or solitude. *Decisional interference* involves the government's incursion into people's decisions regarding their private affairs.[57]

4. **Reductionists.** Some theorists, referred to as "reductionists," assert that privacy can be reduced to other concepts and rights. For example, Judith Jarvis Thomson contends that there is nothing particularly distinctive about privacy and to talk about things as violating the "right to privacy" is not all that useful. Privacy is really a cluster of other rights, such as the right to liberty, property rights, and the right not to be injured: "[T]he right to privacy is everywhere overlapped by other rights."[58] Is there something distinctive about privacy? Or can privacy be explained in terms of other, more primary rights and interests? What does privacy capture that these other rights and interests (autonomy, property, liberty, etc.) do not?

ANITA L. ALLEN, *COERCING PRIVACY*
40 Wm. & Mary L. Rev. 723 (1999)

. . . The final decades of the twentieth century could be remembered for the rapid erosion of expectations of personal privacy and of the taste for personal privacy in the United States. . . . I sense that people expect increasingly little physical, informational, and proprietary privacy, and that people seem to prefer less of these types of privacy relative to other goods. . . .

One way to address the erosion would be to stop the avalanche of technology and commercial opportunity responsible for the erosion. We could stop the

---

[57] Daniel J. Solove, *A Taxonomy of Privacy,* 154 U. Pa. L. Rev. 477 (2006). For a more complete account of Solove's theory, see Daniel J. Solove, *Understanding Privacy* (2008).

[58] Judith Jarvis Thomson, *The Right to Privacy*, 4 Phil. & Pub. Aff. 295 (1975).

avalanche of technology, but we will not, if the past is any indication. . . . In the United States, with a few exceptions like government-funded human cloning and fetal tissue research, the rule is that technology marches on.

We could stop the avalanche of commercial opportunity by intervening in the market for privacy; that is, we could (some way or another) increase the costs of consuming other people's privacy and lower the profits of voluntarily giving up one's own privacy. The problem with this suggested strategy is that, even without the details of implementation, it raises the specter of censorship, repression, paternalism, and bureaucracy. Privacy is something we think people are supposed to want; if it turns out that they do not, perhaps third parties should not force it on them, decreasing both their utility and that of those who enjoy disclosure, revelation, and exposure.

Of course, we force privacy on people all the time. Our elected officials criminalize public nudity, even to the point of discouraging breastfeeding. . . . It is one thing, the argument might go, to force privacy on someone by criminalizing nude sun-bathing and topless dancing. These activities have pernicious third-party effects and attract vice. It would be wrong, the argument might continue, to force privacy on someone, in the absence of harm to others, solely on the grounds that one ought not say too much about one's thoughts, feelings, and experiences; one ought not reveal in detail how one spends one's time at home; and one ought not live constantly on display. Paternalistic laws against extremes of factual and physical self-revelation seem utterly inconsistent with liberal self-expression, and yet such laws are suggested by the strong claims liberal theorists make about the value of privacy. Liberal theorists claim that we need privacy to be persons, independent thinkers, free political actors, and citizens of a tolerant democracy. . . .

For people under forty-five who understand that they do not, and cannot, expect to have many secrets, informational privacy may now seem less important. As a culture, we seem to be learning how to be happy and productive — even spiritual — knowing that we are like open books, our houses made of glass. Our parents may appear on the television shows of Oprah Winfrey or Jerry Springer to discuss incest, homosexuality, miscegenation, adultery, transvestitism, and cruelty in the family. Our adopted children may go on television to be reunited with their birth parents. Our law students may compete with their peers for a spot on the MTV program The Real World, and a chance to live with television cameras for months on end and be viewed by mass audiences. Our ten-year-olds may aspire to have their summer camp experiences — snits, fights, fun, and all — chronicled by camera crews and broadcast as entertainment for others on the Disney Channel.

Should we worry about any of this? What values are at stake? Scholars and other commentators associate privacy with several important clusters of value. Privacy has value relative to normative conceptions of spiritual personality, political freedom, health and welfare, human dignity, and autonomy. . . .

To speak of "coercing" privacy is to call attention to privacy as a foundation, a precondition of a liberal egalitarian society. Privacy is not an optional good, like a second home or an investment account. . . .

A hard task seems to lay before us — namely, deciding which forms of privacy are so critical that they should become matters of coercion. . . .

As liberals, we should not want people to sell all their freedom, and, as liberals, we should not want people to sell all their privacy and capacities for private choices. This is, in part, because the liberal conceptions of private choice as freedom from governmental and other outside interference with decisionmaking closely link privacy and freedom. The liberal conception of privacy as freedom from unwanted disclosures, publicity, and loss of control of personality also closely links privacy to freedom. . . .

Government will have to intervene in private lives for the sake of privacy and values associated with it. . . . The threat to liberalism is not that individuals sometimes expose their naked bodies in public places, display affection with same-sex partners in public, or broadcast personal information on national television. The threat to liberalism is that in an increasing variety of ways our lives are being emptied of privacy on a daily basis, especially physical and informational privacy. . . .

NOTES & QUESTIONS

1. *Should Privacy Be an Inalienable Right?* Allen argues that people regularly surrender their privacy and that we should "coerce" privacy. In other words, privacy must be seen as an inalienable right, one that people cannot give away. What if a person wants to live in the spotlight or to give away her personal information? Why shouldn't she be allowed to do so? Recall those who defined privacy as control over information. One aspect of control is that an individual can decide for herself how much privacy she desires. What would Allen say about such a definition of privacy?

2. *Privacy and Publicity.* Consider also whether a desire for publicity and a desire for privacy can coexist. Does the person who "tells it all" on the Jerry Springer talk show have any less expectation of privacy when she returns home to be with her family and friends or picks up the telephone to make a private call?

3. *Eroding Expectations of Privacy.* Allen contends that our society is changing by becoming more exhibitionistic and voyeuristic. The result is that expectations of privacy are eroding. If people no longer expect privacy in many situations, then why should we continue to protect it?

PAUL M. SCHWARTZ, *PRIVACY AND DEMOCRACY IN CYBERSPACE*

52 Vand. L. Rev. 1609 (1999)

. . . Self-determination is a capacity that is embodied and developed through social forms and practices. The threat to this quality arises when private or government action interferes with a person's control of her reasoning process. . . . [P]erfected surveillance of naked thought's digital expression short-circuits the individual's own process of decisionmaking. . . .

The maintenance of a democratic order requires both deliberative democracy and an individual capacity for self-determination. . . . [T]he emerging pattern of information use in cyberspace poses a risk to these two essential values. Our task now is to develop privacy standards that are capable of structuring the right kind of information use. . . .

Most scholars, and much of the law in this area, work around a liberal paradigm that we can term "privacy-control." From the age of computer mainframes in the 1960s to the current reign of the Internet's decentralized networks, academics and the law have gravitated towards the idea of privacy as a personal right to control the use of one's data. . . .

. . . [One flaw with the "privacy-control" paradigm is the "autonomy trap."] [T]he organization of information privacy through individual control of personal data rests on a view of autonomy as a given, preexisting quality. . . .

As a policy cornerstone, however, the idea of privacy-control falls straight into the "autonomy trap." The difficulty with privacy-control in the Information Age is that individual self-determination is itself shaped by the processing of personal data. . . .

To give an example of an autonomy trap in cyberspace, the act of clicking through a "consent" screen on a Web site may be considered by some observers to be an exercise of self-reliant choice. Yet, this screen can contain boilerplate language that permits all further processing and transmission of one's personal data. Even without a consent screen, some Web sites place consent boilerplate within a "privacy statement" on their home page or elsewhere on their site. For example, the online version of one New York newspaper states, "By using this site, you agree to the Privacy Policy of the New York Post." This language presents the conditions for data processing on a take-it-or-leave-it basis. It seeks to create the legal fiction that all who visit this Web site have expressed informed consent to its data processing practices. An even more extreme manifestation of the "consent trap" is a belief that an initial decision to surf the Web itself is a self-reliant choice to accept all further use of one's personal data generated by this activity. . . .

The liberal ideal views autonomous individuals as able to interact freely and equally so long as the government or public does not interfere. The reality is, however, that individuals can be trapped when such glorification of freedom of action neglects the actual conditions of choice. Here, another problem arises with self-governance through information-control: the "data seclusion deception." The idea of privacy as data seclusion is easy to explain: unless the individual wishes to surrender her personal information, she is to be free to use her privacy right as a trump to keep it confidential or to subject its release to conditions that she alone wishes to set. The individual is to be at the center of shaping data anonymity. Yet, this right to keep data isolated quickly proves illusory because of the demands of the Information Age. . . .

NOTES & QUESTIONS

1. *Privacy and Personhood.* Like Schwartz, a number of theorists argue that privacy is essential for self-development. According to Jeffrey Reiman, privacy "protects the individual's interest in becoming, being, and remaining

a person."[59] The notion that privacy protects personhood or identity is captured in Warren and Brandeis's notion of "inviolate personality." How does privacy promote self-development?

Consider the following: "Every acceptance of a public role entails the repression, channelizing, and deflection of 'private' or personal attention, motives, and demands upon the self in order to address oneself to the expectations of others."[60] Can we really be ourselves in the public sphere? Is our "public self" any less part of our persona than our "private self"?

2. ***Privacy and Democracy.*** Schwartz views privacy as essential for a democratic society. Why is privacy important for political participation?

3. ***Privacy and Role Playing.*** Recall Westin's view of selfhood:

> Each person is aware of the gap between what he wants to be and what he actually is, between what the world sees of him and what he knows to be his much more complex reality. In addition, there are aspects of himself that the individual does not fully understand but is slowly exploring and shaping as he develops. Every individual lives behind a mask in this manner; indeed, the first etymological meaning of the word "person" was "mask," indicating both the conscious and expressive presentation of the self to a social audience. If this mask is torn off and the individual's real self bared to a world in which everyone else still wears his mask and believes in masked performances, the individual can be seared by the hot light of selective, forced exposure.

Is there a "true" or "core" or "authentic" self? Or do we perform many roles and perhaps have multiple selves? Is there a self beneath the roles that we play?

Daniel Solove contends that "[s]ociety accepts that public reputations will be groomed to some degree. . . . Society protects privacy because it wants to provide individuals with some degree of influence over how they are judged in the public arena."[61] To what extent should the law allow people to promote a polished public image and hide the dirt in private?

4. ***Control over Information.*** Schwartz criticizes the conception of privacy as control over information. Why? What are the problems of viewing privacy as a right to control personal information?

SPIROS SIMITIS, *REVIEWING PRIVACY IN AN INFORMATION SOCIETY*

135 U. Pa. L. Rev. 707 (1987)

. . . The increased access to personal information resulting from modern, sophisticated techniques of automated processing has sharpened the need to abandon the search for a "neutral" concept in favor of an understanding free of abstractions and fully aware of the political and societal background of all

---

[59] Jeffrey H. Reiman, *Privacy, Intimacy, and Personhood*, in *Philosophical Dimensions of Privacy: An Anthology* 300, 308 (Ferdinand David Schoeman ed., 1984).

[60] Joseph Bensman & Robert Lilienfeld, *Between Public and Private: Lost Boundaries of the Self* 174 (1979).

[61] Daniel J. Solove, *The Virtues of Knowing Less: Justifying Privacy Protections Against Disclosure*, 53 Duke L.J. 957 (2003).

privacy debates. Modern forms of data collection have altered the privacy discussion in three principal ways. First, privacy considerations no longer arise out of particular individual problems; rather, they express conflicts affecting everyone. The course of the privacy debate is neither determined by the caricature of a prominent golfer with a chocolate packet protruding out of his pocket, nor by the hints at the use of a sexual stimulant by a respected university professor, but by the intensive retrieval of personal data of virtually every employee, taxpayer, patient, bank customer, welfare recipient, or car driver. Second, smart cards and videotex make it possible to record and reconstruct individual activities in minute detail.[62] Surveillance has thereby lost its exceptional character and has become a more and more routine practice. Finally, personal information is increasingly used to enforce standards of behavior. Information processing is developing, therefore, into an essential element of long-term strategies of manipulation intended to mold and adjust individual conduct. . . .

. . . [B]ecause of both the broad availability of personal data and the elaborate matching procedures, individual activities can be accurately reconstructed through automated processing. Surveillance becomes the order of the day. Significantly enough, security agencies were among the first to discover the advantages of automated retrieval. They not only quickly computerized their own data collections but also sought and obtained access to state and private data banks. Entirely new investigation techniques, such as computer profiling, were developed, enabling the agencies to trace wanted persons by matching a presumptive pattern of consumption habits against, for instance, the records of utility companies. The successful attempts at computer-based voice and picture identification will probably influence the work of security agencies even more. . . .

Both the quest for greater transparency and the defense of free speech are legitimated by the goal of allowing the individual to understand social reality better and thus to form a personal opinion on its decisive factors as well as on possible changes. The citizen's right to be "a participator in the government of affairs," to use Jefferson's terms, reflects a profoundly rational process. It presupposes individuals who not only disperse the necessary information but also have the capacity to transform the accessible data into policy expectations. Transparency is, in other words, a basic element of competent communicative action and consequently remains indispensable as long as social discourse is to be promoted, not inhibited.

Inhibition, however, tends to be the rule once automated processing of personal data becomes a normal tool of both government and private enterprises. The price for an undoubted improvement in transparency is a no less evident loss in competence of communication. Habits, activities, and preferences are compiled, registered, and retrieved to facilitate better adjustment, not to improve the individual's capacity to act and to decide. Whatever the original incentive for

---

[62] Editors' Note: Smart cards are also known as "chip cards" or "integrated circuit cards." These devices, generally the size of a credit card, feature an embedded circuit for the processing of data. A precursor of the Internet, Videotex enjoyed its heyday from the late 1970s to mid-1980s. Videotex was typically deployed through a centralized system with one provider of information and involved the display of text on a television screen or dedicated terminal. France Telecom's Minitel was the most successful videotext system in the world.

computerization may have been, processing increasingly appears as the ideal means to adapt an individual to a predetermined, standardized behavior that aims at the highest possible degree of compliance with the model patient, consumer, taxpayer, employee, or citizen. Furthermore, interactive systems do not, despite all contrary assertions, restore a long lost individuality by correcting the effects of mass production in a mass society. On the contrary, the telematic integration forces the individual once more into a preset scheme. The media supplier dictates the conditions under which communication takes place, fixes the possible subjects of the dialogue, and, due to the personal data collected, is in an increasingly better position to influence the subscriber's behavior. Interactive systems, therefore, suggest individual activity where in fact no more than stereotyped reactions occur.

In short, the transparency achieved through automated processing creates possibly the best conditions for colonization of the individual's lifeworld.[63] Accurate, constantly updated knowledge of her personal history is systematically incorporated into policies that deliberately structure her behavior. The more routinized automated processing augments the transparency, however, the more privacy proves to be a prerequisite to the capacity to participate in social discourse. Where privacy is dismantled, both the chance for personal assessment of the political and societal process and the opportunity to develop and maintain a particular style of life fade. . . .

The processing of personal data is not unique to a particular society. On the contrary, the attractiveness of information technology transcends political boundaries, particularly because of the opportunity to guide the individual's behavior. For a democratic society, however, the risks are high: labeling of individuals, manipulative tendencies, magnification of errors, and strengthening of social control threaten the very fabric of democracy. Yet, despite the incontestable importance of its technical aspects, informatization, like industrialization, is primarily a political and social challenge. When the relationship between information processing and democracy is understood, it becomes clear that the protection of privacy is the price necessary to secure the individual's ability to communicate and participate. Regulations that create precisely specified conditions for personal data processing are the decisive test for discerning whether society is aware of this price and willing to pay it. If the signs of experience are correct, this payment can be delayed no further. There is, in fact, no alternative to the advice of Horace: Seize the day, put not trust in the morrow. . . .

NOTES & QUESTIONS

1. *Privacy and Democracy.* As Simitis and other authors in this section observe, privacy is an issue about social structure. What is the relationship between privacy and democracy according to Simitis?

---

[63] For both the colonization process and the impact of the individual's lifeworld on communicative action, see Jürgen Habermas, 1 *The Theory of Communicative Action* 70-71 (1983) (defining "lifeworld" as shared understandings about what will be treated as a fact, valid norms, and subjective experience). . . .

2. *Privacy Law and Information Flow.* Generally, one would assume that greater information flow facilitates democracy — it enables more expression, more political discourse, more information about the workings of government. Simitis, however, contends that privacy is "necessary to secure the individual's ability to communicate and participate." How are these two notions about information flow to be reconciled? Consider Joel Reidenberg:

> Data privacy rules are often cast as a balance between two basic liberties: fundamental human rights on one side and the free flow of information on the other side. Yet, because societies differ on how and when personal information should be available for private and public sector needs, the treatment and interaction of these liberties will express a specific delineation between the state, civil society, and the citizen.[64]

Privacy, according to Reidenberg, involves establishing a balance between protecting the rights of individuals and enabling information flow. Do you think these interests always exist in opposition? Consider financial services, communications networks, and medical care. Does privacy impair or enable information flow?[65]

3. CRITICS OF PRIVACY

AMITAI ETZIONI, *THE LIMITS OF PRIVACY*

(1999)

. . . Although we cherish privacy in a free society, we also value other goods. Hence, we must address the moral, legal, and social issues that arise when serving the common good entails violating privacy.

When I mentioned the subject of this book to audiences of friends, students in my classes, and members of the public, initially they were all taken aback. Privacy, they pointed out, is under siege, if not already overrun. Given privacy's great importance to a free people, my listeners stressed, one should seek new ways to shore it up, not cast more aspersions on it.

To begin a new dialogue about privacy, I have asked these and similar audiences if they would like to know whether the person entrusted with their child care is a convicted child molester. I mention that when such screening is done, thousands are found to have criminal records, ones that include pedophilia. I further ask: Would they want to know whether the staff of a nursing home in which their mother now lives have criminal records that include abusing the elderly? I note that 14 percent of such employees are found to have criminal records, some of which include violent acts against senior citizens. And should

---

[64] Joel R. Reidenberg, *Resolving Conflicting International Data Privacy Rules in Cyberspace*, 52 Stan. L. Rev. 1315 (2000).

[65] For additional reading about philosophical theories of privacy, see Judith W. DeCew, *In Pursuit of Privacy: Law, Ethics, and the Rise of Technology* (1997) (surveying and critiquing various theories of privacy); Anita L. Allen, *Uneasy Access: Privacy for Women in a Free Society* (1988) (same); Ferdinand David Schoeman, ed., *Philosophical Dimensions of Privacy* (1984) (anthology of articles about the concept of privacy).

public authorities be entitled to determine whether drivers of school buses, pilots, or police officers are under the influence of illegal drugs? Should the FBI be in a position to crack the encryption messages employed by terrorists before they use them to orchestrate the next Oklahoma City bombing? Addressing such concerns raises the question of if and when we are justified in implementing measures that diminish privacy in the service of the common good. . . .

Communitarianism holds that a good society seeks a carefully crafted balance between individual rights and social responsibilities, between liberty and the common good. . . .

. . . [T]he next step is to apply this principle to actual societies. We can then ask whether a particular society, in a given period, leans too far in one direction or the other. In a society that strongly enforces social duties but neglects individual rights (as does Japan, for instance, when it comes to the rights of women, minorities, and the disabled), strenuously fostering the other side in order to achieve balance would entail the expansion of autonomy. Indeed, even in the West, when John Locke, Adam Smith, and John Stuart Mill wrote their influential works, and for roughly the first 190 years of the American republic, the struggle to expand the realm of individual liberty was extremely justified, and there was little reason to be concerned that social responsibilities would be neglected. However, as communitarians have repeatedly noted, the relationship between rights and responsibilities drastically shifted in American society between 1960 and 1990 as a new emphasis on personal autonomy and individualism gradually overwhelmed other societal considerations. . . .

. . . *[T]he best way to curtail the need for governmental control and intrusion is to have somewhat less privacy.* This point requires some elaboration.

The key to understanding this notion lies in the importance, especially to communitarians, of the "third realm." This realm is not the state or the market (or individual choices), but rather the community, which relies on subtle social fostering of prosocial conduct by such means as communal recognition, approbation, and censure. These processes require the scrutiny of some behavior, not by police or secret agents, but by friends, neighbors, and fellow members of voluntary associations. . . .

. . . [P]ublicness reduces the need for public control, while excessive privacy often necessitates state-imposed limits on private choices. . . .

NOTES & QUESTIONS

1. ***Privacy and the Common Good.*** Is Etzioni correct in viewing privacy as in tension with the common good? In what ways might privacy serve the common good? Consider the following argument from Priscilla Regan:

   . . . The philosophical basis of privacy policy overemphasizes the importance of privacy to the individual and fails to recognize the broader social importance of privacy. This emphasis of privacy as an individual right or an individual interest provides a weak basis for formulating policy to protect privacy. When privacy is defined as an individual right, policy formulation entails a balancing of the individual right to privacy against a competing interest or right. In general, the competing interest is recognized as a social interest. For example, the police interest in law enforcement, the government interest in detecting fraud, and an employer's interest in securing an honest work force are discussed and defined as societal interests. It is also assumed that the individual has a stake in these societal interests. As a result, privacy has been on the defensive, with those alleging a privacy invasion bearing the burden of proving that a certain activity does indeed invade privacy and that the "social" benefit to be gained from the privacy invasion is less important than the individual harm incurred. . . .

Privacy is a *common value* in that all individuals value some degree of privacy and have some common perceptions about privacy. Privacy is also a *public value* in that it has value not just to the individual as an individual or to all individuals in common but also to the democratic political system. . . .

A public value of privacy derives not only from its protection of the individual as an individual but also from its usefulness as a restraint on the government or on the use of power. . . .[66]

2. *Communities and Privacy Norms.* Paul Schwartz has criticized Etzioni's approach to privacy on a number of grounds.[67] First, groups that act as intermediaries between the individual and the State have often proven oppressive of their members, and this intolerance undercuts Etzioni's belief that strengthening the community will further privacy. Second, communities, as norm theorists have pointed out, often generate inefficient norms. The standard examples of such inefficient norms are the overfishing of New England waters by whalers and dueling, which long persisted as a means of resolving disputes in the antebellum South. Beyond inefficiency, communities may generate privacy norms that are wrong for other reasons.

3. *Warren and Brandeis.* Consider once again the characterization of privacy set out by Brandeis and Warren. Does this strengthen or undermine the various communal interests described by Etzioni?

RICHARD A. POSNER, *THE RIGHT OF PRIVACY*

12 Ga. L. Rev. 393 (1978)

People invariably possess information, including facts about themselves and contents of communications, that they will incur costs to conceal. Sometimes such information is of value to others: that is, others will incur costs to discover it. Thus we have two economic goods, "privacy" and "prying." . . . .

[M]uch of the casual prying (a term used her without any pejorative connotation) into the private lives of friends and colleagues that is so common a feature of social life is also motivated, to a greater extent than we may realize, by rational considerations of self-interest. Prying enables one to form a more accurate picture of a friend or colleague, and the knowledge gained is useful in one's social or professional dealings with him. For example, in choosing a friend one legitimately wants to know whether he will be discreet or indiscreet, selfish

---

[66] Priscilla M. Regan, *Legislating Privacy: Technology, Social Values, and Public Policy* 213, 225 (1995).

[67] Paul M. Schwartz, *Internet Privacy and the State*, 32 Conn L. Rev. 815, 838-43 (2000).

or generous, and these qualities are not always apparent on initial acquaintance. Even a pure altruist needs to know the (approximate) wealth of any prospective beneficiary of his altruism in order to be able to gauge the value of a transfer to him.

The other side of the coin is that social, like business, dealings present opportunities for exploitation through misrepresentation. Psychologists and sociologists have pointed out that even in every day life people try to manipulate by misrepresentation other people's opinion of them. As one psychologist has written, the "wish for privacy expresses a desire . . . to control others' perceptions and beliefs vis-à-vis the self-concealing person." Even the strongest defenders of privacy describe the individual's right to privacy as the right to "control the flow of information about him." A seldom remarked corollary to a right to misrepresent one's character is that others have a legitimate interest in unmasking the deception.

Yet some of the demand for private information about other people is not self-protection in the foregoing sense but seems mysteriously disinterested — for example, that of the readers of newspaper gossip columns, whose "idle curiosity" Warren and Brandeis deplored, groundlessly in my opinion. Gossip columns recount the personal lives of wealthy and successful people whose tastes and habits offer models — that is, yield information — to the ordinary person in making consumption, career, and other decisions. . . . Gossip columns open people's eyes to opportunities and dangers; they are genuinely informational. . . .

Warren and Brandeis attributed the rise of curiosity about people's lives to the excesses of the press. The economist does not believe, however, that supply creates demand. A more persuasive explanation for the rise of the gossip column is the secular increase in personal incomes. There is apparently very little privacy in poor societies, where, consequently, people can easily observe at first hand the intimate lives of others. Personal surveillance is costlier in wealthier societies both because people live in conditions that give them greater privacy from such observation and because the value (and hence opportunity cost) of time is greater—too great to make a generous allotment of time to watching neighbors worthwhile. People in wealthier societies sought an alternative method of informing themselves about how others live and the press provided it. A legitimate and important function of the press is to provide specialization in prying in societies where the costs of obtaining information have become too great for the Nosey Parker. . . .

Transaction-cost considerations may also militate against the assignment of a property right to the possessor of a secret. . . . Consider, for example, . . . whether the law should allow a magazine to sell its subscriber list to another magazine without obtaining the subscribers' consent. . . . [T]he costs of obtaining subscriber approval would be high relative to the value of the list. If, therefore, we believe that these lists are generally worth more to the purchasers than being shielded from possible unwanted solicitations is worth to the subscribers, we should assign the property right to the magazine; and the law does this. . . .

Much of the demand for privacy . . . concerns discreditable information, often information concerning past or present criminal activity or moral conduct at variance with a person's professed moral standards. And often the motive for concealment is, as suggested earlier, to mislead those with whom he transacts.

Other private information that people wish to conceal, while not strictly discreditable, would if revealed correct misapprehensions that the individual is trying to exploit, as when a worker conceals a serious health problem from his employer or a prospective husband conceals his sterility from his fiancée. It is not clear why society should assign the property right in such information to the individual to whom it pertains; and the common law, as we shall see, generally does not. . . .

We think it wrong (and inefficient) that the law should permit a seller in hawking his wares to make false or incomplete representations as to their quality. But people "sell" themselves as well as their goods. They profess high standards of behavior in order to induce others to engage in social or business dealings with them from which they derive an advantage but at the same time they conceal some of the facts that these acquaintances would find useful in forming an accurate picture of their character. There are practical reasons for not imposing a general legal duty of full and frank disclosure of one's material. . . .

. . . [E]veryone should be allowed to protect himself from disadvantageous transactions by ferreting out concealed facts about individuals which are material to the representations (implicit or explicit) that those individuals make concerning their moral qualities.

It is no answer that such individuals have "the right to be let alone." Very few people want to be let alone. They want to manipulate the world around them by selective disclosure of facts about themselves. Why should others be asked to take their self-serving claims at face value and be prevented from obtaining the information necessary to verify or disprove these claims?

NOTES & QUESTIONS

1. *Posner's Conception of Privacy.* What is Posner's definition of privacy? How does Posner determine the value of privacy (i.e., how it should be weighed relative to other interests and values)? In what circumstances is Posner likely to defend a privacy claim?

2. *Irrational Judgments.* One economic argument for privacy is that sometimes people form irrational judgments based upon learning certain information about others. For example, an employer may not hire certain people based on their political views or associations, sexual orientation, mental illness, and prior criminal convictions — even though these facts may have no relevance to a potential employee's abilities to do the job. These judgments decrease efficiency. In *The Economics of Justice*, Posner offers a response:

> This objection overlooks the opportunity costs of shunning people for stupid reasons, or, stated otherwise, the gains from dealing with someone whom others shun irrationally. If ex-convicts are good workers but most employers do not know this, employers who do know will be able to hire them at a below-average wage because of their depressed job opportunities and will thereby obtain a competitive advantage over the bigots. In a diverse,

decentralized, and competitive society, irrational shunning will be weeded out over time. . . [68]

Will the market be able to eradicate irrational judgments?

3. *The Dangers of the "Masquerade Ball."* Consider Dennis Bailey:

> . . . [I]t is interesting to consider the ways in which the world has become like a giant masquerade ball. Far removed from the tight knit social fabric of the village of the past, we've lost the ability to recognize the people we pass on the street. People might as well be wearing masks because we are likely to know very little about them. In other words, these strangers are anonymous to us, anonymous in the sense that not only their names, but their entire identities, are unknown to us — the intimate details of who they are, where they have come from, and how they have lived their lives. . . .
>
> [A]nonymity has become one of the central vulnerabilities of an open society. Freedom may have allowed [9/11 terrorists] al-Mihdhar and al-Hamzi to rent an apartment, use a cell phone, meet with terrorists overseas, and take flying lessons in preparation for 9/11, but anonymity kept hidden the manner in which these individual actions fit together into a larger mosaic of death. [69]

Are we living in a "masquerade ball"? Businesses and the government have unprecedented new technologies to engage in surveillance and gather information. Should the law facilitate or restrict anonymity?

Also consider Steven Nock:

> Any method of social control depends, immediately, on information about individuals. . . . There can be no social control without such information. . . .
>
> Modern Americans enjoy vastly more privacy than did their forebears because ever and ever larger numbers of strangers in our lives are legitimately denied access to our personal affairs. . . . Privacy, however, makes it difficult to form reliable opinions of one another. Legitimately shielded from other's regular scrutiny, we are thereby more immune to the routine monitoring that once formed the basis of our individual reputations. [70]

Does too much privacy erode trust and lessen social control in detrimental ways?

4. *Information Dissemination and Economic Efficiency.* Does economic theory necessarily lead to the conclusion that more personal information is generally preferable? Consider the following critique of Posner by Edward Bloustein:

> We must remember that Posner stated in *Economic Analysis of Law* that economics "cannot prescribe social change"; it can only tell us about the economic costs of managing it one way or another. . . . [Posner's] characterization of the privacy of personal information as a species of commercial fraud . . . [is an] extension[ ] of a social value judgment rather than implications or conclusions of economic theory. . . .Our society, in fact,

---

[68] Richard A. Posner, *The Economics of Justice* (1981). Posner further develops his theories about privacy in Richard A. Posner, *Overcoming Law* 531-51 (1995). Posner first set out his views on privacy in Richard A. Posner, *An Economic Theory of Privacy*, Regulations (May/June 1978).

[69] Dennis Bailey, *The Open Society Paradox* 26-27 (2004).

[70] Steven L. Nock, *The Costs of Privacy: Surveillance and Reputation in America* (1993).

places a very high value on maintaining individual privacy, even to the extent of concealing "discreditable" information. . . .[71]

Also consider Richard Murphy's critique of Posner:

[D]emarcating a relatively large sphere for the private self creates an opportunity for discovery or actualization of a "true" nature, which may have a value beyond the utility of satisfying preferences. . . . As Roger Rosenblatt put it, "Out of our private gropings and self-inspections grow our imaginative values — private language, imagery, memory. In the caves of the mind one bats about to discover a light entirely of one's own which, though it should turn out to be dim, is still worth a life." Unless a person can investigate without risk of reproach what his own preferences are, he will not be able to maximize his own happiness.[72]

When can the circulation of less personal information be more economically efficient than greater information flow?

5. *Why Don't Individuals Protect Their Privacy?* Empirical studies frequently report on growing privacy concerns across the United States. Yet, individuals seem willing to exchange privacy for services or small rewards and generally fail to adopt technologies and techniques that would protect their privacy. If people are willing to sell their privacy for very little in return, isn't this evidence that they do not really value privacy as much as they say they do?

Alessandro Acqusiti and Jens Grossklags have pointed to a number of reasons for this divergence between stated privacy preferences and actual behavior:

First, incomplete information affects privacy decision making because of externalities (when third parties share personal information about an individual, they might affect that individual without his being part of the transaction between those parties), information asymmetries (information relevant to the privacy decision process — for example, how personal information will be used — might be known only to a subset of the parties making decisions), risk (most privacy related payoffs are not deterministic), and uncertainties (payoffs might not only be stochastic, but dependent on unknown random distributions). Benefits and costs associated with privacy intrusions and protection are complex, multifaceted, and context-specific. They are frequently bundled with other products and services (for example, a search engine query can prompt the desired result but can also give observers information about the searcher's interests), and they are often recognized only after privacy violations have taken place. They can be monetary but also immaterial and, thus, difficult to quantify.

Second, even if individuals had access to complete information, they would be unable to process and act optimally on vast amounts of data. Especially in the presence of complex, ramified consequences associated with the protection or release of personal information, our innate bounded rationality limits our ability to acquire, memorize and process all relevant information,

---

[71] Edward J. Bloustein, *Privacy Is Dear at Any Price: A Response to Professor Posner's Economic Theory*, 12 Ga. L. Rev. 429, 441 (1978). For another critique of Posner's approach, see Kim Lane Scheppele, *Legal Secrets: Equality and Efficiency in the Common Law* (1988).

[72] Richard S. Murphy, *Property Rights in Personal Information: An Economic Defense of Privacy,* 84 Geo. L.J. 2381 (1996).

and it makes us rely on simplified mental models, approximate strategies, and heuristics. These strategies replace theoretical quantitative approaches with qualitative evaluations and "aspirational" solutions that stop short of perfect (numerical) optimization. Bounded problem solving is usually neither unreasonable nor irrational, and it needs not be inferior to rational utility maximization. However, even marginal deviations by several individuals from their optimal strategies can substantially impact the market outcome.

Third, even if individuals had access to complete information and could successfully calculate optimization strategies for their privacy sensitive decisions, they might still deviate from the rational strategy. A vast body of economic and psychological literature has revealed several forms of systematic psychological deviations from rationality that affect individual decision making. . . . Research in psychology . . . documents how individuals mispredict their own future preferences or draw inaccurate conclusions from past choices. In addition, individuals often suffer from self-control problems — in particular, the tendency to trade off costs and benefits in ways that damage their future utility in favor of immediate gratification. Individuals' behavior can also be guided by social preferences or norms, such as fairness or altruism. Many of these deviations apply naturally to privacy-sensitive scenarios.[73]

FRED H. CATE, *PRINCIPLES OF INTERNET PRIVACY*

32 Conn. L. Rev. 877 (2000)

Perhaps the most important consideration when balancing restrictions on information is the historical importance of the free flow of information. The free flow concept is one that is not only enshrined in the First Amendment, but frankly in any form of democratic or market economy. In the United States, we have placed extraordinary importance on the open flow of information. As the Federal Reserve Board noted in its report to Congress on data protection in financial institutions, "it is the freedom to speak, supported by the availability of information and the free-flow of data, that is the cornerstone of a democratic society and market economy."

The significance of open data flows is reflected in the constitutional provisions not only for freedom of expression, but for copyrights — to promote the creation and dissemination of expression, and for a post office — to deliver the mail and the news. Federal regulations demonstrate a sweeping preference for openness, reflected in the Freedom of Information Act, Government in the Sunshine Act, and dozens of other laws applicable to the government. There are even more laws requiring disclosure by private industry, such as the regulatory disclosures required by securities and commodities laws, banking and insurance laws, and many others. This is a very basic tenet of the society in which we live. Laws that restrict that free flow almost always conflict with this basic principle. That does not mean that such laws are never upheld, but merely that they face a considerable constitutional hurdle.

---

[73] Alessandro Acquisti & Jens Grossklags, *Privacy and Rationality in Decision Making*, IEEE, Security and Privacy 24 (2005).

This is done with good reason. Open information flows are not only essential to self-governance; they have also generated significant, practical benefits. The ready availability of personal information helps businesses "deliver the right products and services to the right customers, at the right time, more effectively and at lower cost," Fred Smith, founder and President of the Competitive Enterprise Institute, has written. Federal Reserve Board Governor Edward Gramlich testified before Congress in July 1999 that "[i]nformation about individuals' needs and preferences is the cornerstone of any system that allocates goods and services within an economy." The more such information is available, he continued, "the more accurately and efficiently will the economy meet those needs and preferences."

Federal Reserve Board Chairman Alan Greenspan has been perhaps the most articulate spokesperson for the extraordinary value of accessible personal information. In 1998, he wrote to Congressman Ed Markey (D-Mass.):

> A critical component of our ever more finely hewn competitive market system has been the plethora of information on the characteristics of customers both businesses and individuals. Such information has enabled producers and marketers to fine tune production schedules to the ever greater demands of our consuming public for diversity and individuality of products and services. Newly devised derivative products, for example, have enabled financial institutions to unbundle risk in a manner that enables those desirous of taking on that risk (and potential reward) to do so, and those that chose otherwise, to be risk averse. It has enabled financial institutions to offer a wide variety of customized insurance and other products.
>
> Detailed data obtained from consumers as they seek credit or make product choices help engender the whole set of sensitive price signals that are so essential to the functioning of an advanced information based economy such as ours. . . .

In a recent report on public record information, Richard Varn, Chief Information Officer of the State of Iowa, and I examined the critical roles played by public record information in our economy and society. We concluded that such information constitutes part of this nation's "essential infrastructure," the benefits of which are "so numerous and diverse that they impact virtually every facet of American life. . . ." The ready availability of public record data "facilitates a vibrant economy, improves efficiency, reduces costs, creates jobs, and provides valuable products and services that people want."

Perhaps most importantly, widely accessible personal information has helped to create a democratization of opportunity in the United States. Anyone can go almost anywhere, make purchases from vendors they will never see, maintain accounts with banks they will never visit, and obtain credit far from home all because of open information flows. Americans can take advantage of opportunities based on their records, on what they have done rather than who they know, because access to consumer information makes it possible for distant companies and creditors to make rational decisions about doing business with individuals. The open flow of information gives consumers real choice. This is what the open flow of information principle reflects, not just the constitutional importance of information flows, but their significant economic and social benefits as well.

NOTES & QUESTIONS

1. ***The Pros and Cons of the Free Flow of Information.*** In a striking passage, Cate points out that free flows of information create a "democratization of opportunity in the United States." With this phrase, he reminds us that part of the equality at the basis of American life concerns economic opportunity, and that, in his view, a certain kind of flow of personal information will contribute to this goal. While privacy can be problematic, can open access to information also raise difficulties? How should one establish a baseline for open access or restricted access to personal information?

2. ***The Costs of Privacy.*** Can you think of some of the other important values with which privacy might conflict and the costs that privacy can impose? What should the baseline be in measuring costs?

3. ***The Business of Data Trade.*** The trade in personal information is now a valuable part of the U.S. economy. As a single example, Google reached an agreement on April 14, 2007, to purchase DoubleClick, an online advertising company, for $3.1 billion. The deal was driven by Google's interest in behavioral advertising, in which companies use digital data collection techniques to track individuals around the Internet and serve them targeted ads. Should consumers be allowed to sign up for a National Do Not Track List?

4. ***The Benefits of Information Collection and Use.*** Consider Kent Walker:

> Having some information about yourself out there in the world offers real convenience that goes beyond dollars and cents. Many people benefit from warehousing information — billing and shipping addresses, credit card numbers, individual preferences, and the like — with trustworthy third parties. Such storage of information can dramatically simplify the purchasing experience, ensure that you get a nonsmoking room, or automate the task of ordering a kiddie meal every time your child boards a plane. Likewise, most people prefer to use a credit card rather than a debit card, trading confidentiality of purchases for the convenience of deferred payment. . . .
>
> While there's often little individual incentive to participate in the aggregation of information about people, a great collective good results from the default participation of most people. The aggregation of information often requires a critical mass to be worth doing, or for the results to be worth using. (A phone book with only one out of ten numbers would hardly be worth using, let alone printing.) . . .
>
> Another example is Caller ID, which pits different privacy claims against one another. Many people like the notion of an electronic peephole, letting them know who's at the electronic door before they decide whether to pick up the phone. Yet many people block transmission of their own numbers, valuing protection of their privacy. Neither choice is necessarily right, but it's worth recognizing that the assertion of the privacy claim affects the contending desires of others. The classic Tragedy of the Commons aspects are clear. From my selfish perspective, I want access to information about everyone else — the identity of who's calling me, their listed phone number, etc. I want to be able to intrude on others without their knowing who I am (which I can accomplish by blocking Caller ID), and don't want others to be able to intrude

on me unbidden (which I can accomplish by unlisting my phone number). The gain in privacy makes it harder to find the people you want to reach, and harder to know who's calling you.[74]

5. *Privacy as the "Cheshire Cat of Values"?* Many commentators have noted that although people express concern over privacy, their behavior indicates that they do not care very much about privacy. As Jonathan Franzen, the novelist, writes:

> The panic about privacy has all the finger-pointing and paranoia of a good old American scare, but it's missing one vital ingredient: a genuinely alarmed public. Americans care about privacy in the abstract. . . .
>
> On closer examination . . . privacy proves to be the Cheshire cat of values: not much substance, but a very winning smile.
>
> Legally, the concept is a mess. Privacy violation is the emotional core of many crimes, from stalking and rape to Peeping Tommery and trespass, but no criminal statute forbids it in the abstract. . . .
>
> When Americans do genuinely sacrifice privacy . . . they do so for tangible gains in health or safety or efficiency. Most legalized infringements — HIV notification, airport X-rays, Megan's Law, Breathalyzer roadblocks, the drug-testing of student athletes, . . . remote monitoring of automobile emissions . . . are essentially public health measures. I resent the security cameras in Washington Square, but I appreciate the ones on a subway platform. The risk that someone is abusing my E-ZPass toll records seems to me comfortably low in comparison with my gain in convenience. Ditto the risk that some gossip rag will make me a victim of the First Amendment; with two hundred and seventy million people in the country, any individual's chances of being nationally exposed are next to nil.[75]

Do arguments about bounded rationality, as developed in the earlier section, answer Franzen's concerns?

4. THE FEMINIST PERSPECTIVE ON PRIVACY

Has the legal concept of privacy hurt or helped women throughout history? What is the impact of privacy on women today?

STATE V. RHODES

1868 WL 1278 (N.C. 1868)

[The defendant was indicted for an assault and battery upon his wife, Elizabeth Rhodes. The jury returned the following special verdict: "We find that the defendant struck Elizabeth Rhodes, his wife, three licks, with a switch about the size of one of his fingers (but not as large as a man's thumb) without any provocation except some words uttered by her and not recollected by the witness." The lower court found that the defendant "had a right to whip his wife

---

[74] Kent Walker, *Where Everybody Knows Your Name: A Pragmatic Look at the Costs of Privacy and the Benefits of Information Exchange,* 2000 Stan. Tech. L. Rev. 2, 39, 46, 48 (2000).

[75] Jonathan Franzen, *How to Be Alone: Essays* 42, 45-46 (2003).

with a switch no larger than his thumb, and that upon the facts found in the special verdict he was not guilty in law." Judgment in favor of the defendant was entered from which the State appealed.]

The laws of this State do not recognize *the right of the husband to whip his wife,* but our Courts will not interfere to punish him for moderate correction of her, even if there had been no provocation for it.

Family government being in its nature as complete in itself as the State government is in itself, the Courts will not attempt to control, or interfere with it, in favor of either party, except in cases where permanent or malicious injury is inflicted or threatened, or the condition of the party is intolerable.

In determining whether the husband has been guilty of an indictable assault and battery upon his wife, the criterion is the *effect produced,* and not the manner of producing it or the instrument used. . . .

READE J. The violence complained of would without question have constituted a battery if the subject of it had not been the defendant's wife. The question is how far that fact affects the case.

The courts have been loath to take cognizance of trivial complaints arising out of the domestic relations — such as master and apprentice, teacher and pupil, parent and child, husband and wife. Not because those relations are not subject to the law, but because the evil of publicity would be greater than the evil involved in the trifles complained of; and because they ought to be left to family government. . . .

In this case no provocation worth the name was proved. The fact found was that it was "without any provocation except some words which were not recollected by the witness." The words must have been of the slightest import to have made no impression on the memory. We must therefore, consider the violence as unprovoked. The question is therefore plainly presented, whether the court will allow a conviction of the husband for moderate correction of the wife without provocation.

Our divorce laws do not compel a separation of husband and wife, unless the conduct of the husband be so cruel as to render the wife's condition intolerable, or her life burdensome. What sort of conduct on the part of the husband, would be allowed to have that effect, has been repeatedly considered. And it has not been found easy to lay down any iron rule upon the subject. In some cases it has been held that actual and repeated violence to the person, was not sufficient. In others that insults, indignities and neglect without any actual violence, were quite sufficient. So much does each case depend upon its peculiar surroundings.

We have sought the aid of the experience and wisdom of other times, and of other countries.

Blackstone says "that the husband, by the old law, might give the wife moderate correction, for as he was to answer for her misbehavior, he ought to have the power to control her; but that in the polite reign of Charles the Second, this power of correction began to be doubted." . . . The old law of moderate correction has been questioned even in England, and has been repudiated in Ireland and Scotland. The old rule is approved in Mississippi, but it has met with but little favor elsewhere in the United States. In looking into the discussions of the other States we find but little uniformity. . . .

Our conclusion is that family government is recognized by law as being as complete in itself as the State government is in itself, and yet subordinate to it; and that we will not interfere with or attempt to control it, in favor of either husband or wife, unless in cases where permanent or malicious injury is inflicted or threatened, or the condition of the party is intolerable. For, however great are the evils of ill temper, quarrels, and even personal conflicts inflicting only temporary pain, they are not comparable with the evils which would result from raising the curtain, and exposing to public curiosity and criticism, the nursery and the bed chamber. Every household has and must have, a government of its own, modeled to suit the temper, disposition and condition of its inmates. Mere ebullitions of passion, impulsive violence, and temporary pain, affection will soon forget and forgive; and each member will find excuse for the other in his own frailties. But when trifles are taken hold of by the public, and the parties are exposed and disgraced, and each endeavors to justify himself or herself by criminating the other, that which ought to be forgotten in a day, will be remembered for life.

It is urged in this case, that as there was no provocation the violence was of course excessive and malicious; that every one in whatever relation of life should be able to purchase immunity from pain, by obedience to authority and faithfulness in duty. . . . Take the case before us. The witness said, there was no provocation except some slight words. But then who can tell what significance the trifling words may have had to the husband? Who can tell what had happened an hour before, and every hour for a week? To him they may have been sharper than a sword. And so in every case, it might be impossible for the court to appreciate what might be offered as an excuse, or no excuse might appear at all, when a complete justification exists. Or, suppose the provocation could in every case be known, and the court should undertake to weigh the provocation in every trifling family broil, what would be the standard? Suppose a case coming up to us from a hovel, where neither delicacy of sentiment nor refinement of manners is appreciated or known. The parties themselves would be amazed, if they were to be held responsible for rudeness or trifling violence. What do they care for insults and indignities? In such cases what end would be gained by investigation or punishment? Take a case from the middle class, where modesty and purity have their abode but nevertheless have not immunity from the frailties of nature, and are sometimes moved by the mysteries of passion. What could be more harassing to them, or injurious to society, than to draw a crowd around their seclusion. Or take a case from the higher ranks, where education and culture have so refined nature, that a look cuts like a knife, and a word strikes like a hammer; where the most delicate attention gives pleasure, and the slightest neglect pain; where an indignity is disgrace and exposure is ruin. Bring all these cases into court side by side, with the same offence charged and the same proof made; and what conceivable charge of the court to the jury would be alike appropriate to all the cases, except, That they all have domestic government, which they have formed for themselves, suited to their own peculiar conditions, and that those governments are supreme, and from them there is no appeal except in cases of great importance requiring the strong arm of the law, and that to those governments they must submit themselves.

It will be observed that the ground upon which we have put this decision, is not, that the husband has the *right* to whip his wife much or little; but that we will not interfere with family government in trifling cases. We will no more interfere where the husband whips the wife, than where the wife whips the husband; and yet we would hardly be supposed to hold, that a wife has a *right* to whip her husband. We will not inflict upon society the greater evil of raising the curtain upon domestic privacy, to punish the lesser evil of trifling violence. Two boys under fourteen years of age fight upon the play-ground, and yet the courts will take no notice of it, not for the reason that boys have the *right* to fight, but because the interests of society require that they should be left to the more appropriate discipline of the school room and of home. . . . The standard is the *effect produced,* and not the manner of producing it, or the instrument used.

Because our opinion is not in unison with the decisions of some of the sister States, or with the philosophy of some very respectable law writers, and could not be in unison with all, because of their contrariety, — a decent respect for the opinions of others has induced us to be very full in stating the reasons for our conclusion.

REVA B. SIEGEL, *"THE RULE OF LOVE": WIFE BEATING AS PREROGATIVE AND PRIVACY*

105 Yale L.J. 2117 (1996)

. . . The Anglo-American common law originally provided that a husband, as master of his household, could subject his wife to corporal punishment or "chastisement" so long as he did not inflict permanent injury upon her. During the nineteenth century, an era of feminist agitation for reform of marriage law, authorities in England and the United States declared that a husband no longer had the right to chastise his wife. Yet, for a century after courts repudiated the right of chastisement, the American legal system continued to treat wife beating differently from other cases of assault and battery. While authorities denied that a husband had the right to beat his wife, they intervened only intermittently in cases of marital violence: Men who assaulted their wives were often granted formal and informal immunities from prosecution, in order to protect the privacy of the family and to promote "domestic harmony." In the late 1970s, the feminist movement began to challenge the concept of family privacy that shielded wife abuse, and since then, it has secured many reforms designed to protect women from marital violence. . . .

Until the late nineteenth century, Anglo-American common law structured marriage to give a husband superiority over his wife in most aspects of the relationship. By law, a husband acquired rights to his wife's person, the value of her paid and unpaid labor, and most property she brought into the marriage. A wife was obliged to obey and serve her husband, and the husband was subject to a reciprocal duty to support his wife and represent her within the legal system. . . .

As master of the household, a husband could command his wife's obedience, and subject her to corporal punishment or "chastisement" if she defied his authority. In his treatise on the English common law, Blackstone explained that a husband could "give his wife moderate correction." . . .

During the 1850s, woman's rights advocates organized numerous conventions throughout the Northeast and Midwest, published newspapers, and conducted petition campaigns seeking for women the right to vote and demanding various reforms of marriage law. And in time the movement did elicit a response. Legislatures and courts began to modify the common law of marital status — first giving wives the right to hold property in marriage, and then the right to their earnings and the rudiments of legal agency: the right to file suit in their own names and to claim contract and tort damages. . . .

. . . By the 1880s, prominent members of the American Bar Association advocated punishing wife beaters at the whipping post, and campaigned vigorously for legislation authorizing the penalty. Between 1876 and 1906, twelve states and the District of Columbia considered enacting legislation that provided for the punishment of wife beaters at the whipping post. The bills were enacted in Maryland (1882), Delaware (1901), and Oregon (1906). . . .

We are left with a striking portrait of legal change. Jurists and lawmakers emphatically repudiated the doctrine of marital chastisement, yet responded to marital violence erratically — often condoning it, and condemning it in circumstances suggesting little interest in the plight of battered wives. Given this record, how are we to make sense of chastisement's demise? . . .

A key concept in the doctrinal regime that emerged from chastisement's demise was the notion of marital privacy. During the antebellum era, courts began to invoke marital privacy as a supplementary rationale for chastisement, in order to justify the common law doctrine within the discourse of companionate marriage, when rationales rooted in authority-based discourses of marriage had begun to lose their persuasive power. . . .

To quote a North Carolina chastisement opinion:

> We know that a slap on the cheek, let it be as light as it may, indeed any touching of the person of another in a rude or angry manner — is in law an assault and battery. In the nature of things it cannot apply to persons in the marriage state, it would break down the great principle of mutual confidence and dependence; throw open the bedroom to the gaze of the public; and spread discord and misery, contention and strife, where peace and concord ought to reign. It must be remembered that rules of law are intended to act in all classes of society. . . .

In *Rhodes*, the defendant whipped his wife "three licks, with a switch about the size of one of his fingers (but not as large as a man's thumb)"; the trial court ruled that a husband had the right to chastise his wife and so was not guilty of assault and battery. On appeal, the North Carolina Supreme Court upheld the verdict but justified it on different grounds. Opening its opinion with the blunt observation that "[t]he violence complained of would without question have constituted a battery if the subject of it had not been the defendant's wife," the court explained why it would not find the defendant guilty:

> The courts have been loath to take cognizance of trivial complaints arising out of the domestic relations — such as master and apprentice, teacher and pupil, parent and child, husband and wife. Not because those relations are not subject to law, but because the evil of publicity would be greater than the evil involved

in the trifles complained of; and because they ought to be left to family government. . . .

. . . By now it should be clear enough how privacy talk was deployed in the domestic violence context to enforce and preserve authority relations between man and wife. . . .

. . . By the early twentieth century, numerous state supreme courts had barred wives from suing their husbands for intentional torts — typically on the grounds that "the tranquility of family relations" would be "disturb[ed]." . . .

It was not until the late 1970s that the contemporary women's rights movement mounted an effective challenge to this regime. Today, after numerous protest activities and law suits, there are shelters for battered women and their children, new arrest procedures for police departments across the country, and even federal legislation making gender-motivated assaults a civil rights violation. . . .

There is remarkably little scholarship on the social history of privacy discourses; consequently, we know very little about the ways in which conceptions of privacy shaped popular understandings of marriage, or marital violence, in the nineteenth century. But there is no reason to assume that, before demise of the chastisement prerogative, married persons understood a traditional prerogative of marriage, rooted in notions of a husband's authority as master and head of his household, in a framework of "privacy" and "domestic harmony." It seems just as likely that legal elites devised the story linking "privacy" and "domestic harmony" to wife beating in the wake of chastisement's demise (or in anticipation of it). . . .

CATHARINE A. MACKINNON, *TOWARD A FEMINIST THEORY OF THE STATE*

(1989)

The liberal ideal of the private holds that, as long as the public does not interfere, autonomous individuals interact freely and equally. Privacy is the ultimate value of the negative state. Conceptually, this private is hermetic. It means that which is inaccessible to, unaccountable to, unconstructed by, anything beyond itself. By definition, it is not part of or conditioned by anything systematic outside it. It is personal, intimate, autonomous, particular, individual, the original source and final outpost of the self, gender neutral. It is defined by everything that feminism reveals women have never been allowed to be or to have, and by everything that women have been equated with and defined in terms of men's ability to have. To complain in public of inequality within the private contradicts the liberal definition of the private. . . . Its inviolability by the state, framed as an individual right, presupposes that the private is not already an arm of the state. In this scheme, intimacy is implicitly thought to guarantee symmetry of power. Injuries arise through violation of the private sphere, not within and by and because of it.

In private, consent tends to be presumed. Showing coercion is supposed to avoid this presumption. But the problem is getting anything private to be perceived as coercive. This is an epistemic problem of major dimensions and explains why privacy doctrine is most at home at home, the place women experience the most force, in the family, and why it centers on sex. Why a person would "allow" force in private (the "why doesn't she leave" question raised to battered women) is a question given its insult by the social meaning of the private as a sphere of choice. For women the measure of the intimacy has been the measure of oppression. This is why feminism has seen the personal as the political. The private is public for those for whom the personal is political. In this sense, for women there is no private, either normatively or empirically. Feminism confronts the fact that women have no privacy to lose or to guarantee. Women are not inviolable. Women's sexuality is not only violable, it is — hence, women are — seen in and as their violation. To confront the fact that women have no privacy is to confront the intimate degradation of women as the public order. . . .

When the law of privacy restricts intrusions into intimacy, it bars changes in control over that intimacy through law. The existing distribution of power and resources within the private sphere are precisely what the law of privacy exists to protect. . . . [T]he legal concept of privacy can and has shielded the place of battery, marital rape, and women's exploited domestic labor. It has preserved the central institutions whereby women are deprived of identity, autonomy, control, and self-definition. It has protected a primary activity through which male supremacy is expressed and enforced. . . .

This right to privacy is a right of men "to be let alone" to oppress women one at a time. . . .

ANITA L. ALLEN, *UNEASY ACCESS: PRIVACY FOR WOMEN IN A FREE SOCIETY*

(1988)

Critiques of privacy such as MacKinnon's go wrong at the point where the historic unequal treatment of women and the misuse of the private household to further women's domination is taken as grounds for rejecting either the condition of privacy itself or the long-overdue legal rights to effective decisionmaking that promote and protect that condition. Privacy, here broadly defined as the inaccessibility of persons, their mental states, or information about them to the senses and surveillance devices of others . . . does not pose an inherent threat to women. Nor do sex, love, marriage, and children any longer presume the total abrogation of the forms of privacy a woman might otherwise enjoy. On the contrary, women today are finally in a position to expect, experience, and exploit real privacy within the home and within heterosexual relationships. The women's movement, education, access to affordable birth control, liberalized divorce laws, and the larger role for women in politics, government, and the economy have expanded women's opinions and contributed to the erosion of oppressively nonegalitarian styles of home life. These advances have enhanced the capacity of American men and women, but especially and for the first time women, to secure conditions of adequate and meaningful privacy at home paramount to moral personhood and responsible participation in families and larger segments of society. Instead of rejecting privacy as "male ideology" and subjugation, women can and ought to embrace opportunities for privacy and the exercise of reproductive liberty in their private lives.

NOTES & QUESTIONS

1. *Privacy and Gender.* As the *Rhodes* court stated in 1868: "We will not interfere with family government in trifling cases. We will no more interfere where the husband whips the wife, than where the wife whips the husband; and yet we would hardly be supposed to hold, that a wife has a *right* to whip her husband." Is this decision really a neutral one? Does the right to privacy described by Warren and Brandeis apply equally to men and women?[76]

2. *The Uses of the Public/Private Distinction.* Reva Siegel points out the troubling use of privacy to protect the oppression of women in the home, which Catharine MacKinnon has discussed at length elsewhere. Is MacKinnon's negative response to the public/private distinction justifiable given the prior uses of this distinction? Or do you agree with Anita Allen that privacy can and should not be abandoned as a value despite its checkered past?[77]

3. *To What Extent Can Law Change Social Practices?* According to Frances Olsen, "The notion of noninterference in the family depends upon some shared conception of proper family roles, and 'neutrality' [of the State] can be understood only with reference to such roles."[78] This idea suggests that privacy, within or without the family, might also depend on shared views as to proper social roles. Do you agree?

   Olsen also notes: "The theory of the private family, like free market theory, includes the assertion that particularized adjustments of seemingly unfair or inhumane results will not actually serve anybody's long run interests." Specifically, "it is claimed that state intervention to protect the weaker family members from abuse by the stronger is ineffective because powerful, underlying 'real' relations between family members will inevitably reassert themselves." This argument, which one might term the argument from futility, was rejected in the course of the twentieth century by the powerful social movement to stop spousal abuse and mistreatment of children. Are similar arguments from futility being made today about the "inevitable" erosion of privacy?

---

[76] For a feminist critique of the Warren and Brandeis article, see Anita L. Allen & Erin Mack, *How Privacy Got Its Gender*, 10 N. Ill. U. L. Rev. 441 (1990).

[77] For an overview of the feminist critique of privacy, see generally Judith W. DeCew, *In Pursuit of Privacy: Law, Ethics, and the Rise of Technology* 81-94 (1997); Patricia Boling, *Privacy and the Politics of Intimate Life* (1996); Frances Olsen, *Constitutional Law: Feminist Critiques of the Public/Private Distinction*, 10 Const. Commentary 327 (1993); Ruth Gavison, *Feminism and the Public/Private Distinction*, 45 Stan. L. Rev. 21 (1992).

[78] Frances Olsen, *The Family and the Market: A Study of Ideology and Legal Reform*, 96 Harv. L. Rev. 1497, 1506 (1983).

CHAPTER 2

PRIVACY AND LAW ENFORCEMENT

A. THE FOURTH AMENDMENT AND EMERGING TECHNOLOGY

1. INTRODUCTION

(a) Privacy and Security

One of the central tensions in information privacy law is between privacy and security. Security involves society's interest in protecting its citizens from crimes, including physical and monetary threats. One way that government promotes security is by investigating and punishing crimes. To do this, law enforcement officials must gather information about suspected individuals. Monitoring and information gathering pose substantial threats to privacy. At the same time, however, monitoring and information gathering offer the potential of increasing security. Throughout the twentieth century, technology provided the government significantly greater ability to probe into the private lives of individuals.

The prevailing metaphor for the threat to privacy caused by law enforcement surveillance techniques is George Orwell's novel *Nineteen Eighty-Four*. Written in 1949, the novel depicted an all-powerful and omniscient government called "Big Brother" that monitored and controlled every facet of individuals' lives:

> Outside, even through the shut window-pane, the world looked cold. Down in the street little eddies of wind were whirling dust and torn paper into spirals, and though the sun was shining and the sky a harsh blue, there seemed to be no colour in anything, except the posters that were plastered everywhere. The black moustachio'd face gazed down from every commanding corner. There was one on the house-front immediately opposite. BIG BROTHER IS WATCHING YOU, the caption said, while the dark eyes looked deep into Winston's own. Down at streetlevel another poster, torn at one corner, flapped fitfully in the wind, alternately covering and uncovering the single word INGSOC. In the far distance a helicopter skimmed down between the roofs, hovered for an instant like a bluebottle, and darted away again with a curving flight. It was the police patrol, snooping into people's windows. The patrols did not matter, however. Only the Thought Police mattered.

> Behind Winston's back the voice from the telescreen was still babbling away about pig-iron and the overfulfilment of the Ninth Three-Year Plan. The telescreen received and transmitted simultaneously. Any sound that Winston made, above the level of a very low whisper, would be picked up by it, moreover, so long as he remained within the field of vision which the metal plaque commanded, he could be seen as well as heard. There was of course no way of knowing whether you were being watched at any given moment. How often, or on what system, the Thought Police plugged in on any individual wire was guesswork. It was even conceivable that they watched everybody all the time. But at any rate they could plug in your wire whenever they wanted to. You had to live — did live, from habit that became instinct — in the assumption that every sound you made was overheard, and, except in darkness, every movement scrutinized.[1]

Orwell's harrowing portrait of a police state illustrates the importance of limiting the power of the government to monitor its citizens. But consider the reverse as well: Will overly restrictive limitations on the power of the police restrict their ability to protect the public?

Although privacy and security may at times be viewed in conflict, consider the opening words of the Fourth Amendment: "The right of the people to be *secure* in their persons, houses, papers, and effects . . ." (emphasis added). Are the interests in public security and privacy fated to be always at odds? Are there times when the opposition between security and privacy proves a false dichotomy?

(b) The Fourth and Fifth Amendments

In the United States, policing is predominantly carried out by local governments. The Constitution, however, provides a national regulatory regime for police conduct. The Fourth and Fifth Amendments significantly limit the government's power to gather information. The Fourth Amendment provides:

> The right of the people to be secure in their persons, houses, papers, and effects, against unreasonable searches and seizures, shall not be violated, and no warrants shall issue, but upon probable cause, supported by oath or affirmation, and particularly describing the place to be searched, and the persons or things to be seized.

As the Supreme Court has recognized, "[t]he overriding function of the Fourth Amendment is to protect personal privacy and dignity against unwarranted intrusion by the State." *Schmerber v. California*, 384 U.S. 757 (1966).

The Fifth Amendment guarantees that "[n]o person . . . shall be compelled in any criminal case to be a witness against himself. . . ." The Fifth Amendment establishes a "privilege against self-incrimination," and it prohibits the government from compelling individuals to disclose inculpatory information about themselves.

The Fifth Amendment does not apply to all incriminating statements, but to information that is compelled. Further, the information must be "testimonial" in nature, and the Court has held that the Fifth Amendment does not apply to fin-

---

[1] George Orwell, *Nineteen Eighty-Four* 3-4 (1949).

gerprinting, photographing, taking measurements, writing or speaking for identification purposes, and having blood or bodily fluids drawn and tested. *See Schmerber v. California*, 384 U.S. 757 (1966). Finally, the Fifth Amendment does not protect broadly against prying into private secrets; it is limited to information that is incriminating.[2]

(c) Privacy of the Mail

In *Ex Parte Jackson,* 96 U.S. 727 (1877), one of its earliest Fourth Amendment cases, the Supreme Court held that the Fourth Amendment required a warrant to search sealed letters sent via the U.S. Postal Service:

> The constitutional guaranty of the right of the people to be secure in their persons against unreasonable searches and seizures extends to their papers, thus closed against inspection, wherever they may be. Whilst in the mail, they can only be opened and examined under like warrant, issued upon similar oath or affirmation, particularly describing the thing to be seized, as is required when papers are subjected to search in one's own household.

Although the Fourth Amendment protects the contents of a sealed letter, it does not protect the outside of letters, where addressing of information is typically located. As the Court noted in *Ex Parte Jackson,* "the outward form and weight" of letters and sealed packages are unprotected by the Fourth Amendment. Modern caselaw follows this distinction.

Today, federal law also restricts the government's ability to search people's mail. Pursuant to 39 U.S.C. §3623(d):

> No letter of such a class of domestic origin shall be opened except under authority of a search warrant authorized by law, or by an officer or employee of the Postal Service for the sole purpose of determining an address at which the letter can be delivered, or pursuant to the authorization of the addressee.

However, the government can search letters sent from abroad. *See United States v. Various Articles of Obscene Merchandise, Schedule No. 1213,* 395 F. Supp. 791 (S.D.N.Y. 1975), *aff'd,* 538 F.2d 317.

(d) Privacy of Papers and Documents

In *Boyd v. United States*, 116 U.S. 616 (1886), one of the foundational cases defining the meaning of the Fourth and Fifth Amendments, the government issued a subpoena to compel Boyd, a merchant, to produce invoices on cases of imported glass for use in a civil forfeiture proceeding. The Court held that the subpoena violated the Fourth and Fifth Amendments:

---

[2] For more background about the Fifth Amendment, see R. Kent Greenawalt, *Silence as a Moral and Constitutional Right*, 23 Wm. & Mary L. Rev. 15 (1981); Stephen J. Schulhofer, *Some Kind Words for the Privilege Against Self-Incrimination*, 26 Val. U. L. Rev. 311 (1991); William J. Stuntz, *Self-Incrimination and Excuse*, 99 Colum. L. Rev. 1227 (1988); David Donlinko, *Is There a Rationale for the Privilege Against Self-Incrimination?*, 33 UCLA L. Rev. 1063 (1986); Donald A. Dripps, *Self-Incrimination and Self-Preservation: A Skeptical View*, 1991 U. Ill. L. Rev. 329; Michael Dann, *The Fifth Amendment Privilege Against Self-Incrimination: Extorting Evidence from a Suspect*, 43 S. Cal. L. Rev. 597 (1970).

. . . [B]y the proceeding now under consideration, the court attempts to extort from the party his private books and papers to make him liable for a penalty or to forfeit his property. . . .

. . . It is not the breaking of his doors, and the rummaging of his drawers, that constitutes the essence of the offence; but it is the invasion of his indefeasible right to personal security, personal liberty and private property, where the right has never been forfeited by his conviction of some public offence. . . . Breaking into a house and opening boxes and drawers are circumstances of aggravation; but any forcible and compulsory extortion of a man's own testimony or of his private papers to be used as evidence to convict him of crime or to forfeit his goods, is within the condemnation of that judgment. In this regard the Fourth and Fifth Amendments run almost into each other.

In *Gouled v. United States*, 255 U.S. 298 (1921), the Court held that law enforcement officials could not use search warrants to search a person's "house or office or papers" to obtain evidence to use against her in a criminal proceeding. The holdings of *Boyd* and *Gouled* became known as the "mere evidence" rule — the government could only seize papers if they were instrumentalities of a crime, fruits of a crime, or illegal contraband.

The holding in *Boyd* has been significantly cut back. In *Warden v. Hayden*, 387 U.S. 294 (1967), the Court abolished the mere evidence rule. As the Court currently interprets the Fifth Amendment, the government can require a person to produce papers and records. *See Shapiro v. United States*, 335 U.S. 1 (1948). The Fifth Amendment also does not protect against subpoenas for a person's records and papers held by third parties. In *Couch v. United States*, 409 U.S. 322 (1973), the Court upheld a subpoena to a person's accountant for documents because "the Fifth Amendment privilege is a personal privilege: it adheres basically to the person, not to information that may incriminate him." The Fifth Amendment, the Court reasoned, only prevents "[i]nquisitorial pressure or coercion against a potentially accused person, compelling her, against her will, to utter self-condemning words or produce incriminating documents." Similarly, in *Fisher v. United States*, 425 U.S. 391 (1976), the Court upheld a subpoena to a person's attorney for documents pertaining to that person. The Fifth Amendment is not a "general protector of privacy" but protects against the "compelled self-incrimination."

(e) The Applicability of the Fourth Amendment

The Fourth Amendment governs the investigatory power of government officials. It applies every time a government official (not just police) conducts a "search" or the "seizure" of an object or document. Some examples of "searches" include peeking into one's pockets or searching one's person; entering into and looking around one's house, apartment, office, hotel room, or private property; and opening up and examining the contents of one's luggage or parcels. A "seizure" is a taking away of items by the police. A seizure can be of physical things or of persons (arrests). There must be a search or seizure to invoke the protection of the Fourth Amendment.

The Fourth Amendment does not apply simply when the police happen to observe something in "plain view." Whatever law enforcement officials see in plain view is not covered by the protection of the Fourth Amendment. Thus, the initial issue in Fourth Amendment analysis is whether the Amendment applies in the first place.[3]

(f) Reasonable Searches and Seizures

If the Fourth Amendment applies, then it requires that the search be "reasonable." Generally, a search is reasonable if the police have obtained a valid search warrant. To obtain a warrant, the police must go before a judge or magistrate and demonstrate that they have "probable cause" to conduct a search or seizure. Probable cause requires that government officials have "reasonably trustworthy information" that is sufficient to "warrant a man of reasonable caution in the belief that an offense has been or is being committed" or that evidence will be found in the place to be searched. *Brinegar v. United States*, 338 U.S. 160 (1949). Probable cause is more than "bare suspicion." Probable cause must be measured on a case-by-case basis, via the facts of particular cases. *See Wong Sun v. United States*, 371 U.S. 471 (1963). The purpose of a warrant is to have an independent party (judges) ensure that police really do have probable cause to conduct a search.

A search is valid if the warrant is supported by probable cause and the search is within the scope of the warrant. A warrantless search is generally considered to be per se unreasonable; however, there are a number of exceptions to this rule. Under these exceptions, a search is valid even if a warrant was not obtained as long as there was probable cause. For example, a search is not unreasonable if consent is obtained. When exigent circumstances make obtaining a warrant impractical, certain warrantless searches are reasonable.

Even with a warrant, certain searches are unreasonable. For example, in *Winston v. Lee*, 470 U.S. 753 (1985), the removal of a bullet lodged deep in the accused's chest was deemed unreasonable. However, the Court concluded that the taking of blood from a suspect constituted a reasonable search. *See Schmerber v. California*, 384 U.S. 757 (1966).[4]

(g) The "Special Needs" Doctrine

Under certain circumstances, the Fourth Amendment does not require government officials to have a warrant or probable cause to conduct a search. Pursuant to the "special needs" doctrine, searches and seizures are reasonable without a warrant or probable cause if "special needs, beyond the normal need for law enforcement, make the warrant and probable-cause requirement impracticable."

---

[3] There have been extensive writings about the Fourth Amendment's function of protecting privacy. For some background, see Christopher Slobogin, *The World Without a Fourth Amendment*, 39 UCLA L. Rev. 1 (1991); Silas J. Wasserstrom & Louis Michael Seidman, *The Fourth Amendment as Constitutional Theory*, 77 Geo. L.J. 19, 34 (1988); William J. Stuntz, *Privacy's Problem and the Law of Criminal Procedure*, 93 Mich. L. Rev. 1016 (1995); Scott E. Sundby, *"Everyman's" Fourth Amendment: Privacy or Mutual Trust Between Government and Citizen?*, 94 Colum. L. Rev. 1751 (1994); John Kent Walker, Jr., Note, *Covert Searches*, 39 Stan. L. Rev. 545 (1987).

[4] For more background about the Fourth Amendment's requirement of "reasonableness," see Sherry F. Colb, *The Qualitative Dimension of Fourth Amendment "Reasonableness,"* 98 Colum. L. Rev. 1642 (1998); Tracey Maclin, *Constructing Fourth Amendment Principles from the Government Perspective: Whose Amendment Is It, Anyway?*, 25 Am. Crim. L. Rev. 669 (1988).

Griffin v. Wisconsin, 483 U.S. 868 (1987). "The validity of a search is judged by the standard of 'reasonableness . . . under all the circumstances.'" *O'Connor v. Ortega*, 480 U.S. 709 (1987).

The special needs doctrine applies to searches in schools, government workplaces, and certain highly regulated businesses. As an example, the Supreme Court has upheld random drug tests for high school students participating in any competitive extracurricular activities, including academic extracurricular activities. *Board of Education v. Earls*, 536 U.S. 822 (2002). The special needs doctrine applies only when a search is not for a law enforcement purpose. Thus, in *New Jersey v. T.L.O.*, the Court upheld a search of a student's purse by school officials and noted that the search was "carried out by school authorities acting alone and on their own authority" as opposed to searches that might be conducted "in conjunction with or at the behest of law enforcement officials." *New Jersey v. T.L.O*, 469 U.S. 337 (1985).

(h) Administrative Searches

Generally, the need to inspect homes for health and safety violations is outweighed by the individual's privacy interest. *See Camara v. Municipal Court*, 387 U.S. 523 (1967) (holding that warrantless inspections of residences for housing code violations were unreasonable); *See v. City of Seattle*, 387 U.S. 541 (1967) (holding that search of a warehouse for fire code violations was unreasonable).

(i) Checkpoints

The police cannot randomly stop cars to check license and registration. *See Delaware v. Prouse*, 440 U.S. 648 (1979). However, fixed sobriety checkpoints are constitutional. *See Michigan Dep't of State Police v. Sitz*, 496 U.S. 444 (1990). Such a checkpoint search does not require "particularized suspicion." On the other hand, in *Indianapolis v. Edmond*, 531 U.S. 32 (2000), the Court held that checkpoints established to investigate possible drug violations were indistinguishable from a general purpose crime control search and were therefore unconstitutional:

> We have never approved a checkpoint program whose primary purpose was to detect evidence of ordinary criminal wrongdoing. Rather, our checkpoint cases have recognized only limited exceptions to the general rule that a seizure must be accompanied by some measure of individualized suspicion. We suggested in *Prouse* that we would not credit the "general interest in crime control" as justification for a regime of suspicionless stops. Consistent with this suggestion, each of the checkpoint programs that we have approved was designed primarily to serve purposes closely related to the problems of policing the border or the necessity of ensuring roadway safety. Because the primary purpose of the Indianapolis narcotics checkpoint program is to uncover evidence of ordinary criminal wrongdoing, the program contravenes the Fourth Amendment. . . .

The Supreme Court in *Illinois v. Lidster*, 540 U.S. 419 (2004), upheld the constitutionality of so-called "information-seeking highway stops." Following a hit-and-run accident that killed a 70-year-old bicyclist, the police in Lombard,

Illinois set up a checkpoint at the approximate scene of the accident. The police stopped vehicles, asked the occupants of the car whether they had seen anything the previous weekend, and gave each driver a flyer that described the fatal accident and asked for assistance in identifying the vehicle and driver in the accident. The Supreme Court found that "special law enforcement concerns will sometimes justify highway stops without individualized suspicion." It also found that the stop in question was reasonable as well as constitutional. First, the "relevant public concern was grave," involving police investigation of a human death. Second, the stop advanced the grave public concern to a significant degree. "The police appropriately tailored their checkpoint stops to fit important criminal investigatory needs." Third, and "[m]ost importantly, the stops interfered only minimally with liberty of the sort the Fourth Amendment seeks to protect." As the *Lidster* Court concluded: "Viewed objectively each stop required only a brief wait in line — a very few minutes at most. Contact with the police lasted only a few seconds. . . . Viewed subjectively, the contact provided little reason for anxiety or alarm."

In *MacWade v. Kelly*, 460 F.3d 260 (2d Cir. 2006), the New York Police Department instituted a random search program in the subways following a bombing on a subway in London. Police searched people's bags and other items as they entered subway stations. Those wishing not to be searched could leave the station. The court upheld the program under a Fourth Amendment challenge:

> Although a subway rider enjoys a full privacy expectation in the contents of his baggage, the kind of search at issue here minimally intrudes upon that interest. Several uncontested facts establish that the Program is narrowly tailored to achieve its purpose: (1) passengers receive notice of the searches and may decline to be searched so long as they leave the subway; (2) police search only those containers capable of concealing explosives, inspect eligible containers only to determine whether they contain explosives, inspect the containers visually unless it is necessary to manipulate their contents, and do not read printed or written material or request personal information; (3) a typical search lasts only for a matter of seconds; (4) uniformed personnel conduct the searches out in the open, which reduces the fear and stigma that removal to a hidden area can cause; and (5) police exercise no discretion in selecting whom to search, but rather employ a formula that ensures they do not arbitrarily exercise their authority. . . . .
>
> [W]e need only determine whether the Program is "a reasonably effective means of addressing" the government interest in deterring and detecting a terrorist attack on the subway system.
>
> We will not peruse, parse, or extrapolate four months' worth of data in an attempt to divine how many checkpoints the City ought to deploy in the exercise of its day-to-day police power. Counter-terrorism experts and politically accountable officials have undertaken the delicate and esoteric task of deciding how best to marshal their available resources in light of the conditions prevailing on any given day.

(j) *Terry* Stops

In *Terry v. Ohio,* 392 U.S. 1 (1968), the Court carved out another exception to warrants and probable cause. The Court held that a police officer can "stop" an individual if the officer has "reasonable suspicion" that criminal activity is afoot. "Reasonable suspicion" is a standard that is lower than probable cause. A stop must be brief or temporary. If it lasts too long, it becomes a seizure, which requires probable cause. During the stop, the officer may "frisk" an individual for weapons if the officer has reasonable suspicion that the person is armed and dangerous. A frisk is not a full search. The officer cannot search the person for other items — only weapons. If, in the course of searching a person for weapons, the officer finds evidence of a crime, it will still be admissible if it was found within the scope of a valid frisk. For example, in *Minnesota v. Dickerson,* 508 U.S. 366 (1993), a police officer was searching a suspect for weapons and felt an object in the suspect's pocket. The officer did not believe it to be a weapon, but continued to inspect it. The Court concluded that this was an invalid search that extended beyond the limited confines of a frisk.

(k) The Enforcement of the Fourth Amendment

When law enforcement officials violate an individual's Fourth Amendment rights, the individual can seek at least two forms of redress. First, if the individual is a defendant in a criminal trial, she can move to have the evidence obtained in violation of the Fourth Amendment suppressed. This is known as the "exclusionary rule." In *Weeks v. United States,* 232 U.S. 383 (1914), the Court established the exclusionary rule as the way to enforce the Fourth Amendment on federal officials. Later, in *Mapp v. Ohio,* 367 U.S. 643 (1961), the Court held that the exclusionary rule applies to all government searches, whether state or federal. The purpose of the exclusionary rule is to deter law enforcement officials from violating the Constitution.

If the police illegally search or seize evidence in violation of the Constitution, not only is that evidence suppressed but all other evidence derived from the illegally obtained evidence is also suppressed. This is known as the "fruit of the poisonous tree" doctrine. For example, suppose the police illegally search a person's luggage and find evidence that the person is a drug trafficker. Armed with that evidence, the police obtain a warrant to search the person's home, where they uncover new evidence of drug-trafficking along with a weapon used in a murder. The person is charged with drug trafficking and murder. Under the Fourth Amendment, the evidence found in the person's luggage will be suppressed. Additionally, since the search warrant could not have been obtained but for the evidence turned up in the illegal search, the evidence found at the house, including the additional drug trafficking evidence as well as the murder evidence, will be suppressed. However, if the police obtained a warrant or located evidence by an "independent source," then the fruit of the poisonous tree doctrine does not apply. *See Silverthorne Lumber Co. v. United States,* 251 U.S. 385 (1920). Returning to the example above, if the police had evidence supplied from the person's cohort that the person was engaged in drug trafficking out of his home and had murdered somebody, this evidence may suffice to give the police probable cause to have a warrant issued to search the person's house. This evidence is independent from the illegal search, and it is admissible.[5]

---

[5] The exclusionary rule has received significant scholarly attention. A number of scholars question its efficacy and advocate that the Fourth Amendment be enforced through other

The second form of redress for a violation of the Fourth Amendment is a civil remedy. A person, whether a criminal defendant or anybody else, can obtain civil damages for a Fourth Amendment violation by way of 42 U.S.C. § 1983.

2. WIRETAPPING, BUGGING, AND BEYOND

At common law, eavesdropping was considered a nuisance. "Eavesdropping" as William Blackstone defined it, meant to "listen under walls or window, or the eaves of a house, to hearken after discourse, and thereupon to frame slanderous and mischievous tales."[6] Before the advent of electronic communication, people could easily avoid eavesdroppers by ensuring that nobody else was around during their conversations.

The invention of the telegraph in 1844 followed by the telephone in 1876 substantially altered the way people communicated with each other. Today, the telephone has become an essential part of everyday communications. The advent of electronic communications was soon followed by the invention of recording and transmitting devices that enabled new and more sophisticated forms of eavesdropping than overhearing a conversation with the naked ear. One feature of electronic surveillance is that unlike the unsealing of letters, the interception of communications is undetectable. Some of the current forms of electronic surveillance technology include wiretaps, bugs, and parabolic microphones. New legal questions are raised by modern technology such as a cell phone, which can provide information about the physical location of the person using it.

A "wiretap" is a device used to intercept telephone (or telegraph) communications. Wiretapping began before the invention of the telephone. Wiretapping was used to intercept telegraph communications during the Civil War and became very prevalent after the invention of the telephone. The first police wiretap occurred in the early 1890s. In the first half of the twentieth century, wiretaps proliferated due to law enforcement attempts to monitor protests over bad industrial working conditions, social unrest caused by World War I, and the smuggling of alcohol during the Prohibition Years.[7]

A "bug" is a device, often quite miniature in size, that can be hidden on a person or in a place that can transmit conversations in a room to a remote receiving device, where the conversation can be listened to.

A "parabolic microphone" can pick up a conversation from a distance. Typically, a small dish behind the microphone enables the amplification of sound far away from the microphone itself.

---

mechanisms such as civil sanctions. *See* Akhil Reed Amar, *The Constitution and Criminal Procedure* 28 (1997); Christopher Slobogin, *Why Liberals Should Chuck the Exclusionary Rule,* 1999 U. Ill. L. Rev. 363, 400-01 (1999). Other commentators contend that civil sanctions will be ineffective. *See* Arnold H. Loewy, *The Fourth Amendment as a Device for Protecting the Innocent,* 81 Mich. L. Rev. 1229, 1266 (1983); Tracey Maclin, *When the Cure for the Fourth Amendment Is Worse Than the Disease,* 68 S. Cal. L. Rev. 1, 62 (1994).

[6] 4 Blackstone, *Commentaries* 168 (1769).

[7] For more background on the history of wiretapping, see generally Robert Ellis Smith, *Ben Franklin's Web Site: Privacy and Curiosity from Plymouth Rock to the Internet* (2000); Priscilla M. Regan, *Legislating Privacy: Technology, Social Values, and Public Policy* (1995); James G. Carr, *The Law of Electronic Surveillance* (1994); Whitfield Diffie & Susan Landau, *Privacy on the Line: The Politics of Wiretapping and Encryption* (1998).

Electronic surveillance devices were not in existence at the time that the Fourth Amendment was drafted. How, then, should the Fourth Amendment regulate these devices? In 1928, the Supreme Court attempted to answer this question in *Olmstead v. United States*, the first electronic surveillance case to come before the Court.

OLMSTEAD V. UNITED STATES
277 U.S. 438 (1928)

TAFT, C. J. The petitioners were convicted in the District Court for the Western District of Washington of a conspiracy to violate the National Prohibition Act by unlawfully possessing, transporting and importing intoxicating liquors and maintaining nuisances, and by selling intoxicating liquors. Seventy-two others, in addition to the petitioners, were indicted. Some were not apprehended, some were acquitted, and others pleaded guilty. . . .

The information which led to the discovery of the conspiracy and its nature and extent was largely obtained by intercepting messages on the telephones of the conspirators by four federal prohibition officers. Small wires were inserted along the ordinary telephone wires from the residences of four of the petitioners and those leading from the chief office. The insertions were made without trespass upon any property of the defendants. They were made in the basement of the large office building. The taps from house lines were made in the streets near the houses. . . .

The well-known historical purpose of the Fourth Amendment, directed against general warrants and writs of assistance, was to prevent the use of governmental force to search a man's house, his person, his papers, and his effects, and to prevent their seizure against his will. This phase of the misuse of governmental power of compulsion is the emphasis of the opinion of the court in the *Boyd* Case. . . .

. . . The Fourth Amendment may have proper application to a sealed letter in the mail, because of the constitutional provision for the Postoffice Department and the relations between the government and those who pay to secure protection of their sealed letters. . . . It is plainly within the words of the amendment to say that the unlawful rifling by a government agent of a sealed letter is a search and seizure of the sender's papers or effects. The letter is a paper, an effect, and in the custody of a government that forbids carriage, except under its protection.

The United States takes no such care of telegraph or telephone messages as of mailed sealed letters. The amendment does not forbid what was done here. There was no searching. There was no seizure. The evidence was secured by the use of the sense of hearing and that only. There was no entry of the houses or offices of the defendants. . . .

The language of the amendment cannot be extended and expanded to include telephone wires, reaching to the whole world from the defendant's house or office. The intervening wires are not part of his house or office, any more than are the highways along which they are stretched. . . .

Congress may, of course, protect the secrecy of telephone messages by making them, when intercepted, inadmissible in evidence in federal criminal trials, by direct legislation, and thus depart from the common law of evidence. But the courts may not adopt such a policy by attributing an enlarged and unusual meaning to the Fourth Amendment. The reasonable view is that one who installs in his house a telephone instrument with connecting wires intends to project his voice to those quite outside, and that the wires beyond his house, and messages while passing over them, are not within the protection of the Fourth Amendment. Here those who intercepted the projected voices were not in the house of either party to the conversation. . . .

BRANDEIS, J. dissenting. The government makes no attempt to defend the methods employed by its officers. Indeed, it concedes that, if wire tapping can be deemed a search and seizure within the Fourth Amendment, such wire tapping as was practiced in the case at bar was an unreasonable search and seizure, and that the evidence thus obtained was inadmissible. But it relies on the language of the amendment, and it claims that the protection given thereby cannot properly be held to include a telephone conversation.

"We must never forget," said Mr. Chief Justice Marshall in *McCulloch v. Maryland*, "that it is a Constitution we are expounding." Since then this court has repeatedly sustained the exercise of power by Congress, under various clauses of that instrument, over objects of which the fathers could not have dreamed. We have likewise held that general limitations on the powers of government, like those embodied in the due process clauses of the Fifth and Fourteenth Amendments, do not forbid the United States or the states from meeting modern conditions by regulations which "a century ago, or even half a century ago, probably would have been rejected as arbitrary and oppressive." Clauses guaranteeing to the individual protection against specific abuses of power, must have a similar capacity of adaptation to a changing world. It was with reference to such a clause that this court said in *Weems v. United States*, 217 U.S. 349, 373:

> Legislation, both statutory and constitutional, is enacted, it is true, from an experience of evils, but its general language should not, therefore, be necessarily confined to the form that evil had theretofore taken. Time works changes, brings into existence new conditions and purposes. Therefore a principle to be vital must be capable of wider application than the mischief which gave it birth. This is peculiarly true of Constitutions. They are not ephemeral enactments, designed to meet passing occasions. They are, to use the words of Chief Justice Marshall, "designed to approach immortality as nearly as human institutions can approach it." The future is their care and provision for events of good and bad tendencies of which no prophecy can be made. In the application of a Constitution, therefore, our contemplation cannot be only of what has been but of what may be. Under any other rule a Constitution would indeed be as easy of application as it would be deficient in efficacy and power. Its general principles would have little value and be converted by precedent into impotent and lifeless formulas. Rights declared in words might be lost in reality.

When the Fourth and Fifth Amendments were adopted, "the form that evil had theretofore taken" had been necessarily simple. Force and violence were then the only means known to man by which a government could directly effect self-incrimination. It could compel the individual to testify — a compulsion effected, if need be, by torture. It could secure possession of his papers and other articles incident to his private life — a seizure effected, if need be, by breaking and entry. Protection against such invasion of "the sanctities of a man's home and the privacies of life" was provided in the Fourth and Fifth Amendments by specific language. *Boyd v. United States*, 116 U.S. 616 (1886). But "time works changes, brings into existence new conditions and purposes." Subtler and more far-reaching means of invading privacy have become available to the government. Discovery and invention have made it possible for the government, by means far more effective than stretching upon the rack, to obtain disclosure in court of what is whispered in the closet.

Moreover, "in the application of a Constitution, our contemplation cannot be only of what has been, but of what may be." The progress of science in furnishing the government with means of espionage is not likely to stop with wire tapping. Ways may some day be developed by which the government, without removing papers from secret drawers, can reproduce them in court, and by which it will be enabled to expose to a jury the most intimate occurrences of the home. Advances in the psychic and related sciences may bring means of exploring unexpressed beliefs, thoughts and emotions. "That places the liberty of every man in the hands of every petty officer" was said by James Otis of much lesser intrusions than these. To Lord Camden a far slighter intrusion seemed "subversive of all the comforts of society." Can it be that the Constitution affords no protection against such invasions of individual security?

A sufficient answer is found in *Boyd v. United States*, 116 U.S. 616 (1886), a case that will be remembered as long as civil liberty lives in the United States. This court there reviewed the history that lay behind the Fourth and Fifth Amendments. We said with reference to Lord Camden's judgment in *Entick v. Carrington*, 19 Howell's State Trials, 1030:

> The principles laid down in this opinion affect the very essence of constitutional liberty and security. They reach farther than the concrete form of the case there before the court, with its adventitious circumstances; they apply to all invasions on the part of the government and its employees of the sanctities of a man's home and the privacies of life. It is not the breaking of his doors, and the rummaging of his drawers, that constitutes the essence of the offense; but it is the invasion of his indefeasible right of personal security, personal liberty and private property, where that right has never been forfeited by his conviction of some public offense — it is the invasion of this sacred right which underlies and constitutes the essence of Lord Camden's judgment. Breaking into a house and opening boxes and drawers are circumstances of aggravation; but any forcible and compulsory extortion of a man's own testimony or of his private papers to be used as evidence of a crime or to forfeit his goods, is within the condemnation of that judgment. In this regard the Fourth and Fifth Amendments run almost into each other.

In *Ex parte Jackson*, 96 U.S. 727 (1877), it was held that a sealed letter entrusted to the mail is protected by the amendments. The mail is a public service furnished by the government. The telephone is a public service furnished by its authority. There is, in essence, no difference between the sealed letter and the private telephone message. . . .

The evil incident to invasion of the privacy of the telephone is far greater than that involved in tampering with the mails. Whenever a telephone line is tapped, the privacy of the persons at both ends of the line is invaded, and all conversations between them upon any subject, and although proper, confidential, and privileged, may be overheard. Moreover, the tapping of one man's telephone line involves the tapping of the telephone of every other person whom he may call, or who may call him. As a means of espionage, writs of assistance and general warrants are but puny instruments of tyranny and oppression when compared with wire tapping.

Time and again this court, in giving effect to the principle underlying the Fourth Amendment, has refused to place an unduly literal construction upon it. . .

The protection guaranteed by the amendments is much broader in scope. The makers of our Constitution undertook to secure conditions favorable to the pursuit of happiness. They recognized the significance of man's spiritual nature, of his feelings and of his intellect. They knew that only a part of the pain, pleasure and satisfactions of life are to be found in material things. They sought to protect Americans in their beliefs, their thoughts, their emotions and their sensations. They conferred, as against the government, the right to be let alone — the most comprehensive of rights and the right most valued by civilized men. To protect that right, every unjustifiable intrusion by the government upon the privacy of the individual, whatever the means employed, must be deemed a violation of the Fourth Amendment. And the use, as evidence in a criminal proceeding, of facts ascertained by such intrusion must be deemed a violation of the Fifth.

Applying to the Fourth and Fifth Amendments the established rule of construction, the defendants' objections to the evidence obtained by wire tapping must, in my opinion, be sustained. It is, of course, immaterial where the physical connection with the telephone wires leading into the defendants' premises was made. And it is also immaterial that the intrusion was in aid of law enforcement. Experience should teach us to be most on our guard to protect liberty when the government's purposes are beneficent. Men born to freedom are naturally alert to repel invasion of their liberty by evil-minded rulers. The greatest dangers to liberty lurk in insidious encroachment by men of zeal, well-meaning but without understanding. . . .

NOTES & QUESTIONS

1. *Background and Epilogue.* Roy Olmstead, known as the "King of Bootleggers," ran a gigantic illegal alcohol distribution operation on the Pacific Coast during Prohibition. Formerly a police officer, Olmstead had long avoided trouble with state police by bribing them, but federal officials soon caught up with him. The federal investigators, led by Roy Lyle, Director of Prohibition, were wiretapping all of the telephones in Olmstead's home for around five months. The case was widely followed in the press, and it was dubbed "the case of the whispering wires." Olmstead was careful not to leave evidence in his very large home; when the agents searched it, they turned up no evidence. Most of the evidence in the case came from the wiretaps.

Olmstead knew he was being wiretapped; he had been tipped off by a freelance wiretapper the government had hired. But Olmstead believed that because wiretapping was illegal in the state of Washington, the wiretap evidence could not be used against him at trial. He was wrong. At trial, Olmstead was convicted and sentenced to four years in prison. He was later pardoned by President Roosevelt in 1935. In an ironic twist, while Olmstead was in prison, Roy Lyle was arrested for conspiring with rumrunners. Olmstead testified against Lyle at Lyle's trial. While in prison, Olmstead became a Christian Scientist, and after his release, he repudiated alcohol as one of the ills of society.[8]

2. *The Physical Trespass Doctrine, Detectaphones, and "Spike Mikes."* In *Olmstead,* the Supreme Court concluded that Fourth Amendment protections are triggered only when there is a physical trespass. The Court followed this approach for nearly 40 years. In *Goldman v. United States*, 316 U.S. 129 (1942), the police placed a device called a "detectaphone" next to a wall adjacent to a person's office. The device enabled the police to listen in on conversations inside the office. The Court concluded that since there was no trespass, there was no Fourth Amendment violation.

In *Silverman v. United States*, 365 U.S. 505 (1961), the police used a device called a "spike mike" to listen in from a vacant row house to conversations in an adjoining row house. The device consisted of a microphone with a spike of about a foot in length attached to it. The spike was inserted into a baseboard of the vacant row house on the wall adjoining the row house next door. The spike hit the heating duct serving the next door row house, which transformed the heating system into a sound conductor. The Court held that the use of the "spike mike" violated the Fourth Amendment because it constituted an "unauthorized physical encroachment" into the adjoining row house. The Court distinguished *Olmstead* and *Goldman* because those cases did not involve any "physical invasion" or "trespass" onto the defendant's property, whereas the "spike mike" "usurp[ed] part of the [defendant's] house or office." Do you agree with the Court's distinction between *Goldman/Olmstead* and *Silverman* — between surveillance involving physical intrusion (however slight) and surveillance not involving any trespassing on the premises?

3. *Brandeis's Dissent and the Warren and Brandeis Article.* Justice Brandeis's dissent is one of the most famous dissents in Supreme Court history. Note the similarities between Brandeis's 1890 article, *The Right to Privacy*, and his dissent nearly 40 years later in *Olmstead*. What themes are repeated? Recall that *The Right to Privacy* concerned locating common law roots for privacy protection. What is Brandeis saying about the roots of constitutional protection of privacy?

---

[8] Samuel Dash, *The Intruders: Unreasonable Searches and Seizures from King John to John Ashcroft* 74-78 (2004); Robert C. Post, *Federalism, Positive Law, and the Emergence of the American Administrative State: Prohibition in the Taft Court Era*, 48 Wm. & Mary L. Rev. 1, 139-50 (2006).

4. ***Changing Technology and the Constitution.*** Brandeis contends that the Constitution should keep pace with changing technology. But given the rapid pace of technological change and the fact that the Constitution must serve as the stable foundation for our society, can the Constitution keep pace? How adaptable should the Constitution be?

5. ***Wiretapping vs. Mail Tampering.*** Brandeis contends that wiretapping is more insidious than tampering with the mail. Why? How would you compare wiretapping with intercepting e-mail or instant messages?

6. ***State Wiretapping Law.*** In the state of Washington, where the wiretapping in *Olmstead* took place, wiretapping was a criminal act, and the officers had thus violated the law. In a separate dissenting opinion, Justice Holmes noted that:

> . . . [A]part from the Constitution the government ought not to use evidence obtained and only obtainable by a criminal act. . . . It is desirable that criminals should be detected, and to that end that all available evidence should be used. It also is desirable that the government should not itself foster and pay for other crimes, when they are the means by which the evidence is to be obtained. If it pays its officers for having got evidence by crime I do not see why it may not as well pay them for getting it in the same way, and I can attach no importance to protestations of disapproval if it knowingly accepts and pays and announces that in future it will pay for the fruits. We have to choose, and for my part I think it a less evil that some criminals should escape than that the government should play an ignoble part.

Should it matter in Fourth Amendment analysis whether particular federal law enforcement surveillance tactics are illegal under state law?

7. ***The Birth of Federal Electronic Surveillance Law.*** The *Olmstead* decision was not well received by the public. In 1934, Congress responded to *Olmstead* by enacting § 605 of the Federal Communications Act, making wiretapping a federal crime. This statute will be discussed later in the part on electronic surveillance law.

8. ***Secret Agents and Misplaced Trust.*** In *Hoffa v. United States*, 385 U.S. 293 (1966), an undercover informant, Edward Partin, befriended James Hoffa and elicited statements from him about his plans to bribe jurors in a criminal trial in which Hoffa was a defendant. According to the Court:

> In the present case . . . it is evident that no interest legitimately protected by the Fourth Amendment is involved. It is obvious that the petitioner was not relying on the security of his hotel suite when he made the incriminating statements to Partin or in Partin's presence. Partin did not enter the suite by force or by stealth. He was not a surreptitious eavesdropper. Partin was in the suite by invitation, and every conversation which he heard was either directed to him or knowingly carried on in his presence. The petitioner, in a word, was not relying on the security of the hotel room; he was relying upon his misplaced confidence that Partin would not reveal his wrongdoing.

Likewise, in *Lewis v. United States*, 385 U.S. 206 (1966), the defendant sold drugs to an undercover agent in his house. The Court held:

In the instant case . . . the petitioner invited the undercover agent to his home for the specific purpose of executing a felonious sale of narcotics. Petitioner's only concern was whether the agent was a willing purchaser who could pay the agreed price. . . . During neither of his visits to petitioner's home did the agent see, hear, or take anything that was not contemplated, and in fact intended, by petitioner as a necessary part of his illegal business. Were we to hold the deceptions of the agent in this case constitutionally prohibited, we would come near to a rule that the use of undercover agents in any manner is virtually unconstitutional per se. Such a rule would, for example, severely hamper the Government in ferreting out those organized criminal activities that are characterized by covert dealings with victims who either cannot or do not protest. A prime example is provided by the narcotics traffic. . . .

Hoffa and *Lewis* establish that a person does not have a privacy interest in the loyalty of her friends. The government may deceive a person by sending in secret agents to befriend her. Is it problematic that government is permitted to use spies and deception as a law enforcement technique? Consider the following observation by Anthony Amsterdam:

I can see no significant difference between police spies . . . and electronic surveillance, either in their uses or abuses. Both have long been asserted by law enforcement officers to be indispensable tools in investigating crime, particularly victimless and political crime, precisely because they both search out privacies that government could not otherwise invade. Both tend to repress crime in the same way, by making people distrustful and unwilling to talk to one another. The only difference is that under electronic surveillance you are afraid to talk to anybody in your office or over the phone, while under a spy system you are afraid to talk to anybody at all.[9]

9. ***Bugs, Transmitters, and Recording Devices.*** In *On Lee v. United States*, 343 U.S. 747 (1952), Chin Poy, a government informant with a concealed transmitter, engaged On Lee in conversation for the purpose of eliciting that On Lee was a drug dealer. The conversation was transmitted to a law enforcement agent, who later testified at trial about the content of the conversation. The Court held that the Fourth Amendment did not apply:

Petitioner was talking confidentially and indiscreetly with one he trusted, and he was overheard. This was due to aid from a transmitter and receiver, to be sure, but with the same effect on his privacy as if agent Lee had been eavesdropping outside an open window. The use of bifocals, field glasses or the telescope to magnify the object of a witness' vision is not a forbidden search or seizure, even if they focus without his knowledge or consent upon what one supposes to be private indiscretions. It would be a dubious service to the genuine liberties protected by the Fourth Amendment to make them bedfellows with spurious liberties improvised by farfetched analogies which would liken eavesdropping on a conversation, with the connivance of one of the parties, to an unreasonable search or seizure. We find no violation of the Fourth Amendment here.

---

[9] Anthony G. Amsterdam, *Perspectives on the Fourth Amendment*, 58 Minn. L. Rev. 349, 407 (1974). For a detailed analysis of undercover agents, see Gary T. Marx, *Under Cover: Police Surveillance in America* (1988).

Does the use of electronic devices distinguish *On Lee* from *Hoffa* and *Lewis* in a material way?

LOPEZ V. UNITED STATES

373 U.S. 427 (1963)

[The petitioner, German S. Lopez, was tried in a federal court on a four-count indictment charging him with attempted bribery of an Internal Revenue agent, Roger S. Davis. The evidence against him had been obtained by a series of meetings between him and Davis. The last meeting was recorded by Davis with a pocket wire recorder. Prior to trial, Lopez moved to suppress the recorded conversation.]

HARLAN, J. . . . [Petitioner's] argument is primarily addressed to the recording of the conversation, which he claims was obtained in violation of his rights under the Fourth Amendment. Recognizing the weakness of this position if Davis was properly permitted to testify about the same conversation, petitioner now challenges that testimony as well, although he failed to do so at the trial. . . .

Once it is plain that Davis could properly testify about his conversation with Lopez, the constitutional claim relating to the recording of that conversation emerges in proper perspective. The Court has in the past sustained instances of "electronic eavesdropping" against constitutional challenge, when devices have been used to enable government agents to overhear conversations which would have been beyond the reach of the human ear. *See, e.g., Olmstead v. United States.* It has been insisted only that the electronic device not be planted by an unlawful physical invasion of a constitutionally protected area. . . . Indeed this case involves no "eavesdropping" whatever in any proper sense of that term. The Government did not use an electronic device to listen in on conversations it could not otherwise have heard. Instead, the device was used only to obtain the most reliable evidence possible of a conversation in which the Government's own agent was a participant and which that agent was fully entitled to disclose. And the device was not planted by means of an unlawful physical invasion of petitioner's premises under circumstances which would violate the Fourth Amendment. It was carried in and out by an agent who was there with petitioner's assent, and it neither saw nor heard more than the agent himself. . . .

Stripped to its essentials, petitioner's argument amounts to saying that he has a constitutional right to rely on possible flaws in the agent's memory, or to challenge the agent's credibility without being beset by corroborating evidence that is not susceptible of impeachment. For no other argument can justify excluding an accurate version of a conversation that the agent could testify to from memory. We think the risk that petitioner took in offering a bribe to Davis fairly included the risk that the offer would be accurately reproduced in court, whether by faultless memory or mechanical recording. . . .

WARREN, C.J. concurring. I also share the opinion of Mr. Justice Brennan that the fantastic advances in the field of electronic communication constitute a great danger to the privacy of the individual; that indiscriminate use of such devices in law enforcement raises grave constitutional questions under the Fourth and Fifth Amendments; and that these considerations impose a heavier responsibility on this Court in its supervision of the fairness of procedures in the federal court system. However, I do not believe that, as a result, all uses of such devices should be proscribed either as unconstitutional or as unfair law enforcement methods. One of the lines I would draw would be between this case and *On Lee.* . . .

The use and purpose of the transmitter in *On Lee* was substantially different from the use of the recorder here. Its advantage was not to corroborate the testimony of Chin Poy, but rather, to obviate the need to put him on the stand. The Court in *On Lee* itself stated:

> We can only speculate on the reasons why Chin Poy was not called. It seems a not unlikely assumption that the very defects of character and blemishes of record which made On Lee trust him with confidences would make a jury distrust his testimony. Chin Poy was close enough to the underworld to serve as bait, near enough the criminal design so that petitioner would embrace him as a confidante, but too close to it for the Government to vouch for him as a witness. Instead, the Government called agent Lee.

However, there were further advantages in not using Chin Poy. Had Chin Poy been available for cross-examination, counsel for On Lee could have explored the nature of Chin Poy's friendship with On Lee, the possibility of other unmonitored conversations and appeals to friendship, the possibility of entrapments, police pressure brought to bear to persuade Chin Poy to turn informer, and Chin Poy's own recollection of the contents of the conversation. . . .

Thus while I join the Court in permitting the use of electronic devices to corroborate an agent under the particular facts of this case, I cannot sanction by implication the use of these same devices to radically shift the pattern of presentation of evidence in the criminal trial, a shift that may be used to conceal substantial factual and legal issues concerning the rights of the accused and the administration of criminal justice.

BRENNAN, J. joined by DOUGLAS and GOLDBERG, J.J. dissenting. . . . [T]he Government's argument is that Lopez surrendered his right of privacy when he communicated his "secret thoughts" to Agent Davis. The assumption, manifestly untenable, is that the Fourth Amendment is only designed to protect secrecy. If a person commits his secret thoughts to paper, that is no license for the police to seize the paper; if a person communicates his secret thoughts verbally to another, that is no license for the police to record the words. *On Lee* certainly rested on no such theory of waiver. The right of privacy would mean little if it were limited to a person's solitary thoughts, and so fostered secretiveness. It must embrace a concept of the liberty of one's communications, and historically it has. "The common law secures to each individual the right of determining, ordinarily, to what extent his thoughts, sentiments, and emotions shall be communicated to others . . . and even if he has chosen to give them expression, he generally retains the power to fix the limits of the publicity which shall be given them." Warren and Brandeis, *The Right to Privacy*, 4 Harv. L. Rev. 193, 198 (1890).

That is not to say that all communications are privileged. On Lee assumed the risk that his acquaintance would divulge their conversation; Lopez assumed the same risk vis-à-vis Davis. The risk inheres in all communications which are not in the sight of the law privileged. It is not an undue risk to ask persons to assume, for it does no more than compel them to use discretion in choosing their auditors, to make damaging disclosures only to persons whose character and motives may be trusted. But the risk which both *On Lee* and today's decision impose is of a different order. It is the risk that third parties, whether mechanical auditors like the Minifon or human transcribers of mechanical transmissions as in *On Lee* — third parties who cannot be shut out of a conversation as conventional eavesdroppers can be, merely by a lowering of voices, or withdrawing to a private place — may give independent evidence of any conversation. There is only one way to guard against such a risk, and that is to keep one's mouth shut on all occasions. . . .

The risk of being overheard by an eavesdropper or betrayed by an informer or deceived as to the identity of one with whom one deals is probably inherent in the conditions of human society. It is the kind of risk we necessarily assume whenever we speak. But as soon as electronic surveillance comes into play, the risk changes crucially. There is no security from that kind of eavesdropping, no way of mitigating the risk, and so not even a residuum of true privacy. . . .

NOTES & QUESTIONS

1. *Is Electronic Surveillance Different?* Should electronic surveillance be treated similarly or differently than regular eavesdropping? Is it consistent to agree that Davis could testify as to what Lopez said via his memory but cannot introduce a recording of what Lopez said?

KATZ V. UNITED STATES

389 U.S. 347 (1967)

STEWART, J. The petitioner was convicted in the District Court for the Southern District of California under an eight-count indictment charging him with transmitting wagering information by telephone from Los Angeles to Miami and Boston in violation of a federal statute. At trial the Government was permitted, over the petitioner's objection, to introduce evidence of the petitioner's end of telephone conversations, overheard by FBI agents who had attached an electronic listening and recording device to the outside of the public telephone booth from which he had placed his calls. In affirming his conviction, the Court of Appeals rejected the contention that the recordings had been obtained in violation of the Fourth Amendment, because "[t]here was no physical entrance into the area occupied by, (the petitioner)." We granted certiorari in order to consider the constitutional questions thus presented.

The petitioner had phrased those questions as follows:

A. Whether a public telephone booth is a constitutionally protected area so that evidence obtained by attaching an electronic listening recording device to the top of such a booth is obtained in violation of the right to privacy of the user of the booth.

B. Whether physical penetration of a constitutionally protected area is necessary before a search and seizure can be said to be violative of the Fourth Amendment to the United States Constitution.

We decline to adopt this formulation of the issues. In the first place the correct solution of Fourth Amendment problems is not necessarily promoted by incantation of the phrase "constitutionally protected area." Secondly, the Fourth Amendment cannot be translated into a general constitutional "right to privacy." That Amendment protects individual privacy against certain kinds of governmental intrusion, but its protections go further, and often have nothing to do with privacy at all. Other provisions of the Constitution protect personal privacy from other forms of governmental invasion. But the protection of a person's general right to privacy — his right to be let alone by other people — is, like the protection of his property and of his very life, left largely to the law of the individual States.

Because of the misleading way the issues have been formulated, the parties have attached great significance to the characterization of the telephone booth from which the petitioner placed his calls. The petitioner has strenuously argued that the booth was a "constitutionally protected area." The Government has maintained with equal vigor that it was not. But this effort to decide whether or not a given "area," viewed in the abstract, is "constitutionally protected" deflects attention from the problem presented by this case. For the Fourth Amendment protects people, not places. What a person knowingly exposes to the public, even in his own home or office, is not a subject of Fourth Amendment protection. But what he seeks to preserve as private, even in an area accessible to the public, may be constitutionally protected.

The Government stresses the fact that the telephone booth from which the petitioner made his calls was constructed partly of glass, so that he was as visible after he entered it as he would have been if he had remained outside. But what he sought to exclude when he entered the booth was not the intruding eye — it was the uninvited ear. He did not shed his right to do so simply because he made his calls from a place where he might be seen. No less than an individual in a business office, in a friend's apartment, or in a taxicab, a person in a telephone booth may rely upon the protection of the Fourth Amendment. One who occupies it, shuts the door behind him, and pays the toll that permits him to place a call is surely entitled to assume that the words he utters into the mouthpiece will not be broadcast to the world. To read the Constitution more narrowly is to ignore the vital role that the public telephone has come to play in private communication.

The Government contends, however, that the activities of its agents in this case should not be tested by Fourth Amendment requirements, for the surveillance technique they employed involved no physical penetration of the telephone booth from which the petitioner placed his calls. It is true that the absence of such penetration was at one time thought to foreclose further Fourth Amendment inquiry, *Olmstead v. United States*, *Goldman v. United States*, for that Amendment was thought to limit only searches and seizures of tangible property. But "[t]he premise that property interests control the right of the Government to search and seize has been discredited." . . . [O]nce this much is acknowledged, and once it is recognized that the Fourth Amendment protects people — and not simply "areas" — against unreasonable searches and seizures it becomes clear that the reach of that Amendment cannot turn upon the presence or absence of a physical intrusion into any given enclosure.

We conclude that the underpinnings of *Olmstead* and *Goldman* have been so eroded by our subsequent decisions that the "trespass" doctrine there enunciated can no longer be regarded as controlling. . . .

The question remaining for decision, then, is whether the search and seizure conducted in this case complied with constitutional standards. In that regard, the Government's position is that its agents acted in an entirely defensible manner: They did not begin their electronic surveillance until investigation of the petitioner's activities had established a strong probability that he was using the telephone in question to transmit gambling information to persons in other States, in violation of federal law. Moreover, the surveillance was limited, both in scope and in duration, to the specific purpose of establishing the contents of the petitioner's unlawful telephonic communications. The agents confined their surveillance to the brief periods during which he used the telephone booth, and they took great care to overhear only the conversations of the petitioner himself. . . .

. . . It is apparent that the agents in this case acted with restraint. Yet the inescapable fact is that this restraint was imposed by the agents themselves, not by a judicial officer. They were not required, before commencing the search, to present their estimate of probable cause for detached scrutiny by a neutral magistrate. They were not compelled, during the conduct of the search itself, to observe precise limits established in advance by a specific court order. Nor were they directed, after the search had been completed, to notify the authorizing magistrate in detail of all that had been seized. In the absence of such safeguards, this Court has never sustained a search upon the sole ground that officers reasonably expected to find evidence of a particular crime and voluntarily confined their activities to the least intrusive means consistent with that end. Searches conducted without warrants have been held unlawful "notwithstanding facts unquestionably showing probable cause." . . . "Over and again this Court has emphasized that the mandate of the [Fourth] Amendment requires adherence to judicial processes," and that searches conducted outside the judicial process, without prior approval by judge or magistrate, are per se unreasonable under the Fourth Amendment — subject only to a few specifically established and well-delineated exceptions. . . .

HARLAN, J. concurring. . . . As the Court's opinion states, "the Fourth Amendment protects people, not places." The question, however, is what protection it affords to those people. Generally, as here, the answer to that question requires reference to a "place." My understanding of the rule that has emerged from prior decisions is that there is a twofold requirement, first that a person have exhibited an actual (subjective) expectation of privacy and, second, that the expectation be one that society is prepared to recognize as "reasonable." Thus a man's home is, for most purposes, a place where he expects privacy, but objects, activities, or statements that he exposes to the "plain view" of outsiders are not "protected" because no intention to keep them to himself has been exhibited. On the other hand, conversations in the open would not be protected against being overheard, for the expectation of privacy under the circumstances would be unreasonable.

The critical fact in this case is that "(o)ne who occupies it, (a telephone booth) shuts the door behind him, and pays the toll that permits him to place a call is surely entitled to assume" that his conversation is not being intercepted. The point is not that the booth is "accessible to the public" at other times, but that it is a temporarily private place whose momentary occupants' expectations of freedom from intrusion are recognized as reasonable.

BLACK, J. dissenting. . . . My basic objection is twofold: (1) I do not believe that the words of the Amendment will bear the meaning given them by today's decision, and (2) I do not believe that it is the proper role of this Court to rewrite the Amendment in order "to bring it into harmony with the times" and thus reach a result that many people believe to be desirable.

While I realize that an argument based on the meaning of words lacks the scope, and no doubt the appeal, of broad policy discussions and philosophical discourses on such nebulous subjects as privacy, for me the language of the Amendment is the crucial place to look in construing a written document such as our Constitution. The Fourth Amendment says that

> The right of the people to be secure in their persons, houses, papers, and effects, against unreasonable searches and seizures, shall not be violated, and no Warrants shall issue, but upon probable cause, supported by Oath or affirmation, and particularly describing the place to be searched, and the persons or things to be seized.

The first clause protects "persons, houses, papers, and effects, against unreasonable searches and seizures. . . ." These words connote the idea of tangible things with size, form, and weight, things capable of being searched, seized, or both. The second clause of the Amendment still further establishes its Framers' purpose to limit its protection to tangible things by providing that no warrants shall issue but those "particularly describing the place to be searched, and the persons or things to be seized." A conversation overheard by eavesdropping, whether by plain snooping or wiretapping, is not tangible and, under the normally accepted meanings of the words, can neither be searched nor seized. . . .

NOTES & QUESTIONS

1. *Who Was Charlie Katz?* David Skalansky describes the background to *Katz*:

> Charlie Katz was a Damon Runyon character plopped into 1960s Los Angeles. Katz was a professional bettor . . . Katz wagered on sports events, sometimes for himself and sometimes on commission for others. He specialized in basketball games, and he had his own, elaborate system for

ranking teams and predicting outcomes. In February 1965, he was living in a poolside hotel room on the Sunset Strip.[10]

Sklanksy describes how the FBI would observe Katz leaving his hotel to place his bets from the telephone booth. An agent stationed outside would radio the news to another agent near the booth. This second agent would turn on a tape recorder placed on top of the telephone booth, observe Katz making his calls, and once Katz was finished and left the telephone booth, turn the recorder off and take it down from the top of the booth.

2. ***The Reasonable Expectation of Privacy Test.*** The *Katz* decision established a widely cited test for whether the Fourth Amendment is applicable in a given situation. That test was articulated not in the majority opinion but in the concurring opinion by Justice Harlan. The rule as articulated in Justice Harlan's concurrence has become known as the "reasonable expectation of privacy test." Under the test, (1) a person must exhibit an "actual (subjective) expectation of privacy" and (2) "the expectation [must] be one that society is prepared to recognize as 'reasonable.'"

According to Christopher Slobogin and Joseph Schumacher:

> For the most part, the Court has been content with fleshing out the meaning of the phrase[] "reasonable expectations of privacy" . . . through [its] application to specific cases. But the Court has also provided two significant guidelines as to how [this phrase] should be interpreted. The first guideline came in *Rakas v. Illinois*, where the majority opinion, by then-Associate Justice Rehnquist, stated that "legitimation of expectations of privacy by law must have a source outside of the Fourth Amendment, either by reference to concepts of real or personal property law or to understandings that are recognized and permitted by society." Most important for present purposes is the last clause of this excerpt, which indicates the Court's willingness to rely on societal understandings in defining "reasonable expectations of privacy." Although this language appeared in a footnote, and was directed solely toward defining the standing concept, it has since been relied upon in the text of several other cases involving the "search" issue, often rephrased in terms of expectations of privacy "society is prepared to recognize as 'reasonable.'"
>
> The second guideline came from the same footnote in *Rakas*. According to the Court, the use of the word "legitimate" or "reasonable" before "expectations of privacy" is meant to convey "more than a subjective expectation of not being discovered." As the Court explained,

> > [a] burglar plying his trade in a summer cabin during the off season may have a thoroughly justified subjective expectation of privacy, but it is not one which the law recognizes as "legitimate." His presence . . . is "wrongful"; his expectation is not "one that society is prepared to recognize as 'reasonable.'"

> In short, the Fourth Amendment does not protect expectations of privacy that only a criminal would have.[11]

---

[10] David A. Sklansky, *Katz v. United States*, in *Criminal Procedure Stories* (Carol S. Steiker, ed., 2006).

[11] Christopher Slobogin & Joseph E. Schumacher, *Reasonable Expectations of Privacy and Autonomy in Fourth Amendment Cases: An Empirical Look at "Understandings Recognized and Permitted by Society,"* 42 Duke L.J. 727, 731-32 (1993).

3. ***Variations on* Katz.** What if the door to the telephone booth in *Katz* had been open? Would the Court still have concluded that the Fourth Amendment applied? What if the cop stood outside the booth, and Katz spoke loud enough for the cop to hear? Suppose the police placed a sound recording device outside the phone booth, and the device could pick up Katz's voice, which would be inaudible to the naked ear outside the phone booth. Would this be a violation of the Fourth Amendment?

4. ***"Conditioned" Expectations of Privacy.*** Before *Katz*, police sometimes tapped phones. How would this behavior affect a person's expectations of privacy when speaking on the phone? Consider the following observation by the Court in *Smith v. Maryland*, 442 U.S. 735, 741 n.5 (1979):

> Situations can be imagined, of course, in which Katz' two-pronged inquiry would provide an inadequate index of Fourth Amendment protection. For example, if the Government were suddenly to announce on nationwide television that all homes henceforth would be subject to warrantless entry, individuals thereafter might not in fact entertain any actual expectation or privacy regarding their homes, papers, and effects. Similarly, if a refugee from a totalitarian country, unaware of this Nation's traditions, erroneously assumed that police were continuously monitoring his telephone conversations, a subjective expectation of privacy regarding the contents of his calls might be lacking as well. In such circumstances, where an individual's subjective expectations had been "conditioned" by influences alien to well-recognized Fourth Amendment freedoms, those subjective expectations obviously could play no meaningful role in ascertaining what the scope of Fourth Amendment protection was. In determining whether a "legitimate expectation of privacy" existed in such cases, a normative inquiry would be proper.

5. **Berger v. New York.** *Berger v. New York*, 388 U.S. 41 (1967), is an important Fourth Amendment case decided after the Supreme Court agreed to hear *Katz* but before it heard oral arguments in that case. In *Berger*, the Court struck down portions of New York's eavesdropping statute as violating the Fourth Amendment. The New York law authorized the installation of electronic surveillance devices for 60 days, and it allowed the surveillance to be extended beyond the 60 days without a showing of present probable cause to continue the eavesdrop. The Court held:

> . . . The Fourth Amendment commands that a warrant issue not only upon probable cause supported by oath or affirmation, but also "particularly describing the place to be searched, and the persons or things to be seized." New York's statute lacks this particularization. It merely says that a warrant may issue on reasonable ground to believe that evidence of crime may be obtained by the eavesdrop. It lays down no requirement for particularity in the warrant as to what specific crime has been or is being committed, nor "the place to be searched," or "the persons or things to be seized" as specifically required by the Fourth Amendment. The need for particularity and evidence of reliability in the showing required when judicial authorization of a search is sought is especially great in the case of eavesdropping. By its very nature eavesdropping involves an intrusion on privacy that is broad in scope. . . .

. . . New York's statute . . . lays down no . . . "precise and discriminate" requirements. . . . New York's broadside authorization rather than being "carefully circumscribed" so as to prevent unauthorized invasions of privacy actually permits general searches by electronic devices, the truly offensive character of which was first condemned in *Entick v. Carrington*, 19 How. St. Tr. 1029, and which were then known as "general warrants." The use of the latter was a motivating factor behind the Declaration of Independence. In view of the many cases commenting on the practice it is sufficient here to point out that under these "general warrants" customs officials were given blanket authority to conduct general searches for goods imported to the Colonies in violation of the tax laws of the Crown. The Fourth Amendment's requirement that a warrant "particularly describ(e) the place to be searched, and the persons or things to be seized," repudiated these general warrants and "makes general searches . . . impossible and prevents the seizure of one thing under a warrant describing another. As to what is to be taken, nothing is left to the discretion of the officer executing the warrant."

We believe the statute here is equally offensive. First, as we have mentioned, eavesdropping is authorized without requiring belief that any particular offense has been or is being committed; nor that the "property" sought, the conversations, be particularly described. The purpose of the probable cause requirement of the Fourth Amendment, to keep the state out of constitutionally protected areas until it has reason to believe that a specific crime has been or is being committed, is thereby wholly aborted. Likewise the statute's failure to describe with particularity the conversations sought gives the officer a roving commission to "seize" any and all conversations. . . . As with general warrants this leaves too much to the discretion of the officer executing the order. Secondly, authorization of eavesdropping for a two-month period is the equivalent of a series of intrusions, searches, and seizures pursuant to a single showing of probable cause. Prompt execution is also avoided. During such a long and continuous (24 hours a day) period the conversations of any and all persons coming into the area covered by the device will be seized indiscriminately and without regard to their connection with the crime under investigation. Moreover, the statute permits, and there were authorized here, extensions of the original two-month period — presumably for two months each — on a mere showing that such extension is "in the public interest." Apparently the original grounds on which the eavesdrop order was initially issued also form the basis of the renewal. This we believe insufficient without a showing of present probable cause for the continuance of the eavesdrop. Third, the statute places no termination date on the eavesdrop once the conversation sought is seized. This is left entirely in the discretion of the officer. Finally, the statute's procedure, necessarily because its success depends on secrecy, has no requirement for notice as do conventional warrants, nor does it overcome this defect by requiring some showing of special facts. On the contrary, it permits uncontested entry without any showing of exigent circumstances. . . . In short, the statute's blanket grant of permission to eavesdrop is without adequate judicial supervision or protective procedures. . . .

As Sklansky points out, the effect of *Berger* combined with two other cases decided immediately before *Katz* — *Warren v. Hayden*, 387 U.S. 294 (1967) and *Camara v. Municipal Court*, 387 U.S. 523 (1967) — was to underscore the "centrality of the warrant requirement to the Fourth Amendment."[12]

UNITED STATES V. WHITE

401 U.S. 745 (1971)

WHITE, J. In 1966, respondent James A. White was tried and convicted under two consolidated indictments charging various illegal transactions in narcotics. . . . He was fined and sentenced as a second offender to 25-year concurrent sentences. The issue before us is whether the Fourth Amendment bars from evidence the testimony of governmental agents who related certain conversations which had occurred between defendant White and a government informant, Harvey Jackson, and which the agents overheard by monitoring the frequency of a radio transmitter carried by Jackson and concealed on his person. On four occasions the conversations took place in Jackson's home; each of these conversations was overheard by an agent concealed in a kitchen closet with Jackson's consent and by a second agent outside the house using a radio receiver. Four other conversations — one in respondent's home, one in a restaurant, and two in Jackson's car — were overheard by the use of radio equipment. The prosecution was unable to locate and produce Jackson at the trial and the trial court overruled objections to the testimony of the agents who conducted the electronic surveillance. The jury returned a guilty verdict and defendant appealed. . . .

Concededly a police agent who conceals his police connections may write down for official use his conversations with a defendant and testify concerning them, without a warrant authorizing his encounters with the defendant and without otherwise violating the latter's Fourth Amendment rights. For constitutional purposes, no different result is required if the agent instead of immediately reporting and transcribing his conversations with defendant, either (1) simultaneously records them with electronic equipment which he is carrying on his person, *Lopez v. United States*; (2) or carries radio equipment which simultaneously transmits the conversations either to recording equipment located elsewhere or to other agents monitoring the transmitting frequency. *On Lee v. United States*. If the conduct and revelations of an agent operating without electronic equipment do not invade the defendant's constitutionally justifiable expectations of privacy, neither does a simultaneous recording of the same conversations made by the agent or by others from transmissions received from the agent to whom the defendant is talking and whose trustworthiness the defendant necessarily risks.

Our problem is not what the privacy expectations of particular defendants in particular situations may be or the extent to which they may in fact have relied on the discretion of their companions. Very probably, individual defendants neither know nor suspect that their colleagues have gone or will go to the police or are

---

[12] David A. Sklansky, *Katz v. United States*, in *Criminal Procedure Stories* (Carol S. Steiker, ed., 2006).

carrying recorders or transmitters. Otherwise, conversation would cease and our problem with these encounters would be nonexistent or far different from those now before us. Our problem, in terms of the principles announced in *Katz*, is what expectations of privacy are constitutionally "justifiable" — what expectations the Fourth Amendment will protect in the absence of a warrant. So far, the law permits the frustration of actual expectations of privacy by permitting authorities to use the testimony of those associates who for one reason or another have determined to turn to the police, as well as by authorizing the use of informants in the manner exemplified by *Hoffa* and *Lewis*. If the law gives no protection to the wrongdoer whose trusted accomplice is or becomes a police agent, neither should it protect him when that same agent has recorded or transmitted the conversations which are later offered in evidence to prove the State's case.

Inescapably, one contemplating illegal activities must realize and risk that his companions may be reporting to the police. If he sufficiently doubts their trustworthiness, the association will very probably end or never materialize. But if he has no doubts, or allays them, or risks what doubt he has, the risk is his. In terms of what his course will be, what he will or will not do or say, we are unpersuaded that he would distinguish between probably informers on the one hand and probable informers with transmitters on the other. . . .

Nor should we be too ready to erect constitutional barriers to relevant and probative evidence which is also accurate and reliable. An electronic recording will many times produce a more reliable rendition of what a defendant has said than will the unaided memory of a police agent. It may also be that with the recording in existence it is less likely that the informant will change his mind, less chance that threat or injury will suppress unfavorable evidence and less chance that cross-examination will confound the testimony. Considerations like these obviously do not favor the defendant, but we are not prepared to hold that a defendant who has no constitutional right to exclude the informer's unaided testimony nevertheless has a Fourth Amendment privilege against a more accurate version of the events in question. . . .

HARLAN, J. dissenting. . . . Since it is the task of the law to form and project, as well as mirror and reflect, we should not, as judges, merely recite the expectations and risks without examining the desirability of saddling them upon society. The critical question, therefore, is whether under our system of government, as reflected in the Constitution, we should impose on our citizens the risks of the electronic listener or observer without at least the protection of a warrant requirement.

This question must, in my view, be answered by assessing the nature of a particular practice and the likely extent of its impact on the individual's sense of security balanced against the utility of the conduct as a technique of law enforcement. For those more extensive intrusions that significantly jeopardize the sense of security which is the paramount concern of Fourth Amendment liberties, I am of the view that more than self-restraint by law enforcement officials is required and at the least warrants should be necessary. The impact of the practice of third-party bugging, must, I think, be considered such as to undermine that confidence and sense of security in dealing with one another that is characteristic of individual relationships between citizens in a free society. It goes beyond the impact on privacy occasioned by the ordinary type of "informer" investigation upheld in *Lewis* and *Hoffa*. The argument of the plurality opinion, to the effect that it is irrelevant whether secrets are revealed by the mere tattletale or the transistor, ignores the differences occasioned by third-party monitoring and recording which insures full and accurate disclosure of all that is said, free of the possibility of error and oversight that inheres in human reporting.

Authority is hardly required to support the proposition that words would be measured a good deal more carefully and communication inhibited if one suspected his conversations were being transmitted and transcribed. Were third-party bugging a prevalent practice, it might well smother that spontaneity — reflected in frivolous, impetuous, sacrilegious, and defiant discourse — that liberates daily life. Much offhand exchange is easily forgotten and one may count on the obscurity of his remarks, protected by the very fact of a limited audience, and the likelihood that the listener will either overlook or forget what is said, as well as the listener's inability to reformulate a conversation without having to contend with a documented record. All these values are sacrificed by a rule of law that permits official monitoring of private discourse limited only by the need to locate a willing assistant. . . .

Interposition of a warrant requirement is designed not to shield "wrong-doers," but to secure a measure of privacy and a sense of personal security throughout our society. The Fourth Amendment does, of course, leave room for the employment of modern technology in criminal law enforcement, but in the stream of current developments in Fourth Amendment law I think it must be held that third-party electronic monitoring, subject only to the self-restraint of law enforcement officials, has no place in our society.

DOUGLAS, J. dissenting. . . . *On Lee* and *Lopez* are of a vintage opposed to *Berger* and *Katz*. However they may be explained, they are products of the old common-law notions of trespass. *Katz*, on the other hand, emphasized that with few exceptions "searches conducted outside the judicial process, without prior approval by judge or magistrate, are per se unreasonable under the Fourth Amendment.". . .

Monitoring, if prevalent, certainly kills free discourse and spontaneous utterances. Free discourse — a First Amendment value — may be frivolous or serious, humble or defiant, reactionary or revolutionary, profane or in good taste; but it is not free if there is surveillance. . . .

Now that the discredited decisions in *On Lee* and *Lopez* are resuscitated and revived, must everyone live in fear that every word he speaks may be transmitted or recorded and later repeated to the entire world? I can imagine nothing that has a more chilling effect on people speaking their minds and expressing their views on important matters. The advocates of that regime should spend some time in totalitarian countries and learn firsthand the kind of regime they are creating here. . . .

NOTES & QUESTIONS

1. **White *vs.* Katz.** Is this case more akin to the bugging in *On Lee* and *Lopez* rather than the wiretapping of *Katz*? Does it matter whether the police heard the conversation simultaneously? Suppose the conversation had been recorded by a hidden recorder and then handed over later to the police.

2. ***Covert Agents and the Misplaced Trust Doctrine.*** *White* suggests that the misplaced trust doctrine in *Hoffa, Lewis, Lopez,* and *On Lee* survives after *Katz.* Under the misplaced trust doctrine, people place their trust in others at their own peril and must assume the risk of betrayal. But should the misplaced trust doctrine survive after *Katz*? Do we have a reasonable expectation that our friends aren't government agents in disguise?

   In a comparative study of how the United States and Germany regulate undercover policing, Jacqueline Ross identifies numerous differences in the two legal systems.[13] She argues:

   > In Germany, undercover policing is a necessary evil in that it harms targets by invading their constitutionally protected right to privacy, along with other fundamental rights. . . . German law responds to these concerns through legislation that carves out special limitations on the most intrusive covert tactics, namely long-term deep cover operations. Viewing covert policing as an invasion of privacy assimilates it to other police powers, like searches and seizures. While these tactics burden civil liberties, they do so permissibly, through police compliance with procedural constraints such as warrant requirements. Because civil liberties may lawfully be compromised in the name of security, thinking of covert surveillance as invasions of privacy allows the legal system to justify the burdens that covert policing imposes on rights. This regulatory approach also entails the use of procedural constraints on how covert tactics may be authorized, alongside substantive limits on what undercover operatives may do.
   >
   > German privacy law protects dignitary interests, while American conceptions of privacy emphasize physical privacy in the home along with decisional privacy or autonomy. Germany's concern with individual dignity is part of the German Constitution's concern with safeguarding the "free development of personality," in direct reaction to the totalitarian oppression and violations of personal dignity under the Nazi regime. Invasions of privacy also have special salience for residents of the five new eastern states who remember the encompassing surveillance practiced more recently in the GDR [German Democratic Republic, also known as East Germany]. Given these concerns, police infiltration is deeply problematic. It interferes with the rights of all persons to control the face they present to the world; it reveals too much about the intimate details of a person's life; and it disrupts personal relationships. Giving constitutional status to these harms means that the government must satisfy certain requirements before inflicting them. Constitutional protection entails a warrant procedure, a showing of need, and statutory limits on the crimes that the government may target in this way.
   >
   > By contrast, the United States legal system does not treat undercover policing as an intrinsic invasion of privacy rights. Undercover policing is not

---

[13] Jacqueline E. Ross, *The Place of Covert Surveillance in Democratic Societies: A Comparative Study of the United States and Germany*, 55 Am. J. Comp. L. 493 (2007).

recognized as a search or seizure under the Fourth Amendment. Because they have no Fourth Amendment significance, undercover investigations require no warrant and no showing of probable cause or even reasonable suspicion as a matter of constitutional law. . . .

Conceiving of covert policing as a threat to privacy creates other problems for the legitimacy of these tactics. Framing the discourse in terms of constitutional rights (like the right to privacy) invites critics to identify other constitutional rights that may be at risk. Accordingly, German courts (unlike their American counterparts) have accepted defense arguments that the use of jailhouse informers to squeeze admissions out of prisoners infringes on prisoners' autonomy, by taking advantage of targets' "psychological compulsion to unburden themselves." Critics also raise special objections to those sting operations by which undercover agents befriend and wring confessions from persons suspected of long-ago, unsolved crimes, arguing that these undercover contacts unfairly circumvent suspects' rights to counsel and their right not to incriminate themselves.

What would be the impact on law enforcement if *White* came out the other way after *Katz*? In other words, suppose that *Katz* eliminated the misplaced trust doctrine. How would the Fourth Amendment apply to covert agents or informers? Would this unduly hamper police investigations of drug rings, mafia activity, and terrorist cells?

3. ***Electronic Surveillance and the First Amendment.*** Justice Douglas contends that electronic surveillance impinges upon and chills freedom of expression for all individuals in society. Is electronic surveillance without a warrant consistent with the First Amendment? What kind of process should be required to make use of the warrant consistent with the First Amendment?

3. THE REASONABLE EXPECTATION OF PRIVACY TEST AND EMERGING TECHNOLOGY

(a) Applying the Reasonable Expectation of Privacy Test

SMITH V. MARYLAND

442 U.S. 735 (1979)

BLACKMUN, J. This case presents the question whether the installation and use of a pen register[14] constitutes a "search" within the meaning of the Fourth Amendment, made applicable to the States through the Fourteenth Amendment.

On March 5, 1976, in Baltimore, Md., Patricia McDonough was robbed. She gave the police a description of the robber and of a 1975 Monte Carlo automobile she had observed near the scene of the crime. After the robbery, McDonough began receiving threatening and obscene phone calls from a man identifying

---

[14] "A pen register is a mechanical device that records the numbers dialed on a telephone by monitoring the electrical impulses caused when the dial on the telephone is released. It does not overhear oral communications and does not indicate whether calls are actually completed." A pen register is "usually installed at a central telephone facility [and] records on a paper tape all numbers dialed from [the] line" to which it is attached.

himself as the robber. On one occasion, the caller asked that she step out on her front porch; she did so, and saw the 1975 Monte Carlo she had earlier described to police moving slowly past her home. On March 16, police spotted a man who met McDonough's description driving a 1975 Monte Carlo in her neighborhood. By tracing the license plate number, police learned that the car was registered in the name of petitioner, Michael Lee Smith.

The next day, the telephone company, at police request, installed a pen register at its central offices to record the numbers dialed from the telephone at petitioner's home. The police did not get a warrant or court order before having the pen register installed. The register revealed that on March 17 a call was placed from petitioner's home to McDonough's phone. On the basis of this and other evidence, the police obtained a warrant to search petitioner's residence. [A search of Smith's home revealed more evidence that Smith was the robber. Smith moved to suppress all evidence obtained from (and derived from) the pen register. The trial court denied his motion, and Smith was convicted and sentenced to six years' imprisonment.] . . .

The Fourth Amendment guarantees "[t]he right of the people to be secure in their persons, houses, papers, and effects, against unreasonable searches and sei-zures." In determining whether a particular form of government-initiated elec-tronic surveillance is a "search" within the meaning of the Fourth Amendment,[15] our lodestar is *Katz v. United States*, 389 U.S. 347 (1967). . . .

Consistently with *Katz,* this Court uniformly has held that the application of the Fourth Amendment depends on whether the person invoking its protection can claim a "justifiable," a "reasonable," or a "legitimate expectation of privacy" that has been invaded by government action. This inquiry, as Mr. Justice Harlan aptly noted in his *Katz* concurrence, normally embraces two discrete questions. The first is whether the individual, by his conduct, has "exhibited an actual (subjective) expectation of privacy," — whether, in the words of the *Katz* majority, the individual has shown that "he seeks to preserve [something] as private." The second question is whether the individual's subjective expectation of privacy is "one that society is prepared to recognize as 'reasonable,' — whether, in the words of the *Katz* majority, the individual's expectation, viewed objectively, is "justifiable" under the circumstances.[16]

---

[15] In this case, the pen register was installed, and the numbers dialed were recorded, by the telephone company. The telephone company, however, acted at police request. In view of this, respondent appears to concede that the company is to be deemed an "agent" of the police for purposes of this case, so as to render the installation and use of the pen register "state action" under the Fourth and Fourteenth Amendments. We may assume that "state action" was present here.

[16] Situations can be imagined, of course, in which *Katz*'s two-pronged inquiry would provide an inadequate index of Fourth Amendment protection. For example, if the Government were suddenly to announce on nationwide television that all homes henceforth would be subject to warrantless entry, individuals thereafter might not in fact entertain any actual expectation or privacy regarding their homes, papers, and effects. Similarly, if a refugee from a totalitarian country, unaware of this Nation's traditions, erroneously assumed that police were continuously monitoring his telephone conversations, a subjective expectation of privacy regarding the contents of his calls might be lacking as well. In such circumstances, where an individual's subjective expectations had been "conditioned" by influences alien to well-recognized Fourth Amendment freedoms, those subjective expectations obviously could play no meaningful role in ascertaining what the scope of Fourth Amendment protection was. In determining whether a "legitimate expectation of privacy" existed in such cases, a normative inquiry would be proper.

In applying the *Katz* analysis to this case, it is important to begin by specifying precisely the nature of the state activity that is challenged. The activity here took the form of installing and using a pen register. Since the pen register was installed on telephone company property at the telephone company's central offices, petitioner obviously cannot claim that his "property" was invaded or that police intruded into a "constitutionally protected area." Petitioner's claim, rather, is that, notwithstanding the absence of a trespass, the State, as did the Government in *Katz*, infringed a "legitimate expectation of privacy" that petitioner held. Yet a pen register differs significantly from the listening device employed in *Katz*, for pen registers do not acquire the contents of communications. This Court recently noted:

> Indeed, a law enforcement official could not even determine from the use of a pen register whether a communication existed. These devices do not hear sound. They disclose only the telephone numbers that have been dialed — a means of establishing communication. Neither the purport of any communication between the caller and the recipient of the call, their identities, nor whether the call was even completed is disclosed by pen registers. *United States v. New York Tel. Co.*, 434 U.S. 159, 167 (1977).

Given a pen register's limited capabilities, therefore, petitioner's argument that its installation and use constituted a "search" necessarily rests upon a claim that he had a "legitimate expectation of privacy" regarding the numbers he dialed on his phone.

This claim must be rejected. First, we doubt that people in general entertain any actual expectation of privacy in the numbers they dial. All telephone users realize that they must "convey" phone numbers to the telephone company, since it is through telephone company switching equipment that their calls are completed. All subscribers realize, moreover, that the phone company has facilities for making permanent records of the numbers they dial, for they see a list of their long-distance (toll) calls on their monthly bills. In fact, pen registers and similar devices are routinely used by telephone companies "for the purposes of checking billing operations, detecting fraud and preventing violations of law." Electronic equipment is used not only to keep billing records of toll calls, but also "to keep a record of all calls dialed from a telephone which is subject to a special rate structure." Pen registers are regularly employed "to determine whether a home phone is being used to conduct a business, to check for a defective dial, or to check for overbilling." Although most people may be oblivious to a pen register's esoteric functions, they presumably have some awareness of one common use: to aid in the identification of persons making annoying or obscene calls. Most phone books tell subscribers, on a page entitled "Consumer Information," that the company "can frequently help in identifying to the authorities the origin of unwelcome and troublesome calls." Telephone users, in sum, typically know that they must convey numerical information to the phone company; that the phone company has facilities for recording this information; and that the phone company does in fact record this information for a variety of legitimate business purposes. Although subjective expectations cannot be scientifically gauged, it is too much to believe that telephone subscribers, under these circumstances, harbor any general expectation that the numbers they dial will remain secret.

Petitioner argues, however, that, whatever the expectations of telephone users in general, he demonstrated an expectation of privacy by his own conduct here, since he "us[ed] the telephone *in his house* to the exclusion of all others." But the site of the call is immaterial for purposes of analysis in this case. Although petitioner's conduct may have been calculated to keep the *contents* of his conversation private, his conduct was not and could not have been calculated to preserve the privacy of the number he dialed. Regardless of his location, petitioner had to convey that number to the telephone company in precisely the same way if he wished to complete his call. The fact that he dialed the number on his home phone rather than on some other phone could make no conceivable difference, nor could any subscriber rationally think that it would. Second, even if petitioner did harbor some subjective expectation that the phone numbers he dialed would remain private, this expectation is not "one that society is prepared to recognize as 'reasonable.'" This Court consistently has held that a person has no legitimate expectation of privacy in information he voluntarily turns over to third parties. In [*United States v.*] *Miller*, for example, the Court held that a bank depositor has no "legitimate 'expectation of privacy'" in financial information "voluntarily conveyed to . . . banks and exposed to their employees in the ordinary course of business." The Court explained:

> The depositor takes the risk, in revealing his affairs to another, that the information will be conveyed by that person to the Government. . . . This Court has held repeatedly that the Fourth Amendment does not prohibit the obtaining of information revealed to a third party and conveyed by him to Government authorities, even if the information is revealed on the assumption that it will be used only for a limited purpose and the confidence placed in the third party will not be betrayed.

Because the depositor "assumed the risk" of disclosure, the Court held that it would be unreasonable for him to expect his financial records to remain private.

This analysis dictates that petitioner can claim no legitimate expectation of privacy here. When he used his phone, petitioner voluntarily conveyed numerical information to the telephone company and "exposed" that information to its equipment in the ordinary course of business. In so doing, petitioner assumed the risk that the company would reveal to police the numbers he dialed. The switching equipment that processed those numbers is merely the modern counterpart of the operator who, in an earlier day, personally completed calls for the subscriber. Petitioner concedes that if he had placed his calls through an operator, he could claim no legitimate expectation of privacy. We are not inclined to hold that a different constitutional result is required because the telephone company has decided to automate.

Petitioner argues, however, that automatic switching equipment differs from a live operator in one pertinent respect. An operator, in theory at least, is capable of remembering every number that is conveyed to him by callers. Electronic equipment, by contrast can "remember" only those numbers it is programmed to record, and telephone companies, in view of their present billing practices, usually do not record local calls. Since petitioner, in calling McDonough, was making a local call, his expectation of privacy as to her number, on this theory, would be "legitimate."

This argument does not withstand scrutiny. The fortuity of whether or not the phone company in fact elects to make a quasi-permanent record of a particular number dialed does not in our view, make any constitutional difference. Regardless of the phone company's election, petitioner voluntarily conveyed to it information that it had facilities for recording and that it was free to record. In these circumstances, petitioner assumed the risk that the information would be divulged to police. . . .

STEWART, J. joined by BRENNAN, J. dissenting. . . . The numbers dialed from a private telephone — although certainly more prosaic than the conversation itself — are not without "content." Most private telephone subscribers may have their own numbers listed in a publicly distributed directory, but I doubt there are any who would be happy to have broadcast to the world a list of the local or long distance numbers they have called. This is not because such a list might in some sense be incriminating, but because it easily could reveal the identities of the persons and the places called, and thus reveal the most intimate details of a person's life.

MARSHALL J. joined by BRENNAN, J. dissenting. . . . Privacy is not a discrete commodity, possessed absolutely or not at all. Those who disclose certain facts to a bank or phone company for a limited business purpose need not assume that this information will be released to other persons for other purposes.

The crux of the Court's holding, however, is that whatever expectation of privacy petitioner may in fact have entertained regarding his calls, it is not one "society is prepared to recognize as 'reasonable.'" In so ruling, the Court determines that individuals who convey information to third parties have "assumed the risk" of disclosure to the government. This analysis is misconceived in two critical respects.

Implicit in the concept of assumption of risk is some notion of choice. At least in the third-party consensual surveillance cases, which first incorporated risk analysis into Fourth Amendment doctrine, the defendant presumably had exercised some discretion in deciding who should enjoy his confidential communications. By contrast here, unless a person is prepared to forgo use of what for many has become a personal or professional necessity, he cannot help but accept the risk of surveillance. It is idle to speak of "assuming" risks in contexts where, as a practical matter, individuals have no realistic alternative.

More fundamentally, to make risk analysis dispositive in assessing the reasonableness of privacy expectations would allow the government to define the scope of Fourth Amendment protections. For example, law enforcement officials, simply by announcing their intent to monitor the content of random samples of first-class mail or private phone conversations, could put the public on notice of the risks they would thereafter assume in such communications. . . .

In my view, whether privacy expectations are legitimate within the meaning of *Katz* depends not on the risks an individual can be presumed to accept when imparting information to third parties, but on the risks he should be forced to assume in a free and open society. . . .

The use of pen registers, I believe, constitutes such an extensive intrusion. To hold otherwise ignores the vital role telephonic communication plays in our personal and professional relationships, as well as the First and Fourth Amendment interests implicated by unfettered official surveillance. Privacy in placing calls is of value not only to those engaged in criminal activity. The prospect of unregulated governmental monitoring will undoubtedly prove disturbing even to those with nothing illicit to hide. Many individuals, including members of unpopular political organizations or journalists with confidential sources, may legitimately wish to avoid disclosure of their personal contacts. Permitting governmental access to telephone records on less than probable cause may thus impede certain forms of political affiliation and journalistic endeavor that are the hallmark of a truly free society. Particularly given the Government's previous reliance on warrantless telephonic surveillance to trace reporters' sources and monitor protected political activity, I am unwilling to insulate use of pen registers from independent judicial review. . . .

NOTES & QUESTIONS

1. ***Pen Registers and Trap and Trace Devices.*** A pen register records outgoing telephone calls. Another device, known as a trap and trace device, records all incoming calls. In *Smith v. Maryland*, the Supreme Court ruled that a use of pen registers or trap and trace devices was not a form of wiretap (akin to that in *Katz*). What are the critical differences between the pen register and trap and device, on the one hand, and the wiretap, on the other?

2. ***Critiques of the* Smith *Decision.*** Consider the following observation by Laurence Tribe about *Smith*:

   > The "assumption of risk" — more aptly, "assumption of broadcast" — notion underling the holding in *Smith* . . . reveals alarming tendencies in the Supreme Court's understanding of what privacy means and ought to mean. The Court treats privacy almost as if it were "a discrete commodity, possessed absolutely or not at all" [quoting Justice Marshall's dissent]. Yet what could be more commonplace than the idea that it is up to the *individual* to *measure out information* about herself *selectively* — to whomever she chooses?[17]

   Patricia Bellia contends that *Smith* conflicts with *Katz*: "In *Katz*, the phone company necessarily carried the defendant's telephone call, and the phone company no doubt had the technical ability to hear the contents of that call. That technical ability, however, was no impediment to the Court's conclusion that Katz had an expectation of privacy in the conversation."[18] Likewise, Susan Freiwald contends: "The *Smith* court ignored the lesson of *Katz*: We do not lose privacy in communications merely because they may be intercepted." She goes on to argue that the Court in *Smith* "avoided normative analysis and failed to consider how much privacy the law should actually grant to

---

[17] Laurence Tribe, *American Constitutional Law* 1391 (2d ed. 1988). For another critique of *Smith v. Maryland*, see Daniel J. Solove, *Digital Dossiers and the Dissipation*, 75 S. Cal. L. Rev. 1083 (2002).

[18] Patricia Bellia, *Surveillance Law Through Cyberlaw's Lens*, 72 Geo. Wash. L. Rev. 1375, 1405 (2004).

information. If the law treats information as private, then it will not be acceptable to acquire it, even when it possible to do so."[19]

Deirdre Mulligan explains that the Court addressed the discrepancies between *Katz* and *Smith* by discussing in *Smith* "at some length the limited information that can be gleaned from a phone number, contrasting it with what may be revealed from a telephone conversation."[20] Does the holding of *Smith* rest on the fact that the numbers were exposed to a third party or on the fact that the numbers revealed limited information about a person or on both of these factors?

3. *State Constitutional Law.* Some states have rejected the *Smith* holding under their constitutions. For example, in *State v. Hunt*, 450 A.2d 952 (N.J. 1982), the New Jersey Supreme Court rejected *Smith* and held that under the New Jersey Constitution, there is a reasonable expectation of privacy in telephone records:

> The telephone has become an essential instrument in carrying on our personal affairs. It has become part and parcel of the home. When a telephone call is made, it is as if two people are having a private conversation in the sanctity of their living room. . . .
>
> The telephone caller is . . . entitled to assume that the numbers he dials in the privacy of his home will be recorded solely for the telephone company's business purposes. From the viewpoint of the customer, all the information which he furnishes with respect to a particular call is private. The numbers dialed are private. . . .
>
> It is unrealistic to say that the cloak of privacy has been shed because the telephone company and some of its employees are aware of this information. Telephone calls cannot be made except through the telephone company's property and without payment to it for the service. This disclosure has been necessitated because of the nature of the instrumentality, but more significantly the disclosure has been made for a limited business purpose and not for release to other persons for other reasons. . . .

In an analysis of state constitutional law, Stephen Henderson concludes that 11 states have rejected the third party doctrine. Ten more states have not explicitly rejected the third party doctrine, but have case law suggesting that they might do so in the future.[21]

4. *Federal Statutory Law.* Sometimes when the Court fails to identify a privacy interest involving some aspect of the collection of personal information, Congress responds by enacting legislation that provides protection by statutory means. That happened after *Smith* with the Pen Register Act, 18 U.S.C. §§ 3121–3127. This statute requires that the government obtain a court order by certifying that the use of a pen register is "relevant to an ongoing

---

[19] Susan Freiwald, *Online Surveillance: Remembering the Lessons of the Wiretap Act,* 56 Ala. L. Rev. 9, 40, 66 (2004).

[20] Deirdre K. Mulligan, *Reasonable Expectations in Electronic Communications: A Critical Perspective on the Electronic Communications Privacy Act,* 72 Geo. Wash. L. Rev. 1557, 1581 (2004).

[21] Stephen E. Henderson, *Learning from All Fifty States: How to Apply the Fourth Amendment and Its State Analogs to Protect Third Party Information from Unreasonable Seizure,* 55 Cath. U. L. Rev. 373, 395 (2006).

investigation." This standard, however, is significantly less stringent than the probable cause required to obtain a Fourth Amendment warrant.

5. *The First Amendment and Pen Register Information.* Daniel Solove argues that the First Amendment should be understood as a source of criminal procedure and should protect pen register information:

> Although the Supreme Court has focused on the Fourth Amendment, obtaining pen register data without a warrant potentially violates the First Amendment. A log of incoming and outgoing calls can be used to trace channels of communication. It is relatively easy to link a phone number to a person or organization. Pen registers can reveal associational ties, since association in contemporary times often occurs by way of telephone or e-mail. As David Cole argues, modern communications technology has made association possible without physical assembly. For example, if the government scrutinized the phone logs of the main office of the Communist Party, it might discover many of the Party's members. The information would not be equivalent to a membership list, but it would probably include identifying data about countless individuals who would not want the government to discover their connection to the Communist Party. If the government were to examine the phone logs or e-mail headers of a particular individual, it might discover that the individual contacted particular organizations that the individual wants to keep private. The pen register information, therefore, implicates First Amendment values.[22]

Solove contends that government access to pen register information can violate the First Amendment, and he goes on to argue that the First Amendment should require a warrant before the government can obtain such information. Does pen register information implicate the First Amendment? If so, what kind of protections should the First Amendment require?

UNITED STATES V. PLACE

462 U.S. 696 (1983)

O'CONNOR, J. The Fourth Amendment "protects people from unreasonable government intrusions into their legitimate expectations of privacy." We have affirmed that a person possesses a privacy interest in the contents of personal luggage that is protected by the Fourth Amendment. A "canine sniff" by a well-trained narcotics detection dog, however, does not require opening the luggage. It does not expose noncontraband items that otherwise would remain hidden from public view, as does, for example, an officer's rummaging through the contents of the luggage. Thus, the manner in which information is obtained through this investigative technique is much less intrusive than a typical search. Moreover, the sniff discloses only the presence or absence of narcotics, a contraband item. Thus, despite the fact that the sniff tells the authorities something about the contents of the luggage, the information obtained is limited. This limited disclosure also ensures that the owner of the property is not subjected to the

---

[22] Daniel J. Solove, *The First Amendment as Criminal Procedure*, 82 N.Y.U. L. Rev. 112, 169 (2007).

embarrassment and inconvenience entailed in less discriminate and more intrusive investigative methods.

In these respects, the canine sniff is *sui generis*. We are aware of no other investigative procedure that is so limited both in the manner in which the information is obtained and in the content of the information revealed by the procedure. Therefore, we conclude that the particular course of investigation that the agents intended to pursue here — exposure of respondent's luggage, which was located in a public place, to a trained canine — did not constitute a "search" within the meaning of the Fourth Amendment. . . .

ILLINOIS V. CABALLES

543 U.S. 405 (2005)

STEVENS, J. Illinois State Trooper Daniel Gillette stopped respondent for speeding on an interstate highway. When Gillette radioed the police dispatcher to report the stop, a second trooper, Craig Graham, a member of the Illinois State Police Drug Interdiction Team, overheard the transmission and immediately headed for the scene with his narcotics-detection dog. When they arrived, respondent's car was on the shoulder of the road and respondent was in Gillette's vehicle. While Gillette was in the process of writing a warning ticket, Graham walked his dog around respondent's car. The dog alerted at the trunk. Based on that alert, the officers searched the trunk, found marijuana, and arrested respondent. The entire incident lasted less than 10 minutes.

Respondent was convicted of a narcotics offense and sentenced to 12 years' imprisonment and a $256,136 fine. . . .

The question on which we granted certiorari is narrow: "Whether the Fourth Amendment requires reasonable, articulable suspicion to justify using a drug-detection dog to sniff a vehicle during a legitimate traffic stop." Thus, we proceed on the assumption that the officer conducting the dog sniff had no information about respondent except that he had been stopped for speeding; accordingly, we have omitted any reference to facts about respondent that might have triggered a modicum of suspicion. . . .

In our view, conducting a dog sniff would not change the character of a traffic stop that is lawful at its inception and otherwise executed in a reasonable manner, unless the dog sniff itself infringed respondent's constitutionally protected interest in privacy. Our cases hold that it did not.

Official conduct that does not "compromise any legitimate interest in privacy" is not a search subject to the Fourth Amendment. We have held that any interest in possessing contraband cannot be deemed "legitimate," and thus, governmental conduct that *only* reveals the possession of contraband "compromises no legitimate privacy interest." This is because the expectation "that certain facts will not come to the attention of the authorities" is not the same as an interest in "privacy that society is prepared to consider reasonable." In *United States v. Place,* 462 U.S. 696 (1983), we treated a canine sniff by a well-trained narcotics-detection dog as "*sui generis*" because it "discloses only the presence or absence of narcotics, a contraband item." Respondent likewise concedes that "drug sniffs are designed, and if properly conducted are generally likely, to reveal only the presence of contraband." Although respondent argues that the error rates, particularly the existence of false positives, call into question the premise that drug-detection dogs alert only to contraband, the record contains no evidence or findings that support his argument. Moreover, respondent does not suggest that an erroneous alert, in and of itself, reveals any legitimate private information, and, in this case, the trial judge found that the dog sniff was sufficiently reliable to establish probable cause to conduct a full-blown search of the trunk.

Accordingly, the use of a well-trained narcotics-detection dog—one that "does not expose noncontraband items that otherwise would remain hidden from public view," *Place*, 462 U.S., at 707, during a lawful traffic stop, generally does not implicate legitimate privacy interests. In this case, the dog sniff was performed on the exterior of respondent's car while he was lawfully seized for a traffic violation. Any intrusion on respondent's privacy expectations does not rise to the level of a constitutionally cognizable infringement.

SOUTER, J., dissenting. I would hold that using the dog for the purposes of determining the presence of marijuana in the car's trunk was a search unauthorized as an incident of the speeding stop and unjustified on any other ground. I would accordingly affirm the judgment of the Supreme Court of Illinois, and I respectfully dissent.

At the heart both of *Place* and the Court's opinion today is the proposition that sniffs by a trained dog are *sui generis* because a reaction by the dog in going alert is a response to nothing but the presence of contraband.[23] Hence, the argument goes, because the sniff can only reveal the presence of items devoid of any legal use, the sniff "does not implicate legitimate privacy interests" and is not to be treated as a search.

The infallible dog, however, is a creature of legal fiction. Although the Supreme Court of Illinois did not get into the sniffing averages of drug dogs, their supposed infallibility is belied by judicial opinions describing well-trained animals sniffing and alerting with less than perfect accuracy, whether owing to errors by their handlers, the limitations of the dogs themselves, or even the pervasive contamination of currency by cocaine. *See, e.g., United States v. Kennedy*, 131 F.3d 1371, 1378 (C.A.10 1997) (describing a dog that had a 71% accuracy rate); *United States v. Scarborough*, 128 F.3d 1373, 1378, n. 3 (C.A.10 1997) (describing a dog that erroneously alerted 4 times out of 19 while working for the postal service and 8% of the time over its entire career); *United States v. Limares*, 269 F.3d 794, 797 (C.A.7 2001) (accepting as reliable a dog that gave false positives between 7 and 38% of the time); *Laime v. State*, 347 Ark. 142, 159, 60 S.W.3d 464, 476 (2001) (speaking of a dog that made between 10 and 50 errors); *United States v. $242,484.00*, 351 F.3d 499, 511 (C.A.11 2003) (noting that because as much as 80% of all currency in circulation contains drug residue,

---

[23] Another proffered justification for *sui generis* status is that a dog sniff is a particularly nonintrusive procedure. *United States v. Place*, 462 U.S. 696, 707 (1983). I agree with Justice Ginsburg that the introduction of a dog to a traffic stop (let alone an encounter with someone walking down the street) can in fact be quite intrusive.

a dog alert "is of little value"). . . . Indeed, a study cited by Illinois in this case for the proposition that dog sniffs are "generally reliable" shows that dogs in artificial testing situations return false positives anywhere from 12.5 to 60% of the time, depending on the length of the search. In practical terms, the evidence is clear that the dog that alerts hundreds of times will be wrong dozens of times.

Once the dog's fallibility is recognized, however, that ends the justification claimed in *Place* for treating the sniff as *sui generis* under the Fourth Amendment: the sniff alert does not necessarily signal hidden contraband, and opening the container or enclosed space whose emanations the dog has sensed will not necessarily reveal contraband or any other evidence of crime. This is not, of course, to deny that a dog's reaction may provide reasonable suspicion, or probable cause, to search the container or enclosure; the Fourth Amendment does not demand certainty of success to justify a search for evidence or contraband. The point is simply that the sniff and alert cannot claim the certainty that *Place* assumed, both in treating the deliberate use of sniffing dogs as *sui generis* and then taking that characterization as a reason to say they are not searches subject to Fourth Amendment scrutiny. And when that aura of uniqueness disappears, there is no basis in *Place*'s reasoning, and no good reason otherwise, to ignore the actual function that dog sniffs perform. They are conducted to obtain information about the contents of private spaces beyond anything that human senses could perceive, even when conventionally enhanced. The information is not provided by independent third parties beyond the reach of constitutional limitations, but gathered by the government's own officers in order to justify searches of the traditional sort, which may or may not reveal evidence of crime but will disclose anything meant to be kept private in the area searched. Thus in practice the government's use of a trained narcotics dog functions as a limited search to reveal undisclosed facts about private enclosures, to be used to justify a further and complete search of the enclosed area. And given the fallibility of the dog, the sniff is the first step in a process that may disclose "intimate details" without revealing contraband. . . .

GINSBURG & SOUTER, J.J., dissenting. . . . In *Terry v. Ohio,* the Court upheld the stop and subsequent frisk of an individual based on an officer's observation of suspicious behavior and his reasonable belief that the suspect was armed. . . . In a *Terry*-type investigatory stop, "the officer's action [must be] justified at its inception, and . . . reasonably related in scope to the circumstances which justified the interference in the first place." In applying *Terry,* the Court has several times indicated that the limitation on "scope" is not confined to the duration of the seizure; it also encompasses the manner in which the seizure is conducted. . . .

Terry, it merits repetition, instructs that any investigation must be "reasonably related in *scope* to the circumstances which justified the interference in the first place" (emphasis added). The unwarranted and nonconsensual expansion of the seizure here from a routine traffic stop to a drug investigation broadened the scope of the investigation in a manner that, in my judgment, runs afoul of the Fourth Amendment. . . .

A drug-detection dog is an intimidating animal. Injecting such an animal into a routine traffic stop changes the character of the encounter between the police and the motorist. The stop becomes broader, more adversarial, and (in at least some cases) longer. Caballes — who, as far as Troopers Gillette and Graham knew, was guilty solely of driving six miles per hour over the speed limit—was exposed to the embarrassment and intimidation of being investigated, on a public thoroughfare, for drugs.

NOTES & QUESTIONS

1. *Detecting Only Illegal Contraband.* Suppose the police had used a special x-ray machine to examine the contents of the bag. Would this be a Fourth Amendment violation under *Caballes*? Why or why not? Suppose that an x-ray device could be developed that would only detect illegal items, such as drugs, child pornography, weapons, or stolen items. Would the use of such a device to examine the contents of a person's bag or home constitute a search?

2. *Is the Fourth Amendment Primarily Protective of the Individual or Society?* Consider the following observation by Anthony Amsterdam:

> [Should the Fourth Amendment] be viewed as a collection of protections of atomistic spheres of interest of individual citizens or as a regulation of governmental conduct[?] Does it safeguard *my* person and *your* house and *her* papers and *his* effects against unreasonable searches and seizures; or is it essentially a regulatory canon requiring government to order its law enforcement procedures in a fashion that keeps us collectively secure in our persons, houses, papers, and effects, against unreasonable searches and seizures?[24]

> Under what view does the Supreme Court seem to be operating? Which view do you think is the most appropriate?

3. *Is Government Observation Different from Observation by Others?* Amsterdam also argues that one's privacy may be violated by being observed by the police but may not be violated by the very same observation from others:

> [I]f you live in a cheap hotel or in a ghetto flat, your neighbors can hear you breathing quietly even in temperate weather when it is possible to keep the windows and doors closed. For the tenement dweller, the difference between observation by neighbors and visitors who ordinarily use the common hallways and observation by policemen who come into hallways to "check up" or "look around" is the difference between all the privacy that his condition allows and none. Is that small difference too unimportant to claim [F]ourth [A]mendment protection?[25]

> Do you agree that our expectations of privacy turn on who is watching rather than simply whether we are being watched? Should the "reasonable

---

[24] Anthony G. Amsterdam, *Perspectives on the Fourth Amendment*, 58 Minn. L. Rev. 349, 367 (1974). For an additional critique of the reasonable expectation of privacy test, see Andrew E. Taslitz, *The Fourth Amendment in the Twenty-First Century: Technology, Privacy, and Human Emotions*, 65 Law & Contemp. Probs. 125 (2002).

[25] Amsterdam, *Fourth Amendment, supra*, at 404.

expectation of privacy" test be changed to the "reasonable expectation of what the police can observe or search" test?

4. ***Bomb Detection vs. Drug Detection?*** The dissents of both Justice Souter and Justice Ginsburg in *Caballes* distinguish a canine search for drugs from one for bombs. Justice Souter argued in a footnote of his dissent that he reserved judgment concerning "a possible case significantly unlike this one":

> All of us are concerned not to prejudge a claim of authority to detect explosives and dangerous chemical or biological weapons that might be carried by a terrorist who prompts no individualized suspicion. Suffice it to say here that what is a reasonable search depends in part on demonstrated risk. Unreasonable sniff searches for marijuana are not necessarily unreasonable sniff searches for destructive or deadly material if suicide bombs are a societal risk.

For Justice Ginsburg, the use of a bomb-detection dog to check vehicles would be closer to sobriety checkpoints that the Supreme Court has upheld. *Michigan Dep't of State Police v. Sitz*, 496 U.S. 444 (1990). Do you agree with these attempts to distinguish dogs that detect bombs from those that detect drugs?

CALIFORNIA V. GREENWOOD

486 U.S. 35 (1988)

[Police investigators searched the plastic garbage bags that Greenwood left on the curb in front of his house to be picked up by the trash collector. The officers found indications of drug use from the search of Greenwood's trash and obtained a warrant to search the house, where they uncovered more evidence of drug trafficking. Greenwood was arrested.]

WHITE, J. . . . The warrantless search and seizure of the garbage bags left at the curb outside the Greenwood house would violate the Fourth Amendment only if respondents manifested a subjective expectation of privacy in their garbage that society accepts as objectively reasonable.

. . . [The Greenwoods] assert . . . that they had, and exhibited, an expectation of privacy with respect to the trash that was searched by the police: The trash, which was placed on the street for collection at a fixed time, was contained in opaque plastic bags, which the garbage collector was expected to pick up, mingle with the trash of others, and deposit at the garbage dump. The trash was only temporarily on the street, and there was little likelihood that it would be inspected by anyone.

It may well be that respondents did not expect that the contents of their garbage bags would become known to the police or other members of the public. An expectation of privacy does not give rise to Fourth Amendment protection, however, unless society is prepared to accept that expectation as objectively reasonable.

Here, we conclude that respondents exposed their garbage to the public sufficiently to defeat their claim to Fourth Amendment protection. It is common knowledge that plastic garbage bags left on or at the side of a public street are readily accessible to animals, children, scavengers, snoops, and other members of the public. Moreover, respondents placed their refuse at the curb for the express purpose of conveying it to a third party, the trash collector, who might himself have sorted through respondents' trash or permitted others, such as the police, to do so. Accordingly, having deposited their garbage "in an area particularly suited for public inspection and, in a manner of speaking, public consumption, for the express purpose of having strangers take it," respondents could have had no reasonable expectation of privacy in the inculpatory items that they discarded. . .

BRENNAN, J. joined by MARSHALL, J. dissenting. . . . Scrutiny of another's trash is contrary to commonly accepted notions of civilized behavior. I suspect, therefore, that members of our society will be shocked to learn that the Court, the ultimate guarantor of liberty, deems unreasonable our expectation that the aspects of our private lives that are concealed safely in a trash bag will not become public.

"A container which can support a reasonable expectation of privacy may not be searched, even on probable cause, without a warrant." *United States v. Jacobsen*, 466 U.S. 109, 120, n.17 (1984) (citations omitted). Thus, as the Court observes, if Greenwood had a reasonable expectation that the contents of the bags that he placed on the curb would remain private, the warrantless search of those bags violated the Fourth Amendment. . . .

Our precedent, therefore, leaves no room to doubt that had respondents been carrying their personal effects in opaque, sealed plastic bags — identical to the ones they placed on the curb — their privacy would have been protected from warrantless police intrusion. . . .

Respondents deserve no less protection just because Greenwood used the bags to discard rather than to transport his personal effects. Their contents are not inherently any less private, and Greenwood's decision to discard them, at least in the manner in which he did, does not diminish his expectation of privacy.

A trash bag, like any of the above-mentioned containers, "is a common repository for one's personal effects" and, even more than many of them, is "therefore . . . inevitably associated with the expectation of privacy." "[A]lmost every human activity ultimately manifests itself in waste products. . . ." *Smith v. State*, 510 P.2d 793, 798 (Alaska 1973). A single bag of trash testifies eloquently to the eating, reading, and recreational habits of the person who produced it. A search of trash, like a search of the bedroom, can relate intimate details about sexual practices, health, and personal hygiene. Like rifling through desk drawers or intercepting phone calls, rummaging through trash can divulge the target's financial and professional status, political affiliations and inclinations, private thoughts, personal relationships, and romantic interests. It cannot be doubted that a sealed trash bag harbors telling evidence of the "intimate activity associated with the 'sanctity of a man's home and the privacies of life,'" which the Fourth Amendment is designed to protect. . . .

. . . Most of us, I believe, would be incensed to discover a meddler — whether a neighbor, a reporter, or a detective — scrutinizing our sealed trash containers to discover some detail of our personal lives. . . .

The mere possibility that unwelcome meddlers might open and rummage through the containers does not negate the expectation of privacy in their contents any more than the possibility of a burglary negates an expectation of privacy in the home; or the possibility of a private intrusion negates an expectation of privacy in an unopened package; or the possibility that an operator will listen in on a telephone conversation negates an expectation of privacy in the words spoken on the telephone. "What a person . . . seeks to preserve as private, even in an area accessible to the public, may be constitutionally protected." *Katz*, 389 U.S. at 351-52. . . .

NOTES & QUESTIONS

1. *Recycling and Surveillance of Garbage.* In dissent in *Greenwald*, a decision from 1988, Justice Brennan states, "Scrutiny of another's trash is contrary to commonly accepted notions of civilized behavior." In the twenty-first century, however, an increasing number of communities have imposed recycling obligations on its citizens. Sanitation departments sometimes oversee the recycling by routinely checking people's trash, and, in the case of noncompliance, imposing fines. Does this development alter the extent of any reasonable expectation of privacy in one's trash vis-à-vis the police?

2. *Surveillance 24/7.* In addition to searching through Greenwood's trash, the police were staking out his home, watching who came and went from his house. Does the Fourth Amendment protect against such surveillance? Imagine that for one year, the police were to stake out a person's home and follow the person wherever he or she went throughout the day. The person would be under 24-hour surveillance, seven days a week. Assume that the police would simply observe the person anytime he or she was in public. Is this more invasive to privacy than a one-time search of particular items, such as one's luggage? Does the Fourth Amendment provide any limitation on the police activities described above?

PLAIN VIEW, OPEN FIELDS, AND CURTILAGE

"[I]t has long been settled that objects falling in the plain view of an officer who has a right to be in the position to have that view are subject to seizure and may be introduced in evidence." *Harris v. United States*, 390 U.S. 234, 236 (1968). This has become known as the "plain view" doctrine. If it is possible for something to be seen or heard from a public vantage point, there can be no reasonable expectation of privacy.

An extension of the plain view rule is the "open fields" doctrine. An individual does not have a reasonable expectation of privacy in the open fields that she owns. In *Oliver v. United States*, 466 U.S. 170 (1984), the defendant placed "No Trespassing" signs throughout his farm and maintained a locked gate around the farm's entrance. The fields could not be seen from any public vantage point. The police trespassed onto the fields and found marijuana. The Court held, however, that there is no reasonable expectation of privacy in open fields, and the defendant's attempt to keep them secluded and shielded from public view was irrelevant.

An exception to the open fields doctrine is the legal treatment of a house's so-called "curtilage." Under the curtilage doctrine, parts of one's property immediately outside one's home do not fall within the open fields rule. This exception does not mean that the curtilage is automatically afforded Fourth Amendment protection; a reasonable expectation of privacy analysis still must be performed. The question of whether an area constitutes a curtilage depends upon "whether the area in question is so intimately tied to the home itself that it should be placed within the home's 'umbrella' of Fourth Amendment protection." *United States v. Dunn*, 480 U.S. 294, 301 (1987).

FLORIDA V. RILEY

488 U.S. 445 (1989)

WHITE, J. . . . Respondent Riley lived in a mobile home located on five acres of rural property. A greenhouse was located 10 to 20 feet behind the mobile home. Two sides of the greenhouse were enclosed. The other two sides were not enclosed but the contents of the greenhouse were obscured from view from surrounding property by trees, shrubs, and the mobile home. The greenhouse was covered by corrugated roofing panels, some translucent and some opaque. At the time relevant to this case, two of the panels, amounting to approximately 10% of the roof area, were missing. A wire fence surrounded the mobile home and the greenhouse, and the property was posted with a "DO NOT ENTER" sign.

This case originated with an anonymous tip to the Pasco County Sheriff's office that marijuana was being grown on respondent's property. When an investigating officer discovered that he could not see the contents of the greenhouse from the road, he circled twice over respondent's property in a helicopter at the height of 400 feet. With his naked eye, he was able to see through the openings in the roof and one or more of the open sides of the greenhouse and to identify what he thought was marijuana growing in the structure. A warrant was obtained based on these observations, and the ensuing search revealed marijuana growing in the greenhouse. Respondent was charged with possession of marijuana under Florida law. . . .

We agree with the State's submission that our decision in *California v. Ciraolo*, 476 U.S. 207 (1986), controls this case. There, acting on a tip, the police inspected the back-yard of a particular house while flying in a fixed-wing aircraft at 1,000 feet. With the naked eye the officers saw what they concluded was marijuana growing in the yard. A search warrant was obtained on the strength of this airborne inspection, and marijuana plants were found. The trial court refused to suppress this evidence, but a state appellate court held that the inspection violated the Fourth and Fourteenth Amendments to the United States Constitution, and that the warrant was therefore invalid. We in turn reversed, holding that the inspection was not a search subject to the Fourth Amendment. We recognized that the yard was within the curtilage of the house, that a fence shielded the yard from observation from the street, and that the occupant had a subjective expectation of privacy. We held, however, that such an expectation was not reasonable and not one "that society is prepared to honor." Our reasoning was that the home and its curtilage are not necessarily protected from inspection that involves no physical invasion. "'What a person knowingly exposes to the public, even in his own home or office, is not a subject of Fourth Amendment protection.'" As a general proposition, the police may see what may be seen "from a public vantage point where [they have] a right to be." Thus the police, like the public, would have been free to inspect the backyard garden from the street if their view had been unobstructed. They were likewise free to inspect the yard from the vantage point of an aircraft flying in the navigable airspace as this plane was. "In an age where private and commercial flight in the public airways is routine, it is unreasonable for respondent to expect that his marijuana plants were constitutionally protected from being observed with the naked eye from an altitude of 1,000 feet. The Fourth Amendment simply does not require the police traveling in the public airways at this altitude to obtain a warrant in order to observe what is visible to the naked eye."

We arrive at the same conclusion in the present case. In this case, as in *Ciraolo*, the property surveyed was within the curtilage of respondent's home. Riley no doubt intended and expected that his greenhouse would not be open to public inspection, and the precautions he took protected against ground-level observation. Because the sides and roof of his greenhouse were left partially open, however, what was growing in the greenhouse was subject to viewing from the air. Under the holding in *Ciraolo*, Riley could not reasonably have expected the contents of his greenhouse to be immune from examination by an officer seated in a fixed-wing aircraft flying in navigable airspace at an altitude of 1,000 feet or, as the Florida Supreme Court seemed to recognize, at an altitude of 500 feet, the lower limit of the navigable airspace for such an aircraft. Here, the inspection was made from a helicopter, but as is the case with fixed-wing planes, "private and commercial flight [by helicopter] in the public airways is routine" in this country, and there is no indication that such flights are unheard of in Pasco County, Florida. Riley could not reasonably have expected that his greenhouse was protected from public or official observation from a helicopter had it been flying within the navigable airspace for fixed-wing aircraft.

Nor on the facts before us, does it make a difference for Fourth Amendment purposes that the helicopter was flying at 400 feet when the officer saw what was growing in the greenhouse through the partially open roof and sides of the structure. We would have a different case if flying at that altitude had been contrary to law or regulation. But helicopters are not bound by the lower limits of the navigable airspace allowed to other aircraft.[26] Any member of the public could legally have been flying over Riley's property in a helicopter at the altitude of 400 feet and could have observed Riley's greenhouse. The police officer did no more. . . . As far as this record reveals, no intimate details connected with the use of the home or curtilage were observed, and there was no undue noise, and

---

[26] While Federal Aviation Administration regulations permit fixed-wing-aircraft to be operated at an altitude of 1,000 feet while flying over congested areas and at an altitude of 500 feet above the surface in other than congested areas, helicopters may be operated at less than the minimums for fixed-wing-aircraft "if the operation is conducted without hazard to persons or property on the surface. In addition, each person operating a helicopter shall comply with routes or altitudes specifically prescribed for helicopters by the [FAA] Administrator." 14 CFR § 91.79 (1988).

no wind, dust, or threat of injury. In these circumstances, there was no violation of the Fourth Amendment.

O'CONNOR, J. concurring in the judgment. Ciraolo's expectation of privacy was unreasonable not because the airplane was operating where it had a "right to be," but because public air travel at 1,000 feet is a sufficiently routine part of modern life that it is unreasonable for persons on the ground to expect that their curtilage will not be observed from the air at that altitude. Although "helicopters are not bound by the lower limits of the navigable airspace allowed to other aircraft,"there is no reason to assume that compliance with FAA regulations alone determines "'whether the government's intrusion infringes upon the personal and societal values protected by the Fourth Amendment.'" Because the FAA has decided that helicopters can lawfully operate at virtually any altitude so long as they pose no safety hazard, it does not follow that the expectations of privacy "society is prepared to recognize as 'reasonable'" simply mirror the FAA's safety concerns. . . .

BRENNAN, J. joined by MARSHALL and STEVENS, J.J. dissenting. Under the plurality's exceedingly grudging Fourth Amendment theory, the expectation of privacy is defeated if a single member of the public could conceivably position herself to see into the area in question without doing anything illegal. It is defeated whatever the difficulty a person would have in so positioning herself, and however infrequently anyone would in fact do so. In taking this view the plurality ignores the very essence of *Katz*. The reason why there is no reasonable expectation of privacy in an area that is exposed to the public is that little diminution in "the amount of privacy and freedom remaining to citizens" will result from police surveillance of something that any passerby readily sees. To pretend, as the plurality opinion does, that the same is true when the police use a helicopter to peer over high fences is, at best, disingenuous. . . .

It is a curious notion that the reach of the Fourth Amendment can be so largely defined by administrative regulations issued for purposes of flight safety.[27] It is more curious still that the plurality relies to such an extent on the legality of the officer's act, when we have consistently refused to equate police violation of the law with infringement of the Fourth Amendment.

The police officer positioned 400 feet above Riley's backyard was not, however, standing on a public road. The vantage point he enjoyed was not one any citizen could readily share. His ability to see over Riley's fence depended on his use of a very expensive and sophisticated piece of machinery to which few ordinary citizens have access. In such circumstances it makes no more sense to rely on the legality of the officer's position in the skies than it would to judge the constitutionality of the wiretap in *Katz* by the legality of the officer's position outside the telephone booth. The simple inquiry whether the police officer had

---

[27] The plurality's use of the FAA regulations as a means for determining whether Riley enjoyed a reasonable expectation of privacy produces an incredible result. Fixed-wing aircraft may not be operated below 500 feet (1,000 feet over congested areas), while helicopters may be operated below those levels. Therefore, whether Riley's expectation of privacy is reasonable turns on whether the police officer at 400 feet above his curtilage is seated in an airplane or a helicopter. This cannot be the law.

the legal right to be in the position from which he made his observations cannot suffice, for we cannot assume that Riley's curtilage was so open to the observations of passersby in the skies that he retained little privacy or personal security to be lost to police surveillance. The question before us must be not whether the police were where they had a right to be, but whether public observation of Riley's curtilage was so commonplace that Riley's expectation of privacy in his backyard could not be considered reasonable. . . .

. . . The Fourth Amendment demands that we temper our efforts to apprehend criminals with a concern for the impact on our fundamental liberties of the methods we use. I hope it will be a matter of concern to my colleagues that the police surveillance methods they would sanction were among those described 40 years ago in George Orwell's dread vision of life in the 1980's:

> The black-mustachio'd face gazed down from every commanding corner. There was one on the house front immediately opposite. BIG BROTHER IS WATCHING YOU, the caption said. . . . In the far distance a helicopter skimmed down between the roofs, hovered for an instant like a bluebottle, and darted away again with a curving flight. It was the Police Patrol, snooping into people's windows.

Who can read this passage without a shudder, and without the instinctive reaction that it depicts life in some country other than ours? I respectfully dissent.

NOTES & QUESTIONS

1. ***Privacy in Public.*** The court quotes from *Katz v. United States* that "[w]hat a person knowingly exposes to the public . . . is not a subject of Fourth Amendment protection." How far does this principle extend? Can there be situations where a person might have a reasonable expectation of privacy even when exposed in public? Recall the public disclosure tort cases in Chapter 2, which indicate that sometimes a person does have a privacy interest even in the event of public exposure or being in a public place.

2. ***Surveillance Cameras.*** The use of surveillance cameras is increasing. Since 1994, in response to terrorist bombings, Britain has been watching city streets through a system of surveillance cameras monitored by closed circuit television (CCTV).[28] In 2002, the National Park Service announced plans to set up a surveillance system at all major monuments on the National Mall in Washington, D.C. Given the frequent use of surveillance cameras, do we still have an expectation of privacy not to be filmed in our day-to-day activities? Consider Marc Blitz:

> People also need privacy and anonymity in many aspects of public life — for example, when they explore controversial films, books, or ideas, have conversations in public places, or seek aid or counsel of a sort they can only find by venturing into the public sphere. Although walls and windows do not shield these public activities from everyone's view, other features of physical

---

[28] For more background about CCTV, see Clive Norris & Gary Armstrong, *The Maximum Surveillance Society: The Rise of CCTV* (1999); Jeffrey Rosen, *A Cautionary Tale for a New Age of Surveillance*, N.Y. Times Mag. (Oct. 7, 2001).

and social architecture, distinctive to public space, do shield them. Crowds and the diversity and separateness of the social circles that people move in allow people to find anonymity; the existence of isolated and unmonitored islands of public space allow them to find seclusion. . . . These privacy-enhancing features of public space cannot easily survive in a world of ubiquitous cameras, and the task of preserving them requires courts to do in a sense the opposite of what *Katz* recommends: They must abandon the task of identifying difficult-to-identify expectations of privacy . . . and instead return to the task of preserving the environment that makes privacy possible.[29]

What precisely are the harms of surveillance cameras? Consider Christopher Slobogin:

> Virtually all of us, no matter how innocent, feel somewhat unnerved when a police car pulls up behind us. Imagine now being watched by an officer, at a discreet distance and without any other intrusion, every time you walk through certain streets. Say you want to run (to catch a bus, for a brief bit of exercise or just for the hell of it). Will you? Or assume you want to obscure your face (because of the wind or a desire to avoid being seen by an officious acquaintance)? How about hanging out on the street corner (waiting for friends or because you have nothing else to do)?
>
> In all of these scenarios, you will probably feel and perhaps act differently than when the officer is not there. Perhaps your hesitancy comes from uncertainty as to the officer's likely reaction or simply from a desire to appear completely law-abiding; the important point is that it exists. Government-run cameras are a less tangible presence than the ubiquitous cop, but better at recording your actions. A police officer in Liverpool, England may have said it best: A camera is like having a cop "on duty 24 hours a day, constantly taking notes."[30]

Are there any other harms you can think of? What are the benefits of surveillance cameras? Should they not be permissible as a low-cost way to extend the reach of police? Do the benefits outweigh the harms? Regarding the benefits of surveillance cameras, consider Jeff Rosen:

> In 2000, Britain's violent-crime rates actually increased by 4.3 percent, even though the cameras continued to proliferate. But CCTV cameras have a mysterious knack for justifying themselves regardless of what happens to crime. When crime goes up, the cameras get the credit for detecting it, and when crime goes down, they get the credit for preventing it.[31]

Would it be possible to design an empirical study that would test the effectiveness of surveillance cameras in preventing crime?

3. *Face Recognition Systems.* In Tampa, a computer software program called "FaceIt" linked to 36 cameras attempts to scan the faces of individuals on public streets to match them against mug shots of wanted fugitives. A similar

---

[29] Marc Jonathan Blitz, *Video Surveillance and the Constitution of Public Space: Fitting the Fourth Amendment to a World that Tracks Image and Identity*, 82 Tex. L. Rev. 1349, 1481 (2004).

[30] Christopher Slobogin, *Public Privacy: Camera Surveillance of Public Places and the Right to Anonymity*, 72 Miss. L.J. 213, 247 (2002).

[31] Jeffrey Rosen, *The Naked Crowd: Reclaiming Security and Freedom in an Anxious Age* 49 (2004).

system was used to scan faces at Super Bowl XXXV in January 2001. The Tampa Police Department argues that "FaceIt" is analogous to a police officer standing on a street holding a mug shot. Philip Agre contends that face recognition systems are different:

> A human being who spots me in the park has the accountability that someone can spot them as well. Cameras are much more anonymous and easy to hide. More important is the question of scale. Most people understand the moral difference between a single chance observation in a park and an investigator who follows you everywhere you go.[32]

Further, contends Agre, the information used and collected by face recognition systems could fall into the wrong hands and be potentially abused by the government to exercise social control. Additionally, such systems can have errors, resulting in the tracking and potential arrest of innocent persons. As a policy matter, do the costs of facial recognition systems outweigh the benefits? Given the information privacy law you have learned so far, assess the legality and constitutionality of facial recognition systems.

The Tampa face recognition system was ultimately scrapped because of high errors and general ineffectiveness.

4. *Who Decides What Constitutes a Reasonable Expectation of Privacy?* Currently, judges decide whether a defendant has a reasonable expectation of privacy in a particular activity. Is this question appropriate for judges to decide? Or should juries decide it? In all of the cases so far, observe the sources that the Court cites to for support that there is no reasonable expectation of privacy. How is a reasonable expectation of privacy to be measured? Is it an empirical question about what most people in society would generally consider to be private? If so, why aren't polls taken? If you're an attorney arguing that there is a reasonable expectation of privacy in something, what do you cite to? How should courts measure what society as a whole thinks is private?

Christopher Slobogin and Joseph Schumacher conducted a survey of individuals, asking them to rate on a scale of 0 to 100 the intrusiveness of certain types of searches or seizures, with 0 being nonintrusive and 100 being extremely intrusive. Several searches that the Court has concluded do not trigger a reasonable expectation of privacy rated in the middle of the scale. The flyover in *Florida v. Riley* rated at 40.32 on this scale; the dog sniff in *United States v. Place* rated at 58.33; the search of garbage in *California v. Greenwood* rated at 44.95; and the use of a beeper to track a car in *United States v. Knotts* rated at 54.46. Certain searches that the Court held do not involve a reasonable expectation of privacy rated highly on the scale, such as examining bank records in *United States v. Miller,* rated at 71.60. In other highly rated searches, the Court has concluded that the Fourth Amendment applies, such as monitoring a phone for 30 days, rating at 87.67 and a body cavity search at the border, rating at 90.14. The body cavity search was the

---

[32] Philip E. Agre, *Your Face Is Not a Bar Code: Arguments Against Automatic Face Recognition in Public Places* (Sept. 9, 2001), http://dlis.gseis.ucla.edu/people/pagre/bar-code.html.

highest rated search, and a search of foliage in a public park was the lowest rated at 6.48. Slobogin and Schumacher conclude that "the Supreme Court's conclusions about the scope of the Fourth Amendment are often not in tune with commonly held attitudes about police investigative techniques."[33]

To what extent should empirical evidence such as this study be used by courts in determining whether or not there is a reasonable expectation of privacy? If such evidence should be used, at what point in the scale should the line be drawn to establish the existence of a reasonable expectation of privacy?

5. ***Should the Reasonable Expectation of Privacy Test Be Empirical or Normative?*** There is an interesting paradox at the heart of the reasonable expectation of privacy test: Legal protection is triggered by people's expectations of privacy, but those expectations are, to a notable extent, shaped by the extent of the legal protection of privacy. Consider the following argument by Daniel Solove regarding the privacy of the postal letters:

> [I]n America, the privacy of letters was formed in significant part by a legal architecture that protected the confidentiality of letters from other people and government officials. In colonial America, mail was often insecure; it was difficult to seal letters; and the wax often used to keep letters sealed was not very effective. There was widespread suspicion of postal clerks reading letters; and a number of prominent individuals, such as Thomas Jefferson, Alexander Hamilton, and George Washington, decried the lack of privacy in their letters and would sometimes even write in code. . . . Despite these realities, and people's expectation that letters would not be confidential, the law evolved to provide strong protection of the privacy of letters. Benjamin Franklin, who was in charge of the colonial mails, required his employees to swear an oath not to open mail. In the late eighteenth and early nineteenth centuries, Congress passed several laws prohibiting the improper opening of mail. And the Supreme Court held in 1877 that despite the fact that people turned letters over to the government for delivery in the postal system, sealed parcels were protected from inspection by the Fourth Amendment. This example illustrates that privacy is not just found but constructed. By erecting a legal structure to protect the privacy of letters, our society shaped the practices of letter writing and using the postal system. It occurred because of the desire to make privacy an integral part of these practices rather than to preserve the status quo.[34]

Solove argues that societies seek to protect privacy with the law when they do not expect privacy but desire to have it. If Solove is right, then what should courts look to when applying the reasonable expectation of privacy test?

---

[33] Christopher Slobogin & Joseph E. Schumacher, *Reasonable Expectations of Privacy and Autonomy in Fourth Amendment Cases: An Empirical Look at "Understandings Recognized and Permitted by Society,"* 42 Duke L.J. 727 (1993).

[34] Daniel J. Solove, *Conceptualizing Privacy*, 90 Cal. L. Rev. 1087, 1142-43 (2002); *see also* Shaun Spencer, *Reasonable Expectations and the Erosion of Privacy*, 39 San Diego L. Rev. 843 (2002).

(b) Sensory Enhancement Technology

DOW CHEMICAL CO. V. UNITED STATES
476 U.S. 227 (1986)

BURGER, C. J. . . . Petitioner Dow Chemical Co. operates a 2,000-acre facility manufacturing chemicals at Midland, Michigan. The facility consists of numerous covered buildings, with manufacturing equipment and piping conduits located between the various buildings exposed to visual observation from the air. At all times, Dow has maintained elaborate security around the perimeter of the complex barring ground-level public views of these areas. It also investigates any low-level flights by aircraft over the facility. Dow has not undertaken, however, to conceal all manufacturing equipment within the complex from aerial views. Dow maintains that the cost of covering its exposed equipment would be prohibitive.

In early 1978, enforcement officials of EPA, with Dow's consent, made an on-site inspection of two power plants in this complex. A subsequent EPA request for a second inspection, however, was denied, and EPA did not thereafter seek an administrative search warrant. Instead, EPA employed a commercial aerial photographer, using a standard floor-mounted, precision aerial mapping camera, to take photographs of the facility from altitudes of 12,000, 3,000, and 1,200 feet. At all times the aircraft was lawfully within navigable airspace.

EPA did not inform Dow of this aerial photography, but when Dow became aware of it, Dow brought suit in the District Court alleging that EPA's action violated the Fourth Amendment and was beyond EPA's statutory investigative authority. The District Court granted Dow's motion for summary judgment on the ground that EPA had no authority to take aerial photographs and that doing so was a search violating the Fourth Amendment. EPA was permanently enjoined from taking aerial photographs of Dow's premises and from disseminating, releasing, or copying the photographs already taken. . . .

The photographs at issue in this case are essentially like those commonly used in mapmaking. Any person with an airplane and an aerial camera could readily duplicate them. In common with much else, the technology of photography has changed in this century. These developments have enhanced industrial processes, and indeed all areas of life; they have also enhanced law enforcement techniques. . . .

. . . Dow claims EPA's use of aerial photography was a "search" of an area that, notwithstanding the large size of the plant, was within an "industrial curtilage" rather than an "open field," and that it had a reasonable expectation of privacy from such photography protected by the Fourth Amendment. . . .

. . . Dow concedes that a simple flyover with naked-eye observation, or the taking of a photograph from a nearby hillside overlooking such a facility, would give rise to no Fourth Amendment problem.

In *California v. Ciraolo*, 476 U.S. 207 (1986), decided today, we hold that naked-eye aerial observation from an altitude of 1,000 feet of a backyard within the curtilage of a home does not constitute a search under the Fourth Amendment.

In the instant case, two additional Fourth Amendment claims are presented: whether the common-law "curtilage" doctrine encompasses a large industrial complex such as Dow's, and whether photography employing an aerial mapping camera is permissible in this context. Dow argues that an industrial plant, even one occupying 2,000 acres, does not fall within the "open fields" doctrine of *Oliver v. United States* but rather is an "industrial curtilage" having constitutional protection equivalent to that of the curtilage of a private home. Dow further contends that any aerial photography of this "industrial curtilage" intrudes upon its reasonable expectations of privacy. Plainly a business establishment or an industrial or commercial facility enjoys certain protections under the Fourth Amendment. . . .

. . . The curtilage area immediately surrounding a private house has long been given protection as a place where the occupants have a reasonable and legitimate expectation of privacy that society is prepared to accept. . . .

Dow plainly has a reasonable, legitimate, and objective expectation of privacy within the interior of its covered buildings, and it is equally clear that expectation is one society is prepared to observe. Moreover, it could hardly be expected that Dow would erect a huge cover over a 2,000-acre tract. In contending that its entire enclosed plant complex is an "industrial curtilage," Dow argues that its exposed manufacturing facilities are analogous to the curtilage surrounding a home because it has taken every possible step to bar access from ground level. . . .

. . . The intimate activities associated with family privacy and the home and its curtilage simply do not reach the outdoor areas or spaces between structures and buildings of a manufacturing plant. . . .

It may well be, as the Government concedes, that surveillance of private property by using highly sophisticated surveillance equipment not generally available to the public, such as satellite technology, might be constitutionally proscribed absent a warrant. But the photographs here are not so revealing of intimate details as to raise constitutional concerns. Although they undoubtedly give EPA more detailed information than naked-eye views, they remain limited to an outline of the facility's buildings and equipment. The mere fact that human vision is enhanced somewhat, at least to the degree here, does not give rise to constitutional problems. An electronic device to penetrate walls or windows so as to hear and record confidential discussions of chemical formulae or other trade secrets would raise very different and far more serious questions; other protections such as trade secret laws are available to protect commercial activities from private surveillance by competitors. . . .

We hold that the taking of aerial photographs of an industrial plant complex from navigable airspace is not a search prohibited by the Fourth Amendment. . . .

POWELL, J. joined by BRENNAN, MARSHALL, and BLACKMUN, J. J. concurring in part and dissenting in part. The Fourth Amendment protects private citizens from arbitrary surveillance by their Government. For nearly 20 years, this Court has adhered to a standard that ensured that Fourth Amendment rights would retain their vitality as technology expanded the Government's capacity to commit unsuspected intrusions into private areas and activities. Today, in the context of administrative aerial photography of commercial premises, the Court retreats from that standard. It holds that the photography was not a Fourth Amendment "search" because it was not accompanied by a physical trespass and because the equipment used was not the most highly sophisticated form of technology available to the Government. Under this holding, the existence of an asserted privacy interest apparently will be decided solely by reference to the manner of surveillance used to intrude on that interest. Such an inquiry will not protect Fourth Amendment rights, but rather will permit their gradual decay as technology advances. . . .

NOTES & QUESTIONS

1. *New Surveillance Technologies.* One of the rationales of *Dow Chemical* is that the device could have been acquired by a member of the general public. Does the case turn on this point? Suppose the police used a special camera that was developed exclusively for law enforcement purposes.

   The *Dow Chemical* Court stated: "It may well be, as the Government concedes, that surveillance of private property by using highly sophisticated surveillance equipment not generally available to the public, such as satellite technology, might be constitutionally proscribed absent a warrant." But does this sentence reflect contemporary technological reality? Mark Monmonier describes the rapid increase in the availability of commercial satellite capacities once the Cold War ended and the U.S. government lifted its restrictions in this area. The public now has cheaper and more detailed satellite images available to it than ever before.[35] As an example, look at maps.google.com, where free high-quality satellite imagery is available for most street maps.

   Recall that in *The Right to Privacy*, Warren and Brandeis complained in 1890 of the then new ability to take candid photographs of individuals. Before the invention of the snap camera, people did not expect to be photographed without their consent. Clearly today the ability to take pictures in public is greatly enhanced. There are video cameras, night-vision cameras, powerful zoom lenses, and satellite images available for sale. Are these new technologies eroding our reasonable expectation of privacy?[36] How should the law respond?

2. *Flashlights.* The use of a flashlight "to illuminate a darkened area simply does not constitute a search, and thus triggers no Fourth Amendment protection." *Texas v. Brown*, 460 U.S. 730 (1983). If this conclusion seems evident, how is a flashlight different from other devices that enhance human senses? Is any device that enhances the human senses merely an extension of ordinary senses? What factors should be considered in determining which sense enhancement devices trigger a search under the Fourth Amendment and which do not?

---

[35] Mark Monmonier, *Spying with Maps* (2002).

[36] For an argument that people do have reasonable expectations of privacy in public, see Helen Nissenbaum, *Protecting Privacy in an Information Age: The Problem of Privacy in Public*, 17 Law & Phil. 559 (1998).

3. ***Beepers and Tracking Devices.*** In *United States v. Knotts*, 460 U.S. 276 (1983), the police placed a beeper in a five-gallon drum of chloroform purchased by the defendants and placed in their car. The beeper transmitted signals that enabled the police to track the location of the defendants' vehicle. The Court held that the Fourth Amendment did not apply to the use of this device because a "person traveling in an automobile on public thoroughfares has no reasonable expectation of privacy in his movements from one place to another." Therefore, "[t]he governmental surveillance conducted by means of the beeper in this case amounted principally to the following of an automobile on public streets and highways." In *United States v. Karo*, 468 U.S. 705 (1984), law enforcement officials planted a beeper in a can of ether that the defendant bought from an informant. The officials tracked the movements of the can of ether through a variety of places, including within a residence. While the movements in *Knotts* were in public, the movements within the residence were not, and this amounted to an impermissible search of the residence:

> The monitoring of an electronic device such as a beeper is, of course, less intrusive than a full-scale search, but it does reveal a critical fact about the interior of the premises that the Government is extremely interested in knowing and that it could not have otherwise obtained without a warrant. The case is thus not like *Knotts*, for there the beeper told the authorities nothing about the interior of Knotts' cabin. The information obtained in *Knotts* was "voluntarily conveyed to anyone who wanted to look. . . ."

4. ***Global Positioning System (GPS).*** GPS is a radio navigation system, developed by the U.S. Department of Defense; it provides continuous worldwide positioning and timing information. GPS functions through use of 24 satellites in earth-based orbit, which are monitored by ground-based control stations. GPS devices raise technological issues similar to those at stake in *United States v. Karo* and *United States v. Knotts*. In interpreting the Washington State Constitution, the Washington Supreme Court in *State v. Jackson*, 76 P.3d 217 (Wash. 2003), concluded that the police need a warrant in order to attach a GPS device to a vehicle to track its movement — even in public:

> It is true that an officer standing at a distance in a lawful place may use binoculars to bring into closer view what he sees, or an officer may use a flashlight at night to see what is plainly there to be seen by day. However, when a GPS device is attached to a vehicle, law enforcement officers do not in fact follow the vehicle. Thus, unlike binoculars or a flashlight, the GPS device does not merely augment the officers' senses, but rather provides a technological substitute for traditional visual tracking. Further, the devices in this case were in place for approximately two and one-half weeks. It is unlikely that the sheriff's department could have successfully maintained uninterrupted 24-hour surveillance throughout this time by following Jackson. Even longer tracking periods might be undertaken, depending upon the circumstances of a case. We perceive a difference between the kind of uninterrupted, 24-hour a day surveillance possible through use of a GPS

device, which does not depend upon whether an officer could in fact have maintained visual contact over the tracking period, and an officer's use of binoculars or a flashlight to augment his or her senses.

Moreover, the intrusion into private affairs made possible with a GPS device is quite extensive as the information obtained can disclose a great deal about an individual's life. For example, the device can provide a detailed record of travel to doctors' offices, banks, gambling casinos, tanning salons, places of worship, political party meetings, bars, grocery stores, exercise gyms, places where children are dropped off for school, play, or day care, the upper scale restaurant and the fast food restaurant, the strip club, the opera, the baseball game, the "wrong" side of town, the family planning clinic, the labor rally. In this age, vehicles are used to take people to a vast number of places that can reveal preferences, alignments, associations, personal ails and foibles. The GPS tracking devices record all of these travels, and thus can provide a detailed picture of one's life.

Does the Washington Supreme Court's decision track the U.S. Supreme Court's reading of the Fourth Amendment in cases like *Karo* and *Knotts*?

KYLLO V. UNITED STATES

533 U.S. 27 (2001)

SCALIA, J. In 1991 Agent William Elliott of the United States Department of the Interior came to suspect that marijuana was being grown in the home belonging to petitioner Danny Kyllo, part of a triplex on Rhododendron Drive in Florence, Oregon. Indoor marijuana growth typically requires high-intensity lamps. In order to determine whether an amount of heat was emanating from petitioner's home consistent with the use of such lamps, at 3:20 A.M. on January 16, 1992, Agent Elliott and Dan Haas used an Agema Thermovision 210 thermal imager to scan the triplex. Thermal imagers detect infrared radiation, which virtually all objects emit but which is not visible to the naked eye. The imager converts radiation into images based on relative warmth — black is cool, white is hot, shades of gray connote relative differences; in that respect, it operates somewhat like a video camera showing heat images. The scan of Kyllo's home took only a few minutes and was performed from the passenger seat of Agent Elliott's vehicle across the street from the front of the house and also from the street in back of the house. The scan showed that the roof over the garage and a side wall of petitioner's home were relatively hot compared to the rest of the home and substantially warmer than neighboring homes in the triplex. Agent Elliott concluded that petitioner was using halide lights to grow marijuana in his house, which indeed he was. Based on tips from informants, utility bills, and the thermal imaging, a Federal Magistrate Judge issued a warrant authorizing a search of petitioner's home, and the agents found an indoor growing operation involving more than 100 plants. Petitioner was indicted on one count of manufacturing marijuana, in violation of 21 U.S.C. § 841(a)(1). He unsuccessfully moved to suppress the evidence seized from his home and then entered a conditional guilty plea. . . .

. . . "At the very core" of the Fourth Amendment "stands the right of a man to retreat into his own home and there be free from unreasonable governmental intrusion." With few exceptions, the question whether a warrantless search of a home is reasonable and hence constitutional must be answered no.

On the other hand, the antecedent question of whether or not a Fourth Amendment "search" has occurred is not so simple under our precedent. The permissibility of ordinary visual surveillance of a home used to be clear because, well into the 20th century, our Fourth Amendment jurisprudence was tied to common-law trespass. Visual surveillance was unquestionably lawful because "the eye cannot by the laws of England be guilty of a trespass." We have since decoupled violation of a person's Fourth Amendment rights from trespassory violation of his property, but the lawfulness of warrantless visual surveillance of a home has still been preserved. As we observed in *California v. Ciraolo*, 476 U.S. 207, (1986), "[t]he Fourth Amendment protection of the home has never been extended to require law enforcement officers to shield their eyes when passing by a home on public thoroughfares." . . .

The present case involves officers on a public street engaged in more than naked-eye surveillance of a home. We have previously reserved judgment as to how much technological enhancement of ordinary perception from such a vantage point, if any, is too much. While we upheld enhanced aerial photography of an industrial complex in *Dow Chemical*, we noted that we found "it important that this is not an area immediately adjacent to a private home, where privacy expectations are most heightened."

It would be foolish to contend that the degree of privacy secured to citizens by the Fourth Amendment has been entirely unaffected by the advance of technology. For example, as the cases discussed above make clear, the technology enabling human flight has exposed to public view (and hence, we have said, to official observation) uncovered portions of the house and its curtilage that once were private. The question we confront today is what limits there are upon this power of technology to shrink the realm of guaranteed privacy. . . .

. . . [I]n the case of the search of the interior of homes — the prototypical and hence most commonly litigated area of protected privacy — there is a ready criterion, with roots deep in the common law, of the minimal expectation of privacy that exists, and that is acknowledged to be reasonable. To withdraw protection of this minimum expectation would be to permit police technology to erode the privacy guaranteed by the Fourth Amendment. We think that obtaining by sense-enhancing technology any information regarding the interior of the home that could not otherwise have been obtained without physical "intrusion into a constitutionally protected area," *Silverman*, 365 U.S., at 512, constitutes a search — at least where (as here) the technology in question is not in general public use. This assures preservation of that degree of privacy against government that existed when the Fourth Amendment was adopted. On the basis of this criterion, the information obtained by the thermal imager in this case was the product of a search.[37]

---

[37] The dissent's repeated assertion that the thermal imaging did not obtain information regarding the interior of the home is simply inaccurate. A thermal imager reveals the relative heat

The Government maintains, however, that the thermal imaging must be upheld because it detected "only heat radiating from the external surface of the house." The dissent makes this its leading point, contending that there is a fundamental difference between what it calls "off-the-wall" observations and "through-the-wall surveillance." But just as a thermal imager captures only heat emanating from a house, so also a powerful directional microphone picks up only sound emanating from a house — and a satellite capable of scanning from many miles away would pick up only visible light emanating from a house. We rejected such a mechanical interpretation of the Fourth Amendment in *Katz*, where the eavesdropping device picked up only sound waves that reached the exterior of the phone booth. Reversing that approach would leave the homeowner at the mercy of advancing technology — including imaging technology that could discern all human activity in the home. While the technology used in the present case was relatively crude, the rule we adopt must take account of more sophisticated systems that are already in use or in development. The dissent's reliance on the distinction between "off-the-wall" and "through-the-wall" observation is entirely incompatible with the dissent's belief, which we discuss below, that thermal-imaging observations of the intimate details of a home are impermissible. The most sophisticated thermal imaging devices continue to measure heat "off-the-wall" rather than "through-the-wall"; the dissent's disapproval of those more sophisticated thermal-imaging devices, is an acknowledgement that there is no substance to this distinction. As for the dissent's extraordinary assertion that anything learned through "an inference" cannot be a search, that would validate even the "through-the-wall" technologies that the dissent purports to disapprove. Surely the dissent does not believe that the through-the-wall radar or ultrasound technology produces an 8-by-10 Kodak glossy that needs no analysis (i.e., the making of inferences). And, of course, the novel proposition that inference insulates a search is blatantly contrary to *United States v. Karo*, 468 U.S. 705 (1984), where the police "inferred" from the activation of a beeper that a certain can of ether was in the home. The police activity was held to be a search, and the search was held unlawful.

The Government also contends that the thermal imaging was constitutional because it did not "detect private activities occurring in private areas." . . . The Fourth Amendment's protection of the home has never been tied to measurement of the quality or quantity of information obtained. In *Silverman*, for example, we made clear that any physical invasion of the structure of the home, "by even a fraction of an inch," was too much, and there is certainly no exception to the warrant requirement for the officer who barely cracks open the front door and sees nothing but the nonintimate rug on the vestibule floor. . . .

---

of various rooms in the home. The dissent may not find that information particularly private or important, but there is no basis for saying it is not information regarding the interior of the home. The dissent's comparison of the thermal imaging to various circumstances in which outside observers might be able to perceive, without technology, the heat of the home — for example, by observing snowmelt on the roof — is quite irrelevant. The fact that equivalent information could sometimes be obtained by other means does not make lawful the use of means that violate the Fourth Amendment. The police might, for example, learn how many people are in a particular house by setting up year-round surveillance, but that does not make breaking and entering to find out the same information lawful. In any event, on the night of January 16, 1992, no outside observer could have discerned the relative heat of Kyllo's home without thermal imaging.

We have said that the Fourth Amendment draws "a firm line at the entrance to the house." That line, we think, must be not only firm but also bright — which requires clear specification of those methods of surveillance that require a warrant. While it is certainly possible to conclude from the videotape of the thermal imaging that occurred in this case that no "significant" compromise of the homeowner's privacy has occurred, we must take the long view, from the original meaning of the Fourth Amendment forward. . . .

Where, as here, the Government uses a device that is not in general public use, to explore details of the home that would previously have been unknowable without physical intrusion, the surveillance is a "search" and is presumptively unreasonable without a warrant. . . .

STEVENS, J. joined by REHNQUIST, C. J. and O'CONNOR and KENNEDY, J. dissenting. . . . [S]earches and seizures of property in plain view are presumptively reasonable. Whether that property is residential or commercial, the basic principle is the same: "What a person knowingly exposes to the public, even in his own home or office, is not a subject of Fourth Amendment protection." That is the principle implicated here.

While the Court "take[s] the long view" and decides this case based largely on the potential of yet-to-be-developed technology that might allow "through-the-wall surveillance," this case involves nothing more than off-the-wall surveillance by law enforcement officers to gather information exposed to the general public from the outside of petitioner's home. All that the infrared camera did in this case was passively measure heat emitted from the exterior surfaces of petitioner's home; all that those measurements showed were relative differences in emission levels, vaguely indicating that some areas of the roof and outside walls were warmer than others. As still images from the infrared scans show, no details regarding the interior of petitioner's home were revealed. . . .

. . . Heat waves, like aromas that are generated in a kitchen, or in a laboratory or opium den, enter the public domain if and when they leave a building. A subjective expectation that they would remain private is not only implausible but also surely not "one that society is prepared to recognize as 'reasonable.'" . . .

Despite the Court's attempt to draw a line that is "not only firm but also bright," the contours of its new rule are uncertain because its protection apparently dissipates as soon as the relevant technology is "in general public use." Yet how much use is general public use is not even hinted at by the Court's opinion, which makes the somewhat doubtful assumption that the thermal imager used in this case does not satisfy that criterion. In any event, putting aside its lack of clarity, this criterion is somewhat perverse because it seems likely that the threat to privacy will grow, rather than recede, as the use of intrusive equipment becomes more readily available. . . .

Because the new rule applies to information regarding the "interior" of the home, it is too narrow as well as too broad. Clearly, a rule that is designed to protect individuals from the overly intrusive use of sense-enhancing equipment should not be limited to a home. If such equipment did provide its user with the functional equivalent of access to a private place — such as, for example, the telephone booth involved in *Katz*, or an office building — then the rule should apply to such an area as well as to a home. . . .

NOTES & QUESTIONS

1. *Thermal Imagers vs. Canine Sniffs.* How does the Court distinguish the thermal imager in *Kyllo* from the camera in *Dow Chemical* and the dog sniff in *Place*? Does this distinction make sense?

2. *Canine Sniffs Revisited.* The Court decided *Illinois v. Caballes*, another dog sniff case, subsequent to *Kyllo*. In *Caballes*, the majority opinion and Justice Souter's dissent all revisited *Kyllo*. For the *Caballes* majority, the distinction between the two cases was that the thermal-imaging device in *Kyllo* was able to detect lawful activities, such as when an individual enjoyed a hot sauna or bath. The *Caballes* majority stated: "The legitimate expectation that information about perfectly lawful activity will remain private is categorically distinguishable from respondent's hopes or expectations concerning the nondetection of contraband in the trunk of his car." Justice Souter, dissenting, argued: "[G]iven the fallibility of the dog, the sniff is the first step in a process that may disclose 'intimate details' without revealing contraband, just as a thermal-imaging device might do, as described in *Kyllo v. United States.*" Is the dog sniff like a thermal-imaging device? Or is it, as the *Caballes* majority argues, simply *sui generis*?

3. *The Limits on Sense-Enhancing Technology.* The *Kyllo* Court notes that there must be some limits on sense-enhancement technology. What is the limiting principle according to the Court? Do you think this is the appropriate limiting principle?[38]

4. *Technology in General Public Use.* The majority based its holding on the fact that a thermal sensor was *"a device not in general public use."* However, a search of eBay reveals different kinds of thermal-imaging devices for sale at a variety of prices. Hence, the thermal sensor device is one that is publicly available. Is this "eBay test" relevant? How should a court decide when a technology is "in general public use"?

5. *The Home.* Justice Stevens argues that "a rule that is designed to protect individuals from the overly intrusive use of sense-enhancing equipment should not be limited to a home." Do you agree? Given the reasoning of the majority, would the Court reach the same result if the thermal imager had been used outside a person's office rather than her home?

6. *The Courts vs. Congress.* Orin Kerr contends that when new technologies are involved, Congress, not the courts, should be the primary rulemaker. In particular, Kerr critiques the generally held view that "the Fourth Amendment should be interpreted broadly in response to technological change." According to Kerr:

> [C]ourts should place a thumb on the scale in favor of judicial caution when technology is in flux, and should consider allowing legislatures to provide the

---

[38] For background into sensory enhancement technology, see Christopher Slobogin, *Technologically-Assisted Physician Surveillance: The American Bar Association's Tentative Draft Standards*, 10 Harv. J.L. & Tech. 383 (1997); ABA Standards for Criminal Justice, Electronic Surveillance § B (3d ed. 1999) (technologically assisted physical surveillance), available at http://abanet.org/crimjust/standards/taps_toc.html.

primary rules governing law enforcement investigations involving new technologies. . . . When technology is in flux, Fourth Amendment protections should remain relatively modest until the technology stabilizes.

Kerr justifies his conclusion by making an argument about the attributes of judicial versus legislative rulemaking:

> The first difference is that legislatures typically create generally applicable rules ex ante, while courts tend to create rules ex post in a case-by-case fashion. That is, legislatures enact generalized rules for the future, whereas courts resolve disputes settling the rights of parties arising from a past event. The difference leads to Fourth Amendment rules that tend to lag behind parallel statutory rules and current technologies by at least a decade, resulting in unsettled and then outdated rules that often make little sense given current technological facts. . . .
>
> A second difference between judicial and legislative rulemaking concerns their operative constraints. . . . Legislatures are up to the task [of adapting to technological change]; courts generally are not. Legislatures can experiment with different rules and make frequent amendments; they can place restrictions on both public and private actors; and they can even "sunset" rules so that they apply only for a particular period of time. The courts cannot. As a result, Fourth Amendment rules will tend to lack the flexibility that a regulatory response to new technologies may require. . . .
>
> The third important difference between judicial rules and legislative rules relates to the information environment in which rules are generated. Legislative rules tend to be the product of a wide range of inputs, ranging from legislative hearings and poll results to interest group advocacy and backroom compromises. Judicial rules tend to follow from a more formal and predictable presentation of written briefs and oral arguments by two parties. Once again, the difference offers significant advantages to legislative rulemaking. The task of generating balanced and nuanced rules requires a comprehensive understanding of technological facts. Legislatures are well-equipped to develop such understandings; courts generally are not.[39]

Peter Swire responds that Congress's privacy legislation was shaped by judicial decisions concerning the Fourth Amendment:

> At least four mutually reinforcing reasons underscore the importance of judicial decisions to how these privacy protections were enacted. First, the Supreme Court decision made the issue more salient, focusing attention on a topic that otherwise would not climb to the top of the legislative agenda. Second, the importance of the decision to the political process was greater because of what social scientists have called the "endowment effect" or "status quo bias." . . . [T]he concept is that individuals experience a loss as more important than a gain of equal size. . . . [T]he perceived "loss" of Fourth Amendment protections . . . would be a spur to legislative action. Third, the opinions of the Supreme Court shaped the legislative debates. Vigorous dissents in each case articulated reasons why privacy protections should be considered important. . . . Fourth, once the issue had moved high enough on

---

[39] Orin S. Kerr, *The Fourth Amendment and New Technologies: Constitutional Myths and the Case for Caution*, 102 Mich. L. Rev. 801, 803-05, 868, 871, 875 (2004).

the agenda to warrant a vote, there were persuasive public-policy arguments that some privacy protections were appropriate.[40]

Daniel Solove also disagrees with Kerr's conclusions: "Where the courts have left open areas for legislative rules to fill in, Congress has created an uneven fabric of protections that is riddled with holes and that has weak protections in numerous places." Further, Solove contends, legislative ex ante rules are not necessarily preferable to judicial ex post rules:

> The problem with ex ante laws is that they cannot anticipate all of the new and changing factual situations that technology brings about. Ex post rules, in contrast, are often much better tailored to specific types of technology, because such rules arise as technology changes, rather than beforehand. . . .

Solove argues that the "historical record suggests that Congress is actually far worse than the courts in reacting to new technologies." In response to Kerr's argument that the legislature is better equipped to understand new technologies than the judiciary, Solove responds that "merely shifting to a statutory regime will not eliminate Kerr's concern with judges misunderstanding technology. In fact, many judicial misunderstandings stem from courts trying to fit new technologies into old statutory regimes built around old technologies."[41]

B. FEDERAL ELECTRONIC SURVEILLANCE LAW

1. SECTION 605 OF THE FEDERAL COMMUNICATIONS ACT

Recall that in 1928, the Court in *Olmstead* declared that wiretapping did not constitute a Fourth Amendment violation. By the time *Olmstead* was decided, more than 25 states had made wiretapping a crime.

Six years later, responding to significant criticism of the *Olmstead* decision, Congress enacted the Federal Communications Act (FCA) of 1934. Section 605 of the Act provided that "no person not being authorized by the sender shall intercept any communication and divulge or publish the existence, contents, substance, purport, effect, or meaning of such intercepted communications to any person." Although § 605 did not expressly provide for an exclusionary rule, the Court in *Nardone v. United States*, 302 U.S. 379 (1937), held that federal officers could not introduce evidence obtained by illegal wiretapping in federal court.

Section 605 had significant limitations. States could still use evidence in violation of § 605 in state prosecutions. Further, § 605 only applied to wire communications and wiretapping, not to eavesdropping on nonwire communications. Thus, bugging was not covered.

In the words of Attorney General Nicholas Katzenback, § 605 was the "worst of all possible solutions." It prevented law enforcement from using information

---

[40] Peter P. Swire, *Katz Is Dead. Long Live Katz*, 102 Mich. L. Rev. 904, 917 (2004).

[41] Daniel J. Solove, *Fourth Amendment Codification and Professor Kerr's Misguided Call for Judicial Deference*, 74 Fordham L. Rev. 747, 761-74 (2005).

gleaned from wiretaps in court — even if pursuant to a warrant supported by probable cause. And it did little to restrict government wiretapping since it was interpreted not to prohibit such activity so long as the evidence was not used in court.

With the absence of Fourth Amendment protections and the limited protections of § 605, the federal government engaged in extensive wiretapping. During World War II, J. Edgar Hoover, the director of the FBI, successfully urged President Franklin Roosevelt to allow FBI wiretapping to investigate subversive activities and threats to national security. During the Truman Administration, the justification for electronic surveillance expanded to include domestic security as well. In the 1950s, the FBI then expanded its electronic surveillance due to national concern about Communism and communist infiltration of government. During the Cold War Era and beyond, Hoover ordered wiretapping of hundreds of people, including political enemies, dissidents, Supreme Court Justices, professors, celebrities, writers, and others. Among Hoover's files were dossiers on John Steinbeck, Ernest Hemingway, Charlie Chaplin, Marlon Brando, Muhammad Ali, Albert Einstein, John Lennon, and numerous presidents and members of Congress.[42]

The FBI also placed Martin Luther King Jr. under extensive surveillance. Hoover believed King was a Communist (which he was not), and disliked him personally. When the FBI's electronic surveillance of King revealed King's extramarital affairs, the FBI sent copies of the tapes to King along with a letter insinuating that he should commit suicide or else the tapes would be leaked to the public. The FBI also sent the tapes to King's wife and played them to President Lyndon Johnson.[43] In reflecting on the FBI's campaign against King, Frederick Schwarz and Aziz Huq note that an important role was played by Hoover's "personal animus against King, and his profound distaste for the social changes pressed by the civil rights movement." Schwarz and Huq also observe: "But without an institutional underpinning, Hoover's bias would not have taken the form of a massive, multiyear surveillance and harassment campaign. The war against King highlights what happens when checks and balances are abandoned."[44]

During this time, state police also conducted wiretapping. To the extent that this wiretapping was regulated, this regulation was purely that of the individual states. Section 605 only applied at the federal level. In an influential study, Samuel Dash, Richard Schwartz, and Robert Knowlton revealed that regulation of wiretapping by the states was often ineffective. There were numerous unauthorized wiretaps and few checks against abuses.[45]

---

[42] Daniel J. Solove, *Reconstructing Electronic Surveillance Law*, 72 Geo. Wash. L. Rev. 1264, 1273-74 (2004).

[43] David J. Garrow, *The FBI and Martin Luther King, Jr.* (1980).

[44] Frederick A.O. Schwarz, Jr. & Aziz Z. Huq, *Unchecked and Unbalanced: Presidential Power in a Time of Terror* 23 (2007).

[45] *See* Samuel Dash, Richard Schwartz, & Robert Knowlton, *The Eavesdroppers* (1959).

2. TITLE III

In 1968, in response to *Katz v. United States* and *Berger v. New York*, Congress enacted Title III of the Omnibus Crime Control and Safe Streets Act of 1968, Pub. L. No. 90-351, codified at 18 U.S.C. §§ 2510–2520. This Act is commonly referred to as "Title III" or, subsequent to its amendment in 1986, as the "Wiretap Act."

Title III extended far beyond § 605; it applied to wiretaps by federal and state officials as well as by private parties. Title III required federal agents to apply for a warrant before wiretapping. The Act criminalized private wiretaps. However, if any party to the conversation consented to the tapping, then there was no violation of Title III.

Title III authorized the Attorney General to apply to a federal judge for an order authorizing the interception of a "wire or oral communication." A judge could not issue a court order unless there was probable cause. Many other procedural safeguards were established.

Title III excluded wiretaps for national security purposes from any restrictions at all. President Nixon frequently used the national security exception to place internal dissidents and radicals under surveillance. However, in *United States v. United States District Court* (the *Keith* case), 407 U.S. 297 (1972), the Court unanimously rejected Nixon's approach, stating that Title III's national security exception does not apply to internal threats but only to foreign threats.

3. THE ELECTRONIC COMMUNICATIONS PRIVACY ACT

(a) Statutory Structure

In 1986, Congress modernized federal wiretap law by passing the Electronic Communications Privacy Act (ECPA).[46] The ECPA amended Title III (the Wiretap Act), and it also included two new acts in response to developments in computer technology and communication networks. Hence, federal electronic surveillance law on the domestic side contains three parts: (1) the Wiretap Act (the updated version of Title III, which ECPA shifted to its first Title); (2) the Stored Communications Act (SCA); and (3) the Pen Register Act.

Many of the provisions of federal electronic surveillance law apply not only to government officials, but to private individuals and entities as well. In particular, cases involving the violation of federal electronic surveillance law by private parties often occur in the employment context when employers desire to use forms of electronic surveillance on their employees.

---

[46] For more background on electronic surveillance law, see Patricia L. Bellia, *Surveillance Law Through Cyberlaw's Lens,* 72 Geo. Wash. L. Rev. 1375 (2004); Deirdre K. Mulligan, *Reasonable Expectations in Electronic Communications: A Critical Perspective on the Electronic Communications Privacy Act,* 72 Geo. Wash. L. Rev. 1557 (2004); Paul K. Ohm, *Parallel-Effect Statutes and E-mail "Warrants": Reframing the Internet Surveillance Debate,* 72 Geo. Wash. L. Rev. 1599 (2004); Susan Freiwald, *Online Surveillance: Remembering the Lessons of the Wiretap Act,* 56 Ala. L. Rev. 9 (2004). *See generally* Symposium, *The Future of Internet Surveillance Law,* 72 Geo. Wash. L. Rev. 1139-1617 (2004).

TYPES OF COMMUNICATIONS

In order to comprehend how each of the three acts comprising ECPA works, it is important to know that ECPA classifies all communications into three types: (1) "wire communications"; (2) "oral communications"; and (3) "electronic communications." Each type of communication is protected differently. As a general matter, wire communications receive the most protection and electronic communications receive the least.

Wire Communications. A "wire communication," defined in § 2510(1), involves all "aural transfers" that travel through a wire or a similar medium:

> (1) "wire communication" means any aural transfer made in whole or in part through the use of facilities for the transmission of communications by the aid of wire, cable, or other like connection between the point of origin and the point of reception (including the use of such connection in a switching station) furnished or operated by any person engaged in providing or operating such facilities for the transmission of interstate or foreign communications or communications affecting interstate or foreign commerce.

An "aural transfer" is a communication containing the human voice at any point. § 2510(18). The human voice need only be a minor part of the communication. Further, the human voice need not always be present throughout the journey of the communication. Therefore, a communication that once consisted of the human voice that has been translated into code or tones still qualifies as an "aural transfer."

The aural transfer must travel through wire (i.e., telephone wires or cable wires) or a similar medium. The entire journey from origin to destination need not take place through wire, as many communications travel through a host of different mediums — wire, radio, satellite, and so on. Only part of the communication's journey must be through a wire.

Oral Communications. The second type of communication under federal wiretap law are "oral communications." Pursuant to § 2510(2), an "oral communication" is a communication "uttered by a person exhibiting an expectation that such communication is not subject to interception under circumstances justifying such expectation." Oral communications are typically intercepted through bugs and other recording or transmitting devices.

Electronic Communications. The final type of communication is an "electronic communication." Under § 2510(12), an electronic communication consists of all non-wire and non-oral communications:

> (12) "electronic communication" means any transfer of signs, signals, writing, images, sounds, data, or intelligence of any nature transmitted in whole or in part by a wire, radio, electromagnetic, photoelectronic or photooptical system that affects interstate or foreign commerce, but does not include —
>
> > (A) any wire or oral communication. . . .

In other words, an electronic communication consists of all communications that do not constitute wire or oral communications. An example of an electronic communication is an e-mail — at least as long as it does not contain the human voice.

Although electronic communications are protected under the Stored Communications Act as well as the Wiretap Act, they are treated differently than wire and oral communications. The most notable difference is that the exclusionary rule in the Wiretap Act does not apply to electronic communications. Therefore, wire or oral communications that fall within the Wiretap Act are protected by the exclusionary rule, but not when they fall within the Stored Communications Act (which has no exclusionary rule). Electronic communications are not protected by the exclusionary rule in the Wiretap Act or the Stored Communications Act.

THE WIRETAP ACT

Interceptions. The Wiretap Act, which is codified at Title I of ECPA, 18 U.S.C. §§ 2510–2522, governs the interception of communications. In particular, § 2511 provides that:

(1) Except as otherwise specifically provided in this chapter any person who —

(a) intentionally intercepts, endeavors to intercept, or procures any other person to intercept or endeavor to intercept, any wire, oral, or electronic communication;

(b) intentionally uses, endeavors to use, or procures any other person to use or endeavor to use any electronic, mechanical, or other device to intercept any oral communication when —

(i) such device is affixed to, or otherwise transmits a signal through, a wire, cable, or other like connection used in wire communication; or

(ii) such device transmits communications by radio, or interferes with the transmission of such communication; or

(iii) such person knows, or has reason to know, that such device or any component thereof has been sent through the mail or transported in interstate or foreign commerce. . . .

(c) intentionally discloses, or endeavors to disclose, to any other person the contents of any wire, oral, or electronic communication, knowing or having reason to know that the information was obtained through the interception of a wire, oral, or electronic communication in violation of this subsection;

(d) intentionally uses, or endeavors to use, the contents of any wire, oral, or electronic communication, knowing or having reason to know that the information was obtained through the interception of a wire, oral, or electronic communication in violation of this subsection. . . .

As this provision indicates, the Wiretap Act applies to the intentional interception of a communication. To "intercept" a communication means to acquire its contents through the use of any "electronic, mechanical, or other device." § 2510(4). The classic example of an activity covered by the Act is the wiretapping of a phone conversation — a device is being used to listen to a conversation as it is occurring, as the words are moving through the wires. The

Wiretap Act applies when communications are intercepted contemporaneously with their transmission. Once the communication is completed and stored, then the Wiretap Act no longer applies.

In *Bartnicki v. Vopper*, 532 U.S. 514 (2001) (Chapter 2), the Court held that § 2511(1)(c) violated the First Amendment by restricting disclosures involving matters of public concern.

Exclusionary Rule. Under the Wiretap Act, "any aggrieved person . . . may move to suppress the contents of any wire or oral communication intercepted pursuant to this chapter, or evidence derived therefrom." § 2518 (10)(a).

Penalties. Violations of the Wiretap Act can result in fines of a minimum of $10,000 per violation as well as up to five years' imprisonment. *See* §§ 2511(4)(a); 2520(c)(2)(B).

Court Orders. Pursuant to § 2518, an application for a court wiretapping or electronic surveillance order must be made under oath and contain a variety of information, including details to justify the agent's belief that a crime has been, is being, or will be committed; specific description of place where communications will be intercepted; description of the type of communication; and period of time of interception. The judge may require the applicant to furnish additional testimony or documentary evidence in support of the application. The judge must find probable cause and that the particular communications concerning that offense will be obtained through the interception. Further, the court must find that alternatives to wiretapping were attempted and failed, or reasonably appear to be unlikely to succeed or to be too dangerous. The order can last for up to 30 days and can be renewed.

Under the Wiretap Act, only certain government officials are able to apply to a court for a wiretapping order — for federal law enforcement agencies, the relevant party is the attorney general, or a deputy or assistant attorney general; for state officials, the relevant party is the principal prosecuting attorney of a state or a local government, or any government attorney. In other words, the police themselves cannot obtain a wiretap order alone. The Wiretap Act also provides an exclusive list of crimes for which a wiretap order can be issued. The list is broad and includes most felonies. A wiretap order cannot be obtained, however, to investigate a misdemeanor.

Minimization. The Wiretap Act requires that interception must be minimized to avoid sweeping in communications beyond the purpose for which the order was sought. Pursuant to § 2518(6): "Every order and extension thereof shall contain a provision that the authorization to intercept shall be executed as soon as practicable, shall be conducted in such a way as to minimize the interception of communications not otherwise subject to interception under this chapter, and must terminate upon attainment of the authorized objective." For example, if law enforcement officials are wiretapping the home phone line of a person suspected of running an illegal gambling operation and the person's daughter is talking on the line to a friend about going to the movies, the officials should stop listening to the conversation.

Notice. After the surveillance is over, copies of the recorded conversations must be turned over to the court issuing the order. The court must notify the party that surveillance was undertaken within 90 days after the denial of a surveillance order or after the completion of the surveillance authorized by a granted surveillance order. § 2518(8)(d).

Exceptions. There are two notable exceptions under the Wiretap Act. First, the Act does not apply if one of the parties to the communication consents. § 2511(2)(c). For example, a person can secretly tap and record a communication to which that person is a party. Thus, secretly recording one's own phone conversations is not illegal under federal wiretap law. If they participate in the conversation, government agents and informants can record others without their knowledge. An exception to the consent exception is when an interception is carried out for the purpose of committing any criminal or tortious act. In that case, even when a party has consented, interception is illegal. § 2511(2)(d).

Second, a communications service provider is permitted "to intercept, disclose, or use that communication in the normal course of his employment while engaged in any activity which is a necessary incident to the rendition of his service or to the protection of the rights or property of the provider of that service." § 2511(2)(a). Also, a service provider may intentionally disclose intercepted communications to the proper authorities when criminal activity is afoot; with the consent of the originator, addressee, or intended recipient; or to any intermediary provider. § 2511(3).

THE STORED COMMUNICATIONS ACT

Stored Communications. Whereas communications in transmission are covered by the Wiretap Act, communications in storage are protected by the Stored Communications Act (SCA), codified at 18 U.S.C. §§ 2701–2711.[47] With many forms of modern communication, such as Internet service, communications and subscriber records are often maintained in storage by the electronic communications service provider. Pursuant to § 2701:

(a) Offense. — Except as provided in subsection (c) of this section whoever —

(1) intentionally accesses without authorization a facility through which an electronic communication service is provided; or
(2) intentionally exceeds an authorization to access that facility; and
thereby obtains, alters, or prevents authorized access to a wire or electronic communication while it is in electronic storage in such system shall be punished as provided in subsection (b) of this section.

The definition of "electronic storage" in the Wiretap Act also applies to the term as used in the SCA. "Electronic storage" means:

(A) any temporary, intermediate storage of a wire or electronic communication incidental to the electronic transmission thereof; and

---

[47] For more background about the SCA, see Orin S. Kerr, *A User's Guide to the Stored Communications Act, and a Legislator's Guide to Amending It,* 72 Geo. Wash. L. Rev. 1208 (2004).

(B) any storage of such communication by an electronic communications service for purposes of backup protection of such communication. § 2510(17).

Section 2701(a) does not apply to "the person or entity providing a wire or electronic communications service" (such as Internet Service Providers) or to "a user of that service with respect to a communication of or intended for that user." § 2701(c).

The SCA also forbids the disclosure of the contents of stored communications by communications service providers. *See* § 2702(a). There are a number of exceptions, including disclosures to the intended recipient of the communication, disclosures with the consent of the creator or recipient of the communication, disclosures that are "necessarily incident to the rendition of the service or to the protection of the rights or property of the provider of that service," and disclosures to a law enforcement agency under certain circumstances. *See* § 2702(b).

Penalties. The SCA has less severe criminal penalties and civil liability than Title I. Under § 2701(b), violations can result in fines of a minimum of $1,000 per violation and up to six months imprisonment. If the wiretap is done for commercial advantage or gain, then a violation can result in up to one year of imprisonment.

Exclusionary Rule. The SCA does not provide for an exclusionary rule.

Judicial Authority for Obtaining Stored Communications. Under the SCA, the judicial process required for obtaining permission to access stored communications held by electronic communications service providers is much less rigorous than under the Wiretap Act. If the government seeks access to the contents of a communication that has been in storage for 180 days or less, then it must first obtain a warrant supported by probable cause. § 2703(a). If the government wants to access a communication that has been in storage for more than 180 days, the government must provide prior notice to the subscriber and obtain an administrative subpoena, a grand jury subpoena, a trial subpoena, or a court order. § 2703(b). The court order does not require probable cause, only "specific and articulable facts showing that there are reasonable grounds" to believe communications are relevant to the criminal investigation. 18 U.S.C. § 2703(d). However, if the government seeks to access a communication that has been in storage for more than 180 days and does not want to provide prior notice to the subscriber, it must obtain a warrant. § 2703(b). Notice to the subscriber that the government obtained her communications can be delayed for up to 90 days. § 2705.

Court Orders to Obtain Subscriber Records. According to § 2703(c)(1)(B), communication service providers must disclose subscriber information (i.e., identifying information, address, phone number, etc.) to the government under certain circumstances:

> (B) A provider of electronic communication service or remote computing service shall disclose a record or other information pertaining to a subscriber to or customer of such service (not including the contents of communications

covered by subsection (a) or (b) of this section) to a governmental entity only when the governmental entity —

> (i) obtains a warrant issued under the Federal Rules of Criminal Procedure or equivalent State warrant;
> (ii) obtains a court order for such disclosure under subsection (d) of this section;
> (iii) has the consent of the subscriber or customer to such disclosure

Communications service providers who disclose stored communications in accordance with any of the above orders or subpoenas cannot be held liable for that disclosure. *See* § 2703(e).

Exceptions. Similar to the Wiretap Act, the SCA also has a consent exception, see § 2702(b), and a service provider exception, see § 2701(c)(1). Unlike the service provider exception for the Wiretap Act, which allows interceptions on a limited basis (those necessary to provide the communications service), the SCA's exception is broader, entirely exempting "the person or entity providing a wire or electronic communications service." § 2701(c)(1).

THE PEN REGISTER ACT

The Pen Register Act, codified at 18 U.S.C. §§ 3121–3127, governs pen registers and trap and trace devices — and their modern analogues. Recall *Smith v. Maryland,* earlier in this chapter, where the Court held that the Fourth Amendment did not extend to pen register information. The Pen Register Act provides some limited protection for such information. Subject to certain exceptions, "no person may install or use a pen register or a trap and trace device without first obtaining a court order." § 3121(a). Traditionally, a pen register was a device that records the telephone numbers dialed from a particular telephone line (phone numbers of outgoing calls). A trap and trace device is the reverse of a pen register — it records the telephone numbers where incoming calls originate.

Definition of "Pen Register." The Pen Register Act defines pen registers more broadly than phone number information:

> [T]he term "pen register" means a device or process which records or decodes dialing, routing, addressing, or signaling information transmitted by an instrument or facility from which a wire or electronic communication is transmitted, provided, however, that such information shall not include the contents of any communication . . . 18 U.S.C. § 3127(3)

Court Orders. If the government certifies that "the information likely to be obtained by such installation and use is relevant to an ongoing investigation," § 3123(a), then courts "shall authorize the installation and use of a pen register or a trap and trace device for a period not to exceed sixty days." § 3123(c). This standard is a low threshold. As Susan Freiwald contends: "[T]he language of the [pen register] court order requirement raises doubt as to its efficacy as a guard against fishing expeditions. . . . The relevance standard in the transaction records provision allows law enforcement to obtain records of people who may be tangentially involved in a crime, even as innocent victims."[48]

Enforcement. There is no exclusionary rule for violations of the Pen Register Act. Rather than a suppression remedy, the Pen Register Act provides: "Whoever knowingly violates subsection (a) shall be fined under this title or imprisoned not more than one year, or both." § 3121(d).

VIDEO SURVEILLANCE

Prior to the enactment of the ECPA, video surveillance was not encompassed within the language of Title III. When it amended federal electronic surveillance law in 1986 by enacting the ECPA, Congress again failed to address video surveillance. Of course, if the government intercepts a *communication* consisting of video images (such as a transmission of a webcam image or an e-mail containing a video clip), then the Wiretap Act applies. If the government accesses an individual's stored video clip, then the SCA applies. However, being watched by video *surveillance* (such as a surveillance camera) does not involve an interception or an accessing of stored images. The video surveillance must be silent video surveillance, or else it could be an "oral" communication subject to the Wiretap Act. In sum, silent video surveillance is not covered under federal electronic surveillance law. *See, e.g., United States v. Biasuci*, 786 F.2d 504 (2d Cir. 1986); *United States v. Koyomejian*, 970 F.2d 536 (9th Cir. 1992); *United States v. Falls*, 34 F.3d 674 (8th Cir. 1994).

In *United States v. Mesa-Rincon*, 911 F.2d 1433 (10th Cir. 1990), the court observed that although federal electronic surveillance law did not apply to video surveillance, the Fourth Amendment did:

> Unfortunately, Congress has not yet specifically defined the constitutional requirements for video surveillance. Nevertheless, the general fourth amendment requirements are still applicable to video surveillance; and suppression is required when the government fails to follow these requirements.
>
> Title III establishes elaborate warrant requirements for wiretapping and bugging. Unfortunately, Title III does not discuss television surveillance in any way. Thus, its requirements are not binding on this court in the context of video surveillance. However, the fact that Title III does not discuss television surveillance is no authority for the proposition that Congress meant to outlaw the practice.

ELECTRONIC SURVEILLANCE LAW AND THE FOURTH AMENDMENT

Electronic surveillance law operates independently of the Fourth Amendment. Even if a search is reasonable under the Fourth Amendment, electronic surveillance law may bar the evidence. Even if a search is authorized by a judge under federal electronic surveillance law, the Fourth Amendment could still prohibit the wiretap.

---

[48] Susan Freiwald, *Uncertain Privacy: Communications Attributes After the Digital Telephony Act,* 69 S. Cal. L. Rev. 949, 1005-06 (1996).

Moreover, procedures for obtaining a court order under the Wiretap Act are more stringent than those for obtaining a search warrant under the Fourth Amendment. As an example of how the Wiretap Act is stricter, under the Fourth Amendment, any law enforcement official can apply for a warrant. Under the Wiretap Act, in contrast, only certain officials (prosecuting attorneys) can apply.

In at least one significant way, federal electronic surveillance law is broader than the Fourth Amendment. Under the Fourth Amendment, search warrants generally authorize a single entry and prompt search. Warrants must be narrowly circumscribed. They are not a license for unlimited and continued investigation. Under the Wiretap Act, however, courts can authorize continuing surveillance — 24 hours a day for a 30-day period. This period can also be extended.

The Supreme Court has held that, pursuant to a warrant or an order under electronic surveillance law, the government can secretly enter one's residence or private property to install electronic surveillance devices, such as bugs. *See Dahlia v. United States*, 441 U.S. 238 (1979). The *Dahlia* Court further concluded that the Fourth Amendment does not require that an electronic surveillance order include a specific authorization to enter covertly the premises described in the order. In other words, the police need not request permission to make a covert entry when applying for an electronic surveillance order, and the order authorizing the use of electronic surveillance need not make any reference to a covert entry.

ELECTRONIC SURVEILLANCE ORDERS

The number of electronic surveillance orders issued under federal wiretap law has greatly expanded. In 1968, there were a total of 174 orders were approved. In 1980, 564 were approved; in 1990, 872 orders were approved; and in 1999, the number of approved orders was 1,350. In 2004, federal and state courts authorized 1,710 intercepts. In 2006, there was an increase to 1,839. The vast majority of requests for electronic surveillance orders have been granted. For example, from 1968 to 1996, about 20,000 requests for electronic surveillance orders were made, and only 28 have been denied.[49]

Wiretap orders over the last decade have increasingly become a phenomenon of state rather than federal courts. In 1997, there were 617 state orders and 569 federal orders. In 2001, the breakdown was 486 federal and 1,005 state orders. In 2006, there were 461 federal orders and 1,378 state orders.

States vary greatly based on the extent to which they wiretap. Indeed, wiretaps are primarily a phenomenon of a handful of jurisdictions. At the federal and state levels in 2006, four states, California (430 orders), New York (377), New Jersey (189), and Florida (98) accounted for 59 percent of all wiretap orders. This pattern of use is likely independent of crime patterns in the United States. Rather, it probably reflects local norms of law enforcement practice, including prosecutorial familiarity with the complex set of legal requirements for obtaining wiretap orders.

---

[49] *See* Title III Electronic Surveillance 1968-1999, http://www.epic.org/privacy/wiretap/stats/wiretap_stats.html.

In a comparative examination of statistics regarding electronic surveillance orders, Paul Schwartz examined trends in the United States and Germany. Schwartz found that in both countries, "law enforcement agencies in certain geographic areas generate a disproportionate amount of surveillance orders."[50] One German scholar, Johann Bizer, has observed that the differences between different German states cannot be explained by varying population structures or political orientation of state governments. Thus, in both Germany and the United States, requests for telecommunications surveillance are driven by local enforcement norms as well as the law. What factors are likely to shape local enforcement norms and encourage or discourage the use of telecommunications surveillance?

Returning to the U.S. wiretap statistics, 92 percent of all wiretaps in 2006 involved mobile devices, such as cell phones and pagers. In 2006, the average per interception order was 2,685 communications involving 122 persons. The average percentage of incriminating intercepts per wiretap order in 2006 was 20 percent, and this last statistic gives one pause. To be as clear as possible, this statistic is not inconsistent with each wiretap order leading to the collection of some incriminating intercepts. It means that on average 80 percent of the communications intercepted per order did not contain anything incriminating.

Is the glass 20 percent full or 80 percent empty? The Wiretap Act requires strict minimization of the collection of extraneous information once surveillance occurs. Are these statistics an indication that too much innocent communication is being monitored? Rarely will everything said by a particular person or on a particular phone line be incriminating. Is it practical to expect a much higher incriminating percentage than 20 percent?

Finally, the Wiretap Act Report details the results of wiretaps in terms of arrests as well as the number of motions made and granted to suppress with respect to interceptions.[51] Wiretaps terminated in 2006 led to the arrest of 4,376 persons and the conviction of 711 persons.[52] Regarding motions to suppress, the Administrative Office does not provide this information in its 2006 summary report, but it may be calculated from documents that prosecutors file with the Office. Of the 283 motions to suppress in 2006, 7 were granted and 61 were reported as pending.

STATE ELECTRONIC SURVEILLANCE LAW

A number of states have enacted their own versions of electronic surveillance law, some of which are more protective than federal electronic surveillance law. For example, several states require the consent of all parties to a conversation. Unless all parties consent, these states require a warrant for a wiretap. In contrast, federal wiretap law allows law enforcement to listen in to a conversation if any party to it consents to the surveillance.

---

[50] Paul M. Schwartz, *German and U.S. Telecommunications Privacy Law: Legal Regulation of Domestic Law Enforcement Surveillance*, 54 Hastings L.J. 751, 759-60 (2003); *see also* Paul M. Schwartz, *Evaluating Telecommunications Surveillance in Germany*, 72 Geo. Wash. L. Rev. 1244 (2004).

[51] 2006 Wiretap Act Report, p. 30 table 6, http://www.uscourts.gov/wiretap06/contents.html.

[52] *Id.* at 39 table 9.

One prominent example of a more protective state law was the indictment on July 30, 1999, of Linda Tripp on two counts of violating Maryland's wiretapping law. At the request of the Office of the Independent Counsel, Linda Tripp had secretly taped a phone conversation she had with Monica Lewinsky about Lewinsky's affair with President Clinton. Tripp then disclosed the contents of that conversation to a news magazine. Possible penalties under Maryland law included up to ten years' imprisonment and a $20,000 fine. Maryland's wiretapping law, in contrast to federal wiretap law, requires the consent of the other party to a communication. Tripp was indicted by a Maryland grand jury. Although Tripp was protected by a federal grant of immunity from prosecution, Maryland was not part of the immunity agreement and could prosecute Tripp. After a judicial ruling suppressing certain evidence, the case against Tripp was dropped.

Massachusetts also has an all-party-consent electronic surveillance law. Consider *Commonwealth v. Hyde,* 750 N.E.2d 963 (Mass. 2001). The defendant Michael Hyde was stopped by the police for a routine auto stop. The police searched the defendant, his passenger, and his car. No traffic citation was issued. Hyde filed a complaint at the police station about the stop, and he provided a hidden audio recording he had made of the encounter. The police subsequently charged Hyde with illegal electronic surveillance in violation of state law, G.L. c. 272, § 99, which provides that "any person who willfully commits an interception, attempts to commit an interception, or procures any other person to commit an interception or to attempt to commit an interception of any wire or oral communication shall be fined not more than ten thousand dollars, or imprisoned in the state prison for not more than five years, or imprisoned in a jail or house of correction for not more than two and one half years, or both so fined and given one such imprisonment." Hyde was convicted and sentenced to six months probation and a $500 fine.

The *Hyde* court concluded:

We conclude that the Legislature intended G.L. c. 272, § 99, strictly to prohibit all secret recordings by members of the public, including recordings of police officers or other public officials interacting with members of the public, when made without their permission or knowledge. . . .

We reject the defendant's argument that the statute is not applicable because the police officers were performing their public duties, and, therefore, had no reasonable expectation of privacy in their words. The statute's preamble expresses the Legislature's general concern that "the uncontrolled development and unrestricted use of modern electronic surveillance devices pose[d] grave dangers to the privacy of all citizens of the commonwealth" and this concern was relied on to justify the ban on the public's clandestine use of such devices. While we recognize that G.L. c. 272, § 99, was designed to prohibit the use of electronic surveillance devices by private individuals because of the serious threat they pose to the "privacy of all citizens," the plain language of the statute, which is the best indication of the Legislature's ultimate intent, contains nothing that would protect, on the basis of privacy rights, the recording that occurred here. In *Commonwealth v. Jackson, supra* at 506, 349 N.E.2d 337, this court rejected the argument that, because a kidnapper has no legitimate privacy interest in telephone calls made for ransom purposes, the secret electronic recording of that conversation by the victim's brother would not be prohibited under G.L. c.

272, § 99: "[W]e would render meaningless the Legislature's careful choice of words if we were to interpret 'secretly' as encompassing only those situations where an individual has a reasonable expectation of privacy." . . .

Further, if the tape recording here is deemed proper on the ground that public officials are involved, then the door is opened even wider to electronic "bugging" or secret audio tape recording (both are prohibited by the statute and both are indistinguishable in the injury they inflict) of virtually every encounter or meeting between a person and a public official, whether the meeting or encounter is one that is stressful (like the one in this case or, perhaps, a session with a tax auditor) or nonstressful (like a routine meeting between a parent and a teacher in a public school to discuss a good student's progress). The door once opened would be hard to close, and the result would contravene the statute's broad purpose and the Legislature's clear prohibition of *all* secret interceptions and recordings by private citizens.

In dissent, Chief Justice Marshall wrote:

> The purpose of G.L. c. 272, § 99, is not to shield public officials from exposure of their wrongdoings. I have too great a respect for the Legislature to read any such meaning into a statute whose purpose is plain, and points in another direction entirely. Where the legislative intent is explicit, it violates a fundamental rule of statutory construction to reach a result that is plainly contrary to that objective. To hold that the Legislature intended to allow police officers to conceal possible misconduct behind a cloak of privacy requires a more affirmative showing than this statute allows.
>
> In our Republic the actions of public officials taken in their public capacities are not protected from exposure. Citizens have a particularly important role to play when the official conduct at issue is that of the police. Their role cannot be performed if citizens must fear criminal reprisals when they seek to hold government officials responsible by recording — secretly recording on occasion — an interaction between a citizen and a police officer. . . .
>
> The court's ruling today also threatens the ability of the press — print and electronic — to perform its constitutional role of watchdog. As the court construes the Massachusetts wiretapping statute, there is no principled distinction to explain why members of the media would not be held to the same standard as all other citizens.

A few years later, Hyde was convicted again of secretly recording a police officer who had pulled him over in a traffic stop. Are all-party electronic surveillance laws too broad? What kinds of exceptions, if any, should be made?

Note as well that these all-party-consent statutes will also regulate surveillance by private sector entities. In *Kearney v. Salomon Smith Barney*, 137 P.2d 914 (S. Ct. Cal. 2006), two California clients sued a financial institution because their telephone calls to brokers in the institution's Georgia office were recorded without their consent. A California statute prohibited recording a telephone conversation without consent of all parties to it. In contrast, a Georgia statute permitted recording a telephone conversation if consent of one party had been granted. The California Supreme Court concluded that "comparative impairment analysis supports the application of California law in this context." It reached this conclusion by assessing the relative harm suffered to each state due to this conflict of law:

[I]n light of the substantial number of businesses operating in California that maintain out-of-state offices or telephone operators, a resolution of this conflict permitting all such businesses to regularly and routinely record telephone conversations made to or from California clients or consumers without the clients' or consumers' knowledge or consent would significantly impair the privacy policy guaranteed by California law, and potentially would place local California businesses (that would continue to be subject to California's protective privacy law) at an unfair competitive disadvantage vis-à-vis their out-of-state counterparts. At the same time, application of California law will not have a significant detrimental effect on Georgia's interests as embodied in the applicable Georgia law, because applying California law (1) will not adversely affect any privacy interest protected by Georgia law, (2) will affect only those business telephone calls in Georgia that are made to or are received from California clients, and (3) with respect to such calls, will not prevent a business located in Georgia from implementing or maintaining a practice of recording *all* such calls, but will require only that the business *inform* its clients or customers, at the outset of the call, of the company's policy of recording such calls. (. . . if a business informs a client or customer at the outset of a telephone call that the call is being recorded, the recording would not violate the applicable California statute.)

When state government officials are engaging in electronic surveillance, they are often subject to much less public scrutiny than their federal counterparts. Charles Kennedy and Peter Swire have concluded that there are likely to be significant differences between federal and state electronic surveillance because of differences in the respective "[i]nstitutions, procedures and training" of law enforcement personnel:

Because state procedures are watched less systematically by the press and civil liberties organizations, abuses at the state level, whether deliberate or the result of inexperience, may not be detected. The under-reporting of state wiretaps . . . is both a symptom of and a contributing factor to this relative lack of oversight. The simple fact is that half of the states have wiretap powers, yet reported no wiretaps in 2001. The utter failure to file the annual wiretap report would be unthinkable at the federal level. In addition, the under-reporting of state wiretaps keeps the use and possible misuse of state wiretaps less visible.[53]

As noted above, moreover, wiretap orders over the last decade have increasingly become a phenomenon of state rather than federal courts. Yet, as Kennedy and Swire observe, we know far less about how state law enforcement agencies make use of their wiretap powers than federal ones. As for the lack of state wiretap reports from many states, the obligation to file a report with the Administrative Office of the U.S. Courts extends only to instances when the states actually make use of these powers. In other words, the Administrative Office does not require reports to be filed if no interception activity took place in the state during a given year.[54] As a simple, initial step at ending the ambiguity about the possible under-reporting of state wiretap orders, should states be

---

[53] Charles H. Kennedy & Peter P. Swire, *State Wiretaps and Electronic Surveillance After September 11,* 54 Hastings L.J. 971 (2003).

[54] Paul Schwartz, *German and U.S. Telecommunications Privacy Law,* 54 Hastings L.J. 751, 760 (2003).

required to file a report even if no surveillance activity takes place in it during a particular year?

4. THE COMMUNICATIONS ASSISTANCE FOR LAW ENFORCEMENT ACT

In *United States v. New York Telephone*, 434 U.S. 159 (1977), the Supreme Court held that 18 U.S.C. § 2518(4) required telecommunications providers to furnish "any assistance necessary to accomplish an electronic interception." However, the issue of whether a provider had to create and design its technology to facilitate authorized electronic surveillance remained an open question.

In the 1980s, new communications technology was developed to enable more wireless communications — cellular telephones, microwave, and satellite communications. As a result of fears that these new technologies would be harder to monitor, the law enforcement community successfully convinced Congress to force telecommunications providers to ensure that the government could continue to monitor electronic communications.[55]

The Communications Assistance for Law Enforcement Act (CALEA) of 1994, Pub. L. No. 103-414, (also known as the "Digital Telephony Act") requires telecommunication providers to help facilitate the government in executing legally authorized surveillance. The Act was passed against strong opposition from some civil liberties organizations. Congress appropriated federal funding of $500 million to telephone companies to make the proposed changes.

Requirements. CALEA requires all telecommunications providers to be able to isolate and intercept electronic communications and be able to deliver them to law enforcement personnel. If carriers provide an encryption service to users, then they must decrypt the communications. CALEA permits the telecommunications industry to develop the technology. Under a "safe harbor" provision, carriers that comply with accepted industry standards are in compliance with CALEA. 47 U.S.C. § 1006(a)(2).

Limits. CALEA contains some important limits. Carriers must "facilitat[e] authorized communications interceptions and access to call-identifying information . . . in a manner that protects . . . the privacy and security of communications and call-identifying information not authorized to be intercepted." § 1002(a)(4)(A). Further, CALEA is designed to provide "law enforcement no more and no less access to information than it had in the past." H.R. Rep. No. 103-827, pt. 1, at 22. Additionally, CALEA does not apply to "information services," such as e-mail and Internet access. §§ 1001(8)(C)(i), 1002(b)(2)(A).

The J-Standard. In *United States Telecom Ass'n v. FCC*, 227 F.3d 450 (D.C. Cir. 2000), the D.C. Circuit attempted to place certain limits on the FCC's interpretation of CALEA. This statute had set up a process by which the

---

[55] For a detailed analysis of CALEA, see Susan Freiwald, *Uncertain Privacy: Communication Attributes After the Digital Telephony Act*, 69 S. Cal. L. Rev. 949 (1996).

telecommunications industry "in consultation with law enforcement agencies, regulators, and consumers, [was] to develop its own technical standards for meeting the required surveillance capabilities." In 1995, the telecommunications industry started to develop this safe harbor standard, which was adopted by the industry in December 1997.

The standard is known as the Interim Standard/Trial Use Standard J-STD-025 (the "J-Standard"). The J-Standard sets forth the standards by which carriers can make communications and call-identifying information available to law enforcement officials. A group of industry associations as well as privacy organizations challenged the J-Standard and petitioned the Federal Communications Commission (FCC) to remove provisions that they argued extended beyond CALEA's authorization. In contrast, the Justice Department and FBI petitioned the FCC to add nine additional surveillance capabilities on its "punch list" to the J-Standard. The FCC refused the requests of the industry associations and privacy advocacy groups, but did add four of the nine items sought by the Justice Department and FBI to the J-Standard. The D.C. Circuit rejected the four challenged items added to the J-Standard and remanded to the FCC to demonstrate compliance with CALEA, including the statutory requirement of the use of "cost-effective means."

An item on the original J-Standard was a requirement that carriers inform law enforcement officials of the nearest antenna tower to a mobile telephone user, giving officials the ability to track the location of mobile telephones. The D.C. court held that the requirement was valid under CALEA:

> Not only did the Commission elucidate the textual basis for interpreting "call-identifying information" to include location information, but it also explained how that result comports with CALEA's goal of preserving the same surveillance capabilities that law enforcement agencies had in POTS (plain old telephone service). "[I]n the wireline environment," the Commission explained, law enforcement agencies "have generally been able to obtain location information routinely from the telephone number because the telephone number usually corresponds with location." In the wireless environment, "the equivalent location information" is "the location of the cell sites to which the mobile terminal or handset is connected at the beginning and at the termination of the call." Accordingly, the Commission concluded, "[p]rovision of this particular location information does not appear to expand or diminish law enforcement's surveillance authority under prior law applicable to the wireline environment."

On remand, the FCC returned the four items that it had earlier approved from the law enforcement "punch list" once again to the J-Standard. *In the Matter of Communications Assistance for Law Enforcement Act*, FCC 02-108 (Apr. 5, 2002). One of these items concerned "post-cut-through dialed digit extraction," which is a list of any digits that a person dials after a call has been connected. The FCC required that a telecommunications carrier "have the ability to turn on and off the dialed digit extraction capability." It therefore mandated a "toggle feature" that would allow a carrier to turn off the capability if it "had reservations about the legal basis for providing all post-cut through digits" while it was, at the same time, providing "other punch list capabilities included in the same software."

Voice over Internet Protocol (VoIP). A new way to make telephone calls is to use a broadband Internet connection to transmit the call. This technique, VoIP, converts a voice signal into a digital signal that travels over the Internet and connects to a phone number. On August 4, 2004, the FCC unanimously adopted a Notice of Proposed Rulemaking and Declaratory Ruling regarding VoIP and CALEA. *In the Matter of Communications Assistance for Law Enforcement Act and Broadband Access and Services*, FCC 04-187 (Aug. 4, 2004). It tentatively declared that CALEA applies to any facilities-based providers of any type of broadband Internet access service — including wireline, cable modem, satellite, wireless, and powerline — and to managed or mediated VoIP services. This conclusion was based on an FCC judgment that these services fall under CALEA statutory language as "a replacement for a substantial portion of the local telephone service." 47 U.S.C. § 1001(8)B)(ii).

The FCC continued its work in this area by issuing an Order in 2005 that built on its previous Notice of Proposed Rulemaking. This rulemaking, upheld by the D.C. Circuit in June 2006, established that broadband and VoIP are "hybrid telecommunications-information services" that fall under CALEA to the extent that they qualify as "telecommunications carriers." Communications Assistance for Law Enforcement and Broadband Access and Services, 20 F.C.C.R. 14989, at ¶ 18 (2005); *American Council on Education v. FCC*, 451 F.3d 266 (D.C. Cir. 2006).

In May 2006, the FCC issued an additional order to address remaining issues to achieve CALEA compliance. Second Report and Order and Memorandum Opinion and Order (Order), FCC 06-56 (May 12, 2006). The FCC's overarching policy perspective concerned giving law enforcement agencies all the resources that CALEA authorizes to combat crime and support homeland security. As FCC Chairman Kevin J. Martin observed in a statement issued as part of the Order, "Enabling law enforcement to ensure our safety and security is of paramount importance." The Order set a May 14, 2007, compliance date for both facilities-based broadband Internet access and interconnected VoIP providers. It also permitted entities covered by CALEA to have the option of using Trusted Third Parties (TTPs) to help meet their CALEA obligations. The role of the TTPs would include processing requests for intercepts, conducting electronic surveillance, and delivering relevant information to law enforcement agencies.

Susan Landau and Whitfield Diffie argue that extension of CALEA requirements to the Internet will ironically make it less secure and create a potential for cyber-terrorism. The problem is that CALEA has now been interpreted to require that modifications be made to Internet protocols, which present the risk of introducing vulnerabilities into the system. In their view, inserting wiretap requirements into Internet protocols will make the Internet less secure. A system that permits "legally authorized security breaches" (such as a wiretap by law enforcement officers) is also more open to unauthorized security breaches (such as hacking and other kinds of unlawful intrusions). They argue:

> On balance we are better off with a secure computer infrastructure than with one that builds surveillance into the network fabric. At times this may press law enforcement to exercise more initiative and imagination in its investigations. On the other hand, in a society completely dependent on computer-to-computer

communications, the alternative presents a hazard whose dimensions are as yet impossible to comprehend.[56]

5. THE USA PATRIOT ACT

On the morning of September 11, 2001, terrorists hijacked four planes and crashed three of them into the World Trade Center and the Pentagon, killing thousands of people. The nation was awakened into a world filled with new frightening dangers. Shortly after the September 11 attacks, a still unknown person or persons sent letters laced with the deadly bacteria anthrax through the mail to several prominent individuals in the news media and in politics. Acting with great haste, Congress passed a sweeping new law expanding the government's electronic surveillance powers in many significant ways.[57] Called the "Uniting and Strengthening America By Providing Appropriate Tools Required To Intercept and Obstruct Terrorism Act" (USA PATRIOT Act), the Act made a number of substantial changes to several statutes, including the federal electronic surveillance statutes.

Definition of Terrorism. Section 802 of the USA PATRIOT Act added to 18 U.S.C. § 2331 a new definition of "domestic terrorism." According to the Act, domestic terrorism involves "acts dangerous to human life that are a violation of the criminal laws of the United States or of any State" that "appear to be intended: (i) to intimidate or coerce a civilian population; (ii) to influence the policy of a government by intimidation or coercion; or (iii) to affect the conduct of a government by mass destruction, assassination, or kidnapping; and . . . occur primarily within the territorial jurisdiction of the United States." According to many proponents of civil liberties, this definition is very broad and could potentially encompass many forms of civil disobedience, which, although consisting of criminal conduct (minor violence, threats, property damage), includes conduct that has historically been present in many political protests and has never been considered to be terrorism.

Delayed Notice of Search Warrants. Under the Fourth Amendment, the government must obtain a warrant and provide notice to a person before conducting a search or seizure. Case law provided for certain limited exceptions. Section 213 of the USA PATRIOT Act adds a provision to 18 U.S.C. § 3103a, enabling the government to delay notice if the court concludes that there is "reasonable cause" that immediate notice will create an "adverse result" such as physical danger, the destruction of evidence, delayed trial, flight from prosecution, and other circumstances. § 3103a(b). Warrants enabling a covert search with delayed notice are often referred to as "sneak and peek" warrants. Civil libertarians consider "sneak and peek" warrants dangerous because they authorize covert searches, thus preventing individuals from safeguarding their rights during the search. Moreover, there is little supervision of the government's

---

[56] Susan Landau & Whitfield Diffie, *Privacy on the Line* 331, 328 (2d ed. 2007).

[57] For background about the passage of the USA PATRIOT Act, see Beryl A. Howell, *Seven Weeks: The Making of the USA Patriot Act,* 72 Geo. Wash. L. Rev. 1145 (2004).

carrying out of the search. Law enforcement officials argue that covert searches are necessary to avoid tipping off suspects that there is an investigation under way.

New Definition of Pen Registers and Trap and Trace Devices. Under the Pen Register Act of the ECPA, §§ 3121 *et seq.*, the definitions of pen registers and trap and trace devices focused primarily on telephone numbers. A pen register was defined under 18 U.S.C. § 3127(3) as

> a device which records or decodes electronic or other impulses which identify the numbers dialed or otherwise transmitted on the telephone line to which such device is attached. . . .

Section 216 of the USA PATRIOT Act changed the definition to read:

> a device *or process* which records or decodes *dialing, routing, addressing, or signaling information transmitted by an instrument or facility from which a wire or electronic communication is transmitted, provided, however, that such information shall not include the contents of any communication* is attached . . . (changes emphasized).

These changes altered the definition of a pen register from applying not only to telephone numbers but also to Internet addresses, e-mail addressing information (the "to" and "from" lines on e-mail), and the routing information of a wide spectrum of communications. The inclusion of "or process" after "device" enlarges the means by which such routing information can be intercepted beyond the use of a physical device. The definition of a trap and trace device was changed in a similar way. Recall that under the Pen Register Act, a court order to obtain such information does not require probable cause, but merely certification that "the information likely to be obtained by such installation and use is relevant to an ongoing criminal investigation." 18 U.S.C. § 3123. The person whose communications are subject to this order need not even be a criminal suspect; all that the government needs to certify is relevance to an investigation.

Recall *Smith v. Maryland* earlier in this chapter, where the Court held that pen registers were not protected under the Fourth Amendment. Does the new definition of pen register and trap and trace device under the USA PATRIOT Act go beyond *Smith v. Maryland*? Are Internet addresses and e-mail addressing information analogous to pen registers?

Private Right of Action for Government Disclosures. The USA PATRIOT Act adds a provision to the Stored Communications Act that provides for civil actions against the United States for any "willful" violations. 18 U.S.C. § 2712. The court may assess actual damages or $10,000 (whichever is greater) and litigation costs. Such an action must first be presented before the "appropriate department or agency under the procedures of the Federal Tort Claims Act."

Reauthorization. When the USA PATRIOT Act was passed, several provisions had sunset provisions and would expire on a particular date. On March 9, 2006, President George W. Bush signed the USA PATRIOT Reauthorization Act, which made permanent 14 of 16 expiring USA PATRIOT Act sections. It created a new sunset of December 31, 2009 for USA PATRIOT Act sections 205 and 215 (which concern "roving" FISA wiretaps and FISA orders for business records), and for FISA's "lone wolf" amendments. This law also expanded the list of predicate offenses for which law enforcement could obtain wiretap orders.

C. DIGITAL SEARCHES AND SEIZURES

1. SEARCHING THE CONTENTS OF COMPUTERS

The Scope of Warrants to Search Computers. In *United States v. Lacy,* 119 F.3d 742 (9th Cir. 1997), the defendant challenged a search warrant authorizing the seizure of his computer hard drive and disks. The defendant contended that the warrant was too general because it applied to his entire computer system. The court upheld the warrant because "this type of generic classification is acceptable when a more precise description is not possible." Several other courts have followed a similar approach as in *Lacy,* upholding generic warrants. In *United States v. Upham,* 168 F.3d 532 (1st Cir. 1999), the court reasoned: "A sufficient chance of finding some needles in the computer haystack was established by the probable-cause showing in the warrant application; and a search of a computer and co-located disks is not inherently more intrusive than the physical search of an entire house for a weapon or drugs." *See also United States v. Hay,* 231 F.3d 630 (9th Cir. 2000) (following *Lacy* and upholding a "generic" warrant application).[58]

However, there are limits to the scope of a search of a computer. In *United States v. Carey,* 172 F.3d 1268 (10th Cir. 1999), an officer obtained a warrant to search a computer for records about illegal drug distribution. When the officer stumbled upon a pornographic file, he began to search for similar files. The court concluded that these actions amounted to an expansion of the scope of the search and would require the obtaining of a second warrant.

In *United States v. Campos,* 221 F.3d 1143 (10th Cir. 2000), the defendant e-mailed two images of child pornography to a person he talked to in a chat room. The person informed the FBI, and the FBI obtained a warrant to search the defendant's home and computer. The agents seized the defendant's computer, and a search revealed the two images of child pornography as well as six other images of child pornography. The defendant challenged the search as beyond the scope of the warrant because the agents "had grounds to search only for the two images that had been sent." However, the court rejected the defendant's contention, quoting from the FBI's explanation why it is not feasible to search only for particular computer files in one's home:

> . . . Computer storage devices . . . can store the equivalent of thousands of pages of information. Especially when the user wants to conceal criminal evidence, he often stores it in random order with deceptive file names. This requires searching authorities to examine all the stored data to determine whether it is

---

[58] For more about computer searches, see Raphael Winnick, *Searches and Seizures of Computers and Computer Data,* 88 Harv. J.L. & Tech. 75 (1994).

included in the warrant. This sorting process can take weeks or months, depending on the volume of data stored, and it would be impractical to attempt this kind of data search on site. . . .

Searching computer systems for criminal evidence is a highly technical process requiring expert skill and a properly controlled environment. The wide variety of computer hardware and software available requires even computer experts to specialize in some systems and applications, so it is difficult to know before a search which expert should analyze the system and its data. . . . Since computer evidence is extremely vulnerable to tampering or destruction (both from external sources or from destructive code embedded into the system as "booby trap"), the controlled environment of a laboratory is essential to its complete analysis. . . .

Computer Searches and Seizures. Searches and seizures for digital information in computers present some unique conceptual puzzles for existing Fourth Amendment doctrine. Thomas Clancy contends:

> [C]omputers are containers. . . . They . . . contain electronic evidence, that is, a series of digitally stored 0s and 1s that, when combined with a computer program, yield such items as images, words, and spreadsheets. Accordingly, the traditional standards of the Fourth Amendment regulate obtaining the evidence in containers that happen to be computers.[59]

But is a computer a single container or is each computer file its own container? Orin Kerr argues:

> A single physical storage device can store the private files of thousands of different users. It would be quite odd if looking at one file on a server meant that the entire server had been searched, and that the police could then analyze everything on the server, perhaps belonging to thousands of different people, without any restriction.[60]

Is copying a computer file or other digital information a seizure under the Fourth Amendment? In *United States v. Gorshkov*, 2001 WL 1024026 (W.D. Wash. 2001), the FBI remotely copied the contents of the defendant's computer in Russia. The court held: "The agents' act of copying the data on the Russian computers was not a seizure under the Fourth Amendment because it did not interfere with Defendant's or anyone else's possessory interest in the data." However, as Susan Brenner and Barbara Frederiksen contend:

> [T]he information contained in computer files clearly belongs to the owner of the files. The ownership of information is similar to the contents of a private conversation in which the information belongs to the parties to the conversation. Copying computer data is analogous to recording a conversation. . . . Therefore, copying computer files should be treated as a seizure.[61]

---

[59] Thomas K. Clancy, *The Fourth Amendment Aspects of Computer Searches and Seizures: A Perspective and a Primer*, 75 Miss. L.J. 193, 196 (2005).

[60] Orin S. Kerr, *Searches and Seizures in a Digital World*, 119 Harv. L. Rev. 531, 556 (2005).

[61] Susan W. Brenner & Barbara A. Frederiksen, *Computer Searches and Seizures: Some Unresolved Issues*, 8 Mich. Telecomm. & Tech. L. Rev. 39, 111-12 (2002).

Password-Protected Files. In *Trulock v. Freeh*, 275 F.3d 391 (4th Cir. 2001), Notra Trulock and Linda Conrad shared a computer but maintained separate files protected by passwords. They did not know each other's password and could not access each other's files. When FBI officials, without a warrant, asked to search and seize the computer, Conrad consented. The court held that the FBI could not search Trulock's files since Trulock had not consented:

> Consent to search in the absence of a warrant may, in some circumstances, be given by a person other than the target of the search. Two criteria must be met in order for third party consent to be effective. First, the third party must have authority to consent to the search. Second, the third party's consent must be voluntary. . . .
>
> We conclude that, based on the facts in the complaint, Conrad lacked authority to consent to the search of Trulock's files. Conrad and Trulock both used a computer located in Conrad's bedroom and each had joint access to the hard drive. Conrad and Trulock, however, protected their personal files with passwords; Conrad did not have access to Trulock's passwords. Although Conrad had authority to consent to a general search of the computer, her authority did not extend to Trulock's password-protected files.

UNITED STATES V. ANDRUS

483 F.3d 711 (10th Cir. 2007)

[Federal authorities believed that Ray Andrus was downloading child pornography to his home computer. Ray Andrus resided at his parents' house. Federal officials obtained the consent of Dr. Andrus (Andrus's father) to search the home. He also consented to their searching any computers in the home. The officials went into Ray Andrus's bedroom and a forensic expert examined the contents of the computer's hard drive with forensic software. The software enabled direct access to the computer, bypassing any password protection the user put on it. The officials discovered child pornography on the computer. Later on, the officials learned that Ray Andrus had protected his computer with a password and that his father did not know the password. Is the father's consent to search the computer valid since he did not know the password?]

MURPHY, J. . . . Subject to limited exceptions, the Fourth Amendment prohibits warrantless searches of an individual's home or possessions. Voluntary consent to a police search, given by the individual under investigation or by a third party with authority over the subject property, is a well-established exception to the warrant requirement. Valid third party consent can arise either through the third party's actual authority or the third party's apparent authority. A third party has actual authority to consent to a search "if that third party has either (1) mutual use of the property by virtue of joint access, or (2) control for most purposes." Even where actual authority is lacking, however, a third party has apparent authority to consent to a search when an officer reasonably, even if erroneously, believes the third party possesses authority to consent. *See Georgia v. Randolph,* 547 U.S. 103 (2006).

Whether apparent authority exists is an objective, totality-of-the-circumstances inquiry into whether the facts available to the officers at the time they commenced the search would lead a reasonable officer to believe the third party had authority to consent to the search. When the property to be searched is an object or container, the relevant inquiry must address the third party's relationship to the object. In *Randolph,* the Court explained, "The constant element in assessing Fourth Amendment reasonableness in consent cases . . . is the great significance given to widely shared social expectations." For example, the Court said, "[W]hen it comes to searching through bureau drawers, there will be instances in which even a person clearly belonging on the premises as an occupant may lack any perceived authority to consent." . . .

It may be unreasonable for law enforcement to believe a third party has authority to consent to the search of an object typically associated with a high expectation of privacy, especially when the officers know or should know the owner has indicated the intent to exclude the third party from using or exerting control over the object.

Courts considering the issue have attempted to analogize computers to other items more commonly seen in Fourth Amendment jurisprudence. Individuals' expectations of privacy in computers have been likened to their expectations of privacy in "a suitcase or briefcase." Password-protected files have been compared to a "locked footlocker inside the bedroom." *Trulock v. Freeh,* 275 F.3d 391, 403 (4th Cir. 2001).

Given the pervasiveness of computers in American homes, this court must reach some, at least tentative, conclusion about the category into which personal computers fall. A personal computer is often a repository for private information the computer's owner does not intend to share with others. . . .

The inquiry into whether the owner of a highly personal object has indicated a subjective expectation of privacy traditionally focuses on whether the subject suitcase, footlocker, or other container is physically locked. Determining whether a computer is "locked," or whether a reasonable officer should know a computer may be locked, presents a challenge distinct from that associated with other types of closed containers. Unlike footlockers or suitcases, where the presence of a locking device is generally apparent by looking at the item, a "lock" on the data within a computer is not apparent from a visual inspection of the outside of the computer, especially when the computer is in the "off" position prior to the search. Data on an entire computer may be protected by a password, with the password functioning as a lock, or there may be multiple users of a computer, each of whom has an individual and personalized password-protected "user profile." . . .

Courts addressing the issue of third party consent in the context of computers, therefore, have examined officers' knowledge about password protection as an indication of whether a computer is "locked" in the way a footlocker would be. For example, in *Trulock,* the Fourth Circuit held a live-in girlfriend lacked actual authority to consent to a search of her boyfriend's computer files where the girlfriend told police she and her boyfriend shared the household computer but had separate password-protected files that were inaccessible to the other. The court in that case explained, "Although Conrad had authority to consent to a general search of the computer, her authority did not extend to Trulock's password-protected files." . . .

In addition to password protection, courts also consider the location of the computer within the house and other indicia of household members' access to the computer in assessing third party authority. Third party apparent authority to consent to a search has generally been upheld when the computer is located in a common area of the home that is accessible to other family members under circumstances indicating the other family members were not excluded from using the computer. In contrast, where the third party has affirmatively disclaimed access to or control over the computer or a portion of the computer's files, even when the computer is located in a common area of the house, courts have been unwilling to find third party authority.

Andrus' case presents facts that differ somewhat from those in other cases. Andrus' computer was located in a bedroom occupied by the homeowner's fifty-one year old son rather than in a true common area. Dr. Andrus, however, had unlimited access to the room. Law enforcement officers did not ask specific questions about Dr. Andrus' use of the computer, but Dr. Andrus said nothing indicating the need for such questions. *Cf. Trulock,* 275 F.3d at 398 (when law enforcement questioned third party girlfriend about computer, she indicated she and boyfriend had separate password-protected files). The resolution of this appeal turns on whether the officers' belief in Dr. Andrus' authority was reasonable, despite the lack of any affirmative assertion by Dr. Andrus that he used the computer and despite the existence of a user profile indicating Ray Andrus' intent to exclude other household members from using the computer. For the reasons articulated below, this court concludes the officers' belief in Dr. Andrus' authority was reasonable. . . .

First, the officers knew Dr. Andrus owned the house and lived there with family members. Second, the officers knew Dr. Andrus' house had internet access and that Dr. Andrus paid the Time Warner internet and cable bill. Third, the officers knew the email address bandrus@kc.rr.com had been activated and used to register on a website that provided access to child pornography. Fourth, although the officers knew Ray Andrus lived in the center bedroom, they also knew that Dr. Andrus had access to the room at will. Fifth, the officers saw the computer in plain view on the desk in Andrus' room and it appeared available for use by other household members. Furthermore, the record indicates Dr. Andrus did not say or do anything to indicate his lack of ownership or control over the computer when Cheatham asked for his consent to conduct a computer search. It is uncontested that Dr. Andrus led the officers to the bedroom in which the computer was located, and, even after he saw Kanatzar begin to work on the computer, Dr. Andrus remained silent about any lack of authority he had over the computer. Even if Ray Andrus' computer was protected with a user name and password, there is no indication in the record that the officers knew or had reason to believe such protections were in place.

Andrus argues his computer's password protection indicated his computer was "locked" to third parties, a fact the officers would have known had they asked questions of Dr. Andrus prior to searching the computer. Under our case law, however, officers are not obligated to ask questions unless the circumstances are ambiguous. In essence, by suggesting the onus was on the officers to ask about password protection prior to searching the computer, despite the absence of any indication that Dr. Andrus' access to the computer was limited by a password, Andrus necessarily submits there is inherent ambiguity whenever police want to search a household computer and a third party has not affirmatively provided information about his own use of the computer or about password protection. Andrus' argument presupposes, however, that password protection of home computers is so common that a reasonable officer ought to know password protection is likely. Andrus has neither made this argument directly nor proffered any evidence to demonstrate a high incidence of password protection among home computer users. . . .

Viewed under the requisite totality-of-the-circumstances analysis, the facts known to the officers at the time the computer search commenced created an objectively reasonable perception that Dr. Andrus was, at least, *one* user of the computer. That objectively reasonable belief would have been enough to give Dr. Andrus apparent authority to consent to a search. Even if Dr. Andrus had no actual ability to use the computer and the computer was password protected, these mistakes of fact do not negate a determination of Dr. Andrus' apparent authority. In this case, the district court found Agent Cheatham properly halted the search when further conversation with Dr. Andrus revealed he did not use the computer and that Andrus' computer was the only computer in the house. These later revelations, however, have no bearing on the reasonableness of the officers' belief in Dr. Andrus' authority at the outset of the computer search.

MCKAY, J., dissenting. This case concerns the reasonable expectation of privacy associated with password-protected computers. In examining the contours of a third party's apparent authority to consent to the search of a home computer, the majority correctly indicates that the extent to which law enforcement knows or should reasonably suspect that password protection is enabled is critical. . . . I take issue with the majority's implicit holding that law enforcement may use software deliberately designed to automatically bypass computer password protection based on third-party consent without the need to make a reasonable inquiry regarding the presence of password protection and the third party's access to that password.

The presence of security on Defendant's computer is undisputed. Yet, the majority curiously argues that Defendant's use of password protection is inconsequential because Defendant failed to argue that computer password protection is "commonplace." Of course, the decision provides no guidance on what would constitute sufficient proof of the prevalence of password protection, nor does it explain why the court could not take judicial notice that password protection is a standard feature of operating systems. Despite recognizing the "pervasiveness of computers in American homes," and the fact that the "personal computer is often a repository for private information the computer's owner does not intend to share with others," the majority requires the invocation of magical language in order to give effect to Defendant's subjective intent to exclude others from accessing the computer. . . .

The unconstrained ability of law enforcement to use forensic software such as the EnCase program to bypass password protection without first determining whether such passwords have been enabled does not "exacerbate[]" this difficulty; rather, it avoids it altogether, simultaneously and dangerously sidestepping the Fourth Amendment in the process. Indeed, the majority concedes that if such protection were "shown to be commonplace, law enforcement's use of forensic software like EnCase . . . may well be subject to question." But the fact that a computer password "lock" may not be *immediately* visible does not render it unlocked. I appreciate that unlike the locked file cabinet, computers have no handle to pull. But, like the padlocked footlocker, computers do exhibit outward signs of password protection: they display boot password screens, username/password log-in screens, and/or screen-saver reactivation passwords.

The fact remains that EnCase's ability to bypass security measures is well known to law enforcement. Here, ICE's forensic computer specialist found Defendant's computer turned off. Without turning it on, he hooked his laptop directly to the hard drive of Defendant's computer and ran the EnCase program. The agents made no effort to ascertain whether such security was enabled prior to initiating the search. . . .

The majority points out that law enforcement "did not ask specific questions" about Dr. Andrus' use of the computer or knowledge of Ray Andrus' use of password protection, but twice criticizes Dr. Andrus' failure to affirmatively disclaim ownership of, control over, or knowledge regarding the computer. Of course, the computer was located in Ray Andrus' very tiny bedroom, but the majority makes no effort to explain how this does not create an ambiguous situation as to ownership.

The burden on law enforcement to identify ownership of the computer was minimal. A simple question or two would have sufficed. Prior to the computer search, the agents questioned Dr. Andrus about Ray Andrus' status as a renter and Dr. Andrus' ability to enter his 51-year-old son's bedroom in order to determine Dr. Andrus' ability to consent to a search of the room, but the agents did not inquire whether Dr. Andrus used the computer, and if so, whether he had access to his son's password. At the suppression hearing, the agents testified that they were not immediately aware that Defendant's computer was the only one in the house, and they began to doubt Dr. Andrus' authority to consent when they learned this fact. The record reveals that, upon questioning, Dr. Andrus indicated that there was a computer in the house and led the agents to Defendant's room. The forensic specialist was then summoned. It took him approximately fifteen to twenty minutes to set up his equipment, yet, bizarrely, at no point during this period did the agents inquire about the presence of any other computers. . . .

Accordingly, in my view, given the case law indicating the importance of computer password protection, the common knowledge about the prevalence of password usage, and the design of EnCase or similar password bypass mechanisms, the Fourth Amendment and the reasonable inquiry rule, mandate that in consent-based, warrantless computer searches, law enforcement personnel inquire or otherwise check for the presence of password protection and, if a password is present, inquire about the consenter's knowledge of that password and joint access to the computer. . . .

NOTES & QUESTIONS

1. *A Question of Perspective?* Orin Kerr contends:

> From a virtual user's perspective, the child pornography was hidden to the father; it was behind a password-protected gate. Under these facts, the father couldn't consent to a search because he would lack common authority over it. From a physical perspective, however, the file was present on the hard drive just like all the other information. Under these facts, the father could consent to the search because he had access rights to the machine generally. . . .
>
> Viewed from the physical perspective, the investigators reasonably did not know about the user profile and reasonably believed that the father had rights to consent to that part of the hard drive.[62]

2. *Checking for Password Protection.* Was the investigators' belief about the father's authority over the computer reasonable? Should the investigators have asked the father more questions about his use of the computer first? Should they have turned on the machine to see if it was password-protected before hooking up the forensic software? What kinds of incentives does this decision engender for officers doing an investigation?

2. ENCRYPTION

Encryption includes the ability to keep communications secure by concealing the contents of a message. With encryption, even if a communication is intercepted, it still remains secure. Encryption works by translating a message into a code of letters or numbers called "cypher text." The parties to the communication hold a *key*, which consists of the information necessary to translate the code back to the original message, or "plain text." Since ancient times, code-makers have devised cryptographic systems to encode messages. But along with the code-makers arose code-breakers, who were able to figure out the keys to cryptographic systems by, for example, examining the patterns in the encoded messages and comparing them to patterns in a particular language and the frequency of use of certain letters in that language. Today, computers have vastly increased the complexity of encryption.

Encryption presents a difficult trade-off between privacy and surveillance. It is an essential technique to protect the privacy of electronic communications in an age when such communications can so easily be intercepted and monitored. On the other hand, it enables individuals to disguise their communications from detection by law enforcement officials.[63] As Whitfield Diffie and Susan Landau observe:

---

[62] Orin Kerr, *Virtual Analogies, Physical Searches, and the Fourth Amendment,* Volokh Conspiracy, Apr. 26, 2007, http://www.volokh.com/posts/1177562355.shtml.

[63] For more background on encryption, see Simon Singh, *The Code: The Evolution of Secrecy from Mary, Queen of Scots to Quantum Cryptography* (1999); Steven Levy, *Crypto: How the Code Rebels Beat the Government — Saving Privacy in the Digital Age* (2002); A. Michael Froomkin, *The Metaphor Is the Key: Cryptography, the Clipper Chip, and the Constitution,* 143 U. Pa. L. Rev. 709 (1995); Robert C. Post, *Encryption Source Code and the First Amendment,* 15 Berkeley Tech. L.J. 713 (2000); A. Michael Froomkin, *The Constitution and Encryption Regulation: Do We Need a "New Privacy"?,* 3 N.Y.U. J. Legis. & Pub. Pol'y 25 (1999).

The explosion in cryptography and the US government's attempts to control it have given rise to a debate between those who hail the new technology's contribution to privacy, business, and security and those who fear both its interference with the work of police and its adverse effect on the collection of intelligence. Positions have often been extreme. The advocates for unfettered cryptography maintain that a free society depends on privacy to protect freedom of association, artistic creativity, and political discussion. The advocates of control hold that there will be no freedom at all unless we can protect ourselves from criminals, terrorists, and foreign threats. Many have tried to present themselves as seeking to maintain or restore the status quo. For the police, the status quo is the continued ability to wiretap. For civil libertarians, it is the ready availability of conversational privacy that prevailed at the time of the country's founding.[64]

The Clipper Chip. The U.S. government has become increasingly concerned that the growing sophistication of encryption would make it virtually impossible for the government to decrypt. In 1994, the government proposed implementing the "Clipper Chip," a federal encryption standard in which the government would retain a copy of the key in a system called "key escrow." By holding a "spare key," the government could readily decrypt encrypted communications if it desired. The Clipper Chip was strongly criticized, and the government's encryption standard has not been widely used.

Encryption and the First Amendment. In *Junger v. Daley*, 209 F.3d 481 (6th Cir. 2000), the Sixth Circuit concluded that encryption was protected speech under the First Amendment:

> Much like a mathematical or scientific formula, one can describe the function and design of encryption software by a prose explanation; however, for individuals fluent in a computer programming language, source code is the most efficient and precise means by which to communicate ideas about cryptography.

Junger relied on the reasoning of *Bernstein v. United States Dep't of Justice,* 176 F.3d 1132 (9th Cir. 1999) (opinion withdrawn), where the Ninth Circuit struck down a licensing scheme on encryption source code as a violation of the First Amendment:

> Bernstein has submitted numerous declarations from cryptographers and computer programmers explaining that cryptographic ideas and algorithms are conveniently expressed in source code. . . . [T]he chief task for cryptographers is the development of secure methods of encryption. While the articulation of such a system in layman's English or in general mathematical terms may be useful, the devil is, at least for cryptographers, often in the algorithmic details. By utilizing source code, a cryptographer can express algorithmic ideas with precision and methodological rigor that is otherwise difficult to achieve. . . .
>
> Thus, cryptographers use source code to express their scientific ideas in much the same way that mathematicians use equations or economists use graphs. . . .

---

[64] Whitfield Diffie & Susan Landau, *Privacy on the Line: The Politics of Wiretapping and Encryption* (1998).

In light of these considerations, we conclude that encryption software, in its source code form and as employed by those in the field of cryptography, must be viewed as expressive for First Amendment purposes. . . .

Orin Kerr takes issue with *Junger*'s holding: "the court viewed source code using the close-up paradigm of what the code looked like, rather than the deeper functional perspective of what the code was actually supposed to do. . . . Just as viewing a Seurat painting from inches away reveals only dots, the *Junger* court's myopic view of source code revealed only communications that looked like speech in form, but lacked the deeper significance required to establish constitutional expression."[65]

Consider *Karn v. United States Dep't of State*, 925 F. Supp. 1 (D.D.C. 1996), where the court came to the contrary conclusion from *Junger*:

> . . . The government regulation at issue here is clearly content-neutral. . . . The defendants are not regulating the export of the diskette because of the expressive content of the comments and or source code, but instead are regulating because of the belief that the combination of encryption source code on machine readable media will make it easier for foreign intelligence sources to encode their communications. . . .
>
> . . . [A] content-neutral regulation is justified . . . if it is within the constitutional power of the government, it "furthers an important or substantial governmental interest," and "the incidental restriction on alleged First Amendment freedoms is no greater than is essential to the furtherance of that interest." . . .
>
> . . . By placing cryptographic products on the ITAR, the President has determined that the proliferation of cryptographic products will harm the United States. . . .
>
> . . . [T]he plaintiff has not advanced any argument that the regulation is "substantially broader than necessary" to prevent the proliferation of cryptographic products. Nor has the plaintiff articulated any present barrier to the spreading of information on cryptography "by any other means" other than those containing encryption source code on machine-readable media. Therefore, the Court holds that the regulation of the plaintiff's diskette is narrowly tailored to the goal of limiting the proliferation of cryptographic products and that the regulation is justified. . . .

Encryption and the Fourth Amendment. Suppose law enforcement officials legally obtain an encrypted communication. Does the Fourth Amendment require a warrant before the government can decrypt an encrypted communication? Consider the following argument by Orin Kerr:

> Encryption is often explained as a lock-and-key system, in which a "key" is used to "lock" plaintext by turning it into ciphertext, and then a "key" is used to "unlock" the ciphertext by turning it into plaintext. We know that locking a container is a common way to create a reasonable expectation of privacy in its contents: the government ordinarily cannot break the lock and search a closed container without a warrant. . . .

---

[65] Orin S. Kerr, *Are We Overprotecting Code? Thoughts on First-Generation Internet Law*, 57 Wash. & Lee L. Rev. 1287, 1292-93 (2000).

When we use a "lock" and "unlock" in the metaphorical sense to denote understanding, however, a lock cannot trigger the rights-based Fourth Amendment. If I tell you a riddle, I do not have a right to stop you from figuring it out. Although figuring out the secret of an inscrutable communication may "unlock" its meaning, the Fourth Amendment cannot regulate such a cognitive discovery. . . .[66]

Encryption and the Fifth Amendment. Can the government compel the production of a private key if it is stored on a personal computer? What if the key is known only to the individual and not stored or recorded?

3. E-MAIL

STEVE JACKSON GAMES, INC. V. UNITED STATES SECRET SERVICE
36 F.3d 457 (5th Cir. 1994)

BARKSDALE, J. Appellant Steve Jackson Games, Incorporated (SJG), publishes books, magazines, role-playing games, and related products. Starting in the mid-1980s, SJG operated an electronic bulletin board system, called "Illuminati" (BBS), from one of its computers. SJG used the BBS to post public information about its business, games, publications, and the role-playing hobby; to facilitate play-testing of games being developed; and to communicate with its customers and free-lance writers by electronic mail (E-mail).

Central to the issue before us, the BBS also offered customers the ability to send and receive private E-mail. Private E-mail was stored on the BBS computer's hard disk drive temporarily, until the addressees "called" the BBS (using their computers and modems) and read their mail. After reading their E-mail, the recipients could choose to either store it on the BBS computer's hard drive or delete it. In February 1990, there were 365 BBS users. Among other uses, appellants Steve Jackson, Elizabeth McCoy, William Milliken, and Steffan O'Sullivan used the BBS for communication by private E-mail. . . . [In addition, Lloyd Blankenship, an employee of Steve Jackson Games, operated a computer bulletin bulletin board system (BBS).] Blankeship had the ability to review, and perhaps delete any data on the BBS.

On February 28, 1990, [Secret Service] Agent Foley applied for a warrant to search SJG's premises and Blankenship's residence for evidence of violations of 18 U.S.C. §§ 1030 (proscribes interstate transportation of computer access information) and 2314 (proscribes interstate transportation of stolen property). A search warrant for SJG was issued that same day, authorizing the seizure of [computer hardware, software, and computer data.]

The next day, March 1, the warrant was executed by the Secret Service, including Agents Foley and Golden. Among the items seized was the computer which operated the BBS. At the time of the seizure, 162 items of unread, private

---

[66] Orin S. Kerr, *The Fourth Amendment in Cyberspace: Can Encryption Create a "Reasonable Expectation of Privacy?,"* 33 Conn. L. Rev. 503, 520-21, 522 (2001).

E-mail were stored on the BBS, including items addressed to the individual appellants. . . .

Appellants filed suit in May 1991 against, among others, the Secret Service and the United States, claiming [among other things, a violation of] the Federal Wiretap Act, as amended by Title I of the Electronic Communications Privacy Act (ECPA), 18 U.S.C. §§ 2510-2521; and Title II of the ECPA, 18 U.S.C. §§ 2701-2711. . . .

As stated, the sole issue is a very narrow one: whether the seizure of a computer on which is stored private E-mail that has been sent to an electronic bulletin board, but not yet read (retrieved) by the recipients, constitutes an "intercept" proscribed by 18 U.S.C. § 2511(1)(a).

Section 2511 was enacted in 1968 as part of Title III of the Omnibus Crime Control and Safe Streets Act of 1968, often referred to as the Federal Wiretap Act. Prior to the 1986 amendment by Title I of the ECPA, it covered only wire and oral communications. Title I of the ECPA extended that coverage to electronic communications. In relevant part, § 2511(1)(a) proscribes "intentionally intercept[ing] . . . any wire, oral, or electronic communication," unless the intercept is authorized by court order or by other exceptions not relevant here. Section 2520 authorizes, *inter alia*, persons whose electronic communications are intercepted in violation of § 2511 to bring a civil action against the interceptor for actual damages, or for statutory damages of $10,000 per violation or $100 per day of the violation, whichever is greater. 18 U.S.C. § 2520.

The Act defines "intercept" as "the aural or other acquisition of the contents of any wire, electronic, or oral communication through the use of any electronic, mechanical, or other device." 18 U.S.C. § 2510(4). . . .

Webster's Third New International Dictionary (1986) defines "aural" as "of or relating to the ear" or "of or relating to the sense of hearing." And, the Act defines "aural transfer" as "a transfer containing the human voice at any point between and including the point of origin and the point of reception." 18 U.S.C. § 2510(18). This definition is extremely important for purposes of understanding the definition of a "wire communication," which is defined by the Act as

> any aural transfer made in whole or in part through the use of facilities for the transmission of communications by the aid of wire, cable, or other like connection between the point of origin and the point of reception (including the use of such connection in a switching station) . . . *and such term includes any electronic storage of such communication.*

18 U.S.C. § 2510(1) (emphasis added). In contrast, as noted, an "electronic communication" is defined as "any *transfer* of signs, signals, writing, images, sounds, data, or intelligence of any nature transmitted in whole or in part by a wire, radio, electromagnetic, photoelectronic or photooptical system . . . but does not include . . . any wire or oral communication. . . ." 18 U.S.C. § 2510(12) (emphasis added).

Critical to the issue before us is the fact that, unlike the definition of "wire communication," *the definition of "electronic communication" does not include electronic storage of such communications. See* 18 U.S.C. § 2510(12). "Electronic storage" is defined as

(A) any *temporary*, intermediate *storage* of a wire or *electronic communication incidental to the electronic transmission thereof;* and

(B) any storage of such communication by an electronic communication service for purposes of backup protection of such communication. . . .

18 U.S.C. § 2510(17) (emphasis added). The E-mail in issue was in "electronic storage." Congress' use of the word "transfer" in the definition of "electronic communication," and its omission in that definition of the phrase "any electronic storage of such communication" (part of the definition of "wire communication") reflects that Congress did not intend for "intercept" to apply to "electronic communications" when those communications are in "electronic storage." . . .

Title II generally proscribes unauthorized access to stored wire or electronic communications. Section 2701(a) provides:

Except as provided in subsection (c) of this section whoever —

(1) intentionally accesses without authorization a facility through which an electronic communication service is provided; or

(2) intentionally exceeds an authorization to access that facility; and thereby obtains, alters, or prevents authorized access to a wire or electronic communication *while it is in electronic storage in such system* shall be punished. . . .

18 U.S.C. § 2701(a) (emphasis added).

As stated, the district court found that the Secret Service violated § 2701 when it

intentionally accesse[d] without authorization a facility [the computer] through which an electronic communication service [the BBS] is provided . . . and thereby obtain[ed] [and] prevent[ed] authorized access [by appellants] to a[n] . . . . electronic communication while it is in electronic storage in such system.

18 U.S.C. § 2701(a). The Secret Service does not challenge this ruling. We find no indication in either the Act or its legislative history that Congress intended for conduct that is clearly prohibited by Title II to furnish the basis for a civil remedy under Title I as well. . . .

NOTES & QUESTIONS

1. *Interception vs. Electronic Storage.* Is unread e-mail in storage because it is sitting on a hard drive at the ISP? Or is it in transmission because the recipient hasn't read it yet? Is the court applying an overly formalistic and strict reading of "interception"?

2. *The Fourth Amendment and E-mail: A Question of Perspective?* Suppose the police sought to obtain a person's unread e-mail messages that were stored with her ISP waiting to be downloaded. *Steve Jackson Games* demonstrates how ECPA would apply — the weaker provisions of the Stored Communications Act rather than the stronger protections of the Wiretap Act apply to e-mail temporarily stored with a person's ISP. *Steve Jackson Games* is a civil case. In the criminal law context, the Stored Communications Act requires a warrant to obtain e-mails stored at the ISP for 180 days or less. If the e-mails

have been stored over 180 days, then the government can obtain them with a mere subpoena.

Would the Fourth Amendment apply? Orin Kerr argues that the answer depends upon the perspective by which one views the Internet. In the "internal perspective," the Internet is viewed as a virtual world, analogous to real space. From the "external perspective," we view the Internet as a network and do not analogize to real space. Kerr provides the following example:

> Does the Fourth Amendment require [the police] to obtain a search warrant [to obtain an e-mail]? . . . The answer depends largely upon whether they apply an internal or external perspective of the Internet.
>
> Imagine that the first officer applies an internal perspective of the Internet. To him, e-mail is the cyberspace equivalent of old-fashioned postal mail. His computer announces, "You've got mail!" when an e-mail message arrives and shows him a closed envelope. When he clicks on the envelope, it opens, revealing the message. From his internal perspective, the officer is likely to conclude that the Fourth Amendment places the same restriction on government access to e-mail that it places on government access to ordinary postal mail. He will then look in a Fourth Amendment treatise for the black letter rule on accessing postal mail. That treatise will tell him that accessing a suspect's mail ordinarily violates the suspect's "reasonable expectation of privacy," and that therefore the officer must first obtain a warrant. Because e-mail is the equivalent of postal mail, the officer will conclude that the Fourth Amendment requires him to obtain a warrant before he can access the e-mail.
>
> Imagine that the second police office approaches the same problem from an external perspective. To him, the facts look quite different. Looking at how the Internet actually works, the second police officer sees that when A sent the e-mail to B, A was instructing his computer to send a message to his Internet Service Provider (ISP) directing the ISP to forward a text message to B's ISP. To simplify matters, let's say that A's ISP is EarthLink, and B's ISP is America Online (AOL). . . .
>
> What process does the Fourth Amendment require? The second officer will reason that A sent a copy of the e-mail communication to a third party (the EarthLink computer), disclosing the communication to the third party and instructing it to send the communication to yet another third party (AOL). The officer will ask, what process does the Fourth Amendment require to obtain information that has been disclosed to a third party and is in the third party's possession? The officer will look in a Fourth Amendment treatise and locate to the black letter rule that the Fourth Amendment permits the government to obtain information disclosed to a third party using a mere subpoena. The officer can simply subpoena the system administrator to compel him to produce the e-mails. No search warrant is required.
>
> Who is right? The first officer or the second? The answer depends on whether you approach the Internet from an internal or external perspective. From an internal perspective, the officers need a search warrant; from the external perspective, they do not.[67]

---

[67] Orin S. Kerr, *The Problem of Perspective in Internet Law,* 91 Geo. L.J. 357, 361-62, 365-67 (2003).

3. ***Previously Read E-mail Stored at an ISP.*** The e-mail stored on the ISP server in *Steve Jackson Games* had not yet been downloaded and read by the recipients. Many people continue to store their e-mail messages with their ISP even after having read them. Does the Stored Communications Act protect them in the same way? The answer to this question is currently in dispute. Daniel Solove observes:

> Because these messages are now stored indefinitely, according to the DOJ's interpretation . . . the e-mail is no longer in temporary storage and is "simply a remotely stored file." Therefore, under this view, it falls outside of much of the Act's protections. Since many people store their e-mail messages after reading them and the e-mail they send out, this enables the government to access their communications with very minimal limitations.[68]

In *Theofel v. Farey-Jones,* 359 F.3d 1066 (9th Cir. 2004), the court concluded that

> [t]he [Stored Communications] Act defines "electronic storage" as "(A) any temporary, intermediate storage of a wire or electronic communication incidental to the electronic transmission thereof; and (B) any storage of such communication by an electronic communication service for purposes of backup protection of such communication." Id. § 2510(17), incorporated by id. § 2711(1). Several courts have held that subsection (A) covers e-mail messages stored on an ISP's server pending delivery to the recipient. Because subsection (A) applies only to messages in "temporary, intermediate storage," however, these courts have limited that subsection's coverage to messages not yet delivered to their intended recipient.
>
> Defendants point to these cases and argue that messages remaining on an ISP's server after delivery no longer fall within the Act's coverage. But, even if such messages are not within the purview of subsection (A), they do fit comfortably within subsection (B). . . .
>
> An obvious purpose for storing a message on an ISP's server after delivery is to provide a second copy of the message in the event that the user needs to download it again — if, for example, the message is accidentally erased from the user's own computer. The ISP copy of the message functions as a "backup" for the user. Notably, nothing in the Act requires that the backup protection be for the benefit of the ISP rather than the user. Storage under these circumstances thus literally falls within the statutory definition.

See also Fraser v. Nationwide Mutual Insurance Co., 352 F.3d 108 (3d Cir. 2003) (suggesting that such e-mail messages were in backup storage under the definition of electronic storage).

4. ***What Constitutes an Interception?*** In *United States v. Councilman,* 373 F.3d 197 (1st Cir. 2004), an Internet bookseller, Interloc, Inc., provided e-mail service for its customers, who were book dealers. Councilman, the vice president of Interloc, directed Interloc employees to draft a computer program to intercept all incoming communications from Amazon.com to the book dealers and make copies of them. Councilman and other Interloc then read the

---

[68] Daniel J. Solove, *Reconstructing Electronic Surveillance Law,* 72 Geo. Wash. L. Rev. 1264 (2004).

e-mails in order to gain a commercial advantage. Councilman was charged with criminal violations of the Wiretap Act. Councilman argued that he did not violate the Wiretap Act because the e-mails were in electronic storage, albeit very briefly, when they were copied. The court followed *Steve Jackson Games* and concluded that the e-mail was in temporary storage and therefore subject to the Stored Communications Act, not the Wiretap Act. However, unlike *Steve Jackson Games,* Interloc accessed the e-mails "as they were being transmitted and in real time."

The *Councilman* case received significant criticism by academic commentators and experts in electronic surveillance law for misunderstanding the fundamental distinction between the interception of a communication and the accessing of a stored communication. An interception occurs contemporaneously — as the communication is being transmitted. Accessing a stored communication occurs later, as the communication sits on a computer. This distinction has practical consequences, since interceptions are protected by the much more protective Wiretap Act rather than the Stored Communications Act. Does such a distinction still make sense? Is the contemporaneous interception of communications more troublesome than the accessing of the communications in *Steve Jackson Games*?

The case was reheard en banc, and the en banc court reversed the panel. *See United States v. Councilman*, 418 F.3d 67 (1st Cir. 2005) (en banc). The court concluded that "the term 'electronic communication' includes transient electronic storage that is intrinsic to the communication process, and hence that interception of an e-mail message in such storage is an offense under the Wiretap Act." The court declined to further elaborate on what constitutes and "interception."

5. *Carnivore.* Beginning in 1998, the FBI began using a hardware and software mechanism called "Carnivore" to intercept people's e-mail and instant messaging information from their Internet Service Providers (ISPs). After obtaining judicial authorization, the FBI would install Carnivore by connecting a computer directly to the ISP's server and initiating the program. Carnivore was designed to locate the e-mails of a suspect at the ISP when the ISP did not have the capacity to do so.

Carnivore was capable of analyzing the entire e-mail traffic of an ISP, although the FBI maintained it was only used to search for the e-mails of a suspect. The program filtered out the e-mail messages of ISP subscribers who are not the subject of the investigation; but to do so, it had to scan the e-mail headers that identify the senders and recipients. The FBI likened e-mail headers to the information captured by a pen register, a device that registers the phone numbers a person dials.

However, Carnivore could be programmed to search through the entire text of all e-mails, to capture e-mails with certain key words. In this way, Carnivore resembles a wiretap. Recall that under federal wiretap law, judicial approval for obtaining pen register information only requires a certification that "the information likely to be obtained by such installation and use is relevant to an ongoing investigation." 18 U.S.C. § 3123. In contrast, judicial approval of a wiretap requires a full panoply of requirements under Title I, including a showing of probable cause.

To eliminate the negative associations with the term "Carnivore," the device was renamed "DCS1000." Many members of Congress viewed Carnivore with great suspicion. Congress held hearings over the summer of 2000 pertaining to Carnivore, and several bills were proposed to halt or limit the use of Carnivore.

The anti-Carnivore sentiment abruptly ended after the September 11, 2001, World Trade Center and Pentagon terrorist attacks. Section 216 of the USA PATRIOT Act of 2001, in anticipation of the use of Carnivore, required reports on the use of Carnivore to be filed with a court. These reports, filed under seal, require (1) the names of the officers using the device; (2) when the device was installed, used, and removed; (3) the configuration of the device; and (4) the information collected by the device. 18 U.S.C. § 3133(a)(3).

The FBI discontinued use of Carnivore because ISPs can readily produce the information the FBI desires without the assistance of the Carnivore device and because commercially available software has similar functionality.

4. ISP RECORDS

UNITED STATES V. HAMBRICK

55 F. Supp. 2d 504 (W.D. Va. 1999)

MICHAEL, J. Defendant Scott M. Hambrick seeks the suppression of all evidence obtained from his Internet Service Provider ("ISP"), MindSpring, and seeks the suppression of all evidence seized from his home pursuant to a warrant issued by this court. For the reasons discussed below, the court denies the defendant's motion.

On March 14, 1998, J. L. McLaughlin, a police officer with the Keene, New Hampshire Police Department, connected to the Internet and entered a chat room called "Gay dads 4 sex." McLaughlin's screen name was "Rory14." In this chat room, Detective McLaughlin encountered someone using the screen name "Blowuinva." Based on a series of online conversations between "Rory14" (Det. McLaughlin) and "Blowuinva," McLaughlin concluded that "Blowuinva" sought to entice a fourteen-year-old boy to leave New Hampshire and live with "Blowuinva." Because of the anonymity of the Internet, Detective McLaughlin did not know the true identity of the person with whom he was communicating nor did he know where "Blowuinva" lived. "Blowuinva" had only identified himself as "Brad."

To determine Blowuinva's identity and location, McLaughlin obtained a New Hampshire state subpoena that he served on Blowuinva's Internet Service Provider, MindSpring, located in Atlanta, Georgia. The New Hampshire state subpoena requested that MindSpring produce "any records pertaining to the billing and/or user records documenting the subject using your services on March 14th, 1998 at 1210HRS (EST) using Internet Protocol Number 207.69.169.92." MindSpring complied with the subpoena. On March 20, 1998, MindSpring supplied McLaughlin with defendant's name, address, credit card number, e-mail address, home and work telephone numbers, fax number, and the fact that the Defendant's account was connected to the Internet at the Internet Protocol (IP) address.

A justice of the peace, Richard R. Richards, signed the New Hampshire state subpoena. Mr. Richards is not only a New Hampshire justice of the peace, but he is also a detective in the Keene Police Department, Investigation Division. Mr. Richards did not issue the subpoena pursuant to a matter pending before himself, any other judicial officer, or a grand jury. At the hearing on the defendant's motion, the government conceded the invalidity of the warrant. The question before this court, therefore, is whether the court must suppress the information obtained from MindSpring, and all that flowed from it, because the government failed to obtain a proper subpoena. . . .

. . . [Under *Katz v. United States,*] the Fourth Amendment applies only where: (1) the citizen has manifested a subjective expectation of privacy, and (2) the expectation is one that society accepts as "objectively reasonable." . . . Applying the first part of the *Katz* analysis, Mr. Hambrick asserts that he had a subjective expectation of privacy in the information that MindSpring gave to the government. However, resolution of this matter hinges on whether Mr. Hambrick's expectation is one that society accepts as "objectively reasonable."

The objective reasonableness prong of the privacy test is ultimately a value judgment and a determination of how much privacy we should have as a society. In making this constitutional determination, this court must employ a sort of risk analysis, asking whether the individual affected should have expected the material at issue to remain private. The defendant asserts that the Electronic Communications Privacy Act ("ECPA") "legislatively resolves" this question. . . .

The information obtained through the use of the government's invalid subpoena consisted of the defendant's name, address, social security number, credit card number, and certification that the defendant was connected to the Internet on March 14, 1998. Thus, this information falls within the provisions of Title II of the ECPA.

The government may require that an ISP provide stored communications and transactional records only if (1) it obtains a warrant issued under the Federal Rules of Criminal Procedure or state equivalent, or (2) it gives prior notice to the online subscriber and then issues a subpoena or receives a court order authorizing disclosure of the information in question. *See* 18 U.S.C. § 2703(a)-(c)(1)(B). When an ISP discloses stored communications or transactional records to a government entity without the requisite authority, the aggrieved customer's sole remedy is damages.

Although Congress is willing to recognize that individuals have some degree of privacy in the stored data and transactional records that their ISPs retain, the ECPA is hardly a legislative determination that this expectation of privacy is one that rises to the level of "reasonably objective" for Fourth Amendment purposes. Despite its concern for privacy, Congress did not provide for suppression where a party obtains stored data or transactional records in violation of the Act. Additionally, the ECPA's concern for privacy extends only to government invasions of privacy. ISPs are free to turn stored data and transactional records over to nongovernmental entities. *See* 18 U.S.C. § 2703(c)(1)(A) ("[A] provider of electronic communication service or remote computing service may disclose a record or other information pertaining to a subscriber to or customer of such service . . . to any person other than a governmental entity."). For Fourth Amendment purposes, this court does not find that the ECPA has legislatively determined that an individual has a reasonable expectation of privacy in his name, address, social security number, credit card number, and proof of Internet connection. The fact that the ECPA does not proscribe turning over such information to private entities buttresses the conclusion that the ECPA does not create a reasonable expectation of privacy in that information. This, however, does not end the court's inquiry. This court must determine, within the constitutional framework that the Supreme Court has established, whether Mr. Hambrick's subjective expectation of privacy is one that society is willing to recognize.

To have any interest in privacy, there must be some exclusion of others. To have a reasonable expectation of privacy under the Supreme Court's risk-analysis approach to the Fourth Amendment, two conditions must be met: (1) the data must not be knowingly exposed to others, and (2) the Internet service provider's ability to access the data must not constitute a disclosure. In *Katz*, the Supreme Court expressly held that "what a person knowingly exposes to the public, even in his home or office, is not a subject of Fourth Amendment protection." Further, the Court "consistently has held that a person has no legitimate expectation of privacy in information he voluntarily turns over to third parties." *Smith v. Maryland*, 442 U.S. 735, 743-44 (1979). . . .

When Scott Hambrick surfed the Internet using the screen name "Blowuinva," he was not a completely anonymous actor. It is true that an average member of the public could not easily determine the true identity of "Blowuinva." Nevertheless, when Mr. Hambrick entered into an agreement to obtain Internet access from MindSpring, he knowingly revealed his name, address, credit card number, and telephone number to MindSpring and its employees. Mr. Hambrick also selected the screen name "Blowuinva." When the defendant selected his screen name it became tied to his true identity in all MindSpring records. MindSpring employees had ready access to these records in the normal course of MindSpring's business, for example, in the keeping of its records for billing purposes, and nothing prevented MindSpring from revealing this information to nongovernmental actors.[69] Also, there is nothing in the record to suggest that there was a restrictive agreement between the defendant and MindSpring that would limit the right of MindSpring to reveal the defendant's personal information to nongovernmental entities. Where such dissemination of information to nongovernment entities is not prohibited, there can be no reasonable expectation of privacy in that information.

Although not dispositive to the outcome of this motion, it is important to note that the court's decision does not leave members of cybersociety without privacy protection. Under the ECPA, Internet Service Providers are civilly liable when they reveal subscriber information or the contents of stored communications to

---

[69] It is apparently common for ISPs to provide certain information that Mr. Hambrick alleges to be private to marketing firms and other organizations interested in soliciting business from Internet users.

the government without first requiring a warrant, court order, or subpoena. Here, nothing suggests that MindSpring had any knowledge that the facially valid subpoena submitted to it was in fact an invalid subpoena. Had MindSpring revealed the information at issue in this case to the government without first requiring a subpoena, apparently valid on its face, Mr. Hambrick could have sued MindSpring. This is a powerful deterrent protecting privacy in the online world and should not be taken lightly. . . .

NOTES & QUESTIONS

1. *Is There a Reasonable Expectation of Privacy in ISP Records?* The court in *Hambrick* concludes that there is no reasonable expectation of privacy in ISP records based on the third party doctrine in *Smith v. Maryland.* In *United States v. Kennedy,* 81 F. Supp. 2d 1103 (D. Kan. 2000), the court reached a similar conclusion:

   > Defendant has not demonstrated an objectively reasonable legitimate expectation of privacy in his subscriber information. . . . "[A] person has no legitimate expectation of privacy in information he voluntarily turns over to third parties." *Smith v. Maryland,* 442 U.S. 735 (1979). When defendant entered into an agreement with [his ISP], he knowingly revealed all information connected to [his IP address]. He cannot now claim to have a Fourth Amendment privacy interest in his subscriber information.

   Is *Smith v. Maryland* controlling on this issue? Is there a way to distinguish *Smith?*

2. *Statutes as a Basis for a Reasonable Expectation of Privacy?* Hambrick was not seeking relief directly under the Stored Communications Act of ECPA. Why not? Instead, Hambrick asserted he had Fourth Amendment protection in his subscriber records. He argued that under the *Katz* reasonable expectation of privacy test, the ECPA "legislatively resolves" that there is a reasonable expectation of privacy in information that Mindspring gave to the government. Should statutes that protect privacy serve as an indication of a societal recognition of a reasonable expectation of privacy? What are the consequences of using statutes such as ECPA to conclude that the Fourth Amendment applies?

3. *Is There a Remedy?* Mindspring couldn't release information to the government without a warrant or subpoena or else it would face civil liability. However, in this case, the government presented Mindspring with a subpoena that Mindspring had no knowledge was invalid. Therefore, it is unlikely that Mindspring would be liable. If the court is correct in its conclusion that 18 U.S.C. § 2703(a)–(c)(1)(B) of the ECPA only applies to the conduct of Internet Service Providers, then is there any remedy against Officer Richards's blatantly false subpoena? Could a police officer obtain a person's Internet subscriber information by falsifying a subpoena and escape without any civil liability or exclusionary rule?

MCVEIGH V. COHEN

983 F. Supp. 215 (D.D.C. 1998)

SPORKIN, J. . . . Plaintiff Timothy R. McVeigh, who bears no relation to the Oklahoma City bombing defendant, seeks to enjoin the United States Navy from discharging him under the statutory policy colloquially known as "Don't Ask, Don't Tell, Don't Pursue." See 10 U.S.C. § 654 ("new policy"). In the course of investigating his sexual orientation, the Plaintiff contends that the Defendants violated his rights under the Electronic Communications Privacy Act ("ECPA"), 18 U.S.C. § 2701 et seq., the Administrative Procedure Act ("APA") 5 U.S.C. § 706, the Department's own policy, and the Fourth and Fifth Amendments of the U.S. Constitution. Absent an injunction, the Plaintiff avers that he will suffer irreparable injury from the discharge, even if he were ultimately to prevail on the merits of his claims.

The Plaintiff, Senior Chief Timothy R. McVeigh, is a highly decorated seventeen-year veteran of the United States Navy who has served honorably and continuously since he was nineteen years old. At the time of the Navy's decision to discharge him, he was the senior-most enlisted man aboard the United States nuclear submarine U.S.S. Chicago.

On September 2, 1997, Ms. Helen Hajne, a civilian Navy volunteer, received an electronic mail ("email") message through the America Online Service ("AOL") regarding the toy-drive that she was coordinating for the Chicago crew members' children. The message box stated that it came from the alias "boysrch," but the text of the email was signed by a "Tim." Through an option available to AOL subscribers, the volunteer searched through the "member profile directory" to find the member profile for this sender. The directory specified that "boysrch" was an AOL subscriber named Tim who lived in Honolulu, Hawaii, worked in the military, and identified his marital status as "gay." Although the profile included some telling interests such as "collecting pics of other young studs" and "boy watching," it did not include any further identifying information such as full name, address, or phone number. . . .

Ms. Hajne proceeded to forward the email and directory profile to her husband, who, like Plaintiff, was also a noncommissioned officer aboard the U.S.S. Chicago. The material eventually found its way to Commander John Mickey, the captain of the ship and Plaintiff's commanding officer. In turn, Lieutenant Karin S. Morean, the ship's principal legal adviser and a member of the Judge Advocate General's ("JAG") Corps was called in to investigate the matter. By this point, the Navy suspected the "Tim" who authored the email might be Senior Chief Timothy McVeigh. Before she spoke to the Plaintiff and without a warrant or court order, Lieutenant Morean requested a Navy paralegal on her staff, Legalman First Class Joseph M. Kaiser, to contact AOL and obtain information from the service that could "connect" the screen name "boysrch" and accompanying user profile to McVeigh. Legalman Kaiser called AOL's toll-free customer service number and talked to a representative at technical services. Legalman Kaiser did not identify himself as a Naval serviceman. According to his testimony at the administrative hearing, he stated that he was "a third party in receipt of a fax sheet and wanted to confirm the profile sheet, [and] who it belonged to." The AOL representative affirmatively identified Timothy R. McVeigh as the customer in question.

Upon verification from AOL, Lieutenant Morean notified Senior Chief McVeigh that the Navy had obtained "some indication[] that he made a statement of homosexuality" in violation of § 654(b)(2) of "Don't Ask, Don't Tell." In light of the Uniform Code of Military Justice prohibition of sodomy and indecent acts, she then advised him of his right to remain silent. Shortly thereafter, in a memorandum dated September 22, 1997, the Navy advised Plaintiff that it was commencing an administrative discharge proceeding (termed by the Navy as an "administrative separation") against him. The reason stated was for "homosexual conduct, as evidenced by your statement that you are a homosexual."

On November 7, 1997, the Navy conducted an administrative discharge hearing before a three-member board. . . . At the conclusion of the administrative hearing, the board held that the government had sufficiently shown by a preponderance of the evidence that Senior Chief McVeigh had engaged in "homosexual conduct," a dischargeable offense. . . .

. . . Plaintiff is now scheduled to be discharged barring relief from this Court. . . .

. . . At its core, the Plaintiff's complaint is with the Navy's compliance, or lack thereof, with its new regulations under the "Don't Ask, Don't Tell, Don't Pursue" policy. Plaintiff contends that he did not "tell," as prescribed by the statute, but that nonetheless, the Navy impermissibly "asked" and zealously "pursued."

In short, this case raises the central issue of whether there is really a place for gay officers in the military under the new policy, "Don't Ask, Don't Tell, Don't Pursue." [This policy was adopted in 1993, and it prohibits the military from investigating sexual orientation unless there is "credible information" that a gay serviceman or servicewoman has the "propensity or intent to engage in homosexual acts."] . . .

The facts as stated above clearly demonstrate that the Plaintiff did not openly express his homosexuality in a way that compromised this "Don't Ask, Don't Tell" policy. Suggestions of sexual orientation in a private, anonymous email account did not give the Navy a sufficient reason to investigate to determine whether to commence discharge proceedings. In its actions, the Navy violated its own regulations. An investigation into sexual orientation may be initiated "only when [a commander] has received credible information that there is a basis for discharge," such as when an officer "has said that he or she is a homosexual or bisexual, or made some other statement that indicates a propensity or intent to engage in homosexual acts." Yet in this case, there was no such credible information that Senior Chief McVeigh had made such a statement. Under the Guidelines, "credible information" requires more than "just a belief or suspicion" that a Service member has engaged in homosexual conduct. In the examples provided, the Guidelines state that "credible information" would exist in this case only if "a reliable person" stated that he or she directly observed or heard a Service member make an oral or written statement that "a reasonable person would believe was intended to convey the fact that he or she engages in or has a propensity or intent to engage in homosexual acts."

Clearly, the facts as stated above in this case demonstrate that there was no such "credible information." All that the Navy had was an email message and user profile that it suspected was authored by Plaintiff. Under the military regulation, that information alone should not have triggered any sort of investigation. When the Navy affirmatively took steps to confirm the identity of the email respondent, it violated the very essence of "Don't Ask, Don't Pursue" by launching a search and destroy mission. Even if the Navy had a factual basis to believe that the email message and profile were written by Plaintiff, it was unreasonable to infer that they were necessarily intended to convey a propensity or intent to engage in homosexual conduct. Particularly in the context of cyberspace, a medium of "virtual reality" that invites fantasy and affords anonymity, the comments attributed to McVeigh do not by definition amount to a declaration of homosexuality. At most, they express "an abstract preference or desire to engage in homosexual acts." Yet the regulations specify that a statement professing homosexuality so as to warrant investigation must declare "more than an abstract preference or desire"; they must indicate a likelihood actually to carry out homosexual acts.

The subsequent steps taken by the Navy in its "pursuit" of the Plaintiff were not only unauthorized under its policy, but likely illegal under the Electronic Communications Privacy Act of 1986 ("ECPA"). The ECPA, enacted by Congress to address privacy concerns on the Internet, allows the government to obtain information from an online service provider — as the Navy did in this instance from AOL — but only if a) it obtains a warrant issued under the Federal Rules of Criminal Procedure or state equivalent; or b) it gives prior notice to the online subscriber and then issues a subpoena or receives a court order authorizing disclosure of the information in question. See 18 U.S.C. § 2703(b)(1)(A)-(B), (c)(1)(B).

In soliciting and obtaining over the phone personal information about the Plaintiff from AOL, his private on-line service provider, the government in this case invoked neither of these provisions and thus failed to comply with the ECPA. From the record, it is undisputed that the Navy directly solicited by phone information from AOL. Lieutenant Karin S. Morean, the ship's principal legal counsel and a member of the JAG corps, personally requested Legalman Kaiser to contact AOL and obtain the identity of the subscriber. Without this information, Plaintiff credibly contends that the Navy could not have made the necessary connection between him and the user profile which was the sole basis on which to commence discharge proceedings.

The government, in its defense, contends that the Plaintiff cannot succeed on his ECPA claim. It argues that the substantive provision of the statute that Plaintiff cites, 18 U.S.C. § 2703(c)(1)(B), puts the obligation on the online service provider to withhold information from the government, and not vice versa. In support of its position, Defendants cite to the Fourth Circuit opinion in *Tucker v. Waddell*, 83 F.3d 688 (4th Cir. 1996), which held that § 2703(c)(1)(B) only prohibits the actions of online providers, not the government. Accordingly, Defendants allege that Plaintiff has no cause of action against the government on the basis of the ECPA. . . .

. . . [However,] Section 2703(c)(1)(B) must be read in the context of the statute as a whole. In comparison, § 2703(a) and (b) imposes on the government a reciprocal obligation to obtain a warrant or the like before requiring disclosure. It appears from the face of the statute that all of the subsections of § 2703 were intended to work in tandem to protect consumer privacy. Even if, however, the government ultimately proves to be right in its assessment of § 2703(c)(1)(B), the Plaintiff has plead § 2703(a) and (b) as alternative grounds for relief. In his claim that the government, at the least, solicited a violation of the ECPA by AOL, the Court finds that there is likely success on the merits with regard to this issue. The government knew, or should have known, that by turning over the information without a warrant, AOL was breaking the law. Yet the Navy, in this case, directly solicited the information anyway. What is most telling is that the Naval investigator did not identify himself when he made his request. While the government makes much of the fact that § 2703(c)(1)(B) does not provide a cause of action against the government, it is elementary that information obtained improperly can be suppressed where an individual's rights have been violated. In these days of "big brother," where through technology and otherwise the privacy interests of individuals from all walks of life are being ignored or marginalized, it is imperative that statutes explicitly protecting these rights be strictly observed. . . .

. . . With literally the entire world on the world-wide web, enforcement of the ECPA is of great concern to those who bare the most personal information about their lives in private accounts through the Internet. . . .

. . . Although Officer McVeigh did not publicly announce his sexual orientation, the Navy nonetheless impermissibly embarked on a search and "outing" mission.

NOTES & QUESTIONS

1. *A Suppression Remedy?* Recall the following statement in *McVeigh*: "The government knew, or should have known, that by turning over the information without a warrant, AOL was breaking the law. . . . While the government makes much of the fact that § 2703(c)(1)(B) does not provide a cause of action against the government, it is elementary that information obtained improperly can be suppressed where an individual's rights have been violated." Is this last statement correct? The Stored Communications Act does not have a suppression remedy; the court is creating an exclusionary rule for the Stored Communications Act. Is this appropriate? Without a suppression remedy for the conduct of the government in this case, what would deter the government from violating the Stored Communications Act?

2. *Postscript.* Subsequent to *McVeigh v. Cohen,* Congress amended §§ 2703(a)-(c) to make it clear that these provisions applied not just to ISPs but also to government conduct. In *Freedman v. America Online, Inc.*, 303 F. Supp. 2d 121 (D. Conn. 2004), two police detectives signed a warrant themselves (rather than bring it before a judge) and served it to AOL. AOL responded by faxing plaintiff's name, address, phone numbers, account status, membership information, and his other AOL screen names. The district court concluded that the government had violated ECPA: "To conclude that the government may circumvent the legal processes set forth in the ECPA by merely

requesting subscriber information from an ISP contradicts Congress's intent to protect personal privacy."

5. IP ADDRESSES AND URLS

UNITED STATES V. FORRESTER

512 F.3d 500 (9th Cir. 2008)

FISHER, J. . . . Defendants-appellants Mark Stephen Forrester and Dennis Louis Alba were charged with various offenses relating to the operation of a large Ecstasy-manufacturing laboratory, and were convicted on all counts following a jury trial. They now appeal their convictions and sentences. . . .

During its investigation of Forrester and Alba's Ecstasy-manufacturing operation, the government employed various computer surveillance techniques to monitor Alba's e-mail and Internet activity. The surveillance began in May 2001 after the government applied for and received court permission to install a pen register analogue known as a "mirror port" on Alba's account with PacBell Internet. The mirror port was installed at PacBell's connection facility in San Diego, and enabled the government to learn the to/from addresses of Alba's e-mail messages, the IP addresses of the websites that Alba visited and the total volume of information sent to or from his account. Later, the government obtained a warrant authorizing it to employ imaging and keystroke monitoring techniques, but Alba does not challenge on appeal those techniques' legality or the government's application to use them.

Forrester and Alba were tried by jury. At trial, the government introduced extensive evidence showing that they and their associates built and operated a major Ecstasy laboratory. . . .

Alba contends that the government's surveillance of his e-mail and Internet activity violated the Fourth Amendment and fell outside the scope of the then-applicable federal pen register statute. We hold that the surveillance did not constitute a Fourth Amendment search and thus was not unconstitutional. We also hold that whether or not the computer surveillance was covered by the then-applicable pen register statute — an issue that we do not decide — Alba is not entitled to the suppression of any evidence (let alone the reversal of his convictions) as a consequence.

The Supreme Court held in *Smith v. Maryland* that the use of a pen register (a device that records numbers dialed from a phone line) does not constitute a search for Fourth Amendment purposes. According to the Court, people do not have a subjective expectation of privacy in numbers that they dial because they "realize that they must 'convey' phone numbers to the telephone company, since it is through telephone company switching equipment that their calls are completed." Even if there were such a subjective expectation, it would not be one that society is prepared to recognize as reasonable because "a person has no legitimate expectation of privacy in information he voluntarily turns over to third parties." Therefore the use of a pen register is not a Fourth Amendment search. Importantly, the Court distinguished pen registers from more intrusive surveillance techniques on the ground that "pen registers do not acquire the *contents* of communications" but rather obtain only the addressing information associated with phone calls.

Neither this nor any other circuit has spoken to the constitutionality of computer surveillance techniques that reveal the to/from addresses of e-mail messages, the IP addresses of websites visited and the total amount of data transmitted to or from an account. We conclude that the surveillance techniques the government employed here are constitutionally indistinguishable from the use of a pen register that the Court approved in *Smith*. First, e-mail and Internet users, like the telephone users in *Smith*, rely on third-party equipment in order to engage in communication. *Smith* based its holding that telephone users have no expectation of privacy in the numbers they dial on the users' imputed knowledge that their calls are completed through telephone company switching equipment. Analogously, e-mail and Internet users have no expectation of privacy in the to/from addresses of their messages or the IP addresses of the websites they visit because they should know that this information is provided to and used by Internet service providers for the specific purpose of directing the routing of information. Like telephone numbers, which provide instructions to the "switching equipment that processed those numbers," e-mail to/from addresses and IP addresses are not merely passively conveyed through third party equipment, but rather are voluntarily turned over in order to direct the third party's servers.

Second, e-mail to/from addresses and IP addresses constitute addressing information and do not necessarily reveal any more about the underlying contents of communication than do phone numbers. When the government obtains the to/from addresses of a person's e-mails or the IP addresses of websites visited, it does not find out the contents of the messages or know the particular pages on the websites the person viewed. At best, the government may make educated guesses about what was said in the messages or viewed on the websites based on its knowledge of the e-mail to/from addresses and IP addresses — but this is no different from speculation about the contents of a phone conversation on the basis of the identity of the person or entity that was dialed. Like IP addresses, certain phone numbers may strongly indicate the underlying contents of the communication; for example, the government would know that a person who dialed the phone number of a chemicals company or a gun shop was likely seeking information about chemicals or firearms. Further, when an individual dials a pre-recorded information or subject-specific line, such as sports scores, lottery results or phone sex lines, the phone number may even show that the caller had access to specific content information. Nonetheless, the Court in *Smith* and *Katz* drew a clear line between unprotected addressing information and protected content information that the government did not cross here.[70]

---

[70] Surveillance techniques that enable the government to determine not only the IP addresses that a person accesses but also the uniform resource locators ("URL") of the pages visited might be more constitutionally problematic. A URL, unlike an IP address, identifies the particular document within a website that a person views and thus reveals much more information about the person's Internet activity. For instance, a surveillance technique that captures IP addresses would show only that a person visited the New York Times' website at http://www.nytimes.com, whereas a technique that captures URLs would also divulge the particular articles the person viewed.

The government's surveillance of e-mail addresses also may be technologically sophisticated, but it is conceptually indistinguishable from government surveillance of physical mail. In a line of cases dating back to the nineteenth century, the Supreme Court has held that the government cannot engage in a warrantless search of the contents of sealed mail, but can observe whatever information people put on the outside of mail, because that information is voluntarily transmitted to third parties. E-mail, like physical mail, has an outside address "visible" to the third-party carriers that transmit it to its intended location, and also a package of content that the sender presumes will be read only by the intended recipient. The privacy interests in these two forms of communication are identical. The contents may deserve Fourth Amendment protection, but the address and size of the package do not. . . .

We therefore hold that the computer surveillance techniques that Alba challenges are not Fourth Amendment searches. However, our holding extends only to these particular techniques and does not imply that more intrusive techniques or techniques that reveal more content information are also constitutionally identical to the use of a pen register. . . .

Alba claims that the government's computer surveillance was not only unconstitutional but also beyond the scope of the then-applicable pen register statute, 18 U.S.C. § 3121-27 (amended October 2001). Under both the old and new versions of 18 U.S.C. § 3122, the government must apply for and obtain a court order before it can install and use a pen register. When the surveillance at issue here took place in May-July 2001, the applicable statute defined a pen register as a "device which records or decodes electronic or other impulses which identify the numbers dialed or otherwise transmitted on the telephone line to which such device is attached." 18 U.S.C. § 3127(3). Notwithstanding the government's invocation of this provision and application for and receipt of a court order, Alba maintains that the computer surveillance at issue here did not come within the statutory definition of a "pen register."

Even assuming that Alba is correct in this contention, he would not be entitled to the suppression of the evidence obtained through the computer surveillance. As both the Supreme Court and this court have emphasized, suppression is a disfavored remedy, imposed only where its deterrence benefits outweigh its substantial social costs or (outside the constitutional context) where it is clearly contemplated by the relevant statute. . . . Alba does not point to any statutory language requiring suppression when computer surveillance that is similar but not technically equivalent to a pen register is carried out. Indeed, he does not even identify what law or regulation the government may have violated if its surveillance did not come within the scope of the then-applicable pen register statute. The suppression of evidence under these circumstances is plainly inappropriate.

Our conclusion is bolstered by the fact that suppression still would not be appropriate even if the computer surveillance was covered by the pen register statute. Assuming the surveillance violated the statute, there is no mention of suppression of evidence in the statutory text. Instead, the only penalty specified is that "[w]hoever knowingly violates subsection (a)" by installing or using a pen register without first obtaining a court order "shall be fined under this title or imprisoned not more than one year, or both." 18 U.S.C. § 3121(d).

NOTES & QUESTIONS

1. ***IP Addresses vs. URLs.*** The *Forrester* court concludes that e-mail headers and IP addresses are akin to pen registers and that the controlling case is *Smith v. Maryland.* Does *Smith* control because IP address and e-mail header information are not revealing of the contents of the communications or because this information is conveyed to a third party? Recall that in a footnote, the court observes that URLs "might be more constitutionally problematic" because a "URL, unlike an IP address, identifies the particular document within a website that a person views and thus reveals much more information about the person's Internet activity." However, although IP addresses do not reveal specific parts of a websites that a person visits, they do reveal the various websites that a person visits. Why isn't this revealing enough to trigger constitutional protections?

2. ***Content vs. Envelope Information.*** A key distinction under ECPA, as well as Fourth Amendment law, is between "content" and "envelope" information. Orin Kerr explains the distinction:

> . . . [E]very communications network features two types of information: the contents of communications, and the addressing and routing information that the networks use to deliver the contents of communications. The former is "content information," and the latter is "envelope information."
>
> The essential distinction between content and envelope information remains constant across different technologies, from postal mail to email. With postal mail, the content information is the letter itself, stored safely inside its envelope. The envelope information is the information derived from the outside of the envelope, including the mailing and return addresses, the stamp and postmark, and the size and weight of the envelope when sealed.
>
> Similar distinctions exist for telephone conversations. The content information for a telephone call is the actual conversation between participants that can be captured by an audio recording of the call. The envelope information includes the number the caller dials, the number from which the caller dials, the time of the call, and its duration.[71]

Under ECPA, content information is generally given strong protection (e.g., the Wiretap Act), whereas envelope information is not (e.g., the Pen Register Act). But is such a distinction viable?

Daniel Solove contends that the distinction breaks down:

> When applied to IP addresses and URLs, the envelope/content distinction becomes even more fuzzy. An IP address is a unique number that is assigned to each computer connected to the Internet. Each website, therefore, has an IP address. On the surface, a list of IP addresses is simply a list of numbers; but it is actually much more. With a complete listing of IP addresses, the government can learn quite a lot about a person because it can trace how that person surfs the Internet. The government can learn the names of stores at which a person shops, the political organizations a person finds interesting, a person's sexual fetishes and fantasies, her health concerns, and so on.

---

[71] Orin S. Kerr, Internet *Surveillance Law After the USA PATRIOT Act: The Big Brother That Isn't,* 97 Nw. U. L. Rev. 607, 611 (2003).

Perhaps even more revealing are URLs. A URL is a pointer — it points to the location of particular information on the Internet. In other words, it indicates where something is located. When we cite to something on the Web, we are citing to its URL. . . . URLs can reveal the specific information that people are viewing on the Web. URLs can also contain search terms. . . .

[Therefore,] the content/envelope distinction is not always clear. In many circumstances, to adapt Marshall McLuhan, the "envelope" *is* the "content." Envelope information can reveal a lot about a person's private activities, sometimes as much (and even more) than can content information.[72]

Orin Kerr disagrees:

Professor Solove appears to doubt the wisdom of offering lower privacy protection for non-content information. He suggests that the acquisition of non-content information should require a full search warrant based on probable cause. . . .

Despite this, Solove's suggestion that the law should not offer lesser privacy protection for non-content information is unpersuasive. The main reason is that it is quite rare for non-content information to yield the equivalent of content information. It happens in very particular circumstances, but it remains quite rare, and usually in circumstances that are difficult to predict ex ante. In the Internet context, for example, non-content surveillance typically consists of collecting Internet packets; the packets disclose that a packet was sent from one IP address to another IP address at a particular time. This isn't very private information, at least in most cases. Indeed, it is usually impossible to know who asked for the packet, or what the packet was about, or what the person who asked for the packet wanted to do, or even if it was a person (as opposed to the computer) who sent for the packet in the first place. Solove focuses on the compelling example of Internet search terms as an example of non-content information that can be the privacy equivalent of content information. This is a misleading example, however, as Internet search terms very well may be contents. . . . Thus, despite the fact that non-content information can yield private information, in the great majority of cases contents of communications implicate privacy concerns on a higher order of magnitude than non-content information, and it makes sense to give greater privacy protections for the former and lesser to the latter.[73]

Solove replies:

Kerr assumes that a compilation of envelope information is generally less revealing than content information. However, a person may care more about protecting the identities of people with whom she communicates than the content of those communications. Indeed, the identities of the people one communicates with implicates freedom of association under the First Amendment. The difficulty is that the distinction between content and envelope information does not correlate well to the distinction between sensitive and innocuous information. Envelope information can be quite sensitive; content information can be quite innocuous. Admittedly, in many cases, people do not care very much about maintaining privacy over the identities of their friends and

---

[72] Solove, *Surveillance Law, supra,* at 1287-88.

[73] Orin S. Kerr, *A User's Guide to the Stored Communications Act — and a Legislator's Guide to Amending It,* 72 Geo. Wash. L. Rev. 1208, 1229 n.142 (2004).

associates. But it is also true that in many cases, the contents of communications are not very revealing as well. Many e-mails are short messages which do not reveal any deep secrets, and even Kerr would agree that this should not lessen their protection under the law. This is because content information has the potential to be quite sensitive — but this is also the case with envelope information.[74]

3. ***The Scope of the Pen Register Act.*** The version of the Pen Register Act in effect when the search took place in *Forrester* was the pre-USA PATRIOT Act version, which defined pen registers more narrowly as "numbers dialed." The USA PATRIOT Act expanded the definition of pen register to include "dialing, routing, addressing, or signaling information . . . provided, however, that such information shall not include the contents of any communication." Prior to the USA PATRIOT Act changes, it was an open question as to whether the Pen Register Act applied to e-mail headers, IP addresses, and URLs. The USA PATRIOT Act changes aimed to clarify that the Pen Register Act did apply beyond telephone numbers. E-mail headers seem to fit readily into the new Pen Register Act definition. But what about IP addresses and URLs? They involve "routing" and "addressing" information, but they may also include "the contents" of communications. Do they involve "contents" or are they merely "envelope" information?

4. ***Text Messages.*** In *Quon v. Arch Wireless Operating Co., Ltd.,* 2008 WL 2440559 (9th Cir. 2008), the court held that accessing text messages can constitute a violation of the Stored Communications Act because the messages were stored by the communication service provider as "backup" protection for the user. The court also concluded that the Fourth Amendment protects text message communications because they are "content" information: "We see no meaningful difference between the e-mails at issue in *Forrester* and the text messages at issue here."

5. ***ECPA and the Exclusionary Rule.*** The *Forrester* court concludes that even if the acquisition of information violated the Pen Register Act, the exclusionary rule is not a remedy under the Act. As discussed earlier in this chapter, many provisions of electronic surveillance law lack an exclusionary rule. In the Wiretap Act, wire and oral communications are protected with an exclusionary rule, but electronic communications are not. Solove argues that "[s]ince e-mail has become a central mode of communication, this discrepancy is baseless."[75] Is it? Can you think of a reason why e-mail should receive lesser protection than a phone conversation, which would be protected by the exclusionary rule under the Wiretap Act? Additionally, the Stored Communications Act and Pen Register Act have no exclusionary remedies for any type of communication.

---

[74] Solove, *Surveillance Law, supra,* at 1288. Susan Freiwald contends that "the current categories of the ECPA do not cover web traffic data. At least one other category of protection is needed. Search terms entered, web-pages visited, and items viewed are neither message contents nor their to/from information." Freiwald, *Online Surveillance, supra,* at 71.

[75] Solove, *Surveillance Law, supra*, at 1282.

Orin Kerr argues the absence of an exclusionary rule in many of ECPA's provisions leads to inadequate judicial attention to ECPA. Without an exclusionary rule, Kerr contends, "criminal defendants have little incentive to raise challenges to the government's Internet surveillance practices." Therefore, many challenges to Internet surveillance practices "tend to be in civil cases between private parties that raise issues far removed from those that animated Congress to pass the statutes." Adding an exclusionary remedy, Kerr argues, would "benefit both civil libertarian and law enforcement interests alike." He writes:

> On the civil libertarian side, a suppression remedy would considerably increase judicial scrutiny of the government's Internet surveillance practices in criminal cases. The resulting judicial opinions would clarify the rules that the government must follow, serving the public interest of greater transparency. Less obviously, the change could also benefit law enforcement by altering the type and nature of the disputes over the Internet surveillance laws that courts encounter. Prosecutors would have greater control over the types of cases the courts decided, enjoy more sympathetic facts, and have a better opportunity to explain and defend law enforcement interests before the courts. The statutory law of Internet surveillance would become more like the Fourth Amendment law: a source of vital and enforceable rights that every criminal defendant can invoke, governed by relatively clear standards that by and large respect law enforcement needs and attempt to strike a balance between those needs and privacy interests.[76]

6. ***The Internet vs. the Telephone.*** Susan Freiwald contends that while the 1968 Wiretap Act (Title III) provided powerful and effective protection for telephone communications, ECPA in 1986 did not do the same for online communications:

> . . . [O]nline surveillance is even more susceptible to law enforcement abuse and even more threatening to privacy. Therefore, one might expect regulation of online surveillance to be more privacy-protective than traditional wiretapping law. That could not be further from the truth. The law provides dramatically less privacy protection for online activities than for traditional telephone calls and videotapings. Additionally, what makes the Wiretap Act complex makes online surveillance law chaotic. Almost all of the techniques designed to rein in law enforcement have been abandoned in the online context. And, while Congress resolved much of its ambivalence towards wiretapping in 1968, current law suggests the outright hostility of all branches of government to online privacy.[77]

In what ways does federal electronic surveillance law protect Internet communication differently from telephone communication? Should the privacy protections differ in these areas?

---

[76] Orin S. Kerr, *Lifting the "Fog" of Internet Surveillance: How a Suppression Remedy Would Change Computer Crime Law*, 54 Hastings L.J. 805, 824, 807-08 (2003).

[77] Susan Freiwald, *Online Surveillance: Remembering the Lessons of the Wiretap Act*, 56 Ala. L. Rev. 9, 14 (2004).

6. KEY LOGGING DEVICES

UNITED STATES V. SCARFO

180 F. Supp. 2d 572 (D.N.J. 2001)

POLITAN, J. . . . Acting pursuant to federal search warrants, the F.B.I. on January 15, 1999, entered Scarfo and Paolercio's business office, Merchant Services of Essex County, to search for evidence of an illegal gambling and loansharking operation. During their search of Merchant Services, the F.B.I. came across a personal computer and attempted to access its various files. They were unable to gain entry to an encrypted file named "Factors."

Suspecting the "Factors" file contained evidence of an illegal gambling and loansharking operation, the F.B.I. returned to the location and, pursuant to two search warrants, installed what is known as a "Key Logger System" ("KLS") on the computer and/or computer keyboard in order to decipher the passphrase to the encrypted file, thereby gaining entry to the file. The KLS records the keystrokes an individual enters on a personal computer's keyboard. The government utilized the KLS in order to "catch" Scarfo's passphrases to the encrypted file while he was entering them onto his keyboard. Scarfo's personal computer features a modem for communication over telephone lines and he possesses an America Online account. The F.B.I. obtained the passphrase to the "Factors" file and retrieved what is alleged to be incriminating evidence.

On June 21, 2000, a federal grand jury returned a three count indictment against the Defendants charging them with gambling and loansharking. The Defendant Scarfo then filed his motion for discovery and to suppress the evidence recovered from his computer. After oral argument was heard on July 30, 2001, the Court ordered additional briefing by the parties. In an August 7, 2001, Letter Opinion and Order, this Court expressed serious concerns over whether the government violated the wiretap statute in utilizing the KLS on Scarfo's computer. Specifically, the Court expressed concern over whether the KLS may have operated during periods when Scarfo (or any other user of his personal computer) was communicating via modem over telephone lines, thereby unlawfully intercepting wire communications without having applied for a wiretap pursuant to Title III, 18 U.S.C. § 2510.

As a result of these concerns, on August 7, 2001, this Court ordered the United States to file with the Court a report explaining fully how the KLS device functions and describing the KLS technology and how it works vis-à-vis the computer modem, Internet communications, e-mail and all other uses of a computer. In light of the government's grave concern over the national security implications such a revelation might raise, the Court permitted the United States to submit any additional evidence which would provide particular and specific reasons how and why disclosure of the KLS would jeopardize both ongoing and future domestic criminal investigations and national security interests.

The United States responded by filing a request for modification of this Court's August 7, 2001, Letter Opinion and Order so as to comply with the procedures set forth in the Classified Information Procedures Act, Title 18, United States Code, Appendix III, § 1 *et seq.* ("CIPA"). [The FBI contended that a detailed disclosure of how the KLS worked would negatively affect national security and that this information was classified. After an in camera, ex parte hearing with several officials from the Attorney General's office and the FBI, the court granted the government's request not to release the details of how KLS functioned. Instead, the government would provide Scarfo and his attorneys with an unclassified summary about how KLS worked. Based on that summary, Scarfo contended that the KLS violated the Fourth Amendment because the KLS had the capability of collecting data on all of his keystrokes, not merely those of his passphrase.]

Where a search warrant is obtained, the Fourth Amendment requires a certain modicum of particularity in the language of the warrant with respect to the area and items to be searched and/or seized. The particularity requirement exists so that law enforcement officers are constrained from undertaking a boundless and exploratory rummaging through one's personal property. . . . Because the encrypted file could not be accessed via traditional investigative means, Judge Haneke's Order permitted law enforcement officers to "install and leave behind software, firmware, and/or hardware equipment which will monitor the inputted data entered on Nicodemo S. Scarfo's computer in the TARGET LOCATION so that the F.B.I. can capture the password necessary to decrypt computer files by recording the key related information as they are entered." The Order also allowed the F.B.I. to

> search for and seize business records in whatever form they are kept (e.g., written, mechanically or computer maintained and any necessary computer hardware, including computers, computer hard drives, floppy disks or other storage disks or tapes as necessary to access such information, as well as, seizing the mirror hard drive to preserve configuration files, public keys, private keys, and other information that may be of assistance in interpreting the password) — including address and telephone books and electronic storage devices; ledgers and other accounting-type records; banking records and statements; travel records; correspondence; memoranda; notes; calendars; and diaries — that contain information about the identities and whereabouts of conspirators, betting customers and victim debtors, and/or that otherwise reveal the origin, receipt, concealment or distribution of criminal proceeds relating to illegal gambling, loansharking and other racketeering offenses.

On its face, the Order is very comprehensive and lists the items, including the evidence in the encrypted file, to be seized with more than sufficient specificity. *See Andresen v. Maryland,* 427 U.S. 463, 480-81 (1976) (defendant's general warrant claim rejected where search warrant contained, among other things, a lengthy list of specified and particular items to be seized). One would be hard pressed to draft a more specified or detailed search warrant than the May 8, 1999 Order. Indeed, it could not be written with more particularity. It specifically identifies each piece of evidence the F.B.I. sought which would be linked to the particular crimes the F.B.I. had probable cause to believe were committed. Most importantly, Judge Haneke's Order clearly specifies the key piece of the puzzle the F.B.I. sought — Scarfo's passphrase to the encrypted file.

That the KLS certainly recorded keystrokes typed into Scarfo's keyboard *other* than the searched-for passphrase is of no consequence. This does not, as Scarfo argues, convert the limited search for the passphrase into a general exploratory search. During many lawful searches, police officers may not know the exact nature of the incriminating evidence sought until they stumble upon it. Just like searches for incriminating documents in a closet or filing cabinet, it is true that during a search for a passphrase "some innocuous [items] will be at least cursorily perused in order to determine whether they are among those [items] to be seized."

Hence, "no tenet of the Fourth Amendment prohibits a search merely because it cannot be performed with surgical precision." Where proof of wrongdoing depends upon documents or computer passphrases whose precise nature cannot be known in advance, law enforcement officers must be afforded the leeway to wade through a potential morass of information in the target location to find the particular evidence which is properly specified in the warrant. . . . Accordingly, Scarfo's claim that the warrants were written and executed as general warrants is rejected. . . .

The principal mystery surrounding this case was whether the KLS intercepted a wire communication in violation of the wiretap statute by recording keystrokes of e-mail or other communications made over a telephone or cable line while the modem operated. These are the only conceivable wire communications which might emanate from Scarfo's computer and potentially fall under the wiretap statute. . . .

The KLS, which is the exclusive property of the F.B.I., was devised by F.B.I. engineers using previously developed techniques in order to obtain a target's key and key-related information. As part of the investigation into Scarfo's computer, the F.B.I. "did not install and operate any component which would search for and record data entering or exiting the computer from the transmission pathway through the modem attached to the computer." Neither did the F.B.I. "install or operate any KLS component which would search for or record any fixed data stored within the computer."

Recognizing that Scarfo's computer had a modem and thus was capable of transmitting electronic communications via the modem, the F.B.I. configured the KLS to avoid intercepting electronic communications typed on the keyboard and simultaneously transmitted in real time via the communication ports. . . . Hence, when the modem was operating, the KLS did not record keystrokes. It was designed to prohibit the capture of keyboard keystrokes whenever the modem operated. Since Scarfo's computer possessed no other means of communicating with another computer save for the modem, the KLS did not intercept any wire communications. Accordingly, the Defendants' motion to suppress evidence for violation of Title III is denied. . . .

NOTES & QUESTIONS

1. ***Did the Court Need to Reach the Main Issue?*** Judge Politan discusses the government's actions in *Scarfo* as if a suppression remedy were available for Scarfo. He finds that a search warrant was not required under the Wiretap Act because of the way in which the FBI's keylogging device worked; the KLS did not function when the modem was operating. But there was a simpler way to deny Scarfo's motion: the Wiretap Act does not provide a suppression

remedy for electronic communications. Did Judge Politan assume that a remedy existed according to some theory similar to the *McVeigh* case? Was he simply eager to rule on the KLS issue?

2. ***Recording Thoughts and Ideas.*** Consider the following argument by Raymond Ku:

> . . . By monitoring what an individual enters into her computer as she enters it, the government has the ability to monitor thought itself. Keystroke-recording devices allow the government to record formless thoughts and ideas an individual never intended to share with anyone, never intended to save on the hard drive and never intended to preserve for future reference in any form. The devices also allow the government to record thoughts and ideas the individual may have rejected the moment they were typed. . . .
>
> . . . [T]he techniques used in the Scarfo case bring us closer to a world in which the only privacy we are guaranteed is the privacy found in the confines of our own minds. [78]

3. ***Old Technologies in New Bottles?*** A common defense of new technological surveillance devices is that they are analogous to existing technologies. Carnivore can be likened to pen registers; the keystroke monitor in the Scarfo case can be analogized to a bug. To what extent are these analogies apt? Are new surveillance technologies, simply old forms of surveillance in new bottles? Or is there something different involved? If so, what is new with these technologies, and how ought they be regulated?

4. ***Magic Lantern.*** The FBI has developed technology through which a keystroke logging device can be installed into a person's computer through a computer virus that is e-mailed to the suspect's computer. The virus keeps track of keystrokes and secretly transmits the information to the government. Thus, the government can install a keystroke logging device without ever having to physically enter one's office or home. Recall your Fourth Amendment analysis of Carnivore. How does Magic Lantern differ with respect to its Fourth Amendment implications? How does your Fourth Amendment analysis of Magic Lantern differ from that of the keystroke logging device in *Scarfo*?

D. NATIONAL SECURITY AND FOREIGN INTELLIGENCE

1. IS NATIONAL SECURITY DIFFERENT?

Should the law treat investigations involving national security differently than other criminal investigations? In Fourth Amendment law, this question has long remained unresolved. In a footnote to *Katz v. United States,* 389 U.S. 347 (1967), the Court stated that perhaps a warrant might not be required in situations involving national security:

---

[78] Raymond Ku, *Think Twice Before You Type*, 163 N.J. L.J. 747 (Feb. 19, 2001).

Whether safeguards other than prior authorization by a magistrate would satisfy the Fourth Amendment in a situation involving the national security is a question not presented by this case.

Justice White, in a concurring opinion, declared:

In joining the Court's opinion, I note the Court's acknowledgment that there are circumstance in which it is reasonable to search without a warrant. In this connection . . . the Court points out that today's decision does not reach national security cases. Wiretapping to protect the security of the Nation has been authorized by successive Presidents. The present Administration would apparently save national security cases from restrictions against wiretapping. We should not require the warrant procedure and the magistrate's judgment if the President of the United States or his chief legal officer, the Attorney General, has considered the requirements of national security and authorized electronic surveillance as reasonable.

Justices Douglas and Brennan, in another concurring opinion, took issue with Justice White:

. . . Neither the President nor the Attorney General is a magistrate. In matters where they believe national security may be involved they are not detached, disinterested, and neutral as a court or magistrate must be. . . .

There is, so far as I understand constitutional history, no distinction under the Fourth Amendment between types of crimes. Article III, § 3, gives "treason" a very narrow definition and puts restrictions on its proof. But the Fourth Amendment draws no lines between various substantive offenses. The arrests on cases of "hot pursuit" and the arrests on visible or other evidence of probable cause cut across the board and are not peculiar to any kind of crime.

I would respect the present lines of distinction and not improvise because a particular crime seems particularly heinous. When the Framers took that step, as they did with treason, the worst crime of all, they made their purpose manifest.

UNITED STATES V. UNITED STATES DISTRICT COURT
(THE *KEITH* CASE)
407 U.S. 297 (1972)

POWELL, J. . . . The issue before us is an important one for the people of our country and their Government. It involves the delicate question of the President's power, acting through the Attorney General, to authorize electronic surveillance in internal security matters without prior judicial approval. Successive Presidents for more than one-quarter of a century have authorized such surveillance in varying degrees, without guidance from the Congress or a definitive decision of this Court. This case brings the issue here for the first time. Its resolution is a matter of national concern, requiring sensitivity both to the Government's right to protect itself from unlawful subversion and attack and to the citizen's right to be secure in his privacy against unreasonable Government intrusion.

This case arises from a criminal proceeding in the United States District Court for the Eastern District of Michigan, in which the United States charged three defendants with conspiracy to destroy Government property. . . . One of the defendants, Plamondon, was charged with the dynamite bombing of an office of the Central Intelligence Agency in Ann Arbor, Michigan.

Title III of the Omnibus Crime Control and Safe Streets Act, 18 U.S.C. §§ 2510-2520, authorizes the use of electronic surveillance for classes of crimes carefully specified in 18 U.S.C. § 2516. Such surveillance is subject to prior court order. Section 2518 sets forth the detailed and particularized application necessary to obtain such an order as well as carefully circumscribed conditions for its use. The Act represents a comprehensive attempt by Congress to promote more effective control of crime while protecting the privacy of individual thought and expression. Much of Title III was drawn to meet the constitutional requirements for electronic surveillance enunciated by this Court in *Berger v. New York,* and *Katz v. United States.*

The Government relies on § 2511(3). It argues that "in excepting national security surveillances from the Act's warrant requirement Congress recognized the President's authority to conduct such surveillances without prior judicial approval." The section thus is viewed as a recognition or affirmance of a constitutional authority in the President to conduct warrantless domestic security surveillance such as that involved in this case.

We think the language of § 2511(3), as well as the legislative history of the statute, refutes this interpretation. The relevant language is that: "Nothing contained in this chapter . . . shall limit the constitutional power of the President to take such measures as he deems necessary to protect . . ." against the dangers specified. At most, this is an implicit recognition that the President does have certain powers in the specified areas. Few would doubt this, as the section refers — among other things — to protection "against actual or potential attack or other hostile acts of a foreign power." But so far as the use of the President's electronic surveillance power is concerned, the language is essentially neutral.

Section 2511(3) certainly confers no power, as the language is wholly inappropriate for such a purpose. It merely provides that the Act shall not be interpreted to limit or disturb such power as the President may have under the Constitution. In short, Congress simply left presidential powers where it found them.

Our present inquiry, though important, is . . . a narrow one. It addresses a question left open by *Katz*:

> Whether safeguards other than prior authorization by a magistrate would satisfy the Fourth Amendment in a situation involving the national security. . . .

We begin the inquiry by noting that the President of the United States has the fundamental duty, under Art. II, § 1, of the Constitution, to "preserve, protect and defend the Constitution of the United States." Implicit in that duty is the power to protect our Government against those who would subvert or overthrow it by unlawful means. In the discharge of this duty, the President — through the Attorney General — may find it necessary to employ electronic surveillance to obtain intelligence information on the plans of those who plot unlawful acts against the Government. The use of such surveillance in internal security cases has been sanctioned more or less continuously by various Presidents and Attorneys General since July 1946.

Though the Government and respondents debate their seriousness and magnitude, threats and acts of sabotage against the Government exist in sufficient number to justify investigative powers with respect to them.[79] The covertness and complexity of potential unlawful conduct against the Government and the necessary dependency of many conspirators upon the telephone make electronic surveillance an effective investigatory instrument in certain circumstances. The marked acceleration in technological developments and sophistication in their use have resulted in new techniques for the planning, commission, and concealment of criminal activities. It would be contrary to the public interest for Government to deny to itself the prudent and lawful employment of those very techniques which are employed against the Government and its lawabiding citizens. . . .

But a recognition of these elementary truths does not make the employment by Government of electronic surveillance a welcome development — even when employed with restraint and under judicial supervision. There is, understandably, a deep-seated uneasiness and apprehension that this capability will be used to intrude upon cherished privacy of law-abiding citizens. We look to the Bill of Rights to safeguard this privacy. Though physical entry of the home is the chief evil against which the wording of the Fourth Amendment is directed, its broader spirit now shields private speech from unreasonable surveillance. Our decision in *Katz* refused to lock the Fourth Amendment into instances of actual physical trespass.

. . . [N]ational security cases, moreover, often reflect a convergence of First and Fourth Amendment values not present in cases of "ordinary" crime. Though the investigative duty of the executive may be stronger in such cases, so also is there greater jeopardy to constitutionally protected speech. . . . The danger to political dissent is acute where the Government attempts to act under so vague a concept as the power to protect "domestic security." Given the difficulty of defining the domestic security interest, the danger of abuse in acting to protect that interest becomes apparent.

The price of lawful public dissent must not be a dread of subjection to an unchecked surveillance power. Nor must the fear of unauthorized official eavesdropping deter vigorous citizen dissent and discussion of Government action in private conversation. For private dissent, no less than open public discourse, is essential to our free society.

As the Fourth Amendment is not absolute in its terms, our task is to examine and balance the basic values at stake in this case: the duty of Government to protect the domestic security, and the potential danger posed by unreasonable surveillance to individual privacy and free expression. If the legitimate need of Government to safeguard domestic security requires the use of electronic surveillance, the question is whether the needs of citizens for privacy and the free expression may not be better protected by requiring a warrant before such surveillance is undertaken. We must also ask whether a warrant requirement

---

[79] The Government asserts that there were 1,562 bombing incidents in the United States from January 1, 1971, to July 1, 1971, most of which involved Government related facilities. Respondents dispute these statistics as incorporating many frivolous incidents as well as bombings against nongovernmental facilities. The precise level of this activity, however, is not relevant to the disposition of this case.

would unduly frustrate the efforts of Government to protect itself from acts of subversion and overthrow directed against it. . . .

[C]ontentions in behalf of a complete exemption from the warrant requirement, when urged on behalf of the President and the national security in its domestic implications, merit the most careful consideration. We certainly do not reject them lightly, especially at a time of worldwide ferment and when civil disorders in this country are more prevalent than in the less turbulent periods of our history. There is, no doubt, pragmatic force to the Government's position.

[W]e do not think a case has been made for the requested departure from Fourth Amendment standards. The circumstances described do not justify complete exemption of domestic security surveillance from prior judicial scrutiny. Official surveillance, whether its purpose be criminal investigation or ongoing intelligence gathering, risks infringement of constitutionally protected privacy of speech. Security surveillances are especially sensitive because of the inherent vagueness of the domestic security concept, the necessarily broad and continuing nature of intelligence gathering, and the temptation to utilize such surveillances to oversee political dissent. We recognize, as we have before, the constitutional basis of the President's domestic security role, but we think it must be exercised in a manner compatible with the Fourth Amendment. In this case we hold that this requires an appropriate prior warrant procedure.

We cannot accept the Government's argument that internal security matters are too subtle and complex for judicial evaluation. Courts regularly deal with the most difficult issues of our society. There is no reason to believe that federal judges will be insensitive to or uncomprehending of the issues involved in domestic security cases. . . . If the threat is too subtle or complex for our senior law enforcement officers to convey its significance to a court, one may question whether there is probable cause for surveillance.

Nor do we believe prior judicial approval will fracture the secrecy essential to official intelligence gathering. The investigation of criminal activity has long involved imparting sensitive information to judicial officers who have respected the confidentialities involved. Judges may be counted upon to be especially conscious of security requirements in national security cases. Title III of the Omnibus Crime Control and Safe Streets Act already has imposed this responsibility on the judiciary in connection with such crimes as espionage, sabotage, and treason, §§ 2516(1)(a) and (c), each of which may involve domestic as well as foreign security threats. Moreover, a warrant application involves no public or adversary proceedings: it is an ex parte request before a magistrate or judge. Whatever security dangers clerical and secretarial personnel may pose can be minimized by proper administrative measures, possibly to the point of allowing the Government itself to provide the necessary clerical assistance. . . .

We emphasize, before concluding this opinion, the scope of our decision. As stated at the outset, this case involves only the domestic aspects of national security. We have not addressed and express no opinion as to, the issues which may be involved with respect to activities of foreign powers or their agents. . . .

Moreover, we do not hold that the same type of standards and procedures prescribed by Title III are necessarily applicable to this case. We recognize that domestic security surveillance may involve different policy and practical considerations from the surveillance of "ordinary crime." The gathering of security intelligence is often long range and involves the interrelation of various sources and types of information. The exact targets of such surveillance may be more difficult to identify than in surveillance operations against many types of crime specified in Title III. Often, too, the emphasis of domestic intelligence gathering is on the prevention of unlawful activity or the enhancement of the Government's preparedness for some possible future crisis or emergency. Thus, the focus of domestic surveillance may be less precise than that directed against more conventional types of crime.

Given those potential distinctions between Title III criminal surveillances and those involving the domestic security, Congress may wish to consider protective standards for the latter which differ from those already prescribed for specified crimes in Title III. Different standards may be compatible with the Fourth Amendment if they are reasonable both in relation to the legitimate need of Government for intelligence information and the protected rights of our citizens. For the warrant application may vary according to the governmental interest to be enforced and the nature of citizen rights deserving protection. . . .

DOUGLAS, J. concurring. While I join in the opinion of the Court, I add these words in support of it. . . .

If the Warrant Clause were held inapplicable here, then the federal intelligence machine would literally enjoy unchecked discretion. Here, federal agents wish to rummage for months on end through every conversation, no matter how intimate or personal, carried over selected telephone lines, simply to seize those few utterances which may add to their sense of the pulse of a domestic underground. . . .

That "domestic security" is said to be involved here does not draw this case outside the mainstream of Fourth Amendment law. Rather, the recurring desire of reigning officials to employ dragnet techniques to intimidate their critics lies at the core of that prohibition. For it was such excesses as the use of general warrants and the writs of assistance that led to the ratification of the Fourth Amendment. . . .

[W]e are currently in the throes of another national seizure of paranoia, resembling the hysteria which surrounded the Alien and Sedition Acts, the Palmer Raids, and the McCarthy era. Those who register dissent or who petition their governments for redress are subjected to scrutiny by grand juries, by the FBI, or even by the military. Their associates are interrogated. Their homes are bugged and their telephones are wiretapped. They are befriended by secret government informers. Their patriotism and loyalty are questioned. . . .

We have as much or more to fear from the erosion of our sense of privacy and independence by the omnipresent electronic ear of the Government as we do from the likelihood that fomenters of domestic upheaval will modify our form of governing.

NOTES & QUESTIONS

1. ***Domestic Security vs. Foreign Threats.*** The *Keith* Court draws a distinction between electronic surveillance in (1) criminal investigations, regulated under Title III (now ECPA); (2) domestic security investigations; and (3) investigations involving "activities of foreign powers and their agents."

Regarding the first category, the *Keith* Court stated that there was no debate regarding "the necessity of obtaining a warrant in the surveillance of crimes unrelated to the national security interest." Regarding the second category, the focus of the *Keith* Court's opinion, its holding was that the Fourth Amendment required the issuing of a warrant in domestic security investigations. It also held that the precise requirements for issuing a requirement to investigate domestic security need not be the same as for Title III criminal surveillance. Finally, it stated that it did not address issues involving foreign powers and their agents. Does this tripartite distinction seem useful as a policy matter?

How does one distinguish between security surveillance (category two) and surveillance for ordinary crime (category one)? Daniel Solove argues that such a distinction ought not to be made: "'National security' has often been abused as a justification not only for surveillance but also for maintaining the secrecy of government records as well as violating the civil liberties of citizens." He further contends that "the line between national security and regular criminal activities is very blurry, especially in an age of terrorism."[80] On the other hand, Richard Posner contends that the word "unreasonable" in the Fourth Amendment "invites a wide-ranging comparison between the benefits and costs of a search or seizure." He proposes a "sliding scale" standard where "the level of suspicion require to justify the search or seizure should fall . . . as the magnitude of the crime under investigation rises."[81] Paul Rosenzweig argues: "In this time of terror, some adjustment of the balance between liberty and security is both necessary and appropriate. . . . [T]he very text of the Fourth Amendment — with its prohibition only of 'unreasonable' searches and seizures — explicitly recognizes the need to balance the harm averted against the extent of governmental intrusion."[82]

2. ***The Church Committee Report.*** In 1976, a congressional committee led by Senator Frank Church (called the "Church Committee") engaged in an extensive investigation of government national security surveillance. It found extensive abuses, which it chronicled in its famous report known as the Church Committee Report:

> Too many people have been spied upon by too many Government agencies and too much information has been collected. The Government has often undertaken the secret surveillance of citizens on the basis of their political beliefs, even when those beliefs posed no threat of violence or illegal acts on

---

[80] Solove, *Surveillance Law,* 72 Geo. Wash. L. Rev. 1264, 1301-02 (2004).

[81] Richard Posner, *Law, Pragmatism, and Democracy* 303 (2003); *see also* Akhil Reed Amar, *The Constitution and Criminal Procedure* 31 (1997) ("The core of the Fourth Amendment . . . is neither a warrant nor probable cause but reasonableness.").

[82] Paul Rosenzweig, *Civil Liberty and the Response to Terrorism,* 42 Duq. L. Rev. 663 (2004).

behalf of a hostile foreign power. The Government, operating primarily through secret informants, but also using other intrusive techniques such as wiretaps, microphone "bugs," surreptitious mail opening, and break-ins, has swept in vast amounts of information about the personal lives, views, and associations of American citizens. . . . Groups and individuals have been harassed and disrupted because of their political views and their lifestyles. Investigations have been based upon vague standards whose breadth made excessive collection inevitable. . . .

The FBI's COINTELPRO — counterintelligence program — was designed to "disrupt" groups and "neutralize" individuals deemed to be threats to domestic security. The FBI resorted to counterintelligence tactics in part because its chief officials believed that existing law could not control the activities of certain dissident groups, and that court decisions had tied the hands of the intelligence community. Whatever opinion one holds about the policies of the targeted groups, many of the tactics employed by the FBI were indisputably degrading to a free society. . . .

Since the early 1930's, intelligence agencies have frequently wiretapped and bugged American citizens without the benefit of judicial warrant. . . .

There has been, in short, a clear and sustained failure by those responsible to control the intelligence community and to ensure its accountability.[83]

The Church Committee Report was influential in the creation of FISA as well as the Attorney General Guidelines.

3. *National Security vs. Civil Liberties.* Eric Posner and Adrian Vermeule argue that the legislature and judiciary should defer to the executive in times of emergency and that it is justified to curtail civil liberties when national security is threatened:

> The essential feature of the emergency is that national security is threatened; because the executive is the only organ of government with the resources, power, and flexibility to respond to threats to national security, it is natural, inevitable, and desirable for power to flow to this branch of government. Congress rationally acquiesces; courts rationally defer. . . .
>
> During emergencies, when new threats appear, the balance shifts; government should and will reduce civil liberties in order to enhance security in those domains where the two must be traded off. . . .
>
> In emergencies . . . judges are at sea, even more so than are executive officials. The novelty of the threats and of the necessary responses makes judicial routines and evolved legal rules seem inapposite, even obstructive. There is a premium on the executive's capacities for swift, vigorous, and secretive action.[84]

4. *The Fourth Amendment and Foreign Intelligence Surveillance. Keith* did not address how the Fourth Amendment would govern foreign intelligence surveillance (category three). Circuit courts examining the issue have

---

[83] *Intelligence Activities and the Rights of Americans* (Vol. 2), Final Report of the Select Committee to Study Government Operations with Respect to Intelligence Activities 5, 10, 15 (Apr. 26, 1976).

[84] Eric A. Posner & Adrian Vermeule, *Terror in the Balance: Security, Liberty, and the Courts* 4, 5, 18 (2006). For another defense of the curtailment of civil liberties for national security, see Richard A. Posner, *Not a Suicide Pact: The Constitution in a Time of National Emergency* (2006).

concluded that at a minimum, no warrant is required by the Fourth Amendment for foreign intelligence surveillance. In *United States v. Butenko*, 494 F.2d 593 (3d Cir. 1974) (en banc), the court justified this conclusion by reasoning that "foreign intelligence gathering is a clandestine and highly unstructured activity, and the need for electronic surveillance often cannot be anticipated in advance." Reaching a similar conclusion in *United States v. Truong Dinh Hung*, 629 F.2d 908 (4th Cir. 1980), the court reasoned: "[T]he needs of the executive are so compelling in the area of foreign intelligence, unlike the area of domestic security, that a uniform warrant requirement would, following *Keith*, 'unduly frustrate' the President in carrying out his foreign affairs responsibilities."

2. THE FOREIGN INTELLIGENCE SURVEILLANCE ACT

In the *Keith* case, the Court explicitly refused to address whether the Fourth Amendment would require a warrant for surveillance of agents of foreign powers: "[T]his case involves only the domestic aspects of national security. We have not addressed and express no opinion as to, the issues which may be involved with respect to activities of foreign powers or their agents but that surveillance without a warrant might be constitutional in cases where the target was an agent of a foreign power."

The Foreign Intelligence Surveillance Act (FISA) of 1978, Pub. L. No. 95-511, codified at 50 U.S.C. §§ 1801–1811, establishes standards and procedures for use of electronic surveillance to collect "foreign intelligence" within the United States. § 1804(a)(7)(B). FISA creates a different regime than ECPA, the legal regime that governs electronic surveillance for law enforcement purposes. The regime created by FISA is designed primarily for intelligence gathering agencies to regulate how they gain general intelligence about foreign powers and agents of foreign powers within the borders of the United States. In contrast, the regime of ECPA is designed for domestic law enforcement to govern the gathering of information for criminal investigations involving people in United States.

Applicability of FISA. When does FISA govern rather than ECPA? FISA generally applies when foreign intelligence gathering is "a significant purpose" of the investigation. 50 U.S.C. § 1804(a)(7)(B) and §1823(a)(7)(B). The language of "a significant purpose" comes from the USA PATRIOT Act of 2001. Prior to the USA PATRIOT Act, FISA as interpreted by the courts required that the collection of foreign intelligence be the primary purpose for surveillance. After the USA PATRIOT Act, foreign intelligence gathering need no longer be the primary purpose. A further expansion of the FISA occurred in 2008 with amendments to that law, which we discuss below.

The Foreign Intelligence Surveillance Court (FISC). Requests for FISA orders are reviewed by a special court of federal district court judges. The USA PATRIOT Act increased the number of judges on the FISC from 7 to 11. 50 U.S.C. § 1803(a). The proceedings are ex parte, with the Department of Justice

(DOJ) making the applications to the court on behalf of the CIA and other agencies. The Court meets in secret, and its proceedings are generally not revealed to the public or to the targets of the surveillance.

Court Orders. The legal test for surveillance under FISA is not whether probable cause exists that the party to be monitored is involved in criminal activity. Rather, the court must find probable cause that the party to be monitored is a "foreign power" or "an agent of a foreign power." § 1801. Therefore, unlike ECPA or the Fourth Amendment, FISA surveillance is not tied to any required showing of a connection to criminal activity. However, if the monitored party is a "United States person" (a citizen or permanent resident alien), the government must establish probable cause that the party's activities "may" or "are about to" involve a criminal violation. § 1801(b)(2)(A).

The number of FISA electronic surveillance orders expanded from 199 orders (1979) to 886 (1999).[85] In 2001, the FISA court approved 934 applications for electronic surveillance orders. None were denied.[86] The USA PATRIOT Act of 2001 eased the standard for obtaining a FISA order. There were 1,228 orders in 2002, 1,727 orders in 2003 (4 were denied), and 1,758 applications in 2004. This represents an increase of 88 percent from 2001.

Surveillance Without Court Orders. In certain circumstances, FISA authorizes surveillance without having to first obtain a court order. § 1802. In particular, the surveillance must be "solely directed at" obtaining intelligence exclusively from "foreign powers." § 1802(a). There must be "no substantial likelihood that the surveillance will acquire the contents of any communications to which a United States person is a party." § 1802(a)(1)(B). Electronic surveillance without a court order requires the authorization of the President, through the Attorney General, in writing under oath. § 1802(a)(1).

Video Surveillance. Unlike ECPA, FISA explicitly regulates video surveillance. In order to have court approval for video surveillance, the FISA requires the government to submit, among other things, "a detailed description of the nature of the information sought and the type of communications or activities to be subjected to the surveillance," § 1804(a)(6); "a certification . . . that such information cannot reasonably be obtained by normal investigative techniques," § 1804(a)(7); and "a statement of the period of time for which the electronic surveillance is required to be maintained," § 1804(a)(10). Video surveillance orders can last for 90 days.

The FISA Amendments Act. In 2008, Congress enacted significant amendments to FISA. The FISA Amendments Act (FAA) was passed in response to the revelation in 2005 that since 9/11 the National Security Agency (NSA) was engaging in an extensive program of warrantless wiretapping of international phone

---

[85] Foreign Intelligence Surveillance Act Orders 1979-1999, http://www/epic.org/privacy/wiretap/stats/fisa_stats.html.

[86] Office of Attorney General, *2001 Annual FISA Report to Congress,* available at www.usdoj.gov/o4foia/readingrooms/2001annualfisareporttocongress.htm.

calls. Subsequently, several lawsuits were brought against the telecommunications companies that participated in the surveillance for violating FISA and ECPA. One of the most controversial aspects of the FAA was a grant of retroactive immunity to these companies. The NSA surveillance program and the ensuing litigation will be discussed later on in this chapter.

In its other aspects, the FAA both expanded the government's surveillance abilities and added new privacy protections. The FAA explicitly permits collection of information from U.S. telecommunications facilities where it is not possible in advance to know whether a communication is purely international (that is, all parties to it are located outside of the United States) or whether the communication involves a foreign power or its agents. David Kris explains, "With the advent of web-based communication and other developments, the government cannot always determine — consistently, reliably, and in real time — the location of parties to an e-mail message."[87] It is also possible to collect information and then examine it (through data mining) to look for links with a foreign power or its agents. The perceived need, Kris states, was for a kind of "vacuum-cleaner" capacity that would enable the government to sift through large amounts of information without meeting FISA's traditional warrant requirements.

FAA amends FISA to permit "targeting of persons reasonably believed to be located outside the United States to acquire foreign intelligence information." § 702(a). The person targeted must be a non-USA person, or certain more restrictive measures apply. §§ 703–04. The critical substantive requirements are that the "target" of the surveillance be someone overseas and that a "significant purpose" of the surveillance be to acquire "foreign intelligence information," which is broadly defined.

The collection of this information must be carried out in accordance with certain "targeting procedures" to ensure that the collection is directed at persons located outside the United States. § 702(c)(1)(A). The acquisition must also involve new minimization procedures, which the Attorney General is to adopt. § 702(e). The Justice Department and the Director of National Intelligence must certify in advance of the surveillance activity that targeting and minimization procedures meet the statutory standards and that "a significant purpose" of the surveillance is to acquire foreign intelligence information. § 702(g)(2). The FAA also states that the government may not engage in a kind of "reverse-targeting" — the government cannot target "a person reasonably believed to be outside the United States if the purpose of such acquisition is to target a particular, known person reasonably believed to be in the United States." § 702(b)(2).

The FISC is to review certifications and the targeting and minimization procedures adopted. If a certification does not "contain all the required elements" or the procedures "are not consistent with the requirements" of the FAA or the

---

[87] David Kris, *A Guide to the New FISA Bill, Part I*, Balkanization (June 21, 2008), at http://balkin.blogspot.com/2008/06/guide-to-new-fisa-bill-part-i.html. Kris is co-author of the leading treatise, J. Douglas Wilson & David Kris, *National Security Investigations and Prosecutions* (2007).

Fourth Amendment to the U.S. Constitution, the FISC is to issue an order directing the government to correct any deficiencies. § 702(i)(3).

As for its expansion of privacy protections, the FAA requires that the FISC approve surveillance of a U.S. citizen abroad based on a showing that includes a finding that the person is "an agent of a foreign power, or an officer or employee of a foreign power." Previously, FISA did not regulate surveillance of targets, whether U.S. citizens or not, when located outside the United States. The FAA also contains new mechanisms for congressional oversight and crafts new audit functions for the Inspector Generals of the Department Justice.

GLOBAL RELIEF FOUNDATION, INC. V. O'NEIL

207 F. Supp. 779 (N.D. Ill. 2002)

. . . [A]gents of the FBI arrived at the corporate headquarters of Global Relief [a U.S.-based Islamic humanitarian relief organization] and the home of its executive director on December 14, 2001 and seized a considerable amount of material they felt was relevant to their investigation of Global Relief's activities. As the defendants have conceded in their briefs, no warrant had been obtained before the FBI arrived either at Global Relief's headquarters or the executive director's residence. Nevertheless, FISA includes a provision which states that, when the Attorney General declares that "an emergency situation exists with respect to the execution of a search to obtain foreign intelligence information" prior to the Foreign Intelligence Surveillance Court acting on the application, a warrantless search is authorized. 50 U.S.C. § 1824(e)(1)(B)(i). When such an emergency situation arises, the government must submit a warrant application to the Foreign Intelligence Surveillance Court within 72 hours of the warrantless search for approval. *See* 50 U.S.C. § 1824(e). In this case, the failure of the FBI agents to present a FISA warrant on December 14 was caused by the Assistant Attorney General's declaration that an emergency situation existed with respect to the targeted documents and material. The defendants did submit a warrant application to the Foreign Intelligence Surveillance Court on December 15, as required by 50 U.S.C. § 1824(e). We have reviewed the warrant that issued and the submissions to the Foreign Intelligence Surveillance Court in support of that warrant.

We conclude that the FISA application established probable cause to believe that Global Relief and the executive director were agents of a foreign power, as that term is defined for FISA purposes, at the time the search was conducted and the application was granted. . . . Given the sensitive nature of the information upon which we have relied in making this determination and the Attorney General's sworn assertion that disclosure of the underlying information would harm national security, it would be improper for us to elaborate further on this subject.

This Court has concluded that disclosure of the information we have reviewed could substantially undermine ongoing investigations required to apprehend the conspirators behind the September 11 murders and undermine the ability of law enforcement agencies to reduce the possibility of terrorist crimes in the future. Furthermore, this Court is persuaded that the search and seizure made by the FBI on December 14 were authorized by FISA. Accordingly, we decline plaintiff's request that we declare the search invalid and order the immediate return of all items seized.

NOTES & QUESTIONS

1. ***Probable Cause.*** Searches under the Wiretap Act require a "super warrant," including a showing of probable cause that an individual has committed or is about to commit an enumerated offense. 18 U.S.C. § 2518(3). What is the required showing of probable cause for a FISA search? FISA requires a judicial finding, as the *O'Neill* case indicates, that probable cause exists to believe that the target is an agent of a foreign power. It also states that no U.S. person can be considered an agent of a foreign power based solely on First Amendment activities.

2. ***Defendants' Rights?*** In *Global Relief Foundation*, the court finds that disclosure of the information that it reviewed in deciding on the validity of the search was not to be revealed to the defendant because it "could substantially undermine ongoing investigations required to apprehend the conspirators behind the September 11 murders and undermine the ability of law enforcement agencies to reduce the possibility of terrorist crimes in the future." However, FISA requires that defendants receive notice about "any information obtained or derived from an electronic surveillance of that aggrieved person" pursuant to FISA when the government seeks to use information at trial or other official proceedings. 50 U.S.C. § 1806(c).

3. ***The Three* Keith *Categories.*** Recall the *Keith* Court's distinction between electronic surveillance in (1) criminal investigations; (2) domestic security investigations; and (3) investigations involving "activities of foreign powers and their agents." Today, ECPA regulates electronic surveillance in criminal investigations (category one above). The Foreign Intelligence Surveillance Act (FISA), as enacted in 1978, regulates electronic and other kinds of surveillance in cases involving foreign powers and their agents (category three).

What then of the *Keith* category of "domestic security investigations" (category two)? Recall that the defendants in the underlying criminal proceeding were charged with a conspiracy to destroy government property. One of the defendants, for example, was charged with "the dynamite bombing" of a CIA office in Michigan. *Keith* makes it clear that it would be consistent with the Fourth Amendment for Congress to create different statutory requirements for issuing warrants for surveillance in cases involving domestic security. But Congress has not enacted such rules, and, as a consequence, law enforcement is required to carry out surveillance of criminal activities similar to those in *Keith* under the requirements of Title III and other parts of ECPA.

This state of affairs remains unaltered by the "lone wolf" amendment to FISA in 2004. That year, Congress amended FISA to include any non-U.S. person who "engages in international terrorism or activities in preparation therefor" in the definition of "agent of a foreign power." This revised definition sunsets on December 31, 2009. The change means that the "lone wolf" terrorist need not be tied to a foreign power, but must be a non-U.S. person engaged in or plotting "international terrorism." FISA defines "international terrorism" as involving, among other things, activities that "[o]ccur totally outside the U.S., or transcend national boundaries in terms of the means by which they accomplished, the persons they appear intended to coerce or intimidate, or the locale in which their perpetrators operate or seek asylum." 50 U.S.C. § 1801(c). As an illustration of the coverage of the "Lone Wolf" amendment, it would not cover Timothy McVeigh, the Oklahoma City bomber.

4. *A New Agency for Domestic Intelligence?* Francesca Bignami notes that in Europe, one agency gathers intelligence on threats abroad posed by foreign governments, and one agency "is charged with gathering intelligence at home, on activities sponsored by foreign powers (counter-intelligence) as well as on home-grown security threats."[88] Both of these agencies are generally overseen not by judiciary, but by legislative and executive branches. Both intelligence agencies generally carry out surveillance under a more permissive set of legal rules than the domestic police. In contrast, in the United States, the FBI is charged with both domestic intelligence investigations and criminal investigations of violations of federal law.

Judge Richard Posner has emerged as the leading critic of the assignment of this double function to the FBI. He contends that the combination of criminal investigation and domestic intelligence at the FBI has not been successful: "If the incompatibility between the law enforcement and intelligence cultures is conceded, then it follows that an agency 100 percent dedicated to domestic intelligence would be likely to do a better job than the FBI, which is at most 20 percent intelligence and thus at least 80 percent criminal investigation and in consequence dominated by the criminal investigations."[89] Posner calls for creation of a "pure" domestic intelligence agency, one without any law enforcement responsibilities and located outside of the FBI. For Posner, the new U.S. Security Intelligence Surveillance can be modeled on the United Kingdom's MI5 or the Canadian Security Intelligence Service. What should the rules be for such a domestic intelligence agency concerning telecommunications surveillance? Should the FISA rules be applied to it?

UNITED STATES V. ISA

923 F.2d 1300 (8th Cir. 1991)

[The FBI obtained an order pursuant to FISA to bug the home of Zein Hassan Isa and his wife, Maria Matias. The FBI suspected Isa, a naturalized U.S. citizen, of being an agent of the Palestine Liberation Organization (PLO). One evening, the

---

[88] Francesca Bignami, *European versus American Liberty*, 48 B.C. L. Rev. 609, 621 (2007).

[89] Richard A. Posner, *Uncertain Shield* 101-02 (2006).

FBI's recording tapes of the bugged home captured Zein and Maria's murder of their 16-year-old daughter, Tina. Zein and Maria became angry at Tina's general rebelliousness and her defiance of their order not to date a particular young man. On the tape, Zein said to Tina: "Here, listen, my dear daughter, do you know that this is the last day? Tonight, you're going to die!" Tina responded in disbelief: "Huh?" Maria held Tina down while Zein stabbed her six times in the chest. While Tina screamed, Zein said: "Quiet, little one! Die my daughter, die!" The FBI turned the tapes over to the State of Missouri, where the Isas resided, where they were used to convict the Isas of murder. The Isas were sentenced to death.[90] Zein Isa argued that the recording should be suppressed because it captured events that had no relevance to the FBI's foreign intelligence gathering.]

GIBSON, J. . . . [A]ppellant argues that his fourth amendment rights were violated because the government failed to comply with the minimization procedures defined in 50 U.S.C. § 1801(h). Specifically, he contends that the tapes turned over to the State of Missouri record a "private domestic matter," which is not relevant material under the Foreign Intelligence Surveillance Act and must therefore be destroyed. In support of this argument, he cites isolated sentences regarding required minimization procedures from the legislative history of the Foreign Intelligence Surveillance Act:

> Minimization procedures might also include restrictions on the use of surveillance to times when foreign intelligence information is likely to be obtained, ... [Furthermore, a target's] communications which are clearly not relevant to his clandestine intelligence activities should be destroyed. S. Rep. No. 95-701, 95th Cong., 2d Sess. 4.

Notwithstanding the minimization procedures required by [FISA], the Act specifically authorizes the retention of information that is "evidence of a crime", 50 U.S.C. § 1801(h)(3), and provides procedures for the retention and dissemination of such information. 50 U.S.C. § 1806(b)-(f). There is no requirement that the "crime" be related to foreign intelligence. . . .

Thus, we conclude that the tapes are "evidence of crime" and that the district court correctly denied appellant's motion to suppress. 50 U.S.C. § 1801(h)(3).

NOTES & QUESTIONS

1. *Use of Information Obtained Through FISA Orders.* As the *Isa* court notes, information obtained via FISA can be used in criminal trials. However, the standard to obtain a FISA order does not require probable cause. Is it appropriate to allow the use of evidence that would ordinarily required a warrant with probable cause to obtain? On the other hand, the FISA order in *Isa* was properly obtained, and the agents unexpectedly obtained evidence of a murder. If the order is obtained properly in good faith, and evidence of a

---

[90] The Eighth Circuit opinion contains a very meager account of the facts on this case. The facts contained in this book are taken from *Terror and Death at Home Are Caught in F.B.I. Tape,* N.Y. Times, Oct. 28, 1991, at A14.

crime is unexpectedly gathered, why should it be excluded from use in a criminal prosecution?

2. *Minimization Procedures and Information Screening "Walls."* As illustrated by *Isa,* FISA allows the use of information properly obtained under FISA to be used in a criminal prosecution. What prevents the government from using the often more lax standards of FISA to gather evidence in a criminal investigation? The standards of FISA are often much less stringent than those of ECPA. Government officials would merely need to say that they are conducting "intelligence gathering" and obtain a FISA order rather than an order under ECPA — and then, if they uncover evidence of a crime, they could use it to prosecute. FISA has some built-in protections against this. For example, it requires that "the purpose" of the surveillance be foreign intelligence gathering. This language was interpreted by courts as the "primary" purpose.

FISA requires that procedures be implemented to minimize the collection, retention, and dissemination of information about United States persons. § 1801(h)(1). Minimization procedures are designed to prevent the broad power of "foreign intelligence gathering" from being used for routine criminal investigations. In a number of instances, however, there are overlaps between foreign intelligence gathering and criminal investigations.

One common minimization procedure is what is known as an "information screening wall." With the "wall," an official not involved in the criminal investigation must review the raw materials gathered by FISA surveillance and only pass on information that might be relevant evidence. The wall is designed to prevent criminal justice personnel from initiating or directing the FISA surveillance. The wall does not prevent the sharing of information; rather, it prevents criminal prosecutors from becoming involved in the front end of the investigation rather than on the back end.

How should terrorism investigations, which involve both intelligence gathering and the collection of evidence for criminal prosecution, fit into this scheme?

THE 9/11 COMMISSION REPORT

Excerpt from pp. 254-75 (2004)

"The System Was Blinking Red"

As 2001 began, counterterrorism officials were receiving frequent but fragmentary reports about threats. Indeed, there appeared to be possible threats almost everywhere the United States had interests — including at home. . . .

Threat reports surged in June and July, reaching an even higher peak of urgency. The summer threats seemed to be focused on Saudi Arabia, Israel, Bahrain, Kuwait, Yemen, and possibly Rome, but the danger could be anywhere — including a possible attack on the G-8 summit in Genoa. . . .

A terrorist threat advisory distributed in late June indicated a high probability of near-term "spectacular" terrorist attacks resulting in numerous casualties.

Other reports' titles warned, "Bin Ladin Attacks May Be Imminent" and "Bin Ladin and Associates Making Near-Term Threats." . . .

Most of the intelligence community recognized in the summer of 2001 that the number and severity of threat reports were unprecedented. Many officials told us that they knew something terrible was planned, and they were desperate to stop it. Despite their large number, the threats received contained few specifics regarding time, place, method, or target. . . .

["Jane," an FBI analyst assigned to the FBI's investigation of the terrorist attack on the USS *Cole*] began drafting what is known as a lead for the FBI's New York Field Office. A lead relays information from one part of the FBI to another and requests that a particular action be taken. . . . [H]er draft lead was not sent until August 28. Her email told the New York agent that she wanted him to get started as soon as possible, but she labeled the lead as "Routine" — a designation that informs the receiving office that it has 30 days to respond.

The agent who received the lead forwarded it to his squad supervisor. That same day, the supervisor forwarded the lead to an intelligence agent to open an intelligence case — an agent who thus was behind "the wall" keeping FBI intelligence information from being shared with criminal prosecutors. He also sent it to the *Cole* case agents and an agent who had spent significant time in Malaysia searching for another Khalid: Khalid Sheikh Mohammad.

The suggested goal of the investigation was to locate Mihdhar, [a member of al Qaeda and a 9/11 hijacker] determine his contacts and reasons for being in the United States, and possibly conduct an interview. Before sending the lead, "Jane" had discussed it with "John," the CIA official on detail to the FBI. . . . The discussion seems to have been limited to whether the search should be classified as an intelligence investigation or as a criminal one. It appears that no one informed higher levels of management in either the FBI or CIA about the case. . . .

One of the *Cole* case agents read the lead with interest, and contacted "Jane" to obtain more information. "Jane" argued, however, that because the agent was designated a "criminal" FBI agent, not an intelligence FBI agent, the wall kept him from participating in any search for Mihdhar. In fact, she felt he had to destroy his copy of the lead because it contained NSA information from reports that included caveats ordering that the information not be shared without OIPR's permission. The agent asked "Jane" to get an opinion from the FBI's National Security Law Unit (NSLU) on whether he could open a criminal case on Mihdhar.

"Jane" sent an email to the *Cole* case agent explaining that according to the NSLU, the case could be opened only as an intelligence matter, and that if Mihdhar was found, only designated intelligence agents could conduct or even be present at any interview. She appears to have misunderstood the complex rules that could apply to this situation.

The FBI agent angrily responded:

> Whatever has happened to this — someday someone will die — and the wall or not — the public will not understand why we were not more effective at throwing every resource we had at certain "problems." . . .

"Jane" replied that she was not making up the rules; she claimed that they were in the relevant manual and "ordered by the [FISA] Court and every office of the FBI is required to follow them including FBI NY."

It is now clear that everyone involved was confused about the rules governing the sharing and use of information gathered in intelligence channels. Because Mihdhar was being sought for his possible connection to or knowledge of the *Cole* bombing, he could be investigated or tracked under the existing *Cole* criminal case. No new criminal case was need for the criminal agent to begin searching for Mihdhar. And as NSA had approved the passage of its information to the criminal agent, he could have conducted a search using all available information. As a result of this confusion, the criminal agents who were knowledgeable about al Qaeda and experienced with criminal investigative techniques, including finding suspects and possible criminal charges, were thus excluded from the search. . . .

We believe that if more resources had been applied and a significantly different approach taken, Mihdhar and Hazmi might have been found. They had used their true names in the United States. Still, the investigators would have needed luck as well as skill to find them prior to September 11 even if such searches had begun as early as August 23, when the lead was first drafted.

Many FBI witnesses have suggested that even if Mihdhar had been found, there was nothing the agents could have done except follow him onto the planes. We believe this is incorrect. Both Hazmi and Mihdhar could have been held for immigration violations or as material witnesses in the *Cole* bombing case. Investigation or interrogation of them, and investigation of their travel and financial activities, could have yielded evidence of connections to other participants in the 9/11 plot. The simple fact of their detention could have derailed the plan. In any case, the opportunity did not arise. . . .

On August 15, 2001, the Minneapolis FBI Field Office initiated an intelligence investigation on Zacarias Moussaoui. . . . [H]e had entered the United States in February 2001, and had begun flight lessons at Airman Flight School in Norman, Oklahoma. He resumed his training at the Pan Am International Flight Academy in Eagan, Minnesota, starting on August 13. He had none of the usual qualifications for light training on Pan Am's Boeing 747 flight simulators. He said he did not intend to become a commercial pilot but wanted the training as an "ego boosting thing." Moussaoui stood out because with little knowledge of flying, he wanted to learn to "take off and land" a Boeing 747.

The agent in Minneapolis quickly learned that Moussaoui possessed jihadist beliefs. Moreover, Moussaoui had $32,000 in a bank account but did not provide a plausible explanation for this sum of money. He traveled to Pakistan but became agitated when asked if he had traveled to nearby countries while in Pakistan. He planned to receive martial arts training, and intended to purchase a global positioning receiver. The agent also noted that Moussaoui became extremely agitated whenever he was questioned regarding his religious beliefs. The agent concluded that Moussaoui was "an Islamic extremist preparing for some future act in furtherance of radical fundamentalist goals." He also believed Moussaoui's plan was related to his flight training.

Moussaoui can be seen as an al Qaeda mistake and a missed opportunity. An apparently unreliable operative, he had fallen into the hands of the FBI. . . . If Moussaoui had been connected to al Qaeda, questions should instantly have arisen about a possible al Qaeda plot that involved piloting airliners, a possibility that had never been seriously analyzed by the intelligence community. . . .

As a French national who had overstayed his visa, Moussaoui could be detained immediately. The INS arrested Moussaoui on the immigration violation. A deportation order was signed on August 17, 2001.

The agents in Minnesota were concerned that the U.S. Attorney's office in Minneapolis would find insufficient probable cause of a crime to obtain a criminal warrant to search Moussaoui's laptop computer. Agents at FBI headquarters believed there was insufficient probable cause. Minneapolis therefore sought a special warrant under the Foreign Intelligence Surveillance Act. . . .

To do so, however, the FBI needed to demonstrate probable cause that Moussaoui was an agent of a foreign power, a demonstration that was not required to obtain a criminal warrant but was a statutory requirement for a FISA warrant. The agent did not have sufficient information to connect Moussaoui to a "foreign power," so he reached out for help, in the United States and overseas. . .

[Based on information supplied by the French government, Moussaoui was linked to a rebel leader in Chechnya.] This set off a spirited debate between the Minneapolis Field Office, FBI headquarters, and the CIA as to whether Chechen rebels . . . were sufficiently associated with a terrorist organization to constitute a "foreign power" for purposes of the FISA statute. FBI headquarters did not believe this was good enough, and its National Security Law Unit declined to submit a FISA application. . . .

Although the Minneapolis agents wanted to tell the FAA from the beginning about Moussaoui, FBI headquarters instructed Minneapolis that it could not share the more complete report the case agent had prepared for the FAA. . . .

NOTES & QUESTIONS

1. *Confusion About the Law Before 9/11.* The 9/11 Commission Report excerpted above indicated that many law enforcement officials were confused about what FISA required and how information could be shared. The 9/11 Commission Report stated that the FBI headquarters concluded that Moussaoui's association with Chechen rebels was not adequate to justify a FISA order because Chechen rebels were not "sufficiently associated with a terrorist organization to constitute a 'foreign power' for purposes of the FISA statute." Does FISA require that a foreign power involve a terrorist organization? Consider the following excerpt from a Senate Report discussing the problems with the Moussaoui investigation:

> *First,* key FBI personnel responsible for protecting our country against terrorism did not understand the law. The SSA at FBI Headquarters responsible for assembling the facts in support of the Moussaoui FISA application testified before the Committee in a closed hearing that he did not know that "probable cause" was the applicable legal standard for obtaining a

FISA warrant. In addition, he did not have a clear understanding of what the probable cause standard meant. . . . In addition to not understanding the probable cause standard, the SSA's supervisor (the Unit Chief) responsible for reviewing FISA applications did not have a proper understanding of the legal definition of the "agent of a foreign power" requirement.[91]

A footnote in the report explained that the FBI agent "was under the incorrect impression that the statute required a link to an already identified or 'recognized' terrorist organization, an interpretation that the FBI and the supervisor himself admitted was incorrect."

According to Senator Arlen Specter (R-PA), the consequences of this misunderstanding of law were grave:

> The failure to obtain a warrant under the Foreign Intelligence Surveillance Act for Zacarias Moussaoui was a matter of enormous importance, and it is my view that if we had gotten into Zacarias Moussaoui's computer, a treasure trove of connections to Al-Qeada, in combination with the FBI report from Phoenix where the young man with Osama bin Laden's picture seeking flight training, added to [the fact that] the CIA knew about two men who turned out to be terrorist pilots on 9/11 . . . there was a veritable blueprint and 9/11 might well have been prevented. . . .
>
> [I]n a way which was really incredulous, the FBI agents didn't know the standard. They didn't know it when they were dealing with the Moussaoui case, and they didn't know it almost a year later when we had the closed-door hearing.[92]

Does this indication regarding law enforcement confusion point to a need for changes in the law, changes in FBI training, or some other action?

2. *What Did the FISA "Wall" Require?* Since information validly obtained pursuant to a FISA court order can be used for criminal prosecution, the FISA "wall" prevented criminal enforcement officials from directing the implementation of FISA orders. Consider the following remarks by Jamie Gorelick, who was part of the 9/11 Commission:

> At last week's hearing, Attorney General John Ashcroft, facing criticism, asserted that "the single greatest structural cause for September 11 was the wall that segregated criminal investigations and intelligence agents" and that I built that wall through a March 1995 memo. This simply is not true.
>
> First, I did not invent the "wall," which is not a wall but a set of procedures implementing a 1978 statute (the Foreign Intelligence Surveillance Act, or FISA) and federal court decisions interpreting it. In a nutshell, that law, as the courts read it, said intelligence investigators could conduct electronic surveillance in the United States against foreign targets under a more lenient standard than is required in ordinary criminal cases, but only if the "primary purpose" of the surveillance were foreign intelligence rather than a criminal prosecution.
>
> Second, according to the FISA Court of Review, it was the justice departments under Presidents Ronald Reagan and George H.W. Bush in the

---

[91] Senate Report No. 108-040.

[92] *The USA Patriot Act in Practice: Shedding Light on the FISA Process,* S. Hearing 107-947 (Sept. 10, 2002).

1980s that began to read the statute as limiting the department's ability to obtain FISA orders if it intended to bring a criminal prosecution. . . .

[N]othing in the 1995 guidelines prevented the sharing of information between criminal and intelligence investigators. Indeed, the guidelines require that FBI foreign intelligence agents share information with criminal investigators and prosecutors whenever they uncover facts suggesting that a crime has been or may be committed. . . .[93]

According to Gorelick, why was the "wall" in place? What function did it serve? What precisely did it require?

3. *FISA and the USA PATRIOT Act.* Prior to the USA PATRIOT Act, FISA applied when foreign intelligence gathering was "the purpose" of the investigation. Courts interpreted "the purpose" to mean that the primary purpose of the investigation had to be foreign intelligence gathering. Criminal enforcement could be a secondary purpose, but not the primary one. The USA PATRIOT Act, § 204, changed this language to make FISA applicable when foreign intelligence gathering is "a significant purpose" of the investigation. 50 U.S.C. §§ 1804(a)(7)(B) and 1823(a)(7)(B). Why do you think that this change was made in the USA PATRIOT Act?

IN RE SEALED CASE

310 F.3d 717 (FIS Ct. Rev. 2002)

[In 2002, Attorney General John Ashcroft submitted to the FISA court new procedures for minimization, which significantly curtailed the screening walls. The procedures were reviewed by the FISA court in *In re All Matters Submitted to the Foreign Intelligence Surveillance Court* (May 17, 2002). The court expressed concern over the new procedures in light of the fact that in September 2000, the government had confessed error in about 75 FISA applications, including false statements that the targets of FISA surveillance were not under criminal investigations, that intelligence and criminal investigations were separate, and that information was not shared with FBI criminal investigators and assistant U.S. attorneys. The FISA court rejected the proposed procedures because they would allow criminal prosecutors to advise on FISA information gathering activities. The government appealed to the Foreign Intelligence Surveillance (FIS) Court of Review, which is composed of three judges on the D.C. Circuit. In 2002, the FIS Court of Review published its first and, thus far, only opinion.]

PER CURIAM. This is the first appeal from the Foreign Intelligence Surveillance Court to the Court of Review since the passage of the Foreign Intelligence Surveillance Act (FISA) in 1978. The appeal is brought by the United States from a FISA court surveillance order which imposed certain restrictions on the government. . . .

---

[93] Jamie S. Gorelick, *The Truth About "the Wall,"* Wash. Post, Apr. 18, 2004, at B7.

The court's decision from which the government appeals imposed certain requirements and limitations accompanying an order authorizing electronic surveillance of an "agent of a foreign power" as defined in FISA. There is no disagreement between the government and the FISA court as to the propriety of the electronic surveillance; the court found that the government had shown probable cause to believe that the target is an agent of a foreign power and otherwise met the basic requirements of FISA. . . . The FISA court authorized the surveillance, but imposed certain restrictions, which the government contends are neither mandated nor authorized by FISA. Particularly, the court ordered that law enforcement officials shall not make recommendations to intelligence officials concerning the initiation, operation, continuation or expansion of FISA searches or surveillances. Additionally, the FBI and the Criminal Division [of the Department of Justice] shall ensure that law enforcement officials do not direct or control the use of the FISA procedures to enhance criminal prosecution, and that advice intended to preserve the option of a criminal prosecution does not inadvertently result in the Criminal Division's directing or controlling the investigation using FISA searches and surveillances toward law enforcement objectives.

To ensure the Justice Department followed these strictures the court also fashioned what the government refers to as a "chaperone requirement"; that a unit of the Justice Department, the Office of Intelligence Policy and Review (OIPR) (composed of 31 lawyers and 25 support staff), "be invited" to all meetings between the FBI and the Criminal Division involving consultations for the purpose of coordinating efforts "to investigate or protect against foreign attack or other grave hostile acts, sabotage, international terrorism, or clandestine intelligence activities by foreign powers or their agents." . . .

[The FISA court opinion below] appears to proceed from the assumption that FISA constructed a barrier between counterintelligence/intelligence officials and law enforcement officers in the Executive Branch — indeed, it uses the word "wall" popularized by certain commentators (and journalists) to describe that supposed barrier.

The "wall" emerges from the court's implicit interpretation of FISA. The court apparently believes it can approve applications for electronic surveillance only if the government's objective is *not* primarily directed toward criminal prosecution of the foreign agents for their foreign intelligence activity. But the court neither refers to any FISA language supporting that view, nor does it reference the Patriot Act amendments, which the government contends specifically altered FISA to make clear that an application could be obtained even if criminal prosecution is the primary counter mechanism.

Instead the court relied for its imposition of the disputed restrictions on its statutory authority to approve "minimization procedures" designed to prevent the acquisition, retention, and dissemination within the government of material gathered in an electronic surveillance that is unnecessary to the government's need for foreign intelligence information. 50 U.S.C. § 1801(h). . . .

. . . [I]t is quite puzzling that the Justice Department, at some point during the 1980s, began to read the statute as limiting the Department's ability to obtain FISA orders if it intended to prosecute the targeted agents — even for foreign intelligence crimes. To be sure, section 1804, which sets forth the elements of an application for an order, required a national security official in the Executive Branch — typically the Director of the FBI — to certify that "the purpose" of the surveillance is to obtain foreign intelligence information (amended by the Patriot Act to read "a significant purpose"). But as the government now argues, the definition of foreign intelligence information includes evidence of crimes such as espionage, sabotage or terrorism. Indeed, it is virtually impossible to read the 1978 FISA to exclude from its purpose the prosecution of foreign intelligence crimes, most importantly because, as we have noted, the definition of an agent of a foreign power — if he or she is a U.S. person — is grounded on criminal conduct. . . .

. . . In October 2001, Congress amended FISA to change "the purpose" language in § 1804(a)(7)(B) to "a significant purpose." It also added a provision allowing "Federal officers who conduct electronic surveillance to acquire foreign intelligence information" to "consult with Federal law enforcement officers to coordinate efforts to investigate or protect against" attack or other grave hostile acts, sabotage or international terrorism, or clandestine intelligence activities, by foreign powers or their agents. 50 U.S.C. § 1806(k)(1). . . . Although the Patriot Act amendments to FISA expressly sanctioned consultation and coordination between intelligence and law enforcement officials, in response to the first applications filed by OIPR under those amendments, in November 2001, the FISA court for the first time adopted the 1995 Procedures, as augmented by the January 2000 and August 2001 Procedures, as "minimization procedures" to apply in all cases before the court.

The Attorney General interpreted the Patriot Act quite differently. On March 6, 2002, the Attorney General approved new "Intelligence Sharing Procedures" to implement the Act's amendments to FISA. The 2002 Procedures supersede prior procedures and were designed to permit the complete exchange of information and advice between intelligence and law enforcement officials. They eliminated the "direction and control" test and allowed the exchange of advice between the FBI, OIPR, and the Criminal Division regarding "the initiation, operation, continuation, or expansion of FISA searches or surveillance." . . .

Unpersuaded by the Attorney General's interpretation of the Patriot Act, the court ordered that the 2002 Procedures be adopted, *with modifications,* as minimization procedures to apply in all cases. . . .

. . . [W]hen Congress explicitly authorizes consultation and coordination between different offices in the government, without even suggesting a limitation on who is to direct and control, it necessarily implies that either could be taking the lead. . . .

That leaves us with something of an analytic conundrum. On the one hand, Congress did not amend the definition of foreign intelligence information which, we have explained, includes evidence of foreign intelligence crimes. On the other hand, Congress accepted the dichotomy between foreign intelligence and law enforcement by adopting the significant purpose test. Nevertheless, it is our task to do our best to read the statute to honor congressional intent. The better reading, it seems to us, excludes from the purpose of gaining foreign intelligence information a sole objective of criminal prosecution. We therefore reject the government's argument to the contrary. Yet this may not make much practical difference. Because, as the government points out, when it commences an electronic surveillance of a foreign agent, typically it will not have decided whether to prosecute the agent (whatever may be the subjective intent of the investigators or lawyers who initiate an investigation). So long as the government entertains a realistic option of dealing with the agent other than through criminal prosecution, it satisfies the significant purpose test.

The important point is — and here we agree with the government — the Patriot Act amendment, by using the word "significant," eliminated any justification for the FISA court to balance the relative weight the government places on criminal prosecution as compared to other counterintelligence responses. If the certification of the application's purpose articulates a broader objective than criminal prosecution — such as stopping an ongoing conspiracy — and includes other potential non-prosecutorial responses, the government meets the statutory test. Of course, if the court concluded that the government's sole objective was merely to gain evidence of past criminal conduct — even foreign intelligence crimes — to punish the agent rather than halt ongoing espionage or terrorist activity, the application should be denied. . . .

It can be argued, however, that by providing that an application is to be granted if the government has only a "significant purpose" of gaining foreign intelligence information, the Patriot Act allows the government to have a primary objective of prosecuting an agent for a non-foreign intelligence crime. Yet we think that would be an anomalous reading of the amendment. . . . That is not to deny that ordinary crimes might be inextricably intertwined with foreign intelligence crimes. For example, if a group of international terrorists were to engage in bank robberies in order to finance the manufacture of a bomb, evidence of the bank robbery should be treated just as evidence of the terrorist act itself. But the FISA process cannot be used as a device to investigate wholly unrelated ordinary crimes.

Having determined that FISA, as amended, does not oblige the government to demonstrate to the FISA court that its primary purpose in conducting electronic surveillance is *not* criminal prosecution, we are obliged to consider whether the statute as amended is consistent with the Fourth Amendment. . . . [I]n asking whether FISA procedures can be regarded as reasonable under the Fourth Amendment, we think it is instructive to compare those procedures and requirements with their Title III counterparts. Obviously, the closer those FISA procedures are to Title III procedures, the lesser are our constitutional concerns. . . .

With limited exceptions not at issue here, both Title III and FISA require prior judicial scrutiny of an application for an order authorizing electronic surveillance. 50 U.S.C. § 1805; 18 U.S.C. § 2518. And there is no dispute that a FISA judge satisfies the Fourth Amendment's requirement of a "neutral and detached magistrate."

The statutes differ to some extent in their probable cause showings. Title III allows a court to enter an *ex parte* order authorizing electronic surveillance if it determines on the basis of the facts submitted in the government's application that "there is probable cause for belief that an individual is committing, has committed, or is about to commit" a specified predicate offense. 18 U.S.C. § 2518(3)(a). FISA by contrast requires a showing of probable cause that the target is a foreign power or an agent of a foreign power. 50 U.S.C. § 1805(a)(3).

We have noted, however, that where a U.S. person is involved, an "agent of a foreign power" is defined in terms of criminal activity. . . . FISA surveillance would not be authorized against a target engaged in purely domestic terrorism because the government would not be able to show that the target is acting for or on behalf of a foreign power. . . .

FISA's general programmatic purpose, to protect the nation against terrorists and espionage threats directed by foreign powers, has from its outset been distinguishable from "ordinary crime control." After the events of September 11, 2001, though, it is hard to imagine greater emergencies facing Americans than those experienced on that date.

We acknowledge, however, that the constitutional question presented by this case — whether Congress' disapproval of the primary purpose test is consistent with the Fourth Amendment — has no definitive jurisprudential answer.

. . . Our case may well involve the most serious threat our country faces. Even without taking into account the President's inherent constitutional authority to conduct warrantless foreign intelligence surveillance, we think the procedures and government showings required under FISA, if they do not meet the minimum Fourth Amendment warrant standards, certainly come close.

NOTES & QUESTIONS

1. *Assessing the Benefits and Problems of the "Wall."* Paul Rosenzweig argues: "Prior to the Patriot Act, a very real wall existed. . . . While information could be 'thrown over the wall' from intelligence officials to prosecutors, the decision to do so always rested with national security personnel — even though law-enforcement agents are in a better position to determine what evidence is pertinent to their case."[94]

Consider Peter Swire:

> The principal argument [in favor of the wall] is that criminal prosecutions should be based on the normal rules of criminal procedure, not on evidence gathered in a secret court system. The norm should be the usual constitutional protections rather than the exceptional circumstances that arise in foreign intelligence investigations. . . .
>
> "[T]he wall" serves essential purposes. . . . [R]emoval of "the wall" may violate the Constitution for investigations that are primarily not for foreign intelligence purposes. At some point an investigation is so thoroughly domestic and criminal that the usual Fourth Amendment and other protections apply. . . . Second, "the wall" may be important in preventing the spread of the secret FISA system over time. As of 2002, seventy-one percent of the federal electronic surveillance orders were FISA orders rather than Title III orders. The Patriot Act reduction of safeguards in the FISA system means that this figure may climb in the future. . . .
>
> . . . [E]arly in an investigation, it may be difficult or impossible for investigators to know whether the evidence will eventually be used for intelligence purposes or in an actual prosecution. For instance, imagine that a FISA wiretap is sought for a group of foreign agents who are planning a bomb

---

[94] Paul Rosenzweig, *Civil Liberty and the Response to Terrorism,* 42 Duq. L. Rev. 663 (2004).

attack. On these facts, there would be a strong foreign intelligence purpose, to frustrate the foreign attack. In addition, there would be a strong law enforcement basis for surveillance, to create evidence that would prove conspiracy beyond a reasonable doubt. On these facts, it would be difficult for officials to certify honestly that "the primary purpose" of the surveillance was for foreign intelligence rather than law enforcement. The honest official might say that the surveillance has a dual use — both to create actionable foreign intelligence information and to create evidence for later prosecution.

Faced with this possibility of dual use, the Patriot Act amendment was to require only that "a significant purpose" of the surveillance be for foreign intelligence. Under the new standard, an official could honestly affirm both a significant purpose for foreign intelligence and a likely use for law enforcement.

Swire is troubled by the USA PATRIOT Act's changing FISA's requirement that "the purpose" of the investigation be foreign intelligence gathering to a looser requirement that "a significant purpose" of the investigation constituting foreign intelligence gathering:

> The problem with the "significant purpose" standard, however, is that it allows too much use of secret FISA surveillance for ordinary crimes. The FISCR interpreted the new statute in a broad way: "So long as the government entertains a realistic option of dealing with the agent other than through criminal prosecution, it satisfies the significant purpose test." The range of "realistic options" would seem to be so broad, however, that FISA orders could issue for an enormous range of investigations that ordinarily would be handled in the criminal system. . . . The Patriot Act amendment, as interpreted by the FISCR, thus allows the slippery slope to occur. A potentially immense range of law enforcement surveillance could shift into the secret FISA system.[95]

In lieu of the standard that "a significant purpose" of the investigation consist of foreign intelligence gathering, Swire recommends that FISA orders should be granted only if the surveillance is "sufficiently important for foreign intelligence purposes." Will Swire's proposed standard ("sufficiently important for foreign intelligence purposes") make a material difference from that of "a significant purpose"?

2. *The Constitutionality of FISA.* At the end of *In re Sealed Case,* the court concludes: "[W]e think the procedures and government showings required under FISA, if they do not meet the minimum Fourth Amendment warrant standards, certainly come close." Is coming close to meeting minimum warrant standards adequate enough to be constitutional?

Prior to the USA PATRIOT Act amendments, a few courts considered the constitutionality of FISA, with all concluding that the statute passed constitutional muster. For example, in *United States v. Duggan,* 743 F.2d 59 (2d Cir. 1984), the Second Circuit concluded that FISA did not violate the Fourth Amendment because

---

[95] Peter Swire, *The System of Foreign Intelligence Surveillance Law,* 72 Geo. Wash. L. Rev. 1306, 1342, 1360-65 (2004).

[p]rior to the enactment of FISA, virtually every court that had addressed the issue had concluded that the President had the inherent power to conduct warrantless electronic surveillance to collect foreign intelligence information, and that such surveillances constituted an exception to the warrant requirement of the Fourth Amendment. The Supreme Court specifically declined to address this issue in *United States v. United States District Court*, but it had made clear that the requirements of the Fourth Amendment may change when differing governmental interests are at stake, and it observed . . . that the governmental interests presented in national security investigations differ substantially from those presented in traditional criminal investigations.
. . .

Against this background, Congress passed FISA to settle what it believed to be the unresolved question of the applicability of the Fourth Amendment warrant requirement to electronic surveillance for foreign intelligence purposes, and to "remove any doubt as to the lawfulness of such surveillance."
. . .

We regard the procedures fashioned in FISA as a constitutionally adequate balancing of the individual's Fourth Amendment rights against the nation's need to obtain foreign intelligence information. . . .

Why should different Fourth Amendment requirements exist for foreign intelligence purposes as opposed to regular domestic law enforcement? Is the distinction between foreign intelligence and domestic law enforcement tenable in light of international terrorism, where investigations often have both a foreign intelligence and domestic law enforcement purpose? Do the USA PATRIOT Act amendments affect FISA's constitutionality?

3. ***After-the-Fact Reasonableness Review?*** In a critique of the FISA warrant-procedure as amended by the PATRIOT Act, a Note in the *Yale Law Journal* proposes that FISA be repealed and that the United States return to use of warrantless foreign intelligence surveillance in which "targets could challenge the reasonableness of the surveillance in an adversary proceeding in an Article III court after the surveillance was complete."[96]

Do you think that the foreign intelligence context is well-suited to the proposed warrantless regime? For the Note, "the possibility after-the-fact reasonableness review of the merits of their decisions in Article III courts (in camera or note) would help guarantee careful and calm DOJ decisionmaking." Is reasonableness a sufficiently strict standard of review? Furthermore, one of the hallmarks of the Fourth Amendment's warrant procedure is before-the-fact review; law enforcement officials must seek judicial authorization *before* they conduct their search. Would after-the-fact review result in hindsight bias? Another consideration is the extent to which warrantless surveillance would allow the government to "bootstrap" an investigation — the government could undertake broad, unregulated surveillance knowing that it could lead to evidence that may be admissible in court.

---

[96] Nola K. Breglio, Note, *Leaving FISA Behind: The Need to Return to Warrantless Foreign Intelligence Surveillance*, 113 Yale L.J. 179, 203-04, 209, 212 (2003).

3. THE ATTORNEY GENERAL'S FBI GUIDELINES

Unlike many government agencies, the FBI was not created by Congress through a statute. In 1907, Attorney General Charles Bonaparte requested that Congress authorize him to create a national detective force in the Department of Justice (DOJ). The DOJ had been using investigators from the Secret Service, but Bonaparte wanted a permanent force. Congress rejected his request due to concerns over this small group developing into a secret police system. Nevertheless, Bonaparte went ahead with his plans and formed a new subdivision of the DOJ, called the "Bureau of Investigation." President Theodore Roosevelt later authorized the subdivision through an executive order in 1908. J. Edgar Hoover began running the Bureau, which was renamed the Federal Bureau of Investigation in 1935.[97]

The FBI grew at a great pace. In 1933, the FBI had 353 agents and 422 support staff; in 1945, it had 4,380 agents and 7,422 support staff.[98] Today, the FBI has 11,000 agents and 16,000 support staff, as well as 56 field offices, 400 satellite offices, and 40 foreign liaison posts.[99]

FBI surveillance activities are regulated through the U.S. Constitution and electronic surveillance laws, as well as by guidelines promulgated by the Attorney General. In 1976, responding to Hoover's abuses of power, Attorney General Edward Levi established guidelines to control FBI surveillance activities.[100] As William Banks and M.E. Bowman observe:

> The most pertinent Levi Guidelines focused on freedom of speech and freedom of the press. First, investigations based solely on unpopular speech, where there is no threat of violence, were prohibited. Second, techniques designed to disrupt organizations engaged in protected First Amendment activity, or to discredit individuals would not be used in any circumstance.
>
> At the same time, Attorney General Levi emphasized that the Guidelines were intended to permit domestic security investigations where the activities under investigation "involve or will involve the use of force or violence and the violation of criminal law." . . .
>
> On March 7, 1983, Attorney General William French Smith revised the Guidelines regarding domestic security investigations. . . .
>
> The Smith Guidelines were intended to increase the investigative avenues available to the FBI in domestic terrorism cases. Where the Levi/Civiletti Guidelines had established a predicate investigative standard of "specific and articulable facts," the Smith version lowered the threshold to require only a "reasonable indication" as the legal standard for opening a "full" investigation. . . . The "reasonable indication" standard is significantly lower than the Fourth Amendment standard of probable cause required in law enforcement. To balance the lowered threshold for opening an investigation, Attorney General Smith emphasized that investigations would be regulated and would "not be based solely on activities protected by the First Amendment or the lawful exercise of other rights secured by the Constitution."

---

[97] Curt Gentry, *J. Edgar Hoover: The Man and the* Secrets 111-13 (1991).

[98] Ronald Kessler, *The Bureau: The Secret History of the FBI* 57 (2002).

[99] Federal Bureau of Investigation, Frequently Asked Questions, http://www.fbi.gov/aboutus/faqs/faqsone.html (Dec. 4, 2003).

[100] *See* United States Attorney General Guidelines on Domestic Security Investigation (1976).

Nonetheless, the Smith Guidelines authorized FBI Headquarters to approve the use of informants to infiltrate a group "in a manner that may influence the exercise of rights protected by the First Amendment." The Smith Guidelines also stated: "In the absence of any information indicating planned violence by a group or enterprise, mere speculation that force or violence might occur during the course of an otherwise peaceable demonstration is not sufficient grounds for initiation of an investigation." . . .

According to the criminal guidelines, a full investigation may be opened where there is "reasonable indication" that two or more persons are engaged in an enterprise for the purpose of furthering political or social goals wholly or in part through activities that involve force or violence and are a violation of the criminal laws of the United States. . . .

In order to determine whether an investigation should be opened, the FBI must also take into consideration the magnitude of the threat, the likelihood that the threat will come to fruition, and the immediacy of the jeopardy. In addition to physical danger, the FBI must consider the danger to privacy and free expression posed by an investigation. For example, unless there is a reasonable indication that force or violence might occur during the course of a demonstration, initiation of an investigation is not appropriate. . . .[101]

In 2002, Attorney General John Ashcroft issued revised FBI guidelines. Whereas under the preexisting guidelines, the FBI could engage in surveillance of public political activity and search the Internet when "facts or circumstances reasonably indicate that a federal crime has been, is being, or will be committed,"[102] Ashcroft's guidelines eliminate this requirement. The FBI is permitted to gather "publicly available information, whether obtained directly or through services or resources (whether nonprofit or commercial) that compile or analyze such information; and information voluntarily provided by private entities." The FBI can also "carry out general topical research, including conducting online searches and accessing online sites and forums."[103]

Daniel Solove argues that Congress should pass a legislative charter to regulate the FBI:

> . . . [E]xecutive orders and guidelines can all be changed by executive fiat, as demonstrated by Ashcroft's substantial revision to the guidelines in 2002. Moreover, the Attorney General Guidelines are not judicially enforceable. The problem with the current system is that it relies extensively on self-regulation by the executive branch. Much of this regulation has been effective, but it can too readily be changed in times of crisis without debate or discussion. Codifying the internal executive regulations of the FBI would also allow for public input into the process. The FBI is a very powerful arm of the executive branch, and if we believe in separation of powers, then it is imperative that the legislative branch, not the executive alone, become involved in the regulation of the FBI. The

---

[101] William C. Banks & M.E. Bowman, *Executive Authority for National Security Surveillance,* 50 Am. U. L. Rev. 1, 69-74 (2000).

[102] The Attorney General's Guidelines on General Crimes, Racketeering Enterprise and Domestic Security/Terrorism Investigations § II.C.1 (Mar. 21, 1989).

[103] The Attorney General's Guidelines on General Crimes, Racketeering Enterprise and Terrorism Enterprise Investigations § VI (May 30, 2002).

guidelines should be judicially enforceable to ensure that they are strictly followed.[104]

Should other government security agencies have more oversight? Does Solove overlook the FBI's internal administrative processes that serve to limit its power?

4. THE HOMELAND SECURITY ACT

In 2002, Congress passed the Homeland Security Act, 6 U.S.C. § 222, which consolidated 22 federal agencies into the Department of Homeland Security (DHS). Agencies and other major components at the DHS include the Transportation Security Administration, Customs and Border Protection, Federal Emergency Management Agency, U.S. Citizenship and Immigration Services, U.S. Coast Guard, and U.S. Secret Service. The Office of the Secretary of DHS includes the Office of the Chief Privacy Officer, the Office of Civil Rights and Civil Liberties, the Office of Counter Narcotics, and the Office of State and Local Government Coordination.

Among other things, the Act creates a Privacy Office. 6 U.S.C. § 222. The Secretary must "appoint a senior official to assume primary responsibility for privacy policy." The privacy official's responsibilities include ensuring compliance with the Privacy Act of 1974; evaluating "legislative and regulatory proposals involving the collection, use, and disclosure of personal information by the Federal Government"; and preparing an annual report to Congress.

5. THE INTELLIGENCE REFORM AND TERRORISM PREVENTION ACT

Information Sharing and Institutional Culture. The 9/11 Commission found that in addition to the legal restrictions on sharing of foreign intelligence information, limitations in the FBI's institutional culture as well as technology had also prevented the circulation of data. In its final report, the 9/11 Commission stated: "The importance of integrated, all-source analysis cannot be overstated. Without it, it is not possible to 'connect the dots.'"[105] The 9/11 Commission called for a restructuring of the United States Intelligence Community (USIC) through creation of a National Intelligence Director to oversee this process.

In an Executive Order of August 27, 2004, President Bush required executive branch agencies to establish an environment to facilitate sharing of terrorism information.[106] Responding to the 9/11 Commission Report, Congress passed the Intelligence Reform and Terrorism Prevention Act of 2004 (IRPTA), codifying the requirements in Bush's Executive Order. The Act mandates that intelligence be "provided in its most shareable form" that the heads of intelligence agencies and federal departments "promote a culture of information sharing."

---

[104] Daniel J. Solove, *Reconstructing Electronic Surveillance Law,* 72 Geo. Wash. L. Rev. 1264, 1304 (2004).

[105] The 9/11 Commission Report 408 (2004).

[106] Exec. Order No. 13356, 69 Fed. Reg. 53599, 53600-01 (Sept. 1, 2004).

The Privacy and Civil Liberties Oversight Board. The IRTPA seeks to establish protection of privacy and civil liberties by setting up a five-member Privacy and Civil Liberties Oversight Board. The Board gives advice to the President and agencies of the executive branch and provides an annual report of activities to Congress. Among its oversight activities, the Board is to review whether "the information sharing practices of the departments, agencies, and elements of the executive branch . . . appropriately protect privacy and civil liberties." The Board is also to "ensure that privacy and civil liberties are appropriately considered in the development and implementation of . . . regulations and executive branch policies." Regarding FISA surveillance, IRTPA mandates that the Attorney General provide more detailed reporting to Congress on governmental surveillance practices and the government's legal interpretations of FISA.

The Privacy and Civil Liberties Board has been the subject of controversy. A year after its creation, in February 2006, the Board still had not met a single time. When the Board issued its first annual report in May 2007, it led to the resignation of Lanny Davis, the Board's only Democratic member. The Bush Administration made more than 200 revisions to the report. The White House defending the actions as "standard operating procedure," and stated that it was appropriate because the board was legally under the President's supervision. In his resignation letter, Davis contested "the extensive redlining of the board's report to Congress by administration officials and the majority of the Board's willingness to accept most [of the edits.]"

Later that year, Congress enacted legislation to strengthen the independence and authority of the Board. It is now an "independent agency" located within the executive branch. No more than three members of the same political party can be appointed to the Board, and the Senate is to confirm all appointments to it. As before, however, the Board cannot issue subpoenas itself. Rather, a majority of Board members have the power to ask the Attorney General to issue a subpoena.[107]

6. THE NSA SURVEILLANCE PROGRAM

In December 2005, a front page article in the *New York Times* first revealed that the National Security Agency (NSA) was intercepting communications where one party was located outside the United States and another party inside the United States.[108] The Bush Administration named this surveillance program the "Terrorist Surveillance Program" (TSP).

Created in 1952, the NSA collects and analyzes foreign communications. As Frederick Schwarz and Aziz Huq explain, "The NSA collects signals intelligence from telegrams, telephones, faxes, e-mails, and other electronic communications, and then disseminates this information among other agencies of the executive branch."[109] Schwarz and Huq also point out that the Church Committee

---

[107] Ronald D. Lee & Paul M. Schwartz, *Beyond the "War on Terrorism": Towards the New Intelligence Network*, 103 Mich. L. Rev. 1446 (2005).

[108] James Risen & Eric Lichtblau, *Bush Lets U.S. Spy on Callers Without Courts*, N.Y. Times, Dec. 16. 2005, at A1.

[109] Frederick A.O. Schwarz Jr. & Aziz Z. Huq, *Unchecked and Unbalanced: Presidential Power in a Time of Terror* 127 (2007).

investigation in 1975-76 found that "the NSA had not exercised its vast power with restraint or due regard for the Constitution." In the past, the NSA had engaged in activities such as collecting every international telegram sent from the United States and maintaining watch lists of U.S. citizens involved in political protests.

After 9/11, the NSA again began secret surveillance activities within the United States. Although the Bush Administration has discussed aspects of the NSA surveillance of telecommunications, the complete dimensions of the NSA activities remain unknown. And while the Department of Justice has issued a white paper justifying these activities,[110] the legal opinions said to declare the program lawful are secret.

Several lawsuits ensued, challenging the legality of the NSA surveillance. Some of these cases were brought against telecommunications companies that cooperated with the NSA in conducting the surveillance. Plaintiffs alleged that these companies violated FISA and ECPA.

Early in 2007, a secret FISC decision denied permission for certain NSA surveillance activities. The FISC judgment was said to concern a NSA request for a so-called "basket warrant," under which warrants are issued not on a case-by-case basis for specific suspects, but more generally for surveillance activity involving multiple targets. One anonymous official was quoted as saying that the FISC ruling concerned cases "where one end is foreign and you don't know where the other is."[111] The Administration leaked information about this ruling and argued that it impeded the government's ability to investigate threats of imminent terrorist attacks.

In the summer of 2007, Congress enacted the Protect America Act to authorize the NSA surveillance program.[112] This statute was subject to sunset in 120 days, and it expired without Congress enacting a new law or renewing it. At that point, without the Protect America Act's amendments, the original FISA once again took effect, until Congress enacted FAA in July 2008.

A major roadblock to amending FISA had been the subject of immunity for the telecommunications companies that participated or participate in TSP or similar programs. President Bush stated that telecommunications immunity was needed to provide "meaningful liability protection to those who are alleged to have assisted our nation following the attacks of September 11, 2001." FISA already did contain immunity provisions, and this language was in effect at the time that the TSP began. *See* 18 U.S.C. § 2511(2)(a)(ii). The cooperation of the telecommunication companies with the NSA must have been outside the existing safe harbor language.

The FAA of 2008, discussed earlier in this chapter, establishes new rules for at least some of this NSA behavior. Title II of the FAA raises a new challenge to

---

[110] United States Department of Justice, *Legal Authorities Supporting the Activities of the National Security Agency Described by the President* (Jan. 19, 2006).

[111] Greg Miller, *Court Puts Limits on Surveillance Abroad*, L.A. Times, Aug. 2, 2007.

[112] The Protect America Act created an exception to FISA's requirements. The exception was found in the statute's § 105A. This part of the law exempted all communications "directed at" people outside of the United States from FISA's definition of "electronic surveillance." Once a communication fell within § 105A, the government could carry it out subject to § 105B and its requirements — rather than FISA and its obligation to seek a warrant from the FISC.

the litigation against the NSA behavior prior to its enactments — it provides statutory defenses for the telecommunications companies that assisted the NSA. Specifically, the FAA prohibits "a civil action" against anyone "for providing assistance to an element of the intelligence community" in connection "with an intelligence activity involving communications" following a specific kind of certification by the Attorney General. § 802. The certification in question requires a determination that the assistance was (1) authorized by the President during the period beginning on September 11, 2001 and ending on January 17, 2007; (2) designed to detect or prevent a terrorist attack; and (3) the subject of a written request from the Attorney General or the head of the intelligence community. A court presented with such a certificate is to review it for the support of "substantial evidence."

Before enactment of FAA, several courts heard challenges to the NSA warrantless wiretapping program. One of the most important issues in this litigation is the state secrets privilege, which is a common law evidentiary rule. The state secrets privilege protects information from discovery when disclosure of it would harm national security. As you read the following judicial decisions, consider the impact of the state secrets privilege as well as what effect the FAA will have on these cases.

AL-HARAMAIN ISLAMIC FOUNDATION V. BUSH
507 F.3d 1190 (9th Cir. 2007)

McKEOWN, J. Following the terrorist attacks on September 11, 2001, President George W. Bush authorized the National Security Agency ("NSA") to conduct a warrantless communications surveillance program. The program intercepted international communications into and out of the United States of persons alleged to have ties to Al Qaeda and other terrorist networks. Though its operating parameters remain murky, and certain details may forever remain so, much of what is known about the Terrorist Surveillance Program ("TSP") was spoon-fed to the public by the President and his administration.

After *The New York Times* first revealed the program's existence in late 2005, government officials moved at lightning-speed to quell public concern and doled out a series of detailed disclosures about the program. Only one day after *The New York Times'* story broke, President Bush informed the country in a public radio address that he had authorized the interception of international communications of individuals with known links to Al Qaeda and related terrorist organizations. Two days after President Bush's announcement, then-Attorney General Alberto Gonzales disclosed that the program targeted communications where the government had concluded that one party to the communication was a member of, or affiliated with, Al Qaeda. The Department of Justice followed these and other official disclosures with a lengthy white paper in which it both confirmed the existence of the surveillance program and also offered legal justification of the intercepts.

The government's plethora of voluntary disclosures did not go unnoticed. Al-Haramain Islamic Foundation, a designated terrorist organization, and two of its attorneys (collectively, "Al-Haramain") brought suit against President Bush and other executive branch agencies and officials. They claimed that they were subject to warrantless electronic surveillance in 2004 in violation of the Foreign Intelligence Surveillance Act ("FISA"), various provisions of the United States Constitution, and international law. The government countered that the suit is foreclosed by the state secrets privilege, an evidentiary privilege that protects national security and military information in appropriate circumstances.

Essential to substantiating Al-Haramain's allegations against the government is a classified "Top Secret" document (the "Sealed Document") that the government inadvertently gave to Al-Haramain in 2004 during a proceeding to freeze the organization's assets. Faced with the government's motions to dismiss and to bar Al-Haramain from access to the Sealed Document, the district court concluded that the state secrets privilege did not bar the lawsuit altogether. The court held that the Sealed Document was protected by the state secrets privilege and that its inadvertent disclosure did not alter its privileged nature, but decided that Al-Haramain would be permitted to file *in camera* affidavits attesting to the contents of the document based on the memories of lawyers who had received copies. . . .

Al-Haramain is a Muslim charity which is active in more than 50 countries. Its activities include building mosques and maintaining various development and education programs. The United Nations Security Council has identified Al-Haramain as an entity belonging to or associated with Al Qaeda. In February 2004, the Office of Foreign Assets Control of the Department of Treasury temporarily froze Al-Haramain's assets pending a proceeding to determine whether to declare it a "Specially Designated Global Terrorist" due to the organization's alleged ties to Al Qaeda. Ultimately, Al-Haramain and one of its directors, Soliman Al-Buthi, were declared "Specially Designated Global Terrorists."

In August 2004, during Al-Haramain's civil designation proceeding, the Department of the Treasury produced a number of unclassified materials that were given to Al-Haramain's counsel and two of its directors. Inadvertently included in these materials was the Sealed Document, which was labeled "TOP SECRET." Al-Haramain's counsel copied and disseminated the materials, including the Sealed Document, to Al-Haramain's directors and co-counsel, including Wendell Belew and Asim Ghafoor. In August or September of 2004, a reporter from *The Washington Post* reviewed these documents while researching an article. In late August, the FBI was notified of the Sealed Document's inadvertent disclosure. In October of 2004, the FBI retrieved all copies of the Sealed Document from Al-Haramain's counsel, though it did not seek out Al-Haramain's directors to obtain their copies. The Sealed Document is located in a Department of Justice Sensitive Compartmented Information Facility.

Al-Haramain alleges that after *The New York Times* story broke in December 2005, it realized that the Sealed Document was proof that it had been subjected to warrantless surveillance in March and April of 2004. Though the government has acknowledged the existence of the TSP, it has not disclosed the identities of the specific persons or entities surveilled under the program, and disputes whether Al-Haramain's inferences are correct. . . .

Although we have not previously addressed directly the standard of review for a claim of the state secrets privilege, we have intimated that our review is de novo. De novo review as to the legal application of the privilege and clear error review as to factual findings make sense, as the determination of privilege is essentially a legal matter based on the underlying facts. . . .

The state secrets privilege is a common law evidentiary privilege that permits the government to bar the disclosure of information if "there is a reasonable danger" that disclosure will "expose military matters which, in the interest of national security, should not be divulged." *United States v. Reynolds,* 345 U.S. 1, 10 (1953). The privilege is not to be lightly invoked. . . .

We agree with the district court's conclusion that the very subject matter of the litigation — the government's alleged warrantless surveillance program under the TSP — is not protected by the state secrets privilege. Two discrete sets of unclassified facts support this determination. First, President Bush and others in the administration publicly acknowledged that in the months following the September 11, 2001, terrorist attacks, the President authorized a communications surveillance program that intercepted the communications of persons with suspected links to Al Qaeda and related terrorist organizations. Second, in 2004, Al-Haramain was officially declared by the government to be a "Specially Designated Global Terrorist" due to its purported ties to Al Qaeda. The subject matter of the litigation — the TSP and the government's warrantless surveillance of persons or entities who, like Al-Haramain, were suspected by the NSA to have connections to terrorists — is simply not a state secret. At this early stage in the litigation, enough is known about the TSP, and Al-Haramain's classification as a "Specially Designated Global Terrorist," that the subject matter of Al-Haramain's lawsuit can be discussed, as it has been extensively in publicly-filed pleadings, televised arguments in open court in this appeal,[113] and in the media and the blogosphere, without disturbing the dark waters of privileged information.

Because cases in this area are scarce, no court has put a fine point on how broadly or narrowly "subject matter" is defined in the context of state secrets. Application of this principle must be viewed in the face of the specific facts alleged and the scope of the lawsuit. In this case, the analysis is not difficult because Al-Haramain challenges warrantless surveillance authorized under the TSP. Significantly, until disclosure of the program in 2005, the program and its details were a highly prized government secret.

The first disclosure may have come from *The New York Times,* but President Bush quickly confirmed the existence of the TSP just one day later, on December 17, 2005, in a radio address to the nation. The President's announcement that he had authorized the NSA to intercept the international communications of individuals with known links to Al Qaeda cast the first official glimmer of light on the TSP. Since then, government officials have made voluntary disclosure after voluntary disclosure about the TSP, selectively coloring in the contours of the surveillance program and even hanging some of it in broad daylight.

Two days after President Bush's announcement, Attorney General Gonzales disclosed that the TSP intercepted communications where one party was outside the United States, and the government had "a reasonable basis to conclude that

---

[113] Pursuant to a camera request filed before argument, we permitted C-SPAN to record the proceeding for later broadcast.

one party to the communication is a member of al Qaeda, affiliated with al Qaeda, or a member of an organization affiliated with al Qaeda, or working in support of al Qaeda." Attorney General Gonzales confirmed that surveillance occurred without FISA warrants . . . and that American citizens could be surveilled only if they communicated with a suspected or known terrorist . . . .

In an address to the National Press Club on January 23, 2006, General Hayden volunteered further details about the TSP . . . General Hayden's statements provided to the American public a wealth of information about the TSP. The public now knows the following additional facts about the program, beyond the general contours outlined by other officials: (1) at least one participant for each surveilled call was located outside the United States; (2) the surveillance was conducted without FISA warrants; (3) inadvertent calls involving purely domestic callers were destroyed and not reported; (4) the inadvertent collection was recorded and reported; and (5) U.S. identities are expunged from NSA records of surveilled calls if deemed non-essential to an understanding of the intelligence value of a particular report. These facts alone, disclosed by General Hayden in a public address, provide a fairly complete picture of the scope of the TSP.

. . . [T]he government's many attempts to assuage citizens' fears that *they* have not been surveilled now doom the government's assertion that the very subject matter of this litigation, the existence of a warrantless surveillance program, is barred by the state secrets privilege. . . .

Al-Haramain's case does involve privileged information, but that fact alone does not render the very subject matter of the action a state secret. Accordingly, we affirm the district court's denial of dismissal on that basis.

Although the very subject matter of this lawsuit does not result in automatic dismissal, we must still address the government's invocation of the state secrets privilege as to the Sealed Document and its assertion that Al-Haramain cannot establish either standing or a prima facie case without the use of state secrets. . . .

Having reviewed it *in camera,* we conclude that the Sealed Document is protected by the state secrets privilege, along with the information as to whether the government surveilled Al-Haramain. We take very seriously our obligation to review the documents with a very careful, indeed a skeptical, eye, and not to accept at face value the government's claim or justification of privilege. Simply saying "military secret," "national security" or "terrorist threat" or invoking an ethereal fear that disclosure will threaten our nation is insufficient to support the privilege. Sufficient detail must be-and has been-provided for us to make a meaningful examination. . . . That said, we acknowledge the need to defer to the Executive on matters of foreign policy and national security and surely cannot legitimately find ourselves second guessing the Executive in this arena. . . . [O]ur judicial intuition about this proposition is no substitute for documented risks and threats posed by the potential disclosure of national security information. . . .

It is no secret that the Sealed Document has something to do with intelligence activities. Beyond that, we go no further in disclosure. The filings involving classified information, including the Sealed Document, declarations and portions of briefs, are referred to in the pleadings as *In Camera or Ex Parte* documents. Each member of the panel has had unlimited access to these documents.

We have spent considerable time examining the government's declarations (both publicly filed and those filed under seal). We are satisfied that the basis for the privilege is exceptionally well documented. Detailed statements underscore that disclosure of information concerning the Sealed Document and the means, sources and methods of intelligence gathering in the context of this case would undermine the government's intelligence capabilities and compromise national security. Thus, we reach the same conclusion as the district court: the government has sustained its burden as to the state secrets privilege.

We must next resolve how the litigation should proceed in light of the government's successful privilege claim. . . .

After correctly determining that the Sealed Document was protected by the state secrets privilege, the district court then erred in forging an unusual path forward in this litigation. Though it granted the government's motion to deny Al-Haramain access to the Sealed Document based on the state secrets privilege, the court permitted the Al-Haramain plaintiffs to file *in camera* affidavits attesting to the contents of the document from their memories.

The district court's approach—a commendable effort to thread the needle—is contrary to established Supreme Court precedent. If information is found to be a privileged state secret, there are only two ways that litigation can proceed: (1) if the plaintiffs can prove "the essential facts" of their claims "without resort to material touching upon military secrets," *Reynolds,* 345 U.S. at 11, or (2) in accord with the procedure outlined in FISA. By allowing *in camera* review of affidavits attesting to individuals' memories of the Sealed Document, the district court sanctioned "material touching" upon privileged information, contrary to *Reynolds.* Although FISA permits district court judges to conduct an *in camera* review of information relating to electronic surveillance, there are detailed procedural safeguards that must be satisfied before such review can be conducted. *See, e.g.,* 50 U.S.C. § 1806(f). The district court did not address this issue nor do we here.

Moreover, the district court's solution is flawed: if the Sealed Document is privileged because it contains very sensitive information regarding national security, permitting the same information to be revealed through reconstructed memories circumvents the document's absolute privilege. *See Reynolds,* 345 U.S. at 10 (A court "should not jeopardize the security which the privilege is meant to protect by insisting upon an examination of the evidence, even by the judge alone, in chambers."). That approach also suffers from a worst of both worlds deficiency: either the memory is wholly accurate, in which case the approach is tantamount to release of the document itself, or the memory is inaccurate, in which case the court is not well-served and the disclosure may be even more problematic from a security standpoint. The state secrets privilege, because of its unique national security considerations, does not lend itself to a compromise solution in this case. The Sealed Document, its contents, and any individuals' memories of its contents, even well-reasoned speculation as to its contents, are completely barred from further disclosure in this litigation by the common law state secrets privilege.

The requirements for standing are well known to us from the Supreme Court's decision in *Lujan v. Defenders of Wildlife,* 504 U.S. 555 (1992). Standing requires that (1) the plaintiff suffered an injury in fact, *i.e.,* one that is sufficiently "concrete and particularized" and "actual or imminent, not conjectural or hypothetical," (2) the injury is "fairly traceable" to the challenged conduct, and (3) the injury is "likely" to be "redressed by a favorable decision."

Al-Haramain cannot establish that it suffered injury in fact, a "concrete and particularized" injury, because the Sealed Document, which Al-Haramain alleges proves that its members were unlawfully surveilled, is protected by the state secrets privilege. At oral argument, counsel for Al-Haramain essentially conceded that Al-Haramain cannot establish standing without reference to the Sealed Document. . . . It is not sufficient for Al-Haramain to speculate that it might be subject to surveillance under the TSP simply because it has been designated a "Specially Designated Global Terrorist." . . .

Because we affirm the district court's conclusion that the Sealed Document, along with data concerning surveillance, are privileged, and conclude that no testimony attesting to individuals' memories of the document may be admitted to establish the contents of the document, Al-Haramain cannot establish that it has standing, and its claims must be dismissed, unless FISA preempts the state secrets privilege.

Under FISA, 50 U.S.C. §§ 1801 *et seq.,* if an "aggrieved person" requests discovery of materials relating to electronic surveillance, and the Attorney General files an affidavit stating that the disclosure of such information would harm the national security of the United States, a district court may review *in camera* and ex parte the materials "as may be necessary to determine whether the surveillance of the aggrieved person was lawfully authorized and conducted." 50 U.S.C. § 1806(f). The statute further provides that the court may disclose to the aggrieved person, using protective orders, portions of the materials "where such disclosure is necessary to make an accurate determination of the legality of the surveillance." *Id.* The statute, unlike the common law state secrets privilege, provides a detailed regime to determine whether surveillance "was lawfully authorized and conducted." *Id.*

As an alternative argument, Al-Haramain posits that FISA preempts the state secrets privilege. The district court chose not to rule on this issue. Now, however, the FISA issue remains central to Al-Haramain's ability to proceed with this lawsuit. Rather than consider the issue for the first time on appeal, we remand to the district court to consider whether FISA preempts the state secrets privilege and for any proceedings collateral to that determination.

HEPTING V. AT&T CORP.

439 F. Supp. 974 (N.D. Cal. 2006)

WALKER, J. Plaintiffs allege that AT&T Corporation (AT&T) and its holding company, AT&T Inc, are collaborating with the National Security Agency (NSA) in a massive warrantless surveillance program that illegally tracks the domestic and foreign communications and communication records of millions of Americans. . . .

In determining whether a factual statement is a secret for purposes of the state secrets privilege, the court should look only at publicly reported information that possesses substantial indicia of reliability and whose verification or substantiation possesses the potential to endanger national security. That entails assessing the value of the information to an individual or group bent on threatening the security of the country, as well as the secrecy of the information. . . .

Accordingly, in determining whether a factual statement is a secret, the court considers only public admissions or denials by the government, AT&T and other telecommunications companies, which are the parties indisputably situated to disclose whether and to what extent the alleged programs exist. In determining what is a secret, the court at present refrains from relying on the declaration of Mark Klein. Although AT&T does not dispute that Klein was a former AT&T technician and he has publicly declared under oath that he observed AT&T assisting the NSA in some capacity and his assertions would appear admissible in connection with the present motions, the inferences Klein draws have been disputed. To accept the Klein declaration at this juncture in connection with the state secrets issue would invite attempts to undermine the privilege by mere assertions of knowledge by an interested party. Needless to say, this does not reflect that the court discounts Klein's credibility, but simply that what is or is not secret depends on what the government and its alleged operative AT&T and other telecommunications providers have either admitted or denied or is beyond reasonable dispute.

Likewise, the court does not rely on media reports about the alleged NSA programs because their reliability is unclear. To illustrate, after Verizon and BellSouth denied involvement in the program described in *USA Today* in which communication records are monitored, *USA Today* published a subsequent story somewhat backing down from its earlier statements and at least in some measure substantiating these companies' denials.

Finally, the court notes in determining whether the privilege applies, the court is not limited to considering strictly admissible evidence. . . . [T]he court may rely upon reliable public evidence that might otherwise be inadmissible at trial because it does not comply with the technical requirements of the rules of evidence.

With these considerations in mind, the court at last determines whether the state secrets privilege applies here. . . .

In sum, the government has disclosed the general contours of the "terrorist surveillance program," which requires the assistance of a telecommunications provider, and AT&T claims that it lawfully and dutifully assists the government in classified matters when asked. . . .

[I]t is important to note that even the state secrets privilege has its limits. While the court recognizes and respects the executive's constitutional duty to protect the nation from threats, the court also takes seriously its constitutional duty to adjudicate the disputes that come before it. See *Hamdi v. Rumsfeld,* 542 U.S. 507, 536 (2004) (plurality opinion) ("Whatever power the United States Constitution envisions for the Executive in its exchanges with other nations or with enemy organizations in times of conflict, it most assuredly envisions a role for all three branches when individual liberties are at stake."). To defer to a blanket assertion of secrecy here would be to abdicate that duty, particularly because the very subject matter of this litigation has been so publicly aired. The compromise between liberty and security remains a difficult one. But dismissing this case at the outset would sacrifice liberty for no apparent enhancement of security. . . .

The government also contends the issue whether AT&T received a certification authorizing its assistance to the government is a state secret.

The procedural requirements and impact of a certification under Title III are addressed in 18 U.S.C. § 2511(2)(a)(ii):

> Notwithstanding any other law, providers of wire or electronic communication service, their officers, employees, and agents, . . . are authorized to provide information, facilities, or technical assistance to persons authorized by law to intercept wire, oral, or electronic communications or to conduct electronic surveillance, as defined in section 101 of [FISA] . . . . if such provider, its officers, employees, or agents, . . . has been provided with — . . . .
>
> (B) a certification in writing by a person specified in section 2518(7) of this title [18 U.S.C.S. § 2518(7)] or the Attorney General of the United States that no warrant or court order is required by law, that all statutory requirements have been met, and that the specified assistance is required. . . .

Although it is doubtful whether plaintiffs' *constitutional* claim would be barred by a valid certification under section 2511(2)(a)(ii), this provision on its face makes clear that a valid certification would preclude the *statutory* claims asserted here. See 18 U.S.C. § 2511(2)(a)(ii) ("No cause of action shall lie in any court against any provider of wire or electronic communication service . . . . for providing information, facilities, or assistance in accordance with the terms of a . . . . certification under this chapter.").

As noted above, it is not a secret for purposes of the state secrets privilege that AT&T and the government have some kind of intelligence relationship. Nonetheless, the court recognizes that uncovering whether and to what extent a certification exists might reveal information about AT&T's assistance to the government that has not been publicly disclosed. Accordingly, in applying the state secrets privilege to the certification question, the court must look deeper at what information has been publicly revealed about the alleged electronic surveillance programs. The following chart summarizes what the government has disclosed about the scope of these programs in terms of (1) the individuals whose communications are being monitored, (2) the locations of those individuals and (3) the types of information being monitored:

	Purely Domestic	Domestic-Foreign	
	Communication Content	Communication Content	Communication Records
General Public	Government DENIES	Government DENIES	Government NEITHER CONFIRMS NOR DENIES
Al Qaeda or affiliate member/agent	Government DENIES	Government CONFIRMS	

As the chart relates, the government's public disclosures regarding monitoring of "communication content" (i.e., wiretapping or listening in on a communication) differ significantly from its disclosures regarding "communication records" (i.e., collecting ancillary data pertaining to a communication, such as the telephone numbers dialed by an individual). . . .

Beginning with the warrantless monitoring of "communication content," the government has confirmed that it monitors "contents of communications where . . . one party to the communication is outside the United States" and the government has "a reasonable basis to conclude that one party to the communication is a member of al Qaeda, affiliated with al Qaeda, or a member of an organization affiliated with al Qaeda, or working in support of al Qaeda." The government denies listening in without a warrant on any purely domestic communications or communications in which neither party has a connection to al Qaeda or a related terrorist organization. In sum, regarding the government's monitoring of "communication content," the government has disclosed the universe of possibilities in terms of *whose* communications it monitors and *where* those communicating parties are located.

Based on these public disclosures, the court cannot conclude that the existence of a certification regarding the "communication content" program is a state secret. If the government's public disclosures have been truthful, revealing whether AT&T has received a certification to assist in monitoring communication content should not reveal any new information that would assist a terrorist and adversely affect national security. And if the government has not been truthful, the state secrets privilege should not serve as a shield for its false public statements. In short, the government has opened the door for judicial inquiry by publicly confirming and denying material information about its monitoring of communication content.

Accordingly, the court concludes that the state secrets privilege will not prevent AT&T from asserting a certification-based defense, as appropriate, regarding allegations that it assisted the government in monitoring communication content. The court envisions that AT&T could confirm or deny the existence of a certification authorizing monitoring of communication content through a combination of responses to interrogatories and *in camera* review by the court. Under this approach, AT&T could reveal information at the level of generality at which the government has publicly confirmed or denied its monitoring of communication content. This approach would also enable AT&T to disclose the non-privileged information described here while withholding any incidental privileged information that a certification might contain.

Turning to the alleged monitoring of communication records, the court notes that despite many public reports on the matter, the government has neither confirmed nor denied whether it monitors communication records and has never publicly disclosed whether the NSA program reported by *USA Today* on May 11, 2006, actually exists. Although BellSouth, Verizon and Qwest have denied participating in this program, AT&T has neither confirmed nor denied its involvement. Hence, unlike the program monitoring communication content, the general contours and even the existence of the alleged communication records program remain unclear. . . .

[T]he court recognizes that it is not in a position to estimate a terrorist's risk preferences, which might depend on facts not before the court. For example, it may be that a terrorist is unable to avoid AT&T by choosing another provider or, for reasons outside his control, his communications might necessarily be routed through an AT&T facility. Revealing that a communication records program exists might encourage that terrorist to switch to less efficient but less detectable forms of communication. And revealing that such a program does not exist might encourage a terrorist to use AT&T services when he would not have done so otherwise. Accordingly, for present purposes, the court does not require AT&T to disclose what relationship, if any, it has with this alleged program.

The court stresses that it does not presently conclude that the state secrets privilege will necessarily preclude AT&T from revealing later in this litigation information about the alleged communication records program. While this case has been pending, the government and telecommunications companies have made substantial public disclosures on the alleged NSA programs. It is conceivable that these entities might disclose, either deliberately or accidentally, other pertinent information about the communication records program as this litigation proceeds. The court recognizes such disclosures might make this program's existence or non-existence no longer a secret. Accordingly, while the court presently declines to permit any discovery regarding the alleged communication records program, if appropriate, plaintiffs can request that the court revisit this issue in the future.

Finally, the court notes plaintiffs contend that Congress, through various statutes, has limited the state secrets privilege in the context of electronic surveillance and has abrogated the privilege regarding the existence of a government certification. Because these arguments potentially implicate highly complicated separation of powers issues regarding Congress' ability to abrogate what the government contends is a constitutionally protected privilege, the court declines to address these issues presently, particularly because the issues might very well be obviated by future public disclosures by the government and AT&T. If necessary, the court may revisit these arguments at a later stage of this litigation. . . .

[F]or purposes of the present motion to dismiss, plaintiffs have stated sufficient facts to allege injury-in-fact for all their claims. "At the pleading stage, general factual allegations of injury resulting from the defendant's conduct may suffice, for on a motion to dismiss we 'presume that general allegations embrace those specific facts that are necessary to support the claim.'" *Lujan*, 504 U.S. at 561 (quoting *Lujan v. National Wildlife Federation*, 497 U.S. 871 (1990)). Throughout the complaint, plaintiffs generally describe the injuries they have allegedly suffered because of AT&T's illegal conduct and its collaboration with the government. . . . Here, the alleged injury is concrete even though it is widely shared. Despite AT&T's alleged creation of a dragnet to intercept all or substantially all of its customers' communications, this dragnet necessarily inflicts a concrete injury that affects each customer in a distinct way, depending on the content of that customer's communications and the time that customer spends using AT&T services. Indeed, the present situation resembles a scenario in which "large numbers of individuals suffer the same common-law injury (say, a widespread mass tort)."

NOTES & QUESTIONS

1. *Background on* **Al-Haramain:** *The Sealed Document.* How did the Sealed Document in *Al-Haramain* wind up sealed? Where did it come from? Patrick Radden Keefe has interviewed Al-Haramain's attorneys, including Lynne Bernabei, to whom the Treasury Department had accidently sent the top secret material.[114] Based on these interviews, he explains:

> The document that the Treasury Department turned over to Bernabei appears to have been a summary of intercepted telephone conversations between two of Al Haramain's American lawyers, in Washington, and one of the charity's officers, in Saudia Arabia. The government had evidently passed along proof of surveillance to the targets of that surveillance, and supplied the Oregon branch of Al Haramian — a suspected terrorist organization — with ammunition to challenge the constitutionality of the warrantless-wiretapping program.

Keefe explains that the FBI itself retrieved almost all copies of this document from Bernabei, her fellow attorneys, and her clients. It did not, however, seek to retrieve the copies of these documents that went to two of her clients then living in the Middle East. At some point in the litigation, these copies were sent back to Al-Haramain's attorneys, who turned them over to the district court, which then segregated them from the other evidence.

2. *State Secrets and Standing I:* **Al-Haramain Islamic Foundation.** In *Al-Haramain Islamic Foundation*, the Ninth Circuit decided that the Bush administration had revealed too much about the TSP to claim that the very subject matter of the litigation was a state secret. Yet, it did agree that the Sealed Document, which the Treasury Department had inadvertently provided to the Al-Haramain Islamic Foundation, was protected by the state secret doctrine. The Ninth Circuit also found that the state secrets privilege prevented the plaintiffs, the Al-Haramain Foundation, from reconstructing "the essence of the document through memory." Without reference to the Sealed Document, Al-Haramain could not establish that it suffered injury-in-fact. Hence, it lacked standing.

As a final matter, the Ninth Circuit remanded the case back to the lower court on the issue whether FISA preempts the state secrets privilege. If this statutory framework is found to displace the evidentiary privilege, its "detailed regime" would be used to determine the legality of the NSA surveillance.

3. *State Secrets and Standing II:* **Hepting.** In *Hepting*, the plaintiffs alleged that AT&T was collaborating with the NSA in a massive warrantless surveillance program, namely, the TSP. As customers of AT&T, the plaintiffs alleged that they suffered injury from this surveillance. But what about the state secrets privilege? Recall that in *Al-Haramain*, the plaintiffs' ability to demonstrate an injury turned on access to the Sealed Document or their memories of it. Without access to the documents, the Ninth Circuit found that the Al-

---

[114] Patrick Radden Keefe, *Annals of Surveillance: State Secrets*, New Yorker, Apr. 28, 2008.

Haramain Foundation and other plaintiffs could not show standing. In contrast, the *Hepting* plaintiffs alleged injury due to *non-targeted* surveillance under the TSP.

The *Hepting* court found that the existence of the TSP was itself not a state secret. It found that (1) the Bush administration had disclosed "the general contours" of the TSP, which (2) "requires the assistance of a telecommunications provider," and (3) AT&T helps the government in classified matters when asked. Do you agree that these allegations are sufficient to establish standing?

4. ***State Secrets and Standing III: Other Cases.*** Two federal courts have found plaintiffs lacking in standing in attempted litigation against the NSA surveillance. First, the Sixth Circuit in *ACLU v. NSA*, 493 F.3d 644 (6th Cir. 2007), ruled that the plaintiffs lacked standing under the (1) First Amendment, (2) Fourth Amendment, (3) separation of powers, (4) the Wiretap Act, and (5) FISA. As an illustration of its approach, it rejected the plaintiff's Fourth Amendment standing claim because there was no "evidence that the plaintiffs themselves have been subjected to an illegal search or seizure." As for FISA, the Sixth Circuit declared that the plaintiffs have not shown that they were subject to NSA surveillance; "[T]hus — for the same reason they could not maintain their Fourth Amendment claim — they cannot establish that they are 'aggrieved persons' under FISA's statutory scheme."

In dissent, Judge Ronald Gilman argued that plaintiffs had standing to challenge the program because of "specific present harms" that the attorney-plaintiffs faced due to conflicting duties to their clients in light of the real risk that their communications with them would be overhead. Gilman stated: "The TSP forces them to decide between breaching their duty of confidentiality to their clients and breaching their duty to provide zealous representation. Neither position is tenable." Gillman's dissent also argued that TSP violated FISA and the Wiretap Act

Like the Sixth Circuit in *ACLU v. NSA*, the district court in *Terkel v. AT&T*, 441 F. Supp. 2d 899 (N.D. Ill. 2006), found that the plaintiffs lacked standing. According to the *Terkel* court, the plaintiffs had no standing because of their inability to prove that AT&T had disclosed their records to the government. The *Terkel* court also observed that the case before it differed from *Hepting* in two significant ways. First, the *Terkel* plaintiffs challenged the alleged disclosure of *records* about customer communications and not *contents,* as was the case in *Hepting*. Second, the *Terkel* plaintiffs sought prospective relief only, while the *Hepting* plaintiffs also sought damages for past violations.

The *Terkel* court found that disclosures about past governmental activities were of limited value to the plaintiffs before it. Due to the lack of public disclosure of whether or not AT&T had surrendered records to the NSA, the plaintiffs were unable "to prove their standing to sue for prospective relief." The court declared that "based on the government's public submission," it was "persuaded that requiring AT&T to confirm or deny whether it has disclosed large quantities of telephone records to the federal government could give adversaries of this country valuable insight into the government's intelligence activities." It concluded: "Because requiring such disclosures would therefore adversely affect our national security, such disclosures are barred by the state secrets privilege."

5. ***The* Reynolds *Precedent.*** The birth of the modern states secret privilege is *Reynolds v. United States*, 345 U.S. 1 (1953). In this Cold War era case, the Supreme Court drew on English precedents regarding crown privilege. The *Reynolds* Court found that the "occasion for the privilege is appropriate when a court finds "from all the circumstances of the case, that there is a reasonable danger that compulsion of the evidence will expose military matters, which, in the interests of national security, should not be divulged."

In *Reynolds*, a B-29 military aircraft had crashed and killed members of its crew as well as three civilian observers on board the flight. Their widows sued the government under the Federal Tort Claims Act and sought discovery of the official accident investigation of the Air Force. The Supreme Court found both a "reasonable danger that the accident investigation report would contain" state secrets and a "dubious showing of necessity" by the plaintiffs. It reversed the Third Circuit's decision and sustained the government's claim of privilege.

In 2000, the Air Force declassified the accident report at stake in *Reynolds*. As William Weaver and Robert M. Pallitto summarize, "The material originally requested by the plaintiffs in *Reynolds* has recently been made public through Freedom of Information Act requests, and it contained no classified or national security information."[115] In 2005, the Third Circuit heard a claim from a surviving widow and five heirs of the other, now deceased widows, in the original action. In this case, *Herring v. United States*, 424 F.3d 383 (3d Cir. 2005), the plaintiff's claim was that the officials "fraudulently misrepresented the nature of the [accident] report in a way that caused the widows to settle their case for less than its full value."

The Third Circuit rejected this claim. The plaintiffs failed to show a fraud upon the court related to the Air Force's assertions of military secrets privilege for the contested accident report in the *Reynolds*. It found that the statements of the government officials at the time of the *Reynolds* litigation were "susceptible of a truthful interpretation." For the *Herring* court, the question was not whether the accident report actually contained sensitive information about the mission and the electronic equipment involvement. Rather, it would be enough if these reports could reasonably be read "to assert privilege over technical information about the B-29." The statements could be read in that fashion; "the claim of privilege referred to the B-29 itself rather than solely the secret mission and equipment."

Note as well that the *Reynolds* Court had not examined the documents itself, or sought to release the information to plaintiffs in redacted form. Courts continue to be reluctant to examine information about which the government has claimed the states secret privilege. As Weaver and Pallitto state, "In less than one-third of reported cases in which the privilege has been

---

[115] William G. Weaver & Robert M. Pallitto, *State Secrets and Executive Power*, 120 Pol. Sci. Q. 85, 99 (2005).

invoked have the courts required in camera inspection of documents, and they have only required such inspection five times out of the twenty-three reported cases since the presidency of George H.W. Bush."[116]

6. ***Statutory Reform?*** The state secrets privilege is a common law privilege; and it is one without a formal expression in any federal statute. Weaver and Pallitto observe:

> our own attempts to obtain policies governing assertion of the state secrets privilege met with failure, inasmuch as there appear to be no policy guidelines on the use of the privilege in any major department or agency of the executive branch. Freedom of Information Act requests to some three dozen agencies and their various subcomponents yielded nothing in the way of documentation of guidance for use of the privilege. Any limitations on assertion of the privilege appear to be self-imposed by the individual agencies, and use of the privilege seems to be carried out ad hoc at the discretion of the agency heads and their assistants.[117]

A bi-partisan bill, introduced by Senator Edward Kennedy and co-sponsored by Senator Arlen Specter, S. 2533, would limit the state secret doctrine. The bill would require the government to explain why it is invoking the privilege and to attempt to "craft a non-privileged substitute" for the privileged evidence. It also does much to strengthen the judiciary's power. For example, it instructs the court to review a specific item of evidence to determine whether the claim of the government is valid. Its rule for determining the applicability of the privilege is as follows: "Evidence is subject to the states secret privilege if it contains a state secret, or there is no possible means of effectively segregating it from other evidence that contains a state secret."

Is the state secrets doctrine in need of reform? If so, how ought it to be reshaped?

7. ***Checking the Executive.*** Neal Katyal and Richard Caplan have traced the history of "one of the most important periods of presidentially imposed surveillance in wartime" — President Franklin Delano Roosevelt's (FDR) wiretapping and his secret defiance of a congressional prohibition on wiretapping, enacted in § 605 of the 1934 Communications Act. FDR's secret wiretapping also defied the Supreme Court's decisions in two cases. Nonetheless, FDR in a secret memo authorized the Attorney General to wiretap in cases "involving the defense of the nation." Katyal and Caplan state, "[T]here is evidence suggesting that the wiretapping policy was extensively implemented. . . ."

Katyal and Caplan strongly reject the precedential value of FDR's action as a defense of the Bush Administration's program. They note that the FDR program's precedential value is limited because it was secret, and, moreover, that the fact "that a President — even a great one — acted in a certain way does not mean that future Presidents are justified in following his lead." And they also observe:

---

[116] *Id.* at 101.
[117] *Id.* at 111.

. . . [A]s a matter of constitutional governance, it is exceptionally dangerous to vest a President with the power to break the laws, at least at a time when Congress can act. . . . If the President is unable to persuade Congress to authorize a measure he believes necessary to national security, there is likely to be good reason for that refusal. . . .

[A]n obvious exception to the above analysis [is] for those short-term emergencies in which Congress is incapable of action. . . . But that emergency power must, in a constitutional democracy, be tightly circumscribed. . . . Emergency power would otherwise convert itself into a tool for lawbreaking in perpetuity. So the theory of emergency power might justify the first days of the Administration's NSA program, but certainly not one many months (or years) later. Indeed, Congress passed over a dozen pieces of post 9-11 legislation (including, most obviously, the Patriot Act), within three months of the attacks. The notion that an emergency precluded Congress from altering FISA to permit the NSA program is simply implausible. . . .

Katyal and Caplan go on to argue that Congress has proven ineffective to check the President during times of crisis:

Congress's ineffectiveness stems partially from the fact that it is often dominated by security interests and unable to vote for "liberty" when such decisions will be portrayed as against "security." But it also stems from the reality that the President holds the veto pen. So Congress, even once apprised (and aghast) about a massive electronic surveillance program, cannot easily act. So long as the President claims to ground his surveillance program in some law, no matter how dubious, it will require Congress to pass a new law to trump that interpretation. And because Article I, section 7, requires a bicameral supermajority to override a veto, the only way such legislation can pass is with widespread support in both houses. Given the American political-party system, loyalty to the President alone will stymie such efforts. As a result of Congress's appreciation of this voting problem ex ante, it often does not even try to launch reforms.[118]

To effectively check the Executive Branch, Katyal and Caplan recommend creating "institutional friction" — that is, tensions and rivalries within government. But won't this approach just make the Executive Branch less effective — and in an area with important consequences for national security?

In its defense of the legality of the TSP, the Department of Justice points to "the President's well-recognized inherent constitutional authority as Commander in Chief and sole organ for the Nation in foreign affairs to conduct warrantless surveillance of enemy forces for intelligence purposes to detect and disrupt armed attacks on the United States."[119] Given "[t]he Government's overwhelming interest in detecting and thwarting further al Qaeda attacks," why should the Executive Branch be burdened with more "institutional friction"?

8. *The End of FISA?* William Banks argues: "At a minimum, the unraveling of FISA and emergence of the TSP call into question the virtual disappearance

---

[118] Neal Katyal & Richard Caplan, *The Surprisingly Strong Case for the Legality of the NSA Surveillance Program: The FDR Precedent*, 60 Stan. L. Rev. 1023 (2008).

[119] U.S. Department of Justice, *Legal Authorities Supporting the Activities of the National Security Agency Described by the President* 39-40 (Jan. 19, 2006).

of effective oversight of our national security surveillance. The Congress and federal courts have become observers of the system, not even participants, much less overseers."[120] He proposes: "If FISA is to have any meaningful role for the next thirty years, its central terms will have to be restored, one way or another."

In contrast, John Yoo argues that such surveillance should be permitted where there is a reasonable chance that terrorists will appear, or communicate, even if we do not know their specific identities. Yoo argues that in cases where there is a likelihood, perhaps "a 50 percent chance" that terrorists would use a certain kind of avenue for reaching each other, "[a] FISA-based approach would prevent computers from searching through that channel for keywords or names that might suggest terrorist communications."[121]

A third approach is proposed by Orin Kerr, who would update FISA beyond its current approach, which depends "on the identity and location of who is being monitored.[122] In contrast to this "person-focused" approach, Kerr would add "a complementary set of data-focused authorities" to the statute. Under this second approach, "Surveillance practices should be authorized when the government establishes a likelihood that surveillance would yield what I call 'terrorist intelligence information' — information relevant to terrorism investigations. . . ." Kerr is unwilling to state, however, whether the data-focused approach ("used when identities and/or location are unknown") should or should not require any kind of warrant.

9. The FISA Amendments Act. Considerable controversy accompanied the congressional enactment of the FAA. Senator Russ Feingold stated that the FAA was "not a compromise" but "a capitulation." Further, he declared:

> [T]he FISA Amendments Act, like the Protect America Act, would authorize the government to collect all communications between the U.S. and the rest of the world. That could mean millions upon millions of communications between innocent Americans and their friends, families, or business associates overseas could legally be collected. Parents calling their kids studying abroad, emails to friends serving in Iraq — all of these communications could be collected, with absolutely no suspicion of any wrongdoing, under this legislation. . . .
>
> The bill's supporters like to say that the government needs additional powers to target terrorists overseas. But under this bill, the government is not limited to targeting foreigners outside the U.S. who are terrorists, or who are suspected of some wrongdoing, or who are members or agents of some foreign government or organization. In fact, the government does not even need a specific purpose for wiretapping anyone overseas. All it needs to have is a general "foreign intelligence" purpose, which is a standard so broad that it covers all international communications.[123]

---

[120] William C. Banks, *The Death of FISA*, 91 Minn. L. Rev. 1209, 1297 (2007).

[121] John Yoo, *War By Other Means: An Insider's Accounts of the War on Terror* 112 (2006).

[122] Orin Kerr, *Updating the Foreign Intelligence Surveillance Act*, 75 U. Chi. L. Rev. 238 (2008).

[123] Russ Feingold, Remarks of U.S. Senator Russ Feingold, Opposing H.R. 6304, at http://feingold.senate.gov/~feingold/statements/08/06/20080625f.htm.

In contrast, President Bush, in signing the FAA, stated that it would "ensure that our intelligence community professionals have the tools they need to protect our country in the years to come. The Director of National Intelligence and the Attorney General both report that, once enacted, this law will provide vital assistance to our intelligence officials in their work to thwart terrorist plots."[124]

The FAA also provided retroactive immunity to cooperating telecommunications companies. What impact will the FAA have on *Al-Haramain*? On *Hepting*?

10. Inherent Executive Power. As noted above, the Department of Justice issued a white paper on January 19, 2006 in defense of the NSA warrantless wiretapping. A large part of its defense concerned the inherent authority of the Executive in this area. It states, "In exercising his constitutional powers, the President has wide discretion, consistent with the Constitution, over the methods of gathering intelligence about the Nation's enemies in a time of armed conflict." This power extends to the Executive's "inherent constitutional power to conduct warrantless searches and surveillance within the United States for foreign intelligence purposes."

Others have questioned the President's inherent power to engage in warrantless wiretapping in light of congressional legislation in this area through the Wiretap Act and FISA. The Congressional Research Service (CRS), a nonpartisan research branch of the Library of Congress, notes the importance in resolving this question of the enactment of the Wiretap Act, FISA, and the Wiretap Act's exclusivity language (the Wiretap Act states that FISA is to be "exclusive means" for carrying out the interception of foreign or international communications, 18 U.S.C. § 1511(2)(f)).[125] Thus, Congress did intend "to cabin the President's exercise of any inherent constitutional authority to engage in foreign intelligence electronic surveillance." Yet, the CRS also points to language in the Court of Review's decision in *In re Sealed Case*, which we excerpt above, that suggests that the President continues to have power to authorize electronic surveillance outside of FISA. It concludes, "Whether such authority may exist only to those areas which were not addressed by FISA in its definition of 'electronic surveillance' or is of broader sweep appears to be a matter with respect to which they are differing views."

In contrast, in a letter to Congress, 14 legal experts, including Curtis Bradley, David Cole, Walter Dellinger, Ronald Dworkin, Richard Epstein, William S. Sessions (former FBI director), Geoffrey Stone, Laurence Tribe, and Kathleen Sullivan found that the President did not have inherent power that would allow overriding FISA.[126] The experts find that Congress expressly prohibited the NSA domestic spying program by enactment of FISA, and that FISA's limitations are consistent with the President's role under Article II of

---

[124] The White House, *President Bush Signs H.R. 6304, FISA Amendments Act of 2008* (July 10, 2008), at http://www.whitehouse.gov/news/releases/2008/07/20080710-2.html.

[125] Congressional Research Service, *Presidential Authority to Conduct Warrantless Electronic Surveillance to Gather Foreign Intelligence Information* (Jan. 5, 2006).

[126] Curtis Bradley et al., *On NSA Spying: A Letter to Congress*, N.Y. Rev. Books (Feb. 9, 2006).

the Constitution. The letter observes, the DOJ "fails to offer a plausible legal defense of the NSA domestic spying program. If the administration felt that FISA was insufficient, the proper course was to seek legislative amendment, as it did with other aspects of FISA in the Patriot Act . . . [I]t is also beyond dispute that, . . . the President cannot simply violate criminal laws behind closed doors because he deems them obsolete or impracticable." To what extent, are these arguments against the President's inherent power to override FISA now moot with Congressional granting immunity to the tele-communication companies with FAA in 2008?

CHAPTER 3

PRIVACY AND GOVERNMENT RECORDS AND DATABASES

In the United States, government began to use records widely about citizens after the rise of the administrative state in the early part of the twentieth century. The administrative state's extensive and complex systems of regulation, licensing, and entitlements demanded the collection of a significant amount of personal information. For example, the Social Security system, created in 1935, required that records be kept about every employed individual's earnings. To ensure that each record was correctly identified, the Social Security Administration assigned each individual a unique nine-digit number known as a Social Security number (SSN).

Technology has also been developed that helps government create detailed databases of personal information. Indeed, one of the greatest catalysts for the creation of government records has been technology — namely, the computer. The invention of the mainframe computer in 1946 sparked a revolution in recordkeeping. By the 1960s, computers provided a fast, efficient, and inexpensive way to store, analyze, and transfer information. Federal and state agencies began to computerize their records, often using SSNs as identifiers for these records.[1]

Today, federal agencies maintain thousands of databases. States also keep a panoply of public records, pertaining to births, marriages, divorces, property ownership, licensing, voter registration, and the identity and location of sex offenders. State public records will be covered later in this chapter.

The vast stores of personal information spread throughout government databases have given rise to significant fears that one day this information might be combined to create a file on each citizen. In his influential book on privacy from 1971, Arthur Miller warned of the "possibility of constructing a

---

[1] *See* Alan F. Westin & Michael A. Baker, *Databanks in a Free Society: Computers, Record-Keeping and Privacy* 229 (1972); Priscilla Regan, *Legislating Privacy* 69 (1995); Daniel J. Solove, *Privacy and Power: Computer Databases and Metaphors for Information Privacy*, 53 Stan. L. Rev. 1393, 1400-03 (2001).

sophisticated data center capable of generating a comprehensive womb-to-tomb dossier on every individual and transmitting it to a wide range of data users over a national network."[2] Several times, the federal government has seriously considered the idea of creating a national database of personal information. In the 1960s, for example, the Johnson Administration proposed a National Data Center that would combine data held by various federal agencies into one large computer database. However, the plan was abandoned after a public outcry. Following the terrorist attacks on September 11, 2001, there was a new effort to build a national database based on records contained in state motor vehicle agencies. Unlike the earlier proposal that envisioned a centralized system of records management, the new system would be based on standardized record formats and data linkages to enable information sharing among federal and state agencies.

A. PUBLIC ACCESS TO GOVERNMENT RECORDS

1. PUBLIC RECORDS AND COURT RECORDS

As noted above, states maintain a panoply of records about individuals, many available to the public. These records contain varying kinds of information. Birth records often disclose one's name, date of birth, place of birth, the names and ages of one's parents, and one's mother's maiden name. States also maintain driver's license records, as well as accident reports. Voting records, which can disclose one's political party affiliation, date of birth, e-mail address, home address, and telephone number, are publicly available in many states. Several types of professions require state licensing, such as doctors, attorneys, engineers, nurses, police, and teachers. Property ownership records contain a physical description of one's property, including the number and size of rooms as well as the value of the property. Police records, such as records of arrests, are also frequently made publicly available.

Court records are public in all states, though settlements in civil actions are sometimes sealed. A significant amount of personal data can find its way into court records. In a civil case, for example, medical and financial information often is entered into evidence. The names, addresses, and occupations of jurors become part of the court record, as well as the jurors' answers to voir dire questions. In some states, family court proceedings are public.

For information in court records, privacy is protected by way of protective orders, which are issued at the discretion of trial court judges. Courts also have the discretion to seal certain court proceedings or portions of court proceedings from the public, as well as to permit parties to proceed anonymously under special circumstances.

Privacy in records maintained by state agencies is protected under each state's freedom of information law. Most states have some form of exemption for privacy, often patterned after the federal Freedom of Information Act's (FOIA)

---

[2] Arthur Miller, *Assault on Privacy* 39 (1971).

privacy exemptions. Not all states interpret their privacy exemptions as broadly as the Supreme Court has interpreted FOIA's. Further, certain state FOIAs do not have privacy exemptions.

Until recently, public and court records were difficult to access. These documents were only available in local offices. The Internet revolution has now made it possible to access records from anywhere. Furthermore, private sector entities have consolidated these records into gigantic new databases.

DOE V. SHAKUR

164 F.R.D. 359 (S.D.N.Y. 1996)

CHIN, J. This diversity action raises the difficult question of whether the victim of a sexual assault may prosecute a civil suit for damages under a pseudonym. Plaintiff has brought this action charging that defendants Tupac A. Shakur and Charles L. Fuller sexually assaulted her on November 18, 1993. On December 1, 1994, a jury trial in Supreme Court, New York County, found Shakur and Fuller guilty of sexual abuse and not guilty of sodomy, attempted sodomy and weapons violations. They were sentenced on February 7, 1995 and an appeal is pending.

This civil suit was filed approximately two weeks after Shakur and Fuller were sentenced. The complaint seeks $10 million in compensatory damages and $50 million in punitive damages. Before filing her complaint, plaintiff obtained an order *ex parte* from Judge Sprizzo, sitting as Part I judge, sealing the complaint and permitting plaintiff to file a substitute complaint using a pseudonym in place of her real name. Neither defendant filed a timely answer and thus the Clerk of the Court entered a default.

Shakur has moved to vacate the entry of default. In his motion papers, which have not yet been filed with the Clerk of the Court but which have been served on plaintiff, Shakur identifies plaintiff by her real name. Shakur justifies his use of plaintiff's name by noting that Judge Sprizzo's order allowing plaintiff to file her complaint using a pseudonym was signed after an *ex parte* appearance and merely sealed the complaint. That order did not provide that this entire proceeding was to be conducted under seal. In response, plaintiff claims that Judge Sprizzo's order requires all papers filed with the Court to use plaintiff's pseudonym. In the alternative, plaintiff requests that I issue such an order now.

As a threshold matter, it is plain from the face of Judge Sprizzo's order that he did not decide the issue now before me. Judge Sprizzo's order merely allowed plaintiff to file the *complaint* under seal. Judge Sprizzo did not order that all documents filed in this case be sealed. Nor did Judge Sprizzo hold that plaintiff could prosecute the entire lawsuit under a pseudonym. Nor do I believe that Judge Sprizzo, sitting as Part I judge on the basis of an *ex parte* application, intended to foreclose defendants from being heard on the issue.

Rule 10(a) of the Federal Rules of Civil Procedure provides that a complaint shall state the names of all the parties. The intention of this rule is to apprise parties of who their opponents are and to protect the public's legitimate interest in knowing the facts at issue in court proceedings. Nevertheless, in some circumstances a party may commence a suit using a fictitious name.

It is within a court's discretion to allow a plaintiff to proceed anonymously. *Doe v. Bell Atlantic Business Sys. Servs., Inc.,* 162 F.R.D. 418, 420 (D. Mass. 1995). In exercising its discretion, a court should consider certain factors in determining whether plaintiffs may proceed anonymously. These factors include (1) whether the plaintiff is challenging governmental activity; (2) whether the plaintiff would be required to disclose information of the utmost intimacy; (3) whether the plaintiff would be compelled to admit his or her intention to engage in illegal conduct, thereby risking criminal prosecution; (4) whether the plaintiff would risk suffering injury if identified; and (5) whether the party defending against a suit brought under a pseudonym would be prejudiced.

In considering these and other factors, a court must engage in a balancing process. As the Eleventh Circuit has held,

> The ultimate test for permitting a plaintiff to proceed anonymously is whether the plaintiff has a substantial privacy right which outweighs the "customary and constitutionally-embedded presumption of openness in judicial proceedings." It is the exceptional case in which a plaintiff may proceed under a fictitious name.

Frank, 951 F.2d at 323 (*citing Doe v. Stegall,* 653 F.2d 180, 186 (5th Cir. 1981)).

The present case is a difficult one. If the allegations of the complaint are true, plaintiff was the victim of a brutal sexual assault. Quite understandably, she does not want to be publicly identified and she has very legitimate privacy concerns. On balance, however, these concerns are outweighed by the following considerations.

First, plaintiff has chosen to bring this lawsuit. She has made serious charges and has put her credibility in issue. Fairness requires that she be prepared to stand behind her charges publicly.

Second, this is a civil suit for damages, where plaintiff is seeking to vindicate primarily her own interests. This is not a criminal case where rape shield laws might provide some anonymity to encourage victims to testify to vindicate the public's interest in enforcement of our laws. *See id.* (rape shield laws "apply to situations where the government chooses to prosecute a case, and offer[ ] anonymity to a victim who does not have a choice in or control over the prosecution"). Indeed, the public's interest in bringing defendants to justice for breaking the law — assuming that they did — is being vindicated in the criminal proceedings.

Third, Shakur has been publicly accused. If plaintiff were permitted to prosecute this case anonymously, Shakur would be placed at a serious disadvantage, for he would be required to defend himself publicly while plaintiff could make her accusations from behind a cloak of anonymity.

Finally, the public has a right of access to the courts. Indeed, "lawsuits are public events and the public has a legitimate interest in knowing the facts involved in them. Among those facts is the identity of the parties." . . .

Plaintiff argues that Shakur's notoriety will likely cause this case to attract significant media attention, and she contends that disclosure of her name will cause her to be "publicly humiliated and embarrassed." Such claims of public humiliation and embarrassment, however, are not sufficient grounds for allowing a plaintiff in a civil suit to proceed anonymously, as the cases cited above demonstrate. Moreover, plaintiff has conceded that the press has known her name for some time. Indeed, plaintiff makes it clear that the press has been aware of both her residence and her place of employment. Hence, her identity is not unknown.

Plaintiff's allegation that she has been subjected to death threats would provide a legitimate basis for allowing her to proceed anonymously. Plaintiff has not, however, provided any details, nor has she explained how or why the use of her real name in court papers would lead to harm, since those who presumably would have any animosity toward her already know her true identity. Thus, plaintiff simply has not shown that she is entitled to proceed under a pseudonym in this action.

It may be, as plaintiff suggests, that victims of sexual assault will be deterred from seeking relief through civil suits if they are not permitted to proceed under a pseudonym. That would be an unfortunate result. For the reasons discussed above, however, plaintiff and others like her must seek vindication of their rights publicly.

NOTES & QUESTIONS

1. ***Pseudonymous Litigation.*** *Doe v. Shakur* involved a party's request to proceed under a pseudonym. The court refused this request. The standard for allowing a party to proceed with a fictitious name gives significant room for judicial discretion. Consider *Doe v. Blue Cross & Blue Shield United of Wisconsin*, 112 F.3d 869 (7th Cir. 1997):

> The plaintiff is proceeding under a fictitious name because of fear that the litigation might result in the disclosure of his psychiatric records. The motion to proceed in this way was not opposed, and the district judge granted it without comment. The judge's action was entirely understandable given the absence of objection and the sensitivity of psychiatric records, but we would be remiss if we failed to point out that the privilege of suing or defending under a fictitious name should not be granted automatically even if the opposing party does not object. The use of fictitious names is disfavored, and the judge has an independent duty to determine whether exceptional circumstances justify such a departure from the normal method of proceeding in federal courts. *See United States v. Microsoft Corp.,* 56 F.3d 1448, 1463-64 (D.C. Cir. 1995) (per curiam), and cases cited there, and our recent dictum in *K.F.P. v. Dane County,* 110 F.3d 516, 518-19 (7th Cir. 1997). Rule 10(a) of the Federal Rules of Civil Procedure, in providing that the complaint shall give the names of all the parties to the suit (and our plaintiff's name is *not* "John Doe"), instantiates the principle that judicial proceedings, civil as well as criminal, are to be conducted in public. Identifying the parties to the proceeding is an important dimension of publicness. The people have a right to know who is using their courts.
>
> There are exceptions. Records or parts of records are sometimes sealed for good reasons, including the protection of state secrets, trade secrets, and informers; and fictitious names are allowed when necessary to protect the privacy of children, rape victims, and other particularly vulnerable parties or witnesses. But the fact that a case involves a medical issue is not a sufficient reason for allowing the use of a fictitious name, even though many people are

understandably secretive about their medical problems. "John Doe" suffers, or at least from 1989 to 1991 suffered, from a psychiatric disorder — obsessive-compulsive syndrome. This is a common enough disorder — some would say that most lawyers and judges suffer from it to a degree — and not such a badge of infamy or humiliation in the modern world that its presence should be an automatic ground for concealing the identity of a party to a federal suit. To make it such would be to propagate the view that mental illness is shameful. Should "John Doe"'s psychiatric records contain material that would be highly embarrassing to the average person yet somehow pertinent to this suit and so an appropriate part of the judicial record, the judge could require that this material be placed under seal.

Also consider *Doe No. 2 v. Kolko*, 242 F.R.D. 193 (2006). An adult plaintiff alleged that he was sexually abused as a child by a rabbi at a private Jewish school. The court allowed the plaintiff to proceed anonymously by looking to several factors, including: the public's strong interest in protecting sexual abuse victims; the opinion of the plaintiff's psychologist that the alleged abuse had caused the plaintiff severe psychological and emotional injuries; plaintiff's assertion that he feared retaliation and ostracism if his name was disclosed; a lack of showing that knowledge of plaintiff's identity was widespread; any additional prejudice to defendant's reputation due to pursuit of legal action under pseudonym was minimal due to two similar lawsuits against the rabbi by named plaintiffs; and, finally, a lack of showing that defendants' ability to conduct discovery or impeach plaintiff's credibility would be impaired by allowing plaintiff to proceed anonymously. On the final point, the court noted that defendants would need to make redactions and take measures not to disclose plaintiff's identity, but would otherwise not be hampered by plaintiff's mere anonymity in court papers. These restrictions could also be reconsidered before the case went to trial.

When is it appropriate for a judge to allow a party to proceed under a pseudonym? Does the test give too much discretion to judges to make this determination? If so, how would you draft a rule that limits judicial discretion in approaching this issue?

2. ***Protective Orders.*** Federal Rule of Civil Procedure 26(c) provides that judges may, "for good cause shown," issue protective orders where disclosure of information gleaned in discovery might cause a party "annoyance, embarrassment, oppression, or undue burden or expense." In other words, a protective order serves to place limits on the process of discovery. Most states have protective order provisions similar to the federal one. There is a presumption in favor of access to information through discovery, and the party seeking the protective order must overcome this presumption. Courts will issue a protective order when a party's interest in privacy outweighs the public interest in disclosure.[3] Although the standard for obtaining a protective order is easier to satisfy than the standard for proceeding under a pseudonym,

---

[3] For more information about court records, see Gregory M. Silverman, *Rise of the Machines: Justice Information Systems and the Question of Public Access to Court Records Over the Internet*, 79 Wash. L. Rev. 175 (2004).

the thumb on the scale is on the side of public access. Consider the "good cause shown" standard of Federal Rule of Civil Procedure 26(c). Does it grant too much discretion to a court in granting protective orders?

3. ***Personal Information in Court Records.*** Under some court practices, certain information is categorically excluded from court records. As Natalie Gomez-Velez notes:

> The list of data elements categorically excluded from case records varies from state to state, depending to some extent on the degree to which case records are being made available and the extent to which a particular state precludes public access to certain categories of cases and information. . . .
>
> To a great extent, the federal courts, New York, Indiana, and courts in other states that exclude whole classes of sensitive cases like matrimonial, adoption, juvenile, and family law cases from public access, have fewer problems to solve than courts that permit public access to these kinds of cases.[4]

2. THE FREEDOM OF INFORMATION ACT

Until the second half of the twentieth century, only a few states had created a statutory right of public access to government records. The federal government had no such statute until the passage in 1966 of the Freedom of Information Act (FOIA). President Lyndon Johnson, in signing FOIA into law, stated:

> This legislation springs from one of our most essential principles: A democracy works best when the people have all the information that the security of the Nation permits. No one should be able to pull curtains of secrecy around decisions which can be revealed without injury to the public interest.[5]

Significant amendments to FOIA in 1974 strengthened the Act. *See* Pub. L. No. 93-502. Key provisions established administrative deadlines, reduced fees, imposed sanctions for arbitrary and capricious withholding of agency records, and provided for attorneys' fees and costs.

Right to Access. FOIA grants all persons the right to inspect and copy records and documents maintained by any federal agency, federal corporation, or federal department. Certain documents must be disclosed automatically — without anybody explicitly requesting them. FOIA requires disclosure in the Federal Register of descriptions of agency functions, procedures, rules, and policies. 5 U.S.C. § 552(a)(1). FOIA also requires that opinions, orders, administrative staff manuals, and other materials be automatically released into the public domain. § 552(a)(2).

To obtain a document under FOIA, a requester must invoke FOIA in the request and follow the "published rules stating the time, place, fees (if any), and procedures to be followed." § 552(a)(3)(A). The agency must make a "reasonable

---

[4] Natalie Gomez-Velez, *Internet Access to Court Records — Balancing Public Access and Privacy*, 51 Loy. L. Rev. 365, 434-35 (2005).

[5] 2 *Public Papers of the Presidents of the United States: Lyndon B. Johnson* 699 (1967), quoted in H.R. Rep. 104-795 (104th Cong. 2d Sess.), at 8 (1996).

effort[]" to answer any request that "reasonably describe[s]" the information sought. §§ 552(a)(3)(A)-(C). A requester can submit a request by mail or through an online form. The agency receiving the request is required to respond to the request within 20 business days unless the agency requests extra time based on "unusual circumstances." § 552(a)(6)(A). A requester may ask for expedited processing upon a showing of "compelling need." § 552(a)(6)(E)(i)(I).

There is an administrative appeals process to challenge any agency denial of a request that an agency must detail in its denial letter. § 552(a)(6)(A). The requester has 20 business days to invoke the process. After exhausting any administrative appeals or if any agency fails to adhere to statutory time limits, a requester may also file a complaint against the agency in federal court. § 552(a)(4)(B).

Exemptions. FOIA contains nine enumerated exemptions to disclosure. Pursuant to § 552(b):

(b) This section does not apply to matters that are —

(1)(A) specifically authorized under criteria established by an Executive order to be kept secret in the interest of national defense or foreign policy and (B) are in fact properly classified pursuant to such Executive order;

(2) related solely to the internal personnel rules and practices of an agency;

(3) specifically exempted from disclosure by statute (other than section 552b of this title), provided that such statute (A) requires that the matters be withheld from the public in such a manner as to leave no discretion on the issue, or (B) establishes particular criteria for withholding or refers to particular types of matters to be withheld;

(4) trade secrets and commercial or financial information obtained from a person and privileged or confidential;

(5) inter-agency or intra-agency memorandums or letters which would not be available by law to a party other than an agency in litigation with the agency;

(6) personnel and medical files and similar files the disclosure of which would constitute a clearly unwarranted invasion of personal privacy;

(7) records or information compiled for law enforcement purposes, but only to the extent that the production of such law enforcement records or information (A) could reasonably be expected to interfere with enforcement proceedings, (B) would deprive a person of a right to a fair trial or an impartial adjudication, (C) could reasonably be expected to constitute an unwarranted invasion of personal privacy, (D) could reasonably be expected to disclose the identity of a confidential source, including a State, local, or foreign agency or authority or any private institution which furnished information on a confidential basis, and, in the case of a record or information compiled by a criminal law enforcement authority in the course of a criminal investigation or by an agency conducting a lawful national security intelligence investigation, information furnished by a confidential source, (E) would disclose techniques and procedures for law enforcement investigations or prosecutions, or would disclose guidelines for law enforcement investigations or prosecutions if

such disclosure could reasonably be expected to risk circumvention of the law, or (F) could reasonably be expected to endanger the life or physical safety of any individual;

      (8) contained in or related to examination, operating, or condition reports prepared by, on behalf of, or for the use of an agency responsible for the regulation or supervision of financial institutions; or

      (9) geological and geophysical information and data, including maps, concerning wells.

Redaction. If a portion of a document that falls under an exemption can be redacted (blacked out), then the remainder of the document must be provided to the requester:

> Any reasonably segregable portion of a record shall be provided to any person requesting such record after deletion of the portions which are exempt under this subsection. § 552(b).

The Privacy Exemptions. Two of the exemptions involve privacy concerns. Exemption (6) exempts from disclosure "personnel and medical files and similar files the disclosure of which would constitute a clearly unwarranted invasion of personal privacy." § 552(b)(6). Exemption (7)(C) exempts from disclosure "records or information compiled for law enforcement purposes . . . which could reasonably be expected to constitute an unwarranted invasion of personal privacy." § 552(b)(7)(C). Further, FOIA provides that "[t]o the extent required to prevent a clearly unwarranted invasion of personal privacy, an agency may delete identifying details when it makes available or publishes an opinion, statement of policy, interpretation, or staff manual or instruction." § 552(a)(2). Consider the textual differences between Exemptions (6) and 7(c). Which exemption is more protective of privacy interests?

      The exemptions are permissive; that is, agencies are not required to apply the exemptions. Only the government agency can raise Exemptions 6 and 7(C). The individual to whom the information pertains has no right to litigate the issue if the agency does not choose to; nor does the individual have a right to be given notice that her personal information falls within a FOIA request.[6]

The Law Enforcement Exemption. Exemption § 552(b)(7) depends upon the agency demonstrating "that the files were generated during legitimate law enforcement activity." *Freeman v. United States Dep't of Justice,* 723 F. Supp. 1115 (D. Md. 1988). "Exemption 7(E) may not be used to withhold information regarding investigative techniques that are illegal or of questionable legality." *Wilkinson v. FBI,* 633 F. Supp. 336, 349-50 (C.D. Cal. 1986). However, even if people become "an object of investigation because their names were obtained from an unlawful search," FOIA does not "require that documents generated in

---

[6] For more background about FOIA's privacy exemptions, see James T. O'Reilly, *Expanding the Purpose of Federal Records Access: New Private Entitlement or New Threat to Privacy?*, 50 Admin. L. Rev. 371 (1998); Patricia M. Wald, *The Freedom of Information Act: A Short Case Study in the Perils and Paybacks of Legislating Democratic Values,* 33 Emory L.J. 649 (1984); Anthony T. Kronman, *The Privacy Exemption to the Freedom of Information Act,* 9 J. Legal Stud. 727 (1980).

the investigation . . . be turned over." *Becker v. Internal Revenue Service,* 34 F.2d 398 (7th Cir. 1994).

State FOIAs. Since the passage of FOIA in 1966, a number of states have enacted their own open records statutes. Today, every state has an open records law, most of which are patterned after the federal FOIA. These statutes are often referred to as "freedom of information," "open access," "right to know," or "sunshine" laws.

UNITED STATES DEPARTMENT OF JUSTICE V. REPORTERS COMMITTEE FOR FREEDOM OF THE PRESS

489 U.S. 749 (1989)

STEVENS, J. The Federal Bureau of Investigation (FBI) has accumulated and maintains criminal identification records, sometimes referred to as "rap sheets," on over 24 million persons. The question presented by this case is whether the disclosure of the contents of such a file to a third party "could reasonably be expected to constitute an unwarranted invasion of personal privacy" within the meaning of the Freedom of Information Act (FOIA), 5 U.S.C. § 552(b)(7)(C). . . .

In 1924 Congress appropriated funds to enable the Department of Justice (Department) to establish a program to collect and preserve fingerprints and other criminal identification records. That statute authorized the Department to exchange such information with "officials of States, cities and other institutions." Six years later Congress created the FBI's identification division, and gave it responsibility for "acquiring, collecting, classifying, and preserving criminal identification and other crime records and the exchanging of said criminal identification records with the duly authorized officials of governmental agencies, of States, cities, and penal institutions." Rap sheets compiled pursuant to such authority contain certain descriptive information, such as date of birth and physical characteristics, as well as a history of arrests, charges, convictions, and incarcerations of the subject. Normally a rap sheet is preserved until its subject attains age 80. . . .

. . . As a matter of executive policy, the Department has generally treated rap sheets as confidential and, with certain exceptions, has restricted their use to governmental purposes. . . .

Although much rapsheet information is a matter of public record, the availability and dissemination of the actual rap sheet to the public is limited. Arrests, indictments, convictions, and sentences are public events that are usually documented in court records. In addition, if a person's entire criminal history transpired in a single jurisdiction, all of the contents of his or her rap sheet may be available upon request in that jurisdiction. That possibility, however, is present in only three States. All of the other 47 States place substantial restrictions on the availability of criminal-history summaries even though individual events in those summaries are matters of public record. Moreover, even in Florida, Wisconsin, and Oklahoma, the publicly available summaries may not include information about out-of-state arrests or convictions. . . .

The statute known as FOIA is actually a part of the Administrative Procedure Act (APA). Section 3 of the APA as enacted in 1946 gave agencies broad discretion concerning the publication of governmental records. In 1966 Congress amended that section to implement "'a general philosophy of full agency disclosure.'" . . . The amendment . . . requires every agency "upon any request for records which . . . reasonably describes such records" to make such records "promptly available to any person." If an agency improperly withholds any documents, the district court has jurisdiction to order their production. Unlike the review of other agency action that must be upheld if supported by substantial evidence and not arbitrary or capricious, FOIA expressly places the burden "on the agency to sustain its action" and directs the district courts to "determine the matter de novo."

Congress exempted nine categories of documents from FOIA's broad disclosure requirements. Three of those exemptions are arguably relevant to this case. Exemption 3 applies to documents that are specifically exempted from disclosure by another statute. § 552(b)(3). Exemption 6 protects "personnel and medical files and similar files the disclosure of which would constitute a clearly unwarranted invasion of personal privacy." § 552(b)(6). Exemption 7(C) excludes records or information compiled for law enforcement purposes, "but only to the extent that the production of such [materials] . . . could reasonably be expected to constitute an unwarranted invasion of personal privacy." § 552(b)(7)(C). . . .

This case arises out of requests made by a CBS news correspondent and the Reporters Committee for Freedom of the Press (respondents) for information concerning the criminal records of four members of the Medico family. The Pennsylvania Crime Commission had identified the family's company, Medico Industries, as a legitimate business dominated by organized crime figures. Moreover, the company allegedly had obtained a number of defense contracts as a result of an improper arrangement with a corrupt Congressman.

FOIA requests sought disclosure of any arrests, indictments, acquittals, convictions, and sentences of any of the four Medicos. Although the FBI originally denied the requests, it provided the requested data concerning three of the Medicos after their deaths. In their complaint in the District Court, respondents sought the rap sheet for the fourth, Charles Medico (Medico), insofar as it contained "matters of public record." . . .

Exemption 7(C) requires us to balance the privacy interest in maintaining, as the Government puts it, the "practical obscurity" of the rap sheets against the public interest in their release.

The preliminary question is whether Medico's interest in the nondisclosure of any rap sheet the FBI might have on him is the sort of "personal privacy" interest that Congress intended Exemption 7(C) to protect.[7] . . . Because events summarized in a rap sheet have been previously disclosed to the public, respondents contend that Medico's privacy interest in avoiding disclosure of a

---

[7] The question of the statutory meaning of privacy under the FOIA is, of course, not the same as the question whether a tort action might lie for invasion of privacy or the question whether an individual's interest in privacy is protected by the Constitution. *See, e.g., Cox Broadcasting Corp. v. Cohn*, 420 U.S. 469 (1975) (Constitution prohibits State from penalizing publication of name of deceased rape victim obtained from public records). . . .

federal compilation of these events approaches zero. We reject respondents' cramped notion of personal privacy.

To begin with, both the common law and the literal understandings of privacy encompass the individual's control of information concerning his or her person. In an organized society, there are few facts that are not at one time or another divulged to another. Thus the extent of the protection accorded a privacy right at common law rested in part on the degree of dissemination of the allegedly private fact and the extent to which the passage of time rendered it private. According to Webster's initial definition, information may be classified as "private" if it is "intended for or restricted to the use of a particular person or group or class of persons: not freely available to the public." Recognition of this attribute of a privacy interest supports the distinction, in terms of personal privacy, between scattered disclosure of the bits of information contained in a rap sheet and revelation of the rap sheet as a whole. The very fact that federal funds have been spent to prepare, index, and maintain these criminal-history files demonstrates that the individual items of information in the summaries would not otherwise be "freely available" either to the officials who have access to the underlying files or to the general public. Indeed, if the summaries were "freely available," there would be no reason to invoke the FOIA to obtain access to the information they contain. Granted, in many contexts the fact that information is not freely available is no reason to exempt that information from a statute generally requiring its dissemination. But the issue here is whether the compilation of otherwise hard-to-obtain information alters the privacy interest implicated by disclosure of that information. Plainly there is a vast difference between the public records that might be found after a diligent search of courthouse files, county archives, and local police stations throughout the country and a computerized summary located in a single clearinghouse of information. . . .

We have also recognized the privacy interest in keeping personal facts away from the public eye. In *Whalen v. Roe*, 429 U.S. 589 (1977), we held that "the State of New York may record, in a centralized computer file, the names and addresses of all persons who have obtained, pursuant to a doctor's prescription, certain drugs for which there is both a lawful and an unlawful market." In holding only that the Federal Constitution does not prohibit such a compilation, we recognized that such a centralized computer file posed a "threat to privacy":

> We are not unaware of the threat to privacy implicit in the accumulation of vast amounts of personal information in computerized data banks or other massive government files. The collection of taxes, the distribution of welfare and social security benefits, the supervision of public health, the direction of our Armed Forces, and the enforcement of the criminal laws all require the orderly preservation of great quantities of information, much of which is personal in character and potentially embarrassing or harmful if disclosed. The right to collect and use such data for public purposes is typically accompanied by a concomitant statutory or regulatory duty to avoid unwarranted disclosures. Recognizing that in some circumstances that duty arguably has its roots in the Constitution, nevertheless New York's statutory scheme, and its implementing administrative procedures, evidence a proper concern with, and protection of, the individual's interest in privacy.

In sum, the fact that "an event is not wholly 'private' does not mean that an individual has no interest in limiting disclosure or dissemination of the information." The privacy interest in a rap sheet is substantial. The substantial character of that interest is affected by the fact that in today's society the computer can accumulate and store information that would otherwise have surely been forgotten long before a person attains age 80, when the FBI's rap sheets are discarded. . . .

Exemption 7(C), by its terms, permits an agency to withhold a document only when revelation "could reasonably be expected to constitute an unwarranted invasion of personal privacy." We must next address what factors might warrant an invasion of the interest described [above].

Our previous decisions establish that whether an invasion of privacy is warranted cannot turn on the purposes for which the request for information is made. Except for cases in which the objection to disclosure is based on a claim of privilege and the person requesting disclosure is the party protected by the privilege, the identity of the requesting party has no bearing on the merits of his or her FOIA request. . . . As we have repeatedly stated, Congress "clearly intended" the FOIA "to give any member of the public as much right to disclosure as one with a special interest [in a particular document]."

Thus whether disclosure of a private document under Exemption 7(C) is warranted must turn on the nature of the requested document and its relationship to "the basic purpose of the Freedom of Information Act 'to open agency action to the light of public scrutiny,'" rather than on the particular purpose for which the document is being requested. In our leading case on FOIA, we declared that the Act was designed to create a broad right of access to "official information." *EPA v. Mink,* 410 U.S. 73, 80, (1973). In his dissent in that case, Justice Douglas characterized the philosophy of the statute by quoting this comment by Henry Steele Commager:

> "'The generation that made the nation thought secrecy in government one of the instruments of Old World tyranny and committed itself to the principle that a democracy cannot function unless the people are permitted to know *what their government is up to.*'" (quoting from *The New York Review of Books*, Oct. 5, 1972, p. 7) (emphasis added).

. . . This basic policy of "'full agency disclosure unless information is exempted under clearly delineated statutory language,'" indeed focuses on the citizens' right to be informed about "what their government is up to." Official information that sheds light on an agency's performance of its statutory duties falls squarely within that statutory purpose. That purpose, however, is not fostered by disclosure of information about private citizens that is accumulated in various governmental files but that reveals little or nothing about an agency's own conduct. In this case — and presumably in the typical case in which one private citizen is seeking information about another — the requester does not intend to discover anything about the conduct of the agency that has possession of the requested records. Indeed, response to this request would not shed any light on the conduct of any Government agency or official. . . .

Respondents argue that there is a two-fold public interest in learning about Medico's past arrests or convictions: He allegedly had improper dealings with a corrupt Congressman, and he is an officer of a corporation with defense contracts. But if Medico has, in fact, been arrested or convicted of certain crimes, that information would neither aggravate nor mitigate his allegedly improper relationship with the Congressman; more specifically, it would tell us nothing directly about the character of the Congressman's behavior. Nor would it tell us anything about the conduct of the Department of Defense (DOD) in awarding one or more contracts to the Medico Company. . . . Conceivably Medico's rap sheet would provide details to include in a news story, but, in itself, this is not the kind of public interest for which Congress enacted the FOIA. In other words, although there is undoubtedly some public interest in anyone's criminal history, especially if the history is in some way related to the subject's dealing with a public official or agency, the FOIA's central purpose is to ensure that the Government's activities be opened to the sharp eye of public scrutiny, not that information about private citizens that happens to be in the warehouse of the Government be so disclosed. . . .

. . . The privacy interest in maintaining the practical obscurity of rap-sheet information will always be high. When the subject of such a rap sheet is a private citizen and when the information is in the Government's control as a compilation, rather than as a record of "what the Government is up to," the privacy interest protected by Exemption 7(C) is in fact at its apex while the FOIA-based public interest in disclosure is at its nadir. Such a disparity on the scales of justice holds for a class of cases without regard to individual circumstances; the standard virtues of bright-line rules are thus present, and the difficulties attendant to ad hoc adjudication may be avoided. Accordingly, we hold as a categorical matter that a third party's request for law enforcement records or information about a private citizen can reasonably be expected to invade that citizen's privacy, and that when the request seeks no "official information" about a Government agency, but merely records that the Government happens to be storing, the invasion of privacy is "unwarranted." . . .

BLACKMUN J., joined by BRENNAN, J. concurring in the judgment: I concur in the result the Court reaches in this case, but I cannot follow the route the Court takes to reach that result. In other words, the Court's use of "categorical balancing" under Exemption 7(C), I think, is not basically sound. Such a bright-line rule obviously has its appeal, but I wonder whether it would not run aground on occasion, such as in a situation where a rap sheet discloses a congressional candidate's conviction of tax fraud five years before. Surely, the FBI's disclosure of that information could not "reasonably be expected" to constitute an invasion of personal privacy, much less an unwarranted invasion, inasmuch as the candidate relinquished any interest in preventing the dissemination of this information when he chose to run for Congress. In short, I do not believe that Exemption 7(C)'s language and its legislative history, or the case law, support interpreting that provision as exempting all rap-sheet information from the FOIA's disclosure requirements.

NOTES & QUESTIONS

1. *The Privacy Interest and "Practical Obscurity."* Many courts, including the Supreme Court in other contexts, have held that once information is exposed to the public, it can no longer be considered private. In *Reporters Committee,* however, the Court recognizes a privacy interest in the rap sheets despite the fact that they are compiled from information in public records. The Court concludes that "there is a vast difference between the public records that might be found after a diligent search of courthouse files, county archives, and local police stations throughout the country and a computerized summary located in a single clearinghouse of information." Is the Court stretching privacy too far by claiming it can be violated by altering "practical obscurity"?

    Daniel Solove argues in support of the Court's conception of privacy: "Privacy involves an expectation of a certain degree of accessibility of information. . . . Privacy can be violated by altering levels of accessibility, by taking obscure facts and making them widely accessible."[8] Is such a conception of privacy feasible?

2. *The Interest in Public Access.* The Court also denies access to the rap sheets because "this [FOIA] request would not shed any light on the conduct of any Government agency or official." What kind of use of government records is being sought in *Reporters Committee*? Does this use contribute to the public interest? Does the use comport with the purpose of FOIA?

3. *The Court's Rationale Beyond the FOIA Context.* In a footnote, the Court stated that the reasoning of this case is confined to the FOIA context. As a hypothetical case, imagine that there were no privacy exemptions to FOIA, and the FBI disclosed the rap sheets. The Medicos sue, claiming a violation of their constitutional right to information privacy. What would the result likely be? Can the Court coherently claim that people have a privacy interest in their rap sheet information under FOIA but not in the context of the constitutional right to information privacy?

4. *Exemption 6.* The *Reporters Committee* case concerned Exemption 7(C). Exemption 6 provides that FOIA's disclosure provisions do not apply to *"personnel and medical files and similar files* the disclosure of which would constitute a clearly unwarranted invasion of personal privacy." § 552(b)(6) (emphasis added). Does Exemption 6 only apply to "personnel and medical files"? What does "similar files" mean?

    The Supreme Court answered these questions in *United States Dep't of State v. Washington Post Co.*, 456 U.S. 595 (1982). There, the *Washington Post* requested documents indicating whether two Iranian nationals were holding valid United States passports. According to the Department of State, the two individuals were prominent figures in Iran's Revolutionary Government; several Iranian revolutionary leaders had been strongly criticized in Iran for ties to the United States; and the two could be subject to

---

[8] Daniel J. Solove, *Access and Aggregation: Public Records, Privacy, and the Constitution*, 86 Minn. L. Rev. 1137, 1176-78 (2002).

violence if United States ties, such as passports, were disclosed. The *Washington Post* contended that the language of Exemption 6 simply did not cover these types of documents. The Court disagreed:

> The language of Exemption 6 sheds little light on what Congress meant by "similar files." Fortunately, the legislative history is somewhat more illuminating. The House and Senate Reports, although not defining the phrase "similar files," suggest that Congress' primary purpose in enacting Exemption 6 was to protect individuals from the injury and embarrassment that can result from the unnecessary disclosure of personal information. . . .
>
> . . . Congress' statements that it was creating a "general exemption" for information contained in "great quantities of files," suggest that the phrase "similar files" was to have a broad, rather than a narrow, meaning. This impression is confirmed by the frequent characterization of the "clearly unwarranted invasion of personal privacy" language as a "limitation" which holds Exemption 6 "within bounds." Had the words "similar files" been intended to be only a narrow addition to "personnel and medical files," there would seem to be no reason for concern about the exemption's being "held within bounds," and there surely would be clear suggestions in the legislative history that such a narrow meaning was intended. We have found none.
>
> A proper analysis of the exemption must also take into account the fact that "personnel and medical files," the two benchmarks for measuring the term "similar files," are likely to contain much information about a particular individual that is not intimate. Information such as place of birth, date of birth, date of marriage, employment history, and comparable data is not normally regarded as highly personal, and yet respondent does not disagree that such information, if contained in a "personnel" or "medical" file, would be exempt from any disclosure that would constitute a clearly unwarranted invasion of personal privacy. . . .
>
> . . . "[T]he protection of an individual's right of privacy" which Congress sought to achieve by preventing "the disclosure of [information] which might harm the individual," surely was not intended to turn upon the label of the file which contains the damaging information. . . .
>
> In sum, we do not think that Congress meant to limit Exemption 6 to a narrow class of files containing only a discrete kind of personal information. Rather, "[t]he exemption [was] intended to cover detailed Government records on an individual which can be identified as applying to that individual." When disclosure of information which applies to a particular individual is sought from Government records, courts must determine whether release of the information would constitute a clearly unwarranted invasion of that person's privacy. . . .

5. ***Definition of Agency.*** FOIA requires only that "agencies" respond to requesters. Congress is not a federal agency and is therefore not subject to the Act. Nor is the President or his advisors, whose "sole function" is to "advise and assist" the President. For similar reasons, the National Security Council is not an agency. *Armstrong v. Executive Office of the President*, 90 F.3d 556 (D.C. Cir. 1996).

NATIONAL ARCHIVES AND RECORDS ADMINISTRATION V. FAVISH

541 U.S. 157 (2004)

KENNEDY, J. This is case requires us to interpret the Freedom of Information Act (FOIA), 5 U.S.C. § 552. FOIA does not apply if the requested data fall within one or more exemptions. Exemption 7(C) excuses from disclosure "records or information compiled for law enforcement purposes" if their production "could reasonably be expected to constitute an unwarranted invasion of personal privacy." § 552(b)(7)(C).

In *Department of Justice v. Reporters Comm. for Freedom of Press,* 489 U.S. 749 (1989), we considered the scope of Exemption 7(C) and held that release of the document at issue would be a prohibited invasion of the personal privacy of the person to whom the document referred. The principal document involved was the criminal record, or rap sheet, of the person who himself objected to the disclosure. Here, the information pertains to an official investigation into the circumstances surrounding an apparent suicide. The initial question is whether the exemption extends to the decedent's family when the family objects to the release of photographs showing the condition of the body at the scene of death. If we find the decedent's family does have a personal privacy interest recognized by the statute, we must then consider whether that privacy claim is outweighed by the public interest in disclosure.

Vincent Foster, Jr., deputy counsel to President Clinton, was found dead in Fort Marcy Park, located just outside Washington, D.C. The United States Park Police conducted the initial investigation and took color photographs of the death scene, including 10 pictures of Foster's body. The investigation concluded that Foster committed suicide by shooting himself with a revolver. Subsequent investigations by the Federal Bureau of Investigation, committees of the Senate and the House of Representatives, and independent counsels Robert Fiske and Kenneth Starr reached the same conclusion. Despite the unanimous finding of these five investigations, a citizen interested in the matter, Allan Favish, remained skeptical. Favish is now a respondent in this proceeding. . . .

It is common ground among the parties that the death-scene photographs in [the Office of Independent Counsel's, or] OIC's possession are "records or information compiled for law enforcement purposes" as that phrase is used in Exemption 7(C). This leads to the question whether disclosure of the four photographs "could reasonably be expected to constitute an unwarranted invasion of personal privacy." Favish contends the family has no personal privacy interest covered by Exemption 7(C). . . .

We disagree. The right to personal privacy is not confined, as Favish argues, to the "right to control information about oneself.". . . To say that the concept of personal privacy must "encompass" the individual's control of information about himself does not mean it cannot encompass other personal privacy interests as well. *Reporters Committee* had no occasion to consider whether individuals whose personal data are not contained in the requested materials also have a recognized privacy interest under Exemption 7(C). *Reporters Committee* explained, however, that the concept of personal privacy under Exemption 7(C) is not some limited or "cramped notion" of that idea. 489 U.S. at 763. Records or information are not to be released under the Act if disclosure "could reasonably be expected to constitute an unwarranted invasion of personal privacy." 5 U.S.C. § 552(b)(7). This provision is in marked contrast to the language in Exemption 6, pertaining to "personnel and medical files," where withholding is required only if disclosure "would constitute a clearly unwarranted invasion of personal privacy." § 552(b)(6). The adverb "clearly," found in Exemption 6, is not used in Exemption 7(C). In addition, "whereas Exemption 6 refers to disclosures that 'would constitute' an invasion of privacy, Exemption 7(C) encompasses any disclosure that 'could reasonably be expected to constitute' such an invasion." *Reporters Committee,* 489 U.S., at 756. . . .

Law enforcement documents obtained by Government investigators often contain information about persons interviewed as witnesses or initial suspects but whose link to the official inquiry may be the result of mere happenstance. There is special reason, therefore, to give protection to this intimate personal data, to which the public does not have a general right of access in the ordinary course. In this class of cases where the subject of the documents "is a private citizen," "the privacy interest . . . is at its apex."

. . . Foster's relatives . . . invoke their own right and interest to personal privacy. They seek to be shielded by the exemption to secure their own refuge from a sensation-seeking culture for their own peace of mind and tranquility, not for the sake of the deceased. . . .

. . . We have little difficulty . . . in finding in our case law and traditions the right of family members to direct and control disposition of the body of the deceased and to limit attempts to exploit pictures of the deceased family member's remains for public purposes.

Burial rites or their counterparts have been respected in almost all civilizations from time immemorial. See generally 26 *Encyclopaedia Britannica* 851 (15th ed. 1985) (noting that "[t]he ritual burial of the dead" has been practiced "from the very dawn of human culture and . . . in most parts of the world"); 5 *Encyclopedia of Religion* 450 (1987) ("[F]uneral rites . . . are the conscious cultural forms of one of our most ancient, universal, and unconscious impulses"). They are a sign of the respect a society shows for the deceased and for the surviving family members. The power of Sophocles' story in Antigone maintains its hold to this day because of the universal acceptance of the heroine's right to insist on respect for the body of her brother. *See* Antigone of Sophocles, 8 *Harvard Classics: Nine Greek Dramas* 255 (C. Eliot ed. 1909). The outrage at seeing the bodies of American soldiers mutilated and dragged through the streets is but a modern instance of the same understanding of the interests decent people have for those whom they have lost. Family members have a personal stake in honoring and mourning their dead and objecting to unwarranted public exploitation that, by intruding upon their own grief, tends to degrade the rites and respect they seek to accord to the deceased person who was once their own.

In addition this well-established cultural tradition acknowledging a family's control over the body and death images of the deceased has long been recognized at common law. Indeed, this right to privacy has much deeper roots in the common law than the rap sheets held to be protected from disclosure in *Reporters Committee.* An early decision by the New York Court of Appeals is typical:

It is the right of privacy of the living which it is sought to enforce here. That right may in some cases be itself violated by improperly interfering with the character or memory of a deceased relative, but it is the right of the living, and not that of the dead, which is recognized. A privilege may be given the surviving relatives of a deceased person to protect his memory, but the privilege exists for the benefit of the living, to protect their feelings, and to prevent a violation of their own rights in the character and memory of the deceased. *Schuyler v. Curtis,* 147 N.Y. 434 (1895). . . .

We can assume Congress legislated against this background of law, scholarship, and history when it enacted FOIA and when it amended Exemption 7(C) to extend its terms. . . .

We have observed that the statutory privacy right protected by Exemption 7(C) goes beyond the common law and the Constitution. See *Reporters Committee,* 489 U.S., at 762, n.13 (contrasting the scope of the privacy protection under FOIA with the analogous protection under the common law and the Constitution). . . . It would be anomalous to hold in the instant case that the statute provides even less protection than does the common law.

The statutory scheme must be understood, moreover, in light of the consequences that would follow were we to adopt Favish's position. As a general rule, withholding information under FOIA cannot be predicated on the identity of the requester. See *Reporters Committee, supra,* at 771. We are advised by the Government that child molesters, rapists, murderers, and other violent criminals often make FOIA requests for autopsies, photographs, and records of their deceased victims. Our holding ensures that the privacy interests of surviving family members would allow the Government to deny these gruesome requests in appropriate cases. We find it inconceivable that Congress could have intended a definition of "personal privacy" so narrow that it would allow convicted felons to obtain these materials without limitations at the expense of surviving family members' personal privacy.

. . . [W]e hold that FOIA recognizes surviving family members' right to personal privacy with respect to their close relative's death-scene images. Our holding is consistent with the unanimous view of the Courts of Appeals and other lower courts that have addressed the question. . . .

Our ruling that the personal privacy protected by Exemption 7(C) extends to family members who object to the disclosure of graphic details surrounding their relative's death does not end the case. Although this privacy interest is within the terms of the exemption, the statute directs nondisclosure only where the information "could reasonably be expected to constitute an unwarranted invasion" of the family's personal privacy. The term "unwarranted" requires us to balance the family's privacy interest against the public interest in disclosure. . . .

FOIA is often explained as a means for citizens to know "what the Government is up to." This phrase should not be dismissed as a convenient formalism. It defines a structural necessity in a real democracy. The statement confirms that, as a general rule, when documents are within FOIA's disclosure provisions, citizens should not be required to explain why they seek the information. A person requesting the information needs no preconceived idea of the uses the data might serve. The information belongs to citizens to do with as they choose. Furthermore, as we have noted, the disclosure does not depend on the identity of the requester. As a general rule, if the information is subject to disclosure, it belongs to all.

When disclosure touches upon certain areas defined in the exemptions, however, the statute recognizes limitations that compete with the general interest in disclosure, and that, in appropriate cases, can overcome it. In the case of Exemption 7(C), the statute requires us to protect, in the proper degree, the personal privacy of citizens against the uncontrolled release of information compiled through the power of the state. The statutory direction that the information not be released if the invasion of personal privacy could reasonably be expected to be unwarranted requires the courts to balance the competing interests in privacy and disclosure. To effect this balance and to give practical meaning to the exemption, the usual rule that the citizen need not offer a reason for requesting the information must be inapplicable.

Where the privacy concerns addressed by Exemption 7(C) are present, the exemption requires the person requesting the information to establish a sufficient reason for the disclosure. First, the citizen must show that the public interest sought to be advanced is a significant one, an interest more specific than having the information for its own sake. Second, the citizen must show the information is likely to advance that interest. Otherwise, the invasion of privacy is unwarranted.

. . . In the case of photographic images and other data pertaining to an individual who died under mysterious circumstances, the justification most likely to satisfy Exemption 7(C)'s public interest requirement is that the information is necessary to show the investigative agency or other responsible officials acted negligently or otherwise improperly in the performance of their duties. . . .

We hold that, where there is a privacy interest protected by Exemption 7(C) and the public interest being asserted is to show that responsible officials acted negligently or otherwise improperly in the performance of their duties, the requester must establish more than a bare suspicion in order to obtain disclosure. Rather, the requester must produce evidence that would warrant a belief by a reasonable person that the alleged Government impropriety might have occurred. In *Department of State v. Ray,* 502 U.S. 164 (1991), we held there is a presumption of legitimacy accorded to the Government's official conduct. The presumption perhaps is less a rule of evidence than a general working principle. However the rule is characterized, where the presumption is applicable, clear evidence is usually required to displace it. . . . Given FOIA's prodisclosure purpose, however, the less stringent standard we adopt today is more faithful to the statutory scheme. Only when the FOIA requester has produced evidence sufficient to satisfy this standard will there exist a counterweight on the FOIA scale for the court to balance against the cognizable privacy interests in the requested records. . . . It would be quite extraordinary to say we must ignore the fact that five different inquiries into the Foster matter reached the same conclusion. . . . Favish has not produced any evidence that would warrant a belief by a reasonable person that the alleged Government impropriety might have occurred to put the balance into play. . . .

NOTES & QUESTIONS

1. *Coffins of U.S. Soldiers.* In 2004, Russ Kick obtained 361 photos on a CD-ROM of the coffins of U.S. soldiers who had been killed in combat in Iraq. The photos depicted coffins that were closed and draped with U.S. flags. The Air Force released the photos pursuant to a FOIA-request by Kick for "photographs showing caskets (or other devices) containing the remains of US military personnel at Dover [Air Force Base]."[9] Kick had selected Dover Air Force Base because "they process the remains of most, if not all, US military personnel killed overseas." The Air Force initially denied Kick's request; when he appealed the decision, it reversed and released the photos. The photos of the coffins contain no name tags or any other information that might identify the deceased soldier.

   The Bush Administration criticized the release of the photos. According to a Bush spokesperson: "[T]he sensitivity and privacy of families of the fallen must be the first priority."[10] Is there a privacy interest in the photos? Some are skeptical of efforts to keep the photos secret because of privacy concerns; they contend that the real reason is to deprive the public of images that vividly depict the number of fallen soldiers. Based on FOIA, would the photos be exempt under one of the privacy exemptions?

2. *The Implications of Post-Mortem Privacy.* Apart from the narrow context of FOIA, how will post-mortem privacy interests function in other areas of law? Are there other privacy interests that should or should not exist after one's death?

3. *National Security and Critical Infrastructure Information.* Post 9/11, the federal government has taken a new restrictive approach to FOIA. First, as part of the Homeland Security Act, the Bush Administration oversaw enactment of a new exemption to FOIA in the Critical Infrastructure Information Act of 2002 (CIIA). The CIIA exempts from FOIA disclosure any information that a private party voluntarily provides to the Department of Homeland Security (DHS) if the information relates to the security of vital infrastructure.

   "Critical infrastructure information" is "information not customarily in the public domain and related to the security of critical infrastructure or protected [computer] systems." 6 U.S.C. § 131. In a report prepared for Rep. Henry A. Waxman (Waxman Report), the Minority Staff, Special Investigation Division, Committee on Government Reform, stated:

   > Communications from the private sector to government agencies are routinely released under FOIA (apart from confidential business information). This is an important check against capture of governmental agencies by special interests.

---

[9] The Memory Hole, *Photos of Military Coffins*, at http://www.thememoryhole.com/war/coffin_photos/dover/.

[10] Associated Press, *White House: Military Should Respect Family Privacy on Photos of Coffins*, USA Today, Apr. 23, 2004.

But under the critical infrastructure information exemption even routine communications can be withheld from disclosure.[11]

In an op-ed in the *Washington Post*, Mark Tapscott of the Heritage Foundation asked for clarification of "what constitutes vulnerabilities" of infrastructure in order to prevent the CIIA from being "manipulated by clever corporate and government operators to hide endless varieties of potentially embarrassing and/or criminal information from public view."

The Waxman Report also noted that CIIA exempts from FOIA all information that is marked critical infrastructure information. As a consequence, the CIIA may not permit the redaction that is otherwise normally carried out under FOIA. As the Report states, "None of the information in a submission marked as critical infrastructure information is likely to be disclosed, even when portions of the information do not themselves constitute critical infrastructure information."[12]

Second, beyond the enactment of CIIA, a further move toward a restrictive approach to FOIA was made through the Executive Branch's introduction of the concept of "sensitive but unclassified information." On March 19, 2002, Andrew Card, White House Chief of Staff, issued an important memorandum that instructs federal agencies to deny disclosure of "sensitive but unclassified information."[13] The Card Memorandum urged agencies to safeguard records regarding weapons of mass destruction and "other information that could be misused to harm the security of our Nation and the safety of our people." The Card Memorandum urged agencies to apply FOIA's Exemption 2 or Exemption 4 in withholding such records. Please reread these exemptions reprinted earlier in this section. How do you think they are being extended to apply to "sensitive but unclassified information"?

Consider the following argument by Mary-Rose Papandrea:

> FOIA is riddled with large, undefined exceptions. When information arguably involves national security, courts are too timid to force the executive branch to provide a thorough explanation for continued secrecy. . . .
>
> The "right to know" has encountered additional and more disturbing problems since the terrorist attacks of September 11. Not only has the courts' tendency to defer to the Executive's national security risk assessment become exaggerated, but courts now appear overtly hostile to the very existence of a right of access during a time of crisis. Instead, they suggest that an enforceable right to know is unnecessary because the political process is adequate to force government disclosure.[14]

How should open government be reconciled with national security concerns?

---

[11] U.S. House of Representatives, *Committee on Government Reform, Minority Staff, Special Investigations Division, Secrecy in the Bush Administration* 9 (Sept. 14, 2004).

[12] *Id.* at 10.

[13] Andrew H. Card, Jr., Assistant to the President and Chief of Staff, *Memorandum for the Heads of Executive Departments and Agencies; Subject: Action to Safeguard Information Regarding Weapons of Mass Destruction and Other Sensitive Documents Relating to Homeland Security* (Mar. 19, 2002), at http://www.usdoj.gov/oip/foiapost/2002foiapost10.htm.

[14] Mary-Rose Papandrea, *Under Attack: The Public's Right to Know and the War on Terror*, 25 B.C. Third World L.J. 35, 79-80 (2005).

3. CONSTITUTIONAL REQUIREMENTS OF PUBLIC ACCESS

The Common Law Right to Access Public Records. As the Supreme Court held in *Nixon v. Warner Communications, Inc.,* 435 U.S. 589 (1978): "It is clear that the courts of this country recognize a general right to inspect and copy public records and documents, including judicial records and documents." The right to access public records is justified by "the citizen's desire to keep a watchful eye on the workings of public agencies, and in a newspaper publisher's intention to publish information concerning the operation of government." Thus, under the common law, the Court concluded, there is a general right to access public records and court records. The Court noted that the right to access is not absolute.

Court Records. Courts have a long tradition of allowing open access to court records. In *Nixon v. Warner Communications, Inc.,* 435 U.S. 589 (1978), the Supreme Court stated: "Every court has supervisory power over its own records and files, and access has been denied where court files might have become a vehicle for improper purposes." Access to court records is "best left to the sound discretion of the trial court, a discretion to be exercised in light of the relevant facts and circumstances of the particular case." In *Seattle Times Co. v. Rhinehart,* 467 U.S. 20, 33 (1984), the Court held that "pretrial depositions and interrogatories are not public components of a civil trial. Such proceedings were not open to the public at common law, and, in general, they are conducted in private as a matter of modern practice."

The First Amendment Right to Access. The First Amendment requires that certain judicial proceedings be open to the public. In *Globe Newspaper v. Superior Court,* 457 U.S. 596 (1982), the Supreme Court articulated a test to determine whether the First Amendment requires public access to a proceeding: (1) whether the proceeding "historically has been open to the press and general public" and (2) whether access "plays a particularly significant role in the functioning of the judicial process and the government as a whole." The court in *Globe* concluded that the First Amendment requires public access to criminal trials, and the government can deny access only if "the denial is necessitated by a compelling governmental interest and is narrowly tailored to serve that interest." According to the Court, the First Amendment right to access extends to voir dire in a capital murder trial. *Press-Enterprise Co. v. Superior Court* ("*Press-Enterprise I*"), 464 U.S. 501 (1984). It also extends to pre-trial proceedings. *Press-Enterprise Co. v. Superior Court* ("*Press-Enterprise II*"), 478 U.S. 1 (1986).

Privacy of Litigants and Jurors. A court can permit plaintiffs to proceed under a pseudonym, although "it is the exceptional case in which a plaintiff may proceed under a fictitious name." *Doe v. Frank,* 951 F.2d 320, 323 (11th Cir. 1992). Courts can also provide for jurors to remain anonymous. Is such anonymity appropriate?

Consider the case of Juror Number Four. In a well-publicized criminal trial against Tyco International executive L. Dennis Kozlowski, during the jury's 12 days of deliberating, newspapers identified Juror Number Four by name because she appeared to gesture an "O.K." sign to the defense table. The articles stated that she lived on the Upper East Side of Manhattan and that the apartment building staff found her to be cold and stingy. The newspapers reported that friends described her as opinionated and stubborn. Extensive coverage of the juror continued. As a result of the coverage, the juror received a threatening note, and the judge declared a mistrial. On the one hand, the media was reporting on possible juror misconduct. On the other hand, the media coverage interfered with the trial. Suppose on retrial, the judge were to order that the identities of all the jurors shall not be disclosed. Would such an order be constitutional?

In some jurisdictions, the court records of divorce cases are made public. Is such a policy advisable? This issue is best illustrated by what happened in June 2004, when at the request of the *Chicago Tribune* and a TV station, a judge ordered the unsealing of the divorce records of Illinois Republican Senate candidate Jack Ryan and his wife, actress Jeri Ryan. Both Jack and Jeri had vigorously objected to the unsealing of the records, which they contended would cause harm to them as well as their nine-year-old child. The records revealed Jeri's accusations that Jack had taken her to sex clubs and asked her to perform sex acts that made her uncomfortable. A few days after the release of the records, Jack abandoned his quest for the Senate. Was the release of the records appropriate in this case? Jack was a political candidate, and Jeri was a well-known actress. Does their public figure status affect the analysis? Should it? To what extent should the effect of the release of the information on a couple's children be a factor in the analysis?

LOS ANGELES POLICE DEPARTMENT V. UNITED REPORTING PUBLISHING CORP.

528 U.S. 32 (1999)

REHNQUIST, C.J. California Government Code § 6254(f)(3) places two conditions on public access to arrestees' addresses — that the person requesting an address declare that the request is being made for one of five prescribed purposes, and that the requestor also declare that the address will not be used directly or indirectly to sell a product or service.

The District Court permanently enjoined enforcement of the statute, and the Court of Appeals affirmed, holding that the statute was facially invalid because it unduly burdens commercial speech. We hold that the statutory section in question was not subject to a "facial" challenge.

Petitioner, the Los Angeles Police Department, maintains records relating to arrestees. Respondent, United Reporting Publishing Corporation, is a private publishing service that provides the names and addresses of recently arrested individuals to its customers, who include attorneys, insurance companies, drug and alcohol counselors, and driving schools.

Before July 1, 1996, respondent received arrestees' names and addresses under the old version of § 6254, which generally required state and local law enforcement agencies to make public the name, address, and occupation of every individual arrested by the agency. Cal. Govt. Code § 6254(f). Effective July 1, 1996, the state legislature amended § 6254(f) to limit the public's access to arrestees' and victims' current addresses. The amended statute provides that state and local law enforcement agencies shall make public:

> [T]he current address of every individual arrested by the agency and the current address of the victim of a crime, where the requester declares under penalty of perjury that the request is made for a scholarly, journalistic, political, or governmental purpose, or that the request is made for investigation purposes by a licensed private investigator . . . except that the address of the victim of [certain crimes] shall remain confidential. Address information obtained pursuant to this paragraph shall not be used directly or indirectly to sell a product or service to any individual or group of individuals, and the requester shall execute a declaration to that effect under penalty of perjury. Cal. Govt. Code § 6254(f)(3).

Sections 6254(f)(1) and (2) require that state and local law enforcement agencies make public, inter alia, the name, occupation, and physical description, including date of birth, of every individual arrested by the agency, as well as the circumstances of the arrest. Thus, amended § 6254(f) limits access only to the arrestees' addresses.

Before the effective date of the amendment, respondent sought declaratory and injunctive relief pursuant to 42 U.S.C. § 1983 to hold the amendment unconstitutional under the First and Fourteenth Amendments to the United States Constitution. On the effective date of the statute, petitioner and other law enforcement agencies denied respondent access to the address information because, according to respondent, "[respondent's] employees could not sign section 6254(f)(3) declarations." Respondent did not allege, and nothing in the record before this Court indicates, that it ever "declar[ed] under penalty of perjury" that it was requesting information for one of the prescribed purposes and that it would not use the address information to "directly or indirectly . . . sell a product or service," as would have been required by the statute. *See* § 6254(f)(3).

Respondent then amended its complaint and sought a temporary restraining order. The District Court issued a temporary restraining order, and, a few days later, issued a preliminary injunction. Respondent then filed a motion for summary judgment, which was granted. In granting the motion, the District Court construed respondent's claim as presenting a facial challenge to amended § 6254(f). The court held that the statute was facially invalid under the First Amendment.

The Court of Appeals affirmed the District Court's facial invalidation. The court concluded that the statute restricted commercial speech, and, as such, was entitled to "'a limited measure of protection, commensurate with its subordinate position in the scale of First Amendment values.'" The court applied the test set out in *Central Hudson Gas & Elec. Corp. v. Public Serv. Comm'n of N.Y.*, 447 U.S. 557 (1980), and found that the asserted governmental interest in protecting arrestees' privacy was substantial. But, the court held that "the numerous exceptions to § 6254(f)(3) for journalistic, scholarly, political, governmental, and investigative purposes render the statute unconstitutional under the First Amendment." The court noted that "[h]aving one's name, crime, and address printed in the local paper is a far greater affront to privacy than receiving a letter from an attorney, substance abuse counselor, or driving school eager to help one overcome his present difficulties (for a fee, naturally)," and thus that the exceptions "undermine and counteract" the asserted governmental interest in preserving arrestees' privacy. Thus, the Court of Appeals affirmed the District Court's grant of summary judgment in favor of respondent and upheld the injunction against enforcement of § 6254(f)(3). We granted certiorari.

We hold that respondent was not, under our cases, entitled to prevail on a "facial attack" on § 6254(f)(3).

Respondent's primary argument in the District Court and the Court of Appeals was that § 6254(f)(3) was invalid on its face, and respondent maintains that position here. But we believe that our cases hold otherwise.

The traditional rule is that "a person to whom a statute may constitutionally be applied may not challenge that statute on the ground that it may conceivably be applied unconstitutionally to others in situations not before the Court."

Prototypical exceptions to this traditional rule are First Amendment challenges to statutes based on First Amendment overbreadth. "At least when statutes regulate or proscribe speech . . . the transcendent value to all society of constitutionally protected expression is deemed to justify allowing 'attacks on overly broad statutes with no requirement that the person making the attack demonstrate that his own conduct could not be regulated by a statute drawn with the requisite narrow specificity.'" "This is deemed necessary because persons whose expression is constitutionally protected may well refrain from exercising their right for fear of criminal sanctions provided by a statute susceptible of application to protected expression." . . .

Even though the challenge be based on the First Amendment, the overbreadth doctrine is not casually employed. "Because of the wide-reaching effects of striking down a statute on its face at the request of one whose own conduct may be punished despite the First Amendment, we have recognized that the overbreadth doctrine is 'strong medicine' and have employed it with hesitation, and then 'only as a last resort.'" . . .

The Court of Appeals held that § 6254(f)(3) was facially invalid under the First Amendment. Petitioner contends that the section in question is not an abridgment of anyone's right to engage in speech, be it commercial or otherwise, but simply a law regulating access to information in the hands of the police department.

We believe that, at least for purposes of facial invalidation, petitioner's view is correct. This is not a case in which the government is prohibiting a speaker from conveying information that the speaker already possesses. The California statute in question merely requires that if respondent wishes to obtain the addresses of arrestees it must qualify under the statute to do so. Respondent did not attempt to qualify and was therefore denied access to the addresses. For purposes of assessing the propriety of a facial invalidation, what we have before us is nothing more than a governmental denial of access to information in its possession. California could decide not to give out arrestee information at all without violating the First Amendment.

To the extent that respondent's "facial challenge" seeks to rely on the effect of the statute on parties not before the Court — its potential customers, for example — its claim does not fit within the case law allowing courts to entertain facial challenges. No threat of prosecution, for example, or cutoff of funds hangs over their heads. They may seek access under the statute on their own just as respondent did, without incurring any burden other than the prospect that their request will be denied. Resort to a facial challenge here is not warranted because there is "no possibility that protected speech will be muted." . . .

GINSBURG, J. joined by O'CONNOR, SOUTER, and BREYER, J.J. concurring. I join the Court's opinion, which recognizes that California Government Code § 6254(f)(3) is properly analyzed as a restriction on access to government information, not as a restriction on protected speech. That is sufficient reason to reverse the Ninth Circuit's judgment.

As the Court observes, the statute at issue does not restrict speakers from conveying information they already possess. Anyone who comes upon arrestee address information in the public domain is free to use that information as she sees fit. It is true, as Justice Scalia suggests, that the information could be provided to and published by journalists, and § 6254(f)(3) would indeed be a speech restriction if it then prohibited people from using that published information to speak to or about arrestees. But the statute contains no such prohibition. Once address information is in the public domain, the statute does not restrict its use in any way.

California could, as the Court notes, constitutionally decide not to give out arrestee address information at all. It does not appear that the selective disclosure of address information that California has chosen instead impermissibly burdens speech. To be sure, the provision of address information is a kind of subsidy to people who wish to speak to or about arrestees, and once a State decides to make such a benefit available to the public, there are no doubt limits to its freedom to decide how that benefit will be distributed. California could not, for example, release address information only to those whose political views were in line with the party in power. But if the award of the subsidy is not based on an illegitimate criterion such as viewpoint, California is free to support some speech without supporting other speech.

Throughout its argument, respondent assumes that § 6254(f)(3)'s regime of selective disclosure burdens speech in the sense of reducing the total flow of information. Whether that is correct is far from clear and depends on the point of comparison. If California were to publish the names and addresses of arrestees for everyone to use freely, it would indeed be easier to speak to and about arrestees than it is under the present system. But if States were required to choose between keeping proprietary information to themselves and making it available without limits, States might well choose the former option. In that event, disallowing selective disclosure would lead not to more speech overall but to more secrecy and less speech. As noted above, this consideration could not justify limited disclosures that discriminated on the basis of viewpoint or some other proscribed criterion. But it does suggest that society's interest in the free flow of information might argue for upholding laws like the one at issue in this case rather than imposing an all-or-nothing regime under which "nothing" could be a State's easiest response.

STEVENS, J. joined by KENNEDY, J. dissenting. . . . To determine whether the Amendment is valid as applied to respondent, it is similarly not necessary to invoke the overbreadth doctrine. That doctrine is only relevant if the challenger needs to rely on the possibility of invalid applications to third parties. In this case, it is the application of the Amendment to respondent itself that is at issue. Nor, in my opinion, is it necessary to do the four-step *Central Hudson* dance, because I agree with the majority that the Amendment is really a restriction on access to government information rather than a direct restriction on protected speech. For this reason, the majority is surely correct in observing that "California could decide not to give out arrestee information at all without violating the First Amendment." Moreover, I think it equally clear that California could release the information on a selective basis to a limited group of users who have a special, and legitimate, need for the information.

A different, and more difficult, question is presented when the State makes information generally available, but denies access to a small disfavored class. In this case, the State is making the information available to scholars, news media, politicians, and others, while denying access to a narrow category of persons solely because they intend to use the information for a constitutionally protected purpose. As Justice Ginsburg points out, if the State identified the disfavored persons based on their viewpoint, or political affiliation, for example, the discrimination would clearly be invalid.

What the State did here, in my opinion, is comparable to that obviously unconstitutional discrimination. In this case, the denial of access is based on the fact that respondent plans to publish the information to others who, in turn, intend to use it for a commercial speech purpose that the State finds objectionable. Respondent's proposed publication of the information is indisputably lawful — petitioner concedes that if respondent independently acquires the data, the First Amendment protects its right to communicate it to others. Similarly, the First Amendment supports the third parties' use of it for commercial speech purposes. Thus, because the State's discrimination is based on its desire to prevent the information from being used for constitutionally protected purposes, I think it must assume the burden of justifying its conduct.

The only justification advanced by the State is an asserted interest in protecting the privacy of victims and arrestees. Although that interest would explain a total ban on access, or a statute narrowly limiting access, it is insufficient when the data can be published in the news media and obtained by private investigators or others who meet the Amendment's vague criteria. . . . By allowing such widespread access to the information, the State has eviscerated any rational basis for believing that the Amendment will truly protect the privacy of these persons.

That the State might simply withhold the information from all persons does not insulate its actions from constitutional scrutiny. For even though government may withhold a particular benefit entirely, it "may not deny a benefit to a person on a basis that infringes his constitutionally protected interests — especially his interest in freedom of speech." A contrary view would impermissibly allow the government to "'produce a result which [it] could not command directly.'" It is perfectly clear that California could not directly censor the use of this information or the resulting speech. It follows, I believe, that the State's discriminatory ban on access to information — in an attempt to prohibit persons from exercising their constitutional rights to publish it in a truthful and accurate manner — is equally invalid.

Accordingly, I respectfully dissent.

NOTES & QUESTIONS

1. *Reconciling Privacy and Transparency.* Consider the following argument by Daniel Solove:

> How can the tension between transparency and privacy be reconciled? Must access to public records be sacrificed at the altar of privacy? Or must privacy be compromised as the price for a government disinfected by sunlight?
>
> It is my thesis that both transparency and privacy can be balanced through limitations on the access and use of personal information in public records. . . . We can make information accessible for certain purposes only. When government discloses information, it can limit how it discloses that information by preventing it from being amassed by companies for commercial purposes, to be sold to others, or to be combined with other information and sold back to the government. . . .
>
> . . . [B]y making access conditional on accepting certain responsibilities when using data — such as using it for specific purposes, not disclosing it to others, and so on, certain functions of transparency can be preserved at the same time privacy is protected.[15]

However, does this approach, as Justice Stevens contends in his dissent, impermissibly single out certain types of speakers? What if the California statute limited disclosure of the information to anybody who would use a form of mass communication or widespread publicity to disclose that information? In other words, what if it excluded journalists and the media from access?

2. **Florida Star v. B.J.F.** In *Florida Star v. B.J.F.,* 491 U.S. 524 (1989), the Supreme Court struck down a Florida law that prohibited the press from publishing a rape victim's name that inadvertently appeared in a public record. The Court held: "[W]here a newspaper publishes truthful information which it has lawfully obtained, punishment may lawfully be imposed, if at all, only when narrowly tailored to a state interest of the highest order." Daniel Solove notes:

> Governments can make a public record available *on the condition that* certain information is not disclosed or used in a certain manner. However, governments cannot establish post-access restrictions on the disclosure or use of information that is publicly available. Once the information is made available to the public, the *Florida Star* cases prohibit a state from restricting use.[16]

Is *United Reporting* consistent with *Florida Star*? Suppose Florida passed a law that in order for the press to access its police reports about sexual assaults,

---

[15] Daniel J. Solove, *Access and Aggregation: Public Records, Privacy, and the Constitution,* 86 Minn. L. Rev. 1137 (2002).

[16] *Id.*

journalists would have to agree to not disclose rape victims' names from the reports. Would this law be constitutional?

4. CONSTITUTIONAL LIMITATIONS ON PUBLIC ACCESS

(a) Public Records

Like the federal FOIA, many states have privacy exemptions in their freedom of information laws. But not all states balance privacy and transparency equally. Are there limitations on what information governments can release to the public? Consider the cases below:

KALLSTROM V. CITY OF COLUMBUS [*KALLSTROM I*]

136 F.3d 1055 (6th Cir. 1998)

MOORE, J. . . . The three plaintiffs, Melissa Kallstrom, Thomas Coelho, and Gary Householder, are undercover officers employed by the Columbus Police Department. All three were actively involved in the drug conspiracy investigation of the Short North Posse, a violent gang in the Short North area of Columbus, Ohio. In *United States v. Derrick Russell, et al.,* No. CR-2 95-044, (S.D. Ohio), forty-one members of the Short North Posse were prosecuted on drug conspiracy charges. Plaintiffs testified at the trial of eight of the *Russell* defendants.

During the *Russell* criminal trial, defense counsel requested and obtained from the City Kallstrom's personnel and pre-employment file, which defense counsel appears to have passed on to several of the *Russell* defendants. Officers Coelho and Householder also suspect that copies of their personnel and pre-employment files were obtained by the same defense attorney. The City additionally released Officer Coelho's file to the Police Officers for Equal Rights organization following its request for the file in the fall of 1995 in order to investigate possible discriminatory hiring and promotion practices by the City. The officers' personnel files include the officers' addresses and phone numbers; the names, addresses, and phone numbers of immediate family members; the names and addresses of personal references; the officers' banking institutions and corresponding account information, including account balances; their social security numbers; responses to questions regarding their personal life asked during the course of polygraph examinations; and copies of their drivers' licenses, including pictures and home addresses. The district court found that in light of the Short North Posse's propensity for violence and intimidation, the release of these personnel files created a serious risk to the personal safety of the plaintiffs and those relatives named in the files.

Prior to accepting employment with the City, the plaintiffs were assured by the City that personal information contained in their files would be held in strict confidence. Despite its earlier promise of confidentiality, however, the City believed Ohio's Public Records Act, Ohio Rev. Code Ann. § 149.43, required it to release the officers' files upon request from any member of the public.

The officers brought suit under 42 U.S.C. §§ 1983 and 1988 against the City, claiming that the dissemination of personal information contained in their personnel files violates their right to privacy as guaranteed by the Due Process Clause of the Fourteenth Amendment. . . . In addition to seeking compensatory damages, the officers request an injunction restraining the City from releasing personal information regarding them. . . .

Section 1983 imposes civil liability on a person acting under color of state law who deprives another of the "rights, privileges, or immunities secured by the Constitution and laws." 42 U.S.C. § 1983. The threshold question, therefore, is whether the City deprived the officers of a right "secured by the Constitution and laws." . . .

In *Whalen v. Roe,* the Supreme Court declared that the constitutional right to privacy grounded in the Fourteenth Amendment respects not only individual autonomy in intimate matters, but also the individual's interest in avoiding divulgence of highly personal information. The court echoed these sentiments in *Nixon v. Administrator of Gen. Servs.,* 433 U.S. 425 (1977), acknowledging that "[o]ne element of privacy has been characterized as 'the individual interest in avoiding disclosure of personal matters.'" Although *Whalen* and *Nixon* appear to recognize constitutional protection for an individual's interest in safeguarding personal matters from public view, in both cases the Court found that public interests outweighed the individuals' privacy interests.

This circuit has read *Whalen* and *Nixon* narrowly, and will only balance an individual's interest in nondisclosure of informational privacy against the public's interest in and need for the invasion of privacy where the individual privacy interest is of constitutional dimension. . . . We hold that the officers' privacy interests do indeed implicate a fundamental liberty interest, specifically their interest in preserving their lives and the lives of their family members, as well as preserving their personal security and bodily integrity. . . .

In light of the Short North Posse's propensity for violence and intimidation, the district court found that the City's release of the plaintiffs-appellants' addresses, phone numbers, and driver's licenses to defense counsel in the *Russell* case, as well as their family members' names, addresses, and phone numbers, created a serious risk to the personal safety of the plaintiffs and those relatives named in the files. We see no reason to doubt that where disclosure of this personal information may fall into the hands of persons likely to seek revenge upon the officers for their involvement in the *Russell* case, the City created a very real threat to the officers' and their family members' personal security and bodily integrity, and possibly their lives. Accordingly, we hold that the City's disclosure of this private information about the officers to defense counsel in the *Russell* case rises to constitutional dimensions, thereby requiring us . . . to balance the officers' interests against those of the City.

The district court found that although there was no indication that the Police Officers for Equal Rights organization posed any threat to the officers and their family members, disclosure even to that group of the officers' phone numbers, addresses, and driver's licenses, and their family members' names, addresses and phone numbers "increases the risk that the information will fall into the wrong hands." . . . Since the district court did not indicate its view of the severity of risks inherent in disclosure of information to the Police Officers for Equal Rights organization, we remand to the district court for reconsideration in light of this opinion of issues regarding disclosure of personal information to that organization.

In finding that the City's release of private information concerning the officers to defense counsel in the *Russell* case rises to constitutional dimensions by threatening the personal security and bodily integrity of the officers and their family members, we do not mean to imply that every governmental act which intrudes upon or threatens to intrude upon an individual's body invokes the Fourteenth Amendment. But where the release of private information places an individual at substantial risk of serious bodily harm, possibly even death, from a perceived likely threat, the "magnitude of the liberty deprivation . . . strips the very essence of personhood." . . .

Where state action infringes upon a fundamental right, such action will be upheld under the substantive due process component of the Fourteenth Amendment only where the governmental action furthers a compelling state interest, and is narrowly drawn to further that state interest. Having found that the officers have a fundamental constitutional interest in preventing the release of personal information contained in their personnel files where such disclosure creates a substantial risk of serious bodily harm, we must now turn to whether the City's actions narrowly serve a compelling public purpose.

The City believed Ohio's Public Records Act, Ohio Rev. Code Ann. § 149.43, required it to disclose the personal information contained in the officers' records. Ohio's Public Records Act requires the state to make available all public records to any person, unless the record falls within one of the statute's enumerated exceptions. The State mandates release of state agency records in order to shed light on the state government's performance, thereby enabling Ohio citizens to understand better the operations of their government. In the judicial setting, courts have long recognized the importance of permitting public access to judicial records so that citizens may understand and exercise oversight over the judicial system. We see no reason why public access to government agency records should be considered any less important. For purposes of this case, we assume that the interests served by allowing public access to agency records rises to the level of a compelling state interest. Nevertheless, the City's release to the criminal defense counsel of the officers' and their family members' home addresses and phone numbers, as well as the family members' names and the officers' driver's licenses, does not narrowly serve these interests.

While there may be situations in which the release of the this type of personal information might further the public's understanding of the workings of its law enforcement agencies, the facts as presented here do not support such a conclusion. The City released the information at issue to defense counsel in a large drug conspiracy case, who is asserted to have passed the information onto his clients. We simply fail to see how placing this personal information into the hands of the *Russell* defendants in any way increases public understanding of the City's law enforcement agency where the *Russell* defendants and their attorney make no claim that they sought this personal information about the officers in order to shed light on the internal workings of the Columbus Police Department. We therefore cannot conclude that the disclosure narrowly serves the state's interest in ensuring accountable governance. Accordingly, we hold that the City's actions in automatically disclosing this information to any member of the public requesting it are not narrowly tailored to serve this important public interest. . . .

Injunctive relief involving matters subject to state regulation may be no broader than necessary to remedy the constitutional violation. . . . [T]he constitutional violation arises when the release of private information about the officers places their personal security, and that of their families, at substantial risk without narrowly serving a compelling state interest. Thus, the officers are entitled to notice and an opportunity to be heard prior to the release of private information contained in their personnel files only where the disclosure of the requested information could potentially threaten the officers' and their families' personal security. As discussed above, release of the officers' addresses, phone numbers, and driver's licenses, as well as their family members' names, addresses, and phone numbers, is likely to result in a substantial risk to their personal security. On remand, the district court should consider whether release of other private information contained in the officers' personnel files also poses the same risk. . . . [B]ecause the City's decision to continue releasing this information potentially places the officers and their families at risk of irreparable harm that cannot be adequately remedied at law, the officers are entitled to injunctive relief prohibiting the City from again disclosing this information without first providing the officers meaningful notice.

KALLSTROM V. CITY OF COLUMBUS [*KALLSTROM II*]

165 F. Supp. 2d 686 (S.D. Ohio 2001)

SMITH, J. In this case, the Court is being asked to limit the freedom of the press by preventing the news media from obtaining public information contained in the city's personnel files. City police officers fear its publication may endanger themselves and their families.

To deny members of the press access to public information solely because they have the ability to disseminate it would silence the most important critics of governmental activity. This not only violates the Constitution, but eliminates the very protections the Founders envisioned a free press would provide.

Plaintiffs, who are three Columbus police officers ("Officers"), filed suit against defendant City of Columbus ("City") seeking compensatory damages under 42 U.S.C. §§ 1983 and 1988 and an injunction to prevent further dissemination of their personal information. Specifically, plaintiffs claim defendant violated their rights to privacy as guaranteed by the Due Process Clause of the Fourteenth Amendment by making their personnel records available to a criminal defense attorney pursuant to the Ohio Public Records Act, Ohio Rev. Code § 149.43. In October 1998, intervenors, a group of ten Ohio news organizations, joined the lawsuit without opposition after the City, citing the Sixth Circuit decision in this case, denied their request to see plaintiffs' personnel files. . . .

Using the Sixth Circuit's framework, the Court finds the Fourteenth Amendment does not prevent the City from allowing intervenors to inspect or copy the requested information from plaintiffs' personnel files. . . .

Intervenors have requested the home addresses of each plaintiff; summaries of investigations of plaintiffs' backgrounds; memos and reports of any assaults in which the plaintiffs were either perpetrators or victims; memos and reports related to any motor vehicle accidents in which City vehicles operated by plaintiffs were damaged or caused property damage or personal injury to others; memos and notices related to any disciplinary charges; and, answers to personal history questions. The request specifically excludes information identifying the Officers' banking institutions and financial account numbers; personal credit card numbers; social security numbers; information about any psychological conditions the Officers may have; responses to polygraph examinations; and, "medical records" or any other recorded information exempt from mandatory disclosure under Ohio Revised Code § 149.43. Further, intervenors do not object to the City redacting the names of any minor dependents of plaintiffs unless the dependent is employed by the City, any information made confidential by the Americans with Disabilities Act, 42 U.S.C. § 12101 et seq., or records which the Ohio Public Records Act would not require the City to disclose.

The Court finds plaintiffs do not have a constitutional privacy interest in the information requested by intervenors. Under the Sixth Circuit standard, plaintiffs must show that the release of information they wish to keep private would place them "at substantial risk of serious bodily harm, possibly even death, from a perceived likely threat." *Kallstrom,* 136 F.3d at 1064. The Court could fathom information contained in plaintiffs' personnel files that satisfies this stringent constitutional standard. Yet, that is not the Court's responsibility. The Sixth Circuit requires this Court to look at a "clear development of the factual circumstances" surrounding any future release of personal information from the Officers' personnel files. Plaintiffs have failed to provide any potentially admissible evidence to suggest that the release of any information contained in the three personnel files may place any of the plaintiffs at any risk of serious bodily harm. Nor have they identified a current "perceived likely threat."[17] This is fatal to their claims. By not identifying any real potential danger that could arise from the release of information in their personnel files, plaintiffs have failed to make a showing sufficient to establish the existence of an element essential to their case for which they carry the burden.

Further, the majority of intervenors' request focuses on each plaintiff's disciplinary records, incident complaints from citizens, and other documents detailing how each officer is performing his or her job. Although plaintiffs may wish maintain the confidentiality of their employment histories, the Constitution does not provide a shield against disclosure of potentially embarrassing or even improper activities by public servants.

Finally, plaintiffs' interests in their home addresses also fail to meet the stringent constitutional standard set by the Sixth Circuit. Addresses are part of the public domain. Anyone with an individual's name and either Internet access or the initiative to visit a local government office can scan county property

---

[17] The Court sympathizes with plaintiffs' initial fears of retaliation from the Short North Posse. . . . [H]owever, plaintiffs have not developed clear and factual circumstances, outside of mere speculation, that this threat still exists. The only evidence in the record suggests, fortunately, the threat never developed.

records, court records, or voter registration records for such information as an individual's address, the exact location of his or her residence, and even a floor plan of the home. The Supreme Court has found that "[t]he interests in privacy fade when the information involved already appears on the public record." *Cox Broad. Corp. v. Cohn,* 420 U.S. 469 (1975). In this case, plaintiffs have voluntarily revealed their own identities. For instance, plaintiffs initiated this lawsuit in their own names and describe their profession in the pleadings as "undercover narcotics officers." Plaintiffs also chose to testify without a pseudonym in the Posse trial. As plaintiffs have revealed their identities, their addresses are easily accessible in the public domain.

Even assuming plaintiffs have a constitutional interest in the information contained in their personnel files, the balancing test described by the Sixth Circuit still weighs in favor of disclosure. Where a state action infringes upon a fundamental right, the action will be upheld only where it furthers a compelling state interest and is narrowly drawn to further that state interest. In *Kallstrom,* the Sixth Circuit assumed that the state interests served by allowing public access to agency records were compelling, but held that the City's release of plaintiffs' personnel files to counsel for a criminal defendant did not narrowly achieve these interests.

Ohio's Public Records Act requires the state to make available all public records to any person unless the record falls within one of the statute's exceptions. Ohio Rev. Code § 149.43(B). The state has an interest in releasing its governmental agency records to "ensure accountability of government to those being governed." *See State ex rel. Strothers v. Wertheim,* 80 Ohio St.3d 155 (1997). In *Kallstrom,* the Sixth Circuit acknowledged "there may be situations in which the release of this type of personal information might further the public's understanding of the workings of its law enforcement agencies." *Kallstrom,* 136 F.3d at 1065. This is one of those situations. The information intervenors request details the functioning of the City's police force. The personnel files reveal, among other things, the character and background of the City's police officers, whether the officers are using City property responsibly, and whether the City is enforcing the residency requirement for City employees as required by the City's charter. The state has a compelling interest in releasing this type of information to enlighten the public about the performance of its law enforcement agencies and ensure government accountability. The importance of public access to these files as a restraint on government activity is evident from cases such as the U.S. Justice Department's civil rights action against the City concerning police practices, which is currently pending in this courthouse.

Further, the City's disclosure of public records, including police officer personnel files, is narrowly tailored to achieve this compelling state interest. In *Kallstrom,* the Sixth Circuit failed "to see how placing [the Officers'] personal information into the hands of the *Russell* defendants in any way increases public understanding of the City's law enforcement agency." The press, however, is a different entity. . . .

The full disclosure of these personnel files is necessary to enable the press to do its job. As nothing less than full disclosure will ensure transparency in government, the Court finds full disclosure is narrowly tailored to meet the state's compelling interest. . . .

The intervenors seek a second declaration that the City is violating the First Amendment by denying the news organizations a state law right because they might publish accurate reports of the contents of public records. The Court agrees and grants summary judgment for intervenors on their second ground for declaratory judgment. . . .

Neither the First Amendment nor the Fourteenth Amendment mandates a right of access to government information or sources of information within the government's control. . . . In this case, the doors have been opened by the Ohio Public Records Act. Thus, the issue becomes whether the City can deny intervenors their state law right to these public records because, as members of the news media, they have the ability to disseminate the information contained in plaintiffs' personnel files.

The Supreme Court has held that the government may not single out the press to bear special burdens without violating the First Amendment. *Minneapolis Star & Tribune Co. v. Minnesota Comm'r of Revenue,* 460 U.S. 575 (1983). In *Minneapolis Star,* the Supreme Court found that Minnesota's use tax on paper and ink violated the First Amendment for "singling out the press for taxation" that did not apply to other enterprises. Courts, however, have not been hesitant to extend this rationale beyond taxation. *See, e.g., Legi-Tech, Inc. v. Keiper,* 766 F.2d 728 (2d Cir. 1985) (suggesting denial of press access to a public legislative database would face "hostile scrutiny" as singling out the press for a special burden). . . .

Due to these important considerations, a state-imposed burden on the press is always "subject to at least some degree of heightened First Amendment scrutiny." When the government specially burdens the press, "the appropriate method of analysis thus is to balance the burden implicit in singling out the press against the interest asserted by the State." The burden "can survive only if the governmental interest outweighs the burden and cannot be achieved by means that do not infringe First Amendment rights as significantly."

In its pleadings, the City states its interest as preventing members of the press from accessing plaintiffs' personnel records because news organizations have the ability to disseminate the information to "wide and diverse audiences, including the Short North Posse." Since the second part of the *Minneapolis Star* test is dispositive, the Court finds it unnecessary to balance the City's interest with the burden implicit in singling out the press. The Court concludes the City's decision to single out the press for disparate treatment does not satisfactorily accomplish its stated purpose.

Treating the press differently will not prevent the harm the City is seeking to avoid. The City's denial of the intervenors' public records request because of their ability to disseminate information suggests that the same records would have been provided to anyone who did not have this capability. Any member of the public would have access to these records — including Short North Posse members, their friends, and their families. Silencing the press makes no difference as to whether these people have access to plaintiffs' personal information.

Further, this distinction does not prevent the press from gaining access to the materials. The news organizations could have a surrogate request the records and provide copies to the press. Even a reporter for one of the intervenors could request the records as a citizen, without revealing his or her professional affiliation, and use plaintiffs' personal information in the same manner as if the news organization had requested the records as an entity. Allowing the City to impose these arbitrary burdens threatens to eviscerate the ability of the press to serve as a restraint on government activity, poses inherent dangers to free expression, and presents great potential for censorship or manipulation. . . .

In choosing to deny intervenors' request based on their ability to disseminate the information, however, the City placed a burden on the press that would not have attached to any other request for those public records. The City's arbitrary treatment of the press is not only thoroughly ineffective at achieving its objective, but also highly offensive to the First Amendment. . . .

NOTES & QUESTIONS

1. *How Broad Is the* **Kallstrom II** *Decision?* In his reading of *Kallstrom I*, Paul Schwartz argues that the case showed that "[o]nly the threat of life-threatening harm to officers and their families and the City of Columbus' plan for automatic disclosure of this information" allowed an interest in nondisclosure to triumph.[18] Schwartz also notes that the Sixth Circuit granted merely a limited injunction to the undercover officers that allowed them a chance to object when someone requested their personal data. In this fashion, the *Kallstrom II* court left the door open for release of this information under other circumstances. What is left of the Sixth Circuit's opinion after *Kallstrom II*? Under what basis did the district court in *Kallstrom II* decide that the information should be released to the press?

   In *Barber v. Overton*, 496 F.3d 449 (6th Cir. 2007), the Sixth Circuit revisited the *Kallstrom I* and found that this decision was not implicated by a (mistaken) release of Social Security numbers and birth dates of prison officers to prisoners: "*Kallstrom* created a narrowly tailored right, limited to circumstances where the information was particularly sensitive and the persons to whom it was disclosed were particularly dangerous *vis-à-vis the plaintiffs*" (emphasis in original). In sum, the *Barber* court stated that the release of the information "was not sensitive enough nor the threat of retaliation apparent enough to warrant constitution protection here."

2. *Statutory vs. Constitutional Privacy Exemptions.* Contrast the operation of statutory privacy exemptions to FOIA and exceptions based on the constitutional right to information privacy, as in *Kallstrom I*. How does the presence of the Ohio Public Records Act affect the analysis in *Kallstrom II*?

3. *The Scope of Privacy Exemptions.* In *Moak v. Philadelphia Newspapers, Inc.*, 336 A.2d 920 (Pa. 1975), the court held that the employee records of a police department, which contained the name, gender, date of birth, salary, and other personal information about the employees, did not fall within the privacy exemption to Pennsylvania's Right to Know Law because the records would not "operate to the prejudice or impairment of a person's reputation or

---

[18] Paul M. Schwartz, *Internet Privacy and the State*, 32 Conn. L. Rev. 815, 828-29 (2000).

personal security." Should the privacy of personal information turn on whether it will harm a person's reputation or security?

4. ***Public Records in a Digital World.*** Public records are increasingly being stored in electronic format. The paper records of the past were difficult to access. Now, they can be collected in databases and searched en masse. To what extent should the increased accessibility of records created by the digital age affect open record laws?

In 2001, the Judicial Conference Committee on Court Administration and Case Management issued a report with policies regarding public access to electronic case files. As Peter Winn describes it:

> Before the Judicial Conference Committee on Court Administration and Case Management (Committee) issued the Report, a study of the problem was prepared by the staff of the Administrative Office of the United States Courts. The staff white paper described two general approaches to the problem. One approach was to treat electronic judicial records as governed by exactly the same rules as paper records — what the white paper calls the "public is public" approach. The second approach advocated treating electronic and paper files differently in order to respect the practical obscurity of paper case files, urging that the rules regulating electronic court records reflect the fact that unrestricted online access to court records would undoubtedly, as a practical matter, compromise privacy, as well as increase the risk of personal harm to litigants and third parties whose private information appeared in case files. The white paper suggested that different levels of privileges could be created to govern electronic access to court records. Under this approach, judges and court staff would generally have broad, although not unlimited, remote access to all electronic case files, as would other key participants in the judicial process, such as the U.S. Attorney, the U.S. Trustee, and bankruptcy case trustees. Litigants and their attorneys would have unrestricted access to the files relevant to their own cases. The general public would have remote access to a subset of the full case file, including, in most cases, pleadings, briefs, orders, and opinions. Under this approach, the entire electronic case file could still be viewed at the clerk's office, just as the paper file is available now for inspection, but would not generally be made available on the Internet.
>
> Unfortunately, at least with respect to civil cases and bankruptcy cases, few, if any, of the suggestions contained in the staff white paper were ultimately adopted in the Report. Instead, the Committee adopted the "public is public" approach to the problem, rejecting the view that courts have a responsibility to adopt rules governing the use of their computer systems to try to recreate in cyberspace the practical balance that existed in the world of paper judicial records. In supporting this decision, the Committee took the position that attempting to recreate the "practical obscurity" of the brick and mortar world was simply too complicated an exercise for the courts to undertake. The Report does appear to recognize a limited responsibility on the part of the courts to adopt rules in order to limit the foreseeable harms of identity theft and online stalking. The Report recommends that certain "personal data identifiers," such as Social Security numbers, dates of birth, financial account numbers, and names of minor children, be partially redacted by the litigants. . . .
>
> The Report recommends that criminal court records not be placed online, for the present, finding that any benefits of remote electronic access to

criminal files would be outweighed by the safety and law enforcement risks such access would create. The Report expressed the concern that allowing defendants and others easy access to information regarding the cooperation and other activities of co-defendants would increase the risk that the information would be used to intimidate, harass, and possibly harm victims, defendants, and their families. In addition, the Report noted that merely sealing such documents would not adequately address the problems of online access, since the fact that a document is sealed signals probable defendant cooperation and covert law enforcement initiatives.[19]

In March 2004, the Judicial Conference issued a report recommending that, with certain exceptions, all criminal records be placed online accessible to the public.[20]

(b) Police Records

PAUL V. DAVIS

424 U.S. 693 (1976)

REHNQUIST, J. . . . Petitioner Paul is the Chief of Police of the Louisville, Ky., Division of Police, while petitioner McDaniel occupies the same position in the Jefferson County, Ky., Division of Police. In late 1972 they agreed to combine their efforts for the purpose of alerting local area merchants to possible shoplifters who might be operating during the Christmas season. In early December petitioners distributed to approximately 800 merchants in the Louisville metropolitan area a "flyer," which began as follows:

TO: BUSINESS MEN IN THE METROPOLITAN AREA
The Chiefs of The Jefferson County and City of Louisville Police Departments, in an effort to keep their officers advised on shoplifting activity, have approved the attached alphabetically arranged flyer of subjects known to be active in this criminal field.
This flyer is being distributed to you, the business man, so that you may inform your security personnel to watch for these subjects. These persons have been arrested during 1971 and 1972 or have been active in various criminal fields in high density shopping areas.
Only the photograph and name of the subject is shown on this flyer, if additional information is desired, please forward a request in writing. . . .

The flyer consisted of five pages of "mug shot" photos, arranged alphabetically. [Each page had the heading: "ACTIVE SHOPLIFTERS."]
In approximately the center of page 2 there appeared photos and the name of the respondent, Edward Charles Davis III.
Respondent appeared on the flyer because on June 14, 1971, he had been arrested in Louisville on a charge of shoplifting. He had been arraigned on this charge in September 1971, and, upon his plea of not guilty, the charge had been

---

[19] Peter A. Winn, *Online Court Records: Balancing Judicial Accountability and Privacy in an Age of Electronic Information*, 79 Wash. L. Rev. 307, 322-25 (2004).
[20] http://www.privacy.uscourts.gov/crimimpl.htm

"filed away with leave (to reinstate)," a disposition which left the charge outstanding. Thus, at the time petitioners caused the flyer to be prepared and circulated respondent had been charged with shoplifting but his guilt or innocence of that offense had never been resolved. Shortly after circulation of the flyer the charge against respondent was finally dismissed by a judge of the Louisville Police Court.

At the time the flyer was circulated respondent was employed as a photographer by the Louisville Courier-Journal and Times. The flyer, and respondent's inclusion therein, soon came to the attention of respondent's supervisor, the executive director of photography for the two newspapers. This individual called respondent in to hear his version of the events leading to his appearing in the flyer. Following this discussion, the supervisor informed respondent that although he would not be fired, he "had best not find himself in a similar situation" in the future.

Respondent thereupon brought this § 1983 action in the District Court for the Western District of Kentucky, seeking redress for the alleged violation of rights guaranteed to him by the Constitution of the United States. . . .

Respondent's due process claim is grounded upon his assertion that the flyer, and in particular the phrase "Active Shoplifters" appearing at the head of the page upon which his name and photograph appear, impermissibly deprived him of some "liberty" protected by the Fourteenth Amendment. His complaint asserted that the "active shoplifter" designation would inhibit him from entering business establishments for fear of being suspected of shoplifting and possibly apprehended, and would seriously impair his future employment opportunities. Accepting that such consequences may flow from the flyer in question, respondent's complaint would appear to state a classical claim for defamation actionable in the courts of virtually every State. Imputing criminal behavior to an individual is generally considered defamatory per se, and actionable without proof of special damages.

Respondent brought his action, however, not in the state courts of Kentucky, but in a United States District Court for that State. He asserted not a claim for defamation under the laws of Kentucky, but a claim that he had been deprived of rights secured to him by the Fourteenth Amendment of the United States Constitution. Concededly if the same allegations had been made about respondent by a private individual, he would have nothing more than a claim for defamation under state law. But, he contends, since petitioners are respectively an official of city and of county government, his action is thereby transmuted into one for deprivation by the State of rights secured under the Fourteenth Amendment. . . .

If respondent's view is to prevail, a person arrested by law enforcement officers who announce that they believe such person to be responsible for a particular crime in order to calm the fears of an aroused populace, presumably obtains a claim against such officers under § 1983. And since it is surely far more clear from the language of the Fourteenth Amendment that "life" is protected against state deprivation than it is that reputation is protected against state injury, it would be difficult to see why the survivors of an innocent bystander mistakenly shot by a policeman or negligently killed by a sheriff driving a government vehicle, would not have claims equally cognizable under § 1983.

It is hard to perceive any logical stopping place to such a line of reasoning. Respondent's construction would seem almost necessarily to result in every legally cognizable injury which may have been inflicted by a state official acting under "color of law" establishing a violation of the Fourteenth Amendment. We think it would come as a great surprise to those who drafted and shepherded the adoption of that Amendment to learn that it worked such a result, and a study of our decisions convinces us they do not support the construction urged by respondent. . . .

The second premise upon which the result reached by the Court of Appeals could be rested that the infliction by state officials of a "stigma" to one's reputation is somehow different in kind from infliction by a state official of harm to other interests protected by state law is equally untenable. The words "liberty" and "property" as used in the Fourteenth Amendment do not in terms single out reputation as a candidate for special protection over and above other interests that may be protected by state law. While we have in a number of our prior cases pointed out the frequently drastic effect of the "stigma" which may result from defamation by the government in a variety of contexts, this line of cases does not establish the proposition that reputation alone, apart from some more tangible interests such as employment, is either "liberty" or "property" by itself sufficient to invoke the procedural protection of the Due Process Clause. . . .

Respondent's complaint also alleged a violation of a "right to privacy guaranteed by the First, Fourth, Fifth, Ninth, and Fourteenth Amendments." . . .

While there is no "right of privacy" found in any specific guarantee of the Constitution, the Court has recognized that "zones of privacy" may be created by more specific constitutional guarantees and thereby impose limits upon government power. *See Roe v. Wade*, 410 U.S. 113 (1973). Respondent's case, however, comes within none of these areas. He does not seek to suppress evidence seized in the course of an unreasonable search. *See Katz v. United States*, 389 U.S. 347 (1967). And our other "right of privacy" cases, while defying categorical description, deal generally with substantive aspects of the Fourteenth Amendment. In *Roe* the Court pointed out that the personal rights found in this guarantee of personal privacy must be limited to those which are "fundamental" or "implicit in the concept of ordered liberty" as described in *Palko v. Connecticut*, 302 U.S. 319 (1937). The activities detailed as being within this definition were ones very different from that for which respondent claims constitutional protection matters relating to marriage, procreation, contraception, family relationships, and child rearing and education. In these areas it has been held that there are limitations on the States' power to substantively regulate conduct.

Respondent's claim is far afield from this line of decisions. He claims constitutional protection against the disclosure of the fact of his arrest on a shoplifting charge. His claim is based, not upon any challenge to the State's ability to restrict his freedom of action in a sphere contended to be "private," but instead on a claim that the State may not publicize a record of an official act such as an arrest. None of our substantive privacy decisions hold this or anything like this, and we decline to enlarge them in this manner. . . .

NOTES & QUESTIONS

1. **Wisconsin v. Constantineau.** Five years prior to *Paul*, the Court was more receptive to constitutional protection for reputational harms in *Wisconsin v. Constantineau*, 400 U.S. 433 (1971). There, the Court struck down a law authorizing the posting of names of people who had been designated excessive drinkers in retail liquor outlets. Alcohol was not to be sold to these individuals. The Court reasoned:

> Where a person's good name, reputation, honor, or integrity is at stake because of what the government is doing to him, notice and an opportunity to be heard are essential. "Posting" under the Wisconsin Act may to some be merely the mark of illness, to others it is a stigma, an official branding of a person. The label is a degrading one. Under the Wisconsin Act, a resident of Hartford is given no process at all. This appellee was not afforded a chance to defend herself. She may have been the victim of an official's caprice. Only when the whole proceedings leading to the pinning of an unsavory label on a person are aired can oppressive results be prevented.

Is *Paul* consistent with this case?

2. **Paul v. Davis *vs.* Whalen v. Roe.** *Paul v. Davis* was decided one year prior to *Whalen v. Roe,* 429 U.S. 589 (1977), where the Supreme Court recognized that the constitutional right to privacy involves "the individual interest in avoiding disclosure of personal matters." How does *Paul* square with *Whalen*? Does *Whalen* implicitly overrule *Paul* by recognizing a constitutional right to avoid disclosure of certain information? How can these cases be reconciled?

CLINE V. ROGERS

87 F.3d 176 (6th Cir. 1996)

BATCHELDER, J. . . . The plaintiff-appellant, Jackie Ray Cline ("Cline"), alleges that in 1992, a private citizen contacted the Sheriff's Department of McMinn County, Tennessee ("the County"), and asked Sheriff George Rogers to check Cline's arrest record. According to Cline, Rogers searched state and local records and requested a computer search of National Crime Information Center ("NCIC") records of the Federal Bureau of Investigation ("FBI"). Cline alleges that Rogers disclosed to the private citizen the information Rogers obtained regarding Cline's criminal history, in violation of both Tennessee and federal law.

Cline filed this lawsuit against Rogers, individually and in his official capacity as sheriff. Cline also named the County as a defendant, alleging that improper searches of criminal records is "a routine and customary practice in McMinn County," that the County "lacks adequate controls to ensure that access to criminal records is for authorized purposes only," that the County did not have in place an adequate system to detect misuse of criminal records, that the County had provided inadequate training to prevent such abuse, and that the County had "been indifferent to the civil rights of private citizens by allowing such abuses to continue."

Cline's complaint sought damages under 42 U.S.C. § 1983 for violation of his federal civil rights. . . . [The district court dismissed Cline's complaint, and Cline appealed.]

There is no violation of the United States Constitution in this case because there is no constitutional right to privacy in one's criminal record. Nondisclosure of one's criminal record is not one of those personal rights that is "fundamental" or "implicit in the concept of ordered liberty." *See Whalen v. Roe.* In *Whalen*, the Supreme Court distinguished fundamental privacy interests in "matters relating to marriage, procreation, contraception, family relationships, and child rearing and education" and "individual interest in avoiding disclosure of personal matters."

Moreover, one's criminal history is arguably not a private "personal matter" at all, since arrest and conviction information are matters of public record. *See Paul v. Davis* (rejecting a similar claim based on facts more egregious than those alleged here). Although there may be a dispute among the circuit courts regarding the existence and extent of an individual privacy right to nondisclosure of "personal matters," see *Slayton v. Willingham*, 726 F.2d 631 (10th Cir. 1984); *Fadjo v. Coon*, 633 F.2d 1172, 1176 (5th Cir. Unit B 1981) (both opining that *Paul* has been at least partially overruled by the Supreme Court's decisions in *Whalen* and *Nixon*), this circuit does not recognize a constitutional privacy interest in avoiding disclosure of, e.g., one's criminal record. See *DeSanti*, 653 F.2d at 1090 (regarding disclosure of juvenile delinquents' "social histories"); see also *Doe v. Wigginton*, 21 F.3d 733 (6th Cir. 1994) (disclosure of inmate's HIV infection did not violate constitutional right of privacy).

Because there is no privacy interest in one's criminal record that is protected by the United States Constitution, Cline could prove no set of facts that would entitle him to relief; therefore, the district court correctly dismissed this claim. . .

SCHEETZ V. THE MORNING CALL, INC.

946 F.2d 202 (3d Cir. 1991)

NYGAARD, J. . . . Kenneth Scheetz is a police officer in the City of Allentown. Rosann Scheetz is his wife. In the course of an argument between them in their home in January of 1988, Kenneth struck Rosann. Rosann left the house, but returned approximately a half an hour later. The argument resumed, and Kenneth again struck Rosann.

Rosann called the Allentown police. Two officers responded and prepared a standard "offense/incident" report, consisting of a face sheet and supplemental reports. The "face sheet" of this report[21] stated that Rosann Scheetz had reported a domestic disturbance, that two police cars had responded, and that Rosann had left the home.

In the meantime, Rosann had driven to the Allentown police station, apparently with the intention of filing a Pennsylvania Protection From Abuse

---

[21] The "face sheet" is a public document similar to a police blotter. The parties agree that this document is a public record. The parties dispute whether the "supplemental reports" are public records available under Pennsylvania's Right to Know Law. There is some evidence that these reports were generally available, subject to the approval of a police supervisor.

Petition. The officers who interviewed Rosann prepared two "supplemental reports" and made them part of the file. They reveal that Rosann stated that her husband had beaten her before and had refused counseling. The police gave Rosann three options: file criminal charges, request a protection from abuse order, or initiate department disciplinary action against Kenneth. These supplements also note that Rosann had visible physical injuries, that Rosann did not want to return home and that she was permitted to spend the night in the shift commander's office.

Chief Wayne Stephens filed a third supplement to the report. He had spoken to Kenneth about the incident, and the third supplement memorialized this fact, as well as Kenneth's statement to the Chief that he and his wife were scheduled to speak with a marriage counselor. None of the supplements indicated that the Chief took any disciplinary action against Kenneth.

Shortly after the incident, Kenneth Scheetz was named "Officer of the Year" by Chief Stephens. Several months later, as part of "Respect for Law Week," press releases and photos of Kenneth were released. A dinner and official ceremony were held in Kenneth's honor. The Morning Call ("The Call"), a local newspaper, published a story and photo on this honor.

Terry Mutchler, a reporter for The Call, became interested in investigating the prior incident involving Kenneth and Rosann. Another reporter from the paper had tried to get the police report from the police, who refused to release it. Mutchler's request for a copy of the report from the department was also formally refused. Mutchler nonetheless managed to get a copy of the report.

Mutchler then interviewed Chief Stephens about the incident. Chief Stephens initially denied the incident, but when confronted with Mutchler's information, he claimed that the report was stolen and refused further comment. Chief Stephens did, however, offer his insights into the subject of spousal abuse, stating "people fake it" and "women . . . tear their dresses and rip up their bras and say they were raped." Mutchler also interviewed Deputy Chief Monaghan, who offered assorted rationalizations for why no follow-up had been done on the Scheetz incident. The Scheetzes refused comment on the incident.

The Call published an article by Mutchler titled "Police didn't investigate assault complaint against officer." Eight paragraphs of the article were comprised of quotes from the police report of the beating incident which detailed the injuries Rosann received. The bulk of the article, however, focused on the lack of investigation and follow-up by the police department. Chief Stephens was quoted as saying that the incident had not been investigated. The article also quoted the comments Chief Stephens had made to Mutchler about domestic abuse, as well as Deputy Chief Monaghan's explanations for why no charges were pressed. The last two columns of the article consisted of quotes from Kenneth's superiors praising his work. . . .

. . . Kenneth and Rosann then sued Mutchler, The Call, and "John or Jane Doe." The complaint alleged that Mutchler and The Call had conspired with an unknown state actor (the Doe defendant) to deprive the Scheetzes of their constitutional right to privacy in violation of 42 U.S.C. § 1983. The complaint also raised several pendent state law claims. . . .

The district court granted the defendants' motion for summary judgment in part, denied it in part, granted judgment to the defendants on the § 1983 claim, dismissed the pendent state claims, dismissed the Doe defendant and dismissed all remaining motions as moot. The Scheetzes appeal. . . .

. . . Because we conclude that the Scheetzes have not alleged a violation of a constitutionally protected privacy interest, we will affirm.

The defendants rely on dicta in *Paul v. Davis* to support their argument that "garden variety" invasion of privacy claims are not actionable under section 1983. . . . The Supreme Court rejected the proposition that reputation alone was a liberty or property interest within the meaning of the due process clause. In dicta, the Court went on to consider the alternative argument that the police chiefs' action constituted a violation of the plaintiff's right to privacy. After first noting that privacy decisions had been limited in the past to family and procreative matters, the Court concluded that publication by the state of an official act such as an arrest could not constitute invasion of the constitutional right to privacy.

The very next year, however, the Court held in *Whalen v. Roe*, that the right to privacy extends to both "the individual interest in avoiding disclosure of personal matters, and . . . the interest in independence in making certain kinds of important decisions." *Whalen* recognized that the information contained in medical records is constitutionally protected under the confidentiality branch of the privacy right.

Thus, some confidential information is protected under the confidentiality branch of the right to privacy, the dicta in *Paul* notwithstanding.[22] Accordingly, the Scheetzes in this case contend that the information contained in the police incident report is similarly protected by the federal right.

Although cases exploring the autonomy branch of the right of privacy are legion, the contours of the confidentiality branch are murky. We have recognized that some confidential information, such as medical records, is constitutionally protected under the confidentiality branch of the federal privacy right. Other courts have similarly recognized that § 1983 may be used to redress violations of a constitutional confidentiality right.

Concluding that violations of the confidentiality right of privacy may be actionable under § 1983 does not, however, end our inquiry. Although defendants are wrong in arguing that *Paul* prohibits any privacy § 1983 action, we conclude that they correctly argue that the Scheetzes did not have a constitutionally protected privacy interest in the information they divulged in a police report. . . .

Although the outlines of the confidentiality right are not definite, the information that has been protected in other cases was information that the disclosing person reasonably expected to remain private. In reporting this potential crime to the police, Rosann Scheetz could not reasonably expect the information to remain secret. The police could have brought charges without her concurrence, at which point all the information would have wound up on the public record, where it would have been non-confidential. *See Cox Broadcasting Corp. v. Cohn*, 420 U.S. 469 (1975) (privacy interest fades when information is in the public record). This information is not like medical or financial records (which have been accorded some constitutional protection by this court) where there is a reasonable expectation that privacy will be preserved. When police are

---

[22] *Paul* can be reconciled with *Whalen* since the information at issue in *Paul* (the fact of plaintiff's arrest for shoplifting) is not the kind of information entitled to constitutional protection.

called, a private disturbance loses much of its private character. We conclude that the information Rosann Scheetz disclosed in the police reports is not constitutionally protected. . . .

MANSMANN, J. dissenting. . . . I agree that some of the information contained in the police report, specifically that information contained in the "Offense/Incident Report," is not protected under a constitutional privacy interest. Because the "Offense/Incident Report" is classified as a public document under the police department's policy, that information was not treated as confidential. . . .

Some of the information reported by The Call, however, was contained only in confidential portions of the police report entitled "Investigative Supplements" and was not discernable from the public portion of the report. That information detailed the private facts of the Scheetzes' marital counseling and precise details of their marital disturbance, including a description of Rosann's injuries and her statements. Since this information is clearly confidential, I would then examine the nature of the Scheetzes' privacy interest in keeping it confidential. . . .

. . . The majority suggests that because the information could have been publicly disclosed, the Scheetzes had no privacy interest. While it is true that criminal charges could have been brought without Rosann's concurrence, it does not necessarily follow that in spite of the fact that she declined to press charges or take alternative legal action, and no legal action ensued, Rosann Scheetz could have reasonably expected public disclosure of the confidential information that had remained quietly dormant in confidential police department reports.

This is especially true where the public disclosure occurred 16 months after the incident. *See, e.g., Briscoe v. Reader's Digest Ass'n*, 483 P.2d 34 (Cal. 1971) (common law right to privacy infringed by publication of truck hijacking conviction of 11 years ago); *Melvin v. Reid*, 297 P. 91 (Cal. 1931) (liability for common law invasion of privacy imposed upon producers of movie that revealed prior life of prostitution and crime of woman who had long since taken a new name and established a respectable life). . . .

. . . Because this confidential information had lain undisclosed in the confidential police department files for over a year and Rosann Scheetz had not pursued any legal action, the Scheetzes could reasonably have expected that the confidential information would never be publicly disclosed. In light of this delay, I cannot agree with the majority's otherwise appropriate assertion that "[w]hen police are called, a private disturbance loses much of its private character." Information that has remained confidential over a period of time, absent any legal action, can reasonably be expected to recede from public notice. . . .

NOTES & QUESTIONS

1. ***Privacy as a Way to Conceal a Scandal.*** The information about the police department's treatment of Ken Scheetz's abuse of his wife is highly newsworthy. The information reveals a police department that praised rather than disciplined Ken Scheetz and virtually ignored his wife's complaints of

abuse. Is privacy being used to cover up the scandalous way the police department reacted to Rosann Scheetz's complaint?

2. ***Deterring Reporting of Spousal Abuse.*** Would routine disclosure of complaints of spousal abuse inhibit victims such as Rosann Scheetz from coming forward? Keep in mind that it is Rosann Scheetz, in addition to her husband, who is suing for a violation of her privacy.

3. ***Limits on Police Reports.*** The court concluded that Rosann Scheetz lacked an expectation of privacy in the information because it was included in a police report: "In reporting this potential crime to the police, Rosann Scheetz could not reasonably expect the information to remain secret. The police could have brought charges without her concurrence, at which point all the information would have wound up on the public record, where it would have been non-confidential." Are there limits to what information the police should include in a police report?

4. ***Police Threats to Disclose.*** Consider *Sterling v. Borough of Minersville*, 232 F.3d. 190 (3d Cir. 2000). Marcus Wayman, 18 years old, was in a parked car along with a 17-year-old male friend. The car was parked in a lot adjacent to a beer distributor. F. Scott Wilinsky, a police officer, observed the vehicle and became suspicious that the youths might be attempting to burglarize the beer distributor. Wilinsky called for backup. After investigating, the officers determined that a break-in had not occurred at the beer distributor, but that the youths had been drinking. Wilinsky searched the vehicle and discovered two condoms and asked about the boys' sexual orientation. The boys said that they were gay, and that they were in the lot to engage in consensual sex. The boys were arrested for underage drinking and taken to the police station, where Wilinsky lectured them that homosexual activity was contrary to the dictates of the Bible. Wilinsky then told Wayman that he must inform his grandfather about his homosexuality or else Wilinsky himself would inform Wayman's grandfather. When he was released from custody, Wayman committed suicide. Wayman's mother filed a § 1983 suit against the Borough of Minersville, Wilinksy, and other officers and officials alleging, among other things, a violation of the constitutional right to information privacy. The court reasoned:

> We first ask whether Wayman had a protected privacy right concerning Wilinsky's threat to disclose his suspected sexual orientation. . . .
>
> It is difficult to imagine a more private matter than one's sexuality and a less likely probability that the government would have a legitimate interest in disclosure of sexual identity.
>
> We can, therefore, readily conclude that Wayman's sexual orientation was an intimate aspect of his personality entitled to privacy protection under *Whalen.* . . .
>
> Before we can definitely conclude that a constitutional tort has occurred, however, we must further ask whether Wilinsky's threat of disclosure, rather than actual disclosure, constituted a violation of Wayman's right to privacy. . .
>
> The threat to breach some confidential aspect of one's life . . . is tantamount to a violation of the privacy right because the security of one's

privacy has been compromised by the threat of disclosure. Thus, Wilinsky's threat to disclose Wayman's suspected homosexuality suffices as a violation of Wayman's constitutionally protected privacy interest. . . .

(c) Megan's Laws

In 1994, in New Jersey, a seven-year-old girl, Megan Kanka, was brutally raped and murdered by her neighbor, Jesse Timmendequas, who had two earlier sexual assault convictions. Nobody in Megan's family knew about Timmendequas's prior criminal record. Seventeen days after Megan's death, New Jersey Assembly Speaker Chuck Haytaian declared a legislative emergency. A law was proposed, called "Megan's Law," to establish a system for people to learn of the whereabouts of sexual offenders who were released from prison. The statute passed without committee hearings and without supportive research. Within three months of Megan's death, the law was signed by Governor Christie Whitman and became law. Similar laws appeared in other states. These laws, commonly called "Megan's Laws," set up databases of personal information about sexual offenders so that people can learn their identities and where they live.

In 1996, Congress passed a federal Megan's Law restricting states from receiving federal anti-crime funds unless they agreed to "release relevant information that is necessary to protect the public" from released sex offenders. *See* Pub. L. No. 104-145, codified at 42 U.S.C. § 14071(d)(2). Today, all 50 states have passed a version of Megan's Law. Sex offender registries under Megan's Law often contain information such as the sex offender's Social Security number, photograph, address, prior convictions, and places of employment.

States differ in how they disseminate sexual offender information. In California, booths are set up at county fairs so that individuals can browse through the registry. Some states have 1-800 or 1-900 numbers where people can call in and ask if particular people are sex offenders. At least 16 states have made their registries available on the Internet.

PAUL P. v. VERNIERO

170 F.3d 396 (3d Cir. 1999)

SLOVITER, J. Plaintiff Paul P. sues on his behalf and on behalf of a class of persons who, having been convicted of specified sex crimes, are required to comply with N.J. Stat. Ann. § 2c:7-1 et seq., known as "Megan's Law," which provides for a system of registration and community notification. . . .

In a related action, *E.B. v. Verniero*, 119 F.3d 1077 (3d Cir. 1997), this court rejected the claims of comparably situated persons that the community notification requirements violate the Double Jeopardy Clause or the Ex Post Facto Clause of the United States Constitution. That holding of *E.B.* was predicated on the conclusion that the notification required by Megan's Law does not constitute punishment. . . .

In this case, plaintiffs raise a challenge to Megan's Law that they claim is different from that considered in *E.B.* They argue that the statutory requirement that the class members provide extensive information to local law enforcement personnel, including each registrant's current biographical data, physical description, home address, place of employment, schooling, and a description and license plate number of the registrant's vehicle, and the subsequent community notification is a violation of their constitutionally protected right to privacy.

The statutory scheme is described in detail in *E.B.*, and we refer only briefly to the salient details. We explained the registration requirements as follows:

The registrant must provide the following information to the chief law enforcement officer of the municipality in which he resides: name, social security number, age, race, sex, date of birth, height, weight, hair and eye color, address of legal residence, address of any current temporary legal residence, and date and place of employment. N.J.S.A. 2C:7-4b(1). He must confirm his address every ninety days, notify the municipal law enforcement agency if he moves, and re-register with the law enforcement agency of any new municipality. N.J.S.A. 2C:7-2d to e.

The information provided by the registrant is put into a central registry, open to other law enforcement personnel but not to public inspection. Law enforcement officials then use the data provided to apply a "Risk Assessment Scale," a numerical scoring system, to determine the registrant's "risk of offense" and the tier in which the registrant should be classified. In the case of Tier 1 registrants, notification is given only to law enforcement agents "likely to encounter" the registrant. Tier 2, or "moderate risk," notification is given to law enforcement agents, schools, and community organizations "likely to encounter" the registrant. Tier 3, or "high risk," notification goes to all members of the public "likely to encounter" the registrant. Notifications generally contain a warning that the information is confidential and should not be disseminated to others, as well as an admonition that actions taken against the registrant, such as assaults, are illegal.

The prosecutor must provide the registrant with notice of the proposed notification. A pre-notification judicial review process is available for any registrant who wishes to challenge his or her classification.

The plaintiffs are Tier 2 and Tier 3 registrants who have been certified as a class and whose offenses were committed after the enactment of Megan's Law. . . .

The legal foundation for plaintiffs' claim is the Supreme Court's recognition that there is "a right of personal privacy, or a guarantee of certain areas or zones of privacy," protected by the United States Constitution. *Roe v. Wade*, 410 U.S. 113, 152 (1973). This "guarantee of personal privacy" covers "only personal rights that can be deemed 'fundamental' or 'implicit in the concept of ordered liberty.'" This privacy right "has some extension to activities relating to marriage, procreation, contraception, family relationships, and child rearing and education."

Plaintiffs argue that Megan's Law infringes upon their constitutionally protected privacy interests in two ways. One is by the dissemination of information about them, most particularly by disseminating both their home addresses and a "compilation of information which would otherwise remain 'scattered' or 'wholly forgotten.'" Their other claim is that the community notification infringes upon their "privacy interests in their most intimate relationships — those with their spouses, children, parents, and other family members."

Plaintiffs thus seek to invoke the two categories of privacy interests identified by the Supreme Court in *Whalen v. Roe.* . . .

The parties dispute the extent to which our decision in *E.B.* is dispositive of the privacy issue before us in this case. Plaintiffs contend that no privacy issue was raised, briefed, or argued in *E.B.* and that the discussion in *E.B.* relating to cases on which they rely is dictum. The State defendants, on the other hand, regard "[t]he portions of the *E.B.* decision holding that community notification does not implicate a fundamental privacy interest and the finding of a compelling state interest in protecting the public from recidivist sex offenders," as "control[ling] the decision in this case." We thus turn to examine the *E.B.* decision.

The privacy issue arose in *E.B.* during our analysis of whether community notification mandated by Megan's Law constitutes punishment for purposes of the Ex Post Facto and Double Jeopardy Clauses. In that context, we stated that the "primary sting from Megan's law notification comes by way of injury to what is denoted . . . as reputational interests. This includes . . . the myriad of . . . ways in which one is treated differently by virtue of being known as a potentially dangerous sex offender." *E.B.*, 119 F.3d at 1102. We then referred to the Supreme Court's holding in *Paul v. Davis*, stating:

> Just as Davis sought constitutional protection from the consequences of state disclosure of the fact of his shoplifting arrest and law enforcement's assessment that he was a continuing risk, so registrants seek protection from what may follow disclosure of facts related to their sex offense convictions and the resulting judgment of the state that they are a continuing risk. It follows that, just as the officers' publication of the official act of Davis' arrest did not violate any fundamental privacy right of Davis', neither does New Jersey's publication (through notification) of registrants' convictions and findings of dangerousness implicate any interest of fundamental constitutional magnitude.

We rejected the contention that dissemination of information about criminal activity beyond law enforcement personnel is analogous to historical punishments, such as the stocks, cages, and scarlet letters. We found instead that the dissemination is more like the dissemination of "rap sheet" information to regulatory agencies, bar associations, prospective employers, and interested members of the public that public indictment, public trial, and public imposition of sentence necessarily entail. We noted that although the Supreme Court later recognized in *United States Department of Justice v. Reporters Committee for Freedom of the Press*, 489 U.S. 749 (1989), that the dissemination of "rap sheets" implicates a privacy interest, the Court there was determining whether a "rap sheet" fell under the "privacy interest" protected by an exemption to the Freedom of Information Act ("FOIA"), not that protected by the Constitution. We pointed out that the Supreme Court itself made the distinction between the two types of privacy interest, and we quoted its statement in *Reporters*

Committee, that "[t]he question of the statutory meaning of privacy under the FOIA is, of course, not the same as the question . . . whether an individual's interest in privacy is protected by the Constitution." . . .

. . . Finally, we concluded in *E.B.* that even if a "fundamental right" were implicated, "the state's interest here would suffice to justify the deprivation." . . .

The District Court here concluded that there was no privacy interest in the plaintiffs' home addresses, stating that "[b]ecause such information is public, plaintiffs' privacy interests are not implicated." As to the argument based on the "compilation" of various information, the court held that "[i]t is of little consequence whether this public information is disclosed piecemeal or whether it is disclosed in compilation."

To the extent that plaintiffs' alleged injury stems from the disclosure of their sex offender status, alone or in conjunction with other information, the District Court's opinion is in line with other cases in this court and elsewhere holding specifically that arrest records and related information are not protected by a right to privacy. See *Fraternal Order of Police*, 812 F.2d at 117 (holding that "arrest records are not entitled to privacy protection" because they are public); *Cline v. Rogers*, 87 F.3d 176, 179 (6th Cir.) (holding that "there is no constitutional right to privacy in one's criminal record" because "arrest and conviction information are matters of public record"). . . .

We are not insensitive to the argument that notification implicates plaintiffs' privacy interest by disclosing their home addresses. The compilation of home addresses in widely available telephone directories might suggest a consensus that these addresses are not considered private were it not for the fact that a significant number of persons, ranging from public officials and performers to just ordinary folk, choose to list their telephones privately, because they regard their home addresses to be private information. Indeed, their view is supported by decisions holding that home addresses are entitled to privacy under FOIA, which exempts from disclosure personal files "the disclosure of which would constitute a clearly unwarranted invasion of personal privacy." 5 U.S.C. § 552(b)(6). . . .

Although these cases are not dispositive, they reflect the general understanding that home addresses are entitled to some privacy protection, whether or not so required by a statute. We are therefore unwilling to hold that absent a statute, a person's home address is never entitled to privacy protection. . . .

Accepting therefore the claim by the plaintiffs that there is some nontrivial interest in one's home address by persons who do not wish it disclosed, we must engage in the balancing inquiry repeatedly held appropriate in privacy cases. . . .

The nature and significance of the state interest served by Megan's Law was considered in *E.B.* There, we stated that the state interest, which we characterized as compelling, "would suffice to justify the deprivation even if a fundamental right of the registrant's were implicated." We find no reason to disagree. The public interest in knowing where prior sex offenders live so that susceptible individuals can be appropriately cautioned does not differ whether the issue is the registrant's claim under the Double Jeopardy or Ex Post Facto Clauses, or is the registrant's claim to privacy. . . .

The other argument raised by plaintiffs as part of their privacy claim is that community notification infringes upon their fundamental interest in family relationships. . . . In *E.B.*, we recognized that Megan's Law "impose[s] no restrictions on a registrant's ability to live and work in a community," but that plaintiffs complain of the law's "indirect effects: Actions that members of the community may take as a result of learning of the registrant's past, his potential danger, and his presence in the community." Even if we concede, as the District Court did, that "being subject to Megan's Law community notification places a constitutionally cognizable strain upon familial relationships," these indirect effects which follow from plaintiffs' commission of a crime are too substantially different from the government actions at issue in the prior cases to fall within the penumbra of constitutional privacy protection. Megan's Law does not restrict plaintiffs' freedom of action with respect to their families and therefore does not intrude upon the aspect of the right to privacy that protects an individual's independence in making certain types of important decisions. . . .

During the pendency of this appeal, appellants filed a series of motions under seal, six in all, seeking to supplement the record with evidence of recent incidents which have caused serious adverse consequences to them and their families. . . .

. . . [T]his court has previously held that "[t]he fact that protected information must be disclosed to a party who has a particular need for it . . . does not strip the information of its protection against disclosure to those who have no similar need," and we have required the government to implement adequate safeguards against unnecessary disclosure. Because these motions were filed in this court in the first instance, the District Court has not had the opportunity to consider the information contained therein and to determine whether any action is appropriate in light of our precedent.

[We] will remand this matter so that the District Court can consider whether plaintiffs' interest in assuring that information is disclosed only to those who have a particular need for it has been accorded adequate protection in light of the information set forth in the motions. . . .

NOTES & QUESTIONS

1. *The Privacy Interest.* In *Russell v. Gregoire*, 124 F.3d 1079 (9th Cir. 1997), the court considered a similar challenge under the constitutional right to information privacy to Washington's version of Megan's Law, which involved public dissemination of the offender's photo, name, age, birth date, other identifying information, and a summary of his or her crime. It includes the general vicinity of his or her residence, but not the exact address. Wash. Rev. Code § 9A.44.130(1). The court held that the statute did not run afoul of the constitutional right to information privacy:

> In this case, the collection and dissemination of information is carefully designed and narrowly limited. Even if *Whalen* and *Nixon* had established a broad right to privacy in data compilations, the Act does not unduly disseminate private information about Russell and Stearns.
>
> Moreover, any such right to privacy, to the extent it exists at all, would protect only personal information. The information collected and disseminated by the Washington statute is already fully available to the public and is not constitutionally protected, with the exception of the general vicinity of the offender's residence (which is published) and the offender's employer (which

is collected but not released to the public). Neither of these two items are generally considered "private."

Recall that in *Paul P. v. Verniero,* the court held that the reasoning of *United States Department of Justice v. Reporters Committee for Freedom of the Press*, 489 U.S. 749 (1989), was inapplicable to the constitutional right to information privacy. In *Reporters Committee*, the Court concluded that the disclosure of FBI "rap sheets" (compilations of a person's arrests, charges, and convictions) under the Freedom of Information Act (FOIA) implicated a privacy interest:

> In an organized society, there are few facts that are not at one time or another divulged to another. Thus, the extent of the protection accorded a privacy right at common law rested in part on the degree of dissemination of the allegedly private fact and the extent to which the passage of time rendered it private. . . . Recognition of this attribute of a privacy interest supports the distinction, in terms of personal privacy, between scattered disclosure of the bits of information contained in a rap sheet and revelation of the rap sheet as a whole.

The reasoning of this case suggests that sexual offenders have a privacy interest in their prior convictions. Should the reasoning of *Reporters Committee* apply to the constitutional right to information privacy?

Prior to *Paul P.*, the New Jersey Supreme Court had upheld New Jersey's Megan's Law in *Doe v. Poritz*, 662 A.2d 367 (N.J. 1995). There, the court, relying on *Reporters Committee*, recognized a privacy interest in some of the information divulged by New Jersey's Megan's Law:

> . . . We find . . . that considering the totality of the information disclosed to the public, the Notification Law implicates a privacy interest. That the information disseminated under the Notification Law may be available to the public, in some form or other, does not mean that plaintiff has no interest in limiting its dissemination. As the Court recognized in *United States Department of Justice v. Reporters Committee for Freedom of the Press*, 489 U.S. 749 (1989), privacy "encompass[es] the individual's control of information concerning his or her person." . . .
>
> . . . [T]he Court recognized a "distinction . . . between scattered disclosure of the bits of information contained in a rap sheet and revelation of the rap sheet as a whole." . . . The Court noted, furthermore, that there was a "privacy interest inherent in the nondisclosure of certain information even when the information may have been at one time public." . . .
>
> In exposing those various bits of information to the public, the Notification Law links various bits of information — name, appearance, address, and crime — that otherwise might remain unconnected. However public any of those individual pieces of information may be, were it not for the Notification Law, those connections might never be made. We believe a privacy interest is implicated when the government assembles those diverse pieces of information into a single package and disseminates that package to the public, thereby ensuring that a person cannot assume anonymity — in this case, preventing a person's criminal history from fading into obscurity and being wholly forgotten. Those convicted of crime may have no cognizable privacy interest in the fact of their conviction, but the Notification Law, given the compilation and dissemination of information, nonetheless implicates a

privacy interest. The interests in privacy may fade when the information is a matter of public record, but they are not non-existent. . . .

The court, however, concluded that the state interest outweighed the sexual offender's privacy interest:

> There is an express public policy militating toward disclosure: the danger of recidivism posed by sex offenders. The state interest in protecting the safety of members of the public from sex offenders is clear and compelling. The Legislature has determined that there is a substantial danger of recidivism by sex offenders, and public notification clearly advances the purpose of protecting the public from that danger. . . .

Compare the treatment of *Reporters Committee* in *Paul P.* and *Poritz*. How do the cases differ in the way they deal with the import of *Reporters Committee*?[23]

2. *Postscript to* **Paul P.** Following the Third Circuit's decision in *Paul P.*, the district court on remand held that the Megan's Law regulations in New Jersey did not sufficiently protect against unauthorized disclosures. The plaintiffs had cited to 45 instances where information had been released to unauthorized persons, with one disclosure resulting in the offender's name and address being printed in an article on the front page of a newspaper. Although noting that zero leakage is unattainable, the court stated that the government must avoid "unreasonably impinging on the 'nontrivial' privacy interests" of the plaintiffs and that the current Megan's Law regulations failed to meet this standard. *Paul P. v. Farmer*, 80 F. Supp. 2d 320 (D.N.J. 2000). The state attorney general promulgated new guidelines that were approved by the district court and affirmed on appeal. *See Paul P. v. Farmer*, 227 F.3d 98 (3d Cir. 2000). The new guidelines permit two forms of notice. An "unredacted notice" contains all information. A "redacted notice" omits the specific home address of the offender as well as the name and address of the employer. To receive an unredacted notice, the recipient must sign a form agreeing to be bound by court order and submitting to the jurisdiction of the court. The recipient must agree to share information only with her household and those caring for her children. If the person refuses to sign the receipt, then she can only receive the redacted notice.

In 2000, New Jersey amended its constitution by a referendum that provided that nothing in the New Jersey Constitution shall prohibit the disclosure of Megan's Law information over the Internet. New Jersey subsequently posted its sexual offender data on a website, excluding the offenders' current home addresses.

In *A.A. v. New Jersey*, 341 F.3d 206 (3d Cir. 2003), the Third Circuit upheld New Jersey's Megan's Law against a privacy claim against a public Internet registry posting personal information against convicted sex offenders. The court found that the Internet registry, which contains information about

---

[23] *See also Cutshall v. Sundquist*, 193 F.3d 466 (6th Cir. 1999) (rejecting reliance on *Reporters Committee* and concluding that constitutional right to information privacy is not implicated by Megan's Law).

certain high-risk and moderate-risk sex offenders, was permissible due to the state's compelling interest to prevent sex offenses. Although the convicted sex offenders have a "nontrivial" privacy interest in their home addresses, the court concluded that a need exists to access information in a mobile society. The court stated: "Consider parents with young children who want to purchase a new home in New Jersey. Without the Registry, they would not be notified of the presence of convicted sex offenders, even those with a high risk of re-offense, until they had already purchased their new home which may be in the proximity of a Registrant's home. . . . So too a family planning a vacation at the New Jersey shore."

Like New Jersey, many states are placing their Megan's Law information on the Internet. Is such a practice going too far? Or is it necessary to make accessing the information more convenient? Consider Daniel Solove's critique of posting Megan's Law disclosures on the Internet:

> Megan's Law disclosures may be relevant for certain types of relationships, such as child care. Still, what most Megan's Laws lose sight of the use of the information in question. Megan's Law data is beneficial when disclosed for certain purposes, but not necessarily for all purposes. When placed on the Internet for any curious individual around the world to see, Megan's Law information becomes disconnected from its goals.[24]

3. ***The Breadth of Megan's Laws.*** Megan's Law does not merely involve offenses against children. It encompasses a wide range of sex offenses, which can range from sodomy, prostitution, consensual homosexual acts, masturbation in public places, flashing, and statutory rape. In some states, the disclosure does not indicate what particular sexual offense the offender committed. Is such a general listing appropriate? Is Megan's Law justified under the constitutional right to information privacy for every offense that a state classifies as a sexual offense? Or does the balance weigh in favor of Megan's Law only for specific offenses? If so, how should such offenses be distinguished from ones in which the balance does not weigh in favor of Megan's Law?[25]

4. ***Recidivism Rates.*** One of the justifications for Megan's Law is that sexual offenders have a high recidivism rate and, hence, pose a threat to the community. But sexual offenders have a lower recidivism rate than those who commit other forms of violent crime, such as robbers. In one study of offenders re-arrested within three years for any crime, previously convicted murderers had approximately a 42 percent re-arrest rate; rapists had a 51.5 percent re-arrest rate; other sexual offenders had a 48 percent re-arrest rate; and robbers had a 66 percent re-arrest rate. However, re-arrest rates, without more information, are misleading. Of the 51.5 percent of rapists who were re-

---

[24] Daniel J. Solove, *The Virtues of Knowing Less: Justifying Privacy Protections Against Disclosure*, 53 Duke L.J. 967, 1061 (2003).

[25] For more on the privacy implications of Megan's Laws, see Caroline Louise Lewis, *The Jacob Wetterling Crimes Against Children and Sexually Violent Offender Registration Act: An Unconstitutional Deprivation of the Right to Privacy and Substantive Due Process*, 31 Harv. C.R.-C.L. L. Rev. 89 (1996); Symposium, *Critical Perspectives on Megan's Law: Protection vs. Privacy*, 13 N.Y.L. Sch. J. Hum. Rts. 1 (1996).

arrested within three years after being released, only 7.7 percent were re-arrested for a sex crime. Further, different types of sexual offenders have different recidivism rates.[26]

5. *Family Stigma.* The majority of sexual offenses against children are committed by family members or close friends of the family (estimated at about 92 percent).[27] When a child's parent is released and is listed in the sex offender registry, the child's privacy can also be compromised because the entire family is under the stigma of harboring a sexual offender.

In *Doe v. Quiring*, 686 N.W.2d 918 (S.D. 2004), a young woman, who was the victim of incest by her father, brought suit to have her father's name removed from the sex offender public registry. Among the information that the registry contains is the type of crime that the offender committed. The victim argued that "public access to incest offenders and their crimes through the Registry 'necessarily' involves the 'release of . . . identifying information regarding the victim of the crime.'" Pursuant to South Dakota's Megan's Law: "Nothing in this section allows the release of the name or any identifying information regarding the victim of the crime to any person other than law enforcement agencies, and such victim identifying information is confidential." SDCL 22-22-40. The victim contended that "because the crime of incest involves familial relationships, the very definition of the crime of incest 'so narrows the group of possible victims that identification of the victim is necessarily implicated by the name of the offense.'" The court, however, disagreed:

> [B]ecause the Registry does not reveal the victim's familial relationship, age, physical description, address, or gender, a victim could be any one of a number of less than 21-year-old relatives of the offender. Under these circumstances, we believe that the mere listing of the offender and type of offense is not the disclosure of the "identifying information" that the Legislature intended to prohibit. . . .

In dissent, Justices Meierhenry and Sabers argued:

> Initially, the legislative purpose "of alerting the public in the interest of community safety" is satisfied by identifying the crime as "rape" or "sexual contact." To note the crime specifically as incest only serves to narrow the class of victims to a small number capable of being identified. The size of the class of incest victims is limited to family members. The number of family members under the age of twenty-one is even smaller and, in some cases, may include only a couple of children. Publicly identifying the crime as "incest" significantly increases the risk of providing "identifying information of the victim" and may bring opprobrium on family members who were not victims. It may also have the effect of making victims or family members reluctant to

---

[26] *See* Jane A. Small, *Who Are the People in Your Neighborhood? Due Process, Public Protection, and Sex Offender Notification Laws*, 74 N.Y.U. L. Rev. 1451 (1999). For a contrary view regarding recidivism rates for sex offenders, see Daniel L. Feldman, *The "Scarlet Letter Laws" of the 1990s: A Response to Critics*, 60 Alb. L. Rev. 1081 (1997).

[27] Michele L. Earl-Hubbard, Comment, *The Child Sex Offender Registration Laws: The Punishment, Liberty Deprivation, and Unintended Results Associated with the Scarlet Letter Laws of the 1990s*, 90 Nw. U. L. Rev. 788, 851-52 (1996).

report the crimes knowing the registry will list the crime as incest. Often incest crimes go unreported because of the fear of public exposure and embarrassment created for the family, victim, and perpetrator. Michele L. Earl-Hubbard, *The Child Sex Offender Registration Laws: The Punishment, Liberty Deprivation, and Unintended Results Associated with the Scarlet Letter Laws of the 1990s,* 90 N.W. U. L. Rev. 788, 856 (1996). As one author noted, "Ironically, Megan's Laws may stigmatize the very victims of sex offenses whom they are designed to protect, many of whom are children living in the same house as the sex offender." Daniel J. Solove, *The Virtues of Knowing Less: Justifying Privacy Protections Against Disclosure,* 53 Duke L.J. 967, 1060 (2003).

6. ***Shaming Punishments.*** In colonial America, marking criminals with branding, mutilation, or letter-wearing (such as the scarlet letter) was common. Marks would be burned into the convict's hand or forehead. This was often done because there was no way of imprisoning people. Nathaniel Hawthorne's *The Scarlet Letter* involves a famous example of a shaming punishment where Hester Prynne was made to stitch a red letter "A" to her clothing to punish her for adultery. Does Megan's Law amount to a shaming punishment? Is this form of punishment appropriate?

Amitai Etzioni has praised shaming in the context of Megan's Law. He argues: "[S]haming is particularly communitarian in that it does not occur unless the community approves of the values at stake."[28] In his view, moreover, due to recidivism among sex offenders, a likely alternative to publicizing the presence of the sex offender in the community plus shaming will be "to keep the offender longer in jail" to protect the community. Will antisocial behavior expand in the absence of shaming?

7. ***Shaming in Other Contexts.*** Today, shaming punishments are making a comeback. In a move broader than Megan's Law, some localities are publicizing the names of certain arrestees. For example, in 1997, Kansas City created "John TV," broadcasting on television the names, photographs, addresses, and ages of people who had been arrested for soliciting prostitutes. Similar programs have been started in other cities. Is this activity more or less problematic to you than Megan's Law?

8. ***Is Megan's Law a Punishment?*** In *Smith v. Doe,* 538 U.S. 84 (2003), the Supreme Court examined whether Alaska's Megan's Law violated the constitutional prohibitions on ex post facto laws. An ex post facto law is a law that applies after the fact. In other words, the federal government and the states cannot pass a law that criminalizes past actions. Pursuant to U.S. Constitution art. I, § 9, "No . . . ex post facto Law shall be passed" by the federal government. U.S. Constitution art. I, § 10 provides that "No state shall . . . pass any . . . ex post facto Law."

Alaska's Megan's Law makes public the following information: "name, aliases, address, photograph, physical description, description [,] license [and] identification numbers of motor vehicles, place of employment, date of birth, crime for which convicted, date of conviction, place and court of conviction,

---

[28] Amitai Etzioni, The *Limits of Privacy* 60-61 (1999).

length and conditions of sentence, and a statement as to whether the offender or kidnapper is in compliance with [the update] requirements . . . or cannot be located." Alaska Stat. § 18.65.087(b). The Supreme Court noted that if the sex offender registration and notification law is designed to "impose punishment," then it "constitutes retroactive punishment" and is an impermissible ex post facto law. The Court concluded that "the intent of the Alaska Legislature was to create a civil, nonpunitive regime." Further, the Court concluded that the effect of the law did not "negate Alaska's intention to establish a civil regulatory scheme." In reaching this latter conclusion, the Court dismissed an argument that Megan's Law resembles the "shaming punishments of the colonial period."

> Any initial resemblance to early punishments is, however, misleading. Punishments such as whipping, pillory, and branding inflicted physical pain and staged a direct confrontation between the offender and the public. Even punishments that lacked the corporal component, such as public shaming, humiliation, and banishment, involved more than the dissemination of information. They either held the person up before his fellow citizens for face-to-face shaming or expelled him from the community. By contrast, the stigma of Alaska's Megan's Law results not from public display for ridicule and shaming but from the dissemination of accurate information about a criminal record, most of which is already public. Our system does not treat dissemination of truthful information in furtherance of a legitimate governmental objective as punishment. On the contrary, our criminal law tradition insists on public indictment, public trial, and public imposition of sentence. Transparency is essential to maintaining public respect for the criminal justice system, ensuring its integrity, and protecting the rights of the accused. The publicity may cause adverse consequences for the convicted defendant, running from mild personal embarrassment to social ostracism. In contrast to the colonial shaming punishments, however, the State does not make the publicity and the resulting stigma an integral part of the objective of the regulatory scheme.

The Court reasoned that although the "reach of the Internet is greater than anything which could have been designed in colonial times," the goal of the notification is "to inform the public for its own safety, not to humiliate the offender. . . . The Internet makes the document search more efficient, cost effective, and convenient for Alaska's citizenry."

Justices Stevens, Ginsburg, and Breyer dissented. In Justices Ginsburg and Breyer's dissent, they observed:

> And meriting heaviest weight in my judgment, the Act makes no provision whatever for the possibility of rehabilitation: Offenders cannot shorten their registration or notification period, even on the clearest demonstration of rehabilitation or conclusive proof of physical incapacitation. However plain it may be that a former sex offender currently poses no threat of recidivism, he will remain subject to long-term monitoring and inescapable humiliation.
>
> John Doe I, for example, pleaded *nolo contendere* to a charge of sexual abuse of a minor nine years before the Alaska Act was enacted. He successfully completed a treatment program, and gained early release on supervised probation in part because of his compliance with the program's

requirements and his apparent low risk of re-offense. He subsequently remarried, established a business, and was reunited with his family. He was also granted custody of a minor daughter, based on a court's determination that he had been successfully rehabilitated. The court's determination rested in part on psychiatric evaluations concluding that Doe had "a very low risk of re-offending" and is "not a pedophile." Notwithstanding this strong evidence of rehabilitation, the Alaska Act requires Doe to report personal information to the State four times per year, and permits the State publicly to label him a "Registered Sex Offender" for the rest of his life.

9. *Megan's Law Disclosures for All Crimes?* A growing number of states are furnishing online databases of all of their current inmates and parolees. Do these databases serve the statutory purpose of protecting the community? Should registries of felons stop at sexual offenders? Why not all people convicted of a crime?

10. *How Far Can Disclosure Go?* In May 2001, Judge J. Manuel Banales of Texas ordered 21 convicted sex offenders to post signs in their front yards stating: "Danger! Registered Sex Offender Lives Here." Additionally, the offenders must place bumper stickers on their cars stating: "Danger! Registered Sex Offender in Vehicle." Other offenders were ordered to send letters to all the people who lived within three blocks of their homes. Compliance is monitored by the probation department. "The whole idea is that everybody is looking at you," Judge Banales said to the offenders. "You have no one else to blame but yourself." Under the reasoning of either *Russell* or *Paul P.*, is this court order a violation of the constitutional right to information privacy?

11. *A Prison-Privacy Trade-off?* Suppose that instead of enacting Megan's Laws, society just decided to extend the sentences for sexual offenses and lock up sexual offenders for life. Perhaps if states could not enact a Megan's Law, they would resort to more life sentences for sexual offenders. Most likely, many offenders would choose a regime where they would be released from prison and subject to Megan's Law to a regime where they would spend the rest of their lives in prison. What do you think about this potential trade-off?

B. GOVERNMENT RECORDS OF PERSONAL INFORMATION

1. FAIR INFORMATION PRACTICES

In the 1960s, the increasing use of computers gave rise to a significant public debate about privacy. In particular, commentators expressed opposition to the increasing amount of personal information collected by government agencies and stored in computer databases.

In 1973, the Department of Housing, Education, and Welfare (HEW) issued a highly influential report about government records maintained in computer databases. The HEW Report characterized the growing concern over privacy:

> It is no wonder that people have come to distrust computer-based record-keeping operations. Even in non-governmental settings, an individual's control over the personal information that he gives to an organization or that an organization obtains about him, is lessening as the relationship between the giver and receiver of personal data grows more attenuated, impersonal, and diffused. There was a time when information about an individual tended to be elicited in face-to-face contacts involving personal trust and a certain symmetry, or balance, between giver and receiver. Nowadays, an individual must increasingly give information about himself to large and relatively faceless institutions, for handling and use by strangers — unknown, unseen, and, all too frequently, unresponsive. Sometimes the individual does not even know that an organization maintains a record about him. Often he may not see it, much less contest its accuracy, control its dissemination, or challenge its use by others. . . .
>
> The poet, the novelist, and the social scientist tell us, each in his own way, that the life of a small-town man, woman, or family is an open book compared to the more anonymous existence of urban dwellers. Yet the individual in a small town can retain his confidence because he can be more sure of retaining control. He lives in a face-to-face world, in a social system where irresponsible behavior can be identified and called to account. By contrast, the impersonal data system, and faceless users of the information it contains, tend to be accountable only in the formal sense of the word. In practice they are for the most part immune to whatever sanctions the individual can invoke.

To remedy these growing concerns over the accumulation and use of personal information by the government, the HEW Report recommended that a Code of Fair Information Practices be established:

- There must be no personal-data record-keeping systems whose very existence is secret.

- There must be a way for an individual to find out what information about him is in a record and how it is used.

- There must be a way for an individual to prevent information about him obtained for one purpose from being used or made available for other purposes without his consent.

- There must be a way for an individual to correct or amend a record of identifiable information about him.

- Any organization creating, maintaining, using, or disseminating records of identifiable personal data must assure the reliability of the data for their intended use and must take reasonable precautions to prevent misuse of the data.[29]

---

[29] U.S. Dep't of Health, Educ. & Welfare, Records, *Computers, and the Rights of Citizens: Report of the Secretary's Advisory Comm. on Automated Personal Data Systems* 29-30, 41-42 (1973) ("HEW Report").

Fair Information Practices can be understood most simply as the rights and responsibilities that are associated with the transfer and use of personal information. Since the intent is to correct information asymmetries that result from the transfer of personal data from an individual to an organization, Fair Information Practices typically assign rights to individuals and responsibilities to organizations.

MARC ROTENBERG, *FAIR INFORMATION PRACTICES AND*
THE ARCHITECTURE OF PRIVACY (WHAT LARRY DOESN'T GET)

2001 Stan. Tech. L. Rev. 1

. . . Not only have Fair Information Practices played a significant role in framing privacy laws in the United States, these basic principles have also contributed to the development of privacy laws around the world and even to the development of important international guidelines for privacy protection. The most well known of these international guidelines are the Organization for Economic Cooperation and Development's Recommendations Concerning and Guidelines Governing the Protection of Privacy and Transborder Flows of Personal Data ("OECD Guidelines"). The OECD Guidelines set out eight principles for data protection that are still the benchmark for assessing privacy policy and legislation: Collection Limitation; Data Quality; Purpose Specification; Use Limitation; Security Safeguards; Openness; Individual Participation; and Accountability. The principles articulate in only a couple of pages a set of rules that have guided the development of national law and increasingly the design of information systems.

It is generally understood that the challenge of privacy protection in the information age is the application and enforcement of Fair Information Practices and the OECD Guidelines. While some recommendations for improvement have been made, the level of consensus, at least outside of the United States, about the viability of Fair Information Practices as a general solution to the problem of privacy protection is remarkable. As recently as 1998 the OECD reaffirmed support for the 1980 guidelines, and countries that are adopting privacy legislation have generally done so in the tradition of Fair Information Practices.

While some commentators have made recommendations for updating or expanding the principles, there is general agreement that the concept of Fair Information Practices and the specific standards set out in the OECD Guidelines continue to provide a useful and effective framework for privacy protection in information systems.

Commentators have also noted a remarkable convergence of privacy policies. Countries around the world, with very distinct cultural backgrounds and systems of governance, nonetheless have adopted roughly similar approaches to privacy protection. Perhaps this is not so surprising. The original OECD Guidelines were drafted by representatives from North America, Europe, and Asia. The OECD Guidelines reflect a broad consensus about how to safeguard the control and use of personal information in a world where data can flow freely across national borders. Just as it does today on the Internet. . . .

Viewed against this background, the problem of privacy protection in the United States in the early 1990s was fairly well understood. The coverage of U.S. law was uneven: Fair Information Practices were in force in some sectors and not others. There was inadequate enforcement and oversight. Technology continued to outpace the law. And the failure to adopt a comprehensive legal framework to safeguard privacy rights could jeopardize transborder data flows with Europe and other regions. These factors should all have played a significant role in coding a solution to the privacy problem. . . .

2. THE PRIVACY ACT

Influenced by the HEW Report's Fair Information Practices and inspired by the Watergate scandal, Congress enacted the Privacy Act of 1974 four months after President Nixon resigned from office. In passing the Privacy Act, Congress found that "the privacy of an individual is directly affected by the collection, maintenance, use, and dissemination of personal information by Federal agencies" and that "the increasing use of computers and sophisticated information technology, while essential to the efficient operations of the Government, has greatly magnified the harm to individual privacy that can occur from any collection, maintenance, use, or dissemination of personal information."

Purposes of the Privacy Act. The Privacy Act's stated purposes are, among other things, to: (1) "permit an individual to determine what records pertaining to him are collected, maintained, used, or disseminated by [federal] agencies"; (2) "permit an individual to prevent records pertaining to him obtained by such agencies for a particular purpose from being used or made available for another purpose without his consent"; (3) allow an individual to access and correct his personal data maintained by federal agencies; and (4) ensure that information is "current and accurate for its intended use, and that adequate safeguards are provided to prevent misuse of such information."

Applicability and Scope. The Privacy Act applies to federal agencies. It does not apply to businesses or private sector organizations. Moreover, it does not apply to state and local agencies—only federal ones.

In order to establish a violation of the Privacy Act, a plaintiff must prove several things:

First, the plaintiff must prove that the agency violated its obligations under the Act (most often, that the agency improperly disclosed information).

Second, the information disclosed must be a "record" contained within a "system of records." A "record" must be identifiable to an individual (contain her name or other identifying information) and must contain information about the individual. § 552a(a)(4). The record must be kept as part of a "system of records," which is "a group of any records under the control of any agency from which information is retrieved by the name of the individual or by some identifying number, symbol, or other identifying particular assigned to the individual." § 552a(a)(5).

Third, to collect damages, the plaintiff must show that an adverse impact resulted from the Privacy Act violation and that the violation was "willful or intentional."

Limits on Disclosure. Pursuant to the Privacy Act:

> No agency shall disclose any record which is contained in a system of records by any means of communication to any person, or to another agency, except pursuant to a written request by, or with prior written consent of, the individual to whom the record pertains. 5 U.S.C. § 552a(b).

Responsibilities for Recordkeeping. The Privacy Act establishes restrictions and responsibilities for agencies maintaining records about individuals. Agencies shall maintain "only such information about an individual as is relevant and necessary to accomplish a purpose of the agency required to be accomplished by statute or by executive order of the President." § 552a(e)(1). Additionally, agencies shall "collect information to the greatest extent practicable directly from the subject individual when the information may result in adverse determinations about an individual's rights, benefits, and privileges under Federal programs." § 552a(e)(2). Agencies shall inform individuals who make a request about how their personal information will be used. § 552a(e)(3). Agencies must publish in the Federal Register notices about the systems of records they maintain. § 552a(e)(4). Agencies must also "establish appropriate administrative, technical, and physical safeguards to insure the security and confidentiality of records." § 552a(e)(10).

Right to Access and Correct Records. Pursuant to the federal Privacy Act, upon request, individuals can review their records and can ask that the agency correct any inaccuracies in their records. § 552a(d).

Enforcement. If an agency fails to comply with any provision of the Privacy Act, or refuses to comply with an individual's request to obtain access to her records or correct her records, individuals can bring a civil action in federal court. § 552a(g)(1). The court can enjoin the agency from withholding access of records. § 552a(g)(3). In limited circumstances, monetary damages may be awarded:

> (4) In any suit brought under the provisions of subsection (g)(1)(C) or (D) of this section in which the court determines that the agency acted in a manner which was intentional or willful, the United States shall be liable to the individual in an amount equal to the sum of —
>
> > (A) actual damages sustained by the individual as a result of the refusal or failure, but in no case shall a person entitled to recovery receive less than the sum of $1,000; and
> > (B) the costs of the action together with reasonable attorney fees as determined by the court. § 552a(g)(4).

Law Enforcement Exceptions. Pursuant to § 552a(j), the "head of any agency may promulgate rules . . . to exempt any system of records within the agency from any part of [the Privacy Act] if the system of records" is (1) maintained by the CIA or (2) maintained by a law enforcement agency and consists of (A) identifying and criminal history information compiled to identify criminal offenders or (B) "information compiled for the purpose of criminal investigation, including reports of informants and investigators, and associated with an identifiable individual"; or (C) "reports identifiable to an individual compiled at any stage of the process of enforcement of the criminal laws from arrest or indictment through release from supervision." This exception does not apply to § 552a(b), §§ 552a(c)(1) and (2), and certain portions of § 552(e).

Additionally, § 552(k)(2) allows the head of any agency to promulgate rules to exempt "investigatory material compiled for law enforcement purposes" from the Act's accounting and access provisions. However, "if any individual is denied any right, privilege, or benefit that we would otherwise be entitled by Federal law . . . as a result of the maintenance of such material, such material shall be provided to the individual, except to the extent that the disclosure of such material would reveal the identity of a [government informant]."

FOIA Exception. When FOIA requires that information be released, the Privacy Act does not apply. § 552a(b)(3).

Routine Use Exception. The broadest exception under the Privacy Act is that information may be disclosed for any "routine use" if disclosure is "compatible" with the purpose for which the agency collected the information. § 552a(b)(3).

Information Sharing Among Agencies. The Privacy Act permits one agency to disclose information "to another agency or to an instrumentality of any governmental jurisdiction within or under the control of the United States for a civil or criminal law enforcement activity" if the agency or instrumentality's head makes "a written request to the agency which maintains the record." § 552a(b)(7).

Other Exceptions. In all, there are about a dozen exceptions to the Privacy Act. Other exceptions allow disclosure to the Census Bureau, "to a person pursuant to a showing of compelling circumstances affecting the health or safety of an individual"; to Congress; to the Comptroller General, pursuant to a court order, or to a credit reporting agency. § 552a(b).

State Privacy Acts. Although every state has a statute comparable to the federal FOIA, requiring public access to government records, most states do not have a statute comparable to the federal Privacy Act. Only about a third of states have adopted such a statute.

QUINN V. STONE

978 F.2d 126 (3d Cir. 1992)

HIGGINBOTHAM, J. Appellants Randall Quinn (Quinn) and Marianne Merritt (Merritt) are married to each other and work at the Letterkenny Army Depot (LEAD) in Chambersburg, Pennsylvania as civilian employees. Appellee Michael P.W. Stone is the Secretary of the Army and the second appellee is the Department of the Army. At LEAD, Quinn is a natural resource manager and Merritt is an environmentalist. Quinn is responsible for controlling the deer population on LEAD property by setting the length of the hunting season and determining the types of deer to be killed. . . .

In addition to their professional interest in LEAD's wildlife, Quinn and Merritt are both deer hunters and hunt deer on LEAD property with other hunters. Quinn and Merritt are registered with the Pennsylvania Game Commission and possess valid Pennsylvania hunting licenses. Quinn and Merritt also have "bonus tags" which allow the holder to kill one additional deer during the hunting season. Both also possess valid LEAD hunting permits.

On January 6, 1990, Quinn and Merritt went hunting on LEAD property. At check-in Post 2, both Quinn and Merritt complied with the LEAD procedures whereby all hunters are required to produce their Pennsylvania hunting licenses and LEAD hunting permits. As part of this check-in procedure, the LEAD Security employees annotate a computer-generated hunting roster, which lists all hunters with LEAD hunting permits. Each entry on this roster corresponds to a single hunter and consists of:

 a. the LEAD permit number
 b. the Pennsylvania hunting license number
 c. the name of the hunter
 d. the address of the hunter
 e. the phone number of the hunter.

The hunting roster is computer-generated at the beginning of the hunting day, with the check-in time, check-out time, and kill information added by hand as the day progresses.

The computer-generated LEAD hunting roster for January 6, 1990 incorrectly gave separate addresses and phone numbers for Quinn and Merritt. The roster indicated that Quinn lived at an address in St. Thomas, Pennsylvania and Merritt in Chambersburg, Pennsylvania. Both parties agree that Merritt's listed address was incorrect and out-of-date. Apparently, her prior address was never changed in the LEAD files, even though Merritt had written her new address on her LEAD hunting permit application, her LEAD hunting license, her application for a Pennsylvania hunting license, and her Pennsylvania hunting license for the 1988-89 and 1989-90 hunting seasons.

Two of Security personnel conducting the check-in at Post 2 during the day were Lark Myers (Myers) and Statler. Statler personally observed Quinn and Merritt checking in to hunt. Shortly after Quinn and Merritt checked in, Myers mentioned to Statler that Quinn had previously brought a deer to Myers' fiance's butcher shop to be butchered. Statler questioned how Quinn could still be hunting this season if he had already killed one deer. Statler reviewed the roster and found Quinn's name. Statler then looked for Quinn's wife's name but did not recognize Merritt's name. He then asked Myers what Quinn's wife's name was and Myers told him that she thought Merritt continued to go by the name of Merritt after her marriage to Quinn. Statler again reviewed the hunting roster and found Merritt's entry. Statler noted that the home address listed for Merritt was different from that listed for Quinn and remarked on this to Myers.

Later that morning, Statler reported to David Miller (Miller), an investigator in LEAD Security, the information that Quinn and Merritt were hunting and that they had taken a deer to be butchered earlier during the hunting season. Miller then informed Jody Eyer (Eyer), a part-time Deputy Wildlife Conservation Officer with the Pennsylvania Game Commission, of Quinn's and Merritt's hunting even though Quinn had previously killed a deer that season. Eyer believed that there were grounds to suspect that a hunting violation had occurred since a hunter is generally allowed to kill only one deer a season. Eyer contacted Statler and spoke with him directly. He also reviewed the hunting roster. Eyer turned the case over to Frank Clark (Clark), a full-time PGC Wildlife Conservation Officer, for investigation, although Eyer continued to aid in the investigation.

On January 9, 1990, LEAD's Miller met with PGC's Clark. In this meeting, Clark reviewed the hunting roster generated at Post 2 and noted the discrepancies between Quinn's and Merritt's listed addresses. To Clark, the two addresses raised the possibility that Quinn and Merritt "had used two addresses to illegally obtain two sets of hunting licenses." At this meeting, Clark requested that LEAD review available files to determine the correct addresses. LEAD investigator Fox (Fox) did so but was unable to determine the correct addresses. . . .

[After an extensive investigation, Clark concluded that there "was no evidence to charge Quinn and Merritt with hunting violations."]

The appellants allege that both suffered occupational and health damage as a result of the disclosures. Quinn alleges that he suffered damage to his professional image, reputation, integrity and working relationship with LEAD and PGC personnel. Merritt alleges that her reputation for "law-abidingness and integrity" was damaged. Quinn also alleges suffering from stress, headaches, hypertension, chest pains, sinusitis, nervousness, and inability to sleep. Merritt alleges she suffered stress, nervousness, and inability to sleep. Both allege they suffered emotional anguish.

Quinn and Merritt filed separate actions alleging violations of the Privacy Act, 5 U.S.C. § 552a, and seeking an order directing the Army to purge its files of records relating to the plaintiffs and damages for violations of the Act. The district court granted the defendants' motion to consolidate the actions and on September 18, 1991 granted the defendants' motion for summary judgment. Plaintiffs filed a timely appeal. . . .

This appeal presents several different issues relating to three of the four necessary elements for a damages suit under the Privacy Act. As we explain in this opinion, in order to maintain a suit for damages under the catch-all provision of 5 U.S.C. § 552a(g)(1)(D) for a violation of the Act's central prohibition against disclosure, § 552a(b), a plaintiff must advance evidence to support a jury's finding of four necessary elements: (1) the information is covered by the Act as a "record" contained in a "system of records"; (2) the agency "disclose[d]" the information; (3) the disclosure had an "adverse effect" on the plaintiff (an element which separates itself into two components: (a) an adverse effect standing requirement and (b) a causal nexus between the disclosure and the adverse effect); and (4) the disclosure was "willful or intentional."

The appellees first argue that the district court properly granted summary judgment because the information relating to Merritt on the LEAD hunting roster and on her time card is not information covered by the Act. We disagree.

The Act defines a "record" to mean:

> any item, collection, or grouping of information about an individual that is maintained by an agency, including, but not limited to, his education, financial transactions, medical history, and criminal or employment history and that contains his name, or the identifying particular assigned to the individual, such as a finger or voice print or a photograph.

5 U.S.C. § 552a(a)(4). Further, the Act's prohibition on disclosure relates to "any record which is contained in a system of records." § 552a(b). Fitting the statutory definitions of a protected record, the information allegedly disclosed from both the hunting roster and the time card contained an identifying particular (the plaintiff's name) and was maintained within a system of records.

Appellees propose two separate arguments that the information contained in the hunting roster is not a "record" within the meaning of the Act. First, they argue that stale or incorrect information, such as Merritt's out-of-date address and telephone number, is not covered by the Act because this information is not meaningful. We cannot accept this argument in this case. The Third Circuit has recently re-affirmed that, at the very least, there is a "meaningful" privacy interest in home addresses. *Federal Labor Relations Authority v. U.S. Department of the Navy,* 966 F.2d 747 (3d Cir. 1992) (en banc). As we noted there, the disclosure of home addresses "can identify specific and sometimes personal characteristics about residents." In the light of the other information disclosed in this case, the disclosure of the existence of an out-of-date address, different from the one at which Merritt was currently living, revealed the meaningful information that Merritt had maintained an address apart from Quinn's, an address that might be used to manipulate Pennsylvania's hunting laws. As this case demonstrates, the meaningful privacy interest in a particular piece of information may be lessened by the passage of time, but such an interest is unlikely to be extinguished. We conclude that this out-of-date home address was meaningful information and was protected by the Privacy Act.

Second, the appellees argue that the Act protects only information which discloses a characteristic or quality of an individual. The appellees contend that Merritt's information on the hunting roster did not constitute a "record" because "none of the information disclosed a characteristic or quality about her." Applying this argument also to the time card, appellees argue that "[t]he fact that an individual was working or not on a weekday is not information which discloses a characteristic [or] quality about the person."

At first blush, this argument seems close to the requirement that the information must be meaningful, but appellees here propose a different gloss on the statute than that of meaningfulness. They would read the Act to protect only that category of information which is intimate or personal, information which directly reflects a specific or personal characteristic about a person (as opposed to information which might reveal such specific and personal characteristics but only in conjunction with other pieces of information). . . .

[W]e think that such information does reveal a "quality or characteristic" about that person. Time card information regarding taking time off from work as compensation for overtime, as sick leave, or for vacation can easily be considered descriptive of an individual.

More significantly, we reject appellees' underlying argument that the information covered by the Act as a "record" is limited to the information that directly reflects a characteristic or quality of the individual. . . . [W]e find such an interpretation contrary to the language of the statute. On its face, § 552a(a)(4)'s statutory definition of a record as "any item, collection, or grouping of information about an individual" appears to us to have a broad meaning encompassing *any* information about an individual that is linked to that individual through an identifying particular and is not to be restricted to information that reflects a characteristic or quality of an individual. Moreover, our interpretation is consistent with the thrust of the statutory definition. A "record" may be "any item, collection, or grouping of information about an individual." 5 U.S.C. § 552a(a)(4). While a record can therefore consist of a single piece of information, it may also be a collection or grouping of pieces of information. Thus, even if a piece of information could not meet a "characteristic or quality" test standing alone, it could still be included within a "record" as statutorily defined and protected by the Act if that piece of information were linked with an identifying particular (or was itself an identifying particular) and maintained within a system of records.

We thus . . . conclude in this case that both the information on the hunting roster and time card was information that was covered by the Act.

Even if the information on the hunting roster and on the time card were covered by the Act, appellees make two arguments that this information was not "disclosed" within the meaning of 552a(b). The appellees contend that, while Quinn's home address and telephone number were records, they were not disclosed within the meaning of 5 U.S.C. § 552a(b) because the information had been previously disclosed by Quinn to the Pennsylvania Game Commission. Appellees argue that disclosure contemplates release of information not otherwise known to the recipient.

We agree the Act is not violated where the agency makes available information which is already known by the recipient.

There is no basis, however, in this record to make such an argument. Clearly, there was no prior knowledge of the information on the time card. Likewise, there is no evidence on this record that Eyer and Clark, the investigators in the field, already had any actual knowledge of the home address information. There is, by contrast, evidence that Eyer and Clark received the partially out-of-date information about Quinn's and Merritt's addresses by means of a disclosure of the hunting roster. Without evidence that Eyer and Clark otherwise knew the information disclosed, the appellees' argument fails.

The appellees next contend that no disclosure of information occurs when the information, even if not actually known by the recipient, is otherwise public. Appellees may be making either of two arguments here. To say that information is public can mean either that such information is readily accessible to the members of the public or that each individual member of the public should be presumed to know this information. We reject both arguments.

Appellees have cited to this court no case that stands for the proposition that there is no violation of the Act if the information is merely readily accessible to the members of the public (such as in the local telephone book) and our research has discovered none. We doubt if any court would so hold. To do so would eviscerate the Act's central prohibition, the prohibition against disclosure. For instance, such an argument would short-circuit the delicate balancing courts now engage in between the FOIA and the Privacy Act under 5 U.S.C. § 552a(b)(2). See *FLRA v. U.S. Department of the Navy,* 966 F.2d 747 (3d Cir. 1992) (en banc). To define disclosure so narrowly as to exclude information that is readily accessible to the public would render superfluous the detailed statutory scheme of twelve exceptions to the prohibition on disclosure. We conclude that making available information which is readily accessible to the members of the public is a disclosure under 552a(b), subject, of course, to the Act's exceptions. . . .

We thus conclude that not only was the information contained in the hunting roster and the time card covered by the Act, but it was also disclosed within the Act's terms.

What remains is to examine the Act's "adverse effect" requirement. The Privacy Act's civil remedies section, in relevant part, provides as follows:

> (g)(1) Civil remedies. — Whenever any agency . . .
>   (D) fails to comply with any other provision of this section, or any rule promulgated thereunder, in such a way as to have an adverse effect on an individual,
>   the individual may bring a civil action against the agency, and the district courts of the United States shall have jurisdiction in the matters under the provisions of this subsection.

This section thus gives an individual adversely affected by any agency violation of the Act a judicial remedy whereby the individual may seek damages. Thus, there are two limitations placed on the right to sue. First, the adverse effect requirement of (g)(1)(D) is, in effect, a standing requirement. Allegations of mental distress, emotional trauma, or embarrassment have been held sufficient to confer standing. *Albright v. United States,* 732 F.2d 181 (D.C. Cir. 1984). Second, to state a claim under the Act, the plaintiff must also allege a causal connection between the agency violation and the adverse effect. . . .

Appellees argue that neither of these two requirements were met in this case. First, they argue that Merritt makes no assertion that the release of time card information had an adverse effect on her sufficient to confer standing. Upon any fair reading of the record, however, appellees' argument cannot be sustained. As we have recounted above, both appellants allege that they have undergone stress and emotional anguish. Both also allege that they have suffered occupational losses due to the PGC investigation allegedly caused by the disclosures. We think these allegations sufficient to satisfy the Act's adverse effect standing requirement.

With greater vigor, appellees argue there is no causal connection between the disclosures and the adverse effects. They assert that the PGC's investigation was begun prior to and independent of the disclosure of the hunting roster. Appellees claim that the only information passed along to the PGC was Statler's personal observation that plaintiffs were hunting on Jan. 6, 1990 and Myers' observation that they had previously taken a deer to the butcher's. Defendants also claim that the time card disclosure had no causal connection to the adverse effects suffered by the plaintiffs.

We believe, however, that the record amply shows a causal connection between the disclosures and the alleged adverse effects on Quinn and Merritt by means of the PGC investigation. First, there is sufficient evidence for a jury to find that the PGC investigation was initially caused in significant part by the disclosure of the discrepant addresses. There is evidence that the varying addresses were passed along by LEAD Security employee Statler to Eyer of the PGC from the beginning of the investigation. . . .

A trier of fact could infer that the address discrepancy was part of the impetus for Eyer to turn the investigation over to Clark, the full-time investigator.

We thus cannot agree with the district court that the difference in addresses which initially raised the suspicion of the PGC investigator was "only a small part of his investigation." This piece of information was present from the very beginning of the investigation and may have played a significant role in the crucial decisions to initiate and pursue the investigation.

Second, there is sufficient evidence for a jury to conclude that the disclosure of Merritt's time card information served to fuel and to keep the investigation going even after the discrepancy in the addresses had been resolved. . . .

The issue of the "routine use" exception to the Act's prohibition on disclosure has been argued before this court by both parties. However, the issue was not argued before the district court in support of the defendants' motion for summary judgment and the district court did not consider the issue. We thus consider this issue waived for purposes of this appeal. . . .

We recognize that some persons might feel that a lengthy opinion such as this that explores whether or not it was permissible to reveal matters so mundane as information on a hunting record and a time card is a trivialization of the federal litigation process. However, Congress has made the choice that there are some areas of privacy which must be recognized by the federal government in its management of information and, as we read the present record, the appellants should not be precluded from proving their allegations. The district court's grant of summary judgment in favor of the appellees will be reversed in part and affirmed in part and the case remanded for further proceedings consistent with this opinion.

NYGAARD, J. dissenting. While I agree with most of the conclusions reached by the majority, because I believe that the disclosure of the contents of these records was pursuant to a "routine use," I respectfully dissent.

The Privacy Act states that records are not protected from disclosure if the disclosure is pursuant to a "routine use." 5 U.S.C. § 552a(b)(3). A routine use is defined as "the use of such record for a purpose which is compatible with the purpose for which it was collected." 5 U.S.C. § 552a(a)(7). In addition, the Privacy Act states that the agencies must publish a notice each year in the Federal Register indicating the routine uses for which protected records may be used. 5 U.S.C. § 552a(e)(4). This information must include "the categories of users and the purpose of such use." 5 U.S.C. § 552a(e)(4)(D).

In compliance with the Privacy Act, the DOD published in the Federal Register, "blanket routine uses" which are applicable to every record system maintained by its various branches, including the army.

One of these provisions entitled "Routine Use-Law Enforcement," states:

> In the event that a system of records maintained by this component to carry out its functions indicates a violation or potential violation of law . . . the relevant records in the system of records may be referred, as a routine use, to the appropriate agency, whether federal, state, local, or foreign, charged with the responsibility of *investigating or prosecuting such violation* [.] Fed. Reg., May 29, 1985. (emphasis added.) . . . .

These routine uses fairly cover the facts of this case. The disclosure of the hunting roster information was for use by the Pennsylvania Game Commission's wildlife conservation officers to investigate possible violations of state hunting laws. This was precisely the type of "state law enforcement" the regulations covered.

Here, one of the main purposes for the collection of the information on the hunting roster was to monitor hunting in order to prevent unlawful overkilling of deer. The disclosure was made to help PGC find out if appellants were trying to hunt deer lawfully. . . .

The disclosure of Merritt's time card information to PGC investigator Clark creates a tougher question. . . .

In general, the main reason time cards are collected is to determine employees' work hours in order to compute payroll. It is not to collect information about an employee which can be used against him in a criminal investigation.

Nonetheless, the *main* purpose for which time cards are collected certainly is not the *only* purpose. One of the reasons time card information is collected is to find out if an employee was at work on a given day-the precise reason for which it was used in this case. LEAD disclosed information on Merritt's time card precisely for this purpose. . . .

For this reason, I would affirm the district court's grant of summary judgment as to both Merritt's time card and the hunting roster.

NOTES & QUESTIONS

1. ***Information in the Public Domain.*** The court in *Quinn* holds that even publicly accessible information is protected against disclosure by the Privacy Act because holding otherwise "would eviscerate the Act's central prohibition, the prohibition against disclosure." The court noted that it could find no court to conclude that information already in the public domain would not be protected. Subsequently, some courts have so concluded. For example,

in *Barry v. U.S. Department of Justice*, 63 F. Supp. 2d 25 (D.D.C. 1999), the court concluded that a record widely accessible to the public was not protected by the Privacy Act. It distinguished *Quinn* along with other "decisions involving information that may have been 'public,' but that could be found only in isolated public records." The court concluded that because the record in question was publicly available in a way not "isolated or obscure," it was not protected by the Privacy Act. Did *Quinn* turn on the fact that the addresses were "obscure or isolated"? Should information already available to the public be protected against disclosure by the Privacy Act?

2. *The "Routine Use" Exemption: "The Biggest Loophole."* Consider Robert Gellman:

> The act limits use of personal data to those officers and employees of the agency maintaining the data who have a need for the data in the performance their duties. This vague standard is not a significant barrier to the sharing of personal information within agencies. . . . No administrative process exists to control or limit internal agency uses. Suits have been brought by individuals who objected to specific uses, but most uses have been upheld. . . .
>
> The legislation left most decisions about external uses to the agencies, and this created the biggest loophole in the law.
>
> An agency can establish a "routine use" if it determines that a disclosure is compatible with the purpose for which the record was collected. This vague formula has not created much of a substantive barrier to external disclosure of personal information. . . . Later legislation, political pressures, and bureaucratic convenience tended to overwhelm the law's weak limitations. Without any effective restriction on disclosure, the Privacy Act lost much of its vitality and became more procedural and more symbolic.[30]

Other observers have noted the problematic nature of the Privacy Act's "routine use" exemption. According to the Privacy Act's language, a routine use must be "a purpose which is compatible with the purpose for which it was collected." 5 U.S.C. § 552a(7). Paul Schwartz observes:

> Not only is the "routine use" exemption applied in a fashion that ignores relevant statutory language, such agency practice continues despite prolonged and well-placed criticism of it. As early as 1977, the Privacy Protection Study Commission, a blue-ribbon commission created by Congress at the time of the Privacy Act's enactment, noted its disapproval of overbroad applications of the routine use exemption. In 1983, the House Committee on Government Operations issued a condemnation of such agency practice. Three years later, the Congressional Office of Technology Assessment complained that the routine use exemption had become "a catchall exemption." . . . David Flaherty, in a pathbreaking comparative study of data protection law, *Protecting Privacy in Surveillance Societies*, called the American routine use exemption "a huge loophole." Despite these comments, agencies continue to justify almost any use of information as a "routine use" of the data.[31]

---

[30] Robert Gellman, *Does Privacy Law Work?* in Technology and Privacy: The New Landscape (Philip E. Agre & Marc Rotenberg eds. 1997).

[31] Paul M. Schwartz, *Privacy and Participation*, 80 Iowa L. Rev. 553, 586 (1995).

Only a few courts have placed substantive limits on an agency's proposed "routine use" of personal information. Justin Franklin and Robert Bouchard conclude: "In practice, many of the cases where a 'routine use' defense is raised are resolved in favor of the government."[32]

3. **What Is an "Agency"?** The Privacy Act only applies to federal agencies. In *Tripp v. Executive Office of the President,* 200 F.R.D. 140 (D.D.C. 2001), Linda Tripp sued the Executive Office of the President (EOP), the Department of Defense (DOD), and the FBI. Tripp, the friend of Monica Lewinsky who secretly recorded their conversations to assist Kenneth Starr in his investigation of President Clinton, contended that the EOP, DOD, and FBI leaked confidential information about her to the media in retaliation for her role in the Clinton investigation. The EOP moved to dismiss claiming that it was not an "agency" within the meaning of the Privacy Act. The Privacy Act adopts FOIA's definition of "agency," which "includes any executive department . . . . or other establishment in the executive branch of the Government (including the Executive Office of the President), or any independent regulatory agency." 5 U.S.C. § 552(f). However, the court concluded:

> The plain language of the Privacy Act directs one to look to the FOIA for the definition of "agency." 5 U.S.C. § 552a(1). While on its face, the FOIA states that the definition of "agency" includes the Executive Office of the President, the U.S. Supreme Court, the D.C. Circuit, and Congress, through the FOIA's legislative history, have all made it abundantly clear this does not include the Office of the President.

Unlike the EOP, the FBI and DOD are agencies under the Privacy Act. In 2003, Tripp settled her Privacy Act suit against the Defense Department for $590,000.

4. **What Constitutes a "Record" in a "System of Records"?** The Privacy Act does not apply to all information or records that an agency maintains. Rather, it applies to records contained in a "system of records." A "system of records" is a group of records where data is retrieved by an individual's name or other identifying information. 5 U.S.C. § 552a(a)(4). A "record" is "any item, collection, or grouping of information about an individual . . . that contains his name [or other identifying information]." In *Albright v. United States,* 631 F.2d 915 (D.C. Cir. 1980), the court analyzed whether a videotape of a meeting constituted a "record" under the Privacy Act. The court concluded that it was: "As long as the tape contains a means of identifying an individual by picture or voice, it falls within the definition of 'record' under the Privacy Act."

---

[32] Justin D. Franklin & Robert E. Bouchard, *Guidebook to the Freedom of Information and Privacy Acts* §2:18 (2007).

DOE V. CHAO

540 U.S. 614 (2004)

SOUTER, J. The United States is subject to a cause of action for the benefit of at least some individuals adversely affected by a federal agency's violation of the Privacy Act of 1974. The question before us is whether plaintiffs must prove some actual damages to qualify for a minimum statutory award of $1,000. We hold that they must.

Petitioner Buck Doe filed for benefits under the Black Lung Benefits Act, 83 Stat. 792, 30 U.S.C. § 901 *et seq.,* with the Office of Workers' Compensation Programs, the division of the Department of Labor responsible for adjudicating it. The application form called for a Social Security number, which the agency then used to identify the applicant's claim, as on documents like "multicaptioned" notices of hearing dates, sent to groups of claimants, their employers, and the lawyers involved in their cases. The Government concedes that following this practice led to disclosing Doe's Social Security number beyond the limits set by the Privacy Act. See 5 U.S.C. § 552a(b).

Doe joined with six other black lung claimants to sue the Department of Labor, alleging repeated violations of the Act and seeking certification of a class of "'all claimants for Black Lung Benefits since the passage of the Privacy Act.'" Pet. for Cert. 6a. Early on, the United States stipulated to an order prohibiting future publication of applicants' Social Security numbers on multicaptioned hearing notices, and the parties then filed cross-motions for summary judgment. The District Court denied class certification and entered judgment against all individual plaintiffs except Doe, finding that their submissions had raised no issues of cognizable harm. As to Doe, the court accepted his uncontroverted evidence of distress on learning of the improper disclosure, granted summary judgment, and awarded $1,000 in statutory damages under 5 U.S.C. § 552a(g)(4).

A divided panel of the Fourth Circuit affirmed in part but reversed on Doe's claim, holding the United States entitled to summary judgment across the board. 306 F.3d 170 (2002). The Circuit treated the $1,000 statutory minimum as available only to plaintiffs who suffered actual damages because of the agency's violation, and then found that Doe had not raised a triable issue of fact about actual damages, having submitted no corroboration for his claim of emotional distress, such as evidence of physical symptoms, medical treatment, loss of income, or impact on his behavior. In fact, the only indication of emotional affliction was Doe's conclusory allegations that he was " 'torn . . . all to pieces' " and " 'greatly concerned and worried' " because of the disclosure of his Social Security number and its potentially " 'devastating' " consequences.

Doe petitioned for review of the holding that some actual damages must be proven before a plaintiff may receive the minimum statutory award. . . .

"[I]n order to protect the privacy of individuals identified in information systems maintained by Federal agencies, it is necessary . . . to regulate the collection, maintenance, use, and dissemination of information by such agencies." Privacy Act of 1974. The Act gives agencies detailed instructions for managing their records and provides for various sorts of civil relief to individuals aggrieved by failures on the Government's part to comply with the requirements.

Subsection (g)(1) recognizes a civil action for agency misconduct fitting within any of four categories (the fourth, in issue here, being a catchall), 5 U.S.C. §§ 552a(g)(1)(A)–(D), and then makes separate provision for the redress of each. The first two categories cover deficient management of records: subsection (g)(1)(A) provides for the correction of any inaccurate or otherwise improper material in a record, and subsection (g)(1)(B) provides a right of access against any agency refusing to allow an individual to inspect a record kept on him. . . .

Like the inspection and correction infractions, breaches of the statute with adverse consequences are addressed by specific terms governing relief:

> In any suit brought under the provisions of subsection (g)(1)(C) or (D) of this section in which the court determines that the agency acted in a manner which was intentional or willful, the United States shall be liable to the individual in an amount equal to the sum of —
>
> > (A) actual damages sustained by the individual as a result of the refusal or failure, but in no case shall a person entitled to recovery receive less than the sum of $1,000; and
> > (B) the costs of the action together with reasonable attorney fees as determined by the court. § 552a(g)(4).

Doe argues that subsection (g)(4)(A) entitles any plaintiff adversely affected by an intentional or willful violation to the $1,000 minimum on proof of nothing more than a statutory violation: anyone suffering an adverse consequence of intentional or willful disclosure is entitled to recovery. The Government claims the minimum guarantee goes only to victims who prove some actual damages. We think the Government has the better side of the argument.

To begin with, the Government's position is supported by a straightforward textual analysis. When the statute gets to the point of guaranteeing the $1,000 minimum, it not only has confined any eligibility to victims of adverse effects caused by intentional or willful actions, but has provided expressly for liability to such victims for "actual damages sustained." It has made specific provision, in other words, for what a victim within the limited class may recover. When the very next clause of the sentence containing the explicit provision guarantees $1,000 to a "person entitled to recovery," the simplest reading of that phrase looks back to the immediately preceding provision for recovering actual damages, which is also the Act's sole provision for recovering anything (as distinct from equitable relief). With such an obvious referent for "person entitled to recovery" in the plaintiff who sustains "actual damages," Doe's theory is immediately questionable in ignoring the "actual damages" language so directly at hand and instead looking for "a person entitled to recovery" in a separate part of the statute devoid of any mention either of recovery or of what might be recovered.

Nor is it too strong to say that Doe does ignore statutory language. When Doe reads the statute to mean that the United States shall be liable to any adversely affected subject of an intentional or willful violation, without more, he treats willful action as the last fact necessary to make the Government "liable," and he is thus able to describe anyone to whom it is liable as entitled to the $1,000 guarantee. But this way of reading the statute simply pays no attention to the fact that the statute does not speak of liability (and consequent entitlement to recovery) in a freestanding, unqualified way, but in a limited way, by reference to enumerated damages.

Doe's manner of reading "entitle[ment] to recovery" as satisfied by adverse effect caused by intentional or willful violation is in tension with more than the text, however. It is at odds with the traditional understanding that tort recovery requires not only wrongful act plus causation reaching to the plaintiff, but proof of some harm for which damages can reasonably be assessed. Doe, instead, identifies a person as entitled to recover without any reference to proof of damages, actual or otherwise. Doe might respond that it makes sense to speak of a privacy tort victim as entitled to recover without reference to damages because analogous common law would not require him to show particular items of injury in order to receive a dollar recovery. Traditionally, the common law has provided such victims with a claim for "general" damages, which for privacy and defamation torts are presumed damages: a monetary award calculated without reference to specific harm. . . .

This [conclusion] . . . is underscored by drafting history showing that Congress cut out the very language in the bill that would have authorized any presumed damages. The Senate bill would have authorized an award of "actual and general damages sustained by any person," with that language followed by the guarantee that "in no case shall a person entitled to recovery receive less than the sum of $1,000." S. 3418, 93d Cong., 2d Sess., § 303(c)(1) (1974). Although the provision for general damages would have covered presumed damages, this language was trimmed from the final statute, subject to any later revision that might be recommended by the Commission. The deletion of "general damages" from the bill is fairly seen, then, as a deliberate elimination of any possibility of imputing harm and awarding presumed damages. The deletion thus precludes any hope of a sound interpretation of entitlement to recovery without reference to actual damages.

Finally, Doe's reading is open to the objection that no purpose is served by conditioning the guarantee on a person's being entitled to recovery. As Doe treats the text, Congress could have accomplished its object simply by providing that the Government would be liable to the individual for actual damages "but in no case . . . less than the sum of $1,000" plus fees and costs. Doe's reading leaves the reference to entitlement to recovery with no job to do, and it accordingly accomplishes nothing. . . .

Next, Doe also suggests there is something peculiar in offering some guaranteed damages, as a form of presumed damages not requiring proof of amount, only to those plaintiffs who can demonstrate actual damages. But this approach parallels another remedial scheme that the drafters of the Privacy Act would probably have known about. At common law, certain defamation torts were redressed by general damages but only when a plaintiff first proved some "special harm," *i.e.,* "harm of a material and generally of a pecuniary nature." 3 Restatement of Torts § 575, Comments *a* and *b* (1938) (discussing defamation torts that are "not actionable per se"). Plaintiffs claiming such torts could recover presumed damages only if they could demonstrate some actual, quantifiable pecuniary loss. Because the recovery of presumed damages in these cases was supplemental to compensation for specific harm, it was hardly unprecedented for

Congress to make a guaranteed minimum contingent upon some showing of actual damages, thereby avoiding giveaways to plaintiffs with nothing more than "abstract injuries." . . .

The "entitle[ment] to recovery" necessary to qualify for the $1,000 minimum is not shown merely by an intentional or willful violation of the Act producing some adverse effect. The statute guarantees $1,000 only to plaintiffs who have suffered some actual damages.

GINSBURG, STEVENS, & BREYER, J.J. dissenting. "It is 'a cardinal principle of statutory construction' that 'a statute ought, upon the whole, to be so construed that, if it can be prevented, no clause, sentence, or word shall be superfluous, void, or insignificant.'" The Court's reading of § 552a(g)(4) is hardly in full harmony with that principle. Under the Court's construction, the words "a person entitled to recovery" have no office, and the liability-determining element "adverse effect" becomes superfluous, swallowed up by the "actual damages" requirement. Further, the Court's interpretation renders the word "recovery" nothing more than a synonym for "actual damages," and it turns the phrase "shall be liable" into "may be liable." . . .

The purpose and legislative history of the Privacy Act, as well as similarly designed statutes, are in harmony with the reading of § 552a(g)(4) most federal judges have found sound. Congress sought to afford recovery for "*any* damages" resulting from the "willful or intentional" violation of "any individual's rights under th[e] Act." § 2(b)(6), 88 Stat. 1896 (emphasis added). Privacy Act violations commonly cause fear, anxiety, or other emotional distress — in the Act's parlance, "adverse effects." Harm of this character must, of course, be proved genuine. In cases like Doe's, emotional distress is generally the only harm the claimant suffers, *e.g.,* the identity theft apprehended never materialized. . . .

The Government, although recognizing that "actual damages" may be slender and easy to generate, fears depletion of the federal fisc were the Court to adopt Doe's reading of § 552a(g)(4). Experience does not support those fears. As the Government candidly acknowledged at oral argument: "[W]e have not had a problem with enormous recoveries against the Government up to this point." No doubt mindful that Congress did not endorse massive recoveries, the District Court in this very case denied class-action certification, and other courts have similarly refused to certify suits seeking damages under § 552a(g)(4) as class actions. Furthermore, courts have disallowed the runaway liability that might ensue were they to count every single wrongful disclosure as a discrete basis for a $1,000 award.

The text of § 552a(g)(4), it is undisputed, accommodates two concerns. Congress sought to give the Privacy Act teeth by deterring violations and providing remedies when violations occur. At the same time, Congress did not want to saddle the Government with disproportionate liability. . . .

Congress has used language similar to § 552a(g)(4) in other privacy statutes. See 18 U.S.C. § 2707(c); 26 U.S.C. § 6110(j)(2); 26 U.S.C. § 7217(c) (1976 ed., Supp. V). These other statutes have been understood to permit recovery of the $1,000 statutory minimum despite the absence of proven actual damages. . . .

Doe has standing to sue, the Court agrees, based on "allegations that he was 'torn . . . all to pieces' and 'greatly concerned and worried' because of the disclosure of his Social Security number and its potentially 'devastating' consequences." Standing to sue, but not to succeed, the Court holds, unless Doe also incurred an easily arranged out-of-pocket expense. In my view, Congress gave Privacy Act suitors like Doe not only standing to sue, but the right to a recovery if the fact trier credits their claims of emotional distress brought on by an agency's intentional or willful violation of the Act. For the reasons stated in this dissenting opinion, which track the reasons expressed by Circuit Judge Michael dissenting in part in the Fourth Circuit, I would reverse the judgment of the Court of Appeals.

NOTES & QUESTIONS

1. ***Postscript.*** In subsequent litigation, the district court concluded that Buck Doe was still entitled to attorneys' fees and costs under the Privacy Act because he established that the government had willfully violated the Act. The court awarded $57,520.97 for attorneys' fees and costs. On appeal, in *Doe v. Chao*, 435 F.3d 492 (4th Cir. 2006), the Fourth Circuit held that attorneys' fees and costs could still be recovered despite failing to show actual damages. However, the court concluded that the district court erred in assessing the amount of the award because it failed to "give primary consideration to the amount of damages awarded as compared to the amount sought." On remand, the district court awarded $15,887.50 in attorneys' fees and costs to Doe's counsel.

2. ***Damages Under the Privacy Act.*** One of the difficulties in privacy cases that involve the leakage of personal information is establishing damages. In most cases, people might be made more vulnerable to harms like identity theft, but they might not yet be victimized. Damages for the violation of many Privacy Act violations will involve emotional distress rather than overt physical or psychological harm. By requiring "actual damages" in order to receive statutory damages, does the Court's holding in *Doe v. Chao* make it nearly impossible to recover for a Privacy Act violation? On the other hand, should any violation of the Privacy Act result in automatic damages for thousands of dollars?

   What constitutes "actual damages" under the Privacy Act? The *Chao* Court did not reach an opinion on the issue, noting in a footnote:

   > The Courts of Appeals are divided on the precise definition of actual damages. Compare *Fitzpatrick v. IRS*, 665 F.2d 327, 331 (11th Cir. 1982) (actual damages are restricted to pecuniary loss), with *Johnson v. Department of Treasury, IRS*, 700 F.2d 971, 972-974 (5th Cir. 1983) (actual damages can cover adequately demonstrated mental anxiety even without any out-of-pocket loss). That issue is not before us. . . . We assume without deciding that the Fourth Circuit was correct to hold that Doe's complaints in this case did not rise to the level of alleging actual damages. We do not suggest that out-of-pocket expenses are necessary for recovery of the $1,000 minimum; only that they suffice to qualify under any view of actual damages.

3. ***The Linda Tripp Case.*** Recall the Linda Tripp case above in the notes to *Quinn v. Stone.* The Department of Defense (DOD) settled the case for $590,000. In light of *Doe v. Chao,* should the DOD have settled?

4. ***Willful vs. Negligent Violations of the Privacy Act.*** In *Andrews v. Veterans Administration,* 838 F.2d 418 (10th Cir. 1988), an employee of the Veterans Administration (VA) was responding to a FOIA request for proficiency reports of various nurses. The VA employee attempted to redact the identities of nurses from the reports, but failed to do so properly. As a result, several nurses could be identified on their reports. At trial, the district court concluded that the nurses "suffered some degree of anguish, embarrassment, or other mental trauma" from the disclosure and that the VA employee "acted conscientiously, in good faith, though inadvertently negligently, in releasing the proficiency reports in an inadequately sanitized condition." Furthermore, the district court concluded that the VA was grossly negligent in failing to adequately train the employee about the release of personal information. On appeal, the Tenth Circuit concluded that the disclosure of the information was improper. The identities of the nurses were protected under Exemption 6 of FOIA. However, the VA, despite acting with gross negligence, could not be held liable to the nurses:

> . . . [E]ven if the Privacy Act is violated, no punishment may be imposed unless the agency acted in a manner which was intentional or willful. In this case the district court equated "intentional or willful" with gross negligence. . . .
>
> . . . [T]he term "willful or intentional" clearly requires conduct amounting to more than gross negligence. We are persuaded by the District of Columbia Circuit's definitions of willful or intentional that contemplate action "so 'patently egregious and unlawful' that anyone undertaking the conduct should have known it 'unlawful,'" or conduct committed "without grounds for believing it to be lawful" or action "flagrantly disregarding others' rights under the Act," and we adopt those definitions, and add the view . . . that the conduct must amount to, at the very least, reckless behavior. Those, and similar definitions, describe conduct more extreme than gross negligence.
>
> Applying that standard to this case, our review of the record convinces us that the VA's conduct falls far short of a "willful or intentional" violation of the Privacy Act. Indeed, we find that it falls short of even the gross negligence standard applied by the district court to that conduct. . . .

According to Paul Schwartz, "individuals who seek to enforce their rights under the Privacy Act face numerous statutory hurdles, limited damages, and scant chance to affect an agency's overall behavior."[33] The most common form of improper disclosure of records is due to carelessness rather than willful behavior. Does the requirement that disclosure be done "willfully and intentionally" make damages under the Privacy Act virtually impossible to collect? What if the standard for collecting damages were negligence? Would agencies that must handle millions of records and respond to thousands of FOIA requests be exposed to too great a risk of liability? Consider Robert Gellman:

---

[33] Paul M. Schwartz, *Privacy and Participation,* 80 Iowa L. Rev. 553, 596 (1995).

The Privacy Act contains civil and criminal penalties for violations, but it is far from clear that the enforcement methods are useful. . . . In more than 20 years, federal prosecutors have brought no more than a handful of criminal cases, and perhaps only one, under the Privacy Act.

The basic method for enforcing the Privacy Act is the individual lawsuit. Aggrieved individuals can sue the government for violations. . . . The former General Counsel to the Privacy Protection Study Commission testified that the act was "to a large extent, unenforceable by individuals." The main reasons are that it is difficult to recover damages and that limited injunctive relief is available under the law. Individual enforcement does not offer any significant incentive for agencies to comply more carefully with the Privacy Act's provisions.[34]

5. ***The Interaction Between the Privacy Act and FOIA.*** The Privacy Act does not apply to information that must be disclosed pursuant to FOIA. § 552a(k)(1). However, if one of FOIA's privacy exceptions applies, then the Privacy Act would require that the government refrain from disclosing certain information.

United States Dep't of Defense v. Federal Labor Relations Authority, 510 U.S. 487 (1994), clearly illustrates the interaction between these two statutes. There, two local unions requested the names and home addresses of employees in federal agencies. The agencies disclosed the employees' names and work stations to the unions but refused to release their home addresses. The unions filed unfair labor practice charges with the Federal Labor Relations Authority (FLRA), arguing that federal labor law required the agencies to disclose the addresses. Pursuant to the Federal Service Labor-Management Relations Statute, 5 U.S.C. §§ 7101–7135, agencies must, "to the extent not prohibited by law," furnish unions with data necessary for collective-bargaining purposes. § 7114(b)(4). The agencies argued that disclosure of the home addresses was prohibited by the Privacy Act. The Court agreed with the agencies:

> The employee addresses sought by the unions are "records" covered by the broad terms of the Privacy Act. Therefore, unless FOIA would require release of the addresses, their disclosure is "prohibited by law," and the agencies may not reveal them to the unions.
>
> We turn, then, to FOIA. . . . The exemption potentially applicable to employee addresses is Exemption 6, which provides that FOIA's disclosure requirements do not apply to "personnel and medical files and similar files the disclosure of which would constitute a clearly unwarranted invasion of personal privacy." 5 U.S.C. § 552(b)(6).
>
> Thus, although this case requires us to follow a somewhat convoluted path of statutory cross-references, its proper resolution depends upon a discrete inquiry: whether disclosure of the home addresses "would constitute a clearly unwarranted invasion of [the] personal privacy" of bargaining unit employees within the meaning of FOIA. . . .

---

[34] Robert Gellman, *Does Privacy Law Work?* in *Technology and Privacy: The New Landscape* (Philip E. Agre & Marc Rotenberg eds. 1997).

We must weigh the privacy interest of bargaining unit employees in nondisclosure of their addresses against the only relevant public interest in the FOIA balancing analysis — the extent to which disclosure of the information sought would "she[d] light on an agency's performance of its statutory duties" or otherwise let citizens know "what their government is up to."

The relevant public interest supporting disclosure in this case is negligible, at best. Disclosure of the addresses might allow the unions to communicate more effectively with employees, but it would not appreciably further "the citizens' right to be informed about what their government is up to." Indeed, such disclosure would reveal little or nothing about the employing agencies or their activities. . . .

Against the virtually nonexistent FOIA-related public interest in disclosure, we weigh the interest of bargaining unit employees in nondisclosure of their home addresses. . . .

It is true that home addresses often are publicly available through sources such as telephone directories and voter registration lists, but "[i]n an organized society, there are few facts that are not at one time or another divulged to another." *Reporters Comm.* The privacy interest protected by Exemption 6 "encompass[es] the individual's control of information concerning his or her person." An individual's interest in controlling the dissemination of information regarding personal matters does not dissolve simply because that information may be available to the public in some form. Here, for the most part, the unions seek to obtain the addresses of nonunion employees who have decided not to reveal their addresses to their exclusive representative. . . . Whatever the reason that these employees have chosen not to become members of the union or to provide the union with their addresses, however, it is clear that they have *some* nontrivial privacy interest in nondisclosure, and in avoiding the influx of union-related mail, and, perhaps, union-related telephone calls or visits, that would follow disclosure.

Many people simply do not want to be disturbed at home by work-related matters. . . . Moreover, when we consider that other parties, such as commercial advertisers and solicitors, must have the same access under FOIA as the unions to the employee address lists sought in this case, it is clear that the individual privacy interest that would be protected by nondisclosure is far from insignificant.

Because the privacy interest of bargaining unit employees in nondisclosure of their home addresses substantially outweighs the negligible FOIA-related public interest in disclosure, we conclude that disclosure would constitute a "clearly unwarranted invasion of personal privacy." 5 U.S.C. § 552(b)(6). FOIA, thus, does not require the agencies to divulge the addresses, and the Privacy Act, therefore, prohibits their release to the unions. . . .

Suppose the agencies opted not to litigate and disclosed the addresses of their employees. Would an employee have a cause of action under the Privacy Act for the disclosure of her address? Would that employee likely prevail in such an action? What type of remedy could the employee obtain?

6. *The Complementary Values of the Privacy Act and FOIA.* Although the Privacy Act restricts disclosures and the FOIA promotes disclosures, Marc Rotenberg contends that these statutes promote "complementary values." He observes:

In enacting both the Privacy Act of 1974 and adopting the amendments that same year which significantly strengthened the Freedom of Information Act, Congress sought to ensure that personal information collected and maintained by federal agencies would be properly protected while also seeking to ensure that public information in the possession of federal agencies would be widely available to the public. The complementary goals of safeguarding individual liberty and ensuring government accountability were enabled by legislation that protected privacy on the one hand and promoted government oversight on the other.[35]

7. ***The Accuracy of the National Crime Information Center Database.*** In 2003, the Justice Department stated that the FBI would no longer be required to ensure the accuracy of its National Crime Information Center (NCIC) database, which consists of nearly 40 million criminal records. The NCIC provides access to fingerprints, mug shots, people with outstanding arrest warrants, missing persons, suspected terrorists, and gang members. The NCIC database is used by law enforcement officials around the country. Under the Privacy Act, can the FBI be exempted from maintaining the accuracy of NCIC?

8. ***Government Access to Private Sector Databases.*** The Privacy Act also applies to private companies that contract with the government to administer systems of records. 5 U.S.C. § 552a(m). However, as Christopher Hoofnagle observes, "a database of information that originates at a [commercial data broker] would not trigger the requirements of the Privacy Act." Hoofnagle goes on to observe:

> This limitation to the Privacy Act is critical — it allows [commercial data brokers] to amass huge databases that the government is legally prohibited from creating. Then, when the government needs the information, it can request it from the [commercial data broker].[36]

9. ***Law Enforcement Access to Privacy Act Records.*** After 9/11, there were extensive complaints about restrictions on the ability of agencies to share personal information. To what extent does the Privacy Act permit such information sharing? Examine § 552a(b)(7).

10. ***The First Amendment Restriction.*** Pursuant to the Privacy Act, 5 U.S.C. § 552a(e)(7), agencies shall

> maintain no record describing how any individual exercises rights guaranteed by the First Amendment unless expressly authorized by statute or by the individual about whom the record is maintained or unless pertinent to and within the scope of an authorized law enforcement activity.

In *Becker v. Internal Revenue Service,* 34 F.2d 398 (7th Cir. 1994), three brothers, Thomas, Jeffrey, and Steven Becker, sought to have IRS records

---

[35] Marc Rotenberg, *Privacy and Secrecy After September 11,* 86 Minn. L. Rev. 1115, 1129 (2002).

[36] Christopher Jay Hoofnagle, *Big Brother's Little Helpers: How ChoicePoint and Other Commercial Data Brokers Collect and Package Your Data for Law Enforcement,* 29 N.C. J. Int'l L. & Com. Reg. 595, 623 (2004).

about them expunged pursuant to the Privacy Act. The files pertained to a criminal investigation of their failure to pay taxes and their activities as "tax protestors." Some of the records in the IRS's files pertained to the brothers' First Amendment rights, such as "a flyer advertising a book and a collection of newspaper articles regarding various IRS actions against certain individuals and groups who are alleged tax protesters or cheats."

The district court concluded that maintaining these materials in the Beckers' records "unquestionably implies that they are associated with the tax protesters and cheats described in the newspaper articles" and thus describes "how the plaintiffs exercise their First Amendment rights of speech and association." However, the district court concluded that the documents are "pertinent to and within the scope of an authorized law enforcement activity." Accordingly, the district court concluded, "the IRS may lawfully maintain these records and may withhold this information from plaintiffs under the Privacy Act pursuant to 5 U.S.C. § 552a(k)(2)." Section 552a(k)(2) allows agencies to exempt certain systems of records from individual access. The IRS claimed that it exempted the records because "to grant access to an investigative file could interfere with investigative and enforcement proceedings . . . and disclose investigative techniques and procedures."

The Seventh Circuit, however, concluded that § 551a(k)(2) does not allow agencies to be exempt from the First Amendment activities exclusion. The court noted that these documents were contained in files closed several years ago, and that the Beckers' ultimate objective was to have the records removed from their files, not just to gain access. The court reasoned:

> We conclude that the IRS has not sufficiently justified the maintenance of the documents in the Beckers' files. The IRS asserts that it may maintain these articles for possible future uses. Under some circumstances, this may be a legitimate justification for maintaining documents in a file for an extended period of time. We have examined the material, and any thought that it could be helpful in future enforcement activity concerning the Beckers is untenable. The material consists of newspaper articles dating from the middle to late 1980s, with no reference to the Beckers; any potential advantage to having these documents in the Beckers' files, at some uncertain date, is minuscule (and the IRS does not elaborate on how this material would be helpful). This indefinite use must be viewed in light of the fact that Judge Alesia found the Beckers' First Amendment rights are implicated. As the Senate Report on the Privacy Act pointed out,
>
>> This section's [5 U.S.C. § 552a(e)(7)] restraint is aimed particularly at preventing collection of protected information not immediately needed, about law-abiding Americans, on the off-chance that Government or the particular agency might possibly have to deal with them in the future. S. Rep. No. 1183, 93d Cong., 2d Sess., *reprinted in* 1974 U.S.C.C.A.N. 6916, 6971.
>
> There is a remote possibility that a part of the newspaper articles (describing practices of tax protesters) would be helpful in investigation of persons in general. We are not, however, presented with a situation where documents are maintained in a general file rather than in a specific individual's file.

Because we conclude that the IRS has not carried its burden in establishing that the materials are exempt from Privacy Act requirements, the documents should be expunged. . . .

Consider the following case, which came to a different conclusion regarding the First Amendment restriction:

J. RODERICK MACARTHUR FOUNDATION V. FEDERAL BUREAU OF INVESTIGATION

102 F.3d 600 (D.C. Cir. 1996)

GINSBURG, J. . . . The J. Roderick MacArthur Foundation and its former president Lance E. Lindblom seek to compel the Federal Bureau of Investigation to expunge its records relating to their associational activities and to refrain from maintaining such records in the future. Lindblom invokes both the Privacy Act, 5 U.S.C. § 552a, and the First Amendment to the Constitution of the United States; the Foundation relies solely upon the first amendment. . . .

As president of the Foundation, which provides grants to organizations involved with various political, social, and economic issues, Lindblom occasionally met with foreign leaders and political dissidents. At some point Lindblom's associations caught the attention of the FBI. When Lindblom and the Foundation later got wind of the FBI's interest they asked the Bureau, pursuant to the Freedom of Information Act, 5 U.S.C. § 552(a), for copies of all documents it had relating to them. The FBI informed them that it had a file on Lindblom consisting of 23 pages of materials and that, although the FBI did not have a file on the Foundation, it had located in other files five pages on which the Foundation's name appears. . . . The FBI released redacted copies of several of the documents relating to Lindblom and the Foundation but refused to release others. . . . At least some of the documents that the FBI released from the Lindblom file refer to Lindblom's associational activities. . . .

Section (e)(7) of the [Privacy] Act provides in relevant part that a government agency "shall . . . maintain no record describing how any individual exercises rights guaranteed by the First Amendment unless . . . pertinent to and within the scope of an authorized law enforcement activity." 5 U.S.C. § 552a(e)(7). . . .

Lindblom does not challenge the FBI's having collected information about him, and we assume that the information was pertinent to an authorized law enforcement activity when it was collected. Lindblom's claim is that an agency may not maintain (that is, retain) such lawfully collected information unless there is a current law enforcement necessity to do so. More specifically, he claims that "information which may have been properly collected as part of a legitimate law enforcement investigation may not be permanently kept under the name of the individual, especially when that individual is not the target of the investigation." . . .

Lindblom's primary assertion, that the Act forbids maintenance of information about first amendment activities unless that information serves a "current law enforcement necessity," requires more extended analysis. . . .

Looking at the terms of § (e)(7), we find no support for Lindblom's argument that the Act authorizes an agency to maintain a record describing first amendment activities only if and so long as there is a "current law enforcement necessity" to do so. The noun "record" in § (e)(7) is modified in only two ways: the record must be "[1] pertinent to and [2] within the scope of an authorized law enforcement activity." We do not understand this to mean, as Lindblom would in essence require, that the record must be pertinent to an active investigation; "an authorized law enforcement activity" such as foreign counter-intelligence, is a concept far broader than either an active investigation or a "current law enforcement necessity." . . .

Information that was pertinent to an authorized law enforcement activity when collected does not later lose its pertinence to that activity simply because the information is not of current interest (let alone "necessity") to the agency — a point seemingly lost upon our dissenting colleague. . . .

. . . Lindblom's interpretation of the Act would place new and daunting burdens, both substantive and administrative, upon the FBI and other government agencies, with little or no gain to individual privacy. If a law enforcement agency were required to purge its files of information regarding an individual so requesting whenever it had closed a particular investigation, then its ability to accomplish its mission would inevitably suffer. As we have said before, intelligence gathering is "akin to the construction of a mosaic"; to appreciate the full import of a single piece may require the agency to take a broad view of the whole work. Suppose, for example, that a citizen is contacted by a foreign agent but the FBI, after investigation, determines that the contact is innocent. If the same individual is later contacted by another foreign agent and perhaps thereafter by a third, then what had earlier appeared to be innocent when viewed in isolation may, when later viewed as part of a larger whole, acquire a more sinister air. Simply put, information that was once collected as part of a now-closed investigation may yet play a role in a new or reopened investigation. If the earlier record had been purged, however, then the agency's later investigation could not be informed by the earlier event(s).

Furthermore, if federal law enforcement agencies were required upon request to purge all such records, then they would surely be inundated with requests to do so. Responding to each such request could be difficult and time-consuming. . . . [W]e are reluctant to think that the Congress required so formidable an under-taking, with so little potential benefit, absent a clear statement to that effect. . . .

Accordingly, we hold that the Privacy Act does not prohibit an agency from maintaining records about an individual's first amendment activities if the infor-mation was pertinent to an authorized law enforcement activity when the agency collected the information. The Act does not require an agency to expunge records when they are no longer pertinent to a current law enforcement activity. . . .

The Foundation and Lindblom both claim that the FBI violated the first amendment by creating files on them based upon their associational activity. The FBI responds that it has no file on the Foundation and that its maintenance of lawfully gathered information about Lindblom does not violate his rights under the first amendment. We need not, however, decide whether the FBI violated the Constitution because the appellants lack standing so to claim.

"In order to establish standing under Article III, a complainant must allege (1) a personal injury-in-fact that is (2) 'fairly traceable' to the defendant's conduct and (3) redressable by the relief requested." *Branton v. FCC,* 993 F.2d 906 (D.C. Cir. 1992). The injury-in-fact requirement has two elements: The plaintiff must show that it has suffered "an invasion of a legally protected interest which is (a) concrete and particularized and (b) actual or imminent, not conjectural or hypothetical." *Lujan v. Defenders of Wildlife,* 504 U.S. 555, 560 (1992).

Consider first the case of the Foundation. It claims to have been injured because the FBI's maintenance of records on the Foundation inhibited its pursuit of activities protected by the first amendment. More specifically, the Foundation claims that the FBI's maintenance of records regarding the Foundation (1) may deter potential grantees from seeking money from the Foundation and (2) may make it more difficult for current Foundation employees to find jobs elsewhere in the future. . . .

The affiants declare, among other things, that "in the close-knit philanthropic community, an FBI file potentially limits the future employability of foundation personnel" and that "it is likely that some grantees' behavior will be affected by the maintenance of FBI files on foundations."

These affidavits speak broadly of stigma and harm to the Foundation's reputation. A "potential" limitation upon employees' future "employability" lacks concreteness. The Foundation points to not a single Foundation employee whose job prospects have been dimmed because of the FBI records. Nor does either affidavit indicate even generally how "some grantees' behavior will be affected" by the FBI records on the Foundation. The Foundation does not point to a single grantee or even type of grantee that would be any less likely to seek money from the Foundation because the FBI maintains records on it. This is not enough to establish an injury to the Foundation.

The Foundation's claim of injury also lacks immediacy. Because the Foundation does not allege that it has yet suffered any injury in the form of diminished job prospects for its employees or decreased interest from potential grantees, its only hope for standing rests upon showing that a threatened harm is "*certainly* impending." It is not enough for the Foundation to assert that it might suffer an injury in the future, or even that it is likely to suffer an injury at some unknown future time. Such "someday" injuries are insufficient. . . .

Lindblom also raises a first amendment claim, but he offers no separate arguments or affidavits in support of his standing. . . . Lindblom does not claim that the FBI's interest in him has limited or may limit his prospects for employment. . . . Lindblom has failed to show that he has suffered any injury in his individual capacity, we hold that Lindblom lacks standing to press a constitutional claim against the FBI. . . .

TATEL, J. concurring in part and dissenting in part. . . . The statute defines "maintain" as including both "maintain" and "collect." 5 U.S.C. § 552a(a)(3) (1994). To collect means "to gather together." To maintain means "to keep in existence or continuance; preserve." *Random House Unabridged Dictionary* 403, 1160 (2d ed.1993).In order to give each of these verbs its meaning, I would interpret section (e)(7), as a whole, to require that records be pertinent to "an authorized law enforcement activity" — words undefined in the statute — not only at the time of gathering, i.e., collecting, but also at the time of keeping, i.e., maintaining. In other words, if there is no *current* law enforcement activity to which a record has pertinence, the agency may not maintain it. Not only does this approach avoid effectively reading the word "maintain" out of that term's statutory definition, but it furthers the Act's purpose to protect citizens from the unnecessary collection *and* retention of personal information by the government. . . .

Because Congress chose to use the word "maintain" in section (e)(7), and to define that term as both "maintain" and "collect," we know that Congress must have meant something more than just "collect." . . .

Congress passed the Privacy Act to give individuals some defenses against governmental tendencies towards secrecy and "Big Brother" surveillance. *See* S. Rep. No. 93-1183, at 1 (Privacy Act "is designed to prevent the kind of illegal, unwise, overbroad, investigation and record surveillance of law-abiding citizens produced in recent years from actions of some over-zealous investigators, and the curiosity of some government administrators, or the wrongful disclosure and use, in some cases, of personal files held by Federal agencies."). The fewer unnecessary files describing First Amendment activities the government keeps on law-abiding citizens, the lesser the chance of any future abuse of those files.

NOTES & QUESTIONS

1. *The Scope of the First Amendment Restriction.* Which court, *Becker* or *MacArthur Foundation,* comes to a more convincing interpretation of the First Amendment restriction? Based on the *MacArthur Foundation* court's interpretation, to what would the First Amendment restriction apply?
2. *The Fourth Amendment and Information Collection and Recordkeeping.* Does the Fourth Amendment have any applicability in this context? Or does the Fourth Amendment only focus on information gathering activities?
3. *What Constitutes "Law Enforcement Activity" Under § 552a(e)(7)?* In *Bassiouni v. FBI,* 436 F.3d 712 (7th Cir. 2006), a law professor sought to have his records amended or expunged pursuant to the Privacy Act. Mahmoud Cherif Bassiouni, a DePaul University law professor, obtained access to FBI records about himself. The records listed groups labeled as "terrorist" groups, including the Popular Front for the Liberation of Palestine, a group currently designated by the Department of State as a terrorist group. The records did not conclude that Bassiouni was a member of any of these groups. The FBI stated "that it does not suspect him of ties to terrorist groups." Contending that he was not a member of these groups, Bassiouni demanded that the FBI amend or expunge his records because they were outdated and inaccurate. Among other things, Bassiouni contended that the maintenance of the records was a violation of § 552a(e)(7). The court, however, disagreed because § 552a(e)(7) does not apply to information "pertinent to and within the scope of an authorized law enforcement activity." According to the court:

In this case, the Bureau, through Special Agent Krupkowski's declaration, identifies the ways in which Mr. Bassiouni's file is related to its law enforcement activities. First, the FBI notes its ongoing investigations into the threats posed by terrorist groups, specifically those originating in the Middle East. According to the declaration, "the FBI has amended its investigative priorities, naming as its number one priority to 'protect the United States from terrorist attack.'" Because of the nature of these investigative activities, and because of the breadth of Mr. Bassiouni's contacts with the Middle East, the FBI anticipates that it will continue to receive information about Mr. Bassiouni. The Bureau's file on Mr. Bassiouni will provide context for evaluating that new information.

Perhaps more importantly, the public Krupkowski Declaration states that the records are important for evaluating the continued reliability of its intelligence sources. The Declaration explains that the process of verifying source information, and therefore determining whether a source is reliable, takes place over "years, even decades." . . .

We believe that the purposes identified by the Bureau fall within "authorized law enforcement activity" conducted by the FBI. We note at the outset that the realm of national security belongs to the executive branch, and we owe considerable deference to that branch's assessment in matters of national security. Furthermore, although the Privacy Act certainly does not authorize collection and maintenance of information of private citizens on the "off-hand" chance that such information may someday be useful, it does not require law enforcement agencies to purge, on a continuous basis, properly collected information with respect to individuals that the agency has good reason to believe may be relevant on a continuing basis in the fulfillment of the agency's statutory responsibilities. The Privacy Act does not give any indication that Congress intended law enforcement agencies to begin from scratch with every investigation. Nor do we believe that Congress meant to deprive such agencies of the benefit of historical analysis.

Mr. Bassiouni, however, urges us to reject the proffered law enforcement justifications as inadequate. He maintains, first, that, in order to fall within the law enforcement exception of (e)(7) the FBI must be "*currently* involved in a law enforcement investigation of Plaintiff." However, as we have noted already, no court that has considered the meaning of law enforcement activity in (e)(7) has interpreted the term so narrowly.

3. THE USE OF GOVERNMENT DATABASES

(a) The Computer Matching and Privacy Protection Act

In 1977 the federal government initiated Project Match, a program where it compared computer employee records to records of people receiving benefits through Aid to Families with Dependent Children to detect fraud. This was considered by the government to be exempted from the Privacy Act under the "routine use" exception. According to Priscilla Regan:

> . . . The scope of computer matches . . . raises Fourth Amendment questions. Computer matches are generalized electronic searches of millions of records. Under the Fourth Amendment, the Supreme Court has determined that searches must not be overly inclusive; no "fishing expeditions" or "dragnet investigations" are allowed. Yet in computer matches, many people who have

not engaged in fraud or are not actually suspected of criminal activity are subject to the computer search. This raises questions about the presumption of innocence, as reflected in Fourth and Fifth Amendment case law. If matches are considered a Fourth Amendment search, then some limitations on the breadth of the match and/or justifications for a match are necessary. For example, a government agency could be required to show that a less intrusive means of carrying out the search was not available and that procedural safeguards limiting the dangers of abuse and agency discretion were applied. Additionally, procedural safeguards are required under due process protections. A final constitutional issue is whether matching conflicts with the equal protection clause because categories of people, not individual suspects, are subject to computer matches. Two groups — federal employees and welfare recipients — are most often the subjects of computer matching.

Despite these arguments about the constitutionality of computer matches, the courts have generally not upheld individual privacy claims in cases challenging computer-matching programs. Moreover, there has been little litigation in this area for two reasons. First, the damage requirements of the Privacy Act are so difficult to prove that they serve as a deterrent to its use. . . . Secondly, in large-scale computer matching, single individuals are rarely sufficiently harmed to litigate claims and most individuals are not even aware of the match. . . . [37]

In 1988, Congress passed the Computer Matching and Privacy Protection Act (CMPPA), Pub. L. No. 100-503, to regulate the practice of computer matching. The CMPPA amends the Privacy Act and provides that in order for agencies to disclose records to engage in computer matching programs, they must establish "a written agreement between the source agency and the recipient agency or non-Federal agency stating" the purpose and legal authority for the program, a justification for the program, a description of the records to be matched, procedures for the accuracy of the information, and prohibitions on redisclosure of the records. § 552a(o)(1). These agreements must be available upon request to the public.

The CMPPA establishes Data Integrity Boards within each agency to oversee matching, requires agencies to perform a cost-benefit analysis of proposed matching endeavors, and requires agencies to notify individuals of the termination of benefits due to computer matching and permit them an opportunity to refute the termination. § 552a(p).

Is computer matching a violation of the Fourth Amendment? If you believe that matching contravenes the Fourth Amendment, are the due process rights provided by the CMPPA sufficient to cure the constitutional deficiencies?[38]

---

[37] Priscilla Regan, *Legislating Privacy* 89-90 (1995).

[38] For an interesting account of the psychological effects and other harms caused by endeavors such as computer matching on welfare recipients, see John Gilliom, *Overseers of the Poor: Surveillance, Resistance, and the Limits of Privacy* (2001).

(b) Airline Passenger Screening

THE 9/11 COMMISSION REPORT

Excerpts from pp. 1-4, 392-95 (2004)

Boston: American 11 and United 175. [Mohamed] Atta and [Abdul Aziz al] Omari boarded a 6:00 A.M. flight from Portland [Maine] to Boston's Logan International Airport.

When he checked in for his flight to Boston, Atta was selected by a computerized prescreening system known as CAPPS (Computer Assisted Passenger Prescreening System), created to identify passengers who should be subject to special security measures. Under the security rules in place at the time, the only consequence of Atta's selection by CAPPS was that his checked bags were held off the plane until it was confirmed that he boarded the aircraft. This did not hinder Atta's plans. . . .

While Atta had been selected by CAPPS in Portland, three members of his hijacking team — Suqami, Wail al Shehri, and Waleed al Shehri — were selected in Boston. Their selection affected only the handling of their checked bags, not their screening at the checkpoint.

Washington Dulles: American 77. Hundreds of miles southwest of Boston, at Dulles International Airport . . . five more men were preparing to take their early morning flight. At 7:15, a pair of them, Khalid al Mihdhar and Majed Moqed, checked in at the American Airlines ticket counter for Flight 77, bound for Los Angeles. Within the next 20 minutes, they would be followed by Nani Hanjour and two brothers, Nawaf al Hazmi and Salem al Hazmi.

Hani Hanjour, Khalid al Mihdhar, and Majed Moqed were flagged by CAPPS. The Hazmi brothers were also selected for extra scrutiny by the airline's customer service representative at the check-in counter. He did so because one of the brothers did not have photo identification nor could he understand English, and because the agent found both of the passengers to be suspicious. The only consequence of their selection was that their checked bags were held off the plane until it was confirmed that they had boarded the aircraft. . . .

[Overall, on] 9/11, the 19 hijackers were screened by a computer-assisted screening system called CAPPS. More than half were identified for further inspection, which applied only to their checked luggage.

Under current practices, air carriers enforce government orders to stop certain known and suspected terrorists from boarding commercial flights and to apply secondary screening procedures to others. The "no-fly" and "automatic selectee" lists include only those individuals who the U.S. government believes pose a direct threat of attacking aviation.

Because air carriers implement the program, concerns about sharing intelligence information with private firms and foreign countries keep the U.S. government from listing all terrorist and terrorist suspects who should be included. The TSA has planned to take over this function when it deploys a new screening system to take the place of CAPPS. The deployment of this system has been delayed because of claims it may violate civil liberties.

Recommendation: Improved use of "no-fly" and "automatic selectee" lists should not be delayed while the argument about a successor to CAPPS continues. This screening function should be performed by the TSA, and it should utilize the larger set of watchlists maintained by the federal government. Air carriers should be required to supply the information needed to test and implement this new system. . . .

NOTES & QUESTIONS

1. *False Positives.* The 9/11 Report mentioned the number of "hits" that the CAPPS system made, flagging more than half of the 19 terrorists. Each day, there are approximately 1.9 million airline passengers. Imagine a false positive rate of just 1 percent, which by current estimates of such rates would be quite a good rate. At a 1 percent error rate, 19,000 people would be flagged as false positives. Merely talking about the "hits" rather than the "misses" paints only a partial picture of the effectiveness of the system.

   After 9/11, the airline screening system incorrectly singled out a number of high-profile individuals. For example, Senator Edward Kennedy (D-Mass.) and Rep. Donald E. Young (R-Alaska) were tapped for secondary screening. Cat Stevens, a singer who now goes by the name Yusuf Islam, was placed on the no-fly list. According to *Time* magazine, this incident rested in a spelling mistake: "According to aviation sources with access to the list, there is no Yusuf Islam on the no-fly registry, though there is a 'Youssouf Islam.'" The article goes on, however, to state that the U.S. Transportation Safety Administration "alleges that Islam has links to terrorist groups, which he has denied; British foreign minister Jack Straw said the TSA action 'should never have been taken.'"[39]

   Supporters of computerized airline screening argue that even with a significant number of false positives, CAPPS is useful in singling out passengers for extra scrutiny, since the most extensive screening cannot be done on 1.9 million passengers each day.

   Some argue that if the government were able to collect more data, the false positives would drop. Is the answer obtaining more data? Are screening systems like CAPPS effective security measures? Bruce Schneier, a noted security expert, discusses whether a system like CAPPS might in the end be worth the trade-offs:

   > System like CAPPS will be likely to single out lone terrorists who meet the profile, or a terrorist group whose entire membership fits the profile, or copycat terrorist groups without the wisdom, time, and resources to probe [the system]. But terrorists are a surprisingly diverse group . . . CAPPS works best combined with random screening.

   Schneier also notes two basic problems with CAPPS. First, it can be probed. In other words, "a terrorist organization can probe the system repeatedly and identify which of its people, or which ticket characteristics, are

---

[39] Sally B. Donnelly, *You Say Yusuf, I Say Youssouf* . . . , Time.com, Sept. 25, 2004, www.time.com/time/nation/article/0,8599,702062,00.html.

less likely to be searched." Second, a system "that is more likely to select a certain class of passenger is also less likely to select other classes of passengers."[40] As a consequence, terrorists who do not fit a profile may slip by unnoticed.

2. *The Evolution of Airline Passenger Screening.* Since September 11th, the government has been attempting to design an airline passenger screening program. In 2001, the FAA created two lists — a list of people who were barred from flying and a list of people selected for secondary screening. In 2002, the Transportation Security Administration (TSA) was created, and it took over the security functions from the FAA. The Terrorist Screening Center in the FBI maintains the no-fly list as well as the selectee list. The no-fly list, which had only 16 names on it in 2001, now has over 20,000 names. The precise number remains unknown. The names on these lists are kept secret.

In 2003, the federal government announced the creation of CAPPS II, which was to be the successor to CAPPS. CAPPS II would have classified people according to their "threat level" when flying. Passengers would be classified as green, yellow, or red. Green passengers would be screened normally; yellow ones would be given extra scrutiny; and red passengers would not be allowed to fly.

Critics of CAPPS II criticized the lack of transparency in the system. They objected that the data used in the profiling along with the factors that go into the profiles would not be publicly disclosed. What are the costs and benefits of requiring public disclosure of the types of information and the logic used in the profiling?

In July 2004, the government announced that it was abandoning CAPPS II. Shortly thereafter, the Transportation Security Agency proposed a new screening system called "Secure Flight." This system has also been troubled. It was suspended in 2006, revised, and is not yet operational. One official estimate predicts it will not yet start until 2010. On February 28, 2008, the General Accountability Office reported to Congress on Secure Flight: "While TSA has made considerable progress in the development and implementation of Secure Flight, it has not fully addressed program management issues including (1) developing cost and schedule estimates consistent with best practices, (2) fully implementing its risk management plan, (3) developing a comprehensive testing strategy, and (4) ensuring that information security requirements are fully implemented."[41]

Some argue that the benefit of a computerized airline passenger screening system is that without such a system, more individuals must be subjected to extensive searching. With the system, only those individuals profiled as a risk will be subject to extra scrutiny. Therefore, airline screening systems such as Secure Flight protect privacy by narrowing the number of people who must be intrusively searched. On the other hand, the system has costs in terms of both

---

[40] Bruce Schneier, *Beyond Fear* 164-65 (2003).

[41] GAO, *Aviation Security: Transportation Security Administration Has Strengthened Planning to Guide Investments in Key Aviation Security Programs, but More Work Remains*, GAO-08-456T (Feb. 28, 2008).

privacy and equality. Privacy is affected not just in a search, but in the gathering of data for profiling. Equality is implicated because some passengers, very possibly based on race and nationality, will be treated differently than other passengers. How do you weigh the costs and benefits? What about the people who are banned from flying? What kind of legal challenge would they have?

3. **PNR Data.** Airline passenger screening systems rely on passenger name record (PNR) data, which commercial airlines maintain for each passenger. This record includes financial information, such as credit card numbers, as well as itineraries for travel, phone numbers, and any special meal requests. After 9/11, the government requested that airlines turn over their PNR data. Although sharing the information with the government was not authorized in their privacy policies, many airlines willingly complied. Is it problematic for the government to have PNR data? What can be learned about an individual through PNR data?

In 2005, it was revealed that the FBI was keeping 257.5 million PNR records on people who flew between June and September 2001.[42] To what extent does the Privacy Act restrict the FBI from retaining this information?

(c) Government Data Mining

Data mining involves examining personal information in databases to look for patterns or unusual activity, or to identify links between a suspect and other individuals. Computer matching programs are an example of data mining — they seek to detect fraud by making comparisons in personal information residing in different databases.

Total Information Awareness. In 2002, the press reported that the Department of Defense was developing a project called "Total Information Awareness" (TIA), headed by Admiral John Poindexter. TIA would consist of a database of dossiers of people constructed with information about their finances, education, travel, health, and more. The information would be obtained from various private sector companies. The information would then be used to profile people to single out those engaged in terrorist activities. TIA generated a significant public outcry, and the Senate amended its spending bill early in 2003 to bar funding for TIA until the details of the program were explained to Congress.

In its report to Congress on May 20, 2003, the Department of Defense renamed the program "Terrorism Information Awareness" and stated that the program would be protective of privacy. Later in 2003, the Senate voted to deny funding for TIA. According to some media reports, however, classified part of the federal budget still contain funding for certain aspects of TIA.[43] What laws or constitutional rights would be implicated by TIA or a similar program?

Consider K.A. Taipale:

---

[42] Leslie Miller, *FBI Keeping Records on Pre-9/11 Travelers*, Associated Press, Jan. 14, 2005.

[43] Ira S. Rubinstein, Ronald D. Lee & Paul M. Schwartz, *Data Mining and Internet Profiling*, 75 U. Chi. L. Rev. 261, 265 (2008).

[I]t is my view that the recent defunding of DARPA's Information Awareness Office ("IAO") and its Terrorism Information Awareness program and related projects will turn out to be a pyrrhic "victory" for civil liberties as the program provided a focused opportunity around which to publicly debate the rules and procedures for the future use of these technologies and, importantly, to oversee the development of the appropriate technical features required to support any concurred upon implementation or oversight policies to protect privacy.[44]

Daniel Solove predicted in 2004 that TIA was far from dead:

. . . TIA is only one part of the story of government access to personal information and its creation of dossiers on American citizens. In fact, for quite some time, the government has been increasingly contracting with businesses to acquire databases of personal information. Database firms are willing to supply the information and the government is willing to pay for it. Currently, government agencies such as the FBI and IRS are purchasing databases of personal information from private-sector companies. A private company called ChoicePoint, Inc. has amassed a database of 10 billion records and has contracts with at least 35 federal agencies to share the data with them. . . .

Thus, we are increasingly seeing collusion, partly voluntary, partly coerced, between the private sector and the government. While public attention has focused on the Total Information Awareness project, the very same goals and techniques of the program continue to be carried out less systematically by various government agencies and law enforcement officials. We are already closer to Total Information Awareness than we might think.[45]

Pattern-Based vs. Subject-Based Data Mining. There are at least two general types of data mining. "Subject-based" data mining involves searching the data of a specific identified person. It might involve examining whom that person associates and does business with. "Pattern-based" data mining involves starting with a particular profile for terrorist activity and then analyzing databases to see which individuals' patterns of activity match that profile. Do these forms of data mining present different privacy concerns? If so, what are they? How should each type of data mining be regulated?

DATA MINING: FEDERAL EFFORTS COVER A WIDE RANGE OF USES

U.S. General Accountability Office, excerpt from pp. 2-3 (May 2004)

Federal agencies are using data mining for a variety of purposes, ranging from improving service or performance to analyzing and detecting terrorist patterns and activities. Our survey of 128 federal departments and agencies on their use of data mining shows that 52 agencies are using or are planning to use data mining. These departments and agencies reported 199 data mining efforts, of which 68 were planned and 131 were operational. . . .

The Department of Defense reported having the largest number of data mining efforts aimed at improving service or performance and at managing

---

[44] K.A. Taipale, *Data Mining and Domestic Security: Connecting the Dots to Make Sense of Data*, 5 Colum. Sci. & Tech. L. Rev. 9-12 (2003).

[45] Daniel J. Solove, *The Digital Person: Technology and Privacy in the Information Age* 169, 175 (2004).

human resources. Defense was also the most frequent user of efforts aimed at analyzing intelligence and detecting terrorist activities, followed by the Departments of Homeland Security, Justice, and Education. . . .

Data mining efforts for detecting criminal activities or patterns, however, were spread relatively evenly among the reporting agencies.

In addition, out of all 199 data mining efforts identified, 122 used personal information. For these efforts, the primary purposes were detecting fraud, waste, and abuse; detecting criminal activities or patterns; analyzing intelligence and detecting terrorist activities; and increasing tax compliance.

Agencies also identified efforts to mine data from the private sector and data from other federal agencies, both of which could include personal information. Of 54 efforts to mine data from the private sector (such as credit reports or credit card transactions), 36 involve personal information. Of 77 efforts to mine data from other federal agencies, 46 involve personal information (including student loan application data, bank account numbers, credit card information, and taxpayer identification numbers).

Data mining enables corporations and government agencies to analyze massive volumes of data quickly and relatively inexpensively. The use of this type of information retrieval has been driven by the exponential growth in the volumes and availability of information collected by the public and private sectors, as well as by advances in computing and data storage capabilities. In response to these trends, generic data mining tools are increasingly available for — or built into — major commercial database applications. Today, mining can be performed on many types of data. . . .

MARY DeROSA, DATA MINING AND DATA ANALYSIS FOR COUNTERTERRORISM

Center for Strategic and International Studies (CSIS) 6-8 (2004)

A relatively simple and useful data-analysis tool for counterterrorism is subject-based "link analysis." This technique uses aggregated public records or other large collections of data to find links between a subject — a suspect, an address, or other piece of relevant information — and other people, places, or things. This can provide additional clues for analysts and investigators to follow. Link analysis is a tool that is available now and is used for, among other things, background checks of applicants for sensitive jobs and as an investigatory tool in national security and law enforcement investigations.

A hindsight analysis of the September 11 attacks provides an example of how simple, subject-based link analysis could be used effectively to assist investigations or analysis of terrorist plans. By using government watch list information, airline reservation records, and aggregated public record data, link analysis could have identified all 19 September 11 terrorists — for follow-up investigation — before September 11. The links can be summarized as follows:

Direct Links — Watch List Information

- Khalid Almihdhar and Nawaf Alhazmi, both hijackers of American Airlines (AA) Flight 77, which crashed into the Pentagon, appeared on a U.S.

government terrorist watch list. Both used their real names to reserve their flights. . . .

Link Analysis — One Degree of Separation

- Two other hijackers used the same contact address for their flight reservations that Khalid Almihdhar listed on his reservation. These were Mohamed Atta, who hijacked AA Flight 11, which crashed into the World Trade Center North Tower, and Marwan Al Shehhi, who hijacked UA Flight 175.

- Salem Alhazmi, who hijacked AA Flight 77, used the same contact address on his reservation as Nawaf Alhazmi.

- The frequent flyer number that Khalid Almihdhar used to make his reservation was also used by hijacker Majed Moqed to make his reservation on AA Flight 77.

- Hamza Alghamdi, who hijacked UA Flight 175, used the same contact address on his reservation as Ahmed Alghamdi used on his.

- Hani Hanjour, who hijacked AA Flight 77, lived with both Nawaf Alhazmi and Khalid Almihdhar, a fact that searches of public records could have revealed. . .

Thus, if the government had started with watch list data and pursued links, it is at least possible that all of the hijackers would have been identified as subjects for further investigation. Of course, this example does not show the false positives — names of people with no connection to the terror attacks that might also have been linked to the watch list subjects.

Pattern-based data analysis also has potential for counterterrorism in the longer term, if research on uses of those techniques continues. . . . [D]ata-mining research must find ways to identify useful patterns that can predict an extremely rare activity — terrorist planning and attacks. It must also identify how to separate the "signal" of pattern from the "noise" of innocent activity in the data. One possible advantage of pattern-based searches — if they can be perfected — would be that they could provide clues to "sleeper" activity by unknown terrorists who have never engaged in activity that would link them to known terrorists. Unlike subject-based queries, pattern-based searches do not require a link to a known suspicious subject.

Types of pattern-based searches that could prove useful include searches for particular combinations of lower-level activity that together are predictive of terrorist activity. For example, a pattern of a "sleeper" terrorist might be a person in the country on a student visa who purchases a bomb-making book and 50 medium-sized loads of fertilizer. Or, if the concern is that terrorists will use large trucks for attacks, automated data analysis might be conducted regularly to identify people who have rented large trucks, used hotels or drop boxes as addresses, and fall within certain age ranges or have other qualities that are part of a known terrorist pattern. Significant patterns in e-mail traffic might be discovered that could reveal terrorist activity and terrorist "ringleaders." Pattern-based searches might also be very useful in response and consequence management. For example, searches of hospital data for reports of certain combinations of symptoms, or of other databases for patterns of behavior, such as pharmaceutical purchases or work absenteeism might provide an early signal of a terrorist attack using a biological weapon. . . .

NOTES & QUESTIONS

1. *The TAPAC Committee Report.* The Technology and Privacy Advisory Committee (TAPAC) was appointed by Secretary of Defense Donald Rumsfeld to examine the privacy implications of data mining. In its report, it noted that TIA was "a flawed effort to achieve worthwhile ends. It was flawed by its perceived insensitivity to critical privacy issues, the manner in which it was presented to the public, and the lack of clarity and consistency with which it was described." The report recommended:

> If the data mining is limited to searches based on particularized suspicion about a specific individual, we believe existing law should govern. Because, by definition, there is enough evidence about such a person to warrant further investigation, and that investigation is clearly subject to the protections of the Fourth Amendment, supplemented by federal statutes, we rely on existing law. We understand this category of data mining to include searches seeking to identify or locate a specific individual (e.g., a suspected terrorist) from airline or cruise ship passenger manifests or other lists of names or other non-sensitive information about U.S. persons. . . .
>
> For all other government data mining that involves personally identifiable information about U.S. persons, we recommend below that the government be required to first establish a predicate demonstrating the need for the data mining to prevent or respond to terrorism, and second, unless exigent circumstances are present, obtain authorization from the Foreign Intelligence Surveillance Court for its data mining activities. As we stress, that authorization may be sought either for programs that include data mining known or likely to include information on U.S. persons, or for specific applications of data mining where the use of personally identifiable information concerning U.S. persons is clearly anticipated. Legislation will be required for the Foreign Intelligence Surveillance Court to fulfill the role we recommend.[46]

The TAPAC Report's central recommendation is for a secret Foreign Intelligence Surveillance Act (FISA) court to approve various data mining projects. Is this a viable way to regulate data mining?

2. *The Markle Foundation Reports.* The Markle Foundation, a private sector philanthropic organization, established a Task Force on National Security in the Information Age that has issued two reports about government data mining. In these reports, the Markle Task Force is enthusiastic about the potential benefits of government data mining and recommends moving ahead with projects that will draw on this technique. The Markle Task Force recommends that government have ready access to private sector databases,

---

[46] Technology and Privacy Advisory Committee (TAPAC), *Safeguarding Privacy in the Fight Against Terrorism*, vii-x, 45-49 (2004).

but that the databases not be combined into a centralized database like the one envisioned for TIA:

> Attempting to centralize [databases of personal] information is not the answer because it would not link the information to the dispersed analytical capabilities of the network. Centralization could also lead to information becoming obsolete, since a centralized analytical entity would not have the ability to keep up-to-date much of the information collected from dispersed sources. . . .
>
> Our Task Force's fundamental objective, then, is to identify the technological tools and infrastructure, the policies, and the processes necessary to link these different communities so that important information can be shared among the people who need it, and as rapidly as possible. . . .
>
> Today, the private sector is on the frontline of the homeland security effort. Its members are holders of the data that may prove crucial to identifying and locating terrorists or thwarting terrorist attacks. . . . We therefore start from the premise that the government must have access to that information, which is needed to protect our country, and that through a combination of well-crafted guidelines, careful articulation of the types of information needed for identified purposes, and effective oversight using modern information technology, it will be possible to assure that government gets that information in a way that protects our essential liberties.[47]

Is decentralization sufficient to safeguard privacy? While mentioning privacy and civil liberty concerns, the Markle Foundation Task Force does not suggest much in the way of legal controls, but it mentions the possibility of technology to help protect privacy. The report does not, however, explain what concrete limitations should be established to protect privacy.

3. *The CMPPA and Government Data Mining.* To what extent does the Computer Matching and Privacy Protection Act (CMPPA) regulate government data mining? Consider the view of the Markle Foundation:

> Based upon past applications of the routine use exception [to the Privacy Act], it seems likely that future government initiatives promoting increased interagency information sharing to protect national security will meet with little resistance. A routine use need only meet [two requirements] to be valid: (1) compatible with the purpose of the information collection and (2) published in the Federal Register. . . .
>
> In today's age of information, data mining has the potential to become one of the government's most powerful tools for analyzing information on terrorism. Congress, however, has restricted the kinds of data mining federal agencies can do. In 1977, the Department of Health, Education, and Welfare initiated Project Match to identify federal employees fraudulently receiving welfare payments. . . . Over the next decade, such computer matching became pervasive. In a 1986 study, the Office of Technology Assessment reported that in 1984, eleven cabinet level departments and four independent agencies conducted 110 separate computer matching programs, consisting of 700 total matches and involving seven billion records. . . .

---

[47] Markle Foundation Task Force, *Creating a Trusted Information Network for Homeland Security* 14-15 (2003).

The widespread disclosure of information across agencies promoted Congress to act in 1988. To address these problems, Congress amended the Privacy Act by passing the Computer Matching Act, which precluded government agencies from treating computer matching as a routine use in most cases. Congress, however, explicitly excluded "matches performed for foreign counterintelligence purposes or to produce background checks for security clearances of Federal personnel." . . . Thus, so long as an agency lists something like "analyzing information to improve national security or prevent terrorism" as a routine use for the agency's information, a counterterrorism intelligence agency should be able to data mine the agency's records.[48]

4. ***The Privacy Act and Government Data Mining.*** What, if any, limits would the Privacy Act place on the kinds of government data mining discussed earlier in this section? Do any other laws discussed thus far regulate the practice?

Consider the following observation by Stewart Baker in the Markle Foundation Report regarding the limitations of the Privacy Act:

[The Privacy Act] requirements are just restrictive enough to make it awkward for the government to take direct access of private databases for data-mining analysis. As a result, one of the emerging solutions being adopted by the government is to encourage or even require industry to keep the databases in private hands, run pattern recognition themselves, and report suspicious results to the government. . . . [T]his approach has been used in the anti-money-laundering context. The Administration has discussed adopting similar approaches with respect to other records that might be of interest in counter-terrorism investigations.[49]

UNITED STATES V. SOKOLOW

490 U.S. 1 (1989)

Respondent Andrew Sokolow was stopped by Drug Enforcement Administration (DEA) agents upon his arrival at Honolulu International Airport. The agents found 1,063 grams of cocaine in his carry-on luggage. When respondent was stopped, the agents knew, *inter alia,* that (1) he paid $2,100 for two airplane tickets from a roll of $20 bills; (2) he traveled under a name that did not match the name under which his telephone number was listed; (3) his original destination was Miami, a source city for illicit drugs; (4) he stayed in Miami for only 48 hours, even though a round-trip flight from Honolulu to Miami takes 20 hours; (5) he appeared nervous during his trip; and (6) he checked none of his luggage. A divided panel of the United States Court of Appeals for the Ninth Circuit held that the DEA agents did not have a reasonable suspicion to stop respondent, as required by the Fourth Amendment. 831 F.2d 1413 (CA9 1987). We take the contrary view.

---

[48] Markle Foundation Task Force, *Protecting America's Freedom in the Information Age* 131 (2002).

[49] Markle Foundation Task Force, *Protecting America's Freedom in the Information Age* 169 (2002).

This case involves a typical attempt to smuggle drugs through one of the Nation's airports. On a Sunday in July 1984, respondent went to the United Airlines ticket counter at Honolulu Airport, where he purchased two round-trip tickets for a flight to Miami leaving later that day. The tickets were purchased in the names of "Andrew Kray" and "Janet Norian" and had open return dates. Respondent paid $2,100 for the tickets from a large roll of $20 bills, which appeared to contain a total of $4,000. He also gave the ticket agent his home telephone number. The ticket agent noticed that respondent seemed nervous; he was about 25 years old; he was dressed in a black jumpsuit and wore gold jewelry; and he was accompanied by a woman, who turned out to be Janet Norian. Neither respondent nor his companion checked any of their four pieces of luggage.

After the couple left for their flight, the ticket agent informed Officer John McCarthy of the Honolulu Police Department of respondent's cash purchase of tickets to Miami. Officer McCarthy determined that the telephone number respondent gave to the ticket agent was subscribed to a "Karl Herman," who resided at 348-A Royal Hawaiian Avenue in Honolulu. Unbeknownst to McCarthy (and later to the DEA agents), respondent was Herman's roommate. The ticket agent identified respondent's voice on the answering machine at Herman's number. Officer McCarthy was unable to find any listing under the name "Andrew Kray" in Hawaii. McCarthy subsequently learned that return reservations from Miami to Honolulu had been made in the names of Kray and Norian, with their arrival scheduled for July 25, three days after respondent and his companion had left. He also learned that Kray and Norian were scheduled to make stopovers in Denver and Los Angeles.

On July 25, during the stopover in Los Angeles, DEA agents identified respondent. He "appeared to be very nervous and was looking all around the waiting area." Later that day, at 6:30 p.m., respondent and Norian arrived in Honolulu. As before, they had not checked their luggage. Respondent was still wearing a black jumpsuit and gold jewelry. The couple proceeded directly to the street and tried to hail a cab, where Agent Richard Kempshall and three other DEA agents approached them. Kempshall displayed his credentials, grabbed respondent by the arm, and moved him back onto the sidewalk. Kempshall asked respondent for his airline ticket and identification; respondent said that he had neither. He told the agents that his name was "Sokolow," but that he was traveling under his mother's maiden name, "Kray."

Respondent and Norian were escorted to the DEA office at the airport. There, the couple's luggage was examined by "Donker," a narcotics detector dog, which alerted on respondent's brown shoulder bag. The agents arrested respondent. He was advised of his constitutional rights and declined to make any statements. The agents obtained a warrant to search the shoulder bag. They found no illicit drugs, but the bag did contain several suspicious documents indicating respondent's involvement in drug trafficking. The agents had Donker reexamine the remaining luggage, and this time the dog alerted on a medium-sized Louis Vuitton bag. By now, it was 9:30 p.m., too late for the agents to obtain a second warrant. They allowed respondent to leave for the night, but kept his luggage. The next morning, after a second dog confirmed Donker's alert, the agents obtained a warrant and found 1,063 grams of cocaine inside the bag.

Respondent was indicted for possession with the intent to distribute cocaine in violation of 21 U.S.C. § 841(a)(1). The United States District Court for Hawaii denied his motion to suppress the cocaine and other evidence seized from his luggage, finding that the DEA agents had a reasonable suspicion that he was involved in drug trafficking when they stopped him at the airport. . . .

The United States Court of Appeals for the Ninth Circuit reversed respondent's conviction by a divided vote, holding that the DEA agents did not have a reasonable suspicion to justify the stop. The majority divided the facts bearing on reasonable suspicion into two categories. In the first category, the majority placed facts describing "ongoing criminal activity," such as the use of an alias or evasive movement through an airport; the majority believed that at least one such factor was always needed to support a finding of reasonable suspicion. In the second category, it placed facts describing "personal characteristics" of drug couriers, such as the cash payment for tickets, a short trip to a major source city for drugs, nervousness, type of attire, and unchecked luggage. The majority believed that such characteristics, "shared by drug couriers and the public at large," were only relevant if there was evidence of ongoing criminal behavior and the Government offered "[e]mpirical documentation" that the combination of facts at issue did not describe the behavior of "significant numbers of innocent persons." Applying this two-part test to the facts of this case, the majority found that there was no evidence of ongoing criminal behavior, and thus that the agents' stop was impermissible. . . .

Our decision . . . turns on whether the agents had a reasonable suspicion that respondent was engaged in wrongdoing when they encountered him on the sidewalk. In *Terry v. Ohio,* 392 U.S. 1 (1968), we held that the police can stop and briefly detain a person for investigative purposes if the officer has a reasonable suspicion supported by articulable facts that criminal activity "may be afoot," even if the officer lacks probable cause.

The officer, of course, must be able to articulate something more than an "inchoate and unparticularized suspicion or 'hunch.'" The Fourth Amendment requires "some minimal level of objective justification" for making the stop. That level of suspicion is considerably less than proof of wrongdoing by a preponderance of the evidence. We have held that probable cause means "a fair probability that contraband or evidence of a crime will be found," *Illinois v. Gates,* 462 U.S. 213 (1983), and the level of suspicion required for a *Terry* stop is obviously less demanding than that for probable cause. . . .

In evaluating the validity of a stop such as this, we must consider "the totality of the circumstances — the whole picture." . . .

The rule enunciated by the Court of Appeals, in which evidence available to an officer is divided into evidence of "ongoing criminal behavior," on the one hand, and "probabilistic" evidence, on the other, is not in keeping with the quoted statements from our decisions. It also seems to us to draw a sharp line between types of evidence, the probative value of which varies only in degree. The Court of Appeals classified evidence of traveling under an alias, or evidence that the suspect took an evasive or erratic path through an airport, as meeting the test for showing "ongoing criminal activity." But certainly instances are conceivable in which traveling under an alias would not reflect ongoing criminal activity: for example, a person who wished to travel to a hospital or clinic for an operation and wished to concealed that fact. One taking an evasive path through an airport might be seeking to avoid a confrontation with an angry acquaintance or with a creditor. This is not to say that each of these types of evidence is not highly probative, but they do not have the sort of ironclad significance attributed to them by the Court of Appeals.

On the other hand, the factors in this case that the Court of Appeals treated as merely "probabilistic" also have probative significance. Paying $2,100 in cash for two airplane tickets is out of the ordinary, and it is even more out of the ordinary to pay that sum from a roll of $20 bills containing nearly twice that amount of cash. Most business travelers, we feel confident, purchase airline tickets by credit card or check so as to have a record for tax or business purposes, and few vacationers carry with them thousands of dollars in $20 bills. We also think the agents had a reasonable ground to believe that respondent was traveling under an alias; the evidence was by no means conclusive, but it was sufficient to warrant consideration. While a trip from Honolulu to Miami, standing alone, is not a cause for any sort of suspicion, here there was more: surely few residents of Honolulu travel from that city for 20 hours to spend 48 hours in Miami during the month of July.

Any one of these factors is not by itself proof of any illegal conduct and is quite consistent with innocent travel. But we think taken together they amount to reasonable suspicion. Indeed, *Terry* itself involved "a series of acts, each of them perhaps innocent" if viewed separately, "but which taken together warranted further investigation." . . .

We do not agree with respondent that our analysis is somehow changed by the agents' belief that his behavior was consistent with one of the DEA's "drug courier profiles." A court sitting to determine the existence of reasonable suspicion must require the agent to articulate the factors leading to that conclusion, but the fact that these factors may be set forth in a "profile" does not somehow detract from their evidentiary significance as seen by a trained agent. . . .

We hold that the agents had a reasonable basis to suspect that respondent was transporting illegal drugs on these facts. . . .

MARSHALL & BRENNAN, J.J. dissenting. Because the strongest advocates of Fourth Amendment rights are frequently criminals, it is easy to forget that our interpretations of such rights apply to the innocent and the guilty alike. In the present case, the chain of events set in motion when respondent Andrew Sokolow was stopped by Drug Enforcement Administration (DEA) agents at Honolulu International Airport led to the discovery of cocaine and, ultimately, to Sokolow's conviction for drug trafficking. But in sustaining this conviction on the ground that the agents reasonably suspected Sokolow of ongoing criminal activity, the Court diminishes the rights of *all* citizens "to be secure in their persons," U.S. Const., Amdt. 4, as they traverse the Nation's airports. Finding this result constitutionally impermissible, I dissent.

The Fourth Amendment cabins government's authority to intrude on personal privacy and security by requiring that searches and seizures usually be supported by a showing of probable cause. The reasonable-suspicion standard is a derivation of the probable-cause command, applicable only to those brief detentions which fall short of being full-scale searches and seizures and which are necessitated by law enforcement exigencies such as the need to stop ongoing crimes, to prevent imminent crimes, and to protect law enforcement officers in highly charged situations. By requiring reasonable suspicion as a prerequisite to such seizures, the Fourth Amendment protects innocent persons from being subjected to "overbearing or harassing" police conduct carried out solely on the basis of imprecise stereotypes of what criminals look like, or on the basis of irrelevant personal characteristics such as race.

To deter such egregious police behavior, we have held that a suspicion is not reasonable unless officers have based it on "specific and articulable facts." It is not enough to suspect that an individual has committed crimes in the past, harbors unconsummated criminal designs, or has the propensity to commit crimes. On the contrary, before detaining an individual, law enforcement officers must reasonably suspect that he is engaged in, or poised to commit, a criminal act *at that moment.* . . .

Evaluated against this standard, the facts about Andrew Sokolow known to the DEA agents at the time they stopped him fall short of reasonably indicating that he was engaged at the time in criminal activity. It is highly significant that the DEA agents stopped Sokolow because he matched one of the DEA's "profiles" of a paradigmatic drug courier. In my view, a law enforcement officer's mechanistic application of a formula of personal and behavioral traits in deciding whom to detain can only dull the officer's ability and determination to make sensitive and fact-specific inferences "in light of his experience," *Terry, supra,* particularly in ambiguous or borderline cases. Reflexive reliance on a profile of drug courier characteristics runs a far greater risk than does ordinary, case-by-case police work of subjecting innocent individuals to unwarranted police harassment and detention. This risk is enhanced by the profile's "chameleon-like way of adapting to any particular set of observations." *Compare, e.g., United States v. Moore,* 675 F.2d 802 (CA6 1982) (suspect was first to deplane), cert. denied, 460 U.S. 1068 (1983), *with United States v. Mendenhall,* 446 U.S. 544 (1980) (last to deplane), *with United States v. Buenaventura-Ariza,* 615 F.2d 29 (CA2 1980) (deplaned from middle); *United States v. Sullivan,* 625 F.2d 9 (CA4 1980) (one-way tickets), *with United States v. Craemer,* 555 F.2d 594 (CA6 1977) (round-trip tickets), with *United States v. McCaleb,* 552 F.2d 717 (CA6 1977) (nonstop flight), with *United States v. Sokolow,* 808 F.2d 1366, (CA9) (changed planes); *Craemer, supra* (no luggage), *with United States v. Sanford,* 658 F.2d 342 (CA5 1981) (gym bag), with *Sullivan, supra,* at 12 (new suitcases); *United States v. Smith,* 574 F.2d 882 (CA6 1978) (traveling alone), *with United States v. Fry,* 622 F.2d 1218 (CA5 1980) (travelling with companion); *United States v. Andrews,* 600 F.2d 563 (CA6 1979) (acted nervously), *with United States v. Himmelwright,* 551 F.2d 991 (CA5) (acted too calmly). . . . In asserting that it is not "somehow" relevant that the agents who stopped Sokolow did so in reliance on a prefabricated profile of criminal characteristics, the majority thus ducks serious issues relating to a questionable law enforcement practice, to address the validity of which we granted certiorari in this case. . . .

[T]raveler Sokolow gave no indications of evasive activity. On the contrary, the sole behavioral detail about Sokolow noted by the DEA agents was that he was nervous. With news accounts proliferating of plane crashes, near collisions, and air terrorism, there are manifold and good reasons for being agitated while awaiting a flight, reasons that have nothing to do with one's involvement in a criminal endeavor.

The remaining circumstantial facts known about Sokolow, considered either singly or together, are scarcely indicative of criminal activity. . . . [T]he fact that Sokolow took a brief trip to a resort city for which he brought only carry-on luggage also "describe[s] a very large category of presumably innocent travelers." That Sokolow embarked from Miami, "a source city for illicit drugs," is no more suggestive of illegality; thousands of innocent persons travel from "source cities" every day and, judging from the DEA's testimony in past cases, nearly every major city in the country may be characterized as a source or distribution city. That Sokolow had his phone listed in another person's name also does not support the majority's assertion that the DEA agents reasonably believed Sokolow was using an alias; it is commonplace to have one's phone registered in the name of a roommate, which, it later turned out, was precisely what Sokolow had done. That Sokolow was dressed in a black jumpsuit and wore gold jewelry also provides no grounds for suspecting wrongdoing, the majority's repeated and unexplained allusions to Sokolow's style of dress notwithstanding. For law enforcement officers to base a search, even in part, on a "pop" guess that persons dressed in a particular fashion are likely to commit crimes not only stretches the concept of reasonable suspicion beyond recognition, but also is inimical to the self-expression which the choice of wardrobe may provide.

Finally, that Sokolow paid for his tickets in cash indicates no imminent or ongoing criminal activity. The majority "feel[s] confident" that "[m]ost business travelers . . . purchase airline tickets by credit card or check." Why the majority confines its focus only to "business travelers" I do not know, but I would not so lightly infer ongoing crime from the use of legal tender. Making major cash purchases, while surely less common today, may simply reflect the traveler's aversion to, or inability to obtain, plastic money. . . .

NOTES & QUESTIONS

1. ***Profiling.*** What sorts of criteria would be sufficient to find reasonable suspicion for a *Terry* stop for potential terrorist activity at an airport? Having a one-way ticket? Having only carry-on luggage? One of the difficulties in creating a profile of a terrorist, Anita Ramasastry notes, is that "[t]here is no well-defined and reinforced profile for terrorists. Further, attacks are relatively infrequent, making it harder to reinforce any profiles that do exist."[50]

    Is the use of profiles to detain or search people problematic? Fred Schauer contends that making generalizations is not necessarily problematic, even when doing so leads to some mistakes:

    > Here Justice Marshall [dissenting in *Sokolow*] went right to the heart of the matter. He recognized that the question of the profile is not about profiles as

---

[50] Anita Ramasastry, *Lost in Translation? Data Mining, National Security, and the "Adverse Inference" Problem*, 22 Santa Clara Computer & High Tech. L.J. 757, 773 (2006).

such, but is about *rules*. The issue is whether preexisting and general rules should be employed to determine which people to stop, as the majority was willing to permit, or whether that determination must, as Justice Marshall insisted, be made on a particularistic basis by individual officers using their own best judgment in each case, even if that best judgment can itself be seen as just another version of profiling. Once we understand that the issue is not about whether to use profiles or not but instead about whether to use (or to prefer) formal written profiles or informal unwritten ones, it becomes clear that this is not a question of profiles or not, but a question about discretion. Should individual customs officers have the discretion to create their own profiles, as Justice Marshall preferred, or is it at least permissible, even if not constitutionally mandatory, for formal written profiles to be used as a way of regularizing the process and limiting the discretion of individual officers?

Once we understand the choice as being one between profiles that are constructed in advance and have the potential to be both under- and overinclusive, on the one hand, and profiles that are constructed on a case-by-case basis by law-enforcement officials making, in Justice Marshall's words, "sensitive and fact-specific inferences in light of [their] experience," on the other, we can see that the issue is not about profiling at all, for profiling is inevitable.[51]

Is the use of data mining laudable because it involves a computer searching for written pre-established patterns rather than the ad hoc discretion of airline screening officials at the security checkpoints? Pre-established profiles can eliminate the use of race or other problematic factors that might be used in an official's ad hoc discretion. Then again, even pre-established profiles can employ improper factors.

What factors should be considered to be improper? Should information about a person's associations and group memberships be included? Information about a person's political and expressive activity? Information about a person's religion or race?

Fred Schauer examines the issue of whether race should be a factor in the profile:

> Those who commit acts of airplane terrorism, both before and after September 11, 2001, are disproportionately younger Muslim men of Middle Eastern background. . . .
>
> On the evidence we now have, it is more than plausible to suppose that Middle Eastern ethnicity is a significant contributory factor, such that including it in the algorithm will make the algorithm substantially more effective than excluding it.
>
> Because allowing the use of race and ethnicity imposes a cost on those members of the targeted groups who are in the area of overinclusion — Middle Easterners who have done nothing wrong — it might be preferable to distribute the cost more broadly, and in doing so raise the cost without lowering the degree of security. If excluding the relevant factor of Middle Eastern appearance from the algorithm made it necessary to increase the scrutiny of everyone — if excluding ethnicity while still including everything else increased waiting time at airports an average of thirty minutes per passenger — this might still be a price worth paying. . . . Put starkly, the

---

[51] Frederick Schauer, *Profiles, Probabilities, and Stereotypes* 173-74 (2003).

question of racial or ethnic profiling in air travel is not the question of whether racial and ethnic sensitivity must be bought at the price of thousands of lives. Rather, it is most often the question of whether racial and ethnic sensitivity should be bought at the price of arriving thirty minutes earlier at the airport.[52]

Consider the following document obtained by the Electronic Privacy Information Center from NASA regarding airline passenger data:

> ISLE ran a simple anomaly detection algorithm that it developed as part of this project on a subset of the census database, and it found some interesting anomalies. Many of the anomalies were people from unusual countries. One anomaly was a 22-year-old African American man who was not a college graduate but had over $100,000 in capital gains.
>
> We ran Gritbot on a subset of the census database. It discovered many interesting anomalies, including a woman whose ancestry is Mexican but who speaks Chinese at home, a 16-year-old veteran, and some people who reported their race to be white and their ancestry to be African-American. . . .[53]

Profiles ultimately involve human judgment about what patterns should be singled out as suspicious. One difficulty with data mining is that if the profiles remain secret, how can there be oversight to prevent improper factors from being used? Who decides what factors are appropriate?

2. *An Assessment of Government Data Mining.* Consider the following account of the problems of government data mining by Daniel Solove:

> Usually, the government has some form of particularized suspicion, a factual basis to believe that a particular person may be engaged in illegal conduct. Particularized suspicion keeps the government's profound investigative powers in check, preventing widespread surveillance and snooping into the lives and affairs of all citizens. Computer matches . . . investigate everyone, and most people who are investigated are innocent.
>
> With the new information supplied by the private sector, there is an increased potential for more automated investigations, such as searches for all people who purchase books about particular topics or those who visit certain websites, or perhaps even people whose personal interests fit a profile for those likely to engage in certain forms of criminal activity. Profiles work similarly to the way that Amazon.com predicts which products customers will want to buy. They use particular characteristics and patterns of activity to predict how people will behave in the future. Of course, profiles can be mistaken, but they are often accurate enough to tempt people to rely on them. But there are even deeper problems with profiles beyond inaccuracies. Profiles can be based on stereotypes, race, or religion. A profile is only as good as its designer. Profiles are often kept secret, enabling prejudices and faulty assumptions to exist unchecked by the public.[54]

3. *A Hypothetical Data Mining Problem.* Suppose the FBI receives a tip from a credible source that two young males, both naturalized U.S. citizens, who are Muslim and who were originally born in Saudi Arabia, have rented a U-Haul

---

[52] *Id.* at 181-90.

[53] NASA Documents, available at http://www.epic.org/privacy/airtravel/nasa/

[54] Daniel J. Solove, *The Digital Person: Technology and Privacy in the Information Age* 179-85 (2004).

truck and are planning to use it to detonate a bomb at a crowded building or place in Los Angeles, CA within the next week. The source says he met the two males at his mosque, which has over 1,000 worshippers. This is all the information the FBI agents have. The FBI would like to: (1) obtain the records of the people who attend the mosque; (2) obtain the records of U-Haul. The FBI would like to engage in data mining on the records to narrow their search for the two males. Notwithstanding existing law, should the FBI agents be permitted to obtain the records? If so, what privacy protections should be established?

ARIZONA V. EVANS

514 U.S. 1 (1995)

REHNQUIST, J. This case presents the question whether evidence seized in violation of the Fourth Amendment by an officer who acted in reliance on a police record indicating the existence of an outstanding arrest warrant — a record that is later determined to be erroneous — must be suppressed by virtue of the exclusionary rule regardless of the source of the error. . . .

In January 1991, Phoenix police officer Bryan Sargent observed respondent Isaac Evans driving the wrong way on a one-way street in front of the police station. The officer stopped respondent and asked to see his driver's license. After respondent told him that his license had been suspended, the officer entered respondent's name into a computer data terminal located in his patrol car. The computer inquiry confirmed that respondent's license had been suspended and also indicated that there was an outstanding misdemeanor warrant for his arrest. Based upon the outstanding warrant, Officer Sargent placed respondent under arrest. While being handcuffed, respondent dropped a hand-rolled cigarette that the officers determined smelled of marijuana. Officers proceeded to search his car and discovered a bag of marijuana under the passenger's seat.

The State charged respondent with possession of marijuana. When the police notified the Justice Court that they had arrested him, the Justice Court discovered that the arrest warrant previously had been quashed and so advised the police. Respondent argued that because his arrest was based on a warrant that had been quashed 17 days prior to his arrest, the marijuana seized incident to the arrest should be suppressed as the fruit of an unlawful arrest. Respondent also argued that "[t]he 'good faith' exception to the exclusionary rule [was] inapplicable . . . because it was police error, not judicial error, which caused the invalid arrest.". . . .

"The question whether the exclusionary rule's remedy is appropriate in a particular context has long been regarded as an issue separate from the question whether the Fourth Amendment rights of the party seeking to invoke the rule were violated by police conduct." The exclusionary rule operates as a judicially created remedy designed to safeguard against future violations of Fourth Amendment rights through the rule's general deterrent effect. As with any remedial device, the rule's application has been restricted to those instances where its remedial objectives are thought most efficaciously served. Where the exclusionary rule does not result in appreciable deterrence, then, clearly, its use . . . is unwarranted. . . .

If court employees were responsible for the erroneous computer record, the exclusion of evidence at trial would not sufficiently deter future errors so as to warrant such a severe sanction. First, as we noted in [*United States v. Leon,* 468 U.S. 897 (1984)], the exclusionary rule was historically designed as a means of deterring police misconduct, not mistakes by court employees. Second, respondent offers no evidence that court employees are inclined to ignore or subvert the Fourth Amendment or that lawlessness among these actors requires application of the extreme sanction of exclusion. To the contrary, the Chief Clerk of the Justice Court testified at the suppression hearing that this type of error occurred once every three or four years.

Finally, and most important, there is no basis for believing that application of the exclusionary rule in these circumstances will have a significant effect on court employees responsible for informing the police that a warrant has been quashed. Because court clerks are not adjuncts to the law enforcement team engaged in the often competitive enterprise of ferreting out crime, they have no stake in the outcome of particular criminal prosecutions. The threat of exclusion of evidence could not be expected to deter such individuals from failing to inform police officials that a warrant had been quashed. . . .

In fact, once the court clerks discovered the error, they immediately corrected it, and then proceeded to search their files to make sure that no similar mistakes had occurred. There is no indication that the arresting officer was not acting objectively reasonably when he relied upon the police computer record. Application of the *Leon* framework supports a categorical exception to the exclusionary rule for clerical errors of court employees. . . .

O'CONNOR, SOUTER, AND BREYER, J.J. concurring. The evidence in this case strongly suggests that it was a court employee's departure from established recordkeeping procedures that caused the record of respondent's arrest warrant to remain in the computer system after the warrant had been quashed. Prudently, then, the Court limits itself to the question whether a court employee's departure from such established procedures is the kind of error to which the exclusionary rule should apply. . . .

In limiting itself to that single question, however, the Court does not hold that the court employee's mistake in this case was necessarily the *only* error that may have occurred and to which the exclusionary rule might apply. While the police were innocent of the court employee's mistake, they may or may not have acted reasonably in their reliance *on the recordkeeping system itself.* Surely it would *not* be reasonable for the police to rely, say, on a recordkeeping system, their own or some other agency's, that has no mechanism to ensure its accuracy over time and that routinely leads to false arrests, even years after the probable cause for any such arrest has ceased to exist (if it ever existed). . . .

In recent years, we have witnessed the advent of powerful, computer-based recordkeeping systems that facilitate arrests in ways that have never before been possible. The police, of course, are entitled to enjoy the substantial advantages this technology confers. They may not, however, rely on it blindly. With the benefits of more efficient law enforcement mechanisms comes the burden of corresponding constitutional responsibilities.

GINSBURG & STEVENS, J.J. dissenting. This case portrays the increasing use of computer technology in law enforcement; it illustrates an evolving problem this Court need not, and in my judgment should not, resolve too hastily. . . .

Widespread reliance on computers to store and convey information generates, along with manifold benefits, new possibilities of error, due to both computer malfunctions and operator mistakes. Most germane to this case, computerization greatly amplifies an error's effect, and correspondingly intensifies the need for prompt correction; for inaccurate data can infect not only one agency, but the many agencies that share access to the database. The computerized data bases of the Federal Bureau of Investigation's National Crime Information Center (NCIC), to take a conspicuous example, contain over 23 million records, identifying, among other things, persons and vehicles sought by law enforcement agencies nationwide. NCIC information is available to approximately 71,000 federal, state, and local agencies. Thus, any mistake entered into the NCIC spreads nationwide in an instant.

Isaac Evans' arrest exemplifies the risks associated with computerization of arrest warrants. Though his arrest was in fact warrantless — the warrant once issued having been quashed over two weeks before the episode in suit — the computer reported otherwise. Evans' case is not idiosyncratic. . . .

In the instant case, the Court features testimony of the Chief Clerk of the Justice Court in East Phoenix to the effect that errors of the kind Evans encountered are reported only "on[c]e every three or four years." But the same witness also recounted that, when the error concerning Evans came to light, an immediate check revealed that three other errors of the very same kind had occurred on "that same day." . . .

In the Court's view, exclusion of evidence, even if capable of deterring police officer errors, cannot deter the carelessness of other governmental actors. Whatever federal precedents may indicate — an issue on which I voice no opinion — the Court's conclusion is not the lesson inevitably to be drawn from logic or experience.

In this electronic age, particularly with respect to recordkeeping, court personnel and police officers are not neatly compartmentalized actors. Instead, they serve together to carry out the State's information-gathering objectives. Whether particular records are maintained by the police or the courts should not be dispositive where a single computer data base can answer all calls. Not only is it artificial to distinguish between court clerk and police clerk slips; in practice, it may be difficult to pinpoint whether one official, *e.g.*, a court employee, or another, *e.g.*, a police officer, caused the error to exist or to persist. Applying an exclusionary rule as the Arizona court did may well supply a powerful incentive to the State to promote the prompt updating of computer records. . . .

NOTES & QUESTIONS

1. ***Accuracy.*** Pattern-based data mining is often not a highly accurate way of identifying suspects. Daniel Steinbock explores the arguments relating to data mining's accuracy:

> It must be noted at the outset that, in one sense, accuracy is not a particularly high priority in data matching and data mining. To the extent that their results are used for heightened scrutiny or for terrorist profiling, even the staunchest advocates would not pretend that these indicators are foolproof, but would simply respond that they do not need to be. This is especially true for predictive uses; the goal is simply to sort the higher from the lower risks and, perhaps, to see if a certain threshold of risk has been reached. On the other hand, even with predictive uses, errors in the data will produce a larger number of falsely positive results, thereby imposing unnecessary harms. This effectively externalizes the error costs of the computer-generated decision onto its subjects.[55]

Anita Ramasastry notes that data can often be "lost in translation" when it is taken from other contexts and used for government data mining purposes:

> First, data may not be accurate when provided initially by a consumer or may only reflect a partial truth. Second, data may get mistranslated due to human error (e.g. typing in a birth date incorrectly) when placed into a database. Third, when data is used in a new context, it may not be interpreted in the same way as previously used, because the new party using the data may not understand how the data was originally classified. For example, racial or ethnic classifications in one database may be different than in a new database. Fourth, when data from different sources is combined into a larger database, it may be incorrectly integrated. In other words, data from different people who share the same surname might be incorrectly merged, creating a new profile that is incorrect. Thus, there are multiple ways in which data may be erroneous. Where human agents are involved in compiling or aggregating different data, data sources can be mistranslated.[56]

2. ***Due Process.*** Consider Daniel Steinbock:

> The most striking aspect of virtually all antiterrorist and data mining decisions is the total absence of even the most rudimentary procedures for notice, hearing, or other opportunities for meaningful participation before, or even after, the deprivation is imposed.

Steinbock examines four ways to bring due process to data mining programs:

> One is summary hearings, along the lines of those required in brief school suspensions, prior to denial of access to flights or infringements of other liberty or property rights. A second involves correction opportunities after the initial data matching or data mining consequence, in a fuller process with

---

[55] Daniel J. Steinbock, *Data Matching, Data Mining, and Due Process*, 40 Ga. L. Rev. 1, 82-83 (2005).

[56] Anita Ramasastry, *Lost in Translation? Data Mining, National Security, and the "Adverse Inference" Problem*, 22 Santa Clara Computer & High Tech. L.J. 757, 778 (2006).

disclosure and a right to respond. A third means of redress is after-the-fact compensatory damages for false positives in outcome. This solution allows for less process but makes wrongly identified persons whole, at least monetarily. Finally, given the frequent need for secrecy in data matching and data mining decision algorithms and the difficulty of addressing challenges to them in individual hearings, this Article proposes examination of their validity by independent oversight bodies. Evaluating whether a decisional system meets constitutional demands of due process requires attention to all stages of the process.[57]

3. *Transparency.* Consider Daniel Solove:

> The problem with many data mining programs is that they lack adequate transparency. The reason for the secrecy of the programs is that exposing the algorithms and patterns that trigger identification as a possible future terrorist will tip off terrorists about what behaviors to avoid. This is indeed a legitimate concern. Our society, however, is one of open government, public accountability, and oversight of government officials — not one of secret blacklists maintained in clandestine bureaucracies. Without public accountability, unelected bureaucrats can administer data mining programs in ways often insulated from any scrutiny at all. For example, the information gathered about people for use in data mining might be collected from sources that do not take sufficient steps to maintain its accuracy. Without oversight, it is unclear what level of accuracy the government requires for the information it gathers and uses. If profiles are based on race, speech, or other factors that society might not find desirable to include, how is this to be aired and discussed? If a person is routinely singled out based on a profile and wants to challenge the profile, there appears no way to do so unless the profile is revealed.
>
> The lack of transparency in data mining programs makes it nearly impossible to balance the liberty and security interests. Given the significant potential privacy issues and other constitutional concerns, combined with speculative and unproven security benefits as well as many other alternative means of promoting security, should data mining still be on the table as a viable policy option?[58]

UNITED STATES V. ELLISON

462 F.3d 557 (6th Cir. 2006)

GIBBONS, J. . . . The central issue in this case is whether the Fourth Amendment is implicated when a police officer investigates an automobile license plate number using a law enforcement computer database. While on routine patrol, Officer Mark Keeley of the Farmington Hills (Michigan) Police Department pulled into a two-lane service drive adjacent to a shopping center. Keeley testified that a white van, with a male driver inside, was idling in the lane closest to the stores, in an area marked with "Fire Lane" and "No Parking" signs. Keeley did not issue the van a citation for being illegally parked, nor did he request that

---

[57] Steinbock, Data Mining, supra, at 57.

[58] Daniel J. Solove, *Data Mining and the Security-Liberty Debate*, 74 U. Chi. L. Rev. 343 (2008).

the driver move the van. Rather, he moved into a parking spot to observe the van and entered the vehicle's license plate number into his patrol car's Law Enforcement Information Network ("LEIN") computer. The LEIN search revealed that the vehicle was registered to Curtis Ellison, who had an outstanding felony warrant. Following standard procedure, Keeley radioed for back-up and continued observing the van. After two minutes, another male got into the van, and it drove away. Officer Keeley followed the van until his back-up was nearby, and then activated his lights and stopped the van.

Officer Keeley approached the driver's-side window as his back-up arrived. He advised the driver that he was being stopped for parking in a fire lane and asked for license, registration and proof of insurance. The driver, identified as Edward Coleman, stated that he had only stopped in front of the store to wait for the passenger. At this time the passenger stated that he was the registered owner of the vehicle. Keeley verified the passenger's identity as Curtis Ellison and moved to the passenger side of the van. Keeley notified Ellison that he was being arrested on the outstanding warrant. Ellison stepped out of the van, and during the routine safety pat-down, two firearms were found. Coleman was released with a warning about parking in a fire lane.

Ellison was indicted for being a felon in possession of a firearm in violation of 18 U.S.C. § 922(g). Prior to trial, he made a timely motion to suppress the firearm as the fruit of an illegal search. After holding a hearing, the district court made a factual finding that the van was not parked illegally, and thus, the officer did not have probable cause to run the LEIN check of Ellison's license plate. The court issued a Memorandum Opinion and Order granting the motion to suppress under the "fruit of the poisonous tree" doctrine. . . .

The government argues on appeal that Ellison had no reasonable expectation of privacy in the information contained on his license plate, and thus, no probable cause was required for Officer Keeley to run the LEIN check. . . .

Although the district court did not expressly state that Ellison had a reasonable expectation of privacy in the information contained on his license plate, such a conclusion was necessarily implied by the court's ruling that a Fourth Amendment violation occurred. Thus, the district court could only find that the LEIN search violated the Fourth Amendment if it first concluded that Ellison had a "constitutionally protected reasonable expectation of privacy" in his license plate number. . . .

A tenet of constitutional jurisprudence is that the Fourth Amendment protects only what an individual seeks to keep private. *Katz,* 389 U.S. at 351-52. "What a person knowingly exposes to the public . . . is not a subject of Fourth Amendment protection." It is also settled that "objects falling in the plain view of an officer who has a right to be in the position to have that view are subject to seizure." . . .

No argument can be made that a motorist seeks to keep the information on his license plate private. The very purpose of a license plate number, like that of a Vehicle Identification Number, is to provide identifying information to law enforcement officials and others. . . .

The dissent implies that even if an individual has no expectation of privacy in a license plate number, a privacy interest is somehow created by the entry of this information into a law-enforcement computer database. This argument flies in the face of established Fourth Amendment doctrine. First, despite the dissent's concerns over the information available in a LEIN search, Ellison had no privacy interest in the information retrieved by Officer Keely. The obvious purpose of maintaining law enforcement databases is to make information, such as the existence of outstanding warrants, readily available to officers carrying out legitimate law enforcement duties. The dissent fails to state how using a license plate number-in which there is no expectation of privacy-to retrieve other non-private information somehow creates a "search" for the purposes of the Fourth Amendment. . . . This is not a case where the police used a technology not available to the public to discover evidence that could not otherwise be obtained without "intrusion into a constitutionally-protected area." *Kyllo v. United States,* 533 U.S. 27, 34-35 (2001) (holding that the use of thermal-imaging technology to detect heat inside a private home violates the Fourth Amendment). The technology used in this case does not allow officers to access any previously-unobtainable information; it simply allows them to access information more quickly. As the information was obtained without intruding upon a constitutionally-protected area, there was no "search" for Fourth Amendment purposes. . . .

MOORE, J. dissenting. . . . The majority rests its conclusion that the Fourth Amendment was not implicated by the LEIN search on the relatively uncontroversial fact that the operator of a vehicle has no privacy interest in the particular combination of letters and numerals that make up his license-plate number, but pays short shrift to the crucial issue of how the license-plate information is used. . . . This approach misses the crux of the issue before the court: even if there is no privacy interest in the license-plate number per se, can the police, without any measure of heightened suspicion or other constraint on their discretion, conduct a search using the license-plate number to access information about the vehicle and its operator that may not otherwise be public or accessible by the police without heightened suspicion? . . . .

The use of a computer database to acquire information about drivers through their license-plate numbers without any heightened suspicion is in tension with many of the Fourth Amendment concerns expressed in *Delaware v. Prouse,* 440 U.S. 648, 655-63 (1979). In *Prouse,* the Supreme Court held that an officer may not stop a vehicle to check the operator's license and registration without "at least articulable and reasonable suspicion that a motorist is unlicensed or that an automobile is not registered, or that either the vehicle or an occupant is otherwise subject to seizure for violation of law," despite the fact that the state requires drivers to be licensed and vehicles to be registered. The Court stated that the Fourth Amendment aims "to safeguard the privacy and security of individuals against arbitrary invasions. . . . Thus, the permissibility of a particular law enforcement practice is judged by balancing its intrusion on the individual's Fourth Amendment interests against its promotion of legitimate governmental interests." The Court then explained the constitutional concerns that flow from the unbridled discretion associated with permitting random searches of drivers' information:

To insist neither upon an appropriate factual basis for suspicion directed at a particular automobile nor upon some other substantial and objective standard or rule to govern the exercise of discretion "would invite intrusions upon constitutionally guaranteed rights based on nothing more substantial than inarticulate hunches. . . ." *Terry v. Ohio,* 392 U.S. [1], at 22 [1968]. . . . When there is not probable cause to believe that a driver is violating any one of the multitude of applicable traffic and equipment regulations — or other articulable basis amounting to reasonable suspicion that the driver is unlicensed or his vehicle unregistered — we cannot conceive of any legitimate basis upon which a patrolman could decide that stopping a particular driver for a spot check would be more productive than stopping any other driver. This kind of standardless and unconstrained discretion is the evil the Court has discerned when in previous cases it has insisted that the discretion of the official in the field be circumscribed, at least to some extent. . . .

Although the license-plate search at issue here is arguably less invasive than a license-and-registration check, the constitutional concerns regarding abuse of discretion do not disappear simply because drivers are not stopped to conduct the license-plate search. First, a search can implicate the Fourth Amendment even when the individual does not know that she is being searched. Second, the balancing of Fourth Amendment interests also requires consideration of "psychological intrusion[s] visited upon" the individuals searched in assessing the extent of intrusion that a particular police practice imposes. *See Prouse,* 440 U.S. at 657. The psychological invasion that results from knowing that one's personal information is subject to search by the police, for no reason, at any time one is driving a car is undoubtedly grave.

Because the government incorrectly limits its Fourth Amendment analysis to the plain view of the license plate without exploring the constitutional implications of the subsequent LEIN search, it does not provide any explanation as to the governmental interests promoted by license-plate searches. . . .

In addition, the possibility and the reality of errors in the computer databases accessed by MDT systems lead to great concern regarding the potential for license-plate searches to result in unwarranted intrusions into privacy in the form of stops made purely on the basis of incorrect information. . . .

NOTES & QUESTIONS

1. *The Fourth Amendment and Government Data Mining.* Does the Fourth Amendment provide any limits on government data mining? Lee Tien argues that it does:

   The use of patterns discovered through data mining raises . . . particularity issues. Imagine a database of a million people and a hypothesis that those who meet certain criteria are highly likely to be terrorists. But you don't know whether any of these million people actually do meet these criteria; if you did, you wouldn't need to run the search. The basic problem is lack of particularized suspicion; data about these persons would be "searched" without any reason to believe either that the database contains evidence of terrorist activity or that any person "in" the database is a terrorist. . . .[59]

When the government engages in data mining, it often analyzes information that it already possesses. Is this a search? If the government has information about a person in its records and analyzes it, does this trigger the Fourth Amendment?

In contrast, Richard Posner argues in favor of data mining: "Computer searches do not invade privacy because search programs are not sentient beings. Only the human search should raise constitutional or other legal issues."[60] Consider the following argument in response to Posner: "[T]here is human intervention in data mining even before the first automated search is run; humans will write the software, shape the database parameters, and decide on the kinds of matches that count. And the task of data mining itself is guided by some degree of human interaction."[61] To the extent there is a human element in data mining, how ought it to be regulated? Do the problems of data mining stem solely from the human element?

4. THE DRIVER'S PRIVACY PROTECTION ACT

For decades, many states had been selling to private sector companies their motor vehicle records. Motor vehicle records contain information such as one's name, address, phone number, Social Security number, medical information, height, weight, gender, eye color, photograph, and date of birth. This information was highly desired by marketers, who paid states millions of dollars to obtain these records. In 1994, Congress passed the Driver's Privacy Protection Act (DPPA), 18 U.S.C. §§ 2721–2725, to halt this practice.

Restriction on Disclosure. Pursuant to DPPA:

[A] State department of motor vehicles . . . shall not knowingly disclose or otherwise make available to any person or entity personal information about any individual obtained by the department in connection with a motor vehicle record. 18 U.S.C. § 2721(a).

"Personal information" is defined as data "that identifies an individual, including an individual's photograph, social security number, driver identification number, name, address (but not the 5-digit zip code), telephone number, and medical or disability information." § 2725(3). The definition of "personal information" specifically excludes "information on vehicular accidents, driving violations, and driver's status." § 2725(3).

DPPA applies to state DMVs and their officials and employees. Further, DPPA only applies to motor vehicle records.

---

[59] Lee Tien, Privacy, *Technology and Data Mining*, 30 Ohio N.U. L. Rev. 389, 405 (2004).

[60] Richard Posner, *Privacy, Surveillance, and Law*, 75 U. Chi. L. Rev. 245 (2008).

[61] Ira Rubinstein, Ronald D. Lee & Paul M. Schwartz, *Data Mining and Internet Profiling*, 75 U. Chi. L. Rev. 261 (2008).

Consent. State DMVs can disclose personal information in motor vehicle records if the individual consents. In order to disclose a driver's personal information for marketing or other restricted uses, the driver must affirmatively indicate her consent (opt in). § 2721(b) and (d).

Exceptions. The DPPA contains a number of exceptions. Personal information can be disclosed for purposes of law enforcement, recalls, legal proceedings, and insurance claims investigations. § 2721(b). Additionally, DPPA permits disclosure to licensed private investigative agencies. § 2721(b). Ironically, the event that motivated Congress to pass the DPPA was the murder of actress Rebecca Shaeffer. Her murderer ascertained her address from a private detective, who had received it from the DMV.[62]

Restrictions on Further Dissemination. If private entities obtain motor vehicle record information, they cannot resell or further disseminate that information. 18 U.S.C. § 2721(c). However, if the driver consents to the disclosure of her data, then information may be disseminated for any purpose.

Enforcement. The DPPA establishes criminal fines for any "person" who knowingly obtains or discloses motor vehicle record data in ways prohibited by the DPPA. §§ 2722, 2723(a), 2725(2).

The DPPA, § 2724, provides for a private right to action for violations:

> A person who knowingly obtains, discloses or uses personal information, from a motor vehicle record, for a purpose not permitted under this chapter shall be liable to the individual to whom the information pertains, who may bring a civil action in a United States district court.

Note that this section purportedly applies to any "person who knowingly obtains, discloses or uses personal information, from a motor vehicle record." In other words, it does not just apply to state DMVs but to anybody who uses data from a motor vehicle record. States and state agencies are generally excluded from the DPPA, but the U.S. Attorney General may impose a civil penalty of up to $5,000 per day for state agencies that maintain a "policy or practice of substantial noncompliance" with the DPPA. § 2723(b).

In *Margan v. Niles*, 250 F. Supp. 2d 63 (N.D.N.Y. 2003), the court found that the DPPA provided a cause of action beyond the motor operator whose motor vehicle record was disclosed. The court found that "any individual whose address was obtained from a motor vehicle record is a proper plaintiff." Hence, in *Niles*, the spouse and children of an individual whose address was obtained from a motor vehicle record could "maintain an action under the DPPA where the spouse and children share the same address as that individual." The court also found that a municipality whose agent violated the DPPA could be held vicariously liable under this statute. *See also Luparello v. The Incorporated Village of Garden City,* 290 F. Supp. 2d 341 (E.D.N.Y. 2003).

---

[62] *See* Charles J. Sykes, *The End of Privacy: Personal Rights in the Surveillance Society* 30-31 (1999).

The Scope of Congressional Power. In *Reno v. Condon*, 528 U.S. 141 (2000), the Supreme Court upheld the DPPA against a constitutional challenge that DPPA violated the Tenth and Eleventh Amendments:

> The United States asserts that the DPPA is a proper exercise of Congress' authority to regulate interstate commerce under the Commerce Clause, U.S. Const., Art. I, § 8, cl. 3. The United States bases its Commerce Clause argument on the fact that the personal, identifying information that the DPPA regulates is a "thin[g] in interstate commerce," and that the sale or release of that information in interstate commerce is therefore a proper subject of congressional regulation. We agree with the United States' contention. The motor vehicle information which the States have historically sold is used by insurers, manufacturers, direct marketers, and others engaged in interstate commerce to contact drivers with customized solicitations. The information is also used in the stream of interstate commerce by various public and private entities for matters related to interstate motoring. Because drivers' information is, in this context, an article of commerce, its sale or release into the interstate stream of business is sufficient to support congressional regulation.

Based on *Reno v. Condon*, what is the extent of Congress's power to regulate information maintained by the states? Suppose Congress amended the Privacy Act to apply not just to federal agencies but to all state and local governments as well. Would such an extension of the Privacy Act be constitutional?

CHAPTER **4**

PRIVACY OF FINANCIAL AND COMMERCIAL DATA

A. THE FINANCIAL SERVICES INDUSTRY AND PERSONAL DATA

1. THE FAIR CREDIT REPORTING ACT

Increasingly, companies in the United States make sales based on credit. Since 1980, almost all homes and most new cars are purchased on credit. Well over half of retail items are purchased on credit as well.[1]

As a result of the centrality of different forms of consumer borrowing, credit reporting agencies play an ever-greater role in economic transactions. Credit reporting agencies prepare credit reports about people's credit history for use by creditors seeking to loan people money. Credit reports contain financial information such as bankruptcy filings, judgments and liens, mortgage foreclosures, and checking account data. Some companies also prepare investigative consumer reports, which supplement the credit report with information about an individual's character and lifestyle. Creditors depend upon credit reports to determine whether or not to offer a person a loan as well as what interest rate to charge that person. Credit reports are also reviewed by some landlords before renting out an apartment.

Credit reports contain a "credit score" that is used to assess a person's credit risk. In many cases, a low score will not necessarily mean the denial of a loan, mortgage, or credit card; rather, it means that a higher rate of interest will be charged. As Evan Hendricks notes:

> According to the Fair Isaac Corporation, a leading developer of credit scoring models, one delinquent account can lower a credit score from 70 to 120 points. A consumer with excellent credit (credit score of 720-850) would pay about 7.85% interest rate for a home equity loan, while a consumer with marginal

---

[1] *See generally* Robert Ellis Smith, *Ben Franklin's Web Site: Privacy and Curiosity from Plymouth Rock to the Internet* 313-25 (2000); Steven L. Nock, *The Costs of Privacy: Surveillance and Reputation in America* (1993).

credit (640-659) would pay 9.2% and one with poor credit (500-559) would pay a 12.1% rate. The rate swings for a new car loan are even greater, with good credit risks paying a 5.2% rate, moderate risks paying 11.4% and poor risks paying 17.2%.[2]

Credit reports are not only used in connection with granting credit. Employers use credit reports to make hiring and promotion decisions. The issuance of professional licenses, such as admittance to the bar, also can require the examination of one's credit report.

There are three major national credit reporting agencies: Experian, Equifax, and Trans Union. Each of these three companies has information on virtually every adult American citizen, and they routinely prepare credit reports about individuals.

According to Peter Swire, our financial system has been shifting toward more traceable payment transactions: "The shift from cash to checks to credit and debit cards shows an evolution toward creating records, placing the records automatically in databases, and potentially linking the databases to reveal extremely detailed information about an individual's purchasing history."[3] This evolution is generating new problems for the protection of privacy.

In 1970, Congress passed the Fair Credit Reporting Act (FCRA), Pub. L. No. 90-321, to regulate credit reporting agencies. The Act was inspired by allegations of abuse and lack of responsiveness of credit agencies to consumer complaints. In its statement of purpose, the FCRA states: "There is a need to insure that consumer reporting agencies exercise their grave responsibilities with fairness, impartiality, and a respect for the consumer's right to privacy." 15 U.S.C. § 1681. The FCRA requires credit reporting companies to provide an individual access to her records, establishes procedures for correcting information, and sets limitations on disclosure.

Scope. FCRA applies to "any consumer reporting agency" that furnishes a "consumer report." 15 U.S.C. § 1681b. As a consequence, the scope of the FCRA turns on the definitions of "consumer report" and "consumer reporting agencies." Pursuant to § 1681b(d):

> The term "consumer report" means any written, oral, or other communication of any information by a consumer reporting agency bearing on a consumer's credit worthiness, credit standing, credit capacity, character, general reputation, personal characteristics, or mode of living which is used or expected to be used or collected in whole or in part for the purpose of serving as a factor in establishing the consumer's eligibility for
>
> > (A) credit or insurance to be used primarily for personal, family, or household purposes;
> > (B) employment purposes; or
> > (C) any other purpose authorized under [§ 1681b].

---

[2] Evan Hendricks, *Credit Scores and Credit Reports: How the System Really Works, What You Can Do* 3-4 (2004).

[3] Peter P. Swire, *Financial Privacy and the Theory of High-Tech Government Surveillance*, 77 Wash. U. L.Q. 461 (1999).

A "consumer reporting agency" is defined as

[a]ny person which, for monetary fees, dues, or on a cooperative nonprofit basis, regularly engages in whole or in part in the practice of assembling or evaluating consumer credit information or other information on consumers for the purpose of furnishing consumer reports to third parties, and which uses means or facility of interstate commerce for the purpose of preparing or furnishing consumer reports. § 1681b(f).

Courts have held that "even if a report is used or expected to be used for a non-consumer purpose, it may still fall within the definition of a consumer report if it contains information that was originally collected by a consumer reporting agency with the expectation that it would be used for a consumer purpose." *Ippolito v. WNS, Inc.*, 864 F.2d 440 (7th Cir. 1988); *Bakker v. McKinnon*, 152 F.3d 1007 (8th Cir. 1998).

Permissible Uses of Credit Reports. Pursuant to 15 U.S.C. § 1681(b)(a), a consumer reporting agency can furnish a consumer report only under certain circumstances or for certain uses: (1) in response to a court order or grand jury subpoena; (2) to the person to whom the report pertains; (3) to a "person which [the agency] has reason to believe" intends to use the information in connection with (a) the extension of credit to a consumer; (b) employment purposes; (c) insurance underwriting; (d) licensing or the conferral of government benefits; (e) assessment of credit risks associated with an existing credit obligation; (f) "legitimate business need" when engaging in "a business transaction involving the consumer"; (4) to establish a person's capacity to pay child support.

Credit Reports for Employment Purposes. When an employer or potential employer seeks a credit report for employment purposes, she must first disclose in writing to the consumer that a credit report may be obtained, and the consumer must authorize in writing that the report can be obtained. The person seeking the report from a credit reporting agency must certify that she obtained the consent of the individual and that she will not use the information in violation of any equal employment opportunity law or regulation. § 1681b(b). If the person who obtained the report takes adverse action based in any way on the report, she must provide the consumer a copy of the report and a description of the consumer's rights under the FCRA. § 1681b(b).

Pursuant to § 1681b(g):

A consumer reporting agency shall not furnish for employment purposes, or in connection with a credit or insurance transaction or a direct marketing transaction, a consumer report that contains medical information about a consumer, unless the consumer consents to the furnishing of the report.

Law Enforcement Access. Pursuant to FCRA, "a consumer reporting agency may furnish identifying information respecting any customer, limited to his name, address, former addresses, places of employment, or former places of employment, to a governmental agency." § 1681f. The FBI can obtain "the names and addresses of all financial institutions . . . at which a consumer maintains or has maintained an account" by presenting a written request to a consumer reporting agency. § 1681u(a). Additionally, pursuant to a written request by the FBI, a consumer reporting agency must disclose "identifying information respecting a consumer, limited to name, address, former addresses, places of employment, or former places of employment." The FBI, however, must certify that the information is sought in an investigation to protect against "international terrorism or clandestine intelligence activities" and that the investigation "is not conducted solely upon the basis of activities protected by the first amendment to the Constitution of the United States." § 1681u(b). To obtain additional information from a credit report, the FBI must obtain a court order and meet the same standard as above. § 1681u(c).

Moreover, § 1681v provides a broad release exemption "to a government agency authorized to conduct investigations of, or intelligence or counterintelligence activities or analysis related to, international terrorism." These entities can obtain a consumer report on an individual when the government agency provides "a written certification" to a consumer reporting agency that the information is "necessary" for an agency investigation or other agency activity.

Unauthorized Disclosures of Credit Reports: Prescreening. A typical American receives a flood of credit cards offers each year. These offers follow due to the practice of "prescreening" consumers for such offers, which FCRA permits. A credit reporting agency can furnish a credit report, without the consumer's authorization, if

> (i) the transaction consists of a firm offer of credit or insurance;
> (ii) the consumer reporting agency has complied with subsection (e); and
> (iii) there is not in effect the election by the consumer, made in accordance with subsection (e), to have the consumer's name and address excluded from lists of names provided by the agency pursuant to this paragraph. § 1681b(c).

Subsection (e) of § 1681b provides the consumer with a right to opt out of such unauthorized disclosures. If the consumer notifies the credit reporting agency by phone, the opt out shall last for two years and then expire. If the consumer notifies the credit reporting agency by submitting a signed opt-out form, then the opt out remains effective until the consumer notifies the agency otherwise. § 1681b(e).

Limitations on Information Contained in Credit Reports. Credit reporting agencies are excluded from providing certain information in credit reports, such as bankruptcy proceedings more than ten years old; suits and judgments more than seven years old; paid tax liens more than seven years old; and records of arrest, indictment, or conviction of a crime more than seven years old. § 1681c(a). These limitations do not apply, however, when a company is preparing a credit report used in connection with a credit transaction more than $150,000; underwriting a life insurance policy more than $150,000; or employing an individual with an annual salary more than $75,000. § 1681c(b).

Investigative Consumer Reports. An "investigative consumer report" is "a consumer report or portion thereof in which information on a consumer's character, general reputation, personal characteristics, or mode of living is obtained through personal interviews, with neighbors, friends, or associates." § 1681a(f). The FCRA provides limitations on investigative consumer reports. These reports cannot be prepared unless "it is clearly and accurately disclosed to the consumer that an investigative consumer report including information as to his character, general reputation, personal characteristics and mode of living, whichever are applicable, may be made." § 1681d(a)(1). The consumer, if she requests, can require disclosure "of the nature and scope of the investigation requested." § 1681d(b). Further, if the report contains any adverse information about a person gleaned from interviews with neighbors, friends, or associates, the agency must take reasonable steps to corroborate that information "from an additional source that has independent and direct knowledge of the information" or ensure that "the person interviewed is the best possible source of the information." § 1681d(d).

Accuracy. "Whenever a consumer reporting agency prepares a consumer report it shall follow reasonable procedures to assure maximum possible accuracy of the information concerning the individual about whom the report relates." § 1681e(b).

Disclosures to the Consumer. The FCRA requires that credit reporting agencies, upon request of the consumer, disclose, among other things:

> (1) All information in the consumer's file at the time of the request, except . . . any information concerning credit scores or any other risk scores or predictors relating to the consumer.
> (2) The sources of the information. . . .
> (3) Identification of each person . . . that procured a consumer report [within two years for employment purposes; within one year for all other purposes] . . . .
> (4) The dates, original payees, and amounts of any checks upon which is based any adverse characterization of the consumer, included in the file at the time of disclosure. . . . § 1681g.

Responsiveness to Consumer Complaints. National credit reporting agencies must provide consumers who request disclosures under the FCRA with a toll-free telephone number at which personnel are accessible to respond to consumer inquiries during normal business hours. § 1681g(c).

Procedures in Case of Disputed Accuracy. Pursuant to § 1681i(a)(1):

> If the completeness or accuracy of any item of information contained in a consumer's file at a consumer reporting agency is disputed by the consumer and the consumer notifies the agency directly of such dispute, the agency shall reinvestigate free of charge and record the current status of the disputed information or delete the item from the file. . . .

The consumer reporting agency must provide written notice to a consumer of the results of a reinvestigation within five business days after completing the investigation. § 1681i.

If the information is found to be inaccurate or incomplete or cannot be verified, the consumer reporting agency must promptly delete it from the file. § 1681i. At the request of the consumer, the credit reporting agency must furnish notification that the item has been deleted to "any person specifically designated by the consumer who has within two years prior thereto received a consumer report for employment purposes, or within six months prior thereto received a consumer report for any other purpose." § 1681i(d).

"If the reinvestigation does not resolve the dispute, the consumer may file a brief statement setting forth the nature of the dispute." § 1681i(b).

In any subsequent credit report, the agency must clearly note that the information in question is disputed by the consumer and provide the consumer's statement. § 1681i(c).

Public Record Information for Employment Purposes. If a credit reporting agency furnishes a credit report for employment purposes containing information obtained in public records that is likely to have an adverse effect on the consumer, it must either notify the consumer of the fact that public record information is being reported along with the name and address of the person to whom the information is being reported or "maintain strict procedures designed to insure that whenever public record information which is likely to have an adverse effect on a consumer's ability to obtain employment is reported it is complete and up to date." § 1681k.

Requirements on Users of Consumer Reports. If a user of a credit report takes any adverse action on a consumer based in any way on the report, the user shall provide notice of the adverse action to the consumer, information for the consumer to contact the credit reporting agency that prepared the report, and notice of the consumer's right to obtain a free copy of the report and to dispute the accuracy of the report. § 1681m(a). Whenever credit is denied based on information obtained through sources other than a credit report, upon the consumer's written request, the person or entity denying credit shall disclose the nature of that information. § 1681m(b).

Civil Liability. A person who "willfully fails to comply with any requirement" of the FCRA is liable to the consumer for actual damages or damages between $100 and $1,000, as well as punitive damages and attorneys' fees and costs. § 1681n. Negligent failure to comply with any requirement of the FCRA results in liability to the consumer for actual damages as well as attorneys' fees and costs. § 1681n. The FTC also has the power to enforce the FCRA.

The FCRA states that an action to enforce liability under the Act must be brought within two years "from the date on which the liability arises." § 1681p. However, when the defendant has "willfully misrepresented any information required under [the FCRA] to be disclosed and the information . . . is material to [a claim under the FCRA], the actions may be brought at a time within two years after [the plaintiff's] discovery of the misrepresentation." § 1681p.

The Fair and Accurate Credit Transactions Act. In 2003, Congress passed the Fair and Accurate Credit Transactions Act (FACTA), which amended FCRA. Evan Hendricks explains the impetus for passing the FACTA:

> [K]ey provisions of the FCRA that preempted State law were set to expire on December 31, 2003. These provisions dealt with issues affecting billions of dollars in commerce: pre-approved credit card offers, duties on creditors (furnishers) to report accurately and to reinvestigate, and the sharing of personal data among corporate affiliates. Industry expressed fears that if legislation was not passed and the preemption expired, state legislatures would begin passing conflicting laws that would raise compliance costs, and worse, interfere with profits.
>
> To consumer and privacy groups, legislation was long overdue because the 1996 FCRA Amendments were not getting the job done. All of the long-standing problems related to privacy and fair information practices persisted: inaccuracy, faulty reinvestigations, reinsertion, non-responsiveness, and lax security. More dramatically, identity theft had been crowned the nation's "fastest growing crime," and the biggest harm from identity theft, everyone knew, was to the privacy of credit reports. . . .
>
> Both sides wanted legislation, but not the same legislation. Industry wanted a simple, straightforward bill that would do nothing more than make FCRA preemption permanent.
>
> Consumer privacy groups called for a detailed reform bill that would set a "floor" of new protections, but which would leave the states free to go further.[4]

One-Call Fraud Alerts. The FACTA amends FCRA to enable consumers to alert only one credit reporting agency of potential fraud rather than all of them. That agency must notify the other credit reporting agencies. 15 U.S.C. § 1681c-1.

Business Transaction Data. The FACTA gives victims of identity theft the right to require certain disclosures from the creditors used by the identity thief; these disclosures concern information about the fraudulent transactions carried out in the victim's name. 15 U.S.C. § 1681g(e)(1). To obtain this information from the creditors, however, the victim must provide one form of identification from a list (that the business gets to pick) as well as proof of the claim of identity theft (police report, affidavit). The victim's request must be in writing and must specify the date of the transaction and other transaction data. Business entities can decline this request if they believe in good faith that there is not "a high degree of confidence in knowing the true identity of the individual requesting the information." § 1681g(e)(2). Further, business entities cannot be sued if they make a disclosure in good faith under these provisions. § 1681g(e)(7). Business entities are not required to alter their record-keeping practices to provide the information required by these provisions. § 1681g(e)(8).

Block of Identity Theft Information. The FACTA amends the FCRA to provide:

---

[4] Hendricks, *Credit Scores, supra*, at 307-08.

(a) *Block.* Except as otherwise provided in this section, a consumer reporting agency shall block the reporting of any information in the file of a consumer that the consumer identifies as information that resulted from an alleged identity theft, not later than 4 business days after the date of receipt by such agency of —

(1) appropriate proof of the identity of the consumer;
(2) a copy of an identity theft report;
(3) the identification of such information by the consumer; and
(4) a statement by the consumer that the information is not information relating to any transaction by the consumer.

(b) *Notification.* A consumer reporting agency shall promptly notify the furnisher of information identified by the consumer under subsection (a) —

(1) that the information may be a result of identity theft;
(2) that an identity theft report has been filed;
(3) that a block has been requested under this section; and
(4) of the effective dates of the block. § 1681c-2.

SSN Truncation. If a consumer requests it, credit reporting agencies must not disclose the first five digits of the consumer's SSN. § 1681g(a)(1)(A).

Free Credit Reports. The FACTA requires credit reporting agencies to provide a free credit report once a year at the request of a consumer. § 1681j.

Disclosure of Credit Scores. The FACTA requires credit reporting agencies to disclose to a consumer her credit score. Many credit reporting agencies previously would not divulge a person's credit score. § 1681g.

Statute of Limitations. FCRA's statute of limitation extends to two years after the date when the plaintiff discovers the violation or five years after the date of the violation, whichever occurs earlier.

Preemption. The FACTA preempts state laws that address many business practices. State laws that deal with these topics — even if they provide more protection to consumers — are preempted. However, the FACTA does provide that it does not "annul, affect, or exempt any person subject to the provisions of this title from complying with the laws of any State with respect to the collection, distribution, or use of any information on consumers or for the prevention or mitigation of identity theft, except to the extent that those laws are inconsistent with any provision of this title, and then only to the extent of the inconsistency." 15 U.S.C. § 1681t. Nevertheless, the FACTA has numerous exceptions to this provision. *See* Pub. L. No. 108-159 (2003), §§ 605, 615.

SMITH V. BOB SMITH CHEVROLET, INC.

275 F. Supp. 2d 808 (W.D. Ky. 2003)

HEYBURN, J. Christopher Smith ("Plaintiff") alleges that Defendant Bob Smith Chevrolet, Inc. violated the Fair Credit Reporting Act, 15 U.S.C. § 1681 *et seq.,* and invaded his privacy in violation of Kentucky common law. . . . [B]oth parties have moved for summary judgment on the issue of whether Smith Chevrolet lacked a permissible purpose when it accessed Plaintiff's credit report; Smith Chevrolet moved to dismiss the Kentucky invasion of privacy claim. . . .

The underlying facts concern the disputed sale of a 2001 GMC Suburban. Having decided that he wanted to purchase a car, on December 13, 2000, Plaintiff completed a GMAC credit application to determine his eligibility for financing. On December 23, 2000, Plaintiff went to Smith Chevrolet with the intention of purchasing the Suburban to use on a family Christmas vacation.

After arriving at the dealership, Plaintiff met with a company employee to discuss the terms of the sale. Two factors complicated the sale. First, Plaintiff wanted to trade in his 1997 Mercury Villager. Second, as an employee of General Electric — a General Motors ("GM") supplier — he was entitled to a standard discount upon proof of employment. Although Plaintiff did have the 1997 Mercury Villager to trade-in on December 23, 2000, he did not have the proper documentation needed to secure the discount. Notwithstanding this fact, a Smith Chevrolet representative agreed to sell Plaintiff the Suburban at the GM discounted price provided he proved his entitlement to the full discount at a later date. After calculating the Villager's trade-in value and the GM discount, the two sides agreed on a price and set forth the terms of the sale in a handwritten purchase order. . . .

On January 10, 2001, Plaintiff faxed and mailed proof of his eligibility for the GM discount. Shortly thereafter, Plaintiff's bank issued Smith Chevrolet a check in the amount of the balance due.

About a week or ten days later, another dispute arose which gives rise to the current litigation. At that point Smith Chevrolet claims it realized the employee who generated the typewritten Purchase Agreement inadvertently doubled the amount of Plaintiff's discount. Smith Chevrolet contacted Plaintiff, explained the calculation error and told Plaintiff that he owed the dealership more money. Furthermore, Smith Chevrolet told Plaintiff that, until he paid the difference, it refused to transfer the Suburban's title and pay off the outstanding loan attached on the Villager trade-in. These were both actions Smith Chevrolet had promised Plaintiff it would take when Plaintiff left the lot on December 23, 2000.

Following from this dispute, on February 21, 2000, Smith Chevrolet accessed Plaintiff's consumer report. The decision to access Plaintiff's report was made by Drew Smith, Smith Chevrolet's chief executive officer and part-owner. Smith Chevrolet says it accessed Plaintiff's report to determine whether Plaintiff was (1) continuing to make payments on the Villager's loan and (2) maintaining insurance on the Villager. Plaintiff disputes Smith Chevrolet's motivations in this regard and claims that it simply wanted to invade Plaintiff's privacy.

When the parties could not agree on the amount due, Plaintiff sued Smith Chevrolet in Jefferson Circuit Court for breach of the sale contract. He demanded specific performance so that he could receive the Suburban's title and transfer the Villager loan obligations to Smith Chevrolet. About a year later, a state court jury found in Plaintiff's favor. One day earlier, on May 13, 2002, Plaintiff filed this suit in federal court. . . .

The heart of [Plaintiff's] case is the contention that Smith Chevrolet violated the FCRA when it accessed Plaintiff's credit report on February 21, 2001. Specifically, Plaintiff contends Smith Chevrolet is liable for negligently and willfully violating the responsibilities imposed by the FCRA. *See* 15 U.S.C. § 1681o (creating a private cause of action for negligent violations of the FCRA); 15 U.S.C. § 1681n (creating a private cause of action for willful violations). Both sides have filed motions for summary judgment addressing whether Smith Chevrolet had a "permissible purpose" for accessing Plaintiff's credit report. The facts central to this claim are not in dispute. Smith Chevrolet may access Plaintiff's credit report only if, as a matter of law, its actions are consistent with one of the permissible purposes set forth in 15 U.S.C. § 1681b(a)(3).

The FCRA identifies a limited set of "permissible purposes" for obtaining and using a consumer report. *See* 15 U.S.C. § 1681b(a)(3); *see also* 15 U.S.C. § 1681b(f). Those permissible purposes provide that a person may only access a consumer report if he:

> (A) intends to use the information in connection with a credit transaction involving the consumer on whom the information is to be furnished and involving the extension of credit to, or review or collection of an account of, the consumer; or
> (B) intends to use the information for employment purposes; or
> (C) intends to use the information in connection with the underwriting of insurance involving the consumer; or
> (D) intends to use the information in connection with a determination of the consumer's eligibility for a license or other benefit granted by a governmental instrumentality required by law to consider an applicant's financial responsibility or status; or
> (E) intends to use the information, as a potential investor or servicer, or current insurer, in connection with a valuation of, or an assessment of the credit or prepayment risks associated with, an existing credit obligation; or
> (F) otherwise has a legitimate business need for the information—
> > (i) in connection with a business transaction that is initiated by the consumer; or
> > (ii) to review an account to determine whether the consumer continues to meet the terms of the account.

15 U.S.C. § 1681b(a)(3).

In its summary judgment motion, Smith Chevrolet contends it had three bases for accessing Plaintiff's credit report. The Court now addresses each of these arguments.

First and most persuasively, Smith Chevrolet contends its actions complied with § 1681b(a)(3)(f)(i). That section provides that one may obtain a consumer report if it "has a legitimate business need for the information . . . in connection with a business transaction that is initiated by the consumer. . ." Smith Chevrolet argues that because the transaction was in dispute, it needed to ascertain the value of its collateral. If it appeared that Plaintiff was not current on his payments for the Mercury Villager, then his indebtedness would have increased over and above the amount owed Smith Chevrolet.

As a starting point, the Court begins with the FCRA's text. The applicability of this permissible purpose boils down to whether Smith Chevrolet's use of the credit report was "in connection with a transaction initiated by the consumer," as the statute uses those terms. That restriction to the actual statutory usage is important here because, in the abstract, it is true Smith Chevrolet accessed Plaintiff's credit report in connection with a transaction Plaintiff at one point initiated. The Court concludes, however, that the statute uses the terms "in connection with a transaction initiated by the consumer" more restrictively.

Turning to the text at issue, when Congress defined the term "consumer report," it stated:

> The term "consumer report" means any written, oral, or other communication of any information by a consumer reporting agency bearing on a consumer's credit worthiness, credit standing, credit capacity, character, general reputation, personal characteristics, or mode of living which is used or expected to be used or collected in whole or in part for the purpose of serving as a factor in establishing the consumer's eligibility for—
>> (A) credit or insurance to be used primarily for personal, family, or household purposes;
>> (B) employment purposes; or
>> (C) any other purpose authorized under section 604 [15 U.S.C. § 1681b].

15 U.S.C. § 1681a(d).

This definition suggests that Congress primarily envisioned consumer reports being disseminated for the purposes of assessing "eligibility." Then, in § 1681b(a)(3), Congress listed additional specific permissible purposes pertaining to the extension of credit, collection of an account, employment purposes, the underwriting of insurance for a consumer, determining a consumer's eligibility for a governmental benefit, and the valuation of a consumer's credit risk. The rule of *ejusdem generis* provides that when general words follow an enumeration of specific terms, the general words are construed to embrace only objects similar in nature to those objects enumerated by the preceding specific words. The definition of "consumer report" therefore includes those reports needed to assess a consumer's eligibility for a benefit, as well as other predictable needs — such as collecting money owed under an agreement and assessing a particular consumer's credit or insurance risk — that arise in the midst of a typical business transaction. In fact, in every one of these situations, the consumer report is obtained either to provide a benefit to a consumer or to collect a pre-existing debt.

Tellingly, the two permissible purposes stated in § 1681b(a)(3)(F) can also be read to effectuate these same ends. That is, § 1681b(a)(3)(F)(i) suggests the retention of a credit report for the purpose of furthering a business transaction initiated by a consumer and § 1681b(a)(3)(F)(ii) permits the use of a credit report to determine whether a consumer continues to be eligible for a benefit. It is a basic principle of statutory construction that a statute should be read and construed as a whole. Like the definition of "consumer report" and consistent with the other five specific permissible purposes, these two permissible purposes also suggest that Congress intended to allow access to a consumer report either when that access would benefit a consumer or would facilitate the collection of pre-existing debt.

To be precise, Smith Chevrolet's stated reason for accessing the credit report was not in connection with a standard business transaction that Plaintiff initiated. Instead, and quite significantly in this Court's view, Smith Chevrolet accessed the credit report to determine how much additional money it could collect, apart from what the two parties agreed upon in a standard business transaction. Almost certainly, it did not access Plaintiff's credit report for a reason beneficial to the consumer. Nor did it access the credit report to collect on a pre-existing debt. Rather, it accessed the report for its own business purposes and as part of a new event: the recovery of the duplicative discount. Although this is a fine distinction, it may be an important one. Smith Chevrolet's interpretation of the phrase "in connection with" is limitless. Under its reading, so long as any company had a reason to question any part of a transaction, it could access a consumer's credit report "in connection with a business transaction" that at some point was "initiated by the consumer." That is, five weeks, five months, or five years down the line, Smith Chevrolet could access Plaintiff's credit report if some dispute ever arose about the contracted price. In the Court's view, such an interpretation would give commercial entities an unlimited blank check to access and *reaccess* a consumer credit report long after the typical issues of eligibility, price, and financing were determined. Neither the specific language nor the overall scope of the FCRA can be said to support such an interpretation. . . .

Moreover, nearly every federal court addressing this issue has similarly held that the "legitimate business need" permissible purpose should be narrowly construed in the context of the other five enumerated purposes. . . .

The Court concludes, therefore, that when Smith Chevrolet accessed Plaintiff's credit report it was not, as a practical matter, part of the transaction which Plaintiff initiated. That transaction, in so far as Plaintiff's eligibility and debt was concerned, ended when the parties created a contract for the car's price and Plaintiff paid that price in full. Under any conceivable interpretation of the facts in this case, Smith Chevrolet cannot be said to have a "legitimate business need" for Plaintiff's credit report "in connection with a transaction initiated by the consumer." § 604(a)(3)(F)(i).

Smith Chevrolet also argues that its actions were protected both by §§ 1681b(3)(A) and 1681b(a)(1)(F)(ii) which provide that:

> Any consumer reporting agency may furnish a consumer report under the following circumstances and no other: . . .
>
> (A) to a person which it has reason to believe intends to use the information in connection with a credit transaction involving the consumer on whom the information is to be furnished and involving the extension of credit to, or review or collection of an account of the consumer; or . . .
>
> (F) otherwise has a legitimate business need for the information . . . (ii) to review an account to determine whether the consumer continues to meet the terms of the account.

Smith Chevrolet claims that it had a permissible purpose under both of these provisions because, due to its own error, Plaintiff received twice the discount he was entitled to and so a debt remained. Therefore, Smith Chevrolet says that it was reviewing whether Plaintiff owed any additional debt. And, because reviewing the size of the debt Plaintiff owed is synonymous with "collection of an account" and with determining "whether [Chris Smith] continue[d] to meet the terms of the account," Smith Chevrolet contends it therefore clearly had a permissible purpose.

The problem with this argument is that there was no outstanding debt and, consequently, there was no "account" to collect on. To be sure, Smith Chevrolet thought there *should be* an outstanding debt. Thinking there *should be* a debt, Smith Chevrolet contacted Plaintiff and ordered him to pay. At that point, Plaintiff refused to pay. Only then did Smith Chevrolet access Plaintiff's credit report.

Whether a debt or existing account exists simply cannot be a function of whether Smith Chevrolet alleges the existence of a debt. To do so would allow Smith Chevrolet infinite opportunities to access Plaintiff's credit report, so long as he could come up with a reason for thinking the account should continue in existence. As this Court has explained elsewhere, the FCRA intended to strike a balance between protecting the needs of commerce and the consumer's privacy interest. The Court finds that Smith Chevrolet must have a reasonable belief that the debt existed. Here, Smith Chevrolet's decision to investigate Plaintiff's credit report was not based on a reasonable belief that debt was owed; it was based on a belief that the original transaction was mistaken. Plaintiff had no reason to suspect that any new debt would arise after the initial transaction was completed. For all practical purposes that transaction was closed when the vehicle was delivered and Plaintiff made his payment. To find these permissible purposes applicable in this instance would extend the FCRA's language well beyond its intended purpose. . . .

Both sides have also moved for summary judgment on Plaintiff's claim of willful non-compliance. Section 1681n provides for civil liability in cases where the defendant willfully fails to comply with FCRA. In such a case, punitive damages may be awarded. 15 U.S.C. § 1681n(a)(2). This Court has recently explained the standard for liability under § 1681n, stating that, "[t]o show willful noncompliance with the FCRA, [the Plaintiff] must show that [defendant] knowingly and intentionally committed an act in conscious disregard for the rights of others, but need not show malice or evil motive."

Questions involving a party's state of mind are generally appropriately resolved by a jury rather than on summary judgment. From what the Court can ascertain at this point, the following facts are undisputed. Carol Hodges, a former Finance and Insurance Manager for Smith Chevrolet, has testified that the company did not have "written polices" regarding the acquisition of credit reports. She said that salespeople could freely access consumer credit reports. Hodges also said that the company had some unwritten rules for accessing customer credit reports, but these rules were not strictly followed. In fact, Smith Chevrolet's practices were "haphazard" and "very sloppy." Hodges had no part in the February 21, 2001, events and has no idea if Smith Chevrolet acted responsibly the day it accessed Plaintiff's credit report.

Based on these disputed facts, the Court cannot enter summary judgment on the issue of Smith Chevrolet's state of mind and will therefore deny the parties cross motions for summary judgment as they pertain to § 1681n.

Last, Smith Chevrolet has moved for summary judgment on Plaintiff's invasion of privacy claim. The Supreme Court of Kentucky adopted the principles for invasion of privacy as enunciated in the Restatement (Second) of Torts (1976) in *McCall v. Courier-Journal and Louisville Times Co.,* 623 S.W.2d 882, 887 (Ky. 1981). . . .

NOTES & QUESTIONS

1. ***Legitimate Business Need.*** In *Smith Chevrolet,* a critical element in the court's decision is its finding that the auto dealership must have a "reasonable belief" that the debt existed to access the credit report. But the decision to investigate the credit report was based, in fact, on a belief that the Plaintiff should owe the car dealer more than he did (due to the mistaken double discount). How does the court interpret the FCRA's statutory provision that allows businesses access to consumer credit reports when there is "a legitimate business need for the information"?

2. ***Permissible Uses of Consumer Reports.*** The FCRA contains a provision for civil liability for "obtaining a consumer report under false pretenses or knowingly without a permissible purpose." 15 U.S.C. § 1681n(a)(1)(B). But what, exactly, is a "consumer report"? A consumer report is defined based on the purposes for which it is used. These purposes include credit, insurance, and employment background checks, among others. 15 U.S.C. § 1681b.

   In *Phillips v. Grendahl,* 312 F.3d 357 (8th Cir. 2002), Mary Grendahl became suspicious of her daughter Sarah's fiancée, Lavon Phillips. She believed he was lying about being an attorney as well as his ex-wives and girlfriends. Grendahl contacted Kevin Fitzgerald, a friend who worked for a detective agency. By searching computer databases, Fitzgerald obtained Phillips's Social Security number and previous addresses. He then submitted the data to Econ Control to obtain a report called a "Finder's Report." A Finder's Report includes a person's "address, aliases, birthdate, employer addresses, and the identity of firms with which the consumer had credit accounts and firms that had made inquiries about the consumer."

   When Phillips discovered the investigation, he sued Grendahl, the detective agency Fitzgerald worked for, and Econ Control. The court concluded that the Finder's Report was a "consumer report" under FCRA. It also concluded that the defendants did not have a valid purpose under FCRA for obtaining the report:

   > The only purpose for obtaining the report was to obtain information on Mary Grendahl's prospective son-in-law. Investigating a person because he wants to marry one's daughter is not a statutory consumer purpose under section 1681b(a). Even if getting married can be characterized as a consumer transaction under section 1681b(a)(3), it was not Mary Grendahl, but her

daughter, whom Phillips was engaged to marry. He had no business transaction pending with Mary Grendahl. There was no permissible purpose for obtaining or using a consumer report.

3. ***Liability Under FCRA.*** FCRA creates liability for willfully or negligently failing to comply with its requirements. People can recover actual damages or statutory damages between $100 and $1,000 for willful violations, plus punitive damages and attorneys' fees and costs. § 1681n. People can recover actual damages and attorneys' fees and costs for negligent violations. § 1681n. Willful means that one intentionally commits an act "in conscious disregard for the rights of others." In *Safeco Insurance Co. v. Burr,* 127 S. Ct. 2201 (2007), the Supreme Court held that acting in "reckless disregard" of a consumer's rights under FCRA was sufficient to establish willfulness.

Jeff Sovern notes that the FCRA's fault standard for liability — negligence — is inadequate to allow many victims to pursue relief because victims "are not normally aware of the procedures a credit bureau uses when issuing an erroneous credit report or what constitutes reasonable procedures." Because each individual consumer's losses will not be very high, consumers may not bring valid cases because of high litigation costs. Therefore, Sovern argues, credit reports should "be made strictly liable for attributing the transactions of identity thieves to innocent customers." Sovern also recommends liquidated damages for identity theft cases in order to reduce litigation costs.[5]

4. ***Furnishing Information to a Consumer Reporting Agency.*** In *Lema v. Citibank,* 935 F. Supp. 695 (D. Md. 1996), Citibank issued the plaintiff a credit card. When the plaintiff's account became delinquent, Citibank reported the information to consumer reporting agencies. The plaintiff sued Citibank under FCRA, claiming that the information it supplied to the consumer reporting agencies was inaccurate. The court dismissed the claim:

> The FCRA imposes civil liability only on consumer reporting agencies and users of consumer information. Thus, plaintiff must show that defendants are either of those entities in order to withstand defendants' summary judgment motion. . . .
> Plaintiff alleges only that defendants reported to third parties information regarding transactions between defendants and plaintiff. Defendants did not therefore furnish a consumer report regarding plaintiff, nor did they act as a consumer reporting agency with respect to him.

The court noted that the FCRA, § 1681h, provides qualified immunity for those that furnish allegedly false information to consumer reporting agencies. Plaintiffs can "bring a state law claim of defamation, invasion of privacy or negligence, provided such plaintiff alleges that defendants acted with malice or wilful intent to injure plaintiff."

---

[5] Jeff Sovern, *The Jewel of Their Souls: Preventing Identity Theft Through Loss Allocation Rules,* 64 U. Pitt. L. Rev. 343, 393, 406-07 (2003).

SARVER V. EXPERIAN INFORMATION SOLUTIONS

390 F.3d 969 (7th Cir. 2004)

EVANS, J. Lloyd Sarver appeals from an order granting summary judgment to Experian Information Solutions, Inc., a credit reporting company, on his claim under the Fair Credit Reporting Act (FCRA), 15 U.S.C. §§ 1681 *et seq.*

Experian reported inaccurate information on Sarver's credit report, which on August 2, 2002, caused the Monogram Bank of Georgia to deny him credit. Monogram cited the Experian credit report and particularly a reference to a bankruptcy which appeared on the report. Both before and after Monogram denied him credit, Sarver asked for a copy of his credit report. He received copies both times and both reports showed that accounts with Cross Country Bank were listed as having been "involved in bankruptcy." No other accounts had that notation, although other accounts had significant problems. A Bank One installment account had a balance past due 180 days, and another company, Providian, had written off $3,099 on a revolving account.

On August 29, 2002, Sarver wrote Experian informing it that the bankruptcy notation was inaccurate and asking that it be removed from his report. Sarver provided his full name and address but no other identifying information. On September 11, Experian sent Sarver a letter requesting further information, including his Social Security number, before it could begin an investigation. Sarver did not provide the information, but instead filed the present lawsuit, which resulted in summary judgment for Experian. It was later confirmed that the notation on the Cross Country Bank account was inaccurate and, as it turned out, another Lloyd Sarver was the culprit on that account.

In this appeal from the judgment dismissing his case, Sarver claims summary judgment was improper because issues of fact exist as to whether Experian violated FCRA, §§ 1681i and 1681e(b). . . .

Section 1681i requires a credit reporting agency to reinvestigate items on a credit report when a consumer disputes the validity of those items. An agency can terminate a reinvestigation if it determines the complaint is frivolous, "including by reason of a failure by a consumer to provide sufficient information to investigate the disputed information." § 1681i(a)(3). We do not need to decide whether Sarver's failure to provide the information Experian requested rendered his complaint frivolous; his claim under § 1681i(a) fails for another reason, a lack of evidence of damages. In order to prevail on his claims, Sarver must show that he suffered damages as a result of the inaccurate information. As we have said in *Crabill v. Trans Union, L.L.C.,* 259 F.3d 662, 664 (7th Cir. 2001):

> Without a causal relation between the violation of the statute and the loss of credit, or some other harm, a plaintiff cannot obtain an award of "actual damages."

On this point, the district court concluded that there were no damages. Our review of the record leads us to agree.

Sarver, however, disagrees and claims that he suffered damages when he was denied credit from Monogram Bank of Georgia on August 2, 2002. This letter cannot be a basis for his damage claim, however, because as of August 2,

Experian had no notice of any inaccuracies in the report. Even though Sarver asked for a copy of his report on July 18, he did not notify Experian of a problem until a month and a half later. Experian must be notified of an error before it is required to reinvestigate. As we have made clear, the FCRA is not a strict liability statute. *Henson v. CSC Credit Servs.,* 29 F.3d 280 (7th Cir. 1994).

Sarver also does not show that he suffered pecuniary damages between August 29 (when he notified Experian of the error) and February 20, 2003 (when the Cross Country account was removed from his file). He does not claim that he applied for credit during that time period or that a third party looked at his report. In addition, his claim for emotional distress fails. We have maintained a strict standard for a finding of emotional damage "because they are so easy to manufacture." *Aiello v. Providian Fin. Corp.,* 239 F.3d 876, 880 (7th Cir. 2001). We have required that when "the injured party's own testimony is the only proof of emotional damages, he must explain the circumstances of his injury in reasonable detail; he cannot rely on mere conclusory statements." *Denius v. Dunlap,* 330 F.3d 919, 929 (7th Cir. 2003). Finally, to obtain statutory damages under FCRA § 1681n(a), Sarver must show that Experian willfully violated the Act. There is similarly no evidence of willfulness. Summary judgment was properly granted on this claim.

We turn to Sarver's claim under § 1681e(b), which requires that a credit reporting agency follow "reasonable procedures to assure maximum possible accuracy" when it prepares a credit report. The reasonableness of a reporting agency's procedures is normally a question for trial unless the reasonableness or unreasonableness of the procedures is beyond question. *Crabill,* 259 F.3d at 663. However, to state a claim under the statute,

> a consumer must sufficiently allege "that a credit reporting agency prepared a report containing 'inaccurate' information." However, the credit reporting agency is not automatically liable even if the consumer proves that it prepared an inaccurate credit report because the FCRA "does not make reporting agencies strictly liable for all inaccuracies." A credit reporting agency is not liable under the FCRA if it followed "reasonable procedures to assure maximum possible accuracy," but nonetheless reported inaccurate information in the consumer's credit report.

Henson, 29 F.3d at 284. The Commentary of the Federal Trade Commission to the FCRA, 16 C.F.R. pt. 600, app., section 607 at 3.A, states that the section does not hold a reporting agency responsible where an item of information, received from a source that it reasonably believes is reputable, turns out to be inaccurate unless the agency receives notice of systemic problems with its procedures.

Experian has provided an account of its procedures. The affidavit of David Browne, Experian's compliance manager, explains that the company gathers credit information originated by approximately 40,000 sources. The information is stored in a complex system of national databases, containing approximately 200 million names and addresses and some 2.6 billion trade lines, which include information about consumer accounts, judgments, etc. The company processes over 50 million updates to trade information each day. Lenders report millions of accounts to Experian daily; they provide identifying information, including address, social security number, and date of birth. The identifying information is used to link the credit items to the appropriate consumer. Mr. Browne also notes that Experian's computer system does not store complete credit reports, but rather stores the individual items of credit information linked to identifying information. The credit report is generated at the time an inquiry for it is received.

One can easily see how, even with safeguards in place, mistakes can happen. But given the complexity of the system and the volume of information involved, a mistake does not render the procedures unreasonable. In his attempt to show that Experian's procedures are unreasonable, Sarver argues that someone should have noticed that only the Cross Country accounts were shown to have been involved in bankruptcy. That anomaly should have alerted Experian, Sarver says, to the fact that the report was inaccurate. What Sarver is asking, then, is that each computer-generated report be examined for anomalous information and, if it is found, an investigation be launched. In the absence of notice of prevalent unreliable information from a reporting lender, which would put Experian on notice that problems exist, we cannot find that such a requirement to investigate would be reasonable given the enormous volume of information Experian processes daily.

We found in *Henson* that a consumer reporting agency was not liable, as a matter of law, for reporting information from a judgment docket unless there was prior notice from the consumer that the information might be inaccurate. We said that a

> contrary rule of law would require credit reporting agencies to go beyond the face of numerous court records to determine whether they correctly report the outcome of the underlying action. Such a rule would also require credit reporting agencies to engage in background research which would substantially increase the cost of their services. In turn, they would be forced to pass on the increased costs to their customers and ultimately to the individual consumer.

Henson, 29 F.3d at 285. The same could be said for records from financial institutions. As we said, in his affidavit Mr. Browne proclaims, and there is nothing in the record to make us doubt his statement, that lenders report many millions of accounts to Experian daily. Sarver's report, dated August 26, 2002, contains entries from six different lenders. The increased cost to Experian to examine each of these entries individually would be enormous. We find that as a matter of law there is nothing in this record to show that Experian's procedures are unreasonable.

NOTES & QUESTIONS

1. *A Critical Perspective on* **Sarver.** Consider Elizabeth De Armond:

> In justifying the agency's failure to resolve the anomalies within the records attributed to the plaintiff, the court emphasized the 200 million names and addresses, the 2.6 billion trade lines, and the complexity of the system. This reasoning overlooks that the very complexity of the system reveals the ability of the agency to control the high volume of individuals and records, and that ability should alert the agency to the high risk of misattributing information.

The court ruled that the agency's failure to investigate the inconsistency was not unreasonable because the agency had no notice that the specific lender who had provided information about the impaired accounts was unreliable. However, the question, in order to protect individuals from reckless attribution, should not be whether any single provider is unreliable. The question should have been whether reporting it as the plaintiff's without checking it, given the obvious inconsistency, was reckless. Where the agency was aware of the risk of misattribution from fuzzy matching, and that matching produced a record that was unlike the others, a jury should decide whether the failure to take any steps to verify the anomalous data breached the FCRA's accuracy standard.

The *Sarver* court also reasoned that to require an agency to further investigate the accuracy of a consumer's records when an anomaly appeared would impose "enormous" increased costs. However, the court did not refer to any estimate of the costs or explain why an already complex system capable of making many comparisons among different records could not inexpensively adjust to cross-checking data when reliability was at issue. Furthermore, when an anomaly appears that would work to the consumer's detriment, an agency could simply decline to attribute the negative data should it not want to take the extra effort of verifying it. The decision allows the agency all of the benefits of its database technology with none of the responsibilities.[6]

This criticism raises a baseline issue: who should bear the costs of relative degrees of inaccuracy and accuracy in the credit system? If credit agency's need investigate more kinds of inconsistencies in credit reports, will consumers as a group bear the additional costs?

2. *Is FCRA too Deferential to Industry Interests?* Consider De Armond on the flaws of FCRA:

> [FCRA] inadequately protects individuals from the consequential and emotional damages caused by misattributed acts for several reasons. . . .
>
> The Act's most significant flaw is that it imposes meaningful accuracy requirements only after a false and negative item has been reported, has already been put into the data sea. However, given that digitized data is far more available, accessible, duplicable, and transmittable than old paper records, once a false record has been put into the data sea, it is very hard to ever completely cull it out. . . .
>
> The Act is designed to impose meaningful accuracy standards only after inaccurate information has already been provided by a data provider and reported by a data aggregator. The Act permits the original data provider, called a furnisher under the Act, to furnish nearly any item in a consumer's name without first verifying that it belongs to that consumer. But the Act only prohibits the furnisher from furnishing information that the furnisher either "knows or has reasonable cause to believe" to be inaccurate. A furnisher only has "'reasonable cause to believe that an item of information is inaccurate'" if the furnisher has "specific knowledge, other than solely allegations by the consumer, that would cause a reasonable person to have substantial doubts about the accuracy of the information." . . .

---

[6] Elizabeth D. De Armond, *Frothy Chaos: Modern Data Warehousing and Old-Fashioned Defamation*, 41 Val. U. L. Rev. 1061, 1099-1102, 1108 (2007).

Thus, the agency acquires information that likely has not been subjected to any scrutiny, let alone verified. The agency acquires the information, either electronically or via magnetic tape from the provider, and stores it electronically, where it sits until needed for a report. Just as the Act imposes a relatively weak accuracy requirement on data providers at the point of initial provision, the Act places only loose limits on aggregators that then report the information. When a subscriber requests a report on a particular consumer, the aggregator, the consumer reporting agency, must only follow "reasonable procedures to assure maximum possible accuracy" of the information that it returns to the subscriber. The provision does not in fact require agencies to ensure the maximum possible accuracy of every item of information, or to do much if anything to match, verify, or cross-check the information. . . .

It is only after an individual has learned that an agency has falsely charged him or her with negative data that the individual can require an aggregator to examine the data. . . .

As *Sarver* also points out, the Experian computer system does not store computer credit reports, but only generates them when an inquiry is received. Individual items of credit information are stored linked to identifying information, which allows their retrieval and compilation into a credit report. Should individual items of information be reviewed for accuracy at the initial time that the credit agency collects them?

3. ***What Constitutes Negligence in Investigating Errors in Consumer Reports?***
In *Dennis v. BEH-1, LLC*, 504 F.3d 892 (9th Cir. 2007), Jason Dennis was sued by his landlord, but the parties agreed to drop the lawsuit after reaching a settlement. The parties filed a "Request for Dismissal" with the court clerk, and the court register properly registered the dismissal. Later on, Experian Information Solutions, Inc. stated on Dennis's credit report that a civil claim judgment had been entered against him for $1,959. Dennis contacted Experian to complain about the error. Experian had Hogan Information Services, a third party contractor, verify Dennis's claims. Hogan replied that Experian's information was correct and sent along a copy of the stipulation of settlement between Dennis and his landlord. Experian told Dennis that it would not correct his report. Dennis sued under FCRA, contending that Experian failed to maintain "reasonable procedures" under § 1681e(b) to ensure the accuracy of credit reports and that it failed to adequately reinvestigate the disputed information under § 1681i. The district court dismissed Dennis's case on summary judgment. The court of appeals, however, concluded:

> The district court erred insofar as it held that Dennis couldn't make the prima facie showing of inaccurate reporting required by sections 1681e and 1681i. Experian's credit report on Dennis *is* inaccurate. Because the case against Dennis was dismissed, there could have been no "Civil claim judgment" against him: "A dismissal without prejudice . . . has the effect of a final judgment *in favor* of the defendant." Dennis has made the prima facie showing of inaccuracy required by sections 1681e and 1681i.
>
> The district court also seems to have awarded summary judgment to Experian because Dennis didn't offer evidence of "actual damages" as required by section 1681o(a)(1). Here, too, the district court erred. Dennis testified that he hoped to start a business and that he diligently paid his bills on

time for years so that he would have a clean credit history when he sought financing for the venture. The only blemish on his credit report in April 2003 was the erroneously reported judgment. According to Dennis, that was enough to cause several lenders to decline his applications for credit, dashing his hopes of starting a new business. Dennis also claims that Experian's error caused his next landlord to demand that Dennis pay a greater security deposit. In addition to those tangible harms, Dennis claims that Experian's inaccurate report caused him emotional distress, which we've held to be "actual damages."

The court of appeals reasoned that Hogan failed to understand the meaning of the Request for Dismissal document and that Experian could readily have detected this mistake:

> Experian could have caught Hogan's error if it had consulted the Civil Register in Dennis's case, which can be viewed free of charge on the Los Angeles Superior Court's excellent website. As described above, the Register clearly indicates that the case against Dennis was dismissed. Experian apparently never looked at the Register.
>
> Experian also could have detected Hogan's mistake by examining the document Hogan retrieved from Dennis's court file. Hogan mistakenly believed that this document proved that judgment had been entered against Dennis; in fact, the document confirms Dennis's account of what happened. The document is a written stipulation between Dennis and his landlord that no judgment would be entered against Dennis so long as Dennis complied with the payment schedule. The parties couldn't have been clearer on this point: "If paid, case dismissed. If not paid, judgment to enter upon [landlord's] declaration of non-payment. . . ."

The court of appeals further concluded that it had no need to remand the case for a jury trial regarding Experian's negligence:

> Even accepting as true everything Experian has claimed, no rational jury could find that the company wasn't negligent. The stipulation Hogan retrieved from Dennis's court file may be unusual, but it's also unambiguous, and Experian was negligent in mis-interpreting it as an entry of judgment. Experian is also responsible for the negligence of Hogan, the investigation service it hired to review Dennis's court file. . . .
>
> When conducting a reinvestigation pursuant to 15 U.S.C. § 1681i, a credit reporting agency must exercise reasonable diligence in examining the court file to determine whether an adverse judgment has, in fact, been entered against the consumer. A reinvestigation that overlooks documents in the court file expressly stating that *no* adverse judgment was entered falls far short of this standard. On our own motion, therefore, we grant summary judgment to Dennis on his claim that Experian negligently failed to conduct a reasonable reinvestigation in violation of section 1681i. Whether Experian's failure was also willful, in violation of section 1681n, is a question for the jury on remand.
>
> This case illustrates how important it is for Experian, a company that traffics in the reputations of ordinary people, to train its employees to understand the legal significance of the documents they rely on. Because Experian negligently failed to conduct a reasonable reinvestigation, we grant summary judgment to Dennis on this claim. We remand only so that the district court may calculate damages and award attorney's fees. As to all other

claims under the Fair Credit Reporting Act, we reverse summary judgment for Experian and remand for trial. Dennis is also entitled to attorney's fees for an entirely successful appeal. 15 U.S.C. § 1681*o*(a)(2). . . .

4. ***Defamation, Privacy, and FCRA's Qualified Immunity.*** Can the credit reporting agencies be sued under state tort law for defamation or for invasion of privacy? Regarding defamation, recall that the Supreme Court held in *Dun & Bradstreet, Inc. v. Greenmoss Builders, Inc.,* 472 U.S. 749 (1985), that a credit reporting agency reporting on an individual is engaging in "speech on matters of purely private concern" and, consequently, receives less First Amendment protection than other forms of speech. Therefore, for such cases of defamation, the First Amendment limits established by *New York Times v. Sullivan,* 376 U.S. 254 (1964), and *Gertz v. Robert Welch, Inc.,* 418 U.S. 323 (1974), do not apply. All forms of damages (compensatory, presumed, and punitive) are available without showing "actual malice."

However, FCRA provides qualified immunity to credit reporting agencies and to the furnishers of information to credit reporting agencies:

> Except as provided in sections 1681n and 1681o of this title, no consumer may bring any action or proceeding in the nature of defamation, invasion of privacy, or negligence with respect to the reporting of information against any consumer reporting agency, or any user of information, or any person who furnishes information to a consumer reporting agency, based on information disclosed pursuant to section 1681g, 1681h, or 1681m of this title, or based on information disclosed by a user of a consumer report to or for a consumer against whom the user has taken adverse action, based in whole or in part on the report except as to false information furnished with malice or wilful intent to injure such consumer. § 1681h(e).

Therefore, although the Constitution doesn't require actual malice to establish defamation for the false reporting of credit information, the FCRA does. Actual malice exists if one states false information with knowledge of its falsity or in reckless disregard for the truth.

Establishing malice can be difficult. Consider *Morris v. Equifax Information Services, L.L.C.,* 457 F.3d 460 (5th Cir. 2006):

> While Morris has presented evidence that Equifax knew that Morris claimed that there were false statements in the information that Equifax was publishing about Morris, this evidence does not show that Equifax knew these statements were false. Morris also argues that Equifax had a reckless disregard for whether the statements were false because "Equifax continued to publish the same false information about Morris without lifting a finger to determine whether the information was false or not." To show "reckless disregard," however, Morris must present "sufficient evidence to permit the conclusion that the defendant *in fact entertained serious doubts* as to the truth of his publication." *St. Amant v. Thompson,* 390 U.S. 727 (1968) (emphasis added). In this case, there is no such evidence.

How does a person establish that a credit reporting agency "entertained serious doubts" about the truth of its report? The difficulty is that the reporting is an automated process involving hundreds of millions of people. If a person calls to point out an error, should that be sufficient to show that the credit reporting agency had knowledge? Or does it make it too easy for any person to establish reckless disregard, as it would be established anytime a person merely made an allegation of falsity?

Elizabeth De Armond recommends that notwithstanding the requirement of proving actual malice, defamation and false light can serve as a good way to protect victims of credit reporting mistakes. She argues that credit reporting agencies offer special services to protect people from identity theft if people pay for it, but the existence of these services demonstrates that credit reporting agencies "have the analytical capacity to discern unusual activity in a particular consumer's name, at least if the consumer is willing to pay for it." De Armond contends that "data providers and data aggregators should be well aware that data may not belong to whom it appears. Failing to acknowledge that risk, by verifying identities of doers of the deeds they report, surpasses the standard of recklessness." Specifically, with regard to the *Sarver* case, she argues: "In *Sarver,* where the aggregator, a consumer reporting agency, attributed accounts that indicated the borrower's bankruptcy to the wrong individual, the agency acted recklessly . . . when it repeated the misattribution, even after the plaintiff had notified the agency of its error."[7]

2. THE USE AND DISCLOSURE OF FINANCIAL INFORMATION

(a) The Breach of Confidentiality Tort and Financial Institutions

Under the common law, a doctor can be liable to a patient for breach of confidentiality if she discloses the patient's personal information. A number of jurisdictions extend the tort of breach of confidentiality to disclosures by banks and financial institutions of their customers' financial information. In *Peterson v. Idaho First Nat'l Bank*, 367 P.2d 284 (Idaho 1961), the court held that a bank could be sued for breach of confidentiality for disclosing customer information:

> It is generally stated that the relation between a bank and its general depositor is that of debtor and creditor. . . . But it is also said that in discharging its obligation to a depositor a bank must do so subject to the rules of agency. . . .
>
> All agree that a bank should protect its business records from the prying eyes of the public, moved by curiosity or malice. No one questions its right to protect its fiduciary relationship with its customers, which, in sound banking practice, as a matter of common knowledge, is done everywhere. . . .
>
> To give such information to third persons or to the public at the instance of the customer or depositor is certainly not beyond the scope of banking powers. It is a different matter, however, when such information is sought from the bank without the consent of the depositor or customer of the bank. Indeed, it is an implied term of the contract between the banker and his customer that the banker will not divulge to third persons, without the consent of the customer, express or implied, either the state of the customer's account or any of his

---

[7] De Armond, *supra,* at 1139, 1132, 1130.

transactions with the bank, or any information relating to the customer acquired through the keeping of his account. . . .

It is inconceivable that a bank would at any time consider itself at liberty to disclose the intimate details of its depositors' accounts. Inviolate secrecy is one of the inherent and fundamental precepts of the relationship of the bank and its customers or depositors.

Several other jurisdictions have held likewise. *See, e.g., Barnett Bank of West Florida v. Hooper*, 498 So. 2d 923 (Fla. 1986); *Indiana Nat'l Bank v. Chapman*, 482 N.E.2d 474 (Ind. App. 1985); *Suburban Trust Co. v. Waller*, 408 A.2d 758 (Md. App. 1979); *Richfield Bank & Trust Co. v. Sjogren*, 244 N.W.2d 648 (Minn. 1976); *McGuire v. Shubert,* 722 A.2d 1087 (Pa. Super. 1998).

(b) The Gramm-Leach-Bliley Act

In 1999, Congress passed the Financial Services Modernization Act, more commonly known as the Gramm-Leach-Bliley (GLB) Act, Pub. L. No. 106-102, codified at 15 U.S.C. §§ 6801–6809. The GLB Act was designed to restructure financial services industries, which had long been regulated under the Glass-Steagall Act of 1933. The Glass-Steagall Act, passed in response to the Great Depression, prevented different types of financial institutions (e.g., banks, brokerage houses, insurers) from affiliating with each other. The GLB Act enables the creation of financial conglomerates that provide a host of different forms of financial services.

The law authorizes widespread sharing of personal information by financial institutions such as banks, insurers, and investment companies. The law permits sharing of personal information between companies that are joined together or affiliated with each other as well as sharing of information between unaffiliated companies. To protect privacy, the Act requires a variety of agencies (FTC, Comptroller of Currency, SEC, and a number of others) to establish "appropriate standards for the financial institutions subject to their jurisdiction" to "insure security and confidentiality of customer records and information" and "protect against unauthorized access" to the records. 15 U.S.C. § 6801.

Nonpublic Personal Information. The privacy provisions of the GLB Act only apply to "nonpublic personal information" that consists of "personally identifiable financial information." § 6809(4). Thus, the law only protects *financial* information that is *not public*.

Sharing of Information with Affiliated Companies. The GLB Act permits financial institutions that are joined together to share the "nonpublic personal information" that each affiliate possesses. For example, suppose an affiliate has access to a person's medical information. This information could be shared with an affiliate bank that could then turn down a person for a loan. Affiliates must tell customers that they are sharing such information. § 6802(a). The disclosure can be in the form of a general disclosure in a privacy policy. § 6803(a). There is no way for individuals to block this sharing of information.

Sharing of Information with Nonaffiliated Companies. Financial institutions can share personal information with nonaffiliated companies only if they first provide individuals with the ability to opt out of the disclosure. § 6802(b). However, people cannot opt out if the financial institution provides personal data to nonaffiliated third parties "to perform services for or functions on behalf of the financial institution, including marketing of the financial institution's own products and services, or financial products or services offered pursuant to joint agreements between two or more financial institutions." § 6802(b)(2). The financial institution must disclose the information sharing and must have a contract with the third party requiring the third party to maintain the confidentiality of the information. § 6802(b)(2). Third parties receiving personal data from a financial institution cannot reuse that information. § 6802(c). These provisions do not apply to disclosures to credit reporting agencies.

Limits on Disclosure. Financial institutions cannot disclose (other than to credit reporting agencies) account numbers or credit card numbers for use in direct marketing (telemarketing, e-mail, or mail). § 6802(d).

Privacy Notices. The GLB Act requires that financial institutions inform customers of their privacy policies. In particular, customers must be informed about policies concerning the disclosure of personal information to affiliates and other companies and categories of information that are disclosed and the security of personal data. § 6803(a).

Security. The GLB Act requires the FTC and other agencies to establish security standards for nonpublic personal information. *See* 15 U.S.C. §§ 6801(b), 6805(b)(2). The FTC issued its final regulations on May 23, 2002. According to the regulations, financial institutions "shall develop, implement, and maintain a comprehensive information security program" that is appropriate to the "size and complexity" of the institution, the "nature and scope" of the institution's activities, and the "sensitivity of any customer information at issue." 16 C.F.R. § 314.3(a). An "information security program" is defined as "the administrative, technical, or physical safeguards [an institution uses] to access, collect, distribute, process, store, use, transmit, dispose of, or otherwise handle customer information." § 314.2(b).

Preemption. The GLB Act does not preempt state laws that provide greater protection to privacy. § 6807(b). As will be discussed below, Vermont has made use of this provision and requires opt in, or affirmative consumer consent, before a financial institution can share nonpublic personal financial information pertaining to a consumer to a nonaffiliated third party.

Critics and Supporters. Consider the following critique by Ted Janger and Paul Schwartz:

> The GLB Act has managed to disappoint both industry leaders and privacy advocates alike. Why are so many observers frustrated with the GLB Act? We have already noted the complaint of financial services companies regarding the

expense of privacy notices. These organizations also argue that there have been scant pay-off from the costly mailings — and strong evidence backs up this claim. For example, a survey from the American Banker's Association found that 22% of banking customers said that they received a privacy notice but did not read it, and 41% could not even recall receiving a notice. The survey also found only 0.5% of banking customers had exercised their opt-out rights. . . .

Not only are privacy notices difficult to understand, but they are written in a fashion that makes it hard to exercise the opt-out rights that GLB Act mandates. For example, opt-out provisions are sometimes buried in privacy notices. As the Public Citizen Litigation Group has found, "Explanations of how to opt-out invariably appear at the end of the notices. Thus, before they learn how to opt-out, consumers must trudge through up to ten pages of fine print. . . ." Public Citizen also identified many passages regarding opt-out that "are obviously designed to discourage consumers from exercising their rights under the statute." For example, some financial institutions include an opt-out box only "in a thicket of misleading statements.". . . A final tactic of GLB Act privacy notices is to state that consumers who opt-out may fail to receive "valuable offers." . . .

The GLB Act merely contains an opt-out requirement; as a result, information can be disclosed to non-affiliated entities unless individuals take affirmative action, namely, informing the financial entity that they refuse this sharing of their personal data. By setting its default as an opt-out, the GLB Act fails to create any penalty on the party with superior knowledge, the financial entity, should negotiations fail to occur. In other words, the GLB leaves the burden of bargaining on the less informed party, the individual consumer. These doubts about the efficacy of opt-out are supported, at least indirectly, by the evidence concerning sometimes confusing, sometimes misleading privacy notices. . . . An opt-out default creates incentives for privacy notices that lead to *inaction* by the consumer.[8]

Marcy Peek argues that the GLB Act has actually done more to facilitate information sharing than to protect privacy. Enabling greater information uses so long as customers have a right to opt out has resulted in much more information sharing since "the opt-out right is meaningless in practice; the right to opt out of the trafficking of one's personal information is explained in lengthy, legalistic privacy policies that most people throw away as just more junk mail." More broadly, Peek argues, several laws purporting to protect privacy often "represent a façade of protection for consumers, keeping them complacent in the purported knowledge that someone is protecting their privacy interests." In the end, Peek argues, "corporate power drives information privacy law."[9]

In contrast, Peter Swire argues that the GLB Act "works surprisingly well as privacy legislation":

Recognizing the criticisms to date, and the limits of the available evidence, I would like to make the case for a decidedly more optimistic view of the effect of the GLB notices. Even in their current flawed form and even if not a single consumer exercised the opt-out right, I contend that a principal effect of the

---

[8] Ted Janger & Paul M. Schwartz, *The Gramm-Leach-Bliley Act, Information Privacy, and the Limits of Default Rules*, 86 Minn. L. Rev. 1219, 1230-32, 1241 (2002).

[9] Marcy E. Peek, Information *Privacy and Corporate Power: Towards a Re-Imagination of Information Privacy Law*, 37 Seton Hall L. Rev. 127, 147-49, 137 (2006).

notices has been to require financial institutions to inspect their own practices. In this respect, the detail and complexity of the GLB notices is actually a virtue. In order to draft the notice, many financial institutions undertook an extensive process, often for the first time, to learn just how data is and is not shared between different parts of the organization and with third parties. Based on my extensive discussions with people in the industry, I believe that many institutions discovered practices that they decided, upon deliberation, to change. One public example of this was the decision of Bank of America no longer to share its customers' data with third parties, even subject to opt-out. The detailed and complex notice, in short, created a more detailed roadmap for privacy compliance.[10]

The critics of the GLB Act and Swire appear to be looking at the statute from two different perspectives. The critics are looking at it from a consumer-centric view; Swire sees the positive effect that the statute has on practices within institutions. Is there a way for a statute to have a positive impact in both areas?

(c) State Financial Regulation

The Vermont Opt-in Approach. In contrast to the GLB approach, Vermont permits sharing of personal data by financial institutions with nonaffiliated companies only if companies obtain an individual's consent. This requirement of a positive response before information can be shared is termed an "opt in." State of Vermont, Department, Insurance, Securities & Health Care Administration, Banking Division, Regulation B-2001-01, Privacy of Consumer Financial and Health Information Regulation. This regulation also carefully defines the acceptable form of and process for opt-in notice. For example, when consumers want to revoke their opting in to information sharing, financial institutions cannot force "the consumer to write his or her own letter." Financial institutions also cannot make consumers "use a check-off box that was provided with the initial notice but [that] is not included with subsequent notices."

California's SB1. California's Financial Information Privacy Act, known as "SB1," Cal. Fin. Code §§ 4050–4060, was enacted "to afford persons greater privacy protections that those provided in . . . the federal Gramm-Leach-Bliley Act." § 4051. Specifically, the California legislature found that the Gramm-Leach-Bliley Act "increases the likelihood that the personal financial information of California residents will be widely shared among, between, and within companies" and that "the policies intended to protect financial privacy imposed by the Gramm-Leach-Bliley Act are inadequate to meet the privacy concerns of California residents." § 4051.5.

In contrast to the Gramm-Leach-Bliley Act, which provides people with an opt-out right, SB1, like the Vermont regulation, requires opt in:

> [A] financial institution shall not sell, share, transfer, or otherwise disclose nonpublic personal information to or with any nonaffiliated third parties without

---

[10] Peter P. Swire, *The Surprising Virtues of the New Financial Privacy Law*, 86 Minn. L. Rev. 1263, 1315-16 (2002).

the explicit prior consent of the consumer to whom the nonpublic personal information relates. § 4052.5.

SB1 permits financial institutions to offer incentives or discounts for people to opt in. § 4053.

Financial institutions challenged SB1, arguing that it was preempted by the FCRA. In *American Bankers Association v. Gould*, 412 F.3d 1081 (9th Cir. 2005), the court concluded that "SB1 is preempted [by FCRA] to the extent that it applies to information shared between affiliates concerning consumers' 'credit worthiness, credit standing, credit capacity, character, general reputation, personal characteristics, or mode of living' that is used, expected to be used, or collected for the purpose of establishing eligibility for 'credit or insurance,' employment, or other authorized purpose." The court remanded for the district court to determine which portions of SB1 survived preemption.

On remand, *American Bankers Association v. Lockyer*, 2005 WL 2452798 (E.D. Cal. 2005) (not reported in F. Supp. 2d), the court held that "no portion of SB1's affiliate sharing provision survives" preemption. Among the difficulties for the court was that, as plaintiffs argued before it, "it would be virtually impossible to ascertain in advance whether or not information collected and shared by a financial institution would satisfy a FCRA authorized purpose." The district court explained:

> A financial institution may gather and share information with its affiliates believing in good faith that it is not required to comply with SB1 because the information will be used for an FCRA authorized purpose. If, in fact, the information is not so used, the financial institution would have acted in violation of SB1 exposing it to the penalties thereunder. This creates the untenable situation of forcing California financial institutions to either risk violation of SB1 or comply therewith whether or not the information is for an FCRA authorized purpose.

The North Dakota Opt-in Referendum and Other States. In June 2002, North Dakotans overwhelmingly rejected, by a 73 percent vote, a 2001 state law that had established an opt-out rather than opt-in standard for financial institutions in North Dakota. The Privacy Rights Clearinghouse noted: "The referendum in North Dakota was the first time this issue has been taken directly to voters."[11] New Mexico has also provided an opt-in requirement for financial institutions before sharing of personal consumer data is permitted with nonaffiliated companies.

3. IDENTITY THEFT

Identity theft is one of the most rapidly growing forms of crime. Identity theft occurs when a criminal obtains an individual's personal information and uses it to open new bank accounts, acquire credit cards, and obtain loans in that individual's name. Consider the following example from journalist Bob Sullivan:

---

[11] Privacy Rights Clearinghouse, *North Dakota Votes for "Opt-In" Financial Privacy*, June 21, 2002, at www.privacyrights.org/ar/nd_optin.htm.

Starting in August 1998, Anthony Lemar Taylor spent a year successfully pretending to be the golf superstar [Tiger Woods]. Taylor's $50,000 spending spree included a big-screen television, stereo speakers, a living room set, even a U-Haul to move all the stolen goods. Taylor, who looks nothing like the golf legend, simply obtained a driver's license using Tiger's real name, Eldrick Woods; then, he used Wood's Social Security number to get credit in his name. . . .

When Tiger himself testified during the case in 2001, Taylor, a 30-year-old career criminal, didn't stand a chance. Wood's star power helped the state throw the book at Taylor. . . . The firm, swift justice might have made other potential identity thieves think twice, but for this: Precious few identity thefts are even investigated, let alone prosecuted to the full extent of the law. The average victim has enough trouble getting the police to bother filling out an incident report. . . .

The real world of identity theft . . . is . . . a haunting, paperwork nightmare, one often compared to financial rape, littered with small and large tragedies. . . . Couples can't buy homes because their credit is damaged. Identity theft victims are often denied access to the lowest interest rates and can pay as much as 50 percent more to borrow money. . . . And thousands of people face hundreds of hours of electronic trials against their erroneous credit reports and eventually end with fraudulent debts and endless nightly threatening calls from collection agencies.[12]

According to a 2007 report to the FTC, "approximately 8.3 million U.S. adults discovered that they were victims of some form of ID theft in 2005."[13] According to this report's estimates, the total losses from ID theft in that year were $15.6 billion. Moreover, "victims of all types of ID theft spent hours of their time resolving the various problems that result from ID theft. The median value for the number of hours spent resolving problems by all victims was four. However, 10 percent of all victims spent at least 55 hours resolving their problems."

In an important caveat, however, this report also notes that it may not capture all types of identity theft. In particular, it does not measure "synthetic ID theft." This activity involves a criminal creating a fictitious identity by combining information from one or more consumers. Affected consumers face considerable obstacles in detecting synthetic ID theft; therefore, any survey of identity theft, which depends on consumer self-reporting, is likely to underreport it.

Chris Hoofnagle proposes that policy responses to identity theft are hobbled by a lack of information about the dimensions of the problem.[14] He argues: "We are asking the wrong people about the crime. . . . Victims often do not know how their personal data were stolen or who stole the information." Hoofnagle's solution is to create a reporting requirement on financial institutions, including all lenders and organizations that control access to accounts (such as PayPal and Western Union). There would be three disclosure requirements for these entities: "(1) the number of identity theft incidents suffered or avoided; (2) the forms of

---

[12] Bob Sullivan, *Your Evil Twin: Behind the Identity Theft Epidemic* 35-36 (2004).

[13] Synovate, Federal Trade Commission — 2006 Identity Theft Survey Report (Nov. 2007).

[14] Chris Jay Hoofnagle, *Identity Theft: Making the Known Unknowns Known*, 21 Harv. J. L. & Tech. 97 (2007).

identity theft attempted and the financial products targeted (e.g., mortgage loan or credit card); and (3) the amount of loss suffered or avoided."

Hoofnagle's larger hope is that if statistics were available by individual institution on identity theft, financial institutions would have a "new product differentiator, similar to low interest rates and fee-free access accounts." In other words, consumers would be able to choose to have a financial relationship with one organization rather than another based on its track record in providing safe financial products. Do you think that consumers would respond to such market information and actually switch accounts from one organization to another? Personal information might be stolen from nonfinancial institutions, such as a college, and then used by a criminal for fraud at a bank. How can incentives be provided for nonfinancial institutions to have adequate security?

(a) Identity Theft Statutes

The Identity Theft Assumption and Deterrence Act. Congress responded to the growth of identity theft by passing the Identity Theft and Assumption Deterrence Act in 1998. The Act makes it a federal crime to "knowingly transfer or use, without lawful authority, a means of identification of another person with the intent to commit, or to aid or abet, any unlawful activity that constitutes a violation of Federal law, or that constitutes a felony under any applicable State or local law." 18 U.S.C. § 1028.

The Fair Credit Reporting Act. The Fair Credit Reporting Act (FCRA), as amended by the Fair and Accurate Credit Transactions Act (FACTA), has provisions that address identity theft. We discuss these provisions below.

State Legislative Responses. The vast majority of states now have statutes concerning identity theft. Before 1998, only three states had enacted statutes dealing explicitly with identity theft.[15] Arizona was one of these states; it punishes identity thefts as low-grade felony, but its statute does not address victims' rights and remedies. Ariz. Rev. Stat. Ann. § 13-2008(D). The passage of the federal Identity Theft Assumption and Deterrence Act in 1998 sparked most states to pass their own identity theft legislation — more than 40 states now have identity theft statutes on the books.[16]

Many identity theft statutes focus on defining criminal penalties for the crime. Penalties are tied to the amount of money the thief steals. For example, in Florida, identity theft is a second-degree felony if it results in an injury of $75,000 or more, Fla. Stat. Ann. § 817.568(2)(b), but is only a first-degree misdemeanor if the individual is harassed without having reached the $75,000 threshold. Fla. Stat. Ann. § 817.568(3). New Jersey likewise penalizes identity thefts resulting in injury over $75,000 as a second-degree crime; injuries between $500 and $75,000 constitute a third-degree crime; injuries between $200 and

---

[15] U.S. General Accountability Office, *Report to the Honorable Sam Johnson House of Representatives, Identity Theft: Greater Awareness and Use of Existing Data Are Needed* 7 (June 2002).

[16] *Id.* at 6.

$500 constitute a fourth-degree crime; and injuries less than $200 constitute a disorderly persons offense. N.J.S.A. §§ 2C:21-17(c)(1)–(2). Pennsylvania punishes identity thefts in a similar manner. *See* Pa. Stat. Ann. tit. 18, § 4120(c)(1).

Should penalties be tied to the dollar value of the things the thief wrongfully took or to the mental distress and harm caused to the victims, which might not be correlated to such a dollar value?

California, in contrast to most other states, has some of the most comprehensive and powerful identity theft laws. For example, California permits victims to obtain the fraudulent applications that the identity thief made as well as a record of the thief's transactions in the victim's name. Cal. Penal Code § 530.8; Cal. Civil Code § 1748.95. California also assists victims in stopping debt collectors from continuing to try to collect debts that the thief created. Cal. Civ. Code § 1788.18. The central difference between California's approach and that of other states is that California grants powerful rights to victims to assist them in fixing the damage of an identity theft. California also requires companies to notify consumers of data security breaches where personal information about consumers is compromised. Cal. Civ. Code § 1798.82(a).

Assessing Identity Theft Statutes. Daniel Solove contends that many statutes addressing identity theft focus mainly on enhancing criminal penalties and ignore the real roots of the problem:

> [T]he prevailing approach toward dealing with identity theft — by relying on increasing criminal penalties and by depending upon individuals to take great lengths to try to protect themselves against their vulnerabilities to identity theft — has the wrong focus. . . . The underlying cause of identity theft is an architecture that makes us vulnerable to such crimes and unable to adequately repair the damage. . . .
>
> This architecture is not created by identity thieves; rather, it is exploited by them. It is an architecture of vulnerability, one where personal information is not protected with adequate security, where identity thieves have easy access to data and the ability to use it in detrimental ways. We are increasingly living with what I call "digital dossiers" about our lives, and these dossiers are not controlled by us but by various entities, such as private-sector companies and the government. These dossiers play a profound role in our lives in modern society. The identity thief taps into these dossiers and uses them, manipulates them, and pollutes them. The identity thief's ability to so easily access and use our personal data stems from an architecture that does not provide adequate security to our personal information and that does not afford us with a sufficient degree of participation in the collection, dissemination, and use of that information. Consequently, it is difficult for the victim to figure out what is going on and how she can remedy the situation. . . .
>
> Private sector entities lack adequate ways of controlling access to records and accounts in a person's name, and numerous companies engage in the common practice of using SSNs, mother's maiden names, and addresses for access to

account information. Additionally, creditors give out credit and establish new accounts if the applicant supplies a name, SSN, and address.[17]

Lynn LoPucki and Solove agree that the problem of identity theft is caused by the frequent use of SSNs as identifiers. According to LoPucki:

> The problem is not that thieves have access to personal information, but that creditors and credit-reporting agencies often lack both the means and the incentives to correctly identify the persons who seek credit from them or on whom they report.[18]

LoPucki suggests that the problem is caused by the lack of a reliable means for identification. He proposes a system where the government maintains a database of identification information that people submit, such as biometric data, photographs, and other personal information. Solove argues that more sophisticated identification systems come with other problems, such as an increase in data gathering about people and an inability of people who are the victims of abusive spouses or stalkers to hide. However, both Solove and LoPucki agree that identity theft is, in large part, a problem caused by the system in which credit is granted in the United States.

(b) Tort Law

WOLFE V. MBNA AMERICA BANK

485 F. Supp. 2d 874 (W.D. Tenn. 2007)

DONALD, J. Before the Court is Defendant MBNA America Bank's ("Defendant") Motion to Dismiss Plaintiff's Fourth Amended Complaint made pursuant to Rule 12(b)(6) of the Federal Rules of Civil Procedure. Plaintiff Mark Wolfe ("Plaintiff") filed his Fourth Amended Complaint on September 15, 2006, alleging a claim under the Tennessee Consumer Protection Act of 1977 ("TCPA"), Tenn. Code Ann. § 47-18-104(a)-(b), as well as claims for negligence, gross negligence, and defamation.

Plaintiff, now a twenty-seven year old male, is a resident of the State of Tennessee. In or about April 2000, Defendant received a credit account application in Plaintiff's name from a telemarketing company. The application listed Plaintiff's address as 3557 Frankie Carolyn Drive, Apartment 4, Memphis, Tennessee 38118. Plaintiff did not reside and had never resided at this address.

Upon receipt of the application, Defendant issued a credit card bearing Plaintiff's name to an unknown and unauthorized individual residing at the address listed on the application. Plaintiff alleges that Defendant, prior to issuing the card, did not attempt to verify whether the information contained in the credit account application was authentic and accurate. After receiving the card, the

---

[17] Daniel J. Solove, *Identity Theft, Privacy, and the Architecture of Vulnerability*, 54 Hastings L.J. 1227 (2003). For a response to Solove's proposals for solutions and a defense of his own proposed solution, see Lynn M. LoPucki, *Did Privacy Cause Identity Theft?*, 54 Hastings L.J. 1277 (2003).

[18] Lynn M. LoPucki, *Human Identification Theory and the Identity Theft Problem*, 80 Tex. L. Rev. 89, 94 (2001).

unknown and unauthorized individual charged $864.00 to the credit account, exceeding the account's $500.00 credit limit. When no payments were made on the account, Defendant, without investigating whether the account was obtained using a stolen identity, declared the account delinquent and transferred the account to NCO Financial Systems, Inc. ("NCO"), a debt collection agency. Defendant also notified various credit reporting agencies that the account was delinquent.

In order to collect the debt on the delinquent account, NCO hired an attorney, who discovered Plaintiff's actual address. The attorney, in a letter dated November 29, 2004, notified Plaintiff of the delinquent account and requested payment. Upon receipt of this letter, Plaintiff contacted the attorney to inquire about the account, but was told that he would receive information about the account in thirty (30) days. Plaintiff never received any further information.

In January 2005, Plaintiff applied for a job with a bank, but Plaintiff was not hired due to his poor credit score. Following this denial, Plaintiff contacted Defendant numerous times to dispute the delinquent account but was unable to obtain any "adequate or real explanation" from Defendant. At some point in time, Defendant mailed a notice of arbitration proceedings to the address listed on the credit account application, which subsequently resulted in an arbitration award against Plaintiff. Despite Plaintiff notifying Defendant that his identity was stolen, Defendant continues to list the credit account bearing Plaintiff's name as delinquent and has not corrected the information provided to credit reporting agencies regarding the account. . . .

A motion to dismiss for failure to state a claim only tests whether the plaintiff has pleaded a cognizable claim. . . .

Plaintiff alleges that Defendant had a *duty to verify* "the accuracy and authenticity of a credit application completed in Plaintiff's name before issuing a credit card." . . . Plaintiff alleges that Defendant failed to comply with [its duty to verify], and thus, is negligent and/or grossly negligent.

In Tennessee, negligence is established if a plaintiff demonstrates: "(1) a duty of care owed by the defendant to the plaintiff; (2) conduct falling below the applicable standard of care amounts to a breach of that duty; (3) an injury or loss; (4) causation in fact; and (5) proximate, or legal cause." To establish gross negligence, a plaintiff "must demonstrate ordinary negligence and must then prove that the defendant acted 'with utter unconcern for the safety of others, or . . . with such reckless disregard for the rights of others that a conscious indifference to consequences is implied in law'". . . .

Addressing the first context or duty, Defendant asserts that Plaintiff's negligence and gross negligence claims should be dismissed because Tennessee negligence law does not impose a duty on Defendant to verify the authenticity and accuracy of a credit account application prior to issuing a credit card. Defendant, characterizing Plaintiff's claim as one for the "negligent enablement of identity theft," argues that a duty to verify essentially constitutes a duty to prevent third-party criminal activity. Defendant argues that Tennessee courts have never held that commercial banks have a common law duty to prevent the theft of a non-customer's identity. Defendant further argues that it, like Plaintiff, is a victim of identity theft.

Under Tennessee negligence law, a duty is defined as "the legal obligation a defendant owes to a plaintiff to conform to the reasonable person standard of care in order to protect against unreasonable risks of harm." "Whether a defendant owes a duty to a plaintiff in any given situation is a question of law for the court." The "existence and scope of the duty of the defendant in a particular case rests on all the relevant circumstances, including the foreseeability of harm to the plaintiff and other similarly situated persons." A harm is foreseeable "if a reasonable person could foresee the probability of its occurrence or if the person was on notice that the likelihood of danger to the party to whom is owed a duty is probable."

Because Tennessee courts have not specifically addressed whether Tennessee negligence law imposes a duty to verify on commercial banks, Defendant cites in support of its argument the Supreme Court of South Carolina's decision in *Huggins v. Citibank, N.A.,* 585 S.E.2d 275 (S.C. 2003). In *Huggins,* the plaintiff alleged, among other things, that the defendant bank was negligent for issuing a credit card in the plaintiff's name to an unknown and unauthorized person "without any investigation, verification, or corroboration" of the authenticity and accuracy of the credit account application. The defendant argued that under South Carolina negligence law, it had no duty to verify the accuracy and authenticity of the credit account application because plaintiff was technically a non-customer. The South Carolina Supreme Court, despite finding that "it is foreseeable that injury may arise by the negligent issuance of a credit card," ultimately found that no duty to verify existed because "[t]he relationship, if any, between credit card issuers and potential victims of identity theft is far too attenuated to rise to the level of a duty between them." Noting the similarity between negligence law in Tennessee and South Carolina, Defendant argues that its relationship with Plaintiff, like the parties in *Huggins,* was and is too attenuated to warrant the imposition of a duty to verify.

Upon review, the Court finds the South Carolina Supreme Court's conclusion in *Huggins* to be flawed. In reaching its conclusion, the *Huggins* court relied heavily on the fact that there was no prior business relationship between the parties, that is, the plaintiff was not a customer of the defendant bank. The Court believes that the court's reliance on this fact is misplaced. While the existence of a prior business relationship might have some meaning in the context of a contractual dispute, a prior business relationship has little meaning in the context of negligence law. Instead, to determine whether a duty exists between parties, the Court must examine all relevant circumstances, with emphasis on the foreseeability of the alleged harm. As to the issue of foreseeability, the South Carolina Supreme Court found that "it is foreseeable that injury may arise by the negligent issuance of a credit card" and that such injury "could be prevented if credit card issuers carefully scrutinized credit card applications." The Court agrees with and adopts these findings.

With the alarming increase in identity theft in recent years, commercial banks and credit card issuers have become the first, and often last, line of defense in preventing the devastating damage that identity theft inflicts. Because the injury resulting from the negligent issuance of a credit card is foreseeable and preventable, the Court finds that under Tennessee negligence law, Defendant has a duty to verify the authenticity and accuracy of a credit account application before issuing a credit card. The Court, however, emphasizes that this duty to verify does not impose upon Defendant a duty to prevent all identity theft. The Court recognizes that despite banks utilizing the most reasonable and vigilant verification methods, some criminals will still be able to obtain enough personal information to secure a credit card with a stolen identity. Rather, this duty to verify merely requires Defendant to implement reasonable and cost-effective verification methods that can prevent criminals, in some instances, from obtaining a credit card with a stolen identity. Whether Defendant complied with this duty before issuing a credit card in Plaintiff's name is an issue for the trier of fact. Accordingly, Defendant's motion to dismiss Plaintiff's negligence and gross negligence claims in the first factual context is DENIED.

NOTES & QUESTIONS

1. *Tort Law to the Rescue?* In *Wolfe*, the district court located a duty in tort law that required a bank to take steps to verify identity before issuing a credit card in the plaintiff's name to a person. The court operated under a negligence theory: the bank need not prevent all identity theft (strict liability), but merely to use reasonable verification methods. What kind of practical steps might a bank take to make sure that the person to whom it issues a credit card is, in fact, the intended person? In light of the Lo Pucki-Solove debate (excerpted above) about the flawed system for checking and otherwise verifying identity, how successful are any "reasonable" means likely to be?

(c) The Fair Credit Reporting Act

A significant amount of identity theft involves the credit reporting system. When an identity thief starts creating delinquent debts in a person's name, creditors report the delinquencies to the credit reporting agencies, and the delinquencies begin to appear on the person's credit report. This can severely affect the person's credit score and make it impossible for the person to secure credit. What are the responsibilities of credit reporting agencies in ensuring that the data it reports about individuals really pertains to them rather than to the identity thief who impersonated them?

SLOANE V. EQUIFAX INFORMATION SERVICES, LLC
510 F.3d 495 (4th Cir. 2007)

DIANA GRIBBON MOTZ, J. After Suzanne Sloane discovered that a thief had stolen her identity and ruined her credit, she notified the police and sought to have Equifax Information Services, LLC, a credit reporting service, correct the resulting errors in her credit report. The police promptly arrested and jailed the thief. But twenty-one months later, Equifax still had not corrected the errors in Suzanne's credit report. Accordingly, Suzanne brought this action against Equifax for violations of the Fair Credit Reporting Act (FCRA), 15 U.S.C.A. §§ 1681 *et seq.* A jury found that Equifax had violated the Act in numerous respects and awarded Suzanne $351,000 in actual damages ($106,000 for economic losses and $245,000 for mental anguish, humiliation, and emotional distress). The district court entered judgment in the amount of $351,000. In addition, without permitting Equifax to file a written opposition, the court also awarded Suzanne attorney's fees in the amount of $181,083. On appeal, Equifax challenges the award of damages and attorney's fees. We affirm in part and reverse and remand in part.

On June 25, 2003, Suzanne Sloane entered Prince William Hospital to deliver a baby. She left the hospital not only a new mother, but also the victim of identity theft. A recently hired hospital employee named Shovana Sloan noticed similarity in the women's names and birth dates and, in November and December 2003, began using Suzanne's social security number to obtain credit cards, loans, cash advances, and other goods and services totaling more than $30,000. At the end of January 2004, Suzanne discovered these fraudulent transactions when Citibank notified her that it had cancelled her credit card and told her to contact Equifax if she had any concerns.

Unable to reach Equifax by telephone on a Friday evening, Suzanne went instead to the Equifax website, where she was able to access her credit report and discovered Shovana Sloan's name and evidence of the financial crimes Shovana had committed. Suzanne promptly notified the police, and contacted Equifax, which assertedly placed a fraud alert on her credit file. Equifax told Suzanne to "roll up her sleeves" and start calling all of her "20-some" creditors to notify them of the identity theft. Suzanne took the next two days off from work to contact each of her creditors, and, at their direction, she submitted numerous notarized forms to correct her credit history.

Suzanne, however, continued to experience problems with Equifax. On March 31, 2004, almost two months after reporting the identity theft to Equifax and despite her efforts to work with individual creditors as Equifax had advised, Suzanne and her husband, Tracey, tried to secure a pre-qualification letter to buy a vacation home, but were turned down. The loan officer told them that Suzanne's credit score was "terrible" — in fact, the "worst" the loan officer had ever seen — and that no loan would be possible until the numerous problems in Suzanne's Equifax credit report had been corrected. The loan officer also told Suzanne not to apply for additional credit in the meantime, because each credit inquiry would appear on her credit report and further lower her score.

Chagrined that Equifax had not yet corrected these errors in her credit report, Suzanne refrained from applying for any type of consumer credit for seven months. But, in October 2004, after the repeated breakdown of their family car, Suzanne and Tracey attempted to rely on Suzanne's credit to purchase a used car at a local dealership. Following a credit check, the car salesman pulled Tracey aside and informed him that it would be impossible to approve the financing so long as Suzanne's name appeared on the loan. Similarly, when the Sloanes returned to the mortgage company to obtain a home loan in January 2005, eight months after their initial visit, they were offered only an adjustable rate loan instead of a less expensive 30-year fixed rate loan in part because of Equifax's still inaccurate credit report.

In frustration, on March 9, 2005, more than thirteen months after first reporting the identity theft to Equifax, Suzanne sent a formal letter to the credit reporting agency, disputing twenty-four specific items in her credit report and requesting their deletion. Equifax agreed to delete the majority of these items, but after assertedly verifying two accounts with Citifinancial, Inc., Equifax notified Suzanne that it would not remove these two items. At trial, Equifax admitted that under its "verified victim policy," it should have automatically removed these Citifinancial items at Suzanne's request, but it failed to do so in violation of its own written procedures.

Two months later, on May 9, 2005, Suzanne again wrote to Equifax, still disputing the two Citifinancial accounts, and now also contesting two Washington Mutual accounts that Equifax had previously deleted but had mistakenly restored to Suzanne's report. When Equifax attempted to correct these mistakes, it exacerbated matters further by generating a second credit file bearing Shovana Sloan's name but containing Suzanne's social security number. Compounding this mistake, on May 23, 2005, Equifax sent a letter to Suzanne's house addressed to Shovana Sloan, warning Shovana that *she* was possibly the victim of identity theft and offering to sell her a service to monitor her credit file. Then, on June 7, 2005, Equifax sent copies of *both* credit reports to Suzanne; notably, both credit reports still contained the disputed Citifinancial accounts.

The stress of these problems weighed on Suzanne and significantly contributed to the deterioration of her marriage to Tracey. . . . In May 2005, the credit situation forced Tracey, a high school teacher, to abandon his plans to take a sabbatical during which he had hoped to develop land for modular homes with his father. The Sloanes frequently fought during the day and slept in separate rooms at night. . . . Also, during this period, Suzanne was frequently unable to sleep at night, and as her insomnia worsened, she found herself nodding off while driving home from work in the evening. Even after the couple took a vacation to reconcile in August 2005, when they returned home, they were greeted with the denial of a line of credit from Wachovia Bank. . . .

On November 4, 2005 — following twenty-one months of struggle to correct her credit report — Suzanne filed this action against Equifax, Trans Union, LLC, Experian Information Solutions, Inc., and Citifinancial, alleging violations of the FCRA. After settling a separate suit against Prince William Hospital and the personnel company that placed Shovana Sloan in the hospital's accounting department, Suzanne settled her claims in this action against Experian, Trans Union, and Citifinancial. Equifax, however, refused to settle. Thus, the case proceeded to trial with Equifax the sole remaining defendant. The jury returned a verdict against Equifax, awarding Suzanne $106,000 for economic loss and $245,000 for mental anguish, humiliation, and emotional distress.

Equifax moved for judgment as a matter of law and for a new trial or remittitur on the jury's award of damages for emotional distress. The district court denied Equifax's post-trial motions and then, without permitting Equifax to submit an opposition to Suzanne's request for attorney's fees, ordered Equifax to pay $181,083 in attorney's fees. This appeal followed. . . .

In this case, the jury specifically found, via a special verdict, that Suzanne proved by a preponderance of the evidence that Equifax violated the FCRA by negligently: (1) failing to follow reasonable procedures designed to assure maximum accuracy on her consumer credit report; (2) failing to conduct a reasonable investigation to determine whether disputed information in her credit report was inaccurate; (3) failing to delete information from the report that it found after reinvestigation to be inaccurate, incomplete, or unverified; and (4) reinserting information into her credit file that it had previously deleted. On appeal, Equifax does not challenge the jury's findings that Suzanne proved that it violated the FCRA in all of these respects.

The FCRA provides a private cause of action for those damaged by violations of the statute. *See* 15 U.S.C.A. §§ 1681n, 1681o. A successful plaintiff can recover both actual and punitive damages for willful violations of the FCRA, *id.* § 1681n(a), and actual damages for negligent violations, *id.* § 1681o(a). Actual damages may include not only economic damages, but also damages for humiliation and mental distress. The statute also provides that a successful plaintiff suing under the FCRA may recover reasonable attorney's fees. 15 U.S.C.A. §§ 1681n(a)(3), 1681o(a)(2). . . .

Equifax first argues that because Suzanne assertedly suffered a single, indivisible injury, she should not recover any damages from Equifax or, alternatively, her recovery should be reduced to take account of her prior settlements with other defendants. According to Equifax, the prior settlements have fully, or almost fully, compensated Suzanne for all of her injuries.

Equifax relies on the "one satisfaction rule" to support its argument. *See Chisholm v. UHP Projects, Inc.,* 205 F.3d 731, 737 (4th Cir. 2000) ("[T]his equitable doctrine operates to reduce a plaintiff's recovery from the nonsettling defendant to prevent the plaintiff from recovering twice from the same assessment of liability."). But, in the case at hand, we cannot find, as a matter of law, that Suzanne has suffered from a "single, indivisible harm" that has already been redressed by other parties. . . .

To the contrary, Suzanne provided credible evidence that her emotional and economic damages resulted from separate acts by separate parties. She did not attempt to hold any of the credit reporting agencies responsible for damages arising from either the identity theft itself or the initial inaccuracies that the theft generated in her credit reports. Moreover, although some of Suzanne's interactions with Equifax overlapped with exchanges with other credit reporting agencies, her encounters with Equifax both predate and postdate these other exchanges. . . .

Further, during the period when Suzanne attempted to correct the mistakes made by all three agencies, each agency produced reports with different inaccuracies, and each agency either corrected or exacerbated these mistakes independently of the others. Thus, even during this period, the inaccuracies in Equifax's credit reports caused Suzanne discrete injuries independent of those caused by the other credit reporting agencies.

For all of these reasons, we reject Equifax's argument that Suzanne has suffered from a single, indivisible injury or has been doubly compensated as a consequence of her prior settlements.

Equifax next argues that the evidence does not support any award for economic losses. Equifax claims that only speculation and conjecture support such an award, and so the district court erred in denying Equifax's motion for judgment as to this award.

We disagree. The evidence at trial in this case clearly demonstrates that on numerous occasions Suzanne attempted to secure lines of credit from a variety of financial institutions, only to be either denied outright or offered credit on less advantageous terms that she might have received absent Equifax's improper conduct. At times, these financial institutions consulted credit reports from other agencies, but at other times these institutions relied exclusively on the erroneous credit information provided by Equifax. Based on these incidents, we find that there is a legally sufficient evidentiary basis for a reasonable jury to have found that Equifax's conduct resulted in economic losses for Suzanne. Therefore, the district court did not err in denying Equifax's motion regarding this award.

Additionally, Equifax asserts that the district court erred in refusing to order remittitur of the mental anguish, humiliation, and emotional distress damages award to no more than $25,000. Equifax contends that the jury's award of $245,000 is inconsistent with awards in similar cases and is disproportionate to any actual injury proved at trial. Suzanne, by contrast, contends that the evidence provides more than adequate support for the jury's award. To resolve this question, we set forth the relevant governing principles, apply these principles to the evidence before the jury, and compare the evidence and emotional distress award in Suzanne's case with the evidence and award in all assertedly relevant cases. . . .

We begin with Federal Rule of Civil Procedure 59(a), which provides that if a court concludes that a jury award of compensatory damages is excessive, it may order a new trial nisi remittitur. . . . A district court abuses its discretion only by upholding an award of damages when "the jury's verdict is against the weight of the evidence or based on evidence which is false."

In this case, the district court found that the jury's emotional distress award was "not an unreasonable conclusion from this evidence." The court noted that the jury could base its award on Equifax's specific actions, as distinct from those of the other credit reporting agencies, and that Equifax's actions directly led to the mounting frustration and distress that Suzanne felt for almost two years. As one example of Equifax's specific actions, the court recalled the letter that Equifax sent to Suzanne, many months after she had notified Equifax of the identity theft, bearing the name of the identity thief and warning the thief, not Suzanne, that the thief's personal information was in peril. . . .

Moreover, Equifax does not deny that Suzanne suffered emotional distress. Nor does Equifax contend that Suzanne failed to produce sufficient evidence to sustain some award for this injury. Rather, Equifax simply proposes replacing the jury's number with one of its own invention — offering $25,000 in place of $245,000. Yet when asked at oral argument to explain the basis for the proposed remittitur, Equifax's counsel could offer no legal or factual basis for this amount, conceding that the number had been taken "out of the air." Not only is such an unprincipled approach intrinsically unsound, but it also directly contravenes the Seventh Amendment, which precludes an appellate court from replacing an award of compensatory damages with one of the court's own choosing. In short, the issue before us is neither whether Suzanne offered sufficient evidence at trial to sustain an award for emotional distress nor whether we believe that Equifax's "out of the air" $25,000 represents a fair estimate of those damages, but whether the jury's award is *excessive* in light of evidence presented at trial.

Our previous cases establish the type of evidence required to support an award for emotional damages. We have warned that "[n]ot only is emotional distress fraught with vagueness and speculation, it is easily susceptible to fictitious and trivial claims." *Price v. City of Charlotte,* 93 F.3d 1241, 1250 (4th Cir. 1996). For this reason, although specifically recognizing that a plaintiff's testimony can provide sufficient evidence to support an emotional distress award, we have required a plaintiff to "reasonably and sufficiently explain the circumstances of [the] injury and not resort to mere conclusory statements." Thus, we have distinguished between plaintiff testimony that amounts only to "conclusory statements" and plaintiff testimony that "sufficiently articulate[s]" true "demonstrable emotional distress."

In *Knussman v. Maryland,* 272 F.3d 625 (4th Cir. 2001), we summarized the factors properly considered in determinating the potential excessiveness of an award for emotional distress. They include the factual context in which the emotional distress arose; evidence corroborating the testimony of the plaintiff; the nexus between the conduct of the defendant and the emotional distress; the degree of such mental distress; mitigating circumstances, if any; physical injuries suffered due to the emotional distress; medical attention resulting from the emotional duress; psychiatric or psychological treatment; and the loss of income, if any.

In the present case, Suzanne offered considerable objective verification of her emotional distress, chronic anxiety, and frustration during the twenty-one months that she attempted to correct Equifax's errors. First, her repeated denials of credit and continuous problems with Equifax furnish an objective and inherently reasonable "factual context" for her resulting claims of emotional distress. Suzanne also corroborated her account in two ways. She offered "sufficiently articulated" descriptions of her protracted anxiety through detailed testimony of specific events and the humiliation and anger she experienced as a result of each occurrence. She also provided evidence that the distress was apparent to others, particularly her family; Tracey, for instance, described in detail his wife's ongoing struggles with Equifax and the emotional toll these events took upon her. In addition, substantial trial evidence attested to the direct "nexus" between Equifax's violations of the FCRA and Suzanne's emotional distress. Furthermore, Suzanne's emotional distress manifested itself in terms of physical symptoms, particularly insomnia. . . .

Reviewing this evidence in light of the appropriate factors already set forth, we conclude that substantial, if not overwhelming, objective evidence supports an emotional distress award. Equifax ignores much of this evidence, however, and insists that an award of $245,000 is "inconsistent with awards in other similar cases." But Equifax relies on cases which are in fact not very "similar" to the case at hand and so provide little assistance in assessing the amount of the emotional distress award here. . . .

As Equifax's authorities indicate, finding helpful precedent for comparison here is not a simple task. The recent emergence of identity theft and the rapid growth of the credit-reporting industry present a unique dilemma without clear precedent. When Congress enacted the FCRA in 1970, it recognized the vital role that credit-reporting agencies had assumed within the burgeoning culture of American consumerism. Since the mid-1980s, the introduction of computerized information technology and data-warehousing has led to the national consolidation of the credit-reporting industry into the "Big Three" — Equifax, Experian, and Trans Union — and rendered credit reporting an integral part of our most ordinary consumer transactions. According to recent data, each of these national credit-reporting agencies has perhaps 1.5 billion credit accounts held by approximately 190 million individuals. Each receives more than two billion items of information every month, and together these three agencies issue approximately two million consumer credit reports each day.

Against this backdrop, identity theft has emerged over the last decade as one of the fastest growing white-collar crimes in the United States. . . . Given the rapid emergence of identity theft in the last decade, it comes as no surprise that past precedent fails to fully reflect the unfortunate current reality. . . .

A survey of the other, more recent FCRA cases that involve requests for remittitur of emotional distress awards suggests that approved awards more typically range between $20,000 and $75,000.

This handful of cases, while helpful, differs from the case at hand. For, unlike the plaintiffs in those cases, Suzanne did not suffer from isolated or accidental reporting errors. Rather, as a victim of identity theft, she suffered the systematic manipulation of her personal information, which, despite her best efforts, Equifax failed to correct over a protracted period of time. Of course, Equifax bore no responsibility for the initial theft, but the FCRA makes the company responsible for taking reasonable steps to correct Suzanne's credit report once she brought the theft to the company's attention; this Equifax utterly failed to do. A reasonable jury could conclude that Equifax's repeated errors engendered more emotional distress than that found in these other FCRA cases.

We also believe that some guidance can be gained from case law concerning defamation. Prior to the enactment of the FCRA, defamation was one of several common-law actions used by plaintiffs in response to the dissemination of inaccurate credit information.[19] These common-law causes of action parallel those offered under the FCRA in that they typically involve a defendant found liable for propagating inaccurate information about the plaintiff, and the effects, while unquestionably harmful, are difficult to translate into monetary terms. . . . [C]ourts frequently sustain emotional distress awards in the range of $250,000 in defamation cases.

We do not believe the evidence presented here permits an award of this magnitude because, after all, this case does not involve actual defamation. Moreover, Suzanne presented almost no evidence at trial to suggest that Equifax's violations of the FCRA resulted in harm to her reputation, and it appears that few people beyond Suzanne's family and potential creditors knew of her disastrous credit file. We therefore believe that the maximum award supported by the evidence here must be significantly less than these defamation awards. But, considering the extensive corroboration offered at trial concerning the many months of emotional distress, mental anguish, and humiliation suffered by Suzanne, we believe that the evidence does support an award in the maximum amount of $150,000. We recognize that even this amount is appreciably more than that awarded for emotional distress in most other FCRA cases. But, as explained earlier, the case at hand differs significantly from those cases. A

---

[19] A provision of the FCRA bars consumers from bringing actions "in the nature of defamation, invasion of privacy, or negligence" in certain specified contexts, except as those causes of action arise under sections 1681n and 1681o of the FCRA. 15 U.S.C.A. § 1681h(e).

$150,000 award reflects those differences—the repeated violations of the FCRA found by the jury in its special verdict, the number of errors contained in Equifax's credit reports, and the protracted length of time during which Equifax failed to correct Suzanne's credit file. Accordingly, we reduce the emotional distress award to $150,000 and grant a new trial nisi remittitur at Suzanne's option. . . .

[The court vacated the district court's grant of attorney's fees in the amount of $181,083 because the district court failed to allow Equifax to submit a written opposition to Sloane's motion for attorney's fees. The case was remanded to allow Equifax to file its opposition.]

NOTES & QUESTIONS

1. ***Damages.*** Was the remittitur to $150,000 appropriate? Why should damage awards be limited based on the damage awards in other cases? As the court noted, they involve very different facts than the case at bar.

   Also recall the court's statement that "this case does not involve actual defamation. . . . Suzanne presented almost no evidence at trial to suggest that Equifax's violations of the FCRA resulted in harm to her reputation, and it appears that few people beyond Suzanne's family and potential creditors knew of her disastrous credit file." Why doesn't this case involve "harm to her reputation"? Don't reports on people's creditworthiness affect their financial reputations, that is, their ability to pay back their debts, their trustworthiness and dependability?

2. ***The Harm of Identity Theft.*** When assessing the damages Sloane suffered from her identity theft ordeal, how much of the harm was caused by Equifax's actions? Purportedly, the entire incident of identity theft caused her marital discord, insomnia, and emotional distress. Yet, the identity theft did involve, after all, not only Equifax, but the identity thief, creditors, and other credit reporting agencies. Are the damages assessed to Equifax proportionate to Equifax's contribution to Sloane's ordeal? Or should Equifax be viewed as the "least cost avoider," the party who can internalize the costs of preventing this harm at the least overall cost?

B. COMMERCIAL ENTITIES AND PERSONAL DATA

Thus far, this chapter has examined the use of personal information within the financial sector. This part examines the use of personal information by commercial entities and how the law has attempted different ways to regulate in this area.

1. GOVERNANCE BY TORT

DWYER V. AMERICAN EXPRESS CO.

652 N.E.2d 1351 (Ill. App. 1995)

BUCKLEY, J. Plaintiffs, American Express cardholders, appeal the circuit court's dismissal of their claims for invasion of privacy and consumer fraud against defendants, American Express Company, American Express Credit Corporation, and American Express Travel Related Services Company, for their practice of renting information regarding cardholder spending habits.

On May 13, 1992, the New York Attorney General released a press statement describing an agreement it had entered into with defendants. The following day, newspapers reported defendants' actions which gave rise to this agreement. According to the news articles, defendants categorize and rank their cardholders into six tiers based on spending habits and then rent this information to participating merchants as part of a targeted joint-marketing and sales program. For example, a cardholder may be characterized as "Rodeo Drive Chic" or "Value Oriented." In order to characterize its cardholders, defendants analyze where they shop and how much they spend, and also consider behavioral characteristics and spending histories. Defendants then offer to create a list of cardholders who would most likely shop in a particular store and rent that list to the merchant.

Defendants also offer to create lists which target cardholders who purchase specific types of items, such as fine jewelry. The merchants using the defendants' service can also target shoppers in categories such as mail-order apparel buyers, home-improvement shoppers, electronics shoppers, luxury lodgers, card members with children, skiers, frequent business travelers, resort users, Asian/European travelers, luxury European car owners, or recent movers. Finally, defendants offer joint-marketing ventures to merchants who generate substantial sales through the American Express card. Defendants mail special promotions devised by the merchants to its cardholders and share the profits generated by these advertisements. . . .

Plaintiffs have alleged that defendants' practices constitute an invasion of their privacy [in particular, a violation of the intrusion upon seclusion tort]. . . .

. . . [There are] four elements [to intrusion upon seclusion] which must be alleged in order to state a cause of action: (1) an unauthorized intrusion or prying into the plaintiff's seclusion; (2) an intrusion which is offensive or objectionable to a reasonable man; (3) the matter upon which the intrusion occurs is private; and (4) the intrusion causes anguish and suffering. . . .

Plaintiffs' allegations fail to satisfy the first element, an unauthorized intrusion or prying into the plaintiffs' seclusion. The alleged wrongful actions involve the defendants' practice of renting lists that they have compiled from information contained in their own records. By using the American Express card, a cardholder is voluntarily, and necessarily, giving information to defendants that, if analyzed, will reveal a cardholder's spending habits and shopping preferences. . . .

Plaintiffs claim that because defendants rented lists based on this compiled information, this case involves the disclosure of private financial information and most closely resembles cases involving intrusion into private financial dealings, such as bank account transactions. Plaintiffs cite several cases in which courts have recognized the right to privacy surrounding financial transactions.

However, we find that this case more closely resembles the sale of magazine subscription lists, which was at issue in *Shibley v. Time, Inc.* In *Shibley*, the plaintiffs claimed that the defendant's practice of selling and renting magazine subscription lists without the subscribers' prior consent "constitut[ed] an invasion of privacy because it amount[ed] to a sale of individual 'personality profiles,' which subjects the subscribers to solicitations from direct mail advertisers." The plaintiffs also claimed that the lists amounted to a tortious appropriation of their names and "personality profiles." . . .

The *Shibley* court found that an Ohio statute, which permitted the sale of names and addresses of registrants of motor vehicles, indicated that the defendant's activity was not an invasion of privacy. . . .

Defendants rent names and addresses after they create a list of cardholders who have certain shopping tendencies; they are not disclosing financial information about particular cardholders. These lists are being used solely for the purpose of determining what type of advertising should be sent to whom. We also note that the Illinois Vehicle Code authorizes the Secretary of State to sell lists of names and addresses of licensed drivers and registered motor-vehicle owners. Thus, we hold that the alleged actions here do not constitute an unreasonable intrusion into the seclusion of another. We so hold without expressing a view as to the appellate court conflict regarding the recognition of this cause of action.

Considering plaintiffs' appropriation claim, the elements of the tort are: an appropriation, without consent, of one's name or likeness for another's use or benefit. This branch of the privacy doctrine is designed to protect a person from having his name or image used for commercial purposes without consent. According to the Restatement, the purpose of this tort is to protect the "interest of the individual in the exclusive use of his own identity, in so far as it is represented by his name or likeness." Illustrations of this tort provided by the Restatement include the publication of a person's photograph without consent in an advertisement; operating a corporation named after a prominent public figure without the person's consent; impersonating a man to obtain information regarding the affairs of the man's wife; and filing a lawsuit in the name of another without the other's consent.

Plaintiffs claim that defendants appropriate information about cardholders' personalities, including their names and perceived lifestyles, without their consent. Defendants argue that their practice does not adversely affect the interest of a cardholder in the "exclusive use of his own identity," using the language of the Restatement. Defendants also argue that the cardholders' names lack value and that the lists that defendants create are valuable because "they identify a useful aggregate of potential customers to whom offers may be sent." . . .

To counter defendants' argument, plaintiffs point out that the tort of appropriation is not limited to strictly commercial situations.

Nonetheless, we again follow the reasoning in *Shibley* and find that plaintiffs have not stated a claim for tortious appropriation because they have failed to allege the first element. Undeniably, each cardholder's name is valuable to defendants. The more names included on a list, the more that list will be worth. However, a single, random cardholder's name has little or no intrinsic value to defendants (or a merchant). Rather, an individual name has value only when it is associated with one of defendants' lists. Defendants create value by categorizing and aggregating these names. Furthermore, defendants' practices do not deprive any of the cardholders of any value their individual names may possess. . . .

NOTES & QUESTIONS

1. **Shibley v. Time.** In *Shibley v. Time, Inc.* 341 N.E.2d 337 (Ohio Ct. App. 1975), the plaintiff sued the publishers of a number of magazines for selling subscription lists to direct mail advertising businesses. The plaintiff sued under the public disclosure tort and the appropriation tort. Despite the fact that the purchasers of the lists can learn about the plaintiff's lifestyle from the data, the court dismissed the plaintiff's public disclosure action. The court found that the sale of the lists did not "cause mental suffering, shame or humiliation to a person of ordinary sensibilities." The court also rejected the plaintiff's argument that by selling the lists, the defendants were appropriating his name and likeness because the tort of appropriation is available only in those "situations where the plaintiff's name or likeness is displayed to the public to indicate that the plaintiff indorses the defendant's product or business."

   According to *Shibley* and *Dwyer*, why does the public disclosure tort fail to provide a remedy for the disclosure of personal information to other companies? Why does the tort of intrusion upon seclusion fail? Why does the tort of appropriation fail? More generally, can tort law adequately remedy the privacy problems created by profiling and databases?[20]

2. *A Fair Information Practices Tort?* Sarah Ludington recommends that a new tort should be developed in the common law, one that "would impose on data traders a duty to use Fair Information Practices (based on the principles of notice, choice, access, and security)." Why the common law rather than legislation? Ludington argues:

   > [B]ecause it is now clear that industry lobbying has succeeded while self-regulation has failed, and that legislatures have either failed to act or provided solutions that inadequately address the injuries, individuals must — indeed, should — look to the judiciary to help resolve the misuse of personal information.[21]

---

[20] For an interesting argument about how the tort of breach of confidentiality might provide a weak but potential solution to the problem, see Jessica Litman, *Information Privacy/Information Property*, 52 Stan. L. Rev. 1283 (2000). For a discussion of the use of the tort of appropriation, see Andrew J. McClurg, *A Thousand Words Are Worth a Picture: A Privacy Tort Response to Consumer Data Profiling,* 98 Nw. U. L. Rev. 63 (2003).

[21] Sarah Ludington, *Reining in the Data Traders: A Tort for the Misuse of Personal Information*, 66 Md. L. Rev. 140, 172-73 (2007).

Would the use of the common law to regulate the collection and use of personal data be effective or appropriate? What would be the strengths and weaknesses of such a regulatory approach?

3. ***Defining the Harm.*** What is the harm of commercial entities collecting and using personal information? One might contend that the kind of information that companies collect about individuals is not very sensitive or intimate. How much is a person harmed by sharing data that she prefers Coke to Pepsi or Puffs to Kleenex? Is there a significant privacy problem in revealing that a person has purchased tennis products, designer sunglasses, orange juice, or other things? One might view the harm as so minimal as to be trivial.

Does information about a person's consumption patterns reveal something about that person's identity? Stan Karas argues that "consumption patterns may identify one as a liberal, moderate Republican, radical feminist or born-again Christian. . . . For some individuals, consumption is no longer a way of expressing identity but is synonymous with identity. . . . [T]he identity of many subcultures is directly related to distinctive patterns of consumption. One need only think of the personal styles of punk rockers, hip-hoppers, or Harley-fetishizing bikers."[22]

According to Jerry Kang, data collection and compiling is a form of surveillance that inhibits individual freedom and choice: "[I]information collection in cyberspace is more like surveillance than like casual observation." He notes that "surveillance leads to self-censorship. This is true even when the observable information would not be otherwise misused or disclosed."[23]

Daniel Solove contends that the problem of computer databases does not stem from surveillance. He argues that numerous theorists describe the problem in terms of the metaphor of Big Brother, the ruthless totalitarian government in George Orwell's *1984*, which constantly monitors its citizens. Solove contends that the Big Brother metaphor fails to adequately conceptualize the problem:

> A large portion of our personal information involves facts that we are not embarrassed about: our financial information, race, marital status, hobbies, occupation, and the like. Most people surf the web without wandering into its dark corners. The vast majority of the information collected about us concerns relatively innocuous details. The surveillance model does not explain why the recording of this non-taboo information poses a problem.[24]

In contrast, Solove proposes that data collection and processing is most aptly captured by Franz Kafka's *The Trial*, where the protagonist (Joseph K.) is arrested by officials from a clandestine court system but is not informed of the reason for his arrest. From what little he manages to learn about the court system, which operates largely in secret, Joseph K. discovers that a vast bureaucratic court has examined his life and assembled a dossier on him. His

---

[22] Stan Karas, *Privacy, Identity, Databases,* 52 Am. U. L. Rev. 393, 438-39 (2002).

[23] Jerry Kang, *Information Privacy in Cyberspace Transactions,* 50 Stan. L. Rev. 1193 (1998).

[24] Daniel J. Solove, *Privacy and Power: Computer Databases and Metaphors for Information Privacy,* 53 Stan. L. Rev. 1393 (2001).

records, however, are "inaccessible," and K.'s life gradually becomes taken over by his frustrating quest for answers:

> *The Trial* captures the sense of helplessness, frustration, and vulnerability one experiences when a large bureaucratic organization has control over a vast dossier of details about one's life. At any time, something could happen to Joseph K.; decisions are made based on his data, and Joseph K. has no say, no knowledge, and no ability to fight back. He is completely at the mercy of the bureaucratic process. . . .
>
> The problem with databases emerges from subjecting personal information to the bureaucratic process with little intelligent control or limitation, resulting in a lack of meaningful participation in decisions about our information. . . .
>
> Under this view, the problem with databases and the practices currently associated with them is that they disempower people. They make people vulnerable by stripping them of control over their personal information. There is no diabolical motive or secret plan for domination; rather, there is a web of thoughtless decisions made by low-level bureaucrats, standardized policies, rigid routines, and a way of relating to individuals and their information that often becomes indifferent to their welfare.[25]

Joel Reidenberg points out that the lack of protection of information privacy will "destroy anonymity" and take away people's "freedom to choose the terms of personal information disclosure."[26] According to Paul Schwartz, the lack of privacy protection can threaten to expose not just information about what people purchase, but also information about their communication and consumption of ideas:

> In the absence of strong rules for information privacy, Americans will hesitate to engage in cyberspace activities—including those that are most likely to promote democratic self-rule. . . . Current polls already indicate an aversion on the part of some people to engage even in basic commercial activities on the Internet. Yet, deliberative democracy requires more than shoppers; it demands speakers and listeners. But who will speak or listen when this behavior leaves finely-grained data trails in a fashion that is difficult to understand or anticipate?[27]

4. *Is Privacy Still Possible?* Is privacy still possible in an Information Age? Scott McNealy, CEO of Sun Microsystems, Inc., once remarked: "You already have zero privacy. Get over it." Should we eulogize the death of privacy and move on? Or is it possible to protect privacy in modern times? Consider David Brin:

> . . . [I]t is already far too late to prevent the invasion of cameras and databases. The *djinn* cannot be crammed back into its bottle. No matter how many laws are passed, it will prove quite impossible to legislate away the new surveillance tools and databases. They are here to stay.
>
> Light *is* going to shine into nearly every corner of our lives. . . .

---

[25] *Id.*

[26] Joel R. Reidenberg, *Setting Standards for Fair Information Practice in the U.S. Private Sector*, 80 Iowa L. Rev. 497 (1995).

[27] Paul M. Schwartz, *Privacy and Democracy in Cyberspace*, 52 Vand. L. Rev. 1609, 1651 (1999).

If neo-Western civilization has one great trick in its repertoire, a technique more responsible than any other for its success, that trick is *accountability*. Especially the knack — which no other culture ever mastered — of making accountability apply to the mighty. . . .

Kevin Kelly, executive editor of *Wired* magazine, expressed the same idea with the gritty clarity of information-age journalism: "The answer to the whole privacy question is more knowledge. More knowledge about who's watching you. More knowledge about the information that flows between us — particularly the meta-information about who knows what and where it's going."

In other words, we may not be able to eliminate the intrusive glare shining on citizens of the next century, but the glare just might be rendered harmless through the application of more light aimed in the other direction.[28]

Is greater transparency the solution to the increasing threats to privacy?

REMSBURG V. DOCUSEARCH, INC.

816 A.2d 1001 (N.H. 2003)

DALIANIS, J. . . . [Liam Youens contacted Docusearch and purchased the birth date of Amy Lynn Boyer for a fee. He again contacted Docusearch and placed an order for Boyer's SSN. Docusearch obtained Boyer's SSN from a credit reporting agency and provided it to Youens. Youens then asked for Boyer's employment address. Docusearch hired a subcontractor, Michele Gambino, who obtained it by making a "pretext" phone call to Boyer. Gambino lied about her identity and the purpose of the call, and she obtained the address from Boyer. The address was then given to Youens. Shortly thereafter, Youens went to Boyer's workplace and shot and killed her and then killed himself.]

All persons have a duty to exercise reasonable care not to subject others to an unreasonable risk of harm. Whether a defendant's conduct creates a risk of harm to others sufficiently foreseeable to charge the defendant with a duty to avoid such conduct is a question of law, because "the existence of a duty does not arise solely from the relationship between the parties, but also from the need for protection against reasonably foreseeable harm." Thus, in some cases, a party's actions give rise to a duty. Parties owe a duty to those third parties foreseeably endangered by their conduct with respect to those risks whose likelihood and magnitude make the conduct unreasonably dangerous.

In situations in which the harm is caused by criminal misconduct, however, determining whether a duty exists is complicated by the competing rule "that a private citizen has no general duty to protect others from the criminal attacks of third parties." This rule is grounded in the fundamental unfairness of holding private citizens responsible for the unanticipated criminal acts of third parties, because "[u]nder all ordinary and normal circumstances, in the absence of any reason to expect the contrary, the actor may reasonably proceed upon the assumption that others will obey the law."

---

[28] David Brin, *The Transparent Society* 8-23 (1998).

In certain limited circumstances, however, we have recognized that there are exceptions to the general rule where a duty to exercise reasonable care will arise. We have held that such a duty may arise because: (1) a special relationship exists; (2) special circumstances exist; or (3) the duty has been voluntarily assumed. The special circumstances exception includes situations where there is "an especial temptation and opportunity for criminal misconduct brought about by the defendant." This exception follows from the rule that a party who realizes or should realize that his conduct has created a condition which involves an unreasonable risk of harm to another has a duty to exercise reasonable care to prevent the risk from occurring. The exact occurrence or precise injuries need not have been foreseeable. Rather, where the defendant's conduct has created an unreasonable risk of criminal misconduct, a duty is owed to those foreseeably endangered.

Thus, if a private investigator or information broker's (hereinafter "investigator" collectively) disclosure of information to a client creates a foreseeable risk of criminal misconduct against the third person whose information was disclosed, the investigator owes a duty to exercise reasonable care not to subject the third person to an unreasonable risk of harm. In determining whether the risk of criminal misconduct is foreseeable to an investigator, we examine two risks of information disclosure implicated by this case: stalking and identity theft.

It is undisputed that stalkers, in seeking to locate and track a victim, sometimes use an investigator to obtain personal information about the victims.

Public concern about stalking has compelled all fifty States to pass some form of legislation criminalizing stalking. Approximately one million women and 371,000 men are stalked annually in the United States. Stalking is a crime that causes serious psychological harm to the victims, and often results in the victim experiencing post-traumatic stress disorder, anxiety, sleeplessness, and sometimes, suicidal ideations.

Identity theft, *i.e.*, the use of one person's identity by another, is an increasingly common risk associated with the disclosure of personal information, such as a SSN. A person's SSN has attained the status of a quasi-universal personal identification number. At the same time, however, a person's privacy interest in his or her SSN is recognized by state and federal statutes. . . .

Like the consequences of stalking, the consequences of identity theft can be severe. . . . Victims of identity theft risk the destruction of their good credit histories. This often destroys a victim's ability to obtain credit from any source and may, in some cases, render the victim unemployable or even cause the victim to be incarcerated.

The threats posed by stalking and identity theft lead us to conclude that the risk of criminal misconduct is sufficiently foreseeable so that an investigator has a duty to exercise reasonable care in disclosing a third person's personal information to a client. And we so hold. This is especially true when, as in this case, the investigator does not know the client or the client's purpose in seeking the information. . . .

[The plaintiff also brought an action for intrusion upon seclusion.] A tort action based upon an intrusion upon seclusion must relate to something secret, secluded or private pertaining to the plaintiff. Moreover, liability exists only if the defendant's conduct was such that the defendant should have realized that it would be offensive to persons of ordinary sensibilities.

In addressing whether a person's SSN is something secret, secluded or private, we must determine whether a person has a reasonable expectation of privacy in the number. . . . As noted above, a person's interest in maintaining the privacy of his or her SSN has been recognized by numerous federal and state statutes. As a result, the entities to which this information is disclosed and their employees are bound by legal, and, perhaps, contractual constraints to hold SSNs in confidence to ensure that they remain private. Thus, while a SSN must be disclosed in certain circumstances, a person may reasonably expect that the number will remain private.

Whether the intrusion would be offensive to persons of ordinary sensibilities is ordinarily a question for the fact-finder and only becomes a question of law if reasonable persons can draw only one conclusion from the evidence. The evidence underlying the certified question is insufficient to draw any such conclusion here, and we therefore must leave this question to the fact-finder. In making this determination, the fact-finder should consider "the degree of intrusion, the context, conduct and circumstances surrounding the intrusion as well as the intruder's motives and objectives, the setting into which he intrudes, and the expectations of those whose privacy is invaded." Accordingly, a person whose SSN is obtained by an investigator from a credit reporting agency without the person's knowledge or permission may have a cause of action for intrusion upon seclusion for damages caused by the sale of the SSN, but must prove that the intrusion was such that it would have been offensive to a person of ordinary sensibilities.

We next address whether a person has a cause of action for intrusion upon seclusion where an investigator obtains the person's work address by using a pretextual phone call. We must first establish whether a work address is something secret, secluded or private about the plaintiff.

In most cases, a person works in a public place. "On the public street, or in any other public place, [a person] has no legal right to be alone." . . . Thus, where a person's work address is readily observable by members of the public, the address cannot be private and no intrusion upon seclusion action can be maintained.

[Additionally, the plaintiff brought a cause of action for appropriation.] "One who appropriates to his own use or benefit the name or likeness of another is subject to liability to the other for invasion of his privacy." *Restatement (Second) of Torts* § 652E.

. . . Appropriation is not actionable if the person's name or likeness is published for "purposes other than taking advantage of [the person's] reputation, prestige or other value" associated with the person. Thus, appropriation occurs most often when the person's name or likeness is used to advertise the defendant's product or when the defendant impersonates the person for gain.

An investigator who sells personal information sells the information for the value of the information itself, not to take advantage of the person's reputation or prestige. The investigator does not capitalize upon the goodwill value associated with the information but rather upon the client's willingness to pay for the information. In other words, the benefit derived from the sale in no way relates to the social or commercial standing of the person whose information is sold. Thus, a person whose personal information is sold does not have a cause of action for appropriation against the investigator who sold the information. . . .

NOTES & QUESTIONS

1. *The Scope of the Duty.* The court concludes that Docusearch has a duty to people "foreseeably endangered" by its disclosure of personal information. Is this too broad a duty to impose on those who collect and disseminate personal data? What could Docusearch have done to avoid being negligent in this case? Suppose Jill tells Jack the address of Roe. Jack goes to Roe's house and kills her. Based on *Remsburg*, can Jill be liable?

2. *Tort Liability and the First Amendment.* Does liability for Docusearch implicate the First Amendment?

2. GOVERNANCE BY CONTRACT AND PROMISES

(a) Privacy Policies

Privacy policies are statements made by companies about their practices regarding personal information. Increasingly, companies on the Internet are posting privacy policies, and statutes such as the Gramm-Leach-Bliley Act require certain types of companies (financial institutions, insurance companies, and brokerage companies) to maintain privacy policies.

One of the common provisions of many privacy policies is an "opt-out" provision. An opt-out provision establishes a default rule that the company can use or disclose personal information in the ways it desires so long as the consumer does not indicate otherwise. The consumer must take affirmative steps, such as checking a box, calling the company, or writing a letter, to express her desire to opt out of a particular information use or disclosure. In contrast, an "opt-in" provision establishes a default rule that the company cannot use or disclose personal information without first obtaining the express consent of the individual.

JEFF SOVERN, *OPTING IN, OPTING OUT, OR NO OPTIONS AT ALL: THE FIGHT FOR CONTROL OF PERSONAL INFORMATION*

74 Wash. L. Rev. 1033 (1999)

. . . [F]ew consumers understand how much of their personal information is for sale, although they may have a general idea that there is a trade in personal data and that the specifics about that trade are kept from them. . . .

. . . [C]onsumers cannot protect their personal information when they are unaware of how it is being used by others. . . .

The second reason consumers have not acted to protect their privacy, notwithstanding surveys that suggest considerable consumer concern with confidentiality, has to do with how difficult it is to opt out. . . .

. . . Even if consumers can obtain the information needed to opt out, the cost in time and money of communicating and negotiating with all the relevant information gatherers may be substantial. . . .

Companies may not be eager to offer opt-outs because they may rationally conclude that they will incur costs when consumers opt out, while receiving few offsetting benefits. When consumers exercise the option of having their names deleted, mailing lists shrink and presumably become less valuable. . . .

Because of these added costs, companies might decide that while they must offer an opt-out plan, they do not want consumers to take advantage of it. . . . [C]ompanies that offer opt-outs have an incentive to increase the transaction costs incurred by consumers who opt out. . . .

Companies can increase consumers' transaction costs in opting out in a number of ways. A brochure titled "Privacy Notice," which my local cable company included with its bill, provides an example. This Privacy Notice discussed, among other things, how cable subscribers could write to the company to ask that the company not sell their names and other information to third parties. There are at least four reasons why this particular notice may not be effective in eliciting a response from consumers troubled by the sale of their names to others.

First, the Privacy Notice may be obscured by other information included in the mailing. . . .

The second reason why consumers may not respond to the Privacy Notice is its length. The brochure is four pages long and contains 17 paragraphs, 36 sentences, and 1062 words. . . .

Some companies have gone in the other direction, providing so little information in such vague terms that consumers are unable to discern what they are being told. . . .

A third reason why the Privacy Notice may not be effective stems from its prose. Notwithstanding the Plain Language Law in my home state, computer analysis of the text found it extremely difficult, requiring more than a college education for comprehension. By comparison, a similar analysis of this Article found that it required a lower reading level than that of the Privacy Notice.

Fourth, the Privacy Notice may be ineffective because it does not provide an easy or convenient mechanism for opting out. For example, the Privacy Notice invites consumers who object to the sale of their personal information to write to the cable company in a separate letter. By contrast, cable subscribers desiring to add a new premium channel can do so over the telephone, speaking either to a person or tapping buttons on their telephone, depending on their preference. The more difficult the opt-out process, the less likely consumers are to avail themselves of it. . . .

A third explanation for the failure of consumers to opt out as often as their survey answers might suggest is the consumers themselves. Extensive literature on consumer complaint behavior makes clear that many consumers who are distressed by merchant conduct cannot bring themselves to tell the merchant about it. This inability to communicate might translate into failure by consumers to add their names to opt-out lists. . . .

[Sovern suggests that an opt-in system would be more preferable than an opt-out system.]

One benefit of an opt-in system is that it minimizes transaction costs. While some transaction costs are inevitable in any system in which consumers can opt out or opt in, strategic-behavior transaction costs, at least, can be avoided by using a system which discourages parties from generating such costs. The current system encourages businesses to inflate strategic-behavior costs to increase their own gains, albeit at the expense of consumers and the total surplus from exchange. An opt-in system would encourage businesses to reduce strategic-behavior costs without giving consumers an incentive to increase these costs. Instead of an opt-out situation in which merchants are obligated to provide a message they do not wish consumers to receive, an opt-in regime would harness merchants' efforts in providing a message they want the consumer to receive. . . .

An opt-in system thus increases the likelihood that consumers will choose according to their preferences rather than choosing according to the default. . . .

An opt-in system also increases the prospect that direct mailing would be tailored to what consumers wish to receive, thus benefiting consumers who want to receive some, but not all, solicitations. . . .

The sale of information is troublesome in part because it creates externalities, or costs borne by others. Externalities are created when a person engages in an activity that imposes costs on others but is not required to take those costs into account when deciding whether to pursue the activity. The feelings experienced by consumers whose information is sold and used against their wishes constitute just such externalities. An opt-in system — or an opt-out system in which consumers who object to the trade in their personal information have a genuine opportunity to opt out — can shift costs and thereby "internalize" this externality. To put it another way, consumers could bar the sale of their information unless businesses paid them an amount they deemed adequate, thereby requiring businesses selling personal information to incur a cost otherwise borne by consumers. . . .

A regulated opt-out system is less likely than an opt-in system to solve the problem. Opt-out systems do not give businesses the incentive to minimize consumer transaction costs. Consequently, firms might respond to such regulation by generating formal, legalistic notices that consumers would likely ignore. An opt-out system might thus create only the illusion of a cure.

Accordingly, an opt-in system is preferable, chiefly because it eliminates the incentive firms have to engage in strategic behavior and thus inflate consumer transaction costs. An opt-in system would permit consumers who wish to protect their privacy to do so without incurring transaction costs. Consumers who permit the use of their personal information should also be able to realize their wish easily. Indeed, because firms profit from the use of consumer information, firms would have an incentive to make it as easy as possible for consumers to consent to the use of their personal information. . . . An opt-in system, therefore, seems to offer the best hope of accommodating consumer preferences while minimizing transaction costs. . . .

MICHAEL E. STATEN & FRED H. CATE, *THE IMPACT OF OPT-IN PRIVACY RULES ON RETAIL MARKETS: A CASE STUDY OF MBNA*

52 Duke L.J. 745, 750-51, 766, 770-74, 776 (2003)

To illustrate the costs of moving to an opt-in system, we examine MBNA Corporation, a financial institution that offers consumers a variety of loan and insurance products (primarily credit cards), takes deposits, but operates entirely without a branch network. Incorporated in 1981 and publicly traded since 1991, the company has compiled a stunning growth record in just two decades. As of the end of 2000, the company provided credit cards and other loan products to 51 million consumers, had $89 billion of loans outstanding, and serviced 15 percent of all Visa/MasterCard credit card balances outstanding in the United States.

MBNA's ability to access and use information about potential and existing customers is largely responsible for it becoming the second largest credit card issuer in the United States in less than twenty years. To appreciate the critical role that the sharing of information has played in MBNA's remarkable history, one need only reflect on the challenge of acquiring 51 million customers with no brick-and-mortar stores or branches. Like firms in a variety of businesses, but especially financial services, MBNA harnessed information technology as the engine for establishing and building customer relationships without ever physically meeting its customers. By using direct mail, telephone and, most recently, Internet contacts, the company has reached out to new prospects throughout the population, regardless of where they live, with offers tailored to their individual interests. . . .

At the core of its marketing and targeting strategies is the proposition that consumers who share a common institutional bond or experience will have an affinity for using a card that lets them demonstrate their affiliation each time they use it to pay for a purchase. The affinity for the institution raises the probability that a prospect will be converted to a customer. Equally important, the institution or organization usually maintains a list of members on which MBNA can focus its marketing efforts. Following this "affinity group" marketing strategy, MBNA designs a card product tailored to members of a particular group, negotiates a financial arrangement with the organization for the exclusive rights to market an affinity card to its members, and uses the member list as a source of potential names to contact via direct mail or telemarketing. . . .

Design of new affinity cards is an ongoing process. In 2000 alone, MBNA acquired the endorsements of 459 new groups, including the United States Tennis Association, the Atlanta Braves, National Audubon Society, barnesandnoble.com, and the Thurgood Marshall Scholarship Fund.

Although targeting prospects through affinity groups has proven to be a clever strategy, not every group member is offered a card product. The key to the company's profitability and earnings growth, especially given the rapid growth in the size of the customer base, has been in screening the prospects from each affinity group to identify those likely to be quality customers. Given that MBNA's fundamental business is lending money via an unsecured credit card with a revolving line of credit attached, the company wants to put the card in the hands of customers who will use it, but who will not default on their balances.

Consequently, MBNA uses information to screen prospects both before it makes card offers (the targeting process) and after it receives applications (the underwriting process). . . .

How large a drag does an "explicit-consent" system impose on economic efficiency? According to the U.S. Postal Service, 52 percent of unsolicited mail in this country is never read. If that figure translates to opt-in requests, then more than half of all consumers in an opt-in system would lose the benefits or services that could result from the use of personal information because the mandatory request for consent would never receive their attention. Moreover, even if an unsolicited offer is read, experience with company-specific and industry-wide opt-out lists demonstrates that less than 10 percent of the U.S. population ever opts out of a mailing list — often the figure is less than 3 percent. Indeed, the difficulty (and cost) of obtaining a response of any sort from consumers is the primary drawback of an opt-in approach. . . .

MBNA's core product is the affinity card tailored for and marketed to each of more than 4,700 affinity groups. . . . [T]he foundation of MBNA's affinity strategy is access to the member lists of each of its affinity organizations. This marketing partnership with thousands of member organizations nationwide makes MBNA unique among major credit card issuers and accounts for much of the company's superior financial performance and reputation for outstanding customer service. However, in the absence of an explicit joint-marketing exception in an opt-in law, a third-party opt-in regime could effectively end MBNA's unique direct marketing approach by sharply limiting an organization's ability to share its member list. . . .

Like all major credit card issuers, MBNA uses personal information to increase the chance that its credit card offer will reach an interested and qualified customer. This process greatly reduces the number of solicitations that must be sent to achieve a given target volume of new accounts, thereby reducing the cost of account acquisition. It also reduces the volume of junk mail in the form of card offers sent to consumers who are not qualified. Third-party or affiliate opt-in systems would eliminate MBNA's access to a significant portion of the information that it currently uses to identify which individuals on the member lists it receives would be good prospects for a given credit card or other product. A blanket opt-in system applicable to marketing activities would impose similar limits.

The MBNA direct mail marketing operations obtain and consider about 800 million consumer "leads" during the course of a year. The vast majority of these leads are names that appear on affinity group member lists (e.g., university alumni groups and professional associations), or names of consumers who are customers of institutions that have endorsed MBNA's credit card product. Because this is an annual figure, many names appear more than once because the individuals are on more than one list acquired during the course of a year, or may be considered in conjunction with a specific group's marketing campaign several times during the year. The most creditworthy names among them may receive multiple solicitations during the year.

MBNA does not wish to mail to all names on the list. Not all are equally likely to respond to a solicitation, nor will all meet the credit underwriting standards for a particular card product. In 2000, the MBNA direct marketing budget supported approximately 400 million mailings of card offers. The challenge to the company in managing the acquisition of new accounts is to cull the "lead list" of 800 million prospect names to identify and target the 400 million direct mail solicitations to consumers who are most likely to become new cardholders. Generally speaking, MBNA has developed a set of targeting criteria such that names reaching the final mailing list of 400 million: (1) are most likely to respond to the offer and the use of the credit card, and (2) are most likely to meet MBNA's creditworthiness standards for the card.

MBNA prepares hundreds of distinct solicitations throughout the year for its various affinity groups. As part of the targeting process for each new solicitation, the prospect list is scrubbed via comparison to a series of "suppression files" that the company maintains and routinely updates. These files pull information about either individuals or addresses from a variety of internal and external data sources. A few examples of the specific criteria illustrate the process.

[The authors describe how MBNA has proprietary response models to help it determine which customers are most likely to respond to its offer. It uses credit history information to find individuals who are likely to repay, but, at the same time, do not have "extraordinary creditworthiness" and are, hence, likely to be frequently solicited by card issuers and unlikely to respond to an MBNA offer.]

The bottom line from the culling process is that approximately 40 percent of the eight hundred million names are suppressed. The initial lead list is typically reduced by an additional 10 percent through a combination of eliminating duplicate records, suppressing undeliverable addresses, and dropping customer names that appear on various "do not mail" lists that record customer preferences not to be solicited. . . . The approximately four hundred million names remaining on the lead list receive targeted direct mail offers with the endorsement of the affinity group to which they belong. . . .

MBNA's proprietary response models indicate that its use of information in these three categories to cull likely prospects accounts for approximately a 19 percent reduction in names from the annual prospect list. In other words, by targeting offers under current rules, about 150 million names on the prospect list during the course of a typical annual solicitation cycle do not receive solicitations, because the direct mail piece would otherwise reach a consumer who was either not interested or not qualified for the card product. . . .

[Under an opt-in approach,] approximately 550 million names would remain, instead of 400 million under the current rules. Lacking the information necessary to further distinguish good prospects from poor prospects, the company's targeting efficiency would be impaired.

MBNA would have two choices. It could increase its direct mail volume to send solicitations to all 550 million names remaining on the prospect list after the culling process, or it could arbitrarily remove 150 million names from the list after the culling process so that its direct mail volume remained unchanged at 400 million. Under either scenario, approximately 27 percent of the solicitations (150 million of 550 million) would go to consumers who were less interested in, and/or less qualified for, the offer, and who would have been dropped from the target list had MBNA been allowed to access and use the information on which its presently relies under current privacy rules. . . .

Although MBNA's actual response rate and cost per account booked is proprietary, we can illustrate the impact of the decline by utilizing the credit card industry average response rate to direct mail solicitations for 2000, which was 0.6 percent. For every 100 million solicitations mailed to individuals under the opt-in scenario, only 492 thousand new accounts would be booked, as compared to 600 thousand if the offers were targeted under existing rules, an 18 percent reduction in new accounts for the same expenditure on direct mail solicitations. Of course, the higher cost per account booked is borne not only by MBNA, but by MBNA's customers as well, in the form of higher prices, reduced benefits, diminished service, and higher acceptance standards for new credit products.

But, the negative impact does not stop there. Regardless of whether MBNA's response to opt-in is to mail more solicitations or mail the same number to a less-targeted prospect list, under either scenario, the recipient group of four hundred million individuals will — on average — be more risky and less profitable than MBNA's target group reached under the current rules. As a result, MBNA's delinquency and charge-off rates will rise, relative to its current experience, thereby imposing additional costs that will be passed along to all of MBNA's customers. Card usage will also be affected by booking cardholders who are less likely to use the card.

NOTES & QUESTIONS

1. ***Opt out vs. Opt in.*** Do you agree with Sovern that an opt-in policy is more efficient than an opt-out policy? Do you think that an opt-in policy is feasible? Are the views of Staten and Cate convincing on this score? Do you think opt out or opt in should be required by law?
2. ***Internalizing Costs.*** Staten and Cate claim that MBNA's business model will be threatened by opt in. This business model relies in part, however, on sending out 400 million of mostly unwanted solicitations for credit in order to receive a 0.6 percent response rate. In other words, this model views as an externality the added cost of sorting through mail for 99.4 percent of those individuals solicited. Should MBNA be obliged to internalize these costs?

(b) Contract Law

A privacy policy can be thought of as a type of contract, though the terms are typically dictated by the company and are non-negotiable. Consider the following advice of Scott Killingsworth to the drafters of website privacy policies:

> Considering enforcement leads to the question: what is the legal effect of a privacy policy? As between the website and the user, a privacy policy bears all of the earmarks of a contract, but perhaps one enforceable only at the option of the user. It is no stretch to regard the policy as an offer to treat information in specified ways, inviting the user's acceptance, evidenced by using the site or submitting the information. The website's promise and the user's use of the site and submission of personal data are each sufficient consideration to support a contractual obligation. Under this analysis, users would have the right to sue and

seek all available remedies for breach of the privacy policy, without the need for private rights of action under such regulatory statutes as the FTC Act.[29]

Privacy policies can also be viewed simply as notices that warn consumers about the use of their personal information. Assuming that these notices are subject to change as business practices evolve, how effective are privacy policies as a means to protect privacy?

IN RE NORTHWEST AIRLINES PRIVACY LITIGATION

2004 WL 1278459 (D. Minn. 2004) (not reported in F. Supp. 2d)

MAGNUSON, J. . . . Plaintiffs are customers of Defendant Northwest Airlines, Inc. ("Northwest"). After September 11, 2001, the National Aeronautical and Space Administration ("NASA") requested that Northwest provide NASA with certain passenger information in order to assist NASA in studying ways to increase airline security. Northwest supplied NASA with passenger name records ("PNRs"), which are electronic records of passenger information. PNRs contain information such as a passenger's name, flight number, credit card data, hotel reservation, car rental, and any traveling companions.

Plaintiffs contend that Northwest's actions constitute violations of the Electronic Communications Privacy Act ("ECPA"), 18 U.S.C. § 2701 *et seq.,* the Fair Credit Reporting Act ("FCRA"), 15 U.S.C. § 1681, and Minnesota's Deceptive Trade Practices Act ("DTPA"), Minn. Stat. § 325D.44, and also constitute invasion of privacy, trespass to property, negligent misrepresentation, breach of contract, and breach of express warranties. The basis for most of Plaintiffs' claims is that Northwest's website contained a privacy policy that stated that Northwest would not share customers' information except as necessary to make customers' travel arrangements. Plaintiffs contend that Northwest's provision of PNRs to NASA violated Northwest's privacy policy, giving rise to the legal claims noted above.

Northwest has now moved to dismiss the Amended Consolidated Class Action Complaint (hereinafter "Amended Complaint"). . . .

The ECPA prohibits a person or entity from

> (1) intentionally access[ing] without authorization a facility through which an electronic communication service is provided; or
> (2) intentionally exceeds an authorization to access that facility; and thereby obtains, alters, or prevents authorized access to a wire or electronic communication while it is in electronic storage in such system shall be punished. 18 U.S.C. § 2701(a).

Plaintiffs argue that Northwest's access to its own electronic communications service is limited by its privacy policy, and that Northwest's provision of PNRs to NASA violated that policy and thus constituted unauthorized access to the "facility through which an electronic communication service is provided" within the meaning of this section. Plaintiffs also allege that Northwest violated § 2702

---

[29] Scott Killingsworth, *Minding Your Own Business: Privacy Policies in Principle and in Practice*, 7 J. Intell. Prop. L. 57, 91-92 (1999).

of the ECPA, which states that "a person or entity providing an electronic communications service to the public shall not knowingly divulge to any person or entity the contents of a communication while in electronic storage by that service." 18 U.S.C. § 2702(a)(1). Northwest argues first that it cannot violate § 2702 because it is not a "person or entity providing an electronic communications service to the public." . . .

Defining electronic communications service to include online merchants or service providers like Northwest stretches the ECPA too far. Northwest is not an internet service provider. . . .

Similarly, Northwest's conduct as outlined in the Amended Complaint does not constitute a violation of § 2701. Plaintiffs' claim is that Northwest improperly disclosed the information in PNRs to NASA. Section 2701 does not prohibit improper disclosure of information. Rather, this section prohibits improper access to an electronic communications service provider or the information contained on that service provider. . . .

Finally, Northwest argues that Plaintiffs' remaining claims fail to state a claim on which relief can be granted. These claims are: trespass to property, intrusion upon seclusion, breach of contract, and breach of express warranties.

To state a claim for trespass to property, Plaintiffs must demonstrate that they owned or possessed property, that Northwest wrongfully took that property, and that Plaintiffs were damaged by the wrongful taking. Plaintiffs contend that the information contained in the PNRs was Plaintiffs' property and that, by providing that information to NASA, Northwest wrongfully took that property.

As a matter of law, the PNRs were not Plaintiffs' property. Plaintiffs voluntarily provided some information that was included in the PNRs. It may be that the information Plaintiffs provided to Northwest was Plaintiffs' property. However, when that information was compiled and combined with other information to form a PNR, the PNR itself became Northwest's property. Northwest cannot wrongfully take its own property. Thus, Plaintiffs' claim for trespass fails. . . .

Intrusion upon seclusion exists when someone "intentionally intrudes, physically or otherwise, upon the solitude or seclusion of another or his private affairs or concerns . . . if the intrusion would be highly offensive to a reasonable person." . . . In this instance, Plaintiffs voluntarily provided their personal information to Northwest. Moreover, although Northwest had a privacy policy for information included on the website, Plaintiffs do not contend that they actually read the privacy policy prior to providing Northwest with their personal information. Thus, Plaintiffs' expectation of privacy was low. Further, the disclosure here was not to the public at large, but rather was to a government agency in the wake of a terrorist attack that called into question the security of the nation's transportation system. Northwest's motives in disclosing the information cannot be questioned. Taking into account all of the factors listed above, the Court finds as a matter of law that the disclosure of Plaintiffs' personal information would not be highly offensive to a reasonable person and that Plaintiffs have failed to state a claim for intrusion upon seclusion. . . .

Northwest contends that the privacy policy on Northwest's website does not, as a matter of law, constitute a unilateral contract, the breach of which entitles Plaintiffs to damages. Northwest also argues that, even if the privacy policy constituted a contract or express warranty, Plaintiffs' contract and warranty claims fail because Plaintiffs have failed to plead any contract damages. . . .

Plaintiffs' rely on the following statement from Northwest's website as the basis for their contract and warranty claims:

> When you reserve or purchase travel services through Northwest Airlines nwa.com Reservations, we provide only the relevant information required by the car rental agency, hotel, or other involved third party to ensure the successful fulfillment of your travel arrangements. . . .

The usual rule in contract cases is that "general statements of policy are not contractual." . . .

The privacy statement on Northwest's website did not constitute a unilateral contract. The language used vests discretion in Northwest to determine when the information is "relevant" and which "third parties" might need that information. Moreover, absent an allegation that Plaintiffs actually read the privacy policy, not merely the general allegation that Plaintiffs "relied on" the policy, Plaintiffs have failed to allege an essential element of a contract claim: that the alleged "offer" was accepted by Plaintiffs. Plaintiffs' contract and warranty claims fail as a matter of law.

Even if the privacy policy was sufficiently definite and Plaintiffs had alleged that they read the policy before giving their information to Northwest, it is likely that Plaintiffs' contract and warranty claims would fail as a matter of law. Defendants point out that Plaintiffs have failed to allege any contractual damages arising out of the alleged breach. . . .

[The case is dismissed.]

NOTES & QUESTIONS

1. ***Breach of Contract.*** In *Dyer v. Northwest Airlines Corp.,* 334 F. Supp. 2d 1196 (D.N.D. 2004), another action involving Northwest Airlines' disclosure of passenger records to the government, the court reached a similar conclusion on the plaintiffs' breach of contract claim:

> To sustain a breach of contract claim, the Plaintiffs must demonstrate (1) the existence of a contract; (2) breach of the contract; and (3) damages which flow from the breach. . . .
> . . . [T]he Court finds the Plaintiffs' breach of contract claim fails as a matter of law. First, broad statements of company policy do not generally give rise to contract claims. . . . Second, nowhere in the complaint are the Plaintiffs alleged to have ever logged onto Northwest Airlines' website and accessed, read, understood, actually relied upon, or otherwise considered Northwest Airlines' privacy policy. Finally, even if the privacy policy was sufficiently definite and the Plaintiffs had alleged they did read the policy prior to providing personal information to Northwest Airlines, the Plaintiffs have failed to allege any contractual damages arising out of the alleged breach.

2. ***Damages.*** In *In re Jet Blue Airways Corp. Privacy Litigation*, 379 F. Supp. 2d 299 (E.D.N.Y. 2005), a group of plaintiffs sued Jet Blue Airlines for breach of

contract for sharing passenger records with the government. The court granted Jet Blue's motion to dismiss:

> An action for breach of contract under New York law requires proof of four elements: (1) the existence of a contract, (2) performance of the contract by one party, (3) breach by the other party, and (4) damages. . . .
>
> JetBlue . . . argues that plaintiffs have failed to meet their pleading requirement with respect to damages, citing an absence of any facts in the Amended Complaint to support this element of the claim. Plaintiffs' sole allegation on the element of contract damages consists of the statement that JetBlue's breach of the company privacy policy injured plaintiffs and members of the class and that JetBlue is therefore liable for "actual damages in an amount to be determined at trial." . . . At oral argument, when pressed to identify the "injuries" or damages referred to in the Amended Complaint, counsel for plaintiffs stated that the "contract damage could be the loss of privacy," acknowledging that loss of privacy "may" be a contract damage. It is apparent based on the briefing and oral argument held in this case that the sparseness of the damages allegations is a direct result of plaintiffs' inability to plead or prove any actual contract damages. As plaintiffs' counsel concedes, the only damage that can be read into the present complaint is a loss of privacy. At least one recent case has specifically held that this is not a damage available in a breach of contract action. *See Trikas v. Universal Card Services Corp.,* 351 F. Supp. 2d 37 (E.D.N.Y. 2005). This holding naturally follows from the well-settled principle that "recovery in contract, unlike recovery in tort, allows only for economic losses flowing directly from the breach."
>
> Plaintiffs allege that in a second amended complaint, they could assert as a contract damage the loss of the economic value of their information, but while that claim sounds in economic loss, the argument ignores the nature of the contract asserted. . . . [T]he "purpose of contract damages is to put a plaintiff in the same economic position he or she would have occupied had the contract been fully performed." Plaintiffs may well have expected that in return for providing their personal information to JetBlue and paying the purchase price, they would obtain a ticket for air travel and the promise that their personal information would be safeguarded consistent with the terms of the privacy policy. They had no reason to expect that they would be compensated for the "value" of their personal information. In addition, there is absolutely no support for the proposition that the personal information of an individual JetBlue passenger had any value for which that passenger could have expected to be compensated. . . . . There is likewise no support for the proposition that an individual passenger's personal information has or had any compensable value in the economy at large.

If you were the plaintiffs' attorney, how would you go about establishing the plaintiffs' injury? Is there any cognizable harm when an airline violates its privacy policy by providing passenger information to the government?

3. ***Breach of Confidentiality Tort.*** Would the plaintiffs have a cause of action based on the breach of confidentiality tort?

4. ***Enforcing Privacy Policies as Contracts Against Consumers.*** Suppose privacy policies were enforceable as contracts. Would this be beneficial to consumers? It might not be, Allyson Haynes argues:

> [T]here is a distinct possibility that as website operators grow savvier with respect to the law, they will respond to the lack of substantive privacy protection (and lack of consumer awareness) by including in privacy policies terms that are not favorable to consumers.

On the flip side of consumers seeking to enforce privacy policies as contracts, companies might also desire to hold customers to be contractually bound to the companies' privacy policies. Would a privacy policy be enforceable as a contract against the customer? Haynes contends:

> [P]articularly in cases where consumers are deemed to have assented to privacy policies by virtue of their presence on the site or by giving information without affirmatively clicking acceptance, the consumer has a good argument that he or she did not assent to the privacy policy, preventing the formation of a binding contract, and preventing the website from enforcing any of its terms against the consumer.[30]

(c) FTC Enforcement

Beyond private law actions such as contract and promissory estoppel, the promises that companies make regarding their privacy practices can be enforced by the government through public law. Private law actions are initiated on behalf of harmed individuals, who can obtain monetary or other redress for their injuries. In contrast, public law actions are initiated by government agencies or officials, and they typically involve fines and penalties.

In 1995, Congress and privacy experts first asked the Federal Trade Commission (FTC) to become involved with consumer privacy issues.[31] Since 1998, the FTC has maintained the position that the use or dissemination of personal information in a manner contrary to a posted privacy policy is a deceptive practice under the FTC Act, 15 U.S.C. § 45. The Act prohibits "unfair or deceptive acts or practices in or affecting commerce." An "unfair or deceptive" act or practice is one that "causes or is likely to cause substantial injury to consumers which is not reasonably avoidable by consumers themselves and not outweighed by countervailing benefits to consumers or to competition." § 45(n).

The FTC does not have jurisdiction over all companies. Exempt from the FTC's jurisdiction are many types of financial institutions, airlines, telecommunications carriers, and other types of entities. § 45(a)(2). The Act authorizes the FTC to bring civil actions for penalties up to $10,000 for a knowing violation of the Act. § 45(m)(1)(A). Further, the FTC can obtain injunctive remedies. § 53. The Act does not provide for private causes of action; only the FTC can enforce the Act. Since it began enforcing the Act for breaches of privacy policies in 1998, the FTC has brought a number of actions, most of which have settled. Some of these enforcement cases concern companies not

---

[30] Allyson W. Haynes, *Online Privacy Policies: Contracting Away Control Over Personal Information?*, 111 Penn. St. L. Rev. 587, 612, 618 (2007).

[31] Letter from EPIC Director Marc Rotenberg to FTC Commissioner Christine Varney, Dec. 14, 1995.

keeping their privacy promises. As a more complicated example of a violation of the FTC Act, consider *In the Matter of Vision I Properties.*

IN THE MATTER OF VISION I PROPERTIES

2005 WL 1274741 (F.T.C. 2005)

[Vision I Properties licensed shopping cart software and provided related services to small online retail merchants through a website, www.cartmanager.com. The company's software created customizable shopping cart pages for client merchants' websites. The resulting pages resided on websites managed by Vision I Properties, but resembled the other pages on merchants' websites.

Some of the client merchants using this company's shopping cart software and services published various privacy policies on their websites. In its complaint, the FTC excerpted some of these privacy policies, including one that stated: "PRIVACY POLICY: It's simple. We don't sell, trade, or lend any information on our customers or visitors to anyone."

In fact, however, Vision I Properties in January 2003 rented consumers' personal information collected through its shopping cart and check out pages at client merchant sites. The FTC complaint noted: "Such personal information includes the name, address, phone number, and purchase history of nearly one million consumers. This personal information was used by third parties to send direct mail and make telemarketing calls to consumers who shopped at merchant sites using the software."

For the FTC, it was reasonable for consumers to rely on merchants' privacy policies. Moreover, Vision I Properties did not adequately inform merchants of its information sharing. It did assert, however, in its online license agreement that it would retain "full ownership of all data submitted by either Merchant or Purchaser." The FTC dismissed this statement, however, as (1) "buried in the middle of the online agreement" and also as (2) lacking an explanation of how Vision I Properties intended "to use the information or that such use may conflict with the merchants' privacy policies."

On April 19, 2005, the FTC and Vision I properties settled the case and the FTC issued a Decision and Order.]

DECISION AND ORDER

The Federal Trade Commission having initiated an investigation of certain acts and practices of the Respondent named in the caption hereof, and the Respondent having been furnished thereafter with a copy of a draft Complaint that the Bureau of Consumer Protection proposed to present to the Commission for its consideration and which, if issued by the Commission, would charge the Respondent with violation of the Federal Trade Commission Act. . . .

I.

IT IS ORDERED that Respondent, directly or through any corporation, subsidiary, division, or other device, in connection with the collection of personally identifiable information from or about consumers, shall not make, expressly or by implication, any false or misleading representation regarding the collection, use, or disclosure of personally identifiable information.

II.

IT IS FURTHER ORDERED that Respondent, directly or through any corporation, subsidiary, division, or other device, shall not sell, rent, or disclose to any third party for marketing purposes any personally identifiable information that was collected from consumers through shopping cart software used at a merchant customer's Web site prior to the date of service of this Order.

III.

IT IS FURTHER ORDERED that Respondent, directly or through any corporation, subsidiary, division, or other device, shall not sell, rent, or disclose to any third party for marketing purposes any personally identifiable information collected from consumers through shopping cart or other software used at a merchant customer's Web site after the date of service of this Order unless, prior to the date such information was collected, Respondent took one of the following two actions:

A. Provided to the merchant customer a clear and conspicuous written notice of its information practices and obtained from the merchant customer a written certification stating: (1) that the merchant customer received such notice; and (2) either (a) that its posted privacy policy states that consumers' information may be sold, rented, or disclosed to third parties, or (b) that it provides a clear and conspicuous disclosure, before any personally identifiable information is collected from consumers through Respondent's shopping cart or other software, stating that the consumer is leaving the merchant customer's Web site and entering Respondent's Web site, and that Respondent's site is governed by Respondent's own privacy policy.

The written notice to merchants required by this Paragraph shall be labeled "Important Notice to Merchants from CartManager" and must: (1) state that Respondent intends to sell, rent, or disclose such information; (2) identify the types or categories of any entities to which such information will be disclosed; (3) advise the merchant customer that it may be liable for any misrepresentations it makes about the use or disclosure of information collected from consumers at its Web site, including through software used at the site; and (4) contain no other information; OR

B. Provided a clear and conspicuous disclosure on the page(s) through which it collected such information stating: (1) that the consumer is on Respondent's Web site, and (2) that information provided by the consumer to Respondent will be used, sold, rented, or disclosed to third parties for marketing purposes.

IV.

IT IS FURTHER ORDERED that within five (5) days of the date of service of this Order, Respondent shall pay $9,101.63 to the United States Treasury as disgorgement. Such payment shall be by cashier's check or certified check made payable to the Treasurer of the United States. In the event of any default in payment, which default continues for more than ten (10) days beyond the due date of payment, Respondent shall also pay interest as computed under 28 U.S.C. § 1961, which shall accrue on the unpaid balance from the date of default until the date the balance is fully paid.

V.

IT IS FURTHER ORDERED that Respondent Vision One and its successors and assigns shall, for a period of five (5) years after the last date of dissemination of any representation covered by this Order, maintain and upon request make available to the Federal Trade Commission for inspection and copying a print or electronic copy of all documents demonstrating their compliance with the terms and provisions of this Order, including, but not limited to:

A. A sample copy of each different privacy statement or communication relating to the collection of personally identifiable information containing representations about how personally identifiable information will be used and/or disclosed. Each Web page copy shall be dated and contain the full URL of the Web page where the material was posted online. Electronic copies shall include all text and graphics files, audio scripts, and other computer files used in presenting the information on the Web; *provided, however*, that after creation of any Web page or screen in compliance with this Order, Respondent shall not be required to retain a print or electronic copy of any amended Web page or screen to the extent that the amendment does not affect Respondent's compliance obligations under this Order;

B. A sample copy of each different document containing the disclosures required by Part III.A. of this Order; a list of all merchant customers who received each different document containing such disclosures; all communications by merchant customers in response to such disclosures, including all written certifications received pursuant to Part III.A. and any complaints received from merchant customers; and a sample copy of each different document containing the disclosures required by Part III.B.; and

C. All invoices, communications, and records relating to the disclosure to third parties of personally identifiable information collected through merchant customer Web sites. . . .

VII.

IT IS FURTHER ORDERED that Respondent Vision One and its successors and assigns shall notify the Commission at least thirty (30) days prior to any change in the corporation(s) that may affect compliance obligations arising under this Order, including, but not limited to, a dissolution, assignment, sale, merger, or other action that would result in the emergence of a successor corporation; the creation or dissolution of a subsidiary, parent, or affiliate that engages in any acts or practices subject to this Order; the proposed filing of a bankruptcy petition; or a change in the corporate name or address. . . .

IX.

This Order will terminate on April 19, 2025, or twenty (20) years from the most recent date that the United States or the Federal Trade Commission files a complaint (with or without an accompanying consent decree) in federal court alleging any violation of the Order, whichever comes later. . . .

NOTES & QUESTIONS

1. ***Responsibility for Violating Another Company's Privacy Policy?*** In a typical "broken promise" privacy case, the FTC charges a company with breaking its own promise to provide certain kinds of privacy practices or protections. In contrast, the FTC in *Vision I Properties* was faced with a situation in which the behavior of Vision I broke the privacy promises of other parties (the merchants). Vision I Properties does not seem to be in privity with the end customers; it is a B2B (business-to-business) company rather than a B2C (business-to-consumer) company.

    To be sure, Vision I Properties prevented its merchant customers from delivering on their privacy policies. Yet, Vision I Properties had a provision in its contracts with the merchants explicitly claiming ownership of all information collected with use of its software. By pursuing an action against Vision I Properties, the FTC was claiming that its behavior was an unfair or deceptive trade practice. But if a merchant has a privacy policy, why isn't the burden on the merchant to police the behavior of the B2B entities with whom it contracts? Shouldn't the merchants be liable for lack of care in reading their contracts?

2. ***Damages.*** In the *Matter of Vision I Properties,* the FTC assesses damages of $9,101.63 "as disgorgement." A disgorgement measure of damages looks to the unjust enrichment of a defendant and requires her to surrender a profit improperly or illegally obtained. Is the proper measure of damages in this case the disgorgement of profits that Vision I Properties obtained through its practices in renting the information it collected through its shopping cart software?

3. ***Broken Promises:*** **Liberty Financial.** In *In re Liberty Financial Cos.,* No. 9823522, 1999 FTC LEXIS 99 (May 6, 1999), the FTC charged the operator of a website for child and teen investors with falsely promising that the personal information it collected in a survey would be kept anonymous. The website gathered data about the child and family's finances, but instead of being anonymously maintained, it was kept in an identifiable form. Liberty Financial settled with the FTC, agreeing to refrain from making future misrepresentations, to post a privacy notice on its website, and to obtain

parental consent prior to gathering personal data from children. FTC commissioners approved the settlement 4–0.

4. **_Deceptive Data Collection:_ ReverseAuction.** In *FTC v. ReverseAuction.com, Inc.*, No. 00-CV-32 (D.D.C. Jan. 6, 2000), the FTC charged ReverseAuction.com with improperly obtaining personal information from eBay customers. ReverseAuction then used the information to spam eBay customers promoting its own auction website. The message falsely stated to the recipients that their eBay user IDs would expire soon. The FTC charged that ReverseAuction's practice was both unfair and deceptive.

ReverseAuction settled, agreeing to be barred from making future misrepresentations. Further, ReverseAuction had to notify the consumers who received its spam and inform them that its eBay user IDs will not expire and that eBay did not authorize ReverseAuction's spam. Consumers also can delete their personal information from ReverseAuction's database. ReverseAuction must also display its own privacy policy on its website. FTC commissioners voted 5–0 to approve the settlement. However, two commissioners, Orson Swindle and Thomas B. Leary, agreeing that ReverseAuction acted deceptively, disagreed that ReverseAuction acted unfairly:

> We do not, however, support the unfairness theory in Count One. The Commission has no authority to declare an act or practice unfair unless it "causes or is likely to cause *substantial injury* to consumers which is not reasonably avoidable by consumers themselves and not outweighed by countervailing benefits to consumers or to competition." 15 U.S.C. § 45(n) (emphasis added). . . .
>
> We do not say that privacy concerns can never support an unfairness claim. In this case, however, ReverseAuction's use of eBay members' information to send them e-mail did not cause substantial enough injury to meet the statutory standard. . . .
>
> The injury in this case was caused by deception: that is, by ReverseAuction's failure to honor its express commitments. It is not necessary or appropriate to plead a less precise theory.
>
> . . . The unfairness theory . . . posits substantial injury stemming from ReverseAuction's use of information readily available to millions of eBay members to send commercial e-mail. This standard for substantial injury overstates the appropriate level of government-enforced privacy protection on the Internet, and provides no rationale for when unsolicited commercial e-mail is unfair and when it is not.

One commissioner, Mozelle W. Thompson, issued a separate statement to justify the unfairness theory:

> I believe that ReverseAuction's behavior caused substantial injury to members of the eBay community, that the injury could not have been avoided by those members, and it was not outweighed by countervailing benefits. I believe the harm caused in this case is especially significant because it not only breached the privacy expectation of each and every eBay member, it also undermined consumer confidence in eBay and diminishes the electronic marketplace for all its participants. This injury is exacerbated because consumer concern about

privacy and confidence in the electronic marketplace are such critical issues at this time.

5. ***Retroactive Privacy Policy Changes:*** **Gateway Learning Corp.** When Gateway Learning Corp. collected personal information from its consumers, its privacy policy stated that it would not sell, rent, or loan personal information to third parties unless people consented. Subsequently, Gateway altered its privacy policy to allow the renting of personal information to third parties without informing customers or obtaining their consent. The FTC filed a complaint alleging that this practice was an "unfair" act. *See In re Gateway Learning Corp.,* No. C-4120 (Sept. 10, 2004). Gateway settled with the FTC, agreeing to avoid making deceptive claims or retroactively change its privacy policy without consumer consent. Gateway agreed to pay $4,608, the amount it earned from renting the information.

Suppose a company puts the following line in its privacy policy: "Please be aware that we may change this policy at any time." Would this allow for the retroactive application of a revised policy? Or is there an argument that even with a statement such as this one, the revised policy could not be applied retroactively?

6. ***Privacy Promises and Bankruptcy:*** **Toysmart** *and* **Amazon.com.** In *FTC v. Toysmart.com, LLC,* Civ. Action No. 00-11341-RGS (July 21, 2000), an Internet toy retailer, Toysmart.com, went bankrupt in 2000. One of the company's most important assets was its database of personal information — it had a customer list with over 200,000 individual names. This list included addresses, names and ages of children, purchasing information, and a toy wish list. Toysmart was a member of TRUSTe, an e-commerce industry privacy protection organization that establishes rules for privacy policies and permits companies that follow them to display TRUSTe's privacy seal. Toysmart had agreed to follow TRUSTe's guidelines and had displayed the TRUSTe seal on its website.

In its privacy policy, Toysmart promised: "Personal information voluntarily submitted by visitors to our site, such as name, address, billing information and shopping preferences, is never shared with a third party. All information obtained by toysmart.com is used only to personalize your experience online." To pay back creditors, Toysmart attempted to sell its database of personal information.

The FTC filed a complaint objecting to this practice and argued that such a sale, in light of Toysmart's promises never to sell its customer's personal information, would be a deceptive practice. The FTC approved a settlement by a 3–2 vote restricting how Toysmart could sell its database. The settlement states that:

> The Debtor shall only assign or sell its Customer Information as part of the sale of its Goodwill and only to a Qualified Buyer approved by the Bankruptcy Court. In the process of approving any sale of the Customer Information, the Bankruptcy Court shall require that the Qualified Buyer agree to and comply with the terms of this Stipulation.

The Qualified Buyer shall treat Customer Information in accordance with the terms of the Privacy Statement and shall be responsible for any violation by it following the date of purchase. Among other things, the Qualified Buyer shall use Customer Information only to fulfill customer orders and to personalize customers' experience on the Web site, and shall not disclose, sell or transfer Customer Information to any Third Party.

If the Qualified Buyer materially changes the Privacy Statement, prior notice will be posted on the Web site. Any such material change in policy shall apply only to information collected following the change in policy. The Customer Information shall be governed by the Privacy Statement, unless the consumer provides affirmative consent ("opt-in") to the previously collected information being governed by the new policy. . . .

Is this settlement adequate to resolve the problems raised by the FTC in its complaint? As a postscript, one should note that the settlement attracted the support of Toysmart's creditors, since it would allow the sale of the database to certain purchasers, and hence could be used to pay back the creditors. However, in August 2000, Judge Carol Kenner of the U.S. Bankruptcy Court rejected the settlement because there were currently no offers on the table to buy the database, and it would hurt the creditors to restrict the sale to certain types of purchasers without first having a potential buyer. In February 2001, Judge Kenner agreed to let Toysmart sell its customer database to Disney, the primary shareholder, for $50,000. Disney agreed, as part of the deal, to destroy the list.

The Toysmart bankruptcy also led Amazon.com, the Internet's largest retailer, to change its privacy policy. Prior to the Toysmart case, Amazon's privacy policy provided:

Amazon.com does not sell, trade, or rent your personal information to others. We may choose to do so in the future with trustworthy third parties, but you can tell us not to by sending a blank e-mail message to never@amazon.com.

In its new policy, Amazon.com stated:

Information about our customers is an important part of our business, and we are not in the business of selling it to others. We share customer information only with the subsidiaries Amazon.com, Inc., controls and as described below. . . .

As we continue to develop our business, we might sell or buy stores or assets. In such transactions, customer information generally is one of the transferred business assets. Also, in the unlikely event that Amazon.com, Inc., or substantially all of its assets are acquired, customer information will of course be one of the transferred assets. . . .

Amazon.com's new policy was criticized by some privacy organizations. One of the criticisms was that the policy did not provide an opt-out right. Suppose Amazon.com went bankrupt and decided to sell all of its customer data. Can it sell data supplied by consumers under the old policy? Can the new policy apply retroactively?

7. ***Bankruptcy: Property Rights vs. Contract Rights.*** Edward Janger proposes that a property rights regime (as opposed to the contractual rights of a privacy

policy) will best protect the privacy of personal data when companies possessing such data go bankrupt:

> Property rules are viewed as reflecting undivided entitlements. They allocate, as Carol Rose puts it, the "whole meatball" to the "owner." Liability rules, by contrast are viewed as dividing an entitlement between two parties. One party holds the right, but the other party is given the option to take the right and compensate the right holder for the deprivation (to breach and pay damages). . . .
>
> Propertization has some crucial benefits, but it also has some serious costs. Both the bankruptcy and non-bankruptcy treatment of privacy policies turn on whether a privacy policy creates a right enforceable only through civil damages, or a right with the status of property. If bankruptcy courts treat privacy policies solely as contract obligations [liability rule], the debtor will be free to breach (or reject) the contract in bankruptcy. Any damage claim will be treated as a prepetition claim, paid, if at all, at a significant discount. Consumer expectations (contractual or otherwise) of privacy are likely to be defeated. By contrast, if personal information is deemed property subject to an encumbrance, then the property interest must be respected, or to use the bankruptcy term, "adequately protected."

In other words, Janger contends that giving individuals property rights in their personal data will provide more protection than giving individuals contract rights in the event a company goes bankrupt. Janger further argues that property rights alone will not be sufficient. Property rights must be "muddy" rather than "crystalline":

> . . . A crystalline rule places all of the relevant rights firmly in the hand of the entitlement holder or "owner." A muddier standard leaves the right subject to challenge by a competing claimant. Crystalline rules situate decisionmaking and norm-generating authority in either the legislature or the market. Muddy rules lead to decisions made and legal norms articulated by judges. . . .
>
> . . . [M]uddy standards force parties ex ante to recognize that they might have to justify their contractual terms and negotiating behavior ex post. This attribute of muddy rules operates to enforce behavioral norms in ways that crystalline rules do not. Efforts to resolve norm-based disputes force disclosure of information related to the norm. This norm-based information forcing effect has both public and private implications. Muddy rules may improve the contracting behavior of parties, but muddy rules also serve a more public purpose. Muddy rules force information into the legal system about transactions. They allow judges, and the judiciary, to develop rules incrementally, through common law reasoning, and inform legislative decisionmaking by placing disputes on the record. But muddiness alone is not enough. The benefits of the muddy liability rule may evaporate entirely when a debtor goes bankrupt. These behavior regulating and information forcing effects of muddy rules are maximized only when the muddy rule is given the status of property.[32]

---

[32] Edward J. Janger, *Muddy Property: Generating and Protecting Information Privacy Norms in Bankruptcy*, 44 Wm. & Mary L. Rev. 1801 (2002).

8. *Customer Databases as Collateral.* Xuan-Thao Nguyen points out that companies are using their customer databases as collateral for loans, since these databases are one of their most significant assets:

> Whether intentional or unintentional, many Internet companies ignore their own privacy policy statements when the companies pledge their customer database as collateral in secured financing schemes. This practice renders on-line privacy statements misleading because the statements are silent on collateralization of the company's assets. . . .
>
> The secured party can use the consumer database in its business or sell the consumer database to others. The collateralization of the consumer database and its end result may contradict the debtor's consumer privacy statement declaring that the debtor does not sell or lease the consumer information to others. Though there is no direct sale of the consumer database to the secured party, the effect of the collateralization of the consumer database is the same: the consumer database is in the hands of third parties with unfettered control and rights. Essentially, the collateralization of consumer databases violates the privacy policies publicized on debtors' Web sites.[33]

9. *The FTC as an Enforcer of Privacy: An Assessment.* In 2000, Steven Hetcher assessed the FTC's behavior in enforcing privacy in these terms:

> By the Agency's lights, its promotion of the fair practice principles should satisfy privacy advocates, as the fair information practice principles are derived from pre-existing norms of the advocacy community. Public interest advocates contend to the contrary, however, that privacy policies ill serve their aspirational privacy norms. They argue that privacy policies are typically not read by website users. They are written in legalese such that even if people read them, they will not understand them. Hence, they do not provide notice and thus cannot lead to consent. In addition, there is evidence that many sites do not adhere to their own policies. The policies are subject to change when companies merge, such that one company's policy is likely to go unheeded. Finally, very few privacy policies guarantee security or enforcement. Thus, the provision of a privacy policy by a website does not automatically promote the fair practice principles.
>
> Despite these problems, the FTC has strongly endorsed privacy policies. This raises a puzzle as to why the Agency should do so, given the severe criticism privacy policies have received. Why, for instance, is the FTC not coming out in support of the creation of a new agency to oversee privacy protection? . . .
>
> There is a public choice answer as to why the Agency has promoted privacy policies, despite their problems (and despite the fact that they do not appear to promote the interests of any industry groups whose favor the FTC might be seeking). It is through privacy policies that the FTC is gaining jurisdiction over the commercial Internet. Jurisdiction is power. In other words, the FTC acts as if it has a plan to migrate its activities to the Internet, and privacy policies have been at the core of this plan. . . .[34]

---

[33] Xuan-Thao N. Nguyen, *Collateralizing Privacy,* 78 Tul. L. Rev. 553, 571, 590 (2004).

[34] Steven Hetcher, *The FTC as Internet Privacy Norm Entrepreneur*, 53 Vand. L. Rev. 2041 (2000). *See also* Steven Hetcher, *Norms in a Wired World* (2004); Steven Hetcher, *Changing the Social Meaning of Privacy in Cyberspace*, 15 Harv. J. L. & Tech. 149 (2001); Steven A. Hetcher,

Joel Reidenberg argues that the FTC is the wrong choice to regulate privacy in the United States:

Public enforcement of data privacy relies on an expedient set of actors who are generally mismatched to remedy public wrongs. The public actors do not have specific statutory privacy rights authority. Instead, they exploit derivative powers to play a role in privacy claims. At the federal level, the current enforcement agency is the Federal Trade Commission. In many ways, this agency is an illogical choice for the protection of citizens' privacy. The FTC's mission is to enforce antitrust and certain consumer protection laws:

> The Commission seeks to ensure that the nation's markets function competitively, and are vigorous, efficient, and free of undue restrictions. The Commission also works to enhance the smooth operation of the marketplace by eliminating acts or practices that are unfair or deceptive.

Reliance on the FTC as a primary enforcer of citizen privacy is misplaced. The prevention of privacy wrongs, and particularly the public wrongs, as such, is simply not part of the core mission of the FTC. The FTC is not charged with the enforcement of civil rights, nor is the agency equipped or permitted to handle employment or telecommunications privacy matters. In fact, the FTC only grudgingly accepted involvement with privacy issues. During the mid-1990s, Commissioner Christine Varney persistently raised privacy as an important issue. For many years, the FTC hoped that the market would self-regulate and did not want to intervene aggressively. The FTC even opposed new federal legislation to protect information privacy. . . .

While the FTC seems to be the federal regulator of choice for a light touch in enforcement against privacy wrongs, the states' Attorneys General have taken a more aggressive stance. The National Association of Attorneys General has an Internet Law task force that studies and coordinates the enforcement of privacy. In effect, the states are unwilling to wait for federal results. This more aggressive stance of public enforcement at the state level is illustrated well by an enforcement action brought against DoubleClick. In February 2000, the Electronic Privacy Information Center ("EPIC"), a prominent privacy advocacy group, filed a complaint against DoubleClick with the Federal Trade Commission based on the company's practice of profiling web users without adequate disclosure. EPIC's complaint focused on the lack of disclosure and on profiling as an "unfair and deceptive practice." The FTC eventually closed its investigation with no action. However, a coalition of ten states pursued DoubleClick's practices and compelled DoubleClick to accept a binding agreement regarding privacy policies and disclosure; DoubleClick also accepted a fine of $450,000 to reimburse the states' investigative costs.

Like the federal actions, the state cases that rely on "unfair and deceptive practices" statutory authority do not address the public wrongs directly. When states pursue claims, the results are only able to achieve company specific cessations of particular data processing practices. These remedies address specific harms to individuals rather than the broader harms caused by wide-spread practices.[35]

Norm Proselytizers Create a Privacy Entitlement in Cyberspace, 16 Berkeley Tech. L.J. 877 (2001).

[35] Joel R. Reidenberg, *Privacy Wrongs in Search of Remedies*, 54 Hastings L.J. 877 (2003).

After these writings by Hetcher and Reidenberg, however, the FTC developed an additional role — the agency began to enforce standards of data security. Does this role fit in with Hetcher's analysis ("through privacy policies . . . the FTC is gaining jurisdiction over the commercial Internet") or Reidenberg's ("the FTC seems to be the federal regulator of choice for a light touch in enforcement")?

10. *State Deceptive Trade Practices Acts.* In addition to the FTC Act, which is enforced exclusively by the FTC, every state has some form of deceptive trade practices act of its own. Many of these statutes not only enable a state attorney general to bring actions but also provide a private cause of action to consumers. Several of these laws have provisions for statutory minimum damages, punitive damages, and attorneys' fees. *See, e.g.,* Cal. Civ. Code § 1780(a)(4) (punitive damages); Conn. Gen. Stat. § 42-110g(a) (punitive damages); Mich. Comp. Laws § 445.911(2) (minimum damages); N.Y. Gen. Bus. Law § 349(h) (minimum damages). In interpreting these state laws, many state courts have been heavily influenced by FTC Act jurisprudence. However, as Jeff Sovern notes, many states "have been more generous to consumers than has the FTC," and "even if the FTC concludes that practices pass muster under the FTC Act, it is still at least theoretically possible for a state to find the practices deceptive under their own legislation." Thus, Sovern concludes, "information practices that are currently in widespread use may indeed violate state little FTC Acts. Marketers should think carefully about whether they wish to alter their practices."[36]

3. GOVERNANCE BY SELF-REGULATION

Pure Self-Regulation. Some commentators contend that the best solution to data collection and use is to allow companies to regulate themselves. Fred Cate points out that self-regulation is "more flexible and more sensitive to specific contexts and therefore allow[s] individuals to determine a more tailored balance between information uses and privacy than privacy laws do."[37]

Eric Goldman argues:

Relatively few consumers have bought privacy management tools, such as software to browse anonymously and manage Internet cookies and e-mail. Many vendors are now migrating away from consumer-centric business models. So, although consumers can take technological control over their own situation, few consumers do.

Plus, as most online marketers know, people will "sell" their personal data incredibly cheaply. As Internet pundit Esther Dyson has said: "You do a survey, and consumers say they are very concerned about their privacy. Then you offer them a discount on a book, and they'll tell you everything." Indeed, a recent Jupiter report said that 82% of respondents would give personal information to new shopping sites to enter a $100 sweepstakes.

---

[36] Jeff Sovern, *Protecting Privacy with Deceptive Trade Practices Legislation*, 69 Fordham L. Rev. 1305, 1352-53, 1357 (2001).

[37] Fred H. Cate, *Privacy in Perspective* 26 (2001); *see also* Fred H. Cate, *Privacy in the Information Age* (1997).

Clearly consumers' stated privacy concerns diverge from what consumers do. Two theories might explain the divergence.

First, asking consumers what they care about reveals only whether they value privacy. That's half the equation. Of more interest is how much consumers will pay — in time or money — for the corresponding benefits. For now the cost-benefit ratio is tilted too high for consumers to spend much time or money on privacy.

Second, consumers don't have uniform interests. Regarding online privacy, consumers can be segmented into two groups: activists, who actively protect their online privacy, and apathetics, who do little or nothing to protect themselves. The activists are very vocal but appear to be a tiny market segment.

Using consumer segmentation, the analytical defect of broad-based online privacy regulations becomes apparent. The activists, by definition, take care of themselves. They demand privacy protections from businesses and, if they don't get it, use technology to protect themselves or take their business elsewhere.

In contrast, mainstream consumers don't change their behavior based on online privacy concerns. If these people won't take even minimal steps to protect themselves, why should government regulation do it for them?

Further, online businesses will invest in privacy when it's profitable. . . . When companies believed that few consumers would change their behavior if they were offered greater privacy, those companies did nothing or put into place privacy policies that disabused consumers of privacy expectations. Of course, if companies later discovered that they were losing business because customers wanted more privacy, they would increase their privacy initiatives.

Consumer behavior will tell companies what level of privacy to provide. Let the market continue unimpeded rather than chase phantom consumer fears through unnecessary regulation.[38]

In contrast, Peter Swire contends that privacy legislation need not be antithetical to business interests. According to Swire, privacy legislation should be viewed as similar to the "trustwrap" that Johnson & Johnson placed around bottles of Tylenol after a scare involving cyanide poisoning of the pain reliever.[39] Swire believes that "privacy legislation targeted at online practices" would provide the kind of safety to allow consumers to engage in cyberspace activities with confidence.

Default Rules. In contrast to a pure self-regulatory approach, in which personal information belongs to whatever entity happens to obtain it, Jerry Kang argues that a default rule that individuals retain control over information they surrender during Internet transactions is more efficient than a default rule where companies can use the data as they see fit. According to Kang, the latter default rule would create two inefficiencies for individuals in attempting to bargain around the rule:

. . . First, [the individual] would face substantial research costs to determine what information is being collected and how it is being used. That is because individuals today are largely clueless about how personal information is

---

[38] Eric Goldman, *The Privacy Hoax,* Forbes (Oct. 14, 2002), available at http://www.ericgoldman.org/Articles/privacyhoax.htm.

[39] Peter P. Swire, *Trustwrap: the Importance of Legal Rules to Electronic Commerce and Internet Privacy*, 54 Hastings L.J. 847 (2003).

processed through cyberspace. Transacting parties and transaction facilitators do not generally provide adequate, relevant notice about what information will be collected and how it will be used. What is worse, consumer ignorance is sometimes fostered by deceptive practices.

Second, the individual would run into a collective action problem. Realistically, the information collector — the "firm" — would not entertain one person's idiosyncratic request to purchase back personal information because the costs of administering such an individually tailored program would be prohibitive. This explains the popular use of form contracts, even in cyberspace, that cannot be varied much, if at all. Therefore, to make it worth the firm's while, the individual would have to band together with like-minded individuals to renegotiate the privacy terms of the underlying transaction. These individuals would suffer the collective action costs of locating each other, coming to some mutual agreement and strategy, proposing an offer to the information collector and negotiating with it — all the while discouraging free riders. . . .

Therefore, Kang argues, the appropriate default is to give control of information to the individual:

> With this default, if the firm valued personal data more than the individual, then the firm would have to buy permission to process the data in functionally unnecessary ways. Note, however, two critical differences in contracting around this default. First, unlike the individual who had to find out what information is being collected and how it is being used, the collector need not bear such research costs since it already knows what its information practices are. Second, the collector does not confront collective action problems. It need not seek out other like-minded firms and reach consensus before coming to the individual with a request. This is because an individual would gladly entertain an individualized, even idiosyncratic, offer to purchase personal information. In addition, there will be no general "holdout" problem because one individual's refusal to sell personal information to the collector will not generally destroy the value of personal information purchased from others.[40]

Would Kang's approach serve as a dramatic change for the self-regulatory approach? Couldn't companies regularly bargain around Kang's default rule in order to obtain control of the data from individuals? Does assigning the initial entitlement make a practical difference?

Flexible Regulation. Some commentators contend that a middle ground can be found between traditional legal regulation and self-regulation. Dennis Hirsch argues that environmental law suggests ways to regulate privacy that are flexible and that mix legal regulation with self-regulation:

> Over the past forty years, environmental law has been at the epicenter of an intense and productive debate about the most effective way to regulate. Initial environmental laws took the form of prescriptive, uniform standards that have come to be known as "command-and-control" regulation. These methods, while effective in some settings, proved costly and controversial. In the decades that followed, governments, academics, environmental and business groups, and others poured tremendous resources into figuring out how to improve upon these

---

[40] Jerry Kang, *Information Privacy in Cyberspace Transactions*, 50 Stan. L. Rev. 1193, 1253-54, 1257 (1998).

methods. This work has produced a "second generation" of environmental regulation. . . .

Second generation initiatives encourage the regulated parties themselves to choose the means by which they will achieve environmental performance goals. That is what defines them and distinguishes them from first generation regulations under which the agency has the primary decisionmaking power over pollution control methods. This difference tends to make second generation strategies more cost-effective and adaptable than command-and-control rules. The proliferation of second generation strategies has led some to identify the environmental field as having "some of the most innovative regulatory instruments in all of American law."

Privacy regulation today finds itself in a debate similar to the one that the environmental field has been engaged in for years. On the one hand, there is a growing sense that the digital age is causing unprecedented damage to privacy and that action must be taken immediately to mitigate these injuries. On the other, a chorus of voices warns against the dangers of imposing intrusive and costly regulation on the emerging business sectors of the information economy. Missing thus far from the dialogue is any significant discussion of the more flexible "second generation" regulatory strategies that might be able to bridge this gap. It took environmental law decades to arrive at these alternatives. The privacy field could capitalize on this experience by looking to these environmental policies as models for privacy regulation.[41]

Is the analogy of privacy law to environmental law an apt one? To what extent are the privacy statutes discussed in this book thus far command-and-control rules versus flexible rules? Is Hirsch calling less for self-regulation than for industry input into the form and content of rules?

Regulation by Technology. As part of the self-governance, technology can assist companies as well as consumers in making privacy choices. Privacy on the Internet can be protected by another form of regulatory mechanism — technology. According to Joel Reidenberg, "law and government regulation are not the only source of rule-making. Technological capabilities and system design choices impose rules on participants."[42] Reidenberg calls such forms of technological governance "Lex Informatica."

In the privacy context, Privacy Enhancing Technologies (PETs) have received much attention from scholars and the privacy policy community. Herbert Burkert describes PETs as "technical and organizational concepts that aim at protecting personal identity. These concepts usually involve encryption in the form digital signatures, blind signature or digital pseudonyms."[43]

---

[41] Dennis D. Hirsch, *Protecting the Inner Environment: What Privacy Regulation Can Learn from Environmental Law*, 41 Ga. L. Rev. 1, 8-10 (2006).

[42] Joel Reidenberg, *Lex Informatica: The Formulation of Information Policy Rules Through Technology*, 76 Tex. L. Rev. 553 (1998).

[43] Herbert Burkert, *Privacy-Enhancing Technologies: Typology, Critique, Vision*, in *Technology and Privacy: The New Landscape* 123, 125, 128 (Philip E. Agre & Marc Rotenberg, eds., 1997).

4. GOVERNANCE BY PROPERTY

A number of commentators propose that privacy can be protected by restructuring the property rights that people have in personal information. For example, according to Richard Murphy, personal information "like all information, is property." He goes on to conclude:

> . . . [I]n many instances, privacy rules are in fact implied contractual terms. To the extent that information is generated through a voluntary transaction, imposing nondisclosure obligations on the recipient of the information may be the best approach for certain categories of information. The value that information has ex post is of secondary importance; the primary question is what is the efficient contractual rule. Common-law courts are increasingly willing to impose an implied contractual rule of nondisclosure for many categories of transactions, including those with attorneys, medical providers, bankers, and accountants. Many statutes can also be seen in this light — that is, as default rules of privacy. And an argument can be made for the efficiency of a privacy default rule in the generic transaction between a merchant and a consumer.[44]

Lawrence Lessig also contends that privacy should be protected with property rights. He notes that "[p]rivacy now is protected through liability rules — if you invade someone's privacy, they can sue you and you must then pay." A "liability regime allows a taking, and payment later." In contrast, a property regime gives "control, and power, to the person holding the property right." Lessig argues: "When you have a property right, before someone takes your property they must negotiate with you about how much it is worth."[45]

Other commentators critique the translation of privacy into a form of property right that can be bartered and sold. For example, Katrin Schatz Byford argues that viewing "privacy as an item of trade . . . values privacy only to the extent it is considered to be of personal worth by the individual who claims it." She further contends: "Such a perspective plainly conflicts with the notion that privacy is a collective value and that privacy intrusions at the individual level necessarily have broader social implications because they affect access to social power and stifle public participation."[46]

Consider Pamela Samuelson's argument as to why property rights are inadequate to protect privacy:

> . . . Achieving information privacy goals through a property rights system may be difficult for reasons other than market complexities. Chief among them is the difficulty with alienability of personal information. It is a common, if not ubiquitous, characteristic of property rights systems that when the owner of a property right sells her interest to another person, that buyer can freely transfer to third parties whatever interest the buyer acquired from her initial seller. Free alienability works very well in the market for automobiles and land, but it is far

---

[44] Richard S. Murphy, *Property Rights in Personal Information: An Economic Defense of Privacy*, 84 Geo. L.J. 2381, 2416-17 (1996).

[45] Lawrence Lessig, *Code and Other Laws of Cyberspace* (1999).

[46] Katrin Schatz Byford, *Privacy in Cyberspace: Constructing a Model of Privacy for the Electronic Communications Environment*, 24 Rutgers Computer & Tech. L.J. 1 (1998). For an argument about the problems of commodifying certain goods and of viewing all human conduct in light of the market metaphor, see Margaret Jane Radin, *Contested Commodities* (1996).

from clear that it will work well for information privacy. . . . Collectors of data may prefer a default rule allowing them to freely transfer personal data to whomever they wish on whatever terms they can negotiate with their future buyers. However, individuals concerned with information privacy will generally want a default rule prohibiting retransfer of the data unless separate permission is negotiated. They will also want any future recipient to bind itself to the same constraints that the initial purchaser of the data may have agreed to as a condition of sale. Information privacy goals may not be achievable unless the default rule of the new property rights regime limits transferability. . . .

. . . From a civil liberties perspective, propertizing personal information as a way of achieving information privacy goals may seem an anathema. Not only might it be viewed as an unnecessary and possibly dangerous way to achieve information privacy goals, it might be considered morally obnoxious. If information privacy is a civil liberty, it may make no more sense to propertize personal data than to commodify voting rights. . . .[47]

Daniel Solove also counsels against protecting privacy as a form of property right because the "market approach has difficulty assigning the proper value to personal information":

. . . [T]he aggregation problem severely complicates the valuation process. An individual may give out bits of information in different contexts, each transfer appearing innocuous. However, the information can be aggregated and could prove to be invasive of the private life when combined with other information. It is the totality of information about a person and how it is used that poses the greatest threat to privacy. As Julie Cohen notes, "[a] comprehensive collection of data about an individual is vastly more than the sum of its parts." From the standpoint of each particular information transaction, individuals will not have enough facts to make a truly informed decision. The potential future uses of that information are too vast and unknown to enable individuals to make the appropriate valuation. . . .

[Property rights] cannot work effectively in a situation where the power relationship and information distribution between individuals and public and private bureaucracies is so greatly unbalanced. In other words, the problem with market solutions is not merely that it is difficult to commodify information (which it is), but also that a regime of default rules alone (consisting of property rights in information and contractual defaults) will not enable fair and equitable market transactions in personal information. . . .[48]

In contrast to these skeptics, Paul Schwartz develops a model of propertized personal data that would help fashion a market for data trade that would respect individual privacy and help maintain a democratic order. Schwartz calls for "limitations on an individual's right to alienate personal information; default rules that force disclosure of the terms of trade; a right of exit for participants in the market; the establishment of damages to deter market abuses; and institutions to police the personal information market and punish privacy violations." In his judgment, a key element of this model is its approach of "hybrid inalienability"

---

[47] Pamela Samuelson, *Privacy as Intellectual Property?*, 52 Stan. L. Rev. 1125, 1137-47 (2000).

[48] Daniel J. Solove, *Privacy and Power: Computer Databases and Metaphors for Information Privacy*, 53 Stan. L. Rev. 1393 (2001).

in which a law allows individuals to share their personal information, but also places limitations on future use of the information. Schwartz explains:

> This hybrid consists of a use-transferability restriction plus an opt-in default. In practice, it would permit the transfer for an initial category of use of personal data, but only if the customer is granted an opportunity to block further transfer or use by unaffiliated entities. Any further use or transfer would require the customer to opt in — that is, it would be prohibited unless the customer affirmatively agrees to it.
>
> As an initial example concerning compensated telemarketing, a successful pitch for Star Trek memorabilia would justify the use of personal data by the telemarketing company and the transfer of it both to process the order and for other related purposes. Any outside use or unrelated transfers of this information would, however, require obtaining further permission from the individual. Note that this restriction limits the alienability of individuals' personal information by preventing them from granting one-stop permission for all use or transfer of their information. A data processor's desire to carry out further transfers thus obligates the processor to supply additional information and provides another chance for the individual to bargain with the data collector. . . .
>
> To ensure that the opt-in default leads to meaningful disclosure of additional information, however, two additional elements are needed. First, the government must have a significant role in regulating the way that notice of privacy practices is provided. As noted above, a critical issue will be the "frame" in which information about data processing is presented. . . .
>
> Second, meaningful disclosure requires addressing what Henry Hansmann and Reinier Kraakman term "verification problems." Their scholarship points to the critical condition that third parties must be able to verify that a given piece of personal information has in fact been propertized and then identify the specific rules that apply to it. As they explain, "[a] verification rule sets out the conditions under which a given right in a given asset will run with the asset." In the context of propertized personal information, the requirement for verification creates a role for nonpersonal metadata, a tag or kind of barcode, to provide necessary background information and notice.[49]

Finally, consider what Warren and Brandeis said about privacy as a property claim:

> The aim of [copyright] statutes is to secure to the author, composer, or artist the entire profits arising from publication. . . .
>
> But where the value of the production is found not in the right to take the profits arising from publication, but in the peace of mind or the relief afforded by the ability to prevent any publication at all, it is difficult to regard the right as one of property, in the common acceptation of that term.[50]

---

[49] Paul M. Schwartz, *Property, Privacy and Personal Data*, 117 Harv. L. Rev. 2055, 2056, 2098-99 (2004). *See also* Vera Bergelson, *It's Personal But Is It Mine? Toward Property Rights in Personal Information*, 37 U.C. Davis L. Rev. 379 (2003) (although a collector may have rights in individuals' personal information, a property approach would correctly subordinate these rights to the rights of the individuals).

[50] Samuel Warren & Louis Brandeis, *The Right to Privacy*, 4 Harv. L. Rev. 193 (1890).

5. GOVERNANCE BY STATUTORY REGULATION

Numerous statutes are directly and potentially applicable to the collection, use, and transfer of personal information by commercial entities. Congress's approach is best described as "sectoral," as each statute is narrowly tailored to particular types of businesses and services. The opposite of sectoral in this context is omnibus, and the United States lacks such a comprehensive statute regulating the private sector's collection and use of personal information. Such omnibus statutes are standard in much of the rest of the world. All member nations of the European Union have enacted omnibus information privacy laws.

In the United States, sectoral laws also do not regulate all commercial entities in their collection and use of personal information. Thus far, federal statutes regulate three basic areas: (a) entertainment records (video and cable television); (b) Internet use and electronic communications; and (c) marketing (telemarketing and spam). As you examine the existing statutes, think about the kinds of commercial entities that the law does not currently regulate. Consider whether these entities should be regulated. Also consider whether one omnibus privacy law can adequately apply to all commercial entities. Would the differences between types of commercial entities make a one-size-fits-all privacy law impractical?

The sectoral statutes embody the Fair Information Practices originally developed by HEW and incorporated into the Privacy Act. However, not all statutes embody all of the Fair Information Practices. As you study each statute, examine which of the Fair Information Practices are required by each statute and which are not.

(a) Entertainment Records

THE VIDEO PRIVACY PROTECTION ACT

Incensed when a reporter obtained a list of videos that Supreme Court Justice Nominee Robert Bork and his family had rented from a video store, Congress passed the Video Privacy Protection Act (VPPA) of 1988, Pub. L. No. 100-618. The VPPA is also known as the "Bork Bill."

What Is a Video Tape? Who Is a Video Tape Service Provider? The VPPA is written in technology-neutral terms. It defines a "video tape service provider" as "any person engaged in the business, in or affecting interstate or foreign commerce, of rental, sale, or delivery of prerecorded video cassette tapes or similar audio visual materials. . . ." § 2710(a)(4). This statutory language allows the VPPA to extend to DVDs (as opposed to video cassette tapes) and should also cover online delivery of movies and other content.

Restrictions on Disclosure. The VPPA prohibits videotape service providers from knowingly disclosing personal information, such as titles of videocassettes rented or purchased, without the individual's written consent. The VPPA creates a private cause of action when a videotape service provider "knowingly discloses

. . . personally identifiable information concerning any consumer of such provider." 18 U.S.C § 2710(b)(1).

Destruction of Records. The VPPA requires that records of personal information be destroyed as soon as practicable. § 2710(e).

Exceptions. The VPPA contains several exceptions, permitting videotape providers to disclose "to any person if the disclosure is incident to the ordinary course of business of the video tape service provider." § 2710(b)(2)(E).

The statute provides that "the subject matter of such materials may be disclosed if the disclosure is for the exclusive use of marketing goods and services directly to the consumer." § 2710(b)(2)(D)(ii). Videotape service providers can disclose the names and addresses of consumers if the consumer has been given the right to opt out, and the disclosure does not identify information about the videos the consumer rents. § 2710(b)(2)(D).

The statute also permits disclosure to the consumer, § 2710(b)(2)(A); disclosure with the informed written consent of the consumer, § 2710(b)(2)(B); disclosure to a law enforcement agency pursuant to a warrant or subpoena, § 2710(b)(2)(C); and disclosure for civil discovery if there is notice and an opportunity to object, § 2710(b)(2).

Preemption. VPPA does not block states from enacting statutes that are more protective of privacy. § 2710(f).

Enforcement. The VPPA's private right of action permits recovery of actual damages and provides for liquidated damages in the amount of $2,500. The Act also authorizes recovery for punitive damages, attorneys' fees, and enables equitable and injunctive relief. § 2710(c). The VPPA also includes a statutory exclusionary rule that prevents the admission into evidence of any information obtained in violation of the statute. § 2710(d).

DIRKES V. BOROUGH OF RUNNEMEDE

936 F. Supp. 235 (D.N.J. 1996)

BROTMAN, J. Presently before this Court is a motion for summary judgment brought by the Borough of Runnemede, the Borough of Runnemede Police Department, and Lieutenant Emil Busko. . . .

The present action arises from the investigation of and disciplinary action taken against Plaintiff Chester Dirkes, formerly an officer with the Department. On May 24, 1990, in the course of an investigation into a citizen's death, Plaintiff Dirkes allegedly removed pornographic magazines and videotapes from the decedent's apartment. Based on this allegation, the Camden County Grand Jury returned a one count indictment for misconduct in office against him on May 29, 1991. As a result of the indictment, on May 30, 1991, the Department issued a disciplinary notice to Plaintiff Dirkes and suspended him without pay and benefits. Plaintiff Dirkes' trial commenced on April 20, 1992 and on May 5, 1992, he was acquitted of the sole charge against him.

Following the acquittal, the Borough retained special counsel and resumed its internal affairs investigation against Plaintiff Dirkes. The Department assigned Lt. Busko to investigate the matter. On or about May 7, 1992, Lt. Busko obtained the names and rental dates of certain pornographic videotapes previously rented by Plaintiff Dirkes and his wife, co-plaintiff Marie Dirkes. Lt. Busko received this information from an employee of Videos To Go, the store from which Plaintiffs apparently regularly rent or buy video tapes for their private use. In seeking to obtain this information, Lt. Busko failed to secure a warrant, a subpoena or a court order. He simply requested and received the information from an employee of Videos to Go without question.

The internal affairs memorandum listing the video tape rental information was distributed to the Borough's special counsel, who in turn distributed it in connection with Plaintiff Dirkes' disciplinary hearing and in a proceeding before the Superior Court of New Jersey, Camden County.

On or about March 19, 1993, Plaintiffs filed their complaint with this Court alleging that Defendants violated the provisions of the Videotape Privacy Protection Act of 1988, as codified at 18 U.S.C. § 2710 (the "Act"), as well as Plaintiffs' common law privacy rights. . . . Subsequently, the video information was received into evidence at Plaintiff Dirkes' disciplinary hearing. As a result of that hearing, the Department terminated Plaintiff Dirkes from his employment. . . .

Defendants have moved for summary judgment on Count I of Plaintiffs' complaint, which asserts a violation of the Videotape Privacy Protection Act. . . .

Section 2710(c) of the Act provides broadly that "[a]ny person aggrieved by any act of a person in violation of [§ 2710] may bring a civil action" in an appropriate U.S. District Court. The Act can be violated in one or all of three ways. First, a "video tape service provider" violates § 2710(b) of the Act by disclosing "personally identifiable information" regarding a customer unless the person to whom the disclosure is made or the disclosure itself falls into one of six categories. 18 U.S.C. § 2710(b). Second, § 2710(d) of the Act is violated when personally identifiable information obtained in any manner other than as narrowly provided by the Act is "received in evidence" in almost any adversarial proceeding. 18 U.S.C. § 2710(d). Third, a person subject to the Act violates § 2710(e) by failing to timely destroy a customer's personally identifiable information. 18 U.S.C. § 2710(e). Upon finding any of these violations, a court may, but need not, award a range of relief including actual damages, punitive damages, attorneys' fees, or "such other . . . equitable relief as the Court may determine to be appropriate." 18 U.S.C. § 2710(c).

Because it is undisputed that subsections (b) and (d) have been violated in the instant matter, § 2710(c) authorizes the Plaintiffs to bring a suit. Videos to Go, the video tape service provider in this matter, violated subsection (b) of the Act by disclosing Plaintiffs' video rental information to Lt. Busko. It is undisputed that this disclosure does not fall into one of the six permissible disclosure exceptions delineated in subsection (b)(2) of the Act. A second violation of the Act occurred when Plaintiffs' personally identifiable information was received into evidence at Plaintiff Dirkes' disciplinary hearing. 18 U.S.C. § 2710(d).

Having found that there have been two violations of the Act, the Court must now determine whether Lt. Busko, the Department, or the Borough are proper defendants. As noted earlier, subsection (c) provides that "[a]ny person aggrieved by any act of a person in violation of [§ 2710] may bring a civil action." 18 U.S.C. § 2710(c). While it broadly provides relief for violations of § 2710, this subsection does not delineate those parties against whom an action may be instituted. 18 U.S.C. § 2710(c). In support of its current summary judgment motion, the Defendants argue collectively that they cannot be held liable under the Act because their actions did not violate the Act. For example, only the actions of a video tape service provider can cause a violation of § 2710(b). Because the Defendants are not video tape service providers as that term is defined under the Act, they argue that they cannot be held responsible under the Act.

This Court must reject the Defendants' narrow reading of the statute. Again, the plain language of the Act does not delineate those parties against whom an action under this Act may be maintained. Taking the Defendants' argument to its logical extension, this omission would prevent plaintiffs from bringing a cause of action against anyone. Such an absurd result must be rejected. The clear intent of the Act is to prevent the disclosure of private information. As established by its legislative history, the Act enables consumers "to maintain control over personal information divulged and generated in exchange for receiving services from video tape service providers." S. Rep. No. 100-599, at 8 (1988). This purpose is furthered by allowing parties, like these Plaintiffs, to bring suit against those individuals who have come to possess (and who could disseminate) the private information in flagrant violation of the purposes of the Act. While it need not identify all potential categories of defendants in this opinion, the Court finds that those parties who are in possession of personally identifiable information as a direct result of an improper release of such information are subject to suit under the Act. Because it is undisputed that Lt. Busko, the Department, and the Borough all possess the information as a direct result of a violation of the Act, each is a proper defendant.

Furthermore, the Supreme Court in *Local 28 of Sheet Metal Workers v. E.E.O.C.*, 478 U.S. 421 (1986), reinforced the principle that remedial statutes should be construed broadly. *Local 28* involved a violation of Title VII, a statute designed to address employment discrimination. Upon examining the legislative history of Title VII, the Court determined that "Congress reaffirmed the breadth of the [district] court's remedial powers under § 706(g) by adding language authorizing courts to order 'any other equitable relief as the court deems appropriate.'" This added language is identical to that used in subsection (c)(2)(D) of the Videotape Privacy Protection Act. 18 U.S.C. § 2710(c). It is evident throughout the *Local 28* opinion that the Supreme Court intended to give effect to the legislators' intent to provide as broad remedial powers as possible to the district courts to eliminate the effects of illegal discrimination. This Court will exercise the same broad powers to give effect to the intent of Videotape Privacy Protection Act's U.S. Senate sponsors. The importance of maintaining the privacy of an individual's personally identifiable information mandates that people who obtain such information from a violation of the Act be held as proper defendants to prevent the further disclosure of the information. . . .

For the reasons set forth above, the Court will deny Defendants' motion for summary judgment. . . .

DANIEL V. CANTELL
375 F.3d 377 (6th Cir. 2004)

CUDAHY, J. The plaintiff, Alden Joe Daniel, Jr. (Daniel) was charged with and eventually pleaded guilty to the sexual molestation of three underage girls. Allegedly, part of his *modus operandi* was showing pornographic movies to the underage girls. . . . Therefore, as part of the criminal investigation into his conduct, law enforcement officials sought and were able to obtain his video rental records. . . .

Daniel brings this suit against (1) various police officers, attorneys, and the parents of one of Daniel's victims, as well as (2) the employees and owners of two video stores where Daniel rented pornographic videos. There is no dispute that the defendants making up this second category are proper parties under the Act. The only question which we must answer is whether the defendants not associated with the video stores are proper parties under the Act. We believe that based on the plain language of the Act, this first group of defendants are *not* proper parties. . . .

Section (b) provides that "[a] *video tape service provider* who knowingly discloses, to any person, personally identifiable information concerning any consumer of such provider shall be liable to the aggrieved person for the relief provided in subsection (d)." 18 U.S.C. § 2710(b)(1) (emphasis added). Therefore, under the plain language of the statute, only a "video tape service provider" (VTSP) can be liable. The term VTSP is defined by the statute to mean "any person, engaged in the business, in or affecting interstate or foreign commerce, of rental, sale, or delivery of prerecorded video cassette tapes or similar audio video materials, or any person or other entity to whom a disclosure is made under subparagraph (D) or (E) of subsection (b)(2), but only with respect to the information contained in the disclosure." *Id.* at § 2710(a)(4). Daniel does not allege that the defendants in question are engaged in the business of rental, sale or delivery of prerecorded video cassette tapes. Therefore, the defendants may only be VTSPs if personal information was disclosed to them under subparagraph (D) or (E) of subsection (b)(2).

Subparagraph (D) applies "if the disclosure is solely the names and addresses of consumers." *Id.* at § 2710(b)(2)(D). Moreover, disclosure under subparagraph (D) must be "for the exclusive use of marketing goods and services directly to the consumer." *Id.* at § 2710(b)(2)(D)(ii). For instance, if a video store provided the names and addresses of its patrons to a movie magazine publisher, the publisher would be considered a VTSP, but only with respect to the information contained in the disclosure. No disclosure in this case was made under subparagraph (D). The information provided was not limited to Daniel's name and address. Instead, the disclosure was of Daniel's history of renting pornographic videotapes and included the specific titles of those videos. Additionally, the disclosure was not for marketing purposes but for purposes of a criminal investigation. Therefore, subparagraph (D) is inapplicable in this case.

Daniel properly does not argue that the disclosure falls within subparagraph (E). . . . Subparagraph (E) applies only to disclosures made "incident to the ordinary course of business" of the VTSP. *Id.* at § 2710(b)(2)(E). The term "ordinary course of business" is "narrowly defined" in the statute to mean "only debt collection activities, order fulfillment, request processing, and the transfer of ownership." *Id.* at § 2710(a)(2) . . . In sum, because Daniel has presented no evidence suggesting that a disclosure was made under subparagraph (D) or (E) in this case, the non-video store defendants are not VTSPs under the Act and therefore, are not proper parties to this litigation.

Daniel argues, however, that any person, not just a VTSP, can be liable under the Act based on *Dirkes v. Borough of Runnemede,* 936 F. Supp. 235 (D.N.J. 1996). *Dirkes* did reach this conclusion but only by misreading the Act. The court in *Dirkes* was focused on language in the Act stating that "[a]ny person aggrieved by any act of *a person* in violation of this section may bring a civil action in the United States district court." 18 U.S.C. § 2710(c)(1) (emphasis added). Because the statute states that a suit can be based upon an act of "a person" rather than an act of "a VTSP," *Dirkes* found that any person can be liable under the Act. *Dirkes,* however, ignored the rest of the sentence. A lawsuit under the Act must be based on an "act of a person *in violation of this section.* . . ." 18 U.S.C. § 2710(c)(1) (emphasis added). The statute makes it clear that only a VTSP can be in violation of section 2710(b). *See* § 2710(b)(1) ("A video tape service provider who knowingly discloses . . . personally identifiable information . . . shall be liable. . . ."). Moreover, if any person could be liable under the Act, there would be no need for the Act to define a VTSP in the first place. More tellingly, if any person could be liable under the Act, there is no reason that the definition of a VTSP would be limited to "any person . . . to whom a disclosure is made under subparagraph (D) or (E) of subsection (b)(2)." *Dirkes* would have us ignore this limitation and find that any person can be liable under the Act whether or not a disclosure was made to him under subparagraph (D) or (E). We avoid interpretations of a statute which would render portions of it superfluous.

The court in *Dirkes* found otherwise because the "clear intent of the Act," as demonstrated by its legislative history, "is to prevent the disclosure of private information." Where the plain language of a statute is clear, however, we do not consult the legislative history. . . . In any case, our interpretation of the statute — that only a VTSP can be liable under § 2710(b) — does not conflict with Congress' purpose in adopting the Act. One can "prevent the disclosure of private information" simply by cutting off disclosure at its source, i.e., the VTSP. Just because Congress' goal was to prevent the disclosure of private information, does not mean that Congress intended the implementation of every conceivable method of preventing disclosures. Printing all personal information in hieroglyphics instead of English would also help prevent the disclosure of such information. However, nothing in the legislative history suggests that Congress was encouraging hieroglyphics and, similarly, nothing suggests that Congress intended that anyone other than VTSPs would be liable under the Act. In sum, the Act is clear that only a VTSP can be liable under § 2710(b). Because the non-video store defendants do not fit within the definition of a VTSP, they are not proper parties.

NOTES & QUESTIONS

1. *To Whom Does VPPA Apply?* The key question in *Dirkes* and *Daniel* is whether the VPPA *only* regulates videotape service providers. The *Daniel* court answered this question affirmatively; the *Dirkes* court would apply the VPPA to additional parties, including law enforcement officers. Which interpretation of the statutory language do you find most convincing? Would policy reasons support a broader or narrower application of the statute?

2. *Facebook, Beacon, Blockbuster, and a VPPA Violation?* In April 2008, Cathryn Elain Harris filed a lawsuit against Blockbuster Video (a video tape service provider) and Facebook claiming violations of the VPPA. The complaint objected to Blockbuster reporting its customers' activities to Facebook through the Beacon program.

   Facebook introduced Beacon in November 2007; under it, partner companies shared information with Facebook about Facebook user activity that took place on their websites. Initially, this information became part of one's Facebook profile unless the user opted out. After consumer protest, Facebook changed its policy to require that a Facebook user would have to opt in to Beacon before information was disclosed on her Facebook page. It is not clear, however, whether opting out of Beacon stops partner companies from sharing information with Facebook.

   The Harris complaint alleges that Blockbuster's website is still reporting a user's activities back to Facebook, whether or not the consumer opts out of having the information associated with her Facebook profile. Does the Blockbuster-Beacon-Facebook behavior, if as alleged, violate the VPPA? If so, what measure of damages should be used?

THE CABLE COMMUNICATIONS POLICY ACT

In 1984, Congress passed the Cable Communications Policy Act (CCPA or "Cable Act"), Pub. L. No. 98-549. The Act applies to cable operators and service providers. 47 U.S.C. § 551(a)(1).

Notice and Access. The Cable Act requires cable service providers to notify subscribers (in a written privacy policy) of the nature and uses of personal information collected. § 551(a)(1). Subscribers must have access to their personal data held by cable operators. § 551(d).

Limitations on Data Collection. Cable operators "shall not use the cable system to collect personally identifiable information concerning any subscriber without the prior written or electronic consent of the subscriber concerned." § 551(b)(1).

Limitations on Data Disclosure. Cable operators cannot disclose personally identifiable information about any subscriber without the subscriber's consent:

> [A] cable operator shall not disclose personally identifiable information concerning any subscriber without the prior written or electronic consent of the

subscriber concerned and shall take such actions as are necessary to prevent unauthorized access to such information by a person other than the subscriber or cable operator. § 551(c)(1).

However, cable operators can disclose personal data under certain circumstances, such as when necessary for a "legitimate business activity" or pursuant to a court order if the subscriber is notified. Cable operators may disclose subscriber names and addresses if "the cable operator has provided the subscriber the opportunity to prohibit or limit such disclosure." § 551(c)(2).

Data Destruction. Cable operators must destroy personal data if the information is no longer necessary for the purpose for which it was collected. § 551(e).

Government Access to Cable Information. Pursuant to § 551(h):

A governmental entity may obtain personally identifiable information concerning a cable subscriber pursuant to a court order only if, in the court proceeding relevant to such court order —

(1) such entity offers clear and convincing evidence that the subject of the information is reasonably suspected of engaging in criminal activity and that the information sought would be material evidence in the case; and

(2) the subject of the information is afforded the opportunity to appear and contest such entity's claim.

Note that a court order to obtain cable records requires "clear and convincing evidence," a standard higher than probable cause. There is no exclusionary rule for information obtained in violation of the Cable Act.

Enforcement. The Cable Act provides for a private cause of action and actual damages, with a minimum of $1,000 or $100 for each day of the violation, whichever is higher. The plaintiff can collect any actual damages that are more than the statutory minimum. Further, the Cable Act provides for punitive damages and attorneys' fees. § 551(f).

Cable Internet Service. Section 211 of the USA PATRIOT Act amended the Cable Act, 47 U.S.C. § 551(c)(2)(D), to provide disclosure to a government entity under federal wiretap law when the government seeks information from cable companies except that "such disclosure shall not include records revealing cable subscriber selection of video programming from a cable operator." This provision of the PATRIOT Act will not sunset.

New Cable Services and Products? In March 2008, the *New York Times* reported on a plan by the nation's six largest cable companies to create a joint venture to allow national advertisers to purchase custom as well as interactive ads.[51] The initiative is called Project Canoe. According to the report: "Cable companies have the ability to compile better data on users than Internet companies can gleam, which could make focused ads on television more effective." The kind of marketing planned will direct different targeted ads to the bachelor living in a Manhattan skyscraper and a retiree settled in Florida. In addition, interactive advertising allows TV viewers to use their remote control to "request a brochure or call up more information about a product." The key to Project Canoe is the cable set-top box, which collects "vast amounts of data." In light of the Cable Act, how would you advise executives at Project Canoe regarding their plans?

(b) Internet Use and Electronic Communications

CHILDREN'S ONLINE PRIVACY PROTECTION ACT

Passed in 1998, the Children's Online Privacy Protection Act (COPPA), Pub. L. No. 106-170, 15 U.S.C. §§ 6501–6506, regulates the collection and use of children's information by Internet websites. The COPPA applies to "an operator of a website or online service directed to children, or any operator that has actual knowledge that it is collecting personal information from a child." 15 U.S.C. § 6502(a)(1). COPPA only applies to websites that collect personal information from children under age 13. § 6502(1).

Notice. Children's websites must post privacy policies, describing "what information is collected from children by the operator, how the operator uses such information, and the operator's disclosure practices for such information." § 6502(b)(1)(A)(i).

Consent. Children's websites must "obtain verifiable parental consent for the collection, use or disclosure of personal information from children." § 6502(b)(1)(A)(ii). Websites cannot condition child's participation in a game or receipt of a prize on the disclosure of more personal information than is necessary to participate in that activity. § 6502(b)(1)(C). When information is not maintained in retrievable form, then consent is not required. § 6502(b)(2).

Right to Restrict Uses of Information. If parent requests it, the operator must provide to the parent a description of the "specific types of personal information collected," the right to "refuse to permit the operator's further use or maintenance in retrievable form, or future online collection, of personal information from that child," and the right to "obtain any personal information collected from the child." § 6502(b)(1)(B).

---

[51] Tim Arango, *Cable Firms Join Forces to Attract Focused Ads*, N.Y. Times, C1, Mar. 10, 2008.

Enforcement. Violations of the COPPA are "treated as a violation of a rule defining an unfair or deceptive act or practice" under 15 U.S.C. § 57a(a)(1)(B). Thus, the FTC enforces the law and can impose fines. There is no private cause of action for violations of the COPPA.

States can bring civil actions for violations of the COPPA in the interests of its citizens to obtain injunctions and damages. § 6504.

Preemption. The COPPA preempts state law. § 6502(d).

Safe Harbor. If an operator follows self-regulatory guidelines issued by marketing or online industry groups that are approved by the FTC, then the COPPA requirements will be deemed satisfied. § 6503.

Should the COPPA be extended to apply to everyone, not just children? Should there be a private cause of action under the COPPA? Note that the COPPA only applies when a website has "actual knowledge" that a user is under 13 or operates a website specifically targeted to children. Is this too limiting? Would a rule dispensing with the "actual knowledge" requirement be feasible?[52]

FTC Enforcement Actions. The FTC has engaged in several enforcement actions pursuant to COPPA. These cases have resulted in settlements simultaneously with the filing of complaints. Heavy penalties have been assessed as part of some of the settlements. For example, in September 2006, the FTC announced a settlement with Xanga.com, which included a $1 million civil penalty. The complaint charges that Xanga.com, a social networking website, had actual knowledge of its collection of disclosure of children's personal information. The Xanga website stated that children under 13 could not join its social network, but it allowed visitors to create Xanga accounts even if they provided a birth date indicating that they were younger than that age. Moreover, Xanga did not provide parents with access to and control over their children's information, and did not notify the parents of children who joined the site of its information practices. Finally, the FTC found that Xanga had created 1.7 million accounts for users who submitted age information that indicated they were younger than 13 years old.

In addition, the FTC has fined operators of websites in situations where they lacked actual knowledge that they were collecting information of someone who was under 13. Thus, the FTC found a violation of COPPA when a website was directed to children and provided a pull-down menu for the year of birth that did not include any of the last 12 years.[53]

Assessing the COPPA. Consider the following critique of the COPPA by Anita Allen:

---

[52] For more information about COPPA, see Dorothy A. Hertzel, Note, *Don't Talk to Strangers: An Analysis of Government and Industry Efforts to Protect Child's Privacy Online*, 52 Fed. Comm. L.J. 429 (2000).

[53] U.S. v. Lisa Frank, No. 01-CV-1516 (E.D. Va. 2001), Complaint at ¶ 15, at http://www.ftc.gov/os/2001/10/lfcmp.pdf.

Not all parents welcome the veto power COPPA confers. New power has meant new responsibility. The statute forces parents who would otherwise be content to give their children free rein over their computers to get involved in children's use of Internet sites that are geared toward children and collect personal information. . . .

Prohibiting voluntary disclosures by children lacking parental consent in situations in which they and their parents may be indifferent to privacy losses and resentful of government intervention, COPPA is among the most paternalistic and authoritarian of the federal privacy statutes thus far.[54]

ELECTRONIC COMMUNICATIONS PRIVACY ACT

In several cases, plaintiffs have attempted to use the Electronic Communications Privacy Act (ECPA) to prevent certain kinds of information collection, use, and disclosure by commercial entities. Recall from Chapter 2 that EPCA consists of three acts: (1) the Wiretap Act, 18 U.S.C. §§ 2510–2522, which regulates the interception of communications; (2) the Stored Communications Act (SCA), 18 U.S.C. §§ 2701–2711, which regulates communications in storage and ISP subscriber records; and (3) the Pen Register Act, 18 U.S.C. §§ 3121–3127, which regulates the use of pen register and trap and trace devices. The attempts to use ECPA to regulate commercial entities using personal information primarily seek to use the Wiretap Act or the SCA.

IN RE PHARMATRAK, INC. PRIVACY LITIGATION

220 F. Supp. 2d 4 (D. Mass. 2002)

TAURO, J. Plaintiffs . . . bring this consolidated action against Pharmatrak, Inc. and several pharmaceutical companies. . . .

Plaintiffs allege that Defendants "secretly intercepted and accessed Internet users' electronic communications with various health-related and medical-related Internet Web sites and secretly accessed their computer hard drives in order to collect private information about their Web browsing habits [and] confidential health information without their knowledge, authorization, or consent." Plaintiffs contend that the Pharmaceutical Defendants conspired with Plaintiff Pharmatrak to "collect and share this wrongfully obtained personal and sensitive information." This activity was allegedly accomplished through the use of "web bugs," "persistent cookies," and other devices.

The Pharmaceutical Defendants hired Defendant Pharmatrak to monitor their corporate web sites and provide monthly analysis of web site traffic. . . . Pharmatrak specifically represented to the Pharmaceutical Defendants that these products did not collect "personally identifiable information." Even though the Pharmaceutical Defendants may not have known precisely how Pharmatrak's software worked, Plaintiffs readily admit that "the Pharmaceutical Defendants did authorize Pharmatrak's presence upon their Web sites."

---

[54] Anita L. Allen, *Minor Distractions: Children, Privacy and E-Commerce*, 38 Houston L. Rev. 751, 752-53, 768-69, 775-76 (2001).

Pharmatrak's system operated through the use of HTML programming, JavaScript programming, cookies, and "web bugs." Each of the Pharmaceutical Defendants' web pages were programmed with Pharmatrak code, which allowed Pharmatrak to monitor web site activity. When a computer browser requested information from a Pharmaceutical Defendant's web page, the web page would send the requested information to the user, and the site's programming code would instruct the user's browser to contact Pharmatrak's web server and retrieve a "clear GIF" from it. A clear GIF is a one pixel-by-one pixel or two pixels-by-two pixels graphic image, and is sometimes called a web bug or a "pixel tag." The purpose of a clear GIF was to cause the user's computer browser to communicate directly with Pharmatrak's web server. . . .

Having caused the user's Internet browser to contact Pharmatrak, Pharmatrak then sent a cookie back to the browser. A cookie is an electronic file "attached" to a user's computer by a computer server. Plaintiffs concede that "[c]ookies generally perform many convenient and innocuous functions." Commonly, cookies are used to store users' preferences and other information, which allows users to easily access and utilize personalized services on the web or to maintain an online "shopping cart." Cookies also allow web sites to differentiate between users as they visit by assigning each individual browser a unique, randomly generated numeric or alphanumeric identifier. If an individual browser had already visited the "Pharmatrak-enabled" website, Pharmatrak would recognize the previously placed cookie and could therefore differentiate between a repeat visit and an initial visit. . . .

Plaintiffs allege that the JavaApplet used by Pharmatrak allowed Pharmatrak to monitor the length of time that a particular user viewed one of the Pharmaceutical Defendants' web pages. Plaintiffs also allege that the JavaScript programming allowed Pharmatrak to "intercept the full URL of the tracked Web page visited by the user," as well as "the full URL of the Web page visited by the Internet user *immediately prior* to the user's visit to the Pharmatrak-coded Web page. This prior Web page address is known as a 'referrer URL.'" According to Plaintiffs, Pharmatrak used JavaScript "to extract referring URLs from the client's history, thereby bypassing any security or privacy mechanisms put in place to control the flow of potentially sensitive data." The JavaScript and JavaApplet, therefore, also caused users' computer browsers to communicate with Pharmatrak's server while they intentionally communicated with the Pharmaceutical Defendants' servers.

The examination of Pharmatrak's logs "identified hundreds of people by name." . . . Plaintiffs claim that Pharmatrak collected information which included: names, addresses, telephone numbers, dates of birth, sex, insurance status, medical conditions, education levels, and occupations. Pharmatrak also collected data about email communications, including user names, email addresses, and subject lines from emails. . . .

In sum, Plaintiffs argue that "Pharmatrak's technology permits defendants to collect extensive, detailed information about plaintiffs and Class members." In addition to the personal information discussed above, the information collected allegedly included "Web sites the Internet users were at prior to the time they went to the Pharmaceutical Defendants' Web sites, questions they asked and typed in at those prior sites, information they entered while at the Pharmaceutical Defendants' web sites, and the types of computers they were using."

Title I of the Electronic Communication Privacy Act of 1986 ("ECPA"), Interception of Electronic Communications ("The Wiretap Act"), provides that:

> Except as otherwise specifically provided in this chapter[,] any person who — (a) intentionally intercepts, endeavors to intercept, or procures any other person to intercept, any wire, oral, or electronic communication . . . shall be punished as provided in subsection (4) or shall be subject to suit as provided in subsection (5). 18 U.S.C. § 2511(1)(a).

This criminal statute provides for a private right of action, and is subject the following statutory exception:

> (d) It shall not be unlawful under this chapter for a person not acting under color of law to intercept a wire, oral, or electronic communication where such person is a party to the communication or where one of the parties to the communication has given prior consent to such interception unless such communication is intercepted for the purpose of committing any criminal or tortious act. 18 U.S.C. § 2511(2)(d).

Plaintiffs argue that Defendants intentionally "intercepted plaintiffs' or Class members' electronic communications with the Web sites they visited without plaintiffs' or the Class' [sic] knowledge, authorization, or consent. . . ."

Plaintiffs claim that "Pharmatrak intercepted plaintiffs' transmission of their personal information to the Pharmaceutical Defendants' Web sites without the express or implied consent of either plaintiffs or the Pharmaceutical Defendants." Despite the fact that the Pharmaceutical Defendants may have consented to Pharmatrak's assembly of anonymous, aggregate information, Plaintiffs insist that the web sites never consented to Pharmatrak's collection of personally identifiable information. Absent this specific consent, Plaintiffs argue, the Wiretap Act's statutory exception simply does not apply. . . .

In the present case, Plaintiffs concede that the Pharmaceutical Defendants consented to the placement of code for Pharmatrak's . . . service on their web sites. . . . [C]onsent precludes a claim under the Wiretap Act. The Pharmaceutical companies contracted with Pharmatrak, and authorized Pharmatrak to communicate with any users who contacted the Pharmaceutical Web sites. . . . It is sufficient that the Pharmaceutical Defendants were parties to communications with Plaintiffs and consented to the monitoring service provided by Defendant Pharmatrak.

Plaintiffs are also unable to demonstrate that Defendants acted with a tortious purpose. Plaintiffs have produced no evidence "either (1) that the primary motivation, or (2) that a determinative factor in the actor [Pharmatrak's] motivation for intercepting the conversation was to commit a criminal [or] tortious . . . act." Without a showing of the requisite *mens rea,* Plaintiffs cannot succeed on their claim under the Wiretap Act. . . .

Title II of the ECPA, also known as the "Stored Wire and Electronic Communications and Transactional Records Act," "aims to prevent hackers from obtaining, altering, or destroying certain stored electronic communications." The statute provides:

[W]hoever — (1) intentionally accesses without authorization a facility through which an electronic communication service is provided; or (2) intentionally exceeds an authorization to access that facility; and thereby obtains, alters, or prevents authorized access to a wire or electronic communication while it is in electronic storage in such system shall be punished as provided by subsection (b) of this section. 18 U.S.C. § 2701(a).

Plaintiffs acknowledge that § 2701 was primarily designed to provide a cause of action against computer hackers, and argue that "Defendants' conduct of accessing data in plaintiffs' computers, including the content of plaintiffs' e-mails, constitutes electronic trespassing and falls squarely within the ambit of Section 2701."

Defendants disagree, and claim that they are entitled to summary judgment on at least two separate grounds: (1) Plaintiffs' computers are not facilities which provide electronic communications services, an essential element of § 2701; and (2) any alleged access to "communications" was authorized.

Defendants are correct that an individual Plaintiff's personal computer is not a "facility through which an electronic communication service is provided" for the purposes of § 2701. Plaintiffs find it noteworthy that "[p]ersonal computers provide consumers with the opportunity to access the Internet and send or receive electronic communications," and that "[w]ithout personal computers, most consumers would not be able to access the Internet or electronic communications." Fair enough, but without a telephone, most consumers would not be able to access telephone lines, and without televisions, most consumers would not be able to access cable television. Just as telephones and televisions are necessary devices by which consumers access particular services, personal computers are necessary devices by which consumers connect to the Internet. While it is possible for modern computers to perform server-like functions, there is no evidence that any of the Plaintiffs used their computers in this way. While computers and telephones certainly provide services in the general sense of the word, that is not enough for the purposes of the ECPA. The relevant *service* is Internet access, and the service is provided through ISPs or other servers, not though Plaintiffs' PCs.

Even if the court were to assume that Plaintiffs' computers are "facilities" under § 2701, any access to stored communications was authorized and, thus, Defendants' conduct falls under the exception from liability created by § 2701(c)(2). . . . [T]he Pharmaceutical Defendants are "users" under the ECPA. . . . As users, the Pharmaceutical Defendants could consent to Pharmatrak's interception of Plaintiffs' communications. . . .

In addition, the ECPA does not prohibit Pharmatrak's actions with regard to the placing of cookies on Plaintiffs' computers. Section § 2701 seeks to target communications which are in "electronic storage" incident to their transmission. . . . "Title II only protects electronic communications stored 'for a limited time' in the 'middle' of a transmission, i.e. when an electronic communication service temporarily stores a communication while waiting to store it." Even if such cookies were covered by the ECPA, Pharmatrak created and sent the cookies, and thus any accessing of the cookies by Pharmatrak at a later date would certainly be "authorized." Because Pharmatrak's cookies fall outside the scope of § 2701, Plaintiffs' claim under that section must fail. . . .

NOTES & QUESTIONS

1. ***Postscript.*** On appeal, the First Circuit let stand the district court's holding dismissing the plaintiff's Stored Communications Act claim. *In re Pharmatrak, Inc. Privacy Litigation,* 392 F.3d 9 (1st Cir. 2003). As for the Wiretap Act claim, the court reversed. To prove a violation of the Wiretap Act, the court stated, the plaintiff must prove that "a defendant (1) intentionally (2) intercepted, endeavored to intercept or procured another person to intercept or endeavor to intercept (3) the contents of (4) an electronic communication (5) using a device." The court concluded that the "district court made an error of law . . . as to what constitutes consent." The court reasoned that the "client pharmaceutical companies did not give the requisite consent. The pharmaceutical clients sought and received assurances from Pharmatrak that its . . . service did not and could not collect personally identifiable information. . . . Nor did the users consent." The court remanded as to whether the interception had been intentional.

   Note that there was no consent here because Pharmatrak didn't adequately inform its pharmaceutical clients. Suppose that Pharmatrak told its pharmaceutical clients that it was gathering personal information, but that Pharmatrak did not inform the individual users of the pharmaceutical websites. Would the consent exception apply under these circumstances?

   On remand, the district court concluded that the interception was not intentional, and that at most, Pharmatrak had negligently gathered the personal data. Accordingly, the Wiretap Act claim was again dismissed. *In re Pharmatrak, Inc. Privacy Litigation,* 292 F. Supp. 2d 263 (D. Mass. 2003).

2. ***Does ECPA Prohibit Cookies?*** When a person interacts with a website, the site can record certain information about the person, such as what parts of the website the user visited, what the user clicked on, and how long the user spent reading different parts of the website. This information is called "clickstream data."

   Websites use "cookies" to identify particular users.[55] A cookie is a small text file that is downloaded into the user's computer when a user accesses a web page. The text in a cookie, which is often encoded, usually includes an identification number and several other data elements, such as the website and the expiration date. The cookie lets a website know that a particular user has returned. The website can then access any information it collected about that individual on her previous visits to the website. Cookies can also be used to track users as they visit multiple websites.

   In *In re Doubleclick Inc. Privacy Litigation,* 154 F. Supp. 2d 497 (S.D.N.Y. 2001), a group of plaintiffs challenged DoubleClick's use of cookies under the Stored Communications Act (SCA) and Wiretap Act. In 2001, DoubleClick was the leading company providing online advertising. DoubleClick helps advertisers distribute advertisements to websites based on

---

[55] For a discussion of the *DoubleClick* case, see Tal Zarsky, *Cookie Viewers and the Undermining of Data-Mining: A Critical Review of the DoubleClick Settlement,* 2002 Stan. Tech. L. Rev. 1.

information about specific web surfers. When a person visits a DoubleClick-affiliated website, DoubleClick places a cookie on that person's computer. As the person visits other sites that use DoubleClick, it builds a profile of that person's web surfing activity. DoubleClick then can target ads to specific people based on their profile. For example, suppose a news website uses DoubleClick. A person visits the news website. The website checks with DoubleClick to see if DoubleClick recognizes the person. If the person's computer has a DoubleClick cookie, DoubleClick then looks up the profile associated with the cookie and sends the website advertisements tailored to that person's interests. Suppose Person A likes tennis and Person B likes golf. When Person A goes to the news website, a banner ad for tennis might appear. When Person B visits the same site, a banner ad for golf might appear.

The plaintiffs in the *DoubleClick* case raised an SCA claim and a Wiretap Act claim. Regarding the SCA claim, the Act provides:

> [W]hoever (1) intentionally accesses without authorization a facility through which an electronic information service is provided; or (2) intentionally exceeds an authorization to access that facility; and thereby obtains . . . access to a wire or electronic communication while it is in electronic storage in such system shall be punished. . . . 18 U.S.C. § 2701(a).

Although the court ultimately concluded that the SCA did not apply, its reasoning was very controversial. The court first held that an individual's computer, when connected to the Internet, was a "facility through which an electronic information service is provided." This means that when DoubleClick accessed cookies on people's computers, it was "intentionally access[ing] without authorization a facility through which an electronic information service is provided." However, the consent exception to this provision of the SCA is that "users" may authorize access "with respect to a communication of or intended for that user." § 2701(c). The individuals whose computers were accessed were obviously users, and they did not consent. But the websites that the users visited that used DoubleClick cookies were also "users" in the court's interpretation, and they consented. Only one party needs to consent for the SCA consent exception to apply.

Moreover, the court noted that the SCA only applies to "temporary, intermediate storage of a wire or electronic communication," § 2510(17), and that DoubleClick's cookies were not "temporary" because they exist on people's hard drives for a virtually infinite time period.

Commentators argue that the court's application of the SCA is wrong because a "facility" refers to an Internet Service Provider, not an individual computer. Indeed, this was the conclusion of *In re Pharmatrak.* Consider Orin Kerr:

> [T]he Stored Communications Act regulates the privacy of Internet account holders at ISPs and other servers; the law was enacted to create by statute a set of Fourth Amendment-like set of rights in stored records held by ISPs. The theory of the *Doubleclick* plaintiffs turned this framework on its head, as it

attempted to apply a law designed to give account holders privacy rights in information held at third-party ISPs to home PCs interacting with websites.[56]

Regarding the Wiretap Act claim, DoubleClick conceded, for the purposes of summary judgment, that it had "intercepted" electronic communications. Orin Kerr also takes issue with this concession:

> [T]he Wiretap Act prohibits a third-party from intercepting in real-time the contents of communications between two parties unless one of the two parties consents. This law had no applicability to Doubleclick's cookies, as the cookies did not intercept any contents and did not intercept anything in real-time. The cookies merely registered data sent to it from Doubleclick's servers.[57]

DoubleClick argued that even if it intercepted electronic communications, the consent exception applied, since one party (the websites using DoubleClick) consented. The court agreed. The consent exception, however, does not apply if even with consent the "communication is intercepted for the purpose of committing any criminal or tortious act." 18 U.S.C. § 2511(2)(d). The court concluded: "DoubleClick's purpose has plainly not been to perpetuate torts on millions of Internet users, but to make money by providing a valued service to commercial Web sites."

3. **Web Bugs.** Beyond cookies, another device for collecting people's data is called a "web bug." As one court describes it, web bugs (or "action tags") are very tiny pixels on a website that can record how a person navigates around the Internet. Unlike a cookie, which can be accepted or declined by a user, a web bug is a very small graphic file that is secretly downloaded to the user's computer. Web bugs enable the website to monitor a person's keystrokes and cursor movement. Web bugs can also be placed in e-mail messages that use HTML, or HyperText Markup Language. E-mail using HTML enables users to see graphics in an e-mail. A web bug in an e-mail message can detect whether the e-mail was read and to whom it was forwarded. According to computer security expert Richard M. Smith, a web bug can gather the IP address of the computer that fetched the web bug; the URL of the page that the web bug is located on; the URL of the web bug image; the time the web bug was viewed; the type of browser that fetched the web bug image; and a previously set cookie value. Is the use of a web bug a violation of federal electronic surveillance law?

DYER V. NORTHWEST AIRLINES CORP.

334 F. Supp. 2d 1196 (D.N.D. 2004)

HOVLAND, C.J. . . . Following September 11, 2001, the National Aeronautical and Space Administration ("NASA") requested system-wide passenger data from

---

[56] Orin S. Kerr, *Lifting the "Fog" of Internet Surveillance: How a Suppression Remedy Would Change Computer Crime Law*, 54 Hastings L.J. 805, 831 (2003).

[57] *Id.* at 831.

Northwest Airlines for a three-month period in order to conduct research for use in airline security studies. Northwest Airlines complied and, unbeknownst to its customers, provided NASA with the names, addresses, credit card numbers, and travel itineraries of persons who had flown on Northwest Airlines between July and December 2001.

The discovery of Northwest Airlines' disclosure of its customers' personal information triggered a wave of litigation. Eight class actions — seven in Minnesota and one in Tennessee — were filed in federal court prior to March 19, 2004. The seven Minnesota actions were later consolidated into a master file.

[In this case, t]he complaint alleges that Northwest Airlines' unauthorized disclosure of customers' personal information constituted a violation of the Electronic Communications Privacy Act ("ECPA"), 18 U.S.C. §§ 2702(a)(1) and (a)(3). . . .

The Electronic Communications Privacy Act (ECPA) provides in relevant part that, with certain exceptions, a person or entity providing either an electronic communication service or remote computing service to the public shall not:

- knowingly divulge to any person or entity the contents of a communication while in electronic storage by that service (18 U.S.C. § 2702(a)(1)); and

- knowingly divulge a record or other information pertaining to a subscriber to or customer of such service . . . to any governmental entity (18 U.S.C. § 2702(a)(3)).

In its complaint, the Plaintiffs asserted claims under both 18 U.S.C. §§ 2702(a)(1) and (a)(3) of the ECPA. The plaintiffs have conceded no claim exists under 18 U.S.C. § 2702(a)(1). Consequently, the Court's focus will be directed at the Plaintiffs' ability to sustain a claim against Northwest Airlines under 18 U.S.C. § 2702(a)(3). To sustain a claim under 18 U.S.C. § 2702(a)(3), the Plaintiffs must establish that Northwest Airlines provides either electronic communication services or remote computing services. It is clear that Northwest Airlines provides neither.

The ECPA defines "electronic communication service" as "any service which provides the users thereof the ability to send or receive wire or electronic communications." 18 U.S.C. § 2510(15). In construing this definition, courts have distinguished those entities that sell access to the internet from those that sell goods or services on the internet. 18 U.S.C. § 2702(a)(3) prescribes the conduct only of a "provider of a remote computing service or electronic communication service to the public." A provider under the ECPA is commonly referred to as an internet service provider or ISP. There is no factual allegation that Northwest Airlines, an airline that sells airline tickets on its website, provides internet services.

Courts have concluded that "electronic communication service" encompasses internet service providers as well as telecommunications companies whose lines carry internet traffic, but does not encompass businesses selling traditional products or services online. See *In re DoubleClick Inc. Privacy Litig.,* 154 F. Supp. 2d 497 (S.D.N.Y. 2001). . . .

The distinction is critical in this case. Northwest Airlines is not an electronic communications service provider as contemplated by the ECPA. Instead,

Northwest Airlines sells its products and services over the internet as opposed to access to the internet itself. The ECPA definition of "electronic communications service" clearly includes internet service providers such as America Online, as well as telecommunications companies whose cables and phone lines carry internet traffic. However, businesses offering their traditional products and services online through a website are not providing an "electronic communication service." As a result, Northwest Airlines falls outside the scope of 18 U.S.C. § 2702 and the ECPA claim fails as a matter of law. The facts as pled to not give rise to liability under the ECPA. 18 U.S.C. § 2702(a) does not prohibit or even address the dissemination of business records of passenger flights and information as described in the complaint. Instead, the focus of 18 U.S.C. § 2702(a) is on "communications" being stored by the communications service provider for the purpose of subsequent transmission or for backup purposes.

[The plaintiffs also raised a claim under the Minnesota Deceptive Trade Practices Act. The court held that the claim was barred by the federal Airline Deregulation Act, which preempts state regulation of "a price, route, or service of an airline carrier." 49 U.S.C. § 4173(b)(1).]

NOTES & QUESTIONS

1. *ISPs vs. Non-ISPs.* In this case, Northwest Airlines violated its privacy policy by disclosing its customer records to the government. Suppose Northwest Airlines had been an ISP like AOL or Earthlink. Would it have been liable under the Stored Communications Act?

2. *Other Remedies.* What other potential remedies might the plaintiffs have in this case? The plaintiffs brought an action for breach of contract, which was discussed earlier in this chapter in the section on privacy policies. Besides breach of contract, can you think of any other causes of action that might be brought?

COMPUTER FRAUD AND ABUSE ACT

The Computer Fraud and Abuse Act (CFAA) of 1984, 18 U.S.C. § 1030, provides criminal and civil penalties for unauthorized access to computers. Originally passed in 1984, the statue was amended updated throughout the 1990s. Several states have similar statutes regarding the misuse of computers. As Orin Kerr notes:

> While no two statutes are identical, all share the common trigger of "access without authorization" or "unauthorized access" to computers, sometimes in tandem with its close cousin, "exceeding authorized access" to computers.[58]

---

[58] Orin S. Kerr, *Cybercrime's Scope: Interpreting "Access" and "Authorization" in Computer Misuse Statutes*, 78 N.Y.U. L. Rev. 1596, 1615 (2003).

Scope. The CFAA applies to all "protected computer[s]." A "protected computer" is any computer used in interstate commerce or communication. Whereas the Stored Communications Act of ECPA appears to apply only to ISPs, the CFAA applies to both ISPs and individual computers.

Criminal Penalties. The CFAA creates seven crimes. Among these, it imposes criminal penalties when a person or entity "intentionally accesses a computer without authorization or exceeds authorized access, and thereby obtains . . . information from any protected computer." § 1030(a)(2)(c). It criminalizes unauthorized access to "any nonpublic computer of a department or agency of the United States." § 1030(a)(3). The CFAA also criminalizes unauthorized access to computers "knowingly with intent to defraud" and the obtaining of "anything of value, unless the object of the fraud and the thing obtained consists only of the use of the computer and the value of such use is not more than $5,000 in any 1-year period." § 1030(a)(4). Yet another crime created by the CFAA prohibits knowingly transmitting "a program, information, code, or command" or "intentionally access[ing] a protected computer without authorization" that causes damage to a protected computer. § 1030(5)(A)(i). Punishments range from fines to imprisonment for up to 20 years depending upon the provision violated.

Damage. The term "damage" means "any impairment to the integrity or availability of data, a program, a system, or information." § 1030(e). In many provisions in the CFAA, the damage must exceed $5,000 in a one-year period.

Civil Remedies. "Any person who suffers damage or loss by reason of a violation of this section may maintain a civil action against the violator to obtain compensatory damages or injunctive relief or other equitable relief." § 1030(g). "Damage" must cause a "loss aggregating at least $5,000 in value during any 1-year period to one or more individuals." § 1030(e).

Exceeding Authorized Access. Many provisions in the CFAA can be violated not just by unauthorized access, but also when one "exceeds authorized access." To exceed authorized access means "to access a computer with authorization and to use such access to obtain or alter information in the computer that the accesser is not entitled so to obtain and alter." § 1030(e)(6).

CREATIVE COMPUTING V. GETLOADED.COM LLC

386 F.3d 930 (9th Cir. 2004)

KLEINFELD, J. Truck drivers and trucking companies try to avoid dead heading. "Deadheading" means having to drive a truck, ordinarily on a return trip, without a revenue-producing load. If the truck is moving, truck drivers and their companies want it to be carrying revenue-producing freight. In the past, truckers and shippers used blackboards to match up trips and loads. Eventually television screens were used instead of blackboards, but the matching was still inefficient. Better information on where the trucks and the loads are — and quick, easy access to that information — benefits shippers, carriers, and consumers.

Creative Computing developed a successful Internet site, truckstop.com, which it calls "The Internet Truckstop," to match loads with trucks. The site is very easy to use. It has a feature called "radius search" that lets a truck driver in, say, Middletown, Connecticut, with some space in his truck, find within seconds all available loads in whatever mileage radius he likes (and of course lets a shipper post a load so that a trucker with space can find it). The site was created so early in Internet history and worked so well that it came to dominate the load-board industry.

Getloaded decided to compete, but not honestly. After Getloaded set up a load-matching site, it wanted to get a bigger piece of Creative's market. Creative wanted to prevent that, so it prohibited access to its site by competing loadmatching services. The Getloaded officers thought trucking companies would probably use the same login names and passwords on truckstop.com as they did on getloaded.com. Getloaded's president, Patrick Hull, used the login name and password of a Getloaded subscriber, in effect impersonating the trucking company, to sneak into truckstop.com. Getloaded's vice-president, Ken Hammond, accomplished the same thing by registering a defunct company, RFT Trucking, as a truckstop.com subscriber. These tricks enabled them to see all of the information available to Creative's bona fide customers.

Getloaded's officers also hacked into the code Creative used to operate its website. Microsoft had distributed a patch to prevent a hack it had discovered, but Creative Computing had not yet installed the patch on truckstop.com. Getloaded's president and vice-president hacked into Creative Computing's website through the back door that this patch would have locked. Once in, they examined the source code for the tremendously valuable radius-search feature. . . .

Getloaded argues that no action could lie under the Computer Fraud and Abuse Act because it requires a $5,000 floor for damages from each unauthorized access, and that Creative Computing submitted no evidence that would enable a jury to find that the floor was reached on any single unauthorized access. . . .

The briefs dispute which version of the statute we should apply — the one in effect when Getloaded committed the wrongs, or the one in effect when the case went to trial (which is still in effect). The old version of the statute made an exception to the fraudulent access provision if "the value of such use [unauthorized access to a protected computer] is not more than $5,000 in any 1-year period."[59] The new version, in effect now and during trial, says "loss . . . during any 1-year period . . . aggregating at least $5,000 in value."[60] These provisions are materially identical.

---

[59] 18 U.S.C. § 1030(a)(4) (2001) ("[Whoever] knowingly and with intent to defraud, accesses a protected computer without authorization, or exceeds authorized access, and by means of such conduct furthers the intended fraud and obtains anything of value, unless the object of the fraud and the thing obtained consists only of the use of the computer and the value of such use is not more than $5,000 in any 1-year period.").

[60] 18 U.S.C. § 1030(a)(5)(B)(i) ("[Whoever caused] loss to 1 or more persons during any 1-year period (and, for purposes of an investigation, prosecution, or other proceeding brought by the United States only, loss resulting from a related course of conduct affecting 1 or more other protected computers) aggregating at least $5,000 in value.").

The old version of the statute defined "damage" as "any impairment to the integrity or availability of data, a program, a system, or information" that caused the loss of at least $5,000. It had no separate definition of "loss." The new version defines "damage" the same way, but adds a definition of loss. "Loss" is defined in the new version as "any reasonable cost to any victim, including the cost of responding to an offense, conducting a damage assessment, and restoring the data . . . and any revenue lost, cost incurred, or other consequential damages incurred because of interruption of service."

For purposes of this case, we need not decide which version of the Act applies, because Getloaded loses either way. Neither version of the statute supports a construction that would require proof of $5,000 of damage or loss from a single unauthorized access. The syntax makes it clear that in both versions, the $5,000 floor applies to how much damage or loss there is to the victim over a one-year period, not from a particular intrusion. Getloaded argues that "impairment" is singular, so the floor has to be met by a single intrusion. The premise does not lead to the conclusion. The statute (both the earlier and the current versions) says "damage" means "any impairment to the integrity or availability of data[etc.] . . . that causes loss aggregating at least $5,000." Multiple intrusions can cause a single impairment, and multiple corruptions of data can be described as a single "impairment" to the data. The statute does not say that an "impairment" has to result from a single intrusion, or has to be a single corrupted byte. A court construing a statute attributes a rational purpose to Congress. Getloaded's construction would attribute obvious futility to Congress rather than rationality, because a hacker could evade the statute by setting up thousands of $4,999 (or millions of $4.99) intrusions. As the First Circuit pointed out in the analogous circumstance of physical impairment, so narrow a construction of the $5,000 impairment requirement would merely "reward sophisticated intruders." The damage floor in the Computer Fraud and Abuse Act contains no "single act" requirement.

NOTES & QUESTIONS

1. **DoubleClick, Pharmatrak, *and the* CFAA.** In both the *DoubleClick* and *Pharmatrak* cases, the plaintiffs brought CFAA claims. In both cases, the plaintiffs lost. In *In re Doubleclick Inc. Privacy Litigation*, 154 F. Supp. 2d 497 (S.D.N.Y. 2001), the plaintiffs contended that collectively they suffered more than $5,000 in damages, but the court held that the plaintiffs could not add up their damages. Damages could only be combined "for a single act" against "a particular computer." Since the plaintiffs' CFAA claims concerned multiple acts against many different computers, they could not be aggregated to reach the $5,000 threshold. In *In re Pharmatrak, Inc. Privacy Litigation*, 220 F. Supp. 2d 4 (D. Mass. 2002), the court concluded:

   > Plaintiffs do not allege that their computers were physically damaged in any way, or that they suffered any damage resulting from the repair or replacement of their computer systems. . . .
   >   Plaintiffs have not shown any evidence whatsoever that Defendants have caused them at least $5,000 of damage or loss. . . . Any damage or loss under

the CFAA may be aggregated across victims and across time, but only for a single act. Because Plaintiffs have not shown any facts that demonstrate damage or loss of over $5,000 for any single act of the Defendants, [the CFAA claim is dismissed].

2. **The Megan Meier Case and Lori Drew Indictment.** Megan Meier was a 13-year old girl who became friends with a boy named "Josh Evans" on the social network website MySpace. After a while, Josh started sending Megan mean and nasty comments over the Internet. Tragically, Megan committed suicide. Josh was actually a fake MySpace profile created by Lori Drew, the mother of one of Megan's classmates. Drew created the profile in an apparent attempt to learn information about her daughter from Megan. The case generated significant media attention, as well as public outrage over Drew's actions.

In 2008, Drew was indicted with violating the CFAA. The indictment charged four counts, including the one below:

> On or about the following dates, defendant Drew, using a computer in O'Fallon, Missouri, intentionally accessed and caused to be accessed a computer used in interstate commerce, namely, the MySpace servers located in Los Angeles County, California, within the Central District of California, without authorization and in excess of authorized access, and, by means of interstate commerce obtained and caused to be obtained information from that computer to further tortious acts, namely intentional infliction of emotional distress on [Megan Meier].

The prosecution's theory was that Drew exceeded authorized access to MySpace by violating its terms of service, which mandated that Drew provide "truthful and accurate information" when registering and to "refrain from using any information obtained from MySpace services to harass, abuse, or harm other people." The CFAA § 1020(a)(2)(C) makes it a criminal misdemeanor when one "intentionally accesses a computer without authorization or exceeds authorized access, and thereby obtains . . . information from any protected computer." The CFAA § 1030(c)(2)(B)(2) makes it a felony to exceed authorized access if the offense was committed in furtherance of any tortious act.

Is the prosecutor's theory consistent with the CFAA's language and purpose? What are the implications of prosecutions under the CFAA for violating a website's terms of service? Is the CFAA unconstitutionally vague? A constitutionally vague law is one that either fails to provide the kind of notice that will enable ordinary people to understand what conduct it prohibits; or authorizes or encourages arbitrary and discriminatory enforcement.

3. **Spyware.** Spyware is a new kind of computer program that raises significant threats to privacy. Paul Schwartz distinguishes "spyware" from "adware" in terms of the notice provided to the user. He also explains how these programs come about through the linking of personal computers via the Internet: "Spyware draws on computer resources to create a network that can be used for numerous purposes, including collecting personal and nonpersonal information from computers and delivering adware or targeted advertisements

to individuals surfing the Web. Adware is sometimes, but not always, delivered as part of spyware; the definitional line between the two depends on whether the computer user receives adequate notice of the program's installation."[61] Would the CFAA apply to a company that secretly installs spyware in a person's computer that transmits her personal data back to the company without her awareness? Would the Wiretap Act apply?

4. ***State Spyware Statutes.*** The state of Utah became the first state to pass legislation to regulate spyware. The original Spyware Control Act, Utah Code Ann. §§ 13-40-101 *et seq.*, prohibited the installation of spyware on another person's computer, limited the display of certain types of advertising, created a private right of action, and empowered the Utah Division of Consumer Protection to collect complaints. WhenU, an advertising network, challenged the Act in 2004, arguing that it violated the Commerce Clause of the U.S. Constitution, and it obtained a preliminary injunction against the statute. A revised bill was signed by the Utah governor on March 17, 2005. The revised Act defines "spyware" as "software on a computer of a user who resides in this state that . . . collects information about an Internet website at the time the Internet website is being viewed in this state, unless the Internet website is the Internet website of the person who provides the software; and . . . uses the information . . . contemporaneously to display pop-up advertising on the computer."

Following Utah's lead, California enacted a spyware bill, which was signed by Governor Arnold Schwarzenegger on September 28, 2004. The Consumer Protection Against Computer Spyware Act, SB 1426, prohibits a person from causing computer software to be installed on a computer and using the software to (1) take control of the computer; (2) modify certain settings relating to the computer's access to the Internet; (3) collect, through intentionally deceptive means, personally identifiable information; (4) prevent, without authorization, the authorized user's reasonable efforts to block the installation of or disable software; (5) intentionally misrepresent that the software will be uninstalled or disabled by the authorized user's action; or (6) through intentionally deceptive means, remove, disable, or render, inoperative security, anti-spyware, or antivirus software installed on the computer.

(c) Marketing

TELEPHONE CONSUMER PROTECTIONS ACT

The Telephone Consumer Protections Act (TCPA) of 1991, Pub. L. No. 102-243, 47 U.S.C. § 227, permits individuals to sue a telemarketer in small claims court for an actual loss or up to $500 (whichever is greater), for each call received after requesting to be placed on its "Do Not Call" list:

---

[61] Paul M. Schwartz, *Property, Privacy, and Personal Data*, 117 Harv. L. Rev. 2055 (2004).

A person who has received more than one telephone call within any 12-month period by or on behalf of the same entity in violation of the regulations prescribed under this subsection may, if otherwise permitted by the laws or rules of a court of a State bring in an appropriate court of that State [an action for an injunction and to recover actual damages or $500 for each violation]. § 227(c)(5).

Telemarketers can offer as an affirmative defense that they established "reasonable practices and procedures to effectively prevent telephone solicitations in violation of the regulations prescribed under this subsection." § 227(c)(5). If telemarketer has acted "willfully or knowingly," then damages are trebled. § 227(c)(5).

The TCPA prohibits telemarketers from calling residences and using prerecorded messages without the consent of the called party. 47 U.S.C. § 227(b)(1)(B). The TCPA prohibits the use of a fax, computer, or other device to send an unsolicited advertisement to a fax machine. § 227(b)(1)(C). The Act also requires the FCC to promulgate rules to "protect residential telephone subscribers' privacy rights and to avoid receiving telephone solicitations to which they object." § 227(c)(1). In addition, the FCC is authorized to require that a "single national database" be established of a "list of telephone numbers of residential subscribers who object to receiving telephone solicitations." § 227(c)(3). It is within the discretion of the FCC to determine whether such a database is necessary or feasible.

States may initiate actions against telemarketers "engaging in a pattern or practice of telephone calls or other transmissions to residents of that State" in violation of the TCPA. § 227(f)(1).

In *Destination Ventures, Ltd. v. FCC,* 46 F.3d 54 (9th Cir. 1995), Destination Ventures challenged a provision of the TCPA banning unsolicited faxes that contained advertisements on First Amendment grounds. The court upheld the ban because it was designed to prevent shifting advertising costs to consumers, who would be forced to pay for the toner and paper to receive the ads.

CAN-SPAM ACT

In 2003, Congress enacted the Controlling the Assault of Non-Solicited Pornography and Marketing (CAN-SPAM) Act, Pub. L. No. 108-187, 15 U.S.C. §§ 7701 *et seq.,* to address the problem of spam. Spam is a term to describe unsolicited commercial e-mail sent to individuals to advertise products and services.[62] Companies that send unsolicited e-mail are referred to as spammers. Spam is often mailed out in bulk to large lists of e-mail addresses. A recent practice has been to insert hidden HTML tags (also known as "pixel tags") into spam. This enables the sender of the e-mail to detect whether the e-mail was opened. It can also inform the sender about whether the e-mail message was forwarded, to what e-mail address it was forwarded, and sometimes, even comments added by a user when forwarding the e-mail. This only works if the recipient has an HTML-enabled e-mail reader rather than a text-only reader.

---

[62] For more information on spam, see David E. Sorkin, *Technical and Legal Approaches to Unsolicited Electronic Mail*, 35 U.S.F. L. Rev. 325, 336 (2001).

HTML e-mail is e-mail that contains pictures and images rather than simply plain text. The practice has become known as a "web bug."

Applicability. The CAN-SPAM Act applies to commercial e-mail, which it defines as a "message with the primary purpose of which is the commercial advertisement or promotion of a commercial product or service."

Prohibitions. The Act prohibits the knowing sending of commercial messages with the intent to deceive or mislead recipients.

Opt Out. The CAN-SPAM Act also requires that a valid opt-out option be made available to e-mail recipients. To make opt out possible, the Act requires senders of commercial e-mail to contain a return address "clearly and conspicuously displayed." Finally, it creates civil and criminal penalties for violations of its provisions. For example, the law allows the DOJ to seek criminal penalties, including imprisonment, for commercial e-mailers who engage in activities such as using a computer to relay or retransmit multiple commercial e-mail messages to receive or mislead recipients or an Internet access service about the message's origin and falsifying header information in multiple e-mail messages and initiate the transmission of these messages.

Assessing the Act. A year after enactment of CAN-SPAM, media accounts faulted the law as ineffective. Indeed, reports stressed the increase in spam during this time. According to one anti-spam vendor, 67 percent of all e-mail was spam in February 2004, and 75 percent in November 2004. Some spammers employed new tactics after the passage of the Act, such as using "zombie networks," which involve hijacking computers with Trojan horse programs. Anti-spam activists faulted CAN-SPAM for preempting tougher state laws, failing to provide a private right of action, and providing an opt-out option instead of an opt in.

Consider Paul Schwartz's critique of the CAN-SPAM Act:

> The CAN-SPAM Act of 2003 fails to provide for an individual right of action. It does provide, however, for the FTC's study of "a system for rewarding those who supply information about violations of the Act." This proposed bounty system for those who assist the FTC follows a recommendation by Lawrence Lessig, a leading cyberlaw professor. As the CAN-SPAM Act states, the FTC is to develop "procedures . . . to grant a reward of not less than 20 percent of the total civil penalty collected for a violation of [the] Act to the first person" who both "identifies the person in violation of [the] Act" and "supplies information that leads to the successful collection of a civil penalty."
>
> The bounty system calls for a mix of public and private action to increase enforcement of legal norms. It assumes, however, that the FTC's central weakness in enforcement is either informational or technical. That is, the FTC may lack adequate evidence regarding spam or the technical skills to unmask those who send unsolicited commercial e-mails. Yet the FTC already has a procedure for collecting spam, and by 2003 it was already receiving as many as 130,000 forwarded e-mails a day as a result. Moreover, if the FTC lacks the technical skills to unmask spammers, it might simply hire additional computer scientists. The enforcement of laws against spam, junk faxes, and unauthorized use of personal data is frequently a drawn-out, resource-intensive process, and

the bounty-hunter approach still leaves the central burden on the FTC or other governmental agencies. A final problem with the bounty approach, as presented by Lessig and the CAN-SPAM Act, is that it rewards only a single person per spamming case. A stronger mix of public and private action would encourage broader involvement by private individuals. As Diane Mey, the "Erin Brockovich of the anti-telemarketing movement," notes of the benefit of private rights of action: "[I]f enough people sting them a bunch of little stings, maybe they'll get the message and change their ways."[63]

State Anti-Spam Laws. At least 20 states have anti-spam statutes. For example, Cal. Bus. & Professions Code § 17538.4 mandates that senders of spam include in the text of their e-mails a way through which recipients can request to receive no further e-mails. The sender must remove the person from its list. A provider of an e-mail service located within the state of California can request that spammers stop sending spam through its equipment. If the spammer continues to send e-mail, it can be liable for $50 per message up to a maximum of $25,000 per day. *See* § 17538.45.

A Critique of Anti-Spam Legislation. Consumers don't always dislike marketing messages. As Eric Goldman reminds us, "consumers want marketing when it creates personal benefits for them, and marketing also can have spillover benefits that improve social welfare." Goldman is worried that current legal regulation will block the kinds of filters that will improve the ability of consumers to manage information and receive information that will advance their interests. He points to anti-adware laws in Utah and Alaska as especially problematic; these statutes "prohibit client-side software from displaying pop-up ads triggered by the consumer's use of a third party trademark or domain name — even if the consumer has fully consented to the software." For Goldman, these statutes are flawed because they try to "ban or restrict matchmaking technologies." The ideal filter would be a "mind-reading wonder" that "could costlessly — but accurately — read consumers' minds, infer their expressed and latent preferences without the consumer bearing any disclosure costs, and act on the inferred preferences to screen out unwanted content and proactively seek out wanted content." Goldman is confident that such filtering technology is not only possible, but "inevitable — perhaps imminently."[64] What kind of regulatory approach would encourage development and adoption of Goldman's favored filters while also blocking existing SPAM technology? Will surrendering more privacy help better target marketing and thus clear out our inboxes of unwanted spam?

Spam and Speech. Is spam a form of speech, protected by the First Amendment? In *Cyber Promotions, Inc. v. America Online, Inc.,* 948 F. Supp. 436 (E.D. Pa. 1996), Cyber Promotions, Inc. sought a declaratory judgment that America Online (AOL) was prohibited under the First Amendment from denying

---

[63] Paul M. Schwartz, *Property, Privacy and Personal Data,* 117 Harv. L. Rev. 2055, 2112-13 (2004).

[64] Eric Goldman, *A Cosean Analysis of Marketing,* 2006 Wisc. L. Rev. 1151, 1154-55, 1202, 1211-12.

it the ability to send AOL customers unsolicited e-mail. The court rejected Cyber Promotion's argument because of a lack of state action: "AOL is a private online company that is not owned in whole or part by the government." Today, the Internet is increasingly becoming a major medium of communication. Prior to modern communications media, individuals could express their views in traditional "public fora" — parks and street corners. These public fora are no longer the central place for public discourse. Perhaps the Internet is the modern public forum, the place where individuals come to speak and express their views. If this is the case, is it preferable for access to the Internet to be controlled by private entities?

(d) Federal Privacy Legislation: An Assessment

Consider the privacy statutes you have studied so far. Notice the sectoral approach — each statute addresses a particular industry or type of record or problem. Think about these laws together as a system of regulation for privacy. Do these laws adequately carry out the vision of the HEW Report's Code of Fair Information Practices? What, if anything, is missing from this system of regulation? What areas are not covered and should be?

Priscilla Regan contends that Congress has been slow to respond to privacy issues. According to Regan, those interests opposed to privacy protections (law enforcement entities, private industry, employers) were able to delay, block, and weaken Congress' statutory responses to privacy problems. Regan offers an explanation for this phenomenon:

> . . . Generally, the importance of privacy is rooted in traditional liberal thinking — privacy inheres in the individual as an individual and is important to the individual for self-development or for the establishment of intimate or human relationships. Given that the philosophical justification for privacy rests largely on its importance to the individual as an individual, policy discussions about protecting privacy focus on the goal of protecting an individual value or interest. The result has been an emphasis on an atomistic individual and the legal protection of his or her rights.
>
> But as illustrated in congressional attempts to protect privacy, defining privacy primarily in terms of its importance to the individual and in terms of an individual right has served as a weak basis for public policy. . . .
>
> [P]rivacy's importance does not stop with the individual and . . . a recognition of the social importance of privacy will clear a path for more serious policy discourse about privacy and for the formulation of more effective public policy to protect privacy.[65]

Also consider Paul Schwartz's assessment of privacy law:

> . . . At present, however, no successful standards, legal or otherwise, exist for limiting the collection and utilization of personal data in cyberspace. The lack of appropriate and enforceable privacy norms poses a significant threat to democracy in the emerging Information Age. Indeed, information privacy

---

[65] Priscilla M. Regan, *Legislating Privacy: Technology, Social Values, and Public Policy* (1995).

concerns are the leading reason why individuals not on the Internet are choosing to stay off.

The stakes are enormous; the norms that we develop for personal data use on the Internet will play an essential role in shaping democracy in the Information Age. . . .

. . . [T]he traditional American legal approach to information privacy law emphasizes regulation of government use of personal data rather than private sector activities. From the earliest days of the Republic, American law has viewed the government as the entity whose data use raises the greatest threat to individual liberty. For example, federal and state constitutional protections seek to assure freedom from governmental interference for communications and for the press. This approach means that treatment of personal information in the private sector is often unaccompanied by the presence of basic legal protections. Yet, private enterprises now control more powerful resources of information technology than ever before. These organizations' information processing contributes to their power over our lives. As the Internet becomes more central to life in the United States, the weaknesses and illogic of this existing legal model for information privacy are heightened.[66]

Joel Reidenberg critiques the ad hoc approach the United States has taken toward the protection of privacy:

The American legal system does not contain a comprehensive set of privacy rights or principles that collectively address the acquisition, storage, transmission, use and disclosure of personal information within the business community. The federal Constitution does not address privacy for information transactions wholly within the private sector and state constitutional provisions similarly do not afford rights for private transactions. Instead, legal protection is accorded exclusively through privacy rights created on an ad hoc basis by federal or state legislation or state common law rules. In addition, self-regulatory schemes have been adopted by some industries and by various companies. Although these schemes may offer privacy protection, they do not provide enforceable legal rights and do not seem to have permeated the vast majority of information processing entities.

In general, the aggregation of the federal and state rights provides targeted protection for individuals in answer to defined problems. This mosaic approach derives from the traditional American fear of government intervention in private activities and the reluctance to broadly regulate industry. The result of the mosaic is a rather haphazard and unsatisfactory response to each of the privacy concerns.[67]

Reidenberg asserts that other countries, especially those in the European Union, have taken a more comprehensive approach toward protecting privacy.

In contrast, Marc Rotenberg has a mixed verdict on the development of United States privacy law. Rotenberg contends that Congress has been responsive to emerging privacy concerns by passing privacy laws in response to new challenges. He asserts that the privacy statutes have incorporated many of the Fair Information Practices, which continue to guide and shape privacy law in

---

[66] Paul M. Schwartz, *Privacy and Democracy in Cyberspace*, 52 Vand. L. Rev. 1609, 1611, 1633-34 (1999).

[67] Joel R. Reidenberg, *Privacy in the Information Economy: A Fortress or Frontier for Individual Rights?*, 44 Fed. Comm. L.J. 195 (1992).

the United States. However, Rotenberg also argues that recent efforts to promote self-regulation have slowed the adoption of necessary privacy statutes: "One cannot escape the conclusion that privacy policy in the United States today reflects what industry is prepared to do rather than what the public wants done."[68]

(e) State Statutory Regulation

Many states have passed legislation regulating business records and databases. Many state statutes have stronger protections of privacy than federal statutes. In particular, California has passed a series of strong privacy protections, and it is probably safe to generalize that California has the strongest privacy law in the United States.[69]

Office of Privacy Protection. In 2000, California created an Office of Privacy Protection. "The office's purpose shall be protecting the privacy of individuals' personal information in a manner consistent with the California Constitution by identifying consumer problems in the privacy area and facilitating development of fair information practices." Cal. Bus. & Prof. Code §§ 350–352. The office also is authorized to make recommendations to organizations about privacy policies and practices.

In its report of activity highlights for the fiscal year July 2006–June 2007, the Office of Privacy Protection noted that it responded to 4,777 calls and e-mails. The largest amount of contacts concerned identity theft (53 percent), with the next categories being business practices and privacy laws (14 percent) and online databases (8 percent).[70] The office also noted its implementation of "a train-the-trainers strategy." It provided training in assisting victims of identity theft to community organizations, and in basic privacy awareness to state information security officers. It also developed a law enforcement manual on investigation and prosecution of identity theft for use in law enforcement classes.

Destruction of Consumer Records. Pursuant to Cal. Civ. Code § 1798.81:

> A business shall take all reasonable steps to destroy, or arrange for the destruction of a customer's records within its custody or control containing personal information which is no longer to be retained by the business by (1) shredding, (2) erasing, or (3) otherwise modifying the personal information in those records to make it unreadable or undecipherable through any means.

"Shine the Light" Law. In 2003, California passed SB27, codified at Cal. Civ. Code § 1798.83. This statute allows consumers to obtain from businesses information about the personal data that the businesses disclosed to third parties for direct marketing purposes. People can find out what kinds of personal information were provided to third parties for their direct marketing purposes as

---

[68] Marc Rotenberg, *Fair Information Practices and the Architecture of Privacy (What Larry Doesn't Get)*, 2001 Stan. Tech. L. Rev. 1, 117-19.

[69] The California Office of Privacy Protection maintains a comprehensive summary of California's privacy statutes: http://www.privacy.ca.gov/lawenforcement/laws.htm.

[70] See Office of Privacy Protection, at http://www.privacy.ca.gov/.

well as the "names and addresses of all of the third parties that received personal information from the business." § 1798.83(1). The law applies to businesses with 20 or more employees. § 1798(c)(1). It does not apply to financial institutions. Companies with privacy policies that allow people to opt out of the sharing of their data with third parties are exempt. § 1798(c)(2).

C. DATA SECURITY

1. INTRODUCTION

The Database Industry. The database industry consists of companies that compile, analyze, and trade personal data. These companies are known as data brokers. Journalist Robert O'Harrow, Jr., describes several of the large database companies in detail. For example, Acxiom is "a billion-dollar player in the data industry, with details about nearly every adult in the United States." Acxiom provides information to marketers for profiling consumers, manages credit records, sells data for background checks, and provides data to government agencies. According to O'Harrow:

> It's not just names, ages, addresses, and telephone numbers. The computers in [Acxiom's] rooms also hold billions of records about marital status and families and ages of children. They track individuals' estimated incomes, the value of their homes, the make and price of their cars. They maintain unlisted phone numbers and details about people's occupations, religions, and ethnicities. They sometimes know what some people read, what they order over the phone and online, and where they go on vacation. . . .
>
> When someone makes a toll-free call to a client of Acxiom to inquire about clothing or to buy some shoes, information about who the caller is and where he or she lives pops up on a screen. . . . Using TeleSource, the agent can often find out the kind of home the caller lives in, the type of cars the people in the household drive, whether they exercise.

Another major database company is ChoicePoint, which was formed in 1997 as a spin-off from the credit reporting agency Equifax. O'Harrow observes: "ChoicePoint has a total of about 17 billion online public records, a figure that grows by more than 40,000 every day. . . . All told, the company has more than 250 terabytes of data regarding the lives of about 220 million adults."[71]

LexisNexis is another of the large data broker companies. It is commonly known for its legal research services, but it also processes personal information.

In addition to these large data brokers are numerous companies that compile, analyze, and sell data for marketing purposes. Daniel Solove describes some of these companies:

---

[71] Robert O'Harrow, Jr., *No Place to Hide* 34, 37-50, 145 (2005). For more background, see Chris Jay Hoofnagle, *Big Brother's Little Helpers: How ChoicePoint and Other Commercial Data Brokers Collect and Package Your Data for Law Enforcement*, 29 N.C. J Int'l L. & Commercial Reg. 595, 602-03 (2004).

The most powerful database builders construct information empires, sometimes with information on more than half of the American population. For example, Donnelly Marketing Information Services of New Jersey keeps track of 125 million people. Wiland Services has constructed a database containing over 1,000 elements, from demographic information to behavioral data, on over 215 million people.[72]

Data Security Breaches. Several of the largest database companies have had significant security breaches. In 2003, Acxiom had two security breaches. In the first, a person "took the names, credit card numbers, Social Security numbers, addresses, and other details about an estimated 20 million people." In the second, hackers from Florida improperly gained access to Acxiom's records over a period of a few months.[73] In 2005, LexisNexis announced that unauthorized individuals had improperly accessed personal information on about 32,000 people from its Accurint database, which is part of Seisint that LexisNexis acquired in 2004.

The security breach that garnered the most attention, however, involved ChoicePoint. In 2005, ChoicePoint sent over 30,000 letters to California residents announcing that it had suffered a major security breach. It did so because of California's data security notification law, S.B. 1386, codified at Cal. Civ. Code § 1798.82(a), which required individual notification when a security breach involved people's data. At the time, California was the only state with such a law.

The security breach occurred because an identity theft crime ring set up fake businesses and then signed up to receive ChoicePoint's data. As a result, personal information, including names, addresses, and SSNs of over 145,000 people, were improperly accessed. Over 700 of these individuals were victimized by some form of identity theft.

The fraud was discovered in October 2004 by ChoicePoint, but victims were not notified until February 2005 to avoid impeding the law enforcement investigation. When news of the breach was announced, it sparked considerable public attention. After angry statements by many state attorneys general and a public outcry, ChoicePoint decided to voluntarily notify all individuals affected by the breach, not just Californians.

Beyond the ChoicePoint incident, there has been no shortage of other security breaches. LexisNexis announced that the personal information of about 310,000 people was improperly accessed. Beyond the database industry, several universities disclosed that personal information had been leaked or hacked. Bank of America announced that it lost computer data tapes containing data on about 1.2 million government employees. All told thus far, in 2005, at least 50 different announcements were made regarding data security breaches, implicating the personal data of over 50 million people. Today, data security breaches continue to be announced on a frequent basis.

In response, Congress initiated several hearings and bills to examine the database industry and address information privacy and identity theft issues. Bills

---

[72] Daniel J. Solove, *The Digital Person: Technology and Privacy in the Information Age* 20 (2004).

[73] O'Harrow, *supra,* at 71-72.

with various information privacy protections were proposed and passed in many states. For example, very shortly after the ChoicePoint security breach, numerous states enacted data security breach notification laws.

2. DATA SECURITY BREACH NOTIFICATION STATUTES

California was the first state to require companies that maintain personal information to notify individuals in the event of a security breach where personal information is leaked or improperly accessed. Pursuant to SB 1386, codified at Cal. Civ. Code § 1798.82(a):

> Any person or business that conducts business in California, and that owns or licenses computerized data that includes personal information, shall disclose any breach of the security of the system following discovery or notification of the breach in the security of the data to any resident of California whose unencrypted personal information was, or is reasonably believed to have been, acquired by an unauthorized person. The disclosure shall be made in the most expedient time possible and without unreasonable delay, consistent with the legitimate needs of law enforcement. . . .

The California security breach notice provision received national attention after the ChoicePoint data security breach in 2005. Afterwards, almost all states enacted data breach notification laws. At least 44 other states, the District of Columbia and Puerto Rico have enacted statutes that required governmental agencies and/or private companies to disclose security breaches involving personal information.[74] These laws vary according to the following criteria: (1) the entities that the law covers; (2) the law's trigger for notification; (3) any exceptions to the law's notification requirement; (4) the party to whom disclosure is required under the law; (5) whether there is a substantive requirement for data security; and (6) the presence or absence of a private right of action.[75]

Thirty states follow the California approach and rely on the "acquisition" standard for breach notification. These states generally require notification whenever there is a reasonable likelihood that an unauthorized party has "acquired" person information. Only eight states have adopted a higher standard. These states consider whether there is a reasonable likelihood of "misuse" of the information, or "material risk" of harm to the person. The idea is that a breach letter should not be sent to the affected public unless there is a more significant likelihood of harm.

A mere five states provide a private right of action for individuals whose information has been breached. Finally, only twelve of the state statutes create a substantive duty to take reasonable steps to safeguard data. Typically, these statutes provide open-ended, general standards, such as a requirement to provide "reasonable security procedures and practices appropriate to the nature of the

---

[74] National Conference of State Legislatures, State Security Breach Notifications Laws, http://www.ncsl.org/programs/lis/cip/priv/breachlaws.htm (last visited July 16, 2008. For an analysis of data security breach laws, see Paul Schwartz & Edward Janger, *Notification of Data Security Breaches*, 105 Mich. L. Rev. 913, 924-25 (2007).

[75] For a detailed chart examining these laws, state by state (as of 2007), see Schwartz & Janger, *Data Security, supra,* at 972-84.

information." In California, such standards are supplemented by nonbinding, albeit more specific, recommendations from the Office of Privacy Protection.

As noted, most states rely on the same basic trigger for notification: a reasonable belief of "acquisition" of the leaked data. A minority of states require the likelihood of outside "misuse" of the information. More generally, breach notification letters may lose their effectiveness if consumers become dulled by frequent cautions about harms that never materialize. In this sense, Fred Cate writes "if the California law were adopted nationally, like the boy who cried wolf, the flood of notices would soon teach consumers to ignore them. When real danger threatened, who would listen?"[76]

What kind of breach notification statute would be optimal? Schwartz and Janger contend that notification letters to people whose data was leaked play an important role. Within organizations, notification letters have the potential to (1) create a credible threat of negative costs or other punishments for the firm, (2) improve information flows within the firm, and (3) strengthen the position of the data security and privacy officers at the company. Moreover, breach notification letters can play an important role outside the breached organization. Mandated breach disclosure can trigger legislative and other regulatory activity. Schwartz and Janger argue:

> As information about data security breaches and industry practices becomes public, the public, media, and legislators learn about the kinds of errors that lead to data breaches and the types of mistakes that companies make. This situation creates an opportunity for legislators to suggest new regulations and for governmental agencies to provide pressure as to the appropriate content of existing legal standards.[77]

Schwartz and Janger propose that the critical need is for a "coordinated response architecture," which would include a "coordinated response agent" (CRA) to help tailor notice content and supervise the decision whether to give notice. Notification to the consumer would follow upon a reasonable likelihood of "misuse" of notification-triggering information, and notification to the CRA would require the lower standard of a reasonable likelihood of "unauthorized access." The CRA will help coordinate actions that companies take after a breach, tailor the content of the notification in light of the nature of the data breach, and help prepare comparative statistical information regarding data security events.

3. CIVIL LIABILITY

PISCIOTTA V. OLD NATIONAL BANCORP

499 F.3d 629 (7th Cir. 2007)

RIPPLE, J. Plaintiffs Luciano Pisciotta and Daniel Mills brought this action on behalf of a putative class of customers and potential customers of Old National

---

[76] *See, e.g.,* Fred H. Cate, *Another Notice Isn't an Answer,* USA Today, Feb. 27, 2005, at 14A.

[77] Schwartz & Janger, *Data Security, supra,* at 956.

Bancorp ("ONB"). They alleged that, through its website, ONB had solicited personal information from applicants for banking services, but had failed to secure it adequately. As a result, a third-party computer "hacker" was able to obtain access to the confidential information of tens of thousands of ONB site users. The plaintiffs sought damages for the harm that they claim to have suffered because of the security breach; specifically, they requested compensation for past and future credit monitoring services that they have obtained in response to the compromise of their personal data through ONB's website. ONB answered the allegations and then moved for judgment on the pleadings under Rule 12(c). The district court granted ONB's motion and dismissed the case. The plaintiffs timely appeal. For the reasons set forth in this opinion, we affirm the judgment of the district court. . . .

ONB operates a marketing website on which individuals seeking banking services can complete online applications for accounts, loans and other ONB banking services. The applications differ depending on the service requested, but some forms require the customer or potential customer's name, address, social security number, driver's license number, date of birth, mother's maiden name and credit card or other financial account numbers. In 2002 and 2004, respectively, Mr. Pisciotta and Mr. Mills accessed this website and entered personal information in connection with their applications for ONB banking services.

In 2005, NCR, a hosting facility that maintains ONB's website, notified ONB of a security breach. ONB then sent written notice to its customers. The results of the investigation that followed have been filed under seal in this court; for present purposes, it will suffice to note that the scope and manner of access suggests that the intrusion was sophisticated, intentional and malicious.

Mr. Pisciotta and Mr. Mills, on behalf of a putative class of other ONB website users, brought this action in the United States District Court for the Southern District of Indiana. They named ONB and NCR as defendants and asserted negligence claims against both defendants as well as breach of implied contract claims by ONB and breach of contract by NCR. The plaintiffs alleged that:

> [b]y failing to adequately protect [their] personal confidential information, [ONB and NCR] caused Plaintiffs and other similarly situated past and present customers to suffer substantial potential economic damages and emotional distress and worry that third parties will use [the plaintiffs'] confidential personal information to cause them economic harm, or sell their confidential information to others who will in turn cause them economic harm.

In pleading their damages, the plaintiffs stated that they and others in the putative class "have incurred expenses in order to prevent their confidential personal information from being used and will continue to incur expenses in the future." Significantly, the plaintiffs did not allege any *completed direct* financial loss to their accounts as a result of the breach. Nor did they claim that they or any other member of the putative class *already had been* the victim of identity theft as a result of the breach. The plaintiffs requested "[c]ompensation for all economic and emotional damages suffered as a result of the Defendants' acts which were negligent, in breach of implied contract or in breach of contract," and "[a]ny and all other legal and/or equitable relief to which Plaintiffs . . . are entitled, including establishing an economic monitoring procedure to insure [sic] prompt notice to Plaintiffs . . . of any attempt to use their confidential personal information stolen from the Defendants." . . .

The principal claims in this case are based on a negligence theory. The elements of a negligence claim under Indiana law are: "(1) a duty owed to plaintiff by defendant, (2) breach of duty by allowing conduct to fall below the applicable standard of care, and (3) a *compensable injury* proximately caused by defendant's breach of duty." The plaintiffs' complaint also alleges that ONB has breached an implied contract. Compensable damages are an element of a breach of contract cause of action as well.

As this case comes to us, both the negligence and the contractual issues can be resolved, and the judgment of the district court affirmed, *if* the district court was correct in its determination that Indiana law would not permit recovery for credit monitoring costs incurred by the plaintiffs. . . . We must determine whether Indiana would consider that the harm caused by identity information exposure, coupled with the attendant costs to guard against identity theft, constitutes an existing *compensable injury and consequent damages* required to state a claim for negligence or for breach of contract. Neither the parties' efforts nor our own have identified any Indiana precedent addressing this issue. Nor have we located the decision of any court (other than the district court in this case) that examines Indiana law in this context. We are charged with predicting, nevertheless, how we think the Supreme Court of Indiana would decide this issue. . . .

We begin our inquiry with the Indiana authority most closely addressed to the issue before us. On March 21, 2006, the Indiana legislature enacted a statute that applies to certain database security breaches. Specifically, the statute creates certain duties when a database in which personal data, electronically stored by private entities or state agencies, potentially has been accessed by unauthorized third parties. I.C. § 24-4.9 *et seq.* The statute took effect on July 1, 2006, after the particular incident involved in this case; neither party contends that the statute is directly applicable to the present dispute. We nevertheless find this enactment by the Indiana legislature instructive in our evaluation of the probable approach of the Supreme Court of Indiana to the allegations in the present case.

The provisions of the statute applicable to private entities storing personal information require only that a database owner *disclose* a security breach to potentially affected consumers; they do not require the database owner to take any other affirmative act in the wake of a breach. If the database owner fails to comply with the only affirmative duty imposed by the statute — the duty to disclose — the statute provides for enforcement *only* by the Attorney General of Indiana. It creates no private right of action against the database owner by an affected customer. It imposes no duty to compensate affected individuals for inconvenience or potential harm to credit that may follow. . . .

The plaintiffs maintain that the statute is evidence that the Indiana legislature believes that an individual has suffered a compensable injury at the moment his personal information is exposed because of a security breach. We cannot accept this view. Had the Indiana legislature intended that a cause of action should be available against a database owner for failing to protect adequately personal information, we believe that it would have made some more definite statement of that intent. Moreover, given the novelty of the legal questions posed by information exposure and theft, it is unlikely that the legislature intended to sanction the development of common law tort remedies that would apply to the same factual circumstances addressed by the statute. The narrowness of the defined duties imposed, combined with state-enforced penalties as the exclusive remedy, strongly suggest that Indiana law would not recognize the costs of credit monitoring that the plaintiffs seek to recover in this case as compensable damages.

The plaintiffs further submit that cases decided by the Indiana courts in analogous areas of the law instruct that they suffered an immediate injury when their information was accessed by unauthorized third parties. Specifically, the plaintiffs claim that Indiana law acknowledges special duties on the part of banks to prevent the disclosure of the personal information of their customers; they further claim that Indiana courts have recognized explicitly the significant harm that may result from a failure to prevent such a loss. . . . [One of these cases concerned disclosure to law enforcement that a bank account had been "marked for repossession"; the other, a creditor who was told that the plaintiff's bank account had insufficient funds to cover checks written.]

Whatever these cases say about the relationship of banks and customers in Indiana, they are of marginal assistance to us in determining whether the present plaintiffs are entitled to the remedy they seek as a matter of Indiana law. The reputational injuries suffered by the plaintiffs in [the previous Indiana cases] were direct and immediate; the plaintiffs sought to be compensated for that harm, rather than to be reimbursed for their efforts to guard against some future, anticipated harm. We therefore do not believe that the factual circumstances of the cases relied on by the plaintiffs are sufficiently analogous to the circumstances that we confront in the present case to instruct us on the probable course that the Supreme Court of Indiana would take if faced with the present question.

Although not raised by the parties, we separately note that in the somewhat analogous context of toxic tort liability, the Supreme Court of Indiana has suggested that compensable damage requires more than an exposure to a future potential harm. Specifically, in *AlliedSignal, Inc. v. Ott,* 785 N.E.2d 1068 (Ind. 2003), the Supreme Court of Indiana held that no cause of action accrues, despite incremental physical changes following asbestos exposure, until a plaintiff reasonably could have been diagnosed with an actual exposure-related illness or disease. . . . [E]xposure alone does not give rise to a legally cognizable injury.

Although some courts have allowed medical monitoring damages to be recovered or have created a special cause of action for medical monitoring under similar circumstances, *see Badillo v. American Brands, Inc.,* 16 P.3d 435 (Nev. 2001) (citing cases interpreting the law of seventeen states to allow medical monitoring in some form), no authority from Indiana is among them. Indeed, its recent holding in *AlliedSignal* indicates a contrary approach. To the extent the decision of the Supreme Court of Indiana in that matter provides us with guidance on the likely approach that court would adopt with respect to the information exposure injury in this case, we think it supports the view that no cause of action for credit monitoring is available.

Finally, without Indiana guidance directly on point, we next examine the reasoning of other courts applying the law of other jurisdictions to the question posed by this case. *Allstate Ins. Co.,* 392 F.3d at 952. In this respect, several district courts, applying the laws of other jurisdictions, have rejected similar claims on their merits. In addition to those cases in which the district court held that the plaintiff lacked standing, a series of cases has rejected information security claims on their merits. Most have concluded that the plaintiffs have not been injured in a manner the governing substantive law will recognize.

Although some of these cases involve different types of information losses, all of the cases rely on the same basic premise: Without more than allegations of increased risk of future identity theft, the plaintiffs have not suffered a harm that the law is prepared to remedy. Plaintiffs have not come forward with a single case or statute, from any jurisdiction, authorizing the kind of action they now ask this federal court, sitting in diversity, to recognize as a valid theory of recovery under Indiana law. We decline to adopt a "substantive innovation" in state law, or "to invent what would be a truly novel tort claim" on behalf of the state, absent some authority to suggest that the approval of the Supreme Court of Indiana is forthcoming.

In sum, all of the interpretive tools of which we routinely make use in our attempt to determine the content of state law point us to the conclusion that the Supreme Court of Indiana would not allow the plaintiffs' claim to proceed.

NOTES & QUESTIONS

1. ***Private Rights of Action?*** In *Pisciotta*, the court decides that the Indiana legislature did not create "a cause of action against the database owner for failing to protect adequately personal information." As an example of a statute with such a private right of action, California enacted AB 1950 in 2004, a year after passing SB 1386, its data breach notification law. AB 1950 provides: "A business that owns or licenses personal information about a California resident . . . [to] implement and maintain reasonable security procedures and practices appropriate to the nature of the information, to protect the personal information from unauthorized access, destruction, use, modification, or disclosure." Cal. Civ. Code § 1798.81(b). California law also provides a private right of action in its unfair competition law (which generally permits a private party to bring a lawsuit against any business practice otherwise forbidden by law) and in its breach notification law, § 1798.84 (which provides for a right of action for any "customer injured by a violation of this title"). What is the promise and peril of a private right of action for an organization's failure to maintain reasonable data security?

2. ***Tort Negligence for Data Security Breaches.*** In tort law, under a general negligence theory, litigants might sue a company after a data security incident and seek to collect damages. Thus far, however, class action lawsuits following data breaches have been notably unsuccessful. Among other problems, claimants are facing trouble convincing courts that the data processing entities owe a duty to the individuals whose data are leaked, or that

damages can be inferred from the simple fact of a data breach. For example, a South Carolina court declared in 2003 that "[t]he relationship, if any, between credit card issuers and potential victims of identity theft is far too attenuated to rise to the level of a duty between them." *Huggins v. Citibank*, 585 S.E.2d 275 (S.C. 2003).

3. *Proving Harm from Data Security Breaches.* Suppose a person has been notified that her personal information has been improperly accessed, but she has not yet suffered from identity theft. Should she be entitled to any form of compensation? Has she suffered an injury? One might argue that being made more vulnerable to future harm has made her worse off than before. The individual might live with greater unease knowing that she is less secure. On the other hand, no identity theft has occurred, and it may never occur. How should the law address this situation? Recognize a harm? If so, how should damages be assessed?

In *Forbes v. Wells Fargo Bank, N.A.*, 420 F. Supp. 2d 1018 (D. Minn. 2006), a contractor for Wells Fargo Bank had computers stolen containing unencrypted data about customers, such as names, addresses, Social Security numbers, and account numbers. A group of customers sued for breach of contract, breach of fiduciary duty, and negligence. The court, however, dismissed the case:

> Plaintiffs allege that Wells Fargo negligently allowed Regulus to keep customers' private information without adequate security. To establish a negligence claim, a plaintiff must prove that (1) the defendant owed plaintiff a duty of care, (2) the defendant breached that duty, (3) the plaintiff sustained damage and (4) the breach of the duty proximately caused the damage. A plaintiff may recover damages for an increased risk of harm in the future if such risk results from a present injury and indicates a reasonably certain future harm. Alone, however, "the threat of future harm, not yet realized, will not satisfy the damage requirement."
>
> Plaintiffs contend that the time and money they have spent monitoring their credit suffices to establish damages. However, a plaintiff can only recover for loss of time in terms of earning capacity or wages. Plaintiffs have failed to cite any Minnesota authority to the contrary. Moreover, they overlook the fact that their expenditure of time and money was not the result of any present injury, but rather the anticipation of future injury that has not materialized. In other words, the plaintiffs' injuries are solely the result of a perceived risk of future harm. Plaintiffs have shown no present injury or reasonably certain future injury to support damages for any alleged increased risk of harm. For these reasons, plaintiffs have failed to establish the essential element of damages. Therefore, summary judgment in favor of defendant on plaintiffs' negligence claim is warranted.
>
> Plaintiffs also bring a claim for breach of contract against Wells Fargo. To establish their claim, plaintiffs must show that they were damaged by the alleged breach. *See Jensen v. Duluth Area YMCA*, 688 N.W.2d 574, 578-79 (Minn. App. 2004). For all of the reasons discussed above, plaintiffs have failed to establish damages. Therefore, summary judgment in favor of defendant on plaintiffs' breach of contract claim is warranted.

Why aren't expenditures to reduce risks of future harm created by another recoverable? Suppose a company leaks a toxic chemical, causing a person to have an increased risk of cancer. The person sees a doctor and gets a prescription for a drug that will reduce the likelihood that the chemical will cause cancer. Would the expenses of seeing the doctor and purchasing the drug be recoverable? Is this hypothetical analogous to a data security breach?

4. ***Strict Liability for Data Security Breaches?*** Danielle Citron argues for strict liability for harms caused by data breaches. Computer databases of personal information, Citron contends, are akin to the water reservoirs of the early Industrial Age:

> The dynamics of the early Industrial Age, a time of great potential and peril, parallel those at the advent of the Information Age. Then, as now, technological change brought enormous wealth and comfort to society. Industry thrived as a result of machines powered by water reservoirs. But when the dams holding those reservoirs failed, the escaping water caused massive property and personal damage different from the interpersonal harms of the previous century. *Rylands v. Fletcher* provided the Industrial Age's strict-liability response to the accidents caused by the valuable reservoirs' escaping water. The history of *Rylands*'s reception in Britain and the United States reflects the tension between that era's desire for economic growth and its concern for security from industrial hazards.
>
> Computer databases are this century's reservoirs. . . . Much as water reservoirs drove the Industrial Age, computer databases fuel the Internet economy of our Information Age.

Citron argues that a strict liability regime is preferable to negligence tort liability:

> The rapidly changing nature of information technologies may create uncertainty as to what a negligence regime entails. . . .
>
> Due to the rapidly changing threats to information security, database operators will likely be uncertain as to what constitutes optimal care. Cyber-intruders employ increasingly innovative techniques to bypass security measures and steal personal data, thereby requiring an ever-changing information-security response to new threats, vulnerabilities, and technologies. . . .
>
> A negligence regime will fail to address the significant leaks that will occur despite database operators' exercise of due care over personal data. Security breaches are an inevitable byproduct of collecting sensitive personal information in computer databases. No amount of due care will prevent significant amounts of sensitive data from escaping into the hands of cyber-criminals. Such data leaks constitute the predictable residual risks of information reservoirs.
>
> Consequently, negligence will not efficiently manage the residual risks of hazardous databases. Negligence would neither induce database operators to change their activity level nor discourage marginal actors from collecting sensitive information because such operators need not pay for the accident costs of their residual risk.
>
> The high levels of residual risk suggest treating cyber-reservoirs as ultrahazardous activities — those with significant social utility and significant risk — that warrant strict liability. As Judge Richard Posner has explained,

ultrahazardous activities often involve something "new" that society has "little experience" securing, where neither the injurer nor victim can prevent the accident by taking greater care. This characterized water reservoirs in nineteenth-century England. Strict liability creates an incentive for actors engaging in ultrahazardous activities to "cut back on the scale of the activity . . . to slow its spread while more is learned about conducting it safely."

Classifying database collection as an ultrahazardous activity is a logical extension of Posner's analysis. Just as no clear safety standard governing the building and maintenance of water reservoirs had emerged in the 1850s, a stable set of information-security practices has not yet materialized today. . . .

In this analysis, strict liability has the potential to encourage a change in activity level respecting the storage of sensitive personal information, unless and until more information allows operators to better assess optimal precaution levels and to respond to the persistent problem of residual risk. Because strict liability would force database operators to internalize the full costs of their activities, marginally productive database operators might refrain from maintaining cyber-reservoirs of personal data. Strict liability also may decrease the collection of ultrasensitive data among those who are at greatest risk of security breaches. Moreover, as insurance markets develop in this emerging area, database operators that continue collecting sensitive information will be better positioned to assess the cost of residual risk and the extent to which they can spread the cost of such risk onto consumers.[78]

Are you convinced by the analogy between the database industry and reservoirs? Will strict liability lead to the correct level of investment in security by companies? Could it lead to over-investment in data security?

5. *Assessing the Federal Approach to Data Security.* As discussed above, after the ChoicePoint data security breach in 2005 — along with the numerous other breaches that followed — a majority of states have now passed data security breach legislation. Despite several proposed bills, the federal government has yet to pass a comprehensive data security law. However, some existing federal privacy laws protect data security in the context of particular industries. Consider Andrea Matwyshyn:

The current approach to information security, exemplified by statutes such as COPPA, HIPAA, and GLBA, attempts to regulate information security by creating legal "clusters" of entities based on the type of business they transact, the types of data they control, and that data's permitted and nonpermitted uses. In other words, the current regulatory approach has singled out a few points in the system for the creation of information security enclaves. . . .

The current approach ignores the fundamental tenet of security that a system is only as strong as its weakest links, not its strongest points. . . . It will not prove adequate to only ensure that a few points or clusters in the system are particularly well-secured. . . .

The biggest economic losses arise not out of illegal leveraging of these protected categories of data; rather, losses arise out of stolen personally identifiable information, such as credit card data and social security numbers,

---

[78] Danielle Keats Citron, *Reservoirs of Danger: The Evolution of Public and Private Law at the Dawn of the Information Age,* 80 S. Cal. L. Rev. 241, 243-44, 263-67 (2007).

which are warehoused frequently by entities that are not regulated by COPPA, HIPAA or GLBA. Therefore, creating enclaves of superior data security for data related to children online, some financial information, and some health data will not alleviate the weak information security in other parts of the system and will not substantially diminish information crime. . . . [79]

4. FTC REGULATION

The FTC has acted on numerous occasions to penalize merchants that fail to take reasonable measures to protect customer data. In a typical data security complaint, the FTC argues that the firm's data-handling practices constituted unfair acts or practices in violation of Section 5 of the Federal Trade Commission Act. In settling its enforcement actions, the FTC has required both general and specific pledges of reasonable data security.

The most dramatic of these FTC enforcement actions involved ChoicePoint. In settling the FTC charges, ChoicePoint agreed in January 2006 to pay $10 million in civil penalties and $5 million into a consumer redress fund.[80] The $10 million fine is the largest civil penalty in the FTC's history. ChoicePoint also promised changes to its business and improvements to its security practices.

The stipulated final judgment bars the company from furnishing consumer reports to customers without a permissible purpose and requires it to establish reasonable procedures to ensure that it will provide consumer reports only to those with a permissible purpose. One requirement placed on ChoicePoint is to verify the identity of businesses that apply to receive consumer reports by auditing subscribers' use of consumer reports and by making site visits to certain of its customers.

Finally, the settlement obligated ChoicePoint to establish and maintain a comprehensive information security program and to submit this program for two decades to outside independent audits. It agreed to "establish and implement, and thereafter maintain, a comprehensive information security program that is reasonably designed to protect the security, confidentiality, and integrity of personal information collected from or about consumers." In maintaining this "comprehensive information security program," ChoicePoint promised to engage in risk assessments and to design and implement regular testing of the effectiveness of its security program's key controls, systems, and procedures. It also agreed to obtain an initial and then biennial outside assessment of its data security safeguards from an independent third-party professional. The FTC has reached significant settlements in other data security cases as well. Consider the FTC's settlement in *In the Matter of Reed Elsevier, Inc. and Seisint* below.

---

[79] Andrea M. Matwyshyn, *Material Vulnerabilities: Data Privacy, Corporate Information Security, and Securities Regulation*, 3 Berkeley Bus. L.J. 129, 169-70 (2005).

[80] News Release, FTC, ChoicePoint *Settles Data Security Breach Charges* (Jan. 26, 2006), at http://www.ftc.gov/opa/2006/01/choicepoint.htm.

IN THE MATTER OF REED ELSEVIER, INC. AND SEISINT

2008 WL 903806 (F.T.C. 2008)

[Reed Elsevier acquired Seisint in September 2004 and operated it as a wholly owned subsidiary within LexisNexis, more widely known for providing legal information. Seisint collected and sold information about consumers, and did so under the trade name of "Accurint." According to the FTC's complaint, Seisint used its information "to locate assets and people, authenticate identities, and verify credentials." It also sold products about consumers to "insurance companies, debt collectors, employers, landlords, law firms, and law enforcement and other government agencies." In order to sell these products, Reed Elsevier and Seisint collected and aggregated information about millions of consumers from public and nonpublic sources.

The FTC alleged that in its security practices, Reed Elsevier and Seisint failed to provide "reasonable and appropriate security to prevent authorized access" to sensitive consumer information. It argued, "In particular, respondents failed to establish or implement reasonable policies and procedures governing the creation and authentication of user credentials for authorized customers. . . ." Among other flawed practices, the FTC pointed to the companies' failure to establish or enforce rules that would make it difficult to guess user credentials. It permitted their customers to use the same word as both password and user ID. In addition, it allowed the sharing of user credentials among multiple users at a single customer firm, which lowered the likely detection of unauthorized services. It also failed to mandate periodic changes of user credentials and did not implement simple, readily available defenses against common network attacks.

The consequences of the shortcomings in security practices at Reed Elsevier and Seisint were dramatic. In its complaint, the FTC stated:

> On multiple occasions since January 2003, attackers exploited respondent Seisint's user ID and password structures to obtain without authorization the user credentials of legitimate Accurint customers. The attackers then used these credentials to make thousands of unauthorized searches for consumer information in Accurint databases. These attacks disclosed sensitive information about several hundred thousand consumers, including, in many instances, names, current and prior addresses, dates of birth, and Social Security numbers. Although some of these attacks occurred before respondent REI acquired respondent Seisint, they continued for at least 9 months after the acquisition, during which time respondent Seisint was operating under the control of respondent REI. Since March 2005, respondent REI through LexisNexis has notified over 316,000 consumers that the attacks disclosed sensitive information about them that could be used to conduct identity theft.

These incidents also led to new credit accounts being opened in the name of customers.

On March 27, 2008, the FTC announced a settlement with Reed Elsevier and its Seisint subsidiary.]

AGREEMENT CONTAINING CONSENT ORDER

The Federal Trade Commission has conducted an investigation of certain acts and practices of Reed Elsevier Inc. and Seisint, Inc. ("proposed respondents"). Proposed respondents, having been represented by counsel, are willing to enter into an agreement containing a consent order resolving the allegations contained in the attached draft complaint. . . .

ORDER

For purposes of this order, the following definitions shall apply:

1. Unless otherwise specified, "respondents" shall mean Reed Elsevier Inc., its successors and assigns, officers, agents, representatives, and employees, and Seisint, Inc., and its successors and assigns, officers, agents, representatives, and employees.

2. "Personal information" shall mean individually identifiable information from or about a consumer including, but not limited to: (a) a first and last name; (b) a home or other physical address, including street name and name of city or town; (c) an email address or other online contact information, such as an instant messaging user identifier or a screen name that reveals a consumer's email address; (d) a telephone number; (e) a Social Security number; (f) a date of birth; (g) a driver's license number; (h) credit and/or debit card information, including but not limited to card number and expiration date and transaction detail data; (i) a persistent identifier, such as a customer number held in a "cookie" or processor serial number, that is combined with other available data that identifies a consumer; or (j) any other information from or about a consumer that is combined with (a) through (i) above.

3. "Information product or service" shall mean each product, service, or other means by which respondents individually or collectively provide direct or indirect access to personal information from or about consumers that is comprised in whole or part of nonpublic information; *provided, however*, that this term shall not include information products or services that: (a) provide access solely to personal information that is publicly available information, or (b) permit customers to upload or otherwise supply, organize, manage, or retrieve information that is under the customer's control.

4. "Publicly available information" shall mean information that respondents have a reasonable basis to believe is lawfully made available to the general public from: (a) Federal, State, or local government records, (b) widely distributed media, or (c) disclosures to the general public that are required to be made by Federal, State, or local law. Respondents shall have a reasonable basis to believe information is lawfully made available to the general public if respondents have taken reasonable steps to determine: (a) that the information is of the type that is available to the general public, and (b) whether an individual can direct that the information not be made available to the general public and, if so, that the individual has not done so.

I.

IT IS ORDERED that each respondent, directly or through any corporation, subsidiary, division, or other device, in connection with the advertising, marketing, promotion, offering for sale, or sale of personal information collected from or about consumers made available through any information product or service of LexisNexis ("the information"), in or affecting commerce, shall, no later than the date of service of this order, establish and implement, and thereafter maintain, a comprehensive information security program that is reasonably designed to protect the security, confidentiality, and integrity of the information. Such program, the content and implementation of which must be fully documented in writing, shall contain administrative, technical, and physical safeguards appropriate to each respondent's size and complexity, the nature and scope of each respondent's activities, and the sensitivity of the information, including:

A. the designation of an employee or employees to coordinate and be accountable for the information security program.

B. the identification of material internal and external risks to the security, confidentiality, and integrity of the information that could result in the unauthorized disclosure, misuse, loss, alteration, destruction, or other compromise of the information, and assessment of the sufficiency of any safeguards in place to control these risks. At a minimum, this risk assessment should include consideration of risks in each area of relevant operation, including, but not limited to: (1) employee training and management; (2) information systems, including network and software design, information processing, storage, transmission, and disposal; and (3) prevention, detection, and response to attacks, intrusions, or other systems failures.

C. the design and implementation of reasonable safeguards to control the risks identified through risk assessment, and regular testing or monitoring of the effectiveness of the safeguards' key controls, systems, and procedures.

D. the development and use of reasonable steps to select and retain service providers capable of appropriately safeguarding personal information they receive from respondent, and requiring service providers by contract to implement and maintain appropriate safeguards; *provided, however*, that this subparagraph shall not apply to personal information about a consumer that respondent provides to a government agency or lawful information supplier when the agency or supplier already possesses the information and uses it only to retrieve, and supply to respondent, additional personal information about the consumer.

E. the evaluation and adjustment of respondent's information security program in light of the results of the testing and monitoring required by subparagraph C, any material changes to respondent's operations or business arrangements, or any other circumstances that respondent knows or has reason to know may have a material impact on the effectiveness of its information security program.

II.

IT IS FURTHER ORDERED that, in connection with its compliance with Paragraph I of this order, each respondent shall obtain initial and biennial assessments and reports ("Assessments") from a qualified, objective, independent third-party professional, who uses procedures and standards generally accepted in the profession. The reporting period for the Assessments shall cover: (1) the first one hundred and eighty (180) days after service of the order for the initial Assessment, and (2) each two (2) year period thereafter for twenty (20) years after service of the order for the biennial Assessments. Each Assessment shall:

A. set forth the specific administrative, technical, and physical safeguards that respondent has implemented and maintained during the reporting period;

B. explain how such safeguards are appropriate to respondent's size and complexity, the nature and scope of respondent's activities, and the sensitivity of the personal information collected from or about consumers;

C. explain how the safeguards that have been implemented meet or exceed the protections required by Paragraph I of this order; and

D. certify that respondent's security program is operating with sufficient effectiveness to provide reasonable assurance that the security, confidentiality, and integrity of personal information is protected and has so operated throughout the reporting period.

Each Assessment shall be prepared and completed within sixty (60) days after the end of the reporting period to which the Assessment applies by a person qualified as a Certified Information System Security Professional (CISSP) or as a Certified Information Systems Auditor (CISA); a person holding Global Information Assurance Certification (GIAC) from the SysAdmin, Audit, Network, Security (SANS) Institute; or a similarly qualified person or organization. . . .

VII.

This order will terminate twenty (20) years from the date of its issuance, or twenty (20) years from the most recent date that the United States or the Federal Trade Commission files a complaint (with or without an accompanying consent decree) in federal court alleging any violation of the order, whichever comes later. . . .

NOTES & QUESTIONS

1. *The Terms of Settlement.* This settlement illustrates the FTC's classic approach in its data security settlements of imposing long-term requirements for an information security program. Do you think that the settlement terms in *Reed Elsevier* are appropriate? Does the FTC strike the correct balance in providing some flexibility to the companies in deciding the content of a reasonable security program?

2. *Damages:* **Reed Elsevier** *vs.* **ChoicePoint.** Unlike other companies with whom the FTC has settled claims, Reed Elsevier and Seisint avoided paying

fines. Should the FTC have sought to negotiate the payment of damages in *Reed Elsevier*? In its *ChoicePoint* settlement, discussed above, the FTC negotiated a payment of $10 million in civil penalties and $5 million for civil redress. It found that ChoicePoint violated the FCRA by furnishing credit histories to subscribers without a permissible purpose and violated the FTC Act by making false and misleading statements about its privacy practices. One possible difference in the FTC's ability to obtain damages in *ChoicePoint* concerned the company's FCRA violations. The FTC in its *ChoicePoint* complaint sought monetary civil penalties for each separate violation of the FCRA. A violation of FCRA, according to the FTC, occurred each time ChoicePoint (1) furnished a consumer report to a person without a permissible purpose for it, (2) failed to make a reasonable effort to verify the identity of the prospective user, or (3) furnished a consumer report to any person when it had reasonable grounds for believing the report would not be used for a FCRA permissible purpose. Is there a similar way to create a framework for assessing damages in *Reed Elsevier*?

3. ***Data Leaks:* Eli Lilly.** In *FTC v. Eli Lilly*, No. 012-3214, the FTC charged Eli Lilly, a pharmaceutical company, with disclosing people's health data that it collected through its Prozac.com website. Prozac is a drug used for treating depression. Lilly offered customers an e-mail service that would send them e-mail messages to remind them to take or refill their medication. In June 2001, the company sent e-mail messages to all 669 users of the reminder service announcing that the service was terminated. However, this message contained the e-mail addresses of all subscribers in the "To" line of the message. The FTC alleged that the company's privacy policy promising confidentiality was deceptive because the company failed to establish adequate security protections for its consumers' data. Specifically, the FTC complaint alleged that Eli Lilly failed to

> provide appropriate training for its employees regarding consumer privacy and information security; provide appropriate oversight and assistance for the employee who sent out the e-mail, who had no prior experience in creating, testing, or implementing the computer program used; and implement appropriate checks and controls on the process, such as reviewing the computer program with experienced personnel and pretesting the program internally before sending out the e-mail.

In January 2002, Eli Lilly settled. The settlement requires Eli Lilly to establish a new security program. It must designate personnel to oversee the program, identify and address various security risks, and conduct an annual review of the security program. FTC Commissioners voted 5–0 to approve the settlement.

Consider the settlements in the cases described above. Do you think that these settlements are adequate to redress the rights of the individuals affected?

4. **Microsoft Passport *and* Guess: *Proactive FTC Enforcement?*** Microsoft launched Microsoft.NET Passport, an online authentication service. Passport allowed consumers to use a single username and password to access multiple

websites. The goal of Passport was to serve as a universal sign-on service, eliminating the need to sign on to each website separately. A related service, Wallet, permitted users to submit credit card and billing information in order to make purchases at multiple websites without having to reenter the information on each site.

The FTC initiated an investigation of the Passport services following a July 2001 complaint from a coalition of consumer groups. In the petition to the FTC, the privacy groups raised questions about the collection, use, and disclosure of personal information that Passport would make possible, and asserted that Microsoft's representations about the security of the system were both unfair and deceptive. In its privacy policy, Microsoft promised that ".NET Passport is protected by powerful online security technology and a strict privacy policy." Further, Microsoft stated: "Your .NET Passport information is stored on secure .NET Passport servers that are protected in controlled facilities."

On August 8, 2002, the FTC found that Microsoft had violated § 5 of the FTC Act and announced a proposed settlement with the company. *See In the Matter of Microsoft Corp.,* No. 012-3240. The Commission found that Microsoft falsely represented that (1) it employs reasonable and appropriate measures under the circumstances to maintain and protect the privacy and confidentiality of consumers' personal information collected through its Passport and Wallet services; (2) purchases made with Passport Wallet are generally safer or more secure than purchases made at the same site without Passport Wallet when, in fact, most consumers received identical security at those sites regardless of whether they used Passport Wallet to complete their transactions; (3) Passport did not collect any personally identifiable information other than that described in its privacy policy when, in fact, Passport collected and held, for a limited time, a personally identifiable sign-in history for each user; and (4) the Kids Passport program provided parents control over what information participating websites could collect from their children.

Under the terms of the proposed consent order, Microsoft may not make any misrepresentations, expressly or by implication, of any of its information practices. Microsoft is further obligated to establish a "comprehensive information security program," and conduct an annual audit to assess the security practices. Microsoft is also required to make available to the FTC for a period of five years all documents relating to security practices as well as compliance with the orders. The order remains in place for 20 years.

The FTC took a similar approach in *In re Guess.com, Inc.,* No. 022-3260 (July 30, 2003). Guess, a clothing company, had promised that all personal information "including . . . credit card information and sign-in password, are stored in an unreadable, encrypted format at all times." This assertion of company policy was false, and the FTC initiated an action even before data was leaked or improperly accessed. The case was eventually settled.

In both *Microsoft* and *Guess,* the FTC brought an action before any data security breach had occurred. Is this a form of proactive enforcement? Suppose a company merely makes a general promise to "keep customer data secure." The FTC believes that the company is not providing adequate security and brings an action. How should the adequacy of a company's security practices be evaluated, especially in cases in which privacy policies are vague about the precise security measures taken?

5. **The Gramm-Leach-Bliley Act and the FTC.** Consider the following observation by Daniel Solove:

> [O]ne problem with the FTC's jurisdiction is that it is triggered when a company breaches its own privacy policy. But what if a company doesn't make explicit promises about security? One hopeful development is the Gramm-Leach-Bliley (GLB) Act. The GLB Act requires a number of agencies that regulate financial institutions to promulgate "administrative, technical, and physical safeguards for personal information." In other words, financial institutions must adopt a security system for their data, and the minimum specifications of this system are to be defined by government agencies. . . . [81]

Solove argues that the security practices of many financial institutions are quite lax, as such institutions often provide access to accounts if a person merely supplies her Social Security number. Based on the GLB Act, could the FTC use its enforcement powers to curtail such practices?

D. FIRST AMENDMENT LIMITATIONS ON PRIVACY REGULATION

Although the First Amendment protects privacy, privacy restrictions can come into conflict with the First Amendment. In particular, many privacy statutes regulate the disclosure of true information. The cases in this section explore the extent to which the First Amendment limits the privacy statutes. Before turning to the cases, some background about basic First Amendment jurisprudence is necessary. The cases in this section often focus on commercial speech, and the Court analyzes commercial speech differently than other forms of expression.

First Amendment Protection of Commercial Speech. For a while, the Court considered commercial speech as a category of expression that is not accorded First Amendment protection. However, in *Virginia State Board of Pharmacy v. Virginia Citizens Consumer Council, Inc.*, 425 U.S. 748 (1976), the Court held that commercial speech deserves constitutional protection. However, the Court held that commercial speech has a lower value than regular categories of speech and therefore is entitled to a lesser protection. *Ohralik v. Ohio State Bar Ass'n*, 436 U.S. 447 (1978).

Defining Commercial Speech. What is "commercial speech"? The Court has defined it as speech that "proposes a commercial transaction," *Virginia State Board*, 425 U.S. 748 (1976), and as "expression related solely to the economic interests of the speaker and its audience." *Central Hudson Gas & Electric Corp.*

---

[81] Daniel J. Solove, *The Digital Person: Technology and Privacy in the Information Age* 107-08 (2004).

v. Public Service Comm'n of New York, 447 U.S. 557 (1980). The Court later held that neither of these are necessary requirements to define commercial speech; both are factors to be considered in determining whether speech is commercial. *See Bolger v. Youngs Drug Products Corp.,* 463 U.S. 60 (1983).

The **Central Hudson** *Test.* In *Central Hudson,* 447 U.S. 557 (1980), the Court established a four-part test for analyzing the constitutionality of restrictions on commercial speech:

> At the outset, we must determine whether the expression is protected by the First Amendment. For commercial speech to come within that provision, it at least must concern lawful activity and not be misleading. Next, we ask whether the asserted governmental interest is substantial. If both inquiries yield positive answers, we must determine whether the regulation directly advances the governmental interest asserted, and whether it is not more extensive than is necessary to serve that interest.

In *Board of Trustees of State University of New York v. Fox,* 492 U.S. 469 (1989), the Court revised the last part of the *Central Hudson* test — that speech "not [be] more extensive than is necessary to serve [the governmental] interest" — to a requirement that there be a "fit between the legislature's ends and the means chosen to accomplish the ends, . . . a fit that is not necessarily perfect, but reasonable."

In *Cincinnati v. Discovery Network, Inc.,* 507 U.S. 410 (1993), the Court, applying the commercial speech test in *Central Hudson* and *Fox,* struck down an ordinance that banned news racks with "commercial handbills." The ordinance did not apply to news racks for newspapers. The Court concluded that the ban was not a "reasonable fit" with the city's interest in aesthetics. Moreover, the Court concluded that the ordinance was not content-neutral. The Court held that Cincinnati "has enacted a sweeping ban on the use of newsracks that distribute 'commercial handbills,' but not 'newspapers.' Under the city's newsrack policy, whether any particular newsrack falls within the ban is determined by the content of the publication resting inside that newsrack. Thus, by any commonsense understanding of the term, the ban in this case is 'content based.' . . . [B]ecause the ban is predicated on the content of the publications distributed by the subject newsracks, it is not a valid time, place, or manner restriction on protected speech."

ROWAN V. UNITED STATES POST OFFICE DEPARTMENT

397 U.S. 728 (1970)

[A federal statute permitted individuals to require that entities sending unwanted mailings remove the individuals' names from their mailing lists and cease to send future mailings. A group of organizations challenged the statute on First Amendment grounds.]

BURGER, C.J. . . . The essence of appellants' argument is that the statute violates their constitutional right to communicate. . . . Without doubt the public postal system is an indispensable adjunct of every civilized society and communication is imperative to a healthy social order. But the right of every person "to be let alone" must be placed in the scales with the right of others to communicate.

In today's complex society we are inescapably captive audiences for many purposes, but a sufficient measure of individual autonomy must survive to permit every householder to exercise control over unwanted mail. To make the householder the exclusive and final judge of what will cross his threshold undoubtedly has the effect of impeding the flow of ideas, information, and arguments that, ideally, he should receive and consider. Today's merchandising methods, the plethora of mass mailings subsidized by low postal rates, and the growth of the sale of large mailing lists as an industry in itself have changed the mailman from a carrier of primarily private communications, as he was in a more leisurely day, and have made him an adjunct of the mass mailer who sends unsolicited and often unwanted mail into every home. It places no strain on the doctrine of judicial notice to observe that whether measured by pieces or pounds, Everyman's mail today is made up overwhelmingly of material he did not seek from persons he does not know. And all too often it is matter he finds offensive. . . .

The Court has traditionally respected the right of a householder to bar, by order or notice, solicitors, hawkers, and peddlers from his property. In this case the mailer's right to communicate is circumscribed only by an affirmative act of the addressee giving notice that he wishes no further mailings from that mailer.

To hold less would tend to license a form of trespass and would make hardly more sense than to say that a radio or television viewer may not twist the dial to cut off an offensive or boring communication and thus bar its entering his home. Nothing in the Constitution compels us to listen to or view any unwanted communication, whatever its merit; we see no basis for according the printed word or pictures a different or more preferred status because they are sent by mail. The ancient concept that "a man's home is his castle" into which "not even the king may enter" has lost none of its vitality, and none of the recognized exceptions includes any right to communicate offensively with another. . . .

If this prohibition operates to impede the flow of even valid ideas, the answer is that no one has a right to press even "good" ideas on an unwilling recipient. That we are often "captives" outside the sanctuary of the home and subject to objectionable speech and other sound does not mean we must be captives everywhere. The asserted right of a mailer, we repeat, stops at the outer boundary of every person's domain. . . .

MAINSTREAM MARKETING SERVICES, INC. v. FEDERAL TRADE COMMISSION

358 F.3d 1228 (10th Cir. 2004)

EBEL, J. . . . In 2003, two federal agencies—the Federal Trade Commission (FTC) and the Federal Communications Commission (FCC) — promulgated rules that together created the national do-not-call registry *See* 16 C.F.R. § 310.4(b)(1)(iii)(B) (FTC rule); 47 C.F.R. § 64.1200(c)(2) (FCC rule). The national do-not-call registry is a list containing the personal telephone numbers of telephone subscribers who have voluntarily indicated that they do not wish to receive unsolicited calls from commercial telemarketers. Commercial telemarketers are generally prohibited from calling phone numbers that have been placed on the do-not-call registry, and they must pay an annual fee to access the numbers on the registry so that they can delete those numbers from their telephone solicitation lists. So far, consumers have registered more than 50 million phone numbers on the national do-not-call registry.

The national do-not-call registry's restrictions apply only to telemarketing calls made by or on behalf of sellers of goods or services, and not to charitable or political fundraising calls. Additionally, a seller may call consumers who have signed up for the national registry if it has an established business relationship with the consumer or if the consumer has given that seller express written permission to call. Telemarketers generally have three months from the date on which a consumer signs up for the registry to remove the consumer's phone number from their call lists. Consumer registrations remain valid for five years, and phone numbers that are disconnected or reassigned will be periodically removed from the registry.

The national do-not-call registry is the product of a regulatory effort dating back to 1991 aimed at protecting the privacy rights of consumers and curbing the risk of telemarketing abuse. In the Telephone Consumer Protection Act of 1991 ("TCPA") — under which the FCC enacted its do-not-call rules — Congress found that for many consumers telemarketing sales calls constitute an intrusive invasion of privacy. . . . The TCPA therefore authorized the FCC to establish a national database of consumers who object to receiving "telephone solicitations," which the act defined as commercial sales calls. . . .

The national do-not-call registry's telemarketing restrictions apply only to commercial speech. Like most commercial speech regulations, the do-not-call rules draw a line between commercial and non-commercial speech on the basis of content. In reviewing commercial speech regulations, we apply the *Central Hudson* test. *Central Hudson Gas & Elec. Corp. v. Pub. Serv. Comm'n of N.Y.,* 447 U.S. 557 (1980).

Central Hudson established a three-part test governing First Amendment challenges to regulations restricting non-misleading commercial speech that relates to lawful activity. First, the government must assert a substantial interest to be achieved by the regulation. Second, the regulation must directly advance that governmental interest, meaning that it must do more than provide "only ineffective or remote support for the government's purpose." Third, although the regulation need not be the least restrictive measure available, it must be narrowly tailored not to restrict more speech than necessary. Together, these final two factors require that there be a reasonable fit between the government's objectives and the means it chooses to accomplish those ends. . . .

The government asserts that the do-not-call regulations are justified by its interests in 1) protecting the privacy of individuals in their homes, and 2) protecting consumers against the risk of fraudulent and abusive solicitation. Both of these justifications are undisputedly substantial governmental interests.

In *Rowan v. United States Post Office Dep't,* the Supreme Court upheld the right of a homeowner to restrict material that could be mailed to his or her house.

The Court emphasized the importance of individual privacy, particularly in the context of the home, stating that "the ancient concept that 'a man's home is his castle' into which 'not even the king may enter' has lost none of its vitality." In *Frisby v. Schultz,* the Court [held] . . .

> One important aspect of residential privacy is protection of the unwilling listener. . . . [A] special benefit of the privacy all citizens enjoy within their own walls, which the State may legislate to protect, is an ability to avoid intrusions. Thus, we have repeatedly held that individuals are not required to welcome unwanted speech into their own homes and that the government may protect this freedom.

A reasonable fit exists between the do-not-call rules and the government's privacy and consumer protection interests if the regulation directly advances those interests and is narrowly tailored. . . .

These criteria are plainly established in this case. The do-not-call registry directly advances the government's interests by effectively blocking a significant number of the calls that cause the problems the government sought to redress. It is narrowly tailored because its opt-in character ensures that it does not inhibit any speech directed at the home of a willing listener.

The telemarketers assert that the do-not-call registry is unconstitutionally underinclusive because it does not apply to charitable and political callers. First Amendment challenges based on underinclusiveness face an uphill battle in the commercial speech context. As a general rule, the First Amendment does not require that the government regulate all aspects of a problem before it can make progress on any front. . . . The underinclusiveness of a commercial speech regulation is relevant only if it renders the regulatory framework so irrational that it fails materially to advance the aims that it was purportedly designed to further. . .

As discussed above, the national do-not-call registry is designed to reduce intrusions into personal privacy and the risk of telemarketing fraud and abuse that accompany unwanted telephone solicitation. The registry directly advances those goals. So far, more than 50 million telephone numbers have been registered on the do-not-call list, and the do-not-call regulations protect these households from receiving most unwanted telemarketing calls. According to the telemarketers' own estimate, 2.64 telemarketing calls per week — or more than 137 calls annually — were directed at an average consumer before the do-not-call list came into effect. *Cf.* 68 Fed. Reg. at 44152 (discussing the five-fold increase in the total number of telemarketing calls between 1991 and 2003). Accordingly, absent the do-not-call registry, telemarketers would call those consumers who have already signed up for the registry an estimated total of 6.85 *billion* times each year.

To be sure, the do-not-call list will not block all of these calls. Nevertheless, it will prohibit a substantial number of them, making it difficult to fathom how the registry could be called an "ineffective" means of stopping invasive or abusive calls, or a regulation that "furnish[es] only speculative or marginal support" for the government's interests. . . .

Finally, the type of unsolicited calls that the do-not-call list does prohibit— commercial sales calls — is the type that Congress, the FTC and the FCC have all determined to be most to blame for the problems the government is seeking to redress. According to the legislative history accompanying the TCPA, "[c]omplaint statistics show that unwanted commercial calls are a far bigger problem than unsolicited calls from political or charitable organizations." H.R. Rep. No. 102-317, at 16 (1991). Additionally, the FTC has found that commercial callers are more likely than non-commercial callers to engage in deceptive and abusive practices. . . . The speech regulated by the do-not-call list is therefore the speech most likely to cause the problems the government sought to alleviate in enacting that list, further demonstrating that the regulation directly advances the government's interests. . . .

Although the least restrictive means test is not the test to be used in the commercial speech context, commercial speech regulations do at least have to be "narrowly tailored" and provide a "reasonable fit" between the problem and the solution. Whether or not there are "numerous and obvious less-burdensome alternatives" is a relevant consideration in our narrow tailoring analysis. . . . We hold that the national do-not-call registry is narrowly tailored because it does not over-regulate protected speech; rather, it restricts only calls that are targeted at unwilling recipients. . . .

The Supreme Court has repeatedly held that speech restrictions based on private choice (i.e., an opt-in feature) are less restrictive than laws that prohibit speech directly. In *Rowan*, for example, the Court approved a law under which an individual could require a mailer to stop all future mailings if he or she received advertisements that he or she believed to be erotically arousing or sexually provocative. Although it was the government that empowered individuals to avoid materials they considered provocative, the Court emphasized that the mailer's right to communicate was circumscribed only by an affirmative act of a householder. . . .

Like the do-not-mail regulation approved in *Rowan*, the national do-not-call registry does not itself prohibit any speech. Instead, it merely "permits a citizen to erect a wall . . . that no advertiser may penetrate without his acquiescence." *See Rowan*, 397 U.S. at 738. Almost by definition, the do-not-call regulations only block calls that would constitute unwanted intrusions into the privacy of consumers who have signed up for the list. . . .

NOTES & QUESTIONS

1. *The Do Not Call List and* **Rowan.** To what extent is this case controlled by *Rowan*? Does the Do Not Call (DNC) list go beyond the statute in *Rowan*?

2. *Charitable and Political Calls.* The DNC list permits calls based on charitable or political purposes. There is no way to block such calls. Suppose that Congress decided that all calls could be included. Would a charity or political group have a First Amendment ground to overturn the DNC list?

U.S. WEST, INC. V. FEDERAL COMMUNICATIONS COMMISSION

182 F.3d 1224 (10th Cir. 1999)

TACHA, J. . . . U.S. West, Inc. petitions for review of a Federal Communication Commission ("FCC") order restricting the use and disclosure of and access to customer proprietary network information ("CPNI"). *See* 63 Fed. Reg. 20,326 (1998) ("CPNI Order"). [U.S. West argues that FCC regulations, implementing 47 U.S.C. § 222, among other things, violate the First Amendment. These regulations require telecommunications companies to ask consumers for approval (to "opt-in") before they can use a customer's personal information for marketing purposes.] . . .

The dispute in this case involves regulations the FCC promulgated to implement provisions of 47 U.S.C. § 222, which was enacted as part of the Telecommunications Act of 1996. Section 222, entitled "Privacy of customer information," states generally that "[e]very telecommunications carrier has a duty to protect the confidentiality of proprietary information of, and relating to . . . customers." To effectuate that duty, § 222 places restrictions on the use, disclosure of, and access to certain customer information. At issue here are the FCC's regulations clarifying the privacy requirements for CPNI. The central provision of § 222 dealing with CPNI is § 222(c)(1), which states:

> Except as required by law or with the approval of the customer, a telecommunications carrier that receives or obtains customer proprietary network information by virtue of its provision of a telecommunications service shall only use, disclose, or permit access to individually identifiable customer proprietary network information in its provision of (A) the telecommunication service from which such information is derived, or (B) services necessary to, or used in, the provision of such telecommunications service, including the publishing of directories.

Section 222(d) provides three additional exceptions to the CPNI privacy requirements. [These exceptions permit the companies to use and disclose CPNI for billing purposes, to prevent fraud, and to provide services to the consumer if the consumer approves of the use of such information to provide the service. Any other uses or disclosures of CPNI not specifically permitted by § 222 require the consumer's consent. The regulations adopted by the CPNI Order implementing § 222 divides telecommunications services into three categories: (1) local, (2) long-distance, and (3) mobile or cellular. A telecommunications carrier can use or disclose CPNI to market products within one of these service categories if the customer already subscribes to that category of service. Carriers can't use or disclose CPNI to market categories of service to which the customer does not subscribe unless first obtaining the customer's consent. The regulations also prohibit using CPNI without consent to market other services such as voice mail or Internet access, to track customers that call competitors, or to try to regain the business of customers that switch carriers.] . . .

The regulations also describe the means by which a carrier must obtain customer approval. Section 222(c)(1) did not elaborate as to what form that approval should take. The FCC decided to require an "opt-in" approach, in which a carrier must obtain prior express approval from a customer through written, oral, or electronic means before using the customer's CPNI. The government acknowledged that the means of approval could have taken numerous other forms, including an "opt-out" approach, in which approval would be inferred from the customer-carrier relationship unless the customer specifically requested that his or her CPNI be restricted. . . .

Petitioner argues that the CPNI regulations interpreting 47 U.S.C. § 222 violate the First Amendment. . . .

Because petitioner's targeted speech to its customers is for the purpose of soliciting those customers to purchase more or different telecommunications services, it "does no more than propose a commercial transaction." Consequently, the targeted speech in this case fits soundly within the definition of commercial speech. It is well established that nonmisleading commercial speech regarding a lawful activity is a form of protected speech under the First Amendment, although it is generally afforded less protection than noncommercial speech. The parties do not dispute that the commercial speech based on CPNI is truthful and nonmisleading. Therefore, the CPNI regulations implicate the First Amendment by restricting protected commercial speech. . . .

We analyze whether a government restriction on commercial speech violates the First Amendment under the four-part framework set forth in *Central Hudson* [*Gas & Elec. Corp. v. Public Serv. Comm'n of N.Y.*, 477 U.S. 557 (1980)]. First, we must conduct a threshold inquiry regarding whether the commercial speech concerns lawful activity and is not misleading. If these requirements are not met, the government may freely regulate the speech. If this threshold requirement is met, the government may restrict the speech only if it proves: "(1) it has a substantial state interest in regulating the speech, (2) the regulation directly and materially advances that interest, and (3) the regulation is no more extensive than necessary to serve the interest." As noted above, no one disputes that the commercial speech based on CPNI is truthful and nonmisleading. We therefore proceed directly to whether the government has satisfied its burden under the remaining three prongs of the *Central Hudson* test. . . .

The respondents argue that the FCC's CPNI regulations advance two substantial state interests: protecting customer privacy and promoting competition. While, in the abstract, these may constitute legitimate and substantial interests, we have concerns about the proffered justifications in the context of this case. . . .

. . . Although we agree that privacy may rise to the level of a substantial state interest, the government cannot satisfy the second prong of the *Central Hudson* test by merely asserting a broad interest in privacy. It must specify the particular notion of privacy and interest served. Moreover, privacy is not an absolute good because it imposes real costs on society. Therefore, the specific privacy interest must be substantial, demonstrating that the state has considered the proper balancing of the benefits and harms of privacy. In sum, privacy may only constitute a substantial state interest if the government specifically articulates and properly justifies it.

In the context of a speech restriction imposed to protect privacy by keeping certain information confidential, the government must show that the dissemination of the information desired to be kept private would inflict specific and significant harm on individuals, such as undue embarrassment or ridicule, intimidation or harassment, or misappropriation of sensitive personal information for the purposes of assuming another's identity. Although we may feel uncomfortable knowing that our personal information is circulating in the world, we live in an open society where information may usually pass freely. A general level of discomfort from knowing that people can readily access information about us does not necessarily rise to the level of a substantial state interest under *Central Hudson* for it is not based on an identified harm.

Neither Congress nor the FCC explicitly stated what "privacy" harm § 222 seeks to protect against. The CPNI Order notes that "CPNI includes information that is extremely personal to customers . . . such as to whom, where, and when a customer places a call, as well as the types of service offerings to which the customer subscribes," and it summarily finds "call destinations and other details about a call . . . may be equally or more sensitive [than the content of the calls]." The government never states it directly, but we infer from this thin justification that disclosure of CPNI information could prove embarrassing to some and that the government seeks to combat this potential harm. . . .

Under the next prong of *Central Hudson,* the government must "demonstrate that the harms it recites are real and that its restriction will in fact alleviate them to a material degree.". . . On the record before us, the government fails to meet its burden.

The government presents no evidence showing the harm to either privacy or competition is real. Instead, the government relies on speculation that harm to privacy and competition for new services will result if carriers use CPNI. . . . While protecting against disclosure of sensitive and potentially embarrassing personal information may be important in the abstract, we have no indication of how it may occur in reality with respect to CPNI. Indeed, we do not even have indication that the disclosure might actually occur. The government presents no evidence regarding how and to whom carriers would disclose CPNI. . . . [T]he government has not explained how or why a carrier would disclose CPNI to outside parties, especially when the government claims CPNI is information that would give one firm a competitive advantage over another. This leaves us unsure exactly who would potentially receive the sensitive information. . . .

In order for a regulation to satisfy this final *Central Hudson* prong, there must be a fit between the legislature's means and its desired objective. . . .

. . . [O]n this record, the FCC's failure to adequately consider an obvious and substantially less restrictive alternative, an opt-out strategy, indicates that it did not narrowly tailor the CPNI regulations regarding customer approval. . . .

The respondents merely speculate that there are a substantial number of individuals who feel strongly about their privacy, yet would not bother to opt-out if given notice and the opportunity to do so. Such speculation hardly reflects the careful calculation of costs and benefits that our commercial speech jurisprudence requires. . . .

In sum, even assuming that respondents met the prior two prongs of *Central Hudson,* we conclude that based on the record before us, the agency has failed to satisfy its burden of showing that the customer approval regulations restrict no more speech than necessary to serve the asserted state interests. Consequently, we find that the CPNI regulations interpreting the customer approval requirement of 47 U.S.C. § 222(c) violate the First Amendment.

BRISCOE, J. dissenting. . . After reviewing the CPNI Order and the administrative record, I am convinced the FCC's interpretation of § 222, more specifically its selection of the opt-in method for obtaining customer approval, is entirely reasonable. Indeed, the CPNI Order makes a strong case that, of the two options seriously considered by the FCC, the opt-in method is the only one that legitimately forwards Congress' goal of ensuring that customers give informed consent for use of their individually identifiable CPNI. . . .

. . . U.S. West suggests the CPNI Order unduly limits its ability to engage in commercial speech with its existing customers regarding new products and services it may offer. . . .

The problem with U.S. West's arguments is they are more appropriately aimed at the restrictions and requirements outlined in § 222 rather than the approval method adopted in the CPNI Order. As outlined above, it is the statute, not the CPNI Order, that prohibits a carrier from using, disclosing, or permitting access to individually identifiable CPNI without first obtaining informed consent from its customers. Yet U.S. West has not challenged the constitutionality of § 222, and this is not the proper forum for addressing such a challenge even if it was raised. . . .

The majority, focusing at this point on the CPNI Order rather than the statute, concludes the FCC failed to adequately consider the opt-out method, which the majority characterizes as "an obvious and substantially less restrictive alternative" than the opt-in method. Notably, however, the majority fails to explain why, in its view, the opt-out method is substantially less restrictive. Presumably, the majority is relying on the fact that the opt-out method typically results in a higher "approval" rate than the opt-in method. Were mere "approval" percentages the only factor relevant to our discussion, the majority would perhaps be correct. As the FCC persuasively concluded in the CPNI Order, however, the opt-out method simply does not comply with § 222's requirement of informed consent. In particular, the opt-out method, unlike the opt-in method, does not guarantee that a customer will make an informed decision about usage of his or her individually identifiable CPNI. To the contrary, the opt-out method creates the very real possibility of "uninformed" customer approval. In the end, I reiterate my point that the opt-in method selected by the FCC is the only method of obtaining approval that serves the governmental interests at issue while simultaneously complying with the express requirement of the statute (i.e., obtaining informed customer consent). . . .

In conclusion, I view U.S. West's petition for review as little more than a run-of-the-mill attack on an agency order "clothed by ingenious argument in the garb" of First Amendment issues. . . .

NOTES & QUESTIONS

1. *Is Opt in Narrowly Tailored?* Is the opt-in system involved in *U.S. West* more restrictive than the do-not-mail list in *Rowan* or the DNC list in *Mainstream*

Marketing? Is the privacy interest in *U.S. West* different than in *Rowan* and *Mainstream Marketing*?

2. ***Personal Information: Property, Contract, and Speech.*** Consider the following critique of *U.S. West* by Julie Cohen:

> The law affords numerous instances of regulation of the exchange of information as property or product. Securities markets, which operate entirely by means of information exchange, are subject to extensive regulation, and hardly anybody thinks that securities laws and regulations should be subjected to heightened or strict First Amendment scrutiny. Laws prohibiting patent, copyright, and trademark infringement, and forbidding the misappropriation of trade secrets, have as their fundamental purpose (and their undisputed effect) the restriction of information flows. The securities and intellectual property laws, moreover, are expressly content-based, and thus illustrate that (as several leading First Amendment scholars acknowledge) this characterization doesn't always matter. Finally, federal computer crime laws punish certain uses of information for reasons entirely unrelated to their communicative aspects. . . .
>
> The accumulation, use, and market exchange of personally-identified data don't fit neatly into any recognized category of "commercial speech" . . . because in the ways that matter, these activities aren't really "speech" at all. Although regulation directed at these acts may impose some indirect burden on direct-to-consumer communication, that isn't the primary objective of data privacy regulation. This suggests that, at most, data privacy regulation should be subject to the intermediate scrutiny applied to indirect speech regulation.[82]

3. ***Is Opt In Too Expensive?*** Michael Staten and Fred Cate have defended the *U.S. West* decision by noting the results of the testing of an opt-in system by U.S. West:

> In 1997, U.S. West (now Qwest Communications), one of the largest telecommunications companies in the United States, conducted one of the few affirmative consent trials for which results are publicly available. In that trial, the company sought permission from its customers to utilize information about their calling patterns (e.g., volume of calls, time and duration of calls, etc.) to market new services to them. The direct mail appeal for permission received a positive response rate between 5 and 11 percent for residential customers (depending upon the size of a companion incentive offered by the company). Residential customers opted in at a rate of 28 percent when called about the service.
>
> When U.S. West was actually communicating in person with the consumers, the positive response rate was three to six times higher than when it relied on consumers reading and responding to mail. But even with telemarketing, the task of reaching a customer is daunting. U.S. West determined that it required an average of 4.8 calls to each consumer household before they reached an adult who could grant consent. In one-third of households called, U.S. West never reached the customer, despite repeated attempts. In any case, many U.S. West customers received more calls than would have been the case in an opt-out system, and despite repeated contact

---

[82] Julie E. Cohen, *Examined Lives: Informational Privacy and the Subject as Object*, 52 Stan. L. Rev. 1373, 1416-18, 1421 (2000).

attempts, one-third of their customers missed opportunities to receive new products and services. The approximately $20 cost per positive response in the telemarketing test and $29 to $34 cost per positive response in the direct mail test led the company to conclude that opt-in was not a viable business model because it was too costly, too difficult, and too time intensive.[83]

Robert Gellman, however, generally disputes the findings of industry studies about the costs of privacy protective measures. With regard to opt-in cost assessments, Gellman argues that industry studies often fail "to consider other ways [beyond direct mail and telemarketing] that business and charities can solicit individuals to replace any losses from opt-in requirements. Newspaper, Internet, radio, and television advertising may be effective substitutes for direct mail. There are other ways to approach individuals without the compilation of detailed personal dossiers. None of the alternatives is adequately considered."[84]

4. *Is Commercial Transaction Information Different from Other Speech?* Courts analyzing First Amendment challenges to regulation of data about commercial transactions have typically viewed the dissemination and use of such data as commercial speech, and they have applied the *Central Hudson* test. This test is less protective than regular First Amendment protection. Solveig Singleton contends that data about commercial transactions should be considered regular speech, not commercial speech:

> Is commercial tracking essentially different from gossip? . . .
>
> Gossip and other informal personal contacts serve an important function in advanced economies. In Nineteenth Century America, entrepreneurs would increase their sales by acquiring information about their customers. Customers relied on their neighborhood banker, whom they knew since childhood, to grant them credit. They would return again and again to the same stores for personalized service. . . .
>
> [E]conomic actors must develop new mechanisms of relaying information to each other about fraud, trust, and behavior of potential customers. Towards the end of the Nineteenth Century and throughout the Twentieth Century, formal credit reporting began to evolve out of gossip networks. . . .
>
> The equivalence of gossip and consumer databases suggests that there is no need to treat the evolution of databases as a crisis. Those who argue for a new legal regime for privacy, however, view new uses of information as having crossed an "invisible line" between permissible gossip and violative information collection. While the use of new technology to collect information may make people uneasy, is there any reason to suppose that any harm that might result will amount to greater harm than the harm that could come from being a victim of vicious gossip?[85]

---

[83] Michael E. Staten & Fred H. Cate, *The Impact of Opt-In Privacy Rules on Retail Credit Markets: A Case Study of MBNA*, 52 Duke L.J. 745, 767-68 (2003).

[84] Robert Gellman, *Privacy, Consumers, and Costs: How the Lack of Privacy Costs Consumers and Why Business Studies of Privacy Costs Are Biased and Incomplete* (March 2002), at http://www.epic.org/reports/dmfprivacy.html.

[85] Solveig Singleton, *Privacy Versus the First Amendment: A Skeptical Approach*, 11 Fordham Intell. Prop. Media & Ent. L.J. 97, 126-32 (2000).

Singleton goes on to contend that information collected by businesses in databases is less pernicious than gossip because few people have access to it and it is "likely to be much more accurate than gossip." Is the information in computer databases merely gossip on a more systemic scale? Compare how the First Amendment regulates gossip with how it regulates commercial speech.

5. ***The Value of Privacy.*** What is the value of protecting the privacy of consumer information maintained by telecommunications companies? Is it more important than the economic benefits that the telecommunications companies gain by using that information for marketing? How should policymakers go about answering such questions? Consider James Nehf:

> The choice of utilitarian reasoning — often reduced to cost-benefit analysis ("CBA") in policy debates — fixes the outcome in favor of the side that can more easily quantify results. In privacy debates, this generally favors the side arguing for more data collection and sharing. Although CBA can mean different things in various contexts, the term here means a strategy for making choices in which quantifiable weights are given to competing alternatives. . . .
>
> We should openly acknowledge that non-economic values are legitimate in privacy debates, just as they have been recognized in other areas of fundamental importance. Decisions about the societal acceptance of disabled citizens, the codification of collective bargaining rights for workers, and the adoption of fair trial procedures for the accused did not depend entirely, or even primarily, on CBA outcomes. Difficulties in quantifying costs and benefits do not present insurmountable obstacles when policymakers address matters of basic human dignity. The protection of personal data should be viewed in a similar way, and CBA should play a smaller role in privacy debates. . . .
>
> A similar phenomenon is at work in the formulation of public policy. Policymakers are often asked to compare incomparable alternatives. . . .
>
> By converting all values to money, the incomparability problem is lessened, but only if we accept the legitimacy of money as the covering value. In the privacy debate, the legitimacy of monetizing individual privacy preferences is highly suspect. Benefits are often personal, emotional, intangible, and not readily quantifiable. Preferences on privacy matters are generally muddled, incoherent, and ill-informed. If privacy preferences are real but not sufficiently coherent to form a sound basis for valuation, any attempt to place a monetary value on them loses meaning. The choice of CBA as the model for justifying decisions fixes the end, because the chosen covering value will usually result in a decision favoring data proliferation over data protection. . . .
>
> People make choices between seemingly incomparable things all the time, and they can do so rationally. A person is not acting irrationally by preferring a perceived notable value over an incomparable nominal value, even if she cannot state a normative theory to explain why the decision is right. A similar phenomenon may be seen in the formulation of public policy. Notable values may be preferred over nominal ones in the enactment of laws and the implementation of policies even if policymakers cannot explain why one alternative is better than the other. Moreover, by observing a number of such decisions over time, we may begin to see a pattern develop and covering

values emerge that can serve as guides to later decisions that are closer to the margin.[86]

TRANS UNION CORP. V. FEDERAL TRADE COMMISSION
245 F.3d 809 (D.C. Cir. 2001)

TATEL, J. . . . Petitioner Trans Union sells two types of products. First, as a credit reporting agency, it compiles credit reports about individual consumers from credit information it collects from banks, credit card companies, and other lenders. It then sells these credit reports to lenders, employers, and insurance companies. Trans Union receives credit information from lenders in the form of "tradelines." A tradeline typically includes a customer's name, address, date of birth, telephone number, Social Security number, account type, opening date of account, credit limit, account status, and payment history. Trans Union receives 1.4 to 1.6 billion records per month. The company's credit database contains information on 190 million adults.

Trans Union's second set of products — those at issue in this case — are known as target marketing products. These consist of lists of names and addresses of individuals who meet specific criteria such as possession of an auto loan, a department store credit card, or two or more mortgages. Marketers purchase these lists, then contact the individuals by mail or telephone to offer them goods and services. To create its target marketing lists, Trans Union maintains a database known as MasterFile, a subset of its consumer credit database. MasterFile consists of information about every consumer in the company's credit database who has (A) at least two tradelines with activity during the previous six months, or (B) one tradeline with activity during the previous six months plus an address confirmed by an outside source. The company compiles target marketing lists by extracting from MasterFile the names and addresses of individuals with characteristics chosen by list purchasers. For example, a department store might buy a list of all individuals in a particular area code who have both a mortgage and a credit card with a $10,000 limit. Although target marketing lists contain only names and addresses, purchasers know that every person on a list has the characteristics they requested because Trans Union uses those characteristics as criteria for culling individual files from its database. Purchasers also know that every individual on a target marketing list satisfies the criteria for inclusion in MasterFile.

The Fair Credit Reporting Act of 1970 ("FCRA"), 15 U.S.C. §§ 1681, 1681a-1681u, regulates consumer reporting agencies like Trans Union, imposing various obligations to protect the privacy and accuracy of credit information. The Federal Trade Commission, acting pursuant to its authority to enforce the FCRA, *see* 15 U.S.C. § 1681s(a), determined that Trans Union's target marketing lists were "consumer reports" subject to the Act's limitations. [The FTC concluded that targeted marketing was not an authorized use of consumer reports under the FCRA and ordered Trans Union to halt its sale of the lists.] . . . .

---

[86] James P. Nehf, *Incomparability and the Passive Virtues of Ad Hoc Privacy Policy*, 76 U. Colo. L. Rev. 1, 29-36, 42 (2005).

. . . [Trans Union challenges the FTC's application of the FCRA as violative of the First Amendment.] Banning the sale of target marketing lists, the company says, amounts to a restriction on its speech subject to strict scrutiny. Again, Trans Union misunderstands our standard of review. In *Dun & Bradstreet, Inc. v. Greenmoss Builders, Inc.,* 472 U.S. 749 (1985), the Supreme Court held that a consumer reporting agency's credit report warranted reduced constitutional protection because it concerned "no public issue." "The protection to be accorded a particular credit report," the Court explained, "depends on whether the report's 'content, form, and context' indicate that it concerns a public matter." Like the credit report in *Dun & Bradstreet,* which the Supreme Court found "was speech solely in the interest of the speaker and its specific business audience," the information about individual consumers and their credit performance communicated by Trans Union target marketing lists is solely of interest to the company and its business customers and relates to no matter of public concern. Trans Union target marketing lists thus warrant "reduced constitutional protection."

We turn then to the specifics of Trans Union's First Amendment argument. The company first claims that neither the FCRA nor the Commission's Order advances a substantial government interest. The "Congressional findings and statement of purpose" at the beginning of the FCRA state: "There is a need to insure that consumer reporting agencies exercise their grave responsibilities with . . . respect for the consumer's right to privacy." 15 U.S.C. § 1681 (a)(4). Contrary to the company's assertions, we have no doubt that this interest — protecting the privacy of consumer credit information — is substantial.

Trans Union next argues that Congress should have chosen a "less burdensome alternative," i.e., allowing consumer reporting agencies to sell credit information as long as they notify consumers and give them the ability to "opt out." Because the FCRA is not subject to strict First Amendment scrutiny, however, Congress had no obligation to choose the least restrictive means of accomplishing its goal.

Finally, Trans Union argues that the FCRA is underinclusive because it applies only to consumer reporting agencies and not to other companies that sell consumer information. But given consumer reporting agencies' unique "access to a broad range of continually-updated, detailed information about millions of consumers' personal credit histories," we think it not at all inappropriate for Congress to have singled out consumer reporting agencies for regulation. . . .

NOTES & QUESTIONS

1. **U.S. West *vs.* Trans Union.** Compare *U.S. West* with *Trans Union.* Are these cases consistent with each other? Which case's reasoning strikes you as more persuasive?

2. **Trans Union II.** In *Trans Union v. FTC*, 295 F.3d 42 (D.C. Cir. 2002) (*Trans Union II*), Trans Union sued to enjoin regulations promulgated pursuant to the Gramm-Leach-Bliley (GLB) Act, alleging, among other things, that they violated the First Amendment. Trans Union argued that these regulations would prevent it from selling credit headers, which consist of a consumer's

name, address, Social Security number, and phone number. Trans Union contended that the sale of credit headers is commercial speech. The court concluded that Trans Union's First Amendment arguments were "foreclosed" by its earlier opinion in *Trans Union v. FTC,* which resolved that "the government interest in 'protecting the privacy of consumer credit information' 'is substantial.'"

3. *Free Speech and the Fair Information Practices.* Recall the discussion of the Fair Information Practices from Chapter 3. The Fair Information Practices provide certain limitations on the uses and disclosure of personal information. Eugene Volokh contends:

> I am especially worried about the normative power of the notion that the government has a compelling interest in creating "codes of fair information practices" restricting true statements made by nongovernmental speakers. The protection of free speech generally rests on an assumption that it's not for the government to decide which speech is "fair" and which isn't; the unfairnesses, excesses, and bad taste of speakers are something that current First Amendment principles generally require us to tolerate. Once people grow to accept and even like government restrictions on one kind of supposedly "unfair" communication of facts, it may become much easier for people to accept "codes of fair reporting," "codes of fair debate," "codes of fair filmmaking," "codes of fair political criticism," and the like. . . .[87]

Consider Paul Schwartz, who contends that free discourse is promoted by the protection of privacy:

> When the government requires fair information practices for the private sector, has it created a right to stop people from speaking about you? As an initial point, I emphasize that the majority of the core fair information practices do not involve the government preventing disclosure of personal information. [The fair information practices generally require: (1) the creation of a statutory fabric that defines obligations with respect to the use of personal information; (2) the maintenance of processing systems that are understandable to the concerned individual (transparency); (3) the assignment of limited procedural and substantive rights to the individual; and (4) the establishment of effective oversight of data use, whether through individual litigation (self-help), a government role (external oversight), or some combination of these approaches.] . . . [F]air information practices one, two, and four regulate the business practices of private entities without silencing their speech. No prevention of speech about anyone takes place, for example, when the Fair Credit Reporting Act of 1970 requires that certain information be given to a consumer when an "investigative consumer report" is prepared about her.
>
> These nonsilencing fair information practices are akin to a broad range of other measures that regulate information use in the private sector and do not abridge the freedom of speech under any interpretation of the First Amendment. The First Amendment does not prevent the government from requiring product labels on food products or the use of "plain English" by

---

[87] Eugene Volokh, *Freedom of Speech and Information Privacy: The Troubling Implications of a Right to Stop People from Speaking About You,* 52 Stan. L. Rev. 1049, 1090 (2000).

publicly traded companies in reports sent to their investors or Form 10-Ks filed with the Securities and Exchange Commission. Nor does the First Amendment forbid privacy laws such as the Children's Online Privacy Protection Act, which assigns parents a right of access to their children's online data profiles. The ultimate merit of these laws depends on their specific context and precise details, but such experimentation by the State should be viewed as noncontroversial on free speech grounds.

Nevertheless, one subset of fair information practices does correspond to Volokh's idea of information privacy as the right to stop people from speaking about you. . . . [S]o long as [laws protecting personal information disclosure] are viewpoint neutral, these laws are a necessary element of safeguarding free communication in our democratic society. . . .

. . . [A] democratic order depends on both an underlying personal capacity for self-governance and the participation of individuals in community and democratic self-rule. Privacy law thus has an important role in protecting individual self-determination and democratic deliberation. By providing access to one's personal data, information about how it will be processed, and other fair information practices, the law seeks to structure the terms on which individuals confront the information demands of the community, private bureaucratic entities, and the State. Attention to these issues by the legal order is essential to the health of a democracy, which ultimately depends on individual communicative competence.[88]

4. *Is Information Speech?* Is the collection, use, and/or transfer of personal information a form of speech? Or is it merely trade in property?

Eugene Volokh contends that such information processing constitutes speech:

> Many . . . databases — for instance, credit history databases or criminal record databases — are used by people to help them decide whom it is safe to deal with and who is likely to cheat them. Other databases, which contain less incriminating information, such as a person's shopping patterns . . . [contain] data [that] is of direct daily life interest to its recipients, since it helps them find out with whom they should do business.[89]

Further, Volokh contends: "[I]t is no less speech when a credit bureau sends credit information to a business. The owners and managers of a credit bureau are communicating information to decisionmakers, such as loan officers, at the recipient business."[90]

Daniel Solove recognizes that some forms of database information transfer and use can constitute speech:

> There are no easy analytic distinctions as to what is or is not "speech." The "essence" of information is neither a good, nor is it speech, for information can be used in ways that make it akin to either one. It is the *use* of the information that determines what information is, not anything inherent in the information itself. If I sell you a book, I have engaged in a commercial transaction. I sold the book as a good. However, the book is also expressing

---

[88] Paul M. Schwartz, *Free Speech vs. Information Privacy: Eugene Volokh's First Amendment Jurisprudence,* 52 Stan. L. Rev. 1559 (2000).

[89] Volokh, *Freedom of Speech, supra,* at 1093-94.

[90] *Id.* at 1083-84.

something. Even though books are sold as goods, the government cannot pass a law restricting the topics of what books can be sold. . . .

Volokh appears to view all information dissemination that is communicative as speech. Under Volokh's view, therefore, most forms of information dissemination would be entitled to equal First Amendment protection. . . .

However, Volokh's view would lead to severe conflicts with much modern regulation. Full First Amendment protection would apply to statements about a company's earnings and other information regulated by the SEC, insider trading, quid pro quo sexual harassment, fraudulent statements, perjury, bribery, blackmail, extortion, conspiracy, and so on. One could neatly exclude these examples from the category of speech, eliminating the necessity for First Amendment analysis. Although this seems the easiest approach, it is conceptually sloppy or even dishonest absent a meaningful way to argue that these examples do not involve communication. I contend that these examples of highly regulated forms of communication have not received the full rigor of standard First Amendment analysis because of policy considerations. Categorizing them as nonspeech conceals these policy considerations under the façade of an analytical distinction that thus far has not been persuasively articulated.

I am not eschewing all attempts at categorization between speech and nonspeech. To do so would make the First Amendment applicable to virtually anything that is expressive or communicative. Still, the distinction as currently constituted hides its ideological character. . . .

Dealing with privacy issues by categorizing personal information as nonspeech is undesirable because it cloaks the real normative reasons for why society wants to permit greater regulation of certain communicative activity. Rather than focusing on distinguishing between speech and nonspeech, the determination about what forms of information to regulate should center on policy considerations. These policy considerations should turn on the uses of the information rather than on notions about the inherent nature of the information.[91]

Solove goes on to argue that although transfers of personal information may be speech, they are of lower value than other forms of free speech, such as political speech. He contends that whereas speech of public concern is of high value, speech of private concern is given a lower constitutional value, and hence less stringent scrutiny, as is commercial speech and other lower-value categories of speech.

Neil Richards, however, contends that "most privacy regulation that interrupts information flows in the context of an express or implied commercial relationship is neither 'speech' within the current meaning of the First Amendment, nor should it be viewed as such." He criticizes Schwartz and Solove because "they grant too much ground to the First Amendment critique, and may ultimately prove to be underprotective of privacy interests, particularly in the database context." Richards finds Solove's contextual balancing approach too messy to "provide meaningfully increased protection for privacy in the courts." Richards argues instead for a categorical solution

---

[91] Daniel J. Solove, *The Virtues of Knowing Less: Justifying Privacy Protections Against Disclosure,* 53 Duke L.J. 967, 979-80 (2003).

and contends that much regulation of speech in the commercial context should be seen as falling entirely outside the scope of the heightened First Amendment scrutiny:

> This might be the case because the speech is threatening, obscene, or libelous, and thus part of the "established" categories of "unprotected speech." But it might also be the case because the speech is an insider trading tip, . . . an offer to create a monopoly in restraint of trade, or a breach of the attorney-client privilege. In either case, the speech would be outside the scope of the First Amendment and could be regulated as long as a rational basis existed for so doing. . . .
>
> [I]nformation disclosure rules that are the product of generally applicable laws fall outside the scope of the First Amendment. Where information is received by an entity in violation of some other legal rule — whether breach of contract, trespass, theft, or fraud — the First Amendment creates no barrier to the government's ability to prevent and punish disclosure. This is the case even if the information is newsworthy or otherwise of public concern. . . .
>
> From a First Amendment perspective, no such equivalently important social function [as dissemination of information by the press] . . . is played by database companies engaged in the trade of personal data. Indeed, a general law regulating the commercial trade in personal data by database, profiling, and marketing companies is far removed from the core speech protected by the First Amendment, and is much more like the "speech" outside the boundaries of heightened review.

Richards goes on to equate the First Amendment critique of privacy regulation to *Lochnerism,* where the Supreme Court in *Lochner v. New York,* 198 U.S. 45 (1905), struck down a statute regulating the hours bakers could work per week based on "freedom of contract." *Lochner* was, and remains, highly criticized for being an impediment to New Deal legislation by an activist ideological Court. Richards notes:

> [T]here are some fairly strong parallels between the traditional conception of *Lochner* and the First Amendment critique of data privacy legislation. Both theories are judicial responses to calls for legal regulation of the economic and social dislocations caused by rapid technological change. *Lochnerism* addressed a major socio-technological problem of the industrial age — the power differential between individuals and businesses in industrial working conditions, while the First Amendment critique is addressed to a major socio-technological problem of our information age — the power differential between individuals and businesses over information in the electronic environment. Both theories place a libertarian gloss upon the Constitution, interpreting it to mandate either "freedom of contract" or "freedom of information." Both theories seek to place certain forms of economic regulation beyond the power of legislatures to enact. And both theories are eagerly supported by business interests keen to immunize themselves from regulation under the aegis of Constitutional doctrine. To the extent that the First Amendment critique is similar to the traditional view of *Lochner,* then, its elevation of an economic right to first-order constitutional magnitude seems similarly dubious.[92]

---

[92] Neil Richards, *Reconciling Data Privacy and the First Amendment,* 52 UCLA L. Rev. 1149, 1169, 1180, 1172-73, 1206, 1212-13 (2005).

E. GOVERNMENT ACCESS TO PRIVATE SECTOR RECORDS

1. INFORMATION GATHERING WITHOUT SEARCH WARRANTS

(a) Subpoenas

A subpoena is an order to obtain testimony or documents. Numerous statutes authorize federal agencies to issue subpoenas. In *Doe v. Ashcroft,* 334 F. Supp. 2d 471 (S.D.N.Y. 2004), the court explained:

> For example, the Internal Revenue Service (IRS) may issue subpoenas to investigate possible violations of the tax code, and the Securities Exchange Commission (SEC) may issue subpoenas to investigate possible violations of the securities laws. More obscure examples include the Secretary of Agriculture's power to issue subpoenas in investigating and enforcing laws related to honey research, and the Secretary of Commerce's power to issue subpoenas in investigating and enforcing halibut fishing laws. . . .
>
> Where an agency seeks a court order to enforce a subpoena against a resisting subpoena recipient, courts will enforce the subpoena as long as: (1) the agency's investigation is being conducted pursuant to a legitimate purpose, (2) the inquiry is relevant to that purpose, (3) the information is not already within the agency's possession, and (4) the proper procedures have been followed. The Second Circuit has described these standards as "minimal." Even if an administrative subpoena meets these initial criteria to be enforceable, its recipient may nevertheless affirmatively challenge the subpoena on other grounds, such as an allegation that it was issued with an improper purpose or that the information sought is privileged.

In contrast to an administrative subpoena, an ordinary subpoena may be issued in civil or criminal cases. For criminal cases, the government may obtain a subpoena from the clerk of court. Subpoenas are not issued directly by judges. Instead, "[t]he clerk must issue a blank subpoena — signed and sealed — to the party requesting it, and that party must fill in the blanks before the subpoena is served." Fed. R. Crim. P. 17(a). Failure to comply with a subpoena can lead to contempt of court sanctions. A subpoena can broadly compel the production of various documents and items:

> A subpoena may order the witness to produce any books, papers, documents, data, or other objects the subpoena designates. The court may direct the witness to produce the designated items in court before trial or before they are to be offered in evidence. When the items arrive, the court may permit the parties and their attorneys to inspect all or part of them. Fed. R. Crim. P. 17(c)(1).

If the party served with the subpoena has an objection, she may bring a motion to quash or modify the subpoena. "[T]he court may quash or modify the subpoena if compliance would be unreasonable or oppressive." Fed. R. Crim. P. 17(c)(2). As *Doe v. Ashcroft,* 334 F. Supp. 2d 471 (S.D.N.Y. 2004) explains:

> The reasonableness of a subpoena depends on the context. For example, to survive a motion to quash, a subpoena issued in connection with a criminal trial

"must make a reasonably specific request for information that would be both relevant and admissible at trial." By contrast, a grand jury subpoena is generally enforced as long as there is a "reasonable possibility that the category of materials the Government seeks will produce information relevant to the general subject of the grand jury's investigation." Considering the grand jury's broad investigatory power and minimal court supervision, it is accurate to observe, as the Second Circuit did long ago, that "[b]asically the grand jury is a law enforcement agency."

When do subpoenas violate the Fourth or Fifth Amendments? Subpoenas can compel the production of documents with incriminating information. Recall that in *Boyd v. United States*, 116 U.S. 616 (1886), the Supreme Court concluded that the government was barred from obtaining a person's papers or documents via a subpoena. However, the Court reversed course in *Hale v. Henkel*, 201 U.S. 43 (1906), when it concluded that the administrative state depended upon the government's ability to subpoena business documents. The Court made a "clear distinction . . . between an individual and a corporation."

Later on, in *Couch v. United States*, 409 U.S. 322 (1973), the Court held that tax records could be subpoenaed without violating the Fourth or Fifth Amendments: "[In a] situation where obligations of disclosure exist and under a system largely dependent upon honest self-reporting even to survive . . . [people] cannot reasonably claim, either for Fourth or Fifth Amendment purposes, an expectation of protected privacy or confidentiality." Then, in *Fisher v. United States*, 425 U.S. 391 (1976), the Court expanded its holding in *Couch* to encompass the disclosure not just of corporate documents or tax records but of nearly all private papers. Christopher Slobogin notes that this was an alteration in the Court's jurisprudence because the Court had long maintained a distinction between corporate records and personal papers. Later cases cut back on the breadth of *Fisher*, holding that the act of a party producing a document can constitute a Fifth Amendment violation. *See, e.g., United States v. Hubbell*, 530 U.S. 27 (2000).[93] However, as Christopher Slobogin notes, the "lion's share of subpoenas that seek personal papers . . . are directed at third parties." In the next section, consider the Court's approach to the applicability of the Fourth Amendment to information held by third parties.

GONZALES V. GOOGLE

234 F.R.D. 674 (N.D. Cal. 2006)

[The government sought information for its use in *ACLU v. Gonzales*, No. 98-CV-5591, pending in the Eastern District of Pennsylvania. That case involved a challenge by the ACLU to the Children's Online Protection Act (COPA). Google was not a party to that case, but the government subpoenaed from Google: (1) URL samples: "[a]ll URL's that are available to be located to a query on your company's search engine as of July 31, 2005" and (2) search queries: "[a]ll queries that have been entered on your company's search engine between June 1,

---

[93] For an excellent history of the Supreme Court's jurisprudence regarding subpoenas, see Christopher Slobogin, *Subpoenas and Privacy*, 53 DePaul L. Rev. 805 (2005).

2005 and July 31, 2005 inclusive." Subsequently, the government narrowed its URL sample demand to 50,000 URLs and it narrowed its search query demand to all queries during a one-week period rather than the two-month period mentioned above. Google still raised a challenge, and the government again narrowed its search query request for only 5,000 entries from Google's query log. It continued to seek a sample of 50,000 URLs from Google's search index. Under Federal Rule of Civil Procedure 26, a subpoena sought must be "reasonably calculated to lead to admissible evidence." It may be quashed if the "burden or expense of the proposed discovery outweighs its likely benefit."]

WARE, J. . . . As narrowed by negotiations with Google and through the course of this Miscellaneous Action, the Government now seeks a sample of 50,000 URLs from Google's search index. In determining whether the information sought is reasonably calculated to lead to admissible evidence, the party seeking the information must first provide the Court with its plans for the requested information. The Government's disclosure of its plans for the sample of URLs is incomplete. The actual methodology disclosed in the Government's papers as to the search index sample is, in its entirety, as follows: "A human being will browse a random sample of 5,000-10,000 URLs from Google's index and categorize those sites by content" and from this information, the Government intends to "estimate . . . the aggregate properties of the websites that search engines have indexed." The Government's disclosure only describes its methodology for a study to categorize the URLs in Google's search index, and does not disclose a study regarding the effectiveness of filtering software. Absent any explanation of how the "aggregate properties" of material on the Internet is germane to the underlying litigation, the Government's disclosure as to its planned categorization study is not particularly helpful in determining whether the sample of Google's search index sought is reasonably calculated to lead to admissible evidence in the underlying litigation.

Based on the Government's statement that this information is to act as a "test set for the study" and a general statement that the purpose of the study is to "evaluate the effectiveness of content filtering software," the Court is able to envision a study whereby a sample of 50,000 URLs from the Google search index may be reasonably calculated to lead to admissible evidence on measuring the effectiveness of filtering software. In such a study, the Court imagines, the URLs would be categorized, run through the filtering software, and the effectiveness of the filtering software ascertained as to the various categories of URLs. The Government does not even provide this rudimentary level of general detail as to what it intends to do with the sample of URLs to evaluate the effectiveness of filtering software, and at the hearing neither confirmed nor denied the Court's speculations about the study. In fact, the Government seems to indicate that such a study is not what it has in mind: "[t]he government seeks this information *only* to perform a study, in the aggregate, of trends on the Internet" (emphasis added), with no explanation of how an aggregate study of Internet trends would be reasonably calculated to lead to admissible evidence in the underlying suit where the efficacy of filtering software is at issue. . . .

Given the broad definition of relevance in Rule 26, and the current narrow scope of the subpoena, despite the vagueness with which the Government has disclosed its study, the Court gives the Government the benefit of the doubt. The Court finds that 50,000 URLs randomly selected from Google's data base for use in a scientific study of the effectiveness of filters is relevant to the issues in the case of *ACLU v. Gonzales.*[94]

In its original subpoena the Government sought a listing of the text of all search queries entered by Google users over a two month period. As defined in the Government's subpoena, "queries" include only the text of the search string entered by a user, and not "any additional information that may be associated with such a text string that would identify the person who entered the text string into the search engine, or the computer from which the text string was entered." The Government has narrowed its request so that it now seeks only a sample of 5,000 such queries from Google's query log. The Government discloses its plans for the query log information as follows: "A random sample of approximately 1,000 Google queries from a one-week period will be run through the Google search engine. A human being will browse the top URLs returned by each search and categorize the sites by content." . . .

Google also argues that it will be unduly burdened by loss of user trust if forced to produce its users' queries to the Government. Google claims that its success is attributed in large part to the volume of its users and these users may be attracted to its search engine because of the privacy and anonymity of the service. According to Google, even a perception that Google is acquiescing to the Government's demands to release its query log would harm Google's business by deterring some searches by some users.

Google's own privacy statement indicates that Google users could not reasonably expect Google to guard the query log from disclosure to the Government. . . . Google's privacy policy does not represent to users that it keeps confidential any information other than "personal information." Neither Google's URLs nor the text of search strings with "personal information" redacted, are reasonably "personal information" under Google's stated privacy policy. Google's privacy policy indicates that it has not suggested to its users that non-"personal information" such as that sought by the Government is kept confidential.

However, even if an expectation by Google users that Google would prevent disclosure to the Government of its users' search queries is not entirely reasonable, the statistic cited by Dr. Stark that over a quarter of all Internet searches are for pornography indicates that at least some of Google's users expect some sort of privacy in their searches. The expectation of privacy by some Google users may not be reasonable, but may nonetheless have an appreciable impact on the way in which Google is perceived, and consequently the frequency with which users use Google. Such an expectation does not rise to the level of an absolute privilege, but does indicate that there is a potential burden as to Google's loss of goodwill if Google is forced to disclose search queries to the Government.

---

[94] To the extent that the Government is gathering this information for some other purpose than to run the sample of Google's search index through various filters to determine the efficacy of those filters, the Court would take a different view of the relevance of the information. For example, the Court would not find the information relevant if it is being sought just to characterize the nature of the URL's in Google's database.

Rule 45(c)(3)(B) provides additional protections where a subpoena seeks trade secret or confidential commercial information from a nonparty. . . . Because Google still continues to claim information about its entire search index and entire query log as confidential, the Court will presume that the requested information, as a small sample of proprietary information, may be somewhat commercially sensitive, albeit not independently commercially sensitive. Successive disclosures, whether in this lawsuit or pursuant to subsequent civil subpoenas, in the aggregate could yield confidential commercial information about Google's search index or query log. . . .

What the Government has not demonstrated, however, is a substantial need for *both* the information contained in the sample of URLs and sample of search query text. Furthermore, even if the information requested is not a trade secret, a district court may in its discretion limit discovery on a finding that "the discovery sought is unreasonably cumulative or duplicative, or is obtainable from some other source that is more convenient, less burdensome, or less expensive." Rule 26(b)(2)(i).

Faced with duplicative discovery, and with the Government not expressing a preference as to which source of the test set of URLs it prefers, this Court exercises its discretion pursuant to Rule 26(b)(2) and determines that the marginal burden of loss of trust by Google's users based on Google's disclosure of its users' search queries to the Government outweighs the duplicative disclosure's likely benefit to the Government's study. Accordingly, the Court grants the Government's motion to compel only as to the sample of 50,000 URLs from Google's search index.

The Court raises, sua sponte, its concerns about the privacy of Google's users apart from Google's business goodwill argument. . . .

Although the Government has only requested the text strings entered, basic identifiable information may be found in the text strings when users search for personal information such as their social security numbers or credit card numbers through Google in order to determine whether such information is available on the Internet. The Court is also aware of so-called "vanity searches," where a user queries his or her own name perhaps with other information. . . . This concern, combined with the prevalence of Internet searches for sexually explicit material — generally not information that anyone wishes to reveal publicly — gives this Court pause as to whether the search queries themselves may constitute potentially sensitive information.

The Court also recognizes that there may a difference between a private litigant receiving potentially sensitive information and having this information be produced to the Government pursuant to civil subpoena. . . . Even though counsel for the Government assured the Court that the information received will only be used for the present litigation, it is conceivable that the Government may have an obligation to pursue information received for unrelated litigation purposes under certain circumstances regardless of the restrictiveness of a protective order. The Court expressed this concern at oral argument as to queries such as "bomb placement white house," but queries such as "communist berkeley parade route protest war" may also raise similar concerns. In the end, the Court need not express an opinion on this issue because the Government's motion is granted only as to the sample of URLs and not as to the log of search queries.

The Court also refrains from expressing an opinion on the applicability of the Electronic Communications Privacy Act. . . . The Court only notes that the ECPA does not bar the Government's request for sample of 50,000 URLs from Google's index though civil subpoena.

NOTES & QUESTIONS

1. *URL Samples vs. Search Queries.* The sought-after subpoena in *Gonzales v. Google* concerned information about both URL samples and search queries. What decision did the district court reach for each type of data? Are there different privacy implications for governmental access to the two kinds of information?

2. *Can People Be Identified from Anonymous Search Data?* An incident involving AOL proved that individuals can be identified based on their search queries. In August 2006, AOL revealed that it had released to researchers about 20 million search queries made by over 650,000 users of its search engine. Although AOL had substituted numerical IDs for the subscribers' actual user names, the personal identity of the user could be found based on the search queries. The *New York Times* demonstrated as much by tracking down AOL user No. 4417749; it linked this person's data trail to a 62-year old widow who lived in Lilburn, Georgia, and admitted to the reporter, "Those are my searches."[95]

(b) Financial Information and the Third Party Doctrine

THE BANK SECRECY ACT

The Bank Secrecy Act, Pub. L. No. 91-508, was enacted by Congress in 1970. The Act requires the retention of bank records and creation of reports that would be useful in criminal, tax, or regulatory investigations or proceedings. The Bank Secrecy Act was passed because of worry that shifting from paper to computer records would make white collar law enforcement more complicated.[96] The Act requires that federally insured banks record the identities of account holders as well as copies of each check, draft, or other financial instrument. Not all records and financial instruments must be maintained; only those that the Secretary of the Treasury designates as having a "high degree of usefulness." 12 U.S.C. § 1829b. Further, the Act authorizes the Secretary of the Treasury to promulgate regulations for the reporting of domestic financial transactions. 31 U.S.C. § 1081. The regulations require that a report be made for every deposit, withdrawal, or other transfer of currency exceeding $10,000. *See* 31 C.F.R. § 103.22. For transactions exceeding $5,000 into or out of the United States, the amount, the date of receipt, the form of financial instrument, and the person who received it must be reported. *See* 31 C.F.R. §§ 103.23, 103.25.

---

[95] Michael Barbaro & Tom Zeller, Jr., A Face is Exposed for AOL Searcher No. 4417749, N.Y. Times, Aug. 9, 2006.

[96] H. Jeff Smith, *Managing Privacy* 24 (1994).

CALIFORNIA BANKERS ASSOCIATION V. SHULTZ

416 U.S. 21 (1974)

[A group of bankers as well as depositors challenged the Bank Secrecy Act as a violation of the First, Fourth, and Fifth Amendments. The Court held that the Act did not violate the Fourth Amendment. First, the Court held that the bankers did not possess Fourth Amendment rights in the information because "corporations can claim no equality with individuals in the enjoyment of a right to privacy." Second, as to the Fourth Amendment rights of the individual depositors, the Court concluded that they lacked standing to pursue their claims.]

REHNQUIST, J. . . . The complaint filed in the District Court by the ACLU and the depositors contains no allegation by any of the individual depositors that they were engaged in the type of $10,000 domestic currency transaction which would necessitate that their bank report it to the Government. . . . [W]e simply cannot assume that the mere fact that one is a depositor in a bank means that he has engaged or will engage in a transaction involving more than $10,000 in currency, which is the only type of domestic transaction which the Secretary's regulations require that the banks report. That being so, the depositor plaintiffs lack standing to challenge the domestic reporting regulations, since they do not show that their transactions are required to be reported. . . .

We therefore hold that the Fourth Amendment claims of the depositor plaintiffs may not be considered on the record before us. Nor do we think that the California Bankers Association or the Security National Bank can vicariously assert such Fourth Amendment claims on behalf of bank customers in general. . .

[The Court also rejected a Fifth Amendment challenge to the Act as well as a First Amendment challenge. With regard to the First Amendment challenge, the Court concluded that the "threat to any First Amendment rights of the ACLU or its members from the mere existence of the records in the hands of the bank is a good deal more remote than the threat assertedly posed by the Army's system of compilation and distribution of information which we declined to adjudicate in *Laird v. Tatum*, 408 U.S. 1 (1972)."]

DOUGLAS, J. dissenting. . . . One's reading habits furnish telltale clues to those who are bent on bending us to one point of view. What one buys at the hardware and retail stores may furnish clues to potential uses of wires, soap powders, and the like used by criminals. A mandatory recording of all telephone conversations would be better than the recording of checks under the Bank Secrecy Act, if Big Brother is to have his way. The records of checks — now available to the investigators — are highly useful. In a sense a person is defined by the checks he writes. By examining them the agents get to know his doctors, lawyers, creditors, political allies, social connections, religious affiliation, educational interests, the papers and magazines he reads, and so on ad infinitum. These are all tied to one's social security number; and now that we have the data banks, these other items will enrich that storehouse and make it possible for a bureaucrat — by pushing one button — to get in an instant the names of the 190 million Americans who are subversives or potential and likely candidates.

It is, I submit, sheer nonsense to agree with the Secretary that all bank records of every citizen "have a high degree of usefulness in criminal, tax, or regulatory investigations or proceedings." That is unadulterated nonsense unless we are to assume that every citizen is a crook, an assumption I cannot make.

Since the banking transactions of an individual give a fairly accurate account of his religion, ideology, opinions, and interests, a regulation impounding them and making them automatically available to all federal investigative agencies is a sledge-hammer approach to a problem that only a delicate scalpel can manage. Where fundamental personal rights are involved — as is true when as here the Government gets large access to one's beliefs, ideas, politics, religion, cultural concerns, and the like — the Act should be "narrowly drawn" to meet the precise evil. Bank accounts at times harbor criminal plans. But we only rush with the crowd when we vent on our banks and their customers the devastating and leveling requirements of the present Act. I am not yet ready to agree that America is so possessed with evil that we must level all constitutional barriers to give our civil authorities the tools to catch criminals. . . .

UNITED STATES V. MILLER
425 U.S. 435 (1976)

POWELL, J. . . . [A]gents from the Treasury Department's Alcohol, Tobacco and Firearms Bureau presented grand jury subpoenas issued in blank by the clerk of the District Court, and completed by the United States Attorney's office, to the presidents of the Citizens & Southern National Bank of Warner Robins and the Bank of Byron, where respondent maintained accounts. The subpoenas required the two presidents to appear on January 24, 1973, and to produce [all records of loans as well as savings and checking accounts in the name of Mitch Miller]. . . .

The banks did not advise respondent that the subpoenas had been served but ordered their employees to make the records available and to provide copies of any documents the agents desired. . . .

The grand jury met on February 12, 1973, 19 days after the return date on the subpoenas. Respondent and four others were indicted. . . . The record does not indicate whether any of the bank records were in fact presented to the grand jury. They were used in the investigation and provided "one or two" investigatory leads. Copies of the checks also were introduced at trial to establish the overt acts [in a conspiracy in which the defendants were charged].

In his motion to suppress, denied by the District Court, respondent contended that the bank documents were illegally seized. It was urged that the subpoenas were defective because they were issued by the United States Attorney rather than a court, no return was made to a court, and the subpoenas were returnable on a date when the grand jury was not in session. The Court of Appeals reversed. Citing the prohibition in *Boyd v. United States*, 116 U.S. 616, 622 (1886), against "compulsory production of a man's private papers to establish a criminal charge against him," the court held that the Government had improperly circumvented *Boyd*'s protections of respondent's Fourth Amendment right against "unreasonable searches and seizures" by "first requiring a third party bank to copy all of its depositors' personal checks and then, with an improper invocation of legal process, calling upon the bank to allow inspection and reproduction of those copies." . . . The subpoenas issued here were found not to constitute adequate "legal process." The fact that the bank officers cooperated voluntarily was found to be irrelevant, for "he whose rights are threatened by the improper disclosure here was a bank depositor, not a bank official." . . .

We find that there was no intrusion into any area in which respondent had a protected Fourth Amendment interest and that the District Court therefore correctly denied respondent's motion to suppress. . . .

On their face, the documents subpoenaed here are not respondent's "private papers." Unlike the claimant in *Boyd* [*v. United States*], respondent can assert neither ownership nor possession. Instead, these are the business records of the banks. Respondent argues, however, that the Bank Secrecy Act introduces a factor that makes the subpoena in this case the functional equivalent of a search and seizure of the depositor's "private papers." We have held, in *California Bankers Ass'n v. Shultz*, that the mere maintenance of records pursuant to the requirements of the Act "invade(s) no Fourth Amendment right of any depositor." But respondent contends that the combination of the recordkeeping requirements of the Act and the issuance of a subpoena to obtain those records permits the Government to circumvent the requirements of the Fourth Amendment by allowing it to obtain a depositor's private records without complying with the legal requirements that would be applicable had it proceeded against him directly. Therefore, we must address the question whether the compulsion embodied in the Bank Secrecy Act as exercised in this case creates a Fourth Amendment interest in the depositor where none existed before. This question was expressly reserved in *California Bankers Ass'n*.

Respondent urges that he has a Fourth Amendment interest in the records kept by the banks because they are merely copies of personal records that were made available to the banks for a limited purpose and in which he has a reasonable expectation of privacy. He relies on this Court's statement in *Katz v. United States*, 389 U.S. 347, 353 (1967), that "we have . . . departed from the narrow view" that "'property interests control the right of the Government to search and seize,'" and that a "search and seizure" become unreasonable when the Government's activities violate "the privacy upon which (a person) justifiably relie[s]." But in *Katz* the Court also stressed that "[w]hat a person knowingly exposes to the public . . . is not a subject of Fourth Amendment protection." We must examine the nature of the particular documents sought to be protected in order to determine whether there is a legitimate "expectation of privacy" concerning their contents.

Even if we direct our attention to the original checks and deposit slips, rather than to the microfilm copies actually viewed and obtained by means of the subpoena, we perceive no legitimate "expectation of privacy" in their contents. The checks are not confidential communications but negotiable instruments to be used in commercial transactions. All of the documents obtained, including financial statements and deposit slips, contain only information voluntarily conveyed to the banks and exposed to their employees in the ordinary course of business. The lack of any legitimate expectation of privacy concerning the information kept in bank records was assumed by Congress in enacting the Bank Secrecy Act, the expressed purpose of which is to require records to be maintained because they "have a high degree of usefulness in criminal tax, and regulatory investigations and proceedings." 12 U.S.C. § 1829b(a)(1).

The depositor takes the risk, in revealing his affairs to another, that the information will be conveyed by that person to the Government. This Court has held repeatedly that the Fourth Amendment does not prohibit the obtaining of information revealed to a third party and conveyed by him to Government authorities, even if the information is revealed on the assumption that it will be used only for a limited purpose and the confidence placed in the third party will not be betrayed.

This analysis is not changed by the mandate of the Bank Secrecy Act that records of depositors' transactions be maintained by banks. In *California Bankers Ass'n v. Shultz,* we rejected the contention that banks, when keeping records of their depositors' transactions pursuant to the Act, are acting solely as agents of the Government. But, even if the banks could be said to have been acting solely as Government agents in transcribing the necessary information and complying without protest with the requirements of the subpoenas, there would be no intrusion upon the depositors' Fourth Amendment rights. . . .

Since no Fourth Amendment interests of the depositor are implicated here, this case is governed by the general rule that the issuance of a subpoena to a third party to obtain the records of that party does not violate the rights of a defendant, even if a criminal prosecution is contemplated at the time of the subpoena is issued. Under these principles, it was firmly settled, before the passage of the Bank Secrecy Act, that an Internal Revenue Service summons directed to a third-party bank does not violate the Fourth Amendment rights of a depositor under investigation.

Many banks traditionally kept permanent records of their depositors' accounts, although not all banks did so and the practice was declining in recent years. By requiring that such records be kept by all banks, the Bank Secrecy Act is not a novel means designed to circumvent established Fourth Amendment rights. It is merely an attempt to facilitate the use of a proper and long-standing law enforcement technique by insuring that records are available when they are needed.

We hold that the District Court correctly denied respondent's motion to suppress, since he possessed no Fourth Amendment interest that could be vindicated by a challenge to the subpoenas. . . .

BRENNAN, J. dissenting. . . . The pertinent phrasing of the Fourth Amendment "The right of the people to be secure in their persons, houses, papers, and effects, against unreasonable searches and seizures, shall not be violated" is virtually in haec verba as Art. I, § 19, of the California Constitution "The right of the people to be secure in their persons, houses, papers, and effects, against unreasonable seizures and searches, shall not be violated." The California Supreme Court has reached a conclusion under Art. I, § 13, in the same factual situation, contrary to that reached by the Court today under the Fourth Amendment. I dissent because in my view the California Supreme Court correctly interpreted the relevant constitutional language. . . .

Addressing the threshold question whether the accused's right of privacy was invaded, and relying on part on the decision of the Court of Appeals in this case, Mr. Justice Mosk stated in his excellent opinion for a unanimous court:

It cannot be gainsaid that the customer of a bank expects that the documents, such as checks, which he transmits to the bank in the course of his business operations, will remain private, and that such an expectation is reasonable. The prosecution concedes as much, although it asserts that this expectation is not constitutionally cognizable. Representatives of several banks testified at the suppression hearing that information in their possession regarding a customer's account is deemed by them to be confidential.

In the present case, although the record establishes that copies of petitioner's bank statements rather than of his checks were provided to the officer, the distinction is not significant with relation to petitioner's expectation of privacy. That the bank alters the form in which it records the information transmitted to it by the depositor to show the receipt and disbursement of money on a bank statement does not diminish the depositor's anticipation of privacy in the matters which he confides to the bank. A bank customer's reasonable expectation is that, absent compulsion by legal process, the matters he reveals to the bank will be utilized by the bank only for internal banking purposes. Thus, we hold petitioner had a reasonable expectation that the bank would maintain the confidentiality of those papers which originated with him in check form and of the bank statements into which a record of those same checks had been transformed pursuant to internal bank practice. . . .

The underlying dilemma in this and related cases is that the bank, a detached and disinterested entity, relinquished the records voluntarily. But that circumstance should not be crucial. For all practical purposes, the disclosure by individuals or business firms of their financial affairs to a bank is not entirely volitional, since it is impossible to participate in the economic life of contemporary society without maintaining a bank account. In the course of such dealings, a depositor reveals many aspects of his personal affairs, opinions, habits and associations. Indeed, the totality of bank records provides a virtual current biography. While we are concerned in the present case only with bank statements, the logical extension of the contention that the bank's ownership of records permits free access to them by any police officer extends far beyond such statements to checks, savings, bonds, loan applications, loan guarantees, and all papers which the customer has supplied to the bank to facilitate the conduct of his financial affairs upon the reasonable assumption that the information would remain confidential. To permit a police officer access to these records merely upon his request, without any judicial control as to relevancy or other traditional requirements of legal process, and to allow the evidence to be used in any subsequent criminal prosecution against a defendant, opens the door to a vast and unlimited range of very real abuses of police power.

Cases are legion that condemn violent searches and invasions of an individual's right to the privacy of his dwelling. The imposition upon privacy, although perhaps not so dramatic, may be equally devastating when other methods are employed. Development of photocopying machines, electronic computers and other sophisticated instruments have accelerated the ability of government to intrude into areas which a person normally chooses to exclude from prying eyes and inquisitive minds. Consequently judicial interpretations of the reach of the constitutional protection of individual privacy must keep pace with the perils created by these new devices. . . .

NOTES & QUESTIONS

1. **The Right to Financial Privacy Act.** Two years after *Miller*, in 1978, Congress passed the Right to Financial Privacy Act (RFPA), Pub. L. No. 95-630, which partially filled the void left by *Miller*. The RFPA prevents banks and other financial institutions from disclosing a person's financial information to the government unless the records are disclosed pursuant to subpoena or search warrant. *See* 29 U.S.C. §§ 3401–3422.

2. **State Law.** As discussed throughout this book, many states have rejected the Supreme Court's interpretations of the Fourth Amendment, opting to provide additional protections. In 2004, a New Jersey court rejected the reasoning of *Miller*:

> The discomfort in finding a stranger pouring over one's checkbook, deposit slips and cancelled checks is equal to seeing someone sifting through his or her garbage, or reviewing a list of dialed telephone numbers called from home, like telephones, are an extension of one's desk or home office. Indeed, as in the case of the telephone, technological advances in the form of personal computers with access to the internet and electronic banking services have made those services available to the homes of its depositors. Bank records kept at home could not be seized in the absence of a duly issued search warrant based upon probable cause and they should not be vulnerable to viewing, copying, seizure or retrieval simply because they are readily available at a bank.
>
> Finally, the fact that financial affairs are memorialized in written records of banks or maintained in their electronic data systems to which, as part of its legitimate business, a bank's employees have access, does not suggest that persons have any sense that their private and personal traits and affairs are less confidential when they deal with their bank than when they make telephone calls or put out their garbage. The repose of confidence in a bank goes beyond entrustment of money, but extends to the expectation that financial affairs are confidential except as may be reasonable and necessary to conduct customary bank business. *State v. McAllister*, 840 A.2d 967 (2004).

3. **Pen Registers and Smith v. Maryland.** Recall the Court's reasoning in *Smith v. Maryland* (Chapter 2), where the Court held that the Fourth Amendment was inapplicable to pen registers of phone numbers. How does the Court's rationale in *Smith* compare to that in *Miller*?

4. **The Implications of the Third Party Doctrine.** Daniel Solove contends that *Miller* and *Smith* pose a substantial threat to privacy in the modern world given the dramatic extent to which third parties hold personal information:

> In the Information Age, an increasing amount of personal information is contained in records maintained by private sector entities, Internet Service Providers, phone companies, cable companies, merchants, bookstores, websites, hotels, landlords and employers. Many private sector entities are beginning to aggregate the information in these records to create extensive digital dossiers.
>
> The data in these digital dossiers increasingly flows from the private sector to the government, particularly for law enforcement use. . . . Detailed records of an individual's reading materials, purchases, magazines, diseases and

ailments, and website activity, enable the government to assemble a profile of an individual's finances, health, psychology, beliefs, politics, interests, and lifestyle. This data can unveil a person's anonymous speech, groups and personal associations.

The increasing amount of personal information flowing to the government poses significant problems with far-reaching social effects. Inadequately constrained government information gathering can lead to at least three types of harms. First, it can result in the slow creep toward a totalitarian state. Second, it can chill democratic activities and interfere with individual self-determination. Third, it can lead to the danger of harms arising in bureaucratic settings. Individuals, especially in times of crisis, are vulnerable to abuse from government misuse of personal information. Once government entities have collected personal information, there are few regulations in how it can be used and how long it can be kept. The bureaucratic nature of modern law enforcement institutions can enable sweeping searches, the misuse of personal data, improper exercises of discretion, unjustified interrogation, arrests, roundups of disfavored individuals, and discriminatory profiling.[97]

Because of the third party doctrine in *Miller* and *Smith*, the Fourth Amendment fails to limit the government from gathering personal information maintained by businesses. *Miller* and *Smith* were decided in the 1970s. Should they be reconsidered in light of the extensive computerized records maintained today? What would be the consequences of overruling *Miller* and *Smith*?

(c) The USA PATRIOT Act § 215

Section 215 of the USA PATRIOT Act adds a new § 501 to the Foreign Intelligence Surveillance Act (FISA):

(a)(1) The Director of the Federal Bureau of Investigation or a designee of the Director (whose rank shall be no lower than Assistant Special Agent in Charge) may make an application for an order requiring the production of any tangible things (including books, records, papers, documents, and other items) for an investigation to protect against international terrorism or clandestine intelligence activities, provided that such investigation of a United States person is not conducted solely upon the basis of activities protected by the first amendment to the Constitution.

(2) An investigation conducted under this section shall —
(A) be conducted under guidelines approved by the Attorney General under Executive Order 12333 (or a successor order); and
(B) not be conducted of a United States person solely upon the basis of activities protected by the first amendment to the Constitution of the United States.

Applications for court orders shall be made to a judge and "shall specify that the records are sought for an authorized investigation" and "to protect against

---

[97] Daniel J. Solove, *Digital Dossiers and the Dissipation of Fourth Amendment Privacy*, 75 S. Cal. L. Rev. 1083, 1084-86 (2002).

international terrorism or clandestine intelligence activities." § 501(b). This section also has a gag order:

> (d) No person shall disclose to any other person (other than those persons necessary to produce the tangible things under this section) that the Federal Bureau of Investigation has sought or obtained tangible things under this section. § 501(d).

The American Library Association (ALA) led a spirited campaign against § 215. It issued a resolution stating, in part, that

> the American Library Association encourages all librarians, library administrators, library governing bodies, and library advocates to educate their users, staff, and communities about the process for compliance with the USA PATRIOT Act and other related measures and about the dangers to individual privacy and the confidentiality of library records resulting from those measures.

In 2003, Attorney General John Ashcroft stated that § 215 had never been used to access library records. He further stated: "The fact is, with just 11,000 FBI agents and over a billion visitors to America's libraries each year, the Department of Justice has neither the staffing, the time nor the inclination to monitor the reading habits of Americans. . . . No offense to the American Library Association, but we just don't care." In 2005, the ALA revealed the results of a survey of librarians indicating a minimum of 137 formal law enforcement inquiries to library officials since 9/11, 49 of which were by federal officials and the remainder by state and local officials. The study did not indicate whether any of these were pursuant to § 215.

(d) National Security Letters

Provisions in several laws permit the FBI to obtain personal information from third parties merely by making a written request in cases involving national security. No court order is required. These requests are called "National Security Letters" (NSLs).

The Stored Communications Act. ECPA's Stored Communications Act contains an NSL provision, 18 U.S.C. § 2709. This provision allows the FBI to compel communications companies (ISPs, telephone companies) to release customer records when the FBI makes a particular certification. Before the USA PATRIOT Act, the FBI had to certify that the records were "relevant to an authorized foreign counterintelligence investigation" and that "there are specific and articulable facts giving reason to believe that the person or entity to whom the information sought pertains is a foreign power or an agent of a foreign power as defined in section 101 of the Foreign Intelligence Surveillance Act of 1978 (50 U.S.C. 1801)."

Section 505 of the USA PATRIOT Act amended the National Security Letters provision of ECPA by altering what must be certified. The existing requirements regarding counterintelligence and specific and articulable facts that the target was an agent of a foreign power were deleted. The FBI now needs to certify that the records are "relevant to an authorized investigation to protect against terrorism or clandestine intelligence activities, provided that such an investigation of a United States person is not conducted solely on the basis of activities protected by the first amendment of the Constitution to the United States." 18 U.S.C. § 2709.

This provision also has a gag order:

No wire or electronic communication service provider, or officer, employee, or agent thereof, shall disclose to any person that the Federal Bureau of Investigation has sought or obtained access to information or records under this section. § 2709(c).

Unlike § 215, Ashcroft made no statement about § 505.[98]

The Right to Financial Privacy Act. The Right to Financial Privacy Act (RFPA) also contains an NSL provision. As amended by the Patriot Act, this provision states that the FBI can obtain an individual's financial records if it "certifies in writing to the financial institution that such records are sought for foreign counter intelligence purposes to protect against international terrorism or clandestine intelligence activities, provided that such an investigation of a United States person is not conducted solely upon the basis of activities protected by the first amendment to the Constitution of the United States." 12 U.S.C. § 3414(a)(5)(A). As with the Stored Communications Act NSL provision, the RFPA NSL provision contains a "gag" rule prohibiting the financial institution from disclosing the fact it received the NSL. § 3414(a)(5)(D).

The Fair Credit Reporting Act. Likewise, the Fair Credit Reporting Act provides for NSLs. Pursuant to a written FBI request, consumer reporting agencies "shall furnish to the Federal Bureau of Investigation the names and addresses of all financial institutions . . . at which a customer maintains or has maintained an account." 15 U.S.C. § 1681u(a). Consumer reporting agencies must also furnish "identifying information respecting a consumer, limited to name, address, former addresses, places of employment, or former places of employment." 15 U.S.C. § 1681u(b). To obtain a full consumer report, however, the FBI must obtain a court order ex parte. 15 U.S.C. § 1681u(c). Like the other NSL provisions, the FCRA NSL provisions restrict NSLs for investigations based "solely" upon First Amendment activities. The FCRA NSL also has a "gag" rule. 15 U.S.C. § 1681u(d).

The USA PATRIOT Reauthorization Act. In the USA PATRIOT Reauthorization Act of 2005, Congress made several amendments that affected NSLs. It explicitly provided for judicial review of NSLs. It also required a detailed examination by the DOJ's Inspector General "of the effectiveness and use, including any improper or illegal use" of NSLs. This kind of audit proved its value in March 2006 when the Inspector General issued its review of the FBI's use of NSLs. First, the Inspector General found a dramatic underreporting of NSLs. Indeed, the total number of NSL requests between 2003 and 2005 totaled

---

[98] Mark Sidel, *More Secure, Less Free?: Antiterrorism Policy and Civil Liberties After September 11*, at 14 (2004).

at least 143,074. Of these NSLs requests, as the Inspector General found, "[t]he overwhelming majority . . . sought telephone toll billing records information, subscriber information (telephone or e-mail) or electronic communication transaction records under the ECPA NSL statute." [99]

The Inspector General also carried out a limited audit of investigative case files, and found that 22 percent of them contained at least one violation of investigative guidelines or procedures that was not reported to any of the relevant internal authorities at the FBI. Finally, the Inspector General also found over 700 instances in which the FBI obtained telephone records and subscriber information from telephone companies based on the use of a so-called "exigent letter" authority. This authority, absent from the statute, was invented by the FBI's Counterterrorism Division. Having devised this new power, the FBI did not set limits on its use, or track how it was employed. Witnesses told the Inspector General that many of these letters "were not issued in exigent circumstances, and the FBI was unable to determine which letters were sent in emergency circumstances due to inadequate recordkeeping." Indeed, "in most instances, there was no documentation associating the requests with pending national security investigations."[100]

NSL Litigation. In *Doe v. Ashcroft*, 334 F. Supp. 2d 471 (S.D.N.Y. 2004), a federal district court invalidated 18 U.S.C. § 2709 (*Doe I*). It found that § 2709 violated the Fourth Amendment because, at least as applied, it barred or at least substantially deterred a judicial challenge to an NSL request. It did so by prohibiting an NSL recipient from revealing the existence of an NSL inquiry. The court also found that the "all inclusive sweep" of § 2709 violated the First Amendment as a prior-restraint and content-based restriction on sweep that was subject to strict scrutiny review. Additionally, the court found that in some instances the use of an NSL might infringe upon people's First Amendment rights. For example, suppose that the FBI uses an NSL to find out the identity of an anonymous speaker on the Internet. Does the First Amendment limit using an NSL in this manner? Does the First Amendment restriction on the NSL provisions, which prohibits NSLs for investigations based "solely" upon First Amendment activities, adequately address these potential First Amendment problems?

Shortly after *Doe I,* another district court invalidated 18 U.S.C. § 2709(c), which prevented a recipient of an NSL to disclose information about the government's action. *Doe v. Gonzales*, 386 F. Supp. 2d 66, 82 (D. Conn. 2005) (*Doe II*).

While appeals in *Doe I* and *Doe II* were pending, Congress enacted the USA PATRIOT Reauthorization Act of 2005, which made several changes to § 2709 and added several provisions concerning judicial review of NSLs, which were codified at 18 U.S.C. § 3511. Following enactment of these provisions, plaintiffs challenged the amended nondisclosure provisions of §§ 2709(c) and 3511. The same district court that issued the *Doe I* opinion then found §§ 2709(c) and

---

[99] Office of the Inspector General, *A Review of the Federal Bureau of Investigations Use of National Security Letters* x-xiv (Mar. 2007).

[100] *Id.* at xxxviii, xxxiv.

3511(b) to be facially unconstitutional. *Doe v. Gonzales*, 500 F. Supp. 2d 379 (S.D.N.Y. 2007) (*Doe III*).

The newly enacted § 3511 provided for judicial review of NSLs. As a result, the *Doe III* plaintiffs did not challenge it on Fourth Amendment grounds as in *Doe I*. Instead, they argued, and the court agreed, that the nondisclosure provisions of § 2709(c) remained an unconstitutional prior restraint and content-based restriction on speech. The court also concluded that § 3511(b) was unconstitutional under the First Amendment and the doctrine of separation of powers. Among its conclusions, the court noted that Congress in amending § 2709(c) allowed the FBI to certify on a case-by-case basis whether nondisclosure was necessary. Yet, this narrowing of the statute to reduce the possibility of unnecessary limitation of speech also means that the FBI could conceivably engage in viewpoint discrimination. As a consequence, the amended statute was a content-based restriction as well as a prior restraint on speech and, therefore, subject to strict scrutiny.

2. INFORMATION GATHERING WITH SEARCH WARRANTS

Under the Fourth Amendment, a search warrant may be issued if there is probable cause to believe that there is incriminating evidence in the place to be searched. This is not limited to places owned or occupied by the criminal suspect. In certain instances, incriminating documents or things may be possessed by an innocent party. What if that innocent party is a journalist or news entity, and the search implicates First Amendment rights? Consider the following case:

ZURCHER V. THE STANFORD DAILY
436 U.S. 547 (1978)

[A demonstration at the Stanford University Hospital turned violent when police tried to force demonstrators to leave. A group of demonstrators attacked and injured nine police officers. The officers were able to identify only two of the assailants. The *Stanford Daily*, a student newspaper, published articles and photographs about the incident. The District Attorney obtained a search warrant to search the *Daily*'s offices for negatives, film, and pictures about the incident. After the search, the *Daily* brought suit under 42 U.S.C. § 1983, alleging that the search was unconstitutional.]

WHITE, J. . . . The issue here is how the Fourth Amendment is to be construed and applied to the "third party" search, the recurring situation where state authorities have probable cause to believe that fruits, instrumentalities, or other evidence of crime is located on identified property but do not then have probable cause to believe that the owner or possessor of the property is himself implicated in the crime that has occurred or is occurring. . . .

Under existing law, valid warrants may be issued to search *any* property, whether or not occupied by a third party, at which there is probable cause to believe that fruits, instrumentalities, or evidence of a crime will be found.

Nothing on the face of the Amendment suggests that a third-party search warrant should not normally issue. . . .

As the Fourth Amendment has been construed and applied by this Court, "when the State's reason to believe incriminating evidence will be found becomes sufficiently great, the invasion of privacy becomes justified and a warrant to search and seize will issue." . . .

As we understand the structure and language of the Fourth Amendment and our cases expounding it, valid warrants to search property may be issued when it is satisfactorily demonstrated to the magistrate that fruits, instrumentalities, or evidence of crime is located on the premises. The Fourth Amendment has itself struck the balance between privacy and public need, and there is no occasion or justification for a court to revise the Amendment and strike a new balance by denying the search warrant in the circumstances present here and by insisting that the investigation proceed by subpoena *duces tecum*, whether on the theory that the latter is a less intrusive alternative or otherwise. . . .

[The *Daily* argues] that searches of newspaper offices for evidence of crime reasonably believed to be on the premises will seriously threaten the ability of the press to gather, analyze, and disseminate news. This is said to be true for several reasons: First, searches will be physically disruptive to such an extent that timely publication will be impeded. Second, confidential sources of information will dry up, and the press will also lose opportunities to cover various events because of fears of the participants that press files will be readily available to the authorities. Third, reporters will be deterred from recording and preserving their recollections for future use if such information is subject to seizure. Fourth, the processing of news and its dissemination will be chilled by the prospects that searches will disclose internal editorial deliberations. Fifth, the press will resort to self-censorship to conceal its possession of information of potential interest to the police.

It is true that the struggle from which the Fourth Amendment emerged "is largely a history of conflict between the Crown and the press," and that in issuing warrants and determining the reasonableness of a search, state and federal magistrates should be aware that "unrestricted power of search and seizure could also be an instrument for stifling liberty of expression." Where the materials sought to be seized may be protected by the First Amendment, the requirements of the Fourth Amendment must be applied with "scrupulous exactitude." . . . Where presumptively protected materials are sought to be seized, the warrant requirement should be administered to leave as little as possible to the discretion or whim of the officer in the field. . . .

Aware of the long struggle between Crown and press and desiring to curb unjustified official intrusions, the Framers took the enormously important step of subjecting searches to the test of reasonableness and to the general rule requiring search warrants issued by neutral magistrates. They nevertheless did not forbid warrants where the press was involved, did not require special showings that subpoenas would be impractical, and did not insist that the owner of the place to be searched, if connected with the press, must be shown to be implicated in the offense being investigated. Further, the prior cases do no more than insist that the courts apply the warrant requirements with particular exactitude when First Amendment interests would be endangered by the search. As we see it, no more

Preface

What this book is about

The study of the animal mind is one of the most exciting areas in the cognitive sciences. The feats of navigation performed by bees and pigeons, tales of talking parrots and counting rats, self-aware chimpanzees and tool-using crows not only fascinate the nonspecialist, they raise important issues in psychology and biology. How do bees or pigeons find their way home? Can other animals navigate as well as they do, and if not, why not? Do parrots really talk? What use would counting be to rats in the wild anyway? Do monkeys and apes, which look so much like us, think like us too? What is the relationship between the human mind and the minds of other species?

Questions like these raise issues that are intrinsically interdisciplinary. Because of this they have traditionally been covered inadequately in most textbooks, although they are often the subject of popular and semipopular treatments. Introductions to animal cognition for psychology students have usually reviewed laboratory studies of rats, pigeons, and monkeys from an anthropocentric point of view. Evolutionary issues or observations of behavior outside the laboratory have typically been over-simplified or not discussed at all. On the other hand, introductions to animal behavior or behavioral ecology include at most a brief survey of research on animal learning and cognition, even though the authors may point out that the sorts of cognitive processes generally studied by psychologists play a role in ecologically relevant behavior. A zoologist wishing to know more soon feels mired in the psychologist's specialist terminology. Equally specialized terms await the psychology student wanting to know more about evolution and behavioral ecology. Phylogeny, MVT, and ESS are just as baffling to the uninitiated as US, RI, and fixed interval schedule.

I wrote the first edition of this book in the belief that the future of research on comparative cognition, behavioral ecology, and behavioral neuroscience lies in increased interdisciplinary training and communication. I tried to capture a vision of an approach to the evolution of the mind in which it is natural, indeed necessary, to integrate the answers to questions traditionally asked in psychology laboratories with the answers to questions about ecology and evolution. I tried to make it accessible to students and researchers from both psychology and biology, or with backgrounds in neither. It was for the increasing numbers of people trained in the cognitive sciences who are finding that their discipline must embrace consideration of species other than humans and that the study of cognition in any species is incomplete without consideration of evolution and ecology.

Equally, it was for behavioral ecologists and ethologists who find themselves wanting to answer essentially psychological questions about behavior.

Why a second edition?

The decade since the first edition of *Cognition, Evolution, and Behavior* was written has seen an explosion of new developments in almost every area it covers. Many of them are around the boundary that traditionally divided comparative psychology from the biological study of behavior, the very boundary that *Cognition, Evolution, and Behavior* focused on bridging. There is now every sign that a truly integrative cross-disciplinary research program on comparative cognition has finally taken off. As a happy result, many parts of the first edition are outdated. This second edition integrates new developments and insights with earlier material. To mention a few examples, associative learning has seen new challenges to what has been the domi-nant theory in the area for almost a half century. New studies of whether animals are aware of their memories or have "episodic like" memory—questions hardly touched by serious researchers before 1998—raise fundamental issues about the promises and limits of what we can learn from comparing verbal and nonverbal species. Comparative studies of numerical cognition, spatial cognition, and animal commu-nication have taken important new directions and seen more theoretical integration with work on child development and with neuroscience. The study of social learning and animal culture has exploded. Analyses of social cognition in field and laboratory, including the contentious topic of whether other species have theory of mind, have been extended to species as diverse as dogs, hyenas, goats, ravens, and fish. Spirited debates about whether any animals can be said to teach their conspecifics or to have culture have been fueled by prominent new discoveries, not only with primates but with other species. Likewise, studies of tool using—both fieldwork documenting its occurrence and analyses of what tool-users know—now include birds as well as a range of primates. As with studies of social cognition, the possibility of convergence in evolutionarily diverse species promises important insights into the conditions for evolution of human-like behavior and understanding. We are seeing the development of a much more detailed, nuanced, and biologically informed view of how and why species are both the same and different cognitively, including of course what humans share with other species and how we may be unique.

How this book is organized

Like the first edition of *Cognition, Evolution, and Behavior,* this one aims to be a comprehensive cross-disciplinary account of contemporary research on animal cog-nition in the broadest sense, from perception to the bases of culture, and to be accessible to students and specialists alike. The general approach and organization are the same as for the first, but with 15 rather than 13 chapters. The old Chapter 1 is divided into two to permit explicit discussion of classic foundational issues such as the role of Morgan's Canon that are so clearly still at stake today. New discussions of the relationship between brain evolution and cognition justify a separate Chapter 2 for background on evolution and on the brain that was originally part of Chapter 1. As before, the order of subsequent substantive chapters implies a "bottom-up" approach to cognition, starting with perception and simple forms of learning along with some basic concepts from ethology and building up to so-called higher or more complex processes. The central chapters (Chapters 3–14) are now divided into three sections, each with a short introductory overview: "Fundamental Mechanisms" (perception, learning, categorization, memory), "Physical Cognition" (space, time, number, physical causation), and "Social Cognition" (social knowledge, social learning, communication).

One major change is the placement of timing and counting in separate chapters, recognizing how new research and theorizing have transformed the study of numerical cognition into a key area of comparative research in its own right. At the same time, material on subjects where there have been few new developments has been condensed. For example, optimal foraging is now part of a comprehensive treatment of instrumental behavior that also includes economic decision-making, tool use, and planning. In another reorganization, the three chapters on aspects of social cognition now begin with a chapter on the nature of social knowledge. This draws on the depth and breadth of new information about social understanding in wild animals from baboons to birds to provide a background for burgeoning laboratory research on social cognition and cooperation.

As in the first edition, the final chapter (here Chapter 15) reflects on what the preceding chapters teach us about some overarching issues. Here these include what comparative studies reveal about "the modularity of mind" and whether comparative cognition research can be said to have any single well-defined set of methods or theoretical approach. This chapter also looks at new contributions to what has arguably been the central discussion in comparative studies of the mind since their beginnings in the late 19th century: how are humans different from other species, and why? In the concluding chapter of *The Origin of Species* Darwin (1859) prophesied, "In the future I see open fields for far more important researches. Psychology will be securely based on the foundation . . . of the necessary acquirement of each mental power and capacity by gradation. Much light will be thrown on the origin of man and his history." He would no doubt be pleased to see that, along with all the other amazing fields opened up by his insights, this one is yielding such a rich harvest.

Acknowledgments

In addition to all those individuals and institutions already thanked for their contributions to the first edition and to whom I am unendingly grateful, many others deserve thanks for help with this one. Members of the extended international community of researchers too numerous to name generously shared unpublished material, often along with much-appreciated encouragement for this project. Ken Cheng and the other members of the Center for the Integrative Study of Animal Behaviour at Macquarie University provided a stimulating Visiting Fellowship and opportunity to discuss some early chapters. John Ratcliffe, Jeff Katz and his students, and Bill Timberlake commented on various preliminary drafts. Derek Penn, Nick Mackintosh, Judy Stamps, and Tom Zentall reviewed the entire text for Oxford, in some cases in great detail. Their comments and suggestions were incredibly helpful, even if I did not take all the advice they offered.

For practical matters, I thank Alissa Bello for help with the references, and especially Caroline Strang for so cheerfully and efficiently doing so many editorial tasks, among them obtaining all the permissions to reproduce previously published material. I am grateful to NSERC for continued support, the University of Toronto library system for instant access to everything a modern scholar could wish for, and the folks at End Note for kindly updating the formatting of the first edition. Most of all, thanks to Catharine Carlin at Oxford for her unfailing support and enthusiasm and to Dr. Margaret C. Nelson, a true collaborator without whose splendid illustrations neither the first edition nor this one would be nearly so attractive or useful. Once again, the book is dedicated to past and future students of animal cognition, especially all the students and postdocs in my lab from whom I have learned so much over the years.

Sara Shettleworth
Toronto, Ontario, Canada

Contents

Cognition, Evolution, and Behavior

1
Cognition and the Study of Behavior

Walnut trees shade the streets of Davis, California. They also provide food for the crows that roost near Davis. Crows crack walnuts by dropping them from heights of 5–10 meters or more onto sidewalks, roads, and parking lots. Occasionally they drop walnuts in front of approaching cars, as if using the cars to crush the nuts for them. Do crows intentionally use cars as nutcrackers? Some of the citizens of Davis, as well as some professional biologists (Maple 1974, in Cristol et al. 1997) were convinced that they do, at least until a team of young biologists at UC Davis put this anecdote to the test (Cristol et al. 1997). They reasoned that if crows were using cars as tools, the birds would be more likely to drop nuts onto the road when cars were coming than when the road was empty. Furthermore, if a crow was standing in the road with an uncracked walnut as a car approached, it should leave the nut in the road to be crushed rather than carry it away.

Cristol and his collaborators watched crows feeding on walnuts and recorded how likely the birds were to leave an uncracked walnut in the road when cars were approaching and when the road was empty. They found no support for the notion that crows were using automobiles as nutcrackers (Figure 1.1). In other respects, however, the birds' behavior with walnuts was quite sophisticated (Cristol and Switzer 1999). For example, by dropping nuts from buildings on the Davis campus, Cristol and Switzer verified that English walnuts did not have to be carried so high before breaking as the harder black walnuts and that they broke more easily when dropped onto pavement than onto soil. The crows' behavior reflected these facts (Figure 1.1). A crow dropping a nut also took into account the likelihood that a greedy fellow crow might steal a dropped nut before it could be retrieved: the fewer crows waiting on the ground nearby, the higher they took walnuts before dropping them.

The story of the nutcracking crows encapsulates some key issues in the study of cognition in animals. Foremost is how to translate a hypothesis about essentially unobservable internal processes into hypotheses about behavior in a way that permits different explanations to be distinguished. Here, this meant asking, "What will crows do if they are using cars as tools that they will not do if they are merely dropping nuts onto the road as a car happens by?" A second issue has to do with the kinds of hypotheses people entertain about the processes underlying animal behavior. The people in Davis and elsewhere (Nihei 1995; Caffrey 2001) who saw nutcracking as an expression of clever crows' ability to reason and plan were engaging in an

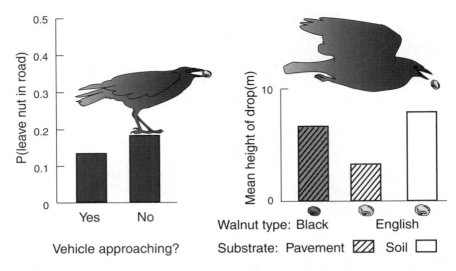

Figure 1.1. Left: Proportion of crows dropping a walnut in the road when flying away as a function of whether or not a vehicle was approaching (data from Cristol et al. 1997). Right: Mean height to which crows carried black or English walnuts before dropping them onto pavement (cross-hatched bars) or onto soil (English walnuts only) (data from Cristol and Switzer 1999).

anthropomorphism that is common even among professional students of animal behavior (see below, Section 1.3.2; Kennedy 1992; Wynne 2007a, 2007b). As we will see, such thinking can be a fertile source of ideas, but research often reveals that simple processes apparently quite unlike explicit reasoning are doing surprisingly complex jobs. Free-living crows were observed doing something suggestive of interesting information processing and decision making. Their behavior was then examined with more systematic observations and experiments. Among other things, these revealed how closely the crows' behavior matched environmental requirements. Numerous cognitive processes underlie the crows' nutcracking, and each of these could be analyzed further. For example, how do crows judge the height from which they drop nuts? Do they have to learn to adjust their behavior to the kind of nut, the kind of substrate, and the number of nearby crows? Several species of crows, gulls, and other birds break hard-shelled prey by dropping them (Cristol and Switzer 1999), and one might also ask what ecological conditions or evolutionary history favor this behavior.

1.1   What is comparative cognition about?

1.1.1   What is cognition?

Cognition refers to the mechanisms by which animals acquire, process, store, and act on information from the environment. These include perception, learning, memory, and decision-making. The study of comparative cognition is therefore concerned with how animals process information, starting with how information is acquired by the senses. The behavior examined for evidence of cognition need not be learned, and it need not be studied in the laboratory by psychologists. In this book how birds classify songs in the field will be considered alongside how animals can be taught to classify artificial stimuli in the laboratory (Chapter 6). Possible natural examples of tool use like the crows' nutcracking will be examined along with tests of what captive animals understand when they use tools (Chapter 11). The dance communication of bees and the alarm calling of chickens will be considered alongside the use of human gestures, words, and symbols by parrots and chimpanzees (Chapter 14). How ants find their way in the desert and how rats find their way in mazes will both be examined for what they reveal about the principles of spatial cognition (Chapter 8).

Not all agree that such an inclusive definition of cognition is useful. *Cognitive* is often reserved for the manipulation of declarative rather than procedural knowledge (e.g., Dickinson 2008). Declarative knowledge is "knowing that" whereas procedural knowledge is "knowing how," or knowing what to do. The declarative knowledge that a chipmunk might gain from moving about its territory could be maplike: "Home burrow is south of that big rock." Or the chipmunk might store information about its territory as procedural knowledge such as "Turn left at the rock." The first kind of representation implies more flexible behavior than the second, but in both cases behavior results from processing and storing information about the world. A related distinction is that between first-order and higher-order processes, only the latter of which may be regarded as interestingly cognitive. First-order processes operate directly on perceptual input, as when a stimulus triggers a response or creates a trace in memory. Second-order processes operate on first-order processes, as in evaluating the strength of one's memory for an event (Heyes 2008; Penn, Holyoak, and Povinelli 2008).

For many psychologists, mental representations of the world or computations on them are the essence of cognition. However, it is almost never possible to tell without experimental analysis what kinds of processes are reflected in a given behavior. Moreover, functionally similar behavior, such as communicating, recognizing neighbors, or way finding, may be accomplished in different ways by different kinds of animals (Dyer 1994). Much interesting adaptive behavior results from processing limited information in simple ways, and the richness of the representations underlying behavior varies considerably across species and behavior systems. Because comparing the ways in which different species solve similar information-processing problems is an important part of the comparative study of cognition, it should embrace all sorts of information processing and decision-making.

1.1.2   *Animal* cognition or *comparative* cognition?

Referring to the field of research discussed in this book as *comparative* rather than *animal* cognition is similarly inclusive. Some classic assessments of psychological research on animals (Beach 1950; Hodos and Campbell 1969; Dewsbury 1998) are complaints that most studies labeled "comparative" are mere "animal psychology" because they deal with only a single nonhuman species or at most implicitly compare that one species with humans. As we will see, the situation in the early twenty-first century is dramatically different. More species are being studied and compared with one another, and findings are interpreted with increasing biological sophistication. But there is still a good deal of research aimed at analyzing particular processes in depth in one or a few species. It is especially prominent in the section of this book on Basic Processes (Chapters 3–7). But thorough analyses of cognitive processes in limited species form the foundation for comparative work, as when comparisons of memory in food storing and nonstoring birds (Chapters 2 and 7) draw on method and theory developed in studies with pigeons. Therefore "animal cognition" research is part of the overarching enterprise referred to in this book as research on comparative cognition aimed at understanding cognition across the animal kingdom, including how it works, what it is good for in nature, and how it evolved.

1.1.3   Consciousness and animal cognition

People intuitively distinguish between merely responding to events and being aware of them, as when someone driving along a busy highway while deep in conversation says, "I wasn't conscious of the passing miles." Perceptual awareness can be distinguished from reflective consciousness, which might be evidenced when the driver mentally compares possible routes to her destination, perhaps evaluating her own ability to recall their details (self-reflective consciousness).

Within psychology, the rise of behaviorism in the early 1900s threw introspective studies of consciousness into disrepute. The cognitive revolution of the 1960s and 1970s continued this tradition. Studying cognition meant inferring how information is processed from analyzing input-output relations without regard for the extent or kind of concomitant awareness. But in the last decade or so of the twentieth century, the study of consciousness in humans and other species became not only scientifically respectable but an active area of research. One impetus for this work was the discovery of striking phenomena such as "blindsight" (Box 1.1) and priming in memory (Chapter 7), which reveal distinct conscious and unconscious processes in

---

Box 1.1 Vision with and without Awareness

Neurological patients with "blindsight" react to objects in the visual field without reporting awareness of them (Weiskrantz 1986). If such patients, who have damage in area V1 of the visual cortex, are shown an object in the affected part of the visual field, they report seeing nothing. However, when they are forced to point to the object's location or guess its characteristics, they perform above chance. Thus these people seem to have vision without awareness. Visual detection apparently can be dissociated from visual awareness in monkeys, too (Cowey and Stoerig 1995, 1997). Three monkeys with lesions to area V1 were trained in two different tasks (Figure B1.1). One was analogous to asking them "Do you see it?" and the other, to asking them "Where is it?" The lesions affected only the right half of each monkey's visual field, so each monkey's performance to stimuli there could be compared to its performance when stimuli were shown in the field with normal vision. To control the part of the retina stimulated, displays were presented briefly while the monkey was fixating a spot in the middle of a computer screen.

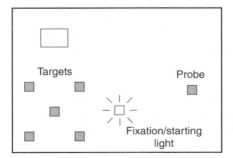 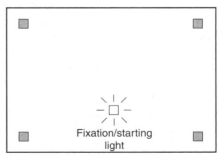

Figure B1.1. Stimulus displays for testing blindsight in monkeys. Redrawn from Cowey and Stoerig (1995) with permission.

To train the monkeys to report "I see it," a stimulus was presented any of five positions in the lower part of the normal field, and on some trials no stimulus was presented (Figure B1.1, left). In the former case, the monkey was rewarded for touching the location where the stimulus had appeared. In the latter, it was rewarded for reporting "no" by touching a white rectangle at the top of the screen. When the monkeys were reporting presence/absence correctly on about 95% of the trials, they were tested with occasional probes in the "blind" half of the visual field. They reported "no stimulus" about 95% of the time. Importantly, a normal control monkey did transfer correct responding to this novel location. In the other task, a brief flash appeared in one of the four corners of the screen on every trial (Figure B1.1, right). The monkeys had simply to touch the location where it had appeared, in effect reporting where they saw it. In this task, performance was highly accurate for both the normal and the "blind" visual field. These data are consistent with other evidence that primates have separate visual pathways for perception and action (Goodale and Milner 1992). Like people with comparable brain damage, the monkeys appear to have vision without awareness in the affected part of the visual field, suggesting that their normal vision is accompanied by awareness.

In this example, nonverbal responses that the monkeys were trained to make substituted directly for humans' verbal reports ("I see it," etc.). When people with blindsight took the same nonverbal tests as the monkeys, their responses paralleled their verbal reports of awareness (Stoerig, Zontanou and Cowey 2002).

everyday cognition. Debates about the extent to which people are aware of their own cognition (metacognition; Chapter 7) have also placed a new emphasis on how subjects consciously experience their memories, percepts, or the like as distinct from how they act on them. Progress in analyzing the neural basis of behavior in such experiments through brain imaging and studies of cognitively impaired people have encouraged attempts to investigate the same processes in animals (e.g., Terrace & Metcalfe 2005). If some pattern of brain activity turns out to be necessary and sufficient for verbal reports of conscious awareness, thinking, remembering, or the like, what does it mean if this same pattern can be identified in an animal?

A central methodological problem here is that because evidence for consciousness in humans generally consists of what people say about their mental experiences, seeking it in nonverbal species requires us to accept some piece of the animal's behavior as equivalent to a person's verbal report. For example, in the experiment described in Box 1.1, we must accept that the monkeys' "I see it" response indexes a subjective state equivalent to a person's experience of seeing. Clearly we can never know whether this is correct or not, since we can never know the animal's private state. Therefore, the point of view of most researchers studying animal cognition is that how animals process information can, and should, be analyzed without making any assumptions about what their private experiences are like. That is, the best we can do is to seek *functional similarities* between behaviors taken as evidence for given processes in humans and behaviors of animals (Staddon 2000; Hampton 2005; Heyes 2008). This approach takes support from evidence that people act without being aware of the reasons for their actions, that is, without using reflective consciousness, more often than is commonly realized. We may, for example reach for the reddest tomato on the bush and only later explain why (Carruthers 2005). A related view (Macphail 1998) is that human babies nor nonhuman animals can have reflective consciousness because it requires language.

The view that consciousness in animals is not a subject for research either because it is inaccessible to scientific study or because animals lack language was emphatically rejected by scientists calling themselves cognitive ethologists (Ristau 1991a). Stimulated by the writings of the distinguished biologist Donald Griffin (1976, 2001), cognitive ethologists claim that much behavior suggests that animals have conscious intentions, beliefs, and self-awareness, and that they consciously think about alternative courses of action and make plans (Griffin and Speck 2004). Studies of animals communicating, using tools, and apparently deceiving one another figure prominently in these discussions because they seem to reveal flexible behaviors governed by intentions to achieve specific goals. However, it is difficult to find a situation for which the notion that an animal has a conscious belief or intention or is consciously manipulating information unambiguously predicts what it does (Dawkins 1993; but see Griffin 2001). Nevertheless, the early years of the twenty-first century have seen an upsurge of provocative and sometimes controversial research addressed to exactly these issues.

Of course, some anthropomorphic mentalistic terms have traditionally been accepted to refer to processes underlying animal behavior. For example, training a rat that a tone predicts a shock is usually referred to as fear conditioning. The rat is said to fear the tone, and indeed it may be in the same physiological state as a person describing himself as fearful. Similarly, a hungry rat trained to press a lever for food could be said to be doing so because it desires food and believes that lever pressing will give it food. On one view (Chapter 11 and Dickinson 2008) the goal-directedness of bar pressing or other instrumental responding, that is, evidence that it is controlled by belief and desire, is what is meant by its being under cognitive control. Belief, desire, fear, or other mental or emotional states may be ascribed to animals on the basis of well-defined behavioral criteria, that is, on the basis of functional similarity, without implying that the animals are undergoing humanlike conscious experiences.

Thinking about how consciousness might have evolved is not much help here. On the one hand, if we accept that human beings are conscious it seems that some other species, perhaps among primates, must share at least perceptual awareness with humans (see Terrace and Metcalfe 2005). Saying that only humans are conscious in any way seems like rejecting evolutionary continuity (but see Penn, Holyoak, and Povinelli 2008). On the other hand, because evolution has acted via the results of what creatures do, not directly on what they experience privately while doing it, it seems there must be something promoting survival and reproduction that a conscious animal can do and one lacking consciousness cannot, but so far there are no clear candidates for that "something" (Dawkins 1993, 2006). This same problem of an apparent evolutionary gap between humans and other living species arises in discussions of the evolution of human language and abstract conceptual abilities (Chapter 15 and Penn, Holyoak, and Povinelli 2008). Despite the apparent successes of teaching aspects of language to apes, most would now conclude that language is unique to humans, and the conditions under which it could evolve are an active area of debate (Chapter 14). Anthropological studies of human evolution and of primate behavior in the wild are likely to add fuel to these discussions for some time to come.

1.1.4   A word about *intelligence*

It is sometimes said by cognitive ethologists (Griffin 1992) and popular writers (e.g., Barber 1994) that animals must be thinking because they behave so intelligently. Indeed, to the nonspecialist one of the most persuasive arguments that animals think as we do is that it is impossible to imagine another explanation for their "clever" behavior (Blumberg and Wasserman 1995; Wynne 2004a). On the whole, however, *intelligence* is not a useful term for describing animal behavior, for two reasons. First, intelligence is generally used to describe global ability in people, whereas the cognitive abilities of animals (and perhaps people as well) are to a large extent modular (Box 2.3). For instance, a Clark's nutcracker that can retrieve thousands of pine seeds months after caching them (Box 1.4) is not necessarily "smart" in other ways. It is particularly good at encoding and retaining certain kinds of spatial information, but it may remember other kinds of information no better than other birds. Within this context, *intelligence* is sometimes used nowadays to refer to the collection of specific cognitive abilities that a species may have (cf., Emery 2006; Pearce 2008).

A second reason to use *intelligence* carefully is that it should be defined formally with respect to a specified goal (McFarland and Bosser 1993). A robot is intelligent with respect to a goal of efficiency if it minimizes use of its battery while when crossing a room. It is intelligent with respect to the goal of remaining intact if it avoids collisions. On this view, biological intelligence should be defined in terms of fitness (Box 1.2 and Kacelnik 2006) or goals such as choosing a good mate that contribute to fitness, and even plants can be intelligent (Trewavas 2002). Sometimes, as we will often see in this book, intelligent behavior may be produced by very "unintelligent" means.

Box 1.2 Natural Selection and Fitness

Evolution, the change in the characteristics of organisms over generations, occasioned much debate before Charles Darwin (1859) and Alfred Russel Wallace explained how it happens. Fossils indicated that very different kinds of animals and plants had existed in the past. Explorers, including Darwin and Wallace themselves, documented how animals and plants in different parts of the world are both similar and different. What Darwin and Wallace did, independently at about the same time, was to show how both the changes in organisms over time and the relationships among them can be explained by a natural cause. That cause is *natural selection,* and it is the inevitable outcome of three fundamental properties of all living things.

1. Offspring inherit their parents' characteristics. Bean seeds produce more bean plants, robin eggs produce more robins, and many of their features will be more like those of their parents than others of the same species. We now know a great deal about the genetic mechanisms involved, but the principle of *inheritance* is independent of such knowledge, which Darwin and Wallace did not have.
2. There is *variation* among individuals within the same species, even when they are closely related.
3. *Selection* takes place. A sea turtle lays hundreds of eggs, an oak tree drops hundreds of acorns, yet the world is not overrun with sea turtles or oak trees. Only those best able to survive in the current environment will live to reproduce. This principle is sometimes summarized as "the survival of the fittest." In technical terms, *fitness* refers to an organism's ability to leave copies of its genes in the next generation, not to what people get at the gym. A male who sires ten healthy offspring is fitter than one who sires two. Because relatives share some of one's own genes, fitness can be enhanced through helping them as well as direct offspring (Chapter 5).

Evolution is the inevitable consequence of inheritance, variation, and selection. Gradually, over many generations, individuals with characteristics that made their ancestors best able to survive and reproduce will come to predominate. Individuals that migrate or are carried into new environments may evolve such different characteristics that eventually their descendents will form a new species, unable to breed with individuals of the ancestral species (see Grant and Grant 2008). Throughout the last part of the twentieth century evolutionary theorists, including most of the founders of behavioral ecology, emphasized selection at the level of the individual, indeed the individual's genes. On this view, the genes best able to program the organisms bearing them to develop into individuals that propagate successfully will be the ones that persist over generations (R. Dawkins 1976, 1995).

However, the logic of inheritance, variation, and selection applies to units at all levels, most importantly for contemporary theorizing, even to groups of individuals. After being emphatically rejected for nearly 40 years, evolution through selection at the level of groups is now becoming accepted as part of a broad theory of multilevel selection (Wilson and Wilson 2007, 2008). Group and individual selection may pull in different ways, but the characters that benefit the group at the apparent expense of the individual may still be advantageous over the long run. Among other things, the force of group selection helps to explain some of the unique features of human psychology such as a tendency to cooperate and empathize with unrelated others (Chapter 12 and Wilson and Wilson 2007, 2008).

Finally, labeling behavior *intelligent* is pretty frankly both anthropomorphic and anthropocentric. Recent demonstrations that species differ in behavioral flexibility, or propensity to adopt novel foraging behaviors (Box 2.2), have revived discussions of overall animal intelligence (cf., Roth & Dicke 2005). This is especially so because the correlation of flexibility with overall brain size and/or size of the forebrain in some animal groups (Box 2.2) satisfies the everyday equation of intelligence with "braininess." The naively anthropocentric nature of such discussions is underlined by a comparison of pigeons and people in a test of complex reaction time (Vickrey and Neuringer 2000). In such a test the subject is confronted with an array of lights; a randomly chosen one, the target, lights up on each trial and the subject's task is to touch it as quickly as possible. Human subjects take longer to respond as the number of lights in the array increases, but people with high IQ show the smallest increase. It is claimed this is because high IQ reflects a general ability to process information fast. On this analysis, " less intelligent" species should be affected more strongly by increasing numbers of targets than humans. In fact, however, pigeons show a smaller effect than very intelligent humans (students at the highly selective U.S. Reed College) tested in the same way, maintaining a fast response speed as target number increases. As the authors of this study observe, "the counterintuitive conclusion follows that pigeons are more intelligent than people. An alternative view assumes that different *intelligences* or factors are employed in different situations by different individuals, groups, and species" (Vickrey & Neuringer, 2000, 291).

1.2   Kinds of explanation for behavior

1.2.1   Tinbergen's four questions

The pioneering ethologist Niko Tinbergen (1963) emphasized that the question, "Why does the animal do that?" can mean four different things, sometimes referred to as "Tinbergen's four whys." "Why?" can mean "How does it work?" in the sense of "What events inside and outside the animal cause it to behave as it does at this moment?" This is the question of the proximate cause (or simply cause) of behavior. Perceptions, representations, decisions, as well as the neural events that accompany them, are all possible proximate causes of behavior (Hogan 2005). One might also ask about development in the individual, that is "How do experience and genetic makeup combine to cause the animal to behave as it does?" "Why" can also mean "What is the behavior good for; what is its survival value?" This is the question of function or adaptive value. Finally, one can ask how a particular behavior evolved, as inferred from the phylogeny of species that show it (Chapter 2) together with evidence about its current function (Cuthill 2005). Causation, development, function, and evolution are not levels of explanation but complementary accounts that can be given of any behavior. As Tinbergen emphasized, a complete understanding of behavior includes answers to all four questions. However, it is important to be clear on how they differ from one another and to avoid confusing the answer to one with the answer to another.

Consider as an example some possible answers to the question raised at the beginning of this chapter, "Why do crows drop walnuts?" The proximate cause of nut dropping would be sought in some interaction of the bird's internal state, most likely hunger, with external stimuli like the presence of walnuts, other crows, and hard surfaces. Proximate causes can be specified at levels right down to events at the level of genes and neurons, but often causal mechanisms are inferred from input-output relations at the level of the whole animal (Hogan 2005). This is generally true with the sorts of cognitive mechanisms discussed in this book. Explanations of the immediate causes of behavior do not include teleology, or reference to conscious purposes or goals (see Hogan 1994a). The future cannot cause what is happening in the present. The crow does not drop walnuts "to get food" though it is possible that she does so because similar behavior in the past was followed by a tasty snack, that is, because of past reinforcement. Examining the bird's history of reinforcement would be part of a developmental explanation, as would an account of any other factors within the crow's lifetime that affected its nut dropping.

The immediate function, or adaptive value, of behavior is what it is good for in the life of the individual. Cracking walnuts clearly functions in obtaining food, but questions about the function of the crow's behavior can also asked at finer levels of detail. For instance, the functional question, "Why carry a nut so high and no higher?" was tackled by testing whether the height to which nuts are carried matched the type of nut and where it was dropped (Figure 1.1, see also Zach 1979).

Tinbergen's fourth question, "How did it evolve?" usually has to be tackled by trying to look at the behavior's phylogenetic history using methods described in Chapter 2. For the crows' nutcracking, this would include discovering whether close relatives of American crows also drop hard-shelled prey items and whether specific ecological conditions are associated with prey-dropping (Cristol and Switzer 1999). Occasionally it has been possible to observe evolution happening in the wild as natural populations have changed rapidly in response to changes in selection pressures (e.g., Endler 1986). Some of these examples involve behavior at least implicitly. For instance, in a famous long-term field study, Rosemary Grant and Peter Grant observed the beaks of seed-eating finches on the Galapagos Islands changing in response to drastic changes in rainfall (Grant and Grant 2008). In years of drought, only the birds most skilled at cracking the few remaining seeds could survive and reproduce. Beak depth, an indication of seed-cracking power, contributed importantly to survival in the medium ground finch (*Geospiza fortis*). Because beak depth is heritable, changes in the population's distribution of beak depths could be detected in a few generations (Figure 1.2). The birds' behavior must have changed, too, perhaps through learning. Rather than ignoring the hardest seeds, as they did in times of plenty, the successful individuals evidently became skilled at finding and cracking them.

In terms of Tinbergen's four questions, cognition is one of the proximate causes of behavior. Because studying cognition may include analyzing how information and ways of responding to it are acquired, studying cognition may also involve studying development. Throughout this book we will be concerned with the adaptive value

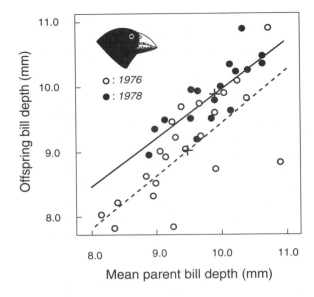

Figure 1.2. Upper panel: Inheritance of bill depth (height of the bill in the drawing) in medium ground finches in two different years. Slope of the line relating offspring to parent bill depth—a measure of heritability—was almost the same in both years. Variation and selection of bill depth are illustrated in the two lower panels. In 1978 there was a drought, and the finches could subsist only by cracking the hardest seeds, accounting for the greater survival of those with deeper bills. Redrawn from Boag and Grant (1984) and Boag (1983) with permission.

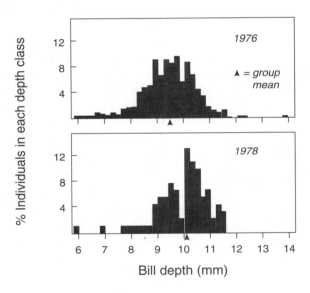

and evolution of cognitive mechanisms. But speaking of cognition doesn't imply that animals are aware of the effects that their actions have on fitness. Evolution produces machines that reproduce themselves (Box 1.2). A robin builds a nest and lays eggs. It responds to eggs by incubating them. As a result of the parents' keeping the eggs at a temperature they have evolved to develop at, young robins hatch with nervous systems so constructed that they open their beaks and beg when an adult approaches the nest. The adult's nervous system responds to gaping by inserting food, and so on. The bird isn't responding to "my young," let alone planning to have lots of grandchildren, but to stimuli that are generally reliable correlates of offspring like gaping mouths in its nest. Behavioral mechanisms, including cognitive processes such as memory for the location of the nest and tuning of the adults' perception to the signals emitted by the young, are selected if they increase their bearer's representation in future generations, but such mechanisms need not—and seldom, if ever, do—include foresight into the effects of behavior on fitness (Chapter 11).

1.2.2   "Learned" and "innate" behavior

Learning is often contrasted with genetic or innate control of behavior. What this dichotomy overlooks is that learning is possible only for an animal whose genes and prior environment have resulted in development of an individual ready to be affected by experience in a certain way. No behavior is either strictly learned or entirely innate. An excellent illustration of how preexisting selective processes in the animal interact with specific experiences to produce learning comes from classic comparisons of song learning in two species of sparrows (Marler and Peters 1989). Like many other songbirds (Box 13.2), male song sparrows (*Melospiza melodia*) and swamp sparrows (*Melospiza georgiana*) need to hear species-specific song early in life in order to sing it when they mature. The two species are closely related, but swamp sparrows sing a much simpler song.

Marler and Peters played song sparrow songs and swamp sparrow songs to isolated young males of both species in the laboratory. Thus, all the birds had the same acoustic experience. But their behavior as adults revealed that they had learned different, species-appropriate things from it (Figure 1.3). Swamp sparrows learned only swamp sparrow songs, and song sparrows had a strong preference to learn song sparrow songs. The interaction of species with experience is still seen even when the birds are raised in the laboratory from the egg or very early nestling stage, showing that it probably does not result from birds hearing their father's song. Because birds of each species sometimes do produce sounds characteristic of the other species, it seems unlikely that the species difference in song production results from a motor constraint. In the wild, these two species may live within earshot of each other, so early-developing selectivity in perception and/or learning likely functions to ensure that each one learns only its own species song. Indeed, young birds still in the nest respond most to their own species song, as shown by the way heart rate changes when they are played different sounds (Marler and Peters 1989).

This example comes from a specialized behavior shown by only a few of the world's species, but it makes a very important general point: cognitive mechanisms are adaptations to process and use certain kinds of information in certain ways, not mechanisms for information processing in general. As for the theme of this section, insofar as it implies that genes can work without an environment to work in, the term *innate* is never appropriate in modern biology (Bateson and Mameli 2007). However, we do sometimes need a term for the many behaviors that appear in development ready to serve their apparent function before they can have done so. For instance, selecting the species-typical song for learning clearly serves the function of allowing the adult male, many months later, to sing in a way that his conspecifics are most responsive to. Hogan (1994b) has suggested the term *prefunctional* for such cases, because it does not imply that the genes have worked in isolation nor that prior experience is irrelevant. However, because this term implies that we know the function of the behavior, *predisposition* or *preexisting bias* may be preferable.

Finally, to say that some behavior or cognitive process develops prefunctionally is not to say that it is unmodifiable (Dawkins 1995). As the comparison of song and swamp sparrows illustrates, how much and in what ways behavior can be modified

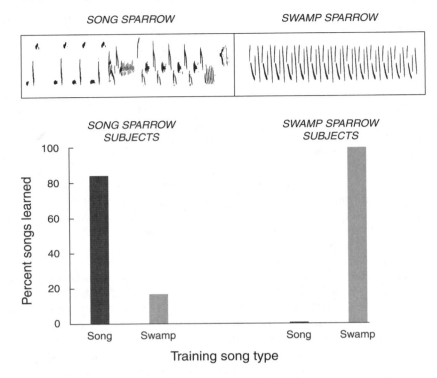

Figure 1.3. Song sparrows and swamp sparrows exposed to both song sparrow and swamp sparrow songs when young learn primarily the songs of their own species. Top panel shows sonagrams (sound frequency vs. time) of songs from normal adults of the two species. Redrawn from Marler and Peters (1989) with permission.

itself reflects events earlier in development. This example also shows how a stereo-typed behavior seen in most normally developing members of a species can result from learning. However, although it makes a key point for this book in showing how experience can have species-species effects, it misleadingly implies that effects of experience (here, the songs) and genes (the species of sparrow) can always be neatly separated. Developmental biologists are increasingly documenting gene by environment interactions and interdependencies as well as epigenetic effects, in which environmental effects on the genes of one generation are passed on to the next (Sokolowski & Levine in press). Some of these discoveries have implications for behavior; undoubtedly more such will be uncovered in the future.

In conclusion, structure as well as behavior, the animal's *phenotype,* results from a continuous and seamless interplay of genes and environment that is itself selected. The extent to which behavior patterns or cognitive capacities are modifiable by experience varies so much as to make the terms *learned* and *innate* (or *nature* and *nurture*) obsolete (Bateson and Mameli 2007). The fact that individuals within a species (i.e., with a common *genotype*) may develop different physical and/or behavioral phenotypes in different environments is known as *phenotypic plasticity*. The ability of individuals to learn details of their own environment that are unpredictable on an evolutionary timescale is but one aspect of the more general phenomenon of adaptive phenotypic plasticity (Dukas 1998; for a brief review see Agrawal 2001; for further discussion of the topics in this section see Marler 2004).

1.3   Approaches to comparative cognition

Psychologists and biologists have traditionally taken different approaches to studying learning and cognition in animals. These two contrasting traditions have been called, among other things, the study of general processes and the study of adaptive specializations (Riley and Langley 1993) or the General Social Science Model and evolutionary psychology (Cosmides and Tooby 1992). Psychologists have tended to ask, "Can animals do what people do, and if so how do they do it?" whereas biologists tend to ask, "Why, in all Tinbergen's four senses, do animals do what they do in the wild?" Thus the contrast between traditional psychological and biological approaches is one between anthropocentric, or human-centered, and ecological, animal-centered, approaches. It is also one between a field centered on mechanism, just one of Tinbergen's four questions, and one in which "Nothing makes sense except in the light of evolution" (see e.g., Plotkin 2004)

1.3.1   The anthropocentric approach

Comparative psychology began with Darwin's claim—profoundly shocking at the time—that humans are similar to other species in mental as well as physical characteristics. Chapter 3 of his second book, *The Descent of Man and Selection in Relation to Sex* (Darwin 1871), touches on almost every problem that has been studied by comparative psychologists since. In it, Darwin claimed that other animals differ cognitively from humans in degree but not in kind. That is to say, animals share human abilities such as reasoning, memory, language, and aesthetic sensibility, but generally they possess them to a lesser degree (see Chapter 15). His emphasis was on continuity among species rather than diversity, the other side of the evolutionary coin (Rozin and Schull 1988). Acceptance of continuity has led to using animals in psychology as little furry or feathery people, model systems for studying general processes of learning, memory, decision-making, even psychopathology and their neural and genetic underpinnings. Thus this approach can be characterized as *anthropocentric* because it is concerned primarily with issues related to human psychology.

Around the beginning of the 1900s psychologists' study of cognitive processes in animals began to focus on associative learning (see Boakes 1984). Some researchers in the first part of the twentieth century did study issues such as animal reasoning or insight learning (Dewsbury 2000), but animal cognition as a recognized subfield did not take off until the 1970s (Hulse 2006). Its practitioners were concerned to distinguish themselves from S-R psychologists, who explained behavior in terms of connections between stimuli and responses established by classical or instrumental conditioning and eschewed speculation about unobservable processing of information. Psychologists studying animal cognition, in contrast, used behavior as a window onto processes of memory and representation (Wasserman 1984). Initially, much of their research used learned behavior of rats and pigeons in the laboratory to analyze processes that were being successfully studied in people, such as memory for lists of items, concept formation, and attention (cf., Hulse, Fowler, and Honig 1978).

Research on animal cognition based on the anthropocentric approach has three important characteristics. First, it focuses on memory, representation, and other kinds of information processing that can be identified in people. Second, such research is implicitly comparative, in that other species like parrots or pigeons are compared with humans, but the choice of species is often based more on convenience than on evolutionary considerations. Finally, traditional discussions of anthropocentric research were pervaded by the incorrect and misleading notion of a phylogenetic scale or *scala naturae* (Hodos and Campbell 1969). This is the idea that evolution is a continuous ladder of improvement, from "lowly" worms and slugs, through fish, amphibians and reptiles, to birds and mammals. Humans, needless to say, are at the pinnacle of evolution in this scheme. But present-day species cannot be lined up in this way (Chapter 2). People are not more highly evolved fish, birds, rats, or even chimpanzees. Correct inferences about the relationship between cognitive or brain processes in humans and those in nonhumans depend on a detailed appreciation of the biology of "animal models" (Preuss 1995 ; Papini 2008). Nevertheless, studying a few very diverse species, as in the research sketched in Box 1.3, may be the best way to reveal processes general to all species (Bitterman 2000; Papini 2002). Exactly this approach to genome mapping has provided stunning support for generality: species as

---

Box 1.3 Traditional Comparative Psychology: An Example

In the 1960s and 1970s, M. E. Bitterman and his associates carried out an extensive program of research comparing the performance of goldfish, painted turtles, pigeons, rats, and monkeys on a number of standard laboratory tasks (Bitterman 1965, 1975). Later, this work was extended to honeybees (see Bitterman 2000). Their overall aim was to test the assumption that the "intelligence" of "lower" animals differed only in degree and not in kind from that of "higher" animals. Of course, as Bitterman (1975, 2000) recognized, these species are not on an evolutionary ladder but at the ends of separate branches of the tree of life (Figure B1.3). Therefore, commonalities must reflect either their presence in some very ancient common ancestor or convergence due to similar environmental pressures

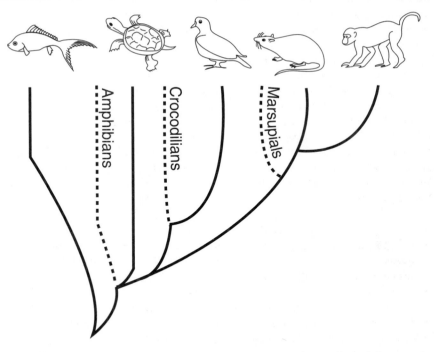

Figure B1.3. A simple phylogeny (see Chapter 2) of the species tested by Bitterman and his colleagues in comparative studies of learning. Neither the recency with which one group is thought to have diverged from another nor its left-right arrangement in such a diagram necessarily implies anything about "intelligence." Redrawn from Bitterman (1975) with permission.

Bitterman devised ingenious versions of standard apparatuses to present the same kinds of tasks to these very different species. Fish pushed paddles for a reward of worms; pigeons pecked lighted disks for a few grains of corn; turtles crawled down small runways. In one series of experiments, the animals were compared on their ability to learn *successive reversals* of simple visual and spatial discriminations. In successive reversal (Chapter 6) an animal is first rewarded for choosing a certain one of two simultaneously presented stimuli, say red rather than green. After a number of trials, the rewarded stimulus is reversed, for example, the animal must choose green rather than red, and so on. "Intelligent" behavior is to improve over successive reversals, eventually performing perfectly after just one trial on each new problem. Within each species, performance on visual discriminations (e.g., red vs. green for species with color vision or black vs. white for those without) was also compared to performance on spatial (e.g., left vs. right) discriminations. Monkeys, rats, and pigeons improved on both visual and spatial reversals, fish improved on neither, and turtles improved on spatial but not visual reversals. What results from this kind of selection of species and problems can reveal about "the evolution of intelligence" is discussed further in Chapter 2 (see also Papini 2002, 2008).

diverse as fruitflies, mice and humans are turning out to share unexpected numbers of genes and basic developmental processes (see Robinson 2004; Papini 2008). In addition, the rigorous methodology and the principles developed with traditional psychological studies of animals are essential to more biologically focused research (e.g., Timberlake, Schaal, and Steinmetz 2005).

1.3.2 Anthropocentrism, anthropomorphism, and Morgan's Canon

Documenting human-like "mental powers" of animals was central to the agenda of early defenders of Darwinism. Similarity between human and animal minds would surely be the most convincing evidence of evolutionary continuity between humans and other species. Accordingly, some of Darwin's supporters, primary among them George Romanes (1892) set out to collect anecdotes appearing to prove animals could think and solve problems the way people do. Their approach was not just anthropocentric but frankly *anthropomorphic,* explaining animals' apparently clever problem solving in terms of human-like thinking and reasoning. But as we have seen in the case of the nutcracking crows, just because an animal's behavior looks to the casual observer like what a person would do in a similar-appearing situation does not mean it can be explained in the same way. Such reasoning based on analogy between humans and other animals must be tested with experiments that take into account alternative hypotheses (Heyes 2008).

Fortunately for progress in understanding animal cognition, critics of extreme anthropomorphism were not slow to appear. E. L. Thorndike's (1911/1970) pioneering experiments on how animals solve simple physical problems showed that gradual learning by trial and error was more common than human-like insight and planning (Galef 1998). C. Lloyd Morgan also observed animals in a systematic way but is now best known for stating a principle commonly taken as forbidding unsupported anthropomorphism. What Morgan (1894) called his Canon states, "In no case may we interpret an action as the outcome of the exercise of a higher psychical faculty, if it can be interpreted as the outcome of the exercise of one which stands lower in the psychological scale." Morgan's Canon is clearly not without problems (Sober 2005). What is the "psychological scale"? Don't "higher" and "lower" assume the phylogenetic scale? In contemporary practice "lower" usually means associative learning, that is, classical and instrumental conditioning or untrained species-specific responses. "Higher" is reasoning, planning, insight, in short any cognitive process other than associative learning.

For an example of how Morgan's Canon might be applied today, suppose, contrary to the data in Figure 1.1, that crows had been found to drop nuts in front of cars more than on the empty road. An obvious "simple" explanation is that they had been reinforced more often when dropping a nut when a car was coming than when the road was empty and thereby had learned to discriminate these two situations. A "higher," anthropomorphic, explanation might be that having seen fallen nuts crushed by cars the insightful crows reasoned that they could drop the nuts themselves. The contrast between these explanations suggests a straightforward test: observe naïve crows to see if the discrimination between approaching cars and empty roads develops gradually (supporting the "simple" explanation) or appears suddenly, without any previous trial and error (supporting the "higher" explanation). Unfortunately, competing explanations do not always make such readily discriminable predictions about observable behavior. Even when they do, experiments designed to pit them against each other may not yield clear results. Then agnosticism may be the most defensible policy (Sober 2005).

In practice, the field of comparative cognition as it has developed in the past 30–40 years has a very strong bias in favor of "simple" mechanisms (Sober 2001; Wasserman and Zentall 2006a). The burden of proof is generally on anyone wishing to explain behavior in terms of processes other than associative learning and/or species-typical perceptual and response biases. To many, anthropomorphism is a dirty word in scientific study of animal cognition (Mitchell 2005; Wynne 2007a, 2007b). But dismissing anthropomorphism altogether is not necessarily the best way forward. "Anthropodenial" (de Waal 1999) may also be a sin. After all, if other species share common ancestors with us, then we share an a priori unspecifiable number of biological processes with any species one cares to name. Thus in some ways, as Morgan apparently thought (Sober 2005), the simplest account of any behavior is arguably the anthropomorphic one, that behavior analogous to ours is the product of a similar cognitive process. Note, however, that "simple" has shifted here from the cognitive process to the explanation (Karin-D'Arcy 2005), from "simpler for them" to "simpler for us" (Heyes 1998).

Where do these considerations leave Morgan's Canon? A reasonable modern interpretation of the Canon (Sober 2005) is that a bias in favor of simple associative explanations is justified because basic conditioning mechanisms are widespread in the animal kingdom, having been found in every animal, from worms and fruitflies to primates, in which they have been sought (Papini 2008). Thus they may be evolutionarily very old, present in species ancestral to all present-day animals and reflecting adaptations to universal causal regularities in the world and/or fundamental properties of neural circuits. As species diverged, other mechanisms may have become available on some branches of the evolutionary tree, and it might be said to be the job of comparative psychologists to understand their distribution (Papini 2002).

But for such a project to make sense, it must be clear what is meant by associative explanations and what their limits are. Associative learning, discussed in depth in Chapter 4, is basically the learning that results from experiencing contingencies, or predictive relationships, between events. At the theoretical level, such experience in Pavlovian (stimulus-stimulus) or instrumental (response-stimulus) conditioning has traditionally been thought of as strengthening excitatory or inhibitory connections between event representations. Thus one might say that any cognitive performance that does not result from experience of contingencies between events and/or cannot be explained in terms of excitatory and/or inhibitory connections is nonassociative. Path integration (Chapter 8) is one example: an animal moving in a winding path from home implicitly integrates distance and direction information into a vector leading straight home. As another, on one view of conditioning (Section 4.5.2) the flow of events in time is encoded as such and computed on to compare rates of food presentation during a signal and in its absence. Other nonassociative cognitive processes which might be (but rarely if ever have been) demonstrated in nonhumans include imitation, that is, storing a representation of an actor's behavior and later reproducing the behavior; insight; and any kind of reasoning or higher-order representations or computations on event representations. As we will see throughout the book, discriminating nonassociative "higher" processes from associative ones is seldom straightforward, in part because the learning resulting from associative procedures may have subtle and interesting cognitive content. In any case, the goal of comparative research should be understanding the cognitive mechanisms underlying animal behavior in their full variety and complexity rather than partitioning them into rational or nonassociative vs. associative (Papineau and Heyes 2006).

In conclusion, neither blanket anthropomorphism nor complete anthropodenial is the answer (Mitchell 2005). Evolutionary continuity justifies anthropomorphism as a source of hypotheses. When it comes to comparing human cognition with that of other species, it is most likely that—just as with our genes and other physical characters—we will find some processes shared with many other species, some with only a few, and some that are uniquely human. One of the most exciting aspects of contemporary research on comparative cognition is the increasing detail and subtlety in our picture of how other species' minds are both like and not like ours.

1.3.3   Biological approaches to animal behavior

While experimental animal psychology was flourishing in North America, ethology was developing in departments of zoology in Europe (Burkhardt 2005). Guided by Tinbergen's four questions and the vision of developing a biological science of behavior distinct from psychology, ethologists emphasized the behavior of animals in the wild. They studied a wide range of species: insects, birds, and fish as well as mammals. Behavior was seen to be as much a characteristic of a given species as its coloration or the structure of its body (Lorenz 1941/1971; Tinbergen 1959). In an effort to break free of sentimental attitudes toward animals, ethologists emphasized the same objective behaviorist approach as Skinner and other experimental psychologists. For instance, at the very beginning of his textbook *The Study of Instinct* Tinbergen (1951, 4) warns, "Because subjective phenomena cannot be observed directly in animals it is idle either to claim or to deny their existence. Moreover to ascribe a causal function to something that is not observable often leads to false conclusions."

In the 1960s and 1970s the ethological study of the adaptive value and evolution of behavior developed into the field of behavioral ecology (Krebs and Davies 1993; Cuthill 2005). Behavioral ecology, or sociobiology (Wilson 1975), is characterized by an attempt to predict behavior from first principles of evolutionary biology using explicit models of the consequences of behavior for fitness. Like ethologists, behavioral ecologists focus on behavior of animals in the field and study a wide variety of species, but initially they were concerned almost exclusively with the functional and evolutionary "why" questions. Early research in behavioral ecology aimed to discover simply whether or not behavior had the properties predicted by evolutionary models. For example, did redshank or some other bird choose food items optimally? As the field developed, and at about the same time as some psychologists (e.g., Kamil 1988; Shettleworth 1993) were advocating analyses of ecologically meaningful aspects of cognition, behavioral ecologists began to appreciate the role of cognitive mechanisms in producing or failing to produce the predicted behaviors (e.g., Stamps 1991; Huntingford 1993; Dukas 1998; Chittka and Thomson 2001). They began to ask, for example, about the processes of perception, learning, and choice that lead the redshank to select its prey and how these play a role in the bird's making, or failing to make, optimal choices (Chapter 11). The integration of cognitive psychology with the study of how animals solve ecologically important problems was referred to as *cognitive ecology* (Real 1993; Dukas 1998; Healy and Braithwaite 2000). *Sensory ecology* (Dusenbery 1992) and *neuroecology* (Bolhuis and Macphail 2001; Sherry 2006), were coined for the study of how sensory systems and brain architecture, respectively, are matched to species-specific environmental requirements.

1.3.4   Convergence and synthesis: Comparative cognition in the twenty-first century

Ethologists, behavioral ecologists, and traditional comparative psychologists emphasize different questions about animal behavior and tend to do their research in different settings and on different species, but their fields are clearly related. It stands to reason that data and theory of each of these fields should illuminate issues being studied by the others. Within psychology, this point of view led to what has been called the ecological or synthetic approach to comparative cognition (Kamil 1988; Shettleworth 1993). Unlike the anthropocentric or general process approach, the ecological approach emphasizes studying how animals use cognition in the wild, for example in foraging or finding their way around. Species are chosen on the basis of behavior indicating some particularly interesting cognitive processing such as the ability to home over long distances, use tools, keep track of relationships in a large social group, or remember the locations of large numbers of food items (Box 1.4). The ecological approach includes explicitly comparative studies designed to analyze the evolution and adaptive value of particular cognitive abilities. The species compared may be close relatives that face different cognitive demands in the wild and therefore are expected to have diverged in cognitive ability. Alternatively, species may be compared that are not very close relatives but face similar cognitive demands in the wild. Such species are expected to have converged in the ability of interest. Data about natural history and evolution are an integral part of this kind of comparative psychology, but so are theories and methods developed with the anthropocentric approach. This approach is increasingly shared by biologists trying to understand cognitive processes underlying behaviors they observe in wild animals (e.g., Bluff et al. 2007; Cheney and Seyfarth 2007).

Cognitive ecology, sensory ecology, cognitive ethology, neuroecology, evolutionary psychology, ecological comparative psychology: whatever these enterprises are called, they all have in common the assumption that cognition is best understood by being studied in the context of evolution and ecology, that is, as a biological science. Together they have been converging into a vigorous interdisciplinary field of comparative cognition research. Kamil (1998) suggested that *cognitive ethology* should be reclaimed from those who use it to refer to studies of conscious processes in animals to refer to this synthetic research program. Reasonable though this

Box 1.4 Food Storing Birds and the Ecological Approach

Some species of birds store food in the wild and use memory to find it again. One of the most remarkable is the Clark's nutcracker (*Nucifraga columbiana*) of the American Southwest (Figure B1.4). Nutcrackers bury thousands of caches of pinon pine seeds in the late summer and dig them up from beneath the snow throughout the winter and into the next spring (Balda and Kamil 2006). Early observers of food-storing in corvids (jays, crows, and nutcrackers) and parids (chickadees and titmice) found it incredible that these birds might be able to remember the locations of caches. Perhaps they were just raising the general level of availability of food for all birds in the area. But food-storing would be unlikely to evolve unless the individuals doing it have greater fitness than lazy individuals which simply eat the food stored by others (Andersson and Krebs 1978). As this argument suggests, food storing birds do retrieve their own caches, and they use memory to do it (Shettleworth 1995).

Figure B1.4. A Clark's nutcracker burying a seed. A bird generally caches several seeds in each site. From a photograph by R. P. Balda.

The fact that food-storers must remember the locations of a large number of items for days, weeks, or months suggests that along with the specialized behavior of caching food they may have evolved an enhancement of some aspect of memory. For example, maybe they can remember more items of spatial information for longer than other birds. Within both the corvids and the parids, some species store more food than others, so this hypothesis can be tested by comparing memory within each bird family. Corvids or parids that store more do tend to have better spatial memory, and the hippocampus, a part of the brain involved in spatial memory, is bigger relative to brain and body size in food storers than in nonstoring species. Both the data and the thinking behind these conclusions have proven controversial, as discussed in Chapter 2. Nevertheless, research on food-storing birds is still a good example of how information from evolutionary biology, field studies, neurobiology, psychological theories about memory, and techniques for testing memory in the laboratory can all be integrated to provide new insights.

suggestion may be, it does not seem to have been widely adopted (Allen 2004), and the term *comparative cognition* is generally used here. The present trend toward interdisciplinary research is a major departure from a century or more in which psychological research with animals (including often the human animal) has been largely divorced from, or even hostile to, the rest of the biological sciences and the framework provided by evolution (Richards 1987; Plotkin 2004). For more than 50 years, comparative psychologists (e.g., Beach 1950; Hodos and Campbell 1969) have been complaining about the detrimental effects of this divorce on psychological research with animals. Is the field itself evolving at last? There is plenty of evidence that it is. To some extent this evolution reflects the fact that psychology in general is becoming better integrated with the rest of the biological sciences, impelled by the apparent success of neuroscience and genetics in illuminating mechanistic under-pinnings of behavior (e.g., Lickliter and Honeycutt 2003). But it also reflects the excitement generated by a variety of specific research programs that approach ques-tions about animal cognition in a comprehensive biological framework.

For example, the last 20 years or so have seen the development of a lively cross-disciplinary field of research and theorizing on comparative social learning and possible precursors of human culture (Zentall and Galef 1988; Heyes and Galef 1996; Reader and Laland 2003; Galef and Heyes 2004; Richerson and Boyd 2005). Anthropocentrism has been turned on its head as studies of animal tool using, theory of mind, cultural transmission of skills, episodic memory and other capacities tradi-tionally thought to be unique to humans are seen as relevant to understanding human cognitive evolution and development (e.g., Gomez 2005; Penn et al. 2008). The study of spatial behavior is increasingly interdisciplinary, embracing field and laboratory research on brain, behavior, and ecology of species as diverse as honeybees, ants, rats, and people (Gallistel 1990; Healy 1998; Jeffery 2003). Behavioral ecologists are embracing mechanistic studies at the level of the brain (Giraldeau 2004). Textbooks of animal behavior (e.g., Dugatkin 2004; Bolhuis and Giraldeau 2005) include sections on learning and animal cognition. The International Comparative Cognition Society, which began in 1994 as a small group of experimental psycholo-gists mainly working with rats and pigeons, now represents researchers from psy-chology, biology, and anthropology studying most of the species and issues discussed in this book. As we see throughout the book, such convergence of researchers from different traditions, accustomed to focusing on different ones of Tinbergen's ques-tions, can lead to misunderstanding and controversy, as when cognitive psychologists and behavioral ecologists disagree about what counts as *teaching* (Chapter 13), but it has also immeasurably broadened and enriched the field.

1.3.5   Comparative cognition and other areas of the behavioral and brain sciences

The comparative study of cognition intersects with many other areas of the beha-vioral and brain sciences. These include neuroscience, genetics, evolutionary psychol-ogy, developmental psychology, anthropology, conservation, and animal welfare. The research perhaps most closely connected to that discussed in this book concerns the neurobiological and molecular mechanisms of learning and cognition. By far the majority of studies of learning in animals at the present time are being done in this context (Domjan and Krause 2002). As Skinner wrote in *The Behavior of Organisms,* "a rigorous description at the level of behavior is necessary for the demonstration of a neurological correlate" (Skinner 1938, 422; Timberlake, Schaal, and Steinmetz 2005). So, for example, when researchers engineer a mouse strain that develops neurological symptoms of Alzheimer's disease (Chen 2000), deciding whether those mice show memory impairments analogous to those seen in human Alzheimer's sufferers depends crucially on having appropriate behavioral tests of memory, as well as knowledge of mouse behavior (Gerlai and Clayton 1999). Here, however, we will be concerned with research on neuroscience and genetics only when it impinges on the understanding of cognitive processes as such.

Evolutionary psychology is also closely related to some topics in the present book. Evolutionary psychology is based on the premise that principles of cognition and behavior in humans are adaptations to social and environmental demands throughout evolution (Barkow, Cosmides, and Tooby 1992; Barrett, Dunbar, and Lycett 2002; Dunbar and Barrett 2007). For example, reasoning ability may have evolved at least in part to deal with social obligations in early hominid groups (Cosmides 1989). Evolutionary psychology has generated some controversial findings (see Buller 2005). One of its weak points is that its hypotheses often have to be based on conjectures about the conditions present early in human evolution. In this respect, research on the evolution of cognition in other animals is on much firmer ground because other species' present-day environments are likely much more representative of their past environments than is the case for humans. Hypotheses about evolution and adaptation can also be tested more directly in other species than in humans by comparing groups of present-day species. Thus research with nonhuman species can provide well-grounded hypotheses for testing in humans as well as a model for how such hypotheses should be tested (Daly and Wilson 1999). Indeed, the subject of this book might be described as evolutionary psychology "in the round" (i.e., in the broad sense, see Heyes 2000).

Some contemporary researchers directly address questions about the evolution of human cognition through studies with other species, for example seeking to combine insights from genetics, neurobiology, anthropology, child development, field studies of primate behavior, and laboratory tests to understand the fundamental question of what makes us different from even our closest living relatives, the chimpanzees and other primates (Chapter 15 and Gunter et al. 2005). This is particularly true in the study of spatial, numerical, and social cognition (Chapters 8, 10, and 12). Communication between comparative and developmental researchers is partly explained by the fact that those who study very young children share a problem faced by those studying animals—their subjects can't talk—making methods easily transferred between fields. It is also commonly assumed that any cognitive abilities chimpanzees share with us are most likely to be those shown by very young children (cf., Matsuzawa 2007).

Finally, the results of research on comparative cognition can have implications for conservation and animal welfare. For example, when members of an endangered species are raised in captivity to be released in the wild, it may be important to understand what they would have learned normally and figure out how to impart such knowledge to captive-reared individuals. This can include what predators to avoid (Griffin, Blumstein, and Evans 2000; Griffin 2004) and what cues indicate a suitable habitat (Stamps and Swaisgood 2007). When it comes to animal welfare, there is a widespread sentiment that the more research shows that animals are like us, the more we should value and protect them (but see Wynne 2004b). Whatever one's point of view in this controversial area, knowledge about animal behavior and cognition can be applied to better understand and thus improve the welfare of both wild and captive animals (see Fraser and Weary 2005; Dawkins 2006).

1.4   Summary

Studying cognition means analyzing how animals acquire, process, and use information. Most people who study comparative cognition remain agnostic as to whether animals process information consciously or not. Some animals may be conscious in some sense, but we cannot know because consciousness refers to a private subjective state. Furthermore, it is often difficult to specify any behavior uniquely resulting from consciousness. How animals process information and behave adaptively can be understood, and on the whole should be studied, without reference to consciousness. Nevertheless, some researchers are of the opinion that some animals are undoubtedly conscious, and scientists should be trying to understand the nature of their conscious states.

Four questions, often referred to as Tinbergen's four whys, can be asked about any behavior. These are questions about immediate causation, development in the individual, present-day function, and evolution. The four questions are complementary; each contributes to a complete understanding of behavior. Cognitive mechanisms such as perception and memory are among the immediate causes of behavior; learning is part of behavioral development. Cognitive processes are also part of an animal's adaptation to its environment and therefore must have evolved through natural selection.

Cognition in nonhuman species has traditionally been approached differently by psychologists than by biologists. Psychologists have tended to take an anthropocentric approach, seeking to understand humanlike performance in other species and perhaps interpreting their findings by reference to an assumed phylogenetic scale. Anthropocentrism is not the same as anthropomorphism, or interpreting animal behavior as if it was caused by humanlike thought processes. Explicit anthropomorphism is thought to have been rejected with the adoption of Morgan's Canon early in the 1900s, but cannot be done away with entirely. The ecological or biological approach to cognition consists of analyzing the kinds of information processing animals do in situations of ecological importance like foraging, choosing mates, finding their way around. With this approach, species are compared with reference to evolutionary and ecological relationships. After a long history in which comparative psychology developed largely independently of biological studies of behavior, contemporary research on comparative cognition is increasingly integrating these two approaches and making rich connections with other biological sciences.

Further reading and websites

The whole field of comparative cognition is covered in recent books including introductory texts by Wynne (2001) and Pearce (2008), the books edited by Balda, Pepperberg, and Kamil(1998); Heyes and Huber (2000); Wasserman and Zentall (2006b); and Bekoff, Allen, and Burghardt (2002), and the March, 2009, special issue of *Behavioural Processes* (vol. 80, no. 3). Hauser's (2000) *Wild Minds* and Wynne's (2004a) *Do Animals Think?* are excellent popular books by researchers in the field. Donald Griffin regularly updated his proposals about animal consciousness (Griffin 1976) almost until the end of his life (Griffin 2001). The animal behavior texts by Bolhuis and Giraldeau (2005) and Lucas and Simmons (2006) both cover topics included in this book, as does *Congitive Ecology II* (Dukas and Ratcliffe, 2009). Papini's (2008) *Comparative Psychology* provides comprehensive background on the evolution of brain and behavior. *Behavioural Ecology* (Danchin, Giraldeau, and Cezilly 2008) is a comprehensive overview of that field.

From Darwin to Behaviorism (Boakes 1984) and the books by Richards (1987), Plotkin (2004), and especially Burkhardt (2005) are recommended for the history of thought and research in comparative psychology and ethology. *Tinbergen's Legacy*

(Verhulst and Bolhuis 2009) reprints Tinbergen's 1963 paper along with the contemporary discussions of the four questions that were originally published in 2005 in *Animal Biology*. For animal consciousness, the writings of Dennett (1996), Allen and Bekoff (1997), Carruthers (e.g., 2005), and Sober (e.g., 2005) are useful; the chapter by Heyes (2008) is exceptionally clear on this and other issues. Kennedy's (1992) little book is a stimulating analysis of what he saw as the insidious influence of anthropomorphism. The discussions accompanying Wynne's (2007a) paper make clear that it is still controversial.

Most of the active scientists whose research is discussed in this book have lab websites with further information about their work. Many such websites and online editions of journals have links to video illustrations. These can be both entertaining and wonderful aids to understanding. The Animal Behavior Society and the Comparative Cognition Society both have comprehensive websites with links to researchers' sites, news, and events in the area. Given the ease with which these resources can be located, on the whole this book does not include specific references to online material.

2
Evolution, Behavior, and Cognition: A Primer

Thanks to the admonitions of writers like Hodos and Campbell (1969) and Beach (1950), comparative psychologists have largely stopped interpreting species differences in terms of the *scala naturae*. Arguably, however, more sophisticated evolutionary thinking has yet to take its place (Papini 2002). This chapter introduces contemporary approaches to studying evolution and adaptation. It begins with an overview of ways to test hypotheses about adaptive value and then sketches the ways in which information about present-day species is used to learn about phylogeny, or patterns of descent. Section 2.3 introduces a framework for thinking about how evolution shapes behavior and summarizes some of the challenges in testing comparative hypotheses about cognition. Major trends in vertebrate brain evolution, summarized in Section 2.4.1, might be expected to provide some clues about cognitive differences among major groups of animals. Indeed, some hypotheses about the causes of brain evolution are hypotheses about what brains and parts of brains allow animals to do in foraging and social life. Research on the relationship between food storing and hippocampus size in birds (Section 2.4.2) is an example of research connecting the evolution of a brain part with ecology. The debate it has occasioned about the relationship between functions and mechanisms of cognition and the brain is evaluated in the final part of the chapter.

2.1   Testing adaptation

"Drab coloration is an adaptation for reducing detection by visual predators." "Bats' sonar is an adaptation for detecting flying insects in the dark." "Reasoning ability is an adaptation to conditions in early hunter-gatherer societies." To say that some characteristic of an animal's structure, behavior, or cognition is an adaptation is to assert that it has evolved through natural selection. But selection has occurred in the past, so how can we ever test such a statement? Aren't hypotheses about adaptation no better than Kipling's *Just-So Stories* (Gould and Lewontin 1979) like "The Elephant's Child," which explains that elephants have long trunks because a hungry crocodile once stretched the nose of a curious young elephant? Perhaps just-so stories can be concocted for most situations, but in fact serious ideas about adaptation are testable using direct observation and experiment, model building, or the comparative method. In the best possible cases, all three approaches can be used in a complementary way.

2.1.1   Testing present function

A character can serve a function in the present without having been selected for that function, that is, without being an adaptation for it. Function may change over evolutionary time (Williams 1966). To take a nonevolutionary analogy, in big cities like Rome or New York one sometimes sees groups of tourists all wearing identical hats. Hats are designed (adapted) to protect the head. Originally, tour organizers may have found it convenient to give out souvenir hats that were all the same, but that having happened, the hats now serve the function of allowing members of a group to identify one another and stick together.

Evolution and present-day function are not unrelated, however. Demonstrations that a behavior serves a particular function increase confidence in the hypothesis that that function has contributed to its evolution (Cuthill 2005). A classic example of an experimental test of current function comes from Tinbergen's (Tinbergen et al. 1963) studies of eggshell removal in gulls. Soon after their eggs hatch, black-headed gulls (*Larus ridibundus*) pick up the empty eggshells, fly off, and drop them some way from the nest. Why should a bird leave its vulnerable chicks for even a few seconds to engage in this behavior? Maybe the white insides of broken shells attract predators. To test this hypothesis, Tinbergen and his colleagues distributed single gull eggs around the dunes where the black-headed gulls nest. Some of these decoy eggs had broken eggshells placed nearby; others were isolated. The eggs near broken shells disappeared sooner, eaten by crows and herring gulls, than the less conspicuous isolated eggs (Figure 2.1). Thus removing broken eggshells from the nest functions to protect offspring from the predators found where the gulls nest. This suggests a comparative hypothesis: gull species nesting in areas without this same predation pressure should not remove empty shells from their nests. Kittiwakes (*Rissa tridactyla*) provide a natural test of this hypothesis. These gulls nest on small ledges on steep cliffs, inaccessible to most predators. Kittiwakes' behavior differs from that of ground-nesting gull species in

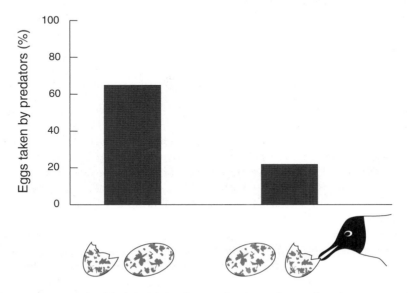

Figure 2.1. Proportion of 60 black-headed gull eggs taken by predators when the eggs were placed in the dunes near a broken eggshell (left bar) or alone, mimicking the situation in a nest from which the owner had removed broken shells (Tinbergen et al. 1963, Table 16).

several ways that can be seen as adaptations to nesting on cliffs (Cullen 1957). Among other things, they do not remove broken eggshells from their nests.

2.1.2   Adaptation as design

Many features of animals' structure and behavior seem so perfectly suited to their function that they seem unlikely to have arisen by chance. The eyes of vertebrates, the sonar of bats, the nest building and parental behavior of birds: all seem designed to accomplish their ends. Often, designs in biology are remarkably like what engineers would build to achieve the same goals. These considerations seem to compel the conclusion that intricate structures and behaviors like eyes, ears, and eggshell removal must be evolved adaptations. In pre-Darwinian days, however, such arguments from design were used as evidence for a divine creator (see Dennett 1995). Darwin's genius lay in deducing how natural causes produce the same end (Box 1.2).

A major contribution of behavioral ecology has been the use of formal optimality models to study adaptation (Chapter 11). Working out the optimal behavior for a given situation is a way of specifying the best design. One beauty of precise optimality arguments is that in principle they can be shown to be false. For example, the schooling behavior of fish had been thought to save energy for each individual by allowing it to swim in the eddies from its neighbors. However, detailed consideration of the hydrodynamics of swimming fish shows that in fact individuals of some species do not position themselves in so as to benefit as much as they could from the way the water is moved by other fish in the school. Thus, although hydrodynamic advantage may have contributed to the evolution of schooling behavior, other selective forces must have been involved (see Dawkins 1995). This is an example of how a model's predictions can fail because the modeler failed to take into account all the relevant factors. Such failures may lead to more complex models incorporating tradeoffs among competing selection pressures. In any case, evolution has not necessarily always produced the absolute optimum. Among other reasons, selection can work only on preexisting variations among individuals, including the variations thrown up by random mutations.

2.1.3   The comparative method

At most, experimental tests of function or observations of natural selection in action like the studies of Galapagos finches described in Chapter 1 can be done on only a few species. For a look at the broad sweep of evolution, at whether an important selection pressure has produced similar patterns across many species, the comparative method is essential. We have already met an informal example in the study of eggshell removal by gulls nesting in different habitats. In general, a comparative test of the adaptive value of a character consists of obtaining data from a large number of species and relating the degree to which they display the character with the degree to which the hypothesized selection pressure is present (Harvey and Pagel 1991; for an introduction see Sherry 2006). It must be applied together with good information about evolutionary relationships (i.e., *phylogeny*, Section 2.2) so similarity due to common selection pressures can be distinguished from similarity due to descent from common ancestors. Conclusions about adaptation may therefore change with changes in the amount and quality of information used to construct the associated phylogeny.

Animals live in all sorts of places and in an amazing variety of kinds of social groups. Some are solitary and cryptic except during mating. Others, like the wildebeest of the African plains or the caribou of the American Arctic, form enormous herds. Breeding may take place promiscuously, or between members of monogamous pairs or, among other possibilities, in a *polygynous* mating system, in which a few males may each control access to a harem of many females. Why have all these different social arrangements evolved? One approach to answering this question is to see if social structure can be related to ecology. Vulnerability to predators, what food a species eats and its spatial and seasonal distribution, the availability of nesting sites—all these and other variables can be related to social organization in a variety of animal groups. For example, in African ungulates, body size, habitat, group size, and mating system are related in the way shown in Table 2.1 (Jarman 1974). Smaller species need high-quality food because they have a high metabolic rate. They primarily seek fruits and buds in the forest. Because these foods are relatively sparse, the animals cannot form large groups, and there is no opportunity for one male to monopolize many females. Rather, the small-bodied forest species are found alone or in pairs. The large-bodied species graze relatively unselectively on the plains, on food that is locally very abundant but which varies seasonally in distribution with rainfall. Thus species like wildebeest tend to form large herds that migrate long distances with the seasons. Being in a group opens the opportunity for one male to monopolize several females. Hence, polygyny rather than monogamy tends to be found in the large grassland species.

Table 2.1 Relationship between ecology and social behavior in African ungulates. Reproduced from Krebs & Davies (1981); data from Jarman (1974).

| | Exemplary species | | Body weight (kg) | | | Habitat | |
	Diet	Group size	Reproductive unit			Antipredator behaviors	
Group I	Dikdik Duiker	3–60	Forest	Selective browsing: fruit, buds	1 or 2	Pair	Hide
Group II	Reedbuck Gerenuk	20–80	Brush, riverine grassland	Selective browsing or grazing	2 to 12	Male with harem	Hide, flee
Group III	Gazelle Kob Impala	20–250	Riverine woodland, dry grassland	Graze or browse	2 to 100	Males territorial in breeding season	Flee, hide in herd
Group IV	Wildebeest Hartebeest	90–270	Grassland	Graze	Up to 150 (thousands on migration)	Defence of females within herd	Hide in herd, flee
Group V	Eland Buffalo	300–900	Grassland	Graze unselectively	Up to 1000	Male dominance hierarchy in herd	Mass defence against predators

By itself, especially as summarized in a paragraph, this account seems like a *Just-So Story*. Several things make it much more than that. For one, a similar account can be given of social structure in other animal groups, including birds and primates (Cuthill 2005; Danchin, Giraldeau, and Cezilly 2008). This is what would be expected if social structure is the outcome of fundamental selection pressures like the distributions of food and predators and not just associated with ecology in ungulates by chance. For another, more detailed comparative analyses have tended to uphold the conclusions from categorical analyses like that summarized in Table 2.1. Consider one correlate of social structure, sexual dimorphism in body size, that is, the degree to which males and females are different sizes (Clutton-Brock and Harvey 1984). In a variety of animal groups, males tend to be about the same size as females in species that form breeding pairs, whereas males tend to be larger than females in polygynous species. One possible explanation of this relationship is that large males have an advantage in defending females from rival males. Among primates, polygynous species may live in one-male or multi-male groups. Each male dominates more females in one-male groups. Sexual dimorphism in primates, measured as ratio of male weight to female weight, is related to mating system just as this discussion predicts (Figure 2.2).

Results like those shown in Figure 2.2 and Table 2.1 must not be distorted by unequal degrees of relatedness among the species being considered. If the species within each ecological category are more closely related to each other than they are to species in other ecological categories, differences among categories could reflect descent from a common ancestor rather than common selection pressures. One way to deal with this problem is to look at different groups of species. For instance, the same relationship between sexual dimorphism and breeding system is found in several independently evolved animal groups, suggesting that it is indeed related to the degree to which males compete for females.

Although Figure 2.2 shows a significant positive relationship between sexual dimorphism in body size and number of females per male in the breeding group, the error bars indicate that considerable variation is still unaccounted for. Correlations between characters and ecology across large numbers of species almost always use data from many sources, and inevitably some data points will represent larger numbers of more careful observations than others. However, if enough species

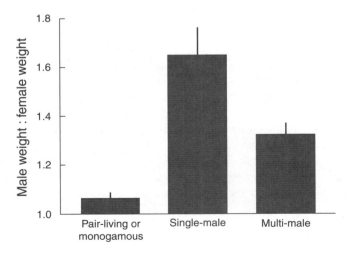

Figure 2.2. Body size dimorphism in primates, measured as the ratio of male to female body weight, as a function of whether the breeding group has a single male and female, a single male defending a group of females, or multiple males and females. Redrawn from Clutton-Brock and Harvey (1984) with permission.

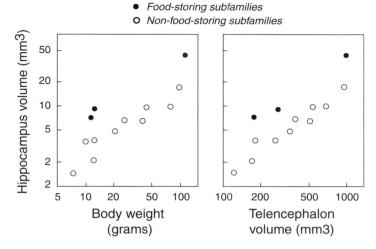

Figure 2.3. Hippocampal volume correlated with body weight (left panel) and volume of the telencephalon in birds. Redrawn from Sherry et al. (1989) with permission.

are sampled, random errors should balance each other out and genuine relationships reveal themselves. The variables examined also need to be good measures of the ecological factors being considered. For instance, ratio of females to males in the breeding group might not be the best measure of intermale competition, the factor hypothesized to favor large-bodied males, and body size is probably influenced by factors other than social structure, such as whether the animals live in trees or on the ground (Clutton-Brock and Harvey 1977).

Obvious exceptions to an overall relationship can be instructive. Figure 2.3 shows an example based on the *allometric* relationship among the sizes of body parts. Allometry refers to the principle that animals with bigger bodies have, on average, bigger body parts. A plot of the size of any structure against total body size has a characteristic slope, with most points clustered close to the overall regression line. In Figure 2.3 volume of the hippocampus, a brain structure important for memory, particularly spatial memory, in mammals and birds is plotted against body weight and against volume of the telencephalon (most of the rest of the brain) for a large number of genera of European birds. Three points stand out as being substantially above the overall regression lines indicating that three groups of birds have larger hippocampi than expected for their body and brain sizes. These all contain species that store food for the winter and retrieve it using long-lasting spatial memory. These and other data summarized in Section 2.4.2 indicate that food storing evolved together with a relatively large hippocampus.

2.2 Mapping phylogeny

Correlation is not evolutionary causation. The association between food storing and a relatively large hippocampus does not tell us about the sequence of events in evolution. Maybe food-storing species evolved an unusually large hippocampus for some unknown reason and it then allowed them to benefit from storing food. Or maybe rather than ask why some birds have such a large hippocampus relative to brain and body size we should be asking why other birds have such a small one (Deacon 1995). Such questions have to

Table 2.2

	Bird	Bat	Monkey
Wings?	Yes	Yes	No
Body Covering	Feathers	Fur	Fur
Reproduction	Lays Eggs	Live Young	Live Young
Lactates?	No	Yes	Yes

do with what ancestral species were like and how and why they changed, but suggestions of the answers to them can be found by looking at present-day species, given some reasonable assumptions about how evolution works. This is the study of phylogeny, or the reconstruction of the tree of life, the branching relationships among species during evolution (Stearns and Hoekstra 2005).

Suppose we have a bat, a bird, and a monkey. The bat is like the bird in having wings, but it is like the monkey in having fur instead of feathers, lactating, and giving birth to live young instead of laying eggs (Table 2.2). On the basis of these four characters, we would classify bats as more closely related to monkeys—that is, having a more recent common ancestor—than to birds because bats and monkeys have more characters in common. Moreover, although bats and birds both have wings, they differ embryologically and in details of structure. Thus they are *homoplasies* (or *analogies*), not *homologies,* that is, they have evolved from different ancestors and converged on a similar shape due to common selection pressures of an aerial way of life rather than being descended from a common winged ancestor. Differences between the bat's limbs and the monkey's reflect a third evolutionary outcome, *divergence* from a comparatively recent common (mammalian) ancestor (for further discussion see Papini 2002; Papini 2008).

Biological classification is hierarchical. Figure 2.4 shows three ways of representing the nested relationships among species. A phylogenetic tree represents the divergence among species over time. The times at which species diverged from an ancestral state can be tied down by examining the fossil record and/or from molecular evidence based on species differences in DNA and/or other molecules and assumptions about the rate of random mutation of DNA. Figure 2.5 shows the phylogeny of primates

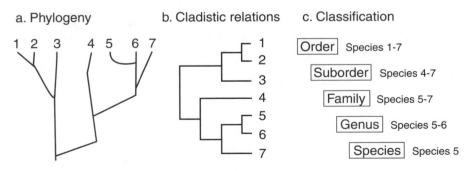

Figure 2.4. For seven fictitious species, the relationship between a phylogenetic tree (divergence as a function of time), a cladistic classification, and—for species 5—the traditional classification in terms of species, genus, and so forth. As an example of how to read panel b, species 1 and 2 share a character they do not share with species 3, while all three of them share a character not shared with species 4–7. Redrawn from Ridley (1993) with permission.

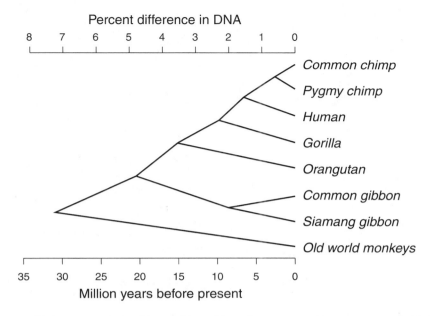

Percent difference in DNA

Figure 2.5. Phylogenetic relationships of old-world monkeys, apes, and humans as revealed by DNA hybridization. Greater similarity in DNA (top axis) indicates more recent divergence (bottom axis). Redrawn from Ridley (1993) with permission.

based on molecular evidence. Many diagrams of primate phylogenies betray our continuing belief that humans are the "highest" primates by putting them at the top (Hodos and Campbell 1969; Nee 2005). In fact, the arrangement of species branching from a particular node is largely arbitrary. What matters is the nodes (i.e., connections), not which ones are higher on the page or further to the right or left. Figure 2.5 puts chimpanzees at the top to emphasize the sequence in which the species diverged from common ancestors.

The classification of organisms into *clades*, or groups descended from a common ancestor, can be based on characters of present-day species alone. Nowadays an important part of this process is comparison of gene sequences and proteins and use of sophisticated statistical techniques that take into account large numbers of characters (see Pagel 1999). But the simple example in Table 2.2 is enough to show the logic of phylogenetic reconstruction. Without knowing anything about genes or the fossil record, we could infer from the table that bats and monkeys share an ancestor that had fur, gave birth to live young and lactated (i.e., a mammalian ancestor) that was not ancestral to birds. Such inferences rely on the notion that any particular evolutionary change is improbable. For a new species to evolve, an advantageous rather than a deleterious or lethal mutation has to occur and spread. It is therefore more likely that shared characteristics were present in a common ancestor than that they evolved several times independently. Representations of cladistic classification can display the characters that have changed as species diverged, as in Figure 2.6. Finally, although the classification of organisms into species, genera, families, and so on is also hierarchical, traditional classifications of species groups do not always correspond so closely to the other classifications as in Figure 2.4c.

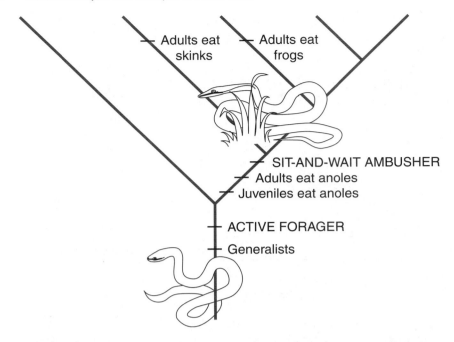

Figure 2.6. Cladogram for colubrid snakes on the island of Hispanola based on their feeding behavior. The species of interest (the four rightmost branches) and a comparison group of close relatives (the outgroup, left branch) all evolved from active generalist foragers. Evolutionary changes inferred from shared characters are indicated along the branches. Time is not explicitly represented in this type of diagram, unlike that in Figure 2.5. Redrawn from Brooks and McLennan (1991) with permission.

2.3   Evolution, cognition, and the structure of behavior

Studying cognition entails inferring mental organization from observing behavior, but behavior reflects sensory, motor, and motivational as well as cognitive mechanisms. This section introduces a general framework for thinking about the organization of behavior which is useful for thinking about how evolution affects behavior and cognition.

2.3.1   Behavior systems

Behavior is organized into functional systems like hunger, fear, and sexual behavior, called instincts by Tinbergen and other classical ethologists. These are hierarchical organizations of motor patterns that share some proximate causal factors (Timberlake 1994; Hogan 1994b). For example, an animal's hunger system includes the behavior patterns that change in frequency, intensity, or probability when it has been deprived of food and/or is in the presence of food. For a chicken, these might be walking around, scratching the ground, and pecking. A behavior system also includes relevant stimulus processing (perceptual) mechanisms and central mechanisms that coordinate external and internal inputs (Figure 2.7). In the case of the hunger system in a chicken, a central motivational mechanism integrates the bird's state of depletion or satiation with visual information to determine whether or not it will peck at what it

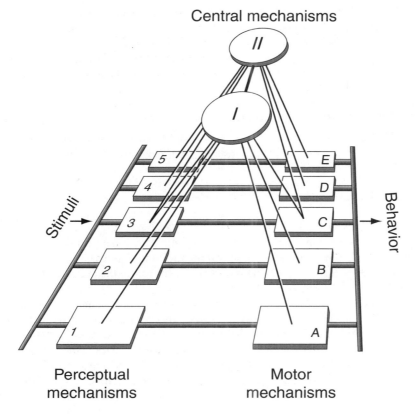

Central mechanisms

Stimuli

Behavior

Perceptual mechanisms

Motor mechanisms

Figure 2.7. The structure of behavior systems. Stimuli are processed by perceptual mechanisms (1–5) and may affect motor mechanisms directly, as in reflexes (horizontal lines) or through the mediation of central mechanisms, of which two (I and II) are indicated. Each interconnected set of perceptual, central, and motor mechanisms forms a behavior system, so two behavior systems are shown here. Some motor mechanisms, such as C, which might be walking or pecking, may belong to more than one behavior system. Redrawn from Hogan (1988) with permission.

sees (Hogan 1994b). Cognitive mechanisms are part of this organization, too. Whether the chicken pecks at the thing in front of it may be influenced by what it is attending to and past learning about the consequences of pecking.

As just described, behavior systems are defined causally (Hogan 1994b), in terms of internal and external causal factors rather than immediate outcome or apparent goal. However, the causal organization of behavior must make functional sense. An animal that ignored food while starving or approached predators rather than hiding or running away would be unlikely to have as many offspring as one that ate when hungry and fled from danger. Animals that ignore food when deprived or behave in a friendly manner toward predators have been weeded out by natural selection not because they are "too stupid" to forsee the dire consequences of their acts but because they leave fewer copies of their genes than do individuals whose motivational and cognitive mechanisms result—blindly—in their being better-nourished and less preyed upon. This relationship is depicted in Figure 2.8. Natural selection shapes cognition in an indirect way. Cognition—processing environmental information—results in behavior. That behavior has an immediate consequence such as ingesting

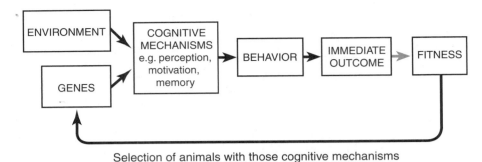

Figure 2.8. How cognition and behavior are shaped by natural selection. Adapted from Shettleworth (1987) with permission.

food, depositing sperm in a fertile female, strengthening a nest. In the long run, such consequences have a measurable impact on the individual's fitness and thereby on the representation of genes contributing to development of the mechanisms that generate that behavior.

With few exceptions, like nest-building and burrowing, behavior does not leave fossils. But the evolution of behavior can nevertheless be inferred from phylogeny, as indicated in Figure 2.6. In terms of the organization of behavior systems shown in Figure 2.7, species differences could evolve in sensory, motor, or central mechanisms. For instance, the range of energies detectable by the senses could expand or contract, new motor patterns could appear, and/or the central coordination of input and output could change. The evolution of behavior can be traced at a more detailed level, too. For instance, species differences in motor patterns may be analyzed into differences in muscular and skeletal anatomy and patterns of firing in nerve cells (Lauder and Reilly 1996). Species differences in visual sensitivity related to differences in the kind of light prevalent in different environments might be related to differences in photopigments and the genes for producing them (see Chapter 3).

The loss of bat-avoidance behavior by moths on Tahiti is an example of evolutionary change nicely accommodated by this way of thinking about behavior. The raison d'être for hearing in most moths is to avoid bats, which search for moths in the dark using ultrasonic cries. Accordingly, a moth's simple auditory system is tuned to ultrasonic frequencies because moths can avoid bats by dropping immediately to the ground when they hear one. Although bats have apparently never been present on the Pacific island of Tahiti, the auditory nerves of the moth species that arrived on Tahiti millions of years ago (*endemic* species) still fire to bat cries. Nevertheless, when bat cries were played to endemics in flight, they did not drop to the ground like individuals of more recently arrived species. Assuming that the endemics are still capable of altering their flight in response to other stimuli, this pattern of findings indicates that in the absence of selection the sensory input has been decoupled from the motor avoidance response (Fullard, Ratcliffe, and Soutar 2004).

Many morphological (i.e., structural) differences among species result from relatively small changes in developmental programs, that is, from changes in when specific genes are turned on and off (see Stearns and Hoekstra 2005). A speeding up or slowing down of growth in one part relative to others can result in dramatic

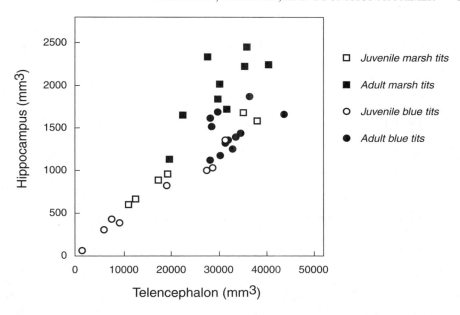

Figure 2.9. Growth of hippocampus and telencephalon (most of the rest of the brain) in marsh tits, a food-storing species, and blue tits, which do not store food. Redrawn from Healy, Clayton, and Krebs (1994) with permission.

changes in shape. The brains of food-storing birds provide one example related to cognition (Figure 2.9). In baby marsh tits (food-storers) and baby blue tits (non-storers), the whole brain grows rapidly in the first few weeks after hatching. At this stage, the hippocampus develops relative to the rest of the brain in the same way in both species. By around 6 weeks after hatching, when the babies are feeding themselves and the marsh tits are starting to store food, brain growth has slowed down. However, the marsh tits' hippocampus continues to grow, so that the typical food-storers' larger hippocampal size relative to the rest of the brain appears by the time memory for storage sites is needed (Healy, Clayton, and Krebs 1994). Magpies (food-storing corvides and jackdaws (nonstoring corvids) show the same pattern (Healy and Krebs 1993). In the case of marsh tits, experience using spatial memory also contributes to the species difference in hippocampus, but blue tits are not influenced by experience in the same way as marsh tits (Clayton 1995).

Darwin was deeply impressed by how behavior as well as structure could be artificially selected by animal breeders. And in *The Origin of Species* he speculated on how complex and intricate behaviors like the comb-building behaviors of honey bees could have evolved in small steps. Nowadays, genetic engineering can be used to demonstrate that particular genes contribute to particular behaviors or cognitive processes and to analyze the mechanisms by which they do so (Mayford, Abel, and Kandel 1995; Fitzpatrick et al. 2005). Natural selection can provide molecular geneticists with opportunities to dissect how genetic changes have produced species differences, including differences in cognition and behavior. Bringing together information derived from genetic engineering with phylogenies of real species offers exciting possibilities for research on the mechanisms of evolutionary change (see Fitzpatrick et al. 2005; Grant and Grant 2008).

2.3.2   Evolution and cognition

Most tests of adaptation mentioned in Section 2.1 involve comparing different species or groups of species: ground-nesting vs. cliff-nesting gulls, solitary vs. social species of ungulates, and so on. Naturally, any such comparison must be done carefully. For example, when correlating social group size and male body size, it is important to be sure the values going into the analysis are representative of the species and to take account of other variables that might be confounded with the variables of interest. Comparing cognition across species encounters its own particular difficulties, which largely arise from the fact that behavior is influenced by a host of processes that are not specifically cognitive. As a result, conclusions like "species A has more of ability X than species B" always need to be viewed critically. The same is true in comparisons of genetically manipulated animals. This section introduces some of the general problems in doing comparative research on cognition, taking as an example research on male-female differences in spatial memory in different species of rodents. This is not to imply that such problems have not been addressed in this area; as we will see, many have been dealt with rather well.

In many monogamous animals, the male and female occupy a territory together, whereas in some polygynous species females have relatively small territories where they rear their young, while males range over larger areas, visiting several different females for mating. These observations suggest that in monogamous species males and females need similar abilities to find their way around and remember the locations of resources in the pair's territory, whereas in polygynous species males need a better-developed ability to process and remember spatial information than do females. This hypothesis about the relationship between spatial cognition and mating system has inspired research on sex differences in brain and spatial cognition in several groups of rodents (Gaulin 1995; Jacobs 1995; Sherry 2006). It is arguably the most coherent and best-supported of several proposed evolutionary explanations for the sex differences in spatial cognition observed in a variety of mammals, including humans (see Jones, Braithwaite, and Healy 2003).

The specific hypothesis here is that males and females do not differ in spatial ability in monogamous species whereas there is a difference in favor of males in polygynous species. But to evaluate it, we cannot necessarily just test males and females of a number of different species all in the same way because a test standardized in terms of physical variables may affect different species differently. For instance, animals that become frightened and stay close to the walls in a big open space might take longer than bolder animals to learn to swim straight to the dry platform in the middle of a pool of water. Recent research on animal personality (Box 2.1) has provided plenty of evidence for stable within- and between-species differences in behavior that could influence the outcome of cognitive tests as this example suggests. If the animals are rewarded with food, we need to be sure all species are equally hungry and equally fond of the reward provided. If we compare them on discrimination learning, we need to know that they process the stimuli involved in the same way, that is, we need to know something about their sensory systems. Such considerations underline the importance of what Macphail (1982, 1987) called *contextual variables*. Within any species, many aspects of the experimental context, some much less obvious than timidity or reward size, can affect what animals do. Therefore, any species difference on a single task could reflect different effects of contextual variables on performance rather than the cognitive ability that performance is supposed to measure.

Box 2.1 Animal Personality?

Anyone who has had pets will know that animals seem to differ in characteristics such as boldness, aggressiveness, and sociability. In people these would be referred to as personality traits. For nonhuman species the term *behavioral syndromes* (Sih et al. 2004; Bell 2007) is often used to refer to the analogous observation that suites of related behaviors seem to vary together across individuals. In one very well studied case, for instance, wild great tits (*Parus major*) that are quickest to move through a novel environment tend to be quickest to explore a novel object and most aggressive toward conspecifics (Dingemanse and Reale 2005). In effect, human personality is also measured by behavior, even if only on paper-and-pencil tests, so *animal personality* (Dingemanse and Reale 2005) or *temperament* (Reale et al. 2007) is increasingly used in this comparatively new area of research in behavioral ecology. Candidates for behavioral evidence of a given characteristic such as boldness, aggressiveness, or sociability must be repeatable within tests of the same individual and correlated across related tests. Validating tests of animal personality is not always easy or straightforward, and methods for doing so are still debated (Miller, Garner, and Mench 2006). Nevertheless, with great tits and a few other species there is considerable evidence both that individual differences are heritable and that they show up in both behavior and reproductive success in the wild (Dingemanse and Reale 2005).

The existence of cross-situational individual differences in behaviors with fitness consequences creates difficulties for evolutionary models that assume all individuals exhibit the same range of variation in behavior. Strong personality traits might be maladaptive. For instance, an animal that is consistently shy may fail to discover new resources being exploited by its bolder conspecifics. How can two or more behavioral syndromes coexist in a species or population and why do they take the form they do? For example, why is boldness vs. shyness a dimension of individual difference in so many species? One proposal (Wolf et al. 2007) is that many aspects of animal personality represent a fundamental tradeoff between risk-seeking and risk-avoiding life history strategies. A bold, quick, aggressive approach to life can increase fitness by permitting early reproduction but it is also dangerous; less bold and risky behaviors delay reproduction, but they may have an advantage when conditions are relatively stable or when there will be more opportunities for reproduction in the future (i.e., when the time horizon is long). When the environment varies on an appropriate scale, both risk-seeking and risk-avoiding personality types can persist because either one can be successful depending on circumstances (Dingemanse and Reale 2005; Wolf et al. 2007).

Research on animal personality has implications for comparative research on cognition because many of the differences that have been documented among individuals, populations, or species involve behaviors that often play a role in cognitive tests. One obvious example is that because willingness to move around in a novel environment and explore the things in it is a prerequisite for many traditional tests of learning, boldness or tendency to explore may predict fast acquisition of new tasks even though it is not necessarily correlated with learning ability as such. As another example, fearfulness (Miller et al. 2006) might be positively correlated with speed of acquisition in an avoidance task, but negatively correlated in a maze-learning task. Attempts to test general learning ability, or animal IQ (if there is such a thing), have controlled for such motivational or behavioral predispositions by using a variety of tasks, as done by Matzel and colleagues with mice (Matzel et al. 2003).

One proposed solution to this problem is *systematic variation* (Bitterman 1965). This means testing the animals under several values of relevant contextual variables. For instance, the difficulty of the task should be varied over a wide range. Gaulin and Fitzgerald (1989) did just that by using seven different mazes to compare spatial learning in monogamous prairie voles (*Microtus ochorogaster*) and polygynous meadow voles (*M. pennsylvanicus*). Meadow vole males performed better than meadow vole females on all the mazes, but, as predicted, there was no sex difference in the prairie voles (Figure 2.10). Importantly, the mazes seem to be a fair test of species differences in that both species score about the same on average on any given maze. They are also not so hard that most animals fail or so easy that everyone does perfectly, which is important because "floor" or "ceiling" effects, respectively, could obscure group differences.

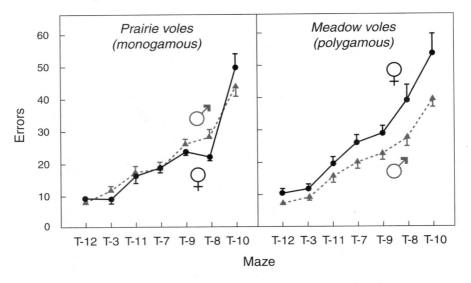

Figure 2.10. Number of errors made by male and female voles of two species in a series of increasingly difficult mazes. Data from Gaulin and Fitzgerald (1989) redrawn from Gaulin (1995) with permission.

Systematic variation has two sides. In cases like that originally discussed by Bitterman (1965), one species fails to show some effect shown by another or shows it to a much smaller degree. Clearly, if it is already known that the strength of this effect in species that show it is influenced by some contextual variable, then this same variable should be manipulated with the second species to be sure it was not just at an unfavorable level initially. Here, systematic variation amounts to trying to reject the null hypothesis that no factor other than differences in cognition is responsible for differences in performance (Kamil 1988). To return to our case study, it might be suggested that sex differences in activity are responsible for sex differences in performance in spatial tasks. This possibility has been rendered implausible by showing that males' and females' activity levels are similar under a range of conditions (Gaulin, FitzGerald, and Wartell 1990). But a skeptic might then suggest another confounding factor, further systematic variation would have to be done, and so on ad infinitum. Kamil's proposed solution to this problem is, instead of systematically varying factors within a given task, to vary the tasks. For instance, if food-storing and nonstoring species differ in ability to process and remember spatial information, these differences ought to be detectable in a variety of different spatial tasks. There may of course be tasks or species for which contextual variables are overwhelmingly important, but if enough tasks are used, the results should converge on a single conclusion. Kamil and his colleagues have used this approach with considerable success to compare memory for spatial information in food-storing vs. nonstoring species of birds (Box 1.4; Chapter 7).

The other side of systematic variation is emphasized by Papini (2008): if an independent variable affects species in the same way, even if their levels of performance generally differ quantitatively, this is evidence for a shared process. Figure 2.10 provides an example. Although male meadow voles perform better than females, their errors still increase with maze complexity. Systematic variation appears frequently throughout this book as a way to discover whether very different species, exhibiting behaviors as different as speaking vs. pressing a key vs. digging up a worm, have access to the same kinds of cognitive processes. The tests of blindsight in monkeys described in Box 1.1 are an example. This approach is also, as in Chapter 7, referred to as testing for functional similarity. Most importantly, examples of what can be learned from systematic variation underline the principle that conclusions about species differences in cognition must always be based on more than a single test.

Ideally, a thorough comparative test of an ecological hypothesis includes tests on which the species are predicted not to differ, or—even better—to differ in the opposite direction. Such tests can help to rule out the possibility that one group performs better than another because of some general factor like how well they adjust to the lab. In food-storing species of corvids (the crow family, including jays and nutcrackers; Box 1.4), some species are highly social while others are not. Therefore, the pattern of species differences in social cognition may differ from that in spatial cognition (Balda and Kamil 2006). Sex differences in spatial behavior related to space use in the wild may be present only in the breeding season (Galea et al. 1994; Sherry 2006). Such seasonal or developmental changes within individuals of the same species offer excellent opportunities for testing adaptive relationships among cognition, brain, and natural behavior with minimal confounds from contextual variables. An example is the comparison of spatial and other kinds of memory in white-footed mice exposed to summerlike vs. winterlike photoperiods (Pyter, Reader, and Nelson 2005). However, even comparisons within a species may be subject to motivational or other confounds. For example, the time available for feeding may differ when animals live in days of different lengths, and/or the animals in short days may reduce their activity or metabolic rate.

A general problem with applying the comparative method to behavior and cognition is getting enough independent comparisons. One solution to the practical difficulties of testing large numbers of species is to build up a sample gradually by comparing two species at a time, in this case one monogamous species with one closely related polygynous species, but we need to be able to find a sufficient number of lineages in which monogamy arose separately. Research relating spatial ability to mating systems has been done on, among other rodents, voles (*Microtus*) and mice (*Peromyscus*), and of course the hypothesis could also be tested on birds with appropriate mating systems (Jones, Braithwaite, and Healy 2003).

Exceptional spatial ability may be associated with other exceptional demands on spatial learning and/or memory in the wild. For instance, birds that migrate might be expected to use memory and spatial learning more than relatively sedentary populations, not necessarily because they actually need learning to migrate, but because they need to acquire spatial and other information about each of the places where they spend a few months at the ends of their travels, and perhaps at stopovers along the way. They might also form long-term memories for the areas where they regularly spend part of the year, so as not to waste time relearning their stable features. There is some evidence consistent with this hypothesis (e.g., Cristol et al. 2003; Mettke-Hofmann and Gwinner 2003). Not only amount but kind of spatial learning might be expected to be associated with different ecological demands. For example, individuals living in different kinds of habitats might rely on different kinds of spatial cues. In one test of this notion, Odling-Smee and Braithwaite (2003) found that stickleback fish from ponds relied more on landmarks than fish of the same species from fast-moving streams.

2.4   Evolution and the brain

2.4.1   Patterns of vertebrate brain evolution

To look for patterns in a large sample of species, it is a lot easier to measure brains than to measure behavior and infer cognitive structures. As a result, compared to what we know about the distribution of any cognitive ability across the animal kingdom, we know vastly more about the brain, at least in vertebrates. Figure 2.11 shows the relationship of brain weight to body weight in the major groups of vertebrates. The polygons enclosing data from each taxonomic group (*taxon*) indicate that brain size can vary considerably even for animals of a given group with a given body weight, as illustrated for mammals in teh lower panel of Figure 2.11. There is a trend for larger brains during vertebrate evolution. For instance, birds are thought to have evolved from a primitive reptile, and the polygon for birds is entirely above that for reptiles, indicating that in general birds have larger brains than reptiles of equivalent size. On the whole, mammals have the largest brains for their body weight, but small mammals overlap considerably with birds. Within mammals, humans are the species farthest in perpendicular distance above the group regression line (details of each taxon in Chapter 4 of Striedter 2005).

Within a lineage, why do some species have larger brains relative to their body weights than others? Brains are metabolically costly to maintain (Laughlin 2001), so there must be some advantage to having a large brain. Not surprisingly, hypotheses about the function of relatively large brains have focused on the assumed connection between brains and cognitive abilities. For instance, the "foraging intelligence hypothesis" of primate brain size proposes that fruit-eating species need excellent spatial and temporal learning abilities for tracking the locations and ripeness of items that are scattered widely throughout the forest whereas leaf eaters do not need such abilities. The "social intelligence hypothesis" (Chapter 12) suggests that animals living in large groups in which individuals have differentiated and ever-changing social roles need to keep track of the identities of large numbers of individuals and their interactions. Tests of the various versions of these hypotheses have relied on comparative studies relating primates' brain size to proxies for cognitive abilities such as type of foraging niche or social group size (review in van Schaik and Deaner 2003; Healy and Rowe 2007).

Among birds, parrots and corvids have the biggest brains for their body sizes. As we will see, some corvids may have social and tool-using abilities comparable to those of some primates. These, along with relatively large brains, appear to represent convergent evolution in separate vertebrate lineages (Emery and Clayton 2004). Relatively new are the comparative studies of primates and birds described in Box 2.2 indicating that brain size is related to propensity for innovation. To the extent that foraging on ephemeral food sources, managing social relations, and acquiring novel behaviors call on common abilities, these explanations for the evolution of large brains need not be mutually exclusive (Striedter 2005). In any case, most accounts of relative brain size in terms of complex behaviors are still largely speculative pending more direct evidence about the neural substrates of the behaviors in question (Healy and Rowe 2007).

The foregoing discussion addresses the whole brain, but the relationship of relative hippocampus size to food-storing in birds depicted in Figure 2.3 suggests that maybe we should be looking at how individual parts of the brain evolve in association with specific behaviors or ecological variables. Whether brain

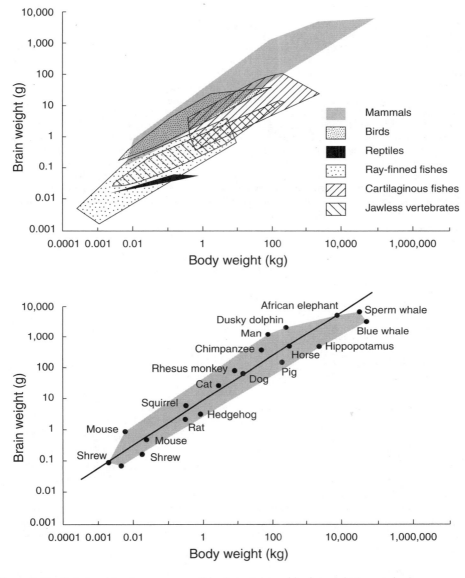

Figure 2.11. Relationships between overall brain weight and body weight in vertebrates, on logarithmic scales. Top panel: data for major groups as the minimal polygon which encloses each one's data. Redrawn from Striedter (2005) with permission. Lower panel: data for selected species of mammals surrounded by its minimal polygon. The dark slanted line is the overall regression line for mammals. The perpendicular distance of a species' data from this line (formally, the *residual*) is a measure of how much it deviates from the average allometric relationship for mammals. Redrawn from Roth and Dicke (2005) with permission.

evolution is *concerted* or *mosaic,* that is, whether brain size evolves as a whole or through selection on particular parts, is a contentious question in comparative neuroanatomy (see discussions accompanying Finlay, Darlington, and Nicastro 2001 and Striedter 2006). Figure 2.11 is consistent with concerted evolution because it shows an evolutionary trend toward larger brains.

Box 2.2 Innovation and the Brain: General Intelligence after All?

About ten years ago, Louis Lefebvre and colleagues (Lefebvre et al. 1997; reviews in Reader and Laland 2003; Lefebvre, Reader, and Sol 2004) suggested that the limitations of laboratory studies for obtaining data on cognition in large numbers of species could be overcome by looking at the many reports of innovative behavior in natural history journals. Such innovations usually take the form of foraging behaviors described as novel or unusual for the species, such as eating a new food or using a new foraging technique. For example, magpies might be seen digging up potatoes (Lefebvre et al. 1997). Raw frequencies of such reports can be corrected for obvious biases such the general rate of publication on those species and then combined for groups of species, correcting for number of species per group, to get a measure of innovation rate for, for example, all corvids, parrots, or pigeons (see Figure B2.2 for details). This measure of "intelligence" in the field correlates with available data on learning in the same species in the laboratory (Lefebvre, Reader, and Sol 2004). An alternative approach (Ramsey, Bastian, and van Schaik 2007) is to infer that innovation must have occurred when populations of a species differ in ways that cannot be ascribed to local ecological factors (cf. discussion of animal cultures in Section 13.5). Either way, an innovation is a *product* of some unidentified behavioral process(es). These processes are generally assumed to be similar to those that contribute to human intelligence or inventiveness.

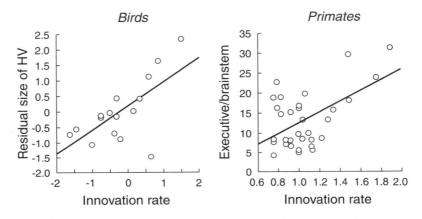

Figure B2.2. Relationship between size of parts of the brain and innovation. For birds (left), residuals (see Figure 2.11) are used as a relative measure of both innovation rate and size of the neostriatum plus hyperstriatum ventrale (HV), areas involved in learning. For primates (right) the "executive brain" (see text) is measured relative to volume of the brainstem. Innovation rates are based on the number of innovations reported for a species relative to overall number of articles about that species (details in Reader and Laland 2002). Redrawn from Lefebvre, Reader, and Sol (2004) with permission.

Analysis of hundreds of reports of innovative feeding behaviors in birds shows that rate of innovation in a bird order is correlated with overall size of the brain and with size of the forebrain (Figure B2.2). Innovation rate is potentially significant for evolution because it also predicts whether a species will become established when introduced into a new environment (Sol et al. 2005). Data from primates examined in a similar way also show a positive relationship between innovation rate, as well as tool using and social learning frequency, and "executive brain ratio" (volume of the forebrain and striatum relative to the brainstem, Figure B2.2; Reader and Laland 2002; see also Reader and Laland 2003). The association of innovation or general behavioral plasticity with overall brain size seems more consistent with the old assumption (Chapter 1) that animals have a "general intelligence" than with the idea that cognition and the brain are largely modular (Box 2.3; Lefebvre and Bolhuis 2003). These ideas are not necessarily incompatible. For humans, it has been suggested that IQ measures a flexibility needed for dealing with evolutionarily novel situations that is not afforded by coexisting modular systems (Kanazawa 2004).

Innovation may be related to overall brain size precisely because innovative behavior is a heterogeneous category any instance of which involves one or more of a concatenation of factors. Indeed, large brain areas such as forebrain that are associated with innovation rate are involved in multiple behaviors (Sherry 2006; Healy and Rowe 2007). For example, to profit from a chance encounter with a new way of getting food, it helps to be able to learn quickly, presumably using a rather general ability to associate events and their consequences. But to do something new in the first place, especially if that requires interacting with a new object, food, or location, it helps to be not too neophobic, and in fact Webster and Lefebvre (2001) showed in a series of laboratory and field tests that of the species of birds they studied, those rated as most innovative were indeed least neophobic. Thus part of innovativeness may be general boldness, perhaps an aspect of personality (Box 2.1), rather than cognitive ability per se. Similarly, general mechanisms of reinforcement may explain why innovative feeding behaviors may persist and spread when food is scarce. For these sorts of reasons, it seems unlikely that innovations are the products of a single specialized cognitive process.

Historically, brain evolution was thought to be a matter of adding new, more advanced, structures to primitive ones in a linear fashion leading up to primates and humans. Hence the prevalence of prefixes such as "paleo," "neo," and "archeo" to label structures in traditional brain anatomy. It is now recognized that all vertebrate brains have the same basic parts, although their relative sizes and detailed structures are characteristic of each vertebrate group (Avian Brain Nomenclature Consortium 2005). Within a lineage, larger brains are not just scaled up versions of smaller ones. Bigger brains need a more modular organization (Box 2.3), and this well might lead to cognitive differences between big- and small-brained species within a group, for example, primates vs. rodents or parrots vs. canaries. The proportion of the brain occupied by particular structures such as the neocortex also tends to differ in a systematic way in larger-brained species, apparently consistent with mosaic evolution. However, on one theory (Finlay, Darlington, and Nicastro 2001) most of this variation is consistent with concerted evolution because it reflects the way in which common processes of very early brain development produce larger brains. Indeed, a recent survey (Striedter 2005) finds that the majority of the evidence is consistent with concerted evolution in that within a given taxon, and after taking into account developmental constraints, the relative size of a given structure generally does not show very dramatic deviations across species. "Not very dramatic" means not more that about a 2- or 3-fold difference in size relative to the rest of the brain. Within this context, the hippocampus–food storing story is "wonderful" (Striedter 2005, 173) as a potential example of at least mildly mosaic evolution. It is also an instructive case study of the challenges of trying to connect brain, behavior, and cognition in a rigorous way.

2.4.2   Hippocampus and food storing in birds

The *principle of proper mass* (Jerison 1973) as a tenet of comparative neuroanatomy says that the more important a function is for a species, the more brain area will be devoted to it. This principle is most sensibly interpreted as applying to the size of a structure relative to other parts of the brain in comparisons of reasonably close relatives (Striedter 2005). Sensory and motor areas provide some spectacular

Box 2.3 Modularity in Development, Evolution, and Cognitive Science

Anyone who has written a computer program or assembled a chest of drawers from IKEA is acquainted with modularity. Modularity, or organization as somewhat independently functioning but interconnected subunits, is a fundamental aspect of complex systems (Simon 1962). Indeed, Simon (1962) argued vividly that complex systems cannot develop or function effectively unless they consist of a hierarchical organization of parts. Not surprisingly then, it has been claimed that modularity "is a universal property of living things and a fundamental determinant of how they evolve." (West-Eberhard 2003, 56; see also Schlosser and Wagner 2004). Hogan's (1994a) definition of a behavior system (Section 2.3.1) as a "set of sensory, motor and central mechanisms that function as a unit in some situations" could be taken to suggest that animal behavior as a whole is modular, and indeed, the discussion by West-Eberhard just cited goes on to include modularity of behavior and to connect modularity at all levels to fundamental processes in development. In turn, developmental modules may function as basic units of evolution (Schlosser and Wagner 2004; Callebaut and Rasskin-Gutman 2005).

Notwithstanding its status as a basic feature of biological systems, *modularity* is fraught with debate and disagreement in cognitive science. Most of this centers on the properties of "the modularity of mind" proposed by Jerry Fodor (1983) in his book of the same name (Barrett and Kurzban 2006). In Fodor's sense, a module is among other things an informationally encapsulated perceptual system: it acts exclusively on a restricted kind of input unconsciously but in an apparently intelligent way. What this means is illustrated in a simple way by the Muller-Lyer illusion

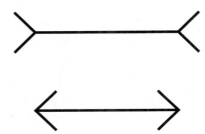

Figure B2.3. The Muller-Lyer illusion.

(Figure B2.3). The upper line appears longer than the lower one, presumably because some feature of the drawing is a trigger (Gigerenzer 1997) for a visual perceptual system that makes implicit inferences about the relative sizes and distances of objects. *Encapsulation* refers to the fact that the system is impenetrable to information from other systems, in this case the "higher level" information obtained from measurement: measuring the lines and discovering that they are equal does not abolish the illusion. Modules are *domain specific* in that the computations or "rules of operation" (Sherry and Schacter 1987) implicit in the output of a particular module are applied only to that module's own limited kind of information. Fodor also suggested that cognitive modules are primarily perceptual, as in the example of the Muller-Lyer illusion, whereas central processing, that is, reasoning and decision making, is not. In addition, he suggested (but did not necessarily require, Coltheart 1999) that modules are fast, hardwired (i.e., neurally specific), and innately specified.

Many of the debates about cognitive modularity (e.g., Bolhuis and Macphail 2001; Flombaum, Santos, and Hauser 2002; Cheng and Newcombe 2005) seem to arise from a fixation on whether particular candidate cognitive modules meet all of Fodor's strict criteria (which are not always easy to decipher) rather than on the question, to what extent and in what ways, if any, is cognition modular? If instead we take domain-specificity of cognitive processing as definitional, the extent to which any candidate modular cognitive mechanism is central, is entirely encapsulated, depends on experience for its development, relies on a localized area in the brain, and so forth, becomes an empirical question (Coltheart 1999; Barrett and Kurzban 2006). Functionally modular cognitive mechanisms need not be associated with localized brain processes or be comparatively independent of experience for their development (for an extended discussion see Barrett and Kurzban 2006; Bateson and Mameli 2007). As we will see, extracting and storing information from the flow of events does not follow the same rules for all types of events, and thus learning mechanisms, (or memory systems, Sherry and Schacter 1987) are to some extent domain specific, that is, modular (Gallistel 1998; Shettleworth 2000; Gallistel 2003). Particularly good examples come from learning about space, time, and number (Chapters 8–10).

This is not to say that the concept of modularity is unproblematical. For example, if we identify a module as a domain-specific kind of information processing, how do we distinguish domains or a "kinds of information processing"? Evolutionary psychologists have promoted the metaphor of the mind as a Swiss Army knife, that is, a general-purpose tool made up entirely of special-purpose devices. But is there a module for everything? If a cheater-detection module (Chapter 12), or a face-processing module (Kanwisher 2006), why not hundreds of other modules beside (Fodor 2001; Buller 2005)? In learning theory the modularity debate takes the form of a debate about adaptive specializations *versus* general processes of learning (Section 2.5.2), but forthcoming chapters provide illustrations of how association formation is not the only way of acquiring information. At the same time, however, many candidate modular learning and memory systems share some fairly general properties such as sensitivity to duration and frequency of events. Thus modularity should not be emphasized at the expense of common features or connectedness. If nothing else, candidate modules are connected by virtue of being contained within the same individual. Modules may share sensory input systems, and, no matter how specific the triggering information, decision making, and behavioral output of a modular cognitive subsystem, central decision making of some sort is needed to set the animal's priorities for action. West-Eberhard (2003) recommends keeping the focus on connectedness and modularity at the same time by eschewing the term *module* and referring instead to developmental systems as more or less modular (see also Callebaut and Rasskin-Gutman 2005). Perhaps this recommendation can be applied to cognitive modularity as well.

illustrations. For instance, the superior colliculus, a visual processing area, is nine times larger in a 13-lined ground squirrel (a diurnal species) than in a laboratory rat (nocturnal), and in the blind mole rat, which spends its life underground, it is 38 times smaller than in a hamster. In the very dextrous raccoon, the sensory and motor areas devoted to the paws are greatly enlarged compared to those in other nonprimates (see Streidter 2005). Although these examples are exceptional in quantitative terms, because sensory systems are clearly evolved to allow each species to discriminate the stimuli most important to it (Chapter 3) it is not surprising to find sensory specializations reflected in species-specific tweakings of sensory organs and associated brain areas. However, suggestions that an analogous principle applies to cognition and the brain—in particular to an association between demand for spatial memory in the wild and size of the hippocampus— have been surprisingly controversial (Bolhuis and Macphail 2001; Macphail and Bolhuis 2001; Bolhuis 2005). Cognition is surely not exempt from evolutionary processes, so why should this be?

Figure 2.3 shows that among North American families of birds the three families with food-storing species all have, on average, larger hippocampi than expected for the size of the rest of their brains. The relationship between food storing and performance in tests of spatial memory is discussed in Chapter 7; here we delve into the relationship between food storing and hippocampus suggested by Figure 2.3. One can ask a number of questions about it. For example, what exactly does a bigger relative hippocampus consist of in neuroanatomical terms? How does a comparatively large hippocampus impact on the rest of the brain? How does it improve ability to retrieve stored food? For instance does a relatively large hippo-campus increase the capacity or the durability of memory? These questions are still largely unanswered (see Bolhuis 2005), but some progress has been made in more detailed application of the comparative method to test the basic relationship shown in the figure.

Figure 2.3 classifies birds simply as food-storing or not, but in fact dependence on stored food varies considerably within both parids and corvids. For example, the Clark's nutcracker (Box 1.4) stores one type of food, pinyon pine seeds, very intensely during late summer and depends on its stores throughout the winter. The jackdaw, another corvid, does not store at all, and some other corvids store only moderately. Similarly, the great tit and blue tit do not store, whereas the willow tit and black capped chickadee store a great deal. These variations suggest looking within families at hippocampal volume as a function of dependence on storing. This has been done a number of times for both corvids and parids, with results coming out first one way (e.g., Hampton et al. 1995; Basil et al. 1996) and then another (Brodin and Lundborg 2003) as successive analyses have been more and more refined. It turns out that, for unexplained reasons, North American corvids and parids tend to have smaller hippocampi than European species, but when this continent effect is controlled for in cross-species comparisons, relative hippocampus size does correlate with food hoarding status in both corvids and parids (Lucas et al. 2004; Healy, de Kort, and Clayton 2005). Birds that store a lot also tend to have bigger brains overall than expected for their body size, perhaps reflecting sensory or motor specializations in behaviors for storing and retrieving food (Garamszegi and Eens 2004).

These analyses have all assumed that each species fits into a single category of hoarding intensity. However, some food storers such as black-capped chickadees have a very wide distribution, from rather moderate climates to areas with severe winters. One might expect differences between populations in such species. Accordingly, when chickadees from Alaska are compared to those from the lowlands of Colorado in tests in the laboratory, the Alaska birds store more, show better spatial but not color memory, and have larger hippocampi relative to brain size (Pravosudov and Clayton 2002). Since the birds in this study were taken from the wild, it is not known whether this hippocampal difference is present early in development or results from differences in food hoarding or other experiences in the wild. There are also many unanswered questions about details of hoarding-related changes in the brains of the chickadees in this and related studies (Bolhuis 2005; Sherry 2006).

Research on food-storing birds is but one set of tests of the more general hypothesis that spatial memory and hippocampus size should be related to demands on spatial memory in the wild (Sherry, Jacobs, and Gaulin 1992). Much of the work relating spatial learning and memory to territory size and migration discussed in Section 2.3.2 includes studies of the hippocampus (see Sherry 2006). An example involving sex differences comes from cowbirds. The females of several species of cowbirds lay their eggs in other birds' nests (i.e., they are nest parasites). The females of the brown-headed cowbird (*Molothrus ater*), a North American species, spend a good deal of their time in the breeding season prospecting for nests where potential hosts are about to lay. They need to remember the locations of many nests so as to be able to deposit an egg quickly when the host parent is absent at just the right time in its breeding cycle. Male brown headed cowbirds share none of this work, so they might be expected to have smaller hippocampi than females. And indeed the predicted sex difference is found for hippocampus relative to the rest of the brain in cowbirds, whereas there is no sex difference in two closely related species that are not nest parasites (Sherry et al. 1993). Making this story even more interesting, three other species of cowbirds are found in Argentina, only one of which behaves like the brown headed cowbird. In another, male and female prospect for nests together, and the third is not a nest parasite. Hippocampi of these three species show the pattern of species and sex differences in relative size predicted from the notion that participating in finding host nests requires exceptional memory (Reboreda, Clayton, and Kacelnik 1996). However, unlike the examples involving food storing or territory size, there is as yet little information on spatial memory in any of these birds in standardized laboratory tests (see Sherry 2006).

2.5   What does all this have to do with comparative psychology?

2.5.1   Function and mechanism and the comparative method

The kind of research summarized in the last section was dubbed *neuroecology* by Bolhuis and Macphail (2001). It has been criticized by these authors (see also Macphail and Bolhuis 2001; Bolhuis 2005) for supposedly confusing answers to Tinbergen's question about mechanism (e.g., how does cognition or the hippocampus work?) with answers to the question about function (e.g., what is spatial memory or the hippocampus good for?). This theoretical critique has tended to be combined with a defense of the overwhelming role of general processes in learning and memory and/ or with claims that hippocampus, food-storing, and spatial memory are at best only weakly related.

Clearly, correlating features of the brain with food storing or any other ecologically relevant behavior does not show us directly *how* the brain works but rather what it allows the animal to do. Nevertheless, knowing what something does can provide valuable clues as to how it works. Figure 2.12 is an example borrowed from Richerson and Boyd (2005). To quote Sherry (2005, 449), "Causal explanations must meet design criteria that are set by the function of behavior." Therefore, the study of adaptation (or current function), with which we began this chapter, has a role in the study of cognition and the brain. A critical application of the comparative method–a solid data set with many cases of independent evolution and checks that other areas of the brain are not also correlated with the same behavior or ecological factor—provides strong evidence that particular behavioral and neural characters evolved together. Additional data could perhaps give us a picture of the sequence of events in evolution. For example, de Kort and Clayton (2006) suggest that a phylogeny of corvids shows ancestral corvids were moderate cachers, and therefore that food caching has become more intense in some species while being lost in others. And of course the correlational evidence characteristic of the comparative method is rarely interpreted in isolation. For example, behavioral and lesion studies of individual species clearly show that the hippocampus is involved in spatial memory and cache retrieval. In the example in Box 2.2, we know very little about what innovativeness or behavioral flexibility means in terms of specific cognitive and brain mechanisms, so this is a case in which findings from the comparative method may suggest new kinds of naturalistic tasks that could be used to compare species behaviorally.

The idea that cognitive science can advance by analyzing the information processing tasks that organisms are designed to do has been profitably applied to the study of perception (Marr 1982; Shepard 1994). Among the most prolific and eloquent proponents of the view that thinking about the evolved function of cognition is the best way to understand how it works are the evolutionary psychologists Leda Cosmides and John Tooby (e.g., Cosmides and Tooby 1995; Tooby and Cosmides 1995). One prediction of this adaptationist point of view is that distinguishable cognitive mechanisms or modules (Box 2.3) will evolve whenever the information-processing problems a species has to solve require different, functionally incompatible, kinds of computations (Sherry and Schacter 1987). These modules will be

Figure 2.12. What is this? For the answer, see Figure 2.14 at the end of the chapter.

domain-specific, that is, each one will operate only on a restricted appropriate set of inputs, for example information about physical causation, time, space, or social relationships (see Gallistel 1998; Shettleworth 2000).

A second key prediction of the adaptationist viewpoint is no organism is the proverbial tabula rasa, or blank slate. Rather, animals' nervous systems are preorganized to process information in species-appropriate ways. Not only such specialized learning abilities as bird song (Chapter 1) but also associative learning, memory storage, attention, and problem solving as well as perception are matched to specific environmental requirements. Thus, cognitive scientists should be seeking to understand the structure of information-processing in terms of the structure of the world. For example, Cosmides (1989) claims that the ability to solve the Wason selection task, a logical problem, reflects an ability that was selected because it helped in detecting cheaters on social contracts. This notion predicts that people should reach the logically correct solution more often with problems about detecting cheaters than with formally identical problems about other material. Although many data are consistent with this hypothesis, it has not gone unchallenged (Chapter 12). The same kind of argument has been applied to experimental tests of the adaptive value of Pavlovian conditioned responding (Chapter 4). Such research is implicitly based on the argument from design: "X appears to be designed specifically to do Y; if it is, then animals with X should be better at Y than at some superficially similar but adaptively irrelevant task, Z."

The evolutionary psychologists' approach is essentially the same as the approach to cognition taken in this book. However, it faces several problems. Some stem from the indirectness of the relationship between cognition and fitness depicted in Figure 2.7. As Lehrman put it, "Nature selects for outcomes, not processes of development" (Lehrman 1970; Shettleworth 1983; Rozin and Schull 1988). Function does not uniquely determine the details of causation (Hogan 1994a; Bolhuis 2005). For instance, if the adaptive problem solved by eggshell removal is reducing predation, why didn't gulls evolve eggshells that were cryptically colored inside? The answer to this sort of question may lie in constraints from other aspects of the species' biology. The way in which eggshells are produced in the gull's oviduct may not readily allow for a change in the color of their interior, whereas gulls need motor patterns for picking things up and carrying them in foraging and nestbuilding, and these could be used equally well to carry eggshells. To take an example from cognition, many animals need to be able to return to a home to care for their young or to gain protection from predators. Thus they need a cognitive device for remembering and relocating places, but its details may differ from species to species. For example, dead reckoning (path integration) is accomplished very differently by rats and ants (Chapter 8). Similarly, because animals are selected to care for their own offspring rather than unrelated young, species with parental care must have mechanisms for recognizing their own offspring, in some sense. This can mean nothing more sophisticated than spending a couple of weeks stuffing food into any gaping mouth in your nest, but animals with young that run around while their parents are still feeding them need another mechanism, such as mutual learning of identifying cues. Thus although the prediction that offspring should be favored does not tell us how a particular species recognizes its young, a closer look at the species' biology may make functional sense of the mechanisms by which it does so. Conversely, identifying the function of a process discovered in the laboratory can raise new mechanistic questions that would not have been asked otherwise (Sherry 2005).

2.5.2   Adaptive specializations and general processes

If an ability is an adaptation to certain ecological requirements, it should vary quantitatively across species with those requirements. More spatial information to process means more capacious spatial memory (section 2.3.2); reliance on olfaction for foraging at night means relatively bigger olfactory bulbs (in birds anyway, see Healy and Guilford 1990); more complex social groups may mean better-developed social cognition (Chapter 12). These statements describe adaptive specializations of characters that species share. Such variations are readily observed in characters like beaks in birds (Figure 2.13). A bird that drinks nectar needs a long narrow beak, one that lives on hard seeds needs a beak like a nutcracker, one that tears flesh needs a hooked beak. Of course such changes are rarely confined to a single character but must be accompanied by adaptations of the digestive system, prey-catching behavior, habitat preference, and so on. As Darwin argued, evolutionary change can be seen as resulting from gradual modifications from some ancestral state. As a result, the characters of any given species are both unique, or adaptive specializations, and general, or shared with many other species.

Unfortunately, in the study of learning adaptive specialization has too often been set in opposition to general processes (Macphail and Bolhuis 2001). There is a historical reason for this. *Adaptive specialization* was introduced into discussions of learning by Rozin and Kalat (1971) in a landmark paper about flavor aversion learning and other newly described phenomena that seemed to reveal qualitatively new kinds of learning. For example, rats learned aversions to flavors that were followed by illness even when a single experience of illness had followed sampling of the flavor by many hours. Flavor aversion learning seemed to be comprehensible only by thinking of animals in the laboratory *qua* animals rather than *qua* model humans or general learning machines. In fact, conditioned flavor aversion and related findings turned out to have the same properties as other examples of associative learning, but with quantitatively special—and functionally suitable—parameters (Chapter 4). Thus they illustrate in a very compelling way how general processes of learning are expressed in a species- and situation-specific way, that is, with quantitative specializations. Just as with the debates about concerted vs. mosaic evolution of the brain, or general intelligence vs. modularity, the truth about general processes vs. adaptive specializations is "both."

Figure 2.13. Some adaptations of birds' bills for different modes of feeding. From left to right, a seed cracker, nut cracker, meat tearer, generalized forager, flower prober, and earth prober. After Welty (1963) with permission.

In any case, opposing generality and specialization is biologically incorrect. Commonality and diversity are two sides of the same coin (Rozin and Schull 1988), and one should not be emphasized at the expense of the other. People interested in general processes have tended to compare species widely separated on the evolutionary tree, for example pigeons and rats as in Box 1.3, whereas the study of adaptive specializations is associated with comparison of close relatives chosen for having different behaviors in the wild. As Papini (2002) has argued, both approaches have much to reveal about the phylogenetic distribution and evolution of learning mechanisms, just as they are doing with genetics and neurobiology.

Thinking in terms of function and evolution, of convergences and divergences of both close and distant relatives, is a tremendously powerful tool in comparative psychology. For example, we learn in Chapter 10 that monkeys but not pigeons solve a test of transitive inference in a way that suggests they form a representation of an ordered set of items. That is, when exposed to training designed to teach them, in effect, "green is better than red," "red is better than blue," "blue is better than yellow," "yellow is better than purple," monkeys behave appropriately (i.e., choose red) when presented with the novel red and yellow pair and pass further tests that pigeons fail. Is this simply a mammal-bird difference, a difference in general intelligence perhaps? But asking what transitive inference might be good for in the real world suggests that it is useful for animals that form social hierarchies, regardless of whether they are mammals or birds. And here the general study of animal behavior becomes integrated with investigations of the generality of this cognitive process in suggesting species to study. The corvids include species with and without dominance hierarchies, thus providing subjects for one test of whether the ability to "do" transitive inference is confined to primates or is convergently evolved in species living in groups that need a certain kind of social intelligence (Kamil 2004; Paz-y-Mino C. et al. 2004). Thus integrating investigations of mechanistic and functional questions about cognition does not mean confusing the answers to different sorts of questions but rather developing a science in which information about how cognition may be used informs investigations of how it works.

2.6   Summarizing and looking ahead

Just as Chapter 1 introduces the study of comparative cognition, this chapter introduces the study of evolution and adaptation. A claim that any character is adaptive can be tested in three ways: by modeling, to discover how well the character serves a hypothesized function; with the comparative method, to test whether variations in the character across many species are related to variations in ecology; and by experiment. Ideally two or more of these methods can be used together. Using the comparative method requires good inferences about the phylogeny of the species being compared. Evolutionary psychologists claim that

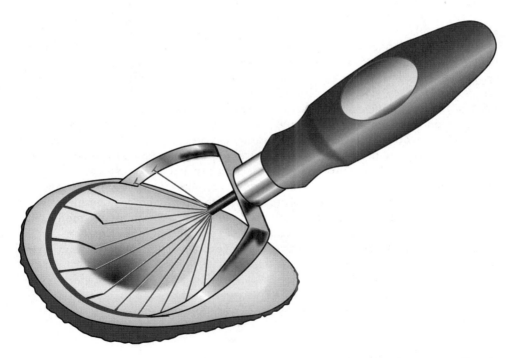

Figure 2.14. The object in Figure 12.12 is an avocado slicer. The sharp curved edge separates the pulp from the outside of the avocado and the thin wires make neat, equal-sized, slices. Richerson and Boyd (2005) used this example of how knowing what something designed to do helps to understand its structure.

understanding how cognitive mechanisms evolved and what they are for can help us to understand how they work. However, testing evolutionary hypotheses about cognition can be difficult because cognitive processes affect fitness indirectly, through the medium of behavior.

We have encountered three sets of contrasts in this chapter that seem intuitively to have much in common: Mosaic vs. concerted evolution, modularity vs. connectedness, adaptive specialization vs. general process. All seem to express a tension between a focus on parts with their specific properties and a focus on a whole with what its parts have in common. In the long (or maybe not so long) run, the kinds of processes they refer to may be linked mechanistically; developmental modularity is already being linked with evolution (West-Eberhard 2003; Schlosser and Wagner 2004). In any case, the conclusion to be drawn from discussion of each of these contrasts is that the truth is usually a mixture of both. It may be human nature to focus on only particularities or only wholes, but "It would be difficult to overemphasize the importance of agility in being able to appreciate both the modularity and the connectedness of biological organization" (West-Eberhard 2003, 83).

Further readings

Most of the topics in this chapter are covered in greater depth for students in Papini's (2008) *Comparative Psychology* and the behavioral ecology text by Danchin, Giraldeau, and Cezilly (2008). For understanding the theory of evolution there is no substitute for reading at least part of *The Origin of Species* (Darwin 1859) or *The Descent of Man and Selection in Relation to Sex* (Darwin 1871). Stearns and Hoekstra (2005) is a current introductory text. Evolutionary theory and its application to behavior have been the subject of some outstanding books for the general reader. Richard Dawkins's (1976) *The Selfish Gene* is already a classic exposition of the basics of behavioral ecology. *Darwin's Dangerous Idea* (Dennett 1995)is a philosopher's discussion of evolutionary theory and its wider implications. *The Beak of the Finch* (Weiner 1994) is a very readable account of studies of evolution in action on the Galapagos, now updated by Rosemary Grant and Peter Grant's (2008) own account of their work and its implications.

For brain evolution, Streidter's (2005) clear and fascinating text is highly recommended, as is Healy and Rowe's (2007) thoughtful review of comparative studies of the relationship between brain size and complex cognition. Two thoughtful reviews by Sherry (2005, 2006) analyze the debate surrounding neuroecology and review recent developments. For an extended discussion of the debate about modularity along the same lines as Box 2.3, the review by Barrett and Kurzban (2006) is recommended. It also incorporates considerations from human evolutionary psychology.

Part I

Fundamental Mechanisms

Cognitive mechanisms are generally defined functionally, that is, by what they do, but the specificity of these functions varies tremendously. For instance, principles of perception, memory, or discrimination learning are pretty much the same regardless of the kind of information being perceived, remembered, or discriminated, whereas by definition principles of numerical, spatial, or social cognition apply only in particular cognitive domains. But the mechanisms involved in assessing numerosity, traveling in space, interacting with others, and so on cannot be understood in isolation from domain-general principles of perception, learning, and memory. Although cognition may be modular to some extent (Box 2.3), it is impossible to appreciate what may be unique to individual cognitive domains without first appreciating some fundamental principles that cut across some or all of them.

Accordingly, Chapters 3–7 lay the groundwork for the parts of the book dealing with specifically physical and social cognition. Chapter 3 describes fundamental mechanisms of perception in the context of their evolution and ecology. Chapters 4–6 introduce basic mechanisms of learning: how animals associate events, recognize single objects, and learn to discriminate among things and classify them. Chapter 7 looks at basic principles of memory, concluding with controversial attempts to discover whether other animals have conscious memories as humans do. Some of the issues discussed in these five chapters are among the oldest and most-studied in comparative psychology, but as we will see they continue to inspire new discoveries and lively debates.

3
Perception and Attention

To a bat or an owl, a summer evening is full of sounds of which we are only dimly aware. A honeybee sees patterns on flowers that are invisible to us. That every kind of animal has its own *umwelt* or self-world, formed by the kinds of information its senses can process, was one of the fundamental insights of the founders of ethology. The ethologist Von Uexküll (1934/1957) attempted to capture this insight in pictures of how the world might seem to other species (Figure 3.1). A great deal is now known about how animals process sensory information even if most contemporary behavioral scientists do not attempt to translate it into such depictions of subjective experience.

The study of comparative cognition begins with sensation and perception for two reasons. First, it is important to keep in mind that adaptive behavior can result from specializations in perception as much as from higher-level learning or decision processes. Second, perception provides some excellent examples of modularity and adaptation in information processing. This chapter begins with a few illustrative examples of sensory specialization, then looks at how perception can be studied in animals and introduces the important ideas of signal detection theory. Armed with this information, we can see how "receiver psychology" (Guilford and Dawkins 1991; Endler and Basolo 1998; Rowe and Skelhorn 2004) has influenced the evolution of animal signals. And at the end of the chapter we look at how sensory information is filtered by attention and how attentional processes can explain the classical ethological phenomenon of search image formation.

3.1 Specialized sensory systems

Every animal must be able to respond appropriately to its own food, mates, young, and predators. The cues it can use are determined by the environment characteristic of its species (Dusenbery 1992). Species active at night have a different set of cues available to them from those active during the day; those that live underground, different cues from those that live in the treetops; creatures of the deep sea, different cues again from creatures of clear streams. Sensory systems and their sensitivities tend to be matched to lifestyle and environment.

The sensory specializations we find most impressive are those allowing animals to respond to forms of energy that an unaided human cannot detect. The ultrasonic

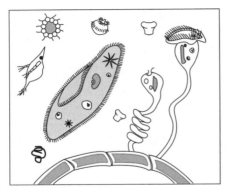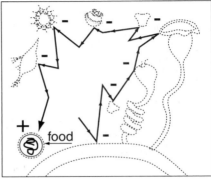

Figure 3.1. Von Uexküll's conception of the *umwelt* of a paramecium (the large gray blob in the left panel). The environment in all the complexity perceived by humans is depicted on the left, the same environment as perceived by the paramecium on the right, with + and—_ showing what attracts and repels it, respectively. Redrawn from von Uexküll (1934/1957) with permission.

hearing of bats is one well-studied example (Figure 3.5). Many bat species find prey in the dark using a kind of sonar. They continually emit ultrasonic cries, and the echoes from flying insects enable the bats to locate their prey in complete darkness. Some snakes locate live prey by homing in on warm objects, using infrared detectors in their snout. The platypus feeds underwater at night using sensitive receptors in its bill to detect the electric fields generated by movements of its prey (Manger and Pettigrew 1995). Using mechanisms that are still somewhat mysterious, some birds, mammals, reptiles, and other animals navigate by means of the intensity and/or inclination of the Earth's magnetic field (Wiltschko and Wiltschko 2006).

Many animals with color vision, such as honeybees and most birds, have a different pattern of wavelength sensitivity from humans. Thus they do not necessarily see prey items or potential mates (or images we create to mimic them) the way we do (Box 3.1). For example, wavelength sensitivity of many birds extends into the ultraviolet (UV), and some feathers reflect UV light (Cuthill et al. 2000). This discovery has led to some striking observations which illustrate very compellingly how we need to understand an animal's species-specific perceptual world to understand its behavior. For example, blue tits and starlings are bird species in which males and females look the same color to humans. But to a blue tit or starling, males look very different from females because they have conspicuous patches of UV-reflecting feathers, patches which are larger or better developed in males. In such species, females may base mate choice on the brightness of these patches, rejecting males treated with UV-blocking sunscreen in favor of untreated males (review in Cuthill et al. 2000). To take an example from prey-catching, kestrels locate places where voles can be found using the UV reflectance of the urine that the voles deposit as they run along their habitual trails (Viitala et al. 1995). Honeybees also have UV vision, which they use to discriminate among flowers (Section 3.5.1).

The foregoing are but a few examples of striking species differences in what animals sense. The sensitivity of particular systems also may differ among closely related species or even individuals of the same species. For example, optimal visual sensitivity is different for fish dwelling at different depths because the distribution of wavelengths illuminating objects changes with depth as sunlight is filtered by seawater. Sensitivity may change with age if the same fish lives at different depths at

Box 3.1 Color Vision

Color resides not in objects but in the observer's perception of wavelength differences and similarities. To a color blind animal, objects differ visually only in brightnesss. What this means is illustrated by a classic demonstration of color vision in honeybees (Frisch 1914, as cited in Kelber, Vorobyev, and Osorio 2003). Bees trained to find sugar water on a blue or a yellow card showed that they were using wavelength and not brightness by choosing their training color over all shades of grey, from very light to very dark. The first stage in responding to wavelength is the reaction of photopigments to light; in vertebrates these are in the retinal cone cells (cones). Each photopigment has a unique profile of responsiveness as a function of wavelength. Behavioral discriminations are based on a neural comparison of the responses of different photoreceptor types (for further details see Cuthill et al. 2000; Kelber, Vorobyev, and Osorio 2003).

The kind of color vision available to different species is revealed by the relative sensitivities, or absorption spectra, of the animals' photoreceptor types (Figure B3.1). Honeybees, like many other insects (Briscoe and Chittka 2001), have three photoreceptor types all near the blue-green end of the spectrum. One is sensitive in the ultraviolet. Pigeons have three photoreceptor types (retinal cone cells, or *cones*) with sensitivities similar to those of humans' and a fourth with maximum sensitivity in the ultraviolet (UV). Many other birds have UV vision, as discussed in the main text. Humans and many other primates have three cone types, with maximum sensitivities in red, green, and blue wavelengths. Primates are unique among mammals in having color vision, and there is some debate about why such trichromatic color vision evolved (Surridge, Osorio, and Mundy 2003). Red-green discrimination is thought to be useful for detecting ripe fruits in the forest, but it could be equally useful for folivorous (leaf-eating) primates because the freshest and most nutritious leaves tend to be red. Color also plays a role in social communication in some primates (Ghazanfar and Santos 2004), but whether it evolved first in that context or in the context of foraging is still debated. Selection for enhanced visual capabilities, including color vision, may have played a role in the evolution of relatively large brains in primates (Chapter 12; Barton 2000).

Behavioral tests of color matching are important in showing how photoreceptors are actually used: any wavelength can be matched with a mixture of the primary colors for that species (i.e., those at the peak sensitivities for the different photoreceptors). This principle is made use of in video screens that generate colors by activating red, green, and blue phosphors in different proportions for different colors. As a result, most animals do not see the colors on conventional TV the way we do because their peak sensitivities and/or distributions of different receptor types are different from ours (Box 6.1; Oliveira et al. 2000).

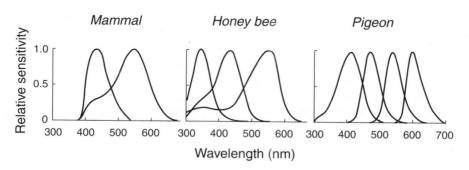

Figure B3.1. Relative wavelength sensitivities of photoreceptors in a representative nonprimate mammal, honeybees, and pigeons. In terms of human perception, red is toward the right on the x-axis. Relative sensitivity, on the y-axis, is the proportion of maximum responsiveness that the given receptor type shows at each wavelength. Human sensitivity is similar to that of pigeons except that we lack the very short-wavelength, UV, receptor. Adapted from Kelber, Vorobyev, and Osorio (2003) with permission.

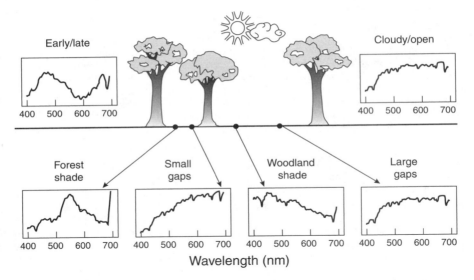

Figure 3.2. The relative intensities of different wavelengths of light in different parts of a forest and under different conditions. Forest shade, for instance, has a relatively high proportion of wavelengths from the middle (greenish) part of the spectrum, whereas small gaps are rich in longer (redder) wavelengths. Redrawn from Endler (1992) with permission.

different stages of its life cycle (Lythgoe 1979). As shown in Figure 3.2, the light environment also differs in different parts of the forest and at different times of day. The nuptial plumage of male forest birds and the times and places at which they display may be matched to the available light in such a way as to maximize the males' conspicuousness (Endler and Thery 1996; Endleret al. 2005). The sound frequencies that travel farthest are determined by factors such as atmospheric conditions and type of vegetation. These physical constraints have affected the evolution of animal sound production and reception mechanisms. For example, the songs of forest birds tend to have a different distribution of frequencies from the songs of birds from open habitats. Regardless of habitat, many birds choose to sing from high, exposed, perches, from which sound travels furthest (Catchpole and Slater 1995; Slabbekoorn 2004).

How much of the environment an animal can see at once depends on where its eyes are. Animals with eyes on the sides of their heads can see a wider arc of their surroundings than animals with frontally placed eyes. The placing of the eyes reflects the extent of binocular vision required by the species diet and the extent to which the animal is predator as opposed to prey, as illustrated in Figure 3.3 with the striking contrast between an owl and a woodcock. The most important things may be near the horizon or above or in front of the animal, and this feature of ecology may be matched by greater visual acuity in some parts of the visual field than others. For example, pigeons view a small area in front of them binocularly. Binocular vision and concomitantly good depth perception are important for accurate pecking at seeds, whereas the lateral field of view is important for detecting predators. Accordingly, pigeons have two "foveas," areas of maximally dense photoreceptors, one in the binocular field and one on which objects to the side are focused (see Roberts et al. 1996). Species of birds with different lifestyles also have different retinal distributions of photoreceptors (Nalbach, Wolf-Oberhollenzer, and Remy 1993). For example,

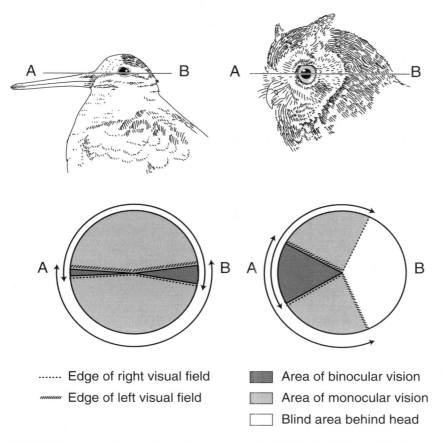

Figure 3.3. Differences in the placement of the eyes and visual fields for different lifestyles, prey animal (wood cock) versus visual predator (owl). Redrawn from Evans and Heiser (2004) with permission.

seabirds tend to have a central horizontal strip of high density photoreceptors. Owls and other birds of prey have the densest photoreceptors in the part of the retina that views the ground. They may have to turn their heads almost upside down to see something approaching from above.

In many situations animals respond to a very narrow range of stimuli. For example, male moths of species like *Bembyx mori* are sexually attracted to a particular molecule contained in a pheromone emitted by the female of their own species (see Hopkins 1983). A hungry baby herring gull pecks at a red spot near the end of its parent's beak and less at other colors in other locations (Tinbergen and Perdeck 1950). The first step in analyzing such an example of selective behavior is to find out whether it can be explained by the responsiveness of the sensory system involved. In the case of the moth, the characteristics of the olfactory system completely account for the male's selective sensitivity. The male moth's antennae are covered with receptors selective for the female's sexual pheromone. In contrast, the herring gull's selective pecking at red spots on beaklike objects reflects processing at a higher level (Delius et al. 1972). Both the female pheromone and the red spot would be classified as sign stimuli (Chapter 6), but one reflects a purely sensory filter, the other a more central processing mechanism.

3.2   How can we find out what animals perceive?

3.2.1   Studying perception in animals

Three approaches can be taken to analyzing perception in animals: *(1)* electrophysiology and related methods of neuroscience, *(2)* studying how natural behavior changes with changes in stimulation, and *(3)* testing learned behavior with the methods of animal psychophysics. Each one of these approaches has its advantages and disadvantages. Two or three of them can be used together to understand selective responsiveness in natural situations.

Recording electrical responses of sensory neurons to controlled stimuli (electrophysiology) is the most direct way to find out what sensory information is potentially available to an animal. In the case of the moths described in the just-preceding section, such methods make clear that the "decision" to approach and court another moth is reached by the olfactory receptors. However, to find out what features of the world are behaviorally significant, it is necessary to go beyond electrophysiology and look directly at behavior. Often, an animal's natural behavior to stimuli of importance to it can be used to test simple sensory discriminations. For example, hamsters, like many other mammals, mark their territories with secretions from special glands. To find out whether they can discriminate among the scent marks of different individuals, Johnston et al. (1993) made use of the fact that a hamster spends a great deal of time sniffing a glass plate scent marked by another hamster. This response decreases as the hamster encounters successive marks of the same kind from the same hamster, that is, the response *habituates* (see Chapter 5). However, once the subject hamster has habituated to the scent from one hamster, it still vigorously investigates scent from a second hamster (Figure 3.4). Such renewed investigation shows that the animal discriminates the second scent from the first. As we will see in later chapters, this is a powerful way to discover what stimuli all kinds of subjects, including humans, discriminate. It is generally called the *habituation/dishabituation method*, but it should be noted that renewal of an habituated response in the presence of a new stimulus is not strictly the same as what is referred to as dishabituation in the analyses of the habituation process discussed in Chapter 5.

The differences animals perceive among behaviorally relevant stimuli can be studied in the field as well as in the laboratory. For example, many territorial songbirds learn the characteristics of their neighbor's songs and where those neighbors typically sing (Box 5.1). A familiar neighbor singing from a new location is treated as

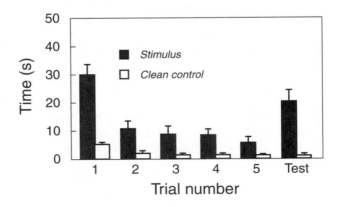

Figure 3.4. Data from a habituation/dishabituation test of olfactory discrimination in male golden hamsters. Time spent sniffing the scented (stimulus) half of a glass plate is compared to time spent sniffing the clean half. The stimulus was the same in Trials 1–5 and different in Trial 6. Redrawn from Johnston et al. (1993) with permission.

a threat and attacked. A novel conspecific song from a loudspeaker is also attacked (Falls 1982), making it possible to present songs in a controlled way in the field to find out what aspects of this complex auditory stimulus birds are sensitive to. Experiments of this kind have shown, for example, that great tits can discriminate among the voices of their neighbors (Weary 1996).

A limitation of using natural responses to natural stimuli is that there are at least two reasons why an animal may respond in the same way to two or more stimuli. It may not be able to discriminate among them or the differences it discriminates may have no behavioral significance for it. In the example above, for instance, a territorial male bird might be equally aggressive toward two very different novel songs, but he might later show that he could discriminate them if one was the song of a neighbor while the other remained relatively novel (for further discussion see Collins 2004; Dooling 2004). Late in the breeding season, when sex hormone levels are lower, he might respond equally little to all songs. A good understanding of the behavior of the species being tested is clearly necessary to ensure that tests of discrimination are being done in a meaningful way. In general, because natural responses to natural stimuli may reflect so many motivational and other variables, electrophysiological or psychophysical methods must be used to study sensory ability separately from responses to the signals of interest.

3.2.2   Animal psychophysics

One of the oldest areas of experimental psychology is *psychophysics,* the study of how information is processed by the senses. For example, what is the smallest amount of light energy, at each wavelength, that can be seen in total darkness? Or, with a given background sound, what increase in sound pressure level is required for subjects to report an increase in loudness? The former is a question about the *absolute threshold*; the latter, about the *relative* or *difference threshold.* Data from psychophysical investigations typically consist of plots of absolute or relative thresholds as a function of a physical stimulus dimension.

A psychophysicist interested in absolute auditory thresholds can tell a human subject, "Press this button whenever you hear a tone." Visual acuity can be tested by instructing a person, "Press the left button when you see stripes; press the right when you see a gray patch." Animals, in contrast, have to be given their instructions by careful training, using the methods of operant or classical conditioning. Figuring out how to ask nonverbal subjects the questions one wants to ask in a way that yields unambiguous answers is one of the biggest challenges in any area of comparative cognition. With operant methods, the animal is placed in a situation where it can obtain reward or avoid punishment only by using as a cue the stimulus the experimenter is interested in. Since animals seem to have an uncanny knack of latching onto subtle irrelevant cues, being sure the animal responds only to the stimulus of interest is not as easy as it sounds. Well-designed psychophysical experiments include stringent controls for possible influences of extraneous cues.

A typical procedure for investigating animal sensory abilities is one used for testing bats' ability to discriminate distances by echolocating (Figure 3.5). The basic idea is to reward a bat for making one response when it detects an object moving rapidly back and forth (a "jittering" target) and another response when the target is stationary. As long as the bat can make the correct choice at above the chance level of 50%, it must be discriminating between the two distances from which it hears the jittering target's echoes, that is, between the two echo delays. Since all bats are not really "as blind as a

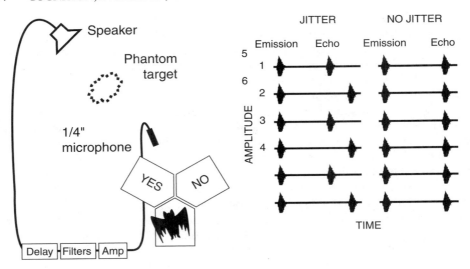

Figure 3.5. Schematic view of a setup for testing temporal discrimination in bats. The bat was reinforced for moving onto the left platform for a jittering target ("yes, jitter present") and onto the right platform when no jitter was present. Redrawn from Moss and Schnitzler (1989) with permission.

bat," the experiment depicted in Figure 3.5 had to eliminate visual cues to motion. This was done by using virtual rather than real targets. The bat's cries were picked up by a microphone near its mouth and broadcast back to it either with a fixed delay, as if reflected by a stationary object, or with alternating short and long delays, as if coming from a jittering object. The bat sat on a Y-shaped platform and was rewarded with a mealworm for crawling onto the left arm when a (virtual) jittering target was presented and onto the right arm for a stationary one. To ensure that the animal learned the required discrimination, training began with large jitters. When the animal performed correctly a large proportion of the time on this easy task, the task was made more difficult, and so on. The bats were eventually making extremely fine discriminations.

This elaborate instrumentation and training procedure may suggest that psychophysical experiments can be done only in the laboratory, but this is not so. Classic field studies of bees' color and shape perception were done by von Frisch (1967) and similar methods have been used with hummingbirds (Goldsmith, Collins, and Perlman 1981). Animals that return repeatedly to one food source as bees and hummingbirds do are particularly good candidates for field tests of sensory abilities because the animal is using the sense for the job it has most likely evolved to do. Not all training methods used in animal psychophysics are so obviously related to the subjects' natural behaviors. It might be assumed that any arbitrary training procedure may be used to tap the capabilities of any sensory system, but the results of psychophysical studies could be influenced by the motivational and response systems used. For example, pigeons attend more to lights than tones when working for food but the reverse is true when they are avoiding shocks (Foree and LoLordo 1973). This could mean that subtle auditory discriminations are easier to teach to frightened than to hungry pigeons. The kind of behavior guided by a given sensory system should be taken into account in psychophysical tests of that system.

3.3.   Some psychophysical principles

All sensory systems have some basic properties in common (Barlow 1982), many of them shared by instruments designed to detect physical energies. As we have already seen, the senses are characterized by specificity in the kinds of energies they detect: the visual system is specific for electromagnetic radiation in a certain range of wavelengths; the auditory system for changes in sound pressure; the olfactory system for airborne chemicals. Moreover, most sensory systems are not equally sensitive to everything they detect. Rather, each system can be characterized electrophysiologically and behaviorally by a tuning curve. The plots of visual sensitivity as a function of wavelength in Box 3.1 are examples.

In addition to quality ("what is it?") an important feature of stimuli is intensity ("how much is it?"). Brightness, sweetness, and loudness are examples of perceptual intensity continua. An important psychophysical principle that emerges from research on perception of intensity or size continua is Weber's Law, which describes the difference threshold (or *just noticeable difference*, the *JND*) between two stimuli as a function of their magnitude. The JND is a constant proportion across a wide range of base values. This proportion, the Weber fraction, depends on the species and sensory channel. For example, suppose a 10-gram weight has to be increased by .5 grams in order for a person consistently to detect the change. Weber's Law says that if we ask for the same judgment starting with a 20-gram weight, the difference threshold will be 1 gram, whereas it would be .25 grams if we started with a 5-gram weight. Examples of Weber's Law in animals' time and number discrimination are discussed in Chapters 9 and 10.

Three other psychophysical principles have important implications for animal behavior. First, sensory neurons tend to respond more to physically more intense stimuli. Therefore, more intense or reliable behavioral responses can be expected to stimuli that are brighter, louder, or bigger in some other way. This seems so obvious and right as hardly to need stating, but animals need not have been designed this way. One could build, say, a sound meter that gave high readings to soft sounds, and none at all to loud ones. An animal built like it would react to things far away from it and ignore predators or conspecifics close by. In fact, the opposite is generally the case, and it does make functional sense that animals should react more intensely to things that are larger and/or closer.

A second general feature of sensory or perceptual systems is a tendency to habituate (or show adaptation) to prolonged unchanging stimulation. We have seen in the last section how this feature has been put to use to test hamsters' odor sensitivity. It has been suggested that the tendency for listeners to habituate explains why some bird species have repertoires of many different songs. Females, it is suggested, will be more stimulated by a constantly changing series of songs than by one song sung monotonously over and over, and indeed in some species males that sing more different songs are more successful in obtaining mates (Collins 2004).

Third, in many systems response to a given stimulus depends on its contrast with the background. A quiet tone is more easily heard in silence than in soft noise. To a person with normal color vision, a red spot looks redder on a green than on an orange background. The tendency of sensory systems to respond more strongly to stimuli that contrast with what surrounds them in time or space appears to have shaped the evolution of animal color patterns, auditory signals, and the like. For example, many animals that are food for other animals resemble the substrate on which they typically rest, that is, they minimize contrast so as to be cryptic rather than conspicuous. Such

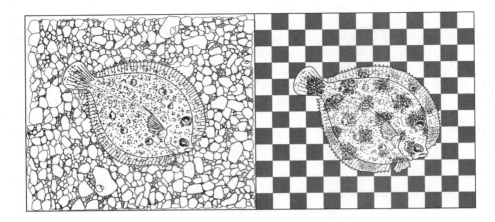

Figure 3.6. Examples of camouflage, showing how a tropical flounder changes its pattern to match the substrate. From photographs in Ramachandran et al. (1996) with permission.

animals sometimes behave so as to enhance their resemblance to their surroundings. For instance, moths that resemble birch bark not only choose birch trees to rest on, they rest so that their stripes are in the same orientation as the black patches on the bark (see Figure 3.18). Flounders, fish that lie flat on the bottom of the sea, provide one remarkable example of how animals can change their appearance to match the substrate (Figure 3.6). Cephalopods (octopus, squids, and cuttlefish) show truly amazing control over not only the color and pattern but the texture of their skin, and the neural and visual control of their elaborate camouflage is beginning to be understood (Hanlon 2007). However, although many details of animal color patterns have long been thought to aid in camouflage, there is surprisingly little experimental evidence for most of these suggestions (Ruxton, Sherratt, and Speed 2004). A recent exception is a demonstration that color patches that break up the outline of a moth's body ("disruptive coloration") do in fact reduce predation by birds compared to the same patches entirely within the body contours (Cuthill et al. 2005).

Far from being cryptic, some animals have what would appear to be the maximum possible contrast with their typical backgrounds. Red rain forest frogs and bright yellow-and-black striped caterpillars seem to be advertising their presence to predators. However, many such warningly colored, or *aposematic*, species sting, prickle, taste bad, or otherwise cause their attackers to reject them. Their bright colors may help predators to learn to avoid attacking them and others like them (see Chapter 6). Contrast with the background is also important in intraspecific communication, as exemplified by the colorful plumage and loud songs of many male birds (see also Section 3.5)

3.4   Signal detection theory

3.4.1   Detecting signals in noise: Theory

In Section 3.3, threshold was mentioned as if it were a definite quantity above which a stimulus is always detected and below which it never is. Even in the best-controlled psychophysical experiment, however, data do not fit this pattern. Observers report detecting a constant stimulus only a proportion of the time. Threshold is calculated as the value detected a fixed proportion of the time, often 75% or 80%. Variation in response to a constant stimulus is thought to be due to inevitable changes in the observer's state, perhaps lapses in attention or spontaneous firing of sensory nerves, and to uncontrollable fluctuations in the stimulus. In addition, data from different observers can vary because people vary in how willing they are to say "it's there" when they are unsure. Thus the idea of an observer with an absolute threshold must be replaced by the idea that a stimulus has a distribution of effects. The observer's problem is to detect that signal against a fluctuating background with which the signal can be confused (noise). An animal's problem in nature is essentially the same: to detect biologically important signals in an environment filled with unimportant stimuli (see Wiley 2006). For both the psychophysical observer and the animal in the field a certain proportion of mistakes is inevitable, and their cost must be kept to a minimum. Signal detection theory quantifies this fundamental tradeoff.

Signal detection theory (Figure 3.7) was originally developed to tell radar operators the best way to decide which blobs to treat as planes on a noisy radar screen. It has been used extensively in the analysis of human psychophysical data (Macmillan and Creelman 2005), but the ideas it embodies apply to any difficult discrimination performed by any creature. Signal detection theory conceptualizes the perceiver as faced with the task of discriminating some signal from a noisy background (which could be another signal). Signal and noise both have a distribution of effects. The

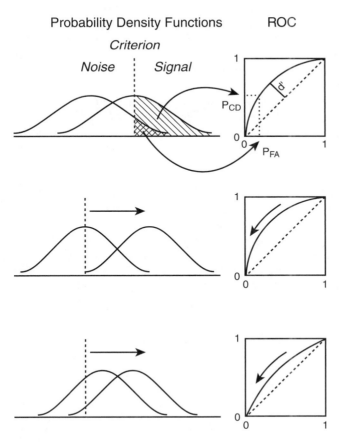

Figure 3.7. The elements of signal detection theory. Hypothetical normal probability distributions of the effect of signal and of noise along some stimulus dimension together with the placement of the criterion for classifying stimuli as "signal" vs. "noise" translate into ROC curves. As the criterion moves from left to right, as shown in the two lower panels, correct detections (CD) and false alarms (FA) move along the ROC curve in the direction of the arrows. As signal and noise become less discriminable, in the bottom panel, performance moves onto an ROC curve with a smaller d.' After Wiley (1994) with permission.

computations are simplest if these distributions are normal with the same variance, as in Figure 3.7. The essential features of these distributions, regardless of their shape, are that *(1)* they overlap, more so the more similar are signal and noise; and *(2)* the value along the stimulus continuum (x-axis) represents the only information about the signal that is available to the perceiver. Thus, many stimuli are inherently ambiguous: the perceiver cannot know whether they represent the noise alone or the signal. All the perceiver can do is to set a decision criterion, a value along the stimulus dimension above which to say "signal" and below which to say "no signal." Once the criterion is set, any of four things can happen: the observer can say "signal" when there is in fact a signal; these responses are termed *correct detections* or *hits*. Inevitably, however, the observer will sometimes say "signal" when there is no signal; such responses are *false alarms*. Saying "no signal" when the signal is in fact absent is a *correct rejection;* "no signal" when a signal is there is a *miss*. Thus there are two kinds of correct responses, and two kinds of errors (Table 3.1). The probability of each is related to the location of the criterion and the overlap between the two distributions as shown in Figure 3.7.

With fixed characteristics of the signal, the background, and the sensory system, correct detections and false alarms change together in a way described by the receiver operating characteristic, or *ROC curve* (Figure 3.7). ROC curves are characterized by their distance from the diagonal that bisects the plot of p(correct detection) versus p(false alarm), represented by the parameter d' ("dee prime"). A perceiver with a lower criterion, saying "signal" more often, has more correct detections but necessarily more false alarms (and concomitantly fewer correct rejections) as well. A conservative observer will make few false alarms but concomitantly fewer correct detections. The optimal location of the criterion depends on the relative payoffs for the four possible outcomes described above. For instance, as the payoff for correct detections rises relative to the penalty for false alarms, the criterion should be lower, that is, the observer should respond more often as if the signal is present. The same thing should happen if the observer learns that signals are relatively common. Observers can move onto a ROC curve further from the diagonal, with higher d' and higher sensitivity, only if the stimuli become more discriminable. This can happen because of changes in the signal, the noise, or the observer's sensory system.

3.4.2   Data

Humans and other species do perform in psychophysical experiments as predicted by signal detection theory. For example, Wright (1972) tested pigeons' ability to discriminate wavelengths in the way depicted in Figure 3.8a. This two-alternative forced-choice experiment was designed to ask the bird whether it perceived both halves of a central pecking key as the same color or as different colors. It pecked a left side key to report

Table 3.1 Possible responses in a signal detection task

		Signal	
		Present	Absent
Response	Yes ("Signal there")	Correct Detection (Hit)	False Alarm
	No ("No signal")	Miss	Correct Rejection

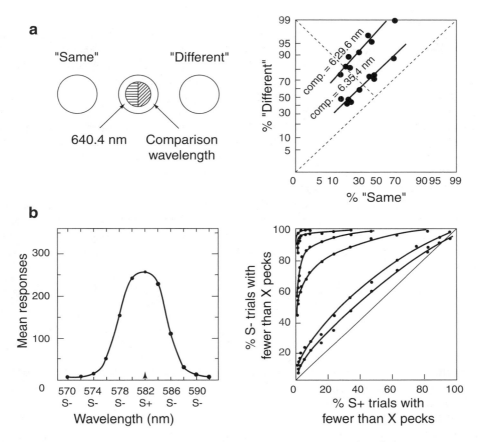

Figure 3.8. a. Method and results of Wright's (1972) experiment on wavelength discrimination in pigeons. The discs are the pecking "keys" referred to in the text. The ROC curves described by the results are plotted as as straight lines on logarithmic coordinates. b. Pigeons' wavelength generalization gradient and derived ROC curves from Blough (1967). Redrawn with permission.

"same" and the right side key to report "different." A bird was occasionally rewarded with food for reporting "same" or "different" correctly. Feedback was always given by briefly turning on a light above the feeder after correct responses but extinguishing all lights in the test chamber after incorrect responses. The bird's criterion for pecking left vs. right was manipulated by varying the probability of reward for correct left vs. right responses. On some sessions it was more profitable to report "same" correctly than it was to report "different," and on other sessions the opposite was true. The pattern of results was exactly as predicted by a signal detection analysis. For each pair of wavelengths, plotting the probability of correctly reporting "different" (i.e., hits) versus the probability of incorrectly reporting "different" (i.e., false alarms) traced out a single ROC curve as the payoffs were varied. For example, when the probability of reinforcement for reporting "different" (pecking the right key) was relatively high, the birds behaved as if adopting a liberal criterion, with a relatively high p(correct detection) accompanied by relatively high p(false alarm). And as indicated in Figure 3.8 a, the more the wavelengths differed, the further from the diagonal was the ROC plot (i.e., the higher the d').

Wright's procedure for varying the birds' criterion required each bird to complete many trials at each combination of wavelengths and reinforcement probability, but human observers can be asked to apply several criteria simultaneously by reporting the certainty with which choices are made. Responses given with high certainty are assumed to have exceeded a more stringent criterion than those given with lower certainty. Animals can reveal their "certainty" about their choices by how quickly or how much they respond. If the choice keys in a psychophysical experiment are lit for a fixed amount of time on each trial, the number of responses made to the chosen alternative in that time behaves like the human observers' report of subjective certainty. For example, Blough (1967) trained pigeons on a difficult wavelength discrimination. A central pecking key lit up for 30-second trials with one of 13 wavelengths. Pecks at 582 nm were reinforced, but pecks at any of 12 other wavelengths ranging between 570 and 590 nm were never reinforced. The birds' rates of pecking traced out a typical *generalization gradient*, with more pecking to stimuli closest to the positive, or reinforced, stimulus (Figure 3.8b). One way to interpret these data is to say that the lower the rate, the more certain the bird was that the stimulus was not 582 nm. For each nonreinforced stimulus, the proportion of trials with fewer pecks than each of a series of criteria did trace out a ROC curve, just as this notion suggests, with stimuli further from 580 nm giving ROC curves of higher d' (Figure 3.8b).

3.4.3   Implications for the evolution of animal signals

The examples presented so far have been framed in terms of psychophysical experiments, but signal detection theory applies to any decision whether or not to respond to a signal. The "decision" need not involve performing a learned response for reward. The criterion can represent the threshold for attacking a possible rival or prey item or for displaying to a female. The threshold might be adjusted through evolution or through individual experience. Likewise, evolution and/or experience might adjust the distributions of signal or noise effects, by altering some aspect of the signaler or the sensitivity of the receiver. The payoffs may be in terms of energy wasted, injury risked, food items or mating opportunities gained or lost. Here we consider an example from animal signaling systems. In later chapters we will see how signal detection theory can be applied to other animal decisions (for further discussion and related models see Getty 1995; Sherman, Reeve, and Pfennig 1997; Bradbury and Vehrencamp 1998; Phelps, Rand, and Ryan 2006; Wiley 2006).

Suppose the perceiver is a female bird in the spring, living in an area inhabited not only by males of her own species but by males of another species that look and sound very similar to her species male. Natural selection will have ensured that she is more likely to mate with a male of her own species than with males of other species. To emphasize how signal detection theory applies here, the following discussion refers to the female's decision to mate or not to mate. This means only that the female performs or does not perform some behavior leading to successful copulation and production of young. It does not necessarily mean that she decides in the same way a human observer in a psychophysical experiment decides how to classify a light or a tone. The female's decision mechanism might be as simple as the evolutionarily determined threshold for performing a display that in turn elicits copulation by the male.

The female's problem can be translated into the language of signal detection theory as shown in Figure 3.9 (see also Wiley 2006). Here the signal and noise distributions represent the sensory effects of some male feature or features such as plumage color or song. The "signal" is the distribution from males of the female's own species; "noise" is signals from the other species. The criterion represents the female's threshold for mating with a male, although in fact successful copulation is not usually the result of a single response on the part of either male or female. Correct detections result in viable, fertile offspring, the ultimate evolutionary payoff. False alarms waste reproductive effort. Because many birds lay just one clutch of eggs in a season and may not live long past their first breeding season, incubating eggs and feeding young that do not eventually put their parents' genes into the next generation does represent a considerable cost, putting pressure on females to adopt high criteria. On the other hand, too many missed detections of conspecific males means that the breeding season may pass or all males become mated before the female mates at all, so some false alarms may be worth the risk. In cases where the costs and benefits of each possible outcome can be quantified, the optimal criterion can be derived (see Chapter 14 in Bradbury and Vehrencamp 1998). An informal analysis nevertheless provides two important insights (Wiley 1994).

First, whatever their criterion, females are stuck with at least some false alarms and missed detections unless something reduces the overlap of the signal and noise distributions, that is, moves the female onto an ROC curve of higher d'. This can occur in two ways. The two distributions can stay the same shape while their means move further apart (Figure 3.9). This might represent the case of males of the two species in our example evolving more differentiated songs or displays, a phenomenon referred to as *character displacement*. The female's discrimination will also improve if the distributions become narrower while the means remain the same. This might represent the case of changes in the female's sensory system that, for example, sharpen her sound or color discrimination ability. She might also pay more attention to the parts of the signal that best differentiate the species. The distributions of sensory effects from the males could also sharpen if the males evolve to broadcast their signals more effectively. For example they might sing from more exposed perches so their songs are degraded less before reaching the female.

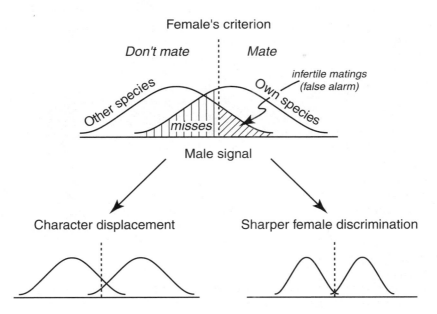

Figure 3.9. Signal detection theory applied to mate choice, showing how false alarms (infertile matings) can be reduced either by males evolving more discriminable characteristics or by females evolving better discrimination.

The second insight afforded by a signal detection analysis of mating signals is that in a situation like that depicted in Figure 3.9, where the signals of two species overlap, the males successful in achieving matings will have a more extreme distribution of signal characteristics than the distribution in the population. That is to say, they will have exaggerated signals, and in fact this is often true (Ryan and Keddy-Hector 1992). As long as the male features that release female sexual behavior are at all similar between species living in a given area (*sympatric* species), the typical payoff matrix for this situation means that females should reject the conspecific males most similar to males of the other species. Therefore the average acceptable male will differ more from males of the other species (or from background noise of whatever sort) than from the average male of the species. If the male characteristics that elicit sexual responses in females are heritable, over generations this process will cause the average male to differ in a more and more extreme way from males of sympatric species and/or from the environmental background.

Exaggerated features elicit greater than normal responses in systems other than sexual behavior. Egg retrieving in the herring gull provides a classic example. An incubating herring gull that sees an egg placed just outside its nest uses its beak and neck to roll the egg into the nest. The Dutch ethologist Baerends and his colleagues (Baerends and Kruijt 1973) presented gulls with pairs of artificial eggs differing in size, color, or speckling and recorded which one of each pair the gulls chose. The preferred size and number of speckles were both greater than the values typical of the study population. The preferred values were combined in a giant, densely speckled egg to create a *supernormal releaser* of retrieval, an egg which the gulls preferred to a normal egg. Comparable effects of supernormality are found in other species of ground nesting birds (Figure 3.10). One might speculate that they appear when selection pressure works to sharpen a discrimination in only one direction. For example, presumably it is important not to retrieve a lot of noneggs. The activity wastes energy (beaks not being very efficient retrieval tools) and extra objects

Figure 3.10. Oystercatcher attempting to incubate a supernormal egg. The egg on the left is a normal oystercatcher egg; the one to its right is a herring gull egg. After Tinbergen (1951) with permission.

cluttering the nest mean less room for eggs and chicks. A discrimination in favor of supernormal eggs may indicate that over evolutionary time the typical nesting habitat contained more small, plain, dull than large, colorful, speckly noneggs, leading to a bias in favor of retrieving the largest, most speckly object in sight. An analogous phenomenon in discrimination learning is peak shift (see Chapter 6 and Ghirlanda and Enquist 2003).

3.5   Perception and evolution: Sensory ecology

Some of the most important sensory information animals have to process comes from other animals. Interactions between predators and prey, parents and offspring, males and females both shape and are shaped by the characteristics of sensory systems. Together with the features of the environment that determine the most effective channels for communication, the senses of their conspecifics and predators influence animals' behavior, appearance, and lifestyle. Unrelenting competition to detect the best habitat, food, and mates constantly selects for animals able to make sharp discriminations. The area of behavioral ecology that deals with these issues is sometimes called *sensory ecology*. Studies at the frontiers of sensory ecology combine physics, neuroscience, and molecular phylogeny with behavioral ecology to understand the evolution and present-day distribution of sensory abilities in terms of the stimuli animals are actually processing in nature (e.g., Bradbury and Vehrencamp 1998; Ghazanfar and Santos 2004; Endler and Mielke 2005; Endler et al. 2005; Fleishman, Leal, and Sheehan 2006). The rest of this section discusses two comparatively simple examples of the interrelationship between perception and the evolution of signals which illustrate how experimental and comparative methods, laboratory and field studies, sensory psychology and behavioral ecology can be integrated to shed light on the evolution and normal functioning of animal signaling systems.

3.5.1   Predators and prey

Most animals are subject to two conflicting selection pressures: be inconspicuous to predators but be conspicuous to selected conspecifics. One of the best illustrations of how the tradeoff between these pressures has influenced signals and behavior involves the color patterns and mating behavior of guppies (Endler 1991; Houde 1997). Guppies (*Poecilia reticulata*) are small South American fish that live in clear tropical streams. Mature males sport colored spots and patches that are used in courtship behavior. Male color pattern is heritable and varies in different populations. In experimental tests of the effectiveness of color patches, females are more likely to mate with males that have larger and brighter blue and orange, red, or yellow patches. Thus female choice creates sexual selection pressure for conspicuous coloration. In contrast, predators create selection pressure for cryptic coloration: duller, smaller, color patches, and patterns that match the background.

The effects of predation have been established in several ways. In the field, guppies are found in streams that have different numbers and kinds of visually hunting, diurnal predators, mostly other fish. Males from populations with more predators are more cryptically colored. Prawns are thought to see poorly in the red end of the spectrum. As might therefore be expected, guppies in areas with heavy predation by prawns have more orange than guppies subject to predators with better red-orange vision (Millar, Reznick, Kinnison et al. 2006). Predictions about the effects of predation have been tested directly by establishing guppies from a single genetic background and distribution of color patterns in laboratory "streams" and exposing them to different numbers and kinds of predators. In guppies' natural habitat of forest streams, the intensity and wavelength of light varies with the time of day (Figure 3.2). Visually hunting predators are most active in the middle of the day, but in both the laboratory and the field, guppies engage in more sexual display early and late in the day, that is, in relatively dim light. Taken all together, the transmission characteristics of tropical streams and the visual capabilities of guppies and their most common predators indicate that at the times of day when they are most likely to be courting, guppies' colors are relatively more conspicuous to other guppies than to guppy predators (Endler 1991; Millar et al. 2006).

The foregoing example illustrates how visual conspicuousness and crypticity are literally in the eyes of the beholder. Detailed sensory physiology may be needed to figure out whether color patterns that appear conspicuous or cryptic to us appear that way to the animals that normally view them (for examples see Endler and Mielke 2005; Fleishman, Leal, and Sheehan 2006). A particularly nice example involves camouflage of crab spiders (Thery et al. 2005). Crab spiders make their living sitting on flowers waiting to grab bees or other pollinators that happen by. But by resting in such an exposed position, the spiders make themselves conspicuous to insectivorous birds. Clearly, they should be colored so as to be inconspicuous to both birds and bees, but this is not easy because bees and birds have different color sensitivities (see Box 3.1). Thery and colleagues (2005) collected crab spiders (*Thomisus onustus*) from the yellow centers of white marguerite daisies and measured the relative intensities of wavelengths across the spectrum, including the ultraviolet, reflected by daisy petals and centers and by crab spiders. The daylight reflectance spectra were then related to the color sensitivities of birds (blue tits, typical predators in the French meadows where the spiders were collected) and honeybees. These computations showed that the spiders' color did not contrast sufficiently with the flower centers for them to be detected by either predator or prey. Their contrast with the petals was well above both birds' and bees' thresholds, which presumably selected for spiders to rest in the center. To make matters even more interesting, individuals of this species of crab spider also match their color to pink flowers, and they are similarly of low contrast to both birds and bees on this background as well (Thery and Casas 2002). To human eyes, Australian crab spiders (*T. spectabilis*) are cryptic on white daisies, but from a honeybees' point of view they are highly visible because they reflect much more UV than the daisy petals. Bees are actually attracted to flowers with these UV-reflecting spiders, apparently expressing a general preference for flowers with contrasting markings (Heiling, Herberstein, and Chittka 2003).

3.5.2   Sensory bias and sexual selection: Frog calls and fish tails

Darwin (1871) was the first to discuss an evolutionary puzzle that is still being debated today: why do males of some species have secondary sexual characters so large or conspicuous that they must be detrimental to survival? Natural selection would be expected to mitigate against cumbersome antlers and extraordinarily long brightly colored tails, so why do such exaggerated characters persist? Darwin's answer was that such ornaments evolve because females prefer them: the force of sexual selection outweighs the forces of natural selection. Roughly speaking, sexual selection occurs due to greater reproductive success of individuals preferred as mates by the opposite sex; in most cases females do the choosing, driving appearance and behavior of males. A central question in this area is "What is the evolutionary cause of the observed patterns of female choice, in particular, females' preference in many species for exaggerated male characters?" There are several answers. As explained next, each may be correct for some situations (Andersson 1994; Maynard Smith and Harper 2003; Searcy and Nowicki 2005).

It is not particularly problematic why females may prefer male characters correlated with large size, good health, or—in species with biparental care—ability to help rear the young. For example, growing bright glossy feathers may be possible only if you can get enough of the right foods to eat and resist diseases and parasites. Such characters may signal that the male has "good genes" that allow him to be strong and healthy and/or provide resources for a female and her offspring. Genes for preferring males that are better fathers would spread because daughters of females with these genes would inherit preference for better fathers, sons would inherit the genes for being better fathers, and by definition better fathers have more offspring than poor ones. A preferred character of this sort might become exaggerated through evolution as discussed in Section 3.4.3, but it and the females' response to it are selected because it indicates male quality.

The "runaway" hypothesis of sexual signal evolution specifically accounts for signals that seem to have no intrinsic relationship to male quality. It is essentially Darwin's suggestion buttressed by mathematical modeling. Informally stated, if at some stage in evolution females by chance preferred an arbitrary male character, females with the preference and males with the character could come to dominate the gene pool, in a runaway positive feedback process. On this scenario, the female preference and the male character evolved together, and the preferred male character need not be correlated with male quality.

But what gets selection on such a character started in the first place? One prominent suggestion is that preexisting features of females' sensory systems or perceptual preferences make such characters especially attractive, a suggestion known as the sensory bias hypothesis (Ryan 1994; for discussion of the many different terms and ideas in this area see Endler and Basolo 1998). Some kind of arbitrary bias is needed to get runaway selection started, but the sensory bias theory has been thought to make at least two unique predictions (Fuller, Houle, and Travis 2005; Searcy and Nowicki 2005). First, female sexual preferences evolved before male characters. This possibility can be tested with comparative behavioral data and phylogenies. Second, a preference expressed in a sexual context may have a function in another context such as feeding or predator avoidance. For instance, male lizards of the species *Anolis auratus* start their sexual display with a rapid up and down motion of the head (Fleishman 1988). Sudden motion attracts attention in many contexts, and for good reason, as it could indicate a live prey item or an approaching predator. The sexual display of the male water mite *Neumania papillator* includes waving his appendages in a way that mimics the motion of prey items, and in fact hungry females are more likely than sated ones to respond to displaying males (Proctor 1992). The strong attraction of both male and female guppies to orange fruits suggests that the orange spots of male guppies similarly exploit a feeding preference (Rodd et al. 2002; but see Millar et al. 2006). By implication, in these cases responsiveness evolved first in the nonsexual context and males have been selected to exploit it in the sexual context. Cladistic analysis (Chapter 2) has supported this conclusion for water mites.

In all the foregoing examples the chief evidence that a more general preference is reflected in sexual signaling is the observation that all members of the species show it. For instance, whether breeding or not both male and female guppies are attracted to orange fruits (Rodd et al. 2002). When instead phylogenetic inference is the main support for a hypothesized preexisting bias, conclusions are very much dependent on the number of species used to collect behavioral data and to construct the phylogeny on which conclusions about signal evolution are based. This important point is illustrated very well by two of the original candidates for signals evolved through sensory bias. One is the swordlike extension on the tails of male swordtail fish (Ryan and Rand 1995; for another example see Garcia and Ramirez 2005). Female sword-tails prefer long swords over short ones (Basolo 1990a; Basolo 1990b). Platyfish are a group of swordless species that share a common ancestor with swordtails (Figure 3.11), and females of a swordless platyfish species prefer males with swords as sensory bias predicts. Now the question for a phylogenetic analysis is whether the most recent common ancestor of swordtails and platyfish had a sword or not. The best phylogeny available when Basolo made her discovery (Figure 3.11top), indicates that swordlessness is ancestral, and therefore preference for swords must have evolved before swords. However, a later phylogeny based more heavily on similarities in DNA (Figure 3.11bottom) seems to indicate that swords were ancestral and have been gained and lost several times within the swordtail-platyfish group (Meyer, Morrissey, and Schartl 1994). But even newer behavioral data reveals that in a species

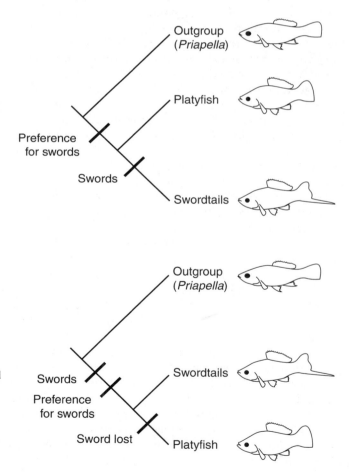

Figure 3.11. Possible alternative pathways for the evolution of swords and sword preference in swordtails and platyfish. The phylogenies are simplified, since each branch actually contains numerous species. Adapted from Basolo (1995a) with permission.

in the outgroup for this phylogeny, that is, the closest relative of both swordtails and platyfish, females also prefer males with swords (Basolo 1995b; but see Basolo 2002), indicating that preference for swords predated any evolution of swords.

The call of the male túngara frog, *Physalaemus pustulosus*, is another male mating signal hypothesized to have evolved through exploiting the sensory bias of females (Ryan and Rand 1993). In this case tests of the sensory bias hypothesis have included physiological studies of the frogs' auditory system as well as behavior and phylogeny. The call of the male túngara frog contains a whine followed by a number of lower-pitched chucks. The whine is necessary and sufficient for mate recognition, but the addition of chucks enhances the attractiveness of the call to females in choice tests in the laboratory. Chucks contain predominantly the frequencies to which the female frog's inner ear is most sensitive, suggesting that chucks might be quite stimulating to females generally, even though males of closely related species do not add chucks to their calls. This proved to be the case with the first set of species studied. Females of the closely related species *P. coloradorum* responded more to *P. coloradorum* calls with added chucks than to unaltered calls. Thus they have a preference for calls with chucks, which they normally do not express because males of their species do not chuck. Phylogenetic analysis based on characters other than male mating calls initially indicated that the chucks are recently evolved, as the sensory bias hypothesis requires (Ryan and Rand 1993). Accordingly, the frog calls became a key example of signal evolution through sensory bias. However, when more species are included in both the phylogeny and the tests of auditory sensitivity and female preference, the pattern is inconsistent with preexisting sensory bias. Instead, female preference and male calls seem to have coevolved, implying that some degree of central decision making is involved in the females' choice (Ron 2008; see also Phelps, Rand, and Ryan 2006). Although this tale may not be all told yet, it illustrates very well the much more general principle that conclusions about the evolution of cognition and/or the role of cognition in evolution depend on testing plenty of species and having good information about the relationships among them. The latter, in particular, depends heavily on how many and which species are included in the analysis (see Ron 2008).

3.6   Search and attention

At any given moment, most of the surrounding environment is irrelevant for current behavior. For example, as you read this book, you may be drinking a cup of coffee and playing your stereo, but neither the taste of coffee nor the sound of music is relevant for the task at hand. For some species, like the *Bembyx* moth, the problem of selecting what parts of the world to respond to has been solved by the evolution of specialized sensory channels and stimulus coding mechanisms ensuring that the moth senses only the few things in the world that matter for survival and reproduction. But such reliable coding limits flexibility. Animals like birds, monkeys, and human beings that can perceive a wide range of stimuli from several sensory modalities need a way to ensure that, for example, they switch appropriately from looking for food at one moment to looking for a safe refuge at another. Attention is one process that does this selecting. Motivational processes may play a role too, for example by changing thresholds for responding to relevant stimuli with physiological state.

Concentrating on reading while doing other things illustrates how attention is used as a filter, deployed in this case in a top-down manner (i.e., through some internal decision process). But attention doesn't necessarily filter out all but one set of cues. A door slamming, or someone calling your name can grab attention (an example of a bottom-up or externally driven switch of attention). In these examples, attention has the beneficial effect of ensuring that the important things of the moment are processed best. But attention also has a cost: if we actually listen to the radio while reading, we'll get less out of the reading (and vice versa) than if we do one thing at a time. Why attention is limited is a much debated theoretical question. Obviously it sometimes solves the problem of animals not being able to do two physically incompatible things at once, such as search for food and watch for predators, but this does not explain why it should not be possible, for example, to search for two kinds of food as efficiently as for one or to read while listening to the radio. This property of attention may reflect basic limitations on the size of the brain due to the metabolic costs of neural tissue (Dukas 2004). Traditional psychological theorizing similarly assumed a limitation on perceptual processing resources or a bottleneck in more central processing, but contemporary theorizing has identified alternative possible mechanisms, some of them better specified (Luck and Vevera 2002). But rather than advancing any general theory, research on attention in nonhuman species has primarily aimed to establish effects similar to those found in people (Section 3.6) and show how attention plays a role in ecologically relevant behavior (Section 3.7).

3.6.1   Visual search: The basics

Much data and theory on attention in humans is based on research with visual stimuli (Luck and Vevera 2002). Comparable experiments with highly visual animals, primarily monkeys and birds, indicate that basic attentional processes are shared across species (reviews in Blough 2001; Zentall 2005b; Blough 2006). Clearly, however, the important things in life are sometimes defined by sound, smell, or other nonvisual stimuli. For example, a father penguin returning to the colony with food needs to be able to pick out his mate's or baby's calls from those of hundreds of others (Aubin and Jouventin 2002). Such *auditory scene analysis* has been extensively studied in the context of animal vocal communication (Hulse 2002). It is also important in understanding how bats distinguish prey-generated echoes from background noise (Moss and Surlykke 2001). However, because the most detailed analyses of animal attentional processes have addressed visual attention, that will be the focus here.

In visual search tasks (Schiffrin 1988; Treisman 1988) as the name implies, the subject searches for something by looking for it. The thing being searched for is referred to as the *target*. It is embedded among other items, the *distractors*. Figure 3.12a shows a typical example for a human subject, a target X among distracting Os, and one that might confront a visual granivorous predator, a black seed among white pebbles. No one reading this book would fail to find the X or the seed in Figure 3.12a, but suppose the figure had been flashed for a fraction of a second or the distractors were much more similar to the target, say Ys instead of Os surrounding the target X. Now the results would start to be interesting. Under these sorts of conditions, with limited viewing time or high similarity between target and distractors, subjects may make mistakes and/or take longer to find the target.

In Figure 3.12a, the target X seems to "pop out" from the background of Os. The same would be true if the target were a yellow X among red Xs or a moving dot among stationary ones. The pop out effect is evident in data from visual search tasks

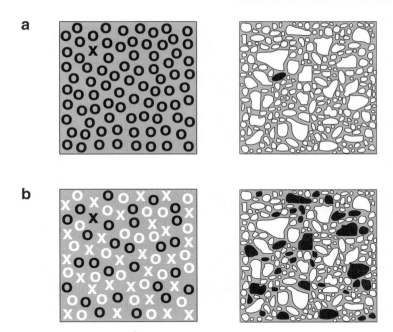

Figure 3.12. Typical stimuli for visual search experiments. a. Targets defined by a difference in one feature (shape or color) "pop out" from the background. b. Conjunctively defined targets, the black X and the black grain, take longer to find. Panels on the right adapted from Dawkins (1971) with permission.

in the fact that with such displays reaction time (latency to detect the target) increases only slightly with the number of distractors (Figure 3.13). In contrast, when the target is defined by the conjunction of two features, for example a black X or among black Os together with white Xs and Os (Figure 3.12b), reaction time increases sharply with the number of distractors. One interpretation of this pattern of data is that when target and distractors differ in just one feature, the objects in the display are processed in parallel, that is, all at the same time. When the target is defined by a conjunction of features, the items have to be processed serially, that is, one by one. With conjunctive targets, the times taken to decide "no, the target is not there" support this interpretation. Every item in the display must be mentally inspected in order to decide the target is absent. It will take twice as long on average to say (correctly) "No target" than to locate the target (Figure 3.13). The fact that the functions relating reaction time to number of distractors are straight lines indicates that processing each additional item takes a constant amount of time (Treisman and Gelade 1980).

3.6.2   Feature integration theory

Treisman's (1988, 1999) interpretation of results like those just described is that elementary features of objects such as shape, color, and motion are registered automatically without needing attention (preattentively). Identifying visual objects consisting of a conjunction of features requires that the object's location in space become the focus of attention and the features perceived there be integrated. Some of the evidence in support of Treisman's feature integration theory comes from experiments in which subjects are briefly shown a circular display of colored letters and asked to

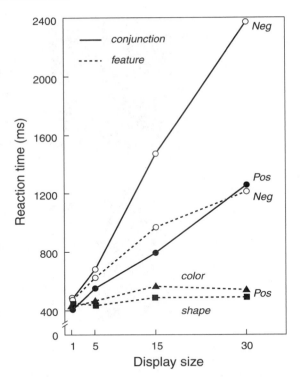

Figure 3.13. Human subjects' latencies to respond correctly in visual search experiments with a target defined by a single feature or a conjunction of features as a function of display size. On positive trials (Pos) the target was present; it was absent on negative (Neg) trials. Redrawn from Treisman and Gelade (1980) with permission.

report the color, the shape, or both the color and shape of the letter in one location. The probability of correctly reporting the conjunction of features is predicted almost perfectly by the probabilities of correctly reporting color and shape separately (Treisman 1988). This pattern of data is consistent with the notion that the object's features are first processed independently rather than as a unit. Moreover, identifying a conjunctive target is strongly associated with reporting its location correctly, as if objects are perceived as a spatial conjunction of independently processed features.

Another way to demonstrate the processes in feature integration is texture segregation. The idea behind texture segregation is that a cluster of identical objects is perceived as a distinct object in itself. As can be seen in Figure 3.14, the distinction between elemental and conjunctive targets is just as evident here as with individual targets: areas defined by a difference in one element, such as a cluster of white objects among black ones, pop out. Areas defined by a conjunction of elements, such as a cluster of white squares and black circles among white circles and black squares, take time to detect. Data from both humans and pigeons support this conclusion (Treisman and Gelade 1980; Cook 2001b).

In the experiments with pigeons (see Cook 2001b; Cook 1992a), birds were trained to peck at displays on a video monitor surrounded by an array of infrared emitters and detectors. This "touch frame" was positioned so that when the bird pecked at the TV screen its beak broke two infrared beams crossing the screen at right angles, and information about the location pecked was transmitted to the computer controlling the stimuli and reinforcers. The screen was covered with rows of small shapes, with one square about a quarter of the screen's area having different shapes from the rest

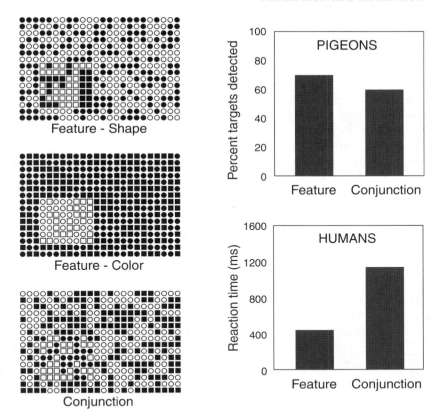

Figure 3.14. Stimuli used to study texture segregation by pigeons and humans and both species' performance with simple ("feature") and conjunctive targets. Data from Cook (1992b); stimuli reproduced from the same article with permission.

(Figure 3.14). The birds were reinforced with food for pecking five times anywhere on this rectangle; one peck elsewhere caused the screen to go dark and postponed the next trial. The pigeons were trained at first with a relatively small number of different small shapes and colors defining the target rectangle and just a few target positions, but they continued to perform well above chance when novel shapes, colors, and positions were introduced. These data alone suggest that, like humans, the pigeons perceived the cluster of distinctive items as "an object" and that they had learned "peck the object," not "peck the training items." Most importantly, targets defined by a difference in a single feature were consistently detected more accurately than targets defined by a conjunction of features. Cook (1992b) tested humans with the same displays as the pigeons. The pattern of results was the same, except that whereas the pigeons showed differences mainly in accuracy of detecting the target areas, people showed differences in reaction time (see Figure 3.14). Nevertheless, these data compellingly indicate that at least this one animal species, evolutionarily and neurologically very different from us, shares the same kind of elemental processing in the early stages of vision (review in Blough and Blough 1997; Blough 2001).

Feature integration can be contrasted with the Gestalt approach to perception, in which perception of the whole is primary and analysis into parts comes later. It also contrasts with the influential approach of J. J. Gibson (1979), which emphasizes the importance of ecologically relevant wholes. For instance, the spatial structure of the environment is immediately evident in the way objects move relative to each other when the observer moves: nearby objects move across the visual field faster than those farther away. The contrast between elemental and holistic approaches pervades theoretical debates about many cognitive processes. Feature integration theory assumes a modular organization of perception in that there is a separate module for processing each stimulus dimension. In evolution, modular organization would permit the ability to process additional dimensions to be added onto an initially simple perceptual system. Similarly, in a modular system the ability to process a feature of particular importance for a given species can be fine-tuned without affecting processing of other features.

3.6.3   Attention in visual search.

In experiments like those just described, visual search is used to test focused attention, that is, the subject searches for one thing at a time. The question being investigated is how the distractors in the visual display do just what their name implies, namely distract the subject from finding the target as rapidly and accurately as possible. If target and distractors are very different, the popout effect occurs and the number of distractors does not matter. But with increasing similarity between target and distractors, even when the subject searches for just one type of target reaction times increase (or accuracy decreases) as the number of distractors (the *display size*) or the similarity of the distractors to the target increases. The data from search for conjunctive targets in Figure 3.13 illustrate effects of display size in humans. Figure 3.15 illustrates comparable effects of similarity and display size for pigeons.

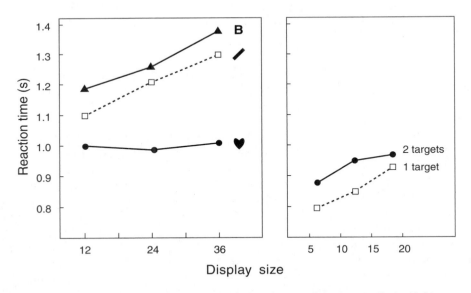

Figure 3.15. Effects of display size (number of items) and target-distractor similarity (left) or memory set size (right) on visual search in pigeons, as measured by time taken to locate the target (reaction time). Left panel redrawn from P. Blough (1992) with permission; the distractors were standard alphanumeric characters, hence the heart shape was the least similar and "popped out." Right panel, one pigeon's data from P. Blough (1989), redrawn with permission.

Figure 3.15 also illustrates the effects of number of possible targets used in a series of trials, the memory set size. In human subjects, too, search slows as the number of potential targets increases. Subjects searching for just one sort of target are like specialist foragers, animals that eat only one kind of thing, whereas subjects for which targets are mixed unpredictably are like generalists, foragers that can eat several kinds of prey. The decrease in performance with a larger memory set size is a cost of being a generalist. If the targets were food items, the benefit to generalists of being able to eat more of what they encounter might have to be traded off against this cost. However, the detrimental effect of memory set size diminishes with extended practice. That is, search becomes automatized as if attention is automatically drawn to items that have frequently been attended to (Schiffrin 1988). With pigeons, too, the effect of display size on search accuracy disappears after extended training, but only with a comparatively small set of potential targets (Vreven and Blough 1998). These findings suggest that generalizing might not have a cost in the wild once animals are familiar with all available items.

The effect of memory set size means that a given target is found more quickly or accurately when it is the only one presented over a series of trials than when it is unpredictably mixed with one or more other targets. Finding one target of a given type *primes* attention to targets of that type. Priming is thought of as a transitory activation or facilitation of processing of the target's features. Priming can occur either sequentially as just described, or associatively. In associative priming, performance is facilitated by presenting a cue that has been associated with the target, either just before or during presentation of the target. For example, in a further part of the study whose results are displayed in Figure 3.15, distinctive borders were added to the stimulus displays. Black and white were paired with A and L, respectively; a striped border, paired equally often with A and L, served as an ambiguous cue (P. Blough 1989; D.Blough 1991). Performance with each letter was better when it was cued than otherwise. If each target is paired consistently with a particular distractor, the distractors themselves may serve as associative priming cues (Blough 1993a).

Priming seems not only to facilitate processing of the primed target, but to inhibit processing of unprimed targets. In P. Blough's (1989) experiments, performance on occasional test trials in which A appeared when L was cued or vice versa was worse than on trials with the ambiguous cue. Pigeons can also be primed to attend to particular areas of a display (Blough 1993b). These data on priming seem to suggest that if foraging is like visual search for prey scattered on a substrate of distractors, as Figure 3.12 was made to suggest, any sources of information about the identity of the prey aid search (Blough 1993a). These include what prey have been found recently (sequential priming), where they have been found (priming by locations), and what substrate they were found on (associative priming). It is not yet clear, however, whether these different sources of priming all work in the same way. When sequential and associative priming are combined, they do not always have the strictly additive effect that would be expected if both enhance the same attentional process (Kamil and Bond 2006).

For animals foraging in the wild, as we see in Chapter 11, what matters is not success or speed on any single trial but overall rate of food intake. A nice demonstration of how attentional priming translates into this currency was a study in which bluejays were trained to search on video displays for two simulated prey items, a brown horizontal bar and a white vertical ellipse in mixtures of different sized brown horizontal bars and white vertical ellipses (Dukas and Kamil 2001). The bird began a trial by pecking a "start" circle surrounding an image of one or both of the possible "prey." A single image reliably cued the item to be found in the upcoming display, presumably allowing the bird to focus its attention on items of the cued color, whereas a double image was an ambiguous cue to item type. As soon as a bird pecked a target once, it received half a mealworm and 3 seconds later the signal for the next trial, whereas pecking a distractor delayed the next trial for 15 seconds. This contingency meant that speed and accuracy at pecking the targets would increase the rate of food intake. Consistent with sequential and/or associative priming, the number of mealworms obtained per minute increased by about 50% when the upcoming prey image was signaled.

3.7   Attention and foraging: The behavioral ecology of attention

3.7.1   Search images

By comparing the kinds of insects birds brought to their young with the kinds available in the trees where the birds foraged, Luc Tinbergen (1960), brother of the more famous Niko referred to elsewhere in this book, discovered that insects are not preyed on when they first appear in the environment. Instead, a new prey type such as a freshly hatching species of caterpillar will suddenly begin to be taken when its abundance increases. This sudden increase in predation, Tinbergen suggested, occurs because predators adopt a specific searching image for that prey type after a few chance encounters. "The birds perform a highly selective sieving operation on the stimuli reaching the retina" (Tinbergen, 1960, 333). Described in this way, adopting a searching image (or *search image*) sounds like an attentional process. Recent experiments have supported this conclusion.

The idea that animals might search selectively, ignoring items that do not match a mental representation of desired prey, is appealing because it agrees so well with introspection. Most people have had the experience of not seeing what is right in front of their noses. Indeed, one of the earliest references to search images in animal behavior is von Uexküll's (1934/1957) description of looking for a familiar earthenware water jug and not seeing the glass one that had replaced it (Figure 3.16).

Figure 3.16. Von Uexküll's depiction of his own search image of an earthen water jug and of a frog's search image of a worm. After von Uexküll (1934/1957) with permission.

Animals, too, von Uexkull suggested, could have a mental image of a prey item that enhances their ability to detect matching items and interferes with detecting others (Figure 3.16). It has generally been assumed that an animal can have only one search image at a time, that is, the search image enhances predation on one cryptic prey type while temporarily inhibiting detection of other types. Crypticity is important because search images are assumed to be useful only for prey that are difficult to find in the first place.

By themselves, Tinbergen's data can be explained in a number of ways. Runs of the same type of prey can be explained by the birds repeatedly visiting the same patch of habitat. If the birds were relatively young, they could have been learning that particular insects were suitable as prey or where or how to hunt for them (Dawkins 1971). Learning the characteristics of novel prey in the first place is not the same as selectively attending to a known prey type. Therefore, most recent experiments on search images have varied the abundance and/or crypticity of items that are familiar to the animals being tested. For example, Bond (1983; Langley et al. 1996) studied pigeons searching for two kinds of grains, black gram and wheat, scattered over multicolored gravel. Because the grains were the same color as some pieces of gravel, they were more difficult for the birds to detect on this background than on a plain gray one. After the birds were familiar with feeding on these grains on the gravel backgrounds, the relative proportions of black gram and wheat were varied randomly between 100% black gram and 100% wheat. The birds behaved as if adopting a search image for the more frequent type, taking proportionately more of it rather than matching the proportion taken to the proportion available (Figure 3.17). However, pigeons do match the proportion taken to the proportion available when the prey items are conspicuous, showing that crypticity is important, not just variations in relative proportion (Langley 1996).

One way to find more prey that are difficult to see is to search more slowly, spending longer scanning each section of the substrate (Gendron and Staddon 1983; Guilford and Dawkins 1987). A tradeoff between speed and accuracy in performing difficult discriminations is common to many species, including honeybees (Dyer and Chittka 2004). Reaction time is a good index of the amount of mental processing a task requires, even when it is performed very accurately (see Blough 2006). In the present example, there is an optimal speed-accuracy tradeoff for each

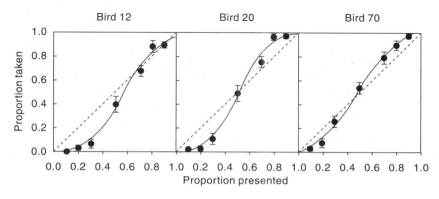

Figure 3.17. Proportion of cryptic grains of one type taken by each of three pigeons as a function of its proportion in a mixture of two types of cryptic grains in the study by Bond (1983). Redrawn with permission.

degree of crypticity that balances the potential benefit of encountering more prey by searching faster against the cost of missing cryptic items by searching too fast (Gendron and Staddon 1983).

The search rate hypothesis predicts that a predator searching slowly should detect all equally cryptic prey equally well. In contrast, an animal with a search image should take one type and ignore the other, even if both types are equally cryptic. Figure 3.17 shows that the two grains used were equally cryptic because when equal numbers were presented (proportion presented = 50%), equal numbers were taken. However, contrary to the search rate hypothesis, the proportion taken did not equal the proportion presented under all conditions. Disproportionate predation on the more abundant type implies that the birds were using a search image for the more frequently encountered grain. This does not mean, however, that animals faced with difficult discriminations in nature might not also search more slowly.

Allowing an animal to search freely for prey items as was done in these studies has some drawbacks as an experimental technique. The animal rather than the experimenter controls the rate and sequence of encounters, and the relative proportion of different items changes as the food depletes. To test the effect of recent experience on choice or detectability of prey it is necessary to present a standard test after differing experiences (Chapter 4). One way to do this is to present prey items one at a time. For example, Pietrewicz and Kamil (1981) tested blue jays (*Cyanocitta cristata*) in an operant task in which they pecked at slides showing two species of moths (blue jays' natural prey items) resting against tree trunks on which they were cryptic. The birds were rewarded with mealworms for indicating correctly that a moth was present. If no moth was present, pecking a central "moving on" key led to the next trial. These pecks generally had longer latencies than pecks to slides with a moth, as if the birds used exhaustive serial search to decide no moth was present. The critical data came from comparing performance in trials following runs of moths of the same type with performance in mixed trials with both species (Figure 3.18). Performance improved within runs as compared to mixed trials. Notably, the birds' accuracy at detecting the absence of a moth improved as well as their accuracy at detecting the presence of a moth, consistent with the notion that attention enhances detection of attended features. These data suggest that the bluejays had a search image for the moth species they had encountered most recently. Because the moths were depicted as they would appear in nature, one species on birch tree trunks and the other on oak trunks, associative priming may have been operating in addition to the sequential priming evident Figure 3.18.

When multiple kinds of prey items can be found on the same substrate, priming presumably occurs when several of the same type are found in succession by chance. Experiments in which pigeons search for grains among gravel have been used to analyze this situation (Reid and Shettleworth 1992; Langley 1996; Langley et al. 1996). Pamela Reid (Reid and Shettleworth 1992) used wheat dyed yellow, green, or brown on a background of green and brown gravel. A free search experiment similar to Bond's established that brown and green were equally cryptic whereas yellow grains were highly conspicuous to the pigeons. To control the birds' experience, Reid then used the apparatus shown in Figure 3.19. Small plaques of gravel, each holding one or two grains, were presented one at a time, and the birds were allowed a single peck at each one. In a run of green or brown after a run of conspicuous yellow grains, the birds' accuracy gradually increased, consistent with their forming a search image for the new cryptic type, just as when they searched freely for grains. However, after a switch from a run of one cryptic type to a run of the other, the birds performed just as

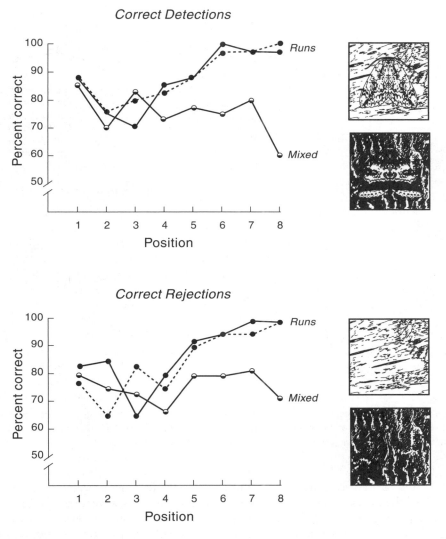

Figure 3.18. Performance of bluejays reinforced for reporting the presence (top panel) or absence (lower panel) of moths in slide images like those on the right in runs of the same moth species or trials with a mixture of two species. Adapted from Pietrewicz and Kamil (1981) with permission.

well as if they had a single cryptic type all along (Figure 3.19). This seems to mean that the birds' "search image" includes some feature distinguishing grains in general from gravel, perhaps shape or texture. Nevertheless, when Reid's pigeons had a choice between brown and green grains, the two cryptic types, after a run of one of them, they tended to choose the color they had just been having. This was not just a general preference for what they had been eating most recently, because the effect depended on the grains being cryptic. Thus the "search image" also seems to include information about the grain's color.

These results naturally lend themselves to interpretation in terms of feature detection and priming. Easy detection of the conspicuous yellow grains is an instance of the popout effect: the target (the grain) differs from the distractors (the bits of gravel) in a

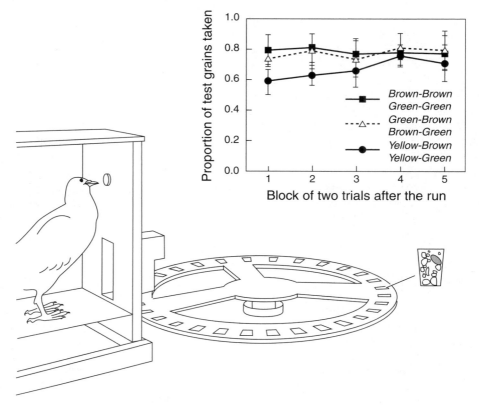

Figure 3.19. Search image effects in pigeons searching for cryptic brown or green or conspicuous yellow grains. Data from a test run of 10 grains after a run of the same or a different color, as indicated. Adapted from Reid and Shettleworth (1992) with permission.

single salient feature (color). The cryptic grains are difficult to detect because they resemble the distractors in color. Because the cryptic items were all grains of wheat, priming with grains dyed one color could enhance detection of other grains with the same shape, size, and texture. The effect on choice shows that the specific color was also primed to some extent. Such a priming effect occurs even if the priming grains are conspicuous, but it is detected only in a test with cryptic grains (Langley 1996). Thus, contrary to the fanciful depictions in Figure 3.16, the "search image" is a collection of independently primed features of the prey. This interpretation suggests that when, unlike the case in Reid's experiments, two cryptic items do not share features allowing them to be detected against their background, the search image/priming effect should be truly specific, with enhanced detection of one item accompanied by reduced detection of the other. Such an effect was observed in a study by Langley (1996) in which pigeons searched computer images of multicolored gravel for a bean or a grain of wheat. By manipulating features of the images, Langley also showed that the importance of color and shape differed for beans versus wheat (see also Plaisted and Mackintosh 1995).The type of background and the type of search task can also influence what features are attended to, as shown in an elegant study by Blough (2002) in which pigeons performed difficult detection and disambiguation tasks with a single set of striped disks. In summary, the "search image," that is, the representation or activation underlying sequential or associative priming, is rarely if ever an actual image of the item being searched for. Rather, what it consists of may vary from one situation and task to another depending on factors such as what distinguishes the item from the substrate and what features it shares with other concurrently available items.

The priming effects we have been discussing are by definition short-lived. Indeed, Bond (1983) suggested that sequential priming decays after a few seconds. But this raises a question about the interpretation of some findings reviewed in this section. For instance, consider that in Reid and Shettleworth's (1992) study two green grains were separated by twice as long on average in mixed green and brown trials as in green-only trials. When pigeons are detecting small black and white patterns against black and white checked backgrounds, a difference in presentation rate by itself can produce differences in discrimination accuracy (Plaisted, 1997). When items in runs were presented at the same rate as items of a single type were occurring in mixed trials, accuracy was no greater than in the matched mixed trials. Plaisted (1997) therefore proposed that search image effects reflect a short-lived priming of independent memory traces for recent items rather than priming of attention to particular item features. However, although this methodological feature should be to taken into account in studies of priming, so far there is no evidence that Plaisted's proposal accounts for results such as those discussed earlier in this section (Bond and Kamil 1999; Blough 2001; Blough 2006; Kamil and Bond 2006).

3.7.2   Search images and prey evolution

Attentional priming has implications for the evolution of species that are prey. For example cryptic prey of a single species should spread themselves out in the environment to reduce the chances of predators encountering them in runs. *Polymorphism,* that is, a tendency for different individuals of the same species to have markedly different colors or patterns, would have the same effect (Croze 1970; Bond 2007). But it is one thing to speculate on how predator psychology has selected for prey appearance and behavior, another thing to demonstrate that this could actually happen. Such a demonstration is provided by a series of studies with bluejays, using procedures similar to those of Pietrewicz and Kamil (1981) but with computer-generated "moths" (Figure 3.20) that "evolve" in response to predation (Kamil and Bond 2006). In the first experiment with this "virtual ecology" (Bond and Kamil 1998; Kamil and Bond 2001) the initial prey population consisted of three "species," digitized images of *Catocala* moths. They appeared on a background of random pixels that could vary from almost smooth grey on which the moths were very conspicuous to a mixture of patches similar to the patches on the moths. Bluejays that had been trained to detect the moths under very cryptic conditions then became the selective agents in the following way. Every day 240 moth images were used. In the first day of the experiment there were 80 of each species (Figure 3.20). At the end of each day, the moths detected by the jays were considered killed, and the remaining moths were allowed to reproduce (actually, here to clone themselves) to provide the population for the next day. In this way the least detectable moths became proportionately more numerous in the next virtual generation.

In three repetitions of this procedure with different initial conditions, the same moth (moth 1 in Figure 3.20)—evidently the most cryptic of the three—came to dominate. This was true even when it was in the minority to begin with, as in the

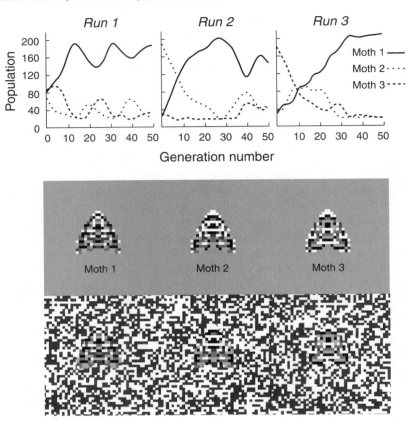

Figure 3.20. Lower panels: the three artificial moth species in Bond and Kamil's (1998) "virtual ecology" shown in both easy (gray background) and hard to discriminate conditions. Upper panel: changes in the virtual population over generations of predation by jays given different compositions of the initial population (Runs 1–3). After Bond and Kamil (1998) with permission.

second and third replications. The jays were showing the same kind of *frequency-dependent selection* evident in Bond's (1983) pigeons (Figure 3.17). A separate study (Bond and Kamil 1999) demonstrated that indeed jays show attentional priming effects with such digital moth displays. As the relatively conspicuous moths 2 and 3 were eliminated, individuals of moth 1 were found more often, priming detection. At the final abundances in each repetition, the intrinsically greater detectability of moths 2 and 3 was balanced by the primed detectability of moth 1.

The next step with this approach was to model evolution more realistically by modeling the genetics of wing patterns and letting the surviving virtual moths from a large and varied initial population "reproduce" via an algorithm that randomly recombined genes for different aspects of wing patterns (Bond and Kamil 2002; Bond and Kamil 2006). The populations that resulted from 100 generations of selection by jays were more cryptic and more diverse in appearance than control populations. Analysis of the sequences of events within sessions of the experiment showed that, just as would be expected, accuracy at detecting one of the more cryptic moths was better the more similar it was to the last moth detected. In summary, then, this approach shows that search image effects are still at work even in a dynamic situation with multiple prey types, and that—just has been commonly hypothe-sized—they can have an important impact on prey evolution.

The results of all these studies with "virtual ecology" imply that the learning and attentional mechanisms of predators can help to maintain polymorphisms in popula-tions of a single species by leading to *frequency dependent selection*, that is, as a type of prey becomes more frequent it is proportionately more preyed on (Bond 2007). The different prey types, which may be morphs of a single type, do not have to differ in crypticity. If one type is rare for any reason, it should have a survival advantage. Thus Figure 3.17 illustrates frequency-dependent predation when the "prey" are different kinds of grains. In a nice demonstration in the wild, male guppies with different tail color patterns were removed from isolated natural pools in Trinidad, recombined into experimental populations in which one tail color pattern or another was comparatively rare, and reintroduced. Males chosen to have a color pattern that was uncommon in their group were most likely to survive until the pool was re sampled 2 to 3 weeks later (Olendorf et al. 2006).

3.7.3   Divided attention and vigilance

An animal that is foraging cannot wait until it is satiated to check for predators but should continuously divide attention between foraging and vigilance. The classic illustration of how hard it is for people to divide attention is the situation at a cocktail party: when many conversations are going on simultaneously, it is very difficult to follow more than one of them at a time. In tests of divided attention in the laboratory (see Luck and Vevera 2002), people are instructed to report on more than one source of information at once. In general, performance on a given task falls when attention must be shared between it and another task. The same is true in animals tested in common laboratory paradigms, most often short-term memory tasks (Chapter 7; Zentall 2005a). Just as in the tests of focused attention discussed up to now in this chapter, the detrimental effect of divided attention may diminish as practice leads to automatization (Schiffrin 1988), consistent with the idea that well-learned tasks demand fewer processing resources.

Birds that feed on the ground have been popular subjects for naturalistic studies of dividing visual attention between feeding and vigilance. Many such birds alternate short periods with their heads down, presumably attending to food-related cues, with short periods of head-up scanning, presumably attending to predator-related and/or social cues. For instance, members of a flock of starlings walking across a field probing the ground for leatherjackets raise their heads between pecks and scan the sky and bushes. The smaller the flock, the more time each individual spends scanning (Elgar 1989). More demanding foraging tasks leave less time for vigilance. For example, when blackbirds are foraging on cryptic baits they take longer between scans and spend a smaller proportion of the time scanning than when they are feeding on conspicuous baits (Lawrence 1984).

However, the assumption that head position defines the focus of attention is problematical. For one thing, as mentioned in Section 3.1, what an animal sees from different viewpoints depends on the structure of its visual system. Many birds have a wide field of view and an area of high density photoreceptors placed to detect things approaching from the side (Figure 3.3). As long as they have a clear field of view, with no low barriers, thick grass, or the like, birds may be able to spot a predator almost as well while feeding with head down as while scanning with head up (Lima and Bednekoff 1999; Fernandez-Juricic, Erichsen, and Kacelnik 2004). And in any case, most studies of divided attention in humans deal with a central filtering mechanism, not where the receptors are directed. Thus, although some animals do continually display brief bouts of vigilance while feeding, at the level of mechanism they may not be doing the same thing as person at a cocktail party who attends at one moment to Joe's voice and at the next to Pete's.

Fish have also been subjects in studies of the tradeoff between feeding and vigilance. Sticklebacks recently exposed to a model predator, a kingfisher, flying overhead, feed more slowly than fish not so exposed. It is not surprising that fear increases vigilance, that is, it redirects attention, just as any motivational state enhances the salience of relevant stimuli (Milinski and Heller 1978; Milinski 1984). Suppressing feeding when preparing to flee has a function in that flight responses direct blood flow and other physiological resources away from digestion and toward the muscles for escaping. Independently of such motivational conflicts, a high feeding rate may indicate that less attention is available for predators. This was nicely demonstrated in an experiment in which guppies feeding on water fleas (*Daphnia*) were exposed to predation by a cichlid fish (Figure 3.21, Godin and Smith 1988). The amount of attention devoted to foraging, as reflected in the speed of capturing prey, was manipulated by varying both the density of *Daphnia* and the guppies' hunger level. The faster the guppies were feeding (i.e., at shorter intercapture intervals in Figure 3.21), the more likely one was to be captured by the cichlid. Animals foraging in a group may also need to monitor social stimuli, experiencing a three-way conflict among feeding, watching for predators, and seeing what companions are doing. For instance, juvenile brown trout feeding with familiar companions fed faster and responded more quickly to a model heron than did trout with novel companions, who instead spent more time in aggressive interactions (Cresswell et al. 2003).

Dividing attention in all these naturalistic situations seems to have clear costs such as lower feeding rate or increased risk of being caught by a predator, but the most direct demonstration of such a cost is perhaps that by Dukas and Kamil (2000). Bluejays were trained to find cryptic items among distractors in a central area and two

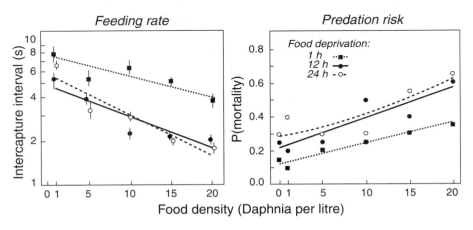

Figure 3.21. Effects of food density on guppies' feeding rate (the inverse of the interval between prey captures, left panel) and predation risk, the number of guppies caught by a predator. Redrawn from Godin and Smith (1988) with permission.

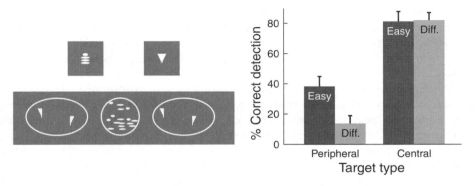

Figure 3.22. Procedure and results from Dukas and Kamil's (2000) demonstration of the cost of limited attention in bluejays. On the left, the two possible "prey items" are shown above a depiction of the video screen on a typical trial, with distracting elements present in the peripheral and central areas. Data, on the right, compare detection rate with prey in the central versus peripheral areas and when the task was relatively easy or difficult ("diff."). Adapted from Dukas and Kamil (2000) with permission.

peripheral areas on a video monitor (Figure 3.22). Birds pecked the center of the screen to cause the three prey-containing areas to appear for 500 milliseconds. They then had another 1000 milliseconds to peck the one area where a prey item had just appeared. Making the display brief and requiring the birds to peck the center of the screen ensured that they were always looking in the same place when the display appeared, much as people are required to look at a central fixation point in analogous tests. And by having competing foraging tasks Dukas and Kamil ensured that they were not measuring a change in vigilance associated with a motivational change, for example from hunger to fear. The jays were expected to devote most attention to the central part of the monitor because an item appeared there on 50% of the trials, whereas one appeared in each peripheral area on only 25% of trials. And indeed, as the central task was made more difficult by increasing the number of distractors, presumably thereby increasing its demands on attention, birds missed more of the peripheral prey (Figure 3.22).

The *confusion effect* may be another manifestation of divided attention in naturalistic situations. The confusion effect refers to the observation that many species of predators have more difficulty capturing prey when confronting a large school, swarm, or flock of similar individuals than when confronting one or a small group of individuals (Miller 1922; Krakauer 1995; Schradin 2000). The probability of an attack ending in prey capture once it has been initiated can decline dramatically with increases in the number of individuals in the group being attacked (Magurran 1990). The confusion effect has generally (cf. Krakauer 1995) been interpreted as caused by the predator dividing its attention among the prey rather than focusing on one until capturing it. The individual in a school of identical conspecifics is the limiting case of a cryptic prey item because it is identical to the "background" of surrounding individuals. On this view it is not surprising that odd individuals or stragglers in a group tend to be the ones captured. Just as in visual search (e.g., P. Blough 1979), the larger the group, the more detectable an odd individual seems to be (Milinski 1990). Notice that the predator confronted with a dense school of prey is assumed to be dividing attention among two or more spatial locations, perhaps because the motion it perceives at each one automatically attracts attention.

The evolutionary determinants of group living and group size are important topics in behavioral ecology (see Chapters 12 and 13). The material in this section suggests that the difficulty of effectively dividing attention confers at least two benefits of living in groups. One is that each individual in a group does not have to take so much attention away from foraging for vigilance because others can warn it of approaching predators. The other is that by being in a group of similar looking individuals the potential prey animal benefits from the ability of the swarm to confuse a predator. The confusion effect may account for several features of swarming or schooling species such as the fact that they tend not to show sexual dimorphism (i.e., males and females look the same), that they crowd together more when threatened, and that mixed species groups tend either to consist of species that look similar or to break up into same-species groups in the presence of a predator (Landeau and Terborgh 1986; Tegeder and Krause 1995).

3.8   Summary

Many universal principles of perception reflect the organization of the physical world (Shepard 1994). Paradoxically, some of the best support for such an adaptationist view of perception is diversity: general mechanisms have been tweaked by evolution in an adaptive way for each species. Animals differ dramatically in the sensory channels they use and in the patterns of sensitivity of those channels. Differences in sensory systems among species can be related to differences in their habitat and lifestyle. Nevertheless, all sensory systems that have been studied share some features, such as greater response to more intense stimuli, sensitivity to contrast, Weber's law, and a tendency to habituate.

Behavioral methods for discovering what animals perceive include testing natural behavior to the stimuli of interest and testing learned behavior using the methods of animal psychophysics. Signal detection theory is a general model of the discrimination of signals from background noise that applies to any situation where an animal has to make a difficult discrimination, and it has implications for the evolution of animal signals. In animal signaling systems, one animal provides a signal to which another animal, of the same or a different species, responds. Perception and the evolution of signals are therefore inextricably linked.

To understand how objects are perceived we have to go beyond sensitivities to individual stimulus modalities or features to ask how features are combined. One influential theory states that objects are perceived as the sum of individual primary features such as color and shape that co-occur at the same time and place. This feature integration theory is supported primarily by the performance of humans in visual search tasks, but some similar data have been reported from other species. To understand how behavior is controlled selectively by only some parts of the environment at any given time, it is necessary to understand attention. Characteristics of attention such as its susceptibility to priming have been studied in visual search tasks in humans and other animals. The apparent ability of foragers to form a search image, enabling them better to detect cryptic prey, may be explained by priming of attention to the features of the prey that best distinguish it from the background. Dividing attention between two or more tasks causes performance on each one to fall. The effects of divided attention can be seen in the tradeoff between foraging and vigilance and in the confusion effect, both of which create a selection pressure for animals to live in groups.

The story of research on search images is a good example of how hypotheses suggested by observations in the field were tested in the laboratory, using a whole range of approaches from the "naturalistic" to the "artificial," from tests in which animals search freely for familiar prey to those with controlled presentation of digital images. Some studies bridge the gap between tests of search image and those of visual search for abitrary targets like letters and shapes. And most recently, this research has come full circle in studies designed to to test hypotheses about how predators' attentional mechanisms drive the evolution of prey populations. Short-lived priming of feature detection is likely responsible for effects originally attributed to a search image for a prey item, but they do not mean that attentional priming is the only mechanism responsible for observations like Tinbergen's (1960). When animals first encounter novel prey items, they must learn to recognize them as prey and learn where to find them and how to capture and handle them, among other things. Each of these processes can be isolated and analyzed experimentally, as we will see in the next two chapters.

Further reading

This chapter has emphasized topics that connect perception with issues in behavioral ecology somewhat at the expense of the substantial work by comparative psychologists on more anthropocentric topics. More about such work can be found in the book edited by Wasserman and Zentall (2006b), the review by Spetch and Friedman (2006), and the online "cyberbook," *Avian Visual Cognition* (Cook 2001a). High-level introductions to basic topics in the psychological study of sensation and perception in humans, including attention, color vision, and signal detection theory, can be found in Volume 1 of *Stevens' Handbook of Experimental Psychology* (Yantis 2002).

Dusenbery's (1992) *Sensory Ecology* is an overview of the physical principles of information transmission, also covered in Bradbury and Vehrencamp's (1998) comprehensive text on the ecology and evolution of animal communication. The books by Maynard Smith and Harper (2003) and Searcy and Nowicki (2005) are both excellent briefer introductions to animal signaling, topics that we come back to in Chapter 14. Lythgoe's (1979) *The Ecology of Vision* is a classic, a rich source of information about adaptations in animal visual systems that has not been replaced. Kelber et al. (2003) is a comprehensive review of the mechanisms and distribution of animal color vision. A brief overview of methods in animal psychophysics is provided by Blough and Blough (1977). The two papers by Wiley (1994, 2006) are excellent introductions to signal detection theory and its implications for issues in animal communication.

4
Learning: Introduction and Pavlovian Conditioning

Like *attention, consciousness,* and other words from ordinary language used in psychology, *learning* is a term that everyone understands even though it eludes satisfactory technical definition (Section 4.2.1; Rescorla 2007). Functionally, learning allows animals to adjust their behavior to the local environment through individual experience. Animals need to know such things as what locally available food is good to eat, where and when to find it, which individuals to avoid and which to approach. This chapter introduces a basic framework for thinking about learning and then considers some ideas about the function and evolution of learning. The longest part of the chapter reviews data and theory about Pavlovian conditioning, perhaps the best-studied form of learning and one of the phylogenetically most widespread. Armed with this framework and some facts about conditioning, we will be in a position to analyze other forms of learning in future chapters. We will also be equipped to assess claims that some animals sometimes behave in ways that cannot be only the products of conditioning but rather require reasoning, a theory of mind, a qualitatively different kind of learning, or the like.

4.1 General processes and "constraints on learning"

As we have seen in Chapter 1, experimental studies of learning and other aspects of cognition in animals were stimulated by Darwin's (1871) claim that animal minds share properties with human minds. Early in their history, studies of learning came to focus on instrumental (operant) and later classical (Pavlovian) conditioning (Jenkins 1979; Boakes 1984), while other kinds of learning and cognitive processes were largely overlooked. The result was an approach referred to as general process learning theory (Seligman 1970), an attempt to account for all learning with the same set of principles. Although there were a few dissenters (Tolman 1949), general process learning theory had a heyday in the 1940s and 1950s and remains tremendously influential.

In the mid-1960s, however, psychologists discovered several puzzling phenomena that the supposedly general learning principles did not seem explain (Seligman 1970; Rozin and Kalat 1971; Shettleworth 1972). The key examples of these "constraints on learning" were conditioned taste aversion (Box 4.1), and autoshaping.

In autoshaping (Brown and Jenkins 1968), pigeons are placed in an operant chamber and a disk on the wall (the pecking key) is lit for a few seconds before food is presented. The pigeon does not have to peck the key, yet after a number of pairings between the keylight and food, pecking develops and persists. This finding seemed related to the Brelands' (Breland and Breland 1961) reports that animals being reinforced with food engaged in counterproductive species-specific food-related behaviors or "misbehaviors." For instance, a raccoon rewarded for depositing coins in a bank began to "wash" and rub the coins together in its paws rather than promptly getting its reward. Attention was also drawn to the difficulty of training rats to perform anything other than natural defensive behaviors when learning to avoid shock (Bolles 1970). To such observations of constraints on what animals could learn (or at least, do) in laboratory paradigms was added information about song learning, imprinting, and other "exceptional" examples of learning observed by ethologists.

Box 4.1 Flavor Aversion Learning

When rats and many other vertebrates sample a flavor and become ill later, they learn to avoid consuming that flavor. As first described by John Garcia and his colleagues in 1966, flavor aversion learning has two remarkable properties. First, it takes place even with delays of hours between sampling the flavor (the CS in this Pavlovian paradigm) and becoming ill (the US; Garcia, Ervin, and Koelling 1966). Second, in rats, learning with illness as a US is specific to flavors. Garcia and Koelling (1966) had rats drink from a tube of flavored solution and also exposed them to a noise and a light each time they licked ("bright noisy tasty water"). Some of the rats were made ill after drinking, whereas some were shocked through the feet as they drank. When tested with the light plus the noise or the flavor alone after conditioning, the poisoned rats avoided drinking the "tasty water" while the rats that had been shocked avoided drinking the "bright noisy water." Figure B4.1 displays data from a later experiment with this basic design but with the mode of presentation of the various CSs and USs

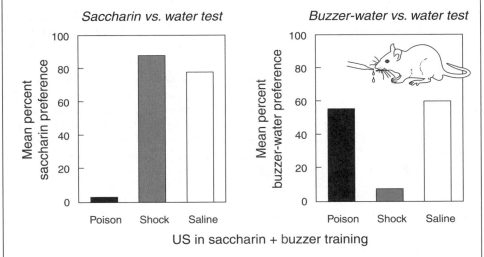

Figure B4.1. Test performance of three groups of rats that had experienced saccharin flavored water infused into their mouths while hearing the sound of a buzzer and had then been shocked, injected with lithium chloride to produce illness (poison US), or given a control saline injection. In the test rats chose between plain water and either saccharin (left panel) or water in a bottle that produced a buzzing sound when licked. Redrawn from Domjan and Wilson (1972) with permission.

better controlled than in the original (Domjan and Wilson 1972). These findings attracted tremendous attention when they were first reported because long-delay learning and CS-US specificity seemed to contradict then-current assumptions about the generality of the laws of learning. Some investigators rushed to test hypotheses that various uninteresting "general process" factors might have been responsible, while others were equally quick to claim far-reaching implications for them (Domjan and Galef 1983). The idea that learning may be especially fast with certain functionally appropriate combinations of events is now generally accepted (Section 4.4.4).

Conditioned taste aversion is a good example of how the details of conditioning in different systems can differ in an adaptive way: if the effects of ingesting something with a certain flavor can only be felt hours later, the learning mechanism for avoiding illness-producing foods should be capable of bridging this temporal gap. Strictly speaking, however, conclusions about adaptation require showing that animals with the hypothesized adaptation have greater fitness than animals lacking it or doing comparative studies. In the case of taste aversion, species that specialize on one or a few foods might have less need to learn flavor aversions than generalist species, that is, those which sample a variety of foods. Although a test of this hypothesis with two species of kangaroo rats (Daly, Rauschenberger, and Behrends 1982) provided only weak support for it, a test with four species of bats had clear positive results. Vampire bats, which consume only blood, showed no evidence of learning a flavor aversion, whereas three species with a varied diet of insects or fruit readily learned under the same conditions (Ratcliffe, Fenton, and Galef 2003).

Around 1970 several articles appeared on the theme that general process theory had overlooked the biological aspects of learning (Bolles 1970; Seligman 1970; Rozin and Kalat 1971; Garcia, McGowan, and Green 1972; Shettleworth 1972). They suggested that the newly discovered phenomena could be understood in terms of the idea that learning evolved for solving problems animals face in nature. However, despite proclamations that a revolution in the study of learning was on its way, the original candidates for "biological constraints" and "adaptive specializations" were gradually absorbed into a liberalized general theory of associative learning (Domjan 1983). At the same time, by not formulating a clear research program with testable predictions, proponents of the "biological constraints" approach failed to stimulate research into related phenomena that might have been better examples of adaptive specialization of learning (Domjan and Galef 1983). The term "constraints" in itself implies a general process that is constrained in particular species and situations. But it is more appropriate to think in terms of evolved predispositions or adaptive specializations than in terms of constraints (Section 2.5 and Hinde and Stevenson-Hinde 1973). Recent developments in the study of behavior and cognition reviewed in Section 1.5 have similarly absorbed "constraints on learning" into a more biologically oriented approach to psychology in general.

4.2   A framework for thinking about learning

4.2.1   What is learning?

Learning, or equivalently memory, is a change in state due to experience. Obviously, this definition includes too much. For instance, 24 hours without food changes a rat's state so it is more likely to eat when given food again, but this change in state is called hunger, not learning. Running 10 kilometers a day improves a person's endurance, but although a person may learn something from doing it, physical training is not normally called learning either. The changes in state referred to as learning seem to involve a change in cognitive state, not just behavioral potential, but this is helpful only if cognitive can be distinguished from other kinds of changes.

So why start with such a broad definition? In the past learning has often been defined too restrictively, in a way that automatically rules out consideration of diverse and novel forms of behavioral plasticity (Rescorla and Holland 1976; Rescorla 2007). For example, saying that learning is the result of reinforced practice equates learning with instrumental conditioning. Specifying that learning must last for at least 24 hours implies that a small effect of experience lasting, say, 20 hours is qualitatively different from one lasting two days. Saying that motivational changes such as increases in hunger can be reversed easily while developmental changes like learning cannot (Hogan 1994b) does not specify where to draw the line between "easy to reverse" and "hard to reverse." Defining learning as a neuronal change (Dukas 2009) rules out potential examples in plants or bacteria but switches the focus from behavior to a less readily observed level. Beginning without too many constraints allows us to consider the broadest possible range of experience-induced cognitive changes.

The changes in state commonly referred to as *learning* (or *memory*, Chapter 7) have the potential to be read out in behavior. But by itself a change in behavior with experience is not diagnostic of learning. To decide whether or not any sort of learning has occurred, it is always necessary to compare two groups of individuals. One has the experience of interest at an initial time, T1. The other, control, group does not have that experience. In effect, therefore, the control has a different experience, and thoughtfully defining that experience is essential to understanding the nature of learning. In any case, the two groups given different experiences at T1 must be compared *on a standard test* at some later time, T2 (Rescorla and Holland 1976; Rescorla 1988b; Rescorla 2007). This simple but important notion is diagrammed in Figure 4.1a. To make it concrete, consider a simple demonstration (Figure 4.1b). Suppose we want to know whether male canaries learn how to sing from other canaries. A first step would be to raise some male canaries in isolation and others in normal social groups. The rearing period, during which the birds are treated differently, is T1. We might well observe that males in social groups begin to sing more or in a different way than isolated males, but we would not know whether this difference in behavior at T1 reflects learning. For instance, maybe being with other birds in itself stimulates young males to sing more or in a different way. This is why the standard test at T2 is necessary. Here, this test might consist of placing each male with a female and recording his vocalizations. We might observe that the socially raised males sang more complex and varied songs than those raised in isolation. We could safely conclude that some learning had occurred, but we could not conclude that the *form* of the songs was learned. Maybe, for instance, the males raised in isolation are frightened of the females and behave differently from males that are familiar with females for that reason. Further comparisons would be necessary to isolate such factors. For instance, in many studies of song learning a possible role for differences in social experience is ruled out by raising all the birds in isolation and playing them tape-recorded songs.

4.2.2   Three dimensions of learning

Three basic questions can be asked about any learning phenomenon (Rescorla 2007): What are the conditions (or circumstances) that bring learning about? What is

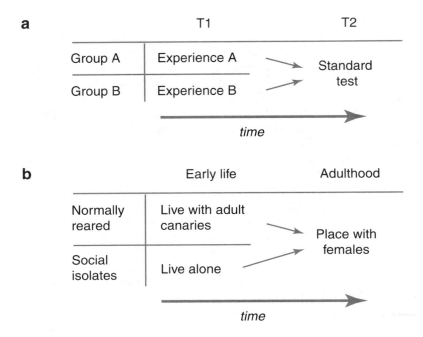

Figure 4.1. a. Essentials of any experiment designed to demonstrate learning. b. The abstract design illustrated by a test of the contribution of early experience to adult behavior in canaries.

learned? How does learning affect behavior? Of course one can ask other questions about learning, too. How widespread among species is it? What function does it serve? How did it evolve? How does it develop within the individual's lifetime? What neural and molecular processes underlie it? However, most experimental analyses of learning at the behavioral level have been directed toward understanding the conditions for learning, the contents of learning, or its effects on behavior.

Conditions for learning

The first step in understanding any instance of learning is to analyze the conditions that bring it about. What kind of experience is necessary for the behavioral change that we are interested in? Does the age, the sex, the species, or the past experience of the subject matter? In our example of song learning in canaries, studying the conditions for learning might involve exposing different groups of birds to various amounts and kinds of auditory input and doing so when they are at different ages. In general, when relevant experience is repeated more often, lasts longer, and/or is more intense, more learning occurs, as measured in some way like how many subjects show the behavioral change of interest, how much of it they show, or how long it lasts. Qualitative features of experience usually matter. For instance, while canaries may learn the song of another canary, they might show less evidence of learning if they have heard the song of a sparrow under similar conditions.

Which of the many possible conditions for learning to investigate is a decision based, if only implicitly, on assumptions about what kinds of events are likely to be important. For example, our experiments on bird song are unlikely to include tests of the effects of barometric pressure, but they are likely to include comparisons of the effects of songs from the bird's own vs. another species. Choice of what to look at is often based on the assumption that in general the function of learning is to allow an animal to fine-tune its behavior to the specific environmental conditions it encounters during its lifetime. If the male canary learns his song at all, he is likely to learn from canaries, not sparrows. However, experiences seemingly having little to do with the function of a behavior may play an important role in its development. For example, if duck-lings do not hear their own vocalizations while they are still in the egg, they do not prefer calls from adults of their species after they hatch (Gottlieb 1978). A strictly functional approach can mislead investigators into overlooking such effects. Indeed, they are not usually classified as "learning" (Hogan 1994a), although the conditions underlying developmental changes may not differ from those underlying "learning."

Some conditions for learning reflect reliable patterns of events in the world. For instance, the more something has occurred in the past, the more likely it is to occur in the future. Thus behavior should be better adjusted to frequently recurring events than to rare ones. An event of great biological importance, like arrival of a fierce predator or a large meal, requires more or faster changes in behavior than a small and insignificant one, and learning is accordingly faster and more complete the larger the reinforcer. Such properties of learning seem so obvious and reasonable that it is easy to forget they are not necessary features of the way behavior or the nervous system changes with experience. They are reminders that evolution has selected for nervous systems that respond adaptively to experience.

Contents of learning

Questions about the contents of learning, that is, what is learned, are of two sorts. Easiest to answer are those at the level of data. For example, we might want to know what features of song our male canaries learned. We could try to find out by varying the notes and phases in the training songs and seeing if this variation is reflected in the subject canaries' singing. The harder questions about what is learned are the theoretical ones. What hypothetical internal cognitive structure accounts for the observed relationships between experience and behavioral change? A classic answer is that experience changes the strength of an association, an excitatory or inhibitory connection between stimuli and/or responses (Dickinson 2007). The contemporary cognitivist's answer (e.g., Gallistel 1990) is more likely to be that experience changes a more complex representation of some aspect of the world. As we see in Section 4.5.2, there is currently some debate about what is learned in conditioning. For other types of learning, the underlying representation is referred to as a cognitive map, a neuronal model, or a template, among other things. For instance, the now-classic model of song learning depicts the effects of experience with song as being stored in an auditory template against which the bird matches its own vocal output (see Box 13.2).

Effects of learning on behavior

If learning is thought of, as it is by radical behaviorists, as nothing more than change in behavior, questions about the contents of learning never arise. They arise only if observable behavioral changes are seen as the readout of underlying cognitive changes. That is, these questions assume a distinction between learning and *performance* based on that learning, between what the animal knows and what it does. For instance, a young male white-crowned sparrow is normally exposed to the songs of adults during his first summer, but he will not begin to sing himself until the next spring. The learned information is stored for months, until singing is stimulated by seasonal hormonal changes (Marler and Peters 1981). We can find out what the animal knows only by observing what it does (though techniques for imaging brain activity may be changing that). Nevertheless, the knowledge exists even when it is behaviorally silent. A theory of how learning translates into performance needs to specify what behavior will occur as a result of learning. For instance, in terms of the model of behavior discussed in Chapter 2, one might ask whether an experience changes a single motor pattern or a whole behavior system. A hallmark of change in a central cognitive representation is that it can be reflected in behavior in a flexible way. For instance, when marsh tits (*Parus palustris*) have stored food in sites in the laboratory, they show that they remember the locations of those sites in two different ways. When they are hungry and presumably searching for food, they return directly to the sites holding hoarded food. In contrast, when they are given more food to store, they go to new, empty, sites (Shettleworth and Krebs 1982). Thus rather than merely returning automatically to the sites with food, the birds seem to have a memory for the locations with food which they can act on in a flexible and functionally appropriate way.

4.3   When and how will learning evolve?

If the world were always the same, learning would be more costly than fixed behavior. In an entirely unpredictable world, there would be no point in learning anything. The predictable unpredictability favoring the evolution of learning exists when some environmental condition important for fitness changes across generations but remains the same within generations (Johnston 1982; Stephens 1991). But this description applies to most forms of phenotypic plasticity (Dukas 1998). For example, in the presence of chemicals from predators, tadpoles of some North American frog species develop longer tails and smaller bodies, making them better able to escape predators (see Miner et al. 2005). Caterpillars of the moth *Nemoria arizonaria* that hatch from eggs laid early in the season eat oak pollen and develop to resemble the oak catkins where they prefer to rest. Their kin hatched from eggs laid later in the season feed on oak leaves, and they resemble and rest on oak twigs (Greene 1989). What the caterpillar finds around it to eat when it hatches reliably predicts how best to be cryptic, and accordingly chemicals in the food induce these differences in morphology and behavior. Such *inducing effects* of the environment are useful when reliable sensory information about local conditions is available from early in the organism's development. Unlike some other forms of phenotypic plasticity, learning is usually (but not always; imprinting, in Chapter 5, may be an exception) potentially reversible, reflecting the fact that a given kind of information may change over time. For example, honeybees readily acquire a preference for the color of flowers that currently have the most nectar, but they learn a new color preference when new plants begin to flower (Dukas 1998).

Functionally, by learning animals acquire sensory information about local conditions that is useful in determining future behavior (Gallistel 2003). The kind of thing that needs to be learned must be the same in every generation, otherwise any given learning ability could not cope with between-generation variation. For instance, the location of food or a nest may vary from generation to generation, but there may always be some advantage in being able to learn and use the kinds of cues that predict such locations. The conditions that bring learning about should be reliable correlates of the state of the world that the animal needs to adjust to. This correlation is encoded in learning mechanisms so that experience brings about relevant, fitness-enhancing, changes in cognitive state and behavior. For instance it would be no good to a blue jay to associate the orange and black pattern of a Monarch butterfly with the emetic effects of ingesting it if this association caused the bird to attack Monarchs more avidly rather than rejecting them.

When learning is a matter of life or death, there is not time to try out all possible solutions to a problem while learning the best one. Animals, including human beings (Cosmides and Tooby 1992), must therefore be preprogrammed to take in only the most relevant information and use it in relevant ways. Lorenz (1965) called this tendency "the innate schoolmarm," emphasizing that learning is not possible without an underlying predisposition to learn. Gould (2002) similarly refers to "learning instincts." This idea leads to the prediction that multiple kinds of learning or memory systems or modules will evolve to deal with functionally incompatible requirements for processing different kinds of information (Sherry and Schacter 1987; Gallistel 1998; Shettleworth 2000; Gallistel 2003). For example, a nocturnal rodent or a desert ant leaving its underground nest to forage must rely on its own internal sense of the distance and direction it has moved from home in order to get back there when returning with food or escaping from a predator. The ability to acquire and act on this vector-like information, the capacity for path integration (Chapter 8), reflects a distinct cognitive module. For conditioning, by contrast, what matters is the relationship between events in time, as when a bee learns that arrival at certain flowers is followed by access to nectar or a jay learns that eating Monarch butterflies is followed by vomiting. Conditioning can of course affect an animal's movement through space, as when the bee approaches a rewarding flower, but unlike the vector information encoded for path integration the information necessary for learning is not inherently spatial.

Although people tend to think of learning as an unalloyed good, behavior dependent on learning does have a cost because almost by definition behavior will be less than optimal while the animal is acquiring the information it needs (T. D. Johnston 1982; Dukas 1998, 2009). For instance, many songbirds experience very high mortality during their first summer, partly because they are learning to forage efficiently on locally available prey. This is illustrated in Figure 4.2 in dramatic age differences in the time free-ranging yellow-eyed juncos (*Junco phaeonotus*) took to consume a mealworm provided by the experimenter. Recently independent juveniles spent most of the daylight hours foraging, yet 3.85% of them died every day (Sullivan 1988). Similarly, young European shags (*Phalacrocorax aristotelis*) may die in winter if they cannot forage fast enough to get sufficient food during the limited hours of daylight (Daunt et al. 2007). The costs of learning may therefore affect multiple aspects of life history in species that must learn about essential resources (T. D. Johnston 1982; Dukas 1998, 2009). For instance, the more that young animals need to learn before they can feed themselves, the longer they will remain dependent on parental feeding and the longer they will have to delay reproduction. Adults should not produce more young than they can feed to the age of independence, or their reproductive effort will be wasted. Thus long-lived animals with complex foraging skills, like chimpanzees and albatrosses, tend to have small families and long periods of association between parent and young (T. D. Johnston 1982).

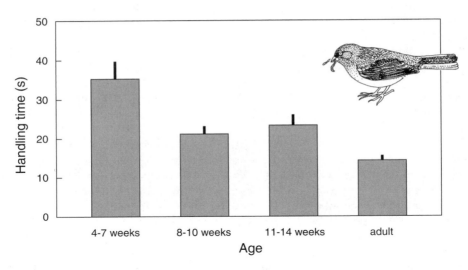

Figure 4.2. Development of foraging efficiency in yellow-eyed juncos, as indicated by reductions in the time taken to ingest a mealworm. Data from Sullivan (1988).

Of course, animals with short life spans such as bees learn too (Dukas 1998; Giurfa 2007). If resources are somewhat patchy in time and space, learning is favored (Krakauer and Rodriguez-Girones 1995), and this may be why bees have evolved such good learning abilities.

Evidence like that from Sullivan's (1988) study of the juncos is consistent with the assumption that learning evolved because it contributes to fitness. The ability to learn is so widespread among species that this assumption seems hardly to demand questioning. It has been tested, however, in a handful of experiments (Hollis et al. 1997; Domjan, Blesbois, and Williams 1998; Dukas and Bernays 2000; Dukas and Duan 2000; Domjan 2005). The logic was to deprive animals of the opportunity to learn about some resource by manipulating their environment and comparing their fitness (or some variable correlated with fitness) to that of animals experiencing the same cues and resources but in a predictive relationship. For example Dukas and Bernays (2000) compared growth rates of grasshoppers in two environments offering two kinds of food. For one group, the more nutritious food always had the same flavor and was on the same side of the cage with the same visual cue nearby. For the other group, the relationship of these cues to the two foods changed with every feeding. Thus these grasshoppers were deprived of the opportunity for learning that would allow them to find the better food efficiently, although after a few days they were able to reject the poorer food and switch once they began to eat it. Nevertheless, the grasshoppers deprived of the opportunity to learn grew more slowly than those provided with learnable cues, and because size is correlated with number of eggs laid, it seems likely that such inability to learn would have decreased their fitness. More direct measures of fitness have been used in some studies of the function of Pavlovian conditioning discussed in Section 4.7.3. Complementary to such studies are demonstrations (e.g., Mery and Kawecki 2002) that selection for learning ability does indeed result in lines better able to learn the kind of task that is the basis for selection. However, as when comparing learning across species (Chapter 3), careful controls are necessary before concluding that learning ability per se is being selected in such studies rather than sensory or motivational factors that improve performance.

4.4   Pavlovian conditioning: Conditions for learning

4.4.1   Background

In the prototypical example of Pavlovian conditioning, a dog stands on a platform with a fistula extending from its cheek, allowing its saliva to be measured drop by drop (Figure 4.3 top). A bell sounds, and shortly afterward the dog gets a morsel of food. The food itself evokes copious salivation, but after several pairings the dog begins to salivate when it hears the bell. The dog has undoubtedly learned something, but what has it learned, and what are the essential features of the experience that brings this learning about?

Historically, the ability of the bell to evoke salivation (a *conditioned response* or *CR*) was attributed to the transfer of control of a reflex (the *unconditioned response* or *UR* of salivation) from the innate eliciting stimulus of food (the *unconditioned stimulus* or *US*) to the initially neutral stimulus of the bell (the *conditioned stimulus* or *CS*). Now, however, learning theorists would be more likely to say that the dog has learned that the bell predicts food (Rescorla 1988a). Its salivation is merely conveniently measured evidence of that knowledge. If the dog were free to move about it might instead approach the feeder or beg and wag its tail at the sound of the bell (Jenkins et al. 1978). Indeed, in most of the currently popular experimental arrangements such as autoshaping (Figure 4.3 bottom), conditioning is measured by changes in behavior of the whole animal. On either interpretation, however, Pavlovian conditioning is seen as a case of *associative learning,* the formation of some sort of mental connection between representations of two stimuli. This statement conflates two meanings of *associative learning.* On a descriptive or operational level the term refers to learning resulting from the procedures involving contingencies among events specified in this upcoming section, that is, it is based on the conditions for learning. On a theoretical level, that dealing with the hypothetical contents of learning, associations are traditionally seen as excitatory or inhibitory links between event representations which do not themselves represent the nature of the link. Thus an encounter with a previously learned CS, A, simply arouses or suppresses a memory of its associate, B. More recently developed views are discussed in Section 4.5. These include suggestions that an association is equivalent to a proposition such as "A causes B" (see De Houwer 2009) and that the performance based on associative learning procedures does not reflect associative links at all.

The rest of this chapter is a bare-bones review of the properties of conditioning, as exemplified by Pavlovian (or classical) conditioning. It is organized in terms of the three aspects of learning introduced in Section 4.2: the conditions for learning, the contents of learning, and the effects of learning on behavior. There are at least four reasons for discussing Pavlovian conditioning before any other examples of learning. First, we know more about it than about any other form of learning. The analysis of Pavlovian conditioning thus illustrates how to answer the three central questions about learning in great depth and thereby provides a model for how other learning phenomena can be studied. Second, although Pavlovian conditioning has been thought of as mere "spit and twitches," some examples of conditioning turn out to have complex and interesting cognitive content (Rescorla 1988a). Thus it belongs in

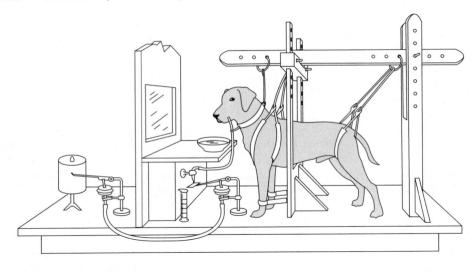

Figure 4.3. Two arrangements for studying Pavlovian conditioning. Upper panel, salivary conditioning in a dog, after Yerkes and Morgulis (1909). Lower panel, autoshaping in a pigeon, after Colwill (1996) with permission. In autoshaping, lighting of the pecking key (the disk on the wall) precedes delivery of food in the opening below it. The pigeon begins to peck the key even though food is given regardless of whether it pecks or not.

any account of animal cognition. Third, discussions of candidates for other forms of learning are usually organized around the question, "How is this different from conditioning?" To answer this question, we need to be familiar with the properties of conditioning. In the context of this book, it is especially important to appreciate the subtlety and complexity of what apparently simple animals can learn from apparently simple experiences. Finally, the basic phenomena of conditioning are phylogenetically very widespread, perhaps more so than any learning phenomena other than habituation (Papini 2008). Pavlovian conditioning allows animals to adjust their foraging, predator avoidance, social behavior, and many other aspects of existence to their individual circumstances. Moreover, the conditions for acquiring Pavlovian conditioning are formally largely the same as those for acquiring instrumental (or operant) conditioning, that is, learning the relationship between behavior and its outcome as opposed to learning the relationship between stimuli. The contents of instrumental learning and the effects on behavior of instrumental procedures may be different, however, as discussed in Chapter 11 in the context of other issues surrounding learning about the consequences of behavior.

A useful characterization of conditioning is that it is the process by which animals learn about predictive relationships between events and behave appropriately as a result (Dickinson 1980; Mackintosh 1983; Rescorla 1988b; Macphail 1996). This functional description makes very good sense of the conditions necessary for classical and instrumental conditioning. It also reflects the philosophical basis of the study of conditioning in associationism, which suggests that effects should be associated with their causes (Hall 1994; Young 1995). Associations have traditionally been thought of as the building blocks of all cognition, but seeing them as resulting from a distinct class of relationships makes associative learning just as adaptively specialized as, for example, learning about spatial or temporal relationships (Gallistel 2003).

The late 1960s and early 1970s saw a huge increase in research on conditioning, made possible by the development of arrangements for studying it that were more practical than the traditional salivary conditioning. For over 25 years this research was guided by the tremendously productive yet simple theory (Rescorla and Wagner 1972) discussed in the next section, which conceptualizes learning as changes in associative strength (R. Miller, Barnet, and Grahame 1995; Siegel and Allan 1996). More recent years have seen the formulation of several alternatives, each of which addresses particular shortcomings of Rescorla and Wagner's model, but all of which—perhaps inevitably–assume implicitly that what is learned is some sort of connection (Pearce and Bouton 2001; R. Miller and Escobar 2002; R. Miller 2006). Because there is as yet no generally accepted new model, this chapter follows other contemporary accounts in presenting the basic facts of conditioning and their interpretation within the context of the Rescorla-Wagner model, while pointing to some of its difficulties and how they are addressed by alternatives.

Nearly all of this section is based on data from vertebrates, mostly rats and pigeons. Invertebrates also show the basic phenomena of conditioning (Dukas 2008; Papini 2008). Indeed, an important body of research deals with the neural basis of learning in the simple nervous systems of species like the sea slug *Aplysia* (Krasne 2002). Fruitflies and nematode worms, along with mice, are now popular subjects for investigations of genetic and molecular mechanisms of learning (Matzel 2002). However, with the notable exception of honeybees (Bitterman 2000; Giurfa 2007; Papini 2008) species other than rats and pigeons have rarely been tested for all the phenomena central to theory development. Moreover, generally even rats and pigeons have been studied in only limited kinds of conditioning arrangements, such as autoshaping in the case of pigeons. A relatively recent development in conditioning research is the inclusion of comparable experiments on both rats and pigeons (e.g., Rescorla 2005)—or in some cases rats and humans (e.g., Arcediano, Escobar, and Miller 2005)—within a single article. Because different forms of conditioning are subserved by different neural circuits even within mammals (Box 4.2), one might wonder about the generality of all the aspects of conditioning described in upcoming pages. Indeed, some of the most revealing and provocative findings about the determinants and function of conditioned responding discussed in Section 4.7 come from research with unconventional conditioning arrangements (e.g., rats chasing ball bearings), behavior systems (e.g., sex and aggression), or species (e.g., Japanese quail, blue gourami fish). Basic mechanisms of conditioning remain powerful candidate explanations for any example of naturalistic learning in any species (e.g., Darst 2006), but given the considerable evidence (see R. Miller and Escobar 2002) that parameters such as choice of CS or amount of training influence details of the outcomes, it would not be surprising if species membership also determines the optimal parameter values, or indeed whether some phenomena occur at all. For example, as discussed in Chapter 11, the extent to which instrumental behavior reflects a representation of reward value rather than "mindless" habitual responding varies predictably within rats with amount of training, but it also varies across species, with fish always behaving habitually (Papini 2002).

Box 4.2 Conditioning, Genes, and the Brain: Commonalities and Contrasts

Although the basic phenomena of conditioning may be universal, their underlying neural and molecular mechanisms can differ across and even within species. For example, two of the best studied brain circuits involved in learning in mammals are those for fear and eyeblink conditioning (Fanselow and Poulos 2005). These are located in the amygdala and cerebellum, respectively. In each case, the essential neural circuit is specialized for detecting the coincidence of relevant CSs and USs within a specific time frame; repeated coincidence engages mechanisms for neural plasticity at the cellular (synaptic) level, but the genes and neurotransmitters or other cellular mechanisms may differ. Figure B4.2 is adapted from the extended discussion of these issues by Papini (2008) to show how learning mechanisms can be the same at one level and differ at others. Across species too, learning phenomena that are the same at the level of behavior can differ dramatically at other levels. Honeybees don't have a cerebellum, an amygdala, or a hippocampus, but they still have a structure, the mushroom body, which integrates multisensory information (see Papini 2008). Bees show not only most basic phenomena of conditioning, but sophisticated spatial memory besides (Chapter 8).

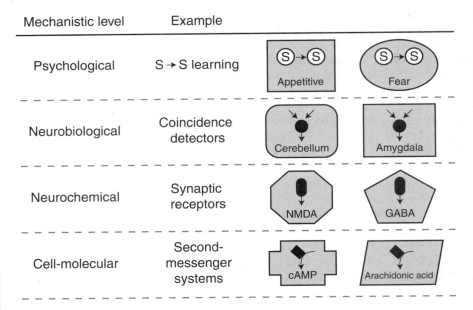

Figure B4.2. The different levels at which learning mechanisms may be compared within or across species. In this example, appetitive and fear conditioning are the same at the psychological level but access coincidence detection in different brain structures, where different neurochemical and molecular mechanisms are involved. Redrawn from Papini (2008) with permission.

The existence of multiple levels for analyzing mechanisms of learning and memory has important implications for thinking about the organization and evolution of learning and of cognition in general. Traditionally when psychologists refer to learning mechanisms they mean purely hypothetical underlying processes, as when competition for associative strength is said to be a mechanism for blocking and overshadowing. This is the principal level for discussing cognitive processes throughout this book. It is the basis for discussing, for example, whether aspects of memory or social behavior are functionally similar across species. However, similarity at the behavioral level does not necessarily represent strict homology in the sense of descent from common ancestors (see Chapter 2). Demonstrating homology requires the same mechanisms be shared right the way down to genes, and this is most likely in close relatives. Similarities of conditioning phenomena at the behavioral level in species that are not close relatives are often homoplasies (or analogies; see Chapter 2), possibly convergently evolved or evolved in parallel in different lineages. All the evidence now available on genetic and neural mechanisms of conditioning suggests that although conditioning can be treated as largely unitary at the behavioral level, the detailed neurobiological and molecular mechanisms for it may have evolved multiple times, perhaps reflecting the widespread functional importance of being able to learn that one event predicts another and at the same time the widespread availability of mechanisms for neural plasticity.

4.4.2   Contingency and surprise

To be sure that one is studying behavior reflecting the animal's experience of a CS predicting a US it is necessary to be able to discriminate this behavior from similar behavior brought about for other reasons. In the terminology of Section 4.2, animals that have experienced a predictive relationship between CS and US at T1 must behave differently at T2 from control animals that experienced some other relationship between CS and US. The best way to do this is to expose the control group to random occurrences of the CS and US. The behavior of these latter, random control, animals will reflect any effects of exposure to CS and US individually in the experimental context (Rescorla 1967). The effects of both positive contingency (CS predicts US) and negative contingency (CS predicts absence of US) can be assessed against this baseline (Figure 4.4).

The importance of the random control group was not always appreciated. Traditionally, temporal contiguity, or pairing, between two events was thought to be the necessary and sufficient condition for conditioning. The most popular control conditions eliminated contiguity by presenting only the CS or only the US or by presenting them systematically separated in time. But this experience has effects of its own. For instance, it can teach the animal that the US never follows the CS, thereby establishing the CS as a *conditioned inhibitor*. An alternative approach often used with invertebrates to establish that they can learn at all is differential conditioning with two CSs. When a US is paired with one CS and concurrently not paired with another, the animal should come to respond differently to the two CSs. However, as a test of CS-US associations, this design is subject to a subtle confounding from possible differential habituation, since habituation may be selectively prevented to a CS that is always quickly followed by a US (Colwill 1996). Colwill (1996) argues that the most conclusive tests of associative learning make use of the fact that, as reviewed in Section 4.5.1, a genuine CR reflects the quality and value of its US.

Even the relatively simple stimuli used in most laboratory experiments on conditioning have many features. For instance, a tone comes from a particular location

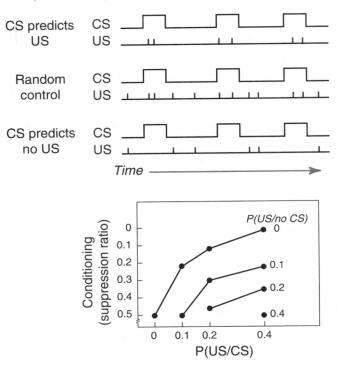

Figure 4.4. Effects of contingency on conditioning. In this example, illustrating the methods and results of Rescorla (1967), shock USs occurred with a constant probability per unit of time in the random control condition. Positive and negative contingencies were created by removing the USs between or during CSs, respectively. The effects of CS and US rates on fear conditioning are plotted as a function of the probability of shock during the CS, with a separate function for each probability of shock when no CS was present. Rats were bar-pressing for food and fear conditioning was indexed as the ratio between bar pressing rate during the CS and ongoing response rate. Zero suppression indicates maximal conditioning; 0.5 is minimal suppression. Redrawn from Rescorla (1988a).

and has a particular loudness and duration. A visual stimulus has brightness, size, shape, and perhaps other features. Are stimuli encoded as a unit or as a sum of features? And what about features that are added after initial learning? It turns out that if an animal has learned, say, that a light predicts food, and a new stimulus, say a tone, now accompanies the light so that the compound light + tone predicts food, learning about the tone, the new element, is reduced or absent (Kamin 1969). Like the contingency effects illustrated in Figure 4.4, this *blocking* effect means the CS must convey new information about the US in order for learning to occur. Mere temporal contiguity between CS and US is not enough. In the case of blocking, if the added CS does convey new information about the occurrence of the US, for example, when the US is now larger or smaller than it was when predicted by the first CS, animals do learn (Mackintosh 1978). Such *unblocking* shows that blocking is not merely due to a failure of attention to the added element. It suggests that animals associate two events only when the second one, the US, is somehow surprising or unexpected.

The notion that surprisingness or prediction error (Dickinson 2007) is essential for conditioning is captured formally in the influential Rescorla-Wagner model (Rescorla and Wagner 1972) referred to earlier. It generates the properties of conditioning

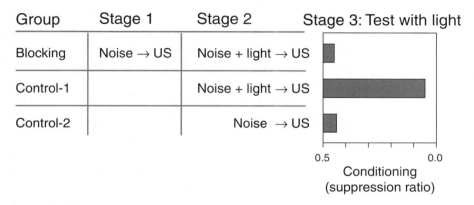

Group	Stage 1	Stage 2	Stage 3: Test with light
Blocking	Noise → US	Noise + light → US	
Control-1		Noise + light → US	
Control-2		Noise → US	

Figure 4.5. Design and results of Kamin's (1969) original demonstration of blocking of fear conditioning in rats. As in Figure 4.4, conditioning was measured by suppression of bar pressing: suppression ratios closer to zero correspond to greater conditioned fear.

reviewed so far and many others besides. A few of its assumptions are worth noting. One is that performance, that is, whatever behavioral index of learning is being measured, is monotonically related to the amount of underlying learning, or *associative strength*. Thus the model makes predictions about the relative level of conditioned responding in two or more conditions within a particular experiment, not absolute strengths of CRs. It also assumes that multifeatured events are treated as the sum of parts, rather than—as in one alternative model (Pearce 1994a)—a unique configuration. Thus the total associative strength, V, of a compound CS is the sum of strengths of its elements. The importance of surprise or prediction error is embodied in the assumption that the amount of associative strength a given CS accrues on a trial with a given US (ΔV) is proportional to the difference between the maximum associative strength that the US can support (the asymptote, λ) and the current associative strength of all CSs currently present (ΣV). The current associative strength of all CSs present corresponds to the degree to which the animal expects the US in the presence of those CSs. Learning is based on the discrepancy between what the animal needs to learn (λ) and what it already knows (see Figure 4.6). The parameters α and β in the equation are

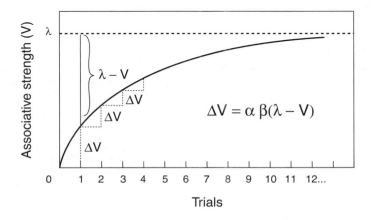

Figure 4.6. How the Rescorla-Wagner model generates a negatively accelerated learning curve.

constants related to the particular CS and US to reflect the fact that performance changes faster with salient or strong stimuli than with inconspicuous or weak ones.

The Rescorla-Wagner model readily accounts for blocking. When a novel stimulus, B, is added to an already-conditioned stimulus, A, the total associative strength of the compound is close to the maximum thanks to element A, so there is little left for B. The model also accounts for the effects of contingency as due to contiguity between CS and US by assuming that an explicit CS is actually a compound of CS and experimental context, that is, such things as the room where the experiment is carried out, the presence of the experimenter, and so on. When the predictive value of the CS is degraded by extra USs, as in Figure 4.4, the context becomes associated with the extra USs and leaves less room for conditioning to the CS. On this view, an animal exposed to random occurrences of CS and US is not an animal that has learned nothing; it may have associated the US with the environment or learned that the CS and US are unrelated.

The Rescorla-Wagner model also accounts for a second important form of competition between cues to the same outcome that was first described by Pavlov (1927), namely *overshadowing*. Because the gain in associative strength by each element of a compound is determined by the total associative strength of all stimuli present at the time, during training with a compound less is learned about either element than if it were trained alone. For example, a rat trained to expect shock after a light and a noise come on together will show less conditioned responding to the light alone than will rats trained for the same number of trials with light alone. The same goes for the tone, provided tone and light are of similar salience (α in the equations). Otherwise, the more salient element will do most of the overshadowing. It can be seen from the Rescorla-Wagner equations that overshadowing should occur only after the first trial of compound training. This prediction is not always fulfilled (Pearce and Bouton 2001).

Sometimes, too, the opposite of overshadowing is found, namely *potentiation*. That is, *more* is learned about a given cue when it is trained with a second cue than when it is trained alone. For example, conditioning to an odor is improved by training it in compound with a flavor rather than alone (Domjan 1983). This makes functional sense in that flavor can be seen as identifying the odors as a property of food and therefore worth learning about (Galef and Osborne 1978). When it was first discovered in taste aversion learning, potentiation was interpreted as a specific adaptation for learning about the properties of foods. However, potentiation occurs with other stimuli and in other conditioning situations (Domjan 1983; Graham et al. 2006). Some instances of potentiation are attributable to associations between elements of a compound CS (within-event learning, see Chapter 5). Thus, for example, rather than being directly associated with poison when they accompany a flavor, odors could be associated directly with the flavor and rejected because the flavor is aversive. Such effects suggest that the original claims that potentiation is a special kind of learning, a violation of the Rescorla-Wagner model, may not have been justified. However, the determinants of potentiation may be different in different situations (Graham et al. 2006), leaving open the possibility that it sometimes results from special mechanisms whereby one element of a compound enhances learning to another, perhaps by enhancing attention to it (LoLordo and Droungas 1989).

4.4.3   Associating CSs

In the most familiar examples of conditioning, the US is food, a painful stimulus, or some other event with preexperimental significance for the animal. Then learning is easy to measure because the animal usually behaves as if expecting the US when the CS occurs. Animals run about, salivate, peck, or gnaw in the presence of signals associated with food; they become immobile ("freeze"), squeak, or try to escape in the presence of danger signals. But preexisting biological significance is not essential for conditioning. In *sensory preconditioning,* two relatively neutral stimuli are presented with the same kinds of arrangements as in conditioning with food, shock, and the like. After such experience, the animal's knowledge about the events' relationship can be revealed by making one of the events behaviorally significant and observing behavior toward the other. For instance, if the animal first learns "tone is followed by light" and then "light is followed by food" it behaves as if making the inference, "tone is followed by food."

Second order conditioning is similar to sensory preconditioning in that initially neutral stimuli are used, but here one of them is given biological significance beforehand. That is, the animal first learns "light causes food" and then "tone causes light." When tested appropriately it behaves as if inferring that "tone causes food." Figure 4.7 depicts the experimental arrangements in these two paradigms. Some arrangements for studying conditioning in humans resemble those for sensory preconditioning in that the stimuli being learned about have little or no preexisting biological significance for the subject. This insight may be the key to understanding why some phenomena seen in first-order conditioning with animals fail to appear in humans (Denniston, Miller, and Matute 1996).

4.4.4 "Belongingness"

In the Rescorla-Wagner model the salience of the CS and US determine the speed of learning, through the parameters α and β, respectively. These values are fixed in the original model, though variants of it suggest experience can decrease (Pearce and Hall 1980) or increase (Mackintosh 1978) CS salience (for discussion of these models see Pearce and Bouton 2001). Contrary to any of these models, it may also matter how particular events are paired up. The best-known example is poison-avoidance learning (Box 4.1). In general, if associative learning is a mechanism for learning true causal relations, then if one event is a priori likely to cause another, it should take less evidence to convince the animal of its causal relationship than if it is a priori an unlikely cause. As this notion suggests, the importance of what has been called belongingness (Thorndike 1911/1970), preparedness (Seligman 1970), relevance (Dickinson 1980), or intrinsic relations between events (Rescorla and Holland 1976) has been demonstrated in a number of situations other than conditioned taste aversion (Domjan 1983). Far from being the evidence for special laws of learning it was once supposed to be, relevance or belongingness of stimuli is now recognized as a general principle of conditioning (R. Miller and Escobar 2002).

	Stage 1	Stage 2	Test
Sensory Preconditioning	A → B	B → US	A
Second Order Conditioning	B → US	A → B	A

Figure 4.7. Procedures for sensory preconditioning and second order conditioning.

Belongingness also plays a role in instrumental conditioning. For instance, pigeons more readily use visual than auditory stimuli as signals for food, but sounds are better than lights as danger signals. In both food-getting and shock-avoidance with pigeons, the "relevant" stimulus has a privileged status in that it cannot be blocked (LoLordo, Jacobs, and Foree 1982). Pigeons trained to press a treadle for grain in the presence of a tone still learned about an added light, whereas prior learning about the light did block the tone. Related effects are discussed in Section 4.7.4. Monkeys selectively develop fear to things like snakes that might be important to fear in the wild. A much-discussed suggestion (Davey 1995; Öhman and Mineka 2001, 2003) is that human phobias are underlain by an evolved predisposition to fear objects that were danger-ous to our ancestors. For instance, people appear more likely to develop phobias toward things like snakes, spiders, mushrooms, or high places than flowers, electric outlets, soft beds, or fast cars. The propensity to develop fear to things that were dangerous in the evolutionary past is reflected in faster acquisition with snakes and the like as CSs in the laboratory, where it is specific to tasks with an aversive US (see Chapter 13 and Ohman and Mineka 2003).

Belongingness could reflect a preexisting connection that gives a head start to learning (LoLordo 1979; Davey 1995). Alternatively, experience of a given US may direct attention to certain kinds of stimuli. For instance, a rat that has recently been sick may subsequently pay particular attention to flavors. This possibility has been ruled out in the case of flavor aversions by exposing all animals to both USs of interest or by giving only a single training trial. However, it might be that illness specifically retrieves a memory of recently experienced flavors, making them available for asso-ciation as in Wagner's model of learning discussed in Chapter 5. This mechanism would allow long delay learning in one trial. The possibility that prior learning plays a role can be addressed by using very young animals or animals with controlled past history. Finally, apparent belongingness may not represent different degrees of learn-ing but differential readiness to exhibit that learning in performance. Evidence of learning might be seen especially readily, for example, if the response evoked by expectation of the US is similar to the response which the CS tends to evoke on its own (Holland 1984; Rescorla 1988a). Each of these and possibly other mechanisms may play a role in different cases. New tests (Rescorla 2008a) indicate that the original example of belongingness in flavor aversion and shock avoidance in rats is a case of enhanced associability between specific pairs of events. Similar experiments (Rescorla 2008b) have analyzed another example: for rats, attractive flavors are more quickly conditioned with positive consequences and bitter or sour flavors with negative consequences. Here, belongingness gives a head start to learning.

Classical associationism did recognize one kind of "belongingness." Namely, similarity and spatial contiguity between stimuli were thought to favor association formation. Of course similarity and spatial contiguity can both be seen as reasonable prior predictors of causal relationships. However, it is not always easy to disentangle them from other factors. For instance, a CS that is similar to a given US may evoke responding via stimulus generalization. But an elegant experiment with pigeons by Rescorla and Furrow (1977) shows that over and above any such effect similarity enhances associability. As indicated in Figure 4.8, all their birds were exposed to all the stimuli used in the experiment; they differed only in whether similar or dissimilar stimuli were paired in the critical second order conditioning phase. Similarly designed experiments have shown that spatial contiguity or a part-whole relation between CS and US can also facilitate second-order conditioning (Rescorla and Cunningham 1979). Although it is difficult to vary the spatial contiguity of CS to US without

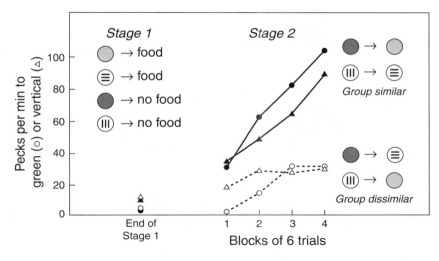

Figure 4.8. Effects of similarity between the stimuli to be associated on speed of second-order autoshaping in pigeons. Data for the end of Stage 1 are the rates of pecking the two stimuli that became CSs in second order conditioning but that predicted no food during Stage 1. The unpatterned stimuli were green and blue, shown here by dark and light shading respectively. After Rescorla and Furrow (1977) with permission.

also varying temporal contiguity, spatial contiguity by itself does appear to influence learning rate (Christie 1996; Rescorla 2008a).

4.4.5   Temporal relationships

Within limits, conditioning is more rapid the more closely in time the US follows the CS. But "close enough" depends on the CS and US. With eyelid conditioning, the CS must precede the US by no more than a second or so, whereas in conditioned taste aversion, flavor can precede illness by twelve hours or more (Box 4.1). In general, as the temporal separation of CS and US increases, conditioning improves at first but then declines (Figure 4.9). A functional reason is easy to see: causes often precede their effects closely in time and seldom follow them. However, it is easy to imagine cases in which a cause follows its effect from the animal's point of view. A stealthy predator might not be noticed until after it has attacked, but this does not mean that the victim (if it's still alive to benefit from its experience) should not learn about its enemy's features. This argument has been advanced as a functional explanation for some cases of successful *backward conditioning* (Keith-Lucas and Guttman 1975; Spetch, Wilkie, and Pinel 1981).

Figure 4.9 indicates that conditioning does not take place when CS and US are simultaneous. However, simultaneous conditioning can be quite robust in second order conditioning or sensory preconditioning, as when a pigeon associates patterns on two halves of a pecking key (Rescorla 1988a). This paradigm may capture how animals learn about the features of events, as discussed in Chapter 5. Another way to explain simultaneous and backward (as well as forward) conditioning is to suggest that conditioning establishes knowledge of the precise temporal relationship between CS and US. Indeed, Pavlov (1927) described evidence for this from the two paradigms

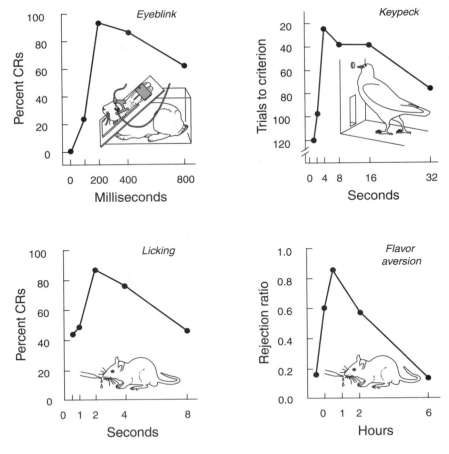

Figure 4.9. Conditioning as a function of the delay between CS and US in different conditioning preparations. Eyeblink conditioning in rabbits, redrawn from from M. Smith et al. (1969) with permission; rabbit redrawn from Domjan and Burkhard (1986) with permission; autoshaping in pigeons, data from Gibbon et al. (1977); conditioned licking with water reinforcement in rats redrawn from Boice and Denny (1965) with permission; flavor aversion in rats from Barker and Smith (1974). After Rescorla (1988b) with permission.

diagrammed in Figure 4.10. In *delay conditioning,* the CS lasted for maybe a minute or more before the food US was presented. Salivation gradually came to occur mainly near the end of the CS. Now such behavior is interpreted as evidence for timing the CS (Chapter 9). *Trace conditioning* is similar except that the CS is relatively brief and the US follows its offset by a fixed time. Hence the name: the animal is in effect conditioned to a memory trace of the CS. Evidence from humans suggests that trace and delay conditioning rely on different brain mechanisms and that trace, but not delay, conditioning depends on conscious awareness of the CS-US relationship (C. Smith et al. 2005). This suggestion has provocative implications for other species, but not all even agree on the importance of consciousness for conditioning in humans (Lovibond and Shanks 2002).

Not only the temporal pattern of events during conditioning trials is important, the time between trials—the *intertrial interval* (or ITI)—matters too. The notion that CSs provide information about the occurrence of USs suggests that when CS and US are

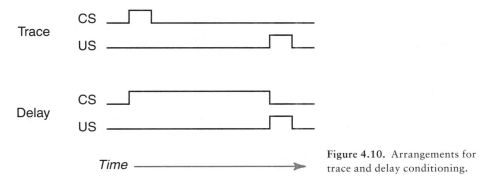

Figure 4.10. Arrangements for trace and delay conditioning.

comparatively rare, the CS is more worth learning about than when CS and US are more frequent. This corresponds to the traditional wisdom that when people learn a task *spaced practice* is more effective than *massed practice*. However, when it comes to animal training, this intuitive notion leads to a somewhat counterintuitive prediction: if for example, one is autoshaping a pigeon by turning on the keylight for 8 seconds and then presenting grain, pecking will actually appear after fewer keylight-food pairings if these trials are separated by, say, 2 minutes than by 20 seconds. It is sometimes hard for students training pigeons to accept that their bird may actually peck sooner if they don't pack the trials in too much, but in fact what matters is the ratio of intertrial time to trial time, at least in the arrangements with pigeons (Gibbon et al. 1977) and rats (Lattal 1999; Holland 2000) where parametric tests have been done. As illustrated in Figure 4.11, a higher I:T ratio, that is, longer ITI (I) relative to trial (T) or CS duration, leads to faster acquisition of responding to the CS. (This ratio is sometimes, e.g., by Domjan, 2003, equivalently referred to as the C:T ratio, where C is the "cycle time," or total ITI + CS time per trial.) A reader who has taken Section

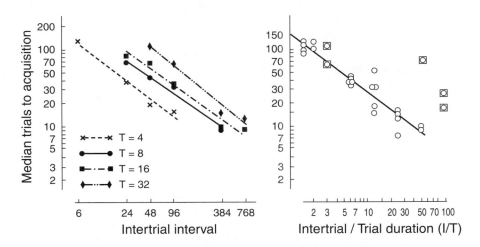

Figure 4.11. Influence of the I:T ratio on acquisition, illustrated by data from autoshaping in pigeons. Left panel shows data from groups of birds trained with the given CS (or T, i.e. keylight) and intertrial interval (ITI) durations. In the right panel the same data are replotted as a function of the I:T ratio; points in boxes were omitted in calculating the solid overall regression line . Redrawn from Gibbon et al. (1977) with permission.

4.2.2 to heart will realize that tests with a standard ITI and CS after different acquisition treatments are needed to clinch this argument. The results of such tests have been consistent with the importance of the I:T ratio for learning (Lattal 1999; Holland 2000; but see Section 4.7.2 and Domjan 2003). The implications of this and the other effects of time summarized in this section for theories of conditioning are discussed in Section 4.5.2.

4.4.6   Prior learning

In blocking, prior learning about one element of a compound CS reduces learning about the other. But the effects of past experience on present learning are more widespread. For example, exposure to a CS by itself before pairing with a US leads to *latent inhibition,* retarded conditioning to that CS. It is as if having learned that the CS signals nothing of importance the animal ceases to pay attention to it. Latent inhibition is similar to habituation, in that mere exposure to an event results in learning, but it is not clear whether the two phenomena reflect the same mechanism (Chapter 5). Exposure to the US alone in the conditioning context also reduces its effectiveness when a CS is later introduced. This can be explained as blocking of the CS by the context: the animal already expects the US, so the CS adds little new information. Conditioning to the context itself is readily observed: animals learn what to expect in particular places, be they conditioning chambers or parts of the natural environment. For example, a pigeon that has received food in a distinctively wallpapered Skinner box becomes more active when placed in that environment than in an equally familiar environment where it has never been fed. Rats learn where a novel object was located in a single trial (Eacott and Norman 2004). At least in birds and mammals, learning about the physical and temporal context of events is powerful and ubiquitous. Thinking about the role of context in learning has led to novel theoretical viewpoints (Chapter 7; Bouton 1993) as well as novel predictions about naturalistic examples of learning (Darst 2006).

If exposure to either the CS or the US alone reduces conditioning, prior exposure to random presentations of both CS and US should have an even more detrimental effect. Of course this is the random control condition. The nature of its effects is captured very well by the name *learned irrelevance* or, in the case of instrumental conditioning, *learned helplessness.* However, it is debatable whether animals actually learn that CS and US have a random relationship or whether their behavior can be accounted for by the sum of effects of CS and US preexposure (Bonardi and Hall 1996; Bonardi and Ong 2003).

4.4.7   Extinction

If conditioned responding results from learning a predictive relationship between two events, then it should be abolished if the animal has opportunity to learn that the relation no longer holds. Traditionally it was given this opportunity by removing the US and observing how the CR waned. However, the logic behind the random control condition for original learning implies that the proper way to teach an animal that CS and US are now unrelated and thereby produce *extinction* of responding is to present CS and US in a noncontingent relationship. In one dramatic demonstration of the effectiveness of this procedure, Gamzu and Williams (1971) extinguished pigeons' autoshaped keypecking by adding extra food between keylight-food pairings, preserving contiguity between the keylight and food but degrading their predictive relationship.

Extinction may appear to involve loss of a learned association, unlearning. Accordingly, Rescorla and Wagner (1972) modeled it by setting the asymptote of conditioning with no US to zero so that already-acquired associative strength decreases over unreinforced trials. However, considerable evidence indicates that, contrary to this depiction, associations are not really lost during extinction (R. Miller and Escobar 2002; Bouton and Moody 2004). *Savings* after extinction, that is, speeding up of relearning compared to initial learning, is one such piece of evidence. Another is *spontaneous recovery,* a partial recovery of extinguished responding when the animal is returned to the experimental situation, say the next day. Originally reported by Pavlov (1927), it has only been studied in any depth relatively recently and may have more than one explanation (see Section 7.3). *Reinstatement* is further evidence that learning is not entirely lost during extinction: simply presenting the US alone in the experimental context after extinction can get responding going again. Such data indicate that rather than losing the original learning during extinction, the animal acquires new learning, perhaps an inhibitory association specific to the temporal and spatial context in which extinction occurs (Bouton and Moody 2004). On this view, as in cases of memory loss which can be remedied by exposure to appropriate retrieval cues, in extinction the effects of original training are retained but need the right conditions in order to be expressed. This view is developed further in Section 7.3.

4.5   What is learned?

Saying that conditioning causes a CS to become associated with a US conceals all kinds of interesting and even contentious questions about what is learned, many of which have only begun to be unpacked relatively recently. Section 4.5.2 summarizes some of the theoretical issues involved. But first we look at some data bearing on a comparatively more straightforward question: what *is* the CS or the US from the animal's point of view, that is, what aspects of it actually enter into learning? Or, how does the animal represent the CS and the US?

4.5.1   Data

Learning about the CS

Any CS has a variety of features. It has a certain duration and intensity, it may have shape, brightness, size, loudness, taste, odor, or texture, and occur in a certain context. What is included in the animal's representation of the CS? This question can be answered by changing features of the CS after conditioning and observing the effect on responding. With CSs that can be varied along a single physical continuum like wavelength or auditory frequency, variations away from the training value often lead to orderly variations in responding as in the generalization gradients in Figure 3.9 (see also Chapter 6). Obviously, some specificity in responding is a prerequisite for concluding that conditioning has occurred at all. For example, if a rat responds in the same novel way to any and all sounds after tone-shock pairings, one would conclude that the animal was *sensitized* rather than conditioned to the tone.

As we have seen, the Rescorla-Wagner model treats separable features of a CS as if they gain associative strength independently. This makes some sense for compounds of discrete CSs from different modalities like the proverbial light + tone. But what about a compound of features from the same modality, say a red cross on a blue pecking key? Why should we think that a pigeon represents this as a blue field with a red cross superimposed on it? Maybe instead it encodes a configuration. If the key with the red cross is paired with food, the bird will come to peck it, and it might peck white keys with red crosses or plain blue keys, too. But maybe this is not because the bird has acquired a red cross association and a separate blue key association. Maybe instead the bird pecks at the red cross or the blue key alone because they are similar to the original training stimulus, that is, through generalizing from the configuration. A formal *configural model* of learning based on this intuition has been quite success-ful in accounting for a large body of data, including some that the elemental Rescorla-Wagner model cannot deal with (Pearce 1994b; Pearce and Bouton 2001). The relative merits of configural vs. elemental accounts of learning with complex stimuli are discussed further in Chapters 5 and 6.

Learning about time

In addition to sensory features, CSs and USs have temporal properties. The impor-tance of temporal factors in conditioning, for example in trace and delay conditioning (Figure 4.10), was traditionally explained with the concept of the stimulus trace. For instance, the silence five seconds after a tone goes off is a different stimulus from the same silence ten seconds later because the aftereffect or trace of the tone changes systematically with time. Similarly, different times within an extended CS can be thought of as different stimuli. However, evidence that animals accurately time short intervals reviewed in Chapter 9 makes an account in terms of direct sensitivity to the durations of CSs, USs, CS-US intervals, and the like seem more natural (Savastano and Miller 1998). For instance, blocking is maximized when the CS-US interval is the same for both the pretrained and the to-be-blocked CS (Barnet, Grahame, and Miller 1993). It may seem more plausible that the CS-US interval itself is appreciated than that the traces of two qualitatively different CSs, with which the US is associated, are most similar after identical intervals, but both accounts explain this effect equally well.

The notion that the temporal relationship between CS and US is itself learned, rather than simply being one of the conditions affecting learning, suggests a novel way of viewing simultaneous and backward conditioning. Perhaps animals learn that CS and US are in fact simultaneous or in a backward temporal relationship but respond-ing is not the same as in forward conditioning because the behavior appropriate to anticipation of an event is not the same as that appropriate to its presence or recent occurrence. As this notion suggests, rats given first order conditioning in which a tone occurred at the same time as shock showed little conditioned suppression of drinking in the presence of the tone CS, but nevertheless they acquired second order condi-tioned suppression when a second-order click CS preceded the tone (Figure 4.12; Barnet, Arnold, and Miller 1991; R. Cole, Barnet, and Miller 1995). There is now considerable evidence that animals learn the specific temporal patterns of events in conditioning experiments (R. Miller and Escobar 2002).

Learning about the US

When Pavlov's dog salivated to a CS for food, what had it actually learned? Did the CS evoke a complete representation of the food's taste, texture, and the like, thereby

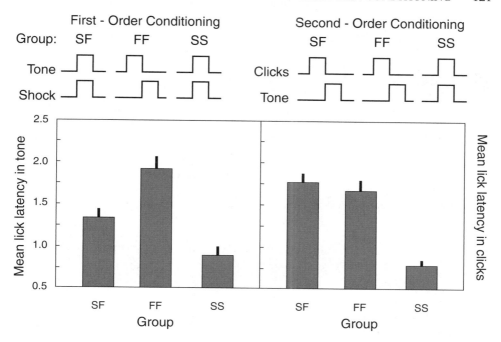

Figure 4.12. Evidence that rats learn the temporal relationship between CS and US. Three groups of rats receiving first-order and then second-order conditioning differed in whether the stimuli to be associated at each stage were simultaneous (S) or in a forward temporal relationship (F), that is, with CS preceding US as depicted above the data panels. Data from Barnet, Arnold, and Miller (1991) redrawn with permission.

causing the dog to salivate? Or did the CS evoke salivation directly? If the dog could talk, would it say "I'm salivating because I'm thinking of food" or would it say "This tone makes me salivate, but I don't know why?" A classic demonstration that animals encode the features of reward comes from instrumental learning, a delayed-response experiment by Tinklepaugh (1928). Monkeys saw a piece of their favorite banana or less-preferred lettuce being hidden. After a retention interval, the animals were allowed to uncover the reward and eat it. When lettuce was substituted for banana on occasional trials, the monkeys showed signs of surprise and anger, indicating that they knew not simply where the reward was but what food it was (Figure 4.13). Watanabe (1996) repeated such observations using an operant task and recorded distinct patterns of cortical activity corresponding to the monkeys' expectations of raisin, apple, cabbage, water, grape juice, and other rewards. The implications of such findings for the cognitive structure underlying instrumental behavior are discussed in Chapter 11.

Questions about how the US is represented can be addressed in Pavlovian conditioning by changing the value of the US after training. If responding is unaffected, the animal must have merely associated the CS with the response or response system activated by the original US. Often, however, responding changes with postconditioning changes in the value of the US in a way that indicates the animal has associated the CS with a detailed representation of the US. For instance, the value of a food to rats may be decreased by pairing it with poison. The rats then show less conditioned

Figure 4.13. Tinklepaugh's monkey Psyche looking for banana when lettuce had been secretly substituted. After a photograph in Tinklepaugh (1928).

responding to a CS previously paired with that food than do control rats given noncontingent poisoning. Such tests must be done without further USs being given (i.e., in extinction) so as to tap the representation established by the original training rather than new learning that the CS signals nasty food (Holland and Straub 1979).

A similar technique can be used to discover which sensory features of the US are encoded. For instance, rats can be trained with two different CSs, each paired with a distinctive type of food, say food pellets and sucrose. If the rat represents both USs merely as "food," "something tasty," or the like, then it should not matter which of them is later paired with poison: conditioned responding should decrease to the CS signaling either one. In fact, however, responding decreases selectively to the CS whose US was devalued (Colwill and Motzkin 1994; Colwill 1996). Selective satiation or deprivation also change US value. For instance, pigeons that are hungry but satiated with water reduce pecking at a CS signaling water but not at one signaling food (Stanhope 1989). However, after extended training responding may continue at a high rate even though the reinforcer has been devalued. Animals apparently learn about both the sensory and the affective or response-eliciting features of USs, perhaps to different degrees in different circumstances (Dickinson 1980; Balleine and Dickinson 2006).

Images of the US

So far, this section indicates that a CS evokes a representation of a particular US, an image of the US in some sense. As this idea suggests, associatively evoked stimulus representations can substitute for the stimuli themselves in new learning (Holland 1990; Hall 1996). In one demonstration (Holland 1990), rats were exposed to pairings of a tone with food until they showed clear evidence of anticipating food in the presence of the tone. The tone was then paired with injections of a mild toxin, a toxin adequate to condition aversion to any distinctive flavor paired with it though not to the tone itself (see Box 4.1). As a result of the tone-toxin pairings, the rats developed an aversion to the food previously paired with the tone. It was as if during these pairings the tone evoked an image of the food and that image was associated with toxin (Dwyer 2003; Holland 2005).

Such learning about absent events turns out to be quite robust, and it need not involve flavor aversions. For example, Holland and Sherwood (2008) trained individual rats with one light signaling a tone and a second light signalling sucrose. After subsequent training in which the "tone light" signaled the "sucrose light," the rats investigated the food cup more during the "tone light" than did control rats. Two previously learned CSs can also serve as surrogates for their associates in inhibitory learning (Holland and Sherwood, 2008). Such findings are important because they suggest that conditioning allows animals to bring absent events to mind and acquire new information about them, a primitive form of thought (Holland 1990; Hall 1996).

4.5.2   What is learned? Theory

S-S or S-R associations?

Historically, the question "What is learned in conditioning?" was posed as "Are associations formed between CS and US (stimulus-stimulus, S-S, associations) or between CS and UR (stimulus-response, S-R, associations)?" The 1940s and 1950s saw numerous experiments designed to determine whether learning consisted of S-S or S-R connections, mainly using instrumental learning. In experiments with mazes, this amounted to the question whether animals learned a rigid response such as turning right or acquired knowledge about the location of the goal, a cognitive map which they could use to reach the goal in different ways as circumstances required (Chapter 8). As usual in controversies of this kind, the answer seemed to be "it depends," in this case on factors like the amount and conditions of training. The S-R versus S-S distinction is often phrased for Pavlovian conditioning as a distinction between *procedural* and *declarative* learning. Does the animal merely learn what to do in the presence of the CS (S-R or procedural learning) or does it form a representation that could be expressed as a proposition, "A is followed by B," and base action on this knowledge in a flexible way (S-S or declarative learning)? The experiments discussed in the last section, in which the value of the CS or the US is changed after training, have shown that either may occur and that S-S learning may include quite a detailed representation of both CS and US.

More than associative strength?

A more fundamental question than whether associations are S-S or S-R is whether what is learned in conditioning is best conceptualized as associations at all. An important condition for learning is the temporal patterning characteristic of contingency between events, so why not conclude that this is what animals learn? Gallistel (1990; Gallistel and Gibbon 2000) suggested that animals record the times of onset and offset of potential CSs and USs and compute whether the statistical likelihood of the US increases during the CS. Responding is determined not by stored associative strength but by an online computation of the statistical uncertainty about whether the US will follow the CS. This analysis is useful because it formalizes the notion of contingency. However, the fact that a theorist can compute contingency in this way does not mean that animals must do the same computations in order for their behavior to reflect the contingencies they experience. Sensitivity to the sorts of experiences afforded by conditioning experiments may have evolved to enable animals to track causal, or contingent, relations among events in the environment, but an animal that blindly forms associations by contiguity in the way described by the Rescorla-Wagner model can track causality or contingency very well without having any representation of causality or contingency as such. There is an important general caveat here: cognitive mechanisms do not necessarily embody literal representations of their functions, and assuming that they do can blind us to what is really going on (see also Chapter 2 and p. 82 in R. Miller and Escobar 2002). In Chapter 12, for instance, we see that some animals may behave as if sensitive to the states of mind of their companions but without representing others' states of mind as such at all.

RET and the comparator model

Nevertheless, Gallistel (1990) and others (R. Miller 2006) have correctly pointed to a serious problem: an association as traditionally conceived has only one dimension, strength. Thus it cannot encode the temporal relationship between CS and US, even though it is clear that animals learn this (section 4.5.1). Moreover, increasing evidence from studies of animal memory (Chapter 7) lends plausibility to the claim that animals remember the details of a large number of the individual episodes experienced in a conditioning experiment. This flies in the face of the implicit assumption that all that is acquired in conditioning is a connection that summarizes past experience with a particular CS and US in a single value of associative strength. The Rescorla-Wagner model and its variants also assume that associations of the same strength acquired in different ways are equivalent. This assumption of *path independence* is clearly not always correct (R. Miller, Barnet, and Grahame 1995; R. Miller 2006). For instance, an equally weak CS-US association could be present early in training or after extinction, but further training would proceed faster after extinction than it did originally, indicating that the animal has retained some effect of the original training that is not evident in performance of the CR.

Such evidence that animals acquire more complex and detailed information than can be encoded in unidimensional associations has stimulated formulation of two distinct alternative models in which animals retain a more or less veridical representation of the events during conditioning, including their temporal properties. Performance is determined by an online comparison of some sort, making these models fundamentally different from the Rescorla-Wagner and related models in which performance directly reflects the strength of learning (Dickinson 2001a; Gallistel and Gibbon 2001; R. Miller and Escobar 2002). That is, they are performance-based rather than acquisition-based models (R. Miller and Escobar 2001). In the comparator model developed by Miller and his group (see R. Miller and Escobar 2002) learning is through simple contiguity. During a blocking experiment, animals do associate the added (blocked) CS with the US. At the test the animal compares the strength or predictive value of the added CS to that of other CSs present or associated with it and finds that the CS trained first has a stronger link to the US. This point of view predicts *backward blocking* (or *retrospective revaluation*). That is, rather than blocking CS B by training A-US and then AB-US, one trains AB-US first and then, in effect, teaches the animal that A was actually the cause of the US by training A-US. Indeed, as the informal description of this procedure suggests, in the final test of B animals may show little conditioned responding, as if they do not attribute the US to it. However, it is possible for a modified acquisition-based model to account for such effects (see R. R. Miller and Escobar 2002).

Similarly, in Gallistel and Gibbon's (2000) rate expectancy theory (RET), performance is based on an ongoing comparison of the rate of USs during the CS with their rate overall, that is, during CSs plus ITIs. This view predicts that the distribution of total CS experience across trials should be unimportant. For example, if training consists of episodes with 100 seconds of ITI and 20 seconds of CS per US, it shouldn't matter whether the animal experiences 100-second ITIs and 20-second CSs, each followed by a US or 50-second ITIs and 10-second CSs, half of which end in a US (i.e., partial reinforcement, which is usually supposed to retard acquisition (Gottlieb 2005). In either case, the relevant rates will be one US per 20 seconds when the CS is present and one US per 120 seconds overall. Several well-controlled tests of such a prediction have, however, produced results more consistent with the traditional trial-based account of acquisition, though sometimes revealing an additional role for time (e.g., Bouton and Sunsay 2003; Domjan 2003; Gottlieb 2005).

Contrary to the traditional assumption that associative strength increases gradually over trials, RET implies that number of trials, that is, CS-US pairings, as such is unimportant. Tests of this prediction have tended to support RET over trial-based approaches. As one example, a review of acquisition data from a variety of species and conditioning paradigms reveals that individual animals abruptly switch from responding hardly at all to responding at close to their asymptotic rate instead of increasing responding smoothly over trials (Gallistel, Fairhurst and Balsam 2004). Group learning curves resemble the theoretical curve of associative strength in Figure 4.6 only because they average individual curves. However, models based on associative strength can account for such findings by postulating a threshold of associative strength above which the animal always responds. In an even more direct test of the importance of number of trials, Gottlieb (2008) compared acquisition of conditioned approach to a food dispenser (magazine) in rats or mice given either 4 or 32 trials, when trials were distributed within and between sessions so as to equate either total ITI or total session length across groups. Little effect of the eightfold increase in trials was evident in training sessions and, most importantly, in a common test at the end of training. According to RET, this is because only a trial or so is necessary to give the animal evidence that the CS predicts the US; the rest of the session shows it that the context alone does not.

Summary

The twenty-fifth anniversary of the Rescorla-Wagner model occasioned major assessments of its successes and limitations (R. Miller, Barnet, and Grahame 1995; Siegel and Allan 1996). In the ensuing years, arguably some problems with it have become more acute (R. Miller 2006). Among the areas considered in this book, conditioning is one for which formal modeling is particularly well developed. The Rescorla-Wagner model has guided discovery of new phenomena and still summarizes much of what we know (Pearce and Bouton 2001), but newer alternatives imply that the analysis of conditioning can and should be better connected with other aspects of animal cognition, in particular timing and memory. As illustrated in the preceding few paragraphs, they have also stimulated researchers to examine some fundamental associationist assumptions. One review (R. Miller and Escobar 2002) characterizes theory development in this area as a continual tension between simple and easily falsifiable models vs. more elaborate models devised to deal with the problems of the simple ones. It remains to be seen whether any single model will eventually prove adequate to all the richness and variety of phenomena that current debates are revealing. This includes phenomena of human causal or contingency learning in associative paradigms, which are largely beyond the scope of this book, but some of which seem more compatible with the acquisition of propositional knowledge than simple excitatory or inhibitory links (De Houwer 2009; Dickinson 2009).

4.6   Conditional control of behavior: Occasion setting and modulation

Consider the following problem, known as a *feature positive discrimination:* In the presence of stimulus A nothing happens, but when A is preceded by another stimulus, X, the US follows A (Figure 4.14). The Rescorla-Wagner model predicts that conditioning will accrue only to X because it is the only reliable predictor of the US. Stimulus A should gain no strength because the US occurs whether or not A is presented. This is indeed what happens if X and A are simultaneous. However, if X and A are presented serially, so that X precedes reinforced occurrences of A while A alone is not reinforced, X does not become an excitor. Rather, it acquires the ability to modulate excitation to A. The serial feature positive discrimination appears to support a different, higher-level, kind of learning from the simple excitatory or inhibitory connections between event representations discussed so far. This kind of learning has been called, alternatively, *facilitation,* by analogy with inhibition, whose conceptual opposite it appears to be (Rescorla 1987), and *occasion setting,* by analogy with the occasion setting function of discriminative stimuli in instrumental learning (Holland 1992), or simply *modulation* (Swartzentruber 1995). A stimulus can be simultaneously an excitor and a modulator, and these functions are somewhat independent.

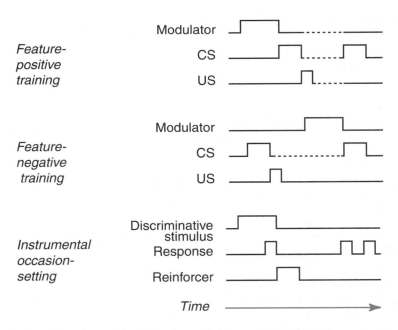

Figure 4.14. Procedures for training Pavlovian modulators and instrumental occasion setters. Each row shows one trial with and one without the modulator/occasion setter.

Two kinds of evidence show that modulation is not the same as simple excitation: First, modulation has different conditions for acquisition and extinction. Second, excitors and occasion setters fail to block each other, indicating that the contents of learning are different. For instance, continuing the example above, the necessary condition for extinction of facilitation is that X predict nonreinforcement of A. Simply presenting the facilitator alone, with no reinforcement and no occurrences of A, does not extinguish its facilitatory function (Rescorla 1986). One of the two traditional paradigms for demonstrating Pavlovian conditioned inhibition (Rescorla 1969) parallels that for training a facilitator: a CS is reinforced when presented alone but nonreinforced when preceded by another stimulus, the conditioned inhibitor. It now appears that conditioned inhibitors trained in this way (as opposed to those trained with simultaneous presentations with the nonreinforced CS) are best viewed as modulators with properties analogous to those of facilitators (i.e., positive modulators Williams, Overmier, and LoLordo 1992; Swartzentruber 1995).

Modulation has been investigated in several different preparations, sometimes with different results (see Pearce and Bouton 2001). What is clear is that facilitation differs from simple conditioning in a number of ways. It seems to develop in parallel with excitation and to serve a kind of higher-level function that is not readily captured by simple associative models of conditioning. Moreover, although it has been useful to study modulation using discrete stimuli, it is clear that environmental contexts are important modulators of associative information in addition to becoming directly associated with CSs and USs (Bouton 1993; Swartzentruber 1995; Pearce and Bouton 2001). The most important feature of modulation or occasion setting is that it allows animals to use associative information in a flexible and appropriate way rather than mindlessly performing a CR whenever a CS appears.

4.7   Effects of learning on behavior

4.7.1   Learning and performance

On the view that Pavlovian conditioning is merely transfer of control of a reflex, S-R learning, behavior automatically results from learning so there is no distinction to be made between learning and performance. However, examples of "behaviorally silent learning" (Dickinson 1980) compel a distinction between learning and performance. As one example, inhibitory learning, that is, below-zero associative strength in Rescorla-Wagner terms, may not become evident until the conditioned inhibitor is presented in combination with an excitor and suppresses conditioned responding (Rescorla 1969). In another example, Holland and Rescorla (1975) presented food to rats following either a tone or a light. The rats soon became more active during the tone, but activity changed very little during the light, suggesting that the rats had learned only about the tone. Nevertheless, when rats trained with the light had second order conditioning in which the tone predicted the light, they became more active to the tone. The light could also block first-order conditioning to the tone. Eventually direct observations (Holland 1977) revealed that the rats' behavior did change during the light, but not in a way that influenced motion of the jiggle cage that Holland and Rescorla (1975) had used to record general activity. In fear conditioning, too, rats show different CRs to tones and lights that support the same underlying learning (Kim et al. 1996). In such cases, learning is "silent" until it is measured appropriately.

If learning is distinct from performance, then *performance rules* are needed to describe how learning is expressed in behavior. The traditional Pavlovian performance rule was *stimulus substitution:* the CS becomes a substitute for the US. A dog salivates when fed, so it salivates to a signal for food. Pigeons that are both hungry and thirsty peck a lighted key signaling food in the same way as they peck at food, whereas they "drink" a key signaling water (Jenkins and Moore 1973). But much of the behavior resulting from Pavlovian conditioning is not strictly stimulus substitution. For example, if rats see another rat passing by on a trolley just before food arrives, they don't try to eat the signal rat but exhibit social behaviors like sniffing its face and crawling over it (Timberlake and Grant 1975). Hamsters, which would not normally interact socially over food, do not develop any social or feeding behavior in such a situation (Timberlake 1983).

Such findings can be roughly described by saying that species-specific behavior appropriate to the US occurs during the CS if there is stimulus support for it. Thus, diffuse visual stimuli paired with food cause pigeons to become active rather than to peck. Shock generally makes rats jump and squeak, but after getting shock from touching a small prod rats throw sawdust over the prod and bury it, whereas they freeze (i.e., become completely inactive) in the presence of diffuse signals for shock to the feet (Pinel and Treit 1978). Behavior in such cases is determined by the nature of the CS itself, not merely by what stimuli happen to be present when it appears. This is shown very clearly by observations of rats' behavior to a compound of a light plus a tone CS for food (Holland 1977). Rats pretrained to the light (i.e., rats for which conditioning to the tone was blocked) behaved in a way appropriate to the light when the light and tone were presented together, whereas rats pretrained to the tone behaved as they normally did with the tone alone. Some differences in CR form can be accounted for as enhanced orienting responses to the CSs involved (Holland 1984), but as we see below the preexisting natural relationship between CS and US may also be important.

4.7.2   Behavior systems

Can all the different kinds of CRs animals display be described in a unified way that allows unambiguous predictions for new species and situations? An approach based on the ethological notion of behavior systems introduced in Chapter 2 reasonably hypothesizes that the CS brings into play the behavior system relevant to the US (Holland 1984; Suboski 1990; Hogan 1994b; Hollis 1997; Timberlake 2001b; Domjan 2005). Because behavior systems can be assessed outside of conditioning situations, this approach offers a powerful causal analysis of conditioned behavior (Shettleworth 1994a). In terms of the model of a behavior system in Figure 2.7, Pavlovian conditioning could result in modification of either perceptual-motor or perceptual-central connections. Perceptual-motor connections correspond to S-R learning: the CS triggers a particular movement, as in stimulus substitution. However, conditioning often seems to result in new perceptual (CS)—central connections that facilitate the whole system of behaviors relevant to the US (Hogan 1994b). Behavior systems may also have a temporal organization, with activities that change with proximity to the relevant goal as illustrated in Figure 4.15 and discussed further below.

Behaviors shown after conditioning have a preexisting organization that influences their performance as CRs. For example, pigeons normally peck only stimuli much smaller than the usual 2.5 cm. diameter pecking key. If a 6-mm. dot, smaller than the pigeon's gape, is on the key in an autoshaping experiment, pecking develops

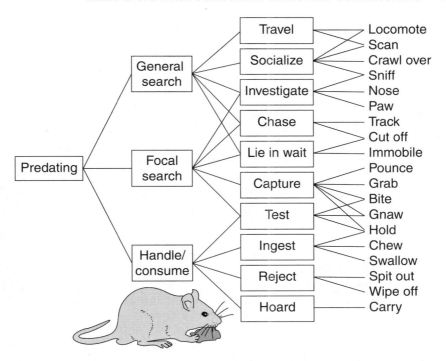

Figure 4.15. The organization of the rat's feeding system. The three functional subsystems indicated are activated in the order shown from top to bottom as the rat searches for and then finds food. Redrawn from Timberlake (1994) with permission.

to it much more quickly than to the blank key (Jenkins, Barnes, and Barrera 1981). In the behavior system view, this illustrates the joint control of a CR by its normal causal factors (the size of spots) and associative ones. The behavior systems account also explains why CRs are not necessarily the same as URs. For instance, when young chicks are placed in a cool environment and exposed to pairings of a lighted pecking key and a heat lamp, they come to peck the key even though they never peck the heat lamp (Wasserman 1973). If the lamp is seen as a surrogate mother hen, the CR of pecking can readily be understood: chicks peck at the mother's feathers and snuggle underneath her as she sits down to brood them (Hogan 1974). The behavior system view also implies that not all species will show the same CRs in a given situation. For instance, how seven species of rodents treat a moving ball bearing that signals food depends on their species-specific predatory behavior (Timberlake and Washburne 1989).

4.7.3   Behavior systems and the function of conditioning

The behavior systems approach offers a causal analysis of what animals do in conditioning experiments, but much research based on it has also been guided by thinking about the functions of conditioning in the natural lives of animals. This thinking has led to some novel predictions and discoveries. For example, on the view that the function of conditioning is to allow animals to learn cause-effect relationships, the CR should optimize the animal's interaction with the US (Hollis 1982; Hollis 1997; Domjan 2005). This is not an answer to Tinbergen's mechanism or development question but to the current function question. It does not mean that CRs are instrumental responses learned through reward and punishment. Indeed, *omission training* experiments show that CRs may occur despite adverse experimental consequences, as if they are involuntary. For instance in autoshaping pigeons go on pecking even if pecking cancels food (Chapter 11). Evidence from conditioning with USs including drugs, shock, and sexual behavior shows that this functional approach makes sense of a wide variety of CRs (Hollis 1997; Domjan 2005). Importantly, this includes cases of conditioning with drugs where the CR is opposite rather than similar to the UR. A CR of vasodilation may occur when the direct response to the drug (the UR) is vasoconstriction, body warming occurs instead of cooling, and so forth. Such CRs maintain homeostasis by counteracting a drugs' tendency to push physiological variables outside normal ranges (Siegel 2005). Such *compensatory* CRs make sense in the same framework as stimulus substitution: both function to optimize interaction with USs.

The notion that the tendency to display particular CRs evolved because they contribute to fitness suggests testable predictions about the present-day function of conditioning. For example, Hollis has shown that sexual and aggressive CRs do in fact give some fish an advantage that is very likely to translate into reproductive success, and in one case she and her colleagues measured reproductive success directly. Male blue gourami fish (*Tricogaster tricopterous*) were trained to expect an encounter with a territorial rival following lighting of a red panel on the side of their tank. The fish evidenced knowledge of the predictive relationship between the panel and the rival's arrival by displaying aggressively during the CS (Figure 4.16). Control males had either unpaired exposure to rivals and the red panel or exposure to rivals alone. When pairs of conditioned and control males were shown the red panel at the same time and then allowed to fight each other, the conditioned males showed more bites and tailbeating responses than their rivals, and they nearly always won the fights (Hollis 1984; Hollis et al. 1995).

A provocative illustration of how conditioning contributes to social behavior comes from a similar experiment with blue gouramis, this time involving competition for food between two nonterritorial males (Hollis et al. 2004). Pairs of males were first observed as they formed dominance relationships, in which the dominant usually

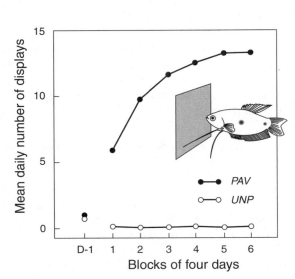

Figure 4.16. Male blue gouramis' aggressive display toward a light paired with a rival (Pav group) and in an unpaired (UNP) control group. Redrawn from Hollis (1984) with permission.

won contests over food. Then the males of each pair were separated and each was exposed to a small light CS signaling food dropped into the tank. Conditioned males oriented toward the light when it came on, approached it, and nipped at the water surface, whereas in control males these behaviors waned with unpaired light-food experience. However, when dominant and subordinate males were put together for tests, on the very first trial subordinate males trained with light-food pairings did not perform their previous suite of CRs. Instead, before the dominant had time to attack they adopted a submissive head-up posture. Thus, by anticipating food in the presence of the dominant, whether that dominant himself was conditioned or not, subordinates reduced the number of attacks and bites they were subjected to. In some cases they were actually able to steal some of the food. This example of behavioral flexibility in conditioning is worth keeping in mind when we come to discuss the cognitive basis of social tactics in Chapter 12.

Breeding males of many species behave aggressively toward any animals approaching their territory, even females. If the male could anticipate the approach of a female and inhibit undue aggression, mating success might be increased. Indeed this has proven to be the case in blue gouramis. Male blue gouramis' sexual behavior can be conditioned with a female as a US using methods similar to those for conditioning aggressive behavior (Hollis, Cadieux, and Colbert 1989; Hollis 1990). After presentations of the CS, conditioned males direct fewer bites and more courtship movements at a test female than do controls; that is to say, the CS prepares them for mating. Moreover, this behavior translates into spectacularly enhanced reproduction. When conditioned and control males remained with females after a single presentation of the CS, the conditioned males spawned sooner and fathered on average over a thousand young, compared to a mean of less than 100 fathered by controls for which the CS had been explicitly unpaired with a female (Hollis et a1.1997). Similarly when male Japanese quail (*Coturnix japonica*) mate in a chamber where they have previously encountered females, they release more sperm than do control males (Domjan, Blesbois, and Williams 1998), and their partners produce more fertilized eggs (Adkins-Regan and MacKillop 2003). Females conditioned in a similar way also produce more eggs after copulating in the presence of the CS for mating (Adkins-Regan and MacKillop 2003; Mahometa and Domjan 2005). And when two males in succession copulate with a female in a context that is a sexual CS for one of them, the conditioned male fathers more of the resulting young, that is, he has an advantage in sperm competition (Matthews et al. 2007).

4.7.4   Behavior systems and the laws of learning

The typical measure of strength of learning is the probability or intensity of a single CR. Thus, the low levels of CR performance with long CS-US intervals (Figure 4.9) or with a low I:T ratio (Figure 4.11) have been taken as evidence of poor learning. But the behavior systems approach suggests that although responses resembling consummatory behavior may not be seen under these conditions, general search activity might increase in the experimental context. This idea has proven useful in accounting for the CRs shown with CSs of different durations in conditioning of fear in rats (Fanselow 1994), feeding in rats (Timberlake 2001b), and sexual behavior in quail (Domjan, Cusato, and Krause 2004). In all three systems, conditioning is evident even with quite long CS-US intervals, but what CR appears depends on the interval. The influence of CS-US interval on CR form has long been recognized, for instance in Konorski's (1967) distinction between preparatory and consummatory CRs. In his terms, preparatory behaviors tend to be shown with long CS-US intervals and consummatory behaviors with short ones. In the behavior systems account, the behaviors within appetitive systems such as feeding or sex are classified functionally as general search (e.g., general activity in search of food or a mate), focal search (e.g., striking and pouncing on prey; grabbing and mounting a female), and consummatory behaviors (e.g., tearing and chewing prey, ejaculating; Timberlake 1994, 2001b). Similarly, the perceived imminence of attack determines which defensive behaviors are shown (Fanselow and Lester 1988). Preencounter behaviors such as reorganization of feeding or increased vigilance occur in places where predators have been encountered before, an animal that has just met a predator engages in postencounter behaviors like freezing or fleeing, but if the predator attacks, the victim shows circastrike behaviors such as vocalizing and striking back at its attacker.

As an example, consider the studies of Domjan and his colleagues (Domjan, Cusato, and Krause 2004; Domjan 2005) with Japanese quail (*Coturnix japonica*). In these studies, male quail typically receive one trial per day in a large chamber with a US consisting of opportunity to copulate with a receptive female kept in an adjacent chamber. Akins (2000; see also Domjan, Cusato, and Krause 2004) trained birds with 1-minute or 20-minute presentations of a CS consisting of a terrycloth-covered object roughly the size and shape of the body and neck of a female quail (see Figure 4.17). At each CS duration, birds for which the CS immediately preceded access to the female were compared to unpaired controls who copulated two hours before CS presentations. Birds trained with the short CS quickly increased the time they spent near the CS object during the first minute it was present, whereas those trained with the long CS increased their activity, or general search, above control levels. Importantly, both CRs appeared within just two or three trials. In Akins's (2000) experiment, both the 20-minute and the 1-minute CSs were exceptionally short relative to the ITI, since the subject birds actually spent the entire 24 hours containing each trial in the conditioning chambers. However, when Burns and Domjan (2001; Domjan 2003) varied the I:T ratio by varying the time the birds spent in the chambers, they still found strong learning at what should have been an unfavorable ratio, but it was evident in general activity rather than approach to the CS. Rats show comparable effects during conditioning with food (Silva and Timberlake 1997). Even in conventional conditioning arrangements, variation in CS-US interval may have different effects on different measures of learning (Delamater and Holland 2008). Such findings cast doubt on the

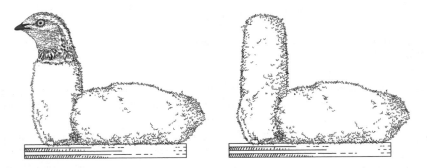

Figure 4.17. More and less quail-like objects used as CSs in sexual conditioning of male quail in the studies by Akins and by Cusato and Domjan. Redrawn from Cusato and Domjan (1998) with permission.

claim (Section 4.4.5) that the I:T ratio is a critical determinant of the strength of conditioned responding (Domjan 2003).

As we have seen, the behavior systems approach predicts that CRs will depend on the species-specific relationship of the CS to the behavior system relevant to the US. In one of the most comprehensive analyses of such effects, Timberlake and colleagues (see Timberlake 2001b) showed, for example, that for rats rolling ball bearings versus conspecifics on trolleys versus diffuse lights and tones all result in predictably different CRs with the same food US. Similarly, in sexual conditioning with quail (Domjan, Cusato, and Krause 2004; Domjan 2005) localized lights, diffuse context cues, and different sorts of quail-sized objects all support different CRs. Earlier, we saw how Holland (1977) found that in rats conditioned with food, lights and tones support different CRs expressive of the same underlying learning, as revealed by blocking and second order conditioning. However, some of the research by Timberlake and Domjan suggests that naturalistic CSs may actually support qualitatively different learning which cannot be blocked by more arbitrary CSs.

As an example, consider some of the findings with quail (for review see Domjan, Cusato, and Krause 2004). Because these birds live naturally in short grassland, a male would often see a female's head and neck as she approaches before getting close enough to copulate. This bit of natural history suggested using as a CS the object with the head and neck of a female quail shown in Figure 4.17 along with a control CS of the same shape and size (Cusato and Domjan 2000). Both objects therefore afford males the opportunity to mount and attempt to copulate. When they were used as CSs, conditioned approach behavior exceeded levels in unpaired controls with either one, but grabbing, mounting, and attempts at cloacal contact with the model exceeded control levels only in the group trained with the more realistic model. By itself the superiority of this model could reflect an effect purely on performance, and the response of naïve males showed that it is indeed more effective in eliciting sexual responses. However, a study of blocking (Figure 4.17; Koksal, Domjan, and Weisman 1994) suggests that it actually supports stronger underlying learning. Quail were first conditioned with a localized light predicting copulatory opportunity. They revealed their learning by approaching the light when it came on. Controls had either unpaired light and copulation experience in the first phase or no training. Then all birds received four trials in which one of the models shown in Figure 4.17 was lowered into the cage at the same time as the 30-second light came on. Blocking and control groups trained with the naturalistic model spent high proportions of the trial near it, that is, the light CS did not block learning with this model, but it did block conditioning to the model lacking the head and neck of a female quail.

Domjan (2005) suggests that conditioning with the more realistic model exemplifies a widespread natural situation in which the CS has a preexisting relationship to the US, perhaps because it is part of the US (as with the quail model) or because it is a natural precursor of the US, as for a baby mammal contact with a mother's nipple is a natural precursor to obtaining milk. The failure of blocking just described, as well as effects of the I:T interval and other evidence that learning with the naturalistic quail CS is especially strong and supports more US-appropriate CRs, suggests that such naturalistic contingencies support learning that obeys different principles than learning with the traditional arbitrary CSs (Timberlake 2001a; Domjan, Cusato, and Krause 2004). Quite separately from the behavior systems approach, on the basis of other evidence Miller and colleagues (Oberling et al. 2000; R. Miller and Escobar

2002) suggest that in general stimuli of high inherent or acquired biological significance are protected from overshadowing and blocking. In their terms, high biological
significance is equivalent to strong preexisting responses to the candidate CS.
Although this may boil down to the same thing suggested by behavior systems, it
seems less satisfactory because it lacks the same connection with the functional
organization of behavior, a connection which has been used to predict and explain
some intriguing phenomena.

4.8   Concluding remarks

This chapter began with some general ideas about the function and evolution of
learning. The section on Pavlovian conditioning sketched three different sets of
ideas that closely connect theories of the mechanism of conditioning with
assumptions about its function. Traditionally, conditioning is seen as a mechanism for associating effects with their causes. This view has roots in philosophy.
It is echoed today in associative accounts of experiments on human causal
reasoning (Baker, Murphy, and Mehta 2001) and is the basis for modeling the
effect of conditioning as a change in associative strength. Such models implicitly
assume that the content of associative learning is excitatory and inhibitory links
between event representations with no representational content themselves. The
RET model emphasizes the importance of conditioning for tracking patterns of
arbitrary events through time and proposes a mechanism by which animals
explicitly do this. The behavior system approach, as we have just seen, focuses
instead on natural signaling relationships. In nature, CSs may be precursors to,
or even parts of, USs and the function of conditioning is to optimize interaction
with those USs. Each of these views inspires distinctive kinds of experiments
instantiating situations in which learning has its assumed function. But the
mechanism of learning need not directly reflect this function. In all cases, the
function of learning is ultimately to allow animals to adjust behavior appropriately to forthcoming events. It remains to be seen whether and, if so, how
different contemporary views about how this happens can be harmonized.

In addition to the basic facts about Pavlovian conditioning, this chapter has
two lessons to keep in mind for the rest of the book. One is that the conditions
for learning, the contents of learning, and the effects of learning on behavior are
central to a behavioral analysis of any kind of learning. The review of Pavlovian
conditioning that takes up most of the chapter shows how these three basic
questions have been addressed in one very well studied case. It thus provides a
model for analyzing other forms of learning. Secondly, even in this apparently
simple form of learning, animals show evidence of subtle and interesting cognitive processing. For instance, rats or pigeons learn about multiple features of
CSs and USs, the context in which they occur, and the temporal relationships
between them. Access to some of this information is conditionally controlled by
the context, so that only the information most relevant in the current situation
controls behavior. Thus associative learning is not a stupid, low-level, process to
be contrasted with more "cognitive" mechanisms. It is important to keep in
mind the power of conditioning to produce subtle and sophisticated adjustments
to the local environment when evaluating claims that some examples of adaptive
behavior require other mechanisms for their explanation.

Further reading

A comprehensive introduction to Pavlovian and instrumental conditioning is the text by Bouton (2007). The textbooks by Eichenbaum (2008) and by Gluck, Mercado, and Myers (2008) combine introductory surveys of research on conditioning and learning with introductions to related neurobiological research. Higher-level reviews of all these topics can be found in volume 3 of Stevens' *Handbook of Experimental Psychology* (Gallistel 2002). An excellent comparative survey of learning and its neurobiological basis can be found in the relevant chapters of Papini's (2008) text. The function and evolution of learning, with particular reference to insects, is also discussed in the chapters by Dukas (2008, 2009).

5
Recognition Learning

To recognize is *to know again,* "to perceive to be identical with something previously known" (*Oxford English Dictionary,* 3rd edition). Therefore, in a sense all learning involves recognition. This chapter is about how animals learn about objects, other animals, and events they experience in the absence of obvious relationships with other events. Such learning seems to reflect what people usually mean by *recognition.* When I ask, "Do you recognize that woman?" I mean "Have you seen her before?" Psychologists' experiments on recognition memory (Chapter 7) capture this meaning. In behavioral ecology, *recognition* can refer to classifying objects or other animals appropriately on first encounter. For instance, *kin recognition* means treating relatives differently from other conspecifics, regardless of whether they have been encountered before. This corresponds to a second definition, "to know by means of some distinctive feature."

Kin recognition is discussed at the end of this chapter. First, however, we consider three examples of simple recognition learning: habituation, perceptual learning, and imprinting. In each case we ask two familiar questions: What are the conditions for learning? What is the content of learning, that is, what kind of representation underlies it? Habituation has been an important part of the "simple systems" approach to learning from its inception because it appears more amenable to neurobiological analysis than associative learning (R. F. Thompson and Spencer 1966; Papini 2008). Until relatively recently psychologists barely regarded habituation as genuine learning (J. D. Harris 1943), but we see in this chapter that animals are learning the characteristics of things in their world all the time, even when those things do not signal food, predators, sex, or other conventional reinforcers. Increased appreciation of this fact has led to new ways of testing nonverbal creatures for spatial, numerical, and social knowledge, as described in later chapters.

5.1   Habituation

When a frog's back is tickled, the frog reflexively wipes the spot that was tickled. If the same place is touched repeatedly, the wiping reflex becomes less and less vigorous. When a male white-throated sparrow hears the song of a neighbor on the edge of his territory, he approaches and flies back and forth, finally perching on a branch to sing a territorial song. Over the breeding season he becomes less aggressive toward familiar neighbors but still shows his aggressive display toward strangers and toward familiar neighbors in new places (Box 5.1). The waning of the frog's wiping reflex and

Box 5.1 Habituation, Association, and Individual Recognition

Males of many songbird species hold territories in the breeding season and exclude conspecific males from them (Collins 2004). Singing and aggressive interactions are prominent near territory boundaries, especially early in the breeding season. Birds that can learn who their neighbors are and focus time and energy on repelling new arrivals will have more time for other activities. As this functional notion suggests, birds do in fact respond less to familiar neighbors as the season advances. The learning involved includes both habituation and association (Falls 1982; Catchpole and Slater 1995). White-crowned sparrows habituate to the same song played repeatedly from the same location (Petrinovich and Patterson 1979). However, birds may also associate the songs of a particular singer with the place where he usually sings. For instance, white throated sparrows behave just as aggressively toward a neighbor's song played from a new location as toward a stranger's song played from that location (Figure B5.1; Falls and Brooks 1975). Male bullfrogs (*Rana catesbeiana*) behave similarly: aggressive responses habituate to repeated croaks from a single neighbor in a fixed location and dishabituate when a different frog calls from that location or the same frog calls in a new location. Bullfrogs discriminate between familiar and novel neighbors whether they call from the original or the novel location, apparently recognizing them as individuals (Bee and Gerhardt 2002).

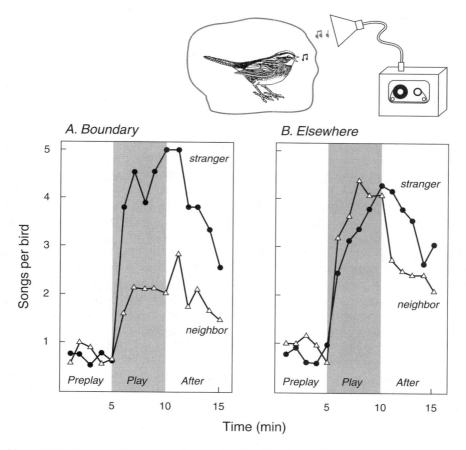

Figure B5.1. Response (songs per minute) of male white-throated sparrows to the recorded songs of neighbors or strangers presented either at the territorial boundary shared with the neighbor (A) or elsewhere in the subject bird's territory. Data from Falls and Brooks (1975), redrawn with permission.

Males of some bird species have repertoires of up to hundreds of different songs, which may function partly to prevent females habituating to them (Catchpole and Slater 1995; Collins 2004). If neighbor-stranger discrimination depends on associating the neighbor's songs with the direction from which they are usually heard, neighbor-stranger discrimination might be less sharp in species with large repertoires, but this is not always so. Songs within an individual's repertoire may have some shared characteristics, permitting generalization among them. Such individual differences have been documented in great tits in both the field and operant tests in the laboratory, where birds trained to discriminate between the songs of different males generalize to unfamiliar songs of the same individuals (Weary and Krebs 1992; but see Searcy, Coffman, and Raikow 1994).

The ability to identify a particular individual by any of several distinctive features presumably develops through associating those features, as in examples of perceptual learning in the main text. For example, a male hamster habituated to the vaginal scent of a familiar female (see Figure 3.4) also proves to be habituated to her flank gland scent (Johnston and Bullock 2001; for a similar effect in ground squirrels see Mateo 2006). Males that have never met the stimulus female do not transfer habituation between scents, showing that habituation does not simply generalize from one scent to the other. To transfer between two of a female's odors a male needs to interact with her, even if through a screen. Contact with the female's body while she is anesthetized also suffices, perhaps because warmth, touch, or some other chemicals from the female potentiate associations among her odors. This mechanism would mitigate against associating odors that occur together by chance, as when two different individuals have passed by the same place (Johnston and Peng 2008).

Cross-modal associations, as between faces and voices, may also play a role in individual and species recognition. Some birds seem to associate the song of another species with its appearance (Matyjasiak 2004; D. Grant and Grant 2008). When rhesus macaques trained to discriminate among colony mates in photos were played the vocalizations of those animals, an individual's voice seemed to access the same representation as the pictures (Adachi and Hampton 2008). In Chapter 12 we will see that social primates acquire elaborate networks of associations among the characteristics of social companions.

the waning of the sparrow's aggressive display have both been studied as examples of habituation even though the behaviors differ greatly in complexity and wane over different time courses. In both cases behavior changes in such a way that time and energy are not wasted in unnecessary or inappropriate behavior.

Habituation is a widespread form of behavioral plasticity, found even in one-celled organisms and in many behavior systems (W. Thorpe 1956; Papini 2008). It also appears to be the simplest: exposure to a single event is certainly the most elementary of experiences. However, this apparently elementary experience can have some quite complex effects, both long-term and short-term. Responses may increase or decrease in intensity when they are repeatedly elicited, and sometimes a single response does first one and then the other. Moreover, exposure to a single event can produce perceptual learning, latent inhibition, and/or imprinting. This section is organized around the same topics as Chapter 4. We look first at the conditions for habituation learning, its contents, and the effects of learning on behavior and then consider three theories about the content of learning in habituation.

5.1.1   Conditions for learning

Habituation is identified operationally as a decrease in responding resulting from repeated stimulation. (Confusingly, the procedure involved is also called *habituation*.) The response measured can be anything from a simple reflex to behavior of a whole animal. However, changes in behavior due to fatigue of receptors or effectors

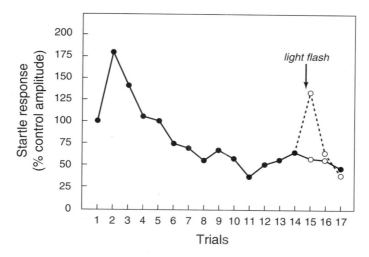

Figure 5.1. Habituation and dishabituation of rats' startle response to a sudden sound. Rats whose data are represented by the dotted line received a flash of light just before the fifteenth sound. Redrawn from Groves and Thompson (1970) with permission.

are not accepted as habituation. Fatigue can be eliminated as the cause of decreased responding by demonstrating *dishabituation:* a novel stimulus restores responding to the original habituating stimulus. Figure 5.1 shows an example from rats in which presentation of a light restored the startle response to a sound. (Startle is a primitive defensive response to sudden strong and therefore potentially dangerous stimuli. In mammals, the whole body reacts as the animal instantly tenses its muscles and draws its head and limbs close to its body. The reaction is conveniently measured by placing the animal in a motion-sensitive cage.)

Experience with a single event is described by the answers to a few simple questions: What is it? How long and intense is it? How often does it occur? How many times has it occurred? What was the animal's age and motivational state during exposure? These same questions define the key parameters of other forms of recognition learning.

Stimulus quality

Specificity is one of the defining features of habituation. Completely general response decrement would be attributed to receptor adaptation or response fatigue. However, habituation does generalize to stimuli similar to the habituating stimulus. Taking the stimulus-specificity of habituation as a given implies that in dishabituation the animal is classifying the new stimulus as different from the old one. Because the behaviors that habituate do not have to be trained initially, this so-called *habituation-dishabituation paradigm* is a powerful tool for studying basic memory and classification processes in nonverbal organisms, including human infants. The data on hamsters' odor discrimination in Figure 3.4 is one example. A large body of literature on infants' cognition rests on the fact that babies orient toward novel visual and auditory stimuli. Orienting (looking and/or modifying sucking rate) habituates to repeated stimuli but is shown at a higher level when a novel stimulus appears. Thus for example, a baby hears "ba ... ba ... ba" and then "pa ... pa" to test if she discriminates between speech sounds. Similar tests have been used with monkeys and rats to study spatial, numerical, and social discriminations (Chapters 8, 10, 12, and 14). Notice, however, that stronger responding to a novel stimulus than to the original habituating stimulus is not the same as the enhancement (i.e., dishabituation) of responding to the *original* stimulus illustrated in Figure 5.1. Strictly speaking then, the popular habituation-dishabituation test should be called something like the habituation-discrimination test.

Number of stimulations

It almost goes without saying that the more an eliciting stimulus is presented, the more the response decreases. In a classic article, R. F. Thompson and Spencer (1966) claimed that responding was a negative exponential function of number of stimulations. This suggests that, like associative learning, the learning in habituation reduces the discrepancy between "expected" and actual events in a manner proportional to the discrepancy. However, the exact form of habituation curves depends on how responding is measured (Hinde 1970b; Figure 5.2). Unlike theories of associative learning, theories of habituation have not always differentiated the underlying learning, the theoretical habituation process, from performance of the habituated response. However, the phenomenon of *habituation below zero* (R. F. Thompson and Spencer 1966; Hinde 1970b) suggests that a learning-performance distinction may be needed for habituation, too. Continuing stimulation after responding stops results in slower recovery than simply habituating to zero, suggesting that learning continues in the absence of measurable responding.

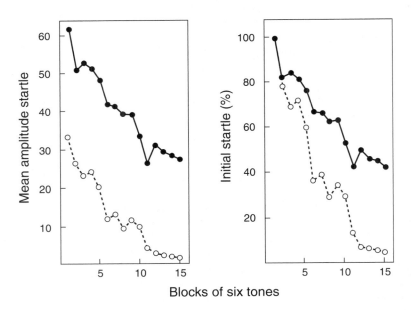

Blocks of six tones

Figure 5.2. How choice of absolute (left) or relative response measures can influence the pattern of data, illustrated with effects of amphetamine on habituation of startle in rats. The panel on the left suggests that the drug (filled circles) raises the level of responsiveness without affecting the rate of habituation, whereas that on the right suggests that the drug slows habituation. Redrawn from Davis and File (1984) with permission.

Increasing numbers of presentations also reduce generalization to similar stimuli. For example, Gillette and Bellingham (1982, cited in Hall 1991) habituated rats to drinking a novel fluid flavored with salt (NA) and sucrose (S). The rats drank little of this novel fluid at first but gradually increased their consumption. Generalization was measured by the rats' willingness to drink NA or S alone. The rats drank *less* NA or S the more they had been habituated to the mixture. That is, the more they had been exposed to NA+S the better they discriminated this compound from its elements. This is just the opposite of what would be expected if the compound was simply the sum of elements and indicates that exposure results in learning about the stimulus, that is, perceptual learning (Hall 1991).

Timing and intensity

Responding typically declines faster during massed than during spaced presentations of the eliciting stimulus. But as discussed in Chapter 4, such an observation is not enough to infer differences in learning. Differences in learning at T1 (i.e., during the train of stimuli) must be assessed by a common test at a later time, T2. Here, the more profound decline has been seen after spaced training (Figure 5.3; M. Davis 1970). The same idea applies to the effects of stimulus intensity (M. Davis and Wagner 1969). R. F. Thompson and Spencer (1966) claimed that habituation is "more rapid and/or pronounced" with weaker stimuli. But when responding is measured in a standard test after exposure to different schedules and intensities of stimulation, the results can be surprising. For instance, a relatively loud tone evokes a smaller startle response in rats habituated with a

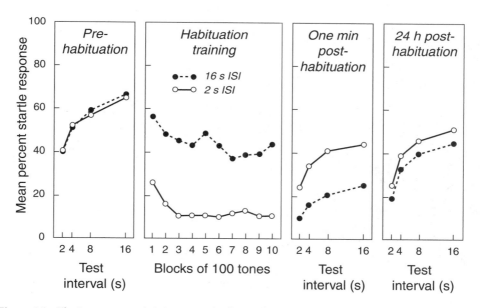

Figure 5.3. The importance of giving a standard test after different habituation experiences. Two groups of rats were pretested (left panel) and then habituated to tones presented with an interstimulus interval (ISI) of either 2 or 16 seconds and tested 1 minute or 24 hours later at a variety of ISIs (M. Davis 1970). Note how leftmost and rightmost panels depict the same test before and after the habituation experience. Redrawn with permission.

series of tones of gradually increasing loudness than in rats exposed to an equal number of tones of the same loudness as the test tone (M. Davis and Wagner 1969).

The interval between T1 and T2

W. Thorpe (1956) stipulated that only a "relatively permanent" response decrement counts as habituation. In fact, however, repeated stimulation can have two distinct effects, one short-term and one lasting for days or weeks (Staddon and Higa 1996). Even simple response systems such as gill withdrawal in *Aplysia* show long-term retention of habituation (Figure 5.4). However, long-term habituation is also gradually forgotten, and generalization gradients broaden as time passes, as if the animal forgets details of the habituating stimulus (Hall 1991).

State variables: Sensitization

Repeated stimulation can increase responding as well as decreasing it, especially if the stimulus is moderately aversive. In the experiment shown in Figure 5.1, the rats were actually more startled by the second and third tones than by the first one, although startle later declined. This biphasic curve is typical of the results of many experiments

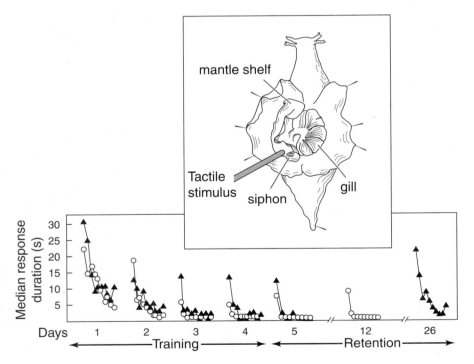

Figure 5.4. Long-term and short-term habituation of *Aplysia's* siphon withdrawal to a jet of water applied to the siphon (tactile stimulus). No trials were administered between the last training day and the tests on Day 5 and Day 12 (group represented by open circles) or Day 26, yet habituation was retained. At the same time, habituation developed within each day. Redrawn from Carew, Pinsker, and Kandel (1972) with permission.

on habituation. The initial increase seems to reflect an independent process of *sensitization,* a general enhancement of responsiveness to a whole class of stimuli, not just the one being habituated. Sensitization often has a shorter time course than habituation, as in Figure 5.1.

The sensitizing effect of moderately strong stimuli may be responsible for some instances of "dishabituation." Functionally, it seems as if a potentially dangerous stimulus alerts the animal, making it more responsive to whatever comes next. Associative potentiation of the rat's startle response (Davis et al. 1993) fits this description: rats startle more when they are in the presence of a signal associated with shock. However, dishabituation can reflect a separate process from sensitization. Siphon withdrawal in the sea slug *Aplysia* wanes when the siphon is repeatedly squirted with a jet of water (Figure 5.4). If the animal's tail is touched or shocked, siphon withdrawal is enhanced in both habituated and untrained animals. In an elegant series of experiments, Marcus, Nolen, Rankin, and Carew (1988) showed that sensitization and dishabituation can be dissociated in Aplysia in three independent ways, thus lending support to a two-process theory of habituation (Groves and Thompson 1970). For instance, the best dishabituating stimulus is a touch to the tail or a relatively weak shock, whereas strong shocks or many shocks to the tail are the best sensitizing stimuli. Sensitization of this response in *Aplysia* has been the subject of a rare study of the phylogeny of learning at the neural level (see Papini 2002).

5.1.2   Diversity of effects on behavior

Examples of habituation like startle in the rat or the wiping reflex in frogs seem to involve little more than changes in specific reflex circuits. But complex behaviors of whole animals like the territorial behavior of birds described in Box 5.1 also habituate. As another example, rats or hamsters released into a large open enclosure (an "open field") approach and sniff objects in it, exploring them. Exploration wanes over time, but if some of the objects are moved to new places, the animals explore them again. Renewed exploration specific to the relocated objects shows that their original locations were learned. As another example, when wild vervet monkeys hear the call of a member of their troop broadcast from a loudspeaker, they gradually stop looking toward the hidden speaker. Habituation transfers to acoustically dissimilar calls with the same referent (e.g., both are given when another group of vervets is approaching). It seems the animal is not habituating to the physical stimulus so much as to the reception of a certain kind of information (see Chapter 14).

5.1.3.   Contents of learning: Three models

Over 60 years ago, one of the first reviews of habituation concluded, "It will be obvious, . . . that no 'mechanism' of habituation will be found. There are quite probably several mechanisms . . . any single explanatory principle would have to be too general to be satisfactory" (J. D. Harris 1943, 388). This conclusion is just as apt today. In this section we consider three models of habituation. The two classic ones differ in that one is a simple model of changes in S-R connections, and the other assumes incoming stimuli are compared to a more complex representation. The third, more recent, model depicts habituation as a form of associative learning (for further discussion see Hall 1991; Macphail 1993).

Sherrington's reflex model

The simplest model of habituation dates from Sir Charles Sherrington's studies of animals with severed spinal cords in the late nineteenth century. Because this surgery removes influences from the brain, habituation in spinal animals necessarily reflects changes in specific reflex pathways, S-R connections. As in S-R accounts of associative learning, this model does not distinguish between learning and performance: learning, the decrement in connection strength, is directly reflected in decreased responding. As a general account of habituation this is simply a restatement of behavioral observations in neural terms and as such is relatively impoverished. It does not predict any new phenomena or specify the precise form of the decrement in connection strength. However, this model can be elaborated in several ways to account for phenomena such as dishabituation and sensitization (e.g., Horn 1967; Davis and File 1984). It is a reasonable account of some examples of habituation such as siphon withdrawal in *Aplysia*. Nevertheless, a simple S-R account is not very useful for understanding habituation of more complex behaviors or possible changes in the representation of stimuli during habituation.

Sokolov's neuronal model

A more complex model couched in neural terms is Sokolov's (1963) comparator model. Here learning consists of building up a representation of the features of a stimulus, the *neuronal model*. How this takes place is not specified but it could involve the kind of within-event learning discussed in Section 5.2. Incoming stimuli are compared to existing neuronal models before being acted on. If there is a match, the initial response to the stimulus is inhibited, that is, behavioral habituation is observed. If the incoming stimulus is discrepant from the neuronal model, an *orienting response* (OR) occurs and the neuronal model is modified to reduce its discrepancy from the incoming stimulus. This scheme therefore distinguishes between learning (modification of the neuronal model) and performance (the OR based on detection of a discrepancy).

Some examples of habituation seem to require such a comparator account. One is the *missing stimulus effect* (Sokolov 1963). If an animal is habituated to stimuli coming at regular intervals and then one stimulus is omitted, the habituated response reappears at the time the omitted stimulus was due. Similarly, hamsters that have learned the locations of objects through exploration spend extra time in the location from which a familiar object has just been removed (Poucet et al. 1986). The simple reflex model has trouble with such effects because the absence of a stimulus has significance only by comparison to expected input (but see Hall 1991). However, the comparator model also has its troubles. In particular, an increasing series of stimulus intensities should not result in greater response decrement than a series of presentations of the same intense stimulus (Davis and Wagner 1969; Groves and Thompson 1970). The neuronal model should match the test stimulus better when that stimulus has been presented all along than when different stimuli have been presented.

Sokolov proposed a specific neural embodiment of his model: the neuronal model is built up in the cortex, and it inhibits activity in the reticular formation, but this system cannot apply to habituation in spinal animals or in *Aplysia*. There may be different neural mechanisms for behavioral habituation in different systems. For potential generality there is a lot to be said for more abstract "black box" models like the one discussed next.

Wagner's SOP model

Accounting for an apparently simple kind of learning in terms of a more complex one may seem unappealing, a violation of Lloyd Morgan's Canon. Yet one influential model of habituation does just that: in this model, habituation results from associating the habituating stimulus with the context in which it appears (Wagner 1978, 1981). This account integrates habituation with associative learning and with standard features of short-term memory. (Hence its acronym, *SOP,* for *standard operating procedure* of memory.) In the SOP model (Figure 5.5) incoming stimuli are compared to the contents of active or *working memory.* Working memory has two levels or states. The highest level of activation, A1, corresponds to the focus of attention or "rehearsal." The contents of A1 are directly read out in behavior appropriate to the stimulus being processed. If stimuli from food are in A1 the animal will be engaged in food-related activities; if a sudden loud noise is being processed, the animal will startle. Behavior appropriate to incoming stimuli will be observed whenever the incoming stimulus is not already represented in one of the levels of active memory (A1 or A2).

Representations (nodes) in A1 fade into the A2 state, corresponding to representation in working memory just outside the immediate focus of attention, and thence into long term or inactive memory (I). The behavioral readout of A2 is therefore behavior appropriate to the memory of a very recent event. Representations can also be activated into A2 associatively, that is, the animal can be reminded of them. The distinction between the two states of active memory captures the notion that remembering something and experiencing it are not the same and may evoke correspondingly different behaviors. If an event is already represented in A2, this will interfere with its ability to be evoked into A1. In this way, expected events (associatively activated into A2) evoke a smaller response than unexpected ones. Short-term memory has limited capacity so that new, unexpected, stimuli displace stimuli currently

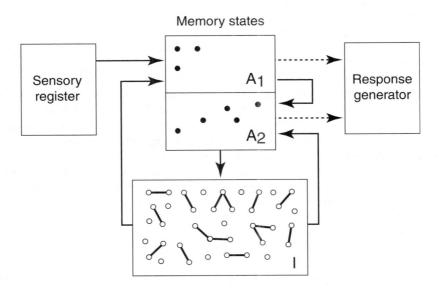

Figure 5.5. Wagner's SOP model of habituation as depicted by Roitblat (1987), indicating memory nodes (circles) and associative links (lines). Redrawn with permission.

being processed or *rehearsed* in A1. Associative learning occurs only when the stimuli to be associated are processed simultaneously in A1. On this view associatively activated representations (represented only in A2) should not be able to function as USs, contrary to the evidence about US images in Chapter 4. Short-term habituation occurs because the more recently a stimulus has been primed into A1 the more it occupies A1 and/or A2. This limits the ability of new occurrences of that stimulus to command processing in A1 and evoke behavior. Long-term habituation reflects association of the habituating stimulus with its context. Thus this model differs from the other two in distinguishing between long-term and short-term habituation.

The SOP model generates a number of novel predictions which have inspired clever tests. For example, habituation should be retarded by presenting "distractors" between occurrences of the target stimulus in a sort of dishabituation paradigm. Whitlow (1975) did this by presenting tones to rabbits and measuring vasoconstriction in the ear (essentially the extent to which the rabbits "pricked up their ears" to the sounds). He presented tones at various intervals to test the prediction that responding is evoked if incoming stimulation does not correspond to the representation currently active in short-term memory. When the same tone was presented twice in succession, the response to the second tone was reduced at intertone intervals up to 150 seconds. However, if two successive tones differed, the response to them was the same, even when the intertone interval was as little as 30 seconds. The stimulus-specific response decrement could be eliminated by presenting a distractor—flashing a light and touching the rabbit—between successive presentations of the target stimulus (see Figure 7.10).

In Wagner's model, the animal becomes less responsive to the target because it learns to expect it in the experimental context (i.e., the representation is associatively evoked into A2 by the context). Thus habituation should be context-specific. Furthermore, it should be possible to "extinguish" habituation by exposing the animal to the context in the absence of the habituating stimulus. Latent inhibition reflects the same mechanism as habituation in this model because if a stimulus is not well represented in A1 it is less available to be associated with another stimulus. Tests of the prediction that both latent inhibition and habituation should be specific to their original training context have had mixed results (McLaren and Mackintosh 2000; Hall 2003). For example, latent inhibition generally fails to transfer to new but familiar contexts, whereas habituation does transfer. Functionally, whether or not habituation transfers should perhaps depend on the animal and the context. For instance, contact with the body of another animal is innocuous as long as you are in a herd or a communal burrow, but it's potentially dangerous when you are alone.

In conclusion, the SOP model is appealing because it applies to a broader range of phenomena than the earlier simpler models. It allows for complex behavior and for short-term as well as long-term habituation, and it has links with standard memory models and associative learning theory. In the years since it was first proposed it has been elaborated to encompass a wider variety of phenomena from conditioning by allowing both CSs and USs to have multiple components in the style of the models discussed in the next section (see Brandon, Vogel, and Wagner 2003).

5.2   Perceptual learning

Perceptual learning refers to learning the characteristics of stimuli as distinct from learning their relationship to other stimuli. The classic demonstration of perceptual learning is an experiment by E. Gibson and Walk (1956). Young rats were exposed to large triangles and circles on the walls of their home cages until they were 90 days old. Then they were trained to approach one of these patterns and avoid the other. Rats familiar with the stimuli learned the discrimination much faster than rats for which the stimuli were novel. This finding seems opposite to what would be expected if exposure to the shapes produced latent inhibition. A way to understand it is to realize that learning depends on both *discriminability* and *associability* of stimuli. Associability corresponds to α or salience in the Rescorla-Wagner model (Chapter 4). Exposure to a stimulus may reduce its associability with reward and at the same time enhance its discriminability from similar stimuli, as shown by the following experiment (Hall and Honey 1989).

Rats were exposed to a horizontally and a vertically striped plaque in a runway or their home cages. Then they had a go/no go discrimination in the runway with one of the plaques as the reinforced stimulus (i.e., they were rewarded for running when the designated plaque was at the end of the runway but not when it was absent). The preexposed rats learned the discrimination more slowly than a control group that had been preexposed only to the runway (Figure 5.6). This illustrates latent inhibition (Section 4.4.6): preexposure slowed associating the familiar plaque with reward. After learning the presence-absence discrimination with one of the striped plaques, the rats were tested in the runway with the other one. The control rats generalized their relatively fast running to the second plaque, which they had not seen before. The preexposed groups generalized less, that is, they discriminated better between the patterns. In more recent experiments, such effects have been explored using liquids made up of different

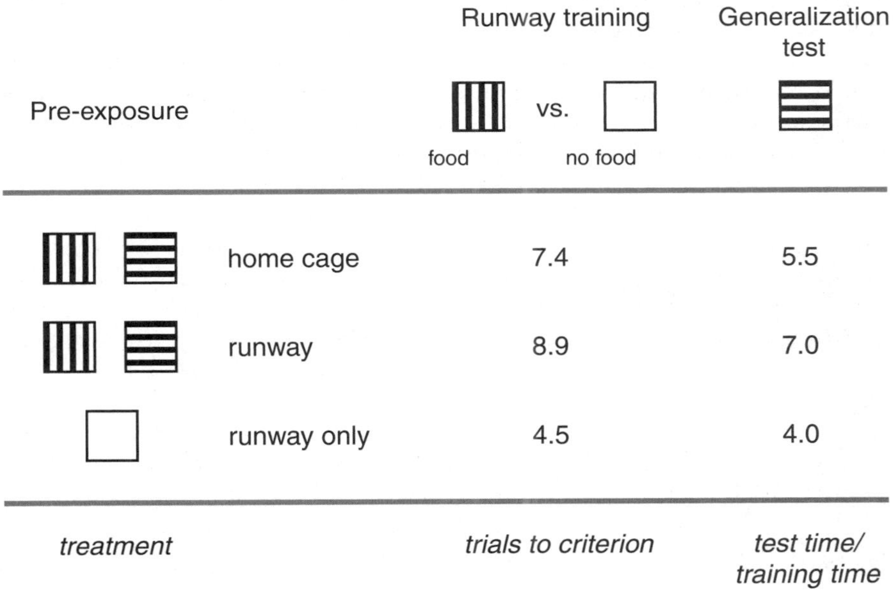

Pre-exposure	treatment	Runway training food vs. no food	Generalization test
⦀ ☰	home cage	7.4	5.5
⦀ ☰	runway	8.9	7.0
☐	runway only	4.5	4.0
	treatment	*trials to criterion*	*test time/ training time*

Figure 5.6. Procedure and results of Hall and Honey's (1989) demonstration that preexposure both reduces associability and enhances discriminability. Faster discrimination learning is indicated by fewer trials to criterion. In the generalization test, the striped plaque not used for training was presented in extinction and its effects measured as the ratio of running times to running time at the end of training; hence, the higher the ratio the less the generalization, that is, the rats ran more slowly to the test plaque than to the reinforced plaque.

components. For instance, two flavored solutions such as saline and sucrose may be made more similar by adding a third flavor such as lemon to both of them (McLaren and Mackintosh 2000).

5.2.1   A model of stimulus representation

William James (1890, 511) described what seems to go on during perceptual learning as follows:

> How does one learn to distinguish claret from burgundy? ... When we first drank claret we heard it called by that name, we were eating such and such a dinner, etc. Next time we drink it, a dim reminder of all those things chimes through us as we get the taste of the wine. When we try burgundy our first impression is that it is a kind of claret; but something falls short of full identification, and presently we hear it called burgundy. During the next few experiences, the discrimination may still be uncertain—"which," we ask ourselves, "of the two wines is this present specimen?" But at last the claret-flavor recalls pretty distinctly its own name, "claret," "that wine I drank at So-and-so's table" etc.; and the name burgundy recalls the name burgundy and someone else's table ... After a while ... the adhesion of each wine with its own *name* becomes ... inveterate, and ... each flavor suggests instantly and certainly its own name and nothing else. The names differ far more than the flavors, and help to stretch the latter further apart.

James's idea—that things initially difficult to discriminate become more discriminable by means of associations among their unique features—is captured in a general model of stimulus representation proposed by McLaren, Kaye, and Mackintosh (1989; McLaren and Mackintosh 2000). The model starts from the assumption (Estes 1950) that stimuli are composed of a number of discrete elements. In James's example, the elements of each wine include its name, its flavor, and the occasions on which it was drunk. Elements are assumed to be sampled randomly each time the stimulus is encountered (Figure 5.7a). In earlier versions of stimulus sampling theory

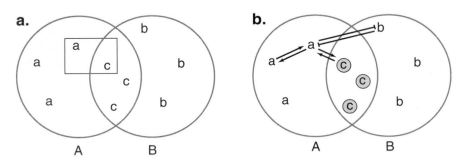

Figure 5.7. The model of perceptual learning proposed by McLaren, Kaye, and Mackintosh (1989). a: Circles represent two stimuli, A and B, that have some common elements (c's) as well as unique ones (a's and b's). A subset of elements (inside the rectangle) is sampled when A appears. b: The situation that develops after exposure to A and B, with reference to representative elements. Each a element develops excitatory associative links with other a elements and with the common elements, c. Inhibitory links develop between a and b elements. Meanwhile, the most frequently encountered elements, the c's, acquire the most latent inhibition (gray circles). After McLaren, Kaye, and Mackintosh (1989) with permission.

(e.g., Estes 1950; Pearce 1987) each stimulus element is a little CS independently associated with the US. But this approach becomes much more interesting and powerful if elements also become associated with each other as suggested by James. Each stimulus element activates a unit or node in a hypothetical network of such nodes (Hall 2002). When a stimulus is presented the nodes corresponding to stimulus elements being sampled are activated both externally, by the element itself, and internally, through associatively modifiable links with other nodes. Learning reduces the discrepancy between internal and external inputs to a node by strengthening connections among the nodes most often activated together, that is, those corresponding to features of the same stimulus. As a result, eventually a subset of elements will tend to activate nodes corresponding to the whole set (Figure 5.7b). The taste of claret will immediately remind one of the name, the occasions on which it was drunk, and so on. In effect, the network of associated nodes is a neuronal model of the stimulus.

This Jamesian account indicates how stimuli become "unitized," but to explain how at the same time wines that share features might become more discriminable from one another, McLaren et al.'s explanation calls upon latent inhibition. Exposure to stimuli with common elements will give most latent inhibition to their common elements, since by definition those elements appear most often. Then when one of these familiar stimuli is to be associated with a US, strongest associations will develop to the unique elements. In addition, sets of nodes corresponding to elements unique to the different stimuli will develop inhibitory connections with each other, as indicated in Figure 5.7b. In James's example, burgundy reminds the inexperienced taster of claret, that is, claret elements are activated internally. Inhibition develops between elements unique to burgundy and those unique to claret because the expectation of "claret" is not activated externally when burgundy is presented. At the same time elements common to the two wines such as a red color will undergo latent inhibition. These ideas suggest that perceptual learning will be more evident relative to latent inhibition with stimuli that are initially less discriminable, that is, have more common elements. The relevant data are consistent with this prediction (McLaren and Mackintosh 2000; Hall 2003).

5.2.2. Within event learning

The model just reviewed hinges on the assumption that separable features of a single event are associated with each other just as CSs are associated with USs. There is considerable evidence for this assumption from experiments on *within event learning*. The logic of such experiments is to create events with separable elements, expose animals to this compound, then give one element a new significance and measure behavior to the other. An experiment on within event learning is thus much like a sensory preconditioning experiment (Figure 4.7) except that the stimuli to be associated occur simultaneously. If the animal views them as features of the same event, then its behavior to one element should reflect conditioning with the other (Rescorla and Durlach 1981).

For example, rats might first drink two compound flavors such as sweet+sour and salty+bitter. In the second phase of the experiment, an element of one compound—say sweet—is paired with poison, and as a control a single element of the other compound—say salt—is presented alone. In the final phase, when the rats choose between the two elements not encountered in the second phase (i.e., sour vs. bitter), they prefer to drink the flavor not paired with the poisoned one, that is, bitter. Parallel results have been obtained using lights and tones for rats and visual stimuli for pigeons (Rescorla and Durlach 1981). Such within event learning increases rapidly and monotonically with number of exposures to the compound. Learning about simultaneous events can even be superior to learning about successive events (see Rescorla and Durlach 1981). And, as one would expect, within-event learning can be extinguished by presenting one or the other element of the event by itself. However, although retraining after extinction is normally quicker than original acquisition with Pavlovian or instrumental conditioning (the phenomenon of *savings*), retraining of within event learning is difficult or impossible after extinction. This finding is consistent with the view that animals originally treat the compound stimulus as a single unanalyzed unit or configuration. On this view (Pearce 1994b) the acquired value of one element transfers to the other through generalization because the individual elements are similar to their compound. Exposure to the elements in isolation sets up representations of these as separate events, and associative changes, involving them are no longer related back to the compound.

Although other processes may sometimes be involved in perceptual learning, this model shows that within-event associations can effectively account for much of what is known about how animals form representations of the events and objects they are simply exposed to (McLaren and Mackintosh 2000; Hall 2003). This same learning process is likely involved in coming to recognize individuals through multiple distinctive cues, as discussed in Box 5.1. In Chapter 6 we will see that it may also be involved in explicit discrimination and category learning.

5.3   Imprinting

Precocial birds like chickens, ducks, and geese can run around within a few hours after hatching. In natural conditions they are kept from running away from their mother at this time, when they still need her for warmth and protection, by rapidly developing a preference for following her rather than other large moving objects. In experiments, they have become attached to moving balls, dangling sponges, flashing lights, stuffed ferrets, and many other objects instead, through the learning process known as *imprinting*. Although it had been described by Douglas Spalding in the 1870s, Konrad Lorenz's (1935/1970) discussion of imprinting was responsible for an outpouring of research on it in the 1950s and 1960s (see Bateson 1966). Lorenz described how birds that had been removed from others of their own species early in life would court and try to mate with members of the species that had raised them, including Lorenz himself. Lorenz claimed that the process responsible for acquisition of such social preferences was a kind of learning distinct from "ordinary learning," by which he meant Pavlovian or operant conditioning (Lorenz 1970, 377). He based this claim on four apparently special characteristics. *(1)* Imprinting could occur only during a *critical period*, early in life. *(2)* After this, it was irreversible. *(3)* Imprinting influences behavior that is not, and often cannot be, shown at the time of learning, that is, adult sexual behavior. *(4)* From experience with a particular individual, normally the mother, the animal learns characteristics of its species.

It soon became apparent (cf. Bateson 1966; Bolhuis 1991) that Lorenz's description of a gosling instantaneously and irreversibly imprinted with a lifelong preference for people after one brief glimpse is far too simple. The phrase *critical period* was replaced by *sensitive period* or *sensitive phase*, implying that the onset and offset of sensitivity were gradual. And, as Lorenz (1935/1970) had acknowledged, the nature of the imprinting stimulus was important. Rather than being irreversible, early preference for an inadequate artificial stimulus could sometimes be replaced by preference for a more naturalistic one. And the differences between imprinting and "ordinary learning" turned out to be not so great after all.

Imprinting was depicted as a "special," "preprogrammed" kind of learning because it is shown only by certain species at certain times in their lives (e.g., Staddon 1983). But it is actually no more "preprogrammed" than any other kind of learning, and it shares many properties with other examples of recognition learning. Most of this section is about *filial imprinting,* acquisition of social preferences in young birds, because most work has been done in this area. Formation of sexual preferences (Section 5.3.2) may involve some different processes.

5.3.1 Conditions and contents of learning

Laboratory tests of imprinting

When a chick or duckling is exposed to an effective imprinting object, it spends more and more time close to it, twittering softly and snuggling up to it. It spends less and less time shrilly peeping ("distress calling") and trying to escape. Demonstrating that such changes are due to experience with the object rather than simply maturation requires two potential imprinting stimuli, A and B. Some animals are exposed to A in the imprinting situation and some to B. Then all animals are given a choice between A and B. For example, Bateson and Jaekel (1976) placed chicks in a running wheel facing a red or a yellow flashing light. The chicks could run toward the light but they did not get any closer to it. After varying amounts of experience with one of the lights, the chicks were tested in another running wheel on a track with the red light at one end and the yellow light at the other (Figure 5.8). When the chick ran toward one light it was transported toward the other, but it could continue to run toward its preferred light even when carried to the opposite end of the track by its efforts. Preference was measured as proportion of all wheel revolutions in a particular direction. Other tests of imprinting take advantage of the fact that a bird will learn an instrumental response to see an object on which it has been imprinted (e.g., Hoffman 1978; Figure 5.9). Such an object also suppresses distress calling when it appears.

Length of exposure

Notice that when birds are trained in a running wheel as in Figure 5.8, running is not instrumentally reinforced because they never get any closer to the imprinting object. Thus sheer exposure to an object is sufficient for a preference to develop. In fact, if exposed to them for long enough, chicks imprint to patterns on the walls of their pens (see P. Bateson 1966). Just as with any other learning phenomenon, length of exposure, type of stimulus, and the state of the animal must all be considered together. A few minutes' exposure to a conspicuous moving object during the first day or two after hatching may have effects only matched by an inconspicuous stationary object after many days' exposure (ten Cate 1989). The effects of length of exposure may depend on the species. Lorenz (1935/1970) described two extremes of imprintability. A greylag gosling that had once seen people would never afterward associate with geese, but curlews would always flee

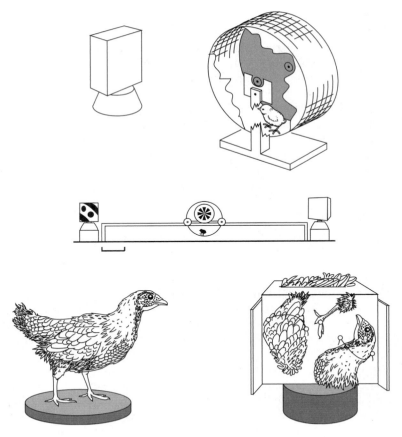

Figure 5.8. Running wheels for imprinting chicks (top row) and testing their preferences (middle), and some of the stimuli used by Bateson, Horn, and their colleagues. Redrawn from Horn (1985) and Bateson and Wainwright (1972) with permission.

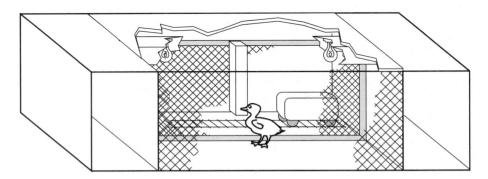

Figure 5.9. Apparatus used for imprinting ducklings and testing instrumental responding reinforced by presentation of the imprinting stimulus. The ducking pecks the square pole in the middle of his compartment to illuminate the compartment in which the imprinting object moves back and forth. Redrawn from Eiserer and Hoffman (1973) with permission.

from people no matter how much they had been exposed to them. Yet Lorenz's assertion that imprinting is instantaneous and irreversible has nearly always been tested on species other than greylag geese, such as domestic chicks and ducklings (see Goth and Hauber 2004).

Type of stimulus

Lorenz (1935/1970) claimed that adults of the bird's own species were more effective imprinting objects than artificial stimuli. Species-specific stimuli do seem to be special for both domestic chicks and ducklings, but not exactly in the way one might expect. Domestic chicks prefer stuffed hens of the junglefowl (their wild ancestors; see Figure 5.8). A preference for fowllike objects develops in the first 2 to 3 days of life as a result of certain nonspecific experiences. It sums with learned preferences. Rearranged stuffed junglefowl (Figure 5.8), stuffed ducks, or even ferrets (a potential predator) are approached as much as junglefowl, perhaps because they have eyes (Johnson and Horn 1988; Bolhuis 1996). These findings indicate that in natural conditions imprinting to the mother is supported, or canalized, by preferences for species-specific stimuli which ensure that the young bird is initially attracted to the mother rather than to other moving objects (see ten Cate 1994). The role of filial imprinting may be to establish not species identification, as suggested by Lorenz, but identification of a particular individual—the mother—within that species (Bateson 1979).

The sensitive period

Many aspects of behavioral development have a sensitive period, a time when they are most susceptible to environmental influence (see Hogan and Bolhuis 2005). Filial imprinting needs to take place only at the beginning of life because its immediate function is to keep the young bird with its mother at this vulnerable time. Accordingly, filial imprinting in chicks and ducklings takes place most readily between a few hours and a few days after hatching. By itself, however, a sensitive period does not make imprinting qualitatively different from associative learning: how learning depends on age is a different question from what kind of experience causes it. Intuitively, the sensitive period reflects a developmental timetable in which imprintability develops at a certain point in ontogeny and further maturational processes end it. This *clock model* (ten Cate 1989) probably accounts for the onset of the sensitive period, but it does not explain its end.

On the alternative account, variously called the *competitive exclusion* (Bateson 1981; 1987), *capacity* (Boakes and Panter 1985), or *self-termination model* (ten Cate 1989), imprinting is fundamentally different from most other forms of learning because once an animal is fully imprinted to one object it cannot become imprinted to any other object. That is, imprinting as intrinsically self-terminating (Bateson 1990), as if there were a fixed number of neural connections that it could occupy. Once these have been used up the animal may still learn to recognize other stimuli such as food or siblings, but these do not, in Bateson's terms, "gain access to the executive system" for filial behavior. This model thus distinguishes between S-S learning—learning the characteristics of the imprinting object—and S-R learning—connecting the features of the object to the filial behavior system.

Is imprinting a kind of conditioning?

The observation that conspicuous moving or flashing objects lead to faster imprinting than stationary ones suggests that imprinting is a form of Pavlovian conditioning in which the static features of the object function as the CS and visual motion as the US. This suggestion leads to a number of testable predictions that contrast with those of the most explicit alternative, namely, that imprinting is a form of perceptual learning in which the animal simply learns the features of the imprinting object and approaches it because it is familiar (see van Kampen 1996). On the perceptual learning view, moving objects are effective because they are more conspicuous than stationary objects. Once the conspicuous features of the mother have acquired value through exposure in the sensitive period her inconspicuous features can go on being learned about. As this discussion suggests, the phenomena of perceptual learning reviewed earlier in the chapter are found with imprinting objects. For instance, in an analog of the experiment depicted in Figure 5.6, chicks imprinted to a visual pattern and later trained on a heat-reinforced discrimination between two patterns learned faster if the imprinting stimulus was one of the to-be-discriminated patterns (Honey, Horn, and Bateson 1993).

The conditioning analysis of imprinting is supported by evidence that imprinting objects are reinforcing. For example, chicks and ducklings will perform an instrumental response to get a view of an imprinting object (Bateson and Reese 1969; Hoffman and Ratner 1973) even before imprinting can have taken place. Since Pavlovian USs such as food also reinforce instrumental behavior, it seems reasonable to conclude that some feature of the imprinting object, such as motion, functions as a US in imprinting. Consistent with this view is evidence that an object whicht does not initially evoke any filial behavior comes to do so when the bird has seen it moving but not stationary (Hoffman 1978). In addition, features of the imprinting object should block or overshadow each other, as indeed they do in experiments using objects with separable parts (review in van Kampen 1996). However, the conditioning model also predicts that imprinting to a moving object will extinguish if the object is kept stationary. This does not happen, and on the perceptual learning view it should not. Also contrary to the conditioning model is the fact that filial behavior eventually develops to a sufficiently conspicuous stationary object (Eiserer 1980; Figure 5.10).

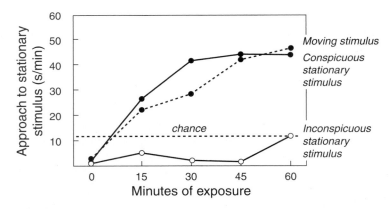

Figure 5.10. Mean time (in seconds per minute of test) ducklings spent approaching a stationary imprinting stimulus during three kinds of experience with it. Redrawn from Eiserer (1980) with permission.

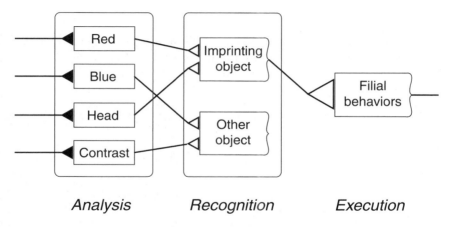

Figure 5.11. The "ARE" (Analysis, Recognition, Execution) model of imprinting. In this example the imprinting object is distinguished by being red and having a head. After P. Bateson (1990) with permission.

The contents of learning: A hybrid model

On the perceptual learning theory, what is learned in imprinting is a representation of the features of the imprinting object. On the conditioning model, it is an association of the neutral features of the imprinting object with its US-like features. Clearly, each theory uniquely explains some features of imprinting and omits others. For example, the perceptual learning model does not distinguish recognizing the imprinting object from recognizing anything else familiar. The conditioning model does not account for possible later effects of the imprinting experience like gradual learning of the imprinting object's features. Because perceptual learning about an object can be going on at the same time as associating the object with a US, both could be correct. This solution is proposed by the competitive exclusion model (P. Bateson 1990; Hollis, ten Cate and Bateson 1991; van Kampen 1996; P. Bateson 2000), according to which imprinting results in two kinds of learning: recognition of the individual imprinting object (perceptual learning) and connections of its representation to "the executive system" for filial behavior (S-R learning). It consists of three systems, corresponding to the perceptual, central, and motor aspects of any behavior system (Figure 2.7). Here these are analysis of incoming stimuli into features, recognition of familiar features, and execution of filial behavior patterns (Figure 5.11).

Conditions for learning: Summary

Filial imprinting is influenced by the same kinds of conditions that influence other learning about single events. Exactly how these factors matter differs among species (Goth and Hauber 2004). The discussion of whether imprinting is an example of classical conditioning (i.e., whether the conditions of learning include a positive contingency between neutral and US-like features) reduces to the question whether manipulations of the hypothesized CS-US relationship influence imprinting as predicted by conditioning theory. Clearly there is no single US such as motion, since young birds deprived of exposure to a conspicuous moving object will imprint to almost anything else eventually. One solution is to conclude that the "real" US is some feature shared by all effective imprinting objects such as arousing a particular affective state (Bolhuis, de Vos, and Kruijt 1990). This doesn't say much except that objects that support imprinting support imprinting. It also doesn't seem to explain non-conditioning-like aspects of imprinting such as failure to extinguish.

5.3.2   Effects of learning on behavior: Sexual imprinting

Like Pavlovian conditioning and some examples of habituation, imprinting endows a stimulus with control over a whole behavior system (van Kampen 1996). The behavior system is filial or attachment behavior, behavior that functions to keep the young bird close to its mother and the mother close to it. But one of Lorenz's claims for the uniqueness of imprinting was that it also influences behaviors which have not yet appeared at the time of learning, namely sexual behaviors. Contrary to Lorenz's claim, however, one might expect sexual preferences for conspecifics to develop without any specific experiences because mating with members of one's own species is essential to fitness.

Examples of sexual imprinting show that experience can in fact influence mate choice. The classic observation is Lorenz's (1935/1970; Immelmann 1972) report that hand-reared birds prefer to court humans even after years of social experience with their own species, including successful courtship and mating. But filial imprinting need not be directly responsible for sexual preferences. In filial imprinting the young bird needs to learn the characteristics of a particular individual, normally its mother, whereas species characteristics are what matter for mating. However, early learning about the mother could produce a generalized preference for individuals of the same species later on. If the mother is not present when the young are ready to mate, as in species where the young disperse from the natal area, the bird may choose the closest match it can find. In addition, fine details of the mother's appearance may be forgotten between infancy and maturity while salient features, characteristic of species members generally, are not (Zolman 1982). Moreover, the preference for the mother developed early in life need not be specifically sexual. The adolescent male may simply approach females of his species because they resemble his mother and thereby learn that they can provide sexual interactions (Bischof 1994).

The optimal outbreeding hypothesis

Attempts to distinguish sexual and filial imprinting experimentally have shown that filial and sexual imprinting can be dissociated in time. Vidal (1980) exposed domestic cockerels of three different ages to an object that could support both filial and sexual behavior. At sexual maturity, the birds that had been exposed to the model at the youngest age and shown most filial behavior showed the least sexual behavior to it. Those exposed latest and showing least filial behavior toward the model, showed most sexual behavior toward it. Sexual imprinting also occurs after filial imprinting in quail and ducks while birds are still in the family group but beginning to develop adult plumage (Bateson 1979). This timing may function to allow animals to learn the characteristics of siblings so they can choose mates slightly different from them. This combination of learning and choice mechanisms would promote an optimal degree of outbreeding, allowing animals to avoid the deleterious effects of breeding with very close relations without outbreeding so much as to dilute adaptations to local conditions. The representation of "close relative" should be based on siblings rather than mother alone because the siblings provide a larger sample of close relatives, one which includes characteristics of the father's family.

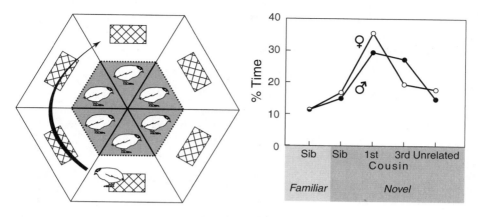

Figure 5.12. Overhead view of apparatus for testing sexual preference in quail and results when the stimulus animals were related to the subject as indicated. A pedal in front of each window (hatched rectangles) records how long the subject walking in the outer runway spends there. Redrawn from P. Bateson (1982) with permission.

Evidence consistent with the optimal outbreeding hypothesis comes from studies in which quail raised in family groups were exposed to siblings, cousins, and non-kin in the multiple choice apparatus shown in Figure 5.12. Birds of both sexes spent most time near first cousins (Bateson 1982). When quail of different degrees of relatedness were housed together after being raised in families, those housed with cousins layed fertile eggs sooner than those housed with siblings or more distant relatives (Bateson 1988), showing that preferences evident in the choice apparatus could have a real impact on reproduction. Mice and great tits also prefer mates slightly different from animals they were raised with (Barnard and Aldhous 1991; Boyse et al. 1991), but it is not clear how widely the optimal outbreeding hypothesis applies (Cooke and Davies 1983; Burley, Minor and Strachan 1990).

The content of learning

The optimal discrepancy model raises the question how information about different family members is represented: does the bird form a representation of a prototypical family member or does it store information about each individual (or exemplar) separately? This is a general question about category learning (Chapter 6). Prototype theory predicts that after training with a number of specific instances of a category, the *prototype* or central tendency will be preferred to any other instance, even if it is novel. Ten Cate (1987) tested this notion for "double imprinting" in zebra finches. (Notice that zebra finches are *altricial,* that is, they hatch naked and helpless. They do not need very early filial imprinting to keep them with the mother but may form sexual preferences while still in the family group.) If male zebra finches are raised by their own parents for about the first thirty days and then housed with Bengalese finches, some of them become "ditherers" (ten Cate 1986). They direct sexual behavior about equally to both zebra finches and Bengalese finches, although they prefer either to a novel species (Figure 5.13). Have such birds formed two separate representations of acceptable sexual partners or a single composite representation? Ten Cate (1987) tried to find out by offering them a choice between a zebra finch–Bengalese finch hybrid and a zebra finch or a Bengalese finch. If we assume that

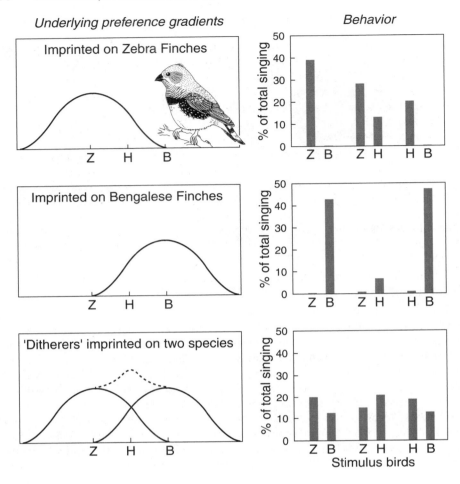

Figure 5.13. Panels on the left show hypothetical generalization of sexual preference in male zebra finches imprinted to zebra finches (Z), Bengalese finches (B), or on both species. In the latter case, the sum of the two preference gradients (dotted line) is maximal for a bird resembling a zebra finch–Bengalese finch hybrid (H). Panels on the right show sexual preference in pairwise tests with a zebra finch, a Bengalese finch, and a hybrid, measured as proportion of songs directed to each stimulus bird. Redrawn from ten Cate (1987) with permission.

the hybrid combines features of both species, prototype theory predicts that ditherers should prefer it to either a zebra finch or a Bengalese finch. But the same outcome is predicted by exemplar learning if generalization gradients from the two separate standards overlap enough (Figure 5.13). Ditherers did prefer the hybrid, and the results with birds imprinted on just one species indicated that such a preference could not result from summation of two separate generalization gradients (Figure 5.13). Thus the birds seemed to acquire a representation of a prototype. This research is a good example of how a framework for thinking about the development of representations may be transferred from one context (conditioning theory) to another (imprinting), although the conclusions from this study may not always apply (Vos, Prijs, and ten Cate 1993).

Sexual imprinting?

Some effect of experience on sexual preferences has been found in every species in which it has been looked for (ten Cate and Vos 1999), but in most cases the relative contributions of experiences and species-specific predispositions are unknown. Acquisition of sexual preferences would be a better term than sexual imprinting to summarize the effect of experience on what species an individual chooses to mate with because it is not a unitary learning phenomenon. In some cases (e.g., Gallagher 1977; Vidal 1980; ten Cate, Los, and Schilperood 1984) mere exposure to animals with certain characteristics influences later choice. In others, individuals have protracted and complex interactions with siblings and parents while sexual preferences may be being formed, making it next to impossible to isolate the experiences which are critical (if indeed any are) to later mate choice. For example, when young zebra finches are raised by foster parents consisting of a zebra finch and a Bengalese finch, the zebra finch parent directs more feeding and aggressive behavior toward the young zebra finches than does the Bengalese finch. The young may therefore pay more attention to the zebra finch parent and learn more about its appearance (ten Cate 1994). In addition, a preference developed during early life may be replaced by a preference for the first species the animal breeds with (Bischof 1994).

Species differences

Not all birds are raised by their own parents. For example, cowbirds and cuckoos are among species that are *brood parasites,* laying their eggs in other birds' nests and leaving them to be raised by their unfortunate foster parents (Box 5.2). Megapodes, large chicken-like birds of Australia and nearby islands, bury their eggs in the ground and the young hatch and dig their way out by themselves. How such birds recognize individuals of their own species for flocking and mating has been attracting attention more recently than the "classic" imprinting species (Goth and Hauber 2004). Indeed, functional notions about imprinting suggest many possibilities for comparative studies which have hardly been exploited.

Box 5.2 A Cost of Recognition

European cuckoos (*Cuculus canorus*) lay their eggs in other birds' nests. When the young cuckoo hatches, it pushes the eggs or young of its host out of the nest, thereby monopolizing all the host's parental effort while reducing the host's reproductive success to zero (Davies and Brooke 1988). It would seem that the small songbirds parasitized by cuckoos should be able to recognize their own eggs and/or offspring so they can discriminate against cuckoos. Some such birds do learn what their own eggs look like and reject eggs that are too different (Davies and Brooke 1988; Lotem, Nakamura, and Zahavi 1995). However, cuckoos' eggs are very good mimics of their hosts' eggs; different races (*gentes*) of cuckoos specialize on different host species and lay eggs that closely resemble the eggs of those hosts. Thus potential hosts faces a difficult signal detection problem, and their behavior can be understood in terms of the costs of and benefits of accepting versus rejecting unusual eggs in the nest (Figure B5.2; Davies, Brooke, and Kacelnik 1996). Ejecting an egg entails some risk of breaking or rejecting one's own egg. When the probability of parasitism is low, the host's expected reproductive success is highest with a relatively lax criterion for rejection, but when the probability of parasitism is high, the benefit of rejecting outweighs the cost, and potential hosts should discriminate more strongly against deviant eggs. Some birds adjust their criterion on a short-term basis: seeing a stuffed cuckoo on the edge of the nest increases reed warblers' tendency to reject a model cuckoo egg (Davies, Brooke, and Kacelnik 1996).

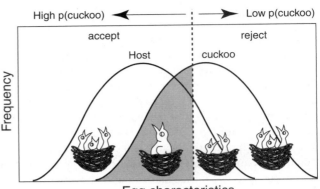

Figure B5.2. The decision to accept or reject eggs in the nest as a signal detection problem. Payoffs are represented as raising a full brood of one's own (three small nestlings), a reduced brood, or a cuckoo (single big nestling). The optimal placement of the decision criterion depends on the probability of cuckoos in the environment as indicated. After Davies, Brooke, and Kacelnik (1996) with permission.

Why doesn't this reasoning also apply to offspring recognition? One possibility is that any mechanism for rejecting parasites such as cuckoos requires that the hosts learn what their own offspring look like in the first place. A learning process like imprinting on the first brood of offspring raised would go wrong whenever the first clutch was parasitized: the parent would learn to accept cuckoos and reject all future offspring of its own (Lotem 1993). Here is a case where not learning is better than learning. Moreover, a small bird like a reed warbler can discriminate against cuckoos without recognizing them as something not their own young simply by abandoning its nest when the nestling has been there too long. The cartoon in Figure B5.2 with one large baby cuckoo nearly filling a nest built for several baby warblers is an accurate depiction of the relative sizes of cuckoo and host offspring. The big baby cuckoo takes longer to fledge than a brood of smaller birds, and it turns out that reed warbler hosts abandon young that have been in the nest unusually long. This is true whether there is only one offspring or as many as four (Grim 2007).

Bird species in which individuals nest close together and/or the young may wander should have mechanisms for parent-offspring recognition. Sometimes animals must make what seem to be incredibly difficult discriminations, as when penguins can find their offspring in a colony of hundreds or thousands (Aubin and Jouventin 2002). Such feats need not involve specializations in recognition learning ability. Cues to identity of the eggs or young could be very salient and/or the animals could have perceptual specializations for discriminating individual differences. Learning to recognize eggs and offspring has been studied comparatively in colonial and solitary-nesting gulls and swallows (Beecher 1990; Storey et al. 1992). In swallows, colonial and solitary species differ in the signals given off by the young rather than in adult perception or learning.

5.3.3   Imprinting: Conclusions

The essence of filial imprinting is that through mere exposure to a stimulus during a sensitive period the animal both learns its features and comes to preferentially direct filial behavior to it. The feature-learning part of imprinting seems to be the same as any perceptual learning, but its behavioral effects are specific to filial behavior. This makes filial imprinting distinct from a mere preference for the familiar, which is widespread among animals and reflects the fact that something previously experienced without aversive consequences is probably safer than something unknown. The fact that the imprinting experience endows the imprinting object with privileged access to the filial behavior system parallels the way in which conditioning endows CSs with control over feeding, sexual, fear, or other behavior systems (Chapter 4). What remains as unique to filial imprinting is its rapid occurrence through mere exposure early in life and—at least with naturalistic objects—the difficulty of reversing it. As well, its restriction to a comparatively few species gives it one property of a specialized learning module.

When it comes to sexual imprinting it is probably preferable to think in terms of a set of processes involved in acquisition of sexual preferences rather than a single imprinting-like process. We look a little further at some of these processes in the next section. The term *imprinting* has been extended to other preferences that appear to be formed early in life, most notably habitat preferences (see Davis and Stamps 2004). When young animals disperse from the place where they were born, choosing to settle in a place that is similar to the natal habitat makes sense because by virtue of its similarity such a place is likely to have the necessary resources for living and breeding. And indeed, there is experimental evidence from diverse species that animals prefer habitats like their natal habitats (Davis and Stamps 2004). However, "habitat preference" could actually be preference for any of a number of resources in the habitat, acquired in any of a number of ways, For example, the animal might settle where there an abundance of familiar food. Accordingly, the label *habitat imprinting* has been replaced by the more neutral term *natal habitat preference induction* (Davis and Stamps 2004).

5.4   The behavioral ecology of social recognition: Recognizing kin

Recognizing your mother and recognizing an appropriate mate are but two kinds of social recognition. Even some invertebrates such as wasps and hermit crabs show evidence of recognizing specific individuals, dominance hierarchies imply an ability to recognize individuals by rank (review in Tibbetts and Dale 2007), and many animals show social recognition in a variety of other contexts as well (Chapters 12 and 13). But the form of recognition most discussed by behavioral ecologists is *kin recognition*, that is, social recognition in which animals respond selectively to their relatives. Inbreeding avoidance, mentioned in the last section, requires discriminating against relatives, but in *nepotistic* situations animals help their relatives. For example, rather than leaving their parents' territory and starting their own families, Florida scrub jays and young of some other birds remain at home and help to feed their younger siblings (Woolfenden and Fitzpatrick 1984). Helping at the nest tends to occur when good territories are so scarce that young inexperienced birds are unlikely to be able to breed successfully on their own. The scrub jays' helping at the nest is an example of behavior that benefits close relatives and is therefore subject to *kin selection* (W. Hamilton 1963). Kin selection arises because what really counts in evolution is the *inclusive fitness* of an act, its effects on the actor's individual fitness plus its effects on the fitness of the actor's relatives in proportion to their relatedness (Box 1.2). For example, because siblings share half their genes with each other, behavior that increases two siblings' reproductive success more than it reduces the reproductive success of the altruist increases the altruist's inclusive fitness. This reasoning explains how scrub jays could be selected to stay at home and help when conditions are unfavorable for independent breeding.

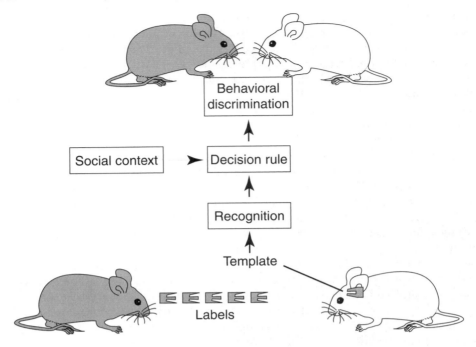

Figure 5.14. The elements of a recognition system. The white mouse recognizes the grey one as having the relevant label for a behavioral response. Adapted from Waldman, Frumhoff, and Sherman (1988) with permission.

Kin recognition has received a lot of attention from behavioral ecologists because it is expected whenever fitness is increased by directing resources selectively toward relatives. Figure 5.14 is a general depiction of social recognition systems that helps in thinking about the information processing it requires. A fundamental requirement is that the individuals to be discriminated must emit a distinctive signal (a "label") that species members can perceive. Signals for discriminating kin should be reliable cues to the bearer's genetic identity (Neff and Sherman 2002), but as we see in a minute this does not mean they have to be correlated with the animal's genetic makeup as such. Perception of the signal must trigger an internal representation that corresponds to "relative," the "template" in the figure. This sort of representation for the central tendency of a category is referred to as a *prototype* in Chapter 6, but *template* is used here to retain the flavor of the model in Figure 5.14.

Having detected whatever cues identify their kin, the perceiver directs some behavior selectively to them. The behavior shown and the threshold for showing it may depend on the social context (Reeve 1989; Mateo 2004). The distinction between detecting kin and discriminating in their favor is nicely underlined by a comparison of golden-mantled and Belding's ground squirrels (Mateo 2002). As discussed later in this section, the very social Belding's ground squirrels discriminate in favor of kin in a variety of situations whereas golden-mantled ground squirrels show little evidence of recognizing kin other than mothers and offspring. Nevertheless, in habituation-dishabituation tests, golden-mantled ground squirrels discriminate among the odors of grandmother, aunt, half-aunt, and non-kin in a graded way just as Belding's ground squirrels do (Figure 5.15; Mateo 2002). In terms

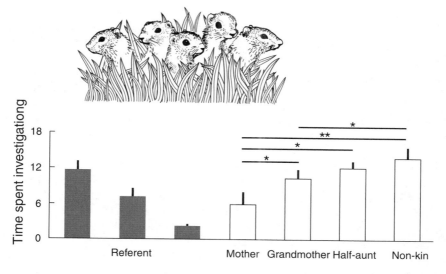

Figure 5.15. Time (mean seconds) Belding's ground squirrels spent investigating an object with the odor of an unfamiliar animal (referent) during successive presentations and the same measure from subsequent presentation of the odor of an individual related to the referent animal as indicated. Bars mark siginificant differences. Data from Mateo (2002), redrawn with permission; drawing after a photograph in Krebs and Davies (1993), with permission.

of Figure 5.14, they evidently possess kin labels and a recognition template, but the ability to discriminate along the dimension of relatedness does not modulate nepotistic behavior.

Kin recognition may be indirect: the altruist responds to a contextual stimulus normally correlated with kinship. For instance, parents of altricial young like many songbirds or small rodents are usually safe in responding to anything they find in their nest as if it is their offspring, for example by feeding it. Cuckoos, cowbirds, and other avian nest parasites exploit this rule by laying their eggs in other birds' nests. When the young cuckoo hatches, it pushes its foster siblings out of the nest, and the host birds unwittingly put all their reproductive effort into feeding the young cuckoo (Box 5.2). Following a simple rule like "treat everything in the nest as your offspring" does not require kin recognition nor learning the features of the offspring as such. Discrimination might be tied to location, so that a relative encountered elsewhere is treated as a stranger. For this reason, not all agree on whether indirect recognition should be regarded as a form of kin recognition (Tang-Martinez 2001; Mateo and Holmes 2004). Clearly, however, it functions to allow animals to discriminate in favor of kin and that sense is as good a kin recognition mechanism as any other.

When family members are together in the same nest or territory at a predictable time in the life cycle, the stage is set for learning that permits recognition outside that spatial context. In imprinting, for instance, newly hatched chicks and ducklings behave as if following the rule: "The first large moving object you see is your mother." This rule works because the mother is virtually certain to be near the nest when the babies hatch. The same kind of principle allows young animals to learn characteristics of their siblings while in the nest and later behave altruistically toward them. Such experience-based kin recognition has been studied extensively in ground squirrels and other rodents, where it is based on odor (R. Johnston 2003; Mateo 2003), and in some birds, where it is more often based on auditory or visual cues (e.g., Beecher 1990; Nakagawa and Waas 2004; Sharp. et al. 2005). In Belding's ground squirrels (*Spermophilus beldingi*), males disperse from the area where they were born, but adult females establish burrows close to their natal area (Holmes and Sherman 1982). Therefore, females often interact with their own offspring, their sisters, and the sisters' offspring, but males do not. As kin selection thinking predicts, closely related females behave altruistically toward each other in defense against predators and territorial disputes. For example, females are more likely to alarm call in the presence of sisters and offspring, a behavior that may increase their own risk of being caught by the predator.

The role of experience in kin recognition in this species has been investigated by means of *cross-fostering experiments* (see Mateo and Holmes 2004; Holmes and Mateo 2007). In such experiments, babies from one nest are raised in the nest of a foster mother along with babies to which they are unrelated. (Until the time when the young are ready to start leaving the nest, mothers accept foster babies and rear them as their own, that is, they use a location rule as a guide to kinship at this stage.) Kin recognition can then be tested by allowing two animals to meet in a neutral arena and recording the incidence of aggression and other behaviors. Such studies show that Belding's ground squirrels treat the animals they were raised with as kin. The learning involved could be sheer familiarization, as in habituation or perceptual learning. It could be imprinting-like, conferring a special social significance to stimuli experienced during a sensitive phase of development, or it could involve associating features of others in the nest with some US-like events (Tang-Martinez 2001; Mateo 2004).

When there are multiple siblings in the nest, the learning is essentially category learning, discussed in Chapter 6. Thus the resulting representation or recognition template might include features of each sibling or be like a prototype or average of "sibling" (Mateo and Holmes 2004). In general, it is difficult to distinguish these possibilities behaviorally, and notwithstanding some speculations about whether prototypes or exemplar memory are involved in kin recognition (Mateo 2004), there seems to be no relevant evidence one way or the other. Consistent with either kind of representation, ground squirrels generalize their learned representation of kin, treating new individuals like kin if they are similar to those in their natal nest. For example, unrelated females raised with each others' siblings are less aggressive toward each other as adults than are pairs of unfamiliar animals not raised with each others' relatives (Holmes 1986). Such generalization is based on the similarity of odors from genetically similar individuals (Holmes and Mateo 2007; Cheetham. et al. 2007). Indeed, tests in which ground squirrels were allowed to investigate odors from different individuals, much like the tests with hamsters described in Chapter 3, show that odors are perceived as more similar the more closely related the individuals they come from (Figure 5.15; R. Johnston 2003; Mateo 2003).

If odors carry cues to genetic relatedness (see Cheetham. et al. 2007), then unfamiliar individuals can be recognized as kin. For example, females respond altruistically to those genetically similar to themselves even if they have never encountered each other or their siblings before (Holmes 1986). Such behavior suggests that individuals respond to some signal directly linked to genes similar to their own. It could result from a single gene, or "recognition allele," controlling production of signal, recognition, and discriminative behavior, but this sort of single-gene control of multiple behavioral mechanisms is considered unlikely (Grafen 1990; Mateo 2004). A more likely, but controversial, possibility is that direct recognition of kin is based on comparing their characteristics to your own, a mechanism known as *self-referent phenotype matching* (Hauber and Sherman 2001). For example, because female Belding's ground squirrels may mate with more than one male, litters can contain both full siblings (same father and mother) and half siblings (same mother, different father). Who is who can be determined by DNA fingerprinting. Females raised with full and half sisters behave most altruistically toward their full sisters (Holmes and Sherman 1982), implying that genetic similarity is playing a role over and above familiarity.

A critical test of self-referent phenotype matching requires raising an animal apart from its relatives from birth and then seeing if it discriminates kin from non-kin (Hauber and Sherman 2001; see also Mateo and Holmes 2004). This has been done with positive results in golden hamsters (Mateo and Johnston 2000), peacocks (Petrie, Krupa, and Burke 1999), and cowbirds (Hauber, Sherman, and Paprika 2000). None of these experiments makes clear, however, whether the animal is matching cues from the stimulus animal to a learned representation of some aspect of itself or to on-line perception of its own characteristics. For example because cowbirds develop in the nest of another species, they could use self-referent phenotype matching to recognize which species to mate with when adult. When nestling cowbirds began to grow feathers, Hauber, Sherman, and Paprika (2000) colored some black and left others normal grayish-brown. When tested for preference between black-dyed and normal gray adults, colored birds preferred black females, whereas controls preferred undyed females. However, experimental birds were still black and the controls still gray at this time. Additional groups in which the subject birds were colored just before the test could help to unravel the roles of past experience versus perception of present appearance (see Tang-Martinez 2001).

5.5   Forms of recognition learning compared

Animals learn about events they are simply exposed to in the absence of specific contingencies with other events. The examples of recognition learning that have been analyzed most extensively are habituation, perceptual learning, and imprinting. In each case, the features of a stimulus likely become associated with each other so that exposure to one feature recalls other features, as described in Section 5.2 on perceptual learning. With the exception of the sensitive period in filial imprinting similar conditions are important for each kind of recognition learning. However the resulting behavioral changes are qualitatively different and are evident in more or less specific behavior systems. Perceptual learning is traditionally assessed by testing whether an arbitrary relationship is learned more readily with a familiar than with a novel stimulus. In habituation, a preexisting response decreases in probability or intensity. In imprinting, sexual or filial preferences develop. Comparator models have been prominent in accounts of recognition learning: present input is compared to a stored representation and responding is based on the discrepancy between them. Notwithstanding largely untested differences in the kinds of representations they imply, the models of the cognitive processes involved in recognition in habituation, imprinting, and kin discrimination are essentially the same, as can be seen by comparing Figures 5.5, 5.11, and 5.14.

The section of the chapter on social recognition describes some natural situations involving recognition of other individuals. In a few of them, something is known about what cues are used and how they acquire their significance. In most of these cases, too little is known about the conditions and contents of recognition learning to compare it in detail to the examples described earlier in the chapter. However, there seems to be no reason to question that the same sorts of learning are involved. For instance, in Belding's ground squirrels, phenotype matching of the individual's odor might be involved in initial recognition of kin, but distinctive features such as appearance and voice may later be associated with this feature to permit individuals to be recognized at a distance (see Box 5.1). The results of the many studies of how animals readily learn about the objects to which they are exposed in the laboratory make it plausible that similar learning contributes to the complex social knowledge underlying some animal societies (Chapter 12).

Further reading

Chapter 5 of Papini's (2008) text includes a comprehensive and well-illustrated introduction to habituation, including recent work on its neurobiology. Ethological observations of a wide range of examples are described by Hinde (1970a, Chapter 13). The book by Hall (1991), still the standard review of habituation and perceptual learning, develops an argument for an integrated model of habituation, latent inhibition, and perceptual learning. Hall (2001) updates it.

Lorenz's (1935/1970) own account of his work in imprinting is still very much worth reading. The most comprehensive review of imprinting remains that by Bolhuis (1991). There has been comparatively little recent behavioral work on filial imprinting (Bateson 2000), but it has continued to be studied at the neural level, as summarized by Horn (2004). A new direction in research on sexual imprinting is comparative work on species recognition by brood parasites, reviewed by Goth and Hauber (2004). The chapter by Sherman, Reeve, and Pfennig (1997) is a general discussion of recognition mechanisms. Mateo (2004) and R. Johnston (2003) provide substantial reviews of recent work, and Holmes and Mateo (2007) give a nice overview of research on kin recognition with particular reference to rodents. Tibbetts and Dale (2007) discuss individual recognition from a functional perspective, with many examples including wasps, lobsters, and cetaceans.

6
Discrimination, Classification, and Concepts

6.1 Three examples

1. A male stickleback with a bright red belly, ready to mate, swims about in a tank. A grayish model fish with a swollen "belly" appears, and our subject begins to display courtship movements. Their vigor increases when the model assumes a diagonal posture with its head up. A short time later, another model, with a red, unswollen, belly, is introduced. The male darts toward it, ready for a fight (Figure 6.1).

2. A female baboon hears another female in her troop make a threatening grunt and looks in the direction of the sound. The grunt is answered by the scream of a low ranking female from the caller's own family, and the listener resumes foraging. The next day, she hears the same female grunt, but this time the grunt is followed by the scream of a dominant female, and our listener looks toward the sounds for several seconds.

3. A pigeon pecks at a small photograph of Harvard Yard containing trees, buildings, people. After a few seconds, a hopper of grain appears and the pigeon eats. Now the scene changes to a treeless Manhattan street. The bird emits a few desultory pecks, then turns away and paces about. After a minute or so, a picture of a leafy suburban garden appears and the bird begins pecking again.

These animals are *discriminating* among model fish, sounds, or pictures. In operational terms, they are exhibiting *stimulus control*. At the same time they are *classifying* or *categorizing* complex stimuli, in that they give one response to some stimuli and different responses to others. This chapter asks what mechanisms underlie such behavior. When animals respond differently to different classes of things, does this mean they have an underlying concept? Does the stickleback, for example, have a concept of "mate" or "rival male"? Or can their behavior be explained as responses to a few simple stimuli? What do these apparently different explanations mean? And how does discriminative behavior develop?

Clearly, the issues here overlap with those in the chapters on perception, learning, and recognition. In general, in this chapter animals are discriminating among stimuli that they readily perceive as different. Chapter 5 was concerned with discriminative

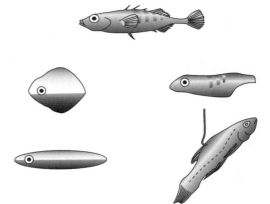

Figure 6.1. Model fish used to discover what stimuli control sexual and aggressive behaviors of male sticklebacks. Top: a normal male stickleback. Models on the left have red undersides, like normal males. On the right is a model with the swollen belly characteristic of egg-laden females and a dead tench presented in the upright posture of a courting female stickleback. Redrawn from Tinbergen (1951) with permission.

behavior acquired through simple exposure, whereas much of this chapter concerns explicit *discrimination training,* in which some stimuli are paired with one consequence and others, with another. Ideas about learning and event representation introduced in Chapters 4 and 5 are key to understanding the effect of such training, and they are elaborated here.

We start, however, with natural stimuli and discriminations that are not explicitly trained, as in Examples 1 and 2. Experience may contribute to what animals do in these situations, but the focus is on what aspects of natural objects control discriminative responding and how they do so, not on how it develops. Section 6.2 introduces classical ethological phenomena and ideas, and Section 6.3 reviews more recent analyses of how animals classify signals in the wild. Traditional discrimination training experiments used simple stimuli like tones and lights. Section 6.4 reviews the principles they reveal, and Box 6.3 discusses the role these principles play in the arms race between predators and prey. We then return to classification of complex stimuli in experiments on learned discriminations between categories of things like Example 3. Is animals' behavior in such experiments evidence that they have a concept or are they just clever memorizers? What does it mean to have a concept anyway?

As this preview suggests, animal discrimination and classification have been the subject of two rather separate research traditions. Laboratory research by psychologists has been—and continues to be—dominated by studies with pigeons like that depicted in Example 3. These are designed to test theories of visual category learning, many of them derived from studies with humans. Research like that depicted in Examples 1 and 2 is more concerned with discovering whether and how animals classify natural signals and other stimuli in biologically meaningful ways. Examples of what may be learned by integrating these approaches will be highlighted throughout the chapter.

6.2   Untrained responses to natural stimuli

6.2.1   Sign stimuli

One of the key observations of classical ethologists was that, like the stickleback in Example 1, animals respond selectively to objects in their environment. Among the wide range of stimuli that an animal's sense organs can detect, some elicit one behavior, some another. Patently perceptible features of natural objects are apparently ignored in some contexts. For example, male sticklebacks in breeding condition attack crude models with red bellies that lack most other fishlike characteristics. The red belly is a *sign stimulus*. Subtle features of sign stimuli can be important, however, particularly their configuration (see Ewert 2005). For instance, the red on the model is more effective if it is on the "belly," not the "back."

Sign stimuli may have their effects on very young animals or as soon as the animal can perform the appropriate responses, for example when it is ready to breed for the first time. Many of the stimulus-response connections appropriate for species-specific feeding, breeding, and other behaviors exist prefunctionally, but this need not mean that learning cannot occur later on nor that environmental conditions before they are first performed have no influence. That is, although the traditional concept of sign stimulus may have included innateness, the important fact that some stimuli selectively elicit highly specific responses survives the demise of the innate/learned distinction (see Chapter 1).

One way in which experience affects sign stimuli is to bring about control by subtle features of an object that are not effective originally. One well-analyzed example involves pecking at the parent's bill by gull chicks. Adult herring gulls have a red spot near the end of the lower mandible, and chicks' pecking at this spot stimulates the adult to regurgitate food. The red color of the spot is a sign stimulus (Hailman 1967). Newly hatched herring gulls seem to ignore features of model gull heads like shape and color and respond only to the presence of a red bill-like area (Figure 6.2). However, older chicks are also influenced by more subtle features like the shape of the head and peck more at more realistic models, reflecting a process Hailman (1967)

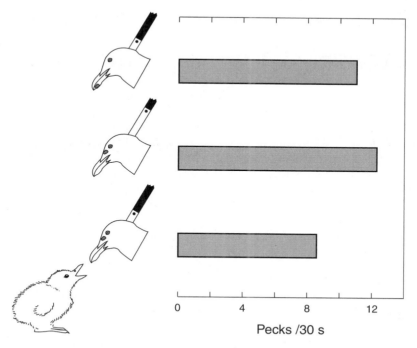

Pecks /30 s

Figure 6.2. Effects of the placement of the red spot normally at the end of the parent's bill as in the top model and the point at which the model pivots (black dots) on pecking by herring gull chicks. Redrawn from Hailman (1967) with permission.

called *perceptual sharpening*. As in perceptual learning (Chapter 5), initially ineffective features of an object become associated with an effective feature so that objects
originally treated as similar are differentiated. Indeed, young gulls learn to discriminate their own parents from other gulls by associating their visual and auditory
features with the food reinforcement they provide (Griswold et al. 1995).

6.2.2   Multiple cues: Heterogeneous summation and supernormality

More than one feature of a natural stimulus may influence a given response. For example, a
model's "posture" and its way of moving as well as its color determine how vigorously a
male stickleback attacks it. Separable cues may have a precisely additive effect, a phenomenon known as *heterogeneous summation* (see Margolis et al. 1987; Ewert 2005). In an
elegant example Heiligenberg (1974) measured aggression in the cichlid fish,
Haplochromis burtoni, by observing how much one fish attacked smaller fish of another
species living in its tank. The modest baseline level of attack could be temporarily raised or
lowered by presenting a model conspecific outside the tank. A model with a black eye bar
raised the level of attack; a similar model with orange spots but no eye bar reduced attack
(Figure 6.3). These effects summed algebraically: a model with both a black eye bar and

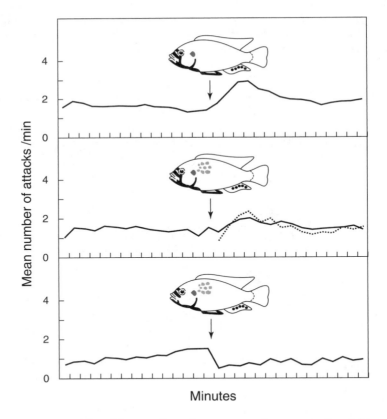

Figure 6.3. Summation of the inhibitory effect of orange spots (bottom panel) and the excitatory
effect of a black eye bar (top panel) on attack rate of male cichlids, *Haplochromis burtoni*. Dotted
line in the central panel is the sum of the curves in the two other panels; the solid line represents the
data. Redrawn from Heiligenberg (1974) with permission.

orange spots caused little change in the attack rate. Sometimes stimuli with more extreme values than those found in nature are most effective. Baby herring gulls peck more at a red knitting needle than at the red spot on a parent's beak (Hailman 1967). As another example, incubating herring gulls retrieving eggs from outside the nest prefer eggs that are larger or more speckled than normal. Such extra-attractive characteristics can be combined in a single model to create a *supernormal stimulus* or *supernormal releaser* like that shown in Figure 3.10 (see also Section 6.4.2.; N. Tinbergen 1951; Baerends 1982).

Heterogeneous summation is analogous to the additivity of CSs in conditioning (Chapter 4). However, as in conditioning, separable cues are not always precisely additive (Partan 2004; Partan and Marler 2005). Features may form a configuration, psychologically different from the sum of its parts (Ewert 2005). Also as in conditioning (see Fetterman 1996), relative rather than absolute values of cues may be important. For instance, the optimal stimulus for begging in baby thrushes is a small "head" near the top of a larger "body." When a model has two "heads" near the top, more begging is directed toward the one that has the more nearly natural relative size (N. Tinbergen 1951). Some stimuli may not elicit responding in themselves but rather modulate responding to another stimulus, just as with occasion setting in conditioning.

The evolution, function, and use of multiple cues raises questions for behavioral ecologists (Fawcett and Johnstone 2003; Maynard Smith and Harper 2003), particularly in the context of mate choice (Candolin 2003; Phelps, Rand, and Ryan 2006). For instance, why do so many male birds invest in multiple signals such as brightly colored and long feathers plus singing plus displaying? All of these are not only energetically costly to produce but make males conspicuous to predators. Why do some male bowerbirds build elaborate avenues of sticks and decorate them with colored objects? Not only are such signals costly to males, females have been assumed to incur a cost in time and/or psychological resources when evaluating more than one feature of a signal. However, a consideration of "receiver psychology" (Rowe 1999) suggests that accuracy of detection, recognition, and discrimination should be enhanced rather than degraded by simultaneous presentation of multiple cues. Furthermore, multiple sexual signals can have several functions (Candolin 2003). They may signal different aspects of a male's quality or different features important in mate choice, particularly species membership versus individual identity (but see Phelps, Rand, and Ryan 2006). They might also be simultaneous redundant signals of the same thing, where "receiver psychology" may favor their evolution (Rowe 1999). In any case, sometimes different signals are used at different points in the mate choice process, as when a female is attracted by song from a distance and then responds to visual signals as she approaches the singing male. Such sequential use of cues is undoubtedly important functionally but it is less interesting mechanistically than simultaneous processing of multiple cues.

Multiple signals are also important in other forms of social recognition and in prey choice (Rowe 1999; Fawcett and Johnstone 2003; Partan 2004). Enhanced response to simultaneous cues in more than one modality, as to the song and sight of a displaying male, is an example of multisensory integration, a topic of active research in cognitive neuroscience (Calvert, Spence, and Stein 2004) and has attracted interest on that account (Partan 2004). So far, however, more attention has been given to documenting and classifying examples of such phenomena (e.g., Partan and Marler 2005) than to probing whether they have any special mechanistic properties (see Candolin 2003). Research like that on unimodal multicomponent signals described in Section 6.3 might be helpful in showing how different components are weighted in determining a response, perhaps by combining psychophysical theories about how different sources of information should be weighted (see Section 8.2.2) with evolutionary models of optimal cue use (Fawcett and Johnstone 2003; Phelps, Rand, and Ryan 2006).

6.2.3 Conclusions

Ethological terms like *sign stimulus* and *releaser* summarize important facts about animal behavior, but few researchers still use them. One reason is that the analysis of sign stimuli was intimately related to the Lorenzian model of motivation, now considered by many to be oversimplified and unrealistic (but see Hogan 2005). Sign stimuli were assumed to release accumulated *action-specific energy* via a species-specific decision mechanism, the *innate releasing mechanism* or *IRM*. One objectionable feature of this scheme was the term *innate*. As discussed in Chapter 1, this term fell out of use as all involved in debating it accepted that both environmental and genetic factors contribute to all behavior. Nevertheless, whatever it is called, untrained discriminative behavior shares many features with explicitly trained discriminations. These include the following.

1. Not all features of a relevant situation or object control behavior equally, even though all might be perceptible by the animals involved.
2. Features that do influence behavior have may have additive effects as CSs do. Conditional control and control by configurations or relationships may also be seen (Partan and Marler 2005).
3. Stimuli other than those that occur in nature may be more effective than natural objects. This describes supernormality as well as peak shift in trained discriminations (Section 6.4.2).
4. Discriminative behavior may be specific to relevant motivational states. For example, a male stickleback does not behave so differently toward males and females when he is not in reproductive condition. Similarly, stimuli associated with food may no longer evoke CRs in sated animals, evidence that the CS evokes a representation of the features of the US which then controls action (see Section 4.5.1).

6.3   Classifying complex natural stimuli

6.3.1   Classifying multidimensional signals in the field

Features of a sign stimulus are not always precisely additive, nor are they as simple as a red belly or a black stripe. For example, bird songs are complex temporal patterns of sound frequencies analyzable into notes and phrases. One approach to understanding behavior toward such complex stimuli represents them as points in a multidimensional stimulus space. For example, Nelson and Marler (1990) tested the hypothesis that birds identify the songs of their species by relying on the features that best distinguish them from the songs of other species found in the same habitat, the local *sound environment*. They studied two North American songbirds, the field sparrow (*Spizella pusilla*) and the chipping sparrow (*S. passerina*) by analyzing a number of parameters of the songs of these and 11 other species commonly singing around them in upstate New York. Many *exemplars* (i.e., specific examples) of each species' song were described along dimensions such as maximum and minimum sound frequency, number of notes, and note and song duration. When the average song of each species and its range of variation were placed in the multidimensional *signal space* so defined, three variables were sufficient to differentiate chipping sparrow song from those of the other species, while four additional variables were needed for field sparrow song, that is, this song overlapped with more of the other songs in the signal space (Figure 6.4).

To discover whether field sparrows actually use the features that best discriminate their species-typical song in signal space, Nelson and Marler observed the birds' aggressive responses to songs played in the middle of their territories. A standard species-typical song with median values of all features was compared to a song differing in just one feature. The feature being tested, note duration for example, was altered until the test signal reliably elicited less territorial threat than the normal song. The difference from normal defined the *just meaningful difference* (*JMD*) for that feature. In general, birds responded less to an altered song when its features took on values about 2.5 standard deviations away or more from the average value for the species. The just meaningful difference is most likely larger than the psychophysical just noticeable difference (JND, Chapter 3), that is, the birds could probably be trained to make much finer discriminations.

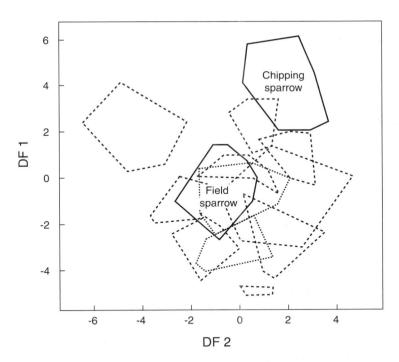

Figure 6.4. Two-dimensional space of song characteristics showing the extent to which chipping sparrow and song sparrow songs are similar to those of 11 other species found in the same habitat. Polygons enclose all songs sampled for each species. Dimension DF1 is positively correlated with song duration and number of notes; DF2 is correlated positively with minimum frequency and negatively with internote interval and note duration. Redrawn from Nelson and Marler (1990) with permission.

To find out how features were weighted in the birds' decisions, Nelson and Marler used two altered songs in each test. For example, a song with its maximum frequency altered by one JMD was pitted against one with its duration altered by one JMD. If the bird directed more aggressive behavior toward the song with altered duration than toward the song with altered frequency, it could be concluded that duration was less important than frequency in the classification of song as "field sparrow" versus "other species". Sound frequency was the most important feature for field sparrows, consistent with the hypothesis that birds should be most responsive to features that best differentiate their song from others in the same sound environment (see Figure 6.4). Other features were ranked in a way consistent with the hypothesis that species recognition is based on the least variable features of species-specific signals.

6.3.2   Birds classifying signals in the laboratory

A thorough multidimensional analysis requires large amounts of data from standardized tests, and these may be difficult to obtain in the field. Operant tests in the laboratory overcome this limitation. In one useful paradigm, the animal performs one response to present a steady background stimulus against which a second stimulus sometimes appears. The animal is reinforced for performing a second response when the different stimulus appears, and its latency to report "different" is taken as evidence of the ease with which it perceives the difference. A relatively large set of stimuli is used, maybe a dozen or more, and each appears sometimes as background and sometimes as the alternated stimulus. The data are converted into a representation of psychological distances among the stimuli in a multidimensional space: pairs of stimuli for which "different" is reported quickly are far apart, while pairs for which the latency is long are close together, that is, perceived as similar. Each cluster of stimuli in such a space defines a psychological category (for further discussion see Blough 2001). Unlike the method of category discrimination training discussed in Section 6.5, this procedure allows the animal to show how it classifies the stimuli on its own rather than imposing a classification scheme on it. The two approaches can be combined, as in the studies with bird song discussed in Section 6.5.5.

Dooling and his collaborators exploited this technique to study how birds classify vocalizations of their own and other species (Dooling et al. 1990; Dooling et al. 1996). For example, Dooling, Brown, Klump, and Okanoya (1992) tested canaries, zebra finches, budgerigars and starlings with the contact calls of canaries, zebra finches, and budgerigars. For each species of subjects, the sounds formed three clusters in multidimensional stimulus space corresponding to the three species' calls (Figure 6.5). When it came to detecting differences within species, the canaries, zebra finches, and budgerigars were each quickest at detecting differences between individuals of their own species. Psychophysical studies indicate that this species-specific advantage does not reflect differences in auditory perception but rather more central processing, in which calls are compared to a representation of a species-typical call and close matches are treated as belonging to the subjects' own species (Dooling 2004).

A similar study with primates (Brown, Sinnott, and Kressley 1994) showed that humans and Sykes's monkeys (*Circopithecus albogularis*) classified monkey and bird alarm calls as predicted on functional grounds. In the wild, the monkeys should respond similarly to all monkey species' alarm chirps because any of them could signal a predator, but they should ignore the acoustically similar chirping of forest birds.

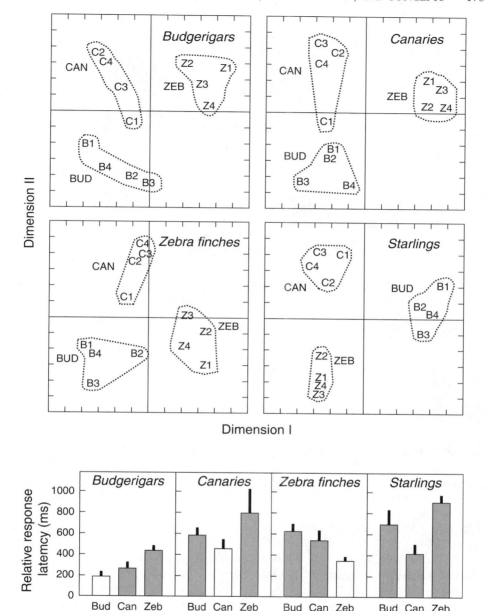

Figure 6.5. Top: Plots similar to that in Figure 6.4 showing how budgerigars, canaries, zebra finches, and starlings classified the songs of four canaries (C1–C4), four budgerigars (B1–B4) and four zebra finches (Z1–Z4). Lower panels: Latency with which birds of the four species tested responded when the test stimulus changed from one song to the song of another individual of the same species. Response to vocalizations of the subject's own species shown in white. Redrawn from Dooling et al. (1992) with permission.

Accordingly, Sykes's monkeys classified alarm chirps of their own and another sympatric monkey species as more similar to each other than either was to a sample of bird calls. People tested in the same way classified the bird calls as more similar to those of

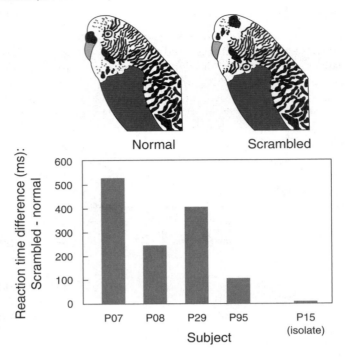

Figure 6.6. Normal and scrambled budgerigar faces used to test face perception in budgerigars. Data are the increase in latency when individual budgerigars were required to discriminate between scrambled faces compared to their latency to discriminate between two normal faces. The isolate was raised apart from other budgerigars. Redrawn from Brown and Dooling (1993) with permission.

monkeys and the monkey calls as more different from one another than the monkeys did. As another example of a species-specific advantage in auditory classification, birds of a number of species outperform humans when tones in one range of frequencies are to be discriminated from higher and lower tones. The birds discriminate the category boundary much more sharply than the humans do, showing evidence of the absolute pitch presumably used in song learning and recognition in the wild (Weisman et al. 2006).

Such comparative data on classification raise many questions. For example, would monkeys raised in the laboratory classify bird and monkey calls in the same way as monkeys that had lived in the wild? Conversely, would a naturalist with a lot of experience in the monkeys' habitat classify the calls as monkeys do? In Chapter 14 we see that many animals learn functional categories consisting of the alarm calls of other species in their habitat and thereby warn each other of a common danger. To what extent is the monkeys' response in these experiments due to this kind of experience as opposed to a perceptual specialization? We also need to be sure that animals treat sounds in an artificial context like an operant chamber as species-specific signals. There is some evidence that birds working for food in the laboratory do treat recorded species-specific vocalizations as vocalizations in that zebra finches learn an operant discrimination between zebra finch songs faster than birds not in reproductive condition (Cynx and Nottebohm 1992). Similarly, captive cottontop tamarins (*Saguinus oedipus*, a small monkey) reply to recorded tamarin long calls just as they do to the actual calls (Miller, Iguina, and Hauser 2005).

From a nonhuman perceiver's point of view, visual images in photographs and video may not match the real things very well (Box 6.1). Nevertheless, Brown and Dooling (1992, 1993) have successfully used colored slides in a procedure like the one used with auditory stimuli to analyze how budgerigars classify the faces of budgerigars and other birds. The birds classified slides of natural budgerigar faces on the basis of features that would be socially significant in the wild. They did not seem to be influenced by purely pictorial features like the proportion of the slide occupied by the image, suggesting that they were processing the slides as bird faces. Moreover, as with vocalizations, there was a species-specific advantage: budgerigars detected a difference between budgerigar faces quicker than one between zebra finch faces, although people judged zebra finches to differ more. In addition, studies with scrambled budgerigar faces indicated that the configuration of features into a face was important.

Box 6.1 How Do Animals See Pictures?

Following Herrnstein's (1979) demonstration that pigeons could acquire and generalize a discrimination between pictures with trees and pictures without trees (Example 3 at the beginning of the chapter), Herrnstein and de Villiers (1980) asked how pigeons perform when slides of fish—a natural category irrelevant to present-day pigeons—are used instead. This experiment is interesting only on the assumption that pigeons recognize objects and scenes in back-projected colored slides as such. If all the pigeon sees is an array of colored blobs, discrimination learning should not be affected by whether the slides depict objects natural or unnatural to pigeons' environment, or indeed whether they depict objects at all, and it was not. In retrospect, the notion that slides of objects and scenes are more naturalistic or ecologically valid stimuli than simple patterns and colors because animals see them as depicting places and things in the real world appears naive and misguided (Fetterman 1996; Delius et al. 2000; Fagot 2000).

How animals behave toward still or moving pictures has been addressed in two remarkably separate bodies of work. Some psychologists have continued on from Herrnstein using operant techniques to study aspects of picture perception in animals, mostly pigeons but also monkeys (Fagot 2000). One approach is to see if a learned discrimination transfers between arbitrary objects or scenes to images of them, or the reverse, to test whether objects and pictures are in some sense equivalent. The results have been mixed (Delius et al. 2000; Fagot, Martin-Malivel, and Depy 2000; Watanabe 2000). For example, pigeons trained to find food in a distinctive part of a large room seemed to transfer this discrimination to slides of different parts of the room (Cole and Honig 1994), but exposure to a particular outdoor location did not speed learning of a discrimination between slides of it and a second outdoor location (Dawkins et al. 1996; but see Wilkie 2000). A number of factors mitigate against transfer (D'eath 1998), including that slides or video may not capture color as seen by pigeons (see Box 3.1), and that they may be at unnatural viewing distances for the real objects they depict (Dawkins and Woodington 1997). Tests of transfer between objects and pictures of them also fail to take into account that real objects provide many cues to depth and distance unavailable in pictures (see Dawkins et al. 1996, for further discussion). Other research (Spetch and Friedman 2006) has looked at whether purely pictorial features important for object recognition in humans are also used by pigeons to classify drawings of objects. The results may or may not reveal something about general mechanisms of object recognition.

In a novel and potentially useful approach to testing whether animals relate pictures to representations of the real thing Aust and Huber (2006) trained pigeons to discriminate slides with versus without people using slides which never showed a particular part of the body, either hands or heads. If the birds saw the slides as representing parts of people, they should generalize to slides showing the missing part, for example, to a head alone for the group trained on headless people, but they should not generalize if they saw the slides as meaningless patterns. The birds did generalize to some extent, pecking more at slides with the missing part than to novel slides without any part of a person, and various controls suggested that no simple visual features of the slides could account for this. A nice further control would be a similar experiment manipulating parts of something pigeons are unfamiliar with.

Meanwhile, behavioral ecologists and ethologists have had a lively debate about the use of video playbacks in one twenty-first-century version of sign stimulus research with diverse species including spiders, lizards, fish, and birds. Videos of sexual, aggressive, and other behaviors have tremendous potential for revealing the cues animals use in social interactions because the behaviors and features of the animal in the video can be controlled and manipulated, even in an interactive way. However, not only do moving pictures have all the limitations of still pictures already mentioned, in addition some animals' flicker fusion frequency is higher than humans,' which means that what we see as smooth motion is likely perceived as jerky and perhaps aversive (see Adret 1997; D'eath 1998). Recent technical advances in producing and displaying computerized images have overcome many of these problems. Studies making use of them have shown, for example, that Japanese quail recognize a video image of a particular individual they saw "in person" earlier (Ophir and Galef 2003) and that Jacky dragons, a species of small lizard, display aggressively to a video rival exactly as to a real one (Ord et al. 2002). Increasingly robots are used to reveal the stimuli important in social interactions as they can even be deployed in the field. One way to be sure their visual properties are realistic from the perceiver's point of view is to cover them with real skin or feathers as done by Patricelli, Coleman, and Borgia (2006).

In summary, the best answer to the question asked by this box is, "It depends"—on the species of animal and the kind of discrimination being tested. Jumping spiders court conspecifics and attack prey that they see on TV, apparently not discriminating a video image from the real thing (Clark and Uetz 1990). Even with older types of video, chickens behave as if seeing real conspecifics and predators, apparently reacting to simple sign stimuli such as shape or motion. When used with appropriate caution, slides and video images of real-world things and events can be extremely useful for answering certain questions about how animals discriminate and classify things of importance in nature. The work on face recognition in budgerigars and other species described earlier in this chapter is one example; another is that on vocal communication in chickens discussed in Chapter 14.

Independently of this kind of research, numerous studies of category learning in pigeons like Example 3 (see Section 6.5) have used images of human faces as stimuli. Some of this work has looked at the importance of parts and their configurations in the birds' ability to respond differently to different sets of photographs such as male versus female faces. Face images have generally been used here simply as arbitrary patterns that can be varied in a systematic way with readily available morphing algorithms. Arguably, the results of such studies have only tenuous relevance to either pigeons' or humans' natural classifications, especially given some of the findings described next.

Monkeys, chimpanzees, and sheep can discriminate between individual conspecifics' faces in photographs (Kendrick et al. 1995; Parr et al. 2000). In humans, facial features in a normal configuration are thought to tap into a specialized face-recognition system. Some evidence for this is the observation that individuals' faces become more difficult to recognize when they are upside down. However, baboons trained to respond differently to images of two different familiar caretakers' faces showed no evidence for differential processing of upright versus inverted faces. Rather, they appeared to treat them as meaningless shapes (Martin-Malivel and Fagot 2001). Consistent with this conclusion are the results of a clever comparative study in which both humans and baboons classified black and white images as the faces of humans or baboons (Martin-Malivel et al. 2006). Once subjects succeeded with a set of 60 training images, they were exposed to computer-generated human-baboon morphs and degraded faces. Analysis of how such images were classified as a function of how they were degraded revealed that the baboons used the information in the images as would an observer treating the images as abstract shapes, whereas the humans referred them to preexisting concepts of baboon and human faces. Unlike tests varying features, such as eyes, that should be important for recognition, this method does not rest on any assumptions about what features are used. However, notwithstanding the conclusion suggested by this experiment, under some circumstances individuals of various primate species, including chimpanzees and rhesus macaques, do treat images of conspecific faces as such. For example, chimpanzees and rhesus match the facial expressions naturally associated with distinctive vocalizations to those vocalizations (Parr et al. 2000; Ghazanfar and Logothetis 2003; Parr 2003).

6.4   Discrimination learning

Discrimination learning traditionally refers to the results of procedures in which animals are reinforced for performing a different, arbitrary, response to each of two or more stimuli. Training with a single stimulus requires discrimination learning too, since the animal has to discriminate the experimental context plus the reinforced stimulus from the context alone. Methods of training with two or more stimuli (Box 6.2) have led to a distinctive body of data and theory with implications for the nature of animal category or concept learning. The discrimination training procedures described in Box 6.2 may suggest that they all involve instrumental training, that is, associating responses rather than stimuli with their consequences. However, procedures the experimenter views as instrumental may be effective because of the Pavlovian contingencies embedded in them. For example, as we have seen in Chapter 4, approaching a stimulus paired with food and retreating from one not paired with expected food are natural outcomes of Pavlovian conditioning procedures. Contemporary discussions typically apply to discrimination training in general. In any case, although theories about the content of instrumental learning are not discussed until Chapter 11, for present purposes it is necessary to know only how instrumental procedures are used to discover how animals discriminate and classify stimuli.

Box 6.2 Methods for Discrimination Training

Stimuli to be discriminated may be *simultaneous* or *successive*. For example, in a simultaneous black-white discrimination in a T-maze a rat chooses between a black arm and a white one, with black sometimes on the left, sometimes on the right. The rat might receive food in the white arm, no food in the black arm. Gradually it learns to enter the white arm regardless of which side it is on. In a comparable successive black-white discrimination the rat is placed in a black alley on some trials and a white alley on others. It finds food only at the end of the white (or the black) alley. In this *go/no go* discrimination, performance is assessed by comparing running speeds or latencies to reach the end of the white vs. black alleys.

Correction procedures can be helpful in exposing animals to to-be-learned contingencies: if the animal makes an unrewarded choice at the beginning of the trial, it is "corrected" by removing opportunity for all but the rewarded response. In simultaneous discriminations, there is always a correct, rewarded, response, and this may make these procedures more sensitive for detecting the early stages of learning with difficult discriminations because the animal never has to withhold responding.

Much of the older literature on discrimination training (see Mackintosh 1974) used rats in alleys and mazes, as described above. Now computer-controlled operant chambers are widely used because they allow automated testing of large numbers of animals for large numbers of trials. Pigeons are popular subjects because their visual acuity and color vision means they can be trained on tasks involving large numbers of visual stimuli. Operant procedures may have *discrete trials* as in the T-maze and runway, but *free operant* procedures are also used. In these, one or another of the stimuli to be discriminated is always available and response rates are compared in the different stimulus-reward conditions. A successive free-operant discrimination procedure is also referred to as a *multiple schedule*. Simultaneous free-operant discriminations are *concurrent schedules*. *Intermittent reinforcement* may be scheduled with a different frequency or pattern in the presence of each stimulus and response rates compared. It is not necessary that one of the stimuli be completely unrewarded; with sufficient exposure animals can learn quite subtle differences between reinforcement contingencies paired with different stimuli. They sometimes learn all sorts of other things the experimenter may not intend, too. For instance, in a successive free-operant discrimination with intermittent reinforcement in the presence of one stimulus and no reinforcement (extinction) in the presence of the other, animals can use the presence or absence of reinforcement in the first few seconds of each stimulus presentation as a cue to whether to keep responding during that stimulus.

Once animals have acquired a discrimination they may be tested to see which aspects of the discriminative stimuli control responding, as in the studies of generalization in Section 6.4.2. But animals don't stop learning just because the experimenter is giving a test. Reinforcing the animal for any response it makes in the test may teach it to respond indiscriminately, but never reinforcing it for responding to the novel test stimuli is no better. A common solution to this dilemma is to reinforce responding intermittently during the training phase, as in the study by Blough described in Section 6.4.2. Intermittent or *partial reinforcement* for correct responses increases *resistance to extinction* (i.e., the animal will keep responding longer without reinforcement) and makes it possible to sneak in occasional unreinforced test stimuli without the animal learning not to respond to them, thereby increasing the number of tests that can be given.

6.4.1   Acquisition

Simple discriminations

Even in a novel environment a frightened rat runs into a black compartment rather than into a white one. It clearly discriminates black from white already, yet if experimentally naive rats are trained in a black-white discrimination with food reward, many trials may elapse before they perform differently from chance. This is not surprising if we consider that the situation is initially completely novel. Before the animal can become interested in eating and learn how to get food, its tendency to explore the novel environment and/or its fear of it has to habituate. This learning may occupy a separate phase of pretraining, or feeder training (sometimes called *magazine training*). In two-choice situations, animals commonly adopt *position habits* during the acquisition phase, or *presolution period*. For instance, a rat being trained on a simultaneous black-white discrimination may always choose the stimulus on the left. Historically, this kind of consistent response to incorrect features was called *hypothesis testing,* as if the animal was testing the hypothesis "left is correct." Considerable debate was devoted to the question whether animals learn anything about the correct features during this phase (see Mackintosh 1974).

Not surprisingly, physical similarity between the stimuli to be discriminated influences the speed of discrimination learning. A discrimination between two shades of grey is learned more slowly than one between black and white. If the stimuli to be discriminated differ in several features, providing redundant cues, acquisition is faster than if they differ in only one feature (Mackintosh 1974). Animals may learn a difficult discrimination faster if they first learn an easy related one, as in the study of bats' auditory sensitivity described in Chapter 3.

Relative validity

Consider the following experiment on eyelid conditioning in rabbits (Wagner et al. 1968; Figure 6.7). (In eyelid conditioning, a CS signals a puff of air or a mild shock to the eyelid; the rabbit closes the nictitating membrane over its eye in anticipation of the US.) Two groups of rabbits were each exposed to two tone CSs, T1 and T2. Both tones were always presented in compound with a light, L. In the *uncorrelated group,* T1 + L and T2 + L were each followed by the US on 50% of trials. In the *correlated group* , T1 + L was always reinforced and T2 + L was never reinforced. Notice that the light was followed by the US half the time for both groups. If the number of pairings of light with the US is all that matters in learning to discriminate the light from the context alone, all the rabbits should respond similarly on test trials with the light alone. In fact, however, only the animals in the uncorrelated group showed substantial numbers of CRs to the light alone. This group blinked rather little to either of the tones alone (Figure 6.7). In contrast, rabbits in the correlated group responded to T1 and not to T2 or L alone. This pattern of results and others like it in instrumental paradigms (Mackintosh 1983) is accounted for by the notion that what matters for learning is the predictive value of a CS relative to that of other potential CSs in the situation (see Chapter 4). Here the light always predicts the US for the uncorrelated group, regardless of which tone is present. For the correlated group, T1 predicts the US perfectly and the light is irrelevant.

The tendency to learn most about the best predictors has ecological implications. Dukas and Waser (1994) exposed bumblebees (*Bombus flavifros*) to patches of artificial flowers, each decorated with two colors. For example, a bee might find yellow + blue, yellow + purple, white + blue, and white + purple flowers. Bees for which a single

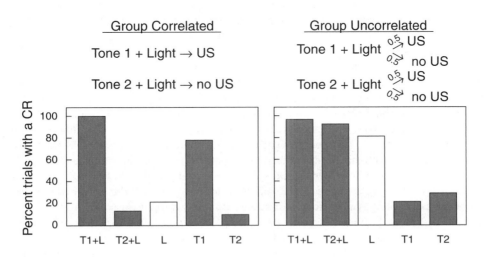

Figure 6.7. Method and results of the relative validity experiment of Wagner et al. (1968).

color reliably predicted nectar (e.g., only white + blue and white + purple rewarded) gradually increased the proportion of visits they made to rewarded flowers, but those for which no single color was a reliable predictor (e.g., only white + blue and yellow + purple rewarded) did not improve their foraging efficiency in over 300 visits. Bumblebees in the latter group would have had to learn the significance of each configuration of colors, a solution to discrimination training discussed next.

Compounds as configurations

Suppose stimulus A is reinforced and stimulus B is reinforced, but their compound, stimulus AB, is not reinforced. According to the Rescorla-Wagner model (Chapter 4) it is impossible for animals to learn to respond to A and to B but not to AB. The AB compound should support more responding than either A or B alone, not less. Nevertheless, rats and pigeons can learn such a configural discrimination. To explain how they do, elemental theories have to assume that the compound, AB, contains an extra, configural, element. In effect this corresponds to the animal's knowledge that AB is a distinct entity more than the sum of its parts. In this way the separately reinforced A and B can still be excitatory but the hypothetical configural element can gain enough inhibitory strength to cancel their combined effects.

In contrast to this approach, Pearce's (1994a, 1994b) configural theory mentioned in Chapter 4 suggests that a compound is treated as a unique stimulus, albeit one with some similarity to both A and B. Generalization between the compound and its elements makes the configural discrimination difficult, but not impossible. To account for behavior in this particular discrimination problem, there is not much to choose between configural and elemental models. Pearce's theory provides a better account of performance in some more complex discriminations involving three or four elements in different combinations, but on the other hand, there are some situations for which an elemental account does a better job (review in J. A. Harris 2006). Each account may be correct for some subset of discrimination learning situations (Pearce and Bouton 2001). Or perhaps some new model will provide a better account than any existing one (cf. J. A. Harris 2006). But both elemental and configural approaches suffer from vagueness in the specification of similarity. How do we identify the "elements" that two stimuli may or may not have in common or quantify the similarity between two compounds with common features (Fetterman 1996; D. S. Blough 2001)?

6.4.2   Generalization and peak shift

No stimulus is exactly the same twice. A red belly may be on a small or a large male or seen at different angles and distances, but it is still a sign of a male in breeding condition. If nothing else, the internal state of the perceiver or the orientation of its receptors changes from one encounter with an object to the next. *Generalization* from one thing to others that are physically similar to it makes it possible to behave consistently to events that are the same in consequential ways. The experience of eating a particular seed or butterfly is a good indication of what will follow from eating other seeds or butterflies of the same kind, so there is a sense in which the universal tendency to generalize expresses a creature's estimate that a new thing is the same kind as a thing previously learned about (Shepard 1987, 1994). As this functional account implies, generalization is seen with all sorts of discriminative behavior, whether trained in the laboratory or not (Ghirlanda and Enquist 2003). Generalizing from one thing to another does not necessarily mean the animal cannot tell them apart. In nature, there is a tradeoff between generalizing and discriminating (McLaren 1994). For instance, fear responses are likely to generalize widely because the cost of ignoring the slightest sign of a predator is likely to be greater than the cost of making a startle response to a falling leaf. Reflecting such functional tradeoffs, the extent of generalization may depend on the behavior system and the strength of motivation underlying responding.

Learned behaviors seldom generalize completely, even when they might be expected to. For example, suppose a pigeon is reinforced intermittently when a pecking key is lighted with green light but not when the key is dark. If it receives food intermittently, perhaps on a *variable interval (VI) schedule,* it will peck steadily whenever the light is on. (On a VI schedule, food can be earned with a specified average frequency but at intervals varying from very short to very long.) All it has to learn is a discrimination between light on and light off, but when the wavelength of the light is now varied, the pigeon's pecking rate will vary in an orderly way with wavelength (Figure 6.8).

After discrimination training, generalization may be tested along a dimension shared by S+ and S-. In the example above, suppose the pigeon is reinforced for pecking when the key is illuminated with one wavelength and not reinforced, or reinforced less often, for pecking at another wavelength. Now testing with stimuli varying in wavelength will reveal the highest rates of pecking not to the reinforced wavelength but to one displaced away from the unreinforced wavelength (Figure 6.8). This is *peak shift,* found with many species and stimulus dimensions (Ghirlanda and Enquist 2003; Lynn, Cnaani, and Papaj 2005; ten Cate and Rowe 2007; but see Spetch and Cheng 1998). Peak shift is generally more marked the closer together are the positive (S+) and negative (S-) stimuli (but see Baddeley, Osorio, and Jones 2007). Notice that in Figure 6.8 training a wavelength discrimination increased the rate of pecking to S+ compared to what it was in the simple discrimination between light on and light off. This increase in rate is related to the phenomenon of *behavioral contrast:* behavior in the presence of a stimulus correlated with an unchanging schedule of reinforcement depends on the reinforcement rate during other stimuli that may be present. If more frequent reinforcement is sometimes available,

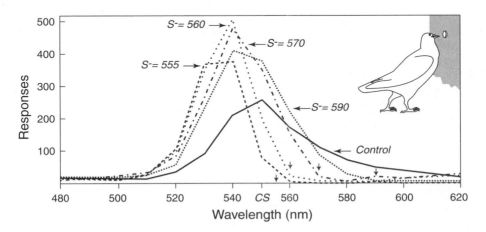

Figure 6.8. Wavelength generalization and peak shift in pigeons. The control group was simply reinforced for pecking at a key illuminated by 550 nm (CS). The other four groups were reinforced at this wavelength and extinguished at one other, S-, wavelength as indicated. Redrawn from Hanson (1959) with permission.

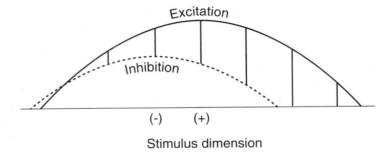

Figure 6.9. How additive gradients of excitation and inhibition can generate peak shift. The net excitation from reinforcement at S+ minus inhibition from extinction at S- is represented by the length of the vertical lines. The longest such line is not at S+ but to its right. Redrawn from Spence (1937) with permission.

responding in the constant schedule will be lower than when that schedule is contrasted with lower reinforcement rates, as if an unchanging schedule is evaluated relative to other current options.

Gradients of excitation and inhibition

From the time of Pavlov, theories of discrimination learning have been based on the notion that reinforcement results in excitatory connections between stimuli or responses and reinforcers, whereas nonreinforcement results in inhibitory ones. This notion provides a simple mechanistic account of peak shift if we assume that both excitation and inhibition generalize and that behavior toward a stimulus reflects its net excitation (i.e., excitation minus inhibition), as shown in Figure 6.9. This model, the classic Hull-Spence model, takes generalization for granted rather than trying to explain it from first principles. An alternative (Blough 1975) provides a possible mechanism for generalization by viewing the S+ and S- as each consisting of a number of elements separately associated with the US, as in the model of perceptual learning in Chapter 5. If elements individually acquire associative strength, it follows that discriminations will be learned more slowly between similar than between dissimilar stimuli. Elements common to S+ and S- will alternately gain and lose associative strength, retarding the emergence of a difference in net associative strength between S+ and S-, the more so the more common elements there are. Table 6.1 shows how this approach accounts for peak shift.

Table 6.1 An elementalist analysis of peak shift

Stimuli	1	2	3 (S+)	4 (S-)
Elements	0 1 1 2	1 2 2 3	2 3 3 4	3 4 4 5
+	+	+ + +	+ + + +	+ + +
-		-	- - -	- - - -
Net =/-	+1	+2	+1	-1

Stimuli 1–4 are composed of various proportions of elements 1–5, as indicated. If 3 is the positive stimulus in discrimination training and 4 is the negative stimulus, stimulus 2 will acquire greater net positive strength than stimulus 3. After Mackintosh (1995), reproduced with permission.

Because *inhibition* implies suppression below a "zero" level, it cannot be distinguished from absence of excitation without a moderate baseline level of behavior. One solution to this problem is a *summation test*: compound the putative inhibitory stimulus with an excitor to test whether it reduces responding more than does an untrained stimulus (Rescorla 1969). Another is to test whether excitation is acquired more slowly to the supposed inhibitor than to a neutral stimulus (the *retardation test;* Rescorla, 1969). Blough (1975) conducted a summation test in which a whole range of stimuli were reinforced at a low level to generate a stable baseline of behavior. Pigeons pecked a key with a single colored line on it which could be illuminated by any of 25 wavelengths (Figure 6.10). Each time the key lit up, pecking produced food on a fixed-interval (FI) 20-second schedule; that is, when 20 seconds had elapsed since the beginning of the trial, the next peck would be reinforced. In general, food was only given on about 10% of the trials, but pecking was maintained by presenting a gray square sometimes paired with food (*a secondary reinforcer*) at the end of every trial. This procedure resulted in an increasing rate of pecking with the time a stimulus was on and similar average rates to all 25 stimuli. Generalization of excitation was studied on this baseline by giving extra reinforced presentations of a selected wavelength to increase its excitation. Similarly, inhibitory gradients resulted from extra nonreinforced presentations of a selected wavelength. Because intermittent reinforcement was continued at the other wavelengths, this procedure permitted prolonged assessment of generalization.

The sharpness of the gradient obtained in this procedure depends on when it is measured during the 20-second fixed interval (see Figure 6.10). Early in the interval responding is at its most selective. The pecking rates to all wavelengths increase throughout the interval so the excitatory gradient is nearly flat near the time of reinforcement. No other evidence is needed that generalization reflects more than lack of ability to discriminate. Here one might say that the more there is to gain from responding, as at the end of the FI, the more responding generalizes. An interesting feature of the gradients in Figure 6.10 is the "shoulders" in the inhibitory gradients on either side of the nonreinforced value. They can be generated by the elemental model in a similar way to the enhanced responding that accompanies peak shift (see Blough 2001).

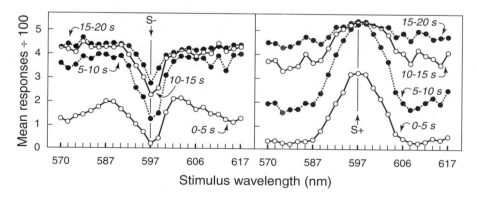

Figure 6.10. One pigeon's excitatory and inhibitory wavelength generalization gradients in Blough's (1975) experiment. Separate gradients are shown for each 5-second period of the 20-second stimulus, timed up from zero with food at the end of 20 seconds. Redrawn from Blough (1975) with permission.

Supernormality and peak shift

Peak shift is like supernormality in untrained discriminations in that stimuli with more extreme values than those normally present evoke the most responding. This similarity has stimulated discussions about possible mechanistic and/or functional commonalities between the two phenomena (Cheng 2002; Ghirlanda and Enquist 2003; Lynn, Cnaani, and Papaj 2005). The examples of supernormality described in Section 6.2.2, however, seem to differ from peak shift as depicted in Figures 6.8–6.10 in being open-ended. That is, a wide range of stimuli with characteristics more extreme than normal evoke greater responding than normal. Such responses might be the outcome of natural selection against responding to values below some criterion, for instance, objects too small to be eggs (Staddon 1975; Baerends 1982). But this is not the whole story. An important difference between features such as wavelength, in the examples in Figures 6.8 and 6.10, and features such as size and number is that the latter vary in intensity. Unlike the case with wavelength or orientation, changing an object along an intensity dimension means there is more or less of it, and even in generalization tests with explicitly trained responses, the shape of the gradient can vary with the type of continuum tested (Ghirlanda and Enquist 2003). Peak shift in any kind of discrimination may be the outcome of the kind of decision process depicted in signal detection theory (Chapter 3 and Lynn, Cnaani, and Papaj 2005). With overlapping sensory effects of two sets of stimuli such as S+ and S- (or eggs and not-eggs), the animal can be more certain that the stimulus is S+ when it differs more from S- than usual. One intriguing suggestion is that 'difference' is judged relative to the original discrimination. A small difference is more relevant after training on a difficult discrimination (Baddeley, Osorio, and Jones 2007).

6.4.3   Other processes in discrimination learning

In the wild animals must be learning new discriminations all the time. For instance, as the seasons progress and new seeds and insects appear, a young bird may need to learn how to discriminate them from the substrate, where they are most abundant, and how to handle them. Birds that migrate have to learn about new food items at stopovers along the way and in their final wintering grounds (Mettke-Hofmann and Gwinner 2003). Long-lived animals may have to learn new things about neighbors and territories in each breeding season. One might therefore wonder whether discrimination learning becomes easier with experience. That is, do animals "learn to learn"? This amounts to asking whether animals acquire anything during discrimination training besides excitatory and inhibitory connections to specific positive and negative stimuli. This question has been investigated in a number of ways (see Mackintosh 1974), but here we focus on discrimination reversal learning and learning sets. Studies of these phenomena have also yielded some noteworthy comparative data.

Serial reversal learning

Discrimination reversal learning is just what it says: after being exposed to a given S+ and S- for a number of trials an animal is now exposed to the same stimuli with their significance reversed. So if black was initially positive in a black-white discrimination, black becomes negative. In *serial reversals* the animal is exposed to a series

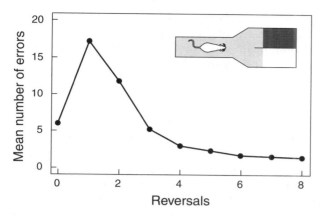

Figure 6.11. Mean total errors before making 18 correct choices out of 20 for rats trained on serial reversal of a black-white discrimination in a choice apparatus like that shown. After Mackintosh et al. (1968) with permission.

of reversals. The significance of the stimuli may change at the beginning of each experimental session. Rats typically perform worse in the first few reversals of a given problem, but they eventually perform better than they did on the first discrimination (Figure 6.11). Optimal performance is one error per reversal. This can be attained by adopting a *win stay—lose shift* strategy: always try the response that was last rewarded, and if that is no longer rewarded, shift to the other response, otherwise stay. Monkeys seem to learn this strategy, but rats do not. Instead, two other things seem to happen. First, a long series of daily reversals causes *proactive interference* (*PI*, see Chapter 7) in memory. The rat has had so many reversals that it cannot remember at the beginning of one day which response was rewarded yesterday, so it performs at chance. (At the beginning of each early reversal, performance is below chance; at this stage the rat evidently does remember the last problem.) Second, performance increases from 50% correct, or chance, more quickly in late than early reversals, suggesting that rats gradually learn what stimuli to pay attention to in the experimental situation.

Rumbaugh and his colleagues (Rumbaugh and Pate 1984; Rumbaugh, Savage-Rumbaugh, and Washburn 1996) compared primates on a version of reversal learning in which animals were first trained to a criterion of either 67% or 84% correct with a given pair of objects and then given ten trials with the significance of the objects reversed. This procedure was repeated with a series of new pairs of objects. An animal influenced only by past reinforcement with given objects should reverse more slowly the higher the original criterion, whereas one that has learned the principle of reversal might be expected to do just the opposite because the better it knows the current contingencies the easier it should be to tell when they reverse. In a comparison of 13 primate species, most of the prosimians tested showed the former pattern, the apes showed the latter, and the monkeys were intermediate (Rumbaugh, Savage-Rumbaugh, and Washburn 1996).

Some common tasks for studying children's cognitive development essentially require reversal learning. For example, in Piaget's classic test of object permanence, the child sees an object hidden in one place, A, and successfully retrieves it. But when the same object is now hidden in another place, B, a very young child will continue reaching for it in A, failing to reverse the previously successful response. But even while committing this *A not B error* in responding, the child may be looking toward B, as if knowing where the object is but being unable to inhibit the old behavior. The disappearance of this error somewhere between the ages of 1 and 2 years is but one of many kinds of evidence for the growth of inhibitory control during human development. Indeed, the same trend, along with evidence for its link to development of the prefrontal cortex may be seen in non-human primates (Hauser 2003). Differences in reversal learning among primates such as those reported by Rumbaugh and colleagues could be related to species differences in this area of the brain.

Learning set

Tests for *learning set* are like discrimination reversals in that the animal is trained on many discrimination problems in succession, but the stimuli are different in each problem. As in reversal learning, general factors like learning to ignore irrelevant cues can improve performance over problems. The optimal strategy for learning set is again win stay—lose shift because an animal can do no better than choose randomly on the first trial of each problem and then stay with the alternative chosen first if it was rewarded, otherwise shift. Proportion correct choices on the second trial is a measure of the extent to which this strategy has been acquired. The ability to acquire a learning set has been used to compare animals in "intelligence." This is an appealing kind of test because "learning to learn" does seem intelligent from an anthropocentric point of view. In addition, the shape of the curve representing number of errors as a function of successive problems seems to be a meaningful measure of learning regardless of its absolute level. Whether individuals of a particular species learn the first problems slowly or quickly, one can still ask whether they improve over problems and whether they eventually attain the optimum of perfect performance on the second trial of each new discrimination.

The view that learning set is a good test of animal intelligence was encouraged by early data from mammals (Figure 6.12). The ordering of species, with rhesus monkeys performing better than New World squirrel monkeys, which performed better than cats, and rats and squirrels doing worst, is consistent with the assumption that animals can be ordered on a single ladder of intellectual improvement. However, this naive interpretation (see Chapter 2) is not even supported by further data on learning set. Data of other mammals do not fall where they would be expected to (Macphail 1982), and at least one bird species, blue jays, acquire a win stay/lose shift strategy like rhesus monkeys do (review in Kamil 1985). In both blue jays and monkeys, staying or shifting depends—as it would be expected to—on memory for the first trial of a problem. Accuracy on the second trial of a new discrimination falls as the time between trials (the *inter trial interval* or *ITI*) lengthens so that the outcome of the first trial is forgotten.

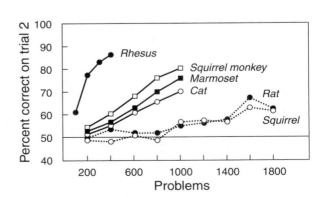

Figure 6.12. Visual discrimination learning set performance of six mammalian species, redrawn from Warren (1965) with permission.

The results of learning set experiments with rats deal a further blow to the idea that learning set performance is a unitary reflection of a species' "intelligence": the sensory modality of the stimuli to be discriminated has an overwhelming effect on rats' performance. The rat data in Figure 6.12 come from an experiment with visual stimuli: in over 1000 problems, the rats' accuracy on second choices hardly rose above chance. But with spatial cues rats acquire a learning set within fewer than 50 problems (Zeldin and Olton 1986), and with olfactory cues they do so even faster (Eichenbaum, Fagan and Cohen 1986; Slotnick, Hanford, and Hodos 2000). The many procedural differences among experiments with different cues could have contributed to the differences in results, but they are consistent with evidence that rats have excellent memory for olfactory and spatial cues (Chapter 7).

Attention

In the Rescorla-Wagner model (Chapter 4), the learning rate parameter α is a measure of the salience of a CS. Salience is assumed to be determined by physical features of the CS—for instance a dim light has lower salience than a bright light— and by the animal's species-specific sensory abilities. For instance, odors are probably more salient than colors for rats, while the reverse is likely true for most birds. But some elaborations of the Rescorla-Wagner model have assumed that in addition associability or salience of stimuli, α in the equation for learning, can change with experience (for a review see Pearce and Bouton 2001). Intuitively, it might seem that as a stimulus acquires predictive value it would be attended to more: good predictors deserve more attention, so α should increase as associative strength increases (Mackintosh 1973). But it is equally plausible that well-learned predictors are responded to automatically, so α of a CS should decrease as its associative strength increases (Pearce and Hall 1980). There is some evidence consistent with each of these views, suggesting that each one is correct in some yet-to-be-specified circumstances.

Experience may change attention not just to particular stimuli but to whole stimulus dimensions or modalities. For example, Blough (1969) reinforced pigeons intermittently for pecking in the presence of a single combination of tone frequency and wavelength out of 49 such compounds made up of 7 tones and 7 wavelengths. The birds could perform well only by paying attention to both tone and light. That they did so was shown by steep generalization gradients along both tone frequency and wavelength (Figure 6.13). But when one feature of the reinforced stimulus was made irrelevant by keeping it constant for several sessions, the gradient along that dimension flattened dramatically, indicating that the birds were paying less attention to it.

Several other sorts of data have also been thought to point to changes in attention during discrimination training (Mackintosh 1974, 1983). For instance, performance on a color discrimination is better following previous training on another color discrimination than following training on, say, an orientation discrimination. In such experiments, possible effects of simple stimulus generalization from one discrimination to the next need to be ruled out by varying the positive and negative stimuli for different animals and by making them as dissimilar as possible from one discrimination to the next. If an animal trained with red positive and green negative showed positive transfer to a discrimination with orange positive and blue negative, an appeal to stimulus generalization would be more appropriate than an appeal to increased attention to wavelength. Despite the intuitive appeal of

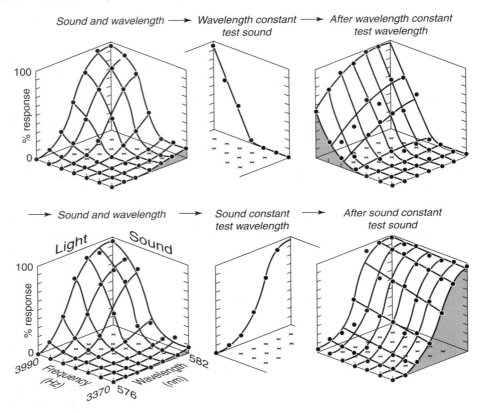

Figure 6.13. Generalization along the dimensions of wavelength and sound frequency following reinforcement at a single combination of wavelength and frequency. A single pigeons' rate of pecking is shown as proportion of rate to the reinforced wavelength and tone frequency. After Blough (1969) with permission.

the notion that animals learn what to pay attention to, it has proven remarkably difficult to obtain unambiguous evidence for changes in attention in conventional discrimination learning because of the difficulty of ruling out such specific transfer effects (Mackintosh 1983). Procedures like Blough's together with tests of short-term memory have been more illuminating (Riley and Leith 1976; see Chapter 7). Nevertheless, this does not mean that animals do not learn what to attend to in discrimination learning experiments. The ability to acquire new discriminations does improve with experience, probably for a variety of reasons. The processes involved may be important in variable environments in nature.

6.5   Category discrimination and concepts

Example 3 at the beginning of this chapter depicts a classic series of experiments (Herrnstein, Loveland, and Cable 1976; Herrnstein 1979) in which pigeons were trained to classify photographic slides according to their membership in categories such as "tree" and "non-tree." Typically, birds were trained with about 40 S+ slides, all having exemplars of the category, and 40 S− slides, lacking exemplars. The slides were presented in random order on a multiple schedule, so that each one was on for a minute or so. A bird was reinforced intermittently for pecking at S+ slides and not reinforced for pecking at S- slides. A correction procedure might be used in which each negative slide remained on until a certain number of seconds had elapsed without pecks, thus extending the period of extinction for poorly learned negative slides. The data consisted of response rates before the first reinforcer in positive slides and during a comparable period for negative slides. In general, pigeons learn remarkably quickly with such a procedure to classify photographs representing a large number of human-defined natural categories including water, fish, and people as well as trees (see Chapters 16–21 in Wasserman and Zentall 2006b; Zentall et al. 2008). Most importantly, they generalize to new instances. For example, birds that respond at a higher rate to trees than to non-trees continue to do so when shown slides they have never seen before (Herrnstein 1979).

This research attracted attention because the results seem to suggest that the birds "have a concept" in the same way humans do. Indeed, one of the first articles about it (Herrnstein, Loveland, and Cable 1976) was titled "Natural concepts in pigeons." However, what animals are doing in such experiments is best referred to operationally, as *category discrimination*. That is, they are behaving differently to different categories of items. One can then ask whether any special processes underlie this behavior. Besides possibly illuminating mechanisms of human performance in comparable situations (Mackintosh 2000; Ashby and Maddox 2005), the results are of interest from an ecological point of view because objects to be discriminated in nature are, like the slides in Herrnstein's experiments, more complex and variable than the stimuli typical of traditional discrimination learning experiments.

The pigeons in Herrnstein's experiment are discriminating on the basis of membership in a *perceptual category*, as distinct from a *functional category*. The former is defined by perceptual features of its members, whereas the latter is defined by some other property such as being edible or being related to a dominant female. For example, screwdrivers belong in a perceptual category of *long thin objects* along with pencils and carrots, but they also belong in the functional category *tools* along with hammers and saws. In effect, all members of a functional category have a common associate, for example, edibility or Female A as a relative. Categories may also be *relational*; that is, a set of two or more things belongs to the category if it instantiates a specified relationship such as identity or mother and offspring.

As may be apparent, much psychological research on animal category learning is decidedly anthropocentric (Zentall *et al.* 2008). The key question is what representational ability is implied by performance such that of Herrnstein's pigeons. We will see that perceptual or functional category learning requires no more than the species-general ability to associate surface features of stimuli with reward and/or with one another; no special ability for abstraction or conceptualization need be invoked. When it comes to relational categories, however, in particular same versus different, it's another story. Although both primates and pigeons can be trained, sometimes with great difficulty, to categorize displays as to whether the items in them are all the same or not, they seem to do so on the basis of perceptual variability. This makes their performance very different from that of people, most of whom classify such displays categorically—either the same or different, not more or less variable (Castro, Young, and Wasserman 2006)—and who possess a domain general concept of sameness. That is, people can represent second-order relationships, those abstracted from the first-order or perceptual features of stimuli. This sensitivity has been suggested to characterize a pervasive mental discontinuity between humans and all other species (see Chapter 15; Penn, Holyoak, and Povinelli 2008).

6.5.1   Perceptual category discrimination: Memorizing and generalizing

When photographs of real-world scenes and objects are the stimuli in a category discrimination experiment, animals do not have to see them as representing real things in order to classify them correctly. Indeed, it is questionable whether pigeons see the photographs in experiments like Herrnstein's as anything other than arrays of colored blobs (Box 6.1). Monkeys trained to discriminate slides with people from those without people proved to be responding partly to red patches: slides showing a slice of watermelon or a hyena carrying a dead flamingo were treated like slides of people (D'Amato and Van Sant 1988). Thus learning perceptual category discriminations may have little to do with human-like conceptual representations of the things depicted. Rather, much of what is going on can be accounted for as simple discrimination learning and stimulus generalization.

Because memorizing 80 or more individual slides seems quite a feat, the possibility that pigeons solve category discriminations by doing so was initially discounted. However, it turns out that pigeons can memorize many more than 80 slides. Vaughan and Greene (1984) trained birds with a total of 160 S+ and 160 S- slides. This was a *pseudocategory* discrimination: slides were assigned to the positive and negative sets regardless of perceptual similarity or natural category membership. Nevertheless, within a few sessions with each new set of 40 positive and 40 negative slides appearing twice per session, the birds were pecking more to most positives than to most negatives. Moreover, they still performed the final discrimination with 320 slides well above chance after a rest of more than two years. Pigeons trained similarly for 2 to 3 years with an ever-increasing pool of pictures were estimated to remember over 800 individual slides (Cook et al. 2005).

Pigeons are also sensitive to fine details like those differentiating one photograph of a scene from another taken a few minutes later (S. Greene 1983). But memorization is not the whole story. Pigeons generally learn faster and perform better with categorical groupings than with pseudocategories (S. Watanabe, Lea, and Dittrich 1993). But members of a perceptual category like "tree" or "fish" have more in common as visual stimuli (e.g., patches of green, certain kinds of contours) than members of a random collection of things. Thus stimulus generalization among category members will tend to improve performance with categories while, if anything, the same process will impede learning of pseudocategories.

The earliest experiments on category discrimination consisted largely of demonstrations that pigeons and a few other species could learn most—though apparently not all—category discriminations (S. Watanabe, Lea, and Dittrich 1993). However, to understand what such performance is based on, a more analytical approach was needed. Wasserman and his colleagues (review in Wasserman and Astley 1994) pursued such an approach by, in effect, asking pigeons, "What category does this slide belong to?" and giving them four possible answers. This is like the "name game," in which an adult shows pictures to a young child and asks, "What is it?" The pigeon viewed a central slide representing a member of one of four categories, for example cats, flowers, cars and chairs (Figure 6.14). After being required to peck at the slide a number of times, ensuring that it was processed, the bird chose among four keys, one at each corner of the viewing screen. A peck at the upper right, red, key might be reinforced if the slide showed a cat, a peck at the lower left, green, key, reinforced if

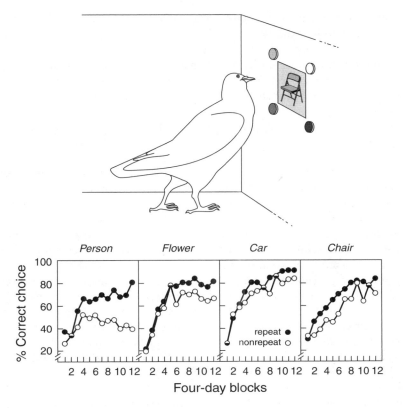

Figure 6.14. Apparatus for training four-way categorization in pigeons and performance on slides never seen before (nonrepeat) compared to performance on slides repeated from session to session. Data redrawn from Bhatt et al. (1988) with permission.

the slide showed a car, and so on. With 10 instances of each category, pigeons chose correctly about 80% of the time within 10 days of training, seeing each slide just once a day (note that chance performance is only 25% correct).

This procedure was used in a series of experiments which documented how pigeons' discrimination among categories of photographs is based on a combination of memorizing exemplars and generalizing from them. For instance, when the number of training slides per category was varied from 1 (i.e., a discrimination among only four slides) to 12, pigeons learned more slowly the more slides per category, consistent with a role for memorizing individual slides. On the other hand, when tested with new slides after reaching 70% correct on training slides, they performed better the more exemplars of each category they were trained with. This result should not be surprising. The more, say, cat slides the bird has been exposed to, the more likely a new cat slide will be similar to one seen before. Perhaps the best evidence for the joint contribution of memory and stimulus generalization was an experiment in which pigeons were able to learn a category discrimination even though each slide was shown only once (Figure 6.14). The birds evidently learned enough from a single trial with each slide to permit generalization to new slides of the same category. This could mean that only the common features of each category were learned, since these would be repeated from exemplar to exemplar. However, when novel slides were intermixed with slides being shown for the second time, performance was worse on novel than on familiar slides. Thus, the birds apparently memorized features or combinations of features unique to single slides as well as features common to many slides. Pigeons can also learn to classify a given set of images in two ways concurrently (Lazareva, Freiburger, and Wasserman 2004), a laboratory analogue of the multiple classification of social companions described in Chapter 12.

6.5.2 The contents of perceptual category learning: Exemplars, features, or prototypes?

What has an animal learned when it can accurately classify stimuli into perceptual categories? One answer was suggested in the preceding section: the animal simply learns the characteristics of every slide as a whole (Wasserman and Astley 1994; Chase and Heinemann 2001). Associative strength is acquired to each individual stimulus, and by definition there is more stimulus generalization within than between perceptual categories. However, a theory based on learning of elements makes similar predictions to exemplar learning here. The elemental approach starts from the observation that perceptual category membership is defined by the possession of certain features. For instance, trees are likely to be green, have leaves and/or branches, dark vertical trunks, be outdoors, and so on. But obviously many nontrees—for instance celery stalks—have one or more of these features, too. Furthermore, natural categories may be *polymorphous;* that is, not all category members have all the same features, although each has at least a subset of them. For instance, birch trees have a trunk and leafy branches with white bark, pine trees have a trunk with dark-colored bark but needles in place of leaves. An elemental analysis of categories proposes that nevertheless a set of features can be found such that the conjunction of some number of them separates category members from other things. The number and identity of conjoined features may vary from instance to instance, as with trees.

A more analytical approach than using collections of photographs is to create categories of artificial stimuli (Figure 6.15). Reinforcement for responding to each feature can depend on the other features with which it appears, much as with objects forming natural categories (e.g., in a tree–no tree discrimination, a leafy oak tree is positive, but a leafy celery stalk, negative). Pigeons can learn category discriminations with stimuli like those depicted in Figure 6.15 (Huber and Lenz 1993; Lea, Lohmann, and Ryan 1993; Huber and Lenz 1996), but they do not always learn as quickly as they learn to categorize colored slides of natural scenes. One reason may be that, unlike the case with natural categories, the artificial categories have been designed so that no one feature or cluster of features is more predictive of category membership than others. For instance, each artificial seed in Figure 6.15 is described by values of each of five features (spotted/plain, fat/thin, stripe curved/straight, horizontal/vertical, rounded/pointed). Because category membership depends on any three or more features being shared with the perfect exemplar, each feature is equally important. In contrast, in many natural categorization problems such as that depicted in Figure 6.4 some features predict category membership better than others.

Huber and colleagues (Huber and Aust 2006) analyzed something more like a natural categorization problem with controlled stimuli by using computer-manipulated images of human faces. Like other research summarized below, this work supports the conclusion that pigeons use both elements and configurations of elements, depending on the task. An even more stripped-down and well-controlled approach to creating

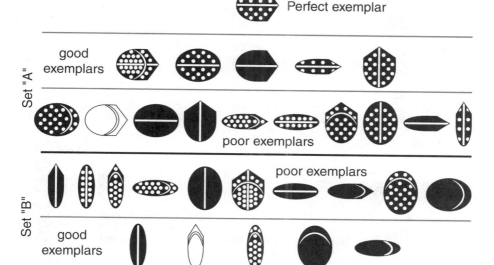

Figure 6.15. "Artificial seeds" for category discrimination experiments. The perfect exemplar of Set A is fat, dotted, horizontal, with a straight stripe present and a curved stripe absent. The perfect exemplar of set B has the opposite value of each of the five features. "Good" and "poor" exemplars have only 4 or 3 features, respectively, in common with the perfect exemplar of their category. Redrawn from Lea, Lohmann, and Ryan (1993) with permission.

naturalistic categories is to create overlapping sets of stimuli that vary continuously along two dimensions, such as height and width (Shimp et al. 2006). Just as in the stimulus space defining songs from two bird species (Figure 6.4), categories are defined probabilistically, with items near a central value being more likely than more deviant ones. For example, a "high wide" category might include a few "low narrow" exemplars. Reasoning familiar from signal detection theory (Chapter 3) predicts the optimal choice of the response corresponding to each category. Pigeons do choose close to optimally with a variety of categorization rules. For example, as in Figure 6.13, when the relevance of one dimension changes relative to the other, pigeons' weighting of it changes accordingly,

Both exemplar-learning and element-learning accounts of category discrimination are fundamentally associative: exposure to each instance changes associative strength of the whole exemplar or its features, respectively, and performance to other exemplars and nonexemplars is based on stimulus generalization. A somewhat different account, derived from human concept learning (Ashby and Maddox 2005), is that exposure to individual exemplars results in the formation of a representation of a category *prototype*, a sort of ideal exemplar, the central tendency of all exemplars. The prototypical bird, for instance, is more like a robin or a sparrow than a penguin or an ostrich. Categorization of exemplars is based on comparing them to the prototype.

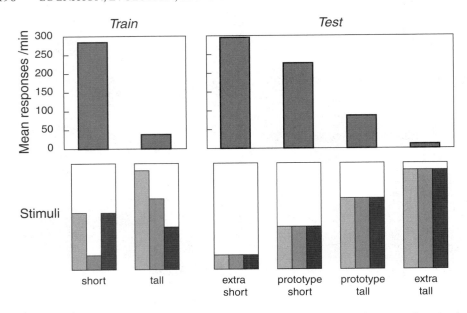

Figure 6.16. Stimuli and data from Pearce's (1989) experiments on artificial category learning by pigeons. After Pearce (1989) with permission.

Prototype theory makes two predictions that at first sight appear to be unique, but they can equally well be generated by associative theories. One prediction is that categorization of the prototype stimulus itself should be more accurate than categorization of any exemplars, even if the prototype has never been seen before. Pearce (1988, 1989) tested this prediction using categories consisting of patterns of three colored bars (Figure 6.16). Individual bars varied in height from 1 to 7 units, and patterns were classified in terms of the total height of their components. Patterns with a total of 9 units were positive; a total of 15 units defined a negative pattern. Individual bars could be 1 to 5 units high in positive patterns and 3 to 7 units high in negative patterns. Thus, some individual stimulus elements (here, bars 3, 4, or 5 units high) could appear in a pattern belonging to either category.

One would suppose that the prototypical positive pattern would be one composed of three 3-unit bars; similarly, the negative prototype is three 5-unit bars. Pearce's pigeons saw neither of these patterns in training, but they were tested with the prototypes and other novel patterns after learning the category discrimination (Figure 6.16). Response rates were not highest to the prototype "short" pattern and lowest to the "tall" one. Instead, the birds showed the most extreme response rates to extra-short and extra-tall patterns. This result can best be described as peak shift. The birds appear to have treated the individual bars as the stimulus elements, which gained excitatory or inhibitory strength as they were paired with reinforcement or nonreinforcement, respectively. Because bars 1 unit high could occur in positive but not negative patterns, they would be more strongly associated with reinforcement than bars of length 3, which could occur in both positive and negative patterns. Similarly, most inhibition would accrue to bars of length 7.

This associative, element-based account of Pearce's results implies that a *prototype effect* (best discrimination between the central tendencies or prototypes of the

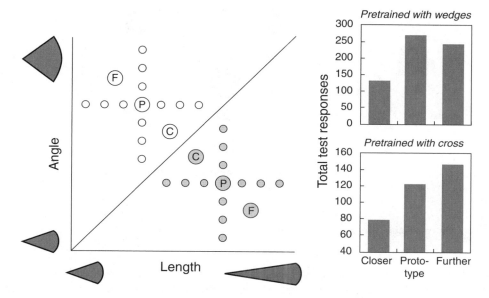

Figure 6.17. Two-dimensional space defining the stimuli used by Mackintosh (1995). Pigeons were trained in two different ways to discriminate stimuli above the diagonal line from stimuli below it. Small disks represent the stimuli used in training; larger disks, the stimuli used in testing, that is, the category prototype (P) and stimuli closer to (C) and farther from (F) the category boundary than the prototype. After Mackintosh (1995) with permission.

categories) might still be found with certain categories and training procedures. Mackintosh (1995, 2000) reported just such an effect (Figure 6.17). As in Pearce's experiment, pigeons were trained to discriminate two artificial categories without being exposed to the prototypes of those categories. Testing with new stimuli revealed a prototype effect if the birds had been trained initially to peck at all 12 stimuli that defined the positive stimulus class. By itself, this training results in greatest associative strength to the stimuli with the central values of the set, that is, the prototype. Peak shift was obtained when the birds had only pecked at a black cross before category discrimination training began.

In general *prototype* suggests a specific configuration, not just a set of features. In Pearce's experiments with the rows of colored bars, for example, the average height of the whole row defined category membership (for the experimenters, if not for the pigeons). But by designing categories of three colored bars such that no one element appeared more frequently in one category than the other, Aydin and Pearce (1994) obtained a prototype effect, which they attribute to the pigeons learning each display as a configuration. Similarly, Huber and Aust (2006) concluded that pigeons use both facial elements and their configuration to categorize simplified images of human faces. Because a combination of elements in a certain configuration is what characterizes a specific image, or category exemplar, it might appear that this is no different from an exemplar-based account. However, it differs from pure exemplar learning theory in specifying the dimensions for generalization from learned exemplars, namely elements and their spatial arrangement. A mathematical model of configural learning (Pearce 1994a) accounts for Aydin and Pearce's findings and related ones.

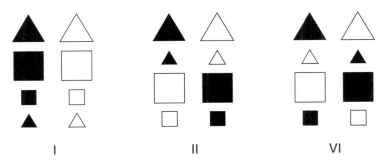

Figure 6.18. Example of three tasks used by Smith, Minda, and Washburn (2004) to compare category learning by rhesus macaques and people. In each set, one response is rewarded for stimuli on the left, the other for stimuli on the right. Both species find Task I easiest; humans find Task II intermediate and Task VI hardest. All tasks other than Task I are equally hard for macaques. Redrawn from Smith, Minda, and Washburn (2004) with permission.

The discussion so far suggests that, just as in humans (Ashby and Maddox 2005), what is learned from category discrimination training is flexible and depends to some extent on how the categories are constructed. If a difference along just one dimension defines a category boundary, animals will base responding on one element (Shimp et al. 2006), whereas if all elements are shared between categories and their configuration must be used, it will be (Aydin and Pearce 1994; Huber and Aust 2006), and if categories are defined arbitrarily, at least pigeons will memorize the significance of every exemplar. Rule-based category representations, however, may be unique to humans (J. Smith, Minda, and Washburn 2004). To take an example from a simple perceptual category, Task II in Figure 6.18, triangles and squares that are either black or white and either big or small can be classified according to the rule " "It's an A if it's a black triangle or a white square; otherwise it's a B." No single feature predicts category membership here, but this classification is easier for people to learn than more arbitrary groupings of the same stimuli in which the significance of the exemplars must be memorized separately, as in Task VI in Figure 6.18. Rhesus macaques, however, find all such tasks similarly difficult, as would be expected if they must learn all by memorizing the exemplars. However both macaques and humans, find Task I the easiest classification to learn, that is, one based on a single common element, "A's are black, B's are white' (J. Smith, Minda, and Washburn 2004). This is a nice example of how imposing different kinds of classifications on a single stimulus set can reveal species differences.

6.5.3   Functional categories and equivalence classes

Members of a functional category may be perceptually similar—consider *writing implements* for example—but they have more than perceptual attributes in common. In the laboratory, functional (or associative) categories are typically designed so the members share only an associate: a reinforced response, or a specific stimulus, reinforcer or US. We have already seen that some animals can learn such arbitrary groupings (pseudocategories) by brute-force memorization. But members of genuine functional categories are connected by their associate(s) in such a way that performance toward all category members is affected by changing the significance of one of them. The common associate serves as a common element that mediates generalization among category members. This is what Hull called *mediated* or *secondary generalization* (see Delius, Jitsumori, and Siemann 2000; Urcuioli 2006). Research using three different paradigms—and to some extent different explanatory frameworks—has shown that animals can learn functional categories and provided some information about how they do so.

Conceptual knowledge in humans links members of a category so that, for example, learning that "tools are cheap here" immediately changes our behavior toward all members of the class *tool* (Lea 1984). What this implies for animal category learning is illustrated by an experiment in which pigeons learned a pseudocategory discrimination with 40 unrelated positive slides and 40 unrelated negative slides (Vaughan 1988). When the birds were reliably pecking more to most of the positive than to most of the negative slides, their significance was reversed so the birds were now reinforced for pecking the originally negative slides and not for pecking the original positives. When the birds were once more responding appropriately, the significance of the two categories was reversed again, and so on. Finally, after 20 or more reversals, reversing the contingency with a few slides was enough to result in responding to the remaining slides that was appropriate to the new contingencies, as if all members of a category were *functionally equivalent*.

With relatively large categories of items as in Vaughan's experiment, repeated reversals are generally needed to develop functional equivalence (Delius et al. 2000). This is not true in the two other paradigms that have been used to investigate functional equivalence, perhaps because the categories involved are small. Indeed, the *many-to-one* (MTO) matching to sample procedure illustrated in Table 6.2 is essentially the minimal category learning procedure. In brief, on each trial of an MTO matching experiment, the animal first sees a *sample* stimulus and is then given the choice of two *comparison* stimuli, say X and Y. Importantly, each set of comparisons is used with two or more possible samples. For instance, choice of X is reinforced after samples A or B, choice of Y after samples C or D. To test for functional equivalence of

Table 6.2 Many to one matching and mediated conditioning as tests of acquired equivalence.

Many-to-one matching to sample					
Initial training		Reassignment		Acquired equivalence ?	
Sample	*Choice**	*Sample*	*Choice*	*Sample*	*Choice***
A	$\underline{X}$ vs. Y	A	X vs. $\underline{Y}$		
B	$\underline{X}$ vs. Y			B	X vs. $\underline{Y}$?
C	X vs. $\underline{Y}$	C	$\underline{X}$ vs. Y		
D	X vs. $\underline{Y}$			D	$\underline{X}$ vs. Y?
Mediated conditioning (Ward-Robinson and Hall 1996)					
A – grape pellets		A – shock			
B – grape pellets				panel push to B?	
C – nothing				panel push to C?	
Control group					
A – nothing		A – shock			
B – nothing				panel push to B?	
C – grape pellets				panel push to C?	

*Note: reinforced option is underlined
** No reinforcement given; underlined choice would be evidence of acquired equivalence

A with B and of C with D, training proceeds with reversed contingencies for, say, A and C. Once these are learned, if the pairs of stimuli have become equivalent in the first phase, B and D will now be responded to in a way more appropriate to the new than to the old contingencies, as indeed they are (Urcuioli 2006).

Logically equivalent procedures have been used with Pavlovian conditioning, as shown in Table 6.2 (Hall 1996). For example, in Ward-Robinson and Hall's (1999) experiment with rats, CSs A and B signaled grape-flavored food pellets for the critical group whereas C signaled nothing. In Phase 2, A was now followed by shock while B and C were not presented. The effects of this experience on evaluation of B and the control CS C were then tested by presenting B and C while the rats were pressing a panel for plain food pellets. Responding on such a baseline typically increases during a food-associated CS and decreases during a shock-associated CS. As predicted if Phase 1 training had made A and B functionally equivalent, rats panel-pressed less during B than during the neutral C, whereas the reverse was true for the control rats treated as shown in Table 6.2.

Ward-Robinson and Hall (1999) explain their results as an instance of *mediated conditioning*. In effect, at the end of Phase 1, A and B both evoke a representation of grape pellets. In Phase 2, shock occurs when this representation is activated, serving to link the grape pellet representation to shock. Then when B is presented in the test, the common association with grape pellets, now with its further link to shock, mediates reduced responding. In a more direct test of such mediated conditioning, the same rats later received grape pellets for bar pressing. The rats in the experimental group bar pressed less than those in the control group for which CS C, previously unpaired with pellets, rather than CS B had signaled shock in Phase 2. Notice that grape pellets themselves had never been paired with shock, only their representation. On the reasonable assumption that a stimulus can evoke a representation of an upcoming reinforced response (called *prospective coding* in the matching to sample literature; see Chapter 7) a similar argument explains functional equivalence in matching to sample, but it may not be the whole story (see Urcuioli 2006).

In Chapter 14 we learn that diana monkeys and some other animals show common behavior to alarm calls of their own species, alarm calls of other species, and predator vocalizations. This seems to be an example of many-to-one matching, or classification. Acoustically different signals are to some extent functionally equivalent, but whether the behavioral equivalence is mediated by a representation of a predator per se or of the response to be made to it is a matter of debate, part of a more general discussion of how animal communications have their effects (Chapter 14; Seyfarth and Cheney 2003a).

More than functional equivalence is implied by *equivalence classes*, or *Sidman equivalence*, after Murray Sidman, who first specified their characteristics on the basis of studies of verbal labeling in children. Members of an equivalence class are entirely logically equivalent, just as the word *dog*, a picture of a dog, and a real dog are in some sense equivalent. This equivalence emerges from simple experience of learning to match members of such a class to another without special additional training, making it what Sidman (e.g., 2000) calls an *emergent relation*. Members of equivalence classes satisfy tests of logical transitivity, symmetry and reflexivity as well as equivalence in the sense discussed so far. Symmetry means that having been trained to choose comparison B when A is the sample in matching to sample, without further training a subject chooses A if B is the sample. Transitivity implies that training to choose B when A is presented and C when B is presented will result in C being chosen when A is presented (and as well, A is chosen when C is presented).

And reflexivity means logically A = A. These kinds of performance emerge in language-competent children, but there is little evidence from other species—mainly pigeons—for the spontaneous emergence of the full package after training on one part of it (Jitsumori et al. 2002; Zentall, Clement, and Weaver 2003; Urcuioli 2006). An exception may be the sea lion trained extensively with a matching procedure similar to Vaughan's (Schusterman and Kastak 1998; Schusterman, Kastak, and Kastak 2003). However, just as in any cross-species comparisons, it is important to ask whether the procedures used are entirely comparable across species, and they may not be (Hall 1996).

As perhaps with same/different concept learning, discussed in next section, attempts to demonstrate Sidman equivalence in animals may be an example of disproportionate attention being devoted to a phenomenon influentially claimed to exist only in humans but without much thoughtful comparative or functional analysis. Nevertheless, what makes Sidman equivalence potentially important comparatively is its assumed similarity to conceptual abilities expressed in human language. As Hall (1996) points out, to the extent that equivalence class formation or functional categorization results from simple associative learning mechanisms, it should be phylogenetically very widespread. The apparent failure of pigeons to show full equivalence in Sidman's sense despite extensive testing implies that it requires something more.

6.5.4 Abstract or relational categories

Humans can classify things according to properties that emerge out of relationships among things. Do any animals use abstract categories (Herrnstein 1990)? One of the candidates most discussed in a comparative context is the same/different or matching concept (see Mackintosh 2000; Cook and Wasserman 2006). For instance, do animals trained to match to sample have a generalized ability to match? Pigeons trained with just a few stimuli (e.g., red and green) do not match novel samples (e.g., yellow and blue) but apparently memorize conditional rules ("If the sample was red, choose red; if green, choose green"). In contrast, various corvids such as rooks acquire a matching concept, transferring to novel colors, after similar treatment (Wilson, Mackintosh, and Boakes 1985; Mackintosh 1988). Monkeys and chimpanzees, too, match novel stimuli after exposure to just one matching problem, though the monkeys' transfer is not complete (D'Amato, Salmon, and Colombo 1985; Oden, Thompson, and Premack 1988). Pigeons do eventually acquire generalized matching if they are trained for thousands of trials with a large set of stimuli (review in Katz, Wright, and Bodily 2007).

However, matching to sample, in which the animal responds first to the sample and then chooses between the sample and a comparison, is a test of relative familiarity rather than identity, "Which did I just respond to?" rather than "Are these two things the same?" (Macphail, et al. 1995; Mackintosh 2000). Genuine same-different discrimination means classifying displays categorically as to whether items in it are all the same or not. This kind of discrimination, particularly whether pigeons can learn it, has arguably received undue attention (see Mackintosh 2000), partly because Premack (1983) claimed that only language-trained chimpanzees are capable of it. That is, given AX as a novel sample they choose BY over BB. However, chimpanzees with other kinds of experience also match "same" and "different" displays spontaneously (R. K. R. Thompson, Oden, and Boysen 1997; review in Zentall et al. 2008). Moreover, young chimpanzees implicitly categorize pairs of objects as the same or different without any special training (see

R. Thompson 1995). Given a pair of identical objects to handle, they are then more interested in a pair of nonidentical objects than in a pair of new objects that are identical to each other. Such behavior is also seen in young children but not in monkeys (Zentall et al. 2008).

A similarly low-level perceptual process or implicit knowledge is apparently responsible for pigeons' as well as monkeys' ability to categorize stimuli like those in Figure 6.19 as same or different (Cook and Wasserman 2006; Zentall et al. 2008). Pigeons were exposed to category discrimination training with pecks to one side key reinforced in the presence of a display of 16 identical elements; pecks to a second side key were reinforced in the presence of a display of 16 elements each different from the others. After being trained to 83% correct with 16 arrays of each kind, pigeons averaged 71% correct on arrays composed of novel symbols (Wasserman, Hugart, and Kirkpatrick-Steger 1995). Further analysis indicates that both pigeons and monkeys discriminate among such arrays on the basis of their variability, a feature measured continuously as entropy (see Cook and Wasserman 2006; Zentall et al. 2008; Wasserman and Young 2009). The more

"Same"

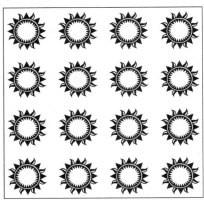

"Different"

Figure 6.19. Examples of stimuli used to train pigeons in same/different discriminations. After Wasserman, Hugart, and Kirkpatrick-Steger (1995) with permission.

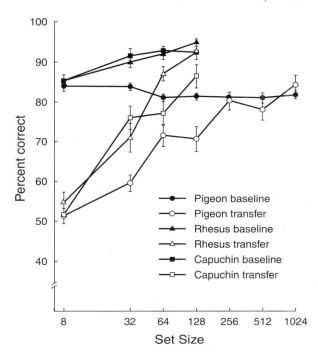

Figure 6.20. Progress of same/different classification learning with two items per display for pigeons, rhesus macaques, and capuchin monkeys as size of the set of possible items increased. The same stimuli and procedures were used for all species. All eventually classify novel stimuli as accurately as familiar ones ("transfer" data). Redrawn from Katz and Wright (2006) with permission.

different items in the display, that is, the more variable, the more likely it will be classified as different. But the human concept of *same* versus *different* is categorical: either things are the same or they are not, and in a task like the one for the pigeons, most—but not all—people behave accordingly (Castro, Young, and Wasserman 2006). Monkeys, however, are more likely to respond "different" the more different items there are (Smith et al. 2008). Reliance on variability in the displays probably accounts for why pigeons do poorly when the displays are reduced to two elements each, but they do eventually learn, albeit slower than monkeys (Figure 6.20). Importantly, all species represented in Figure 6.20 come to transfer perfectly to new displays, implying that they learn to rely on a feature that is independent of specific stimuli (Katz and Wright 2006; Katz, Wright, and Bodily 2007).

Consideration of this line of research suggests that the line between abstract concepts and direct perception of relationships is not easy to draw. Implicit knowledge of some abstract relationship may be embedded in a highly specific perceptual module without the animal being able to access it to control explicit, arbitrary, discriminative responses. Biological motion (R. K. R. Thompson 1995) and connectedness (Hauser 1996) might be other examples that are perceived directly. This same issue arises in discussions of whether animals have other kinds of conceptual knowledge about the physical and social worlds. They may behave as if having it but without showing the full suite of behaviors associated with explicit knowledge of, for example, the properties of objects or of others' minds (for further discussion see Hauser 2003; Vonk and Povinelli 2006). The capacities other species share with humans may be the building blocks of the fully elaborated, domain-general, consciously and verbally accessible, human capacities. Consistent with this interpretation, the continuous same/different discrimination process seen in pigeons and monkeys is still evident in humans doing the same task: even while correctly classifying arrays of items categorically, they are slower to respond "different" when the display has only a few different kinds of items than when each is different from the others see (see Wasserman and Young 2009). Nevertheless, the results of attempts to train nonhuman species on explicit use of a general concept *same* versus *different* are consistent with Penn, Holyoak, and Povinelli's (2008) claim that higher-level relational concepts are unique to humans.

6.5.5 Category learning, concepts, and natural behavior

The methods of category learning experiments can be used to discover whether and how animals categorize ecologically relevant stimuli. For example, cryptic palatable caterpillars tend to be neat eaters, leaving the leaves they have bitten with smooth contours like the contours of undamaged leaves, but unpalatable species are more likely to be messy eaters, turning leaves into ragged tatters. Captive black-capped chickadees can learn to search for insects on trees with damaged leaves (Heinrich and Collins 1983). Palatable caterpillars have enhanced their crypticity by evolving neat feeding behavior under pressure from the learning abilities of bird predators, an influence of learning on evolution to add to those mentioned in Box 6.3. P. Real et al. (1984) trained bluejays to respond differently to a slide silhouette of a cherry leaf damaged by a "neat" caterpillar than to one damaged by a "messy" caterpillar (Figure 6.21). After training on one exemplar of each type, the birds generalized to new exemplars. Furthermore, the responding associated with the "neat" leaves generalized to silhouettes of undamaged leaves. The shapes of these leaf silhouettes seem to be very salient, at least for bluejays (Cerella 1979).

Category learning procedures like those illustrated in Section 6.3 have been used extensively to understand how birds classify vocalizations (e.g., Sturdy et al. 1999; Braaten 2000). For instance, Bloomfield et al. (2003) tested whether black capped chickadees (*Poecile atricapilla*) classify the very similar calls of their species and the closely related Carolina chickadee (*P. carolinensis*) by species by training the birds on a category discrimination in which one of the sets of calls to be discriminated had calls from both species while the other had calls from only one. For example, all positive stimuli might be black capped chickadee calls but some negative stimuli came from each species. If the birds were sensitive to the between-species difference, they should more quickly learn the correct response for the different-species negative calls, which they did.

Not only perceptual but functional and relational categorization skills could be useful in the wild. As suggested in Example 2 at the beginning of the chapter, categorizing other group members by social relationship may be particularly important. An often-cited study by Dasser (1988a, 1988b) used a standard category

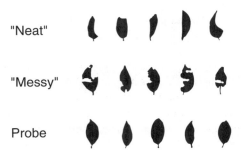

Figure 6.21. Stimuli used by Real et al. (1984). The leftmost "neat" and and "messy" leaves were used in training; other stimuli in those rows are examples of leaf patterns used in generalization testing. The bottom row shows probes representing undamaged leaves. Redrawn from Real et al. (1984) with permission.

Box 6.3 Evolution and Discrimination Learning: Models and Mimics

Brightly colored or patterned, noisy, or otherwise conspicuous prey tend to be bad-tasting or illness-producing, suggesting that their conspicuous features are warning predators to leave them alone. Although warning (*aposematic*) colors or other signals may be avoided when novel, potential predators usually must learn to avoid them. Many aposematic species have palatable *mimics*, palatable species that acquire protection from their resemblance to the unprofitable *model* species. For instance, some flies look like bees (Figure B6.3), some harmless snakes look like poisonous coral snakes, orange and black Viceroy butterflies have wing patterns remarkably close to those of poisonous Monarch butterflies. These are examples of *Batesian mimicry;* cases in which two or more unpalatable species resemble one another have traditionally been referred to as *Mullerian mimicry.*

The influence of predators' perception, learning, and memory on the evolution of mimicry and on relationships among populations of models and mimics has been widely discussed and investigated (for a comprehensive review see Ruxton Sherratt, and Speed 2004; Darst 2006). Consideration of basic learning principles generates a number of straightforward predictions about relationships between models and mimics. For instance, because stronger punishment should lead to faster

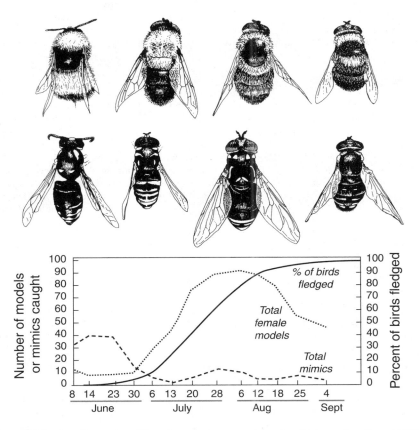

Figure B6.3. Top. Examples of Batesian mimicry complexes in which species of syrphid flies have evolved the appearance of stinging wasps and bees (Hymenoptera). In each row the insect on the left is the model bee or wasp; all the rest are different fly species (mimics). After a photograph in Waldbauer (1988) with permission. Bottom: Seasonal asychrony of stinging hymenoptera and their mimics in northern Michigan and the relationship of model and mimic abundance to the presence of naive predators, fledgling insectivorous birds. Redrawn from Waldbauer and LaBerge (1985) with permission.

learning and greater resistance to extinction, more aversive models should confer protection on larger numbers of mimics (Skelhorn and Rowe 2006). Because a stronger aversion should generalize more widely, more aversive or more numerous models should support cruder mimicry, and when two unpalatable species are present (i.e. in Mullerian mimicry), palatable (Batesian) mimics will be protected by the sum of generalization from both (Darst and Cummings 2006). Such predictions have been tested in numerous laboratory experiments with birds, often domestic chicks eating colored food flavored with quinine. However, careful analysis of natural predator-prey systems can also produce impressive support for them. For example, if predators can remember for a reasonably long time, a bird that has learned to avoid one species of insect in the fall may avoid a species that resembles it the next spring. The life histories of some mimics fit well with this scenario: they appear in the spring when they are avoided by experienced birds, but disappear by the time young, inexperienced birds have begun to forage on their own, which is when models appear (Figure B6.3; Waldbauer 1988).

Cryptic prey may benefit from being dispersed because this reduces the likelihood that predators will develop a search image for them (Chapter 3). In contrast, aposematic species should perhaps be aggregated. A group presents a stronger signal than does a single individual, and this would improve initial learning and later recognition by predators. Considering how warning coloration could evolve leads to the same prediction because a conspicuous bad-tasting individual will, by definition, probably be noticed by a naive predator and killed. Therefore it cannot pass on its characteristics to its offspring, but if the victim's relatives are nearby the predator may retain a memory of its bad experience long enough to give them a selective advantage. Thus warning coloration may evolve through kin selection. Laboratory experiments testing whether or why noxious prey are actually better avoided when aggregated (see Ruxton Sherratt, and Speed 2004) illustrate the intimate relationship between evolutionary and psychological issues in this area.

As Chapter 3 suggests, conspicuousness, distastefulness, and resemblance are all relative to the perceptual systems of the predators involved. Different kinds of warning signals confer protection against different kinds of predators. For example, many species of tiger moths are distasteful to both birds and bats. The species occurring in Southern Ontario vary in both visual conspicuousness and whether they produce ultrasonic clicks when stimulated by the calls of foraging bats. The former species tend to be diurnal and to be most abundant early in the season, when foraging by breeding migratory birds is at its peak. The latter, clicking, species tend to be nocturnal and to appear later in the season, when bats are doing most of their foraging. Thus contrary to suggestions that clicking and visual conspicuousness combine in an extraeffective multimodal warning signal for birds (which anyway would hardly hear the clicks), here different warning signals have evolved under pressure from different predators (Ratcliffe and Nydam 2008).

discrimination procedure to ask whether Java monkeys (*Macaca fascicularis*) could discriminate pairs of other monkeys on the basis of whether they were mother and offspring. One of the two subjects was trained in a discrimination task in which positive slides showed a mother-daughter pair from the subject's social group and negative slides showed a pair of unrelated monkeys. After training with five slides of a single mother-offspring pair and five different unrelated pairs, the subject monkey responded correctly to 14 out of 14 sets of slides showing new pairs of monkeys. Another monkey performed comparably on a matching to sample procedure. It is not clear whether perceptual similarity between mothers and offspring played any role here as it may in chimpanzees (Vokey et al. 2004) or whether performance reflected only knowledge of relationships gained in the subjects' social group, a kind of functional category. This could be tested by comparing performance with familiar versus unfamiliar mother-offspring pairs.

Animals that live in complex social groups may need to classify others simultaneously by dominance relationship and family (kinship group) as well as in other ways discussed in Chapter 12. Example 2 at the beginning of the chapter depicts a study designed to capture such multifeatured classification (Bergman et al. 2003) . Groups of related baboon females (*matrilines*) share a relative dominance ranking within their troop, but there are also dominance ranks within each matriline. This means that, from the point of view of a baboon listener, a submissive scream from a given female is to be expected if that individual was just threatened by a higher ranking member of her own matriline, but not if she was threatened by a lower ranking member of that matriline, because the latter sequence would represent a reversal in rank. Such rank reversals within families, however, are mere family squabbles, of less moment to an eavesdropper from another family than are reversals of rank between families, as these can presage social upheavals affecting the whole troop. Accordingly, a baboon hearing a submissive scream from one individual in response to a threat by an individual in a lower-ranking matriline should really take notice, as measured by how long she looks toward the source of the sound (a recorded simulation from a hidden loudspeaker in this experiment). Durations of looking were as predicted if baboons classify their social companions hierarchically, by family (rank reversals of which elicited relatively long looks) and by rank within family (reversals of which elicited shorter looks, slightly but not significantly longer than those elicited by control threat-scream sequences simulating a genuine dominance relationship). A critique of this study (Penn, Holyoak, and Povinelli 2008) suggests that the rank distance in within- versus between-family dyads for these mock inter-actions were a critical determinant of the results, but these were controlled appro-priately (Cheney, personal communication, October, 2008). Japanese macaques recruiting allies for aggressive interactions seem to recognize the same sort of hier-archical classification (Schino, Tiddi, and Di Sorrentino 2006). They solicit help from higher ranking individuals, but only if they are not within the same family as their opponent.

Schusterman and colleagues (cf. Schusterman, Kastak, and Kastak 2003) have argued that classifying different members of the same family together is like learning an equivalence set. However, equivalence sets do not seem to capture the way in which individuals are simultaneously classified into, for example, both different families and social relationships within those families such as mother-infant, and dominant-subordinate. Rather, as Seyfarth and Cheney (2003a) have argued, this sort of multifaceted classification is more like the spontaneous chunking shown by rats and monkeys when required to remember many items of information (Chapter 7). For example, when rats have to remember the locations of 12 food items consisting of four pieces each of three food types, they behave as if organizing the information into categories corresponding to the food types. Seyfarth and Cheney's (2003a) analysis of the learning reflected by natural social classification is an out-standing example of how data on basic cognitive mechanisms from laboratory research can be integrated with information about natural behavior. Given the growing interest in comparative social cognition documented in Chapter 12, there are many possibilities for further development of such an integrative approach.

A relationship like mother-offspring or social dominance is abstracted from and in turn predicts many different behaviors of specific individuals. For example, a young monkey suckles from its mother, runs to its mother when frightened, is groomed and defended by its mother, and so on. In effect, different behavioral interactions belong together as signs of a particular relationship, and once that relationship is encoded as such on the basis of a limited number of observations, novel behavioral interactions can be predicted. Bovet and Washburn (2003) tackled the question whether captive rhesus monkeys perform this kind of classification by showing three monkeys short videos of other, unfamiliar, monkeys in a dominance interaction such as fighting, chasing, or giving a bared-teeth display. A film was stopped at the last frame and the monkey was reinforced for moving a joystick to make a cursor touch the image of the dominant monkey of the pair. Novel films continually introduced into the training set served on their first presentation as tests of generalization to new monkey pairs. When the monkeys were reliably able to indicate the dominant individual in one kind of interaction, for example, chasing, training moved on to another interaction, for example, the subordinate monkey moves away as the dominant approaches. Two of the monkeys showed some transfer across sets of films, as if using a concept of dominance. Transfer was far from complete, perhaps because the subjects actually had rather little social experience themselves and the images were small. However, this experiment suggests a tremendously effective way to probe the nature of animals' natural social knowledge.

6.6   Summary and conclusions

Any animal must respond differently to different things in its world, food and nonfood, mate and enemy. This chapter started by discussing discriminative behavior that is not obviously trained, as studied in classical ethology. Behavior toward complex natural objects generally turns out to be controlled by one or a few simple features, the ethologists' sign stimuli. The effective features have additive effects (heterogenous summation) and this may mean that objects never found in nature are more effective than natural objects (supernormality). Animals may discriminate among signals of their own species more accurately than among similar signals of other species, reflecting perceptual specializations and/or experience.

The discussion of how discriminations are learned among arbitrary stimuli in the laboratory in sections 6.4 and 6.5 parallels that of how natural discriminations are controlled, starting with classic studies of simple discrimination training and concluding with discrimination among categories of complex stimuli. It reveals similar principles as well, particularly when it comes to stimulus generalization and peak shift (which resembles supernormality) and in the additive effects of separable stimuli. The Rescorla-Wagner model (Chapter 4) provides a good account of how features that best predict reward or nonreward gain most control over discriminative behavior. Discrimination training also may have effects that cannot readily be explained as changes in excitatory or inhibitory strength. These include the acquisition of learning sets and possible changes in attention during successive reversal training.

Although discrimination among complex polymorphous categories like natural scenes and objects depicted in photographs was originally labeled "concept learning," no such special process seems to be required. To some extent the mechanism for learning to classify stimuli is flexible. Under some conditions some animals, such as pigeons, may simply memorize every item and its associated response, but category discriminations may also be solved by learning the features that distinguish the categories or by learning the central tendency or prototype of the category. Learning of functional categories (equivalence classes) approaches a little closer to what is thought of as concept learning, in that a common history of reinforcement binds perceptually disparate items together and mediates generalization among them. What nonhuman animals have so far not proven to learn is a truly abstract relational concept, one that transcends first-order or perceptual features of stimuli. This may be a kind of categorization that humans do not share with other species.

Equivalence class learning seems to play a role in social cognition and communication in nature, although other processes may also be involved. It would be surprising if equivalence classes, as well as the other kinds of categories that animals can learn in the laboratory, do not have counterparts in natural behavior. It is interesting to speculate on whether particular ways of classifying stimuli might be selected for in particular situations. For example, Nelson and Marler (1990) suggest that for songbirds, classifying songs on the basis of a species-specific prototype may be less useful than classification based on similarity to memorized exemplars because the latter can be fine tuned to the local sound environment.

This chapter contains some lessons that will be important to bear in mind later, when we get to comparative research on some abstract concepts that animals might have, including number and serial order (Chapter 10). We also look at tests of social and physical concepts, such as theory of mind (Chapter 12) and physical understanding (Chapter 11). The acid test of a concept is always generalization to novel stimuli that share only the abstract or conceptual relationship under test with the training stimuli. Defining stimuli for such tests is not necessarily easy. Just as with the pigeons trained to discriminate trees from nontrees, it is critical to bear in mind that effective behavior can be based on cues and kinds of representations very unlike those that people would use to solve the same task and try to imagine what they might be.

Further reading

Tinbergen's (1951) *The Study of Instinct* is highly recommended as an introduction to ethology. Dooling et al. (1990) provide a good introduction to the use of multi-dimensional scaling to study natural perceptual categories, as does the chapter by Nelson and Marler (1990). Fetterman (1996) thoughtfully discusses the issue of "what is a stimulus," especially as it applies to psychological research on category learning. For reviews of recent work on the psychology of discrimination learning and classification in animals, excellent sources are the online "cyberbook" *Avian Visual Cognition* (R. Cook 2001a) and the book edited by Wasserman and Zentall (2006), particularly Chapters 16–21. In the former collection, the contribution by D. S. Blough (2001) is especially recommended. Zentall et al. (2008) is a useful short review of recent work on categorization, but for an in-depth review of the research started with the same/different paradigm in Figure 6.19 see Wasserman and Young (2009). Mackintosh (2000) is an excellent overview from an associationist viewpoint. Ghirlanda and Enquist (2003) as well as Cheng (2002) discuss phenomena and theories of generalization from both psychological and behavioral ecological perspectives. *Avoiding Attack* (Ruxton, Sherratt, and Speed 2004) contains a clear and well-illustrated discussion of the various forms of mimicry along with other aspects of the arms race between predators and prey.

7

Memory

Forming a search image, acquiring a conditioned response, recognizing one's mother: all are examples of learning. But they are also examples of memory because new information is being retained from one occasion to the next. Nevertheless, in psychology *learning* and *memory* define separate bodies of research. Research on learning has traditionally dealt with how information about relationships between events is acquired, as measured by fairly long-lasting changes in behavior. Research on memory, in contrast, deals with how information is stored, retained and retrieved. The cognitive changes of interest often take place rapidly, may not be very long lasting, and may be read out in a variety of behaviors. But parts of this description apply to examples of "learning." For instance, flavor aversions can form in one trial, and Pavlovian conditioning may influence a whole behavior system (Chapter 4). Thus there is good reason to question the traditional dichotomy between *learning* and *memory*. It is simply disregarded in contemporary research on the neuroscience of memory in which studies of changes in the brain during learning are labeled as studies of memory (Section 7.5.3).

From early in the twentieth century until the 1960s, most research on memory was done with human subjects even though much of the theorizing that drove it came from associative models based on research with other species. The "cognitive revolution" of the 1960s turned the tables. Research on human memory began to focus on the nature of information processing and representation. Research on animals followed (Chapter 1). Early research on animal memory was often quite anthropocentric, designed to discover whether representatives of convenient species like Norway rats or pigeons behaved like people when they were tested in a parallel way. Some of this research took on a life of its own, directed more at the nature of particular species' performance in particular paradigms than at the nature of memory generally. In the early twenty-first century, studies of human and of nonhuman memory are increasingly reconnected in research on the neurobiological and genetic mechanisms of memory (Dudai 2004; Pickens and Holland 2004; Roediger, Dudai, and Fitzpatrick 2007; Eichenbaum 2008), and in the research on metacognition and episodic-like memory discussed at the end of this chapter, among other ways.

We start by looking at whether the properties of memory can be predicted by considering what memory is used for and sketching a framework for asking questions about memory. Studying memory in animals poses the same problems as studying perception: whereas adult humans can be asked "What do you perceive?" or "What do you remember?.," subjects of other species have to be asked in other ways, some of which are described in Section 7.2. Section 7.3 summarizes the main conditions that affect memory. Section 7.4 reviews several research programs testing the notion that species differ in how much or how long they can remember. Theories about the contents and mechanisms of memory are discussed in Section 7.5. Recent years have seen clever experiments designed to test for memory processes that, in humans, are accompanied by distinctive states of awareness. The challenges posed by this research, on metacognition and episodic-like memory, and the important general principles it illustrates are discussed in Section 7.6.

7.1   Functions and properties of memory

7.1.1   What are memory and forgetting for?

What determines which information is stored, how it is expressed in behavior, and how long it is retained? These questions map into functional questions: what information is useful, what is it useful for, and how long is it useful? The first two of these were addressed in Section 4.3, on the function and evolution of learning. With respect to memory, the principal functional question is how quickly memories should be acquired and how long they should be retained, or, on the flip side, how quickly forgotten.

As William James (1890, vol. 1, 679) wrote, "forgetting is as important a function as remembering." Not forgetting may have a cost in inappropriate behavior when conditions change. Keeping memories perfectly accurate for long periods may also have a cost in neural circuits and genetic machinery for their maintenance and repair (Dukas 1999). Given that forgetting is therefore to be expected (see also Kraemer and Golding 1997), the rate of forgetting should evolve to track the rate at which the environment changes: the more quickly old information becomes useless, the more quickly it should be forgotten. In other words the probability of retrieving a particular memory should track the probability that it is needed (Anderson and Schooler 1991). Two variables predicting the likelihood that information will be needed now are how often it was needed in the past and how long ago it was last needed. These correspond to *practice* and *retention interval,* respectively, in tests of memory. To discover whether the effects of practice and retention interval do match the properties of the environment, Anderson and Schooler (1991) looked at three sources of data on the temporal distribution of information in the world. One was words in the headlines of the *New York Times.* These reflect demands on memory use because when a word like *Iraq* or *Beatles* appears, the reader has to retrieve a memory of its significance in order to interpret the headline. A given word was less likely to appear the longer since it last appeared and the less often it had appeared in the past (Figure 7.1). Data from experiments on memory retrieval as a function of time and number of past exposures in humans and other species resemble these functions (Figure 7.1; Wixted and Ebbesen 1991). Because Anderson and Schooler's is a proposal for why forgetting has evolved as it has, changing the probability that information is needed within an animal's lifetime (e.g., Sargisson and White 2004) should not necessarily affect memory duration.

With some success, Anderson and his colleagues (Anderson and Milson 1989; Anderson and Schooler 2000) have explored ways in which the properties of memory in humans can be related to the properties of information-retrieval systems (see also

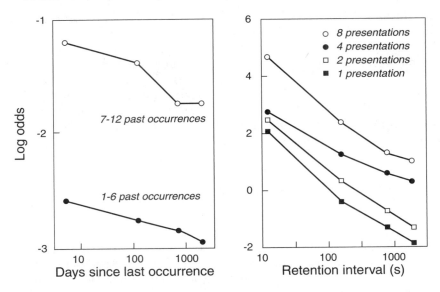

Figure 7.1. Left panel: The odds of a word appearing in the headline of the *New York Times* related to the days since it last occurred and the number of times it occurred in the past. (*Odds* is defined as follows: if p is the probability of an event, $q = p/(1 - p)$ is the odds of that event.) The right panel shows forgetting curves from a study of human memory that have an analogous pattern. Figure 7.5 shows analogous data for pigeons. Redrawn from Anderson and Schooler (1991) with permission.

Nairne, Pandeirada, and Thompson 2008). But our ancestors were not reading *The New York Times,* so to consider Anderson and Schooler's (1991) results relevant to the evolution of memory, one has to assume that headlines in a late twentieth-century Western newspaper reflect a general property of events in the world. There have been few comparable attempts to test how well the properties of memory in other species match the properties of their environment. As one example, foraging theorists have discussed what memory window should be used for estimating fluctuating quality of food patches (see Chapter 11 and Box 7.1). Averaging over too long a time may not allow effective tracking of patch quality, but with too short a memory window behavior will be unduly influenced by local fluctuations.

Box 7.1 Forgetting and Temporal Weighting

When a resource frequently changes in value, if it has not been sampled for a while an animal should respond as if the resource has the average of its past values. For instance, if 2/3 of the time Patch A has food while B has none, and 1/3 of the time the reverse is true, and the forager has not sampled either patch recently, its best bet is to visit A regardless of which patch was better on its last visit. Under some conditions, this *Temporal Weighting Rule* (Devenport et al. 1997) predicts behavior indistinguishable from the result of forgetting, but in situations for which its predictions differ, behavior fits those predictions.

One illustration is a field study of ground squirrels and chipmunks (Devenport and Devenport 1994). Two platforms that could be loaded with sunflower seeds were set up in an area that golden-mantled ground squirrels (*Spermophilus lateralis)* and least chipmunks (*Tamias minimus*) had been trained to visit. One platform, A, was always baited until the animals reliably chose it first. Then the second platform, B, was immediately baited instead until animals were visiting it first. Choice of A vs. B was tested either 1 hour or 24 hours later. Animals tested immediately always chose B first, but animals tested 24 hours later chose B only about 50% of the time. This finding that could of course reflect either forgetting or temporal weighting. It could also be interpreted as spontaneous recovery (see Chapter 4) of the tendency to visit A which had been extinguished when baiting of B began. The same is not true of the results of a further experiment with three platforms—A, B, and C. A was baited twice as often as B, and C was never baited. Here the temporal weighting rule predicts that B will be chosen immediately after a trial in which it was baited, but A will be chosen after a delay. This pattern of choice has been found not only in this study with chipmunks and ground squirrels (Figure B7.1), but also in laboratory studies with pigeons (Mazur 1996) and rats (Devenport et al. 1997; Devenport 1998).

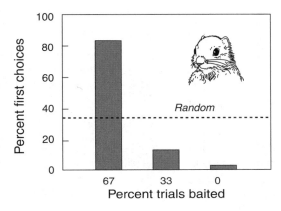

Figure B7.1. Percent of trials on which free ranging ground squirrels chose each of three feeders first 24 hours after the last trial as a function of the overall percent of previous trials on which each one had been baited. Data from L. D. Devenport and J. Devenport (1994).

The procedure in these experiments is essentially successive reversal learning. The discussion of successive reversals in Chapter 6 suggested that interference in memory is responsible for the fact that extended reversal training results in random choice of two equally rewarded alternatives at the beginning of each new session. Spontaneous recovery of the response not most recently reinforced may also play a role (Mazur 1996; Rescorla 1996; Devenport et al. 1997; Devenport 1998). Currently, the temporal weighting rule itself is one current candidate for an account of spontaneous recovery (Rescorla 2004). In any case, along with the study of Cheng and Wignall (2006) discussed in the main text, research designed to test the temporal weighting rule shows how changes in behavior with time since training do not necessarily reflect loss of memory.

A functional approach suggests that some things should be remembered longer than others. In a seminal paper, Sherry and Schacter (1987) developed the notion that acquiring, storing, and using different kinds of information demands adaptively different memory systems (or cognitive modules). The existence of two kinds of spatial memories—path integration and landmark memory—in desert ants, *Cataglyphis fortis*, provides a nice test of this idea within a single species and behavior system. The path integration system records position on the current journey by keeping track of an animal's current distance and direction from home on the basis of internally generated cues, thereby enabling it to return straight there when it finds food or is frightened by a predator (Chapter 8). Because successive foraging trips may have different lengths and directions, the path integration system would not be expected to retain information for more than a few hours, longer than an ant could stay away from the safety of its nest. In contrast, the system for learning visual landmarks should integrate information about stable features of the environment over successive trips. As these functional ideas predict, ants trained without landmarks and then captured and held before being allowed to home could not home accurately after 2 to 4 days, whereas ants that had equivalent experience in the presence of landmarks showed no forgetting after 20 days (Ziegler and Wehner 1997). The ants' path integration system uses only information from the current trip (Cheng, Narendra, and Wehner 2006; Narendra, Cheng, and Wehner 2007). Averaging information over successive journeys of different lengths would not be useful as it could lead the ant somewhere between the currently required distance and the one before.

Sometimes animals should retain information they have not needed for many months or even years. For example, fur seal mothers and offspring recognize each others' vocalizations when they return to the breeding grounds after a year or more away (Insley 2000). Birds' memories for their neighbors' songs (Box 5.1) are retained from year to year and used if they return to the same territories after migration (P. McGregor and Avery 1986; Godard 1991; Stoddard. et al. 1992). This song memory is distinct from that used in learning song in the first place (Box 13.2). After five months in hibernation Belding's ground squirrels still discriminate odors of littermates from those of strangers, but they do not appear to recognize the odors of unrelated individuals that they had recognized before hibernation (see Section 5.4 and Mateo and Johnston 2000b). Mateo and Johnston suggest that unrelated individuals may not be so important to remember through hibernation. This is an intriguing example of possible adaptive differences in memory, but the apparent difference in forgetting could reflect the fact that kin recognition is a matter of matching other individuals' odors to one's own (see Chapter 5) and thus does not depend on memory. If dependent on memory, it could reflect greater prehibernation exposure to littermates than to unrelated individuals

Animals that return annually to the same breeding or feeding grounds as the fur seals do should retain information that is useful there rather than pay the cost of relearning. For this reason some migratory species might be expected to have especially good long-term memory, a prediction put to the test by Mettke-Hofmann and Gwinner (2003) in a comparison of migratory garden warblers (*Sylvia borin*) and closely related nonmigratory Sardinian warblers (*S. melanocephala momus*). All the birds were exposed to seasonal changes in day-night cycle while held in captivity in Germany. When the garden warblers would have been starting toward Africa, each bird was exposed to two large cages ("rooms") adjoining its home cage. One was furnished with artificial geranium plants and one with artificial ivy. Only one of the rooms had food. Separate groups of birds were tested for their memory of the better "habitat type" at six retention intervals ranging from four days to one year. At the three longest intervals (5.5 months or more), as predicted the migrants showed a significant preference for the vegetation type associated with food whereas the nonmigrants did not. The case for species differences in memory here would be stronger if all birds had been tested at end of the training phase to be sure they learned the task to the same degree initially. A similar approach has been used to test population differences in memory in sedentary and migratory populations of a single species (cf. Cristol. et al. 2003). Pravosudov, Kitaysky, and Omanska (2006) found a difference in both spatial memory and hippocampal volume in favor of migratory as opposed to nonmigratory white-crowned sparrows (*Zonotrichia leucophrys*), but they tested the birds only after a 20-minute retention interval. All these studies are subject to the usual problems with comparative studies of memory discussed later in the chapter and therefore are more suggestive than conclusive, but they illustrate the rich possibilities for future studies.

7.1.2   Properties of memory

The same three questions can be asked about memory as were asked about learning in Chapter 4. *(1)* What are the conditions under which information is retained? Answering this question involves describing those conditions (Section 7.3) and understanding why they have the effects they do (Section 7.5). *(2)* What are the contents of memory? This question, about the nature of representation in memory, can be answered at different levels of detail. For example, we might infer that the location of food is remembered by observing that a hungry animal goes back to where it last found food. But the content of that memory might be the position of the food relative to nearby landmarks, the path to the food, or something else. *(3)* What are the effects of memory on behavior? Traditionally, it was assumed that a memory can be accessed in a variety of ways. For example, a subject shown a list of words can later be asked to find them in a larger list or write them down or call them out. A rat can indicate which arms of a maze it remembers by selectively returning to those arms or by avoiding them. However, humans can access some memories only through certain kinds of behavior but not verbally, as discussed in Section 7.6. And just as with learning, memory is distinguished theoretically from performance, so it is important to keep in mind that the behavior taken as expressing memory can occur for other reasons (Bouton and Moody 2004; Thorpe, Jacova, and Wilkie 2004).

7.2   Methods for studying memory in animals

Figure 7.2 shows a standard conception of the structure of memory. Input is first processed in sensory registers and stored temporarily in a *short-term store* (or *short-term memory, STM*), where it is accessible to decision processes. The short-term store also includes information called up from the *long-term store* (or *long-term memory, LTM*). Current input and stored information about its significance together with motivation control response output. Some of the contents of the short-term store are quickly lost, while others become part of long-term memory. One focus of research

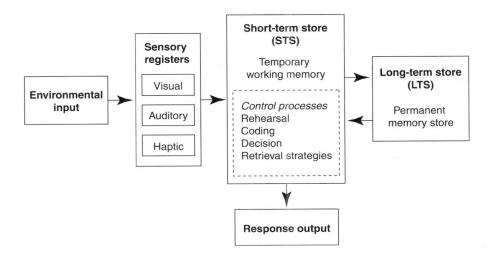

Figure 7.2. The hypothetical flow of information through memory. Redrawn from Baddeley (1995) with permission.

on human memory has been the nature of these memory stores and their relationship. The most closely parallel behavioral work with nonhuman species is that of Wagner and his associates using habituation, discussed in Chapter 5.

Those who work with animals sometimes distinguish between *working memory* and *reference memory*. Working memory here does not necessarily mean the same thing as working memory in humans (Baddeley 1995). Working memory in experiments with animals is defined operationally as memory for events on a specific trial, whereas reference memory is memory for the unchanging characteristics of a task (Honig 1978). For example, a test of memory might require the animal to learn "food comes out of that hole in the wall" or "you will get food if you choose the color you saw most recently." This information about what happens on every trial is part of reference memory. Information like "the most recent stimulus was a red square" is part of working memory. As we will see, the duration of working memory may depend on the task.

With humans, *recognition* or *recall* can be tested. That is, a person can be presented with a stimulus and asked "Have you experienced this before?" (recognition) or simply instructed to "Tell me what you remember" (recall). Recognition is typically better than recall of the same material, possibly because there are more *retrieval cues* in the test of recognition (Section 7.3.3). Most tests of animal memory are tests of recognition (but see C. Menzel 1999). Often the same items are used over and over, so the animal is really being trained in a *recency discrimination*. That is, rather than discriminating something familiar from something novel, it has to discriminate the stimulus presented most recently from other familiar stimuli presented earlier in the same session or in previous sessions (Wright 2006). Still, in tests of memory for lists of words, human subjects are essentially asked whether familiar words were presented in the experiment, not whether they have ever seen them before. Recognition memory is often distinguished from *associative memory*, memory for whether reward or nonreward accompanied an event in the past. When the same items are used repeatedly, recognition may be difficult to disentangle from effects of reinforcement history (Macphail, Good, and Honey 1995). Repeated presentations of the same items may also drive down performance and obscure effects that are apparent with items that appear no more than once per session, that is, *trial-unique* items (Wright 2006)

7.2.1 Habituation

The logic of habituation experiments is simple: if behavior toward an eliciting stimulus changes from one occasion to the next, and if motivational and sensory causes of the change can be ruled out, information about the earlier presentation must have been stored in memory. A strength of habituation as a test of memory is that it can be used with species and stimulus-response systems where training is difficult or perhaps impractical because large numbers of animals are to be tested, as in neurobiological studies. Its corresponding weakness is that it can be used as an assay of memory only for events that naturally evoke a well-defined response. As discussed in Chapter 5, much recent work has made use of the fact that animals may reveal what they have spontaneously encoded about events and objects by looking at them or exploring them when they change. For example, up to an hour after encountering an object in a particular location and context rats given a test like that depicted in Figure 7.3 show evidence of memory for the particular configuration of object, place, and context, a possible example of episodic memory (Section 7.6; Eacott and Norman 2004).

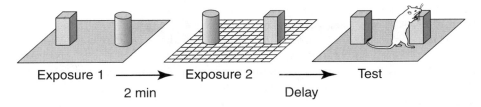

Exposure 1 ⟶ Exposure 2 ⟶ Test
2 min   Delay

Figure 7.3. Procedure for testing encoding of place, context, and identity during habituation. In each distinct "exposure" context, the two objects are arranged differently. Some time ("delay") after rats have explored them in each context, they encounter two copies of one object in one of the exposure contexts. Preferential investigation of the object that is in a new location for that context is evidence for episodic-like memory. After Eacott and Norman (2004) with permission.

7.2.2   Delayed response tasks

Hunter (1913) was one of the first to use a delayed response test of memory for animals (Boakes 1984). He trained rats, raccoons, and dogs in appropriately sized versions of the apparatus shown in Figure 7.4 to approach the door under a light to obtain food. The light was over a different door on each trial so that the animal had to approach the light regardless of its location. Then the animal was restrained in the start area while the light was turned on briefly. If it could still choose the correct door when released after the light went out, it must have retained information about the location of the light during the delay, the *retention interval*. Hunter wanted to discover whether animals had "ideas,"

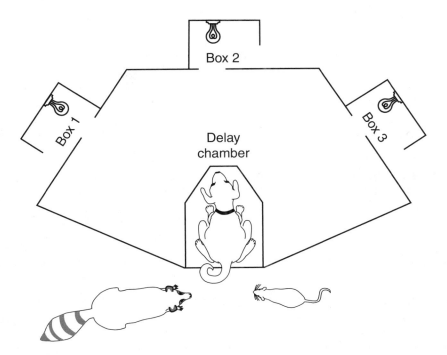

Box 2

Box 1

Box 3

Delay
chamber

Figure 7.4. Schematic view of Hunter's apparatus for studying delayed response. The size was adjusted for the different species. After Maier and Schneirla (1935/1964) with permission.

representations of objects or events that were not present at the time of responding. But some animals performed well by facing the correct door during the delay. Disrupting this orientation by removing the animal from the start area during the delay could reduce choice to chance levels.

Figure 7.5 depicts a modern version of Hunter's task, the *delayed matching to sample* procedure, as it might be used for pigeons in an operant chamber. A trial begins with display of a *sample*, the to-be-remembered stimulus. The bird is generally required to peck the sample a number of times to turn it off and advance to the next stage of the trial. This ensures that the animal has actually seen the sample and gives the experimenter some control over the duration of exposure to it. Primary reinforcement such as food is usually not given for responding to the sample, so if the animal chooses a stimulus like it in the test phase this is despite earlier nonreward. The sample is separated from the test phase of the trial by a retention interval (*RI*). At the end of the RI the animal is presented with a choice between the stimulus it saw before,

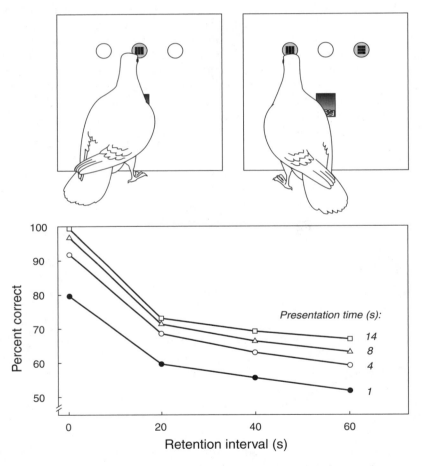

Figure 7.5. Typical delayed matching to sample procedure for pigeons. Here the pigeon is reinforced (by grain appearing in the opening below the keys) for pecking the pattern that matches the pattern pecked in the first part of the trial. Redrawn from Wright (1991) with permission. Lower panel: Effects of retention interval and duration of sample exposure on pigeons' matching to sample performance. Redrawn from Grant (1976) with permission.

say red on the key, and a *comparison stimulus,* say green. Because these stimuli are on two side keys whereas the sample was on the center key, memory for the sample's location cannot influence choice in the test. If the bird chooses correctly, it will be reinforced; if it chooses incorrectly it may proceed directly to the intertrial interval or it may be punished or corrected. For example, the lights in the testing chamber may go out for a few seconds, or the trial may be repeated until the bird makes the correct choice. In any case, an intertrial interval (*ITI*) ensues and then a new trial begins. The identity of the sample and the location of the choices on the side keys change randomly from trial to trial. A typical daily session might include 100 or more trials, and the same small set of stimuli (often just two) is used over and over. What the animal is exposed to, then, is a rapid-fire series of events: "Red." ... "Was it red or green?" ... "Green." ... "Was it red or green?" ... "Green." ... "Was it red or green?" ... Small wonder that pigeons' performance in this type of task is typically quite poor in absolute terms, even after thousands of trials of training. Figure 7.5 shows an example. Of course, the precise slope and height of forgetting curves depend on details of the testing procedure like those discussed in Section 7.3 (van Hest and Steckler 1996; White, Ruske, and Colombo 1996; Wright 2006).

Memory for a sample can also be tested by reinforcing choice of the comparison that differs from it, that is, *delayed nonmatching to sample* or *oddity.* Despite its name, pigeons generally do not acquire a concept amounting to "choose the comparison stimulus that matches (or doesn't match) the sample" in these procedures, although some animals do (Chapter 6). Indeed, pigeons do just as well at *symbolic matching* as at literal matching (for examples see Zentall et al. 1989). In symbolic matching, each sample is associated with one or more arbitrary comparisons. For example, choice of a horizontal line is reinforced following a red sample, whereas choice of vertical is reinforced following green. There are many other variants on the basic delayed matching test. In *delayed alternation,* an animal is reinforced for responding to the stimulus it didn't just respond to. For instance, a rat may be allowed to visit one arm of a T-maze, then replaced in the start box and required to visit the opposite arm. After doing so, it must visit the first arm again, and so on.

7.2.3 The radial maze

In typical delayed matching tasks, memory of a single sample is not retained for more than a few seconds or minutes. Imagine, then, the sensation created by an article entitled "Memory for places passed: Spatial memory in rats" (Olton and Samuelson 1976) reporting that rats could retain information about all the arms they had visited in an 8-arm *radial maze* for at least several minutes. As devised by Olton and Samuelson, a radial maze (Figure 7.6) consists of eight flat, unwalled arms, elevated (so rats don't climb off), each about a meter long, radiating out from a central platform. The maze is placed in a normal, lighted, laboratory room, with pieces of furniture, windows, doors, posters on the walls, in short, numerous objects to provide the rat with cues about where it is on the maze. At the start of a trial, a small piece of food is concealed at the end of each arm. The rat is placed on the central platform and allowed to remain on the maze until it has collected all the food. Once rats have been accustomed to the maze, they collect all the bait very quickly and seldom revisit already-emptied arms while doing so. Various control procedures have shown that they do not use odors either from the remaining food or from their own tracks

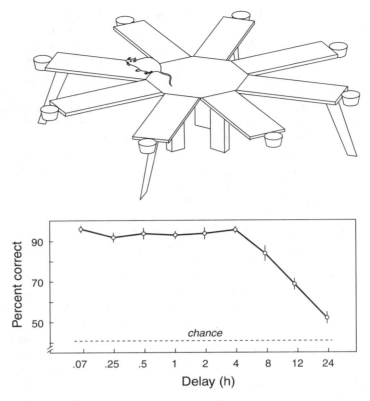

Figure 7.6. A rat on an eight-arm radial maze with a food cup at the end of each arm, redrawn from Roitblat (1987) with permission. Data are mean (+ SE) proportion correct choices out of the first four choices following a retention interval during which rats were removed from the maze, having already visited four arms. Redrawn from Beatty and Shavalia (1980) with permission.

down the arms. Individual rats generally do not repeat the same pattern of visits from one trial to the next, nor do they follow an obvious rule in choosing successive arms (Olton and Samuelson 1976; W. Roberts 1984). Thus, they are exhibiting working memory for the locations already visited on the current trial.

In most tests of human memory, the experimenter chooses the items to be remembered, but in the radial maze as just described the animal chooses them because it controls the order of arms it visits. The to-be-remembered items can be controlled in the radial maze, however, by placing doors around the center platform and opening only one or a few at a time. This simple modification also allows control over the interval over which the experimenter-selected "items" must be remembered. In a typical procedure that does this, a rat is placed on the maze with four doors open. Once the rat has collected food from these arms, a retention interval ensues, which the rat may spend off the maze. Then all eight doors are opened and only the arms not visited in the first phase of the trial are baited. With this procedure, rats perform better than chance at retention intervals up to 24 hours (Figure 7.6). Radial mazes and equivalent arrangements have become standard for testing working memory in all sorts of species, including hummingbirds collecting nectar from artificial flowers in the field (Healy and Hurly 1995, 2001).

7.2.4 Delayed matching, the radial maze and foraging

In Figure 7.5, one item is completely forgotten in a few seconds. In Figure 7.6, four items are retained for hours. Why do pigeons perform so much worse on operant delayed color matching than rats do on the radial maze? A number of reasons immediately suggest themselves: rats versus pigeons, "natural" versus "unnatural" tasks, spatial versus nonspatial tasks, rich multiple cues versus impoverished single cues. Less obviously, the typical testing regimes differ drastically. Rats are generally given just one trial of eight choices a day on a radial maze, whereas a daily session of operant delayed matching consists of many trials. No wonder the animal performing the operant task is sometimes more confused about which stimulus it saw last! The two tasks typically differ enormously in difficulty as *relative recency discriminations,* in terms of the potential for *interference* between one trial and the next (Section 7.3). Moreover, in delayed matching of colors the stimuli to be discriminated differ in only one respect, whereas the arms of a radial maze typically differ in many respects. The richness of cues also helps to make the spatial task easier. Operant delayed matching tasks incorporating both spatial and color cues give much better performance than those with more impoverished cues (Wilkie and Summers 1982; Zentall, Steirn, and Jackson-Smith 1990). Conversely, folding the arms of a radial maze together so they all point the same way degrades rats' perfomance (Staddon, 1983).

The variety of cues available and the fact that the animal travels from place to place rather than being passively exposed to the to-be-remembered items makes the radial maze resemble some natural foraging problems. Animals that consume nectar, such as bees and hummingbirds, feed from sites are not replenished immediately. Some apparently adopt a systematic pattern of visits rather than relying on working memory. For example, bumblebees (e.g., Hartling and Plowright 1979) collect nectar from closely spaced blossoms by following a fixed movement rule: "start at the bottom and always move to the next higher inflorescence," but they may also learn the locations of rewarding flowers (J. Burns and Thomson 2006). Some nectar feeding birds appear to follow an habitual "trapline" (Kamil 1978; Gill 1988; but see Healy and Hurly 2001). Because different kinds of flowers refill at different rates, nectar feeders might be expected to adjust their intervisit intervals on the basis of experience. Hermit hummingbirds seem to do this (Gill 1988). After being exposed for a few days to two "species" of artificial flowers, one of which refilled 10 minutes after being depleted and one after 20, rufous hummingbirds (*Selasphorus rufus*) learned to time their visits to each species appropriately (Henderson,. et al. 2006), a natural example of the interval timing discussed in Chapter 9.

Scatter hoarding animals retrieving their stores also face the problem of remembering where they have collected food and not going back. Sherry (1984) allowed black-capped chickadees to retrieve part of a batch of stored food one day and the rest the next day. On the second test, the birds visited storage sites still holding food rather than those they had already visited (see also Shettleworth and Krebs 1982). Reinforcement would seem to dictate that an animal should return to a place where it got food, not go somewhere else, so this behavior, like that of rats in radial mazes (Maki 1987) and hummingbirds collecting nectar, indicates that the animal is responding to food as information, not reinforcement. Shifting away from a recently rewarded site rather than revisiting it immediately (i.e., a *win-shift* rather than a *win-stay* strategy) might be an adaptation to foraging on food sources that can be depleted in one visit, but of course the forager should return to such a food source when it has had time to refill. Thus win-shifting might be replaced by the opposite propensity after a suitable time, and indeed one species of Australia honeyeater does show such an effect (Burke and Fulham 2003).

7.3   Conditions for memory

Not surprisingly, the conditions that influence memory are similar to those that influence association formation (Chapter 4) and recognition learning (Chapter 5). The more salient, long-lasting, or frequent an event, the better it is remembered. In the study of memory, attention has been directed not only at the conditions present at T1 (the time of input or *encoding*) but also at the conditions between T1 and T2, that is, during the retention interval, and at how the conditions at T2, the time of test, influence the *retrieval* of memories. The relationship of a target event to events in the past may also matter, as in the example of proactive interference in Figure 7.8. And as with learning, because the effect of experience may be expressed only under certain conditions or only in some behaviors, competence must be distinguished from performance (Bouton and Moody 2004; Thorpe., Jacova, and Wilkie 2004).

The primary index of memory is the influence of events at T1 on behavior at T2. However, showing that two treatments at T1 lead to different behavior in a standard test at T2 does not allow one to distinguish effects on encoding, that is, on how well the information was stored in the first place, from effects on retention. This theoretical distinction explains why many investigations of the conditions for memory include tests at a variety of retention intervals. Two of the possible patterns of data are shown in Figure 7.7. In Figure 7.7a, two treatments at T1 have resulted in the same performance in immediate tests but performance later declines at different rates, that is, initial encoding is evidently the same but retention differs. In Figure 7.7b, immediate performance differs, but it declines in parallel in the two hypothetical groups. Whether this was called a difference in forgetting rate would depend on theoretical considerations, such as whether forgetting should be measured in absolute or relative terms.

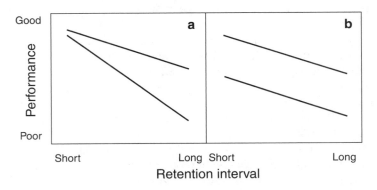

Figure 7.7. Hypothetical forgetting curves showing possible combinations of effects of two treatments on performance after various retention intervals.

7.3.1   Conditions at T1

Amount and distribution of experience.

Grant (1976) trained pigeons to match samples of colors at retention intervals up to 60 seconds long. The birds' exposure to the samples was varied from 1 second up to 14 seconds. The pattern of data, in Figure 7.5, was like that in Figure 7.7b: longer exposure, which presumably produces more complete encoding, led to an equal increment in performance at all retention intervals. The time between entire trials, that is, episodes in which information is presented and then tested, is also important. *Spacing* of trials in which different information is presented, that is, lengthening the intertrial interval (ITI), improves performance. For instance, in delayed matching to sample with colors, pigeons averaged 90% correct with an ITI of 20 seconds but only 73% correct with an ITI of 2 seconds (Maki, Moe, and Bierley 1977). When rats had eight successive trials on a radial maze in one day, performance was worse from the second trial onward than on the first (Figure 7.8). This is an example of *proactive interference,* discussed in Section 7.3.2.

Kind of items to be remembered

Some events, such as those closely related to survival, may be intrinsically more memorable than others (Nairne, Pandeirada, and Thompson 2008). The similarity of the current event to other to-be-remembered events is also important. In studies of human memory, a distinctive item such as a flower name in a list of vehicles is remembered especially well, a phenomenon known as the *von Restorff effect* (R. Hunt 1995). Similarly, when W. Roberts (1980) trained pigeons to match either

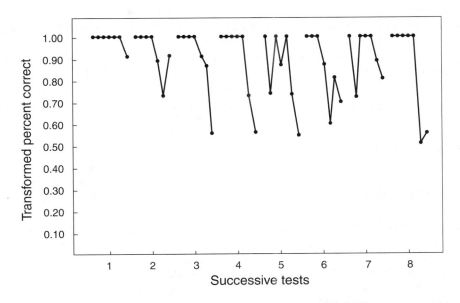

Figure 7.8. Performance (% correct on choices 2–8) on eight successive radial maze tests within the same day, an example of proactive interference. Data within each test are from the seven visits following the first one (which is necessarily always correct). Scores are transformed so that zero is chance. Redrawn from Olton (1978) with permission.

colors or lines and then exposed them to sessions in which a single trial with lines followed every three trials with colors, the birds matched samples of lines more accurately than under control conditions in which line trials were less distinctive. Another effect on memorability in both people and nonverbal animals (monkeys) is the *generation effect;* active participation in generating to-be-remembered items leads to better memory than passive exposure (Kornell and Terrace 2007). An event can be surprising and hence memorable because of previous conditioning; for instance, food is surprising after a CS that has always predicted no food (Wagner 1978; Grant, Brewster, and Stierhoff 1983). Increasing the number of discriminable features of to-be-remembered events improves performance, as in the radial maze versus operant tests of memory. Warningly colored prey (Box 6.3) often have several distinctive features and these may have evolved because they enhance memorability (Guilford and Dawkins 1991; Rowe 1999). For example, bees are bright yellow and have conspicuous black stripes and they buzz.

Divided attention

Having multiple distinctive features may enhance memorability of an object as a whole, but the flip side is what happens to the memorability of a single feature like the bees' yellow color when it is accompanied by other memorable features. Research on divided attention in matching to sample addresses this question. Most experiments on this topic have used pigeons as subjects and color and shape or orientation as the to-be-remembered features, as in Figure 7.9. The essence of such experiments is to ask the pigeon about one feature, for example, "what color was it" or "what shape was it," and compare accuracy on trials with a sample consisting of one feature (or *element*) to accuracy on trials with a compound sample. On the latter trials either element may be tested, so the bird should remember both. With two visual features, pigeons typically match an element more poorly on compound than on element trials, as if any one element is processed less well when the animal divides attention between it and another element (Figure 7.9). Research on divided attention in matching to sample has had to address a large number of possible confounds in findings like those in Figure 7.9, but when they are eliminated the results are still largely consistent with divided attention (Zentall 2005b).

Divided attention effects are not found with all combinations of features (Sutton and Roberts 1998; Zentall 2005b). One feature may completely preempt processing: pigeons can symbolically match samples of sound to visual stimuli, but performance falls to chance when a sample of sound is accompanied by a to-be-remembered visual signal (Kraemer and Roberts 1985). On the other extreme, multiple features may be processed with no interference. Dark-eyed juncos and black-capped chickadees matching the color and/or location of samples on a touchscreen show no divided attention effect for location, although color matching does suffer in both species when location is also being processed (Shettleworth and Westwood 2002). Pigeons, however, can match both the duration and the color or location of a visual stimulus as well as they match each feature alone (Sutton and Roberts 1998), but performance on a more demanding duration matching task does fall when attention must be divided with color or location (Sutton and Roberts 2002). The evidence that location and time memory do not suffer when visual identity is being processed concurrently is consistent with suggestions in Section 7.6 that animals form memories for unique conjunctions of temporal, spatial, and identity information.

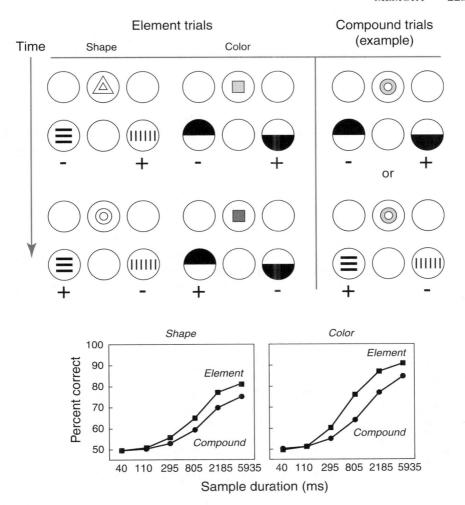

Figure 7.9. Symbolic matching to sample procedure used by Langley and Riley (1993) to test for divided attention in pigeons, together with their results. Two examples of compound trials are shown in which the sample is the same colored shape but memory for the shape (top) or color (bottom) is tested, unpredictably to the pigeon. Data redrawn from Langley and Riley (1993) with permission.

Chunking

As we have seen, several events that have to be remembered at once, as in the radial maze, are better remembered if they are more distinguishable from one another. At the same time, however, large numbers of items are better remembered if they can be grouped into subsets, *chunks* of similar items. For example, people recall more of a long list of words if the words can be grouped into categories such as names of cars, flowers, animals. Pigeons learning to peck several displays in a fixed sequence do so more quickly if the displays are chunked by the experimenter, for example with three colors to be pecked first followed by two patterns (Terrace 1991). Rats behave as if they spontaneously chunk information on a radial maze. Dallal and Meck (1990) exposed rats to a 12-arm radial maze with cheese, chocolate cereal, and pellets of rat chow each on four arms. Rats acquired accurate performance more quickly when the same food was assigned to each arm on every trial than when the locations of the different food types were not predictable from trial to trial. The rats in the former condition chunked their visits by food type, going first to cheese, then cereal, then to the least preferred pellets, but this might have reflected the rat's preferences rather than anything about their memories. To check on this possibility, Macuda and Roberts (1995) tested rats that had learned a maze with fixed food types as in Dallal and Meck's (1990) study by selecting four arms for them to visit at the start of each trial, then allowing a free choice among all 12 arms of the maze. In the whole chunk condition, the four arms selected in the first part of the trial all had the same type of food; in the broken chunk condition, they included arms with all three of the foods. Rats in the whole chunk condition had to remember only one item of information whereas in the broken chunk condition they had to remember all four individual visited arms. As this notion predicts, rats in the whole chunk condition performed more accurately.

The potential for chunking in these experiments was enhanced by providing obvious subsets of items, but monkeys, as well as people, also show evidence of spontaneously chunking remembered information at the time of test. When monkeys have learned to touch a sequence of seven or more simultaneously displayed items in a fixed sequence (a simultaneous chain, see Chapter 10), they typically touch the first few in quick succession, then pause before quickly completing the sequence, as if executing the list in two chunks (Terrace 2001).

7.3.2   Events before and during the retention interval: Interference

Performance at T2 may fall if the retention interval contains events similar to the to-be-remembered target event, an effect called *retroactive interference* (*RI*). An example from habituation is shown in Figure 7.10. The response measured was

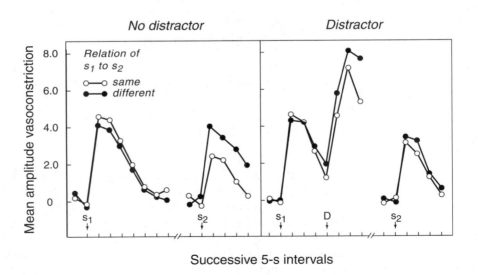

Figure 7.10. Demonstration of retroactive interference produced by a distractor stimulus (D) between successive presentations of a tone to which rabbits are being habituated. Reaction to the tone is measured as the temporal pattern of vasoconstriction in the ear. Redrawn from Whitlow (1975) with permission.

vasoconstriction in rabbits' ears, corresponding to the rabbits' pricking up their ears to a novel sound. Memory for the habituating sound was evidenced in the fact that the rabbits responded less to the second sound in a trial if it was the same as the first sound than if it was different. Interference with memory for the habituating sound was produced by presenting a *distractor* stimulus such as a brief flash of light shortly after the habituating stimulus. In this case, the rabbits apparently forgot the first tone; response to the second tone was undiminished whether or not it was the same as the first one. Comparable effects over longer time courses have been demonstrated in pigeons and monkeys performing delayed matching to sample (Jarvik, Goldfarb, and Carley 1969; W. Roberts and Grant 1978). For example, if the lights in the testing chamber are usually off, turning them on during the retention interval disrupts pigeons' matching (Maki, Moe, and Bierley 1977).

Spatial memory seems less susceptible to interference. For example, taking the rat off the maze or introducing other experiences during the retention interval between the first and last four choices has no effect on performance on a radial maze (S. Roberts 1981). Pigeons performing delayed alternation in a T-maze are also resistant to retroactive interference (Olson and Maki 1983). Similarly, if marsh tits (*Parus palustris*) store two batches of seeds in laboratory "trees," memory for the second batch stored interferes little if at all with memory for earlier stores (Shettleworth and Krebs 1982; see also Crystal and Shettleworth 1994). In contrast, Clark's nutcrackers show clear interference effects on what is probably a more sensitive test, with storage sites close together on the floor of an aviary (J. Lewis and Kamil 2006), perhaps an example of increased interference among more similar memories. Further research would be needed to test the possibility that species and/or memory systems also differ in susceptibility to interference.

In *proactive interference* (PI), memory for later events is degraded by memory for earlier ones. Figure 7.8 shows PI between trials: performance declines on successive visits to a radial maze when they are closely spaced in time. PI can also be produced by events within a trial, as when the sample in a delayed matching trial is immediately preceded by a different sample. Proactive interference can build up over a long time. For example, monkeys' accuracy at matching to sample with the same set of stimuli in every session fell over many sessions, but it shot up when a new set of stimuli was introduced (Wright 2006). This may also be another example of the more general beneficial effect of novelty on processing.

Finally, as discussed further in the next section, experiences may interfere with performance without affecting memory per se. A nice example is provided by a study of honeybees (Cheng and Wignall 2006). Bees that learned to find sugar water on the left of a green landmark retained this memory for at least an hour in the absence of intervening experience, but if bees learned to go to the right of a blue landmark during the hour's retention interval, their performance on the first task fell to chance. This does not mean memory was impaired by learning another task, because bees that learned to visit a blue rather than a yellow card for sugar water during the retention interval performed as well on a test of the original task as bees with no intervening experience. Rather, because of response competition bees trained on two tasks with opposite requirements make many wrong choices on the test. If the test with the green landmark was arranged so it was impossible to choose a location to the right of it but only locations above, below, and to the left, performance was nearly as high as before training on the second task of the procedure (Figure 7.11). Of course the results of this study hardly mean that honeybees never forget, but in their natural foraging they may well need memories for several concurrently available nectar sources, and unlike in

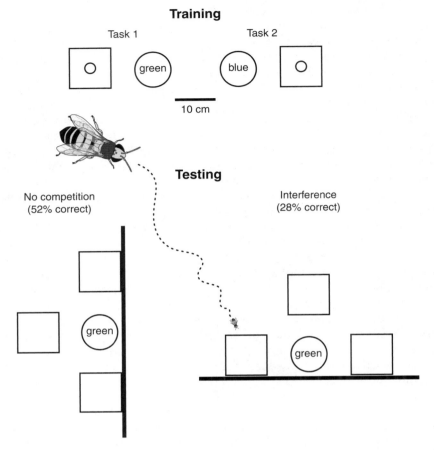

Figure 7.11. Procedure used by Cheng and Wignall (2006) to control the presence versus absence of a competing response from Task 2 during a test of memory for Task 1, learned earlier. In the training phase, the large circles represent cylindrical landmarks, and the small circles are dishes of sugar water. The heavy lines represent the edge of the outdoor table on which the experimental setup was placed. Which of the squares (pieces of red cardboard) a bee landed on indicated its choice.

Cheng and Wignall's (2006) experiment these might not share a spatial context. Box 7.1 describes another situation in which changes in performance over time reflect the presence of several memories.

7.3.3   Conditions at T2: The importance of context

Temporal and spatial context may predict what memories will be useful and therefore ought to be retrieved (Anderson and Schooler 1991). As suggested by the discussion of conditioning to the context in Chapter 4, any and all elements of the external and internal environment present at the time of encoding can provide *retrieval cues* later on (Bouton and Moody 2004). When animals learn first one thing then something incompatible the resulting behavior is a product of both interference and context (Bouton 1993; Bouton and Moody 2004). For example, spontaneous recovery following extinction (Section 4.4.7) reveals that the memory of conditioning is not erased. Rather, animals have two competing memories and evidence one or the other, according to the current context. Immediately after extinction, the temporal context is like that in which extinction took place, but as time passes and both training and extinction are in the past, memory of the original training resurfaces (see also Box 7.1). Another way to show that memory of training is intact is to give noncontingent presentations of the original reinforcer, part of the original training context, just before a test. These reminders tend to reinstate the trained behavior.

Memory for context itself becomes less specific with time. This can have an apparently paradoxical effect: a response that is highly context-specific soon after training later becomes stronger, not weaker, in a novel context. In the example in Figure 7.12, mice that had a single shock in a distinctive chamber gradually developed more freezing (i.e., immobility, evidence of fear) in a novel chamber while showing no forgetting in the original chamber (Wiltgen and Silva 2007; see also Winocur and Moscovitch 2007). It is worth noting that in fear conditioning, animals must be exposed to the to-be-conditioned context for a short time before shock is given, apparently forming a representation of the context to which shock is associated. This is indicated by the absence of learning in the nonexposed group in the right panel of Figure 7.12. The difference between the other groups indicates that it is this representation that becomes less specific over time.

Context includes the time of day at which the to-be-remembered experience occurred. When time of training and time of testing are both controlled for, animals tested at the time of day when they were trained may show better retention than those tested at a different time (McDonald et al. 2002; Cain et al. 2004). Effects of time of day on memory retrieval exemplify the more general phenomenon of *state-dependent learning*, also seen when learning acquired under the influence of a drug is less evident in the drug-free state (Gordon and Klein 1994). At the same time, however, behavior in experiments on memory may change when the context changes for reasons unrelated to changes in the memories being tested (Wilkie, Willson, and Carr 1999; C. Thorpe., Jacova, and Wilkie 2004). For example, animals placed in a new environment may explore it before performing a previously reinforced response, and the resulting delay in responding may wrongly be interpreted as evidence of forgetting (Devenport 1989).

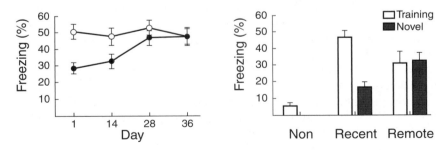

Figure 7.12. Left: proportion of the test spent freezing by separate groups of mice given a single shock in a distinctive chamber and tested at the given retention intervals in the training chamber (open circles) or a novel one. Right: proportion of time freezing in the training or a novel context by groups of mice exposed to the training context either not at all (non), 1 day before (recent), or 36 days before a single shock in the training context. After Wiltgen and Silva (2007) with permission.

7.4   Species differences in memory?

In Chapter 3 of *The Descent of Man and Selection in Relation to Sex,* Darwin (1871) claimed that memory is one of the "mental powers" that humans share with other animals. The behavior of his own dog provided one example. When Darwin returned from his voyage on the *Beagle* after an absence of five years and two days, the dog ran out of the barn when Darwin called and greeted his master as if he had never been away. This and Darwin's other anecdotes suggesting that animals can sometimes remember for a very long time are among the first contributions to a still-growing body of research comparing the persistence and capacity of memory in different species. Given the discussion in Chapter 2, readers should be skeptical that establishing any species differences will be possible, let alone easy. Nevertheless, from the early days of research on animal cognition, there has been a whole series of research programs designed to do just that. Here we review three sorts of tests of the notion that some animals remember things differently from other animals. The first is of mainly historical interest as an illustration of the problems that afflict comparative research on any aspect of cognition. The other two are exemplary ongoing programs of great depth and sophistication, one testing predictions about differences among closely related species with different foraging and social ecologies and the other testing a wide range of species for memory processes shared with humans.

Some examples of long-lasting memories in nature were mentioned earlier in the chapter, but tasks learned in the laboratory can also be remembered for a long time. The effects of simple instrumental training procedures may be retained for months or years (Vaughan and Greene 1984). More remarkably, large numbers of discriminations between complex visual stimuli can be remembered for long periods. For example in one of Vaughan and Greene's (1984) studies of pigeons' discriminations between large numbers of photographic slides, reviewed in Chapter 6, above-chance performance on 160 discriminations (320 slides) was retained for over two years. More recent evidence suggests that pigeons' memory capacity in such a paradigm is actually closer to 800 items (Cook. et al. 2005), and baboons trained similarly over several years learned which response to make to over 3500 pictures (Fagot and Cook 2006). Another example of persistent, large-capacity memory in birds is Clark's nutcrackers' memories for the locations of their buried caches. In the field, these birds bury several thousand caches of pine seeds in the late summer and retrieve them up to six months or more later (Box 1.4 and Section 7.4.2). Nutcrackers performed above chance levels in the laboratory when retrieving 18–25 caches 285 days (9–10 months) after making them. Performance was worse at this retention interval than at 183 days (6 months), a more realistic interval from the point of view of what happens in the field (Balda and Kamil 1992).

Remembering 25 locations for 9 months is not as impressive as remembering 320 slides for 2 years. Does this mean that the excellent memory of food storing birds is a myth, that they are outclassed by ordinary laboratory pigeons? Clearly not. Absolute memory duration is not a meaningful measure when comparing species tested in two such different tasks as those experienced by the pigeons and the nutcrackers. For instance, one involves spatial information, the other two-dimensional visual patterns. Perhaps most important, the food-caching bird has just a brief encounter with each to-be-remembered site, as it pokes its beak into a hole to bury the pine seeds, whereas Vaughan and Greene's pigeons were trained extensively. The pigeons had the first set of slides for a total of 52 sessions, in each of which every slide was shown twice for a minimum of 10 seconds each time. Clearly, the conditions for memory formation differed considerably from those experienced by the nutcrackers. While both sets of data can be taken, along with the story of Darwin's dog, as evidence that animals may have remarkably durable memories, they tell us nothing about whether one animal remembers more or for longer than another.

7.4.1 Comparative tests of delayed responses

The first major research program designed to compare memory in different species in a systematic way was begun by Hunter (1913), using the delayed response task described in Section 7.2. Its purpose was to compare species in "intelligence" by measuring the maximum delay at which performance remained above chance. But this enterprise was beset by the same problems as the comparative studies of successive reversal and learning set reviewed in Chapter 6. As summarized by Maier and Schneirla (1935/1964, 449, Table 30), the early research showed that rats, cats, dogs, raccoons, and five species of primates could all perform correctly without observable orienting responses during the delay, but the maximum delay possible varied drastically among studies. For example, for chimpanzees it ranged between 2 minutes and 48 hours, but rats were hardly worse, with a range between 11 seconds and 24 hours. Obvious differences among the procedures did not seem to account for such variations. Maier and Schneirla (1935/1964, 453) therefore concluded, "differences in results obtained in the various experiments on delayed reaction are artifacts and not measures of a special ability to delay a reaction. As a result, the delayed reaction cannot be regarded as a measure of some higher process." More recent research has not altered this conclusion (Macphail 1982). Comparing species on the shape of an entire forgetting curve, as in Figure 7.13, does not eliminate the problem. Making the task easier or harder for a particular species simply raises or lowers its curve relative to those of other species. The influence of such contextual variables serves to underline Macphail's (1982, 275) conclusion that "delayed response tasks will not provide

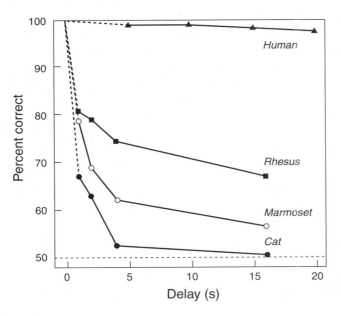

Figure 7.13. Forgetting curves for four mammalian species on a spatial delayed response test. Chance performance is 50% correct. Redrawn from Miles (1971) with permission.

unique rankings of species and cannot be used as a measure of general intelligence." Nor, we may add, of some hypothetical generalized ability to remember.

7.4.2   Spatial memory in food-storing birds

Comparing memory in food-storing and nonstoring species of birds, introduced in Chapters 1 and 2, also involves testing different species in similar situations, so why isn't it just as hopeless a task as attempting to rank species in memory on delayed response tests? What makes it different is that in the ecological or synthetic approach to animal intelligence (Kamil 1988) a profile of species differences and similarities is predicted from ecology and phylogeny, and in the best applications of this approach the species involved are tested in more than one way. Importantly, this includes situations where different patterns of abilities are predicted. Multiple tests of the ability in question are used to be sure that any species ranking is not the product of contextual variables peculiar to one of the tests. Tests of different abilities are used because if, for example, Species A is predicted to have better spatial memory than Species B, and they are never compared on anything other than tests of spatial memory, it is impossible to know whether A outperforms B because it has a specifically better spatial memory, because it has better memory in general, because it adapts better to the laboratory, or for some other reason (Lefebvre and Giraldeau 1996; Shettleworth and Hampton 1998).

A uniquely thorough example of this approach is the program of research on four food-storing corvid species that live in the mountains of the American Southwest (Table 7.1; see Box 1.4; Balda and Kamil 2002, 2006). The star of this show is Clark's nutcracker (*Nucifraga columbiana*), which makes a few thousand pine seed caches every fall and retrieves them throughout the winter and following spring. At the other extreme is the Western scrub jay (*Aphelacoma coerulescens*), a bird of lower elevations that is much less dependent on stored food. Pinyon jays (*Gymnorhynus cyanocephalus*) are intense food-storers but somewhat less so than Clark's nutcrackers; unlike the comparatively solitary nutcrackers they form large flocks. Mexican jays (*A. ultramarina*) are also quite social but are only moderate storers (Balda and Kamil 2006). The latter three species are thought to have diverged from a common ancestor that migrated into North America from the south, whereas the ancestors of nutcrackers, more closely related to European corvids, came across the Bering Strait. Nutcrackers and pinyon jays have some convergently evolved morphological adaptations for gathering and transporting seeds that the other two species lack. Research on the spatial memory of these four species was designed to test the hypothesis that

Table 7.1 Relative ranks of four corvid species studied by Balda and Kamil (2006) on food storing, hippocampus, and performance in tests of memory

	Clark's nutcracker	pinyon jay	Mexican jay	scrub jay
reliance on storing	1	2	3	4
relative hippocampal vol.	1	2	3	2
cache retrieval accuracy	1	2	?	3
radial maze performance	1	1	2	2
spatial delayed nonmatching	1	2	2	2
color delayed nonmatching	2	1	1	2

Same rank indicates no significant difference was found between the given species on the test in question.

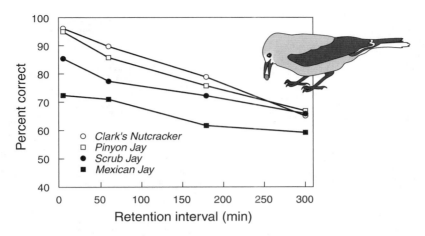

Figure 7.14. Performance of four species of corvids on a radial maze–like task as a function of retention interval between the first and last four choices. Retention intervals were randomly intermixed, unpredictably to the birds. Percent correct is based on the last four choices. Redrawn from Kamil, Balda, and Olson (1994) with permission.

reliance on stored food predicts duration and/or capacity of spatial memory. In tests ranging from retrieving stored food in the laboratory to delayed spatial nonmatching to sample in an operant chamber, the ranking of species fairly consistently supports this hypothesis (Table 7.1; Balda and Kamil 2006).

On a radial maze–like task in which the birds had to remember sites in a large room for up to 24 hours, nutcrackers and pinyon jays consistently performed better than birds of the other two species. However, as shown in Figure 7.14, their advantage was greatest at the shortest retention intervals. This is surprising because the species are assumed to differ in the wild in their ability to retain information for a very long time. This might mean that the species differ in initial processing of spatial information rather than ability to retain it (Kamil, Balda, and Olson 1994). However, differences in initial processing alone should be reflected in forgetting curves that are parallel rather than converging, as in Figure 7.5. In any case, the fact that species differences consistent with the requirements for spatial memory in the wild appear in situations other than food-storing tells us something about the organization of memory in these birds. The mere fact that they retrieve their caches a remarkably long time after making them need not mean they excel in memory in any given way. Encoding spatial information more accurately (Gibson and Kamil 2005), retaining it longer, or being able to keep more items of spatial information in memory could all, singly or together, be selected because they enhance the ability to retrieve stored food. Noncognitive modifications could play a role, too, such as more efficient food storing behavior or ways of storing that make cache sites more memorable.

Nutcrackers, pinyon jays, and scrub jays were also trained on spatial delayed nonmatching to sample in a two-key operant chamber (Olson et al. 1995). The retention interval was increased gradually for each individual as long as it was performing above a standard criterion level so that each bird had the opportunity to show the best it could do: birds with good memory had the retention interval increased faster than birds with poor memory. The nutcrackers performed vastly better than any of the other three species, which performed similarly to each other

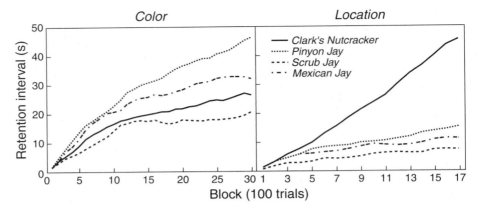

Figure 7.15. Performance of four corvid species on operant delayed matching with samples of color or location. Performance is retention interval attained as a function of trials when the retention interval was increased for each bird whenever it performed above a criterion level. Redrawn from Olson et al. (1995) with permission.

(Figure 7.15). The Clark's nutcrackers also remembered more items than scrub jays in an operant test of spatial memory capacity (Olson 1991). Importantly, in one test of whether the observed species differences are specific to spatial memory or reflect some contextual variable that favors nutcrackers and pinyon jays, the same birds were trained on delayed nonmatching with colors (Olson et al. 1995). Pinyon jays and Mexican jays rather than nutcrackers learned this task fastest and achieved the longest retention intervals (Figure 7.15).

The four species studied by Balda and Kamil differ in sociality as well as reliance on stored food. Because sociality is thought to require its own suite of cognitive adaptations (Chapter 12), the relative performance of the same species can be predicted for rather different cognitive tests. For example, because pinyon jays and Mexican jays travel in groups while caching, they were predicted to be better able than nutcrackers to remember the locations of caches they saw a conspecific making. Indeed, after a two-day retention interval, pinyon jays and Mexican jays retrieved caches they observed as accurately as caches they made themselves, but nutcrackers did not (Templeton, Kamil, and Balda 1999). Pinyon jays also outperform scrub jays on a test of transitive inference, which is thought to require the same ability used in learning a social hierarchy, an ability needed by pinyon jays but not scrub jays (see Chapter 10; Bond, Kamil, and Balda 2003).

The prediction that reliance on food storing is associated with exceptional spatial memory has also been tested with some European corvids and with birds of the family *Paridae*, the chickadees and titmice (Shettleworth 1995). Comparative studies of parids' spatial memory have not revealed species differences so large or so consistent as those among corvids, perhaps reflecting the fact that cognitive and neural mechanisms underlying the ability to retrieve stored caches differ in different groups of species. Food storing has evolved independently in parids and corvids, so perhaps it has recruited somewhat different mechanisms. Also corvids show the most long-term storage in the wild, so they might show more extreme species differences in memory (Brodin 2005). However, one consistent finding across parids and corvids is that in a variety of laboratory tests food-storing species tend to remember spatial cues better than and choose them in preference to color and/or pattern cues, whereas nonstorers treat the two classes of cues about equally (Shettleworth and Hampton 1998; Shettleworth and Westwood 2002). As discussed in Chapter 2, the general notion that greater use of spatial information in the wild should be correlated with enhanced spatial ability (and a larger hippocampus) has also been tested by examining possible differences between males and females, migratory and nonmigratory species, and in other ways. However, so far only with the four American corvid species do we have such a rich and detailed comparison of ecologically relevant cognitive abilities across such a variety of tasks.

7.4.4   List learning in pigeons, rats, monkeys, and people

The *serial position effect* is a classic observation in studies of human memory: items at the beginning and end of a list are typically remembered better than items in the middle. The typical U-shaped curve describing accuracy as a function of position in the list thus contains both *primacy* (better performance with items at the beginning) and *recency* effects (better performance for items at the end). Because the serial position effect is well established in humans, testing for it in other species is frank anthropocentrism. Nevertheless, comparative work on list learning illustrates how asking a rather nonecological question about more or less arbitrarily chosen unrelated species can lead to important insights into general mechanisms of memory. This is the research of Wright and his colleagues on *serial probe recognition* of visual stimuli in pigeons, monkeys, and people (Wright 2006). In serial probe recognition, the subject sees a series of visual images, the to-be-remembered list, followed after a retention interval by a single probe image. If the probe is the same as an item in the list, the subject is reinforced for making one response, say pecking the right key; if it is different from any item in the list, another response is reinforced. Only one item is probed after each list, so that memory for the first, second, and following list positions is tested in a standard way.

In pigeons, monkeys, and people tested with visual items, recency is evident at the shortest retention interval tested. Recency gradually gives way to primacy as the retention interval lengthens (Figure 7.16). The classic U-shaped serial position curve therefore appears only at intermediate retention intervals. The three species differ, however, in the range of retention intervals over which this dynamic pattern appears. "Long" for pigeons is 10 seconds; for the monkeys, 30 seconds; and for humans it takes 100 seconds for recency to be replaced by primacy. The time scale also depends on the task. Rats tested on the radial maze were required to discriminate between one of four arms already entered and an unentered arm show the same sort of dynamic serial position curves displayed in Figure 7.16, but over 16 minutes (Bolhuis and van Kampen 1988; Harper, McLean, and Dalrymple-Alford 1993).

A striking feature of the data in Figure 7.16 is that as time passes the items from the beginning of the list are responded to more accurately. For instance, on the first item pigeons are at chance on an immediate test but about 80% correct after 10 seconds. One way to understand this effect, as well as the whole pattern of dynamic changes, is to suggest that at short retention intervals the early items suffer from retroactive interference from the last items, which are still held in primary or short-term memory at that time. Such retroactive interference evidently dissipates rapidly, perhaps as items move from short-term to long-term memory. Storage in long-term memory has been thought to be accomplished by *rehearsal*. In humans rehearsal may be just what the word implies: the person silently repeats the item, thereby giving it longer

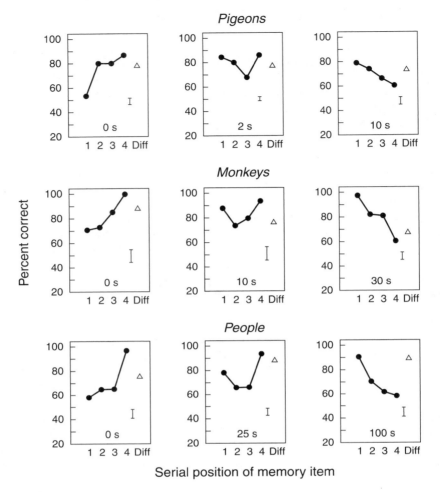

Figure 7.16. Serial probe recognition in pigeons, monkeys, and people with lists of four items as a function of the position of the tested item in the list and the retention interval between the last item and the test (interval indicated in each panel). Triangles are accuracy of indicating "different" on trials in which the probe was an item that had not appeared in the just-presented list. Small vertical bars are standard errors for tests of positions 1–4. Redrawn from Wright et al. (1985) with permission.

exposure. The importance of rehearsal for long-term storage can be demonstrated by inserting *distractors* between items, curtailing rehearsal by making the subject process new material, as in the example in Figure 7.10.

The straightforward notion of rehearsal does not explain the emergence of a primacy effect because performance on the early items improves in absolute terms as time passes. If the items were available to be rehearsed at the shortest retention intervals, they should have been recognized at this retention interval. In addition, because photographs of kaleidoscope patterns were used for the people, they were presumably no better off than the pigeons and monkeys in terms of being able to name and verbally rehearse the to-be-remembered items. To show more directly that the serial position effect in humans can be dissociated from effects of rehearsal, Wright and colleagues (Wright 1989; Wright. et al. 1990) turned to testing the effects of the interval between successive items in the list, *the interstimulus interval* or *ISI*. People perform better with verbal material as the interstimulus interval is lengthened, presumably because there is greater opportunity to rehearse each item as it comes along. On this reasoning, the effect of interstimulus interval should depend on the items being verbally rehearsed. As this idea predicts, people who had learned names for a set of kaleidoscope patterns later performed better on list learning with those patterns and showed a prominent interstimulus interval effect, lacking in a control group also preexposed to the patterns but without learning names for them. Nevertheless, both groups had similar serial position functions, with sharp primacy effects. These findings, like the data from other species, indicate that rehearsal in the sense of verbally repeating the name of an item cannot be the general cause for the primacy effect. As an example of the comparative study of cognition, this research is unusual because it started from an anthropocentric question (do other species show serial position effects like people?) but wound up answering a general question about memory mechanisms by making people behave like nonverbal animals.

Studies of rhesus monkeys' memory for lists of sounds also suggest that rather than rehearsal, dynamic serial position curves reflect the intrinsic time courses of retroactive and proactive interference (RI and PI) among items within a list. Remarkably, serial position curves for auditory lists change with retention interval in the opposite way to those for lists of visual items even when both are tested similarly. This within-species difference in the serial position curve, like the cross-species differences, apparently reflects a quantitative difference in common mechanisms rather than a qualitative one. PI is strongest immediately after a list of sounds is presented and dissipates with time while RI increases (Wright and Roediger III 2003; Wright 2006). Why this should be is somewhat mysterious, but functionally it means that if a monkey is forming a memory for a natural sequence of multimodal events, either the auditory or the visual component of each memory will always be available although the other may be temporarily suppressed.

7.5 Mechanisms: What is remembered and why is it forgotten?

Nowadays studying the mechanisms of memory most often means studying neural and molecular mechanisms, but ultimately of course the findings must explain behavior. In this section we look at some memory mechanisms that have been addressed with primarily behavioral studies. An important historical theme is whether memories consist simply of the persistence of the neural activity that occurs when events are perceived, that is, *stimulus traces,* or whether the direct effect of experience is transformed in some way for storage in memory. Similarly, is forgetting the passive fading of a trace or a more active process? Finally, how do memories sometimes become more stable with time, in the process of consolidation?

7.5.1   Retrospective and prospective coding

A stimulus trace is a *retrospective code.* Intuitively, performance based on stimulus traces results from mentally "looking back" (retro-specting) at recent traces. In a *prospective code,* in contrast, information is transformed at the time of input into some representation of what is to be done at the time of test, that is, the code looks forward or pro-spects. In simple red/green matching to sample, for instance, retrospective coding of the red sample is a trace corresponding to the experience of red, whereas prospective coding of the same sample amounts to an instruction, "choose red on the test." Extensive investigations of the conditions favoring one form of code or the other in short-term or working memory have been done with pigeons in matching to sample tasks. In *many-to-one* matching, each of several samples is associated with the same correct choice. For example, Grant (1982) trained pigeons to choose a red comparison stimulus after samples of red, 20 pecks, or a brief presentation of food, and to choose green following a sample of green, one peck, or no food. When one, two, or three samples were presented in succession before the retention interval, birds performed more accurately with multiple samples regardless of whether they were the same (e.g., two food presentations) or just associated with the same comparison (e.g., one presentation of food and one of the red key).

This finding suggests that samples associated with a common comparison are coded in the same way, that is, prospectively. However, pigeons may not always code information prospectively in matching to sample, let alone in general. Among other reasons, initial learning of any kind requires retrospective coding. It is impossible to form a prospective code without information about what the memory will be used for, so the most primitive memory code must be retrospective. Only when the same items are tested over and over in the same kind of way, either during an individual's lifetime or during evolution, is prospective coding possible. Thus, as with many issues in psychology, the best question is not, "Is coding retrospective *or* prospective?" but rather "*Under what conditions* is coding retrospective and under what conditions prospective?" One condition favoring retrospective coding is the use of highly discriminable samples. For pigeons, colors on the pecking key are much more salient than lines of different orientations. Colors seem to be coded retrospectively even under conditions favoring prospective coding of less discriminable stimuli such as lines (Zentall et al. 1989). Under some conditions, the type of code used appears to switch within a trial (Cook, Brown, and Riley 1985; Brown, Wheeler, and Riley 1989; Zentall, Steirn, and Jackson-Smith 1990).

It is not clear what prospective coding of short-term memories would be good for outside the laboratory because it is hard to think of natural situations in which an animal would repeatedly encounter the same kind of information and its later choices depend on what had happened earlier. Nevertheless, the distinction between prospective and retrospective processes has wider applicability (Wasserman 1986). For instance, prospection can be seen as the ability to anticipate and make plans, issues discussed in Chapter 11. In any case, experiments on time-place learning discussed in Chapter 9 arguably better approximate studies of prospective memory in humans than do studies of coding in working memory. As Thorpe, Jacova, and Wilkie (2004) point out, in studies of prospective memory with people, subjects are told to remember to do something at a certain time or when a certain cue appears, as in everyday life when making a date to meet for lunch.

7.5.2   Directed forgetting

One way to test whether memory is a passive recording of a trace or a more active process is to see whether remembering can be brought under stimulus control. People can be told to remember some things and forget others, and such instructions do influence later recall (see Zentall et al. 1997). In *directed forgetting* experiments with nonverbal species, distinctive stimuli inserted into the retention interval play the role of instructions to remember or forget. Such cues are presented after the sample stimuli so they can affect only processing of their memories. But "forget" and "remember" trials may differ in many other ways. For example, if there is never a test of any kind after a cue to forget, that cue will signal absence of reinforcement. The animal may therefore stop attending to the keys until the next trial and behave as if not remembering the sample when memory is unexpectedly probed on "forget" trials. For such reasons, most early tests of whether memory processing can be brought under stimulus control were inconclusive (Zentall et al. 1997).

In tests of directed forgetting with human subjects, people are typically given several items of information and told which to remember; implicitly, this means forget the others. A way of giving pigeons these instructions is diagrammed in Figure 7.17 (Roper, Kaiser, and Zentall 1995). The bird's memory is always tested; what varies from trial to trial is whether the test is of memory for the first of two stimuli presented (a color sample stimulus) or the second (a sample for a symbolic matching test). The appearance of one of the symbolic matching samples, the dot or circle in the example, in effect tells the bird it can forget whether red or green was just presented. With this procedure pigeons do perform worse when memory for the first sample is probed after a forget cue than after a remember cue (Figure 7.17, bottom), apparently reallocating processing from one sample to another.

7.5.3   Consolidation and reconsolidation

Since the time of the ancient Greeks, people have realized that new memories need time to stabilize, reflecting a process known as *consolidation* (Dudai 2004). Two separate consolidation processes are now recognized at the neurobiological level. Cellular or *synaptic consolidation* takes place in the first minutes to hours after learning and depends on protein synthesis, a universal property of memory acquisition in nervous systems. In mammals, memories dependent on the hippocampus undergo a longer term or *systems consolidation* lasting days or even years during which they become represented outside the hippocampus (see Winocur and Moscovitch 2007). As these characterizations indicate, nowadays consolidation—in nonhuman species, at least—is most often studied via manipulations of the nervous system (see Dudai 2004), but behavioral studies, including some with with humans (Wixted 2004), also provide evidence for it.

In one example with mice, (Boccia et al. 2005) the target memory was acquired in a single trial of *step-down avoidance learning* (notice the irrelevance of the distinction between "memory" and "learning" typical of this kind of work). In this task an animal is placed on a small platform elevated above an electrified grid floor. Because the animal is shocked when it steps off, even after a single trial it tends to stay much longer on the platform than a naive animal, and it may retain the memory of the shock for days. The mice spent five minutes in a novel open field with small holes in the floor that mice investigate by poking their noses in ("hole board") either immediately after one trial of avoidance training or three hours later (Figure 7.18). When placed on the platform in the avoidance apparatus one, two, and three days later, the mice exposed to the hole board immediately after original learning stepped down nearly as quickly as unshocked mice, as if they had no memory of the shock. Learning about the novel environment evidently prevented consolidation of memory for the avoidance task. Mice that experienced the hole board three hours after learning all stayed on the platform for the entire five minute test, as did controls unexposed to the hole board (Figure 7.18) Thus here memory is consolidated within the first three hours. What

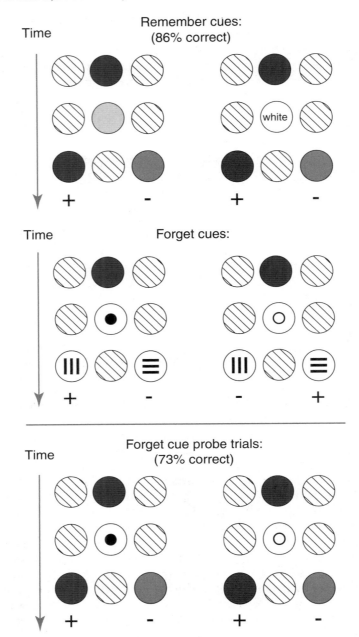

Figure 7.17. Examples of trials in the directed forgetting procedure of Roper, Kaiser, and Zentall (1995). The "forget" cues (small white and black disks) are themselves samples for a subsequent symbolic matching test. Redrawn from Roper, Kaiser, and Zentall (1995) with permission.

interferes with consolidation is not experience of the hole board per se but the new learning it instigates. Mice well habituated to the hole board and then placed on it immediately after avoidance training showed no decrement in memory. Izquierdo and colleagues (1999) report parallel findings with rats. These authors also found that

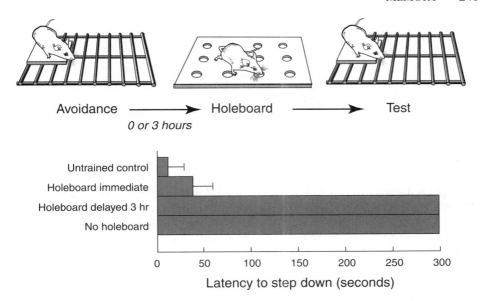

Figure 7.18. Exposure to a novel environment (the holeboard) prevents consolidation of fear memory in mice. Procedure and results of the experiment described in the text (Experiment 1 Boccia et al. 2005) adapted with permission. A longer latency to step onto the grid in the test indicates greater fear. A further control showed that for immediate exposure to abolish fear memory as shown, the holeboard must be novel.

consolidation of memory for the open field is not disrupted by avoidance training, suggesting that it is consolidated more quickly.

The discussion so far seems to suggest that synaptic consolidation is a one-time event, but to the contrary recently formed memories sometimes become labile again when they are retrieved and require *reconsolidation*. In a continuation of the study shown in Figure 7.18 memory for shock was tested 24 hours after training; no shock was given. Then the mice were exposed to the hole board for the first time either immediately or three hours later. Experience on the hole board disrupted memory when it occurred immediately after the test but not three hours later. When mice exposed to the hole board immediately after the memory test were later exposed to noncontingent shock, that is, in a reactivation treatment, they still behaved as if having lost their memories. These findings suggest that on the first test, a day after training, the apparently consolidated memory returns to the same labile state as immediately after training. Whether this is strictly true, whether susceptibility to reconsolidation lasts indefinitely, whether it characterizes all sorts of memories, and related questions are the subject of lively debate and much research, most of it using neurobiological methods (Tronson and Taylor 2007).

7.6   Memory and consciousness

In traditional studies of memory, consciousness is not an issue. Memory is inferred when a creature's behavior at one time (T2) is influenced by experience at an earlier time (T1), as when a mouse is slow to step onto a shock grid again or a person recalls a word from a list. But recent years have seen increased interest in aspects of human memory linked to states of consciousness. Examples include explicit (conscious) as opposed to implicit (unconscious) memory, episodic versus semantic memory, remembering an event as opposed to merely knowing that it happened, and awareness of the strength of one's own memories (metamemory). Perhaps inevitably, researchers have looked for evidence of these processes in other species, partly because "animal models" promise better understanding of their neurobiology. But even if a particular memory process in humans is accompanied by a distinctive subjective experience, researchers testing other species can measure only nonverbal behavior, that is, what the cognitive process in question allows animals to do but not how it feels. The issue therefore becomes the extent to which other species show behavior that is *functionally similar* to that of humans, in the mathematical sense of changing similarly with independent variables (Heyes 2008; Hampton 2009). This is essentially no different from showing that basic memory processes are the same across species, as in the comparative study of serial position effects (Figure 7.16).

As an example of memory processes accompanied by different subjective experiences, consider the distinction between implicit and explicit memory in humans. *Implicit memory* is memory without awareness; *explicit memory* is memory we are aware of in that we can report on it verbally. Some of the now-classic demonstrations that normal adults reliably form memories they are unaware of come from studies of word fragment completion (e.g., Tulving, Schacter, and Stark 1982; Tulving 1985; Schacter 1995). People are shown a few letters of a word and asked to fill in the blanks, as in _s_s_in (for *assassin*). Subjects are more successful if the fragments can be completed as words they have recently studied for an unrelated test, even though they may not recognize the completed items as ones they saw recently. Conscious recognition (explicit memory) and implicit, nonconscious memory or *priming* can be dissociated in at least three ways (Tulving 1985). First, individual subjects do not necessarily explicitly remember the same items that show priming; surprisingly, explicit and implicit memory are statistically independent. Second, priming and explicit memory may decay over different time courses (Figure 7.19). Third, some brain-damaged patients with little or no explicit memory for new experiences show normal priming. Similar effects with material such as line drawings of objects

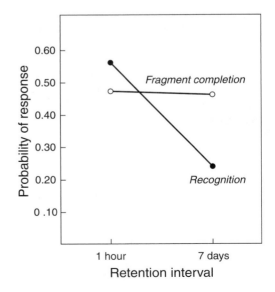

Figure 7.19. Dissociation of word fragment completion and explicit recognition of words presented under the same conditions. Redrawn from Tulving, Schacter, and Stark (1982) with permission.

suggesting that priming with words is but one manifestation of a more general unconscious *Perceptual Recognition System* (or PRS, Tulving and Schacter 1990), perhaps an evolutionarily primitive memory system (Tulving 1995). This hypothesis suggests that animals should also show priming in memory, a notion tested so far in only one experiment (Brodbeck 1997).

The next two sections summarize the more substantial and sometimes controversial research asking whether nonhuman species share other memory processes that are accompanied by distinctive states of awareness in humans, namely metamemory and episodic memory. This is our first extended discussion of some key issues prominent in comparative research on other anthropocentric topics such as physical understanding (Chapter 11) and theory of mind (Chapter 12). These issues are of two kinds, methodological or practical and theoretical. Methodological issues surround deciding what constitutes functional similarity. This is easiest when the process under study is well understood in people, especially when human subjects and other species can be given the same nonverbal tests, as in the comparative study of serial position effects (Section 7.4.3). Even when they cannot, the distinctive procedures and patterns of data providing evidence for the given process should be well defined to begin with. Ideally a variety of tests is available, allowing researchers to seek converging evidence from multiple situations. When instead the process under study is more familiar in folk psychology than in research laboratories, appropriate tests for nonhuman species may not be easy to agree on and how to interpret the results even less so. For example (Chapter 11), most tests of what physical understanding (if any) underlies primates' or birds' use of tools are based more on folk psychological intuition about what people would do in similar circumstances than on actual data. And when experiments are designed to collect such data, they can have counterintuitive results (Silva and Silva 2006).

The principal theoretical issue is that by itself functional similarity between human and animal behavior (or behavior of any two species) is not necessarily decisive evidence for a common underlying process. As with the nut dropping crows in Chapter 1, functional similarity can have multiple possible causes. Consistent with Morgan's Canon (Chapter 1), evidence that some process involving consciousness, understanding, or the like underlies behavior generally consists of evidence eliminating or rendering unlikely the possibility that it results from simpler mechanisms of learning and behavioral control. The latter can be referred to as publicly observable causes, in that behavior is predicted from external cues without the assumed mediation of some unobservable cognitive state (a private cause of behavior, Hampton 2009). The most powerful experimental designs for distinguishing public from private causes place predictions from candidate processes into opposition (Heyes 2008). But even when data are more consistent with a private cause, it is a final theoretical leap to the conclusion that functionally similar behavior reflects the same private cause in different species. One twist here is that students of human cognition are increasingly coming to appreciate that our own accounts of what we do as resulting from conscious thought and rational decision making may in fact be after-the-fact explanations of reactions to simple cues of the sort that other species might also respond to (Koriat, Hilit, and Nussison 2006; Carruthers 2008).

7.6.1   Metacognition

People tend to know how well they remember things. Such *metamemory* has two functions, monitoring memory strength and controlling information-seeking. For example, metamemory allows someone decide whether he remembers the way to a friend's house or needs to consult a map. *Metacognition* additionally includes knowing how well one is able to make perceptual discriminations, as in "I'm sure that green matches the curtains." Formal tests of metacognition require both a primary memory or perceptual discrimination task and metacognitive reports. The metacognitive reports should reflect accuracy on the primary task, as they tend to in tests of human subjects (Nelson and Narens 1990; Metcalfe and Kober 2005).

Because the function of metacognition seems to be facilitating efficient behavior, it might be shared by nonhuman species, and indeed, since the late 1990s researchers have tested for it in pigeons, rats, monkeys, chimpanzees, and a dolphin (J. Smith, Shields, and Washburn 2003; Terrace and Metcalfe 2005; Hampton 2009). However, on some interpretations metacognition entails higher-order representation because cognitive processes are themselves being represented, and this makes its presence in nonhuman species very unlikely (Carruthers 2008; see also Penn, Holyoak, and Povinelli 2008). In that people feel aware of their own memory strength or perceptual certainty, metacognition in humans also involves phenomenal consciousness (Koriat 2007). These features of metacognition mean that purported demonstrations of it in other species have attracted a good deal of critical scrutiny.

Hampton's (2001) experiment

We begin with a test of metamemory in rhesus macaques (Hampton 2001) that provides perhaps the strongest evidence to date that animals can respond to private cues predictive of accuracy on a memory test. Two monkeys performed on a four-alternative delayed matching to sample procedure with an extra step (Figure 7.20). At the end of the retention interval, before the sample and distractors, one or two symbols appeared. On two-thirds of trials, two symbols gave the monkeys a choice between taking the memory test and escaping from it. Choosing to take the test played the role of a person's reporting "I know I remember the sample on this trial." Completing the test correctly was reinforced with a peanut, but taking it and failing got nothing, whereas escaping was reinforced immediately with a piece of monkey chow, less preferred than the peanut. Assuming they prefer chow for sure to a peanut with less than certainty, monkeys with metamemory should escape more often the weaker their memories. Such animals should also perform less accurately on the one-third of memory tests they were not allowed to escape than on tests they chose because these "forced trials" include trials with poor memory, which the animal would have escaped if it could. Of course, if such forced trials were comparatively rare, animals might perform poorly on that account alone, that is, because of generalization decrement, so they were mixed randomly with choice trials throughout (but see J. Smith, Shields, and Washburn 2003; J. Smith et al. 2006).

In effect, the procedure diagrammed in Figure 7.20 reinforces animals for using some correlate of memory strength as a discriminative stimulus and at the same time, in the forced trials, potentially verifies that this cue is being used. But clearly a number of potential publicly observable cues could directly predict success on the memory test. An obvious one is the length of the retention interval. Animals could certainly learn that after a long delay escaping is more profitable than taking the memory test, although at first glance it is not clear how use of this cue could result in differences between chosen and forced memory tests. In any case, Hampton's study was designed so that monkeys could not use delay as a cue because they were trained initially with a

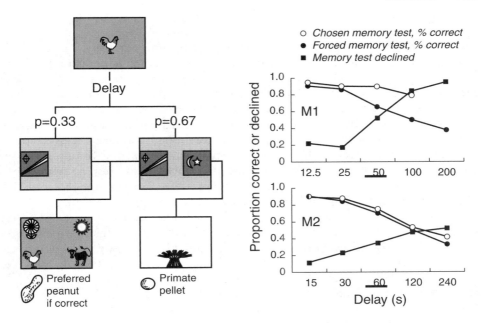

Figure 7.20. Procedure and data from the test of metamemory in monkeys by Hampton (2001) described in the text. In the left panel, each square represents what the monkeys saw at the given stage in a trial, from top to bottom. For example, the rooster at the top is a sample stimulus, and the left most panel in the middle row would be a forced memory test. The two panels on the right show data from two monkeys, M1 and M2. The initial training delay is underlined .

single moderate retention interval at which they were about 70% correct on forced memory tests (Figure 7.20). In contrast, when escaping was available both monkeys were over 80% correct on memory tests they did not escape, that is, they behaved as if reporting fairly accurately on the strength of their memories. To address the possibility that the monkeys' behavior, motivation, or distractions during the retention interval were used as public cues predicting success on the memory test, Hampton then manipulated memory directly by the clever expedient of occasionally omitting the sample. Now, when the monkeys could have no memory of a recent sample, escaping immediately increased dramatically. Finally, the retention interval (RI) was varied across values both shorter and longer than the one the monkeys had been trained on. Again the results were consistent with the animals assessing their memory strength on a trial by trial basis (Figure 7.20). The longer the RI, the worse they did on forced tests, the more they escaped, and the more matching accuracy on chosen tests exceeded that on forced tests. Moreover, this pattern of data appeared within the first 100 such trials.

These findings imply that the monkeys are responding to some private cue that predicts success on the test of memory, and in that sense they are aware of the strength of their memories. But whether this cue shares any of the subjective qualities of a person's awareness of having a strong or a weak memory is impossible to say. The monkeys' behavior does not necessarily entail a higher-order representation, that is, *meta* cognition in the strictest sense (Carruthers 2008). It might, for example, be based on the vividness of a mental image of the sample (Hampton 2005).

Confidence ratings

Metacognitive judgements are sometimes expressed after completing a test, as in "I aced that exam!" Such confidence ratings have been captured in operant tasks by requiring animals to make an additional choice after completing a primary test of memory, in effect rating their confidence in whether they were correct. The "high confidence" option is reinforced if the animal was correct but not otherwise; the "low confidence" option always gives a mediocre reward. Rhesus macaques respond as if having metacognition in such tasks, with choice of the high confidence icon positively correlated with accuracy on the test of memory (Kornell, Son, and Terrace 2007; see also Shields et al. 2005). Consistent with the possibility that this response expresses a subjective sense of memory strength, monkeys transferred appropriate choice of high versus low confidence responses from a series of two perceptual discrimination tasks in the same apparatus to a memory task. This and other such examples of transfer (Shields et al. 2005; Washburn, Smith, and Shields 2006) reveal that the metacognitive reponses must be mediated by something common to all the tasks, but it is not necessarily the subjective feeling of certainty emphasized by Smith and colleagues (e.g., J. Smith, Shields, and Washburn 2003; J. Smith and Washburn 2005; Beran et al. 2006). A strong candidate for a public cue is some feature of the monkeys' own behavior such as response latency in the primary task (Son and Kornell 2005) or expectation of reinforcement, an implicit but not explicit index of memory strength. Indeed, human subjects' metacognitive judgements may be also based on such factors (Metcalfe and Kober 2005; Koriat 2007).

Information-seeking: Metamemory or behavioral conflict?

In everyday life, we often employ metamemory implicitly in the control of information-seeking, as when feeling it's necessary to look in the phone book before dialing. Rhesus macaques were tested for such an ability with a naturalistic task in which they watched the experimenter put a treat into one of four opaque tubes and then had one chance to retrieve it (Hampton, Zivin, and Murray 2004). In preliminary trials they learned that with a little effort they could peer into the tubes to locate the reward before choosing. On probe trials with baiting done behind a screen, monkeys peered down the tubes before choosing more often than when they had seen the tubes baited. Looking increased their rate of success over that on trials on which they chose a tube without looking first. Most importantly, they began looking appropriately right away, before they could have learned to use the screen as a discriminative stimulus. Similar behavior is shown by apes (chimpanzees and orangutans) as well as children (Call and Carpenter 2001), but it is more difficult to demonstrate in capuchins, a species of new world monkey (Basile et al. 2008; Paukner, Anderson, and Fujita 2006). Analogously, in a difficult serial learning task rhesus monkeys chose costly "hints" early in learning new lists but not later on (Kornell, Son, and Terrace 2007).

Unlike in other procedures discussed so far, in the tubes task the opportunity to make the metacognitive response occurs simultaneously with the test. Therefore, the animals' behavior could reflect competing tendencies among responses learned to currently present cues (Hampton 2009). With baiting visible, monkeys have acquired a strong tendency to pull the tube that has just been baited. Looking into one or more tubes and then pulling was also specifically trained, but because it is reinforced only after a delay, looking is not such a strong response as pulling when the baited tube is known. But the tendency to

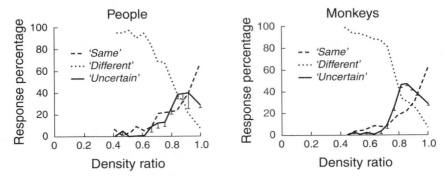

Figure 7.21. Display used to test metacognition in monkeys and people. If the two rectangles at the top of the screen had the same pixel density, touching them was rewarded; if they were different, touching the D was rewarded. Touching the star signified "uncertain" and led to an easy trial after a short delay. The lower panels show average data from 6 people and two rhesus macaques. Adapted from Shields, Smith, and Washburn (1997) with permission.

pull a specific tube is weak when the tubes are presented after an unseen baiting, so the looking response is expressed.

Several other tests of both metamemory and perceptual certainty share with the tubes task the property that a metacognitive "escape" or "uncertain" response is presented simultaneously with the test of cognition (J. Smith et al. 2008; Hampton 2009). Some of the first tests of animal metacognition to be reported involved difficult perceptual tasks in which the animal classified stimuli as bright or dim, high or low, or the like (see J. Smith, Shields, and Washburn 2003). A third "uncertain" option was presented along with the two response options associated with the two stimulus classes. The uncertain response, leading to a delayed or otherwise reduced reinforcement, was usually chosen most when the stimulus to be classified was near the threshold of discriminability. An elegant feature of some of these studies was that human subjects were given the same tests and showed the same pattern of data as the other species tested (e.g., Shields, Smith, and Washburn 1997; Shields et al. 2005). Figure 7.21 shows an example from a diffucult perceptual task (Shields et al. 1997). When people choose the "uncertain" option in such studies, they say they experience a feeling of uncertainty, but whatever the subjective states of the animals here, behavior consistent with metacognition in these tests can be completely accounted for in terms of learned contingencies and the resulting competing response tendencies (J. Smith et al. 2008).

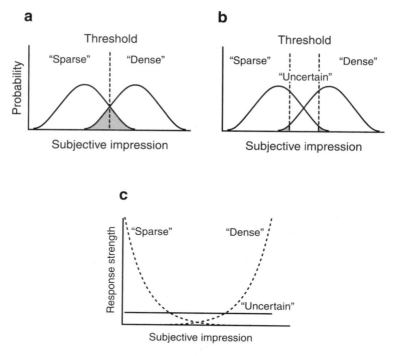

Figure 7.22. Signal detection analysis of a difficult perceptual task. a. Subjects forced to classify the density of pixels as "sparse" or "dense" set a criterion in the middle, but because their subjective impressions of the stimuli overlap, they will inevitably make the proportion of errors indicated by the shaded areas. b. When subjects are allowed an escape or "uncertain" option, using it in the region where the distributions overlap decreases the proportion of errors in trials they choose to complete. c. The response strengths for the three options in situation b when escaping is followed by a reinforcer smaller than that given for classifying the stimuli correctly. Panel c after J. Smith et al. (2008) with permission.

Figure 7.22 shows how the argument goes for a difficult perceptual discrimination. As we know from signal detection theory (Chapter 3), stimuli have a range of subjective effects. The more difficult a discrimination, the more these will overlap. With symmetrical distributions and equal reward for classifying all stimuli correctly, the threshold is located as in Figure 7.22a. Inevitably subjects will make errors, corresponding to the shaded areas of the figure. When an escape or "uncertain" response that receives a mediocre reward is available whatever stimulus is present, it will be the strongest response near the threshold subjective value (Figure 7.22c). In this situation, subjects behave as if partitioning the stimulus continuum as in Figure 7.22b, a situation that results in a higher proportion of correct responses on chosen than on forced trials.

Conclusions

As an account of behavior consistent with metacognition, the analysis in Figure 7.22 (developed by J. Smith et al. 2008) applies most directly to perceptual discriminations in which the escape or "uncertain" option is presented simultaneously with the primary task, as in Figure 7.21. For it to be applicable to a metamemory task, memory strength must be treated as a stimulus continuum, but this amounts to assuming animals are sensitive to the strength of their own memories, which is supposedly being tested in the first place. In any case, although there is now a substantial body of data from monkeys, rats, and a dolphin from a variety of tests of metacognition, nearly all of them are subject to interpretation as direct responses to publicly available cues (J. Smith. 2008; Hampton 2009). The chief exception is Hampton's (2001) experiment. It is one of the few in which the metacognitive response was made before the direct cognitive test so that the animal could respond nonrandomly only by consulting some private cue, a situation impossible to arrange in tests of perceptual certainty.

One response to this state of affairs (J. Smith et al. 2008) is to suggest that "true" animal metacognition must be pursued in situations devoid of differential reinforcement for expressing subjective uncertainty. This suggestion flies in the face of the notion that testing animals for an unknown and difficult-to-observe capacity requires a situation in which reward is contingent on using the capacity, as in the study of bats' echolocation discussed in Chapter 3. Another response is to accept that only very limited paradigms can isolate responses to private cues, or at least have done so up to now (Hampton 2009). Animals may behave in the adaptive ways characteristic of creatures with metacognition without any higher order representation. The same may be true of people to a greater extent than is usually appreciated (Koriat 2007). An important implication of the analysis in this section is that blanket terms such as *metacognition* can mislead investigators (e.g Sutton and Shettleworth 2008) into thinking that disparate tests provide converging evidence for a single process when different mechanisms underlie successful performance in each one. For instance, meta-cognitive responses in perceptual tasks can be accounted for as direct responses to external cues (Figure 7.22), but this account is harder to sustain for some tests of metamemory, and it would seem to be ruled out entirely when the metacognitive response is made before the test of cognition.

In summary, nearly all the data from tests of metacognition to date can be accounted for in terms of learned responses to external, or "public," cues, although they are also consistent with the animals reporting on a subjective state. One suggestion that the former is not the whole story comes from the fact that pigeons do not behave consistently as if they have any metacognitive ability even though they have been tested with both perceptual and memory tasks with tests of metacognition presented before, concurrently with, and after the choices on the primary task (Inman and Shettleworth 1999; Sole, Shettleworth, and Bennett 2003; Sutton and Shettleworth 2008). Since public associative cues, response competition, sensitivity to reinforcement contingencies and other basic behavioral mechanisms are clearly within the grasp of pigeons, these findings suggest that maybe monkeys have access to some additional process. If studies continue to give results consistent with such a species difference one next step will be to discover whether it is characteristic of mammals versus birds, or whether perhaps the birds discussed in the next session can also show evidence of using private cues in tests of metamemory.

7.6.3   Episodic memory

Episodic memory is memory for specific episodes in one's personal past, as distinguished from *semantic memory,* or memory for facts and ideas. For example, memory for the experience of dinner at Luigi's Restaurant last Saturday night is episodic whereas knowledge about what is involved in having dinner at a restaurant in general is semantic. When it was first discussed (Tulving 1972) episodic memory was defined primarily as a memory for a personal experience, that is, what happened, where, and when. Subsequently, supported by evidence that some people with hippocampal damage have semantic but not episodic memory, the definition of episodic memory evolved to emphasize its conscious component, a feeling of reexperiencing the remembered event (*autonoetic consciousness,* Tulving 2002). It is now (Tulving 2005) further claimed to be part of a uniquely human faculty of "mental time travel," the ability to mentally project oneself into the future as well as into the past (W. Roberts 2002; Suddendorf and Corballis 2007, 2008a; Addis, Wong, and Schacter 2007). We return to this idea at the end of the section, but behavior indicative of future planning is discussed primarily in Chapter 11 in the context of control by delayed reinforcers. This section summarizes current approaches to studying animal episodic memory (for further details see Crystal 2009).

Episodic-like memory in scrub jays

The study of episodic memory in animals began with a landmark experiment by Clayton and Dickinson (1998, 1999) showing that Western scrub jays (*Aphelecoma californica*) remember the location, time, and identity of items they store. They referred to the birds' memory as *episodic-like* because it satisfies the original definition of episodic memory (Tulving 1972) as a memory for what, where, and when of a unique experience but (necessarily) without any evidence of autonoetic consciousness. Jays stored peanuts and waxmoth larvae ("waxworms"), a greatly preferred food, in the sand-filled compartments of plastic ice cube trays placed in their home cages. Each tray was surrounded with a unique arrangement of colored Lego bricks to make it spatially distinct. In several pairs of caching episodes the birds cached peanuts in one side of a tray and waxworms in the other, sometimes in one order and sometimes in the other (Figure 7.23). The two episodes were separated by 120 hours with the opportunity to retrieve items from both sides of the tray four hours after the second caching episode, that is, 124 hours after the first.

In a series of such trials the birds learned that when worms had been cached 124 hours ago they had rotted and become distasteful whereas four hours after caching they were still fresh. Peanuts were always fresh. Thus if the birds could remember where they had cached each type of item and how long ago, they should search for worms when worms had been cached more recently and for peanuts otherwise. This is what they began to do within as few as four matched pairs of caching episodes, and they continued to choose appropriately in tests with no items in the trays, when they could not be using odors or other direct cues (Figure 7.23). Control birds for which worms did not rot always searched for worms first, showing that worms were not simply selectively forgotten. A series of studies with variations of this design (see de Kort, Dickinson, and Clayton 2005) showed that the scrub jays' memory for their caches also integrates location, time, and identity information and can be used flexibly, properties which Clayton and colleagues suggest further qualify it as episodic-like. For example (Clayton, Bussey, and Dickinson 2003), the jays' choices change appropriately when they receive new information about the decay rate of an item during the retention interval.

The findings with scrub jays stimulated analogous studies with mammals, partly in the hope of finding a tractable animal model for neurobiological work (see Morris

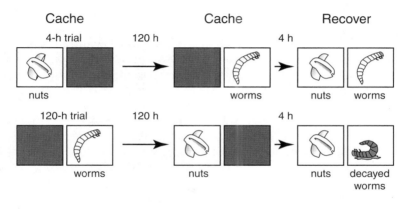

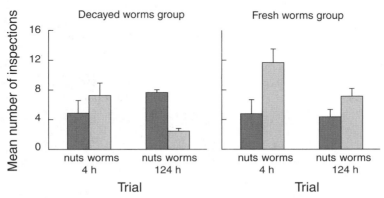

Figure 7.23. Procedure and results for Clayton and Dickinson's (1998) test of episodic memory in scrub jays. Each bird had both types of trials diagrammed at the top; birds in the control group encountered only fresh worms in the recovery phase. Dark squares signify a half of the storing tray unavailable for caching. Lower panels: mean number of inspections directed toward the peanut and worm halves of the tray by birds in the two groups during recovery following both types of trials. After Clayton and Dickinson (1998) with permission.

2001; Eichenbaum et al. 2005; Dere et al. 2006). In the most successful, Babb and Crystal (2006a) demonstrated that rats could remember where in a radial maze a distinctive food (chocolate) had been at a particular time in the past. The first time rats visited the maze on any given trial, a different four of its eight arms were open; three held rat chow and one held chocolate, greatly preferred by the rats. After a retention interval of one or 25 hours, a rat was returned to the maze with all arms open. Rat pellets were in the arms blocked in the first part of the trial; in addition if the retention interval had been 25 hours, chocolate had "replenished," that is, it was back where it had been before. Accordingly, the rats became more likely to visit the chocolate arm within the first four arms visited after the long but not the short retention interval. Once they were performing well, chocolate was degraded by making the rats mildly ill after eating chocolate in their home cages during a 25-hour retention interval. They were much less likely to revisit the chocolate arm on the next test, showing that their memory of the first part of the trial included a representation of a specific food in a specific location (see also Babb and Crystal 2006b; Crystal 2009).

Unexpected questions

Not all agree that the experimental approach pioneered with the scrub jays and adapted for rats is the best or only nonverbal test of episodic memory. One limitation is that the animals are exposed over repeated trials to limited kinds of sequences of events. Correct responding in the tests indisputably requires remembering what was where and how long ago, but the animals' training can be seen as teaching a complex conditional matching to sample task based on trace strength and/or time since the study episode (Zentall et al. 2001; W. Roberts 2002; Eichenbaum et al. 2005; W. Roberts et al. 2008). In contrast, episodic memory in people involves the spontaneous encoding of unique experiences later reported on by answering an unexpected question (Zentall 2005a). Zentall and colleagues (Zentall et al. 2001) cleverly demonstrated that pigeons can "answer an unexpected question" by first training them to "report" whether they had just pecked or not; that is, occurrence or nonoccurrence of pecking was the discriminative stimulus for a color choice. When the opportunity to "report" was introduced into a second context following pecks induced in another way, the birds made the choice previously associated with pecking on about 70% of the first four trials. However, although this study may have captured one aspect of episodic memory, it was memory that had lasted only a few seconds whereas episodic memories in people may be long-term memories (Hampton and Schwartz 2004).

Habituation and episodic-like memory

This drawback is not shared by the test of habituation depicted in Figure 7.3, which can be interpreted (Eacott and Norman 2004) as tapping episodic-like memory in rats. This interpretation depends on the idea that the temporal aspect of human episodic memory is experienced not so much as a specific time ("in July 2003"), but as a context of other experiences ("during my trip to Kenya"). In the situation used by Eacott and Norman (2004; see Figure 7.3), rats' spontaneous exploratory behavior showed that they remembered which side of a chamber and against which colored background (context) a particular object was on up to 30 minutes ago. These findings were obtained after fairly brief exposures; allowing the rats to explore each of the training configurations for longer would likely result in longer-lasting memories. In any case, this paradigm shares two important features with the "unexpected question" paradigm for pigeons. The animals show what they have encoded spontaneously, and because no specific reinforcement is involved they cannot be encoding the experiences in the first phase of trials in preparation for being asked about them later. This and related habituation paradigms have been used effectively in neurobiological studies of episodic like memory in rats and mice (Dere et al. 2006; Crystal 2009).

Remembering versus knowing

In tests of recognition memory in the laboratory, people may be asked whether they remember seeing an item before or merely know it was shown. "Remembering" in this context is identified with episodic recollection whereas "knowing" is simply a sense of familiarity. The everyday counterpart of remembering versus knowing is the difference between a rich recollection of a previous encounter with someone and merely knowing one has seen them somewhere before. When the results of forced choice tests of recognition are represented as ROC curves (Box 7.3), the data can be decomposed into "remember" and "know" components, although this interpretation is somewhat controversial (Yonelinas and Parks 2007). The same pattern can be reproduced in rats' olfactory recognition (Box 7.3; Fortin, Wright, and Eichenbaum 2004). Moreover, consistent with evidence from humans and with the results from serial probe recognition described in Box 7.2, hippocampal lesions selectively affect the "remember" component. What the hippocampus does in rats other than record episodic memories (if that) is at least as controversial as how best to test nonverbally for episodic memory, so this evidence is hardly conclusive. However, because people require an intact hippocampus for episodic memory, dependence on the hippocampus can be seen as one of the necessary if not sufficient properties of episodic-like memory in another mammal (Eichenbaum et al. 2005; Ferbinteanu, Kennedy, and Shapiro 2006). In summary then, the findings described in Boxes 7.2 and 7.3 together with others such as data from Eacott and Norman's (2004) habituation paradigm indicate that rats' memory for recently presented items shares many functional properties with human episodic memory (Hampton and Schwartz 2004; Eichenbaum et al. 2005; Ferbinteanu, Kennedy, and Shapiro 2006; Crystal 2009).

Box 7.2 Olfactory Memory in Rats

Although rats are nocturnal, lack color vision, and have rather poor visual acuity (Prusky and Douglas 2005), traditional studies of rats' discrimination learning (Chapter 6) relied heavily and anthropocentrically on visual cues. But rats are much better able to discriminate among and learn about flavors and odors, and recent studies have capitalized on this ability to study their memory, often with the aim of analyzing its neural basis. A very effective and simple procedure involves allowing the rat to dig in a small sand-filled bowl to find food buried at the bottom. Odors are introduced by mixing common household spices or other substances into the sand. Perhaps partly because they come into direct contact with the odors while digging for food, rats quickly learn to discriminate familiar from novel odors and can discriminate up to 10 or more sequentially presented odors from other familiar odors presented on previous days (see Box 7.3). Visual cues and textures on the bowls are also effective cues in such a digging task (Botly and De Rosa 2007) as are the materials in the bowls (Sauvage et al. 2008).

A continuous non–matching to sample task with odors (Wood, Dudchenko, and Eichenbaum 1999) consists of letting rats encounter one sand-filled cup at a time, each in a different random location in an open field. If its odor differs from the odor of the last cup presented, it holds food and the rat digs; if the odor is the same, there is no food and rats learn to withhold digging and turn away. Then another cup is presented, and the same rule holds, and so on. (Note that various controls, such as unbaited probe trials, are always included in such studies to show that the rats are not smelling the food in baited bowls.) In a more elaborate variant of this task diagrammed in Figure B7.2, a series of five odors, A–E, is presented, a different selection from 20 familiar odors on each trial (Fortin, Agster, and Eichenbaum 2002). Memory for items in the sequence can be tested in a serial probe recognition procedure in which the rat is given a choice between an odor from the current sequence (unrewarded) and an odor not in the sequence (rewarded). As shown in Figure B7.2, recognition is excellent, with a clear recency effect, that is, better performance for items at the end of the sequence.

Memory for relative position in the sequence can also be tested by presenting two odors from the sequence and rewarding choice of the earlier one. Rats display excellent memory for sequential order in this test. Not surprisingly, performance is better with odors farther apart in the sequence. Rats trained in the sequence memory task and then given hippocampal lesions showed normal recognition memory but their discrimination of relative position was severely impaired (Figure B7.2). Thus the lesioned rats had nearly normal memory traces in that they could discriminate odors in the present list from those in earlier lists about as well as intact rats, yet their near-chance performance in the sequential order task suggests that this task calls upon a different mechanism than comparing trace strengths (see also Kesner, Gilbert, and

Barua 2002). One possibility discussed in Section 7.6.3 is that the list is encoded as a series of events much like an episode. Whether this analogy is accepted or not, the way in which lesions dissociate simple recognition from memory for sequential order is a nice example of how the results of neurobiological research can inform theory at the level of "black box" mechanisms.

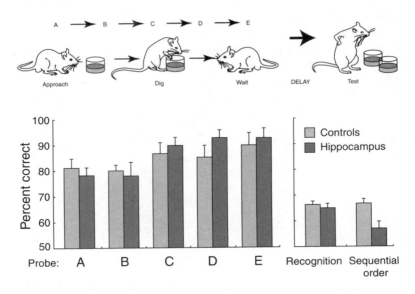

Figure B7.2. Procedure and data from tests of rats' memory for sequences of odors. In the exposure phase, the rat encounters five odors, A–E, 2.5 minutes apart. In the test (top right), recognition is tested by offering one odor from the list and one not in the most recent list; choice of the latter is rewarded. Memory for sequential order is tested by offering two odors from the list and rewarding choice of the one presented first. From Fortin, Agster, and Eichenbaum (2002) with permission.

Box 7.3 Familiarity, Recollection, and Signal Detection

Just as in tests of perception, in tests of memory the behavior taken as evidence of an underlying cognitive process can occur for other reasons. The pigeon in a delayed matching experiment might prefer to peck a red key rather than a green one regardless of which was the sample, or a rat might prefer to visit some arms of a radial maze rather than others. Signal detection analysis (Chapter 3) again provides a way to distinguish such response biases from effects on memory. In studies of human recognition memory, ROC curves can be generated when subjects study a list of words and are tested by presenting words from the list along with an equal number of words not in the list. Subjects classify each word as "new" or "old." Saying "old" to words in the list is a hit; "old" for a new word is a false alarm, as if subject is making a discrimination among memory traces that overlap in strength much as perceptual effects do (see Figure 7.22).

Data along a given ROC curve may be collected either by varying subjects' criteria (e.g., "say 'old' only if you're very sure") or by collecting confidence ratings along with "new" versus "old" responses. Figure B7.3 shows an example. Unlike the ROC curves in Chapter 3, it is asymmetrical. With a high criterion, saying "old" only when they are very sure, nearly all subjects' "old" responses are correct and very few are false alarms. This asymmetry has been interpreted as meaning that performance is the sum of two separate processes: recollection or episodically remembering the item, which is an all-or-none or threshold process, and familiarity or "knowing," which by itself describes a symmetrical ROC curve (Yonelinas and Parks 2007). In normal adults, different instructions may dissociate these processes; in amnesic patients, only the second process may be evident.

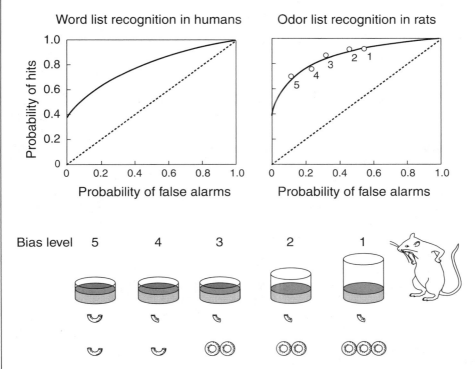

Figure B7.3. Typical ROC curve from tests of word recognition in which people rate test words as "old" (i.e., in the studied list) or "new" and data from rats in a test of odor recognition. Rats are reinforced for digging in a test cup with an odor not in the list and digging in a standard alternative cup for "old" odors. For the five bias levels, the rats' criterion was varied as indicated in the diagram. For example, at bias level 1, a high level of false alarms (choosing "old") results from a relatively large reward (three whole cereal pieces) for digging in the neutral cup versus a small reward in a tall test cup, difficult to dig in. Adapted from Fortin, Wright, and Eichenbaum (2004) with permission.

In a forced choice test of odor recognition using a procedure similar to that diagrammed in Figure B7.2, rats encountered ten odors in succession and were tested 30 minutes later with these and ten other odors (Fortin, Wright, and Eichenbaum 2004). They were rewarded for digging in test cups with new odors and for digging in an alternative, neutral, cup when an "old" odor was present in the test cup. The criterion was varied by varying both the height of the test cup and the amount of reward for choosing the "old odor" cup as diagrammed in Figure B7.3. Intact rats' recognition data (Figure B7.3) described an asymmetrical ROC curve much like normal humans.' As discussed in the main text, these findings can be taken to support claims that rats have episodic-like memory.

Signal detection theory has been applied to many other issues in the study of animal as well as human memory (Marston 1996). Examples include the work of Wixted (1993) on pigeons' delayed matching with samples of food and no food and Blough's (1996) analysis of the sources of errors in delayed matching tasks. Shettleworth and Krebs (1982) used ROC curves to show that both caching site preferences and memory contribute to marsh tits' retrieval of stored seeds in the laboratory.

Conclusions: Elements of episodic memory?

All the experimental approaches sketched in this section involve testing memory for the "what, where, and when" of some unique recent event. Some paradigms go beyond demonstrating that animals pass a single test to documenting further functional similarities between the animals' behavior and human reports of episodic memory. The variety of approaches that has developed might be taken as welcome evidence of a search for convergent data, but they also reflect the fact that no one approach to date has captured all aspects of human episodic memory in another species. This diversity is consistent with the broad use of the term among students of human memory. For instance, Tulving (e.g., 2005) describes episodic memory in terms of vividly recollected personal experiences, but studies of comparatively short-term memory for lists of items in the laboratory (e.g., Kohler, Moscovitch, and Melo 2001) are also described as testing episodic memory. Accordingly, both the original Clayton and Dickinson paradigm, with memories lasting hours or days, and studies with rats remembering odors or locations of objects for a few minutes are legitimate candidates for animal analogues. Arguably (Crystal 2009) the disparate tests for episodic-like memory each tap one or more of its elements. Other elements include whether the features of an episode are integrated in memory or treated as separate items of information (Skov-Rackette, Miller, and Shettleworth 2006) and whether the temporal component, if any, is time of day, time in the past, or something else (Roberts. et al. 2008).

We will see elsewhere that breaking some global ability such as counting (Chapter 10), theory of mind (Chapter 12), or communication (Chapter 14) into components and asking which are shared among which species, to what degree, and why (in functional and mechanistic senses) can be a more productive approach to comparative research than asking all-or-nothing questions about whether animals have the ability in question or not. The study of animal episodic-like memory has progressed in this way. It leads to the provisional conclusion that a variety of species, even some invertebrates (Pahl. et al. 2007), share with humans a propensity to encode the "what, where, and when" of unique events and that some of these memories share other functional properties of human episodic memory. It is possible, however, that by eschewing speculation about subjective experience, researchers testing animals are missing the essence of episodic memory, which is that by allowing people to mentally reexperience events it supports "time travel" not only into the past, but into the future, to imagine and plan for entirely new kinds of events in a way that is impossible on the basis of learned responses to old events (Suddendorf and Corballis 2008a). Indeed, episodic memory has most likely evolved so people can imagine and plan for the future, not so they can relive the past. On this view (Suddendorf and Corballis 2008a), the functional similarities between nonhuman and human memory reviewed in this section fail to capture a key—and uniquely human—feature of episodic memory. We revisit this discussion in Chapter 11.

7.7   Summary and conclusions

Memory is the most general term for the process that allows animals to base their behavior on information from individual past experience. The questions we can ask about memory therefore parallel those asked about learning in Chapters 4 and 5: what are the conditions under which memories are acquired, the contents of memory, and the effects of memory on behavior? Accordingly, many of the conditions affecting memory parallel those affecting learning. These include frequency, duration, and number of exposures to the to-be-remembered events, proactive and retroactive interference from previous, similar experiences, and the similarity between the current context and that in which the memory was acquired. Most such conditions are thought to be important regardless of what is to be remembered, suggesting that even if it is possible to identify different memory systems in some sense (Sherry and Schacter 1987) they will have a number of common properties. Much contemporary research on animal memory is devoted to analyzing its neural and genetic basis, often using simple paradigms introduced in this and earlier chapters.

Since before the beginning of experimental studies of animal cognition, people have wondered whether some animals have better memories than others. Section 7.4 examined several research programs inspired by this question, including early comparative studies of delayed response, recent ecologically based comparisons of closely related species that rely on spatial memory to differing extents in the wild, and comparisons of serial position effects in pigeons, monkeys, rats, and people. Any attempt to collect meaningful comparative data on memory faces a number of challenging problems such as to how to deal with possible contextual variables. The research reviewed here has revealed at most quantitative differences among species in capacity and durability of memory.

Finally, Section 7.6 introduces attempts to devise nonverbal tests for processes that are accompanied by distinctive subjective states in humans, here metacognition and episodic memory. In a number of situations animals show behavior consistent with metacognition, but nearly all the data to date can be explained in terms of sensitivity to publicly observable cues rather than to private states. Research on episodic memory has largely focused on tests that capture one or more of its key elements, especially formation of an integrated memory for the "what, where, and when" of a unique experience, referred to as episodic-like memory. A variety of species, in a variety of situations, show at least elements of episodic memory. The important notion of functional similarity, or focusing on what cognitive processes allow animals to do rather than on the subjective states that accompany them, is illustrated very well with research on metamemory and episodic-like memory. It will also come in handy in future chapters.

Further reading

The development of contemporary research on animal memory and other aspects of cognition can be traced in a series of edited books. Medin, Roberts, and Davis (1976); Hulse, Fowler, and Honig (1978); and Roitblat, Bever, and Terrace (1984) are among the landmarks. Chapters in Wasserman and Zentall (2006b) review more recent work. *The Science of Memory: Concepts* (Roediger, Dudai, and Fitzpatrick 2007) contains brief discussions of all aspects of memory by major researchers in the field. Eichenbaum's (2008) text is a good introduction to neurobiological mechanisms of memory in all species. Bouton and Moody (2004) discuss the interface between conditioning and memory, Balda and Kamil (2006) comprehensively review the research on food-storing corvids, and Wright (2006) does the same for serial order memory. For discussion of metacognition, see the book edited by Terrace and Metcalfe (2005) and the "forum" of pieces by many of the major players in the 2009 edition of the online *Comparative Cognition and Behavior Reviews*.

Part II

Physical Cognition

Each of the next three chapters discusses how animals acquire and use information about a specific aspect of the physical world: space (Chapter 8), time (Chapter 9), and number (Chapter 10). Spatial, temporal, and numerical cognition each involve some domain-general processes as well. For instance, Weber's Law appears in each of Chapters 8–10 as do basic principles of learning, memory, and discrimination. But understanding navigation, timing, and counting also requires some domain specific theoretical concepts and perhaps cognitive mechanisms. Effective spatial behavior inherently involves acquiring and using vector-like information, that is, information about distances and directions. Historically, debate has revolved around suggestions that such information is stored in a maplike representation. This debate continues, as we will see. More recently there have also been suggestions that multiple kinds of spatial information are combined in ways not captured by current models of associative learning. Similarly, analyzing how animals respond to the universal cycle of day and night requires particular concepts such as pacemakers and entraining agents and models of its own which may or may not be applicable to timing events at shorter intervals. And the study of numerical cognition is a burgeoning model for comparative research in the way it integrates complementary experiments with human adults, children, and diverse nonverbal species. The over simple anthropocentric question, "Can animals count?" is now replaced by a clear evolutionary framework in which numerical cognition is seen as consisting of several subprocesses that may be shared among species to different extents.

As its title indicates, Chapter 11, "Cognition and the consequences of behavior: Foraging, planning, instrumental learning, and using tools," differs from the other chapters in this section in discussing a seemingly diverse set of topics. But for each of them the key issue is understanding how a specific kind of activity is influenced by its outcome. In the section on foraging we see how functional models, primarily the predictions of optimal foraging theory, have been brought together with data and theory about the control of instrumental behavior. Then we look more deeply at the kind of learning and representation underlying behavior that is acquired and maintained because of its consequences, along the way returning to and enlarging upon the discussion of associative learning theory in Chapter 4. Finally in the sections on planning and tool use we look at two kinds of behavior traditionally thought to be uniquely human but increasingly found in other species and ask whether they depend on any special processes. Do tool-using apes and birds, for example, understand how tools work?

8
Getting Around: Spatial Cognition

Limpets are small mollusks that live on coastal rocks where they are exposed to the air at low tide. As it grows, each limpet erodes a scar on the rock that matches the irregular outline of its shell. By clinging tightly to this spot during low tide, the limpet can protect itself from dehydration (and from predators, as anyone who has tried to pry one loose can testify), but to find food it must forage over the rock while the water is high (Cook et al. 1969).

Many mobile animals face the same problem as the limpet: food and other resources are separated from places of refuge, and the animal has to be able to travel between them without getting lost. There is a premium on making this trip efficiently rather than wandering at random until the goal is found, which in the limpet's case might be too late to prevent drying out. The limpet's problem is a miniature one in space and time compared to the orientation problems solved by other species (Figure 8.1), but they all have certain features in common. Each individual or group of individuals is locating its own home, hoards, or other resources. Therefore, they need some sort of acquired representation of the goal's location or how to get to it. Some animals, like the limpet, create such a representation in the external world in the form of a chemical trail (Chelazzi 1992). Under some circumstances, animals can find their way by directly approaching cues emanating from their goals or learning sequences of responses. However, we will be most concerned with how animals acquire and use information that is inherently spatial, that is, information about distances and directions. Mathematically, this is vector or shape information. And although long-distance navigation may involve amazing feats of perception, learning, and memory (see Box 8.1), we will be almost entirely concerned with travels of a meter or less to at most a few kilometers.

Because acquiring and acting on spatial information appears to have different computational requirements from learning to predict temporal sequences of events, we might expect to find adaptively specialized, domain-specific mechanisms of spatial learning and/ or performance, different from those for associative learning (F. Dyer 1998; Gallistel 2003). This issue can be addressed in terms of the three fundamental questions about learning from Chapter 4—the conditions for learning, the contents of learning, and its effects on behavior. Spatial performance rules can be thought of as servomechanisms. That is, they generate behavior that reduces the discrepancy between the animal's current position and a remembered target position (Cheng 2000). Although mechanisms for

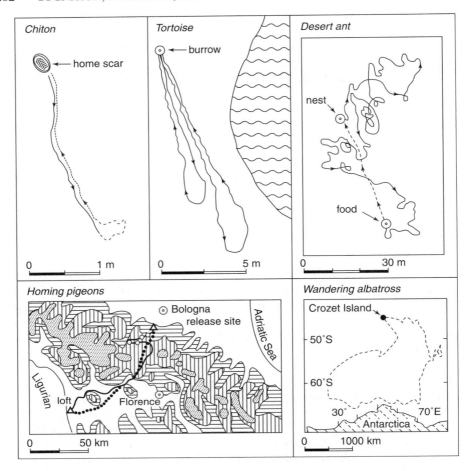

Figure 8.1. Homing paths of individuals from five species, illustrating the wide range of spatial scales over which journeys out from a central place and back may take place. After Papi (1992b). Tortoise from Chelazzi and Francisci (1979); albatross from Jouventin and Weimerskirch (1990). Redrawn with permission.

Box 8.1 Long-Distance Migration

The astonishing ability of animals from all taxa to find their ways over hundreds or thousands of kilometers is a subject in itself (see Alerstam 2006; Holland, Wikelski, and Wilcove 2006). It has been given a huge boost in recent years by sophisticated satellite tracking systems for recording not only the position but the activities, temperatures, and so forth, of migrating animals. The sensory and neural mechanisms required can also be studied in some of the same species (Frost and Mouritsen 2006). Notwithstanding their vastly different scales, however, long-distance and short-distance travels are largely analyzed with the same basic conceptual framework (Bingman and Cheng 2005). Distance, direction, and position information are important however far one is going, and the degree to which it is maplike is an issue whatever its scale.

Probably the longest-standing subjects in studies of the mechanisms for long-distance migration are birds. Among the many species of small birds that migrate at night, even captive hand-reared individuals exhibit nocturnal activity, so-called migratory restlessness, at the time of year when they would normally migrate (see Gwinner 1996). In indoor cages at night they tend to hop toward the compass direction in which their conspecifics are flying at that time of year. Manipulating the early experience of such birds has revealed a kind of interaction between predisposition and experience that might be called *calibration*. Calibrating a physical measuring instrument means comparing its readings to those of an independent standard and adjusting it so its readings match the standard's. An electronic thermometer might be calibrated against a mercury thermometer, for example. Analogously, one orientation mechanism may be changed by experience so that its outputs more closely match those of a second, independent, mechanism. The primary examples involve calibrating celestial cues against magnetic information.

For example, the primary directional cues for nocturnal migrants are the Earth's magnetic field and, on clear nights, the stars, but the pattern of stars varies with geographic location, time of night, and season, and it changes over geologic time. Insight into how birds nevertheless use the stars to tell direction comes from classic experiments by Emlen (1970) with indigo buntings (*Passerina cyanea*). He raised three groups of birds indoors out of sight of the sky, but late in their first summer two of those groups were exposed to the "night sky" in a planetarium. For one, the stars rotated normally, around the North star, whereas for the other the center of rotation was the bright star Betelgeuse. When all the birds then spent autumn nights in the planetarium under stationary star patterns typical for the time of year, the birds with no experience of the sky were not well oriented, but those exposed to the normal sky oriented Southward, indicating that they had somehow learned to use the stationary star patterns during earlier exposure to the normal night sky. The third group treated Betelgeuse as the North star, flying "south" with respect to it, indicating that the star or star pattern near the center of rotation of the night sky is used to give direction. Magnetic information interacts with this information during normal development (see Able and Bingman 1987; Able and Able 1990; Weindler, Wiltschko, and Wiltschko 1996).

Some species change direction in midjourney, following routes that take them around inhospitable places like the Alps and the Sahara. Young birds raised in captivity show evidence of population-specific genetic programs that specify the duration of migratory restlessness and its direction with respect to the magnetic field (Helbig 1994, 1996). Figure B8.1 shows an example in which two European populations of a single species, the blackcap (*Sylvia atricapilla*), migrate in different directions, and one changes course part way while the other does not. Such inborn tendencies to head in a certain compass direction at a certain season are likely important for the many species in which animals migrating for the first time are not accompanied by experienced adults. This likely includes sea turtles and at least one insect, the Monarch butterfly (Holland, Wikelski, and Wilcove 2006). At the same time, the success of programs for reintroducing migratory bird species to their ancestral flyways by training them to follow ultralight aircraft (www.operationmigration.org) indicates that some species learn details of their migratory routes.

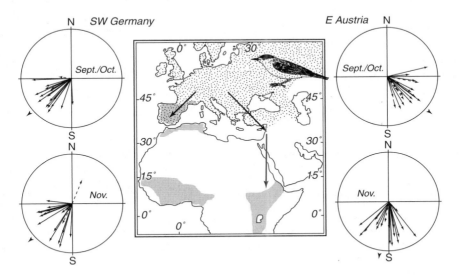

Figure B8.1. Breeding (dotted) and wintering areas (grey) of two populations of European blackcaps with their major migration routes. Arrows inside the circles represent orientation of hand raised birds from the two populations tested in funnel cages early and late during the period when they would normally be migrating. Each vector is the mean orientation of a single bird; the longer the arrow the stronger the directional tendency. Redrawn from Helbig (1994) with permission.

reading out where to go from information about where one is are far from simple (Biegler 2006), the effects of spatial learning on behavior are generally taken for granted: the animal reaches the goal in the presence of the appropriate cues. Much more attention has been devoted to the content of spatial learning. In practical terms, this means discovering what features of the goal control behavior. The most controversial question about the content of spatial learning is "Do animals have cognitive maps?" That is, is spatial orientation in complex environments controlled by an overall representation of distances and directions that allows the animal to select an efficient route when displaced to a new location? This question turns out to be difficult to answer, for two reasons. First, although a map is a powerful metaphor for spatial knowledge, different investigators may mean different things by *cognitive map*. Second, before we can consider whether any animal might have a cognitive map in any sense, we need to consider all the simpler mechanisms animals can use to find their ways to goals (Section 8.1). and how they may be combined (Section 8.2). Section 8.3 discusses how animals acquire spatial knowledge, especially whether any processes different from associative learning are involved. Then, in Section 8.4, we will assess the evidence for cognitive maps.

8.1   Mechanisms for spatial orientation

8.1.1   Dead reckoning

A foraging desert ant (*Cataglyphis fortis*) wanders here and there, taking a long and tortuous path in its search for food, but as soon as it finds a prey item it heads straight back to its nest over a hundred meters away (see Figure 8.1). These ants return to the vicinity of the nest using *dead reckoning*, an internal sense of the direction and distance of the nest from their current position. That they know both distance and direction can be shown by catching an ant in a matchbox just before it starts its homeward journey and releasing it several hundred meters away. It does not head for the nest but takes a path parallel to that which it would have taken from the point of capture. For instance, if the nest was originally to its south, the ant still heads south even if the nest is now to the east (Wehner 1992, 2003). Moreover, when it has gone about the right distance, the ant begins to circle around as if looking for the nest in the place where it should be (Figure 8.2). This behavior shows that the ant must be performing *path integration* on the outward journey. That is, it behaves as if continuously integrating (in the mathematical sense) information about its changes in distance and direction to compute the vector that links it to the nest.

In fact, ants use an approximation in which each direction taken, as perceived by its solar compass (Box 8.2) is weighted by the distance for which it is maintained (Muller and Wehner 1988). The orientation of the straight path reveals the ant's representation of the homeward direction, and the point at which it begins to circle around reveals its representation of the distance from start to nest. Once the ant arrives near where the nest should be, it continues to perform the same implicit computations. Although taking a roughly spiral path, it continually returns to the point where it began searching, as if keeping track of its position with respect to the most likely nest position. This localized search seems to be programmed to overcome the inherent errors of path integration in that the further an ant has traveled from the nest, the wider its spiraling loops when it returns to the nest's vicinity (Wehner and Srinivasan 1981; Merkle, Knaden, and Wehner 2006). This behavior increases the chances that the nest is found, which is vital because the hot sand surface can be lethal to ants that do not escape underground quickly enough.

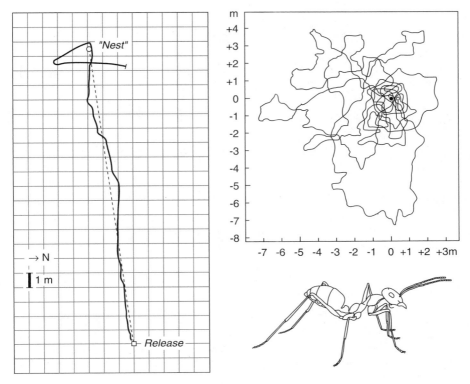

Figure 8.2. Homing in desert ants (*Cataglyphis albicans*). Left: Path of an individual that has just found food and is displaced to unknown territory. The open circle shows where the nest would have been relative to the release site if the ant had been in its home territory. Right: The spiraling path taken by the ant once it arrives near where the nest should be, recorded over one hour. Data redrawn from Wehner and Srinivasan (1981) with permission; ant from Wehner (1992) with permission.

Box 8.2 The Sun Compass

The sun is useless as a landmark because it moves continuously relative to the Earth, but many diurnal animals use it for directional information, that is, they have a *sun compass*. For example, the desert ants in Section 8.1.1 use both the sun and patterns of polarized light it creates in the sky for directional information when computing their paths home from food (Wehner and Müller 2006). If an ant is trained to a food source on a featureless patch of desert at one time of day and then kept in the dark for a few hours, it heads roughly homeward when released even though its direction relative to the sun's position is different from what it was during training. That they are still relying on the sun rather than some subtle landmarks is shown by the fact that ants prevented from seeing the sun in this experiment head off in random directions (Wehner and Lanfranconi 1981).

Reading direction from the sun regardless of the time of day requires both a stored representation of how the sun moves across the sky at the current location and season (an *ephemeris function*) and an internal circadian clock (Chapter 9). The sun's position overhead is converted to a compass direction (i.e., direction relative to North) by computing the sun's *azimuth*. This means taking the imaginary arc connecting the sun with the closest point on the horizon and measuring the angle on the surface of the earth between that point and North (Figure B8.2a). This kind of computation is implied by statements like "The sun is in the South" at noon in the Northern hemisphere. But although the sun *is* in the South at noon, because the sun's elevation at a given time of day changes with the time of year, the sun's azimuth changes at different rates at different times of year and at different times of day (Figure B8.2a). Thus to use the sun for directional information, animals must acquire some

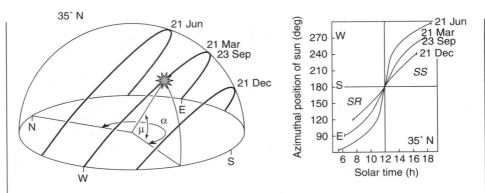

Figure B8.2a. How the apparent path of the sun across the sky (arcs) varies with time of year at a particular latitude, 35° North. Angle α on the surface of the earth is the sun's azimuth; μ is the sun's elevation. Ephemeris functions (right) give the sun's azimuth as a function of time of day and time of year. After Wehner (1992) with permission.

representation of the local ephemeris function and continually update it. This process has been studied in honeybees by restricting the experience of newly hatched foragers when they first leave the hive (F. Dyer and Dickinson 1994). The results indicate that, in a kind of process general to many kinds of learning, bees begin life with a crude default ephemeris function, a best guess about the conditions they are likely to meet, and experience fine-tunes it (F. Dyer and Dickinson 1996).

To show definitively that an animal is using a sun compass it is necessary to shift its internal clock and test whether orientation shifts accordingly. (As discussed in Chapter 9, shifting the clock means keeping the animal under an altered day-night light cycle for several days.) The logic of clock shift experiments is depicted in Figure B8.2b with a hypothetical example using bees. Homing pigeons have also been tested extensively in such experiments (Papi and Wallraff 1992). Of course in laboratory studies of small-scale spatial learning, animals cannot use a sun compass because the

Figure B8.2b. The logic of clock shift experiments, showing how to tell which way a clock-shifted animal will head. In this example, a bee trained to find food in the position indicated has its clock shifted back 3 hours by turning the lights on 3 hours later in the morning. At 9 AM it experiences the time as 6 AM. When it flies from the hive it will maintain the same angle to the sun as when heading to the goal at 6 am before clock shifting.

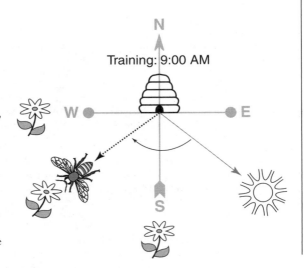

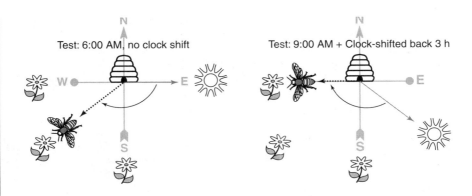

Figure B8.2b. (Continued)

sun is not visible. However, some birds have proved to use the sun compass in learning simple spatial discriminations outdoors under sunny skies. These include homing pigeons (Bingman and Jones 1994; Chappell and Guilford 1995), scrub jays (W. Wiltschko and Balda 1989), and black-capped chickadees (Sherry and Duff 1996). For example, when scrub jays were clock-shifted by 6 hours between storing and retrieving seeds in an outdoor arena, the birds relied on their sun compass in spite of the fact that distant landmarks were visible outside the arena. However, the relative importance of the sun compass vs. other spatial information will vary with species and circumstances as suggested by the discussion of pigeons' homing in the main text.

Dead reckoning is one of the most basic and ubiquitous ways in which animals keep track of their location with respect to a known position. (*Dead reckoning* is a navigators' term; it is generally used interchangeably with *path integration*.) It has been studied most in insects such as ants, bees, and spiders (Wehner and Srinivasan 2003). Indeed, although possible examples of dead reckoning in humans were noted by Darwin (1873), its role in spatial learning by rats and other small mammals was almost completely overlooked before Mittelstaedt and Mittelstaedt (1980) described it in gerbils (*Meriones unguiculatus*). In the situation they studied, mother gerbils and their pups had a nest at the edge of a large circular arena. If the pups were taken from the nest and placed in a cup somewhere in the arena, the mother soon began to search for them. When she found the pups, she picked one up in her mouth and ran almost straight back to the nest, even in total darkness and even if her outward path had zigzags and detours. If the nest was moved by rotating the edge of the arena while the mother was at the stationary cup, she returned to the starting point of her journey like the desert ant, ignoring any cues emanating from the nest in its new location. In contrast, if the cup was rotated briskly while the mother gerbil was in it, she compensated for the rotation and headed straight back to the nest as before. But if the cup was rotated slowly or slowly moved sideways, the gerbil did not compensate and was misoriented. The effect of rotation speed reflects that fact that in mammals information about changes in angular orientation is processed by the vestibular system, which senses accelerations and decelerations above a certain threshold (McNaughton, Knierim, and Wilson 1995; Wallace et al. 2002).

More extensive studies like these have been done by Etienne and her colleagues with golden hamsters (*Mesocricetus auratus*) hoarding food from the center of an arena back to their nest and increasingly with rats (Etienne and Jeffery 2004). Geese carried in a cart up to a kilometer or so from their home also appear to home by dead reckoning (Saint Paul 1982). They obtain information about displacement from the patterns of visual flow. If they cannot see out of the cart for parts of the outward journey, they act as if discounting this part of the trip. This intriguing little study has apparently never been followed up, and few further observations relevant to path integration in birds have been reported. Pigeons show little evidence of relying on visual flow for position information in a laboratory task (Sutton and Shettleworth 2005). In contrast, a great deal is known about how ants and bees compute distances and directions of travel from visual and other cues (Boxes 8.2 and 8.3). Reliance on nonvisual, vestibular, cues for direction is especially appropriate for nocturnal species like hamsters and rats. However, although the sensory inputs are very different in mammals and insects, the implicit computations on them are similar. For example, when forced to take an outward journey consisting of two segments connected at a given angle, ants, spiders, bees, and several species of mammals make similar angular errors when heading home (Etienne and Jeffery 2004).

Box 8.3. Odometers of Honeybees and Desert Ants

We see in the main text that honeybees and desert ants behave as if having an *odometer,* a mechanism for measuring distance traveled. But bees generally fly whereas ants walk, and the odometers of the two species use correspondingly different information. For flying honeybees, distance is measured by *optic flow,* the angular motion of images past the eyes. Evidence comes from experiments such as the one diagrammed in Figure B8.3a, in which bees flew down a tunnel decorated with vertical black and white stripes to find sugar water (Srinivasan et al. 1996). With the food at a fixed location, bees learn where to expect it as evidenced by their circling around over the usual place of food in unrewarded tests. When image motion was eliminated by replacing the vertical stripes by horizontal ones for the tests, the bees searched equally at all distances. When the tunnel was wider or narrower than usual, the bees searched at a greater or lesser distances respectively (Figure B8.3a). To understand why the effect of the tunnel's width, that is, the distance of images from the eyes, means that angular image motion is important, think of how nearby objects cross your visual field faster than those farther away when you are in a moving car. Changing the density of the pattern inside the tunnel also changes the rate of image motion, and accordingly, in natural landscapes the bees' subjective estimates of distance as revealed in their dances (Section 14.2.1) is greater when they have flown over a richly patterned landscape than when they have flown the same distance over water (Tautz et al. 2004).

Desert ants walk across rather featureless terrain. Accordingly they estimate distance using about the only cue available, the number of steps they have taken. In the most direct demonstration that the ant's odometer is in fact a pedometer, ants that had walked along a straight channel from the nest to food were captured before starting home and fitted with stilts made of pig bristle or made to walk on stumps by painlessly removing the last segment of their legs (Wittlinger, Wehner, and Wolf 2007). Then they were released in a long parallel test channel and—as in the tests with bees—the point at which they began circling around searching for the nest was recorded. The altered ants walked in a remarkably normal way. As a result those with stilts went too far, and those with stumps not far enough (Test 1 in Figure B8.3b). In contrast, ants that had stilts or stumps throughout a whole round trip estimated the nest location accurately (Test 2 in Figure B8.3b).

Normally ants compute a straight homeward path by path integration over a winding outward journey as in Figure 8.2. What if part of the journey is over hilly terrain? Remarkably, the ant's pedometer compensates for hills, perhaps relying on gravity sensors in the joints (Grah, Wehner, and Ronacher 2005). Ants that either left the nest over a hilly channel and were transferred to a flat

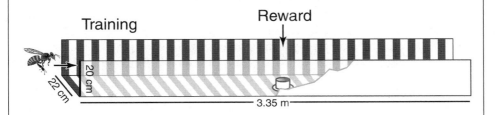

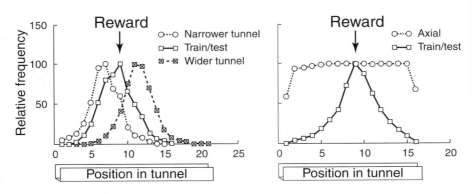

Figure B8.3a. Setup and results of experiment testing influence of visual flow on distance estimation in honeybees. The data are proportions of searches, normalized to 100 at the peak place of searching. The measure of position in the tunnel is number of vertical stripes. All bees were trained to the same position, the one used for trials marked "train/test" but then tested with wider and narrower tunnels or axial stripes in the same tunnel (right panel). Adapted from Srinivasan et al. (1996) with permission.

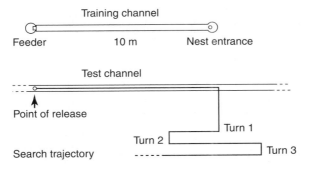

Figure B8.3b. Data from test of odometry in ants on stilts and stumps that was otherwise analogous to the study with bees in B8.3a. Adapted from Wittlinger, Wehner, and Wolf (2006) with permission.

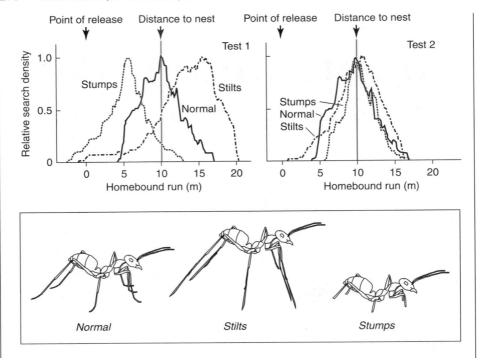

Figure B8.3b. (Continued).

channel to home or the reverse searched for the nest at the correct distance over the ground (Wohlgemuth, Ronacher, and Wehner 2001). And when ants that had traveled around a bend and over a steep "hill" to find food were released on open ground, they headed in the correct direction to find the nest and searched for it at the correct distance from the release point (Grah, Wehner, and Ronacher 2005). That is, they behaved like ants that had traveled to the same feeder over flat ground, not ants that had walked the same number of steps.

The similarities between Figures B8.3a and B8.3b imply that bees and ants compute distances using essentially the same implicit countinglike process but on qualitatively different inputs. We know very little about whether and how any mammals, for example nocturnal rodents, sense distance traveled as such. Most laboratory studies of path integration in rats or hamsters test primarily its directional component: in a confined space, animals can choose which way to head but have little choice in how far to go.

Dead reckoning is a mechanism for *egocentric* spatial localization, that is, the animal is localizing things in the environment with respect to itself. *Allocentric* (or *geocentric*) mechanisms locate the animal with respect to some external frame of reference such as landmarks or environmental geometry. We have already seen one of the major disadvantages of egocentric mechanisms: if the animal is slowly "blown off course," as by the experimenter moving it, path integration does not necessarily compensate. It also accumulates error. For instance, the more the hamsters have been turned around or have turned themselves around while collecting food from the center of the hoarding arena, the less accurately they return to the nest (Etienne, Maurer, and Saucy 1988).

This makes dead reckoning most useful for comparatively brief round-trip excursions, as does the way it seems to be reset at the start of each new journey (Biegler 2000). A major advantage of dead reckoning is its availability from the first trip into a new part of the environment, before there has been time to learn reliable external cues. This makes it a potential basis for learning other cues. Dead reckoning is not only a one-trial affair, though. When hamsters repeatedly traveled in the dark on a circuitous path to a pile of food, they could still find it when forced to make a novel detour (Etienne et al. 1998), evidently using the vector computations of the dead reckoning system (Figure 8.3).

8.1.2   Beacons

In Mittelstaedt and Mittelstaedt's (1980) experiments, we might have expected odors or sounds from the nest itself to act as a *beacon* for the mother gerbil returning with a wandering pup. Beacons are sometimes referred to in the psychological literature as *proximal cues,* that is, cues close to the goal, as distinct from *distal cues,* the landmarks to be discussed in the next section. (*Local* vs. *global* cues is much the same distinction.) Often animals can use either proximal or distal cues, depending on which are available. A now-classic demonstration was devised by Morris (1981; see Figure 8.4). A rat is placed in a circular pool of water in which it swims until it finds a small dry platform, a plexiglas cylinder standing somewhere in the pool. For some rats, the cylinder is black and visible above the water. Thus the platform can function as a beacon, and because rats would rather be dry than swim, they soon learn to approach it wherever it is in the pool. For other rats, the water is made opaque by the addition of milk, and the platform is transparent and slightly below the water surface. These rats must use distal cues, objects in the room surrounding the pool, to find the platform, and they also quickly learn to approach it, provided it stays in the same place from trial to trial. When the platform is removed on test trials, these rats still head directly to the correct location and swim around it as if searching for the platform (see Figure 8.4). This behavior has typically been taken as evidence for

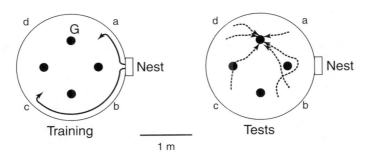

Figure 8.3. Hamsters use long-term memory of a location found by dead reckoning. In training a hamster was repeatedly lured from the nest around the edge of the arena along the two paths shown and then found its own way to the one baited cylinder (G) in darkness. In the tests animals were lured by each of the two possible paths from the nest to each of the four release sites, a–d. Subsequent paths of one hamster to the goal are shown. The paths from the familiar release sites, a and c, are only from trials with the novel path from the nest. After Etienne et al. (1998) with permission.

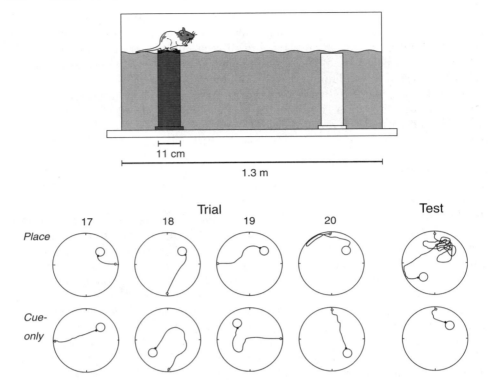

Figure 8.4. The Morris water escape task ("water maze"). At top, a cross section of the pool with a black visible platform and a white platform designed to be invisible to a swimming rat. Bottom: performance on trials 17–20 and a single test trial of one rat trained with the invisible platform always in the same place until the test ("place" condition) and one rat trained with the visible platform in a new place on each trial ("cue only" condition). After Morris (1981) with permission.

learning the specific place where the platform is, but it may often reflect instead learning what direction to head relative to distal cues (Hamilton et al. 2008).

Information from beacons is not inherently spatial because it is not vector information but rather information about value. Cues from a desired object or place, almost by definition, draw the animal to them. A classic subject in ethology is the analysis of simple mechanisms which bring this about (Fraenkel and Gunn 1961). Learned as well as unlearned features attract the animal to the goal: a fundamental effect of conditioning (Chapter 4) is that animals approach CSs associated with positive USs. For mammals, the intuition that beacons and landmarks demand different kinds of cognitive processing is supported by evidence from behavioral neuroscience (N. White and McDonald 2002). Rats with hippocampal lesions can still learn to approach a beacon like the dry platform in the swimming task, but they cannot learn tasks in which a goal is identified only by its spatial relationship to landmarks. But while finding a goal by approaching cues attached to it may be computationally simple, it has a major practical drawback: the animal must stay within range of those cues. In most natural environments, an animal that had to be able to see, smell, or hear its nest or possible food sources at all times would have its travels severely limited.

8.1.3   Landmarks

When features of a goal are not immediately perceptible from a distance, other objects in fixed locations, that is, *landmarks,* can guide the animal to it. A classic demonstration of landmark use is Tinbergen's (1932/1972) study of homing in the digger wasp (*Philanthus triangulum*). These wasps lay their eggs in a number of burrows, which they provision with bees. Each bee that a wasp collects requires a separate foraging trip, so the female wasp has to learn the location of each of her burrows. This learning takes place during a brief orientation flight. When leaving the nest for the first time, the wasp turns and faces the nest entrance and flies around in ever-increasing loops, apparently inspecting the entrance and the objects around it (Figure 8.5a). If the objects surrounding an established nest are altered while the wasp is inside, a new orientation flight will be elicited the next time she departs (T. Collett and Lehrer 1993; Lehrer 1993).

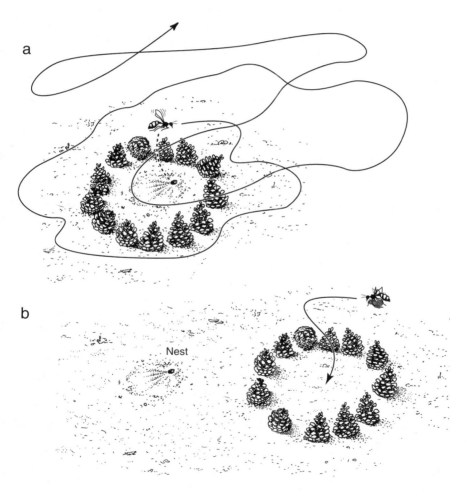

Figure 8.5. Control of orientation in the digger wasp (*Philanthus triangulum*) by nearby landmarks, a circle of pine cones. In a the wasp is shown making an orientation circle over the nest entrance before departing. After N. Tinbergen (1951) with permission.

To discover whether digger wasps were locating their nests using nearby land-marks, Tinbergen made a circle of pinecones around a nest while the wasp was inside and allowed it a number of trips in which to learn about them. Then they moved the pinecone circle to one side of the nest while the wasp was out foraging (Figure 8.5b). Although the nest entrance was still visible, returning wasps nearly always landed in the pinecone circle and searched for the nest entrance there. Only when the experimenters moved the pinecones back did she reenter the nest. To discover which nearby landmarks the wasps learned about, Tinbergen and Kruyt (1938/1972) made landmark circles from two kinds of objects and tested the wasps with separate circles of each kind, one on each side of the nest. Wasps preferentially used as landmarks objects that were large, nearby, and three-dimensional. Such a preference makes functional sense. Large three-dimensional objects are more likely to be visible from a distance than small flat ones, and if perception of distances and directions obeys Weber's Law (Chapter 3), objects close to a goal localize it more accurately than objects farther away. Thus it is not surprising that similar preferences have been found in other animals, including European jays (*Garrulus glandularius*) (Bennett 1993) and honeybees (Cheng et al. 1987). Mechanistically, they likely reflect overshadowing during landmark learning (see Section 8.3). A landmark at a given distance supports more accurate localization the nearer it was to the goal in a training array composed of several landmarks (Goodyear and Kamil 2004).

How are landmarks used? Template matching and local views

One way to compute how to move toward a goal is to compare one's current view of the surroundings with a "snapshot" stored in memory of how the world looks from the goal. Honeybees appear to use such a mechanism. Bees were trained to find sugar water in a particular location in a laboratory room and tested with the familiar landmark array expanded or contracted. When a single landmark defining the goal's location was doubled in size, bees searched twice as far away from it as usual, that is, at the distance where the landmark would look the same as from the goal; conversely, when the landmark was half as big, bees halved the distance at which they searched (Cartwright and Collett 1983). The bee makes the matching task easier for itself by facing important landmarks in a standard compass direction, which it gets from its magnetic sense (T. Collett and Baron 1994). The animal apparently does not need to memorize how the goal looks from all directions. Chickens apparently behave similarly (Dawkins and Woodington 2000).

Figure 8.6 depicts a demonstration (Stürzl et al. 2008) that image-matching can be used to find a goal in a simple laboratory task. Food is buried in one corner of a rectangular enclosure with three black walls and one white one (panel a). Panoramic (i.e., 360°) images centered roughly at the intersection of wall and floor and taking in 115° vertically are recorded at the goal (figure 8.6b) and at other points throughout the arena. Computing the total pixel-by-pixel difference between the image at any location and the image at the goal gives a map of the arena indicating which way the creature relying on such images should move from each point to maximally reduce the difference between the current and the desired image (Figure 8.6c.) The arrows from most starting positions converge on the goal but there will be a substantial number of erroneous choices of the diagonally opposite corner, the "geometric errors" discussed in Section 8.1.5.

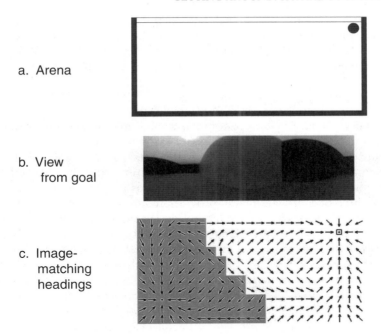

a. Arena

b. View
   from goal

c. Image-
   matching
   headings

Figure 8.6. a. Rectangular arena with one white and three black walls. Black dot indicates the location of buried food (the goal). b. Panoramic image of the arena as seen from the goal (the 360° view is unwrapped with the goal corner to right of center). c. Map of predicted headings for a creature moving at each point to maximally reduce the discrepancy between the current view and that at the goal. Note that from the majority of locations a creature following the arrows will arrive at the correct corner or its geometric equivalent. After Stürzl et al. (2008) with permission.

Figure 8.6 depicts a situation in which the animal is always within sight of the goal, but animals need to get close enough to the goal to use nearby landmarks in the first place. In principle this could also be accomplished by image matching. For example, a bee could have an "album of snapshots" (Cartwright and Collett 1987) from different locations within familiar terrain, each associated with a vector from that location to the hive. In rodents, this kind of mechanism is known as the *local view hypothesis* (Leonard and McNaughton 1990) "A location is nothing more than a set or constellation of sensory/perceptual experiences, joined to others by specific movements." (Leonard and McNaughton 1990, 366; see also McNaughton, Knierim, and Wilson 1995). Navigation based on learned links between local views is in effect what goes on in experiments in which people "move around" in a virtual environment by moving a joystick to reveal sequences of views simulating what one would see when moving around a neighborhood. With experience in realistic and complex virtual environments, people can plan novel routes using the same brain areas involved in "real" navigation (Hartley, King, and Burgess 2004).

Tinbergen's wasps must have used features of the terrain beyond the nest to find their way to within sight of the pinecone circles, but if an animal encounters similar landmarks or local views in different parts of its territory, it has to know which one is which. This problem can be solved by spatial context learning or occasion setting. For example, honeybees use distant landmarks or memory of the recent route to recognize ambiguous nearby landmarks. Bees were trained to find artificial nectar in each of two small featureless huts. Within each hut, the position of the food was specified by an identical array of four landmarks, but it was on the left of the landmarks in one hut and on the right in the other. The bees learned to search in the appropriate position, apparently remembering the global spatial context (Collett and Kelber 1988).

How are landmarks used? The vector sum model

Rather than using a whole visual panorama, animals may encode information about individual landmarks. But although a single beacon is sufficient to localize a goal, a single symmetrical landmark indicates only the distance to the goal. Without directional information, it can do no better than search in a ring around the landmark. Two discriminably different landmarks unambiguously specify a single position, and an array of three of more landmarks provides redundant information. To discover how information from such multiple landmarks is combined, animals can be trained to find a goal with two or more landmarks present, and then one or more of the landmarks is moved, in a so-called transformation test (Cheng and Spetch 1998).

Sometimes animals behave as if learning about only one of several available landmarks. For example, when gerbils were trained to search between two landmarks which were then moved further apart, the gerbils concentrated their searching in two spots, each at the correct distance and direction from one of the landmarks (T. Collett, Cartwright, and Smith 1986). In contrast, pigeons trained to search in a constant location in front of a wide stripe on the wall of a large rectangular box behaved as if averaging information from the conspicuous stripe and other features of the box (Cheng 1989). When the single landmark was shifted along the wall of the box in unrewarded test trials, the position where the birds pecked most shifted along with it, but typically not as much, that is, the birds averaged information from the landmark with some other feature, possibly the corners or visible features of the room outside the box (Figure 8.7). If the landmark was moved perpendicular to the wall of the box, searching shifted toward or away from the wall, but not as much as when the landmark was moved the same distance sideways. The nearby wall of the box seemed to be weighted relatively heavily in the bird's determination of how close to the wall to search. Black-capped chickadees (Cheng and Sherry 1992) and Clarks' nutcrackers (Gould-Beierle and Kamil 1996) also behaved similarly on comparable tests.

How are landmarks used? The multiple bearings model

But what exactly is being averaged? Are whole vectors averaged or are distances and directions computed separately? Cheng (1994) found some evidence that pigeons behave as if separately computing distance and direction from a single landmark. In a natural situation with landmarks more distant than features in a typical laboratory room, directional (or *bearing*) information by itself can be used to localize a goal surprisingly precisely, as illustrated in Figure 8.8. Bearing from a landmark to a goal, as in "the big pine tree is 40° northwest of my nest," does not change with distance, whereas judgment of goal-landmark distance, following Weber's Law, is less precise for more distant objects. Moreover, even if bearings are remembered with slight error, a goal surrounded by multiple landmarks, even quite distant ones, can be localized to the small area where the remembered bearings intersect (Figure 8.8). If animals' spatial judgments reflect these properties of the world, a number of predictions follow (Kamil and Cheng 2001). For instance, when an animal has learned to find a goal that is at a certain relative position, such as in the middle, between two

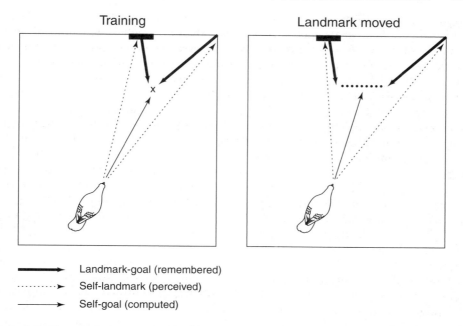

Training   Landmark moved

⟶ Landmark-goal (remembered)
⋯⋯▸ Self-landmark (perceived)
⟶ Self-goal (computed)

Figure 8.7. Hypothetical vectors involved in computation of the distance and direction to a goal (x) during training with a conspicuous landmark (black bar). The corner of the search space is treated as a second landmark. The self to landmark and landmark to goal vectors sum to produce the self to goal vector (the distance and direction resulting from summing two vectors is found by placing them head to tail). When the landmark is moved the animal will search somewhere along the dotted line, searching further toward the left the more heavily the black bar landmark is weighted relative to the corner of the box.

landmarks that vary in separation, direction errors should increase more slowly with interlandmark distance than distance errors.

Clark's nutcrackers are a particularly good species on which to test such predictions because they almost certainly need to rely on multiple and perhaps somewhat distant landmarks to relocate their buried caches under snow. Nutcrackers do behave as predicted by this multiple bearings hypothesis (Kamil and Cheng 2001) in several kinds of tests (Kamil and Jones 2000; Kamil and Goodyear 2001). Besides showing greater distance than direction errors, they more easily learn to locate a goal with a

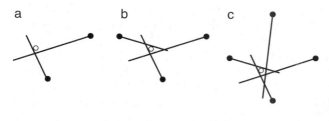

a   b   c

Figure 8.8. a. If an animal remembers only the compass directions (bearings) from the goal (open dot) to two landmarks and positions itself as near as possible to their intersection, even with small error in memory it can arrive reasonably close to the goal. b, c. Using more than two bearings confines search in a smaller area. After Kamil and Cheng (2001) with permission.

constant bearing to two landmarks than one at a constant distance from the line joining them. Pigeons are much less accurate than nutcrackers in laboratory tasks requiring them to use landmarks to search for buried seeds and do not show a clear difference between use of bearings and distances (Jones et al. 2002; Spetch et al. 2003). Although it is always difficult to be sure the training conditions are equated across species in such studies (but see Jones et al., 2002), the fact that this pattern of results has been found in more than one task and laboratory suggests that the nutcrackers have not only the exceptional spatial memory documented in Chapter 7 but exceptional ability at spatial localization.

A related finding that at first appeared to reflect a species difference in use of landmarks turned out instead to reflect differences in training methods. Spetch and colleagues (Spetch, Cheng, and MacDonald 1996; Spetch et al. 1997) found that pigeons trained to find the middle between two landmarks or in a square array of four landmarks in an arena or on a touchscreen behaved as if using only one landmark. When the landmarks were moved further apart in unrewarded tests, birds searched at the training distance from one of them. People behave in such tests as if they had learned "find the middle" (Figure 8.9). In this context, a report (Kamil and Jones 1997) that Clark's nutcrackers also behave as if learning a concept of middle might seem yet further evidence of the tendency of corvids to abstract concepts rather than memorize specific visual patterns as pigeons do (Mackintosh 1988). However, the pigeons in Spetch and colleagues' studies were trained with only a single interland-mark distance, whereas the nutcrackers were trained with multiple distances between the landmarks. The procedure used for the nutcrackers would be expected to teach the birds to weight both landmarks equally in determining distance, whereas relying on just one is a workable strategy for landmarks that never move. As this discussion predicts, when pigeons were trained like the nutcrackers with a variety of interland-mark distances, they also searched in the middle in the tests (Jones. et al. 2002).

8.1.4   Routes

"The animal got home because it had learned a route." As an explanation of accurate orientation, this statement is not very useful because "learning a route" can mean two different things. On the one hand, "learning a route" can refer to a mechanism of egocentric orientation in which an animal records the movements it makes in traveling between two places. This is usually referred to as *response learning* in psychology, to distinguish it from *place learning,* that is, use of landmarks. In the 1950s, considerable effort was devoted to testing whether rats learned mazes primarily as chains of responses or whether they learned about the relationships among places. Clark Hull is usually identified with the first view, and E. C. Tolman with the second. Like many controversies in psychology, this one was resolved—insofar as it ever was—by accepting that the answer to the question, "What does a rat learn in a maze?" is "It depends." Some conditions favor place learning and others, response learning (Restle 1957). Moreover, sometimes place and response learning go on in parallel and either one is used as the situation requires (Section 8.3.3).

A classic example of response learning comes from Konrad Lorenz's (1952, 109) depiction of how his pet water shrews followed their

path-habits, as strictly bound to them as a railway engine to its tracks and as unable to deviate from them by even a few centimetres.... The shrews, running along the wall, were accustomed to jump on and off the stones which lay right in their path. If I

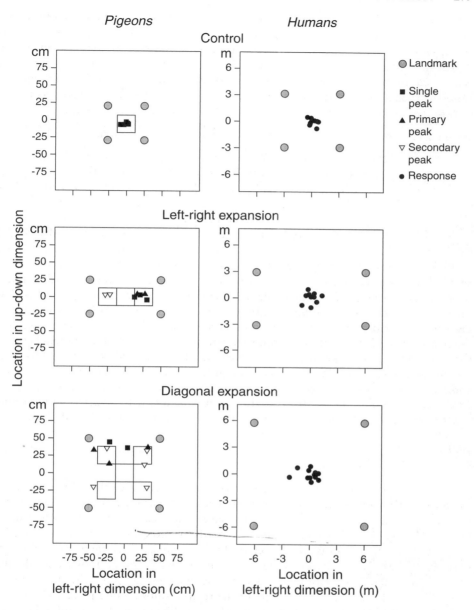

Figure 8.9. Setup and results of experiments testing how pigeons and humans use landmarks when trained to find the middle of a square array of landmarks in an open field. Redrawn from Spetch et al. (1997) with permission.

moved the stones out of the runway, . . . the shrews would jump right up into the air in the place where the stone should have been; they came down with a jarring bump, were obviously disconcerted and started whiskering cautiously left and right, just as they behaved in an unknown environment.

Gallistel (1990, 96–98) reviews analogous examples from the behavior of rats in mazes. As he points out, the animal must be keeping track of its distance and direction from the starting point (otherwise, it would not know where to jump), and it must use other cues to orient itself at the start. For the nearly blind water shrew, these must be tactile and/or olfactory cues gained by "whiskering." The disadvantage of sacrificing continuous monitoring of the environment for speed is that changes in the environment are not detected immediately. However, as Lorenz (1952, 111) pointed out, the shrew's brand of route learning has some advantages. It

compensates the shrew for being nearly blind and enables it to run exceedingly fast without wasting a minute on orientation. On the other hand, it may, under unusual circumstances, lead the shrew to destruction . . . water shrews have broken their necks by jumping into a pond which had been recently drained. In spite of the possibility of such mishaps, it would be short-sighted if one were to stigmatize the water shrew as stupid because it solves the spatial problems of its daily life in quite a different way from man . . . by learning by heart every possible spatial contingency that may arise in a given territory.

In discussions of orientation in natural environments, route learning often refers to reaching a goal using a series of landmarks, that is, a series of stimulus-response (S-R) associations. This kind of orientation can be illustrated with examples of guides for hikers (O'Keefe and Nadel 1978). A person may be instructed "after crossing the bridge, turn left and proceed along the bank of the stream until you reach a hedge. Turn right and climb the hill." Similarly, an animal may learn its way around familiar territory by memorizing distances and directions of travel with respect to landmarks. When homing pigeons are repeatedly released from the same location a few kilometers from their loft, individuals adopt different routes, but each one takes the same route time after time (Biro, Meade, and Guilford 2004; but see Wiltschko, Schiffner, and Siegmund 2007). When honeybees (F. Dyer 1994, see Section 8.3) and desert ants (T. Collett and Collett 2004) repeatedly visit the same foraging site they too learn routes with respect to landmarks in addition to using path integration (see Section 8.2.3).

8.1.5   Environmental geometry

In 1986, Ken Cheng published a remarkable discovery. He had devised a simple test of spatial working memory in which rats found food in a large rectangular box placed within a dark room, were removed from the box for about a minute and then replaced in an identical box differently oriented in the room to dig for the now-buried food. In test trials, no food was present and digging was recorded. The rats showed good memory for locations of food which they had experienced just once, in that they dug in the correct place at above chance levels. But amazingly, they dug nearly as often at the diagonally opposite point in the box like the hypothetical view-matching creature in Figure 8.6. Notice that in diagonally opposite locations the animal's relationship to the box's geometry is the same. For example, a short wall may be on the left, a long wall on the right. And some correlate of geometry, the box's shape, seems to be what the rats are paying most attention to (Cheng 1986; Chapter 6 in Gallistel 1990). For if geometrically identical locations are made more discriminable, for instance by coloring one long wall white and the others black as in the enclosure depicted in Figure 8.6, the rats still make diagonal errors. Similarly, placing distinctive panels with different patterns and odors in the corners still does not eliminate the tendency to make primarily diagonal errors.

Cheng took pains to force his rats to rely on spatial cues within the boxes. They were in a dark and relatively featureless room. Testing the rat in a different box differently oriented in the room meant it could not rely on dead reckoning to return it to the same location in space after it had been removed from the first box. These conditions are crucial for control by geometry. When Cheng's experiments are repeated but with the room visible outside the box and the test and exposure boxes in the same location within the room, rats search almost exclusively in the correct location and make no more diagonal than other kinds of errors. When they are disoriented by making the room dark, not always having the exposure and test boxes in the same place, and being gently rotated between exposure and test, the same rats make as many diagonal errors as correct responses (Margules and Gallistel 1988, Experiment 3).

Cheng's (1986) findings turn out to have remarkable generality across vertebrates. Young chickens, pigeons, black-capped chickadees, two species of fish, and monkeys also encode the locations of goals relative to the geometry of an enclosure, even in the presence of features like corner panels or a colored wall that disambiguate the geometry (Cheng and Newcombe 2005). Like rats (Wall et al. 2004), these animals can eventually perform well in a reference memory task with food in the same place on every trial relative to such features. But even when a feature is the best cue to the goal, they still learn the relationship of the goal to the box's geometry, as shown by searching in geometrically correct locations when the features are removed. Geometry even takes precedence over featural information when young children are tested similarly to rats in a working memory task. Hermer and Spelke (1994) showed college students and 20-month-old toddlers the location of an object in a room and then asked them to find it after they had shut their eyes and turned themselves around ten times. If the room was white and featureless, the students and the toddlers behaved just like Cheng's rats—not surprisingly, since they had no cues to disambiguate the correct corner from its diagonal. When the room was given one blue wall, the students searched mostly in the correct place, but the toddlers were just as confused as before. Like Cheng's rats, they could be provided with salient features in the room (a teddy bear, a toy truck) that they could use for orientation, but when they were disoriented by being rotated before searching, they still fell back on purely geometric information.

By the time children are about six, they use featural cues as adults do (Cheng and Newcombe 2005). Moreover, when adults' attention is occupied with a second cognitive task during the retention interval in a test like Hermer and Spelke's, they fall back once more on geometry (Hermer-Vazquez, Spelke, and Katsnelson 1999). In Cheng's (1986) original discussion, the fact that shape of the environment seems to take priority over features of the very surfaces that define that shape was interpreted as meaning that environmental geometry is processed in a dedicated cognitive module, impenetrable to other spatial information. On this view, developmental changes in use of geometry show that although humans share the geometric module with other vertebrates, language allows them to overcome its limitations (Hermer and Spelke 1994; Wang and Spelke 2002). But the claim that language is critical here is controversial (Cheng and Newcombe 2005; Newcombe and Ratliff 2007). For example, the importance of featural cues relative to geometry depends on the size of the enclosure. Children (Learmonth et al. 2008) as well as chicks and fish are more likely to use features in a relatively large space, in some cases possibly because the features are simply larger (Chiandetti and Vallortigara 2008; N. Y. Miller 2009). Thus even if—as discussed further in the next section—most vertebrates have a geometric module, its output may be combined in adaptive ways with other information (Newcombe and Ratliff 2007).

Of course not only enclosures but also configurations of landmarks have a shape, like the linear and square arrays of landmarks in Figure 8.9. However, the animals were not disoriented in those studies so they are not strictly comparable to the studies of enclosure geometry being discussed here. The limited evidence available indicates that disoriented rats and people do not encode the shape of an array of objects as such (Wang and Spelke 2000; Skov-Rackette and Shettleworth 2005). So why should the global shape of the surrounding environment be so important, and what about it are animals encoding anyway? One answer to the first question is that sensitivity to overall geometry is a mechanism for reorientation, or getting a heading (Wang and Spelke 2002). A not uncommon experience of disorientation and reorientation occurs when one emerges from an unfamiliar subway exit into the street and does not at first know which way is which. The claim is that the overall shape of the surroundings permits reorientation, after which specific environmental features can be identified.

What is geometry?

What it is about shape that is encoded is still unclear. In a rectangular enclosure a rat could encode its position relative to a box's geometry as a certain distance from a corner with a long wall on the right and a short wall on the left. That is, it might encode comparatively local spatial information about absolute or relative (Kelly and Spetch 2001) wall lengths and their left-right position or *sense* and perhaps also the angle at which they meet (Tommasi and Polli 2004). In contrast, using more global spatial information, the animal might extract the principal axes of the space and locate the goal relative to them, for example, at one end of the long axis and to the right (Figure 8.10). (In a symmetrical shape like a rectangle, the long axis is simply the line that divides it in half lengthwise.) Testing what is used requires transforming the space in some relevant way once the animal has learned to use geometric cues.

In one such test, Pearce, Good, Jones, and McGregor (2004) trained rats to find the dry platform in one corner of a rectangular water tank and then gave them unrewarded tests in a kite-shaped tank made by taking the rectangle apart along one diagonal, flipping one of the resulting halves over and putting the enclosure back together (see figure 8.10). Thus it now had two right-angled corners, only one of which had the same

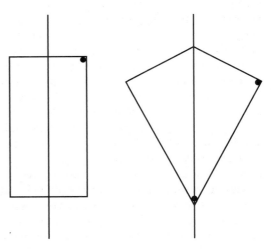

Figure 8.10. Layouts of the training (left) and testing enclosures in the experiment by Pearce et al. (2004) described in the text, showing principal axes (long vertical lines). Black dots in the kite-shaped arena indicate where rats spent most time searching for the platform in trials without the platform after training to go to the corner of the rectangle with the back dot. After Cheng and Gallistel (2005) with permission.

adjoining long and short walls with the same sense as the training corner. Much of the rats' time was spent searching for the platform in this corner, as if they had learned purely local cues. However, they searched about as much at the newly created sharp-angled corner, a finding better explained by the more global, principal axis, account (Cheng and Gallistel 2005). This latter account can also explain the results of an experiment in which young chicks were tested in transformations of a rhomboid-shaped enclosure (Tommasi and Polli 2004), although again the original authors favored a more local account of what their subjects had learned. However, local geometric features and global axes are not the only possibilities. The image matching mechanism depicted in Figure 8.6 does pretty well with several studies involving transformations of kite-shaped arenas even though it does not assume animals have any geometric information as such (Cheung et al. 2008). In summary, then, although the basic phenomena of geometry learning have proven remarkably robust, how best to account for them remains controversial (see Cheng 2008).

8.2   Modularity and integration

8.2.1   Spatial modules?

Section 8.1 makes clear that animals often have a wealth of cues for orientation available simultaneously—far and near landmarks, cues emanating from important goals (beacons), environmental shape, the *idiothetic* (self-generated or internal) cues used in path integration, memory for the chain of responses that got them from one place to another. These serve as input to distinct servomechanisms demanding different implicit computations. For instance, dead reckoning is a working memory process that takes as input some correlate of distance and direction traveled and outputs an approximation of the vector back to the starting place. The process revealed in geometry-learning experiments uses unknown parameters of the sur-rounding space to locate the animal relative to a global heading. Orienting by land-marks takes as input perceived self-landmark vectors and returns a vector from the current position to the remembered location of some goal. From a functional point of view then, spatial information processing consists of modular subprocesses.

But as discussed in Box 2.2, claims of modularity in the cognitive sciences are nearly always controversial because candidate modules seldom fit all Fodor's (1983) classic criteria. A debatable feature of possible spatial modules is the extent to which they are encapsulated, or impenetrable to anything other than their own specific kind of input (see e.g., Cheng and Newcombe 2005). What originally led Cheng (1986) and others (e.g., Gallistel 1990; Wang and Spelke 2002) to emphasize the modularity of spatial processing was not differences in implicit computations so much as striking observa-tions of apparently stupid behavior in which one kind of spatial information is used to the exclusion of others that animals are manifestly sensitive to. The displaced desert ant runs right past its nest, the mother gerbil searches a blank wall even within range of the smells and cries of her babies, the water shrew jumps over a nonexistent stone, the rat turns its back on a conspicuous landmark that defines the correct corner and digs on the opposite side of the box. Such behavior suggests the animals are using one encapsulated module at a time. Indeed, in natural environments redundant cues are normally not dissociated, so relying on just one at a time is likely to work and—as with Lorenz's water shrews—may be more efficient than processing lots of cues at once. Reliance on one cue at a time may also reflect the path of evolution. More sophisticated and flexible orientation may have evolved by the addition of new modules rather than the modification of old ones. But in any case, under many circumstances animals equipped with multiple spatial modules or servomechanisms combine their outputs. In Fodorian terms, modular spatial mechanisms provide input to central decision making (Cheng 2005; Cheng and Newcombe 2005). In this section we consider ways in which multiple spatial inputs are combined to reach a decision about which way to go. A basic research strategy here is to place cues in conflict with one indicating one goal location and one, another. Does the animal search at one place, at the other, or somewhere in between? The relative weightings of different sources of information may change with the conditions. If the conflict between them is too great, animals appear to fall back on one and disregard the other. In some situations one set of cues is primary, providing a context in which other cues are used.

8.2.2   Bayesian averaging

In the vector sum model discussed in Section 8.1.3 information from two or more landmarks, that is, within one module, is averaged. However, although the example in Figure 8.7 indicates that some landmarks are weighted more heavily than others, the model does not specify how these weightings are determined. Functionally, more informative landmarks should be weighted more heavily. Elegant quantitative support for this supposition comes from human psychophysical studies investigating how two or more cues are weighted in determining perceptual localization. For example, in the *ventriloquist effect* people perceive the ventriloquist's voice coming from his puppet's mouth, as if the visual cue of a moving mouth overrides the binaural auditory cue to the location of the sound source. This phenomenon has been brought into the laboratory with stimuli consisting of a blob shown on a video screen simultaneously with a sound presented through stereo headphones, an event experienced as a ball hitting the screen (Alais and Burr 2004). Two such stimuli are briefly presented in succession, and people judge which is to the left. As one might expect, the more blurry the blob the greater the variance in judging its location when it is presented alone. More importantly, the more blurry the blob, the more combined blob+sound stimuli are localized toward the (virtual) sound source. In effect, subjects localize the bimodal stimulus at a weighted average of the locations of its components, weighting each component in inverse proportion to its variance. Such weighting on the basis of prior knowledge of probability distributions (here, "knowledge" is direct perception of fuzziness or sharpness) is prescribed by Bayes' law, according to which it is the optimal way to estimate any metric value. It applies widely in comparable situations (Cheng et al. 2007). Other aspects of Bayesian decision making are of broad interest in psychology (Chater, Tenenbaum and Yuille 2006), but they are beyond the scope of this book.

Although Bayes' Law provides quantitative functional predictions for weighting two or more information sources relevant to localizing a single goal, few data on animal landmark use are adequate to test it precisely because this requires data on the variance in judgments when each information source is presented alone (see Cheng et al. 2007). But a number of studies have provided data consistent with it. For example, on the reasonable assumption that distance judgments obey Weber's Law (i.e., their variance increases with the distance being judged), landmarks should be weighted less the further they are from a goal. An elegant illustration of this principle comes from a study of Clark's nutcrackers relocating their caches (Vander Wall 1982). Birds buried pine seeds throughout a 1.5 meter long oval arena with several prominent landmarks

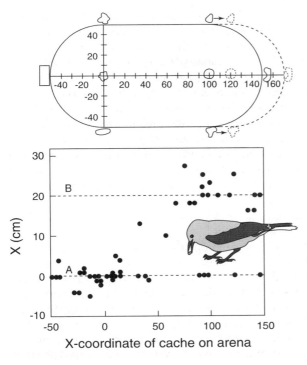

Figure 8.11. Setup and results of experiment to investigate response of Clark's nutcrackers to moved landmarks. Scale on diagram of the arena is in centimeters. Data are the distance between the location of the nutcrackers' probes for hidden seeds and the actual left-right position of the caches, as indicated on the map of the arena. Lines A and B represent, respectively, the loci of probes if the birds ignored the moved landmarks or followed them entirely. Redrawn from Vander Wall (1982) with permission.

at each end. The arena was then expanded by shifting all the landmarks at the right hand end 20 centimeters to the right (Figure 8.11). Thus caches near the right end of the arena were nearer to shifted landmarks than were caches on the left end. Birds probed farther from the stationary position of their caches and closer to a position shifted 20 centimeters the closer those caches were to the shifted landmarks. The graded effect shown in Figure 8.11, with searches in the middle of the arena shifted an intermediate distance, indicates that the moved landmarks were averaged with stationary ones, with landmarks close to a cache weighted more heavily than those further away.

Bayesian averaging should also apply when information from two spatial modules is being combined. One likely example comes from a study of honeybees in which directional information provided by a line of landmarks was put into conflict with direction given by the sun compass (Chittka and Geiger 1995). Many bees followed the landmark at displacements up to about 15°, but, as in some examples coming up next, they ignored the landmarks when they were moved too far. In Bayesian terms, averaging does not make sense if the possible positions indicated by the separate cues do not overlap because the prior probability that the goal is located between them is zero (further discussion in Cheng et al. 2007).

8.2.3   Parallel processing and hierarchical use

Rather than averaging the outputs of different spatial servomechanisms, animals may use them one at a time in a hierarchical manner. This often seems to be true when dead reckoning is involved. In numerous species and situations dead reckoning appears to be obligatory, always going on in the background and available as a backup when other cues fail, even when those cues were originally learned with reference to dead reckoning. One example comes from a study of rats by Whishaw and Tomie (1997). In a lighted room with plenty of landmarks, a rat's home cage was placed below the edge of a circular arena onto which the rat could climb and search for large food pellets which it carried back to the cage to eat. Because the cage was out of sight, rats initially had to use dead reckoning to return home, but with repeated trials from the same starting point they could learn to use landmarks as well. That this is what happened was confirmed by tests with a new starting point. In such tests, rats picked up the food and ran to the usual location of the cage with respect to landmarks. Not finding it there, they returned successfully to the new start location, using dead reckoning. Similarly, hamsters hoarding food immediately revert to dead reckoning when familiar landmarks are not visible (Etienne 2003; Etienne and Jeffery 2004). And as Figure 8.12 shows, when ants have made repeated trips home with food through a channel of a given length and are tested in shorter channels, after they emerge from the channel onto open ground they run in the direction that takes them home by dead reckoning (M. Collett et al. 1998).

As well as a backup, dead reckoning is used implicitly as a reference, in identifying landmarks in the first place (Cheng. et al. 2007). For example, hamsters hoarding food in the dark use a single small light as a landmark to return home. However, if the light is moved too far relative to the nest before the hamsters depart for the hoarding site, some of them ignore it and fall back on dead reckoning (Etienne. et al. 1990). It is as if dead reckoning leads the hamsters to expect the light in a certain position, so they disregard it when it is too far from that position, in effect treating it as a different light. Rats behave similarly (Shettleworth and Sutton 2005). Evidently a familiar landmark is recognized as such from its location with respect to the animal's internal position sense. Interestingly, if hamsters are repeatedly led astray by landmarks, they learn to rely more on dead reckoning and less on landmarks, as if recalibrating their relative weightings (Etienne 1992).

Other information about global spatial position may also determine how landmarks are used. For example, in a working memory task, black-capped chickadees learned the location of a single baited feeder in an array of four differently decorated feeders on the wall of an aviary and then searched for it later in a test of memory. When the array was moved along the wall for the test, they searched first in the feeder closest to the baited feeder's original position in the room (Brodbeck 1994). The birds

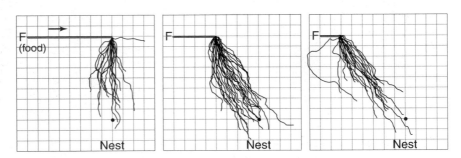

Figure 8.12. Trajectories of individual ants trained to find food at the end of an 8-meter-long channel and released at F in test channels of different lengths some distance away. Thus "nest" is the location where the nest would be relative to the beginning of the homeward trip at F in each diagram. From left to right, the test channel is 8, 4, or 2 meters long. Redrawn from Collett et al. (1998) with permission.

tended to search next in the correct position in the array of feeders. However, when the array was moved too far along the wall, performance fell to chance, as if the birds did not recognize the feeders out of their global spatial context. In the same experiment, local cues such as color on the baited feeder were occasionally placed in conflict with spatial cues by swapping the formerly baited feeder with another feeder in the array for unrewarded probe trials (Figure 8.13). The chickadees went first to the feeder in the formerly baited location, even though it now looked different. Finding no peanut there, they tended to search next in the feeder with the correct color and pattern. Much of the time, these birds used the normally redundant cues hierarchically: global spatial, local array, and color/pattern. In contrast, dark-eyed juncos, which do not store food in the wild, weight color and pattern cues about equally with spatial cues (Brodbeck 1994). The same pattern of species difference is found in an analogous operant task (Brodbeck and Shettleworth 1995) and in two other pairs of food-storing versus non-storing birds (Clayton and Krebs 1994). Analogous tests dissociating local features from spatial cues have revealed differences between men

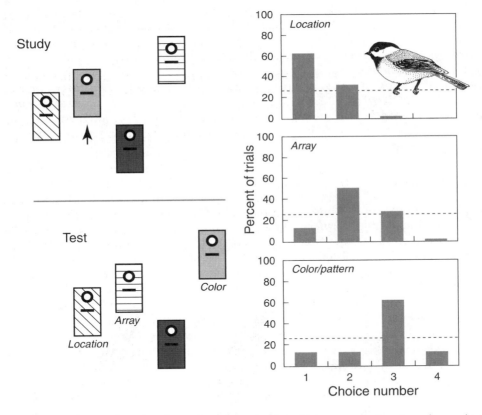

Figure 8.13. Setup and results of experiment investigating which cues to the location of reward are used by black-capped chickadees. On test trials the arrangement of feeders and their location in the room was changed as indicated between the study phase, in which the birds found and ate part of a peanut in one feeder, and the unrewarded test phase. Data are the proportion of trials in which the birds looked first, second, and so on, into the feeder in the formerly rewarded location in the room, in the same position in the array of feeders, or into the feeder of the rewarded color. Redrawn from Brodbeck (1994) with permission.

and women (Jones and Healy 2006) and between children and apes (Haun et al. 2006). Among birds, food storers' greater reliance on spatial cues may be related to their need for spatial memory in the wild (Chapter 7).

Using familiar cues in a hierarchical manner could result from learning some more strongly than others in the first place, because they overshadow other cues. For instance, perhaps chickadees use spatial cues before color cues when given a choice because they remember spatial cues better. However, although this kind of explanation may be correct for this case (Shettleworth and Westwood 2002), it is unlikely to apply in general. The examples involving dead reckoning sketched earlier in this section illustrate the more general principle that egocentric and allocentric orientation mechanisms operate in parallel (Burgess 2006). Possible parallel operation of multiple mechanisms is examined further in section 8.3.3.

8.3   Acquiring spatial knowledge: The conditions for learning

Most recent discussions of the conditions for spatial learning have been strongly influenced by O'Keefe and Nadel's (1978) claim that there is special spatial (*locale*) learning system, distinct from associative learning (the *taxon system*). The locale system is responsible for acquiring a cognitive map of the environment through exploration whereas the taxon system includes response learning, route learning, and classical conditioning, in effect all forms of associative learning. Exploration clearly does have an important role in spatial learning, as we see from research reviewed next. However, recent studies based on ideas about associative learning that largely postdate O'Keefe and Nadel's (1978) book support alternatives to the idea that all kinds of spatial information are spontaneously integrated into a unitary maplike representation.

8.3.1   Exploration

Exploration was a problem for S-R learning theory because it apparently resulted in learning without reinforcement, but in the 1960s the idea that behavior could be spontaneous and continue without reinforcement became more acceptable (Berlyne 1960; Hinde 1970a). The tendency to explore novel objects and environments is one of the best examples of special behaviors that expose animals to the conditions for learning. The rat sniffing a novel object, the young pigeon flying in circles over its loft, or the bee performing an orientation flight (Wei, Rafalko, and Dyer 2002) are actively exposing themselves to objects and spatial relationships that they need to learn about.

Spatial learning begins in the area around an animal's natal nest or burrow. A typical altricial rodent like a ground squirrel ventures out of its burrow a few weeks after birth but stays close to the entrance, maybe just rearing up and looking around from the mouth of the burrow. As the days pass, it makes longer and longer excursions around its mother's territory. Knowledge of the whole territory may be built up by connecting a series of "local charts," detailed knowledge about areas around important sites for food or refuge (see Figure 8.14; Poucet 1993). Indeed, one of the functions of territoriality may be to permit animals to acquire information that allows them to get around more safely and efficiently than they could in unfamiliar areas (Stamps 1995). For terrestrial animals, information from dead reckoning may be primary here, telling the animal where it is relative to its nest or burrow. By integrating the perceived

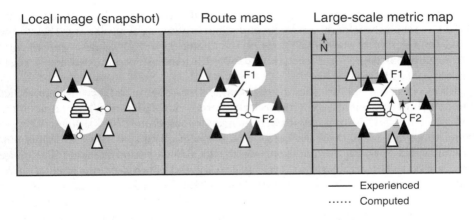

Local image (snapshot)   Route maps   Large-scale metric map

—— Experienced
······ Computed

Figure 8.14. Three ways in which an animal may encode spatial information about the area around its home (the beehive). F1 and F2 are two feeding sites, the black triangles are known landmarks, and the white triangles are unknown ones. White areas are familiar to the animal; thin solid arrows are paths the animal (white dot) can take on the basis of the specified kind of representation. The grid in the large-scale map represents the idea that only in this kind of representation is information about different locations related to a common coordinate system, allowing the animal to compute a novel route (the dotted line). After F. Dyer (1996) with permission.

egocentric coordinates of prominent landmarks with this information, an animal can learn the position of nearby landmarks relative to its home (Gallistel and Cramer 1996; McNaughton et al. 1996).

The acquisition of spatial knowledge in the wild has been studied most in bees and homing pigeons. Pigeon racers have accumulated a vast fund of lore about what is necessary for the birds to learn the location of the loft (Keeton 1974; Wallraff 2005). Training racing pigeons typically begins by letting young birds fly around close to the home loft and then releasing them increasing distances away. In contrast, laboratory studies of exploration and spatial learning typically begin by dumping an animal into a completely novel environment. Even here the tendency gradually to venture further and further from a central place, presumably building up spatial knowledge, can be observed. For instance, rats placed in a large room to live travel over more and more of it in successive nights and gradually organize the space into nesting sites, food stores, runways, and latrines (Leonard and McNaughton 1990).

The two paradigms that have been used most extensively to study learning through exploration are habituation and tests of latent learning in mazes. In Chapters 5 and 7 we have seen how moving objects around, removing them, or introducing new ones elicits investigation of the altered object or location, evidence that the animals knew the features of the environment before it changed. This approach can also reveal what free-ranging animals know about their environment. For instance, wild rats ate less than usual from a familiar feeder displaced as little as a foot, showing they had learned its location quite precisely (Shorten 1954; see also Shillito 1963). And to take a rare example of spatial memory not involving food, free-ranging male thirteen-lined ground squirrels return to locations in their large (average 4.7 hectare) home ranges where they have previously encountered females. If the female has been removed, they spend longer searching for her if she had been about to go into heat the day before. The males also visit a female's territory earlier in the day when she is potentially receptive than otherwise, as if planning their route based on memory of the female's state (Schwagmeyer 1995). Male meadow voles show analogous behavior in the laboratory, with females encountered in a T-maze (Ferkin et al. 2008).

What aspects of exploration are important? Does the animal have to experience different routes through the environment, different views of it, or what? Some of the best examples of attempts to answer such questions come from studies with the Maier three-table task (Maier 1932a). This is essentially a spatial working memory task in which rats must rapidly encode the location of food in a familiar space (Figure 8.15). Three tables in a large well-decorated room are connected by a Y-shaped runway with a central platform. At the beginning of a trial, a rat is allowed to explore the whole apparatus, which is empty of food. It is then placed on the day's goal table with a large pile of food. After the rat has eaten for a few minutes but before it has depleted the food, it is placed on one of the other two tables, from which it may return and finish its meal. Trials are typically run only once a day, with the goal table changed from trial to trial. Experienced rats typically do quite well, even with delays of hours between feeding on a table and testing, but accurate choice of the goal table depends on prior opportunity to explore the maze (Maier 1932a; Stahl and Ellen 1974).

To discover whether rats can link together two parts of space they have never experienced closely together in time, Ellen, Sotere, and Wages (1984) restricted experience in the exploration phase. Three groups of rats had 15 minutes a day to explore the

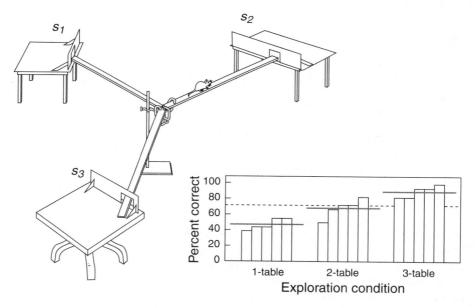

Figure 8.15. Setup for the Maier three-table task, redrawn from Maier (1932b) with permission. Screens are placed so that rats cannot see from the runways whether or not food is on any of the tables. Data redrawn with permission from the experiment of Ellen, Soteres, and Wages (1984) in which rats explored the maze piecemeal, one, two, or three tables at a time before being tested. Results are shown from five rats in each group; solid lines are group means; dotted line is performance level that could occur only 5% of the time or less.

maze, one group exploring only one runway and table per day, one exploring two different connected runways and tables, and one exploring the whole maze. Every three days, the rats were given the standard three-table test. The rats that explored only one runway at a time never performed above chance in 18 such tests, whereas rats given full exploration performed above chance from the outset (Figure 8.15). Thus the information gained from piecemeal exploration does not seem to be knitted together into a unitary representation. Other findings from mazes and swimming pools (e.g., Maier and Schneirla 1935/1964; Sutherland et al. 1987; Save et al. 1996) agree that to treat different places as connected a rat has to travel between them. Seeing they are connected is not enough. Perhaps this finding should not be surprising for an animal that normally does most of its traveling in the dark.

8.3.2   Learning about redundant cues: Competition or parallel processing?

O'Keefe and Nadel (1978) suggested that exploring novel items in a familiar space allows an animal to update its cognitive map in the same way as a cartographer adds a new farmhouse or removes a hedge from a printed map. Incorporating all available cues into a cognitive map would ensure redundancy when primary cues fail, which could be important for tasks like getting home. Indeed, an example of backup mechanisms is illustrated in Figure 8.13. As another example, experienced homing pigeons tested on sunny days use a sun compass, but birds tested under thick cloud cover can home just as well, relying on landmark memory, olfaction, magnetic information and/or infrasound (Keeton 1974). But several of O'Keefe and Nadel's ideas are contradicted by more recent findings in associative learning. One apparent contradiction is the phenomenon of *latent inhibition*, that is, mere exposure to a potential CS may retard later learning about it (Chapters 4 and 5). This is the opposite of what would be observed if the animal is continuously building a cognitive map. However, exposure to a particular spatial context does sometimes retard later learning about locations within it. Just as in associative learning, preexposure enhances discrimination (i.e., perceptual learning occurs) when the locations to be learned about are similar, but latent inhibition occurs when they are very different (Rodrigo et al. 1994; Chamizo 2003). Incorporating redundant cues into a cognitive map is also at odds with the principle of cue competition in associative learning. The Rescorla-Wagner model formalizes this principle, most clearly evidenced in the phenomena of overshadowing and blocking (Chapter 4). So do overshadowing and blocking occur in spatial learning?

Beacons and landmarks

One clear example of cue competition in spatial learning comes from a study of blocking with rats in a water tank by A. Roberts and Pearce (1999). The time spent in the quadrant of the tank where the platform was usually found was compared in two groups of rats (Figure 8.16). Both groups had been trained with a beacon attached to the platform and landmarks visible around the tank, but the blocking group were first trained with curtains drawn around the tank so they learned about the beacon alone. This initial training was expected to block learning about the added landmarks, and Figure 8.16 shows that indeed it did. Further controls with various kinds of swimming experience in the first stage still learned more about the landmarks in stage 2 than rats already trained to use the beacon.

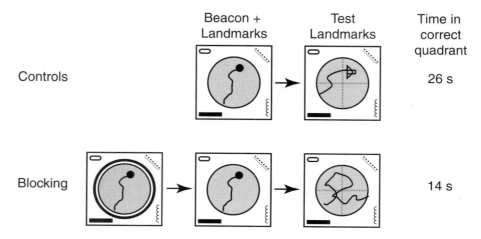

Figure 8.16. Procedure and results of A. Roberts and Pearce's (1999) test of blocking in the water tank. The heavy line around the outside of the tank represents a curtain; the black dot is the dry platform. The final test lasted 60 seconds; hence the blocking group's test score represents random search, i.e. about 1/4 of the time in the quarter of the tank with the platform.

As might be expected, landmarks closest to a goal overshadow more distant landmarks, for example in bees (Cheng et al. 1987), pigeons (Spetch 1995), and rats (Morris 1981; Redhead et al. 1997; Chamizo 2003). Landmarks can also block each other. For example, learning to use a set of three landmarks to locate the hidden platform in a swimming pool blocks rats' learning about a fourth landmark added later on (Rodrigo et al. 1997). Blocking and overshadowing have also been found between intramaze cues (floor texture) and extramaze cues (i.e., landmarks in the room) in a radial maze (Diez-Chamizo, Sterio, and Mackintosh 1985; March, Chamizo, and Mackintosh 1992). Of course such findings are not necessarily incompatible with observations of animals using normally redundant cues in a hierarchical manner. Overshadowing and blocking do not need to be complete. If some cues are simply learned more strongly than others, one would expect those learned best to be used first when available. In any case, landmarks and beacons tap only a subset of spatial processing modules. Tests of overshadowing and blocking may have different results when different spatial modules are brought into play.

Geometry and landmarks

As we saw in Section 8.1.5, when animals are disoriented relative to the outside world, they initially rely on information about the location of a goal relative to the shape of an enclosure and ignore more informative features. Some discussions of the geometric module have suggested that geometry is used for reorientation, perhaps supporting learning about features but not competing with it (e.g., Cheng 1986; Wang and Spelke 2002). That notion suggests that geometric cues should not be overshadowed or blocked by other cues. One test of this idea is illustrated in Figure 8.17. Rats were trained in a rectangular enclosure with a sawdust-filled bowl in each corner and a reward buried in the bowl near a black landmark. Rats learned to go directly to the bowl near the landmark, but they learned about geometry at the same time, as the vast majority of errors during acquisition consisted of digging in the diagonally opposite, that is, geometrically equivalent, bowl. In addition, like

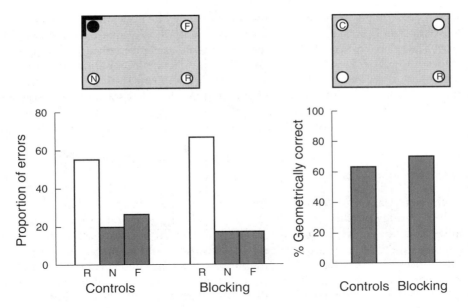

Figure 8.17 Training with a landmark (the black corner) does not block geometry learning. Rats in the blocking group were pretrained with the black corner panel in a square enclosure, yet they still made a high proportion of geometric (rotational, R) errors when transferred to a rectangle (left panel; errors summed over all of training). In a test without the landmark at the end of training, they chose the geometrically correct corners C and R, as often as controls not pretrained with the landmark (right panel). Data from Experiment 3 in Wall et al. (2004).

other species tested in a similar way (Cheng and Newcombe 2005), the rats preferred the geometrically correct corners in a test without the landmark at the end of acquisition, showing they had learned about the geometry as well as the more informative landmark. Moreover, learning based on the shape of the rectangle was not blocked by prior training with the landmark in a square (i.e., geometrically uninformative) enclosure (Wall et al. 2004).

Tests of overshadowing and blocking in water tanks of various shapes have also revealed little evidence of cue competition. Indeed, sometimes a cue at a goal facilitates learning of geometry (e.g., Pearce et al. 2001; N. Y. Miller and Shettleworth 2007). But although these findings suggest that learning the location of a goal relative to the geometry of an enclosure goes on independently of learning about its location relative to features within the enclosure, a deeper analysis reveals that cue competition is still at work (N. Y. Miller and Shettleworth 2007, 2008). Searching for a goal is an instrumental task, so the animal's choices determine the frequency with which the cues at each location searched are paired with reward or nonreward. For instance, when rats begin to learn that the salient black landmark signals reward in the situation in Figure 8.17, they start choosing the marked corner more often. When they do choose that corner they also experience a pairing of its geometry with reward. The learning based on these pairings is reflected both in the relatively large proportion of geometric errors early in training and in geometrically correct choices during tests without the landmark. The same process leads the blocking group to learn about the geometry of the rectangle. Geometry and features are competing for learning, but this is typically not evident in choices because if a location is chosen on the basis of the total associative strength of its cues relative to the total at all locations, one location can be quite strongly preferred over the others even while none of the individual cues is at asymptote. For example, the corner by a landmark in a square enclosure can be chosen a large proportion of the time even if its associative strength is not high enough to block geometric cues when transferred to the rectangle. One prediction of this model, then, is that conventional cue competition will reveal itself in choices under some conditions, including after prolonged training in either stage of an experiment like that in Figure 8.17. The shape of the enclosure and the distribution of features within it will also influence the results, as indeed it does (Miller and Shettleworth 2007).

Dead reckoning and beacons

The characterization of dead reckoning as an obligatory process, a basis for learning the locations of stable allocentric cues yet always going on in the background implies that the idiothetic cues for dead reckoning do not compete with learning landmarks and/or beacons. Indeed, if they did how would animals ever learn about stable allocentric cues? But although some of the findings described in Section 8.2.3 imply that dead reckoning operates independently of beacon and landmark learning, only one study (Shettleworth and Sutton 2005) has tested this implication with a study of overshadowing and blocking. Rats found food pellets in a large circular arena and carried them back to eat in a home cage that was concealed behind one of 16 identical doors on the periphery of the arena. In some conditions the correct door was surrounded by a black panel, functioning as a beacon, and in other conditions no exteroceptive cue identified it so the rats had to home by dead reckoning. To ensure that the rats could not locate the home on the basis of cues outside the arena, the home cage and black panel were in varying locations in absolute space, and the rats were disoriented before entering the arena. Rats trained with the beacon homed no more accurately than rats trained with a "beacon" at random locations relative to the home door, and the two groups homed equally accurately in tests without the beacon. That is, beacon learning did not overshadow the cues used in dead reckoning. And as might be expected on functional grounds, rats that already had extensive experience homing on the basis of dead reckoning alone learned as much about the beacon when it was added as rats that had it from the outset, that is, dead reckoning did not block beacon learning.

Places and responses

Extensive literature also points to a noncompetitive interaction between spatial learning systems in the case of "place" (or landmark) and response learning (sometimes referred to in this context as *habit* learning). Figure 8.18 shows a classic setup for testing whether rats that learn to make a particular turning response to arrive at a particular place in a T-maze have learned the response or the place. Notice, however, that the test consists of forcing the rat to choose between making the rewarded response and going to the rewarded place. A choice consistent with one kind of learning does not mean that the other kind has not also occurred. The typical finding in such tests is that early in acquisition place learning is evident, but later the habitual response prevails (Restle 1957; Packard and McGaugh 1996). This finding in itself suggests cue competition is not going on. If it was, how could response learning develop when place learning was already allowing the animal to locate the reward? Neurobiological data also lend support to the idea that rather than competing, place

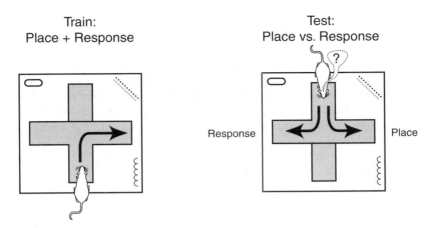

Figure 8.18. Test of whether rats trained in a T maze as indicated in the left panel learn where to find reward or what response to make. The two possibilities are dissociated as indicated in the setup on the right. The dark bar is a block that confines the rat to one part of the maze. The random shapes around the edge are objects in the room that can serve as landmarks.

and response learning go on in parallel, in different brain regions, the hippocampus and caudate nucleus respectively (White and McDonald 2002).

This was beautifully demonstrated in a study using a setup like that depicted in Figure 8.18 in which rats were given the place versus response test early or late in place + response training and while the hippocampus or caudate was temporarily disabled with injections of lidocaine (Packard and McGaugh 1996). Rats with the hippocampal place-learning system disabled chose randomly in the early test but chose on the basis of the trained response in the later test, consistent with the observation that response learning emerges gradually. In contrast, rats with the caudate habit system disabled chose the rewarded place in both the early and late tests. Thus response learning did not emerge at the expense of place learning: it remained intact and could be revealed when the competing behavioral tendency was removed. The same issue was addressed without pharmacological manipulations by testing rats in a radial maze arranged so that response learning and place learning could be dissociated (Gibson and Shettleworth 2005). The results suggested that prior response learning interferes with learning about landmark (place) cues introduced later. This may have occurred because rats for which a habitual response continues to lead to reward when place cues are added simply pay less attention to, or spend less time exposed to, those cues than controls.

Redundant cues in spatial learning: Conclusions

The picture of spatial learning sketched here is not that of a single system in which cues compete for a limited amount of predictive value like CSs in conditioning. Landmarks compete for learning with beacons and geometric cues and with each other, but dead reckoning goes on in parallel yet somehow in support of learning about allocentric cues. At least in mammals, response or habit learning is another parallel system. The existence of parallel systems allows for the redundancy which functional considerations suggest is particularly important for spatial tasks like getting home. Ultimately whether different mechanisms evolve so as to compete would be expected to reflect the relative costs and benefits of relying on minimal sufficient predictors versus processing redundant information. In addition, the costs and benefits of any one mechanism may be balanced by the costs and benefits of others. For instance, well-learned responses demand little attention and permit fast travel in familiar places, but a slower, more attention demanding system such as exploration and landmark learning is called for when conditions change. Evolutionary pressure to optimize over different criteria may account for the widespread existence of multiple spatial learning systems. Whether the multiple kinds of memories that result are integrated into a cognitive map in any sense is the question for the next section.

8.4   Do animals have cognitive maps?

8.4.1   What is a cognitive map?

In Chapter 4, "How does the animal represent the CS?" meant simply, "What features of the CS are encoded or remembered?," a rather minimal kind of representation. In contrast, the representation embodied in a cognitive map is typically assumed to encode distances and directions and to enable mental operations on them. To take an example we will shortly consider in more detail, an animal that can encode the distance and direction of two feeding sites from a home base and whose nervous system is capable of implicit computations analogous to the operations of vector algebra can move directly between the two feeding sites without going home in between (Figure 8.14, "metric map").

Distances and directions are the *metric properties* of space. Blueprints, city plans, road maps, and globes are useful because they represent distances and directions accurately. But plenty of useful maps do not preserve such vector information. A familiar example is a subway route map. Such a map is useful for planning a trip on the subway because it shows which station is on which route and what order they can be reached in. Such a *network map* can be used without its representing distances between stations or angles between connecting routes. Indeed, because these may not be represented accurately, a tourist wanting to explore the city on foot would be foolish to use a it as a guide. In contrast to the subway map, a map that preserves distance and direction information, a *vector* map, allows the planning of novel routes to unseen goals. How useful it is, though, depends on the density of identifiable locations represented. For example, a tourist starting from an obscure side street armed only with a vector map of the city landmarks has to wander around until finding a place marked on the map. This potential limitation of real Euclidean paper maps has traditionally been overlooked. It is an assumed unlimited flexibility that has distinguished a cognitive map from "mere" reliance on one or more kinds of spatial cues. As Section 8.2 shows, however, single cues or combinations of them can guide animals very effectively. This means that it is almost impossible to find indisputable evidence that any animal is using a cognitive map in the sense of a global representation of space equivalent to an overhead view that preserves distances and directions among an infinity of locations. Whether *cognitive map* always means the same thing is a problem too, as we see by surveying some of the landmarks in its history.

Tolman

E.C. Tolman introduced the term *cognitive map* into psychologists' debate about place versus response learning. Rather than simply acquiring chains of stimulus-response connections, Tolman claimed, rats in mazes acquire "something like a field map of the environment" (Tolman 1948, 192). Stimuli influence behavior not through S-R connections, but through the mediation of the cognitive map. Cognitive maps could be broad and comprehensive or "narrow strip maps," confined to knowledge of specific routes. The most compelling data Tolman cited in support of his hypothesis were from tests of *latent learning* and ability to take novel shortcuts in mazes. In a typical latent learning experiment, a rat was allowed to explore a maze without receiving any reward. For instance, food might always be present in one location but the rat would be satiated. If the rat ran straight to the food when it was hungry later on, its behavior could not have resulted from the reinforcement of S-R connections because it had not been getting any reinforcement. Therefore, it must have learned the location of the food and generated appropriate behavior on the basis of this knowledge. Similarly, an animal that took an efficient novel shortcut when displaced to a new location or when its usual path to a goal was blocked must have acquired knowledge about the goal as a place.

Much of the behavior just described is now largely taken for granted in the view of conditioning as a representational process described in Chapter 4, so in a sense Tolman's view of learning as S-S connections has prevailed. It is no longer problematical, for instance, that animals approach or avoid places on the basis of knowledge about their value. Indeed, this is the basis of the popular *conditioned place preference* test. In this paradigm an animal is first exposed to each of two distinctive chambers in each of which a different biologically significant event occurs, for example food in a grey square chamber and opportunity to run in a wheel in a striped round chamber. The relative value it gives to them is then measured by removing the rewards, connecting the two chambers and seeing where the animal spends more time. And in at least some of Tolman's experiments, tests of rats' specifically spatial knowledge did not go beyond demonstrating such S-S learning. For instance, if cues near the goal were still visible from a novel starting point, rats could approach them without any maplike knowledge, as in the experimental arrangement depicted in Figure 8.19 (Tolman, Ritchie, and Kalish 1946).

O'Keefe and Nadel

Although Tolman's views are important in the history of psychology, he actually said rather little about the properties of cognitive maps and how they might be acquired. After a lapse of 30 years, this gap began to be filled by John O'Keefe and Lynn Nadel (1978) in their influential book *The Hippocampus as a Cognitive Map*. They developed the view that some organisms, including humans, rats, and migratory birds, possess cognitive maps, in the sense of a unitary, allocentric, connected spatial representation in which experience locates objects and events. Acquisition and use of the cognitive map is supported by the locale system, a cognitive module located in the hippocampus of vertebrates. The locale system contrasts with the taxon system, which supports conditioning and is located elsewhere in the vertebrate brain. The learning supported by the taxon system was seen by O'Keefe and Nadel as relatively inflexible compared to that supported by the locale system, but developments in the last 30 years have undercut this distinction. As in Tolman's account, maps are acquired through exploration (latent learning) and allow more flexible behavior than route learning. However, as in the example mentioned above, some flexibility can result from stimulus generalization, and at least over relatively short distances, path integration allows

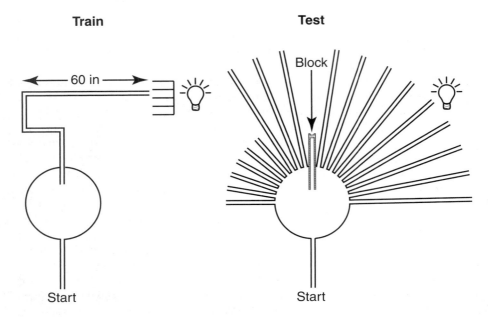

Figure 8.19. Setup used by Tolman, Ritchie, and Kalish (1946) to test place learning in rats. The alleys were arranged as shown on the left for training; for testing they were replaced with the "sunburst" maze shown on the right. Rats tended to choose the new path that led directly toward the goal. Note the light at the goal box. Redrawn from Tolman et al. (1946) with permission.

travel toward unseen goals in a way not fully appreciated when O'Keefe and Nadel first wrote.

Gallistel

Gallistel's (1990) review of spatial behavior in animals has a very different flavor from O'Keefe and Nadel's, partly because by 1990 the cognitive revolution in psychology had made the notion of cognitive mapping more acceptable. In addition, this period witnessed an explosion of relevant research, and Gallistel was the first person writing for people in the cognitive sciences to bring together the new laboratory studies on rats in the Morris swim task and radial maze with biological field work on bees, ants, homing pigeons, and other animals. This integrative approach has been tremendously influential and is now almost taken for granted, as can be seen in numerous more recent reviews (e.g., Newcombe and Huttenlocher 2000; T. Collett 2002; Jeffery 2003). Gallistel's (1990) definition of *cognitive map* is fairly loose (e.g., Chapter 6, 121): any orientation based on implicitly computing distances and directions is evidence of a cognitive map. Dead reckoning, matching "snapshots," or responding to landmarks all count as cognitive mapping, albeit perhaps in a small-scale and limited way. Species may differ in the richness and detail of their cognitive maps, but evidence for them is ubiquitous.

Bennett

Because *cognitive map* means different things to different people and because most frequently used behavioral assays of cognitive mapping have not ruled out well-defined alternatives such as dead reckoning or generalization from familiar local views, it is almost impossible to find unambiguous evidence for it. Discussion of cognitive maps should be replaced with better-grounded specification of how animals (including people) find their way from place to place. This position was stated forcefully by Bennett (1996) and echoed by Mackintosh (2002) in an article titled, "Do not ask whether they have a cognitive map but how they find their way about." To see why this is good advice we need to review the approaches to testing for cognitive maps.

8.4.2   Mapping and short-range orientation

Shortcutting

A central behavioral prediction from any notion of cognitive mapping is that within familiar terrain an animal with a cognitive map should be able to reach a goal by a novel route. It will take a novel shortcut when one is made available, and if it is displaced to a new starting place it will head directly to the goal rather than returning to the familiar start before continuing its journey. Tests of this prediction have a long history, beginning with the work of Tolman, Ritchie, and Kalish (1946) illustrated in Figure 8.19. In laboratory studies like theirs it is easy to guarantee that the offered shortcut is novel, but it is not so easy to be sure that animals are doing anything other than orienting by landmarks (and indeed, that rats use landmarks rather than only S-R habits may have been all that Tolman aimed to establish). As long as landmarks visible from the goal are visible to the animal in the same left-right relationship at the point where it chooses between the shortcut and some other route, the self-to-goal vector computed as in Figure 8.7 will take the animal along the more direct route. Cues at the goal clearly influenced the rats in Tolman et al.'s (1946) original study, because there was a distinctive light right at the goal box (see also Chapuis, Durup, and Thinus-Blanc 1987). In a careful study in which dogs often took the shortest route between two novel locations in a large field (Chapuis and Varlet 1987), this could have been a problem too. The dogs were led first to one location and then another and shown meat in each one before being released from the common starting place for these trips to find the food. As they were shown each piece of food they could have encoded its location with respect to features in the surrounding familiar environment. Indeed, rats can acquire new knowledge about what is where in a single trial in an environment which already supports a network of associations (Tse et al. 2007).

These considerations mean that to test whether animals are using a representation that includes more than local landmark-goal vectors, landmarks perceptible from the goal must not be perceptible when the shortcut is chosen. The importance of this requirement is very well illustrated by a much-discussed series of studies with honeybees. Honeybees are ideal subjects for studies of spatial orientation in natural landscapes because foragers routinely make many round trips each day between the hive and feeding sites hundreds of meters away. Using methods pioneered by Karl von Frisch (1967), marked individuals can be trained to artificial feeding sites selected by the experimenter. Newly emerged foragers gradually become familiar with the area around the hive, as shown by the observation that when bees are released some distance from the hive, the experienced individuals are more likely to find their way back (review in Dyer 1994). Extensive and detailed spatial knowledge thus seems to exist in bees' tiny brains. Discussion of whether it can be described as a cognitive map has centered around a shortcut experiment originally reported by Gould (1986) and repeated by others, sometimes with different results (Wehner and Menzel 1990; F. Dyer 1991, 1994). Bees were trained to only one of two feeders, F1 and F2, equidistant from the hive but out of direct sight of each other. The lines connecting A, B, and the hive formed an approximately equilateral triangle, as in the arrangement depicted in Figure 8.14. The test of whether the bees knew the relationship of a feeding site to the landscape as a whole consisted of capturing marked individuals as they left the hive for one site, say F2, and releasing them at the other. A bee released at a novel location flies up maybe 9 or 10 meters, circling around as if getting its bearings, and then heads off in a definite direction. Data in these studies thus consisted of the compass bearing recorded for each bee when it vanished from view.

Because when tested Gould's bees tended to head toward the site they had been trained to, he concluded that the bees had a "maplike representation" of their local environment. But because their experience was not controlled, it is impossible to know whether the shortcut was truly novel. Moreover, when the bees flew up to get their bearings they could have gotten a view of the landscape sufficiently similar to that near the familiar feeding site to allow them to orient. And indeed, "maplike" orientation in such a test does seem to require this, as shown by Dyer (1991) in a similar study that had one important difference. One of the two critical feeding sites, B, was down in a quarry whereas A was up at the same elevation as the hive. Bees trained to B, in the quarry, and released at A behaved like Gould's bees and headed off from the novel release site toward the feeding site B. But bees trained to feed at A, on the high ground, and released at B, in the quarry, could not easily get a view similar to that which they saw when leaving the hive for A. These bees did not head either for the hive or for A but departed from B in the same compass direction they had been taking when they left the hive. This did not reflect some peculiarity of site B in the quarry; bees trained to fly directly between A and B were able to orient accurately.

As we see presently, this is not the end of the story of cognitive mapping in bees, but Dyer's study remains an important demonstration of why tests of shortcutting must ensure that cues at the goal are not perceptible at the choice point. This was done for rats in the enclosed maze depicted in Figure 8.20 (Singer, Abroms, and Zentall 2006). The three goal boxes were identical, but each arm had a distinctive

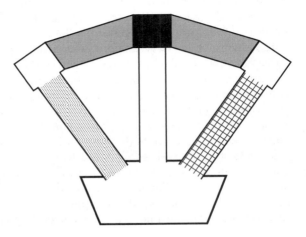

Figure 8.20. The enclosed maze used by Singer, Abroms, and Zentall (2006) to test cognitive mapping in rats. Different shadings signify different textures in the maze arms. The arms linking the three goal boxes (top of the figure) were open only for testing. Redrawn from Singer, Abroms, and Zentall (2006) with permission.

floor covering. Rats found chocolate in the center goal box, and a piece of cereal in a constant one of the side goal boxes. The maze was rotated within the room from day to day to prevent use of extra-maze cues, and food odors within the goal boxes were also controlled. Rats were trained until they visited the two baited arms first on more than 90% of trials and then tested with only the center arm open to the start box and, for the first time, alleys open between the center and side goal boxes. On the first test 15 of 20 rats chose the novel alley to the baited side, and rats continued to choose at above-chance levels over 8 further tests. In an experiment conducted in the same way except that the alleys were unlined and both baited goal boxes had the same food, rats did not perform above chance in the tests, indicating that performance is not based entirely on dead reckoning within the maze. In a more extensive study W. Roberts, Cruz, and Tremblay (2007) found comparable results with an enclosed four-arm maze.

Singer and colleagues suggest that the rats must have had a cognitive map of the maze, but what exactly can "mapping" mean here? In both their study and that of Roberts and colleagues (2007) distinctive cues in the arms or goal boxes identified locations in the maze. We have already seen (Section 8.2) that dead reckoning can be used to locate a familiar goal by a novel route, and that it can be reset by exposure to familiar landmarks (e.g., the distinctive floor and/or food). The experimental design ensured that rats had to base their choices on their internal position sense, and once they were going directly between two arms, they had ample experience of their relative positions based on idiothetic cues. Thus, considering the cues available allows reference to mapping to be replaced with consideration of how specific cues are used in concert.

Planning ahead and taking detours

Shortcutting is but one test of whether animals have an overall map of a familiar environment. Detouring when the shortest route is blocked and choosing an efficient path among multiple goals are two equally classic tests of cognitive mapping. In an example of the latter, Emil Menzel (1978) showed chimpanzees the locations of up to 18 pieces of food in a large outdoor enclosure. The chimpanzee tested was carried around by one experimenter while another hid the food. Other members of the social group, serving as controls for possible influences of olfactory cues or general knowledge of the experimental space, watched from a nearby cage. When all the animals were released into the enclosure shortly afterward, the one that had observed the food being hidden went around collecting it. The animals did not necessarily follow the same path they had been carried along while the food was being hidden nor move at random among the food sites, but took a fairly efficient route. When this tendency was tested with just four or five sites, two or three on one side of the enclosure and the remainder on the other, animals visited the side with most food first in 13 out of 16 cases (Figure 8.21a). However, 13/16 does not differ significantly from the 9.6/16 expected from random choice with 60% of the food on one side. Similarly, marsh tits (*Parus palustris*) do not retrieve seeds stored in an aviary in the order in which they stored them, nor do they retrace the path that they took while storing (Shettleworth and Krebs 1982). But an efficient route need not mean the animal has a representation of the environment as a whole and plans its entire trip within it. Whenever features defining different goals are within sight of each other, the animal will likely approach the nearest or most valuable, making local choices, one at a time, based on currently perceptible cues.

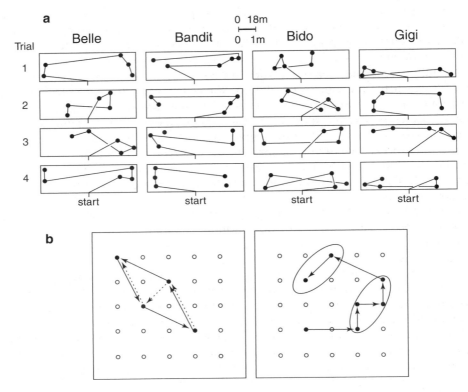

Figure 8.21. a. Paths taken by each of four chimpanzees in their first four trials with five hidden food items. Redrawn from E. Menzel (1978) with permission. The marker indicates the scale in both a and b. b. "Diamond" and "unequal sides" configurations used for testing spatial planning by vervet monkeys. In the diamond configuration, the shortest path among all four corners is the dotted one if the animal is not planning to return to the start (lower right vertex) but the black route if it is. Redrawn from Gallistel and Cramer (1996) with permission.

Nevertheless, cognitive mapping (or at least planning a route beyond the next move) can in principle be distinguished from wholly local choices with certain arrangements of sites. For example, the optimal path for collecting food from the diamond-shaped arrangement shown in Figure 8.21b depends on whether the animal is going to return to the starting point. The animal can make the optimal choice after the second food item only by planning beyond the next two choices. Similarly, when four food items are on one side of an arena and two on the other, the animal must mentally look beyond the first two items to be collected in order to move optimally. Cramer and Gallistel (, 1997; Gallistel and Cramer 1996) report that vervet monkeys behaved as if planning routes in both of these tests. However, without knowing the animals' reinforcement histories in the testing situation, which are not reported, it is difficult to know how to evaluate these data. Moreover, in the four- versus two-item test, the monkeys might simply have remembered the area with four items better if they spent more time there while the sites were being baited. Nevertheless, this approach could be pursued further than it has been (see also Janson 2000).

Some species of jumping spiders are well known for their ability to choose efficient routes and detours in natural conditions. These spiders do not weave a web but pursue their insect prey visually, sometimes watching a victim for a long time while slowly creeping up on it. The spider might move away from the prey initially and climb up a branch from which it can pounce. Tarsitano and Andrew (1999) captured this situation in the laboratory by placing a spider (*Portia labiata*) in the middle of a square enclosure where it could see a prey item above and in front of it. To reach the prey, the spider had to walk diagonally away from it, climb a pole, and traverse a series of two ramps. When spiders were confronted with a choice between two such routes, one to each side, and one of them had a gap in it, 16 of 18 spiders headed in the direction of the unbroken path as soon as they left the start platform. When both routes were complete, they chose the one they had scanned the most while sitting on the start platform; when one route was incomplete, simple algorithms describing scanning ensured they spent most time scanning the complete one. Like the ants we meet shortly, the spiders provide a nice illustration of how apparently demanding feats of navigation can be accomplished by simple mechanisms (see also Cheng 2006).

Knitting together

The idea that animals orient with reference to a cognitive map implies that information gathered in different parts of a journey, even qualitatively different kinds of information, is knitted together into a single allocentric representation. Unlike in the examples of integrating simultaneous cues in Section 8.2, here cues are encountered successively. This occurs in a setup developed by Benhamou (1996) for rats in a water tank and subsequently adopted by Gibson and Kamil (2001; Gibson 2001) for Clark's nutcrackers and people (Figure 8.22). The subject's task is to find a goal hidden at a fixed location in a room full of landmarks. The subject encounters the landmarks on the first part of the

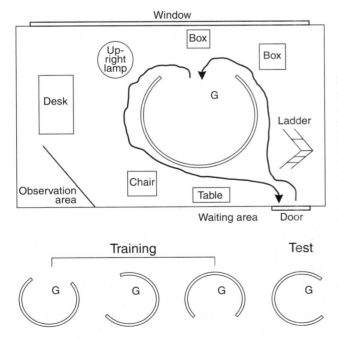

Figure 8.22. Overhead view of the setup used by B. Gibson (2001) to test cognitive mapping in people. The semicircle indicates the opaque enclosure within which the goal (G) was located. The enclosure was rotated from trial to trial to allow about a 270° view of the room from the goal in total. Three of the positions used are shown below the diagram, along with the orientation used for the test. The arrows are the paths people used to enter and leave the enclosure. Redrawn from B. M. Gibson (2001) with permission.

journey, but the goal is within an enclosure that permits only about a 90° view of the room. This enclosure is rotated from trial to trial, so that its entrance has no consistent relationship to the goal, and so that over trials the subject sees different parts of the landmark panorama from the goal. Once subjects can find the goal they are tested with the enclosure in a novel orientation, so they have a new view of landmarks from within it. Neither rats nor nutcrackers oriented accurately in initial tests of this sort, though some nutcrackers eventually learned to do so. Moreover, people behaved similarly if, like nutcrackers, they had to learn for themselves that the goal was at a constant location in the room. Rather than developing a representation of the goal within the room, subjects of all species tested relied much more than they should have on local cues such as the vector between the edge of the enclosure and the goal. In larger-scale space too, people do not do a good job of relating their orientation within an enclosed area such as a room to that within the surrounding environment (Wang and Brockmole 2003).

Some different results have come from another test of knitting together devised by Blaisdell and Cook (2004) for pigeons. As in second-order conditioning in learning of temporal relations (Section 4.4.3), the animal is first exposed to a relationship between two neutral stimuli, simultaneously presented landmarks rather than successively presented tones, lights, or the like. Then it learns to locate food with respect to one of those landmarks, and finally, it is tested with the other. For example, suppose in the first phase A is west of B, and in the second, food is south of A. Knitting together these two experiences would lead the animal to search southwest of B in the test. Generalizing from A to B, a possible alternative strategy, would be expressed as searching directly south of B. Pigeons behave as if connecting the two experiences, whether the landmarks are presented in an open field (Blaisdell and Cook 2004) or on a touchscreen (Sawa, Leising, and Blaisdell 2005). However, in a video simulation of the open field task people at first show generalization between the A and B landmarks (as indeed the pigeons did in the actual open field), but gradually transfer their searching to the site specified by integration (Sturz, Bodily, and Katz 2006). This pattern may reflect learning from initial nonreinforced searches in the test rather than a mapping-like process. However, rats tested in a slightly different way do seem to knit together separately experienced items of landmark information (Chamizo, Rodrigo, and Mackintosh 2006). Rats were trained to find the hidden platform in a water tank in intermixed trials with two sets of three landmarks having one member in common (e.g., landmarks A, B, C and C, D, E). Unlike control rats trained similarly but with nonoverlapping sets of landmarks, those for which the sets shared a member preferred the part of the tank with the platform when tested with a novel combination of landmarks (e.g., A, B, E). The variety of results here indicates that much remains to be done to understand the extent to which animals knit together separately experienced spatial relationships into an overall "map."

Australian desert ants (*Melophorus bagoti*), however, fail entirely and in a surprising way to knit together information obtained in different parts of a journey. The ants are an instructive corrective to anthropomorphism, a reminder of how almost unimaginably strange ways of navigating can be perfectly effective in the natural conditions in which they are normally used. Unlike the Tunisian desert ants we met in Section 8.1, the Australian species live among grass tussocks that provide landmarks, which the ants evidently use along with global path integration somewhat as illustrated in Figure 8.12. By means of a system of barriers, Wehner and colleagues

(Wehner et al. 2006) forced ants to adopt different outward and homeward paths across such terrain to a constant food source. Within a few trips, each ant developed an idiosyncratic round trip route. Having thus shown that they knew the way to the food and home again, the ants were picked up while on the way home with a biscuit crumb and placed down partway along the outward path. What they did then depended on how close to home they were when picked up, but in no case did ants behave as if recognizing where they were on the outward path by either heading back along it or taking a shortcut home. Rather, ants that were still some way from home ran in the direction of the global vector that would have led them home from where they were collected. Ants whose global homing vector was at zero because they were caught just before entering the nest behaved as if lost, searching in circles until they hit the homeward route. To quote the authors' summary, "familiar landmarks are not decoupled from the context within which they have been acquired and are not knitted together in a more general and potentially map-like way. They instruct the ants what to do rather than provide them with map-like information about their position in space" (Wehner. et al. 2006, 75).

Cognitive maps in bees revisited

Dyer's bees tested in the quarry behaved similarly to the ants deprived of familiar landmarks by orienting along the vector that would have taken them to their destination from their original starting point. Indeed, for bees commuting between the hive and a customary feeding site, running off a fixed vector back and forth is very efficient. But what happens when vector information tells displaced bees they should already have arrived? It turns out that at about this point, some maplike knowledge takes over. Menzel and his colleagues (2005) captured experienced bees as they were about to start home from a feeder and quickly fitted them with harmonic radar antennas before releasing them within about 500 meters of the hive but at a different direction from it. The records of displaced bees' entire homeward paths so obtained show that bees trained with a feeder in a stable location flew directly away from the release site in the direction they would have taken to return to the hive (Figure 8.23). Bees that had attended the dance (see Chapter 14) of a bee returning from the stable feeder behaved similarly. After perhaps a few hundred meters this straight flight gave way to a circuitous searching flight, which was then followed by a second phase of straight flight, headed directly to the hive or the feeder. Circling appeared to allow the bees to recognize some features of the landscape from which they knew the homeward vector. Bees that had been trained to a feeder at varying locations immediately began searching flights.

As Cheng (2006) points out, these findings need not mean that bees have an exhaustive knowledge of places around the hive because a bee finding itself with a view similar to that from two familiar locations would presumably still wind up at its goal by generalizing and averaging the resulting vectors. Nevertheless, as R. Menzel et al. (2005) conclude, the bees' behavior implies that they have maplike knowledge in the form of learned vectors from a variety of familiar locations to the hive and/or the feeder, that is, a vector map. That is to say, the bees have evidently learned vectors linking certain known locations and can compute routes home from them, but they do not necessarily have a comprehensive metric map of their territory. Moreover, they apparently do not reverse the process, in that when told a vector along which to head from the hive in the form of another bee's dance, they do not behave as if

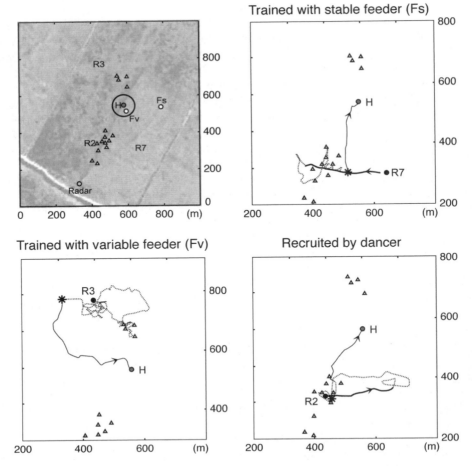

Figure 8.23. Top left: overhead view of the landscape in which bees were tested for maplike knowledge, showing location of the hive (H), the feeder for the stable feeder group (Fs), the tent landmarks (triangles), and several of the experimental release points (R). Remaining panels show paths of one bee from each of the three training groups. Dark lines signify a straight initial flight from the release point. After R. Menzel et al. (2005) with permission.

imagining the location danced about but rather fly to that location even if it is an implausible place for food (see Chapter 14; Wray et al. 2008).

8.4.3   Vertebrates mapping their home ranges

As we have seen, cognitive mapping was originally tested with rats in the laboratory with little or no reference to what the animals might be doing in nature. Indeed, because wild rats are nocturnal and tend to travel along habitual routes and paths (Chitty and Southern 1954), it is not clear what role the visual orientation commonly tested in laboratory rats might have in nature. Ants and bees are more appropriate subjects because their experience can be manipulated in the field and their behavior observed on spatial scales representative of normal foraging trips. As yet no verte-brate has lent itself to such a rich body of work, but a sample of studies of homing pigeons and mammals indicates possibilities for future investigations.

Maps and routes in homing pigeons

Given that people have exploited pigeons' homing ability for thousands of years (Wiltschko and Wiltschko 2003), how pigeons find their way home is still surprisingly controversial (Wallraff 2005). The prevailing view is that they use a "map and compass" mechanism, that is, a way to recognize where they are combined with knowledge of which compass direction to head to reach the home loft. Experiments with clock-shifted birds have established that the directional information may be provided by the sun compass (Box 8.2), but other information is important too. When pigeons start home from unfamiliar locations far from their loft, their "map" is in effect a sense of position relative to home based on olfactory, magnetic, or possibly auditory cues (see Wallraff 2005). Remarkable though it is, this is not a cognitive map in the usual sense. And when pigeons home repeatedly from the same site 7 to 10 kilometers from home, they may not refer to a maplike representation either. Rather, data from tiny GPS trackers carried by flying pigeons show that they may develop stereotyped, idiosyncratic, routes. Somewhat like the Australian desert ants or honeybees, when they are released off their usual routes, they first head not toward home but toward the habitual homeward route (Biro, Meade, and Guilford 2004; Meade, Biro, and Guilford 2006). Under the conditions of this study in the richly detailed countryside around Oxford, the pigeons' usual route seems to be encoded as a series of landmarks or views of the landscape. However, the distances involved and other factors apparently influence whether pigeons develop such stereotyped routes (Wiltschko, Schiffner, and Siegmund 2007). In addition, evidence that clock-shifted birds follow their sun compass rather than a familiar route (Wiltschko, Siegmund, and Stapput 2005) indicates that much remains to be understood about the way in which pigeons integrate different sources of navigational information. When orienting in a familiar landscape, they likely use many more kinds of cues than can ants or bees, relying on different ones according to the circumstances (Keeton 1974; Wallraff 2005).

Meerkats finding boltholes

Meerkats (*Suricata suricatta*) are a species of social mongoose found in the southern African semi-desert. We meet them again in discussing social learning and communication (Chapters 13 and 14), reflecting the fact that one South African population has been intensively studied for many years (cf. Ross-Gillespie and Griffin 2007). Meerkats are primate-like in that they form stable social groups with overlapping generations living in a more or less permanent territory. Animals with such a social system obviously have ample opportunity acquire detailed knowledge about what is where and how to get there. Scattered through its 2–4 square kilometer territory, each group has two or more burrow systems for sleeping and raising young, but they also have numerous boltholes into which they can run for safety when threatened by a predator. By observing what meerkats did in response to naturally occurring and recorded meerkat alarm calls, Manser and Bell (2004) showed that the animals know the locations of boltholes. For example, they headed for the nearest bolthole 83% of the time, whether or not it happened to be one they had recently passed while foraging. Meerkats ignored new, human-made, boltholes, even when these were closest to them when an alarm call was heard. In constrast, if the nearest bolthole was one of their own that the experimenters had covered over with a car mat and sand, the meerkats ran to it and tried to get in. Thus their orientation is based on memory, not visual or olfactory cues from an open bolthole. Since a group may have hundreds of boltholes, these findings suggest that the meerkats have extensive and detailed spatial knowledge of their locations. Perhaps this is not surprising, given that they spend many hours each day moving through the territory digging for invertebrate prey and watching for predators. Exactly how they know the positions of nearby boltholes remains to be determined. Columbian ground squirrels (*Spermophilus columbianus*), another small burrowing mammal of comparatively open spaces, locate escape burrows primarily using global cues from the distal panorama of trees, mountaintops, and the like (Vlasek 2006).

In a further test of meerkats' spatial knowledge, on six occasions Manser (personal communication) captured an adult meerkat foraging with its group and released it about a kilometer away at one of the sleeping burrows within the group's territory. The animals traveled quite directly back to the location where they had been captured, arriving within 40 minutes on average. If the group had already moved on, the lone meerkat began looking around, sniffing the ground, and engaging in similar behaviors indicative of searching. The animals were not obviously using vocal or olfactory cues to find the place where they had been removed from the group, but apparently relying on visual recognition of local or global aspects of the landscape.

Monkeys mapping their home ranges

Like the meerkats, apes and monkeys seem likely to possess large-scale integrated representations of space. Field studies of monkeys and apes that involve following habituated groups on a daily basis have provided an abundance of information about the spatial and temporal distributions of the animals' food and how the animals travel between sleeping sites, water holes, fruiting trees, and other resources (Boinski and Garber 2000; Noser and Byrne 2007). The cognitive demands of tracking temporary and spatially dispersed food sources have been proposed to explain differences in relative brain size among primates, with the fruit-eaters supposedly needing larger brains than leaf-eaters (Chapter 12). Numerous field experiments have shown that various monkey species can learn the locations of artificially provided foods and travel among them in an efficient way (e.g., Janson 1998; Garber 2000). One clever study suggests that Japanese macaques (*Macaca fuscata*) remember the locations of trees with a favorite fruit from year to year. C. Menzel (1991) placed akebi fruit, chocolate, or nothing beside a troop's foraging route at a time of year when akebi fruit were not naturally ripe. Monkeys that discovered akebi often left the troop's foraging route and began looking up into akebi trees, whereas those that found chocolate searched the ground nearby.

Observations of unmanipulated animals are necessary for showing how such learning influences their daily travels. These are often very suggestive but must be interpreted with care (Janson 2000; Janson and Byrne 2007). Mapping where a troop of monkeys goes between leaving its sleeping site in the morning and returning in the evening may suggest the animals are planning their routes, but just as with examples of travel among multiple sites in a smaller space, planning ahead has to be distinguished from moving to the next nearest resource on the basis of locally perceptible cues. For example, to decide whether memory for a fruiting tree's location is being used, it is necessary to know the distance from which it can be detected directly, and that differs for forest and savannah species and with the thickness of vegetation across the year. The animals' nutritional needs relative to different available foods may help explain the sequence in which sites with those foods are visited. Constraints on travel such as needing to arrive at a safe sleeping site by nightfall may need to be taken into account. Noser and Byrne (2007) provide one example of attempting to deal with all these factors. Observed routes can be compared to those predicted on various models of random search (see Janson and Byrne 2007). And ideally, opportunistic observations can help to reveal how the animals' travels reflect what they know. For example, if a predator is encountered at a habitual waterhole, does the troop use another one the next day? In a similar way, the nature and rate of change in travel patterns with the seasons may indicate whether the animals are planning routes with certain goals in mind. For instance, visiting patterns and speed of approach indicate that mangabeys keep track of whether trees are already finished fruiting or are about to produce ripe fruit (Janmaat, Byrne, and Zuberbühler 2006). Such questions have been attracting increasing interest at the same time as they are being addressed in more sophisticated ways. One possibility (Janson and Byrne 2007) is that some primates' spatial knowledge encodes important locations and the routes or vectors between them, but without being a complete Euclidean survey map. Although it would likely represent more and varied types of sites than the vector map of the honeybees, it could be similar in kind.

8.4.4 But do people have cognitive maps?

Research on spatial cognition in human adults and children is a large area in its own right and can be given only a brief mention here (for an introduction see Newcombe and Huttenlocher 2000). As indicated by the scattered mentions of findings with people, much contemporary work in this area is closely integrated with that on other species, especially in looking at spatial behavior in terms of a number of distinct subprocesses and in failing to find evidence for overall cognitive maps. Nowhere is this more evident than in a prominent opinion piece titled "Human spatial representation: Insights from animals" (Wang and Spelke 2002). Wang and Spelke proposed that rather than depending on an enduring allocentric map, much human spatial behavior depends on momentary egocentric representations, specifically dead reckoning, orienting by the geometry of surrounding space, and viewpoint-dependent matching of remembered to current views of the environment. Evidence for each of these processes comes from animal data like that reviewed throughout this chapter and from analogous experiments with people. In one key example, people viewed a room with a few objects in it and were then blindfolded, disoriented, and asked to point to the objects and the corners of the room. Errors in pointing indicated that the objects had not been integrated either into a map of the room as a whole or into a single configuration (Wang and Spelke 2000). Evidence that recognition of a familiar scene takes longer from a novel viewpoint supports the suggestion that encoding is viewpoint-dependent. However, more recent research (Burgess 2006) indicates that human spatial representation has both egocentric and allocentric components, which exist in parallel. In experiments like those just summarized, greater experience, a larger environment, and other factors make allocentric representations more evident. This approach is clearly much in the spirit of other research emphasized in the present chapter in dissecting spatial cognition into distinct parallel but interacting mechanisms and eschewing discussion of overall maps. Whether two systems defined in terms of function, egocentric and allocentric, will provide a useful way forward remains to be seen.

8.4.5   Conclusions

The cognitive map has been seducing investigators for over 60 years, but perhaps it is no more than a metaphor based on human introspection. Just as with theory of mind and other hypothetical mechanisms discussed later in this book, attributing cognitive mapping to an animal may be an unwarranted exercise of anthropomorphism, and one that is not even very useful in explaining human behavior. Translating such an intuitively appealing explanation of apparently intelligent behavior into testable implications in a way that researchers agree on is never easy. When the results of behavioral tests cause theorists to revise ambiguous and slippery concepts, agreement can become almost impossible. In the case of cognitive mapping, there is little if any unambiguous evidence that any creature gets around using a representation that corresponds to an overall metric survey map of its environment. The exceptional cases in which animals satisfy one or another classic criterion for mapping-like behavior by taking novel short cuts in the absence of direct cues from the goal (Singer, Abroms, and Zentall 2006; W. Roberts, Cruz, and Tremblay 2007) or finding their way home when displaced (R. Menzel. et al. 2005) are better explained by reference to what cues the animals are actually using, how they are using them, and how they come to do so than to the ill-defined notion of a cognitive map.

8.5   Summary

The study of spatial orientation is a very active area using a wide variety of species and approaches from fieldwork to neuroscience (Box 8.4). Among areas of research in comparative cognition it is exemplary, perhaps unique, in the way in which data and theorizing have been integrated across species and approaches as for example in the book edited by Jeffery (2003). The richest bodies of data come from three very different groups of animals: small nocturnal rodents (rats and hamsters), diurnal, central-place foraging insects (bees, wasps, and ants), and birds that orient over tens to hundreds of kilometers (homing pigeons and migratory species). The ways in which these animals perceive the world (consider for instance the very different visual systems of rats, pigeons, and bees) and the cues relevant for orientation in their natural environments differ enormously, yet some orientation mechanisms such as landmark learning or path integration and their interactions have been analyzed in a way that cuts across phyla. To some extent, this integrative approach has resulted in a theoretical orientation based on ideas from human psychology being replaced by one rooted in data from nonhuman animals.

Box 8.4 Space in the Brain

The study of what parts of the brain, particularly in mammals, help to control spatial behavior and how they do so is a vast area of contemporary behavioral neuroscience. The fact that the hippocampus is important for spatial memory in both mammals and birds has already been alluded to in Chapters 2 and 7, but in itself this does not tell us much about how brains actually represent space. Until recently the primary relevant information consisted of evidence for *place cells* in the rat hippocampus, single cells that fire when the rat is in a particular location within a laboratory enclosure. However, although the properties of place cells have been studied in some depth, one property seemingly essential for coding space is apparently lacking, topographic organization. That is, cells close together in the hippocampus do not necessarily fire to places close together in space. Moreover, the same cell may have a place field (i.e., area in which it is active) in more than one enclosure (cf. Jeffery 2003).

The last few years have seen major advances in understanding how space is actually coded in the brain (see McNaughton et al. 2006). A major discovery is cells in the entorhinal cortex, *grid cells,* that map space in a periodic pattern whose spatial scale increases in an orderly way across layers of the medial entorhinal cortex. Combined with signals from cells sensitive to the animal's head direction and perhaps self-motion cues, these have the potential to code changes in an animal's position. Just as a unique time could in principle be coded by simultaneously reading the states of multiple oscillators with different frequencies (Section 9.3.2), so a location in space can be represented in terms of overlapping tessellations of tiles ranging from quite small to nearly the size of the space. New paradigms that require rats to navigate by dead reckoning have been used to probe the function of grid cells. In addition, hippocampal place cell recordings from rats moving over much longer distances than in traditional studies (e.g., 18 meters) show that the size of place fields increases across the hippocampus, perhaps providing a means to encode both details of space and general spatial context (see Hasselmo 2008).

This chapter began with descriptions of the wide range of mechanisms animals use for getting around. By itself, each of them has advantages and disadvantages. Dead reckoning is most useful for short journeys back and forth to a central place, especially in an environment with relatively few landmarks, as in the dark or on the desert. Other ways of getting back and forth to a starting place include route learning both in the sense of a memorized sequence of motor patterns (response learning) and in the sense of a sequence of responses to landmarks. Dead reckoning and route learning in either sense leave the animal lost if it is displaced too far off its usual route. However, stimulus generalization between familiar and unfamiliar views of the environment gives route learning some flexibility.

The varieties of spatial information—from landmarks, beacons, dead reckoning, environmental shape—are processed in different cognitive modules which take different kinds of input and output decisions about what distance and/or direction to move relative to different kinds of cues. This raises the question of how the outputs of different spatial modules are combined during the acquisition and use of spatial information. Are different kinds of information processed in parallel, do they compete for learning as in conditioning, or are they integrated in some other way? When are modules used in a hierarchical manner, and why? When spatial cues have acquired their significance, do they compete for control or are their outputs averaged? When does each kind of combination rule operate? For instance, does the system that has been more reliable during evolution or individual experience or that evolved earlier take precedence? A great deal of attention has been devoted to the question of whether any animal integrates different sources of spatial information into a unified allocentric representation of distances and directions, a cognitive map. This question turns out to be difficult to answer, partly because cognitive maps can mean different things to different people. Focusing on the specific cues available to animals and how they are used in specific situations provides better understanding of how animals get around than attempting to prove or disprove use of a cognitive map.

Further reading

Useful recent reviews of most aspects of spatial cognition can be found in the books edited by Jeffery (2003) and Wasserman and Zentall (2006b) and the online "cyberbook" edited by Brown and Cook (2006). Boinski and Garber's (2000) *On the Move* emphasizes field studies of animal movement patterns; the July 2007, special issue of *Animal Cognition* discusses numerous examples from primates. Newcombe and Huttenlocher's (2000) book is an excellent introduction to the development of spatial cognition in children very much in the same spirit as this chapter. The book by Wallraff (2005), the review by Bingman and Cheng (2005), and the special section of the August 11, 2006, issue of *Science* provide more information on homing and migration.

Some of the classics in the area are still well worth reading. These include the first six chapters of Gallistel (1990), with all aspects of animal spatial cognition discussed in the context of human navigation. The first two chapters of O'Keefe and Nadel's (1978) book are an excellent introduction to philosophical and psychological notions about space. A facsimile of this entire book is available free at http://www.cognitivemap.net. For a discussion of exploration, Berlyne (1960) still contains a lot of wisdom and a summary of much psychological and ethological literature.

9
Timing

As sunset gives way to dusk, bats and nighthawks appear, swooping and gliding over city rooftops or above surfaces of lakes, catching insects. Like most other living things, these animals have an internal rhythm, a biological clock with a period of about 24 hours that allows them to become active at the same time each day. Some of the most impressive evidence for such a clock is the nightly appearance of thousands of South American oilbirds pouring out from their roosts deep in caves where no sunlight reaches.

Clocks that time intervals much less than 24 hours are evident in classical and instrumental conditioning. Pavlov (1927) described the first examples. For instance, a dog trained with a three-minute whistle predicting weak acid to its mouth salivated most during the last minute of the whistle. This phenomenon, which Pavlov called *inhibition of delay*, suggests that the dog was timing the signal. Contemporary research on how animals time intervals seconds to minutes long includes some of the most elegant experiments and quantitative models in the study of animal cognition. It is worth knowing about for that reason alone. Timing is also worth knowing about for functional reasons. Information about how animals time events will come in handy in Chapter 11, on foraging and instrumental behavior. For instance, models of foraging suggest that animals need to be sensitive to rates of occurrence. Mathematically, rate is number divided by time, so this idea implies that we need to know how animals time and count (Chapter 10) to understand foraging.

9.1   Circadian rhythms

The regular alternation of day and night is perhaps the most predictable event on Earth. Therefore it is not surprising that nearly every organism that has been studied, including plants, bacteria, and human beings, has an internal model of this daily rhythm. This internal model is evident in a daily cycle of activity and/or physiological state which persists even when organisms are kept in unchanging light or darkness. Circadian rhythms are not usually regarded as part of cognition, but they appear in this book for three reasons. First, the way in which circadian rhythms are synchronized with (or *entrained to*) local day and night is an instructive example of behavioral plasticity in response to experience. Biological rhythms illustrate beautifully the general principle that animals have evolved implicit internal representations of important aspects of the world, representations programmed to be modified in adaptive ways by events that are functionally relevant in nature (Shepard 1984, 1994). Second, in a kind of learning that is important in the wild, animals learn about events that recur on a daily basis, linking them to the state of their circadian clock. Finally, understanding something about timing daily events is necessary for understanding proposals that timing intervals of seconds to minutes involves the same mechanism.

9.1.1   Entrainment: Synchronizing endogenous cycles with environmental cycles

Some animals, like most of us, wake in the morning and sleep at night. Others, like bats and moths, do the reverse. Still other species are most active at dawn and dusk. Although casual observation in nature suggests that daily rhythms of activity are driven by cues from the environment, most daily rhythms run independently of the environment but need continual environmental input to remain synchronized with day and night. The very earliest studies of biological rhythms revealed that daily rhythms of activity and other physiological variables persist, often indefinitely, when animals are isolated from the influence of local day and night. The persistent rhythm cannot be produced by some unknown signals from the earth's rotation reaching into laboratory rooms because these *free-running* rhythms are generally slightly more or less than 24 hours long. Thus, for example, after awhile animals in the laboratory will be active when their conspecifics outdoors are asleep. Because the *endogenous* (i.e., self-generated) daily rhythm is not exactly 24 hours long, researchers refer to *circadian* rhythms, that is, rhythms of approximately (*circa*) a day. Figures 9.1 and 9.2 show examples.

The process by which the underlying rhythm-generator or *pacemaker* is synchronized with environmental signals is referred to as *entrainment*. The signal that entrains the rhythm is referred to as an *entraining agent* or *zeitgeber* (literally "time-giver" in German). The most-studied zeitgeber is light, but other stimuli can also function as entraining agents (Mrosovsky et al. 1989). Our examples are almost all from activity rhythms because these are easily measured in the laboratory and have featured in many studies, but most physiological functions exhibit a daily cycle; it is difficult to find one that does not. The propensity to be entrained is an adaptive feature of the circadian system that adjusts behavior to the local environment. However, the behavioral and physiological variables controlled by the underlying circadian pacemaker can also be influenced in ways other than by entrainment. For example, during a total eclipse of the sun, birds stop singing and sit still, as if dusk were falling. Conversely, a diurnal rodent asleep in its burrow is stimulated to activity if a predator breaks in on it. Such transient changes *mask* underlying rhythms.

Several well-defined criteria characterize entrainment (Dunlap, Loros, and Decoursey 2003): *(1)* The putative entraining agent must act in the absence of other cues. *(2)* It must act to adjust the period of the animal's free-running rhythm to the period of the signal. The unlikely hypothetical case in which a signal repeated every 19 hours caused an animal to become active every 24 hours would not be entrainment because the periodicity of the behavior would not match the periodicity of the signal. *(3)* The entrained rhythm must adopt a stable phase relationship with the imposed cue. For example, if a group of animals is isolated in constant light or constant darkness, the free-running rhythms of different individuals will eventually be out of phase with one another, reflecting individual differences in free-running period. Yet if they are all now exposed to the same light-dark cycle, before very long their activity rhythms will be synchronized with the environment and,

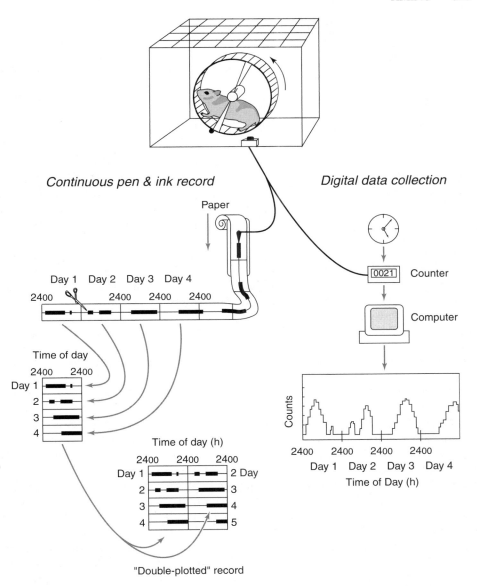

Figure 9.1. Setups for recording rhythms of locomotor activity in hamsters and typical data. (Golden hamsters are used in much contemporary research on mammalian rhythms because they have exceptionally clear and reliable rhythms of running wheel activity.) In the traditional method (left), each revolution of the running wheel results in a pen mark on a continuously running roll of paper. When the records of successive days are mounted one under the other, as at the lower left, regularities in the daily pattern of activity can easily be picked out by eye. This is even easier when each day is "double plotted," as at the bottom. Using a computer to record the activity, as is often done nowadays, may facilitate detailed quantitative analyses. Redrawn from Moore-Ede, Sulzman, and Fuller (1982) with permission.

incidentally, with one another. The original phase relationship of the pacemaker with the entraining agent does not influence the final, species-specific, relationship. *(4)* Entrainment can be distinguished from direct driving of the rhythm (i.e., masking)

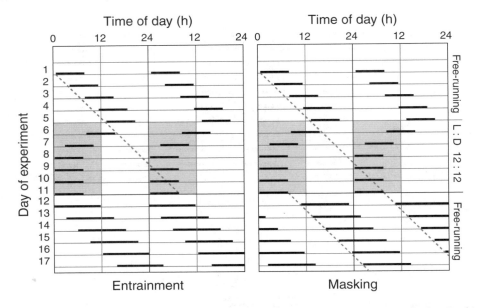

Figure 9.2. The contrast between entrainment and masking. A free running activity rhythm (in this case, one with a period slightly greater than 24 hours, as indicated by its drift to the right) is synchronized by imposition of a 12-hour light—12-hour dark schedule (L:D 12:12; gray rectangles represent the dark period). When the synchronizing cue is removed, the animal on the left shows that it has been entrained; the other's activity returns to where it would have been without the cue, indicating that the underlying rhythm had simply been masked by the L:D cycle.

by putting the animals back into constant conditions and observing the relationship between the phase of the free running rhythm and the phase of the just-removed environmental cycle (Figure 9.2). If the animals in our example are truly entrained, then their activity rhythms will all start their free-running drift in the same place. For example, if laboratory "dawn" and the onset of activity had been at local 10 AM, the animals will still become active about 10 AM on the first day with constant light. However, if the laboratory light cycle is simply masking the effects of the circadian pacemaker, each animal may become active at a different time when constant conditions are instituted. In masking, the time of activity is predicted by extrapolating from the drift in the free-running rhythm before the environmental cue was imposed (Figure 9.2).

Entrainment is a kind of behavioral plasticity in which the animal's internal model of the cycle of day and night is brought into register with true day and night. Like many other kinds of preprogrammed adaptive behavioral plasticity, entrainment of the 24-hour activity rhythm is most sensitive to modification by conditions close to those found in nature. Circadian rhythms can be entrained only to periods of about 24 hours. "About 24 hours" means different things for different species and situations, but a range of three or four hours around 24 hours is typical. Thus, it might be possible to entrain activity to 22- or 26-hour days (i.e., a period of light plus a period of darkness every 22 or 26 hours), but unlikely that the rhythm could be entrained to 19 or 29 hour days.

The fact that a free-running rhythm can be brought into a predictable relationship with a zeitgeber means that a cycle of changing sensitivity to the zeitgeber underlies the measured behavioral or physiological rhythm. This sensitivity can be revealed by

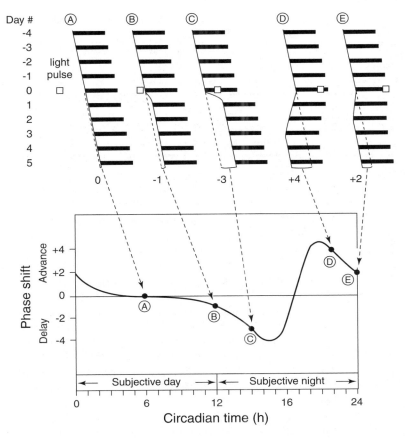

Figure 9.3. A phase-response curve and how it was derived. Data are from five experiments with a nocturnal species. In each, a brief pulse of light is presented at a different phase of the free-running rhythm and the effect on activity in the next few days is measured as number of hours' advance or delay in activity. Redrawn from Moore-Ede, Sulzman, and Fuller (1982) with permission.

experiments in which a single pulse of light 10 or 15 minutes long is presented to animals free-running in constant darkness. The effects of a few minutes of light on one occasion are evident in the ensuing few days, in which the activity rhythm first shifts and then runs freely again. Figure 9.3 shows an example for a nocturnal animal like a golden hamster. In a regular 24-hour cycle of light and dark, the animal would become active at the onset of darkness. When the rhythm is free running, the period of activity reveals this noctural animal's *subjective night; subjective day* is the period of prolonged inactivity. (For a diurnal animal the terms reverse: subjective day is the active period.) In this typical example, a pulse of light early in the subjective night causes the animal to become active later the next day, that is, the phase of the rhythm has been delayed relative to the external 24-hour cycle. Conversely, a pulse of light toward the end of the subjective night advances the rhythm: the animal becomes active earlier the next day. Somewhere toward the middle of subjective night, the effect of a light pulse switches from delaying to advancing. Light has little or no effect in the middle of subjective day. Hamsters' activity rhythms can also be entrained by social stimulation like the regular arrival of a mate or rival or by activity in a novel environment. Such zeitgebers have a characteristic pattern of effects different from those of light (Mrosovsky. et al. 1989).

The fact that the circadian rhythm is most sensitive to light near the beginning and end of subjective night means that in nature dawn and dusk are constantly pushing and pulling animals' endogenous circadian rhythm into synchrony with day and night. In the laboratory, synchrony can be produced by exposing animals to *skeleton photoperiods,* that is, a pulse of light at the beginning of laboratory "day" and another one at the end. This mimics the regime that a nocturnal cave- or burrow-dweller might expose itself to naturally. If it ventures out too early in the evening, its activity will begin later the next day (i.e., its rhythm will be delayed), whereas if it stays active too long, the pulse of light at dawn will advance its activity, causing it to rise earlier the next night. This suggests that an animal that stays in its den for many days on end may become desynchronized with the external day and night (i.e., its rhythm will free run). This is exactly what happens to beavers that stay in their lodges and under the snow-covered ice throughout the Canadian winter (Bovet and Oertli 1974).

The direction and amount of shift in the free-running rhythm produced by a single pulse of light are summarized in a *phase response curve,* a plot of the response of the rhythm to a constant signal as a function of the rhythm's phase when the signal was applied. Figure 9.3 shows an example and how it was derived. A phase response curve (PRC) is analogous to the function relating learning to the CS-US interval or the number of conditioning trials (Chapter 4) in that both describe the effect of an environmental event as a function of systematic variation in its features. Learning is usually thought of as generating new knowledge and behavior whereas entrainment brings a preexisiting cycle into register with a cycle in the environment. However, as we have seen in Chapter 4, conditioning can be seen as bringing a preorganized sequence of behavior, or a behavior system, under the control of certain kinds of environmental events (Timberlake 1994). This provocative analogy summarizes the notion that conditioning does not create the behavior expressive of conditioning any more than entrainment creates the behaviors that change on a circadian cycle. But it is no more than an analogy: entrainment and associative learning otherwise have very different properties.

9.1.2   Effects of regular meal times

A major function of the circadian system is to allow each behavior to be performed at the most appropriate times of day. The most-studied example is feeding. Hummingbirds or bees may find their favorite flowers open only in the morning; kestrels find their rodent prey out of their burrows at some times and not others (Rijnsdorp, Daan, and Dijkstra 1981). Many animals adjust their activities to such periodic feeding opportunities, but how do they do it? There are three possibilities. One is that the circadian oscillator that can be entrained by light is also entrained by regular feeding. A second possibility is that activity in anticipation of regular feedings represents the output of a second endogenous oscillator that is entrained by food (i.e., a food-entrainable, as distinct from a light-entrainable, oscillator). Third, the animal may simply learn at what time of day, that is, at what phase of its circadian clock, to expect food. There is evidence for each of these, although it is not yet clear how the species and/or situation determines which one(s) will be seen.

A landmark study in this area was one in which rats in running wheels were fed two one-hour meals a day, at 10 AM and 4 PM (Bolles and Moot 1973). The rats soon began to show a pattern of anticipatory running that began in the hour or so before

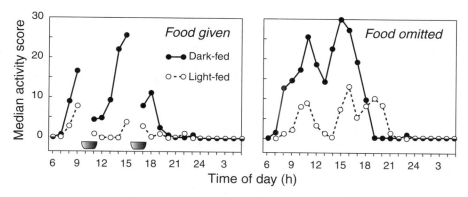

Figure 9.4. Running activity (wheel revolutions per hour) of rats fed twice a day, during the dark or the light phase of the light-dark cycle, and activity in a test with food omitted. Notice that both groups appear to anticipate the food. Redrawn from Bolles and Moot (1973) with permission.

each feeding and increased up to the time when food was given (Figure 9.4). Because hunger was presumably greater near 10 AM, after 17 hours of deprivation, than near 4 PM, the rats must have been using time of day as a conditional cue and not simply running more as they became hungrier. Moreover, when food was omitted on test days, running peaked around the usual time of feeding, then declined and increased again before the next usual mealtime. Thus the rats were apparently learning when their mealtimes were. It could be suggested instead that the two periods of running represent the output of two separate food-entrainable oscillators. However, this kind of interpretation becomes less plausible when there are more separate mealtimes to learn as in the first example of time-place learning in the next section.

The idea that feeding entrains a separate circadian oscillator rather than conditioning anticipation to a particular phase of the rhythm entrained by light is supported by observations that rats in constant darkness, that is, with free-running circadian rhythms, become most active just before feedings if the feedings are at a consistent time of day. The same conclusion is supported by neurobiological studies. Rats with lesions to the suprachiasmatic nucleus of the hypothalamus, which abolish circadian rhythms, still show activity that anticipates daily feedings (review in Mistlberger 1993). However, when they are required to bar press for food, rats do learn about interfood intervals of 17 or 30 hours (Crystal 2001), although they discriminate these intervals less well than those near 24 hours. The implications of this finding for theories of interval timing are discussed in Section 9.3.2.

The relative contributions of entrainment and learning about circadian phase to the effects of periodic feedings vary across species (Mistlberger 1993). Bees appear to have just one circadian oscillator, which can be entrained by food as well as light. Bees kept in constant light and offered sugar water once a day had their activity rhythm entrained to the time of feeding (Frisch and Aschoff 1987). Each experimental nest's daily bout of activity shifted progressively until it began around mealtime, that is, the phase of the rhythm and the zietgeber had a predictable relationship. Furthermore, when feedings stopped, each nest's activity free-ran from its new position in time, satisfying another criterion for entrainment. The few species that have been studied in depth also appear to differ in the number of different daily feeding times they can learn. Bees and birds may be able to learn more different times than rats (Mistlberger 1993).

The preceding brief review indicates that in some species and situations, regular feedings at one or more times of day entrain a distinct circadian oscillator while in others they linked by learning to the circadian rhythm entrained by light. Learning about time of day may take place because the internal 24-hour rhythm acts as a contextual stimulus with which other events like feeding or the arrival of a mate or predator are associated. On this view, learning that food occurs at noon is no different from learning that food occurs in a striped chamber or when a tone is on rather than off. Memories may be better retrieved at the time of day when they were originally formed than at other times, although, like other phenomena reviewed in this section, this "time-stamp" effect varies with species (McDonald. et al. 2002).

9.1.3   Daily time and place learning

A rat in a cage becoming active before the time of feeding is showing that it knows when food is coming. But in nature, food doesn't just drop into a rat's burrow. The animal has to know where to get food, so anticipatory activity may function to get animals to the right place on time. Indeed, one of the first examples of circadian rhythms ever studied was the predictable arrival of bees at the jam pots on a family's outdoor breakfast table (see Gallistel 1990). Because flowers may be producing nectar only at certain times of day, the ability to learn time and place is important to bees, hummingbirds, and other nectar feeders. Carnivores, too, may develop daily routines based on time-place associations. For example when Rijnsdorp, Daan, and Dijkstra (1981) regularly released mice in a field at a time when kestrels (*Falco tinnunculus*) were seldom seen there, the birds' visits to that field became more regular around the release time. Learning about time of day may also allow family members to coordinate their activities with one another. Young rabbits and hares meet their mother for nursing just once or twice a day (Gonzalez-Mariscal and Rosenblatt 1996). Ring dove parents share incubation: the male sits on the nest most of the day and the female the rest of the time (Silver 1990). Each member of the pair leaves off foraging and approaches the nest at a distinctive time of day.

In the prototypical laboratory demonstration of daily time and place learning (Biebach, Gordijn, and Krebs 1989), individual garden warblers (*Sylvia borin*) lived in a large cage which had a central area with four feeding compartments ("rooms") opening off it (Figure 9.5). During each three-hour segment of the daily 12-hour period of light, food was available in a different room. The bird had to start in the central chamber and move into one of the rooms to feed. If it chose the correct room for the current time, it found the door over the food bowl unlocked for a few seconds. After feeding, the bird could return to the central area and make a new choice. Once the birds were apportioning most of their visits appropriately, they had tests with food available in all four places throughout the day. The pattern of visits persisted, indicating that the warblers were not simply going back to the room where they had most recently been fed (Figure 9.5). A further test of whether the pattern of visits was associated with the circadian clock consisted of preventing birds from visiting any of the feeding rooms for one 3-hour period. When visits were permitted again, birds went most to the correct room for the time of day, not the room that would normally follow the one they had been visiting before the block (Krebs and Biebach 1989). Furthermore, when garden warblers or starlings that had learned a time-place pattern were placed in constant dim light with food always available in all four rooms, the pattern persisted for several days (Biebach, Falk, and Krebs 1991; Wenger, Biebach, and Krebs 1991).

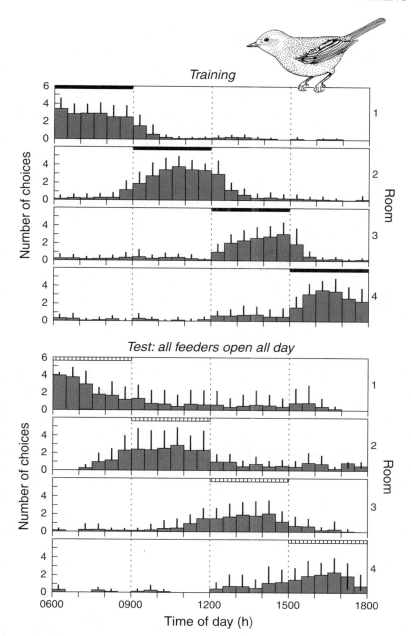

Figure 9.5. Time and place learning in garden warblers, illustrated by the number of entries to each room per half hour throughout the day. During training, food was available for three hours in each of rooms 1 to 4, in that order (dark bars). After Biebach, Gordijn, and Krebs (1989) with permission.

The garden warblers evidently used circadian phase to search primarily in the correct place at each time of day, but clearly this is not the only way to solve a daily time-place learning task. Consider, for example, a task with only two times and places such as has been used for rats, pigeons, and other species (C. Thorpe and Wilkie 2006). Animals might be put into an apparatus with two or more feeding locations at 9 AM and again at 3 PM with reinforcement at location A in the morning and location B in the afternoon. This discrimination could be based on interval timing, using the fact that the first session is, say, 3 hours after the lights come on in the home cage and the second session is 6 hours later. Alternatively, it could be based on *ordinal timing* (Carr and Wilkie 1997), that is, encoding sessions as first or second in the day. This seems more likely when the experimenter schedules feeding opportunities by taking the animal from its home cage and placing it in an apparatus for separate sessions than when the option to visit a possible feeding site is always available, as in nature or in the experiment with garden warblers. And of course ordinal, interval, and/or circadian timing could be combined, for instance using the interval from lights-on to the morning session and encoding the afternoon session ordinally, as "second."

The different behavioral implications of these three mechanisms are illustrated by a study in which rats learned a daily time-place task with three times and locations, A, B, and C (Pizzo and Crystal 2002). A was always correct in the morning and C in the afternoon, but the session in which B was correct was immediately after A for subgroup AB-C, and immediately before C for subgroup A-BC. Once the rats had learned to direct most of their choices to the correct location for each time of day, they were tested with session B moved either late (for subgroup AB-C) or early. If they had been basing their choices in session B on the fact that it was second in the day, behavior should not have been disrupted, but instead rats chose at chance in this test, more consistent with circadian timing. In a further test, the light-dark cycle in the rats' colony room was eliminated, along with other cues such as feeding during the sessions that could have been used for timing the intervals before and between daily sessions. Consistent with reliance on circadian timing, in this brief test the rats still tended to choose the correct site for each session, but consistent with some role for interval timing, they did not perform as well as when all the putative timing cues were present. A variety of other studies of this general type, primarily with rats and pigeons, have shown that daily time-place learning tasks may be solved in many ways, depending on factors such as the discriminability of the time intervals and other relevant cues (Thorpe and Wilkie 2006; Crystal 2006a). Originally, however, interest in daily time-place learning was stimulated by Gallistel's (1990) claim that animal memories consist of linked records of what, where, and when (in the sense of circadian time). It is now clear that animals can indeed base feeding decisions on circadian time and that under some conditions other cues are used as well. A recent example with bees related to episodic memory is the study by Pahl and colleagues (2007).

9.1.4 Summary

Circadian rhythms of activity and rest run freely in constant conditions. They are adjusted to the local environment by the process of entrainment, which has several distinct properties. To decide whether activity that anticipates a regular environmental event reflects entrainment, several questions need to be asked (Aschoff 1986). Is the effect described by a phase response curve, that is, does the possible entraining agent pull the free running rhythm into a predictable relationship with itself? Does the rhythm free run from its new phase when the entraining agent is removed? Does the effect of the putative entraining agent depend on its original relationship to the free running rhythm? For example, the effects of social stimuli on hamsters' subsequent activity depend on when in the circadian activity cycle they occur, indicating that they entrain the rhythm (Honrado and Mrosovsky 1991), whereas in the experiment in Figure 9.5 birds seem to associate each feeding place with the appropriate time of day. Learning about the times and places of food availability, encounters with predators, prey, or conspecifics, probably all play a role in organizing animals' daily routines. When memory for time and place develops in a single trial (e.g., Pahl et al. 2007) it might qualify as episodic-like (Chapter 7).

9.2   Interval timing: Data

In circadian timing, an endogenous oscillator that runs freely in a species-specific way is entrained to periods not too different from 24 hours by light and a few other stimuli. In interval timing, behavior is controlled by events of arbitrary periodicities considerably shorter than a day signaled in arbitrary ways. Whether short-interval timing also reflects one or more oscillators or is best understood in some other way is the subject of Section 9.3. This section summarizes the extensive data that provide the basic material for theories of timing. As we have seen already, concerns about time are intrinsic to the study of learning and memory. Recall, for example, the discussions of the role of time in conditioning (Chapter 4) and of whether animals remember events as occurring at particular times in the past (Chapter 7). But most explicit studies of interval timing have relied on operant conditioning procedures. A large body of such work is in effect psychophysics, asking how time is perceived. Based on that, often with similar experimental procedures, is research asking how perceived time controls behavior, for example when a signal to be timed is interrupted or when several events must be timed concurrently.

9.2.1   The psychophysics of time

The peak procedure, temporal generalization, and Weber's Law

Pavlov's demonstrations of inhibition of delay indicate that animals are sensitive to the time elapsed since a signal began. Operant studies using the *peak interval procedure* or simply *peak procedure* (S. Roberts 1981) tap interval timing in an analogous way. In this procedure, animals are exposed to many daily trials in which food can be earned a fixed time after the onset of a signal. For instance, in a procedure for pigeons, a pecking key lights and the first peck 20 seconds later is reinforced with food. The key then goes dark for an intertrial interval (ITI) of variable duration before lighting again to begin another trial with the same sequence of events. An omniscient pigeon need only peck once per trial, at the end of the programmed interval, but as pigeons are not omniscient and as they are typically fairly hungry in these experiments, they peck many times per trial and do so at a faster average rate as the time for food approaches.

To discover how precisely the animal knows the time of feeding, *empty trials* are added. These are occasional trials, maybe 20% of the total, in which no food occurs and the signal stays on perhaps twice as long as usual. Animals accustomed to this procedure respond most around the scheduled feeding time, as shown in Figure 9.6. Average response rates describe a nearly symmetrical normal distribution with its peak close to the interval being timed. When the interval to be timed is varied across animals or across blocks of sessions, a set of identically shaped curves results. The longer the interval being timed, the greater the spread of the distribution. If the x-axis of these plots is rescaled as proportion of the programmed interval and the y-axis as proportion of maximum response rate, the stretched or compressed response rate

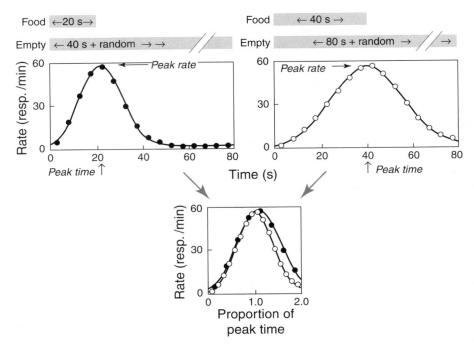

Figure 9.6. Examples of data from rats trained in the peak procedure with reinforcement 20 or 40 seconds after the beginning of the interval on food trials; no food was given on empty trials and the signal lasted longer than usual. The lower part of the figure shows how such data can be superimposed by rescaling the x-axis. The y-axis may also be scaled as proportion of peak rate. Redrawn from S. Roberts (1981) with permission.

graphs can be superimposed on one another (Figure 9.6). This means that for given species and testing conditions a predictable proportion of the maximum response rate is reached a certain proportion of the way though the interval regardless of how long the interval is. If we quite reasonably interpret an animal's rate of instrumental responding for food as an indication of how near in time it perceives the food to be, this result can be seen as an instance of Weber's Law (see Chapter 3). Longer times are perceived and/or remembered with greater variance than shorter times, and that variance is proportional to the duration being timed. This latter property is referred to in discussions of timing as *the scalar property* (Gibbon 1991).

One beauty of research on interval timing is that a variety of procedures produce mutually consistent results. For instance, in a test of temporal generalization responding is reinforced after a signal of one duration but not after other durations. In an early example with rats (Church and Gibbon 1982), the light in the operant chamber was turned off for a few seconds and then a lever slid into the chamber for five seconds. A rat was reinforced with food for pressing the lever if the period of darkness had been, say, four seconds, and not otherwise. This procedure yields a typical generalization gradient (Chapter 6) with its peak centered at the reinforced duration. Longer reinforced durations give broader gradients and, as in the peak procedure, these gradients are superimposed when the x and y axes are rescaled.

An animal tested with temporal generalization or the peak procedure can be seen as comparing a current interval with a memory of reinforced intervals in past trials.

Scalar timing indicates that this comparison is based on the ratio of current elapsed time or signal duration to the remembered interval. Equal ratios (i.e., equal proportions of the reinforced interval) lead to equal response rates or probabilities.

Bisecting time intervals

Further data consistent with ratio comparison come from tests of *temporal bisection*. Consider the following discrimination training procedure for rats. A tone comes on for either two or eight seconds. Then two levers slide into the operant chamber. Pressing the left lever is reinforced if the tone lasted two seconds, and pressing the right lever is reinforced if it lasted eight seconds. In effect, the rats are reporting their judgment of whether the tone is relatively short or long. When they are performing well, they can be tested with tones of intermediate durations. They divide their choices between the two levers in a predictable way, pressing the "long" lever on a higher proportion of trials the longer the tone is (Church and Deluty 1977). What is especially interesting is the duration at which they choose each lever 50% of the time, interpreted as the duration they perceive as halfway between long and short. Arithmetically, 7.5 is halfway between 3 and 12, but if animals compare time intervals by implicitly computing their ratios, the halfway or bisection point from the rats' point of view will be not 7.5 seconds but 6, as in fact it is (Figure 9.7). (The ratio of 12 to 6 is the same as the ratio of 6 to 3.) Another way to describe such findings is to say that the animals bisect the temporal interval at its geometric mean. (The geometric mean of two numbers is the square root of their product, for example, $6 = \sqrt{(3 \times 12)}$).

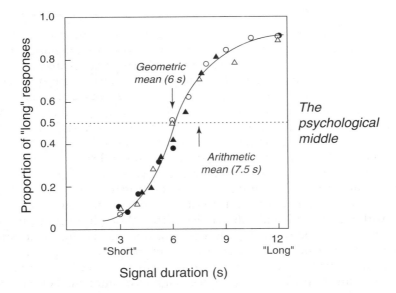

Figure 9.7. Results of a temporal bisection experiment in which rats were trained to press one lever after a 3-second signal ("short") and another after a 12-second signal ("long") and then were tested with intermediate durations. Different symbols represent different sets of test trials. Redrawn from Church and Deluty (1977) with permission.

Linear timing and time left

The foregoing discussion suggests that the length of an elapsing interval is perceived as a linear function of its actual length whereas times are compared in terms of their ratios. For instance, the first 10 seconds of a signal is subjectively the same duration as the last 10 seconds. An alternative possibility is that elapsed time is perceived logarithmically with real time, for example, 10 seconds late in an interval seems shorter than 10 seconds early in the interval (see Figure 9.8). With logarithmic timing, data consistent with the results presented so far would be obtained if perceived or remembered durations were compared arithmetically because equal ratios are equal intervals on a logarithmic scale. Some of the most direct evidence against logarithmic

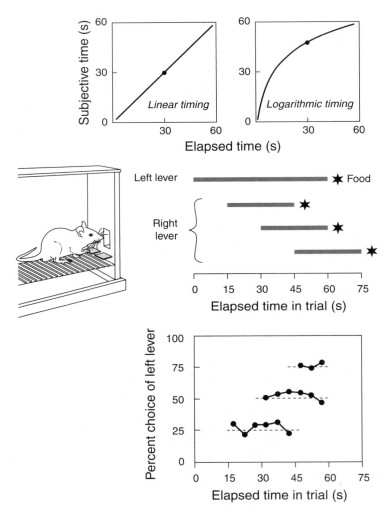

Figure 9.8. Top. How subjective time grows as a function of real time if timing is linear or logarithmic. Middle. Time left procedure for rats. Dark bars represent availability of the designated lever; stars are reinforcement. Bottom. Choice of the left, "time left," lever when the right lever enters 15, 30, or 45 seconds after the trial begins. Data redrawn from Gibbon and Church (1981) with permission.

timing comes from a clever test asking animals at any point at an elapsing interval whether they think the time left in that interval is more or less than a standard interval. The rationale for this *time left procedure* (Gibbon and Church 1981) is explained graphically in Figure 9.8.

In the time left procedure an animal is trained that one signal means food for a given response after one interval and a second signal means food for a second response after an interval half as long. Having learned to time these two signals, the animals are queried while they are working during the long signal, "Would you rather have food after the short signal than after the time left in this signal?" Suppose the long interval is 60 seconds and the short one 30 seconds. Clearly, the way to get food quickest is to choose the short signal when it is presented less than 30 seconds into the 60-second interval and choose what's left of the long signal when it has been on for 30 seconds or more. Around the halfway point, animals should be indifferent between the two alternatives. But if time is measured logarithmically, the last 30 seconds of the elapsing 60-second interval will be subjectively less than the new 30-second alternative, and the animal's choices will switch earlier than halfway through the 60 seconds.

Both rats and pigeons choose as predicted by linear timing (Gibbon and Church 1981; Figure 9.8). People do the same in an equivalent task involving choosing between hypothetical train journeys (Wearden 2002). However, just because the optimal choice can be computed by subtracting the elapsed time in the trial from the total time in the longer interval does not have to mean animals implicitly engage in an analogous process. Choice between two reinforcement schedules is traditionally thought to reflect what the animal has learned about the relative immediacy (inverse of delay) to reward on the alternatives at the time of choice. Variations on the time-left procedure developed within this framework are not so easily described in terms of subtracting representations of times to food (Cerutti and Staddon 2004; Lejeune and Wearden 2006). However, these findings do not necessarily undermine the linearity of timing, which is supported by many other data such as the appropriate location of peak responding in the peak procedure.

9.2.2   Using the clock

Timing with a gap

Sensitivity to the duration of a signal suggests that the onset of the signal starts a clock or timer of some sort (S. Roberts 1981). The results of typical timing experiments with many identical trials imply that this timer resets at the start of each new trial. If the timer were not reset or were only partially reset, successive presentations of the same signal could not be timed equally accurately. This description suggests that the mechanism for interval timing is like a stopwatch that starts running at the start of a new and interesting event and resets at the event's end. So, like a stopwatch, can the timer be stopped and restarted without resetting? The answer to this question has been sought by seeing what animals do when a familiar signal of fixed duration is interrupted earlier than usual and restarted a few seconds later (Figure 9.9). For instance, suppose a rat is pressing a lever for food during a 30-second tone and the tone is interrupted briefly 10 seconds after its onset. When the tone comes on again, will the rat respond at the rate characteristic of 10 seconds into the interval and peak 20 seconds later, or will it start again from zero and peak 30 seconds after the gap in the signal? The former would indicate that the rat's interval timer had been stopped

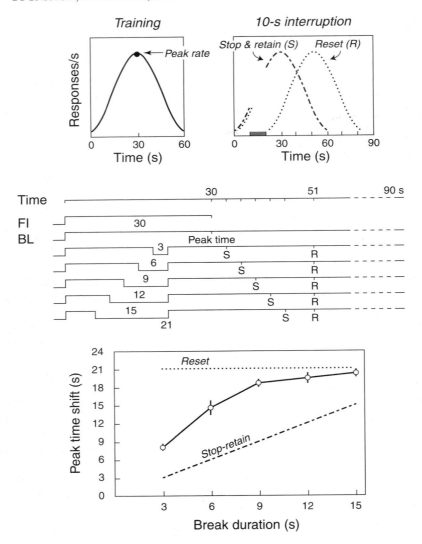

Figure 9.9. Top. Two hypothetical results of training on a 30-second peak procedure and then interrupting the 30-second signal for 10 seconds. The clock timing the interval may either stop during the interruption and retain the duration before the interruption (S) or it may reset (R). Middle. Peak times, in seconds from the start of the interval, predicted by the two models for an experiment with interruptions of different lengths programmed to end at the same point in the interval. FI fixed interval after which food was delivered; BL blank trial, no food. Bottom. Predictions and results for an experiment with pigeons following the design above. Redrawn from Cabeza de Vaca, Brown, and Hemmes (1994) with permission.

and restarted, the latter that it had been reset at the gap. And of course the rat might show peak responding at the usual time after the original onset of the signal, as if its timer kept running through the gap.

At one time it appeared that the results of such experiments depended on the species being tested. Rats resumed timing after a gap (S. Roberts 1981), whereas pigeons reset (W. Roberts, Cheng, and Cohen 1989). However, as often happens in such cases, it turns out that procedural variations can produce the same range of outcomes with one species (Cabeza de Vaca, Brown, and Hemmes 1994; Buhusi, Sasaki, and Meck 2002; Buhusi, Perera, and Meck 2005). Why resetting occurs in some conditions and not others has had several explanations. For example, to time an interrupted signal accurately, it is necessary to retain an accurate memory of the time that elapsed before the gap and add the time after the gap to it. Forgetting the time before the gap leads to apparent resetting. This insight predicts that the extent of resetting should depend in a continuous way on the size of the gap. The longer the gap, the more the first part of the signal is forgotten and the later in the resumed signal is the peak time of responding. This prediction was supported in an elegant series of experiments with pigeons (Cabeza de Vaca., Brown, and Hemmes 1994). But the salience of the gap also turns out to be important. For example, smaller changes in the intensity of a light or tone lead to smaller delays in peak responding, as if timing continues through the gap (e.g., Buhusi, Sasaki, and Meck 2002). Such delays also result if a brief distractor is presented while the signal being timed continues uninterrupted, for example, a noise sounds while a light is being timed (Buhusi and Meck 2006). In the initial experiments in this area, the gap was indistinguishable from an intertrial interval, and because animals in these studies have in effect been trained extensively to erase their memories and start timing afresh at the end of each ITI, resetting after such a gap is to be expected (Zentall 2006). However, the insight that the gap is ambiguous in this way does not appear to account for all the relevant findings. Rather, if timing an ongoing signal is viewed as a working memory task, it can be seen that distracting the animal's attention leads to gradual decay of memory for the time already elapsed, more so the greater the salience of the distractor (Buhusi and Meck 2006). This process-based approach seems more likely to explain what is going on here than is appeal to the metaphor of a stopwatch (see also Staddon and Cerutti 2003).

Timing multiple events

The fact that animals of a given species can time both lights and tones means that different modalities have access to the interval clock. Moreover, timing transfers from one signal to another, novel, signal in a different modality (W. Roberts., Cheng, and Cohen 1989), suggesting that a single timer tracks events within a trial. But animals are also capable of timing two or more concurrent events, as if using multiple timers simultaneously. For instance, pigeons can learn that food occurs at either of two different points within a signal. If food does not appear at the shorter of the two intervals, responding falls, as in the peak procedure, and then rises again as the end of the longer possible interval approaches (Leak and Gibbon 1995). And in laboratory studies of foraging (see Chapter 11), pigeons time the length of foraging bouts while keeping track of the durations of several events within them (e.g., Plowright 1996).

One impressive example of timing multiple events comes from a field study in which rufous hummingbirds (*Selasphorous rufus*) found artificial nectar in an array of eight differently colored feeders (Henderson. et al. 2006). Like real flowers, the experimental "flowers" quickly depleted of nectar but replenished a predictable time later. In this case, four randomly selected flowers in the array replenished after ten minutes and the other four after twenty. The birds learned to time their visits appropriately, as measured by the times between a reinforced visit to a flower and the next visit to that flower. This means not only that they were able to learn the refill rates of eight separate flowers but that throughout the day they were updating their memories of how long ago they had visited each one, in a process that shares elements of the episodic-like memory discussed in Chapter 7. However, because real flowers may take much longer than 20 minutes to replenish (Castellanos, Wilson, and Thomson 2002; Stout and Goulson 2002), to be useful in nature the ability demonstrated by Henderson et al.'s birds might have to be scaled up in numbers and durations of events.

Integrating time with other cues

The hummingbirds' behavior provides but one example of how information about comparatively short intervals is normally combined with other cues, in this case location. A less dynamic form of time and place memory has been documented in numerous laboratory studies analogous to daily time and place learning but using shorter sessions (Thorpe and Wilkie 2006). For example, pressing one lever might be reinforced for the first 15 minutes of a session and pressing another lever reinforced for the next 15 minutes. The integration of interval timing with other information has been explored in a different way by by teaching pigeons and people to respond when a moving shape on a video monitor reached a certain position on the screen (Cheng, Spetch, and Miceli 1996). During training, the shape always moved at the same speed, so subjects could respond to its position, the time since it started to move, or both. When the stimulus moved faster or slower than usual, both the pigeons and the people appeared to respond to both temporal and spatial information and average them when they conflicted. In circadian time-place learning, by contrast, animals learn both the time and the place of important events, but it is not clear what averaging this information could mean.

Chapter 4 provides extensive evidence that animals are always processing information about the durations of interesting events and the intervals between them. Recall, for example, that the distribution of trials in time is critical for conditioning and that temporal information such as when the US occurs during the CS is part of what is learned (see also Arcediano and Miller 2002). Moreover, this information may be acquired in a single trial of fear conditioning (Davis, Schlesinger, and Sorenson 1989) and almost as quickly in other conditioning settings (Balsam, Drew, and Yang 2002). Temporal information appears to be especially powerful when used as an explicit associative cue, for example not being readily blocked (Williams and LoLordo 1995). These facts are relevant to evaluating theories of interval timing in Section 9.3.

9.2.3   Summary

The two most important properties of interval timing are (1) subjective time grows linearly with real time and (2) timing obeys Weber's Law (or has the scalar property, Lejeune and Wearden 2006). Perception of time therefore shares both linearity and conformity to Weber's Law with perception of other features of the world such as space. Interval timing also shares with spatial cognition its sensitivity to multiple sources of information (Cheng 1992).

The most analytical experiments on interval timing have been done with rats and pigeons. Many of the procedures used have been adapted for humans, with similar results (Wearden 2002; Meck 2003). Comparable data from a rodent, a bird, and a primate along with data from other species (Lejeune and Wearden 1991) are suggestive of pretty wide phylogenetic generality among vertebrates. Bumblebees also show evidence of timing short intervals (Boisvert, Veal, and Sherry 2007). These data consist mainly of patterns of responding on *fixed interval* (FI) *schedules,* which are essentially the same as the peak procedure but without the empty trials. The increases in response rate as reward approaches may not be equally sharp in all species. Turtles, for instance, have a much shallower slope than monkeys or rats, suggesting that they do not perceive interval duration as accurately. However, the apparent precision of interval timing can also vary within a species with motivation (Plowright. et al. 2000) and with the response used to index timing. More effortful, costly, responses may lead to apparent increased accuracy. For instance, pigeons appear to time more accurately when they hop on a perch for food than when they peck (Jasselette, Lejeune, and Wearden 1990). Attempting to capture species differences in a model including both response mechanisms and sensitivity to time leads to the conclusion that species differ in both (Lejeune and Wearden 1991). Ecological hypotheses about species differences in accuracy of interval timing have apparently not been tested.

9.3   Interval timing: Theories

For over 20 years, a particular cognitive model, the information processing or pace-maker-accumulator model (Gibbon and Church 1984), has dominated discussion of the processes underlying performance in tests of interval timing. Indeed, the assumptions of this model are reflected in some of the tests already described. More recently, fundamentally different alternatives have been proposed that account for interval timing without a pacemaker and accumulator and in some cases without explicit sensitivity to time as such. Two are described here. Each has stimulated new experiments with results that the information processing model cannot readily account for.

9.3.1   The information processing model

This model is also known as *Scalar Expectancy Theory* (SET; Gibbon 1991) or the pacemaker-accumulator model. The model's general structure (Figure 9.10) has much in common with the structure of the memory model of habituation (Chapter 5) and models in other realms of cognition (Church and Broadbent 1990) in which behavior is based on comparing a current event to a representation of past events. It has three major components, or modules: a clock that measures current time linearly, a memory for storing durations of past events, and a comparator for comparing current time to remembered time. The clock rests on a hypothetical pacemaker that is assumed to generate pulses at a fairly high rate. The onset of a signal to be timed switches these pulses into an accumulator, a working memory that tracks the duration of the signal. The comparator computes the ratio of the value in the accumulator to the value of reinforced time in reference memory and outputs a decision about whether the current time is acceptably close to the remembered time. Behavior is generated in an all-or-nothing way depending on whether or not the ratio exceeds this decision threshold. This last conclusion is based on the fact that rats and pigeons do not increase responding gradually as the time for reinforcement approaches on single trials of the peak procedure. Rather, responding has a *break-run-break* pattern, that is, at a certain point in the trial the animal switches suddenly from a very low rate of responding to a high steady rate. In empty trials, it maintains this rate until after the time of reinforcement, and then there is another break in responding. The run of responding is seen as beginning at the point where the ratio of current time to remembered time of reinforcement exceeds the threshold, and the break in responding at the end of the run reveals when the ratio falls below the threshold again (Cheng and Westwood 1993; Church, Meck, and Gibbon 1994).

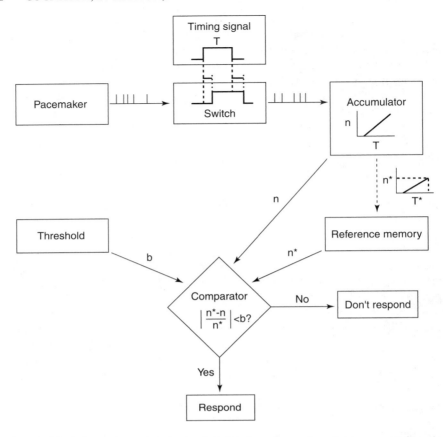

Figure 9.10. The information processing model of timing. n*: number of pulses on reinforced trials, the value stored in reference memory. Redrawn from Church, Meck, and Gibbon (1994) with permission.

In terms of the model, why is timing scalar, that is, why does the variance in temporal generalization, the peak procedure, and the like increase with the length of the interval being timed? The source of this variance cannot be the operation of the switch that causes an event to be timed because the switch is assumed to close just once, at the start of the timed event, and open again at the event's end. Any variability in the latency of the switch's operation would be constant regardless of the length of the interval to be timed. Variability in the speed of the pacemaker, on the other hand, could produce scalar variance because it would influence the total number of pulses in working memory more in long intervals than in short ones. There are other possibilities as well, not all of which are easy to disentangle from one another experimentally.

The pattern of responding on single trials reveals the moment-by-moment dynamics of the decision process (Cheng and Westwood 1993; Church, Meck, and Gibbon 1994). For instance, different, possibly variable, thresholds may be used to decide when to start responding and when to stop. These analyses also indicate that a single sample is taken from the memories of times to reinforcement in reference memory and compared continuously to the time in the accumulator. The notion that a distribution of experienced times to reinforcement is stored in reference memory and sampled on each trial can be distinguished from the possibility that reference memory is an average time to reward, a single quantity updated with each new experience. Storing a continually updated average seems cognitively less demanding than storing a distribution. Nevertheless, as we will see in Chapter 11, a model based on memory for the distribution of intervals accounts very well for a number of kinds of foraging decisions.

9.3.2   The oscillator model

Just as in analogous models of other memory processes, the structures represented in Figure 9.10 are purely hypothetical, analogues to physical structures that could produce outputs matching real data in timing experiments. Such models have served cognitive psychology well, but they are not necessarily biologically realistic. One way to make a biologically more realistic model of timing is to replace the pacemaker plus accumulator with a system of oscillators and status indicators, as originally suggested by Gallistel (1990). The physiology and behavior of most organisms provide evidence of numerous biological oscillators driving repetitive motor patterns like flapping, walking, or licking, and rhythmic functions like heartbeat and breathing (Buhusi and Meck 2005). It is plausible that they include the sorts of oscillators necessary for interval timing. Rather than counting pulses, the oscillator model records the state of each of a set of oscillators of different periodicities, as shown in Figure 9.11. One or more of these may have a period longer than a day, perhaps months, years, or the animal's lifetime. Thus a great appeal of the oscillator model of interval timing is that it unifies timing at all scales in terms of a single set of oscillators.

Figure 9.11 shows why more than the single circadian oscillator is needed to do this job. Because intervals of the order of seconds or a few minutes are just a tiny fraction of a day, timing them accurately with the circadian oscillator would require discriminating tiny changes in the phase of that oscillator. A good solution is to this problem is to record the state of a number of oscillators, each of which oscillates about twice as fast as the next slower one. In this model, interval timing is not counting pulses but recording the times of a signal's onset and offset in terms of oscillator status indicators and computing duration from this information. Accordingly, the oscillator model is compatible with evidence that interval timing involves detecting coincident activity in multiple areas of the brain (Buhusi and Meck 2005).

A key prediction of an oscillator model is that intervals close to the period of one of the oscillators should be more discriminable than slightly longer or shorter intervals, that is, "oscillator signatures" should be detectable as systematic deviations from

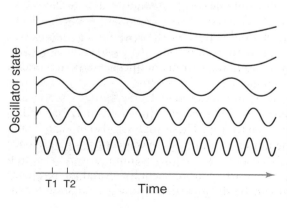

Figure 9.11. Timing with oscillators. Each oscillator has a period half that of the next slower. Unambiguously distinguishing T1 from T2 requires reading the status of all the oscillators (i.e. the height of each sinusoidal line) at both times.

scalar timing. A nice proof of principle for this suggestion comes from training rats with interfood intervals with lengths around the period of a known oscillator, the circadian rhythm (Crystal 2001). Each rat, kept in constant darkness, could earn food within a three-hour period with a fixed intermeal interval between 14 and 34 hours long. (As mentioned in Section 9.1, circadian rhythms do not entrain to the extremes of these intervals, but they can acquire control of instrumental behavior.) For all the intervals, insertions of the rat's head into the food magazine increased during the few hours before food was due, but the data did not superimpose when they were rescaled as proportions of the interfood interval. Instead, as predicted by oscillator theory, the sharpest increases (i.e., best discrimination) were found for the intervals closest to 24 hours.

The applicability of this approach to short interval timing is illustrated by a study in which rats learned a *ramped interval* schedule (Crystal, Church, and Broadbent 1997; Crystal 2006a). This is essentially a fixed interval procedure except that each interfood interval was two seconds longer than the preceding one within a given range between 20 and 160 seconds. When the longest interval in the range was reached, the intervals ramped down again two seconds at a time. Animals do learn such a contingency, as shown by systematically changing pauses between feeding and beginning to respond again. The ramped schedule used here allowed timing of many closely spaced intervals to be assessed. As predicted by oscillator theory, the data showed systematic deviations from a linear relationship between start times and the duration of the interval to be timed. Greatest accuracy was around 10 to 12 seconds and 100 to 120 seconds. The generality of these periodicities to other tests and/or other species remains to be determined (but see Crystal 2006a). To a first approximation, scalar timing remains a good account of many interval timing data (Lejeune and Wearden 2006), but these violations suggest that the underlying measurement of time might not involve a pacemaker and accumulator.

Notwithstanding the appeal of an approach that integrates interval and circadian timing by calling on a common process of biological oscillation, its support by actual biological data is mixed. For example, rather than reflecting a unitary mechanism in the brain, circadian and interval timing are dissociable by brain lesions. In mammals, removing the suprachiasmatic nucleus abolishes daily rhythmicity but leaves interval timing intact, whereas interval timing depends on an intact striatum (see Buhusi and Meck 2005). Furthermore, learning about short intervals is not the same as entrainment of circadian rhythms. For instance, although there is some evidence that temporal patterns of behavior persist when regular reinforcement is discontinued (Crystal 2006b), there is not yet evidence for free-running short-interval timers. At the same time, neurobiological support for the information processing model comes from the fact that some of its components such as clock speed and memory can be dissociated pharmacologically. However, studies of brain activity during timing tasks provide increasing evidence that short-interval timing involves detection of coincident activity in multiple brain regions, more consistent with the oscillator model (Buhusi and Meck 2005; Bhattacharjee 2006).

9.3.3   Timing without a clock: Behavioral theories of timing

Describing the control of behavior by temporal patterns of reinforcement has been a staple of the study of operant conditioning since long before cognitive models appeared (Staddon and Cerutti 2003). The Skinnerian tradition of eschewing explanations of behavior in terms of unobservable internal processes is reflected in the

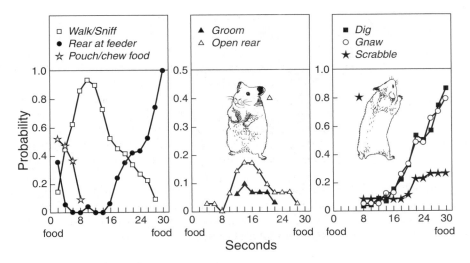

Figure 9.12. Typical behavior of golden hamsters given food every 30 seconds in an open field. Some activities appear reliably just before or after feeding whereas others (the adjunctive behaviors) are performed most in the middle of the interfood interval. Data from one animal, redrawn from Anderson and Shettleworth (1977) with permission; hamsters from Shettleworth (1975) with permission.

behavioral theory of timing (or BeT; Killeen and Fetterman 1988). This approach does not assume that animals count pulses or record states of oscillators, much less that they perform implicit computations on such hypothetical entities. It is an attempt to account for behavior that has seemed to demand a cognitive explanation in purely behaviorist terms, indeed, to account for timing without a clock.

Inspiration for the behavioral theory of timing comes from observations of *adjunctive behaviors* that develop when animals are exposed to food deliveries spaced regularly in time regardless of behavior (*fixed-time schedules*). Immediately after each food delivery, animals tend to engage in behaviors unrelated to food such as grooming and walking about. As the interfood interval progresses, food-related behaviors such as gnawing or pecking in the vicinity of the feeder come to predominate (Figure 9.12). In the language of Chapter 4, activities in the feeding system are performed late in interfood intervals and behaviors from other systems, such as grooming or exploration are performed at other times. In the language of the behavioral theory of timing, the succession of adjunctive behaviors reveals a series of underlying states. Unlike in the example of adjunctive behavior, these states are not specified in terms of feeding or other motivational systems, nor in terms of anticipation of the time of food delivery. Accurate choice or appropriate response rates in operant experiments like the peak procedure or temporal discrimination arises because responding is associated with a particular state in the sequence (Figure 9.13).

When food is more frequent, animals generally appear more excited, switching from one activity to another more often, suggesting that the states succeed each other more rapidly the higher the rate of food presentation. This means that short intervals are timed more accurately than long ones, that is, timing is scalar, just as it should be. This should be true only if the short intervals are generated in a way that increases the average rate of feeding in the experimental context, as when the intertrial interval in

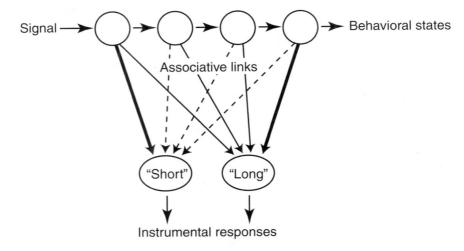

Figure 9.13. The learning to time (LeT) model. Onset of a signal instigates the first in a sequence of behavioral states (top row of circles), each of which may become associated with one or more instrumental responses. Here the responses are identified with a short and a long elapsed time, as in the temporal bisection procedures discussed in the text. After Machado and Keen (1999) with permission.

the peak procedure remains constant while the interval to be timed is shortened. BeT does not predict that the scalar property will be maintained when multiple intervals are being timed concurrently, but in fact it is (Leak and Gibbon 1995). Note too, that no explanation is given for why and how states succeed one another, but in effect their succession plays the role of a pacemaker (Hopson 2003). On a cognitivist view, of course the behavioral "states" are merely the readouts of an internal clock.

The behavioral theory of timing along with its mathematical development as the Learning to Time theory (LeT; Machado 1997) accounts for all the basic phenomena described in Section 9.2. Because it was designed to account for average data, it does not (as yet) account for the timing of breaks and runs in responding on individual trials of the peak procedure, whereas these have a natural interpretation in SET (Church., Meck, and Gibbon 1994). LeT has stimulated a series of studies with the *double bisection* procedure, with dramatically different results from those anticipated by SET. Recall that in temporal bisection an animal is trained to make one response after a comparatively short signal, say a 1-second light, and another response when the same signal has lasted some longer time, say 4 seconds. In tests with intermediate durations, the proportions of trials with each response are seen as revealing the animals' ratings of how similar the duration is to each of the training durations. In terms of SET, onset of the signal causes pulses to flow to the accumulator. At the end of the signal, the total in the accumulator is compared (as a ratio) to the reference memories of the totals associated with each of the choices.

Now consider training two temporal discriminations concurrently. For example, at the end of a 1-second or 4-second white light, pigeons are offered a choice between red and green, with red correct after 4 seconds and green otherwise. On other trials within the same session, the same white signal comes on for 4 seconds or 16 seconds, and the pigeons choose between blue and yellow, with blue correct after the 4 second light. According to SET, if the pigeons are now presented with the 4-second light, or indeed a light of any duration at all, and given the novel choice between red and blue, they should be indifferent because both are associated with the same state of the accumulator. According to LeT, however, choice will depend on the duration of the test signal, as in fact it does (Machado and Pata 2005).

To understand the predictions of LeT, call the two discriminations 1 and 2 and the choices associated with the comparatively short (S) and long (L) intervals respectively S1 and L1, S2 and L2. In our example, L1 and S2 are both associated with the same 4-second signal. According to LeT, onset of the signal initiates a series of behavioral states such as first moving to the left side of the chamber, then turning around, then pecking at the front panel. Such idiosyncratic stereotyped behavioral sequences are often (but not always) observed in pigeons (e.g., Machado and Keen 2003). To understand the double bisection results, we need three states, the initial state, in effect for the first second or two after the light comes on, the intermediate state, and the final state, beginning some time after 4 seconds or so. In discrimination 1, in the presence of the initial state choices of S1 are reinforced and choices of L1 (the 4-second option) are explicitly extinguished. L2 and S2 are neither reinforced nor extinguished during the initial state because the earliest they occur is after 4 seconds of the signal, in discrimination 2. Therefore, when L1 and S2 (the two 4-second options) are presented during the initial state, S2 will be chosen because it has not been extinguished under these conditions whereas L1 has. Extending this argument not only correctly predicts that L1 will be chosen over S2 in the presence of the final state, that is, when the two supposedly equivalent 4-second options are presented after a signal longer than 4 seconds, but also makes interesting (and correct) predictions for choice between other novel pairs (Machado and Pata 2005). However, thinking in terms of times on a clock (as opposed to behavioral states) when the various options are reinforced or not may provide just as good an account. In our last example, after times much greater than 4 seconds choice of S2 should be inhibited because it is never reinforced at such times; hence the alternative, L1, is chosen.

9.3.4   Cognitive and behavioral theories of timing: Conclusions

The oscillator and the LeT/BeT models are not the only alternatives to SET than have been proposed. Other accounts of behavior in timing experiments include Kirkpatrick's (2002) packet theory, models based on neural networks (Hopson 2003), and Staddon's (2005) memory model. Like some neural nets, Staddon's model has no representation of time as such. Important events such as feedings create a memory trace that decays in a predictable way, as in habituation, and the strength of this trace acts as a clock. In the simple example of a fixed-interval 10-second schedule, the next feeding occurs when the trace of the most recent feeding has decayed to a level typical of 10 seconds post-feeding. Multiple traces are needed to generate behavior in more complex situations, not always successfully (Church 1999, 2001; Hopson 2003).

The contrast between explanations at a purely behavioral level and those that call on cognitive mechanisms is exceptionally clear in the area of interval timing. There is currently no consensus about which provides the most comprehensive account of interval timing, but rather respectful acknowledgement that fundamentally different theoretical approaches can satisfactorily account for the major patterns of data, at least within explicit tests of timing (Church 2001; Staddon and Cerutti 2003; Church 2006; Lejeune and Wearden 2006). And the various explanations of timing are not entirely mutually exclusive. For example, it seems possible that when animals are trained with signals predicting food at fixed times, they initially time the signals but once rigid stereotypes develop those behaviors become directly associated with choice responses as depicted in LeT.

Each of the three models discussed in Sections 9.3.1–.9.3.3 can account uniquely well for some subset of data (e.g., nonlinearities in short-interval discriminations for oscillator theory; performance on double bisection for LeT). Evidence from neuroscience may contribute to deciding among candidate mechanisms, for example by increasing the plausibility of a multiple oscillator system. Another consideration that does not seem to have received much attention is functional plausibility. On one view (Gallistel 1990, 2003), sensitivity to time is a core aspect of animal information processing. Spontaneously recording circadian and interval times is obligatory and absolutely fundamental to learning and memory. For example, sensitivity to durations in the seconds to minutes range underlies conditioning (Chapter 4; Gallistel and Gibbon 2000; Arcediano and Miller 2002). From this viewpoint, the behavioral theory of timing (LeT included) is decidedly implausible because it is designed to explain behavior that develops after extensive exposure to rigid and arbitrary sequences of events without assuming any underlying sensitivity to time as such. The stereotyped behavior that may develop under these conditions (e.g., Machado and Keen 2003) hardly seems to provide a primary mechanism for spontaneously recording in some fashion the durations and times of occurrence of interesting events in the messy quotidian flow of experience, even though there is evidence that animals do just that (M. Davis, Schlesinger, and Sorenson 1989; Balsam, Drew, and Yang 2002). The pacemaker-accumulator or oscillator models, and perhaps Staddon's memory-based model, are better able to do this job.

9.4 Summary: Two timing systems?

Notwithstanding attempts to link them in a single system of biological oscillators (Crystal 2006a), circadian and interval timing can be seen as two functionally and causally distinct information-processing systems or modules. (Learning serial order is a third mechanism for organizing behavior in time, as in adopting a daily foraging routine, but, unlike circadian and interval timing, ordinal timing (Carr and Wilkie 1997) does not involve responding to time per se.) The circadian timing system consists of an endogenous oscillator with a period of about a day that is normally entrained by light or one of a few other biologically important events. The circadian oscillator runs freely in the absence of effective entraining agents, and although cells throughout the body have circadian rhythms, in mammals the master oscillator is located in the suprachiasmatic nucleus. A primary function of the circadian system is to adjust the animal's behavior to local day and night. Among other things, it allows animals to learn when and where food is regularly available.

The function of interval timing, in contrast, is to adjust behavior to important events with durations much shorter than a day. Unlike day and night, the durations and times of occurrence of these events are not predictable in advance of individual experience, and they can take on any value. Intervals too short to reasonably discriminate in terms of phase of the 24-hour cycle can be timed accurately. Furthermore, developing a regular sequence of behavior after experiencing a sequence of events that is predictable on the scale of seconds to minutes does not occur through entrainment. In entrainment, the underlying rhythm runs freely and is brought into register with the environmental rhythm as described by a phase response curve. It has a restricted range of entrainable phases. This description does not readily apply to learning of short intervals, although it has hardly had a fair test (see Crystal 2006a).

There is a single generally agreed on model of circadian timing, but several such models of interval timing. One of these, the oscillator model, links circadian and interval timing as different expressions of a single set of oscillators with phases ranging from seconds to multiples of days. However, it does not appear to account for the unique characteristics of the circadian oscillator just reviewed. Although the alternative theories of timing are likely to go on generating challenging data, scalar expectancy theory still appears to provide the most powerful account of all aspects of interval timing. SET reappears in Chapter 11, where it provides a useful account of how animals assess and compare rates while foraging.

Further readings

An authoritative as well as amusing brief introduction to circadian timing is the article by Aschoff (1989), one of the founders of the field. The text by Moore-Ede, Sulzman, and Fuller (1982) is still an excellent introduction to the classic work on biological rhythms. Understanding the genetic control of circadian rhythmicity is one of the greatest success stories in the molecular analysis of behavior; it is described in more recent texts such as *Chronobiology* (Dunlap, Loros, and Decoursey 2003). Chapters 7–9 of Gallistel (1990) discuss both circadian and interval timing from the author's "computational representational" point of view. Thorpe and Wilkie (2006) review time and place learning.

A good introduction to interval timing is the chapter by Russell Church (2002), one of the founders of the field and originators of SET. Church (e.g., 2001, 2006) has also written some thoughtful assessments of the alternative approaches. Staddon and Cerutti's (2003) review of operant conditioning includes a major section on behavioral approaches to interval timing, and Crystal (2006a) reviews studies testing the oscillator model. Arcediano and Miller (2002) summarize the challenges for timing theories from evidence that times are learned during conditioning. Neural bases of timing as well as behavioral studies are discussed in the book edited by Meck (2003) and summarized by Buhusi and Meck (2005; see also Bhattacharjee 2006).

10
Numerical Competence

Readers who know the story of Clever Hans will know that whether animals can count is one of the oldest questions in the experimental study of animal cognition. Clever Hans was a German horse in the early 1900s who answered questions about numbers by tapping with his hoof (Pfungst 1965; Candland 1993). Although a committee of thirteen eminent men was satisfied that Hans really could count, investigations by the young experimental psychologist Oskar Pfungst revealed otherwise. Hans *was* clever, but not in the way he originally appeared to be. He proved to be responding to slight unconscious, movements of questioners who knew the correct answers. Clever Hans's legacy is a name for any effect that reflects responding to cues unintentionally provided by experimenters and a widespread skepticism about any studies in which animal and experimenter interact directly.

Notwithstanding the Clever Hans affair, research on animal counting continued throughout the twentieth century (Rilling 1993), increasing in the 1970s along with research on other aspects of comparative cognition (reviews in Davis and Memmott 1982; Boysen and Capaldi 1993; Shettleworth 1998; Boysen and Hallberg 2000). Toward the end of the century, however, the theoretical focus of research on animals' numerical abilities shifted away from the simplistic "can animals count?" toward a more nuanced view of numerical competence as comprised of several systems shared among species to different degrees, with a language-based system unique to humans. The contemporary study of numerical cognition is a rich area of interaction among comparative and developmental psychologists as well as cognitive neuroscientists, sometimes embodied in the same individual researcher or research team. Much of this progress rests on the fact that babies and monkeys, and to some extent other animals, can be given virtually identical nonverbal tests of sensitivity to number.

To appreciate the way in which the comparative study of numerical abilities has evolved, it is worth briefly reviewing older studies of animal counting. In counting, each member of a set is tagged ("one," "two," "three,"...). These numerical tags are *numerons* (Gallistel 1990). They are applied in a fixed order, but the order in which the items in the set are counted doesn't matter as long as each item gets one and only one tag. The final tag is the *cardinal number* of the set, the number of items in it. True counting implies transfer of the same numeron to sets of all sorts of things in all sorts of arrangements, that is, counting transcends features normally confounded with number such as total extent of items in the set. Numerons need not be words in any human language. Animals' number tags can be "unnamed

Figure 10.1. A jackdaw being tested for the ability to match numbers of items. The small squares are lids on food pots; here if the bird flips over the one with the same number of dots as on the large card it will find food underneath. After a photograph in Koehler (1941).

numbers" (Koehler 1951). The ability of birds to use such tags was studied extensively by Koehler (e.g., 1951; see also Davis and Memmott 1982; Emmerton 2001). For example, he trained parrots, jackdaws, and other birds to match drawings according to the number of items they contained, disregarding size and arrangement (Figure 10.1). He also trained birds to eat a fixed number of items from a pile by shooing them away when they reached the criterion, a demonstration later performed with rats by H. Davis and Bradford (1986). H. Davis (1984) also trained a raccoon to select the one box out of five that had three items of food or three other objects in it, and Capaldi and his colleagues (Capaldi and Miller 1988; Capaldi 1993) showed that rats readily learn to expect food at the end of a runway on two or three trials in a row and no food on a final trial.

In all these examples, "counting" consisted of discriminating a set of one small size from sets of other small sizes, and indeed Koehler reported that his birds failed such tasks when the number involved was greater than six or seven. Some of Koehler's (1951) birds also learned several specific numerosities within this range, for instance matching the number of dots on a card to the number of food items to be taken. However, in all the cases just reviewed, considerable amounts of training were required, consistent with Davis and Memmott's (1982, 547) conclusion that "Counting behavior appears to be a relatively unnatural response in infrahumans, and its acquisition may reflect the boundaries of the animal's associative abilities." But about a decade later, Gallistel (1993) suggested that on the contrary "the common laboratory animals order, add, subtract, multiply, and divide representatives of numerosity. . . . Their ability to do so is not surprising if number is taken as a mental primitive . . . rather than something abstracted by the brain from sense data only with difficulty and long experience." One reason for the difference between these conclusions is that Davis and Memmott focused on explicit counting-like behavior, whereas Gallistel was impressed by natural behaviors implying that animals represent numbers of things and perform mental operations on these representations, for example when discriminating between rates of reinforcement or prey capture. In any case, in nature it is often important to give a bigger response to things that are more numerous because these are likely to be indicative of more food, a more dangerous enemy, a hungrier baby, or a more enthusiastic mate. Sometimes it may be important to discriminate specific small numbers of things (Box 10.1). The capacity for such *numerosity discriminations* does not necessarily mean that an animal can be trained to make arbitrary responses to different numbers of items, but it may be more fundamental and phylogenetically widespread.

Accordingly, much of the new wave of research has focused on numerosity discrimination and the representations underlying it. Under some conditions, the numerosity of small sets, up to three or four items, is represented by a precise small number system based on visual object tracking, that is, identification of separate objects as such. Larger numerosities are represented imprecisely in a

---

Box 10.1 Numbers in the Wild

There are some provocative examples of animals apparently responding to specific small numbers of things in naturalistic contexts, perhaps using the precise small number system discussed in Section 10.2. One such context is nest parasitism, that is, birds laying their eggs in the eggs of another individual (a host) of the same or a different species. For example, the best nests for a cowbird to leave her eggs in are those of hosts that have begun laying but not yet finished. This will ensure that the host starts incubating soon but will carry out the full cycle of incubation needed by the cowbird's eggs. Accordingly, when captive cowbirds are presented with artificial nests holding different numbers, sizes, and/or colors of eggs, they spend more time near and lay more eggs in nests with three versus one "host" egg. This is apparently not sheer preference for more "egg stuff" since they prefer three medium to three large eggs and show little preference when the alternatives are six versus three eggs (White et al. 2007).

Numerosity discrimination may be important to parasites' victims as well. American coot females are sometimes parasitized by other coots and do not eject the parasites' eggs from the nest until after laying has finished. However, because coots use the number of eggs in the nest as a cue to whether to lay more, it is important to discriminate one's own eggs from others.' Coots which do discriminate others' eggs from their own and eventually reject them lay larger clutches than those which do not (Lyon 2003). The nondiscriminators apparently stop laying prematurely because they count the parasite's eggs as their own.

Another natural context for discriminating small numerosities is in responding to species-typical vocalizations. Crows identify other individuals by the number of their caws (N. Thompson 1969). Chickadees' alarm calls contain more "dee" notes the more dangerous the predator they have sighted (Templeton, Greene, and Davis 2005), and listeners respond appropriately, whether they are conspecifics or other small birds in the neighborhood (Templeton and Greene 2007).

Using auditory cues to number of other individuals might be common among social species because responses to rival groups should depend on numbers of companions and rivals present. For example, when lions hear another pride roaring, they should decide whether to respond aggressively or to retreat from the perceived threat by comparing the number of individuals roaring to the number in their own group (McComb, Packer, and Pusey 1994). McComb and her collaborators tested this idea by playing recorded roars from one or three lions to 21 different lion groups. The bigger the group and the smaller the number of individuals heard roaring, the more likely the subjects were to approach the speaker (Figure B10.1). Similarly, the probability and amount of howling shown by a group of black howler monkeys with one,

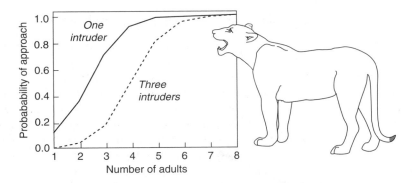

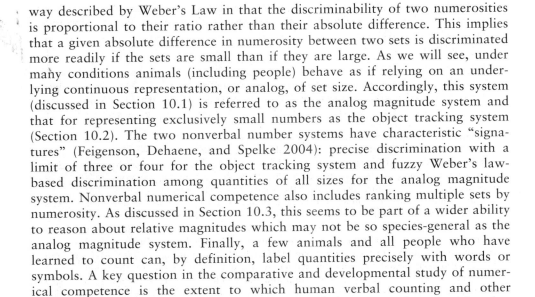

Figure B10.1. Proportion of lionesses approaching a speaker playing recorded roars from another lion pride (simulated intruders) as a function of the number of lions heard roaring and the number in the subjects' pride. Redrawn from McComb, Packer, and Pusey (1994) with permission.

two, or three defenders in response to recorded calls from a group of one, two, or three attackers depends in a graded way on the relationship between the group sizes. This relationship is a measure of the odds that defense will be successful (Kitchen 2004). Finally evidence that a chorus of calls can in fact be unpacked into a representation of a number of individuals comes from a test similar to one conducted with infants (Jordan et al. 2005). Rhesus monkeys heard a recording of two or three conspecifics calling while they looked at two images, one with two vocalizing monkeys and one with three. They looked more at the one showing the correct number of animals, suggesting they have an amodal representation of (at least) small numbers.

way described by Weber's Law in that the discriminability of two numerosities is proportional to their ratio rather than their absolute difference. This implies that a given absolute difference in numerosity between two sets is discriminated more readily if the sets are small than if they are large. As we will see, under many conditions animals (including people) behave as if relying on an underlying continuous representation, or analog, of set size. Accordingly, this system (discussed in Section 10.1) is referred to as the analog magnitude system and that for representing exclusively small numbers as the object tracking system (Section 10.2). The two nonverbal number systems have characteristic "signatures" (Feigenson, Dehaene, and Spelke 2004): precise discrimination with a limit of three or four for the object tracking system and fuzzy Weber's law-based discrimination among quantities of all sizes for the analog magnitude system. Nonverbal numerical competence also includes ranking multiple sets by numerosity. As discussed in Section 10.3, this seems to be part of a wider ability to reason about relative magnitudes which may not be so species-general as the analog magnitude system. Finally, a few animals and all people who have learned to count can, by definition, label quantities precisely with words or symbols. A key question in the comparative and developmental study of numerical competence is the extent to which human verbal counting and other mathematical abilities are built on the nonverbal systems shared with other species (Section 10.4).

10.1   Numerosity discrimination and the analog magnitude system

10.1.1   Discriminating numbers of stimuli

In nature, it must be rare for numerosity as such to vary by itself. For example, more objects occupy more space or take longer to view. More numerous visual objects typically cover more total area and have a longer total edge, or contour length. If more numerous objects are squeezed together in time or space, the gaps between them are smaller than for less numerous ones. Thus a ubiquitous challenge in tests of numerosity discrimination is to disentangle control by numbers of things from control by all the other dimensions of stimuli that usually covary with number. One way to deal with this problem is to acknowledge that number is inevitably confounded with other features and to test for control by number along with control by other potentially relevant features. An example is a test of numerosity discrimination in rats using a procedure essentially the same as the bisection procedure for temporal discrimination described in Chapter 9 (Meck and Church 1983). Responses on one lever were reinforced following two 1-second pulses of tone; responses on a second lever were reinforced after eight pulses (Figure 10.2). Thus, in this stage of training the total duration of the pulse train was perfectly correlated with number of pulses. Once the rats were performing accurately, they had two types of unreinforced test trials. In tests for control by number, the total duration of the stimulus was constant at four seconds and the number of tone pulses varied between two and eight. In tests for control by duration, there were always four tone pulses but the duration of the four tone on–tone off cycles varied between two and eight seconds. The rats' discrimination proved to be controlled by both time and number: their tendency to choose the "long/many" lever (i.e., the one that was correct after 8 pulses/8 seconds) increased with either the duration or the number of tone pulses, as shown in Figure 10.2. Notice that the number at which "two" and "eight" are chosen equally often, that is, the number perceived as halfway between 2 and 8, is not 5 but 4. That is, the numerosity continuum, like the temporal continuum, is bisected at the geometric rather than the arithmetic mean, consistent with Weber's Law.

Data from pigeons show a similar pattern (Emmerton 2001). In a particularly elegant example, pigeons discriminated "many" versus "few" dots in a visual display with a wide range of numerosity pairs (Emmerton and Renner 2006). However, when flashes of light were the stimuli, unlike rats, pigeons were more influenced by time than by number (W. Roberts and Mitchell 1994). Control by number increased relative to control by time when the birds were trained for several sessions with number relevant and time irrelevant. These results, like those from rats, suggest that time and number are processed simultaneously, in parallel. W. Roberts and Mitchell (1994) provided further evidence for this conclusion by training pigeons to use the colors of the choice keys as instructions whether to report the duration or number of the just-presented flashes. The birds learned to respond appropriately even on trials when time and number dictated competing choices. They must have been processing time and number on every trial because the colored choice keys appeared only after the last flash of light. Data like these suggested a model of counting successive stimuli consisting of the information processing model of timing (Figure 9.10) with an added channel for accumulating counts and comparing them with the contents of a reference memory for counts (W. Roberts and Mitchell 1994). If animals

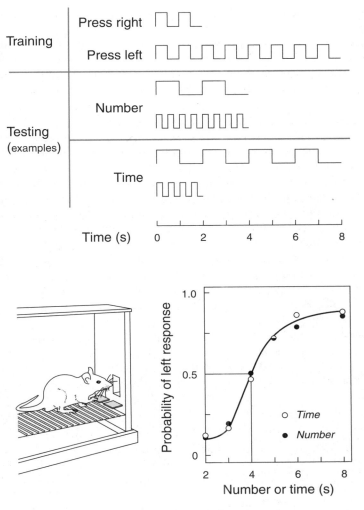

Figure 10.2. Procedure and results demonstrating joint control of rats' choices by duration and number of tone pulses. Data from Meck and Church (1983) with permission.

respond to rates of events by in some sense mentally dividing numbers by times, as in rate expectancy theory (Chapter 4), both channels must be operating all the time.

Further features of the analog magnitude system were documented by Jordan and Brannon (2006) with rhesus macaques, again starting with anchor values of two and eight. The monkeys learned to match samples of two or eight dots to stimuli that matched in number but differed in size, distribution, density, and/or total surface area of the elements. For example, after a sample of two large dots, the monkeys might have to choose two small dots over eight small dots whose total area matched that of the sample dots. Once they were performing well, the monkeys were tested in the typical bisection procedure, with choice between two and eight following samples of intermediate values. As with the rats and pigeons, 50:50 choice occurred nearer 4 than 5. Bisection was again reasonably near the predicted value when the monkeys were further trained with samples of three and twelve. In the final stage of this study, samples had any number of dots from 1 to 9, and the variable of interest was the ratio between the numerosities of the correct match and the distractor. Again in accord with Weber's Law, accuracy and reaction time were predicted by the ratio between the match and the distractor, not their absolute difference. For example, performance was about the same with a sample of 2 and distractor of 4 as with a sample of 4 and a distractor of 8.

10.1.2   Counting responses

Animals also discriminate the numbers of their own responses in a way described by the analog magnitude system. For example, a number of responses on a central key or lever presents two side keys or levers, and the animal is reinforced for choosing the left after one number of responses and the right after a different number of responses. Just as with stimuli, both time and number matter in discriminations of response numerosity and the results obey Weber's Law (Fetterman 1993). Weber's Law implies that greater numerosities are detected with proportionately greater variance. A nice example comes from parallel studies of response counting by rats and humans (Figure 10.3). (Note that number and duration were somewhat confounded here, but related studies have separated number from duration, as discussed by Davis and Memmott 1982). Platt and Johnson (1971) trained rats on what was essentially a *fixed ratio schedule* (i.e., reinforcement was given when the rat had made a fixed number of responses), but when the ratio requirement had been met, the rat had to leave off lever-pressing and put its head into the food tray. If the rat had completed at least the required number of presses, food was given followed by a 10-second timeout with the light off and the lever retracted before the next opportunity to complete the ratio. Premature tray entries started the timeout and restarted the ratio. With requirements from 4 to 24 presses, the probability of a tray entry after different numbers of presses described a set of distributions beautifully in accord with Weber's Law (Figure 10.3), with standard error proportional to the mean. Whalen, Gallistel, and Gelman (1999) obtained similar data from people (Figure 10.3, bottom) by telling them to press a computer key as fast as they could to a target number of presses that varied from trial to trial between 7 and 25. Evidence that the speed requirement encouraged nonverbal counting came from trials showing that fast silent counting to a given target number above about 12 took substantially longer than pressing the key the same number of times. Evidence that subjects were not primarily timing their presses rather than counting came from the fact that timing judgments within the same setting were much more variable than judgments of numbers of presses. The response-counting task, along with a parallel flash-counting task in the same study, therefore seems to tap the same nonverbal analog magnitude system evident in nonhuman species.

10.1.3   Spontaneous numerosity discrimination

None of the studies described so far addresses whether animals spontaneously encode numerosity as Gallistel (1990) suggested because they all involved extensive training. However, at least for some settings and species, numerosity is a more salient aspect of visual stimuli than some other features. Cantlon and Brannon (2007) trained rhesus monkeys in a matching to sample procedure similar to that used by Jordan and Brannon (2006) except that the alternatives in the choice phase always differed in number and in color, shape, or surface area. The correct option matched the sample in both features. For

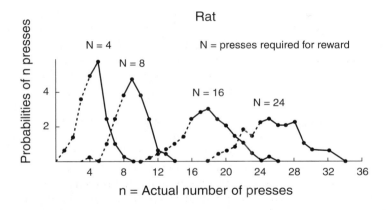

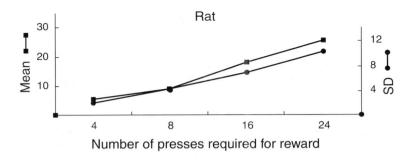

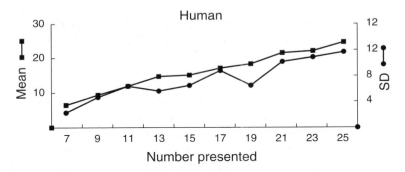

Figure 10.3. Top. Data from separate groups of rats trained by Platt and Johnson (1971) to press a lever N times before switching to a second response, shown as the proportions of trials with different actual numbers of presses. In the middle panel the same data are replotted as mean and standard deviation to show they are correlated as predicted by Weber's Law. The bottom panel shows data of a typical human in a comparable test of nonverbal counting, described in the text. Redrawn from Platt and Johnson (1971) and Whalen, Gallistel, and Gelman (1999) with permission.

example, with a sample of three red stars, the choices might be three red stars and five green stars. Number was placed in conflict with one of the other features in probe trials. For instance, in the example just given, color could be placed in conflict with number by presenting a choice between three green stars and five red stars. With numerosities up to eight, monkeys tended to choose on the basis of numerosity, and accuracies depended on the ratio of sample:distractor numerosities as Weber's Law predicts. The other features did have some effect, however, especially with sample:distractor ratios close to 1 and more so in one monkey without previous numerosity training.

Clearer evidence for spontaneous encoding of numerosity comes from habituation-dishabituation studies with monkeys (cotton-top tamarins; Hauser et al. 2003) and babies (Lipton and Spelke 2003) using auditory stimuli. Subjects were habituated to trains with a fixed number of sounds, syllables from human speech for the tamarins and brief natural sounds for the babies. Trains of different durations but a fixed number of various sounds were presented during the habituation phase, to ensure that habituation was to number and not some other variable such as total duration or sound energy of the train. Orienting to the speaker was then compared for novel trains with the same or a different number of sounds. As shown in Figure 10.4, the study with tamarins explicitly tested for the approximate large number system by including trials with habituation to numerosities of 4 and 8 followed by tests designed to discriminate responding based on absolute or relative difference. The tamarins were sensitive to a 2:3 ratio (i.e., 4 vs. 6 and 8 vs. 12) but not a 4:5 ratio even when, in the case of 8 versus 10, this involved an absolute difference in numerosity that they detected in the 4 versus 6 discrimination.

The precision of babies' discrimination increased with age. Six-month-olds habituated to trains of eight sounds dishabituated to trains of 16 but not 12 sounds, whereas nine-month-olds given the same treatment dishabituated to 12 but not 10 sounds. The consistency of these ratios across absolute number was not tested, but it was tested in a comparable study using visual displays (Xu and Spelke 2000; see also Xu, Spelke, and Goddard 2005). In that experiment, 6-month-olds discriminated 16 from 8 items, and 32 from 16 items, the same 2:1 ratio needed for auditory stimuli in Lipton and Spelke's (2003) study. In comparable tests, adults discriminate ratios down to 1.15:1 (see Feigenson, Dehaene, and Spelke 2004), but they still show the ratio signature of the analog magnitude system. However, the conclusion that these habituation studies all demonstrate sensitivity to number per se is controversial (Mix,

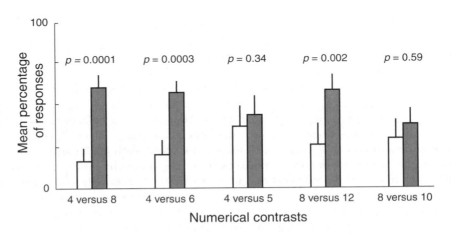

Figure 10.4. Proportion of test trials in which tamarins oriented to the sound train with the same number of elements as in habituation (white bars) and to the train with a novel number, as a function of the contrast between them. Adapted from Hauser et al. (2003).

Huttenlocher, and Levine 2002). Among other problems, continuous variables may not always have been controlled well enough, and when they are, number sometimes turns out to be of no importance. A reasonable conclusion (Hurewitz, Gelman, and Schnitzer 2006) and one consistent with data from other paradigms already presented here is that both number *and* continuous variables are processed but that which is attended to or most important depends on the circumstances. Even when human adults make quick comparisons of the numbers of dots in two displays, they make more errors when number conflicts with size of dots, as when 4 big dots are contrasted with 8 little ones (Hurewitz., Gelman, and Schnitzer 2006).

Another way to test spontaneous numerical representations is to let the subject watch while items of food are hidden in one or more containers. The subject, generally a monkey or baby, then shows how much food it expects by where and/ or how long it searches. In one such study (K. Lewis, Jaffe, and Brannon 2005) mongoose lemurs (*Eulemur mongoz,* a species of prosiminian, that is, on a different branch of the primate evolutionary tree than monkeys and apes) saw grapes placed one by one into a bucket. The bucket had a false bottom that allowed some the grapes to be placed out of the lemur's reach. For a given number that could be retrieved, the lemurs did indeed search longer after retrieving the last grape when they should have expected to find more, but only when as many as half the grapes deposited were unavailable. Thus at ratios of 1:2, 2:4, and 4:8 they increased searching with missing grapes, but not for 2:3 or 3:4. Notice that the ratio limit to discriminability indicates that only the analog magnitude system was called into play, even though some experiments to be described in Section 10.2 indicate that numbers as small as 3 or 4 may be represented with the precise object tracking system.

10.1.4   The analog magnitude scale

The top panel of Figure 10.3 suggests that the analog magnitude representation is linear with number in that equal numerical intervals are shown as equal intervals on the x-axis. Linearity is consistent with the notion (e.g., W. Roberts and Mitchell 1994) that counting is accomplished by the same accumulator system as timing, since Chapter 9 suggested that time is perceived linearly with real time but with scalar variance. Indeed initial discussions of the analog magnitude system suggested that it reflects an accumulator-like mechanism, that is, a process of implicit enumeration, but more recent discussions (e.g., Feigenson., Dehaene, and Spelke 2004) simply assume a monotonically increasing linear or logarithmic representation of set size, as in the visualizations in Figure 10.5. The many data supporting Weber's law for numerosity are equally consistent with this representation being logarithmic with constant variance as with its being linear (Figure 10.5). On the whole, behavioral data cannot discriminate between these mathematically equivalent formulations. However, neurobiological data are more consistent with a logarithmic scale (Nieder 2005). These come from monkeys trained in a matching to sample task in which they have to hold in mind the number of dots in a sample and choose the display with the matching numerosity at test. Single cells in the prefrontal cortex recorded during the delay fire selectively for specific numerosities between one and five, but with tuning curves that are symmetrical on a logarithmic scale (see also Nieder, Diester, and Tudusciuc 2006). Numerosity of simultaneously present items may in fact be perceived directly by the visual system, at least in humans (Burr and Ross 2008).

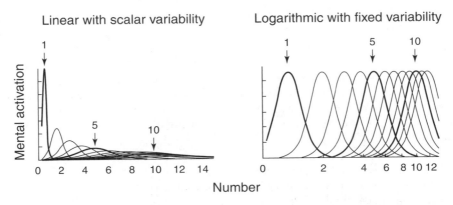

Figure 10.5. Two possible representations of the analogue magnitude scale. Numerical discrimination based on either of these representations obeys Weber's Law. Redrawn from Feigenson, Dehaene, and Spelke (2004).

One study of response number discrimination by pigeons also provides evidence more consistent with a logarithmic than a linear scale (W. Roberts 2005). The pigeons were trained in a typical bisection procedure to discriminate 1 versus 8 or 2 versus 16 pecks. The normal association of number of pecks with time spent pecking was disrupted by presenting the response key briefly at irregular very short intervals to allow only one peck at a time. Tests with intermediate numbers gave the expected result of bisection at the geometric mean. The birds were then trained, in effect, to bisect the interval between smallest and largest number at its arithmetic mean by reinforcing one choice following numbers below the mean and the other following numbers above it. Like the original bisection data, the resulting data were much better fit by a model assuming logarithmic rather than linear scaling.

10.2   The object tracking system

10.2.1   Signature limits

Several hundred rhesus macaques, a species not native to the New World, live and breed in a semi–free ranging state on Cayo Santiago, a small island off Puerto Rico. Because they are habituated to human activities, the monkeys approach and watch when people do interesting things with food. In the study with results depicted in Figure 10.6 (Hauser, Carey, and Hauser 2000) individual monkeys each watched on a single occasion as apple slices were placed one at a time into each of two boxes. Whether the larger number was deposited in the first or the second box, on the left or on the right, by one experimenter or another, was all equated within each condition. When both experimenters had finished hiding food, they retreated and allowed the monkey to approach one box. As the figure shows, the box with the larger number of slices was chosen only when neither number was greater than 4. Notice that ratio does not matter here, nor does absolute difference: monkeys chose the greater number with 2:1, 3:2, and 4:3, but chose randomly with 8:4 and 8:6. A second experiment in which rocks accompanied the smaller number of apple slices showed that the monkeys responded to pieces of food as such, not some other feature like time taken to place

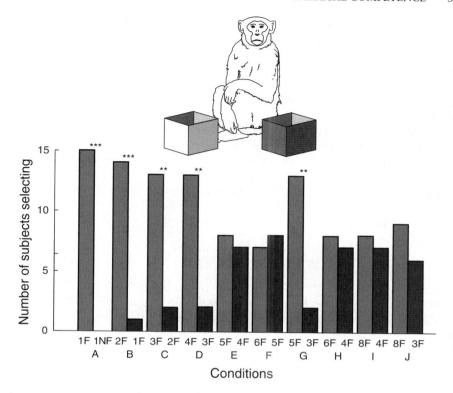

Figure 10.6. Results of Hauser, Carey, and Hauser's (2000) study of free-ranging rhesus macaques, showing number of monkeys out of each group of 15 animals selecting the box in which the given number of items had been deposited. F = food; NF = a non food item, a rock. As noted in the text other researchers have found no preference for 5 over 3 items (Condition G). Light gray = larger number of items; ** = statistically significant difference. Adapted from Hauser, Carey, and Hauser (2000)

items in the boxes. For example, they chose 4 apple slices over 3 apple slices and a rock. In a further experiment replicating aspects of this one (Barner et al. 2008), monkeys showed no preference in either 2:5 or 3:5 conditions, consistent with the conclusion that the system of numerical representation involved here has a set size limit of 4 in adult macaques. However, Barner and colleagues did find a preference in a 1:5 condition, consistent with other data within their study indicating that under some conditions monkeys' choices reflect not a precise representation of set size but a representation of "some" versus "one" (or "none"). The latter kind of representation is especially favored when items are presented as a united set, that is, placed in a container all together on a tray rather than one at a time.

In an adaptation of Hauser, Carey, and Hauser's (2000) method for babies, 10- to 12-month-old infants watched graham crackers being put into two opaque buckets (Feigenson, Carey, and Hauser 2002). About 80% of babies approached the bucket with the greater number for 1:2 and 2:3 but only about 50% did so with 3:4 or even 3:6. Several control conditions indicated that the failures at larger numbers were not due to the greater duration and/or complexity of activity the infants needed to remember. In this paradigm, total amount of cracker was sometimes more important than total number: two regular-sized crackers were rejected in favor of a single very large cracker, and chosen equally with a single double-sized one. Representations of small numbers of individuals as such were perhaps more clearly revealed in a study of searching time (Feigenson and Carey 2005) similar to that with lemurs reviewed in Section 10.1.3 (K. Lewis, Jaffe, and Brannon 2005). Year-old babies watched as balls were placed into a box and were then allowed to search for them. For example, babies that should have expected 3 balls but got only 2 because one was surreptitiously removed were compared to babies that saw 2 balls hidden in how long they spent reaching into the box after finding the second ball. The former group searched longer, revealing discrimination of 2 from 3. Remarkably, both when searching and in a choice test, babies failed a test of 1 versus 4 even though the total number of items to be represented is the same as in 2 versus 3, and both ratio and absolute difference should favor success in 1 versus 4. Like Barner and colleagues (2008), however, Feigenson and Carey (2005) found evidence that sets too large for the object tracking system can still be represented as "some."

10.2.2   Babies and monkeys do arithmetic

Some of the babies' and monkeys' choices in the studies just described may seem paradoxical, but at first glance the results of a series of looking time studies with small numbers of objects are even more remarkable. Figures 10.7 and 10.8 show data from experiments in which 5- to 6-month-old human infants (Wynn 1995) and wild rhesus monkeys (Hauser, MacNeilage, and Ware 1996) watched as objects were placed behind a screen, and their looking time was measured when the screen was removed. For both species, a small number of habituation trials with possible displays or with displays involving no change in numbers of objects (see Figure 10.8) was followed by a test in which responses to possible and impossible displays could be compared across groups. Looking time on various sorts of control trials was measured to assess the possibility that subjects simply look longer at certain static displays, for instance

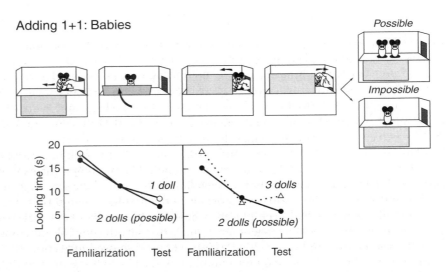

Figure 10.7. "Arithmetic" in infants. Babies sat in an infant seat watching the "puppet show"; in the familiarization phase they were exposed to the individual events later presented in these tests. Redrawn from K. Wynn (1992, 1995) with permission.

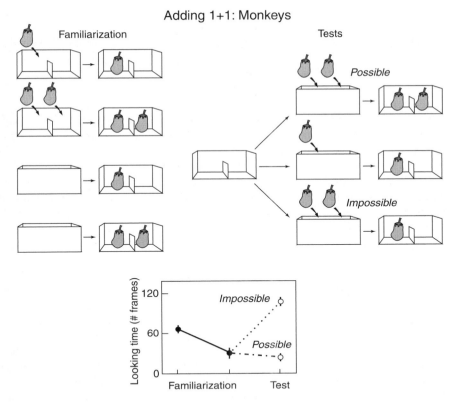

Figure 10.8. "Arithmetic" in free-ranging rhesus macaques. The objects were purple eggplants. Familiarization involved exposure to two of the four sequences on the left. As in Figure 10.7, looking times (measured here in film frames) were scored by observers unaware of which condition the subject was viewing. Redrawn from Hauser, MacNeilage, and Ware (1996) with permission.

those containing more objects. They looked longer at a numerically impossible display such as one corresponding to "1 + 1 = 1," than at a possible one such as "1 + 1 = 2," as if mentally adding and subtracting as objects were inserted or removed from behind the screen (see Wynn 1992). However, the fact that changes in the displays must take place rather quickly (cf. Hauser., MacNeilage, and Ware 1996; Hauser and Carey 1998) is more consistent with the idea that they are tracking a temporary perceptual representation, as discussed in the next section.

As suggested by the examples in Figures 10.7 and 10.8, the original studies of "arithmetic" did not dissociate amount from number. The monkeys, for example, could have been tracking total amount of "eggplant stuff" behind the screen. At least in the case of "1+1," number is more important to the monkeys than total amount: after two small eggplants had been placed behind the screen, monkeys that saw a single large one revealed looked longer than animals that saw the possible outcome of two small ones (Hauser and Carey 2003). However, as discussed in Section 10.1.3, the notion that babies are responding to number as such in looking-time studies is controversial (Mix, Huttenlocher, and Levine 2002). Indeed, in some studies with a "1+1" event like that depicted in Figure 10.7, infants look no more when one big doll emerges from behind the screen than when two small ones do (Mix, Huttenlocher, and Levine 2002). If multiple features of visual objects are encoded in working memory, their relative importance might be expected to vary, just as it does when larger numbers are involved (Hurewitz, Gelman, and Schnitzer 2006). When other features are controlled, infants may fail to respond to small numerosities while continuing to respond to larger ones, perhaps further evidence for two distinct systems (Xu, Spelke, and Goddard 2005). In any case, the conditions necessary to bring out "arithmetic" in these situations are not yet entirely understood. For example, when objects were initially presented as a set (e.g., four lemons in a row) in an experiment like Hauser and Carey's (2003), wild rhesus macaques looked longer at possible than at impossible outcomes with totals up to 4 + 4 (Flombaum, Junge, and Hauser 2005). With size of item controlled, discrimination was based on ratios of set sizes. As another exception, when chimpanzees watched banana pieces placed into two containers one at a time over a period of up to 20 minutes, they reliably chose the container with the greater number at totals up to 6 versus 10 (Beran and Beran 2004). In this study, items were not placed first into one container and then into another, but in a mixed order, and the location of neither the first nor the last item predicted the animals' choices.

10.2.3   What is going on?

Tests of monkeys and babies which reveal small set size limits for numerosity discrimination do not tap numerical representation as such but rather short term memory for visual objects (Feigenson, Dehaene, and Spelke 2004; Barner et al. 2008). A large body of data on human visual attention and memory indicates that objects appearing in the visual field are "tagged" with a spatio-temporal address linking their features into a unified object or "object file" (see Chapter 3), a process also referred to as *parallel individuation* (Barner et al. 2008). Human adults' working memory capacity is 3 or 4 such items (Luck and Vogel 1997), the same size as the implicit representations of set size in monkeys and babies. On this view, in demonstrations of "arithmetic" or searching for missing objects the subject is revealing how it encoded the number of items in a single set by looking or searching longer when the outcome does not match expectation. In choice experiments, two sets are compared not in terms of magnitude as such but in terms of one-to-one correspondence between members of the sets. The larger is the one with, as it were, leftover items. On this interpretation the observed set size limits of 3 for babies and 4 for adult macaques is a limit on items per set, not total items in working memory. Thus babies "pass" with 2 versus 3 but fail 1 versus 4 even though each comparison involves 5 items altogether (Feigenson and Carey 2005). Once one set exceeds the limit for object files, one-to-one correspondence is no longer possible, even though the larger set may still be represented as "some," and chosen over none or one (Barner et al. 2008). Note too that because object files encode multiple features of objects, changes in size or type of objects as well as their number may also increase looking time, and it may be difficult to predict which features will be important (Hurewitz, Gelman, and Schnitzer 2006).

Particularly in earlier discussions of animal numerical competence, discriminating numbers of items in very small arrays has been attributed to *subitizing*, apprehending the number of things in an array immediately, without counting, perhaps by recognizing the distinctive patterns formed by 1, 2, 3, and so on, objects (e.g., Starkey and Cooper 1980; Davis and Perusse 1988). Not everyone agrees that there is a distinct subitizing process (e.g., Gallistel 1990; D. Miller 1993), but if there is it would be used with simultaneously presented arrays of small numbers of items, like those that can be labeled by highly trained animals as described earlier in the chapter. For example, three objects can be arranged on a flat surface in only so many ways, and in its extensive training to identify examples of "three," H. Davis's (1984) raccoon may have memorized most of them.

10.2.4   When is object tracking used?

We have seen evidence for two ways of representing numerosity, each with its distinct signature. In the analog magnitude system, numerosities of unlimited size are discriminated in the fuzzy way described by Weber's Law. In the object tracking system, small numerosities are represented precisely, up to a limit of about 4 for adult humans and macaques and 3 for human infants. Within these small limits, absolute difference matters, not ratio. But object tracking is not the only way of representing small numerosities, that is, it is not *the* "small number system." Under some conditions monkeys or babies simply encode a small set as "some," a quantity greater than one or zero (Barner et al. 2008). And in many cases, numerosities from 1 upward are encoded in common as analog magnitudes. This means that when a range of numerosities is used within a single task, no discontinuity appears around 3 or 4, and discrimination accuracy is predicted by the ratios of the quantities compared regardless of their sizes. An example is Brannon and Terrace's (1998) operant study with rhesus macaques described in the next section. Initial training with numerosities from 1 to 4 transferred seamlessly to larger numerosities, and the ratio rule described data from all numerosities.

In a revealing example, Beran (2007) gave two rhesus macaques a virtual version of the task in which Hauser, Carey, and Hauser (2000; Hauser and Carey 2003) found evidence for the object tracking system with wild monkeys. Beran's monkeys were very experienced with computerized tasks that they accessed freely from their home cages and performed many times a day. They watched as a hand appeared to release small red squares into two containers at the bottom of the computer screen. Reinforcement was given for moving a cursor to the container with more items. Sets varied in size from 1 to 10 items, with controls for total area of the items and total time taken for them to drop. The monkeys' performance fell uniformly as the ratio of set sizes increased, with no evidence that the object tracking system was being used even when both numerosities were small. Like those of Brannon and her colleagues, these findings suggest that the analog magnitude system is called into play for small magnitudes when animals are very experienced with a task, although it is not yet clear how much experience might be necessary, or why experience should matter in the first place.

10.3   Ordinal comparison: Numerosity, serial position, and transitive inference

10.3.1   Ordering numerosities

As we have seen, pigeons and rats implicitly order numerosities in that their probability of rating novel stimuli as having "many" rather than "few" elements increases smoothly as a function of numerosity. Similarly, pigeons given a choice of two or more stimuli each associated with a different delay or amount of food choose them in order from largest to smallest reinforcer (Olthof and Santi 2007). But human numerical competence includes the ability to order an infinity of magnitudes along the real number line. Such explicit ordination has been studied almost exclusively in rhesus macaques and a few other primates. As we will see, numerical ordination tasks seem to tap a more general ability to represent and reason about things that vary in magnitude, whether numerosity of elements, position in an arbitrary sequence, or ranking in a social hierarchy.

Brannon and Terrace (1998, 2000) demonstrated that rhesus macaques could explicitly order numerosities using a version of the simultaneous chaining task to be discussed further in Section 10.3.2. The monkeys saw exemplars of the numerosities 1–4 simultaneously displayed on a touch-sensitive computer screen, as in Figure 10.9. The locations of the different numerosities changed from trial to trial, and in the final stage of training so did the color, shape, size, arrangement, and so forth, of the items in the displays, ensuring that the monkeys based their responses on numerosity alone. Once they had learned to touch four images in order of increasing numerosity even when the images were novel, test trials began with the numerosities 5–9. In this stage just two images appeared on each trial and touching them in order of increasing numerosity was reinforced only if both were familiar. Otherwise test trials were not reinforced. The monkeys performed far above chance even with novel pairs like 6 versus 8. Over all pairs, accuracy increased and latency to touch the first item decreased with numerical distance. In addition to this *numerical* (or *symbolic*) *distance effect,* they showed a *magnitude effect:* at a constant numerical difference, judgments were quicker and more accurate if the numerosities were small (Brannon and Terrace 2000). Note that Weber's Law implies the magnitude effect, for example, that 3 versus 2 is easier than 9 versus 8.

In initial training with 1 to 4, the monkeys evidently acquired a concept of ordinality or relative magnitude or made use of one they already had. Evidence for the latter possibility comes from an unsuccessful attempt to train one monkey to respond to displays of 1 to 4 items in an arbitrary order (Brannon and Terrace 2000). As we see shortly, monkeys can learn sequences of up to 7 arbitrary images in the same sort of procedure, so this monkey's complete failure with an arbitrary order of

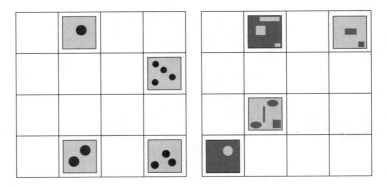

Figure 10.9. Examples of displays used to train macaques to order stimuli by numerosity. The display on the right, with exemplars of the numerosities 1–4 involving items that differ in shape and color, would have been used later in training than the more uniform display on the left. Notice how the locations of specific numerosities in the grid of locations changes from trial to trial. After Brannon and Terrace (2000) with permission.

numerosities (after which he succeeded on the normal order) suggests that monkeys spontaneously not only represent numerosities but order them by magnitude.

In extensions of this work, rhesus macaques transferred ordination skills acquired with numerosities of 1–9 to novel displays with up to 30 items (Cantlon and Brannon 2006). Such monkeys were compared to humans in their ability to order pairs of numerosities between 2 and 30 with controls for nonnumerical features such as density and total surface area of the items. The people were required to answer quickly to discourage counting. As shown in Figure 10.10, monkeys and people showed similar increases in reaction time and decreases in accuracy as the ratio of smaller:larger number approached 1:1. And in a clever adaptation of a human "semantic congruity" task, the same monkeys were trained to use the background color of the touchscreen as a cue whether the smaller or the larger numerosity of a pair between 1 and 9 should be touched first (Cantlon and Brannon 2005). Just like people told to "pick the larger" versus "pick the smaller" of two numerals, at a given numerical distance monkeys were quicker to judge "smaller" than "larger" when both numerosities were small, and quicker to judge "larger" than "smaller" when both were large. Like findings to be described in Section 10.4, these data suggest that human verbal labels for numerosities tap the same nonverbal representation of relative magnitude possessed by other species. As for what those other species might be, information is limited. There has been extensive further work on ordinal judgements with macaques (cf. Terrace 2006) and other primates (Smith, Piel, and Candland 2003; Beran et al. 2005), but little on explicit ordinal judgment of numerosity with nonprimate mammals or birds. The species differences in ranking and reasoning about other magnitude continua reviewed next suggest interesting possibilities for further comparative studies with the paradigm pioneered by Brannon and Terrace.

10.3.2   Ordering arbitrary items: Serial order learning

If arbitrary images replace stimuli related by numerosity, the kind of task depicted in Figure 10.9 becomes a test of *sequence production* or *simultaneous chaining*. The

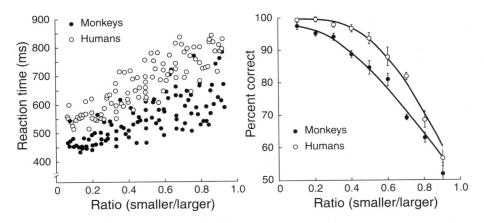

Figure 10.10. Reaction times and proportions of correct responses shown by monkeys and humans touching first the smaller and then the larger of two numerosities as a function of the ratio of the smaller to the larger. Redrawn from Cantlon and Brannon (2006) with permission.

animal's task is to touch or peck five simultaneously presented arbitrary pictures or colors, A–E, in the sequence A–B–C–D–E. Because the stimulus array does not change as the animal responds, it has only self-generated cues to its position in the sequence. And because the spatial arrangement of stimuli changes from trial to trial, the animal cannot memorize a sequence of motor acts. How sequences of responses or stimuli are learned is a classic issue in psychology that touches everything from how rats learn complex mazes to how people learn skills (Terrace 2005, 2006). In principle, such a sequence can be learned without any representation of the sequence as a whole or of items' relative positions within it as such. Animals might acquire a chain of associations so that each item activates a link to the next item in the sequence (Figure 10.11). Pigeons apparently use an even simpler rule. Their performance with subsequences of items such as AB, AC, and CD (reviewed by Terrace 2001) suggests that they learn, "respond first to A, if present, then respond to any other item; if E is present, respond to any other item and then to E." Thus they respond at chance to subsequences like BC that contain only interior items. They also respond equally quickly to the first and to the second items of all subsets, that is, they show nothing analogous to magnitude or distance effects (where magnitude and distance are now defined in terms of position in the sequence.)

Rhesus and cebus monkeys, whose performance in sequence production tasks has been studied extensively (D'Amato and Columbo 1988; Terrace 2001, 2006), behave quite differently from pigeons. They appear to acquire a linear representation of the sequence as a whole, in effect ordered mental slots occupied by specific items (Figure 10.11). Their data from tests with subsets of items parallel those from analogous tests of numerical ordering, as if learning to order unrelated pictures taps the same kind of representation. The latency to respond correctly to the first item increases with its position in the sequence (a magnitude effect), and latency to respond to a given first item decreases as the distance between it and the second item increases (a distance effect). In addition, cebus monkeys (comparable data from rhesus have apparently not been reported) show a "second item effect" (D'Amato and Columbo 1988; Colombo and Frost 2001). The latency to respond correctly to the second item after choosing the first item increases with distance between them (e.g., D is responded to more slowly in AD than in CD tests). On the whole, data from people given the same task show similar patterns (Colombo and Frost 2001). Interestingly, absolute latencies in such experiments as a function of magnitude or distance are substantially longer than those in comparable studies of numerical ordering, perhaps reflecting extra time required to retrieve ordinal information about the arbitrary images (Terrace 2006).

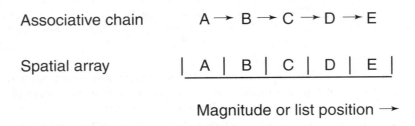

Figure 10.11. Two ways of representing a sequence of actions or events as a function of position: as a chain of associations ("A leads to B leads to C....") or as a linear spatial array.

Of the effects just summarized, the magnitude and second item effects are predicted by learning the list as a chain of associations, since connections should be weaker between items further apart, or further down, in the list. However, the distance effect seems incompatible with an associative representation because it implies that the relative positions of two disparate items are recognized more quickly the further apart they are, as if ordinal position is represented as such. Results of studies in which rhesus monkeys learn multiple lists are consistent with this conclusion. For example they correctly choose first the earlier and then the later item when tested with items from two different lists (Terrace, Son, and Brannon 2003). In one study (Swartz, Chen, and Terrace 1991) monkeys learned four 4-item lists of pictures, A–D, and then had transfer tests in which the familiar items were rearranged to make new lists. They learned the new lists more quickly if the items retained their old relative positions, as for example when A in the new list was A in one of the old lists and it was followed by B from a different old list, and so forth. And monkeys gradually become list-learning experts, learning completely new lists of up to seven items more and more rapidly even when each list is presented in its entirety from the very first trial (Terrace, Son, and Brannon 2003). As Terrace (2006) puts it, this is like figuring out a 7-digit PIN from scratch when the numbers don't even stay put on the keypad. The monkeys' skill implies they have developed a nonverbal strategy for identifying by trial and error first the initial item in the list, then the second, and so on.

10.3.3   Reasoning about quantity: Transitive inference

Nonverbal transitive inference

Transitive inference problems are familiar to every schoolchild. "If Susan is taller than Polly and Polly is taller than Carol, then who is tallest, Susan, Polly, or Carol?" Similarly in animal social life, if A dominates B, and B dominates C, then A probably dominates C. Making such inferences might permit learning one's place without having to fight with everyone in the social group. The functional prediction that follows—that species with a linear dominance hierarchy should be especially successful at transitive inference—has influenced some provocative recent research. However, tests of animals' transitive inference abilities began as tests of "rationality" or "reasoning" based on studies with children using arbitrary stimuli as depicted on the left of Figure 10.12 (McGonigle and Chalmers 1977). The animal learns a set of at least four simultaneous discriminations, construed as forming a series, A>B, B>C, C>D, D>E, where X>Y means that when they appear together X is reinforced and Y is not. Once performing well even when the pair presented varies randomly from trial to trial, the animal is given a choice between the novel pair B and D, each of which has been both reinforced and nonreinforced during training. Not only monkeys (e.g., McGonigle and Chalmers 1977; Treichler, Raghanti, and Van Tilburg 2003) and chimpanzees (Gillan 1981) but also rats (W. Roberts and Phelps 1994; Dusek and Eichenbaum 1997) and pigeons (e.g., von Fersen et al. 1991; Lazareva and Wasserman 2006) reliably choose B over D, but not necessarily for the same reasons. Indeed, the history of research in this area is a good example of how an explanation more or less readily accepted for the performance of primates was deeply (and as it turned out, appropriately) questioned when pigeons showed the same kind of behavior, leading to alternative explanations being devised and tested (Delius and Siemann 1998; Allen 2006).

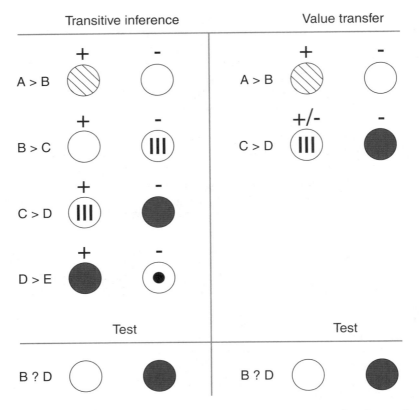

Figure 10.12. Examples of procedures for training and testing pigeons or monkeys in experiments on transitive inference (left side of the figure) or value transfer. The rewarded option in each pair is labeled +.

When people consciously make transitive inferences they seem to rely on a linear, spatial, representation of relative magnitudes; for example, the mind's eye sees Carol, Polly, and Susan standing in order of height. Because other primates seem to use such a linear representation for numerosity and serial order judgements, a reasonable hypothesis is that their transitive inferences rely on a similar representation (Terrace 2005). In addition to correct choice on critical novel pairings, evidence for an overall ordered representation of a series would consist of analogs to the magnitude, distance, and second item effects. A symbolic distance effect has been found in cebus monkeys (D'Amato and Colombo 1990) but as we will see, some such effects are found in other species and may have associative explanations (e.g., Van Elzakker, O'Reily, and Rudy 2003). One effect consistent only with an overall linear representation is inference-like performance when lists are linked, as when one learns the relative speeds of runners in two track teams and then learns that the slowest member of Team 1 outruns the fastest member of Team 2. By analogy, Treichler, Raghanti, and Van Tilburg (2003) taught rhesus monkeys three independent sets of four linked pairs (i.e., involving items A-E, F-J, and K-O) and then linked them by separately teaching "E>F" and " J>K." As a control, either before or afterwards the same monkeys learned three other lists that were not linked. In the experimental condition the monkeys performed substantially better than chance on cross-list pairs from the outset of reinforced testing, whereas in the control condition they began at chance.

Associative explanations of "inference"

Most tests of transitive inference with nonprimates have focused on performance with critical test pairs in a single list, usually B versus D in a 5-item (4-pair) list like that in Figure 10.12. However, there are several ways in which the training procedure might simply give B more associative strength than D. The most subtle arises because, although B and D have similar histories of primary reinforcement, they have appeared in the company of other stimuli with different histories. In particular, B appears not only with C but also with A, which should be very highly valued thanks to never being a negative stimulus in any discrimination in the series. Moreover, D appears sometimes in the company of E, which should be the least-valued stimulus in the series. Thus if B and D gain value by association with the other positive or negative stimuli with which they appear, B should be preferred over D. This sort of indirect acquisition of associative strength is referred to as *value transfer* (von Fersen et al. 1991). Value transfer has been demonstrated directly with the procedure shown on the right of Figure 10.12 (Zentall and Sherburne 1994; Zentall et al. 1996). Pigeons were confronted with negative stimuli, B and D, from two independent simultaneous discriminations, in one of which (A vs. B) the positive stimulus had been reinforced 100% and in the other of which (C vs. D) it had been only partially reinforced. Although both procedures lead to similarly high rates of responding to the reinforced alternative, pigeons reliably pecked more at B than D in the test. However, S+ and S- can interact in more than one way in a simultaneous discrimination (Zentall and Clement 2001), so any preference for B over D remaining despite manipulations designed to equalize value transfer is not conclusive evidence for a linear representation of the series.

Value transfer can be opposed to linear representation by, in effect, bending the linear series on the left of Figure 10.12 around on itself by adding E>A so E and A, together with their associates B and D, no longer have differential value. As value transfer predicts, pigeons did not choose B over D in this "circular" series (von Fersen et al. 1991). However, in an analogous test with rats in which the alternatives were an ordered series of spatial locations, B was still chosen over D, as if the animals had acquired a representation of the relative location of the items in space (Roberts and Phelps 1994). Perhaps this is not surprising when they were ordered in space to begin with; it is not the same as the animal itself generating a spatial representation of inherently nonspatial elements. Overall, tests with circular series have had mixed results (cf. Treichler and Van Tilburg 1996; Delius and Siemann 1998). Consistent with poor performance on a circular series and inconsistent with an overall representation of relationships among items, performance on interior items in a linear series may be strongly influenced by the associative strengths of neighboring items (von Fersen et al. 1991; Van Elzakker, O'Reily, and Rudy 2003). Most unlike what might be expected from pure serial ordering are "end (or anchor) effects": performance is markedly better for the last pair in the series than for interior pairs, reflecting the last item's special status (e.g., Van Elzakker, O'Reily, and Rudy 2003). When monkeys have extensive training in numerical ordering tasks with the same items, an analogous anchor effect becomes one of several determinants of performance (Brannon, Cantlon, and Terrace 2006).

Another line of associative explanation arises from observing that the way animals are typically trained in these tasks leads to reinforcement histories favoring B over D (Wynne 1995; Delius and Siemann 1998). For example, if training starts with "A>B" and successive pairs are added only after the animal meets some criterion on earlier ones in the sequence (as in Bond., Kamil, and Balda 2003), the sheer number of reinforced and nonreinforced choices can vary widely among different items.

Correction trials (Box 6.2) may be used to equate reinforcers to members of a pair, leaving uncontrolled the number of unreinforced choices of each item. A model incorporating this generates transitive choices (Couvillon and Bitterman 1992). Lazareva and Wasserman (2006) tested the dependence of B versus D choices on pigeons' reinforcement history by giving extra D versus E training sufficient to raise each bird's overall ratio of reinforced to nonreinforced first choices of D to a level higher than that for B, but pigeons still chose B on 80% of B versus D tests. Other tests along similar lines, addressed to a variety of associative factors, have had similar results (Wynne 1995; Delius and Siemann 1998). Because there are so many ways in which reinforcement history could produce choices consistent with inference from a linear representation, the basis for any remaining B versus D preference in rats and pigeons is unclear. Tests with lists of more than 5 items (4 pairs) should be most illuminating here because they afford more possibilities for novel pairings of interior items, but even so ambiguities remain. For example, rats trained on a 5-pair series of odors, A-F (Van Elzakker, O'Reily, and Rudy 2003) chose B more often in B versus E than in B versus D tests, but was this a distance effect or did negative value transferred from F reduce choices of E?

Finally, results from studies of "unconscious inference" in human adults show that members of a given species do not necessarily solve transitive inference-like tasks in only one way. Adults have been given a task like that depicted in Figure 10.12, but with Japanese characters. When they are not aware that the pairs form a linked list, their training and test data look much like those of rats and pigeons, but if they are aware of the relationship among the pairs they perform perfectly on all pairs in training and choose correctly in tests with novel pairs (Frank et al. 2005). In a study suggesting that rats may similarly have access to both kinds of representations, Dusek and Eichenbaum (1997) showed that hippocampally lesioned rats could still learn a list of odor pairs but did not perform above chance on B versus D tests whereas intact rats did. They concluded that rats normally rely on a spatial representation of the whole list, but this interpretation is not universally accepted (see Van Elzakker, O'Reily, and Rudy 2003). Moreover, similar effects are not found with pigeons (Strasser, Ehrlinger, and Bingman 2004).

This section of the chapter began with the question whether monkeys and other primates solve transitive inference tasks by reference to the same kind of linear overall representation evident in numerosity and serial ordering tasks. Clearly the associative history of the individual options can generate the choices predicted by transitive inference, but it is still unclear to what extent such factors are actually responsible for monkeys' behavior. We have seen that monkeys solve serial ordering tasks differently from pigeons, but so far the best evidence that the same kind of difference applies in transitive inference tasks is the way in which monkeys respond when separate lists are linked (Treichler, Raghanti, and Van Tilburg 2003), a test not yet reported for other species. In addition, monkeys should be tested with longer lists because these afford the large numbers of interior test pairs necessary for documenting magnitude and distance effects. If transitive inference is an adaptation for a complex social life monkeys and pigeons would be expected to differ just as they differ on sequence production tasks (Section 10.3.2).

Social transitive inference and species differences

Some of the best evidence that transitive inference can be used in social situations comes not from monkeys but from pinyon jays, food-storing corvids that live in stable social groups with linear dominance hierarchies. Paz-y-Mino and colleagues (2004) documented dominance relationships in three groups of captive pinyon jays by observing each pair of birds in a group in a contest over a peanut. Then each experimental bird watched on three occasions as a bird from another group defeated a dominant bird from its own group (Figure 10.13). This experience should have allowed subjects to infer, in effect, "the stranger beats someone who dominates me; therefore the stranger will dominate me." Subjects also saw the same stranger lose a contest with another bird from the stranger's own group on three occasions, thus learning that the stranger could lose as well as win. Control birds saw a stranger both winning and losing contests with others from the stranger's own group, an experience designed to give them no information about their own standing relative to the stranger. And indeed, the first time they encountered the stranger themselves, experimental birds behaved more submissively than controls. Although the effects of observation did not extend beyond the first encounter (and perhaps they should not

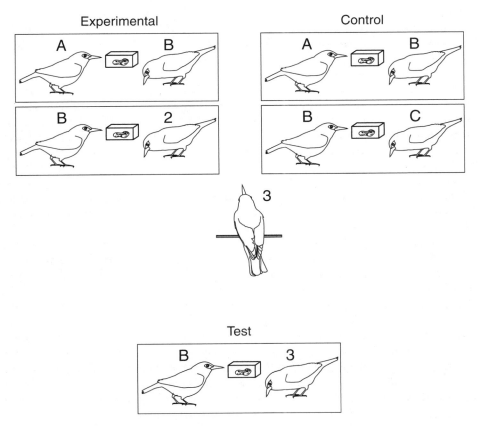

Figure 10.13. Experimental and control conditions in the study of social transitive inference in pinyon jays. Letters and numbers represent birds from two different social groups; relative ranks are represented by their order (e.g., A is dominant to B and 2 to 3). In sketches of the encounters, the bird on the right is behaving submissively to the bird on the left. The box contains a peanut, which would be obtained by the dominant bird. Subjects, here bird 3, watched the encounters like those depicted in the upper part of the figure and were tested as shown. After Paz-y-Mino et al. (2004) with permission.

be expected to), it is noteworthy how quickly the birds appear to have learned the relative rank of the stranger. Also unlike the case in analogous operant tasks, the rankings were learned entirely by observation, without any direct reinforcement of the actions displayed in the test. Hogue and colleagues (Hogue, Beaugrand, and Lague 1996) showed that hens learn about dominance in a similar way, although with a less well balanced design.

Fish as well as birds and mammals learn about other individuals by watching (Chapter 13). Males of a species of cichlid fish, *Astatolapia burtoni,* were exposed to staged encounters among four pairs of neighbors from which they could infer a whole 5-item hierarchy (Grosenick, Clement, and Fernald 2007). Individual neighbors played different roles in the hierarchy for different subject fish. When then confronted with two of these neighbors, one on either side of a tank, subjects were expected to spend more time near the less dominant member of a pair, and this is what they did, for both the A-E (i.e., most and least dominant) and the B-D pair. Four control fish that witnessed neighbors in a nonhierearchical series of interactions showed no preferences. Again, this learning was very quick. In Chapters 12 and 13 we will see more evidence that bystanders or "eavesdroppers" rapidly acquire information about social relationships.

It is worth wondering to what extent the learning by the jays and fish in these experiments is attributable to the same system involved in the slow and laborious food-rewarded instrumental discriminations that provide the basis for transitive choices in the studies reviewed earlier. One study based on the assumption that the same abilities are involved is a comparison of pinyon jays and scrub jays trained on an operant task with a 7-item (6-pair) list (Bond, Kamil, and Balda 2003). Because pinyon jays live in more complex social groups than do scrub jays, they were expected to learn the task faster and perform more like monkeys on novel tests. The first of these predictions was clearly fulfilled in that even with 100 sessions' extra training the scrub jays never reached the same level of performance as the pinyon jays. Birds of both species were well above chance with novel pairs, but when it came to detailed patterns of performance on interior pairs, the pinyon jays tended to behave more as if they had acquired a linear representation of the series of colors than did the scrub jays. However, the results were not unambiguous. As the authors conclude, the case for species differences here would be strengthened (or not) by further work, for example comparing the two species on list linking.

Stronger evidence that social structure predicts performance on operant transitive inference comes from a comparison of ring-tailed lemurs (*Lemur catta*), a very social species, with less social mongoose lemurs (*Euelmur mongoz;* MacLean, Merritt, and Brannon 2008). Although the two species acquired a task with six pairs equally quickly, the ring-tailed lemurs performed better on tests with novel pairs and showed a clear distance effect not evidenced by the mongoose lemurs (Figure 10.14). Importantly, however, after additional exposure to the training pairs (A > B, B > C, etc.) strictly in their sequence in the list, a procedure designed to emphasize their relationship, both species did well equally on novel pairs and showed equivalent distance effects. The authors therefore conclude that the species differ not in transitive inference ability as such but in their predisposition to organize information along a common dimension. How such an ability is related to human domain general ability to reason by transitve inference is open to discussion (see Penn, Holyoak, and Povinelli 2008).

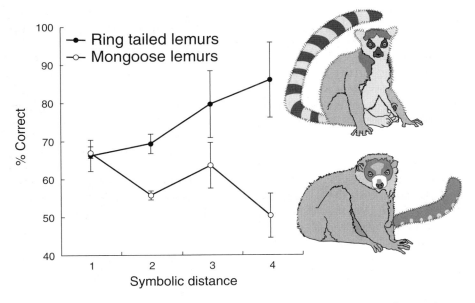

Figure 10.14. Symbolic distance effects compared in two species of lemurs trained on a 7-item transitive inference task. After MacLean, Merritt, and Brannon (2008) with permission.

10.4   Labels and language

We are now back where we began, with animal counting. Given that animals can discriminate numerosities, it is not surprising that a variety of animals can associate specific arbitrary stimuli, including human number words and symbols, with specific numerosities, that is, they can in a sense label numerosities (e.g., Olthof, Iden, and Roberts 1997; Olthof and Roberts 2000; Beran et al. 2005; Olthof and Santi 2007). But does such labeling reveal, or perhaps even convey, any forms of numerical competence that are not evident otherwise? And given that humans and other species share systems for object tracking and numerosity discrimination, is there a special role for counting language in human numerical competence? We address these questions by looking at the uses of number labels by a parrot, a few specially trained chimpanzees and other primates, and people whose language has only a few number words.

10.4.1   Alex the parrot

Alex the African grey parrot was trained for over 20 years to describe his surroundings with English words (Pepperberg 1999). His vocabulary was designed to reveal his ability to categorize objects in terms of features like color, shape, material, and number. After being trained to report the number of items in collections of up to six objects, Alex correctly labeled novel sets of objects on about 80% of trials. He could also say how many objects of a certain type were in a larger array of objects. For example, "How many keys?" on a tray with two keys and four rocks. Like young children, he tended to make errors that consisted of responding with the total number of objects in the array, for example, "six" rather than "two." When there were two keys among four rocks, Alex might have been subitizing, but not when asked the number of yellow keys in a display containing yellow keys, green keys, yellow rocks, and green rocks. Nevertheless, Alex did respond correctly to more than 80% of such questions (Pepperberg 1994). And like the chimpanzees discussed next, Alex could use numbers to answer questions about addition of small quantities, for example, answering "three" when two items are hidden under one cup and one under another. He also appropriately answered "none" to questions for which "zero items" is the correct answer, although he may not have completely understood the mathematical concept of zero (review in Pepperberg 2006).

A nice demonstration that Alex's number words represent precise quantities followed on from his being taught the names for the Arabic numerals 1 to 6. He learned to name the numerals by rote rather than by pairing them with numbers of things. Having done that he could then correctly answer questions that required identifying the names of the numerals with numerosities. For example, he might be shown a 2 and a 4 of equal size and asked "which bigger?" Or he might see 2 candies and a numeral 3 and be asked "which smaller?" This performance implies that he linked the number symbols to numerosities by way of the common vocalization associated with them, much as in mediated generalization (Chapter 6) and some examples of functional reference (Chapter 14).

10.4.2   Counting chimpanzees

Ai: memory span and planning

Matsuzawa and his colleagues have been studying the cognitive abilities of the chimpanzee Ai for many years (Matsuzawa 2007). Ai learned to match arrays of up to 9 objects by selecting the correct numeral on a touchscreen, but unlike children she did not get any quicker with experience learning new numbers. She also learned to touch numerals in order of magnitude when four or more of them appeared in unpredictable locations on the screen. Typically the longest latency in each chain of responses was to the first item, as if Ai was inspecting all the numerals and planning the required sequence of moves before touching the smallest. This supposition was supported by the finding that when all the remaining numerals were replaced by white squares (i.e., masked) as soon as she touched the first one, she still was able to proceed through the correct sequence on a high proportion of trials, even with five items (Kawai and Matsuzawa 2000). The speed and accuracy with which Ai and other chimpanzees can do the task with masking apparently exceeds that of human subjects (Matsuzawa 2007), but of course the chimpanzees may have had more training. Three other chimpanzees and two monkeys were trained to do essentially the same task by moving a joystick to select numerals up to 5 in order. In addition to masking trials, they were subjected to trials in which the locations of two items were swapped after they had begun the sequence, which again should disrupt a planned series of moves. These animals seemed to plan ahead only to the next move in both numerical and arbitrary sequences of items, possibly because selecting moves with a joystick is more attention demanding than just touching them, leaving fewer cognitive resources for planning (Beran et al. 2004).

Numerals and the reversed contingency task

Sally Boysen and her colleagues trained three chimpanzees to label small collections of objects with Arabic numerals (review in Boysen 1993). Their education began with training on one-to-one correspondance, matching numbers of gumdrops to numbers of tokens stuck on cards. Then cardinal numbers replaced the tokens. Eventually the animals could make appropriate choices of arrays when shown Arabic numerals and vice versa. They could use numbers up to 6 or 8 as well as zero. Finally, one animal, Sheba, was allowed to find up to four oranges in any of three places in a room. She reported what she saw by searching the hiding places and choosing the corresponding numeral. The cards with numerals were placed so that Sheba could not see the experimenter while making her choice (Figure 10.15). When oranges were in more than one place, Sheba correctly reported the total number of oranges, apparently adding the numbers found in different locations. To probe further the extent to which numerals represent numbers of things for the animal, Boysen and Berntson (1989) hid cards with numerals. For instance, a *1* might be hidden in one place and a *3* in another. Having seen two numerals, Sheba correctly reported their total. Most remarkably, Sheba's performance was better than chance from the first encounter with this task.

Two of Boysen and Berntson's (1995) number-trained chimpanzees were the first to be studied in a *reversed-contingency task:* in this task the animal is offered a choice between two quantities of food and receives the one it does *not* indicate. In their original experiments whatever the subject selected was given to another chimpanzee in a facing cage, and the subject had what remained. In nearly 100 trials' exposure to this contingency, Sheba and Sarah persistently pointed to the larger quantity more than 50% of the time, and their tendency to make the "wrong" choice was greater the greater the disparity between the two quantities. However, when Sheba had numerals substituted for numbers of treats, she immediately began to indicate the smaller

Figure 10.15. Sheba reports the total number of oranges she found distributed among three hiding places (gray circles). After Boysen and Berntsen (1989) with permission.

amount at greater than chance levels. Five more animals tested similarly performed in the same way (Boysen. et al. 1996). When sessions with real objects alternated with sessions using numerals, all the animals performed so as to maximize their rewards when numbers were used but reverted to suboptimal choice with confronted with the actual treats, even after hundreds of trials. Thus even though numerals represent numbers of objects for the animals, the candies themselves arouse an irrepressible "greedy response" that the numerals do not.

The reversed contingency task has subsequently been tried with tamarins, several other monkey species, and all the great apes (see Vlamings, Uher, and Call 2006). Essentially it requires the animal to inhibit its natural response toward the perceptual features of the two piles of food items and be influenced instead by what the relative quantities represent. Substituting numerals for a direct view of the food clearly reduces its perceptual salience, but the same can be done by teaching the animal an association between colors and amounts of food or by simply covering the food containers before the animal chooses. Alternatively, increasing the cost of choosing the larger amount can reduce the number of suboptimal choices (Vlamings, Uher, and Call 2006). Across primates, there may well be species differences in how easy it is to inhibit the tendency to grab a visible larger amount, perhaps related to foraging ecology and sociality, or (on another level) to executive function in the brain, but documenting it will require further work. For example, a comparison of chimpanzees with the other three species of great apes (gorillas, bonobos, and orangutans; Vlamings, Uher, and Call 2006) found that individuals of all species learned the task and did better with hidden than with visible food, but unlike in some other studies the animals were tested with only two combinations of amounts.

10.4.3   Numerical competence without number language

Notice that so far the studies with "number labels" have not actually revealed much about numerical competence per se. This is not true of a recent study of the Munduruku tribe in the Amazon jungle of Brazil (Pica et al. 2004; see also Gordon 2004). The Munduruku have precise counting words for quantities only up to about four. When shown collections of things and asked "How many?" if there are five or more they give varied and vague answers like "some," "two hands." Yet when asked to make numerosity discriminations in the comparison and addition tasks depicted in Figure 10.16, they perform almost the same as numerate French controls. Asked to compare clouds of up to 80 dots, their judgments are more accurate as a function of the ratio of the quantities being compared, the same Weber's Law principle we saw throughout the first part of the chapter. But counting language does make a difference when it comes to precise comparisons. Asked to name or point to the result of an exact subtraction, the tribes people were correct only when the initial amount was four or fewer, whereas the French controls were nearly perfect up to 8 or so, the largest quantities tested. The answer was always within the same small range; what was critical was precise identification of the initial quantity. Along with other studies of children and human adults like those mentioned earlier in this chapter (see also Barth et al. 2006), the study of the Munduruku shows that people share an imprecise representation of numerosity, and perhaps also a precise representation of numerosities up to about 4, with other species, but in addition it shows that one thing language does is to convey precise representation of larger quantities, presumably through counting (see also Dehaene

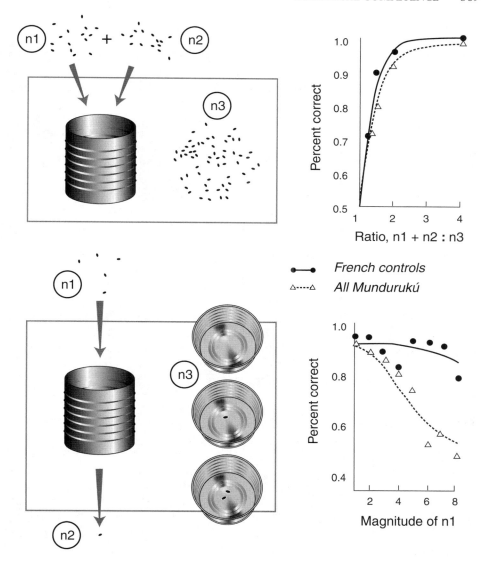

Figure 10.16. Tasks used to test aspects of numerical competence in the Munduruku, with group data compared to that of numerate French adults. In the top task, clouds of n1 and n2 dots successively "fall" into the can and the subject has to judge whether the can holding n1 + n2 items has more or fewer than n3. In the exact subtraction task on the bottom, n1 dots "fall" into the can and n2 "fall out" at the bottom. The subject indicates the number remaining by choosing a can on the right. Adapted from Pica et al. (2004) with permission; samples of the videos presenting these and other tasks to the subjects can be seen in the online supplement to this article.

et al. 2008). Exactly how it does that—for example whether the concept of precise numerosity is built on the small number system—and whether other primitive concepts play a role in mathematical development is a continuing challenge for developmental psychologists (Gelman and Gallistel 2004; Leslie, Gelman, and Gallistel 2008).

10.5   Numerical cognition and comparative psychology

More than any other topic treated in this book so far the comparative study of numerical competence has taken on a whole new look in the last decade. The integrated theoretical and experimental approach that has emerged is exemplary for other areas of comparative cognition. "Can animals count?," the question that informed most traditional research in the area from Clever Hans onward, is in some ways the least productive kind of comparative question because it impels little more than a search for a yes or no answer. Species either do it or they don't, and then what? As this chapter illustrates, researchers now are asking something more like, "What are the components of numerical competence, how may they be characterized, what species share which of them, and why (in neurological, functional and/or evolutionary terms)?" A good deal of progress has been made by thinking in terms of two systems, object tracking for quantities up to about three or four, and Weber's Law based on approximate discrimination among unlimited quantities. However, the exact role and limit, even the existence of, the first of these is still controversial. Discrimination among numerosities seems to imply the ability to order them, but this ability has been studied explicitly mostly with rhesus monkeys. At least in monkeys, the same ability seems to be tapped by learning to order arbitrary items. Whether or not it underlies transitive inference in monkeys remains unclear, as does the relationship of social transitive inference abilities to the performance laboriously elicited in analogous operant tasks. Finally, in the last section of the chapter we see how the numerical abilities of people without language for counting can be understood with the same framework that organizes comparative understanding.

Further reading

Pfungst's account of Clever Hans has been reprinted in English with an introduction by Robert Rosenthal discussing the general problem of inadvertent cueing and other experimenter influences in psychology (Pfungst 1965). Candland (1993) has written an entertaining and thoughtful book for the general reader that puts Clever Hans–related work with chimpanzees in the context of a long history of attempts to probe the "silent minds" of animals and feral children by teaching them to use language. The chapters by Boysen and Hallberg (2000) and by Emmerton (2001) are good reviews of the history of research on primates and birds, respectively, and the chapter by Terrace (2006) comprehensively reviews serial order learning. Excellent recent reviews encompassing more of the research on specifically numerical cognition highlighted in this chapter are those by Hauser and Spelke (2004) Feigenson, Dehaene, and Spelke (2004), Nieder (2005), and Brannon (2006). Irene Pepperberg's work with Alex the parrot is comprehensively described in her 1999 book; the studies of parrot numerical cognition are reviewed in Pepperberg (2006).

11

Cognition and the Consequences of Behavior: Foraging, Planning, Instrumental Learning, and Using Tools

A rat that has learned to press a lever for sucrose gets sick in its home cage after drinking sucrose. Next time it is placed in the operant chamber, it does not press the lever.

A chimpanzee emerges from the jungle near a termite mound carrying a slender stick. It slides the stick into a hole in the mound and extracts a mouthful of insects.

The rat and the chimp are exhibiting instrumentally learned behavior, behavior acquired and maintained because of its consequences. We have already encountered instrumental learning, in Chapters 6 (categorization), 9 (timing), and elsewhere, but now we look at the functional and mechanistic principles underlying it. A theme that unites the diverse topics of this chapter is the different senses in which behavior can be described as rational and how they are related (Kacelnik 2006). Just as with Tinbergen's four questions (Chapter 1), these senses are easily confused, with functional issues sometimes mistaken for mechanistic ones and the reverse. In functional terms, we expect behavior to be biologically rational in that it should increase fitness rather than decreasing it: the rat that has learned sucrose makes it sick should no longer press the bar to get it. Rational behavior in economics is similarly defined in terms of function, in this case maximizing utility. Research on instrumental learning and behavior from functional perspectives is the subject of Section 11.1, which introduces optimal foraging models and economic decision-making. Studies of instrumental learning and choice in these contexts have shed light on cognitive mechanisms, and vice versa, but their primary focus is testing functional predictions.

In psychology and philosophy being rational means being able to give a reason for action (Kacelnik 2006). Human folk psychology typically explains the sorts of behavior discussed in Sections 11.2–11.4—acting now for a future benefit, changing a response as its consequences change in value, using tools in given ways—as resulting from explicit causal reasoning. For instance, I shop today because I am planning a party for tomorrow, when the stores will be closed. But behavior may satisfy functional criteria for rationality without resulting from humanlike representations and decision processes. That is, biological rationality may be accomplished by proximate mechanisms that are not psychologically rational. Just as with metacognition (Chapter 7) or spatial mapping (Chapter 8), much research on the topics in this chapter reflects a fundamental tension between anthropomorphic, folk-psychological explanations and "simpler" ones, usually based on associative learning. Here the challenge is to translate intuitive predictions based on how people reason (or believe they reason) about causes and effects into unambiguous nonverbal tests. How can we tell, for instance, what a chimpanzee getting termites with a stick understands about how the tool works?

11.1   Foraging

A starling walking across a pasture pokes its beak into the ground and pulls out a leatherjacket (*Tipula* larva). When it has three larvae lined up in its beak, it flies off, carrying the load of prey to its nestlings (Figure 11.1). Watching starlings foraging for larvae, a behavioral ecologist would ask "What *should* these animals do, and do they do it?" However, as the study of foraging in behavioral ecology evolved, it incorporated and in turn contributed to answering the psychologist's question, "*How* do these animals do whatever they do?" Indeed, the study of foraging is one of the best examples of how functional and mechanistic approaches to behavior can be integrated (Real 1991; Dukas 1998 ; Stephens, Brown, and Ydenberg 2007; Shapiro, Siller, and Kacelnik 2008). This section begins with a brief overview of foraging theory. Then we look at a sample of classic foraging problems illustrating interactions between tests of optimality models and studies of information-processing and decision making (for a more through review see chapter 9 in Shettleworth 1998). Finally we look at recent work flowing from the analogy between foraging and consumer choice (Section 11.1.5).

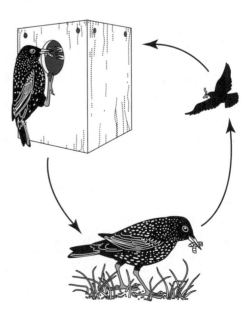

Figure 11.1. Foraging by starlings and other birds while feeding young consists of cycles of traveling to suitable patches of the environment, collecting prey, and flying back to the nest.

11.1.1   Foraging theory

Optimality models in behavioral ecology start with the assumption that behavior has been selected that maximizes fitness (Stephens and Krebs 1986; Parker and Maynard Smith 1990). Because fitness (Box 1.2) is often difficult to measure directly, foraging models usually deal in a more easily measured *currency* that is assumed to contribute to fitness. Very often this is net rate of energy intake, that is, energy consumed minus the energy expended to obtain it, a currency that does demonstrably influence fitness (e.g., Lemon 1991). The formal characterization of a foraging situation also includes *constraints* on the forager. For example, consider a visual forager like a lapwing walking across a meadow scanning the ground for insects (Figure 11.2). How far should the bird move between scans? Walking consumes energy, so the cost of moving increases linearly with the number of steps the bird takes. However, the chance of spotting a new prey item increases as the bird moves away from the area it has just scanned. If the bird can scan a circular area, it should move just the diameter of one scan before stopping to scan again (O'Brien, Browman, and Evans 1990; Parker and Maynard Smith 1990). As illustrated in Figure 11.2, the tradeoff between the cost of moving and the benefit of scanning a new patch can be quantified to compute the course of action that maximizes the lapwing's net rate of energy intake. In this example, the bird's visual system imposes psychological constraints, and the structure of the world in the form of the bird's physiology and the distribution of prey imposes physical constraints.

11.1.2   When to leave depleting patches: The marginal value theorem

In the first of the classic foraging models we consider, prey are in distinct *patches* separated by areas without prey, and the predator depletes patches as it feeds. (All food items are *prey* in this context even if they are grass or seeds.) As items become sparser the forager will experience diminishing returns, so it must decide when to leave the current patch and travel to the next one. The situation confronting starlings collecting leatherjackets to feed their young (Figure 11.1) is formally identical because it takes longer to collect each larva the more it already has in its beak. Thus even if the patch does not deplete appreciably, the rate of gain decreases the longer the starling searches for prey between trips back to the nest.

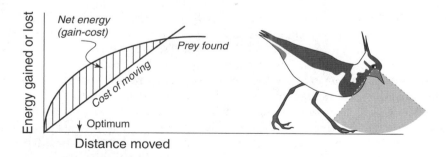

Figure 11.2. Graphical calculation of the optimal size of move for a foraging lapwing. The optimum is the point where the distance between energy intake and energetic cost of moving (the net energy intake) is maximal. After Parker and Maynard Smith (1990) with permission.

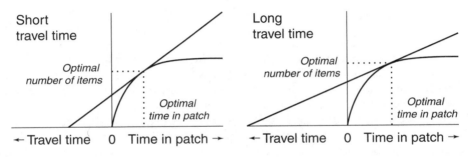

Figure 11.3. Graphical calculation of optimal patch residence time according to the marginal value theorem. Energy gain is in the vertical dimension. The slope of the diagonal line in each panel is the maximum net rate of energy intake in an environment with the given travel time and gain function (items vs. time in patch). The slope will necessarily be less if the animal stays a longer or shorter time.

Intuitively, a forager should stay longer in one patch if the next patch is likely to be far away than if it is close by. For the starling collecting leatherjackets, it makes sense to gather a large load when far from the nest, but to start home with a small load when close to the nest. The solution to the problem of maximizing energy gain in depleting patches, shown in Figure 11.3 is known as the *Marginal Value Theorem*, abbreviated *MVT* (Charnov 1976). To a first approximation, this is a good account of what animals do (Stephens and Krebs 1986; Nonacs 2001). To maximize its overall rate of energy intake, a forager should leave a patch when the rate of energy gain in that patch falls to the average rate in the habitat. Before this time, the forager is by definition doing better than it can do elsewhere. Afterward, it could do better on average by leaving. In order to behave in this way, a forager has to keep track of its current rate of intake. If prey come in discrete similar-sized units like leatherjackets in a field, this means accumulating information about times between prey captures. The forager also needs information about the average intake rate in the rest of the habitat.

The foregoing analysis suggests that foraging close to optimally might mean storing information about travel times and intercapture intervals, in which case the data about timing in Chapter 9 might help to explain what animals do. However, sometimes simpler mechanisms can do the same job. For instance, a flowering plant with multiple blossoms on a single stalk is a patch for a foraging bumblebee. The bee can search it efficiently by using a simple *rule of thumb,* "start at the bottom, move up, and leave when you reach the top" (Pyke 1979), that is, it can respond to a simple reliable cue in a fixed way. *Nemeritis canescens* (now known as *Venturia canescens*) is a parasitoid wasp that lays eggs in the larvae of flour moths. The female wasp searching for hosts in a granary walks about on the substrate. When she encounters a patch of chemicals secreted by the host, she stays in it by turning back whenever she comes to the edge of the patch. The wasp's behavior can be modeled as a process in which responsiveness to the host chemical (reflected in the tendency to turn back into the patch upon reaching the edge) habituates with time in the patch but increases with each oviposition (Waage 1979). A single oviposition has maximum effect; the effect of the next one depends on how much later it occurs, as shown in Figure 11.4. This simple mechanism keeps the wasp longer in a good patch because abundant prey frequently push responsiveness back up, but it allows her to leave after long

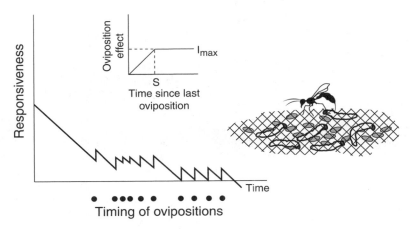

Figure 11.4. Model of patch residence time in *Nemeritis*. The inset shows the increase in responsiveness as a function of time since the last oviposition. When responsiveness to the current patch falls to zero, the wasp leaves. Redrawn from Waage (1979) with permission.

enough without encountering prey. However, other populations of these wasps which lay their eggs in fallen fruits seem to use a different rule (Driessen et al. 1995), a finding which raises the interesting question of whether and how these wasps change their ways of responding in different environments.

The simple combination of sensitization and habituation that governs the wasp's behavior can be contrasted with decision making based on memories for interprey intervals and travel times. Because memory for times is not perfectly accurate but follows Weber's Law (Chapter 9), timing acts as a psychological constraint preventing animals from behaving precisely optimally. The best examples of how it does so come from a program of research on starlings by Kacelnik and his colleagues that combined experiments in the field and in an operant simulation of patch choice in the laboratory (Kacelnik and Cuthill 1987). Here, the "patch" was a pecking key in the middle of one wall of a long cage, and the birds "traveled" from one patch to another by flying between two perches a number of times (Figure 11.5). Completing the travel requirement reset the patch to the shortest interprey interval, as if the bird had arrived in a new patch. If the "patch" delivers a varying number of prey (crumbs from a feeder) at equal intervals and then depletes entirely, the bird should depart as soon as the current interval exceeds the remembered standard interprey interval. But because timing obeys Weber's law, the time of leaving the patch has a variance proportional to the interprey interval (Brunner, Kacelnik, and Gibbon 1992, 1996).

Pecking rate peaked at the value of the interprey interval, with a broader distribution of response rate versus time at longer intervals just as in experiments with the peak procedure (Section 9.2). In addition, the birds waited longer after the expected time for an item before leaving a patch with a long interprey interval, as if their decision took into account the greater error in their ability to detect depletion of a less dense patch (Figure 11.6). The situation in this experiment was not exactly the same as the one addressed by the marginal value theorem because the experimental patch offered prey at fixed intervals and depleted abruptly, but it mimics the situation experienced by animals that prey on swarms of insects. For example, spotted flycatchers (*Muscicapa striata*) stay at a perch while a swarm of insects is within range, sallying out to capture prey at roughly constant intervals. They leave for another

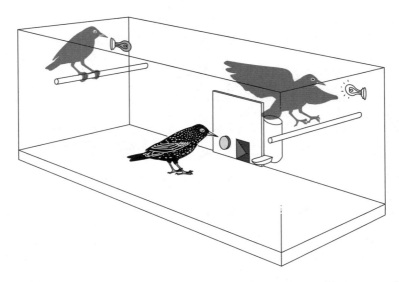

Figure 11.5. Setup used to study patch choice in captive starlings. To travel between patches, the starling hops from the perch with the light off to the one with the light on; the light at that perch then goes out and the opposite light goes on, and so on until the travel requirement is completed. Water is available from the device beside the feeder and pecking key. Redrawn from Brunner, Kacelnik, and Gibbon (1992) with permission.

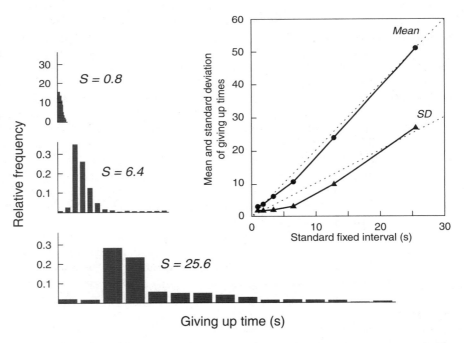

Figure 11.6. Relative frequency of giving up times of different lengths (in seconds) at three of six standard interprey intervals tested. The inset shows the means and standard deviations of the distributions at all six values. Dotted lines are regressions fit to the data. Redrawn from Gibbon and Church (1990) with permission.

perch after a time without prey that is approximately 1.5 times the regular interprey interval (Davies 1977; see Kacelnik, Brunner, and Gibbon 1990).

11.1.3   When to attack

In the classic model of prey choice within patches the forager encounters items successively, and it can accept each one as encountered or reject it and go on searching (Figure 11.7). Acceptance entails devoting a *handling time* to the item, time which cannot be devoted to searching. Pulling the sting off a bee, shelling a nut, extracting nectar from a flower, tearing apart a carcass: all require handling time. In the simplest case the predator recognizes prey types immediately and ranks them in terms of the energy they yield per unit of handling time (E/H). Energy per unit of time foraging can be maximized by accepting all prey items when prey density is low but accepting only the better items (i.e., those with the highest E/H) when prey density is high. If there are just two item types, the predator's behavior toward the poorer items should reflect the density of better items: reject poor items when good items are abundant, otherwise accept them. There is a threshold of good item abundance at which the forager should switch from rejecting to accepting poor items. This policy makes good intuitive sense: when the world is a good place as regards food, mates, homes, a creature can afford to be choosy, but when times are tough, it should take whatever comes along.

The simple optimal prey selection model has qualitative but not always precise quantitative support from redshank selecting worms in mudflats (Goss-Custard 1977), great tits picking mealworms off a conveyor belt in the laboratory (Krebs,. et al. 1977), pigeons pecking key colors paired with different delays to reinforcement (Fantino and Abarca 1985; Shettleworth 1988), and many other tests (Sih and Christensen 2001). An almost universal deviation from optimality is that acceptance

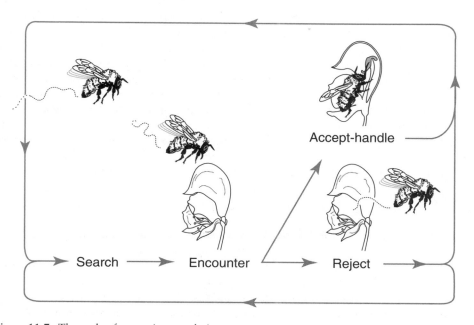

Figure 11.7. The cycle of events in prey choice.

of relatively poor items is seldom all or nothing: at an intermediate abundance of better items some poor ones will be taken and others rejected. Given that perception and memory generally have some degree of error, this is not surprising.

Just as in patch departure, animals may use rules of thumb, relying on simple cues that generally predict prey quality like size (Barnard and Brown 1981). But learning about prey profitability, for example one's own competence at handling a kind of prey, can lead to individual and developmental differences in prey preferences (e.g., Sullivan 1988). A similar variety of mechanisms contributes to assessing prey abundance. For example, prey catching is a reflex in the mantid *Hierodula crassa* (Charnov 1976), but the animal's tendency to strike at flies is modulated by the fullness of its gut. Only nearby flies are attacked when the gut is full; more distant prey become attractive as the gut empties. The apple maggot fly's acceptance of fruit in which to lay her eggs can be modeled like the wasp's oviposition (Figure 11.4), as reflecting a threshold which changes with recent ovipositions and host encounters (Mangel and Roitberg 1989). In contrast, animals trained on operant analogues of prey learn both the delays to food associated with each of two or more signals ("items") and the intervals between them. Animals trained on such schedules do accept nearly all the better "items" offered, and the effects of changing the frequency or profitability of items are seen in the choice of poor items. At the moment of encounter with an item, the animal is choosing between the handling time (or delay to food) associated with that item and a second, variable, delay to food composed of the average time to another item plus the expected time to handle that item. Accordingly, behavior on such schedules, studied mostly with pigeons, is consistent with the mechanistic models of timing and choice discussed in the next section (Shettleworth 1988).

Models of optimal prey selection make one prediction not anticipated by information about behavior on conventional reinforcement schedules: as the time available for foraging, the *time horizon*, grows short, animals should become less choosy, accepting more poor items even when better items are abundant (Lucas 1983). It is easy to see why. If the time available for foraging is about to run out, there may not be enough time to encounter any more items, so the best bet is to take the item at hand. Observations with natural prey items conform to this prediction. For instance, in 3-minute and 6-minute foraging bouts, shrews accepted both large and small mealworm pieces, whereas they rejected small pieces in 9-minute bouts (Barnard and Hurst 1987). In an operant analogue of prey choice, pigeons that had 10-minute sessions in one distinctively decorated operant chamber and 20-minute sessions in another accepted fewer poor items in the first 10 minutes of 20-minute sessions (i.e., when the time horizon was relatively long) than in a 10-minute session (Plowright and Shettleworth 1991). These observations provide reason to question the tradition of treating length of conditioning sessions as a variable of no interest, to be determined mainly by convenience.

11.1.4   Choosing among patches: Matching, sampling, and risk

When patches don't change, foragers face a situation much like that in traditional studies of *concurrent schedules of reinforcement*. As the name implies, on such a schedule two or more reinforcement schedules run concurrently, each associated with a different lever, pecking key, or the like, and at any moment the animal can choose which one to respond to. Historically students of behavior on concurrent schedules have been most interested in the *steady state*, that is, behavior after many sessions of exposure to the same conditions. When both schedules are *fixed* or *variable ratios* (i.e., reinforcement for exactly or on average every *n*th response) the steady state is the relatively uninteresting one of nearly exclusive choice of the more favorable response: reinforcer ratio. Much more influential have been studies of behavior with concurrent *fixed* or *variable interval* (*FI* or *VI*) schedules. On a VI schedule interreinforcement intervals are randomly distributed with a mean specified by the VI value. Thus on VI 20 seconds, reinforcement is available on average every 20 seconds, but with interreinforcement intervals that may range from effectively zero to much longer than 20 seconds. Once it becomes available, a reinforcer typically remains available until the animal responds, as in a repleting patch in which there are no competitors. Such a situation is experienced by wagtails foraging for dead insects washing up along riverbanks (Houston 1986) or traplining territorial hummingbirds (Chapter 9).

Reinforcers can be maximized on a concurrent VI VI (*conc VI VI*) schedule by continually switching back and forth, checking each alternative in turn to see whether a reinforcer has become available there (Houston and McNamara 1981). This is what animals do, even when direct reinforcement for switching has been reduced by imposing a *changeover delay* so reinforcers cannot be collected until a few seconds after switching. But more than just working on both options, animals match the proportion of time spent or number of responses made at an alternative to the proportion of reinforcers obtained there (Herrnstein 1961). This relationship, illustrated in Figure 11.8, has been found so consistently in so many species and situations that it is referred to as *the Matching Law* (review in Williams 1988; Staddon and Cerutti 2003). Animals match behavior not only to numbers of reinforcers but also to reinforcer amounts or delays, in general to any correlate of reinforcer value. Indeed, because matching can be assumed to obtain very generally, preference on conc VI VI schedules is used to assess the relative values animals place on different commodities (e.g., Hamm and Shettleworth 1987; Deaner, Khera, and Platt 2005).

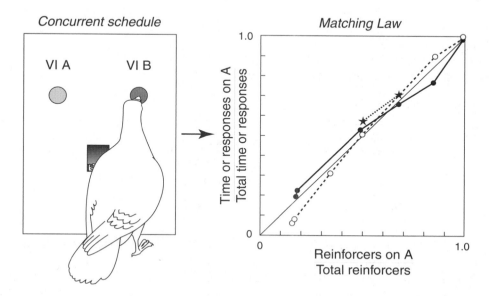

Figure 11.8. Typical experimental setup for studying behavior on concurrent schedules of reinforcement and data illustrating the matching law. Solid diagonal line is perfect matching. Each symbol represents data from a different pigeon. Data redrawn from Herrnstein (1961) with permission.

How do animals match?

Much research has been devoted to understanding what mechanism is responsible for matching, but there is still no completely satisfactory answer (Williams 1994; Staddon and Cerutti 2003). For example, if animals match because matching actually maximizes reinforcers, responses should be allocated in some other way if maximizing requires it. However, when pigeons are required to respond on a seldom-reinforced alternative to advance the schedule on a more frequently reinforced one, they still match relative responding to relative reinforcers obtained even though by doing so they earn fewer reinforcers than they could (Mazur 1981; Williams 1988). The mechanism that brings about matching on concurrent VI VI schedules may have evolved because it results in maximizing fitness under natural conditions, but it does not seem to consist of comparing total intake after allocating choices in different ways and adopting the policy that gave the most food (Houston 1987).

A more successful approach is the SET (Scalar Expectancy Theory) model of choice (Gibbon et al. 1988). Each delay to food experienced is assumed to be remembered in the fuzzy way described by Weber's Law. Faced with a choice between two or more alternatives, an animal is assumed to sample from the distribution of remembered delays associated with each alternative and choose the alternative with the shortest sample on that trial (Figure 11.9). In effect this is a model of maximizing

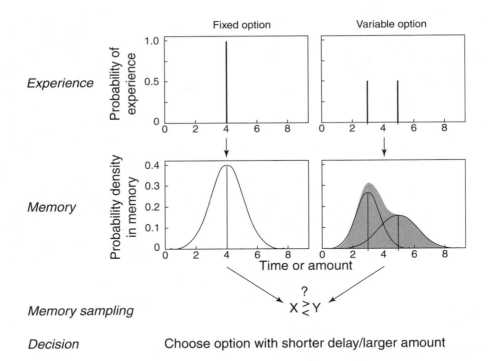

Figure 11.9. The scalar expectancy account of choice between a fixed schedule of reinforcement and a variable schedule with the same mean amount or delay. For simplicity, in this example the variable schedule has two equiprobable values. Reinforcer value decreases with delay but increases with amount. Thus if the units on the x-axis correspond to actual delays and amounts, short delays or small amounts will be overrepresented in the summed probability distribution (gray). After Bateson and Kacelnik (1995) with permission.

rate under a psychological constraint. It does predict matching on concurrent VI VI schedules (Gibbon. et al. 1988). It also explains why animals prefer a variable delay to food (VI schedule) to an FI schedule with the same mean, a finding that cannot be explained as maximizing. As shown in Figure 11.9 for the simplest kind of case, because the memory distribution for a VI has an overrepresentation of short intervals, a sample taken at random is more likely to represent a relatively short interval than is a random sample from the equivalent FI schedule. As this account predicts, pigeons do not prefer a VI schedule constructed so that its memory distribution more closely resembles that from a fixed schedule giving the same mean number of reinforcers per session (Gibbon et al. 1988). The same approach explains why the reverse is true with amounts: a fixed amount is preferred to a variable amount with the same mean (Figure 11.9).

On a roughly equivalent alternative account shortly discussed in more detail, the value of a reward declines disproportionately (hyperbolically or proportionally with 1/time, Mazur 2001) as it is delayed from the moment of choice. Such *discounting* means that the average value of reward in the VI is greater than in the FI. Consistent with the data on temporal bisection in Chapter 9, both accounts predict that a mixture of two equiprobable intervals like that in Figure 11.9 should be psychologically equivalent to a fixed interval with their geometric mean. Mazur (1984) examined such equivalences by training pigeons in a *titration procedure*. Trials occurred in cycles consisting of forced exposure to the current values of a fixed and a variable option followed by opportunities to choose between them. If birds preferred the FI in those trials, it would be made slightly longer in the next cycle whereas if they preferred the VI, the FI would be shortened. This procedure eventually homes in on an FI value psychologically equivalent to the given VI. For example, consistent with scalar timing or hyperbolic discounting, the birds were indifferent between a mixture of 2-second and 18-second delays and a fixed 6-second delay.

The discussion so far assumes that choice between schedules is based on an accumulation of experience, implying that matching develops slowly. However, under some conditions animals respond extremely quickly to changes in times between rewards. Experimentally naive mice show matching as soon as they learn to use two food hoppers that deliver pellets at different rates (Gallistel et al. 2007). And rats exposed to concurrent VI VI schedules of positively reinforcing brain stimulation that change once per session switch their preference within as little as one interreward interval (Mark and Gallistel 1994). They also track random fluctuations in the times between rewards on each schedule. Functionally, frequent changes in the environment should favor immediate tracking, or a short *memory window*, whereas stability should favor storing long-term experience (Cowie 1977), but it is unclear whether this informal functional prediction provides an account of these findings.

Sampling and choice

How much experience should be used to estimate the quality of reward schedules is one example of the more general functional problem of information use in foraging. This is not necessarily one single problem but a set of problems requiring different models (Stephens 2007). An example that brings together an optimality model with the SET model of choice is depicted in Figure 11.10. Here, the animal chooses between a constant mediocre patch and a fluctuating patch where prey occasionally become very abundant. At other times, prey are scarce in the fluctuating patch, and

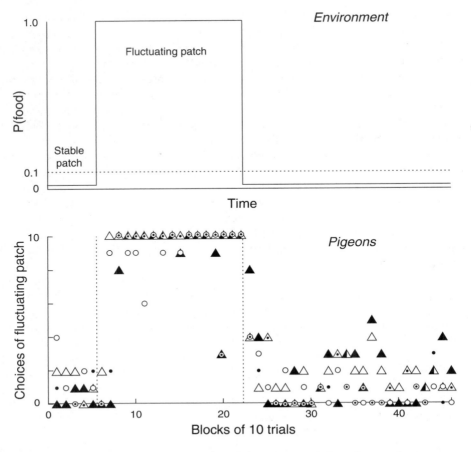

Figure 11.10. Contingencies ("Environment") and data ("Pigeons") from the experiment on environmental tracking described in the text. The four symbols in the lower part of the figure represent data from four different birds. Choices of the fluctuating patch while p(food) = 0 there are sampling responses. Redrawn from Shettleworth et al. (1988) with permission.

the forager is better off in the mediocre patch. If there are no cues to the state of the fluctuating patch, intake is maximized by occasionally visiting the fluctuating patch to sample its state. If it is better than the constant patch, the animal can stay there until prey become sparse again. The optimal behavior in this situation (Stephens 1987) is to sample at fixed intervals—for instance, every tenth foraging trip—rather than at random. This makes sense because sampling too soon will not allow enough time for the patch to change state whereas waiting too long could result in missing some of the good state. Sampling should increase when the constant patch becomes worse or the fluctuating patch's good state becomes better: in both cases there is more to be gained by sampling.

In a test of these predictions (Shettleworth et al. 1988; see also Stephens 2007), pigeons were trained in a long operant chamber with a "patch" at each end. The "fluctuating patch" switched fairly frequently between a schedule delivering no food (extinction) and one delivering food at a high rate. Although the birds sampled occasionally as predicted and switched to the fluctuating patch when it was good (Figure 11.10), behavior deviated from the predictions of the optimal sampling model in three ways. *(1)* Sampling occurred at random, not at regular intervals. *(2)* Sampling frequency did not change when the reinforcement probability in the good state varied. *(3)* When the fluctuating patch was good, the birds occasionally visited the constant patch, a sort of "reverse sampling" that reduced their reward rate. The SET model nicely accounts for all these findings. For instance, visits to the fluctuating patch are random because random samples are taken from memory, and sampling behavior occurs when the shorter memory sample comes from the fluctuating patch. Thus although this situation can be described as one in which animals are collecting information by sampling, here "sampling" is not some special category of behavior reinforced by the information it brings. Rather, the pigeons learned the reinforcement schedules associated with each option and chose accordingly. Box 11.1 discusses other situations in which sampling is optimal.

Box 11.1 Foraging for Mates and Homes

Although optimal foraging and its relationship to psychological studies of food-rewarded behavior are emphasized in the main text, optimality modeling has also been applied to searching for and choosing other resources such as mates and nests. Sexual selection theory predicts that, especially in species in which each offspring demands substantial investment by its mother, females should search for and choose the best males to mate with. But choosiness has a cost in that if the female spends too long searching for a mate, the breeding season may pass or the chances of raising offspring successfully before winter may decline. On one model of optimal mate choice (review in R. Gibson and Langen 1996; Sherman, Reeve, and Pfennig 1997), *best of n,* the female inspects *n* males and then mates with the best. The optimal number is determined by the time and energy costs of searching (Janetos 1980). This seems to require that females remember all the sequentially inspected males equally well, that is, without forgetting or primacy or recency effects. An alternative model with less unrealistic assumptions about memory is that the female mates with the first male she encounters who surpasses some threshold value. The threshold should be determined by the average quality of males in the environment: a male of poor quality in absolute terms may be acceptable if most males are even poorer. Both of these models imply that quality is recognized perfectly and immediately. But as we know from Chapter 3, imperfect recognition is more likely, in which case repeated visits to each male might improve a female's estimate of his quality. This assumption is embodied in a third model of optimal mate choice, the Bayesian assessment model (Luttbeg 2002).

Because which model predicts the highest fitness depends on such factors as how much time is available and the cost of assessment (Luttbeg 2002), species differences in mate choice might be expected. Females of many species do have encounters with more than one male before mating, and as predicted by the best of n and the comparative Bayesian models, males who have been inspected and rejected are sometimes reinspected and accepted (Gibson and Langen 1996; Weigmann et al. 1996). The threshold model also permits choosing a previously rejected male if the threshold is continuously adjusted on the basis of experience. Consistent with this, data from birds (e.g., Collins 1995) and fish (e.g., Bakker and Milinski 1991) reveal a contrast effect: a mate of a given quality is more likely to be preferred the lower the quality of previously encountered males. Another factor that may complicate the picture is that rather than sampling males for herself, a female may copy the mate choice of earlier-arriving females (Chapter 13 and Sherman, Reeve, and Pfennig 1997).

For species that disperse from their natal territory, choosing a place to settle presents the same functional and mechanistic problems as mate choice in that a single decision has large implications for fitness (Mabry and Stamps 2008). In one attempt to infer the decision rules being used, Mabry and Stamps (2008) radio-tracked dispersing brush mice over several days as they visited areas around their natal nest before settling in a nest of their own. The mice most commonly behaved as if using a comparative assessment mechanism, visiting each of a relatively small number of areas several times before settling in one. Since a potential territory likely has multiple relevant features, such as the presence of food, shelter, and competitors, it is perhaps to be expected that animals would need time to assess them. What and how animals learn about habitat quality offers many possibilities for future investigation (Mabry and Stamps 2008). Because more than one feature of a potential mate or territory may be relevant for optimal choice, the economic model discussed in Section 11.1.5 also applies to choice of mates and territories, although as yet little is known about whether these choices are also context-dependent (Bateson and Healy 2005; Royle, Lindstrom, and Metcalfe 2008).

Risk

Preference for a VI schedule over an FI that delivers food at the same mean rate, discussed earlier in this section, is a puzzle if one assumes that foragers are maximizing net rate of energy intake. But variance should matter under some conditions. For example, as a small bird nears the end of a winter day, what it can find in an unvarying patch may not be enough to get it through the night. Its only chance for survival might be in a risky (i.e., variable) patch that occasionally yields a bonanza. This argument leads to the *energy budget rule*: an animal below its energy budget should choose a risky option over a certain option with the same mean, that is, it should be *risk prone*. Otherwise, the forager should be *risk averse* (Stephens 1981; McNamara and Houston 1992). Risk sensitivity is expected in the context of any interruption like the end of the breeding season, the beginning of migration, or the arrival of predators (McNamara and Houston 1992).

Risk sensitivity has been sought in species that include bees, shrews, pigeons, starlings, and juncos (Kacelnik and Bateson 1996; Brito e Abreu and Kacelnik 1999) as well as in people (Weber, Shafir, and Blais 2004). As in Mazur's (1984) experiment already described, in such studies animals typically have "forced" trials with a fixed and a variable option (e.g., 4 items of food on the left and a 50:50 mix of 1 item and 7 items on the right). Subsequent free choices between the options reveal whether the animal is *risk prone* (i.e., prefers the variable option), *risk averse,* or indifferent to risk. As we have seen, animals generally prefer variable over fixed delays to food (i.e., they are risk prone in delay) but with variance in amount they are generally risk averse or indifferent (reviews in Kacelnik and Bateson 1996; Bateson and Kacelnik 1998; Kacelnik and Brito e Abreu 1998). Figure 11.9 shows how the SET approach explains these outcomes.

Risk sensitivity implies that animals do not represent rates of intake only as long term averages (i.e., $\Sigma E/\Sigma T$). A possibility consistent with SET is that instead they store and average short term rates, that is, the average of item-by-item E/T. This makes less demand on memory than long-term averaging because an animal has direct information about the most recent interprey interval and prey size each time it collects a food item. Memory for short intervals may also be favored because it is more accurate than memory for longer ones (see Chapter 9 and Stephens, Kerr, and Fernández-Juricic 2004). In a careful series of experiments using variance in both amount and delay, starlings' choices were consistent with maximizing short-term rates with only the times during the trials taken into account, that is, without the intertrial intervals (Bateson and Kacelnik 1995; 1996, 1997). Expected times to the next feeding(s) seem to determine "risky" choice, not unpredictability of the outcome in itself. Given a choice between two sequences of interreward intervals with equal variance but different degrees of predictability, starlings preferred the predictable string mainly when it began with a comparatively short delay to food, as if discounting later rewards in the sequence (Bateson and Kacelnik 1997). Such steep discounting of future rewards seems inconsistent with the suggestion that animals plan ahead discussed in Section 11.2.

The energy budget rule seems to imply that the way in which outcomes are valued or compared changes with how close the animal is to meeting its energetic requirements, a factor not usually taken into account in psychological theories of choice. In fact, however, experimental tests of the energy budget rule have not given much evidence to support it (Kacelnik and Bateson 1996; Brito e Abreu and Kacelnik 1999). Regardless of energy budget, animals prefer variable delays to food over a fixed delay equal to their mean, but effects of energy budget have sometimes been found in experiments with variance in amounts of food (e.g., Ito, Takatsuru, and Saeki 2000). Effects of energy budget seem to be found more often with small than with big animals, which makes functional sense because a small animal is less likely to have the reserves to survive a temporary shortfall than is a large one. However, such an effect of body mass remains to be documented in a proper comparative test (Brito e Abreu and Kacelnik 1999). In any case, it is difficult to change correlates of energy budget such as the rate of food intake during an experiment without changing experimental parameters that might by themselves influence choice. For example, in the original test of the energy budget rule (Caraco, Martindale, and Whittam 1980), juncos on a negative energy budget were tested later in the day and with longer intertrial intervals than birds supposedly on a positive energy budget, and to equalize overall rates of intake larger amounts of food were followed with longer delays until the next trial, thereby confounding variability in amount with variability in delay. To some extent such problems were overcome by testing birds at two temperatures in a later study (Caraco et al. 1990). The birds tended to be risk averse at the higher temperature and risk prone at the lower one. In the next section and in Section 11.3 we see that the subjective value of food can depend on the circumstances in which it has been experienced. Such *incentive learning* might also lead to apparent energy budget effects in some circumstances.

11.1.5 Foraging and economic decision-making

At first glance there is a compelling parallel between optimal foraging theory and economic theory. Foraging theorists depict animals as maximizing fitness; economists depict individuals as maximizing *utility*. But utility is not fitness; it is a presumed currency of subjective value that economic decision makers are assumed to be maximizing in a consistent way. Still, because evolution would almost by definition be expected to select for creatures that value whatever increases their fitness, under natural conditions maximizing subjective utility and maximizing fitness ought to come to the same thing. This suggests that looking at animal behavior in situations comparable to those studied by economists should produce parallel outcomes and perhaps new insights into the evolution or mechanisms of economic behavior. Indeed, research on the neural mechanisms of economic decision making is thriving in the new field of neuroeconomics (Glimcher and Rustichini 2004; Sanfey et al. 2006). Such research analyzes how probability and value are represented in primate brains, using imaging with humans and single cell recordings with monkeys performing instrumental choice tasks.

Some important contemporary research in economics deals with psychological mechanisms for evaluating and deciding among options. Surprisingly often people rely on rules of thumb, referred to in this context as *heuristics,* simple decision rules that work pretty well in natural conditions but violate utility maximizing in contrived ones (Todd and Gigerenzer 2007). Thus, as in the study of foraging, behavior that meets a functional criterion of rationality occurs in the absence of psychological rationality. Further evidence that economic choices do not necessarily involve literal representation of the variables being maximized comes from the irrational choices reliably shown in certain circumstances. As discussed next, attempts to capture such apparently irrational economic choices with animals in a foraging context has led to a productive analysis of the underlying psychological mechanisms (for other examples see Chen, Lakshminarayanan, and Santos 2006; Padoa-Schioppa, Jandolo, and Visalberghi 2006).

Comparative evaluation

A key assumption of economics is that people maximize utility *in a consistent way.* Among other things, this means that choices are transitive and *independent from irrelevant alternatives.* The latter means that A is preferred to B whether or not other options are present. This principle may be violated when the options differ on two dimensions as illustrated in Figure 11.11. Here we are concerned with preferences between a target item, T, and a competitor, C, that is more attractive than T on one dimension and less on another, such as costing less but being smaller. In many examples with real products, introducing a third option, the *decoy* (D), that is the same as the target on one dimension and lower-valued (i.e., less preferred) on the

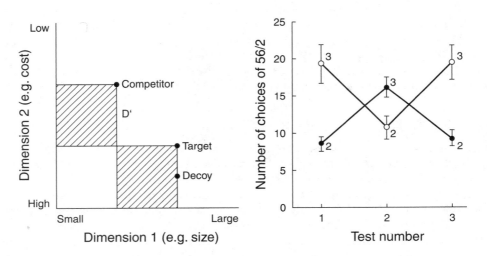

Figure 11.11. Left: the target, competitor, and decoys described in the text in the two-dimensional space of cost versus size. Note that the cost axis represents cost from high to low; thus items higher in this dimension are lower-priced and therefore valued more. The asymmetrically dominated decoy effect will occur for decoys D or D' respectively within the adjacent shaded areas. Adapted from Bateson, Healy, and Hurly (2003). Right: mean number of times gray jays chose the target, 2 raisins 56 centimeters down a tube, in a binary choice (2) and a trinary choice (3) with the decoy, 2 raisins at 84 centimeters, present. Each line represents means of birds tested three times but in different orders, as indicated. Redrawn from Shafir, Waite, and Smith (2002) with permission.

other (e.g., equally large but more costly; see Figure 11.11) increases choice of the target relative to the competitor (i.e., T/T+C increases; the *asymmetrically dominated decoy effect*). Similarly, in this example choices of C relative to T may increase in the presence of a more costly but equally small decoy D'. The absolute number of choices of a target may even increase in the presence of an asymmetrically dominated decoy, a clear violation of rationality which raises the question of how psychological mechanisms of evaluation could depend on context in this way. In this example (shown in Figure 11.1) one possibility is that the larger but more expensive T appears less costly when contrasted with the even more costly but equally large D.

Because most studies of animal choice present only two options while nature presents many (not always a good thing; Hutchinson 2005), these findings with people suggest it is important to discover whether irrelevant alternatives can have similar effects on other species. If they do, the next question is whether this reflects a cognitive mechanism that is optimal in some other context. In a particularly straightforward test of the effect of irrelevant alternatives, Shafir, Waite, and Smith (2002) let tame free-ranging gray jays (*Psorieus canadensis*) collect raisins to hoard from wire-mesh tubes. The birds had to hop into a tube to collect the raisins, a potentially costly activity because being inside a tube increases vulnerability to predation. The binary choice of interest was 1 raisin 28 centimeters inside one tube versus 2 raisins 56 centimeters inside another; the decoy was 2 raisins at 84 centimeters. During blocks of trials with the decoy, choices of 2 raisins at 56 centimeters rose not only in relative but also in absolute terms. As Figure 11.11b indicates, this effect appeared in two separate groups of birds for which binary and trinary choices were administered in different sequences. It is apparent even when the two groups of birds are compared in the third test, by which time all of them had had the same experience and presumably hoarded about the same number of raisins.

The gray jays in this study could immediately perceive the options, like human consumers or people in experiments who only need to be told them. When animals have to be trained more extensively, the options at different stages of the experiment may change energetic state in ways that by themselves influence preference. This was demonstrated in an elegant experiment by Schuck-Paim, Pompilio, and Kacelnik (2004) in which starlings chose between pecking keys that signified 5 food items delayed 10 seconds versus 2 food items delayed 4 seconds. Notice that short-term E/T is the same for both options, that is, 1 item per 2 seconds, so there is no particular reason to prefer one or the other. However, because choices were separated by a 1-minute intertrial interval, the 5 item/10 second option gave the higher rate of intake over an experimental session. Birds preferred it, though not exclusively. The decoys were 5 food items delayed 20 seconds or 1 food item delayed 4 seconds. As in some experiments reviewed earlier, short blocks of trials contained forced exposure to each of the current options followed by choice trials. Importantly, each decoy was tested in a separate series of trials that included both trinary choices and each possible binary choice. As a result the birds' overall intake was higher in sessions with the 5 item/20 second decoy than in those with the 1 item/4 second decoy. Moreover, reduced hunger by itself reduced preference for the 5-item option in a group of birds exposed only to the critical binary choice. Controlling for overall intake by giving extra free feedings eliminated any differential effect of the two decoys in trinary choices. Such effects of hunger could have been involved in previous related studies such as one with hummingbirds (Bateson, Healy, and Hurly 2003; Schuck-Paim., Pompilio, and Kacelnik 2004). Moreover, it turns out that adding options to a choice task, even if some of them are identical in value, can change preferences (Schuck-Palm and

Kacelnik 2007). As Schuck-Paim, Pompilio, and Kacelnik (2004) conclude, when adapting paradigms from economics for animals it is important to ensure the tests do not introduce extraneous variables.

Sunk costs

A person who has already put a lot of effort into trying to obtain something may act as if this goal into which so many costs have been sunk has more value than it otherwise would. In behavioral ecology such a *sunk costs* effect is called the *Concorde fallacy*, after the supersonic airliner which Britain and France persisted in building even when it became apparent that it could never be operated economically. In human psychology, overvaluing the object of a past investment is attributed to an attempt to reduce cognitive dissonance. Like the effect of asymmetrically dominated decoys, the sunk costs effect seems to be an example of irrationality: the mere fact that one has sunk effort into getting something does not increase its intrinsic value. But animals can behave in the same way (Kacelnik and Marsh 2002). Starlings completed either 4 or 16 flights across a cage like that shown in Figure 11.5. When the required number of flights was completed, a distinctively colored key lit up and one peck on it delivered a standard amount of food. When the starlings chose between the two colors on occasional trials with no preceding flight requirement, they preferred the color that had followed 16 flights. Clement and colleagues (2000) found a similar effect in pigeons with work defined as number of key pecks. Likewise, in a simple laboratory task people prefer the stimuli that follow a more effortful response, suggesting that contrast effects explain some aspects of cognitive dissonance (Klein, Bhatt, and Zentall 2005). One interpretation of such findings (Kacelnik and Marsh 2002) is that stimuli are valued in proportion to the improvement in state associated with them in the past. For example in the study with starlings, because four flights does not have a very great energetic cost, the reward is not perceived as improving the bird's state very much compared to the situation after 16 flights.

This general notion turns out to predict a variety of striking cases of "irrational" preferences between objectively identical rewards previously experienced when the subject was in different states. Both starlings (Marsh, Schuck-Paim, and Kacelnik 2004) and desert locusts (Pompilio, Kacelnik, and Behmer 2006) prefer food-related cues experienced when they were hungry. In the locusts this may occur because hunger directly modulates the perception of food. Such effects can be quite extreme: starlings that experienced a 10 second delay to food while only slightly hungry and a longer delay to the same amount of food when quite hungry preferred the stimulus associated with the longer delay, up to 17.5 seconds, whether tested hungry or sated (Pompilio and Kacelnik 2005). Pigeons prefer stimuli (secondary reinforcers) that follow the absence rather than the presence of reinforcement (Friedrich, Clement, and Zentall 2005). This and related effects can be attributed to the original experience of the relevant stimuli being associated with positive contrast (Zentall and Singer 2007), a psychological label for the positive value of an improvement in state. The way in which the psychological value of reward depends on past experience will be taken up again when we discuss incentive motivation in Section 11.3. In the present context, however, we can conclude that as with context dependent choices, research on analogues to sunk costs and similar phenomena in animals has shown that decisions with suboptimal outcomes in these contexts can result from general mechanisms of reinforcement and choice.

11.2   Long-term or short-term maximizing: Do animals plan ahead?

11.2.1   Delayed reinforcement, impulsiveness, and temporal discounting

The psychological literature on learning and choice suggests that animals seldom anticipate events more than a few seconds or minutes in the future (W. Roberts 2002). Even a small delay between response and reinforcer has a devastating effect on rate of learning (see Bouton 2007). Learning with delayed reinforcers can be improved in various ways, for example by introducing one or more stimulus changes between response and reinforcer, but the delays that can be bridged in this way are generally minutes at the most. Even the knowledge that free food will come later does not decrease rats' willingness to work quite hard for food available in the present (Timberlake 1984). In Section 11.1 we have seen other evidence of apparent insensitivity to long-term gain, for instance in the suggestion that animals choose among options on the basis of the delay to the next scheduled reward, that is, short-term rather than long-term E/T. Nowhere is this more evident than in so-called self-control experiments, experiments which in fact demonstrate exactly the opposite, namely *impulsiveness,* also referred to as *preference for immediacy* or *temporal myopia* (W. Roberts 2002).

By analogy with situations in which people might exhibit self control by, say, rejecting a beer now in the interest of a safe drive home later, subjects in experiments on self control choose between a short delay to a relatively small reward and a longer delay to a larger reward. In the typical design, diagrammed in Figure 11.12, the total durations of trials are equated across options by adjusting the delay between reward and the beginning of the next trial. Thus the long delay/large reward option gives more reward per trial and thereby maximizes intake over a session even when it gives the same E/T as the small reward/short delay option if T is measured from trial onset to reward. Most animals that have been tested strongly prefer a short/small option. For example, given the choice between 2 seconds of eating after a 2-second wait and 6

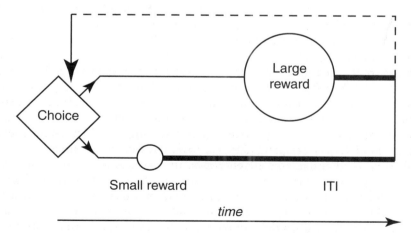

Figure 11.12. Procedure for a self-control experiment. A trial begins with a choice between a small reward after a short delay and a larger reward after a longer delay. Regardless of which is chosen lengths of trials are equated by varying the intertrial interval that separates receipt of reward from the next choice (ITI, the heavy line).

seconds of eating after a 6-second wait, pigeons and rats choose the short/small option on 97% and 80% of trials respectively (Tobin and Logue 1994), but cyno-mologous monkeys show self control with similar parameters (Tobin et al. 1996) as do human adults (Tobin and Logue 1994).

Although humans are not necessarily very good at delaying gratification in real-life economic situations (Fehr 2002), the dramatic failures of other species to show even modest self control (or, equivalently, patience) in laboratory tests suggests that we may be better at it than most other animals. In a direct test of this notion, Jeffrey Stevens and colleagues (Stevens, Hallinan, and Hauser 2005; Rosati et al. 2007) tested humans, marmosets, tamarins, chimpanzees, and bonobos with the delay to the larger reward titrated until a long/large option was chosen as often as an immedi-ate/small one. Most interestingly, when chimpanzees and university students chose between two food items immediately and six items delayed two minutes, the chim-panzees chose the delayed reward on over 70% of trials, whereas the students chose it on fewer than 20% of trials. When money was substituted for food, however, the students' chose the delayed reward on nearly 60% of trials. The authors conclude from the differences between monkeys on the one hand and apes and humans on the other that "core components of the capacity for future-oriented decisions" are shared across the ape/human lineage (Rosati et al. 2007, 1663).

The effect of money versus food on humans' choices should serve as a reminder that conclusions about species differences here, as elsewhere, must be based on multiple tests. When food is involved, species differences in impulsiveness may be related to body weight, with smaller animals being more impulsive (Tobin and Logue 1994), or to feeding ecology, with animals that catch active prey like moving insects being more impulsive (Stevens, Hallinan, and Hauser 2005). The ability to delay reward may also be important in social contexts. In theory, some reciprocal social exchanges involve performing a costly altruistic act in anticipation of the favor being returned hours or days later (see Chapter 12), but the few relevant data provide little evidence that reciprocal social exchanges could be based on such self control (Stevens and Hauser 2004). For example, chimpanzees wait at most eight minutes to exchange a small piece of cookie for a large one (Dufour et al. 2007). But all the data mentioned here are from animals waiting (or not) for food. Self-control might be more evident with resources that are unlikely to disappear or be lost to competitors, such as a water hole or a safe shelter within an animal's territory.

A psychological explanation for impulsiveness is that rewards are discounted in value the more they are delayed. Discounting can be tracked in a titration procedure (see Section 11.1.4) to discover how much immediate food is psychologically equiva-lent to a given amount of delayed food. Consistent with self-control experiments, this procedure reveals very steep discounting functions for rats and pigeons. For example, to a pigeon food delayed 2–4 seconds is worth less than half the same amount of immediate food (Green. et al. 2004). An informal functional explanation is that psychological discounting is an adaptation to the uncertainty of the future: delayed rewards should be devalued in proportion to the probability that they will decay, be lost to competitors, or the like. As the adage has it, "a bird in the hand is worth two in the bush." But the discounting functions just described seem more extreme than any natural situation demands. One alternative explanation is that the short term rate maximization they reflect does lead to maximizing long term intake rates in natural situations, as when choosing whether to stay in a patch or move on (Stephens., Brown, and Ydenberg 2004). Thus discounting is consistent with evidence in Section 11.1 that animals can behave much as predicted by models based on maximizing long-term E/T even when responding on the basis of shorter-term currencies. In any case, none of the evidence summarized here indicates that animals anticipate events days or even hours in the future.

11.2.2   The Bischof-Kohler hypothesis and cognitive time travel

Learning and memory allow animals to behave in ways that prepare them for the future, but without any explicit representation of the future (or the past) as such. For example, conditioned responses express present knowledge about stimuli experienced in the past. Similarly, animals may respond adaptively to recurring daily or seasonal cues by migrating, hibernating, building nests, or caching food, but members of each new generation do so before experiencing the consequences of their behavior and thus presumably without foreseeing those consequences. The Monarch butterflies that fly from Canada to Mexico each fall are the grandchildren or even more distant descendents of the last Monarchs that made the trip South, and they find the wintering grounds without ever having contact with experienced individuals. Food caching bird species whose development has been studied begin to cache early in development even when hand-raised (Clayton 1994), and as adults food-storers express a compulsion to cache without regard to consequences (de Kort. et al. 2007).

Given the power of selection together with learning to produce future-oriented behaviors that do not demand interpretation as planning, what would behavioral evidence for future planning look like? This question hardly arose in comparative cognition research until recently, when Suddendorf and Corballis (1997) drew attention to a claim by Bischof and Kohler that animals, unlike adult humans, are cognitively "stuck in the present" (see also W. Roberts 2002). They dubbed this claim, that no animal engages in *mental time travel,* recreating the past and imagining the future, the Bischof-Kohler hypothesis. By itself such a hypothesis is meaningless, even empty, because we have no direct access to animals' mental events. But this consideration has not discouraged attempts to demonstrate planning for the future in nonhuman species. As with studies of animal episodic -like memory (Chapter 7), the convincingness of these demonstrations depends on how well they fit a clear set of behavioral criteria.

Suddendorf and Busby (2005) proposed that to be evidence of planning, a behavior or combination of behaviors must be novel (thus ruling out conditioned responses, migration, and the like), and it must function in the service of a motivational state other than one the animal is in at the time of performing it. For instance, like a shopper heading to the supermarket after an ample dinner, an animal that can plan would amass resources against future hunger or thirst even while sated. This criterion helps to rule out behaviors acquired or maintained through long-delayed reinforcement, assuming they would not continue without the relevant motivation. Another criterion that rules out gradual learning with delayed reinforcement is that the behavior should be shown reliably as soon as the required information is provided. Finally, planninglike behavior should not be domain-specific but be capable of being expressed in more than one context.

Even human children do not show behavior that fits all these criteria until they are four or five years old (Suddendorf and Busby 2005), but so far no other animals ever do. For instance, planning a route among familiar sites can be seen (cf. Chapter 8 and Janson 2007) as choosing among present stimuli, the cues visible from the animal's present location, which are associated with different delays, energy expenditures, and/or amounts of reward. In a study conceived as a test of the Bischof-Kohler hypothesis, Naqshbandi and Roberts (2006) allowed monkeys or rats to choose between two quantities of food, dates for the monkeys and raisins for the rats. The animals naturally preferred the larger amount, but eating so many dates or raisins at once demonstrably made the animals thirsty. To test whether they could foresee their future thirst while sated with water, they were then exposed to a regime in which water was removed from their cages when the foods were offered but returned sooner on trials when the smaller amount was chosen. With the monkeys, choice of the larger number of dates did fall after about 6 trials and in the one monkey tested it recovered when baseline conditions were reinstated. Rats did not show a comparable effect, but they showed only a weak and variable preference for the larger quantity in the first place. In any case, the fact that preference changed gradually, if at all, means this example fails the test of planning and suggests that delayed reinforcement or punishment was operating in some way.

In an experiment very much like one suggested by Tulving (2005) as a test of mental time travel for children, Mulcahy and Call (2006) tested whether bonobos and orangutans save tools for future use. The animals first learned to use a tool to get grapes from a dispenser. Then while the apparatus was blocked they had opportunity to choose one object from a collection of objects in the test room and take it to an adjoining chamber, where they waited for an hour before being readmitted to the test room with the apparatus available. All animals tested took a tool on some occasions, but their performance was very spotty. For instance, one orangutan took a tool four times in a row on the first eight trials and then not again till trial 14. An anthropocentric view point, that is, folk psychology, would seem to predict that once an animal understood that planning ahead is helpful it would plan on every trial. Moreover, in this task how often a particular tool is taken at random most likely depends on the alternative objects offered and how often they have been paired with food or otherwise used in the recent past, and this was neither well specified nor investigated here. And finally, because using the tool resulted in a treat of grapes that the animals presumably always desired, planning for a future need was not tested (Suddendorf 2006).

Somewhat stronger evidence comes from a similar study (Osvath and Osvath 2008) in which two chimpanzees and an orangutan nearly always chose a tube for sucking juice from a container an hour before opportunity to use it. Whether the animals were planning or simply taking the object most strongly associated with food was addressed by making a piece of favorite fruit one of the options. All animals still chose the tube first on at least half the trials. Moreover, when a second choice of fruit versus tube was given after an animal already had a tube, all animals chose the fruit. They also showed appropriate choice of a stick tool. A next step with studies of this kind would be to offer multiple functional tools and seek evidence that choice anticipates a specific future task. However if such behavior were found, it would be necessary to show how it was different from a conditional discrimination based on present cues to what tool can be used next.

In any case, the candidate that so far fits the largest number of criteria for planning comes not from choice of tools but from food storing in scrub jays (Raby et al. 2007). The birds in this study lived in large cages with three compartments ("rooms"; Figure 11.13). After first acquiring information about which room had food in the morning, they behaved as if planning for breakfast by caching food items in the evening where they were most likely to be needed. For example, in Experiment 1 they first experienced three cycles of a treatment in which they received "breakfast" of pine nuts in the morning in one end room; in the other end room, no breakfast was

| Caching tray | Food bowl | Caching tray |

Figure 11.13. Diagram (not to scale) of the setup used by Raby et al. (2007) to test future planning in scrub jays. Seeds were in the food bowl and the caching trays present in the end "rooms" in the evening only for the final test. Otherwise uncachable powdered food was in the food bowl in the evening and the birds were closed into one room or the other for the night, where they either had breakfast or not in the morning. After Raby et al. (2007) with permission.

provided until 2 hours after daylight. In the test, for the first time whole pine nuts were provided in the central room in the evening along with sand-filled trays for caching in the two end rooms. The birds cached three times as many pine nuts in the "no breakfast room" as in the "breakfast room." Importantly, all the data came from this first test, before the birds had experienced the consequences of their choices. Similarly, birds learned to expect breakfast in both rooms in the second experiment, peanuts in one and dog kibble in the other. On their first opportunity to cache peanuts and dog kibble in the evening, they distributed their caches so as to provide each room with more of the food it usually lacked.

Although this study was greeted (e.g., by Shettleworth 2007) as an advance over earlier ones with primates, it lacks a control for the possibility that scrub jays were expressing a natural tendency to spread out caches of a given food type irrespective of information about how this would determine what they had to eat the next day (Premack 2007; Suddendorf and Corballis 2008b; but see Clayton. et al. 2008). For an animal that caches different kinds of items (and that, as we saw in Chapter 7, can remember what it cached where), a strategy of distributing items of each type as widely as possible would help to defeat predators that might raid just one of those types. In any case, the birds' hoarding here is not clearly behavior for a future need because although they could both eat and cache during the test they may have been somewhat hungry. Correia and colleagues (Correia, Dickinson, and Clayton 2007) used stimulus-specific satiety to address this issue. Birds were sated on one of two foods, peanuts or dog kibble, by prefeeding them with it just before opportunity to cache both foods. Such prefeeding selectively suppresses not only consumption but caching of the prefed item. Here, however, some birds were additionally prefed the alternative item just before opportunity to recover their caches. If they could foresee that they would not want this item at the time of retrieval, they should suppress caching of it initially rather than of the item they were just prefed. Although the findings of this study appear under a title proclaiming positive results, the birds cached so little in the test trials, some of them not at all, that the best conclusion here is "provocative but not proven." Moreover, even if more substantial data were consistent with those published so far, they can be interpreted as a novel and subtle adaptation of the food-hoarding system rather than evidence for a more domain general "mental time travel" (Premack 2007; Suddendorf and Corballis 2008b).

As with episodic memory (Chapter 7), an important impetus for the set of studies reviewed here is the wish to understand the neural substrate of human mental time travel. Mentally recreating the past and imagining the future turn out to share neural underpinnings in normal adults, and patients with impaired episodic memory may also have difficulty thinking about the future (Addis, Wong, and Schacter 2007). None of this seems very surprising. Both conscious and unconscious memory presumably were selected in the first place because they allow past experience to influence future behavior. Indeed, it seems plausible that the adaptive value of episodic memory, in the sense of "mental time travel" into the past, lies entirely in allowing its possessor to imagine and thus plan for the future. Autonoetic consciousness and concomitant future planning may indeed be uniquely human (Suddendorf and Corballis 2008a), but other animals clearly share with humans multiple kinds of future-oriented behavior (W. Roberts et al. 2008; Raby and Clayton 2009). Notwithstanding the challenge laid down by the Bischof-Kohler hypothesis, a more productive way forward may be to look for the components of planning, which species show them, and under what conditions (Raby and Clayton 2009).

11. 3   Causal learning and instrumental behavior

11.3.1   Theories of instrumental learning

Just as a bird storing food looks as if it is planning, an animal performing an instrumentally trained activity such as a rat pressing a lever gives a compelling impression that it "knows what it is doing." Only recently has evidence been sought (and found) that this is more than an impression. This section is about the causal knowledge underlying activities like rats' bar pressing. It will provide a context for analyses of tool using in Section 11.4, but first a little history is in order.

The Skinnerian or behavior analysis approach to operant conditioning, many findings from which have appeared earlier in this chapter, was largely atheoretical. It was and still is (see Staddon and Cerutti 2003) the descriptive study of behavior's control by the environment, particularly as instantiated by schedules of reinforcement. Traditionally, however, beginning with Thorndike (1911/1970) instrumental performance was thought to reflect S-R learning: responses become connected to situational stimuli through the stamping in action of reinforcement. This account provides no role for a representation of the reinforcer in instrumental performance; in an important sense an S-R animal does *not* "know what it is doing." But, as discussed more in a moment, performance of an instrumental action can be modulated by information about the current value of its reinforcer. Moreover, although the S-R account suggests that mere contiguity with a reinforcer suffices to stamp in a response, the reinforcer needs to be contingent on the response just as a US needs to be contingent on a CS for Pavlovian conditioning (Chapter 4).

In an elegant demonstration of this principle, Balleine and Dickinson (1998) trained rats to press a lever for one of two reinforcers, food pellets or starch solution, and in separate sessions to pull a chain for the other reinforcer. When the rats were performing both responses at high rates, the contingency between one response and reinforcement was degraded by introducing free presentations of its reinforcer. For example, a rat trained to pull the chain for pellets would receive additional pellets at times when it had not just pulled the chain while its lever-pressing sessions continued normally. Response rate gradually fell almost to zero for the response whose contingency was degraded whereas it remained high for the alternative response. This effect depended on the extra reinforcers being the same as the normal reinforcer for the response in question. Thus rats pulling the chain for pellets continued to pull when given noncontingent starch reinforcers.

The foregoing findings would be expected if associative learning is a general mechanism for learning simple causal relationships between events regardless of their nature, and indeed, animals learn response-reinforcer associations through the same laws of learning as in Pavlovian conditioning (Mackintosh 1983; Dickinson 1994). But this can make it difficult to know whether behavior in an instrumental conditioning experiment is in fact the expression of instrumental learning. Operationally the distinction between Pavlovian and instrumental conditioning is perfectly clear: in Pavlovian conditioning the experimenter arranges a contingency between a relatively neutral stimulus and a reinforcer; in instrumental conditioning, the contingency is between some aspect of the animal's behavior and a reinforcer. However, any instrumental conditioning setup inevitably includes external stimuli, and a resulting Pavlovian contingency could be what actually controls behavior. For instance, when a rat is reinforced with food for running down a runway, does it run because the act of running predicts food or because running is the CR (i.e., approaching) resulting from associations between stimuli at the far end of the runway and the food found there? Key pecking by pigeons, an archetypal Skinnerian operant, turns out to be a Pavlovian CR that develops from experience of a key light—food contingency (i.e., in autoshaping, see Chapter 4). Furthermore, if the food is omitted each time the bird pecks but presented after each lighting of the key without pecks (an *omission procedure*), pigeons peck anyway, though less than without omission (D. Williams and Williams 1969).

One way to be sure that performance of a particular response is free of Pavlovian influences is to show that both the response and its opposite—for example pushing a lever up and pushing it down—can be trained by making a given reinforcer contingent on them. This is true, perhaps uniquely, of lever pressing in rats (Dickinson and Balleine 2000). Accordingly, the cognitive structures underlying instrumental performance have been most thoroughly analyzed using this and similar responses (Dickinson and Balleine 1994, 2000). The results of this analysis suggest that instrumental performance can be understood as an inference from the information contained in a response-reinforcer association together with information about the current value of the reinforcer. In effect, bar pressing reflects both a belief "bar pressing causes food" and a desire for food. Belief is induced by experience of the response-reinforcer contingency. Desire is surprisingly less straightforward, as discussed next.

11.3.2   Instrumental incentive learning

In Section 4.5.1 we saw that when a food US is revalued after Pavlovian conditioning by pairing it with poison or by changing the animal's hunger for that food, CRs to the CS signaling that food change accordingly. Similar effects are observed in instrumental conditioning. For example, Colwill and Rescorla (1985) trained individual rats to both pull a chain for sucrose and press a lever for food pellets (or the reverse pairings). The rats were then made ill after consuming one of the reinforcers in their home cages. In a subsequent test during extinction they immediately reduced their rate of performing the response that had previously gained the now-undesirable reinforcer (figure 11.14). At the beginning of the test the belief that a particular

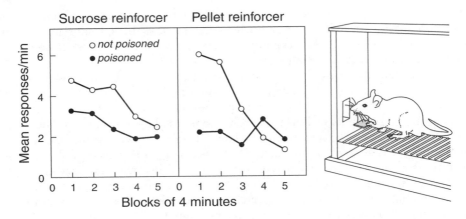

Figure 11.14. Results of the final, extinction, stage of an experiment demonstrating response-reinforcer associations in instrumental learning. Different groups of rats, each trained to make one response for sucrose and another for pellets, had experienced mild poisoning following ingestion of either sucrose or pellets and were tested in extinction. Redrawn from Colwill and Rescorla (1985) with permission.

response gave a particular food was intact (although the absence of any food soon changed that), but rats no longer desired the poisoned food. Notice that testing in extinction revealed the representation that controlled pressing originally; any reduction in responding could not reflect new learning that one response led to a disgusting food. Notice, too, that responding for the poisoned reinforcer was not entirely abolished, at least when the reinforcer was sucrose (see also Dickinson et al. 1995). Residual responding in experiments of this kind is evidence of S-R learning, and it is greater following greater amounts of training. Overtrained responses become habits, independent of the value of their original reinforcer.

In Pavlovian conditioning, revaluation effects resulting from pairing a US with poison or changing the animal's motivation appear immediately. In instrumental conditioning, however, they depend on past experience with the reinforcer, experience that leads to *instrumental incentive learning* (Dickinson and Balleine 1994, 2002). Animals have to experience the changed hedonic value of a reinforcer before responding for it changes appropriately. For example, in experiments like that of Colwill and Rescorla (1985) in the poisoning phase it is important to have multiple trials during which rats taste the food after it has become undesirable (see Dickinson and Balleine 2002). Remarkably, hunger and satiety work in the same way. In an elegant demonstration, Balleine (1992) trained rats to bar press for food pellets while somewhat sated and then tested different subgroups in extinction while they were either hungry or sated. Hungry rats pressed more than sated rats only if they had previously consumed pellets when they were hungry. Similarly, rats trained when hungry reduced their response rate when sated only after prior exposure to the food reinforcer in the sated state. Like the revaluation resulting from poisoning, these effects are specific to the foods eaten in the relevant state (Balleine 1992; Dickinson and Balleine 2002). On one view (Dickinson and Balleine 2000; Dickinson 2008) this instrumental incentive learning relies on a primitive form of phenomenal consciousness, namely awareness of the hedonic value of the reinforcer. This combines with causal knowledge about the response-reinforcer relationship (in effect, the rat's belief that pressing causes food), to generate responding. This interpretation implies that experience with associative relationships results in connections that are more than excitatory or inhibitory links between representations but rather themselves have representational content, a possibility investigated next.

11.3.3   Reasoning and causal learning

As we have seen in Chapter 4 (and see Rescorla 1988a), although associative learning can be viewed as an adaptation for acquiring causal knowledge, that is, some representation functionally equivalent to "A causes B," this need not mean animals represent causation as such. The effects of conditioning can be modeled as excitatory and inhibitory connections between event representations. Some, but arguably not all, human causal learning is well described by the same associative models discussed in Chapter 4 (Shanks 1994; Dickinson 2001b; Penn and Povinelli 2007a). However, the reasoning evident in deducing relationships among events in daily life or conducting scientific experiments seems to encompass an understanding of the nature of causes as such. Such causal understanding and how it develops has become an active area of research in cognitive and developmental psychology (Gopnik and Schulz 2004; Gopnik and Schulz 2007). One simple illustration of qualitatively different kinds of causes ("causal models" in terms of this literature) is depicted in Figure 11.15 (Waldmann, Hagmayer, and Blaisdell 2006). In the scenario on the top left, two fictitious hormones ("sonin" and "xanthan") have a common cause in a third one

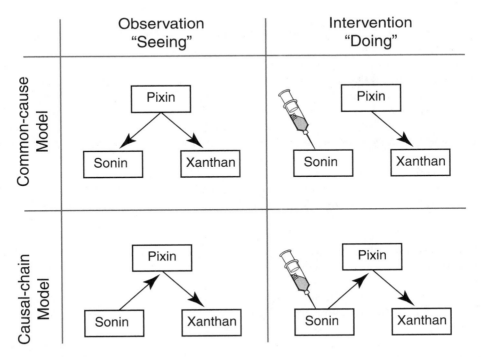

Figure 11.15. Tests of two kinds of causal reasoning by humans. Subjects are exposed to the causal relationships among fictitious biochemicals depicted on the left and then asked whether "xanthan" will be present when "sonin" is injected, as represented on the right. After Waldmann, Hagmayer, and Blaisdell (2006) with permission.

("pixin"). Therefore, if one intervenes by injecting sonin, xanthan should not be present (top right). In contrast, if the same three hormones are part of a causal chain (bottom left) such that sonin causes release of pixin which in turn causes release of xanthan, the same intervention should lead to the presence of xanthan. People do understand the difference between a causal chain model and a common cause model, as evidenced when they are exposed to one of the relationships on the left of Figure 11.15 and then asked whether they expect xanthan to be present following intervention with sonin (Waldmann., Hagmayer, and Blaisdell 2006).

Blaisdell and colleagues (2006) devised a clever arrangement for testing whether rats behave in an analogous way. "Common cause" rats first learned through Pavlovian conditioning that a light could be followed by ("cause") either a tone or food. In the "intervention" phase, pressing a novel lever produced the tone. These rats should not expect food when hearing the tone because the light had not occurred, at least if we assume the separate light-tone and light-food pairings did not induce an association between tone and food. In contrast, rats that had learned a tone-light-food causal chain should expect food when their bar-pressing pro- duced the tone. Expectation of food was measured by the number of times the rat poked its head into the opening above the food hopper during the 10-second tone. As predicted, the "causal chain" rats poked more, as if they understood that their action should cause food to appear, whereas the common cause rats understood that their action was unlikely to cause food. Additional groups in this and related experiments (Leising et al. 2008) successfully controlled for obvious alternative explanations such as differences in how recently the various elements of prior learning had been acquired.

Research on analogues to reasoning in the context of conditioning-like paradigms is still relatively new. There are candidates in purely Pavlovian paradigms, too (Beckers et al. 2006; Penn and Povinelli 2007a). Even if claims that these findings defy explanation in terms of established models of associative learning withstand additional scrutiny, the mechanism involved remains to be specified (Waldmann. et al. 2008). Models such as those depicted in Figure 11.15 are normative, that is, abstract functional descriptions of causal reasoning. Findings like those of Blaisdell, Leising, and Waldmann (2006) open the question of how experience induces beha- vior that approximates their outputs. What, if anything, is involved beyond networks of excitatory and inhibitory connections?

But why might such a reasoning-like process have evolved in an animal some- times referred to (e.g., by Dickinson 2008) as "the humble rat"? Do any natural situations require discriminating between interventions in causal chains versus common cause models? Some suggestions come from Tomasello and Call's (1997, Chapter 12) discussion of the limits to primates' causal understanding, where they imagine scenarios that require reasoning about interventions after observing causal chains. Importantly, Tomasello and Call conclude that primates would be very unlikely to make what to people are obvious deductions. For example, when an animal sees the wind shaking a branch and causing fruit to fall, why does it not reason "I could shake the branch myself to get fruit"? Similarly, if an animal sees a rock fall down a slope and cause a group of its conspecifics to scatter, why does it not reason that it could roll a rock to drive competitors away from some desired resource?

The structure of these situations resembles that of an instrumental secondary reinforcement experiment in which pairings of a CS with food increase a response that produces the CS (as in the control condition in Blaisdell et al. 2006). One difference is that in the scenarios described by Tomasello and Call "reasoning" would consist of spontaneous inferences about one's own behavior based on experience in the past rather than acquired in the situation at hand. These scenarios also resemble tests of the ability to copy another's actions. For example, suppose animal B sees animal A rather than the wind shaking the fruit-laden branch. As we learn in Chapter 13, most animals are not very good imitators, that is, given this experience they would not shake the branch themselves. Tomasello and Call suggest that reasoning about the shaking branch or the rolling rock requires understanding *why* causes have their effects. The latter case, they suggest, involves understanding the minds of conspecifics, a matter taken up in Chapter 12. The former involves physical understanding, the topic of the next section. Both require in some sense interpreting sequences of events as the results of unseen causes (thoughts and emotions of others; gravity and other physical forces). On one compelling and forcefully stated view (Povinelli and Vonk 2003; Vonk and Povinelli 2006; Penn and Povinelli 2007a), this kind of causal understanding is unavailable to species other than humans.

11. 4   Using and understanding tools

Tool use has been defined as "the use of an external object as a functional extension of mouth or beak, hand or claw, in the attainment of an immediate goal" (van Lawick-Goodall 1970). Making and using tools is often seen as a landmark in human evolution, but in fact all sorts of animals use tools (Beck 1980). Some crabs attach anenomes to their claws, where the anenomes' stings repel the crab's enemies. Sea otters break mollusk shells on stone "anvils" that they hold on their chests. Egyptian vultures crack ostrich eggs by throwing stones at them, and chimpanzees use bunches of leaves as sponges to collect water from crevices. Some animals make the tools they use. New Caledonian crows nibble strips off the stiff edges of pandanus leaves and use them to extract insects from holes (Hunt 1996; Bluff et al. 2007; see the cover of this book for a photograph of one of these crows with a twig tool). Chimpanzees make a variety of tools from sticks, leaves, and grass (McGrew 1992; Whiten et al. 2001).

As a functional category of behavior, tool use is hazy around the edges (St Amant and Horton 2008). For instance, only from an anthropocentric viewpoint does it make sense to distinguish one gull's dropping stones onto mussels (tool use) from another's dropping mussels onto stones (not tool use, see Beck 1980, 1982). Both are performing a food-reinforced chain of behavior involving stones. And to take another avian example, New Caledonian crows' ability to choose appropriate materials for tools and manipulate them to extract food from holes is arguably less impressive than the discriminative and motor skills shown by myriads of other bird species in building their nests (Hansell 2000). But in humans, using tools is also thought to entail at least an implicit understanding of how and why tools work, a simple "folk physics." Furthermore, like early hominids, chimpanzees in different geographic areas have distinctive types and uses of tools (Whiten et al. 2001) suggesting that tool use is transmitted socially and, more controversially, that apes have a primitive form of culture (Chapter 13). Provocative terms like "folk physics for apes" (Povinelli 2000) and "chimpanzee cultures" (Whiten et al. 2001) have attracted attention to animal tool use, and new findings about tool use by birds have increased it. Alongside of field work, clever laboratory analogues of situations observed in the field have been devised to allow a critical, controlled, look at two complementary questions. (1) How is tool use acquired? Is it, as might appear to the skeptic, entirely instrumental learning by trial and error or is some form of social influence required? Is insight ever involved? (2) What do animals understand about tools? Do they, for example, immediately recognize—in a way not explicable as stimulus generalization from past experience—what tool is needed in a given situation? We begin, however, with a brief look at the evolution and function of tool use.

11.4.1   What kinds of animals use tools?

Hundreds of observations of primates (Reader and Laland 2002) and birds (Lefebvre, Nicolakakis, and Boire 2002) using tools have been reported, not to mention candidates from other taxa, but routine use of genuine tools by one or more populations is established for only two species of birds and a few primates. A "genuine" tool is one the animal manipulates, like a stick used to extract prey from holes. "Borderline tools" (Lefebvre., Nicolakakis, and Boire 2002) are objects that are used but not actually manipulated, like the balls of mammal dung that burrowing owls place around their nests to attract the beetles which they eat (Levy, Duncan, and Levins 2004). One obvious ecological prerequisite for using genuine tools to get food is that the animal rely to some extent on *extractive foraging*, that is, eating things that have to be extracted from a hard shell or a hiding place inside a tree trunk or the like. Thus the fact that gorillas feed primarily on leaves probably accounts for the apparent rarity of tool use in this species compared to chimpanzees and orangutans (but see Breuer, Ndoundou-Hockemba, and Fishlock 2005). Among birds, it is noteworthy that the two species showing most widespread use of tools for extractive foraging, New Caledonian crows and woodpecker finches, are island species. For example, the woodpecker finch of the Galapagos does with twigs and cactus spines what a woodpecker does with its bill. Presumably in a mainland habitat it would be outcompeted by species equipped with stout bills for extracting the same kinds of prey more efficiently. The absence of competitors may open up a niche that can be exploited by evolving a behavioral specialization.

Differences among populations of tool-using species also provide some clues to ecological conditions favoring the evolution of tool use. A prime example comes from capuchin monkeys (*Cebus* species*)*. Although capuchins readily make and use tools in captivity, researchers in the forests of South America had seldom seen them using tools in the wild (Visalberghi and Fragaszy 2006). But it turns out that several groups of these monkeys in more arid, open, areas in northeastern Brazil routinely use stones to crack nuts (Waga et al. 2006). Some groups carry hard palm nuts to habitual "anvils," where heavy stones are left lying around; a monkey may stand up bipedally holding a stone a quarter of its own weight and drop the stone onto a nut (Fragaszy et al. 2004). The reasons why these populations use tools so much more than the forest monkeys probably include both the scarcity of foods other than palm nuts and the fact that the low density of trees means the monkeys spend a lot of time on the ground, where a stone, a nut, and a hard surface are more likely to be encountered together and to remain together through repeated nut-cracking attempts than in a tree (Waga et al. 2006).

Mainly because tool making and using was traditionally assumed to be uniquely human, it is widely assumed to require some kind of exceptional cognitive ability. In any case, activities such as appropriately bringing together nut, anvil, and stone tool or selecting and modifying sticks to make a tool of a required length and thickness seem unusually cognitively demanding. These considerations suggest that tool use should be associated with enlargement of the brain or some part of it. Comparative surveys of both birds (Lefebvre, Nicolakakis, and Boire 2002) and primates (Reader and Laland 2002) have indeed found evidence for such associations. For example, correcting for such confounds as overall frequencies of observation (see Box 2.2), genuine tool use in birds has been reported most often in corvids, other passerines, and parrots, groups among those with the largest relative neostriatum and whole brain. "Borderline" tool use is related more to overall innovation rate but not to brain measures. In primates, tool use, innovation (see Box 2.2), and social learning are all related to size of the "executive brain," that is, neocortex and striatum. Neither of these surveys provides much insight into precisely what neural specialization, if any, is associated with tool using nor do they look at differences among closely related species that differ in their propensity to use tools. In any case, whether or not it requires a specialized conceptual ability, using tools might not be expected to be associated with a single localized neural specialization because it can involve perceptual, motor, and/or learning abilities.

11.4.2   What do tool users understand?

Understanding what? The trap tube as a case study

A foot-long horizontal transparent tube with a peanut in the middle was placed in the cage of a group of four capuchins. When sticks were provided, monkeys used them to obtain peanuts by inserting a stick into one end of the tube and pushing the peanut out (Visalberghi and Trinca 1989). To use sticks effectively, the monkeys need not have understood anything about the requirements of the situation, such as needing a stick neither too thick nor too short and an unbroken surface between the peanut and the exit from the tube. On the face of it, poking a stick into the tube is instrumental behavior reinforced with food and acquired through trial and error. To test whether the animals understood anything other than "pushing the tool into the tube causes food," Visalberghi and her colleagues gave the capuchins clever modifications of the tube task. In what has become a benchmark test for understanding of tools, a trap was introduced in the middle of the tube (Figure 11.16, Visalberghi and Limongelli 1994). Now inserting the stick at the end closer to the reward (a candy in this experiment) pushed the reward into the trap. Three out of four capuchins given the trap tube never got the candy more than half the time in 140 trials. The fourth began to succeed almost every time after 90 trials. This individual was then given further tests designed to probe what it had learned. For instance, the tube was rotated so the trap was on top. Now the stick could be inserted on either end, but the monkey persisted in carefully selecting the end farther from the candy and frequently monitoring the movement of the candy as she slowly slid the stick into the tube. Thus this successful animal was using a distance-based associative rule.

Five captive chimpanzees were tested similarly to the capuchins (Limongelli, Boysen, and Visalberghi 1995; also see Povinelli 2000). These animals, experienced in a variety of laboratory tasks, all used sticks to get rewards from the plain tube right away. However, in 140 trials with the trap tube, only two of them ever performed above chance, and that not until after 70–80 trials. To see whether they were using a distance-based rule, these two animals were tested with a new trap tube that had the hole displaced from the center so that inserting the stick on the end nearest the reward could push it into the trap. Both animals were successful in this task almost from the beginning, showing that they took into account the position of the reward relative to the trap.

Figure 11.16. A capuchin monkey about to make an error in a trap tube task. After a photograph in Visalberghi and Limongelli (1994) with permission.

One of the successful chimpanzees anticipated the effects of the stick on the reward, as she rarely even began by inserting it on the wrong side. The other animal was more likely to begin with the stick on the wrong side, then withdraw and reinsert it. Still, these behaviors can be seen as reflecting learned rules based on the position of the reward relative to the hole, something like "Insert the stick on the side of the trap away from the candy" or "Push the stick only if it is moving the reward away from the trap."

By now, in addition to capuchins and chimpanzees, other great apes (Visalberghi, Fragaszy, and Savage-Rumbaugh 1995; Mulcahy, Call, and Dunbar 2005), several other primates (Santos et al. 2006), human children (e.g., Horner and Whiten 2007), woodpecker finches (Tebbich and Bshary 2004), a New Caledonian crow (Bluff et al. 2007), and—for good measure—human adults (Silva, Page, and Silva 2005; Silva and Silva 2006) have been tested on the trap tube task or variants of it. For example, in the "trap table task" (Povinelli 2000; Santos et al. 2006) an animal chooses between two tools for pulling food across a table toward itself, one of which is positioned to draw the food into a hole (Figure 11.17). Only human adults and children above the age of 4 or 5 immediately avoid the trap (Silva and Silva 2006; Horner and Whiten 2007). Individuals of other ages and species eventually learn to avoid it but take about as many trials as the capuchins. As suggested in the description of the successful capuchins and chimpanzees in the original studies, animals can learn to use any of a number of cues to avoid the trap. Nothing requires that they "understand gravity" or even the necessity to avoid holes or make the reward slide over an unbroken surface.

Beyond the trap tube

A serious problem here is that presenting successful animals with a tube with the trap rotated to the top is a test with very limited power. Understanding that the tube is no

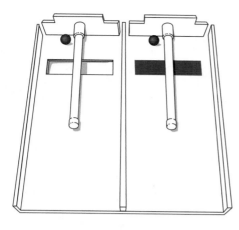

Figure 11.17. The trap table task. The subject, who would be positioned at the bottom of this figure, chooses between two rakelike tools, one of which (on the left here) will pull the reward into a trap. The alternative pulls the reward across a similarly-sized solid rectangle. After Povinelli (2000) with permission.

longer functional would be evidenced by inserting the tool at random on either end, but the same behavior would result from generalization decrement, that is, treating the altered tube as part of a new problem. More importantly, there is no cost to choosing a particular side when the trap is on top because the reward comes out regardless (Machado and Silva 2003). Indeed, unless it brings the reward sooner, human adults avoid using a tool near a nonfunctional trap, as if unthinkingly applying an algorithm "avoid traps" (Figure 11.17; Silva, Page, and Silva 2005; Silva and Silva 2006). Just as with other sorts of concept learning (Chapter 6), what is needed is a test in which conceptual understanding (here of the physical causal structure of the situation) predicts an outcome opposite to that expected from reliance on familiar cues (Machado and Silva 2003).

A design which does this was pioneered by Seed, Tebbich, Emery, and Clayton (2006), who trained rooks to avoid traps in the setups labeled A and B in Figure 11.18. Because rooks do not naturally use tools, the stick "tool" was preinserted into a tube and the birds had only to pull on the correct end to

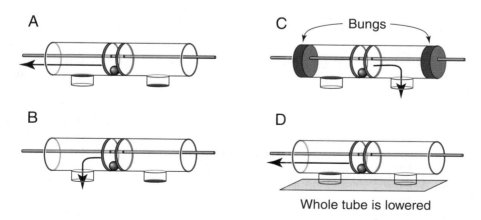

Figure 11.18. Trap tubes presented to rooks by Seed et al. (2006). Notice that in both A and B, pulling the stick to the left will release the reward. Tubes C and D each combine the "safe" ends of Tubes A and B, but require pulling in opposite directions as indicated. After Seed et al. (2006) with permission.

obtain the reward. Animals trained to a criterion of 80% correct on tube A or tube B immediately performed at a similarly high level on the other tube of the pair. However, because the trap looks the same in both cases this finding tells us only that the birds had learned to pull on the side away from the trap. Whether they had also learned something about the characteristics of traps was tested with tubes C and D. Each of them incorporated the "nontrapping" sides of tubes A and B, but arranged in such a way that success required taking into account how the reward would move when the stick was pulled. Six of 7 birds performed at chance on 20 trials with each of these tubes, but one performed almost perfectly from the outset.

What the successful rook had learned was not probed further, but a similarly designed task was used with chimpanzees (Seed et al. 2009). Initially these animals didn't use a tool but learned to slide a reward toward the exit from a transparent "trap box" by pushing it along with a finger. Training on two tasks was followed by tests in which responding based on cues predictive of success in the initial tasks were opposed to responding based on understanding traps. The animals learned both initial tasks much more quickly than previous animals required to use tools in tasks with traps, but as with the rooks only one subject (here, out of six) showed immediate transfer to the probe tasks. Then seven experienced animals along with eight naive animals were given a new version of the trap box to be used with a stick tool or a finger. This turned out to be difficult for naive animals: only one, using a finger, performed above chance in 150 trials. All experienced animals using a finger solved it within 30 trials, and two who had to use a tool also solved it within the time allowed.

This experiment supports two primary conclusions. One is that under some conditions chimpanzees apparently learn more than responses to arbitrary cues, as evidenced by the superior performance of the experienced animals in the final task. They may represent something about the functional properties of such things as a solid shelf or a barrier which allows them to transfer to new tasks with the similar elements. Notice this is not the same as understanding *why* these properties are important in terms of gravity or the tube. Here transfer to the second set of tasks was probably facilitated by the fact that the experienced chimpanzees had already learned four versions of the trap box. As we saw in Chapter 6, a concept or category is taught by exposing subjects to multiple exemplars, and this has rarely been done in other studies of tool use (Machado and Silva 2003). Indeed, a study with just two tasks, a trap tube and a "trap platform," found no evidence of transfer (Martin-Ordas, Call, and Colmenares 2008).

The second conclusion is that whether apes can succeed in avoiding traps while getting food may depend on how the task is presented. Tasks that test the same conceptual ability from a human viewpoint may make different cognitive demands on a chimpanzee. A finger may be easier to use than a stick because attending to movements of a stick leaves fewer resources for other aspects of the task (Seed et al. 2009). Similarly, choosing to rake in food from the solid side of a table with a trap is very much easier when a single tool is positioned in the middle of the table and subjects choose only where to direct it than when there is a tool on each side (as in Figure 11.17) and subjects choose which to pull (Girndt, Meier, and Call 2008). Indeed, with a single rake apes that failed a two-rake version chose the side without the trap on about 80% of trials from the very beginning. Again, a difference in attentional demands may be involved. When two rakes are positioned around food, the animal must inhibit its tendency to grab one before noting the relationship of the food to the trap (Girndt, Meier, and Call 2008). Finally, avoiding a trap may be easier when raking food than when pushing it out because pulling food toward oneself is more natural (Mulcahy and Call 2006b). Demonstrations that such conceptually irrelevant factors can be crucial have two interpretations. On the one hand, under the "right" conditions apes can solve tasks with traps much more readily than first appeared (e.g., in Povinelli 2000). On the other, if apes understood the task, these details should not matter so much. There are, however, some reasonable mechanistic explanations of why one versus two tools or the need to use any tool affects performance. The next step will be to put these explanations to the test.

What makes a good tool? Shape, size, and contact

Less demanding and arguably more central to tool use in general than avoiding traps is to discriminate between objects that are good and bad tools in the first place (Fujita, Kuroshima, and Asai 2003), for example matching the shape, thickness and/or length of tools to task requirements. In one test of this ability, capuchins, chimpanzees, bonobos, and an orangutan were given food in a tube and sticks tied into a thick bundle or a stick with smaller sticks inserted into its ends, in an *H* shape (Visalberghi, Fragaszy, and Savage-Rumbaugh 1995). All the animals untied the bundle or removed one of the small sticks from the *H* but only the apes appeared to do so out of an ability to anticipate the results of their actions. For example, the capuchins sometimes tried to push the whole bundle of sticks into the tube, but the apes never did. Two New Caledonian crows chose a stick from a "toolbox" to use for extracting meat from a transparent tube. They often took the longest stick available, which worked every time, but on trials when they did not, the length taken matched the length required pretty well. And when accessing meat through a small hole in a tube, the crows removed twigs from a branch to make a tool of the appropriate width, only rarely trying one that was too thick (review in Bluff et al. 2007). Woodpecker finches, however, often tried a stick that was too short before taking a better one from a "toolbox," but this is not so different from what they do in the wild (Tebbich and Bshary 2004). In any case, visually matching length of tool to depth of hole may have no function in the wild because the prey is usually concealed in the dark hole. This may explain why two wild New Caledonian crows offered grubs at different depths in experimenter-made visible holes behaved much like the woodpecker finches (Hunt, Rutledge, and Gray 2006).

Another test of the ability to choose good tools on the basis of their immediately perceptible characteristics is *the support problem,* a classic test of physical understanding first used by Piaget (see also Box 11.2). Very young children recognize that an out-of-reach object resting on (i.e., supported by) a cloth can be obtained by pulling on the cloth. In the version for monkeys and apes with options like those depicted in Figure 11.19 the animal chooses which of two cloths to pull to obtain an apple. An effective cloth can be perceived immediately as one with an unbroken surface, however irregular, between the working end and the treat. Cotton-top tamarins learn to discriminate between broken and unbroken cloths, even when the differences between them are quite subtle (Hauser, Kralik, and Botto-Mahan 1999). However, in tests focused on the relationship between the goal object and the cloth, chimpanzees do not immediately discriminate between cloths that actually support an object and those which simply surround or touch it, as in the examples in Figure 11.19 (Povinelli 2000).

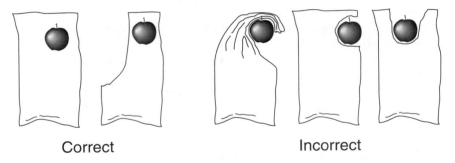

Correct   Incorrect

Figure 11.19. Stimuli used for testing chimpanzees on the support problem. As in the task in Figure 11.17, animals had a choice between an effective "tool" for pulling in reward such as one of the Correct options here, and an ineffective one such as the cloths on the right which surround or touch the apple but do not support it. After Povinelli (2000) with permission.

Box 11.2 Object Permanence in Animals?

Like the support problem discussed in the main text, many of the cognitive tests for young children devised by Jean Piaget are ideal for comparative studies because they rely on simple nonverbal behaviors. One of the most widely used with animals is object permanence (Dore and Dumas 1987; Gomez 2005). When a very young infant sees an attractive object disappear behind a barrier, she does not search for it. "Out of sight is out of mind." An older infant searches for an object that disappears behind one barrier (A), but if it is moved to a second hiding place (B) while the infant watches, it will be searched for in the first (the "A not B error"). Eventually, around two years of age, children search for objects that are displaced invisibly, for instance while carried in a container. Such behavior is taken as evidence for a concept of object permanence, a simple component of physical cognition, namely, the knowledge that an object still exists when out of sight and the ability to represent its unseen trajectory.

Object permanence develops through six stages, and not all species attain the sixth one (Dore and Dumas 1987; Gomez 2005). Clearly, however, animals could search for disappearing objects without representing their continued existence. The sight of an object disappearing behind an occluder could elicit search behaviors prefunctionally or an animal might learn what to do to retrieve it. For instance, when young domestic chicks watched a mealworm being pulled through a tube and disappearing behind a screen, they did not immediately follow it, but they eventually learned by trial and error to find the hidden worm (Etienne 1973; but see Regolin, Vallortigara, and Zanforlin 1995). As in tests of other abstract concepts, immediate accurate performance in a novel situation is necessary to rule out stimulus generalization of previously reinforced behaviors (Dore and Dumas 1987). Here this means animals that have reached a given stage of object permanence should display evidence of it with novel objects and occluders. In addition, because details such as the relative positions of the hiding places or their configuration can improve or interfere with performance (e.g., Call 2001; Collier-Baker and Suddendorf 2006), conclusions about a species' competence should be based on multiple tests.

Of course there are many natural situations in which animals search for hidden objects. Predators continue tracking prey that have gone into cover; nutcrackers dig up seeds they have buried. Such behaviors may not reveal what animals believe about disappearing objects so much as how well they remember an object's last location (e.g., Dore et al. 1996). But passing an invisible displacement test also seems to imply reasoning: "It's not in the container so it must be behind the screen." Watson and colleagues (2001) used the setup diagrammed in Figure B11.2 to test whether dogs use reasoning or an associative rule to find an invisibly displaced object. Both dogs and 4- to 6-year-old children first saw visible displacements: the experimenter showed a treat in a cup, then walked behind the three screens, stopping at each one to conspicuously either leave the treat or hold it up and replace it in the cup. Nearly all the subjects understood the task right away in that they searched for the treat only when the cup was empty at the end of the experimenter's excursion, although the children were more likely to visit the correct screen first. Then subjects had an invisible displacement test, in which the experimenter moved behind all three screens without showing the treat and then displayed the empty cup. Both children and dogs proceeded to search the three screens in order (the treat was actually not behind any). Consistent with reasoning that if the treat was not behind the first or second screen it must be behind the third, the children speeded up as they searched. In contrast, the dogs slowed down, consistent with some extinction of the previously reinforced searching. The conclusion that they were using an associative rule is supported by evidence from other studies with dogs (Collier-Baker, Davis, and Suddendorf 2004).

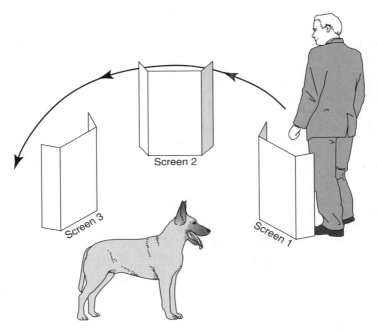

Figure B11.2. Setup used to test dogs and children for their understanding of invisible displacement. In the actual experiment a second person restrained the subject until the experimenter had completed the circuit of the screens and returned to the start area. Adapted from Watson et al. (2001) with permission.

Perception of surrounding or containment is also important for discriminating between effective and ineffective hook tools or canes (Figure 11.20), a test used with chimpanzees (Povinelli 2000) and five species of monkeys and lemurs (Hauser and Santos 2007), as well as with young children (Povinelli 2000; Cox and Smithsman 2006). Interestingly, once animals learn to use a cane of a particular color, thickness, and material, they transfer readily to other tools with the same functional properties even if different in color and texture. For example, tamarins trained with thin blue canes choose a novel thin red cane over an ineffective blue cane (Hauser 1997). Using an object as a tool may focus attention on its functionally relevant features and/or tool-users may be predisposed to attend to such features.

Figure 11.20. A cotton-topped tamarin choosing a hook tool (cane) that surrounds the desired treat over an ineffective tool. After a photograph in Hauser and Santos (2007) with permission.

Normally a tool must be placed in the correct relationship with the goal object, so one might wonder whether tool-using species are better at bringing this relationship about, a skill that seems to require planning a sequence of motor acts (Cox and Smithsman 2006). This issue was addressed by testing capuchins with canes and related tools in a similar way to Hauser's (1997) tamarins (Cummins-Sebree and Fragaszy 2005). Like the tamarins, the capuchins seemed indifferent to the sheer familiarity of a tool's irrelevant features such as color and attended to its functional properties. But unlike the tamarins, which do not use tools in the wild, the capuchins sometimes chose a tool that had not been prepositioned around the food and moved it into position. Their success with such tools improved with practice. These findings are consistent with the capuchins having some sort of specialization for tool-using, perhaps not so much a perceptual or conceptual one as a tendency to engage in certain kinds of exploratory behavior (Cummins-Sebree and Fragaszy 2005). However, as the authors of this study recognized, more thorough comparative work is needed to control for possible differences in, for example, the animals' past experience and their sizes relative to the tools.

Concluding remarks

Shape, size, and orientation do not exhaust the functionally relevant features of tools. Sensitivity to a tool's material has been examined by offering a choice between a floppy and a rigid pulling tool (Povinelli 2000; Santos et al. 2006). But unlike continuity or containment, rigidity cannot be perceived before the tool is chosen. The animal has to recall past experiences with the material, and this requirement may account for failures in such tests. Indeed, it is a mystery why the vervets and tamarins tested by Santos and colleagues (2006) generally rejected a flimsy rope for pulling in food unless some aspect of their past experience predisposed them against it.

Information about what materials animals choose for making tools and how they make those tools also potentially sheds light on the features they regard as important, though again such information cannot be interpreted without knowing the animals' past history, For example, videos of wild chimpanzees arriving at termite nests carrying stout sticks for excavating and/or thin wands for extracting termites as the case requires (Sanz, Morgan, and Gulick 2004) are wonderfully compelling evidence for flexible use of multiple tools and possibly even planning, but tell us nothing about how the behavior develops.

11.4.3   How does tool use develop?

A provisional conclusion from the foregoing section is that using tools involves perceptual and motor skills which tool using species may be predisposed for, but there is no evidence that it involves understanding the unseen causes by which tools work. In this section we look briefly at the development of tool using, in part to see whether this information sheds any new light on what tool users know. Three kinds of learning have been proposed to contribute to the acquisition of tool use: instrumental learning, imitation or some other form of social learning, and insight. Of course insight implies suddenly arriving at understanding without apparent prior practice so solid evidence for it might be thought to settle the question of understanding. However, even if—as does seem to be the case—either or both of the other two mechanisms plays the major role in the development of skilled tool use, this does not rule out the possibility that animals acquire some physical understanding once they begin engaging with tools (Bluff et al. 2007).

Instrumental learning must play some role in the development of skilled tool use—it would be surprising if it did not. Animals should acquire the ways of choosing and manipulating tools that give reward the fastest and most efficiently. An example from the laboratory is the observation that capuchins improved over sessions in placing a hook tool to rake in food (Cummins-Sebree and Fragaszy 2005). But reinforcement works on species-specific predispositions to pick up potential tools like sticks and engage in other behaviors that seem to be precursors of tool use (Schiller 1957; Tebbich et al. 2001; Bluff et al. 2007). This has been best documented in captive young woodpecker finches and New Caledonian crows. They do not need to see adults using tools to start using tools themselves, although social influence may have a role in attracting crows' attention to particular kinds of tools. New Caledonian crows make tools by biting strips off stiff *Pandanus* leaves, and naive socially isolated birds show the rudiments of this behavior. However, the presence of differently shaped tools in different parts of New Caledonia suggests that social learning plays a role in tool manufacture (see Bluff et al. 2007), a possibility we return to in Chapter 13.

The role of social factors in the development of tool manufacture and use by apes and other primates is more difficult to disentangle because of their protracted development and the impossibility of ethically raising them in social isolation. Social learning and the possibility that population-specific forms of tool using in apes are "cultural," that is, socially transmitted, are discussed in Chapter 13. Many of the experiments on imitation and other forms of social learning in apes and monkeys have involved tool-using tasks. As we learn there, true imitation—copying an act from seeing it done—is rare in any species, but numerous other forms of social influence can help to get tool using started, after which the physical requirements of the situation can shape the behavior through individual learning.

Insight

"Aha, I've got it!" In people, this experience accompanies insight, sudden solution of a problem without apparent previous trial and error. The most famous cases of apparent insight in another species were described by Wolfgang Köhler (1959) in the chimpanzees he studied on the island of Tenerife during World War I. They used sticks, strings, and boxes in novel ways to obtain food placed out of reach. For instance, two sticks were joined together to rake bananas into the cage; a box was moved across the cage and used to reach fruit suspended high on the wall. When first confronted with such a problem, animals would usually try the direct solution, jumping up and down under a suspended banana or fruitlessly reaching arms and legs between cage bars. These attempts might be abandoned and the animal might start doing something else when suddenly it would jump up, grab the necessary tool, and immediately solve the problem, as if having experienced an insight into what was required.

Subsequent researchers have emphasized that "insightful" behavior does not appear immediately but may follow many ridiculously (from a human viewpoint) incompetent failures (Povinelli 2000; Machado and Silva 2003). Moreover, experience builds it from species-typical motor patterns (Schiller 1957; review in Beck 1980). Chimpanzees spontaneously carry and climb on boxes, pull strings, play with sticks and put two sticks together. Such experience contributes to solving problems like Köhler's, as does perceptual and motor maturation. Similarly, observations of birds pulling up a dangling string with food on the end reveal a central role for species-typical feeding motor patterns (Vince 1961).

Some insight into precisely how experience with the elements of a solution contributes to "insightful" behavior is provided by a not entirely tongue-in-cheek demonstration that pigeons can solve the banana-and-box problem (Epstein et al. 1984; see also Nakajima and Sato 1993). The pigeons were first trained in two separate parts of the problem. In some sessions they were reinforced with grain for climbing onto a small stationary box and pecking a facsimile of a banana, wherever it was in the testing chamber. Jumping toward the banana was extinguished. In separate interleaved sessions the birds were trained to push the box toward a spot on the wall of the same chamber, with spot and box in varying initial locations. Control birds were trained to climb and peck the banana but did not learn to push the box toward a target. In the critical session, the banana was placed out of reach and the box was available in the chamber, but no spot was present. The birds trained to push directionally all behaved like Köhler's chimpanzees: at first they stretched beneath the banana and looked back and forth between banana and box, but within a minute or so they began to push the box into place under the banana. When the box was in place they climbed onto it and pecked the banana (Figure 11.21).

Films of the pigeons reportedly gave viewers a strong impression of humanlike thoughts and emotions (Epstein. et al. 1984), but a step-by-step analysis of the contingencies involved shows that the behavior can be explained otherwise. Looking back and forth between banana and box at first resulted from their eliciting conflicting responses (Epstein 1985). But because flying and jumping at the banana had already been extinguished, pushing the box quickly became the dominant response. Because both banana and spot had been associated with grain, mediated

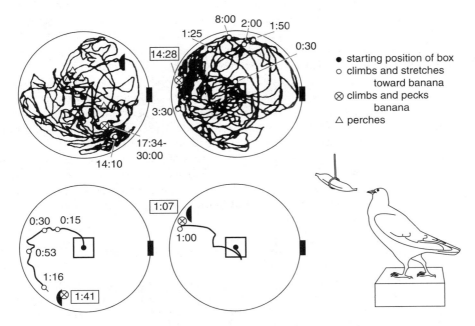

Figure 11.21. Movement of the box during the first 30 minutes of the test of insight in pigeons. Top row: data from two birds trained to push the box, but in no particular direction; bottom row: data from two birds trained to push the box toward a spot on the wall, which was absent in this test. The arena was 69 centimeters in diameter. Times are minutes and seconds from the beginning of the test; time in a rectangle is the time to solution. Redrawn from Epstein et al. (1984) with permission.

generalization (Chapter 6) could account for the banana becoming the target of pushing when the spot was absent. Finally, the birds climbed onto the box when it was under the banana thanks to what Epstein and colleagues call *automatic chaining*. By chance, pushing the box had reinstated a situation (banana within reach) supporting the previously reinforced pecking response. Whether the comparable behavior of Köhler's chimpanzees can be accounted for in a similar way is impossible to say, since their histories were not as thoroughly known.

Epstein and colleagues' account of the pigeons' behavior shows how knowledge of animals' past history and a careful analysis of the stimuli present and the responses they elicit can account for apparently novel or insightful behavior. One mechanism that may have played a role, *resurgence,* has subsequently been well documented (Lieving and Lattal 2003; Reed and Morgan 2007). Resurgence refers to the observation that when two responses are trained in sequence such that the first is extinguished before or during training of the second, the first response reappears during extinction of the second. It is not as well recognized as a source of flexible behavior as it deserves to be. Awareness of resurgence and automatic chaining together with a dispassionate description of actual behavior might take some of the mystery out of other examples of apparently purposeful tool manufacture or use, including examples of using a tool to get another tool ("metatools" Mulcahy, Call, and Dunbar 2005; Taylor et al. 2007).

One much-cited case is the observation that Betty the New Caledonian crow bent a straight wire into a hook and used it as a tool to pull a miniature bucket of meat out of a little well (Weir, Chappell, and Kacelnik 2002). The first time she did this, Betty had already used hooked wires on the bucket, but she was left with only a straight one, and she initially tried to use it. Having failed, she eventually thrust the wire at the base of the transparent well, wedging it in in such a way that it bent when she pulled on it. Now it apparently looked sufficiently similar to hooks she had used in the past to serve as a stimulus for lowering into the well, a successful response for getting the food. Betty was subsequently provided with straight wire on a number of occasions, on most of which she made some sort of bend and got the food, but generally not before trying with the straight wire. However, as Weir, Chappell, and Kacelnik (2002; see also Bluff et al. 2007) acknowledge, only the first trial is relevant as possible evidence of insight or purposeful tool manufacture. Subsequent bends can all be accounted for by reinforcement history. Clearly more subjects are needed, both here and in a further test (Weir and Kacelnik 2006) in which Betty made effective tools by bending and unbending strips of aluminum.

11.4.4 Tool use and causal understanding: Conclusions

Although it has been widely recognized for nearly half a century that making and using tools is not a uniquely human activity, research on nonhuman animal tool use has not yet completely broken free of the snares of anthropomorphism (Wynne 2007a, b). The area lacks a well-developed theory of the abilities required to recognize, use and/or make tools, leaving researchers struggling to grasp what animals understand when they use tools (as in Bluff et al. 2007). In terms of the topic of this chapter, there is no good evidence that anything other than mechanisms of associative instrumental learning discussed in Section 11.3 underlies tool using by any nonhuman species. The role of understanding in humans can be questioned, too (Silva and Silva 2006; but see Penn and Povinelli 2007a). As discussed at length by Povinelli and various colleagues (e.g., Povinelli 2000; Vonk and Povinelli 2006; Penn and Povinelli 2007a), interpreting the world in terms of unseen causes maybe uniquely human. But that is not to say that tool use involves no cognitive specializations. As we have seen, some animals seem quite good at recognizing the functionally relevant features of tools, and this could reflect a predisposition to perceive the affordances of certain classes of objects, if not a preexisting category of tools as a kind of object distinct from foods, landmarks, and other things (Hauser and Santos 2007). Currently the study of animal tool using includes a rich mix of wild and captive animals, natural and contrived tests, birds and primates, species that do and do not naturally use tools. More well-controlled comparative studies could address the question of possible perceptual and representational specializations in tool-using species as well as possible convergence between birds and primates. An example is the parallel studies of apes and corvids by Helme and colleagues (Helme et al. 2006; Helme, Clayton, and Emery 2006). And as in the study of numerical cognition, progress might be made by better contact with theory and data from child development and an attempt to break tool use down into components that may be shared among species to different degrees.

Finally, even though making, using, and culturally transmitting information about tools may be a key component of human civilization, much tool use may not require all that much cognitive complexity. Even people probably learn to use most everyday tools by copying others initially and then perfecting their technique through trial and error. Any folk physics involved is mostly implicit and likely developed though experience with complexes of related tools and tasks—using or seeing others use a hammer, a stone, the heel of a shoe to drive a nail, secure a tent peg, crack a nut, and so on. Poking a stick into a hole and getting out a grub or a candy may not require any more or different understanding than pressing a lever for a food pellet.

11.5   On causal learning and killjoy explanations

In an influential article on cognitive ethology discussed further in the next chapter, the philosopher Daniel Dennett (1983) referred to low-level reflexive accounts of animal deceptive or communicative behavior as "killjoy, bottom of the barrel" explanations. For example, a monkey's alarm call might seem to express an intention to let other monkeys know there is a predator nearby, but maybe it's simply that the sight of a predator when with other animals elicits alarm calling. In these terms, much of this chapter has been an exercise in developing killjoy explanations for kinds of behavior—maximizing long-term intake, planning for the future, learning instrumentally, and using tools—that from an anthropocentric viewpoint seem to demand more complex kinds of understanding. Described from a less value-laden perspective, we have seen the power of basic mechanisms of learning and choice to produce an enormous range of flexible adaptive behaviors without the sorts of explicit understanding people might express in comparable situations. The mechanism underlying rats' behavior in analogues to causal reasoning is still unclear (Waldmann et al. 2008) and not all would agree that animals have no appreciation of qualitatively different causes (Penn and Povinelli 2007a), but whatever the resolution of these debates, an appreciation of how apparent complexity can arise out of cognitive simplicity should be just as much a cause for joy as any validation of anthropomorphism.

Further reading

Overviews of the central issues in this chapter can be found in the book *Rational Animals?* (Hurley and Nudds 2006), especially the chapter by Kacelnik, and in the review by Penn and Povinelli (2007a). *Foraging* (Stephens, Brown, and Ydenberg 2007) and the authoritative text, *Behavioral Ecology* (Danchin, Giraldeau, and Cezilly 2008) provide overviews of current research on optimal foraging. A thorough review of instrumental learning is that by Dickinson and Balleine (2002). Waldmann, Hagmayer, and Blaisdell (2006) and Gopnik and Schulz (2004) provide brief introductions to causal learning, developed further in Gopnik and Schulz (2007) and Waldmann *et al.* (2008). *Decisions, Uncertainty, and the Brain: The Science of Neuroeconomics* (Glimcher 2003) integrates behavioral economics, optimal foraging, animal and human behavior with neuroscience in a clear and readable introduction. For discussions of future planning and related issues, see W. Roberts (2002), Suddendorf and Corballis (2007, 2008a), and Raby and Clayton (2009). Povinelli's (2000) *Folk Physics for Apes* discusses Köhler's (1959) classic work as well as describing the extensive experiments by the author's own group. Tool using by capuchins in field and lab is reviewed by Visalberghi and Fragaszy (2006).

Part III

Social Cognition

Social cognition encompasses all the processes specific to knowing and acting on information about social companions. This includes knowing other individuals' relationship to oneself (e.g., is he friend or foe, dominant or subordinate to me?) and their relationships to one another (e.g., are those two a mated pair, allies, competitors?) For starlings in an anonymous migrating flock or fish in a school such information is of little or no importance, but for animals that form stable groups in which individuals have differentiated social roles, an ability to predict the behavior of known individuals can smooth social relations, allay conflict, and thereby allow more time for feeding, grooming, and resting. Until recently primates were thought to be the only animals with rich networks of social relationships. This assumption led to the theory that the evolution of exceptional cognitive abilities and large brains went hand in hand with the evolution of sociality. Currently, however, the realization that other mammals as well as some birds form groups with similar characteristics are making discussions of this social theory of intellect much more interesting.

In Chapter 12 we begin examining the premise that sociality demands special cognitive abilities of some kind by looking at what individuals know about their social companions. Other animals differ from food, trees, and other parts of the inanimate world in that they have minds. People often explain or predict what others do by attributing mental processes to them: he was angry at someone, trying to deceive me, and so on. Accordingly, a major question in the study of animal social cognition has been whether other animals do the same thing: do animals have theory of mind? Research addressed to this question occupies a large part of Chapter 12. To what extent, if any, is an understanding of other's minds necessary for explaining cooperative, competitive, and/or deceptive behaviors? Again, recent research has expanded to species other than primates, both mammals and birds.

Animals that live in any kind of group can potentially learn from watching their companions, perhaps even be taught or engage in teaching. Chapter 13 looks at what and how animals learn from others, how imitation works, and the controversial proposal that social learning processes have led to animal cultures. Finally, in Chapter 14, we look at communication, intrinsically a social activity, and touch on the possible implications of what we know about animal communication systems for the evolution of human language.

12
Social Intelligence

In traditional studies of learning, social situations were largely neglected. Individual animals were tested in isolation. The same was true in the experimental study of comparative cognition that developed in the 1970s. In classical ethology, social behaviors such as courtship, mating, and aggression were prominent, but they were analyzed in the same way as interactions with the physical world, as sequences of responses to releasing stimuli, here the appearance, vocalizations, and behaviors (displays) of conspecifics (*social releasers*). But more recently, burgeoning information from long-term field studies of primates and other animals along with the cognitive revolution in psychology, theorizing about the evolution of human sociality, interest in human social cognition, even social cognitive neuroscience (Adolphs 2003) and other developments, have transformed the comparative study of social cognition into one of the most lively, fast-moving, interdisciplinary and sometimes controversial areas discussed in this book.

This chapter begins with the *social intelligence hypothesis,* the proposal that living in primatelike social groups requires exceptional cognitive abilities and is therefore associated with high intelligence. Although it was proposed over 40 years ago (Jolly 1966), arguably even earlier (see Cheney and Seyfarth 2007), it is still being debated (cf. Emery, Clayton, and Frith 2007). With only a few exceptions, we still do not know very much about the nature of social knowledge, how it compares across species, and how it is acquired. Is social knowledge qualitatively different from nonsocial knowledge in any way, or is navigating a large social network simply a matter of acquiring an unusually large amount of information? In any case, other individuals are not only social stimuli but have physical features and may administer physical rewards and punishments so their companions can learn about them through domain general mechanisms. Indeed, earlier chapters have included aspects of socially relevant cognition, for example individual recognition (Chapter 5), social concepts (Chapter 6), and reasoning about dominance relationships (Chapter 10). But if there are specifically social forms of cognition, highly social species might be expected to have them to an exceptional degree. To date there are few well controlled tests of this prediction. A promising way forward is with species other than primates, not only mammals such as hyenas and cetaceans (whales and dolphins) but birds and fish.

For human adults, knowing about other individuals means not only being able to predict their behavior but understanding their states of mind, that is, having *theory of mind.* Accordingly, the study of animal social cognition prominently includes tests of the mentalistic underpinnings of social interactions. Do animals, for instance, know that other individuals have beliefs, desires, and intentions? This question is no easier to answer than questions about animal episodic memory (Chapter 7), future planning, or physical understanding (Chapter 11). Section 12.3 lays out a framework for approaching it which is then applied to research on animal theory of mind in Section 12.4. Section 12.5 looks at the evolution of cooperative behavior, asking whether any examples of animal cooperation require specialized cognitive abilities or emotional dispositions. We start, however, with a closer look at the nature of social knowledge.

12.1   The social intelligence hypothesis

As set forth by Jolly (1966) and more influentially by Humphrey (1976), the social intelligence hypothesis (also called the social theory of intellect or the Machiavellian intelligence hypothesis, Byrne and Whiten 1988) proposes that social conditions in primate social groups drove the apparently high general intelligence that monkeys and apes seem to reveal in traditional tests of concept formation, learning set, discrimination reversal, and the like as well as their exceptionally large brains in relation to body size. Characteristic of its time, the original theory assumed that intelligence is general rather than modular. From a contemporary perspective, it might instead be suggested that cognitive adaptations for social life are, or have evolved to be, accessible to problems with nonsocial content (Rozin 1976). In any case, the original version of the social theory of intellect implies that complex social organization and general problem solving ability go together, whereas a modular view (e.g., Gigerenzer 1997) implies that they may be independent. In principle, comparative and phylogenetic data can distinguish among these possibilities. For instance, lemurs have a complex social organization but perform more poorly on tests of physical intelligence than Old World monkeys (Jolly, 1966). Because lemurs are prosimians, closer to ancestral primates than monkeys, this finding is consistent with Jolly's suggestion that social intelligence preceded the evolution of equivalent physical intelligence. But in Chapter 10 we saw evidence consistent with some independence between social and physical intelligence in that some corvids whose excellent spatial memory is consistent with their reliance on stored food are outperformed in socially relevant tasks by less spatially adept species (Balda and Kamil 2006).

An often-proposed alternative to the social theory of intellect might be called the foraging theory of intellect. As an example of how foraging niche might select for high intelligence, consider that tropical forests are a complex mosaic of hundreds of tree species, each with its own schedule of fruit and flower production. Because fruits are typically available for a shorter time than leaves, fruit-eating species may be faced with a harder environmental tracking problem than leaf eaters. In addition, a primate troop of a given size needs a larger home range if they eat fruit than leaves since at any given time there may be less food available in it. The foraging theory of intellect therefore predicts that fruit eaters should show evidence of greater generalized learning ability than leaf eaters. Comparison of howler monkeys (leaf eaters) and spider monkeys (fruit eaters) yields evidence consistent with this hypothesis (Milton 1988), though of course data from two species is hardly conclusive. Comparative data on brain size provide more broadly based evidence that fruit versus leaf eating may be correlated with cognitive differences. In bats, rodents, and primates, fruit-eating species have heavier brains relative to their body weights than their leaf-eating relatives (Barton, Purvis, and Harvey 1995). But it takes a longer gut to digest leaves than fruits, so a difference in brain:body ratios could arise because leaf eaters have relatively big bodies rather than relatively small brains. And type of food could have an indirect effect on brain size in that the young of species that eat things requiring more learning to find or process will remain dependent on their natal social group for longer and thereby have more complex social relationships and/or opportunities for social learning.

The social brain hypothesis

As the preceding brief review suggests, the social theory of intellect has become closely bound up with discussion of correlates for the relatively large brains (more specifically, neocortical areas) of primates (Figure 12.1; overall brain:body weight ratios for some primates can be compared to those for other mammals in Figure 2.11). But although overall brain size may be convenient for comparing species, specific cognitive demands might be most strongly reflected in specific areas of the brain (see Chapter 2; Striedter 2005). We need to know more about whether brain areas involved in learning about the physical versus social environments are the same or not before neuroanatomical comparisons can be strong evidence for or against the social theory of intellect (Healy and Rowe 2007). And in any case, sociality and tracking food availability are only two among a "bewildering" (Healy and Rowe 2007) array of factors that have been proposed as selecting for unusually large brains. For example, on one hypothesis (Barton 2000), much of the enlargement of primate brains is accounted for by visual areas. Unlike other mammals, primates have trichromatic color vision (Box 3.1). Red-green discrimination in particular aids in detecting both ripe fruits and tender young leaves, so although it evidently now also functions in social behavior, as witnessed by the colorful faces and bottoms of many monkeys, color vision may have evolved in the context of foraging. In addition, overall primate brain size can be related to innovation rate, an aspect of physical intelligence (Box 2.2; Lefebvre, Reader, and Sol 2004).

One problem is that except in a few well-studied cases we have only a sketchy idea of what social complexity consists of (Kummer et al. 1997). It is not simply a correlate of group size because not all large groups are socially complex. Animals within a flock

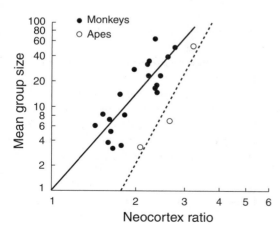

Figure 12.1. Social group size correlated with the ratio of neocortex to the rest of the brain ("neocortex ratio") for monkeys and apes. Each data point is mean for a species. Redrawn from Barrett, Dunbar, and Lycett (2002) with permission.

of birds or a herd of wildebeest may not distinguish among numerous unique individuals and multiple social roles in the way shortly to be described for some primates. However, few if any birds and few nonprimate mammals have been the subjects of the same kind of long-term field studies as some primates. Even within primates, which index is the best proxy for overall social complexity to be correlated with brain measures is disputed. For instance, Figure 12.1 shows a nice relationship between mean overall group size in a species and its ratio of neocortex volume to remaining brain volume, but good correlations have also been shown using other measures such as size of grooming cliques and frequency of deceptive behavior (Dunbar and Shultz 2007). Even worse, this lack of clarity means that attempts to document the social brain hypothesis in other taxa can verge on circularity. Thus the observation (Emery et al. 2007) that larger brains in birds are associated with pair-bonded mating systems, together with the *assumption* that the social brain hypothesis applies to birds, encourages speculation that long-term pair bonds entail special cognitive demands (speculation all too easy to generate from an anthropomorphic perspective). In summary, then, although the social theory of intellect and the associated social brain hypothesis have attracted a lot of attention, thinking in this area is still in flux. The special features of primate brains most likely result from more than one kind of selection pressure (Striedter 2005; Holekamp 2006; Healy and Rowe 2007). Progress will likely come through better information about the roles of different brain areas in social behavior and new statistical techniques allowing multiple factors be considered simultaneously (Dunbar and Shultz 2007) along with more thorough comparisons of social behavior and cognition within groups of related species, both primates and nonprimates.

Why be social anyway?

The species-typical size of animal groups reflects tradeoffs among a multitude of factors related to the nature and distribution of both a species' food and its predators. For example, hamadryas baboons (*Papio hamadryas*) live in the North African semidesert. Food is sparse, and during the day the baboons forage in small bands. However, the safest way for a baboon to sleep is perched on the side of a cliff, and because suitable cliffs are few and far between, as many as 200 baboons gather at night on sleeping cliffs (Kummer 1995). Many birds also congregate to nest or sleep and disperse to forage. In contrast, species dependent on a temporary resource that occurs in large patches, like the grasses of the African plains, forage in large migrating herds or flocks. Still other species are solitary and territorial except for breeding. Other animal social systems were sketched in Chapter 2.

The same costs and benefits determine optimal group size in most species (Section 2.1; Silk 2007a). On the benefit side, an individual foraging in a group can take advantage of others' vigilance and thereby devote more time to feeding (Section 3.7.3). When a predator does attack, the group may be able to confuse it or drive it off. In any case, the effect of the predator on any one individual will be diluted by the presence of others. Individuals foraging together may also help each other find food. They may be attracted to others of their species that are feeding, they may follow each other, as ants follow each other along chemical trails, and they may learn from one another in ways to be described in Chapter 13. But group living may also increase the risk of predation and decrease access to food. For example, a group is more conspicuous to predators than a solitary individual, and animals foraging together may interfere or compete with one another not only for food but also for mates and other resources.

Among some group-living primates, the time-consuming and potentially dama-ging effects of continual squabbling are minimized by observing a strict social hierarchy that defines priority of access to food and other resources. In addition, comparatively friendly relations are maintained among subgroups comprised of kin or others with alliances of some sort. These relationships are often expressed by animals grooming each other or spending time close together; their extent can be an important predictor of individual fitness (Silk 2007b). Among primates and some other animals, all these social arrangements take place in the context of a compara-tively long lifespan and prolonged dependence of the young on their mothers or other adults. Usually members of only one sex, most often males, disperse during adoles-cence while members of the other stay in their natal area for life. Extended families therefore may contain grandmothers, aunts, cousins, and so on of all ages, the oldest of whom have very extensive knowledge of the local social and physical environment. The slow development that underlies this kind of social group also facilitates growth of a large brain (van Schaik and Deaner 2003; Striedter 2005). Perhaps it is not surprising, then, if large brains and complex societies go together.

12.2   The nature of social knowledge

So far we have taken for granted that living in a social group presents distinctive cognitive problems. But what do animals know about their social companions? Is any aspect of social cognition a distinctive *form* of cognition, as opposed to a distinctive, social, *use* of some more general cognitive ability (Gigerenzer 1997)? Tomasello and Call (1997) concluded from their comprehensive review of primate cognition that primates differ from other animals in being able to learn about *third-party relation-ships,* a kind of relationship they claimed is uniquely social. As an example, consider dominance relationships. An animal's knowledge about the dominance hierarchy of which it is a part might be entirely in terms of its own, that is, first-party, relation-ships, perhaps acquired through associating rewards and punishments with particular behaviors directed at particular individuals. For instance, a mid-ranking animal might learn, "If I try to displace Joe from food he moves away and I get the food; if I try to displace Pete, he threatens me." This knowledge implies a third-party relation-ship, namely Pete is dominant to Joe, which could also be acquired just by watching Pete and Joe interact. As we will see, monkeys are sensitive to many kinds of third-party relationships, but we now know that some nonprimate mammals and some birds and fish are, too.

12.2.1   Social knowledge in primates

Much of what we know about primates' social knowledge comes from long-term field studies, sometimes combined with clever field experiments (see Cheney and Seyfarth 1990; Kummer 1995; Cheney and Seyfarth 2007). A sample from such research illustrates the richness of social relationships to which some primates are sensitive.

Relatedness

We saw in Chapter 6 how Dasser (1988a) used operant category learning to test whether Java monkeys had a concept of the relationship *mother-offspring.* Vervet monkeys tested in the field also show evidence of associating particular infants with their mothers (Cheney and Seyfarth, 1990). When vervets hear the cries of a familiar but temporarily unseen infant broadcast from a concealed speaker, they are more likely to look toward that infant's mother than toward some other monkey. Vervets also show evidence that they are sensitive to more remote kinship relationships among troop members. For instance, a monkey that has recently been the subject of aggression is more likely to behave aggressively toward a relative of its attacker than toward an unrelated monkey. Such *redirected aggression* is seen in many nonprimates as well as primates (Engh et al. 2005). However, while all these observations reveal social knowledge, the processes by which it is acquired need not be specifically social. Mothers and infants are normally seen together and thereby may become associated in the minds of their companions. Relatives may look alike (Vokey. et al. 2004) or become associated through proximity, promoting generalization from one to another. Redirected aggression suggests that the negative effects of fighting with an individual generalize less widely to similar individuals than does the tendency to fight that with animal in the first place.

Male-female relationships

Knowing who belongs with whom or what kind of behavior to expect from A as opposed to B may be explicable as the products of learning mechanisms that are not specific to social stimuli. However, an ability to categorize interactions among specific individuals in terms of kinds of social relationships such as mother-offspring, ally, and so on, that is, to use social concepts, would enable ready generalization to completely new individuals if group membership changes (Seyfarth and Cheney 1994). A pioneer in designing experiments to tap such knowledge was the Swiss ethologist Hans Kummer, working with hamadryas baboons in Ethiopia. In this species, males control "harems" of females. When large numbers of males with their females and offspring gather to sleep and rest, the large powerful males seldom fight over access to females. One male's respect for another's possession of a female arises from observing the two interacting, as Bachmann and Kummer (1980) showed in the experiment depicted in Figure 12.2. The subjects were pairs of males from the same troop and females unfamiliar to them. What would the males do when placed together with a female if *(a)* one had previously seen the other interacting in a friendly manner with the female or *(b)* they had both seen the female before but neither had interacted with her? In the first case, as little as 15 minutes observing the pair inhibited any attempt by the second male to interact with the "married" female and her partner. When introduced into the enclosure with them, he sat in the corner with his back turned and groomed himself or looked at the sky or into the bushes. In the control condition, however, both males tried to interact with the female and occasionally fought over her. These results suggest that the observing male processed what he saw as a particular kind of third-party relationship, one that dictated his staying out of the way of the second male. Quite possibly past experience had taught him to refrain from approaching a female in the presence of a possessing male, but this too requires generalizing over a class of interactions among different individuals.

Further evidence that male baboons rapidly encode information about mating associations comes from more recent work by Crockford and her colleagues (2007) with chacma baboons (*P. cyanocephalus*). In this species, males form temporary consortships with sexually receptive females, during which they stay close to a female and repel mating attempts by rival males. Consortships end abruptly after a few hours

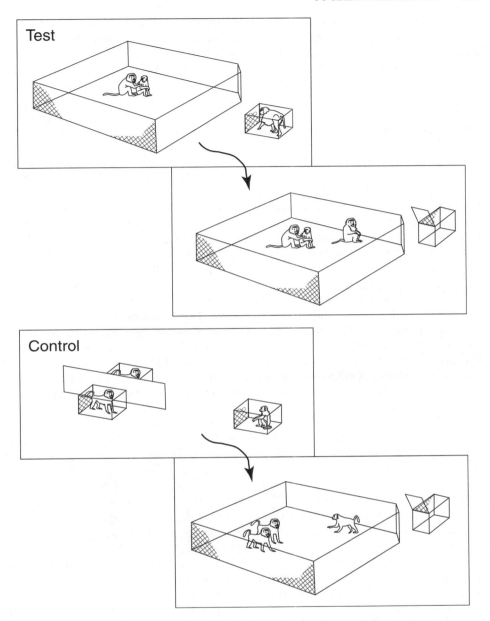

Figure 12.2. Setup and results for a test of male baboons' respect for another male's possession of a female. The Test condition begins with a male watching from the small cage on the right while another male and a female interact. In the Control, first both males see the female in the small cage at the right. Redrawn from Kummer (1995) with permission.

or days while the female is still receptive, opening mating opportunities for others. Males not currently in a consortship were played a recorded copulation call of a female in their group preceded by a grunt from her current or recent consort while both of the consorting animals were well out of sight and earshot. If the consortship was still ongoing and the calls came from the same location or if it had ended and the calls came from different locations, subjects hardly glanced toward the hidden speaker(s). However, if the consortship had been ongoing and the calls came from different locations—as if the consortship had ended—the subject males looked a long time and some even headed toward the speaker from which they had heard the female's call.

Social causation

One might say that the males in the study just described behaved as if performing a kind of causal reasoning: "Those two are have separated because the consortship is over." Another example of such social causal reasoning, this time in chacma baboon females, was provided by Cheney, Seyfarth, and Silk (1995). When a dominant female approaches a subordinate who is holding an infant in an attempt to touch or hold the baby herself, the dominant will often emit a grunt vocalization, and the subordinate may emit a fear bark. If instead a subordinate approaches a dominant, this sequence of vocalizations is never heard. Dominants do not give fear barks to more subordinate individuals. Cheney et al.'s experiment tested whether baboons understand the causal relationship between status of the approaching, grunting, female and fear barking by the female being approached by comparing their reactions to causally consistent and inconsistent sequences of grunts and fear barks (Figure 12.3). In inconsistent sequences, a grunt by a subordinate individual, say F, was followed by the fear bark of a female dominant to her, say C. A consistent sequence matched to this example would also contain F's grunt followed by C's fear bark, but in this case a grunt by an individual dominant to C, say A, preceded C's fear bark. This sequence was causally consistent because C's fear bark could be caused by the approach of A. The consistent sequence contained more vocalizations, so it might

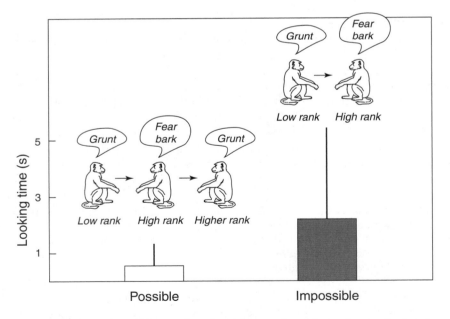

Figure 12.3. Experimental conditions and results of the test of social causal reasoning in baboons. After Hauser (1996) with permission; data from Cheney, Seyfarth, and Silk (1995), redrawn with permission.

be expected to be more salient, and attract more looking, than an inconsistent sequence, the opposite pattern to that expected if the animals are reacting primarily to the information in the sequence.

Each subject heard a consistent sequence on one occasion and an inconsistent sequence on another. On average, subjects looked toward the speaker longer when an inconsistent sequence was played. Because the stimuli were matched for features like the specific vocalizations they contained, these results seem to show that the baboons do recognize a kind of social causation in the sequences of grunts and fear barks. To do so, they need to recognize other individuals' calls and dominance ranks and to know in some sense that fear barks result only from the approach of a dominant toward a less dominant animal. Another possibility, however, is that the specific consistent sequence was simply more familiar. It would be difficult for a study of this kind to escape from such an objection, since it is only through watching and listening to the interactions of other individuals that a subject monkey learns their ranks in the first place.

Alliances and rules of thumb

Monkeys' knowledge about kinship and dominance finds practical expression during agonistic interactions. When two individuals are threatening or fighting each other, bystanders may join relatives or others in *alliances*. Joining may result from *recruitment,* a behavior in which an animal in an agonistic interaction looks back and forth between its opponent and a bystander, the potential recruit. Since rank is power, it makes sense to recruit allies higher ranking than one's opponent. Similarly, a good way to be on the winning side in a fight to join the higher-ranking animal. Both of these choices imply knowledge of third-party relationships, and indeed two species of macaques reveal such knowledge in recruitment and alliances (Silk 1999; Schino, Tiddi, and Di Sorrentino 2006).

Behavior consistent with knowledge of third-party relationships can arise for other reasons (Range and Noë 2005). For example, animals might use rules of thumb like "always recruit the dominant animal" or "always join the winning side" (most likely the more dominant). Relatives may be especially likely to be dragged into each other's disputes simply because they spend a lot of time close together. Unlike in studies with playbacks of social interactions, information about recruitment and alliances is typically extracted from observations of free behavior. Here the only way to control for potential confounds is to start with so much data that subsets of it can be analyzed meaningfully. A good example is the study by Silk (1999) showing that the rank of allies recruited by male bonnet macaques varies with the rank of the opponent (Figure 12.4). We see an example from hyenas in a moment. Still, inevitably a goodly proportion of interactions will be as consistent with rules of thumb as with knowledge of third-party relations (Range and Noë 2005).

Multiple relationships and hierarchies

Taken together, the foregoing information implies that some primates classify their social companions in multiple ways simultaneously, particularly in terms of kinship and dominance, but also in terms of shorter-term relationships like consortship. Evidence for hierarchical classification by family dominance rank and rank within family (Bergman et al. 2003; Schino, Tiddi, and Di Sorrentino 2006) was described in

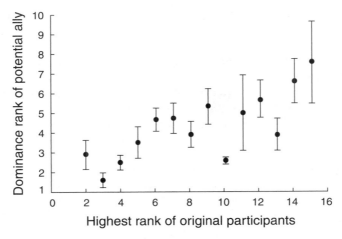

Figure 12.4. Dominance rank of bonnet macaques solicited as allies in an aggressive interaction is higher the higher the rank of the participants. This relationship implies that the animals are sensitive to the relative ranks of third parties, that is, their opponent and potential allies, and not just choosing the highest ranking animal available. After Silk (1999) with permission.

Section 6.5.5 as implying a kind of categorization not yet studied with arbitrary stimuli in the laboratory. As discussed there, learning who belongs to which family has some similarities to learning equivalence classes, but unlike with equivalence classes, the individuals within each class are still differentiated. Seyfarth and Cheney (2003a) have suggested that what is going on is better described as hierarchical chunking of information.

12.2.2   Social knowledge in nonprimates

Elephants, whales, dolphins, and hyenas form long-lasting groups with some of the characteristics of primate societies (see de Waal and Tyack 2003; Bshary and Grutter 2006; Connor 2007). And although it remains to be seen whether any birds or fish form social groups involving such a multiplicity of relationships as those described for primates, some birds and even fish are sensitive to third-party relationships. Not only are studies of social knowledge in such animals fascinating in their own right, but also they provide information that can potentially distinguish among three possible interpretations of the social theory of intellect (Cheney and Seyfarth 2005a). *(1)* Primates exceed all other species in social intelligence. *(2)* Primatelike social cognition is seen in any species with similar numbers and complexity of social relationships. *(3)* Social cognition is similar across species, perhaps because it is qualitatively not different from physical cognition. Accordingly, studies of social cognition in species other than primates are on the increase. This section samples a few that demonstrate knowledge of third-party relationships.

Alliances in hyenas

Spotted hyenas (*Crocuta crocuta*) are carnivores that live in large groups, or clans, similar to primate groups in consisting of individuals from overlapping generations in a network of kin and dominance relationships (Holekamp, Sakai, and Lundrigan

2007). Because carnivores and primates diverged millions of years ago, similarities between them in cognition and brain organization would likely reflect convergent evolution. Like primates, hyenas join conspecifics engaged in agonistic interactions. The knowledge of third-party relationships used in doing so has been analyzed by Engh and colleagues (2005) from extensive records of free behavior just as Silk (1999) has done for monkeys. In the frequent cases where the aggressor was the more dominant of the two original interactants, support by the joining hyena could reflect a rule of thumb ("join the aggressor") rather than knowledge of relative ranks. But in a critical minority of cases a subordinate animal attacked a dominant, and here, too, joiners most often supported the dominant.

Hyenas also show redirected aggression after conflicts. As in primates it is more often directed toward relatives of the former opponent than toward other lower-ranking animals, suggesting that hyenas know about kinship as well as dominance relationships among third parties. These observations may have been biased by relatives of the former opponent being especially likely to be nearby, but they are corroborated by the results of a playback experiment. "Whoops" of hyena cubs not only are recognized by the mothers of the whooping cubs, but they also elicit more looking by the cubs' relatives than by other nearby hyenas (Holekamp et al. 1999). Dominance rank of the cub's mother also influences looking. However, unlike with vervet monkeys, hyenas hearing a cub whooping do not look toward its mother. This could mean they do not recognize the relationship mother-cub, or they may have the requisite knowledge and not express it in looking.

Social transitive inference and eavesdropping and in birds and fish

Some of the best evidence from any species for knowledge of third-party relationships comes from the study of transitive inference in pinyon jays (Paz-y-Mino et al. 2004) discussed in Section 10.3.3. Although the information gained from watching a familiar jay interact with a dominant stranger did not influence more than the first few seconds of the observer's own interaction with the stranger, this is one of the few studies with nonprimate species that rises to the level of Bachmann and Kummer's (1980) experiment with baboons as a well-controlled demonstration that animals can acquire information about third-party relationships by watching. The related study by Grosenick, Clement, and Fernald (2007) provides similar evidence for fish. As discussed in Section 10.3.3, such data suggest that relative information is being encoded as such, perhaps along an analog scale. But the fact that birds and fish learn about the social relationships between pairs of conspecifics was already well established by studies of "eavesdropping" in vocal communication and territorial behavior (see P. McGregor 2005).

The dictionary definition of *eavesdropping* mentions listening in on a secret conversation, but in animal behavior the term refers to extracting any information from the interactions of others, be it auditory, visual, olfactory, or in some other modality (Peake 2005). Importantly—as with *deception, cooperation,* and other terms prominent later in this chapter—this is a functional definition. Deciding whether eavesdropping has occurred does not depend on knowing whether the eavesdropper intended or tried to acquire information, let alone whether it was doing so by stealth, nor does it imply anything about whether the animals eavesdropped upon wanted or intended to provide information. The information acquired by eavesdropping can include absolute features of individuals such as being a good mate or the holder of a certain territory, but some fish and birds also appear to learn about third-party sexual or dominance relationships by eavesdropping.

One example will illustrate the kinds of controls necessary in such studies. Male Siamese fighting fish (*Betta splendens*) are known for showing vigorous aggressive displays as soon as they catch sight of another male. In a study by Oliveira, McGregor, and Latruffe (1998), five males lived in a large tank subdivided as shown in Figure 12.5, with the subject male in the central compartment. After a preliminary exposure to each of his four neighbors, the subject watched (eavesdropped on) a fight between two of them through a one-way glass (i.e., the combatants could not see the eavesdropper). At the same time but unseen by the subject, his two other neighbors had a fight. Following the fights, both of which resulted in a winner and a loser, the

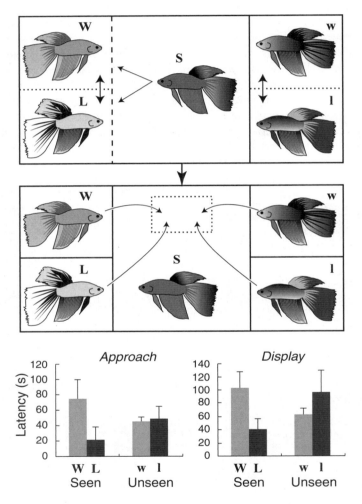

Figure 12.5. Siamese fighting fish learn about third party relationships by eavesdropping. S is the subject; dotted lines = transparent barriers. W, L = winner and loser of fight observed by S; w, l = winner and loser of fight not seen by S. Data refer to the behavior of S in the subsequent one-on-one encounters (lower drawing). Adapted from Oliveira, McGregor, and Latruffe (1998) with permission.

subject encountered each of his four neighbors, one at a time in an order balanced across fishes, in a small transparent compartment in his own tank (Figure 12.5). He spent more time displaying toward the winner than the loser of the fight he had witnessed but showed no discrimination between the unseen combatants. The latter data importantly show that discrimination was not based on intrinsic features of the stimulus fish or aftereffects of their having recently won or lost a fight.

Nevertheless, to discriminate between the winner and loser of a fight an observer need not have encoded the relationship between the combatants as such. He may instead encode the level of aggression and/or submission shown by each individual. A followup study by Peake, Matos, and McGregor (2006) supports this account. In their study, male fighting fish again saw two fish engaged in aggressive behavior, but instead of displaying at one another, each of them was displaying at a mirror between their tanks. When one of the "combatants" was made to appear less aggressive than the other by placing the mirror farther from his tank, the observer treated that fish like a loser. In some studies of social eavesdropping in birds, by contrast, researchers have manipulated what a witness is exposed to while keeping constant the total amount of signaling from each interactant. For example, in some species a relationship between two unseen neighbors is expressed in the degree to which a dominant bird's songs overlap those of a submissive neighbor. Studies in which only song overlap is varied have revealed sensitivity to a relationship as such (review in Peake 2005). Similarly, the pinyon jays in Paz-y-Mino and colleagues' (2004) study on social transitive inference saw each bird they were to encounter later both win and lose fights.

Many of the studies of eavesdropping by birds and fish were done with species such as territorial songbirds that typically interact socially with only their mate and a few close neighbors, perhaps only during the breeding season (see Cheney and Seyfarth 2005a). They therefore suggest that knowledge of third-party relationships is not confined to species living in large stable social groups. But the social lives of birds and fish that have larger and perhaps more complex social networks are also beginning to be examined through a primate-centric lens. For example, young rooks in captive flocks form affiliative relationships expressed through behaviors such as mutual preening and food sharing. Rooks also show redirected aggression, and preliminary evidence suggests that it is directed preferentially against the affiliates of an opponent (Emery, Seed, von Bayern, and Clayton. 2007). We look at other aspects of corvid social cognition later in this chapter, but among birds sophisticated social cognition may not be limited to corvids. Graylag geese (*Anser anser*) form long-term family relationships, and families form flocks with clear dominance relationships among families (Scheiber et al. 2005). Among other evidence of such relationships, family members support each other in aggressive interactions. And in fish, one of the most interesting examples of complex social networks is interspecific, in the relationships among cleaner fish and their clients (Section 12.5; Bshary and d'Souza 2005).

Conclusions

In conclusion, the research on social knowledge in nonprimates sampled here seems consistent with the conclusion that primatelike social cognition is not unique to primates. However, primates may still excel in the multiplicity of qualitatively different relationships to which they are sensitive. For example, a female chacma baboon can be at the same time a mother to a particular youngster, a member of a matriline, a member of a within- and a between-family dominance hierarchy, and in a friendship or consortship with a particular male. Some of her relationships are life-long, others are temporary, some are transitive, others intransitive (Cheney and Seyfarth 2005a, 2007). Yet she and the many other baboons in her troop seem to know all these things about one other. The ability of primates to acquire and deploy such knowledge may or may not be the same ability reflected in their performance in tests of abstract concept learning and transitive inference in the laboratory. In any case, it remains to be seen whether long-term, in-depth studies of any nonprimates comparable to those done on a few primate species will reveal comparably sophisticated social knowledge.

12.2.3 Comparing social and nonsocial intelligence

Having sampled the extensive information about what goes on in primate social groups and similar groups of other animals, we can ask whether social knowledge differs in any way from knowledge about the physical world. This question is distinct from that addressed in the next sections of the chapter, namely does social behavior involve social causal understanding such as theory of mind? Here we ask simply, do social situations have a distinctive abstract structure and/or do they engage distinctive learning mechanisms by virtue of their social content?

To see that neither of these questions need have an affirmative answer, think back to the discussion of associative learning and performance rules in Chapter 4 and consider fear conditioning and conditioned taste aversion in rats. Like other examples of associative learning, both are engaged by predictive temporal relationships between events, but the nature of those events determines both the relevant temporal parameters and the behavioral outcomes of experience. Thus, in fear conditioning a close temporal relationship between an exteroceptive signal and shock engages freezing, escaping, and the like, whereas in conditioned taste aversion, experiencing a flavor minutes to hours before gastric distress engages rejection and other disgust responses. One might similarly try to define a social behavior system or module engaged by predictive relationships among particular social stimuli and ask how the conditions for learning compare to those in conditioning. So far only a handful of provocative examples suggests what such an analysis might yield.

Observations of vervet monkeys in the field suggest that they know much less about the physical than the social world (Cheney and Seyfarth 1990). For instance, vervets may have watched as a snake slithering by left a trail on sandy ground, but show no apprehension on encountering a trail in the absence of a snake. Here associative learning expected on the assumption that a fresh trail means a snake is nearby does not seem to occur. Vervets appear to be good social psychologists but poor naturalists (Cheney and Seyfarth 1990). Cheney and Seyfarth (2007) suggest that in addition to possibly learning more quickly about social than nonsocial events, some primates may be predisposed to attend to and learn about dominance and kinship. They support this suggestion with charming accounts of goat-herding baboons that learned spontaneously which kids belonged to each mother goat. But another legendary baboon learned to help a disabled railway signalman by operating switches on the tracks, seemingly more physical than social learning. And as we see in Chapter 14, various animals learn the meaning of the alarm calls of other species, in that they apparently associate calls with the presence of particular predators and behave appropriately.

Returning to social and nonsocial tasks with similar logical structures, recall the comparative studies of transitive inference in scrub jays and pinyon jays from Chapter 10. The highly social pinyon jays learned faster and performed in a more monkey like way on operant transitive inference with colors. This is consistent with the notion that the operant task taps a social cognitive ability, much as operant spatial memory tasks tap the same ability shown in retrieving hoarded seeds (Chapter 8). However, pinyon jays acquire genuine social transitive inference far more quickly than even the first few items in the physical task, suggesting that the tasks tap different abilities. Clearly, however, this comparison is confounded by all sorts of differences between the social and physical tasks. For instance, one involved observing conspecifics; the other, operant conditioning. Even if it were possible to make the conditions for acquisition more similar, equating the salience of the stimuli involved could be an insurmountable challenge. Other jays interacting may grab another jay's attention more than any physical objects. This consideration creates serious obstacles to deciding whether transitive inference, at least in nonhuman animals, is a specifically social cognitive process engaged only weakly by nonsocial stimuli or whether it is a domain-general ability used with any sufficiently salient stimuli.

What it means to compare social and nonsocial reasoning about identical materials is illustrated by studies of the *Wason selection task* with human subjects (see Cosmides and Tooby 1992). As originally studied by the psychologist Peter Wason, this task requires people to look for violations of a logical rule of the form "If p then q." A subject is given the four cards shown in Figure 12.6A and asked which ones need to be turned over to detect violations of the rule, "If a card has *p* on one side it has *q* on the other." Most people turn over the card with *p* on the front to see if it has *q* on the back. Very few turn over only the one necessary additional card, the one with *not q*. Familiar, less abstract, content doesn't always improve performance, but in the example shown in Figure 12.6B, as many as 75% of subjects can detect whether people are drinking illegally by turning over the correct cards.

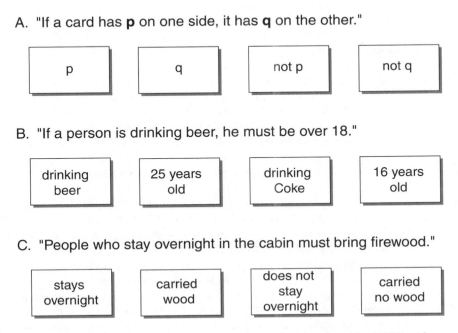

Figure 12.6. Three instantiations of the Wason selection task. After Cosmides (1989) with permission.

According to Cosmides (1989) and others (see J. Evans 2002), the reasoning ability needed here evolved to detect cheaters on social contracts in early hominid society, and the drinking age problem taps into it. Reciprocal altruism depends on participants obeying general rules of the form, "If you take a benefit, you pay a cost." For instance, "If I share my meat with you, you help me gather wood." Cheaters take the benefit without paying the cost, that is, they satisfy the logical condition, "p and not q." The view that reasoning in the Wason task reflects a cognitive adaptation for social exchange has been supported by the results of experiments in which people are asked to reason about identical statements in a social context versus another sort of context. To control for familiarity of content, Cosmides told Harvard students elaborate stories about fictitious tribes and their customs. Similarly, Gigerenzer and Hug (1992) told subjects stories about people visiting a mountain cabin. When solving the Wason task in these contexts, subjects were much more often correct when "If p then q"—for instance "People who stay overnight in the cabin must bring firewood" (Figure 12.6C)—was framed as a social contract than when it was framed as a description of social customs.

The approach to human reasoning exemplified by studies of the Wason selection task has been applied to reasoning in other areas, to see whether other examples of apparent irrationality are actually "ecologically rational," that is they make sense when seen as evolved to solve ecologically relevant problems (Todd and Gigerenzer 2007). However, not surprisingly for a task that was already much studied before any evolutionary theorizing about it, the evolutionary psychologists' view that performance on the Wason task reflects adaptations for social transactions is not universally accepted (cf. J. Evans 2002). Nonetheless, like social versus nonsocial transitive inference in the scrub jay, it shows how one might test the idea that similarly structured problems with different content tap qualitatively different cognitive processes.

12.3   Intentionality and social understanding

12.3.1   Levels of intentionality

"I'll pick up the children from school today," says Max as he leaves for work. We'd normally say that Max's statement conveys an intention. We can predict that he will drive from his office to the school by a certain route at a certain time and that he will change his behavior if the circumstances change. If he is working away from the office, he'll travel by a different route and start out at a different time; if the road is blocked, he'll make a detour; if the car breaks down, he'll walk or take a taxi. That is to say, his behavior will be flexible, directed by the goal of being at the school on time.

A philosopher might say that Max exhibits *intentionality*, but she would not mean that Max has intentions in the everyday, folk-psychological, sense. Intention in the philosophical sense is the property of *aboutness* (Dennett 1987; Allen 1995; Dennett 1996). Intentionality, being about things, is perhaps the defining property of mental states. Beliefs and desires, plans, understandings, and wishes, as well as intentions, are examples of *intentional states*. A belief, for instance, has to be a belief about something. A distinguishing feature of intentional statements is that they do not obey the usual logical rules of substitutability. For instance, Max is Susie's father, and Max is a man born in 1950. It follows logically that Susie's father is a man born in 1950. However, Susie can believe that Max is her father without necessarily believing that a man born in 1950 is her father. If we ask whether nonhumans have intentions, beliefs, desires, or the like we are asking whether they are *intentional systems*. Asking this question means formulating clear criteria for what an animal with a certain sort of intentional state does, just as in the tests of belief, desire, and planning discussed in Chapter 11.

Philosophers distinguish a hierarchy of orders of intentionality (Dennett 1983). In terms of this hierarchy, an animal that does not have beliefs, desires, and the like, that is, one that does not in fact have intentional states, is exhibiting zero-order intentionality. Systems of responses to stimuli have zero-order intentionality. A creature that has beliefs, desires, and the like about the real or imagined physical world or the behavior of others is a first-order intentional system. When its mental states concern the mental states of others, we have graduated to second-order intentionality. Thus if Max *plans* to arrive at the school on time, he has first-order intentionality. If he *believes* that the children *know* he is coming for them today, he is exhibiting second-order intentionality. If he *wants* them to *believe* that he *expects* them to be waiting for him, then he is exhibiting third-order intentionality. Level can be piled on level endlessly in this way, but in dealing with animal behavior, it is enough (usually more than enough) to wonder whether one individual is capable of having beliefs or desires regarding another's beliefs and desires (i.e., second-order intentionality), regarding only others' behavior or physical states of the world (first-order intentionality), or neither of those (zero-order intentionality).

In predicting what Max will do when circumstances or his own beliefs and goals change, we are taking *the intentional stance* (Dennett 1983, 1987). That is, we are using the assumption that he is an intentional being to predict and explain his behavior. Most of the time the intentional stance accounts very well for the behavior of other adult human beings. It often provides useful rough and ready predictions of other species' behavior too, but experiments are needed to test them. In Chapter 11 we saw evidence for a first-order intentional account of rats' bar pressing: a hungry rat presses a bar because it both knows pressing leads to food and wants the food. In the arena of social cognition, folk psychology often suggests that animals have second-order intentionality, that is, knowledge or belief about what other individuals know, believe, desire, or intend, but, as illustrated in Box 12.1, a careful ethological analysis may provide a full account of the behavior involved without invoking any form of social cognition as such.

Box 12.1 Intentional Plovers?

When a fox or other predator approaches a nesting piping plover, she doesn't stay and defend her nest but scuttles off, peeping loudly and dragging one wing on the ground as if injured (Figure B12.1). If the fox follows, the bird keeps displaying till she is some way from the nest, upon which she suddenly takes to the air and flies back to her eggs while the fox continues on its way. The broken-wing display thus functions to deceive the fox, but did the plover intend to lead the fox away by pretending to be injured? Or can her behavior be adequately characterized as a system of complex and flexible responses to stimuli typical of predators?

An ethological causal analysis of the broken-wing display would focus on what constitutes "predator" stimuli and the influence of their distance and direction from the nest, the bird's hormonal state, the presence of eggs, and the like. In principle wants, plans, beliefs, or intentions can be causes of behavior, but they were not recognized in classical ethology. Donald Griffin's (e.g., 1978) proposal for a cognitive ethology (see Chapter 1) was a proposal to make room for such causes. As discussed in the main text, one hallmark of intention is that it generates flexible behavior for achieving a goal. Accordingly, one of the

Figure B12.1. Distraction display of a piping plover. From a photograph by Carolyn Ristau.

first studies inspired by Griffin's proposals sought evidence that nesting plovers show flexible behavior toward human intruders consistent with an intention to lead the intruder away (Ristau 1991b). In 87% of staged encounters in which a person approached the nest, the plover did move in a direction that would not take a follower closer to the nest. A "dangerous" intruder also evoked more display than a "nonthreatening" one. If the plover wants to lead the intruder away, it should monitor the intruder's behavior, for instance starting to display when the intruder is facing it. The plover might also be expected to stop when the intruder stops, and perhaps intensify its display or even approach the intruder as if to attract his attention. These predictions also tended to be borne out.

   Perhaps because we experience ourselves as acting with specific goals in mind, the control of goal-achieving behavior is the subject of many controversies in animal behavior. But a system can be organized to achieve a given goal without any representation of the goal as such (McFarland 1995; A. Clark 1997). For example, wood lice are found in dark damp places, but they get there because wood lice that are dry and/or in the light move about randomly whereas once they are damp and in the dark they move relatively little (Fraenkel and Gunn 1961). This kind of information implies that we need to ask, what is the nonintentional, classical ethological, alternative to an intentional account of the broken-wing display? As we have seen elsewhere in the book, behavior conditional on combinations of external and internal stimuli can be very flexible. Here it is clearly not the case that the sight of an intruder simply releases a broken wing display in which the bird mindlessly moves in a random direction. The sign stimulus releasing the display seems to include the eyes (Box 12.2) and learned signal value of the intruder. Moreover, the direction in which the bird moves is directed in a sophisticated way by the positions of the bird, the intruder, and the nest, not inconsistent with evidence (Chapter 8) that animals implicitly compute distances and directions and add vectors to locate themselves relative to multiple things in the environment. Clearly an explicit model is needed, a set of if-then statements incorporating assumptions about the stimuli that release and direct the display (Hauser 1996). Taking an approach increasingly practical for testing ideas about behavioral mechanisms and even social cognition (Webb 2000; Dautenhahn 2007) a robot operating according to these rules could be constructed and tested to see if it behaves indistinguishably from a plover. Evidence that it does would imply that the behavior so modeled does not require first-order intentionality, let alone a second-order representation of the predator's knowledge about the nest or its belief in the plover's broken wing.

An example closer to those analyzed later in this chapter is the situation depicted in Figure 12.7: a subordinate male baboon moves behind a rock to solicit sexual contact with a female while out of a dominant male's sight, as if aware that the dominant will not know what he's doing there. The numerous cases of such deceptive behavior in primates described by field workers have been taken as evidence of "Machiavellian intelligence" (Whiten and Byrne 1988). But how can we tell whether the subordinate male's behavior is based on a belief about what the dominant sees or knows? Many animals are sensitive to the direction of other animals' gaze (Box 12.2), as if possessing a low-level perceptual module that detects what other animals are looking at (not the same as the mentalistic "what they are *seeing*"). Our subordinate baboon may well be going behind the rock because he has learned that he escapes punishment for approaching certain females if he is out of the dominant's line of sight; that is, his behavior can be explained as a response to observable cues such as where the dominant is facing. First order intentionality is likely involved: the subordinate *wants* to groom the female undisturbed. But because anything the subordinate might do in response to the dominant's seeing or knowing is inevitably a response to his looking or other behavior, second-order intentionality—the subordinate knows *what the dominant sees* or wants *the dominant to believe* he is just sitting doing nothing—is difficult or impossible to prove. Indeed, as discussed in Section 12.4, Povinelli and his colleagues (Povinelli and Vonk 2004; Penn and Povinelli 2007b) have argued at length that no existing data can distinguish between inference about unobservable

Figure 12.7. Cartoon of the representations implied by imputing intentional deception to a subordinate baboon that conceals its activities from a dominant. Here second order intentionality is depicted: the subordinate, on the right, wants the dominant to believe that there is no other baboon behind the rock. After Byrne (1995) with permission.

mental states of others and inference based on their behavior, facial expressions, and so forth. Although, this argument does not deny second-order intentionality to animals so much as assert the extraordinary difficulty of proving it, the same group (see Chapter 15; Penn, Holyoak, and Povinelli 2008) now claim that no animals possess the requisite representational abilities for theory of mind. In any case, saying that animals respond to each other on the basis of behavioral cues rather than mental states inferred from those cues need not imply that animals treat animate beings as they treat physical objects. Indeed, as we see next, certain kinds of motion trigger perception of animacy and intentionality in human babies, and other primates may also possess such a social perceptual module.

12.3.2   Perceiving animacy and intentionality

Infants' and toddlers' implicit knowledge of physical causality has been tested by showing them a cartoon in which, say, a red ball moves in from the left and collides with a stationary green ball and comparing their looking times to physically impossible versus possible sequels to this event. A possible sequel might be Red stopping and Green moving away to the right, as if Red transferred its momentum to Green. A physically impossible sequel might be Red starting back toward the left with Green close behind it. Even very young infants display considerable implicit knowledge of physical causality in such looking time tests (Spelke and Kinzler 2007). More to the present point, the physically impossible sequence just described would be characterized by adults as a social interaction, Green chases Red (Heider and Simmel 1944). Young children, too, attribute intentional states to very simple inanimate objects moving in certain ways (Scholl and Tremoulet 2000).

Animate objects—most importantly conspecifics, predators, and animal prey—differ from inanimate ones in that they are self-propelled, they can be influenced from a distance without physical contact, and they have goals and intentions. Even infants have expectations specific to self-propelled objects (Scholl and Tremoulet 2000), and this has been taken as evidence for a low-level social module triggered by perception of certain kinds of motion (Gigerenzer 1997). Stimuli for one test of this notion are shown in Figure 12.8. Infants watched a small circle "jump over a barrier" and

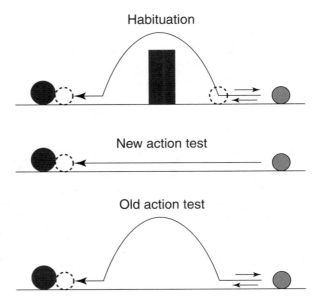

Figure 12.8. Stimuli used to test perception of intentionality in human infants and young chimpanzees. In the habituation phase the small ball moves back and forth briefly then jumps over the barrier. In the test he subject sees one of the lower displays. After Gergely et al. (1995) with permission.

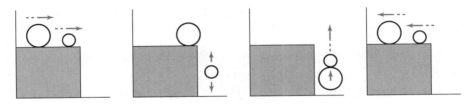

Figure 12.9. Example of a cartoon sequence that would be perceived as depicting intentional, as opposed to purely physical, interactions.

approach a large one. After habituating to this display, they saw one of two test displays in which the barrier no longer separated the two circles. In the old action condition, the small circle still jumped, whereas in the new action condition, it approached the large circle in a straight line. The infants looked longer at the old action than at the new one, but if they had been habituated to the ball jumping without a barrier, this pattern of data was reversed. In effect, they behaved as if representing the moving ball as a rational being approaching a goal and expecting it to take the shortest path available. In one of the few attempts to test for the same kind of encoding in another species, Uller (2004) found similar results in four young chimpanzees.

Not only does self-propelled motion of a lone object trigger a perception of animacy and goal-directedness, displays with more than one such object trigger perception of social interactions (Heider and Simmel 1944; Scholl and Tremoulet 2000; Barrett et al. 2005). Materials from one study with children are sketched in Figure 12.9 (Dasser, Ulbaek, and Premack 1989). In an experimental sequence, the big ball and the small one entered the screen together, the smaller one "fell down the cliff" and bounced around frantically, the big one descended and "helped it up," and they left the screen together. A control sequence consisted of this series of events in reverse order. Children of about three years old looked longer at the experimental than at the control sequence. Furthermore, when the roles of the balls were reversed, children previously shown the experimental sequence looked longer than those previously shown control sequences. Even preverbal infants seem to discriminate between simple shapes (with eyes) that "help" as in the sequence just described, or "hinder." They prefer a "helper" (Hamlin, Wynn, and Bloom 2007).

No tests of primates with similar simplified social stimuli appear to have been reported, but some with pigeons have. Reasoning that interactions between predators and prey should be salient to a vulnerable animal like a pigeon, Goto, Lea, and Dittrich (2002) trained pigeons on a food-rewarded discrimination between displays with four dots moving around at random and displays in which one dot slowly approached one of three others, a display that to people evokes a predator stalking prey. Even after more than 2000 trials, the birds averaged less than 65% correct, suggesting that if pigeons do discriminate intentional from random movement, it is not a salient feature of these displays.

When it comes to perception of intentionality, human gestures have a special status for human babies as young as five or six months (Woodward 1998). In the elegant study of looking times depicted in Figure 12.10, babies saw two toys, here a teddy bear and a ball. The babies were habituated to a hand reaching in from the side and grasping a particular toy. On the test trial the positions of the objects were switched, and the hand reached in again. Now it either grasped the same toy as before, which required a new action, or it performed the old action and grasped the other toy. Babies looked more at the "new object, old action" event, as if they had encoded the

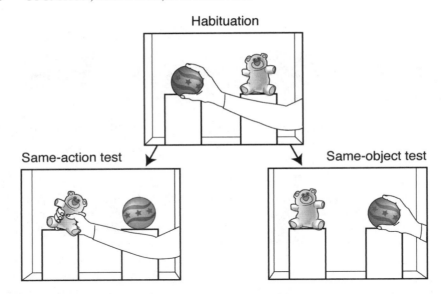

Figure 12.10. Habituation and test events in Woodward's (1998) study of whether infants encode the intentionality of human actions. Redrawn with permission.

action in terms of its goal (grasping a particular toy) and were more surprised to see the goal change than to see a new action performed. This effect did not occur when the hand was replaced by a sponge on a stick or a mechanical claw, suggesting that it is specific to human actions.

In an attempt to see if nonhuman primates behave similarly, a person touched one of two containers or performed an "unintentional" action such as letting their hand flop against it (J. Wood et al. 2007). The animals (cotton-top tamarins, rhesus macaques, and chimpanzees) were then tested to see whether they would look for food in the container that had been touched. Aside from the fact that it is not clear why they would be expected to prefer that container anyway, preferences for the one touched "intentionally" could have been based on past experience seeing people use similar actions to put food into containers (indeed the tamarins tested had been trained extensively to use the intentional action as a cue). In any case, the fact that some animals can apparently predict the outcomes of interactions from a partner's body language and show signs of frustration when the predicted outcome fails to occur does not mean they "understand intentions" in a mentalistic way. The same obviously goes for the infants in similar studies.

In summary, the evidence sketched here shows that animate, potentially socially relevant, objects are discriminated from inanimate ones at a very basic level even by very young infants. The tendency to treat self-propelled objects as goal-directed, a "teleological stance" (Gergely and Csibra 2003), may contribute to the later development of a mentalistic understanding of others' goals and desires but is distinct from it and could be shared with other species. In any case, knowing an individual's goals is distinct from understanding their knowledge or beliefs and from understanding that they have a mental representation of the goal (Perner and Ruffman 2005), but here too, direct perception of simple cues has a role. Individuals of many species acquire knowledge visually, by directing their gaze at things. Accordingly, as shown by a large body of comparative research summarized in Box 12.2,

Box 12.2 Responding to Gaze: Sign Stimulus or Theory of Mind?

The orientation of its head and eyes indicates what visual information an animal is taking in. Accordingly, the eyes of conspecifics or predators can be powerful signals (Coss and Goldthwaite 1995; Emery 2000). For instance, subordinate European jays are more intimidated by a binocular than a monocular glance from a dominant, consistent with the fact that binocular looking is more likely to be followed by attacking (Bossema and Burgler 1980). When rhesus macaque subjects see a video of another rhesus seated between two identical objects looking toward one of them, they appear to attend to the same object (Emery et al. 1997). Sensitivity to a predator's gaze is illustrated by a study in which Hampton (1994) startled captive house sparrows by raising a mask (a model predator) with eyes in different positions or orientations. The birds showed the strongest flight response to a mask with two eyes facing them (Figure B12.2a). The observations described in Box 12.1 suggest that plovers are also sensitive to stimuli correlated with the direction of a potential predator's gaze (see also Watve et al. 2002).

Of greatest interest in this area is *social gaze*, responding to the gaze of conspecifics. Studies described in the main text illustrate how knowing where another individual is looking can be key to success in competitive interactions. In cooperative interactions, too, something worthwhile may usually be learned by following another's gaze. Forward-facing eyes and, in some species, prominent facial markings may make gaze direction a particularly salient social stimulus for diurnal primates (Emery 2000). However, not all species have such conspicuous "whites" of the eyes (sclera) as humans. Thus it is not surprising chimpanzees and some other primates respond primarily to the orientation of the head and/or whole body, even when for practical reasons of experimental control, humans are giving the gaze cues (Emery 2000).

Looking in the same direction as someone else may be an automatic, reflexive, response, rather than evidence of understanding the looker is looking *at* something, that is, of the referential nature of gaze, but the fact that animals also perform effortful responses to get a look at what another individual seems to be gazing at suggests that more is involved. For instance, when chimpanzees are confronted with an experimenter looking at a spot on the wall behind them, they turn around to

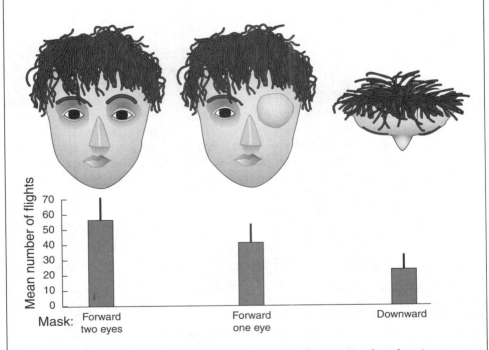

Figure B12.2a. Effect of a simulated predator's direction of gaze (or number of eyes) on escape reactions by captive house sparrows measured as number of flights within an aviary (Hampton 1994). From a photograph by Robert Hampton.

look at it (Figure B12.2b). When confronted with someone looking at a location they cannot see directly, they peer around a partition to get a view of it (Povinelli and Eddy 1996b; Call and Tomasello 2008). Other great apes do the same (Bräuer, Call, and Tomasello 2005). In addition, chimpanzees "check back," that is, alternate looking at the experimenter and the target of his gaze, when they do not see something interesting (reviews in Call and Tomasello 2008; Emery and Clayton 2009). This behavior is also seen in bonobos but to a lesser extent in gorillas and orangutans, consistent with it being an evolutionary precursor of human *shared attention* in which two individuals attend to and communicate about the same thing (Okamoto-Barth, Call, and Tomasello 2007).

Like other behaviors consistent with theory of mind (see main text), some of these more elaborate gaze-following responses are increasingly being documented in birds (Emery 2006) and nonprimate mammals, although they have not yet been analyzed in the same depth (see Okamoto-Barth, Call, and Tomasello 2007). For instance, ravens follow a person's gaze around barriers (Bugnyar, Stöwe, and Heinrich 2004), and goats turn to look in the same direction as another goat (Kaminski et al. 2005). In apes, these behaviors have been taken to support suggestions that the animals "understand seeing," that is, that they have a simple component of theory of mind (Call and Tomasello 2008). This further mentalistic interpretation seems no more demanded here than in the related cases discussed in the main text. Nevertheless, the best answer to the question posed by the heading to this Box is probably "something in between" (Penn and Povinelli in press) in that many animals behave as if knowing that looking normally has a target in ways that seem to go beyond reflexive responses to sign stimuli. Gaze-following is clearly a component of theory of mind, but one precursor to it rather than evidence for it.

Figure B12.2b. A chimpanzee following a person's gaze to the back corner of the cage. The drawing depicts the final stage of a test in which the experimenter begins by facing the chimpanzee and then abruptly switches her gaze. After a photograph in Povinelli (2000) with permission.

animals from birds to apes respond strongly to the direction of another's gaze. Encoding and remembering where others are looking is another basic component of social intelligence that contributes to behavior taken as evidence for theory of mind.

12. 4   Theory of mind

12.4.1   What is theory of mind?

Research on theory of mind stems from a single innovative article (Premack and Woodruff 1978) that inspired a veritable industry of research in developmental and comparative psychology (Carruthers and Smith 1996; Povinelli and Eddy 1996a; Heyes 1998; Wellman, Cross, and Watson 2001; Penn and Povinelli 2007b). As introduced by Premack and Woodruff (1978), having a theory of mind means imputing mental states to others. Theory of mind is evident in intentional deception, using others to gain information by imputing goals, knowledge or belief to them, switching roles, and communicating with intent to inform, among other ways. In the classification of intentional states, theory of mind implies second-order intentionality.

Premack and Woodruff (1978) described a series of tests of whether the chimpanzee Sarah imputed intentions to humans. Sarah, a very special animal with more than 10 years' experience in laboratory tests of cognition, watched short videos in which an actor was thwarted in accomplishing a goal like reaching a banana outside a cage, plugging in a heater, or washing a floor with a hose. The video was stopped and Sarah was allowed to choose between two photographs, one showing the actor about to reach the goal and one not. For instance, the actor might be picking up a long stick to reach the banana or a short one, connecting an intact or a broken hose to a tap. More often than not, Sarah chose the picture showing the action and/or object appropriate to the goal, as if she imputed desires and beliefs to the actor. The fact that she did this in a variety of physically different situations is consistent with behavior arising from a theory of mind. But because she had extensive experience watching people do everyday tasks, she may have been simply choosing the picture that completed a familiar sequence.

Premack and Woodruff sketched several other methods for testing whether a creature's theory of mind extends to imputing knowledge and ignorance to others, but researchers in child development reported the first relevant data (Wimmer and Perner 1983) using what is still (Newton and de Villiers 2007; Penn and Povinelli 2007b) regarded as the acid test of theory of mind, the *false belief test*. Importantly, to pass the false belief test the child must understand that others' beliefs can differ from their own and from the true state of the world. For example, a young child is introduced to a puppet or a person, say a puppet clown. The child and the clown watch as the experimenter hides treat or a toy (Figure 12.11). ("Where is the

Figure 12.11. A false belief test for three- or four-year-old children.

teddy? . . . In the green box.") Then the clown leaves the scene and the child alone sees the experimenter move the object. ("Now where is the teddy? . . . In the purple box.") Then the clown returns and the child is asked, "Where will he look for the teddy?" Surprisingly, until they are about four years old children predict the ignorant stooge will look where they themselves know the object is ("He will look in the purple box"). They do not seem able to separate their own representation of the situation from another's, or at least they are unable to inhibit the tendency to report on their own knowledge. This finding appears in a variety of situations, and has stimulated much research and theorizing about the young child's theory of mind and how it develops (Wellman, Cross, and Watson 2001; Perner and Ruffman 2005).

12.4.2   Do chimpanzees have theory of mind?

Object choice tasks

One way to test whether, like four-year-olds, nonverbal animals appreciate that seeing leads to knowing is to give them the choice of using information provided by two informants, one of whom has been observed getting access to that information while the other has not (Premack 1988). Thus the subject chooses between two objects as in the false belief task, but the demands of this *object choice task* are simpler because there is no need to keep in mind both one's own and another's beliefs or inhibit reporting on the true state of the world. Povinelli and his colleagues pioneered use of object choice tasks with chimpanzees in an influential series of studies. In the initial experiment (Povinelli, Nelson, and Boysen 1990), there were four food containers, each with a handle that the animal could pull to get the food. As a trial began, the containers were behind a screen, and the animal watched as one experimenter baited a single container in view of a confederate (the Knower), while a second confederate (the Guesser) was out of the room. Then the Guesser returned, and Knower and Guesser each pointed to a container as the chimpanzee was allowed to make a choice. A creature whose theory of mind encompasses the understanding that seeing conveys knowledge would obviously choose the container indicated by the Knower, and in fact, all four chimpanzees tested chose correctly some of the time. However, because the experiment went on for 300 trials, the animals had plenty of opportunity to learn a conditional discrimination: choose the person who was in the room when the container was baited. Consistent with this interpretation, choices of the Knower increased across trials. The study therefore concluded with a novel transfer test in which both Knower and Guesser were in the room when the container was baited, but the Guesser had a paper bag over his head. Over all 30 trials of this test, three of the chimpanzees still chose the Knower. However, they chose randomly on the first two such trials (Povinelli 1994), a result more consistent with the conclusion that they quickly learned to choose the person who had not worn a bag than with knowledge attribution. Importantly, object choice does seem to be a good test of theory of mind development in children: in a similar procedure more four-year-olds than three-year-olds consistently chose the Knower (Povinelli and deBlois 1992).

These negative findings were only the beginning of the quest for theory of mindlike abilities in chimpanzees. The next stage was to simplify the Knower/Guesser paradigm into a more direct test of knowledge attribution that did not require remembering where different individuals were looking. In this test, animals need only appreciate that gazing at something (Box 12.2) means seeing it, that is, having some knowledge about the thing being looked at. This approach was taken by Povinelli and

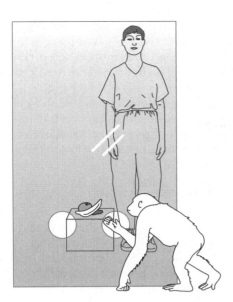 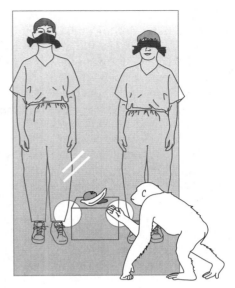

Figure 12.12. Example of Povinelli and Eddy's object choice tests for chimpanzees. Left: control condition. The animal is given the food for directing a begging gesture through the hole in front of the experimenter. Right: the animal will receive food for gesturing toward the experimenter that can see him. After photographs in Povinelli and Preuss (1995) with permission.

Eddy (1996a, 1996b, 1996c) with young chimpanzees. The animals were trained to gesture through a hole in a transparent plexiglas wall toward an experimenter holding food on the other side (Figure 12.12). The wall had two holes, with the experimenter positioned in front of one. The animal received the treat only for reaching through the hole closer to the experimenter. To be sure the animals were attending to what was being offered, occasional probe trials were administered in which one experimenter sat near each hole, one holding a block of wood and the other, a food treat. Both experimenters looked straight ahead, at the plexiglas wall, not attempting to meet the chimpanzee's gaze. Once the animals discriminated very reliably between the two experimenters on probe trials, Povinelli and Eddy started a series of tests in which both experimenters held out food but one could clearly see the chimpanzee as before, whereas the other could not. For instance, the "non-attending" experimenter might be wearing a blindfold, have her hands or a card-board screen over her eyes, or her back to the chimpanzee. Controls for having something unusual on the face included the "attending" experimenter having a blindfold or hands over her mouth or a cardboard screen beside her face. Such tests were intermixed with normal trials and occasional probes with a block of wood versus food. The chimpanzee was always rewarded for begging from the experimenter who could see.

The surprising result of these experiments was that in nearly every type of test the chimpanzees gestured as often to the experimenter who could not see them as to the experimenter who could. This was despite the fact that the animals performed well in the continuing regular trials and probes with the block of wood. The exception to random behavior was that when one experimenter had his back turned, the chimpanzees tended to choose the experimenter who was facing them. Even this did not indicate an understanding of seeing as attention because when both experimenters turned their backs while one looked over her shoulder toward the subject, choice reverted to random. Over trials of all kinds, however, the proportion of choices of the "attending" experimenter gradually crept above 50%, indicating that the chimpanzees were learning, perhaps to choose the person whose eyes were visible.

Povinelli and Eddy concluded that although their subjects were very good at detecting where someone was looking (Box 12.2), chimpanzees do not understand seeing as attention and/or knowledge but can learn to direct behavior selectively to people who are looking at them. Even on the view that experiments like Povinelli and Eddy's cannot in principle establish more than chimpanzees' sensitivity to behavioral cues, their animals' failure to respond more readily, if not spontaneously, to such cues is surprising in the light of the sophisticated social cognition generally attributed to chimpanzees (e.g., by Byrne and Whiten 1988; Whiten and Byrne 1988). Predictably, then, many reasons were found to challenge their conclusion (e.g., Gomez 1996; P. Smith 1996; Tomasello, Call, and Hare 2003). Two questionable aspects of their procedure turn out to be key. First, the animals in Povinelli and Eddy's experiments were confronted with potentially helpful individuals whereas in nature chimpanzees may more often compete than cooperate over food (but see Penn and Povinelli 2007b). Moreover, because the helpful individuals were humans rather than other chimpanzees, the experiments tested the (captive) chimpanzees' theory of the *human* mind, or at least their ability to take behavioral cues from humans. Hare and colleagues tackled both of these issues in a new series of experiments.

Chimpanzees compete for food

In the setup developed by Hare and colleagues (2000) two chimpanzees, one dominant to the other, are in cages on either side of a central area with one or more barriers or containers where food can be placed. In the study depicted in Figure 12.13, two pieces of food are placed in the central cage while the doors to the side cages are closed. One is visible to both animals whereas the other is visible only to the

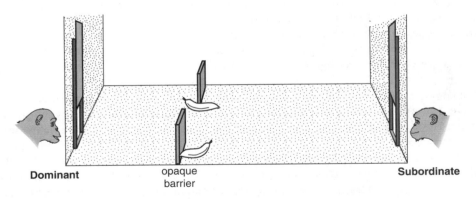

Dominant   opaque   **Subordinate**
                                barrier

Figure 12.13. Test of whether chimpanzees behave as if knowing what another chimpanzee can see in a competition over food. The animals are shown just before being released into the central arena. The subordinate will get a slight head start; the food is closer to the dominant's end to enhance the competition. Adapted from Bräuer, Call, and Tomasello (2007) with permission.

subordinate because the barrier shields it from the dominant's view. When the doors are open, will the subordinate prefer to head toward the piece of food the dominant cannot look at? This question was answered in the affirmative for several variants of the situation in Figure 12.13 (Hare et al. 2000). The same was not true of capuchin monkeys in a similar test (Hare et al. 2003; see also Burkart and Heschl 2007). With the chimpanzees, various controls ruled out possibilities such as the subordinate preferring to eat near a barrier. However, these effects are not evident in all measures of the subjects' behavior and depend on details of the setup that influence the intensity of competition. For example, if the pieces of food are both closer to the dominant or are so close together that one animal can easily reach both, subordinates show no preference (Karin-D'Arcy and Povinelli 2002; Bräuer, Call, and Tomasello 2007).

Not only may chimpanzees respond as if knowing what another can see in a competitive situation, they may remember what others have looked at, leading them to behave as if knowing what others know (Hare, Call, and Tomasello 2001). Food was hidden in a setup like that depicted in Figure 12.13 while the subordinate animal watched. The critical variable was whether the dominant was also watching, that is, whether it could know where the food was and thus be a strong competitor when both animals were released. Subordinates were more likely to obtain the food when the dominant had not seen it hidden. Moreover, subordinates discriminated between a dominant present during the baiting and one that had not seen it, getting the hidden food more often in the latter case as if knowing what a particular animal knew. They did not, however, discriminate in a more demanding situation that required remembering which of two pieces of food the competitor had seen being hidden.

Chimpanzees' sensitivity to others' behavior in these tests may indeed be favored by the situation being one of competition rather than by the fact that it involves conspecifics instead of humans. This conclusion is supported by the finding (Hare and Tomasello 2004) that subject chimpanzees were somewhat more successful in choosing the correct container in a simple object choice task when a human or a chimpanzee "informant" behaved in a competitive rather than in a cooperative manner toward them. Because some of the reaching and pointing cues used by the humans were similar in the two contexts, these findings suggest that competition enhances either the salience of such cues or chimpanzees' motivation to attend to or use them. Notice that this says nothing about theory of mind but a great deal about predispositions to respond to and/or remember certain kinds of behavioral cues. The importance of such predispositions is underlined by the success of dogs in similar tasks.

Dogs take cues from humans

Pet dogs are very good at locating hidden food when a person points to it or gazes toward it (reviews in Hare and Tomasello 2005; Miklosi 2007; Udell and Wynne 2008; Reid 2009). Indeed, they perform substantially better with a variety of human communicative cues than do apes tested in a comparable way. For example, in one study (Bräuer et al. 2006) dogs chose the container a person pointed to in 90% of trials whereas chimpanzees and bonobos chose it only 60% of the time. Several explanations have been proposed for dogs' skill in such tasks: canids versus primates, domesticated versus nondomesticated species, more versus less experience with human cues (Reid 2009). One prominent early study (Hare et al. 2002) indicated that domestication was key. Puppies from a kennel immediately responded to gazing, pointing and the like, but captive wolves with extensive exposure to humans did not. However, when the testing conditions are more rigorously equated across groups, wolves with exposure to people can outperform pet dogs, and stray dogs from shelters perform very poorly (Udell, Dorey, and Wynne 2008). These findings implicate pet dogs' extensive experience with people, especially with their hands as sources of food (Wynne, Udell, and Lord 2008; Reid 2009). But this does not mean the genetic changes accompanying domestication are unimportant. Domestication of dogs may have involved increasing their usefulness to people by selecting for responsiveness to cues from humans. Alternatively, highest reproductive success may have gone to the animals least fearful and aggressive toward humans, with responsiveness to human behavioral cues as a byproduct. Evidence for this hypothesis comes from the finding that foxes selected for 45 generations for low fear and aggression toward people, but not control foxes, behave like dogs in an object choice task with human cues (Hare and Tomasello 2005). Most likely both domestication and experience are important: selection for attentiveness to human actions may have led to a propensity for rapid early learning about human cues (Reid 2009). Clearly more extensive studies are needed of how dogs' and other canids' responsiveness to humans develops from a very early age. In the meanwhile, the discussion has strayed away from theory of mind into analysis of how animals respond to cues from people. One way back toward theory of mind is to look at natural situations in which animals behave as if knowing what their conspecifics see or know.

12.4.3   Food storing birds remember who was watching

Some socially living food-storing birds are able to remember where they saw their companions caching food (Section 7.4.2). To protect its caches from thieves, a storer in such a group should attend to whether others can see it while it is caching and have strategies for reducing the chances that observers later pilfer its caches. A number of food storing species use such strategies (Dally, Clayton, and Emery 2006; Pravosudov 2008). The cognitive processes involved have begun to be analyzed in two of them, ravens and Western scrub jays. The examples summarized here (for others see Clayton, Dally, and Emery 2007) show that food-storing corvids are very good at detecting and remembering what others have watched. As a result they can equal chimpanzees in behavior consistent with theory of mind.

Figure 12.14 depicts the setup for an experiment in which a captive raven cached meat in a large aviary while two flockmates, both subordinate to it, were in separate cages at the side (Bugnyar and Heinrich 2005). One could see the cacher and thus could potentially pilfer the caches, whereas the other's cage was enclosed by curtains. Five minutes after the caching trial the cacher was returned to the aviary either alone or with the observer or nonobserver. As would be predicted if the cacher remembered which bird observed the caching and treated it as a potential pilferer, subjects retrieved more of their caches in an observer's presence than when alone or with a nonobserver. This effect was evident primarily when the second bird was close to caches. That is, subjects were quick to retrieve caches that a knowledgeable competitor was approaching but, if anything, in the presence of an ignorant competitor they selectively retrieved caches at a distance from the second bird. Observers tested alone did in fact know where the caches were and nonobservers did not, as evidenced by differences in their latencies to pilfer the caches. Latencies of observers and nonobservers did not differ significantly in trials when the cacher was present, mainly because the observer was slower to approach the caches in those conditions. Thus cachers may not have been able to detect observers on the basis of their approach behavior but rather needed to remember that they had been watching. Nonetheless,

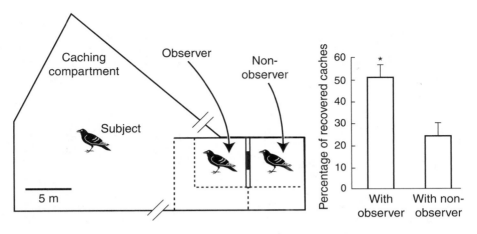

Figure 12.14. Setup for test of whether ravens remember who was watching as they cached. Dotted lines represent transparent barriers. During caching by the subject, the observer and nonobserver were as shown. Data show what happened (as proportion of caches recovered) when the subject was returned to the caching compartment along with the observer or the non observer. After Bugnyar and Heinrich (2005) with permission.

the raven subjects themselves might have been detecting behavioral cues from potential pilferers that were not obvious to people. The same reservation applies to the second experiment in this study, in which the focus was on whether potential pilferers remembered which other ravens had observed caches being made and thus might compete to pilfer them.

In any test of any animal's ability to discriminate between a "knower" and a "guesser," if the roles of knower and guesser are played by animals that do genuinely differ in their knowledge, it is difficult to rule out the possibility that subjects are responding to some subtle differences in those animals' behavior in the test. This problem was tackled by Dally, Emery, and Clayton (2006) in a study with scrub jays that, like Bugnyar and Heinrich's (2005) study with ravens, tested birds' memory for who had witnessed a particular episode of food caching. Here, the birds cached in distinctively marked trays in their home cage. Observers in an adjoining cage never actually competed to retrieve caches but simply watched (or not) at retrieval. The primary measure of whether they were treated as potential competitors was the number of items subjects moved to new locations during retrieval. This recaching behavior is thought to reduce pilfering by observers by overloading or interfering with memory (DallyClayton & Emery, 2006). An earlier study (Emery and Clayton 2001) indicated that scrub jays need experience pilfering the caches of others to show this response to potential pilferers of their own caches, as if projecting their own experience onto others. However, because only small amounts of recaching were shown in this study, and the birds all had extensive past experience in other studies, this provocative finding needs replicating with naive birds pretested for recaching and then assigned randomly to pilfering or control experience.

To return to the study of Dally, Emery, and Clayton (2006), here jays recovering items in private recached more of them when caching had been observed by a dominant bird than by its partner, by a subordinate, or no bird at all. Because these differences occurred in constant conditions, with the subject alone, they are

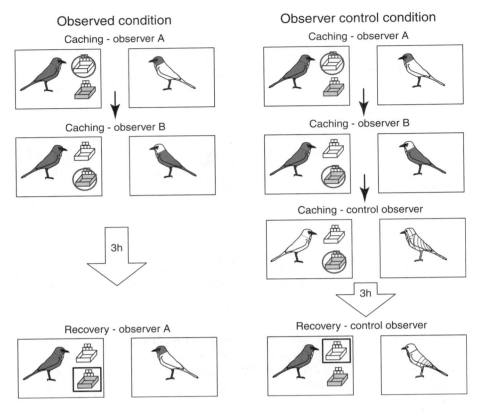

Figure 12.15. The procedure for the experiment with scrub jays by Dally, Clayton, and Emery (2006). Circles around caching trays indicate Plexiglas covers, forcing the subject to cache in just one tray. Square surrounding a tray in the recovery phase indicates the tray in which caching has been observed by the observer present for that test. After Clayton, Dally, and Emery (2007) with permission.

consistent with memory for the type of bird present during caching. To test whether that memory was for a specific individual, in a further experiment jays cached in two different trays, each watched by a different observer, one of which was present while the subject could retrieve from both trays (Figure 12.15). Subjects recached significantly more items from the tray that bird had observed than from the tray observed by a different bird. Of course an observer may have looked in some special way at the tray that it knew had been cached in or otherwise behaved differently toward it than toward the second tray. However, when subjects were watched at recovery by a bird that had seen a *different* subject cache in one of the same trays, recaching was at a low level and did not differ between the trays. These findings indicate that in addition to remembering what, where, and how long ago they cached (Chapter 7), scrub jays remember who was present when they cached in particular places and behave as if aware of other individuals' knowledge. Of course the cacher's behavior could instead have reflected different behaviors by the control and the actual observers, but this difference in itself would mean that scrub jays (in this case observers) know who cached where. In any case, it appears that scrub jays, like ravens and probably other corvids (see Clayton, Dally, and Emery 2007), have detailed social knowledge that they deploy in defending their caches from potential pilferers.

12.4.4   Behavioral abstractions or theory of mind?

The fundamental question about animal theory of mind is whether animals reason about others' mental states or respond to their behavior alone. As Premack and Woodruff (1978) put it, "Is the chimpanzee a behaviorist or a mentalist?" But because inferences about mental states are based on current or remembered behavior it is impossible to be only a mentalist. As we have seen, no existing data demand explanation in terms of theory of mind, but neither do they conclusively rule it out (see also Cheney and Seyfarth 2007; Penn and Povinelli 2007b; Emery and Clayton 2009). Is it even possible in principle to decide whether or not any nonverbal creature has a theory of mind? We look here at three proposed answers to this question, starting with a fresh look at what having a theory of mind entails.

Theory of mind as an intervening variable

We—and perhaps monkeys too—infer that Monkey B wants bananas not only because he looks avidly at Monkey A's banana, but also because he eats bananas whenever possible, he climbs tall trees to get bananas, and so on. The situation parallels that facing motivation theorists deciding, for example, when to describe a rat as thirsty as opposed to merely drinking in response to external stimuli (Whiten 1996). In the traditional language of experimental psychology, a theory of mind or a motivational state is an intervening variable (Sober 1998). The animal as psychologist and the human as animal psychologist have the same problem (Whiten 1994). It becomes defensible to infer such a variable if behavior can be described more economically and predicted more effectively by doing so than by not doing so (Figure 12.16). Thus we cannot tell if Monkey A is imputing desire and belief to B if all we observe is A concealing bananas from B. An animal that has a theory of mind

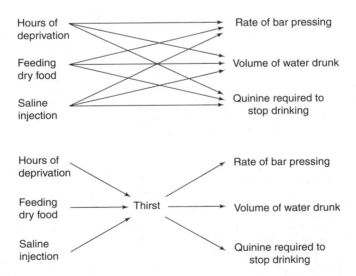

Figure 12.16. *Thirst* as an intervening variable that summarizes efficiently the pairwise relationships between each of three independent variables and three kinds of behavioral observations. If only, say, deprivation and rate of bar pressing had been looked at, the inference of a mediating internal state would complicate rather than simplify matters. Redrawn from N. Miller (1959) with permission.

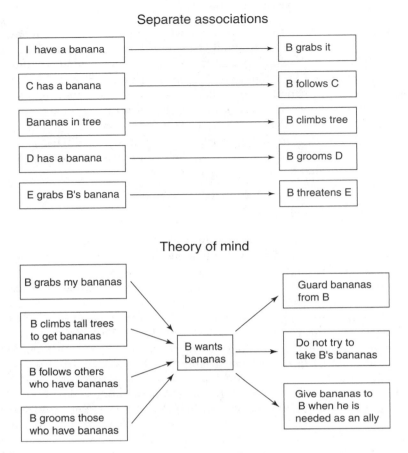

Figure 12.17. Theory of mind as an intervening variable or behavioral abstraction that integrates information in separate associations. After Whiten (1994) with permission.

should act appropriately in a variety of situations, including physically novel ones where simple stimulus generalization from past learning will not work. Such a device would be expected to evolve if it supports fitness-increasing generalization from one social situation to another (Seyfarth and Cheney 1994). For instance, seeing B climb tall trees for bananas and snatch bananas from others gives A no grounds to fear B as a banana thief if she cannot generalize from those physical situations to one in which B is watching when she is eating a banana. Folk psychology assumes that theory of mind mediates this generalization, but the representation in Figure 12.17 is equally consistent with what Povinelli and colleagues (e.g., Povinelli and Vonk 2004) call *behavioral abstraction*. To illustrate this distinction with the false belief test (Figure 12.11), a child who correctly identifies the box where the ignorant stooge will look might explain his answer by saying, "Because that's where he saw it last" (behavioral abstraction) or "Because he thinks it's there" (theory of mind). That is to say, the cognitive structure that connects perception and/or memory of others' behaviors to one's own responses in Figure 12.17 need not be an explicit representation of others' states of mind (Sober 1998; Penn and Povinelli 2007b).

The information in this section so far indicates that through some combination of predispositions for reading and remembering species-specific behaviors and learning like that responsible for mediated generalization (Chapter 6) animals come to categorize behavioral cues together as relevant to given behavior systems or functionally related responses. Just as with physical events, memory for social events engages adaptively relevant behaviors. For example, corvids and chimpanzees treat an individual that gazes at or is remembered as gazing at a desirable piece of food as a competitor or perhaps the owner of the food (Burkart and Heschl 2007). This means that encountering that individual when the food is available to be retrieved engages a species-specific suite of defensive, functionally deceptive, or avoidant behaviors that vary flexibly depending on the spatial setup and the social status of the competitor. Similarly, when the male baboons in Bachmann and Kummer's experiment (Figure 12.2) had seen a particular male and female interacting in a friendly manner, they avoided contact with the couple rather than attempting to gain access to the female.

Inference from self to other

If behavioral abstractions can do the same job as theory of mind in all the tests described so far, maybe a new approach to isolating theory of mind is called for. One such proposed approach rests on a particular interpretation of human theory of mind, namely that it is based on inference—not necessarily explicit—from self to other. Such inference is of the form, "When I look toward something with my eyes open, I see it; when I grab something, I want it; therefore, when others like me do the same things, they must have the same mental states." In a proposed test of chimpanzees based on this notion (Heyes 1998; Penn and Povinelli 2007b), subjects would first be exposed to two distinctively colored visors attached to helmets of some sort. One, for example the red one, would be transparent and the other, for example the blue one, would be opaque. By putting them over its eyes the animal would learn that it can see through the red one but not the blue one. The test phase would resemble Povinelli and Eddy's tests sketched in Figure 12.12 except that people from whom the chimpanzee can beg would be wearing the visors. Choice of the person with the transparent visor would be evidence that the animal imputed its own experience of seeing to another individual.

Informal reports indicate that this has been tried with chimpanzees and they chose randomly (see Penn and Povinelli 2007b), whereas 12- to 18-month-old toddlers behave as if projecting their experience with an opaque or see-through blindfold onto an adult wearing it (Meltzoff 2007). However, not all agree that this would be a powerful test of theory of mind for chimpanzees. The animal need not use the visors' effects on seeing but on its ability to do things while wearing them in order to choose the person who could respond to its request (Andrews 2005; Penn and Povinelli 2007b). Moreover, notwithstanding that "self-recognition" in front of mirrors has been taken as evidence for theory of mind in chimpanzees (Box 12.3), whether the ability to generalize from self to other is predictive of behaviors consistent with theory of mind seems to be an empirical question.

Box 12.3 Monkey in the Mirror

When chimpanzees are exposed to mirrors, at first they treat the reflection like a conspecific, directing threat, greeting, and other social responses to it. Over a few days, social responses wane and self-directed responses emerge. As described by Gallup (1970, 86), who first systematically documented them, these include "grooming parts of the body which would otherwise be visually inaccessible without the mirror, picking bits of food from between the teeth while watching the mirror image, visually guided manipulation of anal-genital areas by means of the mirror," (Figure B12.3). To be sure the animals were referring the reflected image to themselves Gallup devised the *mark test*. The chimps were anesthetized and marked on one eyebrow and the top of the opposite ear with an odorless, non irritating, red dye. After recovering from the anesthesia, the animals showed virtually no behavior directed at the marks until the mirror was reintroduced. Then they touched and rubbed the marks, sometimes looking at their fingers or sniffing them in between touches. Two control chimpanzees that had never seen mirrors did not respond to the marks. In the same study monkeys of various species exposed to mirrors all behaved socially to the mirrors throughout exposure, and none of them touched marks above control levels during the tests. This finding has been repeated many times with a large number of monkey species. Other mammals, birds, and fish also treat mirrors primarily as conspecifics. But among apes, orangutans behave like chimpanzees, the available evidence indicates that bonobos do too, but gorillas do not (reviews in Povinelli and Cant 1995; Tomasello and Call 1997; de Veer and van den Bos 1999; Gallup, Anderson, and Shilito 2002).

How to interpret behavior toward mirrors is controversial. On one view (Gallup 1970; Gallup et al. 2002; Bekoff and Sherman 2004) the chimpanzees' behavior is evidence of self-awareness, and projection of this self-concept onto others underlies theory of mind. Reasons to doubt this interpretation include that—unlike healthy children—not all chimpanzees pass the mark test, the proportion that pass a first test declines with age (Povinelli et al.1993), and self-directed behavior in front of mirrors does not necessarily predict either success in the mark test or "passing" tests of theory of mind. Moreover, theory of mind and behavior toward mirrors are sometimes dissociated in humans; children with autism appear deficient in their understanding of other people's mental states, but their behavior in front of mirrors develops normally (Povinelli 1996).

It is unlikely that nonverbal animals have a fully humanlike sense of self, and critics like Heyes (1994b) have wisely suggested their behavior be called not self-recognition but *mirror-guided body inspection,* a sophisticated kind of visual-kinesthetic matching, self-*perception* rather than self-*conception*. Why the ability to integrate visual, tactile, and proprioceptive input obtained in front of a mirror with the direct visual perception of self would evolve and be confined to great apes and humans is a puzzle. Any animal must use some sense of its own body to move around in the world without bumping into things. Pouncing on prey, leaping from branch to branch, flying through a forest, scratching an itch: all require at least a limited perception of the body's extent. Some birds, for instance, are reluctant to fly through a narrow gap, as if sensing the extent of their wings (Cuthill and Guilford 1990). One suggestion is that locomotion by clambering in early apes required more elaborate representation of the body (Povinelli and Cant 1995). In any case, experience with the mirror must allow the animal to form a visual representation of the parts of its body that it does not normally see, such as its face and ano-genital region, and integrate them with a representation it

Figure B12.3. A chimpanzee engaging in self-exploratory behavior while looking in a mirror. From photographs in Povinelli and Preuss (1995) with permission.

already has based on tactile and proprioceptive feedback. This representation allows detection of a mismatch, as when dye is applied in the mark test, but then the animal must also be motivated to explore the altered parts of its body. It is not always clear whether such motivation is comparable across species in comparative studies in this area (de Veer and van den Bos 1999; Bard et al, 2006).

Nearly 40 years after Gallup's (1970) seminal article, most issues surrounding apes' "self-recognition" in mirrors are unresolved. There are still occasional reports of mirror-directed body inspection in other species (e.g., Plotnik, de Waal, and Reiss 2006; Prior, Schwarz, and Güntürkün 2008). Just as with apes, not all subjects of a given species "pass." With primates, new insights have been contributed by looking at specific elements of mirror-directed behavior in novel ways. Apparently for the first time with any species de Waal and colleagues (2005) directly compared the responses of mirror-naïve animals (capuchin monkeys) to a same-sex stranger in a neighboring cage, a familiar same-sex conspecific, and a mirror. The monkeys immediately showed more positive, friendly, responses and fewer threatening or anxious ones to the mirror than to the stranger. Thus although capuchins do not show mirror self-recognition, for reasons not yet understood the monkey in the mirror is not entirely a stranger either. And in a test of whether learning to use the mirror as a tool would enhance its use in self-grooming, Heschl and Burkhart (2006) trained marmosets to use a mirror to locate things (out-of-sight pieces of food) in the real world. Their skill did not transfer to marks on their heads. Indeed, when the mark was a dab of chocolate cream, rather than touching their own face, most of the animals tried to lick it off the mirror image.

By now, some readers may be inclined to dismiss the vexing question of what animals do in front of mirrors as overblown and misguided. Although animals in the wild may occasionally see their reflections in pools of water, how they behave toward them may not have much adaptive significance. Some intriguing connections have been made between mirror guided body inspection and other aspects of cognition, but it is still not clear that behavior in front of mirrors reflects any fundamental cognitive processes.

Behavioral abstractions

If theory of mind (or behavioral abstraction) allows its possessor economically to encode information and generalize about others' behavior, then any attempt to assess theory of mind must use more than one behavioral test. Moreover, the results of a set of such tests should be statistically nonindependent (Sober 1998). That is, passing one should predict passing others judged to be of similar difficulty. Heyes (1993b) has called this method *triangulation* because it is designed to point to the same conclusion from different metaphorical angles. Just as in any test of a concept (Chapter 6), in triangulation an animal acquires information in one set of conditions and is tested in conditions that are conceptually but not perceptually similar. Penn and Povinelli (2007b) have proposed a new series of false belief tests for chimpanzees based on this logic, using food competition. The proposed setup would be like that in Figure 12.13, but more locations for hiding the food would be available to permit discriminating each of two predicted choices from random behavior. Two locations per trial would be baited, each with a different amount of food. Subordinate subjects are trained to go for the smaller amount in direct competition with a knowledgeable dominant. Then they would experience an elaborate series of tests in which the competitor sees or does not see the food placed and the food is or is not moved or the two food amounts swapped when the competitor is or is not watching. Penn and Povinelli (2007b) suggest that combined results of their proposed tests could distinguish among various possible behavioral rules. Most importantly (see Heyes 2008), some of them would directly contrast predictions from theory of mind with predictions from specific plausible behavioral rules. As Penn and Povinelli acknowledge, however, their proposed protocol is complex and might be difficult to implement for that reason. Whether it ever will be remains to be seen.

Looking in the wrong places?

In the hypothetical tests just discussed, as in those that have actually been done, theory of mind is conceived as a device for predicting the behavior of others. The philosopher Kristin Andrews (2005) has suggested that such tests are "looking in all the wrong places" because humans use theory of mind not to predict others' behavior but to explain it verbally. Indeed, people often do not explicitly reason about others' mental states before acting but react unthinkingly to behavioral cues. This claim is in line with evidence that human theory of mind is closely tied to language, both during development (Perner and Ruffman 2005) and in adults as well. For example, when people watch a cartoon and do an interfering verbal or nonverbal task at the same time, their ability to answer a question about false beliefs of a character in the cartoon is selectively impaired by the verbal task (Newton and de Villiers 2007). This finding is consistent with evidence from tests of implicit memory (Chapter 7) that false beliefs are not tracked automatically, unlike true beliefs/the true state of the world (Apperly et al. 2006).

Andrews (2005) suggests that whether chimpanzees use theory of mind as explanation could be tested nonverbally with a variant of the colored visor experiment. After experience with the distinctive opaque and transparent visors, the chimpanzee would interact with other individuals wearing the visors, but now their color coding is reversed. If, for example, someone with the "transparent" visor behaves as if unable to see, the chimpanzee should find this surprising and perhaps seek an explanation. One acknowledged drawback of this proposal is that it is difficult to specify exactly what animals should do in such a situation and what would count as seeking an explanation. For example, increasing attention or looking are ways of getting information about something unexpected, but they would probably not count as explicit information-seeking.

12.4.5   Conclusions: Misled by folk psychology or denying continuity?

In the absence of evidence that chimpanzees pass a false belief test (see Kaminski, Call, and Tomasello 2008) or any other data agreed to discriminate conclusively between use of behavioral abstractions and reasoning about theory of mind, controversy in this area will surely continue. Are proponents of animal theory of mind being led too far beyond the data by their own folk psychology or are those who conclude that chimpanzees do not reason about mental states denying evolutionary continuity? Morgan's Canon (Chapter 1) is being severely tested here: maybe it's simplest to attribute humanlike theory of mind at least to chimpanzees and other great apes, though it's not clear where this line of reasoning leaves ravens and scrub jays.

One reply to this proposal is that there may be a genuine discontinuity here because human language underlies reasoning about others' states of mind in the first place. But evolutionary continuity is not all or none, especially not when it comes to such a multifaceted ability as theory of mind. Maybe human theory of mind is modular and only some aspects of it are shared by some other species (Lyons and Santos 2006). Indeed, very early on, Premack himself (see Emery and Clayton 2009) suggested three classes or subdivisions of theory of mind: understanding others' attention and perception, their desires and intentions, and their knowledge and beliefs. Much of the research reviewed here seems to have treated animal theory of mind as an all-or-nothing issue, but it is becoming clear that nonhuman species may share some but not all of these separate human competences. For example, the analysis of gaze-following summarized in Box 12.2 shows that many animals follow gaze in subtle ways but without necessarily understanding that the gazer is acquiring knowledge. A prominent suggestion of this kind is that chimpanzees and perhaps some other species understand others' intentions, or "understand others as intentional beings" (Tomasello, Call, and Hare 2003; Tomasello. et al. 2005; Cheney and Seyfarth 2007; Call and Tomasello 2008). However, one can "understand intentions" in the sense of predicting what others are about to do or try to do from behavioral cues such as what they are looking at or moving toward without understanding their underlying mental representations or goals. This latter kind of understanding could be useful in cooperating with others, but the next section—on cooperation—provides no more evidence for it than does this one.

12.5   Cooperation

12.5.1   The evolution of altruism

In behavioral ecology, *altruism* refers to behavior that increases the reproductive success of others at a cost to oneself. When selection can operate between groups, as is increasingly acknowledged (see Box 1.2), cooperative behaviors such as those to be discussed in Section 12.5.3 are expected, but on the view that the main force in evolution is individual selection, altruism is evolutionary puzzle: to be selected, behaviors need to increase the representation of the performer's own genes, not somebody else's. However, with individual selection alone altruism can still evolve under at least three conditions: *kin selection, mutualism,* and *reciprocal altruism* (Trivers 1971). Altruistic behavior directed toward relatives evolves through kin selection as long as those helped bear a large enough proportion of that individual's genes (see Section 5.4). Mutualism refers to cases in which unrelated individuals all concurrently achieve a net benefit from the interaction, as in "you scratch my back while I'm scratching yours." Thus its evolution is similarly unmysterious. When benefits are delayed relative to costs, as in "If you scratch my back now, I'll scratch yours later" or "If you scratch my back now, I'll support you in a fight later," we have reciprocal altruism.

Until relatively recently, kin selection, mutualism, and reciprocal altruism were thought to exhaust the conditions for the evolution of altruism (see West, Griffin, and Gardner 2007). Notice that these are functional terms. Their significance in evolutionary theory must not be confused with their cognitive or emotional implications: altruists need not experience empathy for those helped, nor as we saw in Chapter 5 do those helping kin need to understand relatedness. But each kind of altruism does have specific cognitive (Stevens, Cushman, and Hauser 2005) and emotional (Silk 2007c; de Waal 2008) implications. Kin selection implies discriminative behavior toward kin, which can arise through a variety of recognition mechanisms discussed in Chapter 5. It is easy to imagine that mutualism might be maintained by immediate reinforcement of participants' acts, and this supposition is sometimes correct. Reciprocal altruism has traditionally (e.g., Trivers 1971) been thought to be the most cognitively demanding because reciprocal altruists must recognize each other and remember each other's altruistic acts as if keeping sophisticated mental balance sheets. In addition, interactions of the form "If you scratch my back now I'll support you in a fight later" seem to imply behavior maintained by delayed reinforcement, which as we know from Chapter 11 is not very effective. As these considerations predict, there seem to be few good examples of reciprocal altruism (Stevens, Cushman, and Hauser 2005; Silk 2007d). Cooperative behavior can also be maintained by current punishment (*harassment*) of noncooperators or the threat of future punishment (*sanctioning*) for example, "If you don't scratch my back now, I'll take your food later" (Clutton-Brock and Parker 1995; Stevens, Cushman, and Hauser 2005). Sanctioning requires the same kind of memory for past interactions as reciprocal altruism and is accordingly rare (Stevens, Cushman, and Hauser 2005).

In this section we look first at a few examples of naturally occurring cooperative behavior for which there is at least a hint about underlying mechanisms (for more extensive discussion see Silk 2007d). We then look at new models of the evolution of human sociality showing how cooperative behavior can evolve under conditions not encompassed by classic models of altruism and at some experiments designed to test whether the mechanisms implied by these models are shared with any other primates.

12.5.2   Altruism in the wild

Mutualism

The example of mutualism probably the best-analyzed mechanistically is that among fish and their cleaners (Trivers 1971; Bshary 2006). Cleaner fish species subsist on the ectoparasites they eat from the surfaces of other fish. Cleaners closely approach their "clients," which may be larger predatory fish and even swim in and out of their mouths, but they are seldom eaten. Cleaners may have specialized coloration and behaviors that signal their approach; clients likewise have special behaviors of resting in a trancelike state while being cleaned and then signaling to the cleaner when they are about to depart. The client benefits by getting rid of parasites, and the cleaner gets a meal. Cleaners have fixed stations on the reef, which their clients visit regularly. Contact with cleaners is reinforcing for clients, which learn not the identity of their cleaners as such but the locations where they are found. In the laboratory, fish will learn to enter an area where they are contacted by a cleaner model (Losey 1979).

In the Australian reef fish studied by Bshary and his colleagues, cleaner wrasse, *Labriodes dimidaitus*, sometimes cheat by eating the client's mucus, a food they prefer to parasites. Clients respond by attacking the cleaner and/or swimming away. Bshary and Grutter (2005) simulated this interaction in the laboratory by letting Plexiglas plates coated with food play the role of clients. When both shrimp and fish flakes were offered, cleaners ate the shrimp first, but if an attempt to take shrimp from a plate caused it to "chase" them or "dart away," they learned to take flakes first. On the reef cleaners interact with clients up to 2000 times a day, so there would be plenty of opportunity for the learning demonstrated in this study to shape their behavior, even toward individual clients. Because clients evidently sense when a cleaner is eating mucus and find it aversive, they may also learn which cleaners are reliable. In effect, this would be an example of *direct reciprocity,* that is, one individual reciprocates a known other individual for past benefits or costs. Here it can result from associative learning through positive reinforcement and punishment (being attacked or having mucus eaten) or negative reinforcement (the client

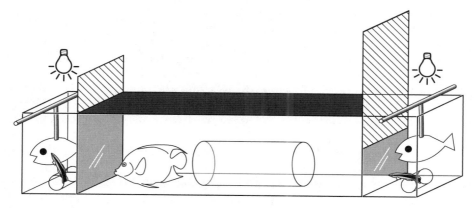

Figure 12.18. Setup in which a client fish, in the central compartment, eavesdrops through one-way mirrors on interactions of two cleaners (the thin black fish) with model clients. In the left end the cleaner appears to be cleaning the model, whereas in the right (nonpreferred) end the cleaner is just swimming around. After Bshary and Grutter (2006) with permission.

withdrawing). Current excitatory strength is in effect a tally of net value of past interactions with a particular client or cleaner. Any learning specializations here lie in the special events that reinforce or punish cleaners and clients.

Clients also learn about cleaners by eavesdropping on their behavior toward other clients (Bshary and d'Souza 2005). On the reef, clients more readily approach a cleaner if it has just been seen cleaning another client without conflict than causing it to dart away. In the laboratory setup shown in Figure 12.18, clients spend more than half their time near the end of a tank where a cleaner is eating from a Plexiglas model fish when the other end of the tank has a cleaner just swimming around, that is, with unknown behavior toward clients. In effect, such preference is an example of *indirect reciprocity,* in that cleaners who do not cheat are reciprocated for their cooperative behavior by eavesdroppers that in turn become their clients. Models like those sketched in Section 12.5.3 show that indirect reciprocity can evolve in species with social networks in which individuals acquire an *image score* or reputation. Those seen to be good cooperators are reciprocated by being cooperated with. So far in the cleaner-client system such image scoring has been shown only to affect immediate choice between waiting a turn at a given cleaning station or going elsewhere. As one might therefore expect, cleaners are more cooperative when they have an audience (Bshary and d'Souza 2005), another likely effect of reinforcement contingencies that has been reproduced in the laboratory (Bshary and Grutter 2006).

Reciprocal altruism in vampire bats?

Unlike mutualism, in reciprocal altruism acts are exchanged over delays. A much-discussed candidate involves vampire bats (*Desmodus rotundus*). Vampires fly out each evening from communal roosts to seek a meal of blood. A substantial blood meal allows a bat to survive another 50–60 hours before feeding again, but not every bat succeeds in getting a meal every night. Unfed bats may starve within 24 hours, but a starving bat can be rescued if a recently fed bat regurgitates blood for it. To test whether feedings were reciprocal, groups of unrelated bats were kept in the laboratory, and each night one was kept without food while the others fed (Wilkinson 1984). When the hungry bat was returned to the group, in 12 of 13 cases it was fed by another bat from the group it had come from in the wild. Moreover, the recipients of regurgitations tended to reciprocate the donation on a later night. These observations suggest that vampire bats recognize unrelated individuals and retain some memory of past interactions with them. However, the relatedness of the bats involved was not always known; because some may have been closely related the possibility remains open that the behavior is kin selected (Stevens, Cushman, and Hauser 2005).

Cooperative sentinels?

Some group-living species appear to resolve the conflict between feeding and vigilance as humans might, by posting sentinels who watch for predators from an exposed location while others forage. At first glance, reciprocal altruism might be in operation here to ensure an equitable sharing of dangerous guard duties. However, it turns out that at least for meerkats not only is a basic assumption of this theory wrong—guards are less vulnerable to predation than their busily foraging companions, not more—but there is no regular rotation of sentinels as would be expected if opportunity to feed is regularly being repaid by time on guard. Instead, meerkats are more likely to guard when they are near satiation (Clutton-Brock et al. 1999). Individuals experimentally given extra food guarded more often and for longer, and individuals that were unusually hungry because they had been babysitting at the burrow temporarily guarded less. Here, then, a simple kind of social organization arises from largely individual processes. A meerkat's top motivational priority is feeding; once fed, it will guard if no one else is on guard at the time.

Reciprocity and alliances in wild primates

As we saw in Section 12.2, members of a primate troop have friendly relationships expressed in mutual grooming and support in agonistic interactions. Such observations suggest the participants are reciprocal altruists who are exchanging grooming for agonistic support (see Silk 2007d). Indeed this does seem to be the case in a group of captive Japanese macaques studied by Schino, Sorrentino, and Tiddi (2007). They analyzed a large number of grooming and agonistic interactions, statistically removing effects of kinship and proximity, and found that not only did monkeys groom most those that had groomed them most, they also groomed most those individuals that had supported them most. Support was similarly predicted by past receipt of both support and grooming. The relevant correlations were apparent over the long term but not when only events in the past 30 minutes were analyzed. The fact that, for example, grooming monkey A today is repaid by A's support tomorrow or the next day seems to imply either learning over long delays or a detailed memory of specific interactions. The improbability of either has been claimed to be a cognitive constraint on reciprocal altruism (Stevens, Cushman, and Hauser 2005). However, as with the cleaner fish, the net effect of past interactions with a particular individual can just as well be encoded as a single current value or attitude, similar to associative strength in models of learning (Chapter 4), resulting in what de Waal (2000) calls *attitudinal reciprocity*. As nicely put by Schino et al. (2007, 186) "it is necessary to assume only that the exchange of services triggers partner-specific emotional variations and that monkeys make their behavioral decisions on the basis of the emotional state associated to each potential partner."

12.5.3   Cooperation and other-regarding behavior

The evolution of human cooperation

Cooperation is a hallmark of human society. Not merely do people behave considerately toward complete strangers, they sometimes make substantial financial and even physical sacrifices for them. Such behavior seems impossible to explain with classic models of the evolution of altruism in which cooperation between unrelated others can arise only when the same individuals interact repeatedly. However, new models of the evolution of human sociality and the results of experiments to test them suggest that a sense of fairness and other foundations of morality have deep evolutionary roots. Such models consider processes at the level of groups of individuals, but without relying on the discredited notion of group selection in which individuals act "for the good of the group" (Wilson and Wilson 2007, 2008). Genes promoting prosocial tendencies in individuals can arise when groups compete in ways argued to be characteristic of the early stages of human evolution. In particular, such conditions may have promoted the evolution of *strong reciprocity,* a tendency to cooperate with anonymous unrelated others and to punish those who do not do the same even when doing so is costly to the punisher (Nowak 2006; review in Gintis et al. 2007).

A good deal of the evidence that people actually have such tendencies comes from simple stripped down social situations, economic games, a key one of which is *the ultimatum game.* The rules are as follows. One individual, the *proposer,* is given a sum of money, say $10, to divide between himself and an anonymous stranger, the *responder.* He can offer the responder any amount from $1 to $10, and if the responder accepts, they both keep whatever is proposed; if the responder rejects, they both get nothing. In either case, they do not interact again. Notice that because the players are anonymous and interact only once, neither one's behavior should be influenced by expectations of the other's approval, reciprocation, or retaliation. Because it should be obvious to both players that the responder will do better by accepting any proposal than rejecting it, selfish proposers should consistently make very low offers and responders should accept them. But contrary to these expectations, proposers generally offer more than the minimum, often near 50% of the total on average, and responders reject very low offers, a costly act that punishes the proposer. Indeed, people report feeling angry at very low offers. There are differences among individuals and also across cultures (see Gintis et al. 2007), but the findings are clearly better described as strong reciprocity than as uniformly self-regarding behavior (i.e., behavior that maximizes the actor's own gain in the short run). These developments have stimulated tests of whether monkeys or apes show such prosocial or other-regarding tendencies, that is do they seem to have a sense of fairness or cooperate with unrelated others? Or is strong reciprocity a uniquely human trait?

Inequity aversion: Do monkeys have a sense of fairness?

One of the first and most controversial tests of other-regarding behavior in primates was a study by Brosnan and de Waal (2003; see also van Wolkenten, Brosnan, and de Waal 2007) with capuchin monkeys. The capuchins had learned to exchange tokens (small rocks) for food. The experimenter would give the monkey a token, and then offer food which the monkey could obtain by handing back the token. In the main experiment, two capuchins in neighboring cages could watch each other engaged in this game; importantly, each could see if its neighbor was getting a grape (a preferred

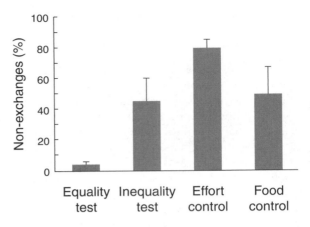

Figure 12.19. Proportion of trials in which subject monkeys refused to exchange a token for a piece of cucumber when a neighbor was getting cucumber (Equality test) or a preferred grape (Inequality test). Control conditions are described in the text. After Brosnan and de Waal (2003) with permission.

food) or a cucumber slice (a nonpreferred food) for its efforts. Isolated capuchins would play for cucumber, but seeing its neighbor get a grape greatly increased a capuchin's tendency to reject cucumber (Equality vs. Inequality tests in Figure 12.19), a phenomenon Brosnan and deWaal called *inequity aversion.*

But what is really going on here? To some extent cucumber is simply less attractive in the presence of grapes irrespective of whether the grapes are being received by another animal (Wynne 2004b). The data from two control conditions in the original study provide evidence for such a contrast effect (Figure 12.19). When a grape was either given to the neighbor for no effort or simply placed in the empty neighboring cage (Effort and Food controls in Figure 12.19), failures to exchange were elevated about as much as when the partner "received unequal pay for equal work." A less immediately obvious source of contrast is that many of the trials in which monkeys rejected cucumber occurred after trials in which those same subjects received grapes (Brosnan and de Waal 2006; Roma et al. 2006). Moreover, although the original report of this effect (Brosnan and deWaal, 2003) was called "Monkeys reject unequal pay," the "work" implied by the title seems trivial. Handing the experimenter a token hardly seems to require more effort than reaching out for food, and accordingly the role of "work" in the effect is also debatable (Fontenot et al. 2007; van Wolkenten, Brosnan, and de Waal 2007). Finally, what is being claimed here? Some discussions of inequity aversion seem to suggest that monkeys have a humanlike emotional reaction to unfairness (cf. Brosnan and de Waal 2003; Wynne 2004b). A more measured interpretation (e.g., Silk 2007c) is that sensitivity to differences between one's own rewards and those available to others could be one of the evolutionary building blocks of human responses to unfairness. Which nonhuman primates show such sensitivity and under what conditions remains to be better understood.

Are chimpanzees altruistic?

Whatever else is going on in tests of inequity aversion, subjects seem averse only to getting less than a companion (Henrich 2004). Getting more than a companion, an equally unfair allotment, does not seem to bother them, whereas tests like the ultimatum game suggest that people are averse to any form of inequity. Another line of research supports the same conclusion. Here, food is out of reach outside a cage, and primate subjects can use a rope or handle to pull it in. If at the same time they can move additional food toward a second animal, do they choose this altruistic act over delivering food to themselves at the same cost? Tests of chimpanzees from several captive groups answer this question resoundingly in the negative (Silk et al. 2005; Jensen et al. 2006; Silk 2007d; Vonk et al. 2008). In each case, chimpanzees could choose to operate either of two pairs of trays. Trays in one pair had a piece of food for the subject and one for a familiar group member in a neighboring cage; the other pair of trays had food for the subject and an empty tray for the neighbor. Subjects were indifferent between these options. They similarly chose only on the basis of personal gain when one choice prevented delivery of food to another (Jensen. et al. 2006).

One of the most clever and elaborate illustrations of chimpanzees' pure self-regard and apparent insensitivity to fairness in such situations is the behavior of pairs of animals in a simplified ultimatum game (Figure 12.20; Jensen, Call, and Tomasello 2007). Again one animal, here in the role of proposer, chose between two pairs of trays. Each pair had 10 raisins, but they were allocated differently between the proposer's tray and the responder's. For example, the choice might be between an 8:2 allotment and 5:5. The proposer could pull one tray closer to both animals, and the responder could then complete the delivery of the chosen raisin allotment to both or reject it. Proposers preferred options with more for themselves, and as long as they got at least one raisin, responders hardly every rejected any offer no matter how inequitable. Control procedures showed that the animals could see what their companion was getting and could discriminate among the amounts of food offered. Unlike in an earlier study that provided some (albeit weak, Stevens, Cushman, and Hauser 2005) evidence for altruistic choices in cotton top tamarins after extensive training (Hauser et al. 2003), here the animals had comparatively few trials with a given condition and companion. Thus, even though the interaction was not anonymous as it usually is with humans in the ultimatum game, it came close to testing the animals' spontaneous preferences, and in any case repeated interactions with known individuals would have been expected to increase displays of fairness. It can be argued that other factors besides species difference such as the desirability of the food reward contributed to the difference between these findings and those that would be expected for humans, but they are consistent with the conclusion that chimpanzees do not

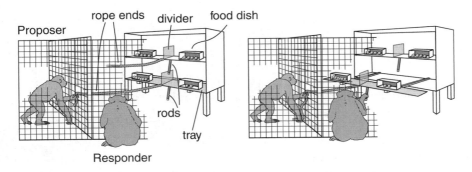

Figure 12.20. Ultimatum game for chimpanzees. On the left, the proposer chooses between the upper and the lower trays, each of which holds pair of food dishes with a different allotment of a fixed number of raisins (here 8). On the right, the proposer has pulled the lower tray so its rod is within reach of the responder, who can complete delivery of the chosen allotment, for example, 6 raisins to the proposer and 2 to himself. After Jensen, Call, and Tomasello (2007) with permission.

share our sense of fairness but are concerned only with maximizing their own economic gains (Jensen, Call, and Tomasello 2007).

Do chimpanzees and monkeys cooperate?

Of course maximizing individual gain is not inconsistent with cooperating in mutualistic situations, particularly those that involve large rewards not easily obtainable by individuals acting alone. Indeed, some chimpanzees are wonderful cooperative hunters. Boesch and Boesch-Acherman (2000) vividly describe how males in the Tai forest go after colobus monkeys, some driving a potential victim down from the trees while others wait on the ground. The animals are clearly cooperating in a complex way, but because skilled hunting takes up to 20 years to develop, it is difficult to say exactly what cognitive skills they are using and how they come to use them. This issue is addressed by experiments in which pairs of apes or monkeys are presented with tasks in which they must act together on an apparatus like that in Figure 12.21 to obtain reward (review in Noë 2006; Silk 2007d). Of course it is not at all surprising if one animal can use another's behavior or the results of it as a discriminative stimulus in a learning task. The questions about specifically social cognition here are therefore something like the following. Do animals ever cooperate spontaneously? If so what animals under what conditions? Even if animals must learn to cooperate, are there specific cognitive prerequisites such as a tendency to attend to others' behavior or to give communicative signals? Or are the prerequisites primarily emotional or temperamental?

Tests of cooperation with brown and tufted capuchins in different laboratories have produced mixed results (see Noë 2006). These tolerant monkeys seem to cooperate in the wild, and they can learn cooperative tasks in the laboratory. Attending to the partner's behavior may contribute to solving them, in that blocking the view of the partner degrades performance (Mendres and de Waal 2000; but see Visalberghi, Pellegrini Quarantotti, and Tranchida 2000). Chimpanzees can also learn to pull such an apparatus together, but they seem to do so entirely through learning the contingencies between their own and the partner's behavior. Unlike in

Figure 12.21. Apparatus for testing cooperation between two chimpanzees. Because the rope is not fixed firmly to the board holding the two food dishes and the ends are too far apart for one animal to reach both of them, getting the food within reach requires two animals to pull simultaneously, one on each end. After Melis, Hare, and Tomasello (2006a) with permission.

one case where the partner was a human (Hirata and Fuwa 2007), they do not attempt to induce cooperation with communicative signals and gestures. Importantly, even when chimpanzees' actions result in separate food for each animal, as would be the case with the apparatus in Figure 12.21, they succeed more often when working together with a partner that they more readily share food with in independent tests (Melis, Hare, and Tomasello 2006b). As this finding predicts, bonobos, which are more socially tolerant, are more successful than chimpanzees on this task (Hare et al. 2007), again supporting the notion that emotional or temperamental rather than specifically cognitive attributes underlie species differences in cooperation.

Empathy and the evolution of helping

The findings sketched so far all seem to point to the conclusion that regard for others' welfare is a uniquely human trait, evolved since humans and apes separated from their common ancestor, possibly in response to the conditions in early human social groups (Silk 2007c). Insofar as regard for another's welfare requires sensitivity to what they are thinking or feeling, this conclusion is entirely consistent with the lack of evidence for theory of mind in chimpanzees. But to some (de Waal 2008) this conclusion flies in the face of countless observations that in naturalistic social groups chimpanzees seem to empathize with others in distress. For example, an animal that has witnessed a fight may appear to console the loser by putting an arm around the loser's shoulders. Moreover, in experimental settings chimpanzees do respond spontaneously to signals that a conspecific or a person needs help, for example handing them an object that they are unsuccessfully reaching toward. Young children do the same thing (Warneken and Tomasello 2006; Warneken et al. 2007).

These situations differ in two important ways from the economic games in which chimpanzees fail to show regard for others: neither food nor learned responses are involved, and natural responses to natural signals are. Evolution may have produced proximate mechanisms for species-specific helpful behaviors in response to specific sign stimuli from body language or vocalizations (de Waal 2008). Responses like those described as consolation or helping may even be accompanied by humanlike affect, but such affect, if present, apparently cannot support functionally similar behavior such as delivering food to another via arbitrary learned responses. Indeed, a wide variety of species show emotional contagion, that is, seeing a conspecific in a certain emotional state arouses the same emotional state in the witness. For example, in the company of a mouse in pain, other mice exhibit a lower threshold to react to a painful stimulus, an effect that could be described as empathy (Langford et al. 2006). As we see in Chapter 13, such reactions can support witnesses' learning what caused their companions' distress.

In conclusion, whether or not animals cooperate or help others depends on not only the species but on what is meant by *helping* or *cooperating*. Animals can learn to cooperate in various ways, but it seems that self-interest generally prevails when small amounts of food are involved. However, some group-living animals actively signal the availability of large amounts of shareable food. Examples include ravens (Heinrich 1989) and the food-calling chickens discussed in Chapter 14. Mechanisms underlying apparent cooperation in such species might repay further analysis. In any case, looking for signs of altruism only in economic, food-related, decisions fails to recognize the importance of what de Waal (2008) calls the altruistic impulse, the spontaneous display of species-typical helpful responses. Rather than resulting from a conscious calculation of benefits to others, helping may be an unconscious reaction to sign stimuli. Such responses are surprisingly important even in human social life. As an example, when a photograph of eyes was placed beside the box where people placed contributions to a coffee pool, payments more than doubled compared to weeks when flowers were present instead (Bateson, Nettle, and Roberts 2006; Milinski and Rockenbach 2007).

12.6   Summary

In the course of the chapter we have seen evidence for a number of specifically cognitive mechanisms, some of them very simple. Many species respond to the gaze of conspecifics and/or predators, perhaps tracking the direction in which they are looking and/or using gaze as a cue to search behind barriers. Some primates and birds also retain this information for use in later competitive encounters. Response to gaze is thus a phylogenetically widespread component of social cognition. Human babies and most likely some other primates (at least) share a second such low-level component of social behavior, namely a propensity to respond to self-propelled objects as if they are animate and goal-directed. In the next chapter we see evidence for another candidate component of social cognition in the responses of mirror neurons in primate brains.

We have also encountered three candidates for higher level components of social cognition. Although it turns out, contrary to earlier suggestions (Tomasello and Call 1997), that sensitivity to third-party social relationships can be demonstrated in nonprimates including fish and birds, some primates classify their social companions in multiple ways simultaneously, perhaps using an ability for hierarchical classification that goes beyond anything yet demonstrated in laboratory studies of categorization in any species. This ability may go along with a particularly fine-tuned ability to decode social relationships. At the same time, however, there is as yet no evidence in any nonhuman species for two other important human social cognitive abilities—theory of mind and a sense of fairness (or a propensity to take other individuals' welfare into account in economic decision-making).

The focus of this chapter has been very much on primates, often on our closest living relatives, the chimpanzees. In the case of social knowledge this reflects the primacy of field research on primates in suggesting that social knowledge and social brains are special. While this conclusion may still prove to be correct, research has been tempering it with studies of species as diverse as hyenas, geese, and fish. Similarly, in research on the mentalistic aspects of social cognition, studies of chimpanzees together with those on young children originally predominated, but research has more recently moved on to look at other primate species as well as birds. To some extent the focus here on chimpanzees and other primates reflects a compelling interest in the question of what makes us human. Indeed, the early years of the twenty-first century have seen a veritable epidemic of attempts to characterize human cognitive uniqueness (e.g., Premack 2007; Penn, Holyoak, and Povinelli 2008). Based on the evidence in this chapter we might conclude that only humans have theory of mind or understand the unseen causes of social events just as they understand unseen physical causes. The final section of this chapter adds to this tentative catalog of species differences the suggestion that only humans govern economic decisions with a sense of fairness or understand the sufferings of others. Chapters 13 and 14 suggest further candidates for human uniqueness. But there are many reasons to doubt that the question "What makes us human?" has a simple answer. We look at it again in Chapter 15.

Further readings

Much of the material in this chapter is covered in more depth in the books edited by Emery, Clayton, and Frith (2007), de Waal and Tyack (2003), P. McGregor (2005), and Dunbar and Barrett (2007); in *Baboon Metaphysics* by Cheney and Seyfarth (2007); and in the review by Emery and Clayton (2009). A comprehensive review of dog behavior and cognition is the book by Miklosi (2007); the research bearing on theory-of-mind-like behaviors in dogs is comprehensively reviewed and analyzed in the article by Reid (2009). The most recent stances of those on two sides of the chimpanzee theory of mind debate are represented in the articles by Call and Tomasello (2008) on the one hand and Penn and Povinelli (2007b) on the other. Healy and Rowe (2007) is recommended for an analysis of the social brain and related proposals, Emery (2000) for a thorough review of social gaze and its neurobiological basis, and de Waal (2008) for a stimulating review of altruism.

13
Social Learning

In the past 50 years or so, forests of Jerusalem pine have been planted in Israel. Here black rats occupy the niche occupied by squirrels in other parts of the world, making their nests in the trees and eating pine seeds. Jerusalem pine seeds are protected by tough overlapping scales tightly wrapped around the central core of the pine cone. To obtain them efficiently, rats must strip the scales off the cones from bottom to top in a spiral pattern (Figure 13.1). Black rats do not learn by themselves to extract the seeds in this way, nor do isolated young rats, but young rats growing up in the pine forests do develop efficient stripping (Terkel 1995).

White-crowned sparrows (*Zonotrichia leucophrys*) are small songbirds, widely distributed in North America. Although they are a single species from Atlantic to Pacific, the songs sung by males during the breeding season vary from one region to another. In California, for example, there is a recognizable Berkeley dialect and a Sunset Beach dialect less than 20 miles away (Marler and Tamura 1964).

Different populations of wild chimpanzees depend on different foods, and they use tools to get some of these foods (Whiten et al. 1999). The chimpanzees of Gombe, in Tanzania, gently poke grass stems into termite mounds to extract the insects. Chimpanzees in the Tai Forest of the Ivory Coast open rock-hard coula nuts by placing them on a stone "anvil" and striking them with a smaller stone, which they may carry around with them. Young chimpanzees accompany tool-using adults and appear to watch them intently.

In all these examples, individuals seem to be learning from others in their social group. But if they are learning from one another, precisely what are they learning, and how are they learning it? Are there specialized mechanisms for social learning and, if so, are they better developed in species that live in groups? Should the localized groups of animals that share pine cone stripping, song dialects, or nut cracking be viewed as animal cultures? What can laboratory studies of social transmission mechanisms tell us about how animal traditions arise and spread?

Observations of animals apparently learning from one another raise both mechanistic and functional questions. In the past, the answers to these questions were pursued in two separate research traditions (Galef 1988; Whiten and Ham 1992). Beginning in the days of Darwin and Romanes, the primary mechanistic, or psychological, question about social learning was whether animals can imitate, that is, whether they can come to perform an action as a result of seeing it done. In contrast, anthropologists and behavioral ecologists have been more interested in discovering

Figure 13.1. Mother black rat and her pup feeding on pine cones. After drawings and photographs in Terkel (1995), with permission.

the conditions under which behaviors spread through populations and are maintained from generation to generation. In this context, mechanisms are important only as they determine the conditions under which behavior is transmitted. The last 20 years or so have seen increasing integration of the many perspectives on social learning (Zentall and and Galef 1988; Heyes and Galef 1996; Galef and Heyes 2004). For example, studies of imitation in chimpanzees and other nonhuman primates now intersect both with evolutionary models suggesting that a "ratcheting up" of culture is possible only in species that imitate (Richerson and Boyd 2005) and with investigations of mirror neurons in primate brains (Section 13.3).

Social learning refers to any learning resulting from the behavior of other animals (Box 13.1). Galef and Giraldeau (2001) characterize the two major approaches to studying it as "top down" (ecological or functional) and "bottom up" (psychological or mechanistic). This chapter begins with the former, with instances of social learning in naturalistic or seminaturalistic situations. In the central part of the chapter, on the

---

Box 13.1 A Social Learning Glossary

Social learning embraces such a potentially bewildering (C. M. Heyes 1993a) variety of different terms that a glossary is useful for keeping track. This one includes those most often encountered in contemporary discussions (Zentall 2006; Hoppitt et al. 2008). Historically, there have been many more, often with overlapping meanings (Galef 1988; Whiten and Ham 1992).

To begin with, any form of social learning requires an *observer* (or *actor)* and a *demonstrator,* who performs the behavior later reproduced in whole or part by the observer. To qualify as learning rather than socially elicited or facilitated behavior, the observer's performance must take place at a later time, away from direct influence of the demonstrator.

Copying. A generic term for doing the same thing as a demonstrator, mechanisms unspecified; for example copying another's choice of mate or foraging patch (Section 13.1).

Social facilitation. Individuals are more likely to perform a behavior when in the company of others performing it. For example, yawning is socially facilitated in people (Provine 2005).

Local enhancement/Stimulus enhancement. Increased likelihood of visiting a place (local enhancement) or contacting a type of stimulus (stimulus enhancement) by virtue of observing others doing it. The enhanced attractiveness of the location or stimulus may or may not be confined to times when demonstrators are present.

Observational conditioning. Associating a cue or object with an affective state or behavior(s) by virtue of watching demonstrators respond to it. For example (Section 13.2), having seen other birds mob an owl, an observer later responds to an owl by mobbing. Sometimes extended to cases in which the observer is directly reinforced following a cue or signal by the demonstrator as when parent babblers "purr" before feeding their young (Section 13.4). However, this seems to be direct conditioning of the observer, that is, CS = purr, US = food, CR = approach.

Imitation. Performing the same action as a demonstrator *by virtue of having seen the action performed.* The action must be novel, thus ruling out such phenomena as "mate choice copying."

Emulation. Copying only elements of a complex action. For example, having seen a demonstrator skillfully use a rake to pull food toward itself, an observer picks up the rake backwards and waves it in the general direction of the food. May be qualified by reference to the element of the sequence apparently emulated, as in *goal emulation* (Section 13.3).

Learning affordances. Learning what can be done with objects or parts of the environment, not necessarily through observing the actions of another animal. For example, an observer seeing a door opened by the wind may learn that it can be opened (*affords opening*).

"bottom up" approach, we see that processes other than imitation play the major role in most natural examples of social transmission. Indeed, much socially influenced learning does not appear to depend on any specialization for social learning as such but rather on species-specific perceptual and motivational mechanisms together with associative learning. Imitation (Section 13.3) may be an exception. At the end of the chapter we return to social learning in natural contexts with two contentious questions: Do animals teach (Section 13.4)? And can animals ever be said to have culture (Section 13.5)?

13.1   Social learning in context

13.1.1   Social transmission of food preferences in rats

One advantage of group living is that individuals foraging together may help each other find food. They may be attracted to feeding conspecifics, or they may follow others, as ants follow each other along chemical trails. Colonies or roosting places may serve as information centers where individuals inform each other about good foraging opportunities in the neighborhood. At one time information exchange was hypothesized to be a major factor in the evolution of sociality, but this *information center hypothesis* is now considered to be without broad empirical support (see Galef and Laland 2005). Nevertheless, information exchange is a potential benefit of sociality, and there are some good examples of animals using information about food sources provided by others in their colonies. Bees communicate the locations of nectar (Chapter 14), and as we see next, rats provide other rats with information about the flavors of edible foods.

Norway rats (*Rattus norvegicus,* the common laboratory rat) are colonial omnivores. They can and will eat almost anything that does not poison them. This means that young rats have a lot of potential foods to learn about, and they start learning before they are born. The flavors of foods eaten by a mother rat late in pregnancy influence the food preferences of her offspring when they begin to feed on solid food (review in Galef 1996b). The pups continue to learn from their mother when they are suckling because the flavors of foods she ingests are present in her milk. In addition when the weanling rats begin to leave the nest to forage, they prefer to forage where other rats are or recently have been feeding. Thus the young rat has at least three ways to become familiar with the flavors of foods being eaten safely by its mother and others in its colony. Combined with a preference for familiar over novel flavors, they almost guarantee that a young rat will eat things that are good for it, or at least not harmful.

In addition to choosing familiar flavors, both young and adult rats choose foods being eaten by their companions over alternatives. This was discovered in experiments designed as depicted in Figure 13.2 (Galef and Wigmore 1983). Pairs of rats lived together for a few days, eating normal laboratory rat chow. Then one rat in each pair, the *demonstrator*, was removed to another cage and deprived of food for 24 hours before being fed cinnamon or cocoa flavored chow. Next, each demonstrator was returned to its familiar companion, the *observer* rat, and demonstrators and observers interacted in the absence of food for 15 minutes. For the following 24 hours the observer, alone once again, had two bowls of food, one flavored with cinnamon and one with cocoa. As shown in Figure 13.2, during this time observers whose demonstrators ate cinnamon consumed more cinnamon-flavored food relative to cocoa flavored food than those whose demonstrators ate cocoa. A large

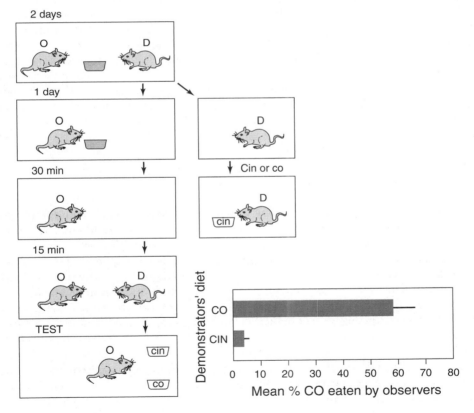

Figure 13.2. Design and results experiments establishing social transmission of food preferences in Norway rats. D = demonstrator; O = observer; CO = cocoa-flavored food; CIN = cinnamon-flavored food. Data are grams of CO eaten as a proportion of total consumption in the first 12 hours of the test in groups whose demonstrators ate CIN (as in the example portrayed) or CO. After Galef and Wigmore (1983) with permission.

number of related experiments has shown, among other things, that observers can be socially induced to choose a familiar food that a demonstrator has eaten recently and to seek out a place where that food is available (Galef 1996b). Thus rats apparently can, in effect, exchange information about what foods are currently available nearby, although the role of these processes in directing food choice in wild colonies is unknown. Such learning is also found in other rodent species (Galef 2007).

How do demonstrators communicate about food? A rat that has just been eating might carry bits of food on its fur and whiskers, but that is not all the observers detect. Observers need to smell the flavor on another rat's breath, more specifically in association with carbon disulfide, a prominent component of rat breath (Galef 1996b). Rats behave in a way that facilitates this learning: when they encounter one another they engage in mouth to mouth contact and sniffing. To borrow a term from embryology (Waddington 1966), development of food preferences in rats is *canalized:* in a kind of fail-safe system often found in development, several separate mechanisms independently and redundantly ensure that young rats will eat what others in their colony are eating.

The social learning mechanisms available to adults are sufficient to transmit colony members' acquired food preferences to succeeding generations (Galef and Allen 1995). In one example colonies of four rats were induced to prefer either Japanese horseradish or cayenne pepper flavored food by making them ill after they ate the alternative diet. The rats in these "founder" colonies were gradually replaced with naive rats until the colonies were made up entirely of rats that had never been poisoned after eating either of the diets. Nevertheless, rats in each colony were still preferring their colony's "traditional" diet. In one experiment, the tradition was maintained over four generations of replacement rats. Preference was still transmitted even when the new colony members never fed in the presence of the older members but just interacted with them in the hours between daily feedings.

13.1.2   Producing and scrounging: Social transmission of feeding techniques in pigeons

Baby rats represent a special case in which social learning is undeniably useful. Without influences from their mother and other adults, they would have to choose foods randomly once they were weaned. But in a group of adult animals encountering unfamiliar resources, not everyone should be engaging in social learning. Indeed, this would be an impossible situation: for there to be anything to learn socially, someone has to be acquiring information for himself, that is, engaging in *individual learning.* Thus when there is new information to be acquired, some should learn for themselves while others copy (Giraldeau, Valone, and Templeton 2002). And if a given individual already has an effective behavior for the situation, copying may not be his best policy. This informal functional notion suggests that animals might not always acquire a novel behavior being exhibited by another group member. The research of Louis Lefebvre, Luc-Alain Giraldeau, and their colleagues with captive and free-ranging pigeons (*Columba livia*) provides some of the best evidence for this suggestion.

Like rats, pigeons are highly social opportunistic foragers that are widely associated with humans because of their ability to flourish in a variety of conditions. Pigeons in the laboratory learn some novel feeding techniques more readily if they have seen them used by another pigeon than otherwise.

One such technique is pecking through a paper cover on a food dish. Pigeons that watch demonstrators both pierce the paper and eat grain perform the task themselves sooner than pigeons given partial demonstrations or no demonstrations (Palameta and Lefebvre 1985). However, when a skilled paper piercer was placed in a laboratory flock of ten birds, only four learned the skill. The others *scrounged* food uncovered by the birds that pierced (Lefebvre 1986). In contrast, when a trained demonstrator was introduced into a free-flying flock in Montreal, 24 birds learned to pierce on their own and only four specialized in scrounging. The sample sizes here are just one captive and one free-living flock, but Lefebvre and Palameta (1988) suggest that one reason for the great difference in proportion of learners is that because individuals could come and go from the urban flock, scroungers sometimes found themselves without anyone to scrounge from and had to learn for themselves to produce food from the apparatus.

In free-ranging flocks different individuals may specialize in different food-finding skills and change roles from producer to scrounger as the situation changes (Giraldeau and Lefebvre 1986). Opportunity to scrounge may reduce performance of a task that has already been learned, but it can also interfere with learning from producers in the first place. When pigeons learned to remove a stopper from an inverted test tube, causing grain to fall out (Figure 13.3; Giraldeau and Lefebvre 1987), eight out of eight observers that watched another pigeon remove the stopper and eat the grain did the same themselves when given the opportunity. If the observers could scrounge some of the demonstrator's grain, however, only two out of eight birds learned in the same number of trials. Just as with paper piercing, when a trained observer was introduced into a laboratory flock, a few birds learned the tube-opening task and became consistent producers, whereas the majority scrounged as long as the producers were present. Taken together, these observations indicate that scrounging influences learning, perhaps because pigeons cannot divide attention between looking for food to scrounge and watching what a demonstrator is doing. Some other species of birds, however, may be able to scrounge and learn at the same time (Lefebvre and Bouchard 2003).

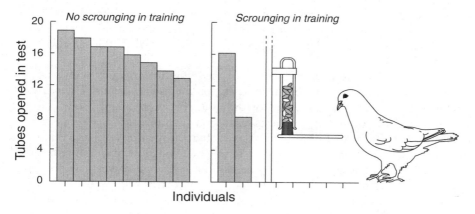

Figure 13.3. Apparatus and results in experiments demonstrating effect of the opportunity to scrounge from the demonstrator on social transmission of a food-finding skill. Data for eight individuals per group, each given 20 opportunities to open a test tube in the test phase. Data redrawn from Giraldeau and Lefebvre (1987) with permission.

13.1.3   Public information, cues, and signals

A young rat approaching a food site frequented by other rats is already familiar with the flavors of some safe foods. This is *private information*. In contrast, the rat excrement and odors of other rats around the site constitute *public information* that quantities of edible food are present, and indeed these cues attract rats (Laland and Plotkin 1993). Similarly, by trial and error a Montreal street pigeon might acquire private information about how to open one of Giraldeau and Lefebvre's feeders, but to find a good foraging patch it could use public information like the sight of a flock of pigeons feeding.

At the end of the twentieth century, uses of public versus private information became a lively topic in behavioral ecology (Danchin et al. 2004; Valone 2007), in parallel with interest in eavesdropping in animal communication (Chapter 12). When animals respond to the behavior of other animals or a byproduct of it to find food or other resources, they are said to be using public information. Using public information does not necessarily require or result in social learning of any kind, but it might. For instance, the young rat feeding in the presence of other rats or their excrement becomes familiar with the flavor of whatever it is eating there. *Eavesdropping* is reserved for cases in which the public information consists of communicative signals, but from a mechanistic point of view there is not necessarily any distinction (Bonnie and Earley 2007; Valone 2007). And like other kinds of public information, signals may arouse specific behaviors or affective states in eavesdroppers without anything necessarily being learned. For example, seeing conspecifics fighting raises testosterone levels in cichlid fish (Oliveira et al. 2001).

In Section 13.2 we analyze how learning from public information might take place. Here a series of studies with stickleback fish will illustrate some potentially cognitively interesting questions about how public and private information interact. In all of them, the fish acquired information about the value of feeding patches in a setup like that illustrated in Figure 13.4. An observer fish confined to a central compartment could see fish feeding in each end of a tank. It could not see the worms that were being delivered on different schedules in the two patches, but it could see the demonstrators feeding and attempting to feed. Both nine-spined and three-spined sticklebacks used public information, in that shortly after demonstrations they chose a patch where fish had been feeding over one where no food had been delivered. However, when both patches had had food, only the nine-spined species chose the one that had delivered food at the higher rate (Coolen et al. 2003; see also Webster and Hart 2006).

Public and private information were opposed in a further study with nine-spined sticklebacks by first letting observers learn for themselves that the richer of two patches was always at a given end of the tank. Between 1 and 7 days later they were exposed to conflicting public information (demonstrators feeding more frequently at the observer's formerly poor patch than at the rich one) and immediately tested. Fish whose private information training had ended the day before behaved as if ignoring the public information, whereas those trained a week before strongly preferred the patch that had just been seen to be better (Fig 13.4). Fish tested at intermediate delays showed no preference (Experiment 2 in van Bergen, Coolen, and Laland 2004). The authors concluded that the fish "will weight public and private information appropriately depending on circumstances." This implies that fish tested at the longest delay still remembered what they learned individually a week before but were reweighting this information. However, because the experiment did not include

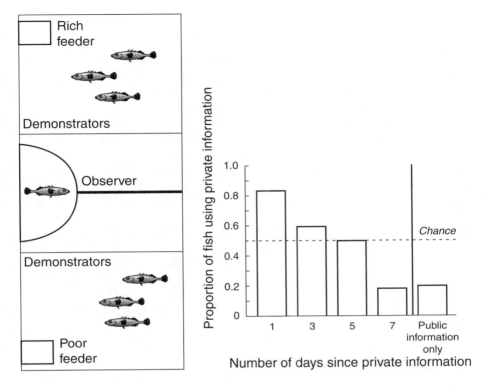

Figure 13.4. Setup in which an observer stickleback acquires public information about two food patches by watching others feed there immediately before it is allowed to choose between the patches. In the observer's own past experience (private information) rich and poor feeders were swapped. Hence, "using private information" means choosing the currently poor feeder. After van Bergen, Coolen, and Laland (2004) with permission.

control fish not exposed to conflicting public information just before testing, the results could as well reflect forgetting of the original private information.

Of course the findings can still be described functionally as showing that recent information is treated as more reliable, but the absence of a forgetting control illustrates how a focus on a functional account can overlook interesting and even important mechanistic questions. (Which is not to say that a focus on mechanism cannot be similarly narrow.) Similarly, the contrast between public information and "social cues" in this context (Coolen et al. 2003) is perhaps not meaningful mechanistically if the former refers to the feeding rate of demonstrators and the latter to their numbers. There seems to be little other than precedent to justify such distinctions among sources of social information (Bonnie and Earley 2007; Valone 2007) nor much reason to think they affect behavior through fundamentally different mechanisms. Indeed, once an animal has learned the value of a site, it may not retain any information about whether it learned from seeing conspecifics there or being there itself.

13.1.4   Copying others' choice of mate

If females are actively choosing mates, some males will be popular simply because they have more of whatever females are basing their choices on: more intense colors, more complex songs, or whatever. But if assessing a potential mate's characteristics takes time, entails a risk of predation, or is otherwise costly, females could reduce their assessment costs by choosing males they see other females choosing (Dugatkin 1996; White 2004). Of course functional copying would result from females using cues that a male has been chosen before, such as the presence of eggs in species where males guard a nest. But remembering the identity of males chosen by other females and later preferring those males would be an example of social learning comparable to that involved when client fish learn about good cleaners or fighting fish and songbirds learn about winners and losers by eavesdropping on their fights (Chapter 12). Indeed, the first examples of mate choice copying involved fish, guppies (review in Dugatkin 1996), but although other fish show mate copying, this example has proven difficult to replicate, perhaps because in guppies mate copying is confined to certain populations (Galef and Laland 2005).

In birds, female black grouse visiting a lek (a communal mating ground) apparently prefer males seen copulating. Stuffed females were placed in males' territories, either on the ground where males could mount and copulate, or on sticks as if sitting in a bush, where males could not copulate. Subject females spent more time in the former than in the latter territories (Hoglund et al. 1995). Both females and males of another bird species, Japanese quail, have been the subjects of perhaps the most extensive investigation of mate copying in any species (White 2004). In the basic demonstration of this phenomenon, a female is first confined equidistant from two males, one of whom is courting a female while the other is alone (Figure 13.5). Later—usually immediately afterward—the subject female is released and the time she spends in defined areas near each male is recorded. "Mate choice" here consists of spending more time near one male than the other, but this measure does predict partner choice when the birds are free to interact.

Clearly there are a number of potential confounds in this simple test. For example, the female might be choosing a male that had been seen courting or a male that had courted recently or the place where such events had occurred. It turns out that what matters is not seeing mating per se but seeing a female near the male (see White 2004). Given that male quail are quite aggressive, a close approach by a female is enough to indicate that a male is willing to mate. Male quail also learn which members of the opposite sex have been chosen by others, but experiments analogous to those with female quail subjects show they prefer a female that has *not* been courted by another male. This sex difference in behavior resulting from essentially similar learning (i.e., in performance rules) means that males do not invest in courting females that are already inseminated.

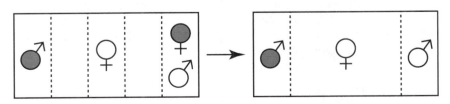

Figure 13.5. Setup for tests of mate choice copying by female quail or other animals. Dashed lines represent transparent barriers.

13.2   Mechanisms: Social learning without imitation

13.2.1   Another example and some distinctions

Not so long ago, milk was delivered to the doorsteps of homes in Great Britain and elsewhere in glass bottles sealed with foil or paper. The milk was not homogenized, so it had a thick layer of cream at the top. In the 1920s and 1930s blue tits began puncturing the bottle tops and stealing the cream (Figure 13.6). Milk bottle opening became relatively common in a few isolated areas, suggesting that it was being transmitted socially within them (Fisher and Hinde 1949; Hinde and Fisher 1951; Lefebvre 1995a). Pecking or tearing open a bottle top is clearly not imitation, since pecking and tearing at bark and seeds are prominent components of tits' foraging behavior, but the birds could have learned from one another where to direct these behaviors. This learning need not have been inherently social, however. Rather, the products of one individual's behavior—opened bottles—could have provided the conditions under which another individual learned for itself. The naive tit drinking from an already-opened bottle would associate bottles with food and then approach closed bottles and engage in food-related behaviors like pecking and tearing, which would be reinforced (Hinde and Fisher 1951).

Sherry and Galef (1984, 1990) showed that indeed milk-bottle opening can develop through this process. They taught captive black-capped chickadees, a North American tit species, to open small cream tubs like those served in restaurants. Then some experimentally naive chickadees watched demonstrators opening cream tubs while chickadees in another group simply learned to feed from opened tubs. Birds in both groups were subsequently more likely to open sealed tubs on their own than chickadees that had observed an empty cage containing a closed cream tub, but the proportion of opening individuals in the two groups did not differ.

The products of a conspecific's behavior may facilitate learning by naive individuals in a number of ways. Adult black rats of the Israeli pine forests, described at the beginning of the chapter, do not directly teach or demonstrate efficient pine cone stripping to their young. Rather, cones partially stripped by experienced rats have their scales exposed in such a way that a young rat gnawing at the cone can easily remove them in an efficient, spiral, pattern, and get at the seeds underneath. Naive rats encountering completely unopened cones gnaw them all over in an inefficient way

Figure 13.6. A blue tit peeling the top off a milk bottle and drinking the cream underneath. Redrawn from Gould and Gould (1994) with permission.

(Aisner and Terkel 1992; Zohar and Terkel 1996). Thus efficient stripping of scales from pine cones, which the rats must develop in order to access their only food in the forest, is socially transmitted when the young rats follow adults around, steal partially opened cones, and continue the stripping themselves (Terkel 1995). This is "social learning" only because the adults create the conditions necessary for it to occur; successful actions emerge through trial and error learning by individuals. In other cases, the products of one individual's behavior attract others to the same sites, allowing those individuals to learn something there. For instance, rats' preference for sites surrounded with fresh rat excrement leads them to become familiar with food eaten by other rats (Laland and Plotkin 1991). This kind of social influence is referred to as *local enhancement* or *stimulus enhancement* (Box 13.1; Galef 1988; Whiten and Ham 1992; Heyes 1994a). The demonstrator's behavior or some product of it attracts the observer to a location or stimulus which it then learns about on its own.

13.2.2   Observational conditioning

In observational conditioning the demonstrator's actions or the affective state and behavior they arouse in the observer are associated with stimuli present at the time. As a result, the observer performs similar species-typical behavior when it encounters those stimuli again by itself. One striking example is provided by the mobbing that small birds direct toward predators. In mobbing, as the name suggests, birds approach a predator in a group, calling in a distinctive way. This behavior functions to alert potential victims in the area to the location of the predator and may also drive the predator away. Some common predators like owls may be mobbed even by naive birds, but mobbing can depend on social learning (Curio 1988). Social transmission of enemy recognition has been studied in European blackbirds in the apparatus depicted in Figure 13.7. A "teacher" sees a stuffed owl in the central compartment. The "pupil" sees and hears the teacher mobbing the owl and is stimulated to engage in mobbing behavior itself. However, in its side of the central compartment the pupil sees not the owl but a harmless bird like a honeyeater or an owl-sized plastic bottle. When the pupil later encounters the training object by itself, it will mob it. The pupil can now "teach" naive blackbirds to mob bottles or honeyeaters. Such mobbing can be socially transmitted across chains of up to six birds (Curio, Ernst, and Vieth 1978).

This is a straightforward case of Pavlovian conditioning. Because the mobbing demonstrator elicits mobbing by the pupil, the pupil acquires an association between the bottle or honeyeater and its own mobbing behavior system (Figure 13.8). Nonassociative controls are necessary to be sure that mobbing is indeed associated specifically with the training object. For example, birds that have mobbed the honeyeater should not mob bottles as strongly, and vice versa (for review see Curio 1988; A. Griffin 2004). Experiments on acquired mobbing have generally begun with a phase in which the subjects are habituated to the bottle or the honeyeater, so later mobbing is clearly the result of having seen the teacher mob. Robust learning to such objects after habituation to them suggests that latent inhibition is not very strong in this system; naive individuals can thus learn about predators even after encountering them while alone. Another possibly specialized feature of this system is that a more predator-like object, a stuffed honeyeater, supports stronger acquired mobbing than a bottle (Curio 1988). Meerkats, monkeys, and some other social mammals also mob predators, but how mobbing develops in these species has not been studied to the same extent as in birds (A. Griffin 2004; Graw and Manser 2007).

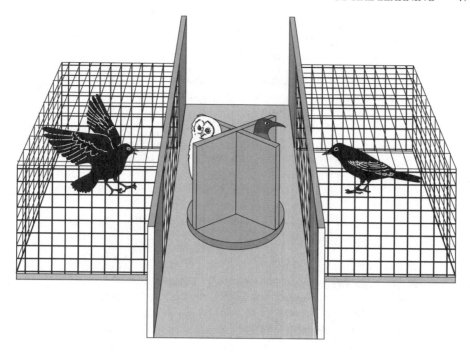

Figure 13.7. Setup for the experiments of Curio and his colleagues in which one blackbird (the one on the left) can "teach" another to mob a harmless object, here a model honeyeater. Redrawn from Gould and Gould (1994) with permission.

Social transmission of predator recognition makes functional sense because individuals that must experience predators for themselves to learn they are dangerous may not survive those experiences. The best-analyzed example involves monkeys' fear of snakes (Mineka and Cook 1988). Monkeys reared in captivity do not exhibit fear the first time they encounter live or toy snakes. If they watch another monkey behaving fearfully toward a snake, they later do the same themselves. As with mobbing, during the learning trial the naive observer exhibits behavior like the model's (in this case responses such as withdrawal, vocalization, and piloerection). If naive monkeys observe a model behaving fearfully toward a snake and neutrally toward another object like a flower, they acquire the same discrimination. For example, if they are later offered raisins that are out of reach beyond a flower or a snake, they reach quickly over the flower but refuse to reach over the snake.

Selective acquisition of fear shows that the animals are not simply sensitized to behave fearfully to any and all relatively novel objects in the experimental situation. However, even though naive monkeys do not show fear to snakes or flowers, they acquire fear much more quickly to snakes than to flowers (Cook and Mineka 1990). Subject monkeys that saw videotapes of demonstrators apparently reacting fearfully to snakes and nonfearfully to flowers acquired fear of snakes, just as if they had seen live demonstrators. However, subjects exposed to tapes edited to depict a monkey fearing flowers but not snakes did not learn to fear either stimulus. This comparison shows simultaneously that snake fear is acquired associatively (it depends on the specific pairing of demonstrator's behavior with a snake) and that the associative process is selective (not any initially neutral object will be feared). Selective learning

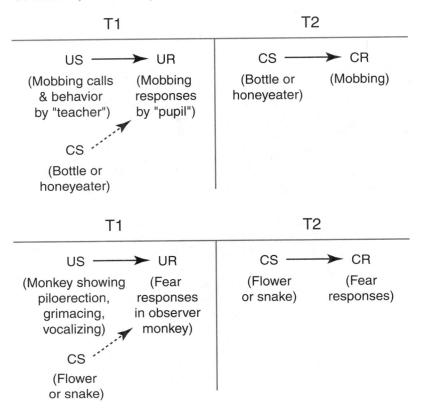

Figure 13.8. Observational conditioning of mobbing or fear as classical conditioning.

about snakes seems to be specific to fear. Monkeys trained with video images of either snakes or flowers paired with food learned equally quickly in both conditions (Cook and Mineka 1990, Experiment 3). However, the stimuli used and the discriminations to be learned were not exactly the same in this experiment as in those involving socially transmitted fear, so this conclusion must be somewhat tentative (Heyes 1994a).

Social learning about aversive events seems to be phylogenetically fairly general (see A. Griffin 2004), as functional considerations suggest it should be. At the same time, the events learned about are species-specific. Several species of birds learn to avoid aversive foods by watching others (Mason 1988; but see Avery 1994). Curio's paradigm (Figure 13.7) has been used to train New Zealand robins to recognize stoats, an introduced predator (Maloney and McLean 1995). Similar training has been used to prepare captive-raised young of endangered species for release in the wild (A. Griffin 2004). Suboski (1990) termed the form of learning here *releaser-induced recognition learning* because in ethological terminology a sign stimulus present at T1 elicits behavior via an innate releasing mechanism. At T2 the animal reveals its recognition of a neutral stimulus that accompanied the releaser. However because the interevent relationships necessary for learning seem to be the same as in simultaneous Pavlovian conditioning (Figure 13.8), it is not clear that any term other than *observational conditioning* (Heyes 1994a) is needed.

Observational conditioning is not confined to aversive USs. Young chicks peck at items they see another chicken or even a motor-driven model beak pecking at, behavior that would normally direct them to food being eaten by a mother hen. If a young chick watches a beak-like object selectively "pecking" dots of one color on the other side of a barrier, it pecks at that same color on its side and retains this discrimination when later tested alone (Suboski and Bartashunas 1984). Similarly, when young junglefowl watch others pecking for food in a distinctively decorated bowl they later peck more in bowls decorated in the same way (McQuoid and Galef 1992). This socially acquired preference was weak and transitory if the bowls were empty in the test, but it was robust and long-lasting if the birds got food in the test. This might be typical of socially acquired preferences (Galef 1995). Because positive reinforcement can perpetuate the behavior once the animal makes the socially induced choice, social learning about positive stimuli need have only a small initial effect to have important consequences.

Most examples of social learning described earlier in this chapter could be described as observational conditioning. The social experiences that influence choice of mates, food patches, flavors, or opponents in a fight are in fact simultaneous pairings of particular individuals, places, or other cues with motivationally signifi-cant stimuli. However, an associative account has implications that need to be tested. At the most basic level, what is the role of contingency between the putative CS and US? Contingency apparently plays a role in socially influenced patch choice in nine-spined (but not three-spined) sticklebacks in that out of two patches where they had seen other fish feeding they preferred the one where food deliveries had been more frequent (Coolen et al. 2003). Cue competition effects might be expected, too, but overshadowing and blocking failed to appear in a study of socially transmitted food preferences in rats (Galef and Durlach 1993). In socially learned mate choice, female zebra finches learn about both a male's identity and an artificial ornament, the color of the band on a male's leg (Swaddle et al. 2005), but whether these cues compete for learning was not tested, for example by manipulating their relative validity. In candidate examples of observational conditioning other than mobbing and snake fear it is unclear how the demonstrators' behavior acts as a US. However, progress in identifying the effective US has been made not only with rats' flavor preferences, but also with mate choice in quail (Ko?ksal and Domjan 1998; White 2004), feeding techniques in pigeons (Palameta and Lefebvre 1985), and feeding patch choice in sticklebacks (Coolen et al. 2005).

In summary, there is plenty of scope for more detailed analyses of what and how animals learn from observing conspecifics engaged in species-typical behavior. In the past such research has been discouraged by confusion over terminology and a ten-dency to dismiss aspects of social transmission other than imitation as both uninter-esting and well understood. As a result there are few such phenomena for which the conditions for learning, the content of learning, and/or the effects of learning on behavior have been clearly delineated. Typical of terms in social learning, and notwithstanding attempts at clarification by Heyes (1994a) and others, *observational conditioning* continues to refer to a confusingly large number of phenomena (cf. Hoppitt et al. 2008). Some of them seem to involve a special learning mechanism, others do not. Learning from watching another animal perform an arbitrary behavior B and receive outcome O could be described as S-S (stimulus-stimulus) learning. It might even follow associative principles, but no performance rule for normal con-ditioning seems able to explain how knowledge that someone else gets O for perform-ing B leads the observer to perform B when it desires O (Papineau and Heyes 2006).

13.2.3   Species differences

Social learning might be expected to vary across species with the conditions of social life. So far, however, we have encountered no evidence for any qualitatively special *kind* of representations or computations. Socially transmitted behavior such as black rats' pine cone stripping and tits' milk bottle opening is best described as *socially influenced learning* in that conspecifics provide the conditions under which the given behaviors are learned by normal associative means. And mate choice copying, socially transmitted food and patch preferences, or enemy recognition all seem to be instances of observational conditioning, as broadly defined. But smelling food together with carbon disulphide or seeing a hen pecking red food results in learning only in species with the appropriate specializations of perception, attention, or motivation. Rats' breath is presumably not interesting to chickens, nor is the sight of chickens pecking interesting to rats. Specializations of learning per se could also play a role, as illustrated by the predisposition of monkeys to acquire fear to snakes but not flowers, stimuli which are apparently equally easy to associate with food (Mineka and Cook 1988). However, with the exception of demonstrations that learning about sexual partners is expressed through different performance rules in male versus female quail (White 2004), there are virtually no thorough comparative studies of any of the sorts of social learning reviewed in this section. But there are a few tantalizing suggestions.

For example, the notion that animals which do not spend much time in family groups should not learn very well from adults was tested by exposing young brush turkey chicks to a brush turkey robot pecking at corn in a red as opposed to a blue dish (Go?th and Evans 2005). In studies like those already mentioned in this section (see Go?th and Evans 2005), young chickens acquire the same discrimination as a model. However, brush turkeys bury their eggs in a mound of rotting vegetation. The young hatch without adults around and have little opportunity for social learning about food. Indeed the young brush turkeys in Goth and Evans's experiment did not prefer the color pecked by the model when tested the next day even though they had approached that color more during the demonstration. Of course data from a single set of conditions are seldom enough to infer a species difference, let alone show what it consists of, but the effect is quite robust in the comparison species, junglefowl and their domestic descendents. The young brush turkeys seem to attend to and copy the choice of the robot so perhaps they forget more quickly than chickens do.

One possible source of species differences in social learning is attentiveness to the activities of other animals, which could perhaps be acquired. Such differences in attention could be responsible for the differences in social learning about the locations of food caches among corvids described in Chapter 8. Indeed, there is some indication of differences in social attention in two other corvids, ravens and jackdaws. This was demonstrated with the setup shown in Figure 13.9 (Scheid, Range, and Bugnyar 2007), one adopted from experiments with primates (e.g., Range and Huber 2007). Both ravens and jackdaws are quite social, but the nature of their sociality differs in a way that the authors argue favors ravens paying more attention to the activities of others, especially their feeding. As predicted, raven subjects spent more time observing a conspecific than did jackdaws. Again, this is only a single set of conditions, and it is important to know whether the results hold up when conditions such as size and ease of access to the viewing ports are varied. Still, this seems a promising method for measuring social attention.

Possible specializations for social learning can be tested very elegantly if the relevant task can be acquired under both social and nonsocial conditions, as in studies

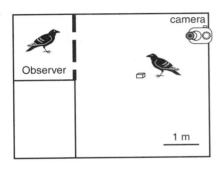 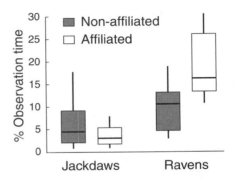

Figure 13.9. Setup for measuring social attention, as used with ravens and jackdaws. Data consist of the proportion of time the camera detected the observer in front of the viewing ports, watching the activities of a feeding conspecific with which it was closely affiliated or not. Adapted from Scheid, Range, and Bugnyar (2007) with permission.

of feeding skills in social versus nonsocial birds by Lefebvre and his colleagues (Lefebvre and Giraldeau 1996). They tested the notion that opportunistic animals such as rats and pigeons, which have fairly generalized food requirements and can take advantage of a wide range of niches, might be more prone to social influences than more conservative species. But because opportunism by definition is the ability to function effectively in a many different environments, opportunistic animals might have generally enhanced learning ability. On this latter hypothesis performance on social learning tasks should correlate positively with performance on nonsocial tasks. Yet another hypothesis is that social learning is most evident in species whose foraging is a matter of *scramble competition,* that is, many individuals feeding at once on limited food sources, as opposed to *interference competition,* where foragers aggressively exclude competitors. Success in scramble competition is a matter of speed, so slow individuals can benefit by learning the techniques being used by their speedier competitors (Lefebvre and Giraldeau 1996). If all these factors are important, then social, opportunistic animals that encounter scramble competitions for food will be the best social learners, whereas solitary species that compete with others by exclusion and have conservative food habits will be the poorest.

All these predictions were addressed by comparing how pigeons and a close relative, the Zenaida dove (*Zenaida aurita*) from Barbados, learn various foraging tasks socially and individually. Pigeons are social and opportunistic and encounter scramble competitions while foraging, so they should excel at social learning. Most Zenaida doves are territorial year-round but tolerate and even forage with birds of other species like grackles (*Quiscalus lugubris*). At first glance, Zenaida doves and pigeons differ in social learning just as the three ecological hypotheses predict. Naive pigeons and doves were equally unlikely to push the lid off a bowl of grain (Figure 13.10, top row), but after watching a conspecific push off the lid and eat the grain underneath, more pigeons than doves pushed off the lid by themselves (Lefebvre, Palameta, and Hatch 1996). However, the pigeons were also quicker to feed from an open bowl of food in the experimental situation, and pigeons pushed off the lid sooner than doves after simply eating from the bowl with no demonstrator present (Figure 13.10, middle row).

These findings suggest that pigeons and Zenaida doves differ not in social learning ability but in some general learning ability or in responses to contextual variables (see Chapter 2). However, the story is still more complicated: Zenaida doves'

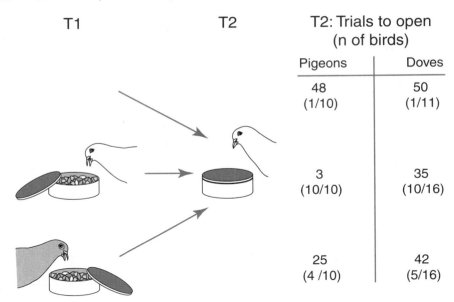

T1	T2	T2: Trials to open (n of birds)	
		Pigeons	Doves
		48 (1/10)	50 (1/11)
		3 (10/10)	35 (10/16)
		25 (4 /10)	42 (5/16)

Figure 13.10. Design and results of experiment by Lefebvre, Palameta, and Hatch (1996) comparing social and individual learning in feral pigeons and Zenaida doves. Each bird had 50 opportunities to open the lid in the test; birds that never opened it were given a score of 50. Numbers in parentheses are the number of birds ever opening the bowl as a fraction of the number of birds in the group.

susceptibility to social influence depends on the species of tutor and on the social situation in which they have been living. In two different feeding tasks, territorial Zenaida doves copied grackles rather than other doves whereas subjects from a gregarious population of Zenaida doves learned more quickly from a dove than from a grackle. These population differences may reflect differences in experience. Gregarious doves could also be shaped more readily than territorial doves to perform a complex food-finding task, suggesting the populations differ in learning ability generally or in something else that influences speed of learning such as neophobia (Dolman, Templeton, and Lefebvre 1996; Carlier and Lefebvre 1997). More extensive comparisons of pigeons and doves, as well as data on several tit species, show that performance on social learning tasks is positively correlated with performance on comparable nonsocial tasks (Lefebvre and Giraldeau 1996). It is also correlated with innovation, both across species and in comparisons of individuals within one species, pigeons (Bouchard, Goodyer, and Lefebvre 2007). Just as innovativeness reflects a concatenation of more general cognitive abilities (Box 2.2) so may "social learning," at least when measured as successfully copying others' behavior in naturalistic conditions. But this analysis begs the question we take up next: whether the narrow but important kind of social learning known as imitation (Box 13.1) is a specialized kind of learning shown by only a few species.

13.3 Mechanisms: Imitation

In imitation, the *form* of a behavior is learned from a demonstrator. Interest in imitation has a long history (cf. Whiten and Ham 1992), but only toward the end of the twentieth century was much progress made in understanding it, as researchers began looking at the development and mechanisms of imitation in humans. As a result candidates for imitation in other species were no longer simply compared to some assumed ideal of human imitation but children and apes were compared directly, often in the same experiments with tasks resembling those chimpanzees are thought to learn socially in the wild. In addition, the discovery of mirror neurons in monkey brains in the late 1990s provided a possible neural mechanism for imitative behavior. All these new findings in turn stimulated new theories about how imitation is possible and its role in the evolution of human culture.

13.3.1   Some history

Imitation is one of the mental faculties Darwin (1871) claimed other species share with humans. Anecdotes about domestic animals apparently imitating complex actions performed by people featured prominently in the evidence for mental continuity collected by Romanes and others. Many of these anecdotes involved cats and dogs learning to open doors and gates by manipulating latches, handles, and door knobs. One of the more colorful of these featured a cat belonging to Romanes's coachman.

> Walking up to the door with a most matter-of-course kind of air, she used to spring at the half-hoop handle just below the thumb-latch. Holding on to the bottom of this half-hoop with one fore-paw, she then raised the other to the thumb-piece, and while depressing the latter, finally with her hind legs scratched and pushed the doorposts so as to open the door.... Of course in all such cases the cats must have previously observed that the doors are opened by persons placing their hands upon the handles, and, having observed this, the animals forthwith act by what may be strictly termed rational imitation.... First the animal must have observed that the door is opened by the hand grasping the handle and moving the latch. Next she must reason, by 'the logic of feelings'—If a hand can do it, why not a paw? (Romanes 1892, 421–422).

"If a hand, why not a paw" captures very well what is cognitively distinctive about imitation. True imitation entails using a representation of a demonstrator's action to generate an otherwise unlikely action that matches the demonstrator's. The cat at the gate is at most matching visually perceptible actions of its own to equally perceptible actions of another, that is, grasping the latch, and so forth. An apparently greater cognitive challenge is reproducing a model's *perceptually opaque* actions, that is, those like facial expressions or whole-body movements that one cannot see or hear oneself perform (Heyes and Ray 2000). In either case, performance of a species-specific activity under the direct influence of another animal does not qualify. Thorndike (1911/1970) made this point with an anecdote about a flock of sheep being driven along a path, each jumping where the one in front of it had jumped, even when the barrier that originally occasioned jumping had been removed. "The sheep jumps when he sees other sheep jump, not because of a general ability to do what he sees done, but because he is furnished with the instinct to jump at such a sight, or because his experience of following the flock over boulders has got him into the habit of jumping at the spot where he sees one ahead of him jump."

What Thorndike emphasized still bears repeating (Galef 1996a): by themselves, observations like those of cats opening latches or sheep all jumping in the same place cannot reveal how such behavior came about. Field data can be enormously suggestive, but experiments, or at least systematic observations of acquisition, are required

Box 13.2 Vocal Imitation: Bird Song Learning

Song learning by birds is the best-studied and most widely distributed example of learning by imitation, yet is it usually omitted from theoretical discussions of animal imitation, largely because the actions copied are not perceptually opaque. That is, the learner hears itself as it hears others. In addition because it is found in only one group of species and involves a system highly specialized both behaviorally and neurally it may seem to have few lessons to teach about imitation in general. But by the same token it is important in the context of this book as an excellent example of a specialized module fine-tuned in species-specific ways.

Song refers to birds' species-typical musical vocalizations, usually emitted primarily by males in the breeding season. Depending on species, males sing from one to over a hundred distinct songs. Song functions in territory defense and advertisement and in attracting mates. Females, of course, must respond selectively to the features of song identifying males of their species, and experience can have a role here too. Vocal learners have been found in oscine birds (a suborder of passeriformes or perching birds, 46% of the approximately 9000 species of birds; Gill 1995), parrots, and hummingbirds. Many are altricial, that is, they hatch naked and helpless, but may develop very rapidly and leave the nest within two or three weeks. In temperate climates, home of most best-studied species, hatching takes place in spring or early summer, when adult males are still singing. Breeding, and hence singing by adults, ends by late summer. Many species migrate for the winter and return to the breeding grounds the next spring, when the young males are ready to breed. This life history means that song learning has two phases, a sensory phase, in which the bird stores auditory information, and a motor phase perhaps many months later, in which this memory guides the bird's song. The onset of the motor learning phase may be evident in *subsong,* quiet, rather formless vocalizations with few identifiable elements of adult song. Shortly before full song appears is a period of plastic song. Plastic song includes many elements identifiable in adult song, but these may drop out as the bird comes to sing one or more (depending on species) crystallized adult songs that may remain in its repertoire for life (Catchpole and Slater 1995). Some species have a third, action-based learning phase, when feedback from other birds influences the male's repertoire.

Contemporary research on the behavioral and neurobiological aspects of bird song learning is the subject of books in itself (e.g., Marler and Slabbekoorn 2004; Zeigler and Marler 2004), but its major themes are evident in research on one of the first species studied in detail, the white-crowned sparrow of North America (*Zonotrichia leucophrys*). Each male white-crowned sparrow has a single, rather simple, song, which he shares with his neighbors. Males in different geographical areas have different songs, that is, there are local dialects (Marler and Tamura 1964). White-crowned sparrows reared in isolation sing abnormal songs, but their songs still develop, from disorganized and variable vocalizations to a single stereotyped song with some species-typical characteristics. Deafened birds also fail to develop normal song, but their vocalizations are more abnormal. The contrast between isolated and early-deafened birds (Figure B13.2a) indicates that progression from subsong to crystallized but atypical song in isolates depends on auditory feedback from the bird's own vocalizations. Feedback may not be important for maintaining the structure of crystallized song, as indicated by the fact that white-crowned sparrows with normal early experience that are deafened as adults continue to sing normally.

White-crowned sparrows taken from the nest at a few days of age and reared in isolation acquire normal song if they hear tape-recorded white-crowned sparrow songs between 10 and 50 days of age (Marler 1970). They acquire the song they hear even if it is not from the same dialect area where they were born, but they do not learn the songs of other species from tape recordings. Just as with imprinting (Chapter 5), the sensitive phase for learning may depend on the stimuli available for learning. For example, white-crowned sparrows learn from live tutors when tapes are no longer effective. They will also learn the songs of other species from live tutors.

The model of song learning suggested by these observations is depicted in Figure B13.2b (Konishi 1965). The bird hatches with a rough representation of its species-typical song, an *auditory template.* During the sensitive period for sensory learning, the template selects in a species-specific way what songs will be learned (see also Section 1.2.2 and Figure 1.3). The hypothetical template is separate from general auditory selectivity: birds can perceive and memorize many songs that they never sing themselves, as in recognizing their neighbors. Early experience hearing song is stored as modifications of the template. During the motor learning phase the bird learns to sing songs he has heard by matching his vocalizations to the refined template. A bird reared in isolation has only the rough, unmodified, template as a guide during the motor phase of learning, as witnessed by the fact that its song has more species-typical characteristics than the song of a bird deafened before the onset of singing.

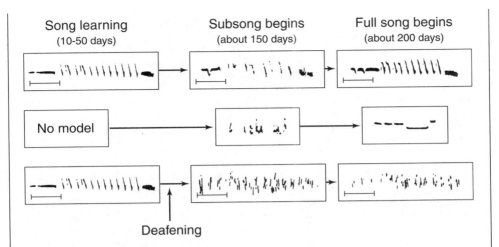

Figure B13.2a. Comparison of song development in normal and isolated male white-crowned sparrows (top two rows) and in birds deafened after hearing normal song during the sensitive period for vocal learning. Left-most sonagrams (plots of sound frequency vs. time) in top and bottom sequences represent the songs heard by the subjects; others represent the songs they sang. After Marler (1976) with permission.

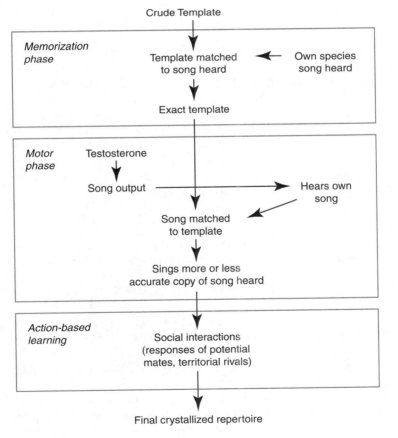

Figure B13.2b. The template model of bird song learning. After Slater (1983) with permission.

485

Species differences in song learning can be described within the framework provided by the template model. The optimal time and stimuli for learning vary across species in ways related to the species ecology (Beecher and Brenowitz 2005), as do the roles of early learning and later experiences. Purely acoustic features may be used to select what is learned, as in swamp and song sparrows (see Figure 1.3), or features of the singer may be important, for example learning may be best from the father or a socially dominant male. Some species, such as starlings, mimic songs of other birds and all sorts of natural sounds, that is, they show very little species-specific selectivity. And song production may not require learning early in life. In the brood-parasitic cowbirds, which are raised by adults of another species, young males sing effective cowbird song but its form is later shaped by the aggressive responses of other males and the sexual responses of females, essentially through operant conditioning (West and King 1988).

Species that learn song have a specialized network of interconnected nuclei, *the song system,* that is involved in song perception, learning, and production, although other parts of the brain may be involved as well (for a brief review see Bolhuis and Gahr 2006). The neurobiological basis of bird song is very well characterized yet a continuing source of new insights. For example, techniques for recording activity of single cells during singing have revealed the equivalent of mirror neurons, cells that fire preferentially to note patterns in the bird's own song when sung by itself or another bird (Prather et al. 2008). Singing has been studied as an example of a highly practiced and precise motor skill that nevertheless shows instructive forms of plasticity (Turner and Brainard 2007). And over the years discoveries about the song system have had wider implications. Seasonal neurogenesis in adult brains, presumably related to the seasonality of singing in some way, was demonstrated in the song system and stimulated a search for neurogenesis in other systems. And like the neurobiological basis of human language, the song system is lateralized and is most plastic early in life.

to know whether behavior has developed through imitation or in some other way. Thorndike's (1911/1970) own experiments were based fairly directly on Romanes's stories about dogs and cats opening latches. But instead of letting animals open gates, Thorndike confined them in "puzzle boxes" that could be opened in various ways to allow the animal to escape and find food. In his experiments on imitation, a cat or a young chick was allowed to learn by itself, by trial and error, how to escape. Then a second, observer animal watched. If observers learned faster than demonstrators, imitation must have occurred. Thorndike's experiments with cats and chicks provided no evidence for imitation, but he did leave open the possibility that monkeys would imitate, a possibility that continues to be debated.

13.3.2   Birds and the two-action test

Because one animal's behavior can come to resemble another's in so many ways, imitation sometimes seems to be what's left over when all other conceivable routes for social learning have been ruled out (Zentall 1996, 2006a). An experimental approach that goes a long way to ruling them out was pioneered by Thorndike (1911/1970). A puzzle box had two escape routes, and a chick watched another chick using one of them. If the observer chick imitated it should follow the same route as the demonstrator rather than the alternative, equally easy, one. In the more refined version developed by Dawson and Foss (1965; see also Galef, Manzig, and Field 1986), this design is known as the *two-action test* (Zentall 1996; Heyes 1996). Two-action tests typically involve an object, sometimes a tool, that can be operated on with either of two responses such lifting versus pushing or twisting versus pulling. Ideally both responses move the object in the same way. Otherwise, observers may copy the model not because they imitated its behavior but because they *emulated* or *learned the affordances* of the object (see Box 13.1).

Emulation tends to be invoked when observers copy demonstrators only crudely. For example, observer chimpanzees learned more quickly to use a tool to rake food into the cage than did controls that had not seen the tool being used, but they did not use the same technique as the demonstrator (Tomasello et al. 1987). *Emulation* has come to have a confusing variety of meanings referring to different kinds of learning thought to underlie the behavior (Box 13.1 and Whiten et al. 2004). Observers may have learned that there is a reward to be obtained or that the object is related to obtaining the reward. An associative analysis (Heyes 2005; Papineau and Heyes 2006) would see the first of these as situation-outcome learning and the second as object-outcome learning. Apparent emulators may have learned the object's affordances, that is, that it can be moved in a certain way, although how this learning could translate into behavior causing that same motion is itself mysterious (Zentall 2004). In any case, some birds as well as primates (Hopper et al. 2008) show affordance learning. For example, when pigeons saw a door move away from a food tray either to the left or to the right, they later more often pushed it in the direction they saw than in the opposite direction (Klein and Zentall 2003). Finally, an observer with theory of mind might infer the demonstrator's intentions and copy those, a process also sometimes referred to as *goal emulation* (see Whiten et al. 2004). However, given the paucity of more direct evidence for theory of mind in nonhuman animals (Chapter 12), there seems to be no good reason to invoke it here whatever the results of tests of imitation. As Heyes (1993a, 1008) put it, "What is apparently essential for imitation is that the imitating animal represent what the demonstrator did, not what it thought." The same can be said of emulation.

Some birds imitate in two-action tests (Zentall 2004). Many of these demonstrations involve a treadle that can be depressed by pecking it or stepping on it. Importantly, pecking and stepping are perceptually opaque responses that differ in topography but cause the lever to move in the same way. In one of the first studies with quail, for example, each subject was trained to eat from the feeder in the demonstrator's compartment before being placed in a neighboring compartment to view a demonstrator either peck or step on the treadle and receive food reinforcers for 10 minutes (Akins and Zentall 1996). When observers were returned to the response half of the chamber immediately after this experience, every bird's first response to the treadle matched the responses it had observed. In the first five minutes of the reinforced test, on average about 90% of the responses to the treadle were imitative responses (Figure 13.11). Of course (see Heyes 1996; Whiten et al. 2004) the birds' behavior does not strictly qualify as imitation because the motor patterns being copied are not novel and unusual behaviors for the species. Nonetheless, considerable progress has been made in analyzing the learning of quail and pigeons in this situation (see Zentall 2004). Importantly (see Box 13.1), imitative behavior does not depend on being tested immediately; in quail it is also evident in a test delayed 30 minutes, more consistent with learning than some sort of temporary facilitation (Dorrance and Zentall 2001).

The robust copying of pecking and stepping sets the stage to discover what the animals actually learn from watching. Because the treadle moves in the same way whether it is pecked or stepped on, the birds must have acquired some representation of the observer's action. Does it matter if the demonstrator is seen to be rewarded for its efforts? Studies with quail indicate that little imitation occurs if either demonstrators are not hungry or observers are not rewarded (Zentall 2004). However, this does

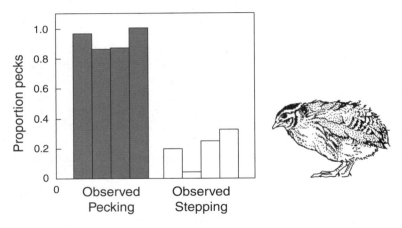

Figure 13.11. Proportion of individual quails' responses to a lever that were pecks during the first five minutes of a two-action test. Redrawn from Akins and Zentall (1996) with permission.

not necessarily mean that observers are learning response-food associations by observation; being hungry and seeing the demonstrator getting food might only increase the observer's attention to the demonstration. Indeed, there is evidence for blind imitation in this kind of situation (i.e., copying the observer regardless of the outcome it is getting), at least with already-trained responses. Pigeons that have been shaped both to peck and to step on a treadle and then watch a demonstrator pecking or stepping subsequently increase their own tendency to perform the same action, whether or not the demonstrator was being rewarded (McGregor et al. 2006). In a similar test in which the demonstrator pecks in the presence of one colored light and steps in the presence of another, pigeons acquire the observed stimulus-response associations (Saggerson, George, and Honey 2005). It is not yet clear whether these findings means that pigeons (and perhaps other birds) always engage in blind imitation or whether imitation is goal-directed under some conditions (McGregor et al. 2006).

As mentioned earlier (Section 13.1.2), social learning is more likely to be adaptive if animals do not always do what others are doing. But the fact that blind imitation occurs when all other factors that might be relevant are tightly controlled does not mean it would lead to maladaptive consequences in nature. For example, in the study of McGregor et al., observers were not rewarded in the test; they might not have copied the demonstrator for long if reward had been available for some alternative behavior. In any case, this series of studies is an important beginning to understanding the conditions for learning by imitation. Further insights come from recent studies of primates.

13.3.3   Chimpanzees and children

Until the last decade or so of the twentieth century, most evidence regarding imitation in monkeys and apes consisted of anecdotes from the field or from captive animals reared in close association with humans (Whiten et al. 2004). Because human children seem to be good imitators, our closest living relatives were assumed to be good imitators too. Indeed, in many languages the same word (e.g., *ape*) refers both to a nonhuman primate and to the act of imitating (Visalberghi and Fragaszy 1990a). The assumption that apes *can* ape led to skepticism about suggestions that they do not ape very readily or exactly and to a lack of experimental tests of imitation in primates. The situation has changed dramatically in the last 15 to 20 years. A recent review lists over 30 studies of apes (Whiten et al. 2004), and that does not include a more recent spate of direct comparisons between chimpanzees and children (e.g., Call, Carpenter, and Tomasello 2005; Horner and Whiten 2005; Herrmann et al. 2007). These studies are important not only for how they illuminate mechanisms of imitation but also for what they imply about human cognitive uniqueness and the abilities that support human culture.

A breakthrough here was an experiment by Whiten et al. (1996). These researchers both gave chimpanzees a two-action test of imitation and tested young children under the same conditions (see also Nagell, Olguin, and Tomasello 1993). Moreover, their task—opening an "artificial fruit"—resembled foraging behaviors chimpanzees might learn by imitation in the wild. The artificial fruit was a transparent plastic box containing a food treat which could be opened by manipulating various handles or bolts (Figure 13.12). In one version the lid was closed by two bolts that could be either poked or twisted out. Captive chimpanzees or 2-, 3-, or 4-year-old children saw a human adult poke or twist the bolts and then were given a similar "fruit" that could be opened using either action. Subjects' behavior was videotaped and scored independently by two observers ignorant of which action the subjects had witnessed. Subjects of both species were significantly more likely to use the action they had seen than the alternative (Figure 13.12). The tendency to imitate was least in the chimpanzees and greatest in the 4-year-old children. The children were more likely than the chimpanzees to copy slavishly even nonfunctional parts of the demonstrator's acts, as if taking for granted that an adult's way of doing things is worth copying. The chimpanzees did direct their behavior at the correct part of the box even when they

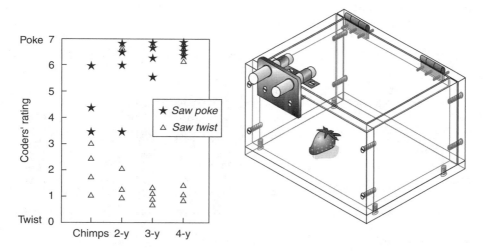

Figure 13.12. Coders' ratings of the performance of chimpanzees and 2-, 3-, and 4-year-old children presented with the artificial fruit at right as a function of whether the subjects had seen a human adult demonstrator poke or twist the bolts. Each data point represents one subject, rated on a 7-point scale as to whether actions on the bolts more resembled poking or twisting. Redrawn from Whiten et al. (1996) with permission.

did not use the same actions they had seen, that is, emulating or showing they had learned the affordances of the apparatus (the bolts come out; the box opens).

One of the first questions these findings raise is whether the chimpanzees would copy more precisely with a chimpanzee rather than a human demonstrator. The answer to this question seems to be "no" (Whiten et al. 2004). Given that the chimpanzees did show some copying of the demonstrated actions, another question is what determines the extent to which they imitate specific actions as opposed to emulate or learn affordances? One suggestion is that imitation plays a greater role in more complex tasks. Conversely, nonsocial processes such as affordance learning appear more important in simple tasks. This latter conclusion is supported by a comparison of two separate studies in which chimpanzees watched devices move by themselves (as if moved by a ghost, hence *ghost conditions*). Using a scaled-up version of Klein and Zentall's (2003) apparatus for pigeons, Hopper and colleagues (2008) had chimpanzees and children watch the door on a box move to the left or the right to reveal food inside (Figure 13.13). The effects of this experience on subjects' subsequent actions on the door were compared to the effects of watching either the door move by itself in the presence of a conspecific who then retrieved the food ("enhanced ghost condition") or a conspecific pushing the door (full demonstration). Chimps and children in all conditions were very likely to push the door in the demonstrated direction on their first opportunity. However, all the children continued to prefer the demonstrated direction, whereas the chimpanzees maintained this preference only if they had seen a chimpanzee doing the pushing. Still, their initial responses are evidence that they learned the affordance of this simple apparatus in which the part to be moved was very close to the food. These results contrast with those obtained when a more complex task was used in a test of social transmission within chimpanzee groups (see Section 13.5 and Hopper et al. 2007). Here a stick had to be used to lift a T-shaped bar on top of a box so that food would roll out at the bottom of the box. Only one of 18 chimpanzees exposed to a ghost condition operated the apparatus successfully in a subsequent 1-hour test. A larger proportion of successes followed demonstrations in which a chimpanzee lifted the T bar. However, this was a

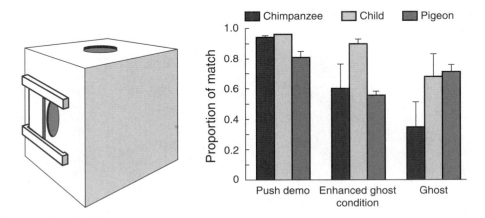

Figure 13.13. Apparatus used for two-action tests of chimpanzees, children and pigeons. Subjects saw the sliding door on the front of the box moved to the left (as shown) or the right. Data are mean proportion of their own attempts to push the door in the same direction. Hole in the top of the box is for inserting the food. After Hopper et al. (2008) with permission.

difficult task in that there were relatively few successes compared to those in an alternative version in which the food was released by poking the tool into a hole.

Although increased task difficulty (and perhaps remoteness of the reward from the object to be moved) seems to reduce affordance learning or emulation, it seems to enhance learning by imitation. Perhaps the most striking evidence for this conclusion comes from another comparison of chimpanzees and children (see also Call, Carpenter, and Tomasello 2005; Horner and Whiten 2005) involving copying several actions in sequence, a capability for which there was already some evidence from chimpanzees (Whiten 1998) and gorillas (Stoinski et al. 2001). Here both chimpanzees and 4-year-old children watched a human adult use a stick to perform one of two sequences of actions on the box shown in Figure 13.14. The only functional part of these sequences involved sliding or lifting the door in the front of the box and pulling out a packet of food with the stick. The demonstrator began, however, by tapping the bolt on top of the box, then moving it aside to reveal a hole and thrusting the stick into the hole. These actions were done in a slightly different way for each of two subgroups, making this as well as the sliding versus lifting of the door a two-action test. In either case they were irrelevant to operation of the box because a barrier separated the top half of the box from the food. Their causal irrelevance was evident in a transparent version of the box but not in an opaque one. Subjects of both species frequently copied the sequence of actions they saw, but the most important result of this study is that whereas the children imitated the irrelevant action of inserting the tool into the top of the box about 80% of the time whether the box was opaque or clear, the chimpanzees did so much more often when the box was opaque (Figure 13.14). If exposed and tested with the clear box, they most often bypassed this part of the sequence and went straight to operations on the door over the food. The authors interpret this finding to mean that when the causal structure of the task was evident the chimpanzees emulated, that is, primarily relied on learning about the results of actions.

It is not clear from this experiment alone, however, whether the animals' ability to see the effects of the irrelevant actions affected learning or performance. Perhaps they learn about both the actions of the demonstrator and the goal that can be obtained

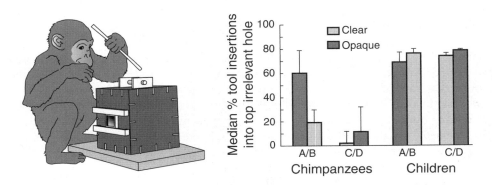

Figure 13.14. Apparatus for testing copying of a sequence of actions by children and chimpanzees, here in the opaque version. Copying the human demonstrator's action of inserting the stick tool into the top of either box, as this subject is about to do, is functionally irrelevant to obtaining reward, which is behind the door on the side. A/B and C/D refer to different orders of presenting an opaque and a clear box, as explained in the text. After Horner and Whiten (2005) with permission.

but goal-related cues take precedence in control of behavior when they are very salient. Animals trained first with the opaque box could learn from observation and personal experience about the food-containing part of the apparatus that lay behind the door; once they could actually see it through the transparent box, direct approach evidently took precedence over imitating earlier parts of the sequence (group A/B in Figure 3.14). Animals trained first with the transparent box continued to go directly to operating the door when given trials with the opaque box (group C/D), but of course by then they had a history of immediate reward for these actions. Interestingly, however, whatever else they did all animals had a significant tendency to move the door in the way they had seen it moved by the demonstrator.

Horner and Whiten (2005) discuss their findings in the spirit of an analysis of human imitation proposed by Wohlschla?ger, Gattis, and Bekkering (2003). This starts from realizing that a demonstration of a complex action on an object has several distinct elements including not only the actions but the object(s), and the outcome of the actions (i.e., the affordances of the object and/or rewards for the demonstrator). Attention to actions may result in imitation, but an observer might instead attend to and learn about the object and/or the outcome. In any case, when the observer confronts the task alone later, memory of one or more of these features will be activated and this in turn will elicit relevant motor programs (for example, copying the action, interacting with the object, trying to obtain the goal directly). Wohlschla?ger and colleagues (2003) propose that the goal of the action always takes highest priority in controlling the observer's behavior. However, priorities vary with the direction of attention, as shown by Bird et al. (2007). People were asked to copy the actions of a model who grasped a pen and placed it into one of two nearby cups. Different elements of this simple demonstration were made more or less distinctive and subjects' copying errors were measured. For example, when the model's hands had differently colored gloves and the cups did not differ in color, subjects made fewer errors in copying which hand to use and more in copying the cup than when the reverse was true.

Bird and colleagues (2007, 1166) conclude that, "the mechanisms that mediate imitation are plastic with respect to the processing of ends and means. Furthermore, the factors influencing which aspects of an action are imitated are task general." Similarly, Horner and Whiten (2005) suggest that chimpanzees attend to different aspects of a demonstration in different circumstances, and imitation, emulation, or something else predominates accordingly. Children, however, seem to have a consistent bias toward imitation (see also Want and Harris 2002). Whether this represents a predisposition present from a very young age and how much it is enhanced by the experience of being constantly shown things by adults is a matter of debate. Moreover, under some conditions young children do not slavishly copy unusual actions of a demonstrator but do the same thing with a different action, as if copying the demonstrator's intention (Gergely and Csibra 2003) or engaging in goal emulation. In any case, an account of variations in chimpanzees' tendency to imitate in terms of variations in attention or memory explains everything and nothing. Experiments with chimpanzees like those of Bird et al. (2007) in which factors known to influence attention are manipulated without otherwise changing the structure of the task being demonstrated will be required to test it.

13.3.4   Do monkeys ape?

Insofar as they have been tested, the other three great ape species (gorillas, orangu-tans, and bonobos) behave similarly to chimpanzees: they imitate to some extent but may copy in other ways too (Whiten et al. 2004). In contrast, there is very little evidence that monkeys of any species imitate in the narrow sense of copying specific actions they have witnessed (Fragaszy and Visalberghi 2004). An exception is the performance of marmosets in a two-action test (Voelkl and Huber 2000). After seeing a demonstrator marmoset use either its mouth or its hand to pull the lid off a film canister and get food inside, observers were more likely to use the action they saw than the alternative. More typical is the finding that capuchin monkeys exposed to conspecifics that were proficient at using a stick to get reward from a tube in the task described in Chapter 11 showed no evidence of imitating them (see Fragaszy and Visalberghi 2004). But notwithstanding their evident failure to copy exactly the actions they have witnessed, many monkey species do show various kinds of social influences on learning (see Fragaszy and Visalberghi 2004). This propensity may lead to social transmission of tool use and other behaviors in some wild monkeys (Section 13.5). In the laboratory, monkeys have provided the only evidence for two novel kinds of imitative learning. In one case, rhesus macaques looked longer at a person who was copying their actions on a novel object than at a second person who handled the object at the same time but did different things with it (Paukner et al. 2005). Thus even though they do not imitate the actions of others very well, monkeys apparently notice when another is imitating them.

In the second novel form of imitation, one of two experienced rhesus macaques watched from an adjoining operant chamber while the other one executed a simultaneous chain that was novel for the observer (Subiaul et al. 2004). In the simultaneous chaining task (Section 10.3), the animal learns to touch a series of arbitrary images in a fixed order. By what the authors call *cognitive imitation,* the observer could learn not the required actions, which in any case varied from trial to trial with the positions of the images on the touchscreen, but the correct sequence of images. Both monkeys in this study showed cognitive imitation in that they completed the first trial of a new sequence with fewer errors after watching the knowledgeable partner than under various control conditions, including exposure to a computer replay of the sequence of images and sounds generated by a knowledgeable partner. Two-year-old children also show cognitive imitation in this task (Subiaul et al. 2007). Learning sequences of actions in this way may have contributed to the performance of subjects in some of the multistage tool-using tasks described earlier.

13.3.5 Other candidates for visual imitation

Although imitation must ultimately be studied with experiments on groups of subjects, it is pretty compelling to see even a single animal do something like put on lipstick or use a tool in a way it has seen humans do. In a sense these are "multiple action tests" because there is a multitude of things the animal might do at the time. The literature on imitation by primates is full of accounts of such behaviors, mostly by chimpanzees and orangutans that have lived closely with people (see Whiten and Ham 1992; Whiten et al. 1996). One of the first of these was the chimpanzee Viki, raised like a child by the psychologists Keith and Cathy Hayes (Hayes and Hayes 1952). The Hayeses demonstrated that Viki had a fairly general ability to imitate novel actions by training her to obey the spoken command, "Do this." Custance, Whiten, and Bard (1995) trained two laboratory-reared chimpanzees in a similar way to the Hayeses but documented the procedures and results more fully. The animals were reinforced for obeying "Do this" using a set of fifteen actions like raising the arms, stamping, and wiping one hand on the floor. After more than three months of intensive training, they reproduced these actions with 80% accuracy or better. In a test with 48 other actions, observers who did not know what the model was doing could classify the chimps' actions at better than chance levels, but the agreement was far from perfect, suggesting that the animals were still not very good generalized imitators.

A host of accounts of orangutans reproducing complex human activities like using hammers and paintbrushes, constructing bridges out of logs, and making fires (!) comes from observations on formerly captive orangutans being rehabilitated for release in the Indonesian jungle (Russon and Galdikas 1993, 1995). Observations of complex imitations are not confined to primates, either. Alex the parrot learned to talk by watching two people, one of whom played the role of parrot and was rewarded by the other for pronouncing and using words correctly (Pepperberg 1999). This situation is thought to reproduce the social situation in which wild parrots acquire vocalizations. However, once Alex began to vocalize himself, he received attention, food, and/or access to the objects he was naming, and in any case vocal imitation is usually treated as a special case (see Box 13.2).

Explicit reward was scrupulously avoided with another parrot, Okichoro, trained by Moore (1992) to vocalize and imitate associated movements. The bird lived alone in a large laboratory room and was visited several times a day by a keeper who performed various stereotyped behavior sequences such as waving while saying "ciao" or opening his mouth and saying "look at my tongue." Gradually Okichoro, observed continuously on closed-circuit TV, began to imitate both the actions and the words of the keeper while he was alone (Figure 13.15). Because each vocalization in effect labeled a specific movement, possible imitation could be isolated from the stream of nonimitative behavior. And unlike pecking or stepping in quail, behaviors such as waving a foot while saying "ciao" are normally highly unlikely. Eventually many cases of imitation were recorded, including some nonvocal mimicry of sounds. For instance, the parrot imitated someone rapping on the door by rapping its beak on a perch. Moore (1996) claims that this is a special category of imitative learning, one of several that have evolved independently.

"Ciao"   "Look at my tongue"   "Nod"

Figure 13.15. Okichoro performing some of his imitations. Each action was accompanied by a vocalization as indicated. After photographs in Moore (1992) with permission.

Although they are entertaining, such examples are prone to the weaknesses that afflict most anecdotal evidence. First, they are often based on a very special single subject. We may not know the animal's history. Was it reinforced for approximations to the purportedly imitated behavior or similar actions in the past? This lack of necessary background information very often characterizes isolated observations in the field, but studying animals in captivity is not always the solution. As with Alex or the orangutans, lengthy and complex experience often precedes the behaviors of interest. Even if every effort was made to control this experience, we rarely know precisely what it was. It may also be difficult to determine how selective the observers were in recording the subject's behavior. For instance, in a "do this" test, as opposed to a two-action test, the alternatives to reproducing the model's behavior may not be clearly specified nor is the time interval within which the animal must imitate as opposed to doing something else (Zentall 1996). Like the proverbial band of monkeys who would reproduce the works of Shakespeare if left long enough in a room full of typewriters, primates raised in homelike environments have many opportunities to perform humanlike actions, and those that are most humanlike and striking are most likely to be the ones reported. For example, how often did the formerly captive orangutans do something *inappropriate* like bite a paintbrush, hold it by the bristles, or hit a nail with it? Finally, the observers— for the very reason they are living closely with the animals in the first place—may be biased like proud parents to anthropomorphize what they see their animals do. Another problem for long-term research with one or a few subjects is the possibility of "Clever Hans" effects (Chapter 10), that is, the possibility that the observer is unintentionally influencing the subjects to produce the desired behavior. Unfortunately, being aware that such effects can occur is not necessarily enough to prevent them, and if the relevant contingencies are not detected by the investigators themselves, they may be difficult or impossible for others to detect in published reports.

The reports of imitation summarized here do not necessarily suffer from all, or even any, of these problems. Moore rigorously avoided Clever Hans effects by collecting data only over closed-circuit TV when the parrot was alone and by stopping data collection on any imitation once it had occurred in the presence of the experimenter. The rehabilitant orangutans imitated some elaborate sequences of behavior that were actively discouraged, like stealing boats and riding down the river (Russon and Galdikas 1993). Nevertheless, when assessing either anecdotes from the field or long-term work with a few subjects in captivity it is important to keep such potential problems in mind.

13.3.6   How is imitation possible?

Mirror neurons

How is it possible for me to perform the same action I see someone else perform, especially when that action is perceptually opaque? For example, when quail see other quail step on a treadle, how is it that they themselves later step rather than peck? This is *the correspondence* (Brass and Heyes 2005) or *translation* (Rizzolatti and Fogassi 2007) *problem*. A solution at the neural level is suggested by one of the most remarkable discoveries of late twentieth-century neuroscience, the *mirror neuron system*. This is a network of cells in the premotor cortex, inferior parietal lobule (IPL) and elsewhere in the brains of rhesus macaques that fire *both* when the monkey performs an action itself *and* when it sees the action performed by another. These actions include not only perceptually transparent actions such as grasping and

Figure 13.16. Mirror neurons distinguish between grasping a food pellet to eat it and grasping a nonfood item to place it in a bowl, as shown by the histograms of firing rate versus time below each drawing (data from Fogassi et al. 2005). Note how the neurons shown fire in the same way whether the actions are done by the monkey itself or by a person and that they fire *before* the action is performed (dark vertical bars), suggesting they could code intention. After Nakahara and Miyashita (2005) with permission.

tearing, but actions of the mouth such as biting and sucking (review in Rizzolatti and Fogassi 2007). Some mirror cells respond to auditory as well as visual correlates of actions, for instance firing both to the sound and the sight of paper being torn. In effect cells in the IPL encode not only the surface features of actions but their intent. The same cells that fire most when the monkey or a person reaches toward an object to grasp it also fire when a person reaches toward an object that the monkey has seen placed behind an occluder, making the grasping action invisible, but they do not fire in the absence of an object to be grasped. And in the example in Figure 13.16, grasping an object to eat it is distinguished from grasping to place it in a bowl, whether the monkey itself or a person does the grasping (Fogassi et al. 2005).

The mirror system evidently includes sensory-motor links between the visual and other cues accompanying performance of an action and its motor representation. Brain imaging shows that humans have a mirror system too (Rizzolatti and Fogassi 2007), and experience influences the strength of its sensory-motor links. For example, watching classical ballet is accompanied by greater activation of the mirror system in ballet dancers than in capoeira dancers, and the reverse (Rizzolatti and Fogassi 2007). Even experience over a relatively short term can have an effect (Catmur, Walsh, and Heyes 2007).

Here then is a remarkably rich neural representation of actions as such, encoding own and others' actions in a unitary way. Mirror neurons seem to be just what is needed to generate imitative behavior, but something must be wrong with this idea because, as we have seen, monkeys are not very good imitators. Instead mirror neurons may play some more general role in social cognition by encoding the actions and intentions of others as, in effect, the same as one's own (Rizzolatti and Fogassi 2007; de Waal 2008; but see Jacob and Jeannerod 2005). Still, the mirror system does seem to play a role in imitation in humans, for example being more activated during imitative than control tasks (Brass and Heyes 2005; Rizzolatti and Fogassi 2007).

One difference between monkey and human mirror systems that may underlie species differences in imitation is that the human system seems to encode specific actions more precisely (Rizzolatti and Fogassi 2007). A second difference may be in the degree to which motor output of the mirror system can be engaged selectively. If viewing another's action generates the same premotor activation as one's own intent to perform that action, then some further mechanism must prevent continual automatic and perhaps even dangerous mimicry. On one view (see Rizzolatti and Fogassi 2007) the primary function of the mirror system in all primates is to permit action understanding, not imitation. The flexible inhibitory mechanisms of the human prefrontal cortex permit its selective use to generate imitative actions, whereas in species that lack such mechanisms imitation needs to be inhibited in general.

Associative sequence learning

Consistent with evidence for an influence of experience on representation in the mirror system is a model of imitation developed by Cecilia Heyes (Heyes and Ray 2000, Heyes, 2005). In the associative sequence learning (ASL) model, imitation is the outcome of general associative mechanisms rather than a specialized ability, and it depends on experience during development (Brass and Heyes 2005). The elements of the model are so-called *vertical associations,* associations between sensory and motor activity correlated with one's own perceptible actions, for example the sight of one's own hand grasping and the motor commands to grasp. When an individual observes a sequence of actions performed by a demonstrator, the sequence is encoded as a set of *horizontal associations,* that is, associations within the sensory side. Now an action that is represented as such a chain of sensory-sensory associations will excite the associated motor representations, and, hey presto, the observer reproduces the sequence of actions it saw.

The ASL model can also explain copying of perceptually opaque actions such as pecking or stepping in quail and pigeons. The ASL model assumes that these flock-living birds will have been in situations where all the individuals present are engaged in the same behavior, for example pecking at grain. Such experience allows a bird to associate its own pecking with the sight of others pecking. When it later sees a demonstrator pecking in a certain experimental context it forms a context-other's pecking association. The vertical association between other's and own pecking in turn activates its pecking behavior. This explains why quail and pigeons are good at copying species-specific behaviors. It also may explain the population differences in sensitivity to different kinds of demonstrators documented by Lefebvre and colleagues (Section 13.2.3; Heyes and Ray 2000). It also suggests that experimental manipulations of social experience should influence what and from whom such birds copy, a suggestion that does not seem to have been tested. However, although it does a good job with copying of familiar actions, the ASL model does not seem to account for the essence of true imitation, namely the copying of novel actions as was done by Okichoro. Decomposing such actions into simpler actions which have been performed with conspecifics would seem to make this "simple" account of imitation quite a bit more complex, perhaps unacceptably so.

13.4   Do nonhuman animals teach?

Animals clearly learn from one another's activities or the products of those activities, even if not by imitation. So do any nonhuman species engage in behavior that could be called *teaching?* In humans, teaching seems to involve theory of mind and intentions to modify the pupil's behavior, but just as with *deception, planning,* and similar terms, when it comes to other species we need a clear operational definition that captures the essentials of the relevant behavior without mentalistic implications. In recent years, the accepted functional definition of teaching has been that proposed by Caro and Hauser (1992). To qualify as teaching, an animal has to meet three requirements. *(1)* It must modify its behavior specifically in the presence of naive individuals in such a way as to facilitate their learning. *(2)* The teacher should incur some immediate cost to itself, or at least no immediate benefit. But of course for teaching to evolve the teacher needs to reap some benefit in the longer term, such as reduced time feeding young or increased inclusive fitness due to having knowledgeable offspring. *(3)* As a result of the teacher's behavior the pupil should learn something earlier in life or more rapidly than it would otherwise or that it would not learn at all.

Discussion of teaching thus shifts the focus from processes in naive individuals in a social group to those in experienced ones. Do the latter respond to correlates of ignorance in others by behaving so as to correct it? How are those responses, if any, tailored to the social learning mechanisms in potential pupils? And even if not theory of mind or intentionality, are any distinctive cognitive processes involved in it?

None of the examples of social transmission of information yet reviewed in this chapter meets Caro and Hauser's first requirement. A bird mobbing an owl is not teaching naive individuals what to mob because as far as is known it would be mobbing whether or not they were present. Similarly, rats transmit flavor preferences by serving as passive vehicles for stimuli that other colony members encounter during routine mouth-to-mouth contact. But perhaps teaching is more likely to evolve when the behaviors to be acquired are more demanding and complex than these. Caro and Hauser (1992) described a number of candidates involving capturing prey that are difficult to subdue or handle. For example, domestic cats bring dead birds and mice back to the nest and present them to their kittens. As the kittens mature, mother cats carry back live prey and allow the kittens to play with it, but if the prey escapes the mother still catches it again. Finally the kittens capture prey by themselves with little intervention from the mother. Cheetahs behave similarly. Osprey, which snatch fish from the water in their talons, have been seen apparently teaching their fledglings to forage. However, in none of these cases was it demonstrated what or how much the young actually learn as a result of the adults' behavior. This gap has been filled by a study of meerkats (*Suricata suricatta;* Thornton and McAuliffe 2006), a unique model demonstration of animal teaching.

13.4.1   Meerkats

Meerkats (or suricates, *Suricata suricatta;* Figure 13.17) are small cooperatively breeding mammals found in the dry parts of Southern Africa. They hold group territories in which the young are mostly produced by a dominant male and female but reared by all members of the group. When meerkat pups are about a month old, they begin to follow foraging groups around, making begging calls which stimulate older animals to bring them prey. These prey include scorpions, which are difficult or even dangerous to handle. Helpers often kill or disable such prey before presenting them to the youngest pups. Scorpions are killed or disabled for the pups to a greater extent than are other prey, but over the next two months all kinds of items are increasingly presented intact, as if the helpers are sensitive to the pups' growing

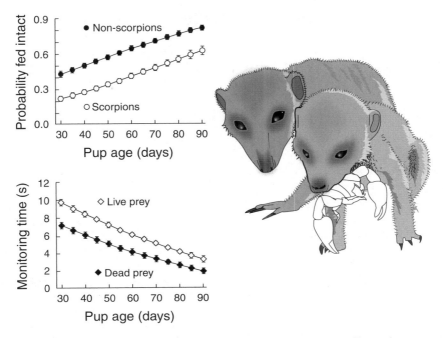

Figure 13.17. An adult meerkat watching a pup eating a scorpion and two effects of pup age on adults' behavior: as pups grow older adults feed more intact prey and spend less time monitoring the pup with the prey. Adult behavior is also appropriate to type of prey throughout. After a photograph provided by Alex Thornton and data in Thornton and McAuliffe (2006) with permission.

competence(Figure 13.17). The pups' age is reflected in their begging calls, and a playback experiment showed that this proxy for pup competence determines the proportions of prey offered in different states. In groups with young pups, calls of older pups elicited more provisioning of intact prey, whereas in groups with older pups, begging calls of young pups increased the number of dead prey provided. In addition to spending foraging effort on obtaining prey for pups, helpers stay nearby for a few seconds after delivering a food item. They stay longer with younger pups, and if a pup of any age does not take an item immediately, they may nudge it, as if drawing the pup's attention. If the prey escapes, the helper recovers it and presents it again.

Thornton and McAuliffe's (2006) extensive observational data together with the playback experiment demonstrate that the helpers' behavior fulfills Caro and Hauser's first two criteria for teaching: it is conditional on the presence (and here, age) of ignorant others and costly in time and effort in the short term. The results of a further experiment show that it also meets the requirement of aiding pup learning. Thornton and McAuliffe (2006) compared three groups of pups matched for age and litter in their treatment of a live but stingless scorpion after three days of supplementary experience with either four live scorpions presented daily by the researchers (a much higher number than normal), four dead scorpions, or equivalent amounts of hardboiled egg. Pups in the first group were markedly more successful in handling the test scorpion, consistent with the experience provided by provisioning "teachers" aiding their learning to subdue and process scorpions. The behavior of the experienced meerkats is therefore comparable to that of mother black rats in that it allows the young to acquire skill in processing a challenging prey item, but the meerkats respond to stimuli indicative of the pups' age (the begging calls) and experience (e.g., whether the scorpion escapes, is attended to, etc.) whereas the role of the mother rats in their pups' learning is mainly to tolerate them nearby and to drop partially eaten pinecones. In neither case however, do we need to invoke adults' understanding of the pups' mental state.

13.4.2   Pied babblers

Another recently described example illustrates how "teaching" may result from a specialization in particular parts of a more species-general kind of behavioral sequence. Pied babblers (*Turdoides bicolor*) are communally breeding birds found at the same study site in South Africa as the meerkats. As in many altricial species, adults feed the young birds in the nest for 2 to 3 weeks, and the family group forages together once the nestlings fledge. Also as in other altricial birds (e.g., Tinbergen and Kuenen 1939/1957), stimuli associated with an adult's arrival at the nest elicit begging by the otherwise quiescent nestlings. Raihani and Ridley (2008) observed that when pied babbler nestlings are 10 to 11 days old, arriving adults begin to emit a "purr" call. When they are about 13 days old, nestlings begin begging in response to purr calls. To show that nestlings' response reflects learning to associate purr calls with food rather than maturation, beginning when the nestlings were 9 days old Rahini and Ridley played purr calls at six nests whenever an adult arrived with food. All them begged in respond to recorded purr calls by the age of 11 days, whereas nestlings in unmanipulated broods did not respond to the same test until Day 13, and begging was seen in only one control that had heard purr calls in the absence of food delivery.

So far, pied babbler purr calling fits the first and third criteria for teaching: it occurs specifically in the presence of "pupils," and they learn something as a result, presumably a Pavlovian association between purr calls and food. It also meets the criterion of being costly to the "teacher." Purr calling is accompanied by fluttering of the wings, and the more that adults display purring and fluttering within a given time, the less weight they gain. But why should the nestlings learn to respond to purring? The adults feed them anyway, or at least they do so without purring for the first 11 days. The likely function of learning that purring signals food becomes apparent after the young leave the nest around the age of 20 days and accompany loose groups of foraging adults around the territory. Adults in such groups purr call more often than in groups that do not have fledglings (Radford and Ridley 2006). They purr when they have found food, in effect calling the young (as well as other adults) to approach, a response that in fact increases the nestlings' foraging success. Sighting a predator also elicits purr calling when fledglings are present, in effect calling them away from danger.

Unlike with the meerkats, where the availability of dangerous and hard to handle but large prey items might create an exceptional pressure for evolution of costly teaching, the situation experienced by the babblers seems much the same as that for other birds in which newly fledged young accompany adults while foraging. What seems special in the babblers, or at least not yet proven for other species, is the context-specific purr call. But food calling in domestic fowl and the ancestral Burmese red junglefowl has many similar properties (see also Section 14.2). In food calling, both hens and roosters pick up a morsel of food in the beak, lower the breast and spread the tail while uttering a distinctive call. Hens food call in the presence of young chicks (Sherry 1977). Food calls attract the chicks, and because chicks tend to peck where they see another bird pecking, the hen's food calling functions to cause the chicks to peck at the food, in effect teaching them what to peck at (see also Nicol and Pope 1996). Moreover, although they have a preexisting tendency to move faster toward a call given to high than to low quality food, chicks can learn the reverse discrimination (Moffatt and Hogan 1992). Thus although by Caro and Hauser's criteria the adult babblers are teaching the young that purring means food, much more could be done to understand whether or why this situation differs from that for many other species in which mobile young accompany foraging adults and use cues to food that they provide.

13.4.3   Teaching in ants?

Ants of the species *Albipennis bithorax* sometime engage in *tandem running* when going from the nest to food: one ant travels behind the other, the follower frequently touching the leader on her legs and abdomen. When leaders were established in a laboratory colony by letting them find food, and naive individuals were then allowed to follow them, leaders were observed to pause when a follower lost contact, as if waiting for the follower to catch up (Franks and Richardson 2006). Moreover, when a follower was removed partway through the trip, leaders waited longer before proceeding the more valuable the food source and the longer the trip had already been in progress (Richardson et al. 2007).

These observations have been interpreted as showing not only that ants teach but as suggesting an additional criterion for teaching, namely that the teacher should be sensitive to feedback from the pupil (Franks and Richardson 2006; Richardson et al. 2007). Be that as it may, leaders clearly meet some of the criteria for teaching in that they behave differently with than without a follower and pay a time cost by doing so. However, it has not yet been directly shown that anything is learned by followers in a tandem run, although some indirect evidence is available (Franks and Richardson 2006; Richardson et al. 2007). It remains to be demonstrated that once a follower has returned to the nest after a tandem run it finds the food again more quickly than a naive individual searching at random. This second trip of ants that have been "taught" the food's location should also be compared to that of ants that originally found it on their own to see whether the benefit, if any, from following is confined to the first trip to the food.

13.4.4   But what about primates?

The folk-psychological assumption that teaching requires cognitive complexity implies chimpanzees and other great apes should teach, but although some apes and monkeys have population-specific behaviors that may be socially transmitted (Section 13.5), there is essentially no evidence than any such behaviors are taught by experienced to inexperienced individuals. For example, in one population in West Africa chimpanzees crack coula nuts with stone hammers and anvils (Figure 13.18). In over 10 years of field work, Boesch (1991) observed hundreds of cases in which chimpanzee mothers "stimulated" or "facilitated" their infants' nut cracking but only two cases that might have been teaching. Stimulation consisted of leaving stone hammers near anvils rather than carrying them off. Facilitation meant providing both hammers and nuts to infants at anvils. Both of these behaviors changed with the ages of the infants. In the two cases of apparent teaching, the mother intervened with an infant attempting to crack a nut and positioned the tool or the nut correctly.

Figure 13.18. Adult chimpanzees cracking and eating coula nuts as a young one watches. After a photograph in Boesch-Achermann and Boesch (1993) with permission.

No indications of teaching or of imitative learning were found in a detailed analysis of the development of nut cracking in another area of West Africa (Inoue-Nakamura and Matsuzawa 1997).

At most, by exposing their infants to nuts and stones, nut-cracking mothers promoted interactions with stones and nuts by providing the conditions for stimulus enhancement. There is also little or no evidence that chimpanzees teach their offspring how to "fish" for termites with sticks. Indeed, although infants spend a lot of time watching their mothers extract termites and even get some of the insects to eat, as with nut cracking they seem to need a good deal of individual practice to become efficient fishers themselves (Lonsdorf 2005). And among the nutcracking capuchins described in Chapter 11, the young themselves make a major contribution to supplying interactions that might serve in social transmission of nut-cracking skills. They prefer to watch the most proficient adult nutcrackers, perhaps because that gives them the most opportunities to scrounge bits of nut (Ottoni and de Resende 2005).

13.4.5   Conclusions

As with deception or planning, demonstrations that candidates for animal teaching meet a clear functional definition are controversial because they seem to lack key components of analogous human competences (Leadbeater 2006; Csibra 2007). Babblers, meerkats, or ants apparently teach others at most one thing. This may not be inconsistent with the functional definition of teaching, but even if further research reveals a species that teaches in several contexts, in human teaching understanding the learner's state of knowledge or ignorance (i.e., using theory of mind) confers an ability to teach everything from tying shoes to doing physics (Premack 2007). In any case, the scattered phylogeny of species with behaviors that function to teach makes it unlikely that such behaviors are homologous with human teaching, that is, evolutionary precursors to it (Galef 2009). This distribution instead raises important questions about what kinds of life history and ecology favor selection for costly behaviors that provide learning opportunities for the young or inexperienced.

The analysis in this section suggests these will be on a continuum with other responses to such individuals, for example specializations in responses to the stimuli that elicit provisioning. There is no evidence so far of any cognitive abilities specific to teaching. And from the learner's point of view, behaviors of "teachers" provide opportunities for learning by trial and error (as in meerkats), observational conditioning (as in pied babblers), acquiring spatial information (as suggested for ants) or by some other general mechanism. In summary there is still no reason to question the conclusion stated many years ago by the ethologist R. F. Ewer (1969, 698), "it is preferable to think in terms of instinctive behavior patterns which produce learning rather than of the 'instinct to teach,' which, in any case, has subjective overtones.... The responses of the mother are simply those which provide the correct situation for evoking the developing repertoire of responses of the young who are thus enabled to educate themselves."

13.5   Animal cultures?

Whatever else it may mean, when applied to humans, *culture* refers to multifaceted groupwide traditions: population-specific behaviors, beliefs, and attitudes, transmitted from one generation to the next through language, teaching, and in many less explicit ways. The socially transmitted behaviors of nonhuman animals described so far such as food preferences in rats or enemy recognition in birds influence so few aspects of their lives as to be scarcely the rudiments of culture. But, in contrast to rats, birds, and most other animals, geographically separated groups of chimpanzees and orangutans show multiple, populationwide differences in acquired behavior that have been suggested to represent evolutionary precursors to human culture. The most substantial relevant data come from a collaboration among researchers doing long-term studies of chimpanzees at seven sites in Africa (Whiten et al. 1999, 2001). For each population, the local team estimated the frequency of occurrence of 65 behaviors, many of which involved tool use or other interactions with objects such as manipulating sticks in different ways to obtain ants or termites, using leaves to sponge up water. When a behavior had not been seen, a judgment was made as to whether there was an ecological explanation for its absence. For instance, termite fishing is impossible without termites. The most interesting cases are those 39 in which a behavior was judged relatively common in some populations but absent in others even though the ecological conditions for its appearance were judged to be present. Given that genetic differences among the populations can be assumed to be unimportant, such patterns suggest the behavior must have been discovered by one or more innovators and then acquired by others in the group by some kind of social transmission (i.e., any one or more of the mechanisms in Box 13.1).

Beginning with the titles of the original reports, these population differences in chimpanzees (Whiten et al. 1999, 2001) and orangutans (van Schaik et al. 2003) have been referred to as "cultural," but this description is much debated (Galef 2004; Laland and Janik 2006; Perry 2006; Whiten and Van Schaik 2007; Galef 2009). There are two basic sources of controversy. One, discussion of which is beyond the scope of this book, is that *culture* has a rich web of connotations in anthropology, archaeology, and a whole range of other disciplines, not to mention in folk psychology, and to some writers these are simply incompatible with the possibility of "animal cultures" no matter how apparently inoffensively and objectively defined. The other is that even if population-specific behaviors in nonhuman species are referred to instead as *behavioral traditions,* conclusive evidence is needed that the behaviors involved really are transmitted socially as the term *tradition* implies rather than learned individually or determined by ecological conditions, and field observations alone rarely if ever can provide such evidence (Galef 2004, 2009).

An analysis of "ant dipping" by chimpanzees shows how ecological factors favoring one behavior rather than another may not be obvious. In dipping for ants, a chimpanzee uses a stick or grass stalk to capture biting ants. The tool is moved back and forth to stimulate the ants to climb up on it. They are then removed either by putting the tool directly into the mouth ("direct mouthing") or by pulling it through the hand and putting the resulting clump of ants into the mouth ("pull through technique"). Ant dipping is a candidate cultural behavior because different techniques as well as different lengths of tools are prevalent in different populations. However, in one population, at Bossou, Guinea, chimpanzees use both techniques as well as both short and long tools. By combining observations of the conditions under which different tool lengths and removal techniques were used with experiments in which the researchers themselves dipped for ants, Humle and Matsuzawa (2002) showed that there are good functional reasons for these variations in dipping. It turns out that there are more and less aggressive species of ants; the ants are also more belligerent at the nest than when migrating along the ground. Using longer tools and the pull through technique limits biting by the ants, and it is the preferred technique for situations where ants are most aggressive. However, an analysis of behavior of ants at two sites with different patterns of ant dipping indicates that some of the population differences in ant dipping are likely to be cultural (Mobius et al. 2008).

A further issue is that no matter how compelling the observations of young animals watching adults using tools or the like (e.g., Figure 13.18), the occurrence of any kind of social learning or social influence on learning in such interactions needs to be tested experimentally. Given the paucity of convincing evidence for social transmission of wild chimpanzees' population-specific behaviors, researchers have turned to demonstrations that tool-using skills can be socially transmitted in captive groups (Whiten, Horner, and De Waal 2005; Horner et al. 2006; Hopper et al. 2007). These studies typically involve apparatuses like that used in two-action tests of imitation, introducing each technique for operating it into a different group of subjects. A third group may be left on their own to see whether one technique or the other, if any, is acquired spontaneously. With an "artificial fruit" having a door that could be lifted or pushed, a transmission chain was formed. Observer 1 learned the technique used by trained demonstrator, then Observer 2 learned it from observing Observer 1, and so on up to a chain of five or six chimpanzees. Some controls who saw food put into the box eventually opened it one way, some the other (Horner et al. 2006). Consistent with these findings, when a single trained demonstrator was introduced into whole group, most individuals learned the tool use task being demonstrated and used the same technique as the demonstrator (Whiten, Horner, and De Waal 2005). However, the robustness of a technique across a transmission chain may depend on the type of task (Hopper et al. 2007).

Monkeys, too, have what appear to be traditional behaviors (Perry and Manson 2003). Indeed, one of the oldest candidates for animal culture is potato washing by Japanese macaques (Box 13.3). More recently, wild white-faced capuchin monkeys have been observed in what are some of the best candidates for socially learned population-specific behaviors. These are rather bizarre and apparently arbitrary "games," such as monkeys taking turns putting their fingers into each others' mouth and getting a firm bite (Perry et al. 2003). It has been possible to trace the spread of some of these behaviors within and between groups. Social transmission of a foraging

Box 13.3 Sweet Potato Washing by Japanese Macaques

One of the most famous candidates for culturally transmitted behavior in free-ranging animals is sweet potato washing by Japanese macaques. A colony on Koshima Island was provisioned with sweet potatoes, and in 1953 a young female, Imo, was first seen taking sand-covered pieces of potato to a stream and washing the sand off before eating them (Kawai 1965; Nishida 1987; Hirata, Watanabe, and Kawai 2001). Over the ensuing years potato washing spread through the colony, first to animals closely affiliated with Imo (Figure B13.3). Although these observations were described in the secondary literature as an innovation invented by a young animal being imitated by social companions (e.g., Bonner 1980; Gould and Gould 1994), more critical thinking about social learning and animal traditions has challenged such conclusions.

One issue is whether the data in Figure B13.3 are actually consistent with social transmission. Any socially transmitted behavior might be expected to arise more or less by chance, spread slowly at first and then more and more rapidly as more models are available for naive individuals to learn from. It has typically been assumed that when, in contrast, individuals learn entirely on their own the number of individuals showing the behavior rises at a constant rate until all members of the group have learned. Clearly, the data shown here are more consistent with the second of these scenarios than with the first. Notice, too, that the time scale is years, suggesting that any social learning was very slow. However, the conclusion suggested by this analysis, due to Galef (1996a), was questioned by adding just one more data point, and by showing that the majority of twenty other cases in the literature on primates also show an accelerating function (Lefebvre 1995b).

The idea that the shape of diffusion functions, of which Figure B13.3 contains a simple example, may be used to discriminate social from individual learning in data from free ranging groups is appealing, but there are many problems with it (Reader 2004). Collecting all the relevant data for a given population may be no easier than collecting any other data on learning in wild animals. In addition, different assumptions about the processes of social and/or individual learning involved generate different diffusion curves. For instance, individual learning can lead to an accelerating function in a population with a normal distribution of learning ability. The number of skilled animals increases slowly when the group is first exposed to the task (for example, the provision of sweet potatoes) because the minority at the "high ability" end of the distribution learn first. It accelerates once enough time has passed for the majority of average ability to acquire the skill and slows down again when only the slowest learners are left (Reader 2004).

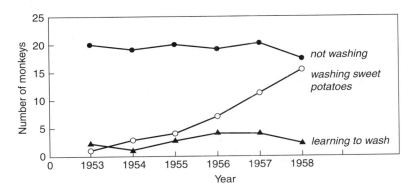

Figure B13.3. The incidence and spread of potato washing among Japanese macaques on Koshima Island between 1953 and 1958. Redrawn from Galef (1996a) with permission.

In any case, because sweet potato washing began over half a century ago, we will never be certain exactly what went on. There are suggestions that once washing had appeared in the colony, the keepers providing the sweet potatoes encouraged the animals to wash them (see Galef 1996a). The activities of knowledgeable individuals with food near water provided conditions under which their companions could discover food washing for themselves, for instance by picking scraps out of the water (M. Kawai 1965). Moreover, washing sandy food is not as unlikely a behavior among monkeys as it might seem. The macaques in the Kashima colony also separated grains of wheat from sand by dropping handfuls of sandy wheat in water, where the grains floated to the top and could quickly be gathered up, and several other examples of apparent cultural transmission involve washing food (Lefebvre 1995b). When Visalberghi and Fragaszy (1990b; see also Visalberghi 1994) provided individual captive tufted capuchins and crabeating macaques with sandy fruit and a tub of water, a number of them showed unambiguous food washing within a few hours. In conclusion, as in the examples in the main text, although potato washing may be a traditional or "precultural" behavior (Kawai 1965), its spread likely involved a variety of different processes.

technique along a chain of animals has also been demonstrated among captive capuchins with similar methods to those used for chimpanzees (Dindo, Thierry, and Whiten 2008).

Conclusions

Notwithstanding the need to look more closely at some of their ecological determinants, it seems likely that at least some of the candidates for traditional behaviors of chimpanzees as well as orangutans are indeed socially transmitted. But does that mean apes have culture in any meaningful way? On one view (e.g., Perry 2006), "cultural primatology" from the early study of Japanese macaques onward reveals a great deal about how culture evolves and what mechanisms maintain it. On another (e.g., Galef 2009), animal traditions are analogous but not homologous to human culture because the processes that perpetuate them do not include the key component of human cultural transmission, namely imitation. Human culture is indeed unique because across generations it "ratchets up": changes introduced in one generation are adopted and further elaborated in the next in a process of cumulative change. On one compelling account (Richerson and Boyd 2005), ratcheting up is possible because people are capable of exactly copying (i.e., imitating) behaviors of those around them and then improving on them by trial and error, reasoning, or other processes, whereas emulation and other social learning mechanisms leave each new generation to relearn much of what was learned by the last. On this view, although humans undoubtedly share some simpler social transmission mechanisms with other species, the propensity to imitate sets us apart even from chimpanzees (see Herrmann et al. 2007) and makes genuine culture possible.

13.6   Summary and conclusions

"Social learning" has a lot in common with "spatial learning" (Chapter 8). Both are essentially functional categories, that is, based on the kind of information acquired rather than on the way in which it is acquired, and both encompass a variety of specific mechanisms. However, individual mechanisms of spatial learning such as path integration, landmark use, and sun compass orientation are relatively well understood, whereas the analysis of separate mechanisms for social learning has been impeded by disproportionate interest in true imitation. The wave of recent research combining observations of naturalistic examples of social learning with experimental analyses of mechanism has led to an appreciation of how species-specific fine-tuning of simple learning mechanisms can lead to social transmission of adaptive behavior in natural social contexts. For example, rats learn about food by smelling other rats' breath because the smell of rat breath has motivational significance for them and because when rats greet each other the nose of one comes close to the mouth of another. A young black rat need never see another black rat stripping the scales off a pine cone; it needs only to be provided with cones than have been partially stripped in the right way (Terkel 1995).

Nonimitative social learning includes stimulus enhancement, observational conditioning, and emulation. None of these is very well understood in terms of the conditions that bring it about, the contents of that learning, and the effects of learning on behavior. Heyes (1994a) suggested that each is roughly analogous to a recognized category of associative or perceptual learning, but the questions she raised, such as the role of contingency and the possible occurrence of overshadowing and blocking in such learning, have still hardly been asked. It is necessary to answer them to know whether these kinds of social learning are distinctive in any way other than in the events that are learned about. There has, however, been considerable progress recently in understanding how imitation occurs and in what species, but emulation and affordance learning still need more study. In most circumstances there may be no need for strict imitation. The job can be done by emulation and the other social learning processes that don't require storing a representation of the demonstrator's behavior as such. Indeed, a tendency to blindly imitate what others do regardless of the positive or negative outcomes for oneself would likely be maladaptive. Thus what may need to be explained is not why most species seem incapable of true imitation but why any *are* capable of it. This explanation may ultimately have to do with the evolution of teaching and human culture.

Further readings

As illustrated in the first part of the chapter, the study of social learning has become exemplary as an area in which researchers from a whole range of different backgrounds—biologists, psychologists, and anthropologists, from mathematical modelers to field workers—are communicating and collaborating in rich and productive ways. Its development can be traced in books edited by Zentall and Galef (1988), Heyes and Galef (1996), and the February, 2004, special issue of *Learning & Behavior* (vol. 32, no.1). The chapter by Galef (1976) was influential in stimulating more recent developments and is still a valuable review of earlier work. The considerable work on social and other aspects of learning in dolphins is reviewed by Herman (2006). The many facets of the animal cultures debate are well represented in the book edited by Laland and Galef (2009). Bird song in all its aspects is reviewed in *Nature's Music* (Marler and Slabbekoorn 2004) and Zeigler and Marler (2004) and introduced more briefly in the book by Catchpole and Slater (1995). For teaching in animals, Caro and Hauser's (1992) review is recommended; the article by Hoppitt et al. (2008) is a brief overview of recent work.

14

Communication and Language

Figure 14.1 depicts a classic ethological example of communication. A male stickleback in breeding condition, with a red belly, swims in a wavering path toward an egg-laden female. When she responds to this "zig zig dance" by swimming toward the male, he heads toward his nest, and she follows. Upon reaching the nest, a little tunnel of vegetation on the substrate, the male pokes his head into the entrance, "showing" it to the female. She enters, and a further series of actions and reactions ends in her depositing eggs in the nest and the male releasing sperm over them.

Courtship in sticklebacks, as in most other animals, involves communication. Behaviors and structures apparently specially designed by natural selection are used by one animal to influence the behavior of others. In effect, the male's red belly and the zig zag dance tell the female something like "I am a male of your species, I have good genes and good health, I am ready to mate, and I want you to mate with me." But of course it is unnecessary to attribute such thoughts to the male. The courtship sequence can be understood as a chain of events in which one animal provides the stimulus for its partner's response, which in turn provides the stimulus for the next response in the chain, and so on.

Figure 14.2 depicts an account of what goes on when people communicate proposed by the philosopher Grice (1957). People generally assume they are modifying not only their listeners' behavior but their understanding. The young man in the figure is not just emitting sounds designed to cause the young woman to enter his car. Rather, he wants her to know that he is an attractive fellow who commands substantial resources and he would like her to come with him. On this view, human communication involves at least third-order intentionality (Section 12.3). In addition, it is referential. Unlike the stickleback's red belly, "Porsche" is not a stimulus that by itself attracts all sexually receptive females of the species. The man is referring to an object, and he intends to activate a representation of that object in his listener's mind.

A cartoon of stickleback behavior might have the male saying "I'm a fit and sexy male. Come with me and lay your eggs in my lovely nest," but few, if any, students of animal behavior would seriously consider a Gricean analysis of the stickleback's courtship. Traditionally, communicative behaviors such as displays or alarm calls were treated as expressions of emotion or motivation. More recently, some communicative behaviors have been interpreted as referring to objects in the world and as being given with intent to modify others' behavior, perhaps even their beliefs. Figure 14.3 depicts what is now a classic example. Vervet monkeys have three

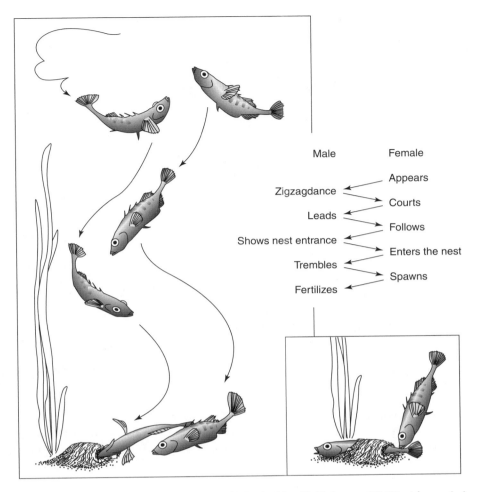

Male   Female

                    Appears
Zigzagdance
                    Courts
Leads
                    Follows
Shows nest entrance
                    Enters the nest
Trembles
                    Spawns
Fertilizes

Figure 14.1. Courtship and spawning in the stickleback. After N. Tinbergen (1951) with permission.

acoustically distinct alarm calls (Seyfarth, Cheney, and Marler 1980). One is given to snakes. Vervets hearing it stand up on their hind legs and look at the ground. A second alarm call is given by a monkey sighting a leopard, and it causes nearby monkeys to run into the trees, out of reach of leopards. The third alarm call is given to aerial predators like eagles that can snatch monkeys out of trees. Vervets hearing it seek shelter at ground level. We could describe the vervets' communication as sequences of stimulus and response, as shown in Figure 14.3a, but would we be leaving out something important? Does an alarm calling vervet intend to modify other monkeys' behavior in definite ways or is he simply emitting a response to a predator stimulus? Do the three calls refer to three different predators? How could we tell? Exploring the possibility of reference and intentionality is an important thread in contemporary research on animal communication discussed further in Section 14.2.

As communications, the stickleback's approach to the female and the man's invitation to his date differ in another way than depicted in Figure 14.3. We would not be inclined to call the behavior sequence in Figure 14.1 *language* because the stickleback is limited to a small number of species-typical communicative acts put

Figure 14.2. An example of human communication indicating the third order intentionality assumed to accompany it. Modified Gomez (1994) with permission.

Will you come for a drive in my new Porsche?

a

Monkey *A*

sees leopard

emits leopard alarm ⟶ hears leopard alarm

Monkey *B*

runs to trees

b

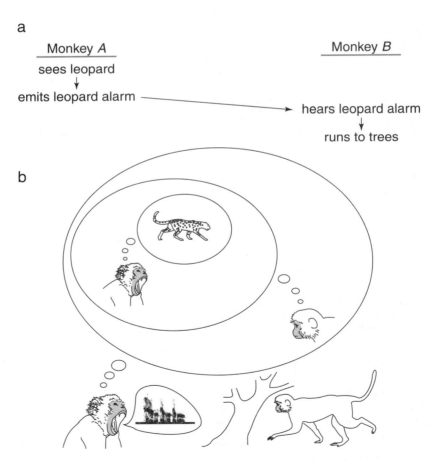

Figure 14.3. Two contrasting accounts of communication about predators by vervet monkeys. Vervets after Seyfarth and Cheney (1992) with permission.

together in a rigid way. Yet some animal communication systems, such as the dancing of honeybees, have been called languages. The vervets' alarm calls function somewhat like words. Discovering whether or in what way any animal communication systems share any properties of human language may help understand how human language evolved. The assumption that species phylogenetically closest to humans should have the most humanlike capacities for communication has inspired a long history of attempts to teach forms of human language to chimpanzees. The results of these efforts have implications for whether some aspects of language should be attributed to a cognitive module possessed only by humans. Section 14.3 reviews this research and Section 14.4 expands on it with more recent developments in the study of language evolution. But first we consider a few general questions about animal communication (for more, see Maynard Smith and Harper 2003).

14.1   Some basic issues

14.1.1   Elements of communication

In communication, one animal influences the behavior of another through the transmission of *signals*. If my dog snarls and bares her teeth at your dog, she is signaling hostility. If your dog runs away because he sees my dog sleeping in the yard, we would be unlikely to say any signaling has taken place. But as we will see in a moment, the line between signaling and other kinds of information transmission is not always easy to draw. Classical ethologists studying communication focused on behavior patterns like the stickleback's zig zag dance that seemed selected specifically for a role in intraspecies interactions. Such behavior patterns are species-specific and occur in particular contexts. They also tend to be stereotyped in form, as in animals' characteristic submissive and aggressive postures (Figure 14.4). Figure 14.4 also illustrates what Darwin (1872/1965) in *The Expression of the Emotions in Man and Animals* called the Principle of Antithesis: signals with opposing meanings tend to be opposite in form. Signals may have evolved this way because antithesis reduces ambiguity. Recording the behavioral context for a candidate signaling behavior and other animals' responses to it are necessary for deciding what, if anything, is being communicated. Observations of freely behaving animals often lead to questions about

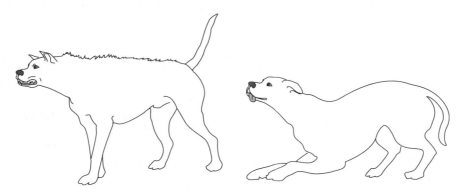

Figure 14.4. Contrast between aggressive and submissive postures, an example of the principle of antithesis. After Darwin (1872/1965).

communication that can best be answered with experiments. For instance, Tinbergen discovered which parts of the courtship sequence function as signals by using dummies, crude models with only some features of live fish (Figure 6.1).

Instances of communication involve not only a physical *signal* such as a sight, sound, or odor, but also a *sender* and a *receiver*. These terms all invite interpretation of animal communication as an active process, but animals may also transmit information about themselves in a more passive way. Red rainforest frogs or aposematic insects are spoken of as signaling that they are unpalatable, and indeed their bright colors and conspicuous patterns are thought to have been selected because predators easily learn to avoid such cues (Box 6.3). As another example, ragged fur, dull plumage, or the like function as signals of poor physical condition in that they may be perceived and responded to as such by potential mates or predators, but it seems unlikely they have been specifically selected as honest signals of quality. Similarly, as we saw in Chapter 12, even though animals that are being eavesdropped on during a social interaction are not specifically signaling to the eavesdropper, the eavesdropper may use their signals as cues for how to behave toward them in the future.

As we saw in Chapter 3, the physical properties of a signal and the receiver's perceptual sensitivity should be matched to each other and to the transmission properties of the environment. Thus a thorough analysis of animal communication integrates physics, ecology, sensory physiology and signal detection theory to explore why signals take the form they do (see Bradbury and Vehrencamp 1998; Owren and Rendall 2001; Wiley 2006). Depending on the species and situation, communication can take place through any of a number of channels, among them visual, olfactory, electrical, tactile, auditory. Here we focus almost entirely on auditory communication. Discussions of communication also consider the *message* of a signal and its *meaning* to the receiver (W. Smith 1977). The message is inferred from how the state of the sender and/or of the environment predicts what signal is given. For instance, does the species or proximity of predator predict the kind or intensity of alarm calling? The meaning of the signal, on the other hand, is inferred from the behavior of the receiver, so it may vary with the receiver's characteristics. For instance, in many species of birds, song is sung primarily by breeding males on their territories (Box 13.2). The song identifies the species of the singer, who he is, where he is, possibly something about his physical condition or the area he grew up in. These can all be considered part of its message. But the meaning of male territorial song is different for rival conspecific males (who may treat it as a challenge for a territorial fight or as a warning to stay away), conspecific females (who may treat it as a signal to approach), and birds of other species (who are likely to be indifferent to it).

14.1.2   The ethology and behavioral ecology of communication

The male stickleback's zig zag dance is a classic example of what ethologists call a *display,* a conspicuous stereotyped movement performed in a special context with an apparent communicative function. The zig zag dance is a example of a display arising from a motivational conflict, in this case between approaching the female and fleeing from her. *Intention movements,* the fragmentary beginnings of an activity that precede its full-blown appearance, are the other main evolutionary source of displays. The male's behavior of "showing the nest" is an example. In both cases, behaviors that normally occur in a given motivational context seem to have evolved into exaggerated and stereotyped, or *ritualized,* forms because exaggerated, stereotyped, displays are less ambiguous. Special coloration and patterning may also have been selected through making displays more noticeable to receivers (Chapter 3).

These ideas about the evolution of displays are supported by ethological studies from Lorenz (1941/1971) onward. Underlying many of them was the notion that communication is a matter of cooperation: signaling systems have evolved because both signaler and receiver benefit. Male and female sticklebacks can both increase their fitness by getting fertile eggs into the nest. The dog that growls and bares its teeth and the dog that runs away both avoid a potentially damaging fight. But ideas about individual selection imply that instead systems of animal communication evolve because animals benefit from manipulating one another (Maynard Smith and Harper 2003). No animal would be selected to give a costly display, one that takes time, consumes energy, and might increase its conspicuousness to predators, simply to share information with a conspecific. Signals must have been selected because they cause the receiver to behave in a way that increases the sender's inclusive fitness. The receiver, on this view, doesn't have to receive any benefit. At the same time, of course, the receiver's response to the signal, along with her perceptual sensitivity to it, will be selected only if it increases *her* net fitness. In contrast to the traditional ethological view, the view of communication stemming from emphasis on individual selection (Maynard Smith and Harper 2003) implies that signals are not necessarily truthful indicators of the sender's state. Instead signaler and receiver are engaged in an arms race. For instance, males may attract more mates and thereby increase their fitness by appearing to be bigger, stronger, and sexier than they really are. However, in species where fathers provide resources for their offspring, females will increase their fitness most by detecting the males that are truly healthy and good providers, since this will increase the chances that the bearers of their genes will be healthy and well provided for. The predator-prey interactions in mimicry systems (Chapter 6) are a case of deceptive interspecific signaling in that palatable prey sport the appearance of unpalatable ones. Here the evolutionary arms race is responsible for the very close resemblances between model and mimic, as well as between cryptic prey and background (Chapter 3). In some cases, however, honest signaling should evolve. For example, sexual selection favors signals like big tails and antlers because they handicap their owners (Zahavi 1975). A peacock that can keep himself in good condition and display vigorously to females in spite of producing and carrying around a huge tail can hardly be bluffing about his quality. Although the handicap principle and honest advertising were originally hotly debated, they are now generally accepted (see Maynard Smith and Harper 2003).

Receivers of signals can be thought of as engaged in "mindreading" (Krebs and Dawkins 1984) in that they may be able to tell what the sender of a signal will do next. For instance, the snarling dog is more likely to attack than to lie down. Mindreading in this sense means using the regularities in behavior in a predictive fashion. But whereas ethologists have to learn the predictive significance of other species' behavior patterns, the animals themselves may respond appropriately to signals like red bellies and territorial songs without much, if any, experience. Dawkins and Krebs's ideas about the evolution and function of communication stimulated a large amount of research and theorizing in behavioral ecology, as well as more than their share of controversy (Hinde 1981; M. Dawkins 1995). One point to take away is that terms like *mindreading, manipulation,* and *deception* do not imply that any animals are thinking about manipulating or deceiving each other any more than a grey moth resting on a grey tree trunk is thinking about deceiving hungry blue jays. They have clear functional meanings in the context of animal communication.

14.1.3   Language and animal communication

Whereas the biological study of animal communication traditionally focused on signals as indicators of the motivational state or behavioral propensity of the sender and on receivers' perception and response, a central issue in comparative cognition has been how nonhuman communication systems compare to human language. But all-or-nothing questions such as "Do any animals have language?" are not the best guides for comparative research. More worthwhile is to identify important features of human language and ask which, if any, of them are shared by the communication system of any other species and why. We look here at some of the components identified many years ago by Hockett (1960; for an update see Fitch 2005), which are still useful guides for comparing human language with the communication systems of other species. Notice that some (unbounded signal set, recursion) are formal characteristics of language whereas others such as reference imply mentalistic or representational skills.

Limited versus unbounded signal set

Most nonhuman species signal about only a few things—sex, aggression, predators, food—using a relatively small set of signals. Some signals are graded in intensity, corresponding for example to different levels of threat, but qualitatively different signals are rather few in number. In contrast, words—the elements of human language—and the ways in which they are put together make language essentially unbounded. *Outsourcing* and *email* are words invented in the 1990s as names for contemporary phenomena. More importantly, language is not just words but combinatorial principles, that is, rules for putting words together to devise new meanings. Therefore once we know what new words like *email* and *outsource* mean, we can immediately talk about them. For instance, we know that "Sue emailed John" and "John emailed Sue" mean two different things despite containing the same words. We also know that "Sue was emailed by John" means the same as "John emailed Sue," even though as a chain of visual or auditory stimuli it is more like "Sue emailed John." In general, animals do not combine their natural signals to create new meaning. In the rare exceptions the resulting signal does not seem logically related to the elements and their order. For example, male putty-nosed monkeys have distinct alarm calls and defensive behaviors for eagles and leopards, but occasionally when no predators are around they spontaneously give the two calls in sequence. These calls seem to predict upcoming initiation of movement by their family group (Arnold and Zuberbühler 2006).

Recursion

The unboundedness of language arises not so much from an ability to form unlimited numbers of associations between words and things or states of the world as from the ability to generate linguistic structure by *recursion* and to recognize and unpack the meaning of recursive structures. Formally, all but the simplest sentences are recursive in some way, that is they consist of patterns within patterns. As one straightforward example, the English sentence, "Jill remembered the time James said that I like cats that catch mice" embeds four subject-verb-object structures within one another, and it's easy to generate further embeddings. On one recently developed view (Hauser, Chomsky, and Fitch 2002), the implicit computational ability underlying recursion is the crucial component of human language not shared with any other species. This controversial (see Pinker and Jackendoff 2005) claim has stimulated attempts to test animals including starlings and tamarins for their ability to learn and discriminate recursive patterns. We look at these in Section 14.4.

Functional reference

In the examples earlier in the chapter, the male stickleback or the snarling dog are communicating that they are sexually aroused and aggressive, respectively. This information allows receivers to predict what the signaler will do next and behave appropriately. But as in Figure 14.2, people also use language to refer to objects and events in the world. The essential behavioral implications of reference are that, first, a signal that refers to a particular object or event is reliably given in its presence and not under other conditions. This criterion separates behavior patterns caused by generalized excitement or anxiety from those performed in the presence of specific arousing or dangerous conditions. Second, and equally important, the receiver of a referential signal behaves consistently in an appropriate manner, even in the absence of the object or event that elicited the signal. Thus an animal hearing a signal for flight flees whether or not it can hear or see something to flee from. Signals that meet these two criteria—*production specificity* on the part of the sender and *context independence* on the part of the receiver (Blumstein 1999)—are *functionally referential* (Evans 1997; Manser 2009). In what way, if any, a receiver's response to a functionally referential signal is mediated by a representation of the thing signaled is a further question discussed in Section 14.2.

Situational freedom (or *displacement*) is one concomitant of reference in human language. No food or danger need be present for us to talk about food or danger that we have experienced in the past or might experience in the future. As readers may suspect from the examples presented so far in this chapter, most animal signals do not exhibit situational freedom. The dance language of bees (Section 14.2.1) is sometimes cited as an exception. Besides allowing communication about objects and events in the past or future, situational freedom permits lying. Accordingly, one might ask whether animals can lie. This question refers not to the possibility that some signals are designed by evolution to deceive but to the cognitively more complex possibility that a signal with a particular message and meaning is occasionally used intentionally in another context for the sender's benefit. On the whole, there is little if any convincing evidence that animals lie, just as there is little evidence that they show other forms of intentional deception (Chapter 12).

Intention

Like the man in Figure 14.2, people generally use language with the intent of informing, changing the cognitive state of receivers. Behaviorally, this means suiting the communication to the audience: a professor gives different lectures to an introductory class and to a professional society. Further, what we say and how we say it are continuously modified by the perceived effects of our communication. If the students are baffled because they know nothing about evolution, the planned lecture on animal signals will be postponed, whereas if they reveal that they learned the basics of signaling systems in another course, the wise professor will move on to the next topic. The idea that animals might also communicate with intent to inform has been investigated in two ways. How the signaler's behavior is influenced by the other animals present, the so-called *audience effect*, has been analyzed in chickens, ground squirrels, and some primates, among other species. Whether signalers alter their behavior according to the response of receivers has also been looked at. On the whole such research has compared solitary signalers to those in a dyad, where the "audience" is the receiver. In principle audience effects might also be found when such a dyad is in the presence of onlookers or eavesdroppers, as in communication networks (P. McGregor 2005; Zuberbühler 2008). In either case, the underlying question is whether sophisticated conditional control by the behavior of receivers can be distinguished from control by the sender's understanding of whether the receivers are getting the intended message. The section on theory of mind in Chapter 12 suggests the answer.

14.2   Natural communication systems

14.2.1   Dancing honeybees

The waggle dance

People have been observing bees and collecting their honey since prehistoric times (Gould and Gould 1988). Aristotle noticed that when sugar water was set out to attract honeybees, no bees might arrive for several days, but once one did arrive others came soon after, apparently following the discoverer to the food. The mechanism underlying this recruitment was not elucidated until the first half of the twentieth century, when von Frisch and his students (von Frisch 1967) perfected methods for training bees to artificial food sources. The area of research opened up by von Frisch, and for which he was awarded a Nobel Prize together with Konrad Lorenz and Niko Tinbergen, is still flourishing (see F. Dyer 2002). Some of his conclusions, however, have had to survive a few challenges.

Von Frisch observed that when a bee returns from finding nectar 100 meters or more away, she may perform a *waggle dance* inside the dark hive on the vertical surface of the honeycomb. Bees returning from close to the hive perform a round dance. The waggle dance consists of a straight run in which the bee waggles her abdomen from side to side while vibrating her wings to make a buzzing sound. At the end of the straight run, she runs quickly back in a semicircle and begins another straight run. This return trip is made alternately to the left and to the right, tracing a figure-eight. Bees that have not recently been foraging successfully attend the dance, crowding around the forager and touching her with their anntennae. The waggle dance contains information about the distance and direction of the food source (Figure 14.5). The angle of the straight run to the vertical corresponds to the angle of the food source to the sun's current azimuth (see Box 8.2). If the food was located in a direct line from the hive toward the sun's azimuth, waggle runs will be oriented straight up on the vertical comb. If the sun is in the south and food is directly west of the hive, dances are oriented on average 90° to the right of vertical, and so on. The duration and length of the waggle run, together with the amount of buzzing accompanying it, corresponds to the distance to the food. The dancer also pauses from time to time and regurgitates a small drop of nectar, providing information about the kind of food. Whether dancing or not, the forager also carries odors from the food picked up by waxy hairs on her body. Finally, returning foragers that have found a resource needed by the colony are most likely to dance, and the vigor with which they dance corresponds to the value of the resource. Bees dance not only after gathering nectar but also after finding pollen, water, tree sap, and potential new nest sites (Seeley 1995).

The waggle dance clearly carries information, but do other bees use it? The designs von Frisch used for testing use of direction and distance information, respectively, are depicted in Figure 14.6. Marked foragers are trained to come to a feeding platform that is gradually moved further and further from the hive. Because they are offered a

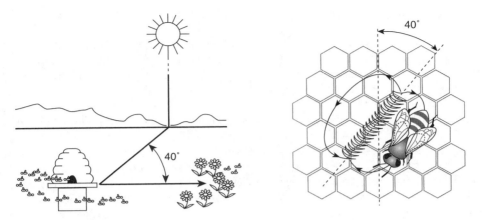

Figure 14.5. The waggle dance of the honeybee showing how its angle to the vertical is related to the angle between the path to the food and the sun's azimuth. Redrawn from Seeley (1985) with permission.

relatively weak sugar solution at this stage, they do not yet dance and recruit other bees. On the test day, the solution is made strong enough to elicit dancing, control platforms are set out along with the training platform, and arriving bees are counted at each one. In the "fan experiment," to test the use of directional information the control feeders were all equidistant from the hive, spread out on both sides of the training feeder. In the "step experiment," to test for the use of distance information the control feeders and the training feeder were in the same straight line from the hive, with control feeders both nearer and farther than the training feeder. In both cases, the majority of recruits turned up at the training location.

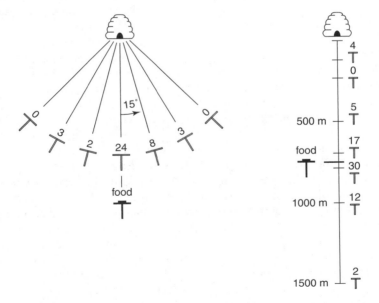

Figure 14.6. Arrangements of training ("food") and control feeders in von Frisch's "fan"(left) and "step" experiments, showing the number of bees arriving at each one in the test. Fan redrawn from von Frisch (1953); step based on data in von Frisch (1967).

The dance language controversy

At first glance, the results of the "fan" and "step" experiments seem clear evidence that recruits use the information in the dance. However, a few cautions are necessary. Recruits are generally much slower to arrive than experienced foragers, and not all the bees attending a dance necessarily find the indicated site. Furthermore, long before he discovered the waggle dance, von Frisch established that bees can find sites recently visited by other bees by odor alone. They use not only the odor of the food itself (e.g., from a flower), but other odors at or near the site including odors deposited by successful foragers. In the late 1960s the clear importance of odor together with the results of some experiments similar but not identical in detail to von Frisch's fan and step experiments led Wenner and others to reexamine the dance language hypothesis (Gould 1976; Wenner and Wells 1990). They concluded that the dance did not function as communication. All von Frisch's results, together with the results of their new experiments, could be explained by the bees' use of odor. In both the fan and the step designs, the target feeder, the one where most bees turn up, is the center of a gradient of odor from the whole array of feeders. In addition, it is the location that has been most visited by bees. When arrays had the target feeder offset from the center and controls were instituted for past bee visits, most recruits still turned up in the center of the array rather than at the feeder signaled by the dancers.

Wenner's attack on the dance language hypothesis was answered by von Frisch himself among others (see Gould and Gould 1988), and in the early 1970s the question of whether or not the waggle dance was communication was *the* controversial issue in ethology. Most biologists now regard it as settled (F. Dyer 2002). Three new kinds of experiments show conclusively that bees use the information in the dance even if, as described at the end of this section, they do not always do so. The first relevant experiment has a simple logic that we meet again in considering referential communication in other species: if a signal functions to communicate, then receivers must respond appropriately to it even in the absence of the environmental conditions that gave rise to it. Otherwise it is impossible to be sure whether they have responded to the signal or directly to the state of the environment. James Gould, then a graduate student, saw that this could be accomplished for the bees' dance by dissociating the direction signaled by dancers from the direction to the food (Gould 1975). In effect, he caused dancing bees to lie and other bees to believe them. He did this by making use of the fact that although bees in the dark orient and interpret dances with respect to the vertical, bees in the light use the sun. For instance, in the dark a dance elicited by food 90° to the right of the sun's azimuth will have a straight run 90° to the right of vertical, but in a lighted hive dancers arriving from the same place will orient 90° to the right of the light. Gould further made use of the fact that bees perceive the overall level of illumination with their ocelli, an array of photoreceptors on the top of the head. Bees whose ocelli are covered with opaque paint behave as if in dim light. Most importantly, at some levels of hive illumination untreated bees reorient their dances and their interpretation of dances to the light while bees with painted ocelli do not. What Gould did was to train some foragers with painted ocelli to a target feeder and cause them to dance in a lighted hive where the attendant bees had unpainted ocelli. The dance was oriented with respect to gravity while the potential recruits interpreted it with respect to the light. In this way Gould dissociated the location actually visited by the dancers, which recruits might have detected via odor, and the location indicated by the dance. Contrary to the odor hypothesis but consistent with the dance language hypothesis, most recruits arrived at the feeder indicated by the dance.

A second experimental approach to testing whether dancing communicates distance and direction employed a traditional ethological tool for presenting signals independently of the environmental conditions that normally elicit them, namely a dummy, here a mechanical bee. A mechanical bee successfully recruits bees that attend its dances, and the recruits use both distance and direction information provided by the model (Michelsen et al. 1992). An even newer technical development has provided a third kind of evidence for use of dance information. Bees that had attended a dance were fitted with transponders for harmonic radar as they left the hive, so their flight paths could be recorded (see Section 8.4.2; Riley et al. 2005). Whether they were released at the hive or at other locations 200 meters away, the recruits flew for roughly the correct distance in the direction indicated by the dance. Then they began to circle around as if searching for other cues to the food's location (Figure 14.7). Odor is normally one such cue, as discussed more below, but the feeders in this experiment were all unscented.

Not only does the experiment of Riley and colleagues (2005) provide direct evidence that the bees, in effect, treat the dance as flying instructions ("go this far in this direction"), it also provides evidence against suggestions that recruits' cognitive maps of the local environment mediate their responses to it. If the bees displaced as indicated in Figure 14.7 had interpreted the dance as telling them about a certain allocentrically defined location, they should have headed toward it rather than directly east and they should have flown farther in that direction before starting to search for the feeder. However, under some conditions experienced bees' maplike knowledge of the local terrain seems to influence how they dance and respond to dances (Section 8.4.2; R. Menzel and De Marco 2006), and a long-standing but sketchily reported experiment is said to indicate the same. This is the "lake experiment" (Gould and Towne 1987; Gould 1990), in which recruits reportedly did not follow dances telling them food was in the middle of a lake, a location in which food was normally very unlikely (the dancers having been trained to a feeder on a boat

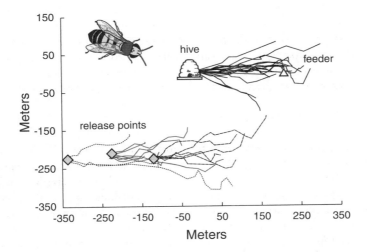

Figure 14.7. Flight paths of honeybees recruited by dancers that had visited the feeder shown (triangle). Some set out from the hive (coordinates 0, 0), and others were released at distant locations (diamonds). Paths were recorded until the bees began to circle around as if searching for cues from the feeder. After Riley et al. (2005) with permission.

which was slowly moved to the middle of the lake). A thorough recent repetition of this study (Wray et al. 2008) provided no evidence that the recruits were mentally traveling to the location signaled by a dance and refusing to follow directions that would take them to the implausible lake.

But exactly what spatial information is encoded in the dance? Foragers forced to follow an indirect route to food, for example around a mountain, seem to "report" the straight line direction to the food, as if using path integration to record the journey (von Frisch 1967; F. Dyer 2002; R. Menzel and De Marco 2006). As for distance, we saw in Box 8.3 that bees measure distance by optic flow. This subjective distance is what the dance communicates. Foragers that have found food in a densely patterned tunnel dance as if food is farther away than it really is, and that is the distance flown by recruits heading out across natural terrain (Esch et al. 2001).

One aspect of local knowledge that does influence recruits' behavior is what they know about the odor carried by the dancer. Although odor does not have the role attributed to it by skeptics who claimed it was the only information imparted in the dance, bees do use it. We have already seen a suggestion (Riley et al. 2005) that when new recruits have flown the vector encoded in the dance to the approximate location of the food, they find the feeder itself using local cues. Normally those would include an odor matching that on the dancer. Experienced bees remember the odor as well as the color of food sources at specific locations. If a familiar location has been without food for a few hours (so bees stop visiting it) and its odor is simply blown into the hive, bees start flying out to visit it (Reinhard et al. 2004). This is evidently a naturalistic example of memory reactivation (Section 7.5). Bees can hold two such odor-location associations in memory at once. They also associate color with odor. When yellow rose-scented and blue lemon-scented feeders were experienced at a variety of locations equidistant from the hive and rose odor was wafted into the hive, the bees selectively visited yellow sites even though they were unscented in the test (Experiment 5 in Reinhard et al. 2004). Such stored personal information may even be used in preference to conflicting public information from a dancer (Grüter, Balbuena, and Farina 2008). For example, if a dancer carries an odor that an experienced but currently inactive forager associates with location A but the dancer is signaling novel location B, in a different direction, the forager will visit A rather than B. The spatial information in the dance may primarily be used by naive bees just beginning to forage or those that have not been foraging recently, whereas the dancer's odor or even its dancing alone serves to reactivate experienced foragers, which then visit sites they already know (Grüter, Balbuena, and Farina 2008).

Conclusions

The dancing of bees differs from the communication systems to be discussed next in that a continuously graded message signals a potentially infinite number of directions and distances. The dance has also (e.g., Roitblat 1987) been claimed to be unique among animal communications in having the human-language property of displacement. This is obviously true in a trivial sense, since the dancer may be displaced in space several hundred meters from the food that caused her to dance. However, if the dance is seen as reporting on a just-completed journey, it is no more displaced than an alarm call given to a just-glimpsed snake. In both cases, too, the communication is symbolic in that the signal bears an arbitrary relationship to the message. It has been suggested that "the dance-communication system of honey bees . . . is exceeded in complexity and information-carrying capacity only by human speech" (Gould and

Towne 1987, 317–318). This conclusion may be overenthusiastic, but there seems no reason to question von Frisch's assertion (see F. Dyer 2002) that the study of the honeybees' dance is a "magic well of scientific discovery" and much is still being drawn from it.

14.2.2   Chickens: Audience effects, functional reference, and representation

Chickens have two kinds of alarm calls (Figure 14.8). Aerial predators such as hawks elicit a scream or whistle, whereas ground predators such as foxes and raccoons elicit a long series of pulses, "cut cut cut cut . . . cuuut." Behavior toward these two classes of predators differs in a functionally sensible way. A chicken sighting a hawk over-head may move toward cover, and it crouches and repeatedly tilts its head to one side, looking up at the sky. When a fox, dog, or raccoon approaches, the chicken stands erect and looks from side to side.

Chickens' alarm calls satisfy the criteria for functional reference. Roosters were presented with video images of either a hawk on an overhead monitor or a raccoon on a monitor at the side of their cage (Figure 14.9). They gave aerial alarm calls to the hawk and ground alarm calls to the raccoon and otherwise behaved appropriately to each one, thus showing production specificity (Evans, Evans, and Marler 1993). The context independence of responses to alarm calling was shown by playing recorded alarm calls to hens isolated in a laboratory cage. The hens moved toward cover only when hearing an aerial alarm, and they crouched and looked up most often in this condition (Figure 14.8). Hens hearing ground alarms did not seek cover, crouch or look up any more than hens hearing background noise. Instead they stood in a tall sleeked posture and looked from side to side. Unlike in the risk-based systems to be discussed in Section 14.2.5, the differences in behavior to aerial and ground predators do not reflect quantitative differences in the threat posed by the predator. For instance, the number

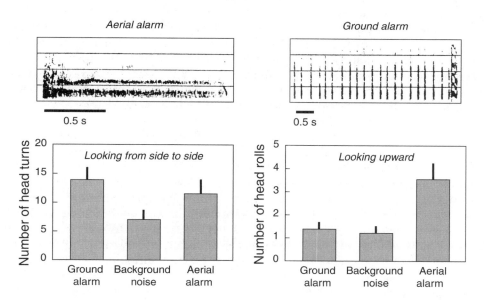

Figure 14.8. Sonagrams and behavioral effects of chickens' aerial and ground alarm calls, compared to effects of background noise. Redrawn from Evans, Evans, and Marler (1993) with permission.

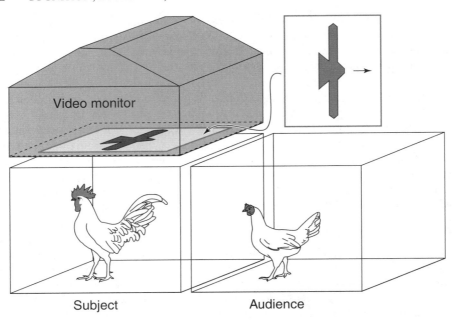

Figure 14.9. Setup for studying effects of the presence of a hen (the audience) on a rooster's alarm calling. Redrawn from Evans and Marler (1992) and Evans, Macedonia and Marler (1993) with permission.

of alarm calls and nonvocal responses increased with the size of an overhead hawk image, but their nature remained the same (Evans, Macedonia, and Marler 1993).

Alarm calling makes sense only if other animals are around to get the message. Indeed, by attracting a predator's attention calling may be costly for a solitary animal. Operationally this means that alarm calling should be modulated by the presence versus absence of an audience. Roosters alarm call more when they can see a live or videotaped hen (Evans and Marler 1995). The characteristics of the audience are also important: roosters alarm call more when the audience is a conspecific than when it is a bobwhite quail (Karakashian, Gyger, and Marler 1988). Notice that the results of these experiments do not demand an intentional interpretation. What is being shown is that aerial alarm calling is affected by characteristics of both the predator and the audience.

Roosters' food calling is also sensitive to the audience. When hens are around, a rooster finding a morsel of food emits a food call and hens are attracted to it, are allowed to eat it, and may subsequently engage in other aspects of courtship with the rooster (Marler, Dufty, and Pickert 1986a, 1986b; Evans and Marler 1994). Here again is a behavior that invites interpretation in terms of intentions to communicate, to attract the hen, and so on, but again it is more simply characterized as conditionally controlled by, among other things, the quality of food and kind of audience. Food calling is also functionally referential (Evans and Evans 1999). Roosters food call not only when they find food in the presence of an audience, but also in the presence of a CS for food; thus in a sense their calls express an expectation of food (Evans and Marler 1994).

On the receiver's side, when a hen hears a food call, but not a ground alarm call, she closely scans the ground as if looking for food. To discover whether she does so because the call represents food, as opposed to eliciting scanning directly, Evans and

Evans (2007) adopted the logic of experiments designed to test whether conditioned responses result from S-S or S-R learning. As described in Chapter 4, such experiments may involve manipulations like devaluing food by poisoning or satiation, to, in effect, change the animal's representation of the US directly without altering the original CS-reinforcer (S-S) or CS-response (S-R) connections. If responding to a CS is mediated by a food representation, that is, if it reflects CS-food rather than CS-response learning, responding decreases immediately when food is devalued. Evans and Evans (2007) reasoned that, similarly, if the hen's response to food calling is mediated by a representation of food, prior information that food is present should decrease it. This prediction was borne out. When hens had recently found and eaten three corn kernels in the experimental chamber, they scanned the ground in response to a food call much less than hens that had not just found corn and no more than hens that heard a ground alarm. Because so little food was given, the hens' lack of responsiveness most likely reflected not satiation but rather the fact that the call gave no new information.

14.2.3   Vervet monkeys: Categorization and intentional communication

In effect, the vervet monkeys' three alarm calls—for eagles and other dangerous raptors, snakes, and leopards (Section 14.1; Figure 14.10)—show how vervets classify predators in much the same way as a pigeon's pecking a different one of four keys in the presence of pictures of different kinds of objects shows how the pigeon is classifying the images (Chapter 6). Vervets make finer discriminations among flying things than chickens do (Figure 14.11). Chickens living outdoors in rural New York State gave a high proportion of their aerial alarms to harmless birds like doves and geese, and even to airplanes and falling leaves, but adult vervets discriminate potentially harmful raptors (hawks and eagles) from equally large but harmless birds such as storks and vultures. This discrimination develops during the first four years or so of life (Seyfarth and Cheney 1986). Infant vervets give the three types of alarms calls in a roughly appropriate manner, for example, eagle alarms to things in the air and snake alarms to long things on the ground. But at first infants do not show much discrimination among things within these classes. For instance, eagle alarms are as likely to nonraptors as to raptors. When juveniles begin to discriminate between the broad

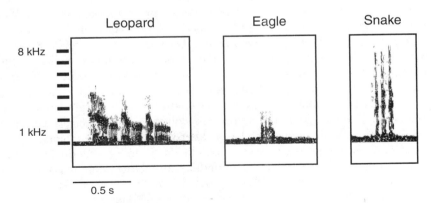

Figure 14.10. Sonagrams of one individual vervet's leopard, eagle, and snake alarms. From Seyfarth, Cheney, and Marler (1980) with permission.

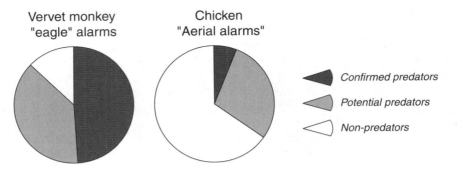

Figure 14.11. Comparison of the specificity of vervet eagle alarms and chicken aerial alarms, in terms of the proportions of calls given to confirmed predators versus other aerial things. Redrawn from Evans and Marler (1995) with permission.

classes of raptors (hawks and eagles) versus nonraptors, they still include raptors that do not prey on monkeys, but later these are more or less ignored. Because these developmental changes take several years, it is impossible to say exactly what experiences contribute to them and how they do so, but teaching by older vervets does not appear to be involved (Cheney and Seyfarth 1990). Adults do not, for example, correct infants when they call inappropriately. Observational learning similar to birds' and other monkeys' observational learning about predators (Chapter 13) may play a role.

The vervets' categorization of predators makes functional sense because each one demands a different response. Eagles strike from above, so monkeys that are high in trees when an eagle is sighted should move down while monkeys on the ground should move into cover. Leopards, in contrast, generally attack monkeys on the ground and can be escaped by climbing trees. Snakes approach along the ground and may be mobbed by the monkey troop. In opportunistic observations in the field, animals' responses to others' calls may be hard to distinguish from responses caused by their own sighting of the predator or other animals' behavior to it, but alarms by themselves elicit appropriate responses when played from concealed loudspeakers in the absence of predators (Seyfarth., Cheney, and Marler 1980).

Vervet alarm calls meet the criteria for functional reference, but do they simply elicit predator-appropriate responses or do they access a representation of a particular type of predator? And since different individuals have different voices, is something about the caller represented as well? To try to find out, Cheney and Seyfarth (1988) turned to habituation-dishabituation experiments. Some of them focused not on alarm calls but on vocalizations used in intergroup encounter. *Wrrs* are emitted when another group is approaching, as are *chutters*, but chutters are more frequent in direct aggressive interactions between groups. Because vervets tend to look toward a calling animal, Cheney and Seyfarth counted the number of seconds looking toward the speaker in films of the period during and immediately after playbacks. Each experiment began with a playback of the target call to get a baseline measure of orienting. On the next day, the subject heard a series of eight habituating calls about 30 minutes apart, during which looking time generally declined. About 30 minutes later, the target call was played again and looking time was compared to baseline (Figure 14.12).

This design was used to test whether habituation transferred from wrrs to an acoustically different call with similar meaning, chutters, and whether the identity

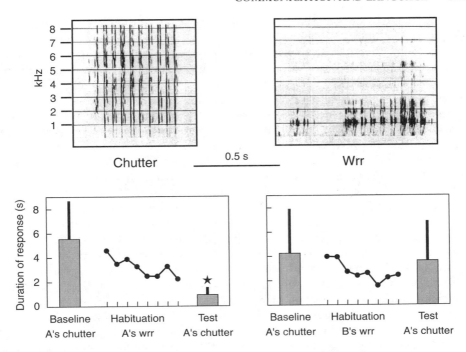

Figure 14.12. Sonagrams of wrr and chutter vocalizations of a single individual and data demonstrating cross habituation between two calls from the same caller. Redrawn from Cheney and Seyfarth (1988) with permission.

of the caller mattered to any transfer of habituation. In effect this design asked, if animal A was unreliable because he repeatedly wrr'd from the bushes and no vervet group appeared, would he be treated as unreliable when he chuttered? A second series of tests asked whether an animal habituated to an eagle alarm would transfer this habituation to leopard alarms, and, again, would it matter if the same or different individuals gave the two kinds of alarms? Regardless of the identity of the caller, habituation did not transfer between eagle and leopard alarms, nor did it transfer from one individual's wrr to another's chutter. However, habituation did transfer from a given individual's wrrs to that same individual's chutters, as if the vervets learned something like "Charlie is unreliable today when it comes to signaling the approach of another group." Because transfer was obtained here but not when the same individual was heard to signal two different predators, it appears that habituation transfers between two acoustically different calls only if they have similar meaning. However, one might still worry that in some sense a wrr and a chutter from a single individual are more similar to each other as acoustic stimuli than are an eagle and a leopard alarm from one individual. But this doubt is laid to rest by evidence that habituation can transfer across acoustically very different calls—a bird's and a monkey's predator alarms (Seyfarth and Cheney 1990).

Superb starlings (*Spreo superbus*) live with the vervets in Kenya and give acoustically distinctive "raptor alarms" to birds that attack them from the air. The starlings also give "terrestrial predator" alarms to a wide variety of ground predators. Vervets respond to both of the starlings' alarm calls, apparently learning to do so (Hauser 1988). As would be expected if the vervets are responding in terms of what the calls signal, habituation transferred between vervet and starling raptor alarms, whereas it did not transfer between vervet leopard alarms and starling raptor alarms. The starling raptor alarm is elicited by aerial predators, not by leopards. However, habituation to the much less specific starling terrestrial predator alarm transferred to both vervet leopard alarms and vervet eagle alarms. As Seyfarth and Cheney concluded from the results of their playback experiments (1990, 764), "The results of these tests are difficult to explain without assuming that vervets have some representation of the objects and events denoted by different call types, and that they compare and respond to vocalizations on the basis of these representations." What is being described here and even more so in the next section is much like many-to-one matching or mediated generalization (Chapter 6), in which arbitrary conditioned stimuli are related to one another via an association with a common US or response. Indeed, Seyfarth and Cheney (e.g., 1997, 2003c) have emphasized that many of their findings are consistent with explanations in terms of associative learning. In any case, as with most observations that meet the criteria for functional reference, we cannot tell exactly what the calls refer to (Manser 2009). A leopard alarm, for instance, could equally well denote a leopard or be an imperative, "run to the trees if you're on the ground and stay in the trees if you're there already."

Whatever the conclusion about the meaning of signals, it is a different question whether they are used with intent to inform. Like chickens, alarm calling vervets show an audience effect. A solitary vervet is unlikely to alarm call. However, there is no indication that an alarm calling vervet takes into account the audience's need to know. The individual that first discovers the snake or the leopard should be more likely to call than one whose fellows are already calling or safe from predation, but extensive observations of vervets in the field yielded no evidence for this (Cheney and Seyfarth 1990). Research on baboons' contact barks (Cheney, Seyfarth, and Palombit 1996) and reconciliatory grunts (Cheney and Seyfarth 1997) leads to the same conclusion (Cheney and Seyfarth 2007). For example, baboons that have become separated from their troop emit "contact barks" but troop members within earshot do not vocalize in response as they should if they understand that the barking animal is trying to locate the group. The evidence relevant to intentional communication in vervets and baboons can thus be summarized as showing that while callers are sensitive to some properties of their audience, they do not take other animals' understanding into account (for review see Seyfarth and Cheney 2003c). This conclusion is of course consistent with the indications in Chapter 12 that monkeys do not have theory of mind.

14.2.4   Diana monkeys: understanding other species' signals

Diana monkeys (*Cercopithecus diana diana*) live in the rainforests of West Africa in groups consisting of a male with several females and their offspring. Male Diana monkeys make acoustically distinct alarm calls in response to leopards, which attack these arboreal monkeys from below, and crowned eagles, which snatch them from above. In the forest it is impossible to observe everything the monkeys do in response to signs of a predator, but because female Diana monkeys respond to male eagle and leopard alarms by calling in characteristic ways themselves, females' vocalizations provide insights into how the monkeys classify sounds from their own and other species. For example, females' calling habituates if the same male alarm call is repeated, but if a series of, say, leopard alarms is followed by an eagle alarm, females call anew in response to the call signifying a new kind of threat. The alarm calls are functionally referential in that they have both production specificity and context independence (Zuberbühler 2003).

Further evidence for functional reference comes from elegant experiments based on the fact that females call appropriately in response to vocalizations of the predators themselves. Zuberbühler, Cheney, and Seyfarth (1999) compared females' responses to an eagle's shriek (a probe stimulus) following each of three habituating experiences (or *primes*): a series of eagle shrieks, a series of male eagle alarms, and a series of male leopard alarms (Figure 14.13). "Eagle" alarm calling to the eagle probe remained at a low level in the first condition, whereas it was high when the females had just heard a series of leopard alarms. In the critical condition, eagle shriek following eagle alarms, calling also remained low, a result that could be described as showing that the females expected to hear an eagle when the male had just "told" them one was around. Analogous results were found with leopard growls as the probe following habituation to eagle alarms, leopard alarms, and leopard growls.

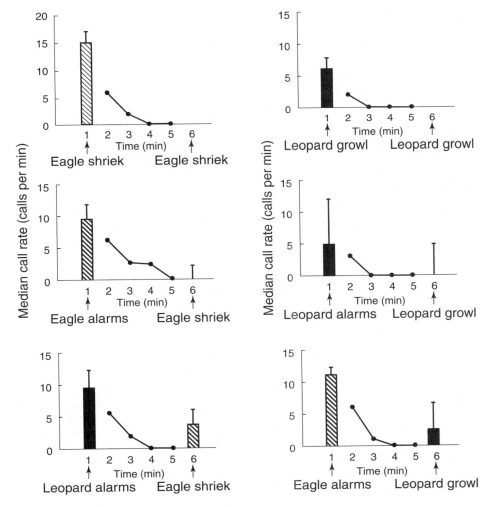

Figure 14.13. Calling of female Diana monkeys to a probe of an eagle shriek (left column) or a leopard growl following habituation to a prime consisting of the same stimulus (e.g., eagle shriek), or male diana monkey alarm calls given to the same predator (e.g., eagle alarm), or a different predator (e.g., leopard alarm). After Zuberbuhler, Cheney, and Seyfarth (1999) with permission.

Notice that with this experimental design the effect of a standardized probe such as the eagle's shriek in Figure 14.13 is compared across groups of subjects that have had different priming stimuli. This is more powerful than simply measuring response to a call before and after habituation as in some related experiments because it controls for the possibility that general responsiveness changes during the habituation treatment (Evans 1997). Much as with Wagner's model of memory (Chapter 5), the results imply that the leopard's growl and the leopard alarm access a common representation because exposure to either one decreases responsiveness to the same probe. In this sense the monkeys represent or remember some correlate of the specific predator signaled (Seyfarth and Cheney 2003c).

Not only primates but birds (Rainey, Zuberbühler, and Slater 2004; Templeton and Greene 2007) and even a reptile, the Galapagos iguana (Vitousek et al. 2007) learn to respond to the alarm calls of sympatric species. Diana monkeys learn some quite subtle things about the vocalizations of other animals they commonly encounter (Zuberbühler 2003). For example, leopards hunt chimpanzees as well as monkeys, and diana monkeys that frequently contact chimpanzees (but not those which do not) make leopard alarms when they hear chimpanzee alarm screams, as if having associated the chimpanzee screams with the presence of a leopard. But diana monkeys are also hunted by chimpanzees, and their response to signs of predatory chimpanzees or humans is not to alarm call but to be silent and cryptic. Accordingly, this is how they behave when they hear chimpanzee social screams or human voices (Zuberbühler 2000b). They learn even more subtle discriminations involving the alarm calls of crested guinea fowl, a species preyed upon by—and giving the same alarm call to—both leopards and humans (Zuberbühler 2000a). By themselves, guinea fowl alarm calls evoke leopard alarms from diana monkeys. But the monkeys call at only a low level if they have been primed with the sound of human voices, as if inferring that humans rather than leopards had caused the guinea fowls' alarms. In contrast, when priming with human voices is followed by the growl of a leopard, they do make leopard alarm calls, showing that signs of people in the area do not evoke cryptic behavior in general.

These findings can be described as showing the monkeys are making causal inferences. They might even fit one of the causal models discussed in Section 11.3.3. However, the monkeys' causal knowledge need not go beyond that implicit in simple associative learning (Zuberbühler 2000a, 2000b). For example, diana monkeys may respond to signs of a leopard by approaching in a group to keep an eye on it from a safe distance. Thus they could well have witnessed encounters between leopards and chimpanzees; even if rare these would provide the conditions for associating chimpanzee alarm screams with the presence of a leopard. Similarly, the way in which the monkeys' response to guinea fowl alarms is conditional on the context could have developed through experiences analogous to those required for occasion setting (Section 4.6). More evidence about the animals' prior experience than can readily be collected in the rainforest would be necessary to test such accounts. A further question is what any of these observations imply about the calls' reference. Different sounds such as leopard growls and alarm calls of monkeys, chimpanzees, and guinea fowl are evidently functionally equivalent (see Chapter 6). Whether the behavioral equivalence is mediated by a representation of a leopard per se or of the response to be made to it is difficult to resolve without experiments like that of Evans and Evans (2007) in which presentation of food was used to directly manipulate chickens' food representations, experiments that may be impossible to do with this system (but see Zuberbühler 2000a).

14.2.5   Ground squirrels and meerkats: Meaning or emotion?

Some species of ground squirrels have different calls and behaviors for snakes and aerial predators, but these are better predicted by the immediacy of threat posed by the predator than by what kind of predator it is (Macedonia and Evans 1993; Blumstein 2007). An aerial predator at a distance is responded to in the same way as a carnivore like a fox or dog, whereas a carnivore close by elicits the calls usually given to an aerial predator. The imminence of predatory threat is reflected in other ground squirrels' responses to the calls, for example in whether they run into their burrows or just stand alert. It is not necessary to interpret such calls as conveying information about the world. Rather they express the caller's emotion, something like "afraid" or "very afraid," and these emotional expressions evoke responses in listeners just as the male stickleback's "expression" of sexual readiness evokes approach in a female stickleback.

The fact that some animal communication is primarily emotional has led to claims that analyses in terms of information are unnecessary and uncalled for (Owren and Rendall 2001). But there are several reasons to see this claim as too extreme (Seyfarth and Cheney 2003b). *(1)* Some systems such as the ground squirrels' alarm calling may primarily involve emotional intensity, but that need not mean all do. *(2)* Emotion and information are not mutually exclusive. A signal that expresses the sender's emotion can still convey information to receivers. In an example suggested by Premack (see Seyfarth and Cheney 2003b), a person might make a certain delighted exclamation when and only when she finds strawberries. This exclamation both expresses the sender's emotion and tells receivers that strawberries are present. *(3)* In principle, signals can be both motivational (or emotional) and referential at the same time. An example of such a system is the alarm calling of meerkats (or suricates, *Suricata suricatta*).

Like the vervets, meerkats live in groups in fairly open terrain (here, the South African semidesert) where they are threatened by snakes, aerial predators, and ground predators such as jackals. Like the vervets too, they have acoustically distinct alarm calls and distinct responses for these three classes of predator, but in addition nearby predators elicit louder, longer, and noisier calls than those farther away. Analysis of the structure of calls given to the three predator types at different distances showed that they cluster according to both predator and distance, or threat level (Figure 14.14; Manser 2001). When recordings from the different categories were played to groups of foraging meerkats, their responses varied appropriately (Manser, Bell, and Fletcher 2001). For instance, in response to aerial alarms they scanned the sky and perhaps ran into the nearest bolthole, whereas in response to snake alarms they gathered together and approached the speaker as if preparing to mob a snake. High-urgency alarms elicited more complete and long-lasting responses than low-urgency alarms, after which the animals might only pause briefly while digging in the sand for invertebrates.

A particularly clear example of how quantitative variation in a single call type elicits parallel variations in a single type of response by listeners comes from alarm calling by black-capped chickadees (Templeton, Greene, and Davis 2005). When chickadees sight a perched owl or hawk or a small mammalian predator such as a cat, they emit "chickadee" alarm calls and gather together to mob the predator. The number of "dee" notes in the calls turns out to vary inversely with the size of predator (Figure 14.15), reflecting the fact that small maneuverable raptors such as kestrels actually pose a greater risk to small birds than do large species such as great horned

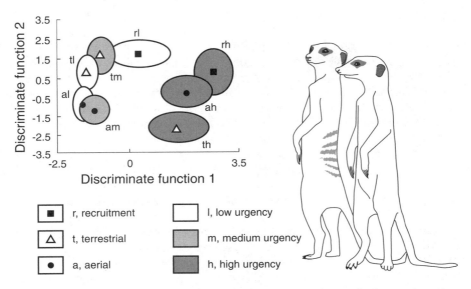

Figure 14.14. Two-dimensional discriminant analysis of meerkat alarm calls showing how they cluster by what is signaled: (terrestrial predator, aerial predator, recruitment (for example, to mob a snake), and by urgency or nearness of the threat to the group. For explanation of how such plots are constructed see Figures 6.4 and 6.5. After Manser (2001) with permission.

owls. Accordingly, playbacks of calls given to small predators evoke more calling and more approaches to the speaker than calls given to large predators. Thus the calls pass the test of functional reference, but they convey only information about risk or emotional intensity. Because they do contain information, other small birds that flock with chickadees learn their significance and join in mobbing the predator (Templeton and Greene 2007).

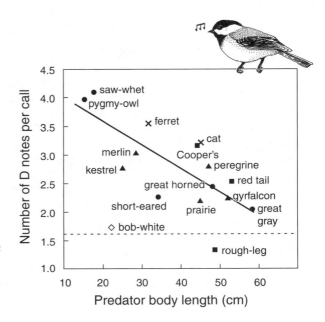

Figure 14.15. Number of "dee" notes in black-capped chickadee alarm calls varies inversely with size of predator, reflecting the fact that smaller owls and hawks are more dangerous to chickadees. After Templeton, Greene, and Davis (2005) with permission.

14.2.6 The evolution of functional reference

Comparing the systems for alarm calling and responding to alarm calls described in the last few sections suggests that the specificity of alarms reflects the specificity of evasive techniques available for different kinds of predators (Macedonia and Evans 1993; Donaldson, Lachmann, and Bergstrom 2007; Manser 2009). For instance, ground squirrels' only escape from predators in open grasslands is underground in their burrows, whereas diana monkeys in the rainforest can either descend from the canopy or climb higher. As a further example, chickens' aerial alarm calls are fairly indiscriminate (Figure 14.11), but since birds generally have very good vision this is unlikely to mean that chickens cannot discriminate among things in the air. Indeed, three species of lapwings make finer discriminations among predators than do chickens (Walters 1990). For instance, Southern lapwings have three different anti-predator responses. These include swooping and pecking at snakes and displaying with wings raised at cattle approaching a nest, presumably with the function of scaring off these predators. The birds' responses to raptors and other large birds depends on the species of predator, on whether the threatening bird is perching or flying, and on whether the lapwing itself has eggs or young in the nest. Walters (1990) suggests that the difference in specificity of antipredator behavior between chickens and lapwings can be related to differences in their habitat and concomitant differences in the relative costs and benefits of correctly detecting predators versus making false alarms. Wild junglefowl, the species ancestral to domestic chickens, live—as their name suggests—in the jungle, where predators are likely to be well concealed until they are nearby. Here it might be important to have a low threshold for alarm calling because any sign of a predator likely means attack is imminent. Making fine discriminations may not be worth the risk in possible decision time lost. In contrast, lapwings live in open habitat where predators can be sighted from afar. If they reacted to anything remotely like a predator they might not have much time left for anything else, and because they can detect distant threats, they have plenty of time to take evasive action.

Comparisons among primates reveal the same relationship between habitat and predator discrimination. For example, Macedonia (1990) compared the antipredator responses of two species of lemurs living in large enclosures. Ring-tailed lemurs (*Lemur catta*), which normally inhabit areas much like those inhabited by vervet monkeys, have different calls and different evasive behaviors for ground versus aerial predators. Each call and type of behavior is characteristic of the type of threat, not its intensity. For instance, calls stimulated by a stuffed owl perched in the lemurs' enclosure or by a hawk silhouette pulled over the enclosure on wires were all aerial alarms, even though the "flying" hawk presumably represented a more immediate danger (Pereira and Macedonia 1991). Ruffed lemurs (*Varecia variegata variegata*) are larger than ringtailed lemurs or vervet monkeys and spend much of their time in dense tree canopy. Although they have more than one alarm call, the responses to these calls are not well differentiated and some of them are given in situations of high arousal not involving predators. Thus their calls do not seem to be functionally referential (Macedonia 1990; Macedonia and Evans 1993). As with ground squirrels, in the ruffed lemurs' habitat imminence may be the only feature of predators that matters. However a comparison of sympatric cape ground squirrels and meerkats (Furrer and Manser 2009) shows that social structure and how a species uses its habitat may also play a role.

All these observations suggest that in evolution as in some category learning experiments, animals come to group multiple stimuli by required response, not necessarily by perceptual similarity. A recent model of the evolution of signaling systems (Donaldson, Lachmann, and Bergstrom 2007) demonstrates exactly this: functional reference evolves when the world is structured so that different classes of situations require different responses. Risk- or intensity-based systems evolve when all that is available is variation in one type of response. Many social species have food calls as well as alarm calls; we have seen an example in fowl. Receivers clearly need to discriminate food calls from alarm calls, but about all food calls have been shown to do is to attract other animals (e.g., Hauser 1998; Pollick, Gouzoules, and De Waal 2005). Thus food calls and alarm calls meet the criteria for functional reference in that the one evokes approach and the other species-specific defensive behaviors, but such a simple system communicates only motivation. A further important factor in signal evolution is social structure (see Hauser 1996; Blumstein 2007). Signaling should evolve as a function of the degree to which the signal can influence kin or long-term companions that may reciprocate in future. Since signaling may be costly if it attracts a predator's attention, we should expect alarm calling to evolve only when single individuals are likely to spot a source of danger before their companions and be in a position to warn relatives or possible reciprocal altruists (Chapter 12).

14.3   Trying to teach human language to other species

Attempts to teach human language to chimpanzees and other animals have a long history (see Candland 1993). To some extent, they are the expression of an enduring human wish to communicate with other species (Candland 1993) or, as the title of one book (Bright 1990) puts it, "The Dolittle Obsession." The last half of the twentieth century saw a series of much-publicized and controversial attempts to teach various forms of human language to chimpanzees and other great apes. Although the accomplishments of these animals seem impressive, there is much about them to debate. The various animal language projects have been extensively reviewed by both proponents and critics (e.g., Wallman 1992; Rumbaugh and Savage-Rumbaugh 1994; Ristau 1996). It is now generally accepted that the earliest projects did not succeed in doing much more than teach chimpanzees a lot of clever tricks. Later projects may or may not have overcome all of the problems of the earlier ones. One animal, Kanzi the bonobo, is reported to have reached a level of comprehension of spoken English comparable to that of a two-year-old child. Arguably, however, taken all together the results of "animal language" studies are most revealing for what the animals did *not* do (Fitch 2005). In any case, the first question that needs to be addressed is what would it mean if members of another species either did or did not acquire a form of human language?

14.3.1   What can we learn?

"Can any animals learn language?"

To begin with, "Can animals learn language?" is the wrong question. As we have seen, several features of language are shared by the natural communication systems of some other species. The candidates for features uniquely characteristic of human language include semanticity, productivity, duality, and recursion (see also Pinker and Jackendoff 2005). The first two are linked in attempts to see whether the animals combine the signs they learn in orderly ways to create new meanings because doing so could imply an understanding of simple linguistic structure. Some of the research with apes has used a system that potentially has duality, that is, in principle the language user could both comprehend and produce the words and sentences of the language. This makes it possible to ask whether subjects actually understand all that they can produce and to probe knowledge of syntax with tests of comprehension. However, syntax is more than discriminative responding to word order. It entails knowledge of the interrelationships among structures in the language. For instance, the native speaker of English knows not only that "Tim gave the apple to Lana" means something different from "Lana gave the apple to Tim." She also knows the relationship of these statements to other grammatical sentences such as "To whom did Tim give the apple?" and "Was the apple given by Tim to Lana?"

Attempts to teach forms of human language to apes were bedeviled by the problem of formulating clear behavioral criteria for language in part because while the research was going on so was research and theorizing about human language. Among other developments were advances in understanding language acquisition in children and language use in deaf users of American Sign Language, which was taught to some of the apes. Closer looks at what actually goes on as children acquire their first words and sentences were stimulated to some extent by the ape language research (Seidenberg and Petitto 1987). Some of these developments made the chimpanzee subjects of language training experiments look less like humans than they first appeared.

"Are apes like young children?"

Even if animals cannot be taught to converse like human adults, some have thought they might at least have a childlike grasp of language. Thus, apes exposed to forms of human language might reasonably be compared to young children in their achievements and how they reach them. The results of such comparisons have much in common with those from the comparisons of swamp sparrows and song sparrows mentioned in Chapter 1 (Figure 1.3): when members of two species are exposed to experiences characteristic of the species-typical development of one of them, they are influenced in very different ways. Each species of sparrow learns only its own song, and similarly, when child and chimpanzee are exposed to the child's species-typical experiences, even if some of those experiences affect both similarly, ultimately the chimpanzee does not develop in the same way as the child.

"Does language acquisition reflect a general learning ability or a specialized module?"

All hearing children except those suffering extreme social deprivation acquire the spoken language used by those around them, and they do so with very little direct teaching. Even deaf children learning to sign develop language in a predictable way across cultures (Pinker 1994). Still, just as in other species, adults have some special ways of behaving around their young that provide conditions conducive to learning. Mothers talk to their babies and toddlers in very simplified, repetitive, language, "motherese." Language development also depends on specifically social cognitive modules, in particular shared attention (cf. Chapter 12; Tomasello et al. 2005). A child knows what an adult is talking about because she knows what the adult is attending to. The similarity of all human languages in abstract structure together with the similarity in the way they are acquired led Chomsky (1968) to the idea of a species-specific Universal Grammar. This is the output of a species-specific Language Acquisition Device, or language module. This nativist view of language was opposed in the 1960s by Skinner's explanation of language as just another operant behavior, a view that is now largely discounted. The fact that language-trained apes, dolphins, or parrots do not learn more than rudimentary elements of linguistic behavior, at best, is one reason why it should be. Nevertheless, any evidence that a component of linguistic competence is acquired by a nonhuman animal, especially one not closely related to humans (see Box 14.1) indicates that at least that component of language can be generated by some sort of general learning ability.

"How did human language evolve?"

The Chomskian view implies that language represents a major discontinuity in evolution. The issue of how something so complex, abstract, and specialized might have evolved is controversial and much discussed by brain anatomists, anthropologists, and human behavioral ecologists, among others (Christiansen and Kirby 2003; Maynard Smith and Harper 2003; Fitch 2005; Fitch, Hauser, and Chomsky 2005; Pinker and Jackendoff 2005). In the present context the issue is simply what, if anything, the effects of exposing apes or other species to language training can tell us about language evolution. A point often made (e.g., Rumbaugh and Savage-Rumbaugh 1994) in support of ape language projects is that the results must be

---

Box 14.1 Fast Mapping by a Dog?

When 2- to 3-year-old children are learning language their vocabulary increases at an amazing rate, in part through a process of rapid word learning known in linguistics as *fast mapping*. Fast mapping is demonstrated experimentally when a toddler is shown a novel object or action labeled with a new word: "This (funny object) is a *dax*." Or the toddler might be shown the novel object along with familiar ones and asked to indicate the *dax*. Importantly, from such minimal experience the young child does not simply form a new sound-object association, but implicitly understands the sound as a *word*, that is, a sound with referential and grammatical properties. For instance, she can use and understand it in new sentences ("Where is the dax now?" "This dax is green.") Fast mapping has been claimed as one specialized component of human linguistic ability (Bloom 2004), but at least one animal, a highly trained border collie named Rico, learns in a way that is superficially similar (Kaminski, Call, and Fischer 2004).

At the time he was tested Rico knew the names of about 200 objects in that he would correctly retrieve them when told to. The demonstration of fast mapping consisted of Rico's owner telling Rico to go into an adjacent room and fetch something from a collection of 8 items, one of which was novel. On 70% of trials when a novel word was used, he fetched the novel item. Retention was tested similarly four weeks later, but now Rico had to choose the target, presumably learned, item from a collection of four completely novel and two or three familiar items. He was correct on three out of six such tests (chance was about 1/8) and chose one of the novel items when he was incorrect.

On one view (Kaminski, Call, and Fischer 2004), Rico's performance demonstrates that one of the building blocks of language is present in other species, at least under conditions of extensive prior experience with words as labels. However, on another (Bloom 2004; Markman and Abelev 2004). Rico's undeniably impressive ability is not the same as learning words. A potential methodological problem is the lack of controls for novelty preference which are usually used with children (Markman and Abelev 2004). Would Rico choose the novel object in a set if simply asked to "fetch"? More importantly, as illustrated in Figure B14.1, does Rico understand the labels he knows referentially or simply as part of a command ("fetch-the-sock")? Can he, for example, learn new words in other ways, as by being shown the object being named, and transfer this knowledge to other contexts (Bloom 2004)?

Whatever the results of further studies with Rico or similarly trained animals, it is worth noting that learning the significance of a novel stimulus in the way he apparently did, namely, by excluding familiar ones, is not unique to this study. A nice example comes from two sea lions trained on matching to sample with two 10-member equivalence classes, essentially numbers and letters (Kastak and Schusterman 2002). For instance, when one of the "numbers" was the sample, the sea lion had to match it with any one one in the "number" class, avoiding an alternative in the "letter" class. Learning by exclusion was demonstrated by following a familiar number sample with a novel symbol and a known letter. The sea lions chose the novel symbol above chance and learned it as a number, whereas if the sample was a letter in this example, a familiar letter comparison would be chosen and the novel symbol avoided. In either kind of case, symbols first encountered in this way then served as samples in normal trials with familiar letters and numbers as comparisons. One animal correctly matched them immediately, and the other with very little experience.

Inference by exclusion is a related ability. In an early example (Premack and Premack 1994) chimpanzees watched as two containers were baited, one with banana and one with apple. With the containers hidden behind a screen, an experimenter removed one of the fruits and ate it in view of the subject. Inferring that the container with that item is empty should lead to choosing the other container. As a group four chimpanzees performed at chance on the first test, although some learning occurred when the test was repeated. A larger group of great apes tested similarly performed above chance on their first trial (Call 2006), but not as well as the four-year-old children tested by Premack and Premack (1994), 90% of whom chose correctly the first time. Other species have also been tested on various paradigms designed to tap inference by exclusion (see Aust et al. 2008) but with little evidence of immediate successful performance.

Figure B14.1. Cartoon depiction of two ways in which Rico could understand names of things in commands such as "fetch the sock": as a word referring to an object (left) or as part of a command for a particular action. After Bloom (2004) with permission.

relevant to human language evolution because the great apes are our closest living relatives (see Hauser 2005). One problem with this line of reasoning is that "closest living relative" has no special status (Pinker 1994). If all extant nonhuman primates went extinct tomorrow, some other mammal would be our closest living relative, but that would not mean that studying it would shed any special light on language evolution. Yet-untold numbers of hominid species have come and gone since the last common ancestor of apes and humans. Because language may have appeared first in a hominid species that is now extinct, at most apes' linguistic abilities can tell us what was present in the most recent common ancestor of apes and humans. They are silent on when, why, and how full human language subsequently evolved. Arguably we will learn more about language evolution by studying other animals' natural communicative and conceptual abilities (Section 14.4).

14.3.2   Washoe, Nim, Sarah, and Lana

The immediate precursors of more contemporary ape language projects were two projects in the 1930s and 1940s in which husband-and-wife psychologists—the Kelloggs and later the Hayeses—raised a young chimpanzee like a child for periods of a few months to several years. Both of these animals, Gua and Viki, could communicate and solve problems, sometimes better than children of the same age, and Viki was eventually shaped to make vocalizations that could be understood as "mama," "papa" and "cup." Overall, however, the results led to the conclusion that chimpanzees could not actually talk, probably because they lacked the neural and anatomical requisites for speech. But clearly this does not mean that they might not be able to communicate linguistically using a medium more within their grasp, and that insight inspired a series of subsequent projects.

In the first of these, Beatrice and Allen Gardner attempted to teach American Sign Language (ASL) to the infant chimpanzee Washoe (Gardner and Gardner 1969). As much research has revealed since the Gardners' work began, ASL is a sophisticated natural language that is acquired and used like spoken language (see Pinker 1994; Ristau 1996). Washoe was surrounded by people who signed but did not speak in the hopes that she would acquire signing spontaneously as deaf children do. Shaping and explicit instrumental reinforcement were also used. After 22 months, Washoe was judged to know 30 signs, and eventually she was reported to use over 100. Much of the data collection on which these numbers were based went on during the course of daily free behavior—going for walks, eating, looking at magazines, playing. Use of signs was recorded from memory after the event. Later Washoe was given structured vocabulary tests in which she signed the names of objects that could not be seen by the person interpreting the signs. Later too, more emphasis was given to the question of whether combinations of signs constituted sentences. Particularly interesting was the possibility that Washoe combined her signs in novel but meaningful ways. For instance, she was reported to sign "water bird" for a swan. The ways in which this report might suffer from all the usual problems with anecdotes need hardly be mentioned.

The Gardners' 1969 *Science* paper marked the beginning of an optimistic out-pouring of projects with nonvocal languages. The optimism lasted until 1979, and the publication, also in *Science,* of a deflationary article by Terrace, Petitto, Sanders, and Bever entitled "Can an ape create a sentence?" (Terrace et al. 1979). These authors had trained an infant chimpanzee, Nim, in ASL using similar methods to the Gardners. Like Washoe, Nim learned to make many different signs and eventually produced them in combinations of two, three, or more (Figure 14.16). His two-sign

Figure 14.16. Nim signing "me" and "hug." From photographs in Terrace et al. (1979) with permission.

combinations did have structure. For instance many combinations consisted of *me* or *Nim* as agent or object of an action, as in "me drink" or "hug Nim." However, when it came to longer utterances, the resemblance to child language vanished. As a young child matures and acquires a larger vocabulary, the mean number of words per utterance increases dramatically. The same was not true of Nim. Even though his vocabulary increased to 125 signs by the end of the 4-year project, the mean length of his "utterances" stayed about the same (Figure 14.17). More important, when he did combine three or more signs, the added signs usually repeated those already given, as in "play me Nim play" or "grape eat Nim eat."

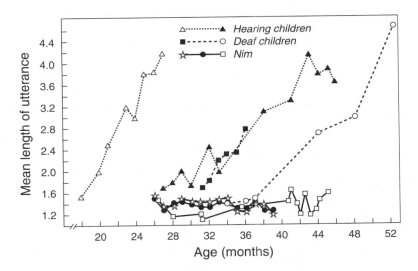

Figure 14.17. Changes in mean length of Nim's utterances over time compared to data from two hearing and two deaf children. Nim's data were recorded in three kinds of circumstances, represented by the three symbols. Redrawn from Terrace et al. (1979) with permission.

Terrace et al.'s most devastating conclusion came from an analysis of filmed interactions between Nim and his trainers. These revealed that very often Nim's signs were simple repetitions of signs that had just been made by the trainer. This same effect was evident in commercially available films of Washoe that Terrace et al. analyzed, much to the consternation of the Gardners (see Ristau and Robbins 1982). The tendency simply to imitate what was just signed is but one of several ways in which the chimpanzee's use of signs is unlike the child's use of language. Children engage in conversation, which means taking turns to exchange information. Children also use language to talk about the world, apparently for sheer pleasure in naming and commenting on things (see Pinker 1994). In contrast, the signing apes tended to "talk out of turn" (Terrace et al. 1979) and seldom used signs other than as instrumental responses. In short, Terrace et al. concluded that the answer to the question posed in the title of their article was a resounding "No." A more recent analysis of extensive filmed records of signing by Washoe and four other chimpanzees trained in the Gardners' program (Rivas 2005) gave results entirely consistent with Terrace et al.'s.

Two other chimpanzee language training projects started in the late 1960s used invented nonvocal languages of visual symbols. The chimpanzee Sarah was trained by Premack (e.g., 1971) to use a system of plastic shapes, and Lana was the first of a continuing series of apes trained by Rumbaugh, Savage-Rumbaugh and associates to use "Yerkish" symbols on computer keys (e.g., Rumbaugh 1977; Savage-Rumbaugh 1986). When the animal communicates by touching plastic shapes or computer keys, it is no longer necessary to rely on trainers who sign, in some cases inexpertly and in nonstandardized ways. There is less ambiguity in the animal's "words" since there is less chance of overinterpreting the choice of a symbol than a movement of the animal's hands. With the computer system it is also possible in principle to record and analyze the subject's entire linguistic input and output (for a thoughtful analysis see Ristau and Robbins 1982; Ristau 1996). On the other hand, confining the animal's linguistic experience to sessions in front of a keyboard limits the possibility for spontaneous communication and makes more apparent the parallels between this form of "language training" and straightforward operant conditioning.

The chimpanzee Sarah was trained with standard operant conditioning methods to associate plastic tokens of various colors and shapes with the objects they "named," in effect learning symbolic matching to sample (Premack 1971). Once Sarah had acquired some vocabulary, the project focused on using the token system to probe her grasp of concepts like *same/different, color of, name of* (Figure 14.18). Rather than a study of chimpanzee language learning it became a test of more general conceptual and problem-solving abilities, such as analogical reasoning (see Premack and Premack 1983). It was claimed that language training had fostered Sarah's apparent abstract reasoning abilities.

In the artificial communication system used first with Lana chimpanzee, the "words" are geometric designs on plastic keys connected to a computer (Figure 14.19; Rumbaugh 1977). Like the animals in other early projects, Lana interacted with the symbol system primarily to get things she wanted. The computer was programmed to activate appropriate dispensers upon receipt of grammatical strings like "Please machine give apple" and "Please machine give drink." Not surprisingly, what Lana learned mirrored the contingencies built into this system. Her behavior could be accounted for as associations between actions, people, or objects and symbols that could be plugged into six stock sentences such as "please (person) (action)" (C. Thompson and Church 1980). Even those who promoted the

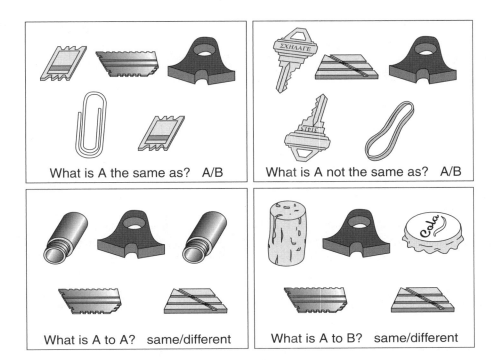

Figure 14.18. Questions about same/different relationships as represented in the system of tokens used to train Sarah the chimpanzee. In the two problems in the top row, Sarah had to choose the correct (matching or nonmatching) object. In the lower pair of questions she had to choose the token corresponding to "same" or "different." From Premack and Premack (1983) with permission.

Figure 14.19. Lana working at her keyboard. From the frontispiece of Rumbaugh (1977) with permission.

Lana project at the time eventually agreed that any training regime in which "words" are used primarily as operants to obtain food and activities does not promote genuine linguistic competence, even if chimpanzees might be capable of it (e.g., Rumbaugh, Savage-Rumbaugh, and Sevcik 1994).

14.3.3   Sherman and Austin, Jack and Jill

Lana was replaced as a student of Yerkish by Sherman and Austin, but work with them emphasized the interrelationships of production and comprehension, the social use of language, and what the symbols meant to the animals. Syntax was less emphasized, perhaps correctly, given the difficulty of distinguishing rudimentary syntax from sequence learning. Sherman and Austin were taught to name foods and other things by being rewarded with something other than the object being named. For instance, Sherman might be shown a banana and asked (in Yerkish symbols, *lexigrams*) "What this?" If he selected the lexigram for *banana* in reply, he received praise or the opportunity to request a different food, but not a piece of banana (Savage-Rumbaugh 1986). Notice that formally this skill is like symbolic matching to sample or category learning: the animal is exposed to a sample, selects a response, and is reinforced. To continue this analogy, Sherman and Austin were also trained in a form of delayed matching to sample, in which they were shown a food or other interesting object in one room and then led back to their keyboard in a different room and asked to describe or request what they had seen. At a later stage, they were encouraged to use lexigrams to specify what they were about to do or wanted to do (Savage-Rumbaugh et al. 1983; Savage-Rumbaugh 1986). For instance, to see if an animal "knew what he was saying" when requesting a tool, he might be presented with the whole tool kit to see if he chose the tool he had asked for, which Sherman and Austin did at better than chance levels. Naming and requesting were combined with other skills in a situation described as "Symbolic communication between two chimpanzees" (Savage-Rumbaugh, Rumbaugh, and Boysen 1978). Sherman and Austin were induced to request and share food with one another through the mediation of lexigrams. Now one animal "informed" the other of the contents of a food container, the second animal requested some of the contents, and if both were correct, they both got some of it to eat. There are parallels here with the attempts to establish the functional reference of natural signals (Section 14.2), in that the animals have to both produce and respond to the signal appropriately.

As the preceding summary implies, many of the elements of Sherman and Austin's behavior can be described as instrumental discriminations. This was underlined by a tongue-in-cheek report of a simulation of Sherman and Austin's performance by two pigeons, Jack and Jill (Epstein, Lanza, and Skinner 1980). With conventional procedures of shaping and selective reinforcement, Jack was trained to ask Jill the color of a light hidden under a curtain by pecking a "what color?" key, and Jill was trained to report it to Jack by pecking a color name. Jack evidenced his understanding of Jill's report by pecking the selected color and then a "Thank you" key (Figure 14.20). When both birds performed correctly, both were reinforced with grain. Borrowing the words of Savage-Rumbaugh, Rumbaugh, and Boysen (1978), Epstein et al. concluded, "We have thus demonstrated that pigeons can learn to engage in a sustained and natural conversation without human intervention, and that one pigeon can transmit information to another entirely through the use of symbols" (Epstein, Lanza, and Skinner 1980, 545). Whether this demonstration captures everything about the processes underlying the chimpanzees' behavior is of course debatable.

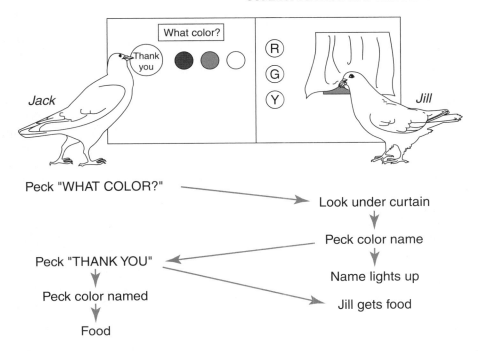

Figure 14.20. Setup and procedure for the demonstration of "communication between two pigeons." After Epstein, Lanza, and Skinner (1980) with permission.

14.3.4   Kanzi the bonobo

Bonobos are so-called pygmy chimpanzees (*Pan paniscus*); previous chimpanzee subjects of language-training projects had all been common chimpanzees (*Pan troglogytes*). Kanzi the bonobo has two accomplishments that set him apart from previously trained apes. First, he learned to use and understand lexigrams through observing his foster mother being taught them (Savage-Rumbaugh et al. 1986). Second, he understands human speech. When Savage-Rumbaugh and her colleagues realized Kanzi had evidently acquired his Yerkish and English comprehension skills simply through observation, much as young children initially comprehend much more than they can produce, they turned to investigating how far he could go if treated more like a young child. He was allowed to roam through a 55-acre wooded area where he could find food and all sorts of experiences, always accompanied by people talking while communicating on portable keyboards about what was happening or about to happen.

Kanzi's understanding of spoken English sentences was directly compared to that of a 2-year-old child in a controlled way (Savage-Rumbaugh et al. 1993). Both Kanzi and Alia, the child, were asked to carry out instructions expressed by simple sentences like "Get the telephone that's outdoors" or "Make the doggie bite the snake." A variety of objects was present, and the two subjects were asked to do several actions with each one rather than just the obvious ones. Importantly, these tests employed some completely novel sentences (see Savage-Rumbaugh and Brakke 1996). Precautions were taken against cuing by the person giving the instructions and selective recording by the raters. For instance, in some tests the other people recording data wore headphones broadcasting loud music so they would not know what Kanzi had been asked to do. Kanzi performed comparably to Alia on these tests. In other tests, his competence at producing sentences with lexigrams was comparable to that of a 1.5-year-old. These results can be taken to indicate that Kanzi learned more than to perform complex operants to get what he wanted but rather could use and understand words and sequences of words as representations of states of the world (Savage-Rumbaugh et al. 1993; Rumbaugh and Savage-Rumbaugh 1994 but see Seidenberg and Petitto 1987).

Does Kanzi's performance represent a species difference between bonobos and chimpanzees? Given the threat to both species in the wild, not to mention the expense and labor involved in raising them with a rich experience of spoken and symbolic language, it is unlikely that the data required to answer this question will ever be collected. However, a few bonobos have been studied, and it does appear that they have a greater propensity to acquire comprehension of spoken English than chimpanzees do (Rumbaugh and Savage-Rumbaugh 1994). So far it is not at all clear why they would be expected to be especially likely to learn human language. Bonobos are not so well studied as chimpanzees in the wild, so it is not clear whether their natural communication system is more languagelike. Evolutionarily they are no more part of the hominid lineage than chimpanzees.

14.3.5   Conclusions

Besides the apes we have considered, a few orangutans and a gorilla have been exposed to various forms of language training (see Ristau 1996). Dolphins and a sea lion have been taught to obey complex systems of gestural or auditory commands (Gisiner and Schusterman 1992; Herman 2006). Although learning to obey such commands can be described as conditional discrimination learning (Schusterman and Kastak 1998), they do have some linguistic properties. Most importantly, perhaps, the sequences of commands learned by the dolphins have a simple syntax, as in "take the hoop to the ball" versus "take the ball to the hoop," and the animals are sensitive to this (Herman and Uyeyama 1999; Kako 1999). And we have already met Alex the parrot, whose ability to talk was exploited more as a way to assess what nonlinguistic concepts he could acquire or express than for its possible relevance to language learning (Pepperberg 1999). He too demonstrated sensitivity to some properties of language, for example once learning a new word in one context (e.g., "rose" as the color of a paper) he transferred it to a new one ("rose wood") and responded correctly to it in new kinds of sentences (Kako 1999). Such findings lend support to proposals that at least some components of human language reflect cognitive competencies shared with other species (Herman and Uyeyama 1999).

Animal language-training projects raise many issues that are common to other areas of comparative cognition. These include the need for unambiguous behavioral criteria when testing another species for an essentially human cognitive process, the problems of Clever Hans and overinterpreted results, the shortcomings of anecdotes and single-subject studies, and the relative roles of general processes of learning versus modularity and species-specificity. The novel issues have to do with what constitutes human language and how it develops in very young children. Much of the controversy here boils down to disagreement over whether or not the subjects are "merely" demonstrating instrumental responding. Paradoxically, even though experience of conditioning procedures is increasingly shown to lead to complex and subtle representations of the world (Chapters 4, 6, 11), interpreting animals' communicative behaviors as resulting from associative learning is taken to rob them of interesting cognitive content. Consider, for example, the experiments of Holland and others reviewed in Chapter 4 in which rats behave as if a Pavlovian CS evokes an image of its associated US, an image that can itself support new learning. Don't these findings mean the CS has acquired a simple kind of meaning for the rat?

Another anomaly is that any demonstration that linguistic output, whether it be vocalizing, pressing symbols, or responding to spoken commands, can be explained as simple discrimination learning is taken as showing that the subjects are not doing what a young child would do in similar circumstances. Yet simple associative learning may well explain some of the young child's early responses to speech, and some of the child's early sentences may be no more complex than Lana's stock sentences (Seidenberg and Petitto 1987). One may note that Kanzi acquired his comprehension of spoken English only after intensive exposure and an extraordinary amount of attention from human companions, but such experience is the norm for young children. If language exposure and "enculturation" through extensive interactions with humans changes apes' cognition as some have claimed (e.g., Premack 1983; Savage-Rumbaugh and Brakke 1996; Tomasello and Call 1997), then maybe some of the same changes are involved in aspects of child language acquisition. Yet the difference remains that the child's early language rapidly develops into an elaborate and unique form of communication that no other primate ever shows. This profound species differences has generated a whole range of experimentation, theorizing, and debate, some of which is sketched in the next section.

14.4   Language evolution and animal communication: New directions

Theorizing about the evolution of human language is a vast and active area in itself, nowadays one that integrates genetics, cognitive neuroscience, and mathematical modeling with more traditional studies of the nature and development of language (Christiansen and Kirby 2003; Fitch 2005; Fisher and Marcus 2006). Most relevant in the context of this book is how information about the communication systems of other species can contribute to this enterprise. The analysis of apparent "fast mapping" in a dog, summarized in Box 14.1, is an example. The neural and behavioral parallels between birds' song learning and humans' language acquisition (Box 13.2) apparently reveal general constraints on learning and producing complex sounds. And unlike in these examples, discovery that any components of language are shared only with apes or only with nonhuman primates would be indicative of some genetic, neural, and/or other factors specific to our own lineage. Not surprisingly then, the wealth of recent information about communication in other species is increasingly being brought to bear on discussions about the nature and evolution of language (Fitch 2005; Jackendoff and Pinker 2005; Weiss and Newport 2006; Hauser, Barner, and O'Donnell 2007).

One focus of these discussions has been the distinction proposed by Hauser, Chomsky, and Fitch (2002) between the human language faculty in the broad sense (*FLB*) and the faculty of language in the narrow sense (*FLN*). FLB includes all the perceptual, motor, and cognitive abilities that contribute to language but are shared with other species and/or used in other domains, whereas FLN includes only those components essential to language and unique to humans. Hauser, Chomsky, and Fitch further proposed that FLN consists solely of recursion, that is, the ability to understand and produce recursive structures. This is essentially an extension of Chomsky's (e.g., 1968) original, seminal, proposal that the essentials of language are in its underlying structure rather than in superficial features like how it is produced. The proposed distinction between FLB and FLN is controversial. A prominent alternative view (Fitch, Hauser, and Chomsky 2005; Pinker and Jackendoff 2005) is that indeed many components of human linguistic ability are shared with other species, but in the evolution of human language they have become uniquely coadapted for communication, that is, no one particular skill corresponds to FLN.

Although even human babies can discriminate recursive auditory structures, Hauser and colleagues' proposal implies that no nonhumans can. This implication has been tested by asking whether animals can discriminate strings of sounds that obey a phrase *structure grammar* from those that obey a simpler *finite state grammar* (Figure 14.21). Recognizing a string that obeys a grammar of the first type requires tracking dependencies across several elements, as in "John, while he was dancing a jig, was singing." Finite state grammar, in contrast, entails only stringing grammatical units together, as in "John was dancing a jig, and he was singing." Formally, the first is an *AABB* string, and the second, *ABAB* (Here the subject, John, is *A*, and *B* is the verb.). Tamarins and Harvard students were exposed to strings of nonsense syllables, the "A" syllables spoken by a female and "B's" by a male (Fitch and Hauser 2004). *A* and *B* were each represented by eight different sounds, with a different pair used in each instance of the string. One subgroup from each species heard strings described by a grammar of each type. The students pressed a key to indicate whether new strings had the same pattern as those they had heard. A habituation/dishabituation paradigm was used for the tamarins. After they were familiarized with their training strings, looking toward the speaker was compared for novel test strings from both grammars. Importantly, the same test stimuli were presented to tamarins from both groups. Those trained with the finite state grammar discriminated ABAB . . . strings from AA . . . BB strings, looking longer toward the speaker for strings with the unfamiliar structure, but those trained with

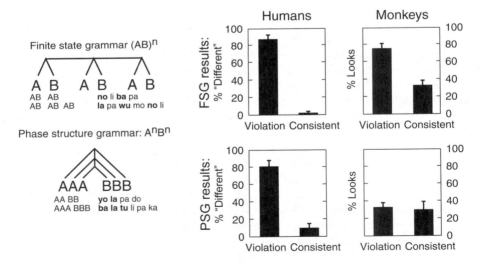

Figure 14.21. Diagrams on left show examples of finite state (nonrecursive) and phrase structure grammars (FSG and PSG) as used by Fitch and Hauser (2004) to test humans and tamarins. Histograms compare the species' ability to detect a difference between the two types of strings as a function of the type they were trained on. Adapted with permission.

the phrase structure grammar did not. As shown in Figure 14.21, the monkeys in this group looked rather little under both conditions, as if they had encoded the training stimuli as unstructured strings of sounds, which were by now rather uninteresting. The students, in contrast, discriminated almost perfectly regardless of training condition.

One problem with a claim that *no* species other than humans can do something is that it is impossible to prove. At the same time, such a claim raises the irresistible and possibly infinite challenge of finding a species and a circumstance in which whatever it is can be demonstrated. When it comes to testing sensitivity to the structure of sound sequences, songbirds would seem to be obvious subjects, and indeed, starlings trained with strings of starling syllables can learn to discriminate between the same two grammars used for the tamarins (Gentner et al. 2006). Starlings were an apt choice for this type of study because in nature they mimic the songs of many other species. However, unlike the tamarins, the starlings had thousands of trials of training with explicit reward for discriminating between the two grammars. Moreover, to succeed with AA . . . BB . . . strings the birds did not need to match corresponding A's and B's correctly as in recognizing the phrase embedded in a sentence. They needed only to detect a match between the numbers of A's and B's (Corballis 2007). That is, they may have learned a rule based on counting, not recursion. Such rule learning has even been demonstrated in rats, which learn and transfer a discrimination between sound patterns (e.g., XXY and YYX versus other sequences of the same sounds; Murphy, Mondragón, and Murphy 2008). Even if starlings pass better tests of sensitivity to recursion this would mean at most that it is independently evolved in one or more species of songbirds, that is, it is analogous not homologous to recursion in humans. Such findings would thus be consistent with the view that the uniqueness of human language is not in any one component but in how its many components are combined (Pinker and Jackendoff 2005; G. Marcus 2006).

Testing tamarins for sensitivity for recursion makes sense on the assumption that other species could possess some of the conceptual or representational components of human language without expressing them in communication. In another example (see Hauser, Barner, and O'Donnell 2007), rhesus macaques were tested to see if they spontaneously make the distinction between singular and plural sets that children make relatively early in language acquisition. Indeed, a relatively uncontroversial one of Hauser, Chomsky, and Fitch's (2002) claims is that comparative studies should be designed to look for such components of language in other species (Pinker and Jackendoff 2005; Hauser., Barner, and O'Donnell 2007). For example, even if hierarchical embedding of sound sequences eludes them, some nonhuman species may show evidence of using concepts with recursive structures in other cognitive domains. Hauser, Chomsky, and Fitch (2002) suggest spatial cognition is one such domain. A stronger candidate, in that it seems to be uniquely present in highly social primates, is hierarchical representation of social relationships (Cheney and Seyfarth 2005b). Consider, for example, the evidence that baboons classify their companions simultaneously by rank and family group (Section 6.5.5; Bergman et al. 2003). Cheney and Seyfarth (2005b) propose that in addition the information baboons acquire from others' vocalizations is referential and propositional, as in "Animal A wants to touch B's baby" or "C is threatening D." They suggest that primate social life favored the evolution of such conceptual abilities and these were eventually reflected in the structure of language, that is, in what primates expressed as well as understood. This and related discussions (e.g., Hauser, Barner, and O'Donnell 2007) have opened a new phase in the comparative study of language that draws on a broad base of laboratory and field studies of animal cognition to make inferences about the distribution of conceptual and other abilities that make human language possible.

14.5   Summary and conclusions

Many of the issues that arise in the study of communication have been considered already in this book. The contrast between ecological and anthropocentric approaches introduced in Chapter 1 is apparent in the contrast between studies of natural communication systems and attempts to teach language to other species. Other examples are how the properties of signals are matched to receivers' perceptual systems (Chapter 3) and how animals categorize stimuli (Chapter 6). Issues relevant to the behavioral ecology and evolution of signaling were touched on in the discussion of reciprocal altruism and kin recognition in Chapter 5 and elsewhere. Issues discussed in Chapter 12 reappear in discussions of whether animals send signals with the intent to modify their receivers' behavior or understanding, to deceive, or to teach, abilities which require theory of mind. So far, there is no better evidence for theory of mind here than in other realms.

In communication as elsewhere, a key issue is how to translate essentially anthropocentric concepts into predictions about observable behavior. In the context of natural communication systems, that has been done in the development of criteria for functional reference. In addition, there are important parallels between functional reference, attempts to study what "words" mean to language-trained apes, and phenomena in the study of what CSs represent in associative learning. The concepts specific to the study of communication include the terminology of *sender, receiver, message,* and *meaning.* Comparisons of animal communication to human language also entail a variety of concepts having to do with the nature of language. One of the most contentious is whether or not any animals have acquired syntax or are sensitive to recursion.

Do honey bees have language? Can apes learn human language? Attempts to answer such questions have engendered controversy in part because they seem to bear so directly on what makes us human. Darwin's (1871) claim of mental continuity between humans and other species has been severely tested when it comes to language. Macphail (1987) suggested that there are essentially no qualitative differences among vertebrates in simple associative learning and all that flows from it, such as category learning, perceptual learning, and the like. To that can be added spatial learning, timing, and numerosity discrimination. What may be unique about humans is the ability to acquire language, and this in turn may make possible self-recognition, theory of mind, consciousness. But the first part of the twenty-first century has seen an explosion of alternative proposals about human uniqueness, many of them drawing on a broad base of comparative research. We briefly evaluate some of them in the next chapter.

Further reading

The part of this chapter on natural communication systems is but a brief survey of a major area of research with vast literature of its own. The authoritative reviews remain the books by Hauser (1996) and Bradbury and Vehrenkamp (1998). The short introduction by Maynard Smith and Harper (2003) focuses on functional aspects of communication. *Animal Communication Networks* (P. McGregor 2005) covers eavesdropping and the like in species from fish to monkeys. Bird song, too, is the subject of whole books (Marler and Slabbekoorn 2004; Zeigler and Marler 2004). Catchpole and Slater is a brief and clear introduction (1995). For bees, Seeley (1995) shows how communication helps regulate a hive's resources.

Pinker's (1994) *The Language Instinct* is a prize-winning account of all aspects of language, giving plenty of attention to evolutionary and comparative issues. The chapters in *Language Evolution* (Christiansen and Kirby 2003) review much of the contemporary work. Candland (1993) provides an illuminating and often entertaining account of the long history of attempts to talk with animals and feral human children. *The Simian Tongue* (Radick 2007) is another book for the general reader, this time on the history of research on "language" in wild primates. It includes an extensive account of the field work by Marler, Cheney, and Seyfarth, whose results are discussed in this chapter.

Few reviews of the animal language training projects are not strongly biased one way or another. Those by Ristau and Robbins (1982) and by Ristau (1996) are exceptions, thoughtfully analyzing the methodology and results of all the early projects. Wallman's (1992) *Aping Language* is a useful but highly critical review of all the twentieth century work. *Kanzi, the Ape at the Brink of the Human Mind* (Savage-Rumbaugh and Lewin 1994) takes a somewhat different point of view.

15
Summing Up and Looking Ahead

In the few years since the first edition of this book was published, understanding of cognition in nonhuman species has been transformed by a plethora of new findings about animal memory, theory of mind, teaching, tool use, numerical cognition, imitation, social intelligence, communication, navigation, causal knowledge, and much more. These findings have been contributed by researchers with varying backgrounds and perspectives, with goals that range from learning how ants navigate in the desert to understanding how the human mind and culture evolved. Theory and data from animal cognition are becoming much better integrated with those from neighboring fields such as child development, primatology, behavioral ecology, cognitive neuroscience, and genetics. Such diversity within the field can be a source of conflict and controversy. For example, the proposal that that chimpanzees' or ravens' social competence reflects nothing more than exquisite sensitivity to cues from conspecifics' behavior may appear entirely reasonable to those trained in ethology or behavior analysis but strain credibility for anyone used to explaining behavior by invoking subjects' understanding of others. Similarly, referring to an ant leading another ant to food as teaching may be unproblematic to behavioral ecologists accustomed to classifying behavior functionally but profoundly questionable for anyone to whom *teaching* implies human pedagogy. Nevertheless, despite the inevitable attendant controversies, continuing engagement between researchers with such different perspectives is essential for the field's continuing progress and enrichment.

This chapter briefly revisits some of the issues introduced in Chapters 1 and 2 in the light of the material in succeeding chapters and reflects on some other issues that have emerged along the way. We begin by summarizing what Chapters 3–14 reveal about cognitive modularity and evolution and then look at some other overarching theoretical issues in the field, concluding with a question that goes right back to Darwin (1871), "Are human beings different from other animals in kind or only in degree?" Arguably this question has been at the core of comparative psychology ever since, but the many recent findings of unexpected competences in other species have inspired an outpouring of new attempts to answer it.

15.1 Modularity and the animal mind

15.1.1 Evidence for modularity: A quick summary

As evolutionary psychologists are fond of saying, the mind is like a Swiss Army knife, a general-purpose tool with many specialized parts. One defining property of a cognitive module is domain-specificity (Box 2.3): a given module processes a restricted kind of information in a functionally appropriate way but is impenetrable to other information. Chapter 3 provided some of the best evidence for modularity with the species-specific tuning of sensory systems. These examples from perception also show how *domain* is a fractal concept. Any category of environmental information can be infinitely subdivided into smaller and smaller nested domains: visual information, then color, shape, motion; spatial information, then vestibular motion sensations, visually localized landmarks, and so on. Deciding when we have more than one distinct cognitive module may depend on implicit assumptions about what differences are theoretically interesting.

Sherry and Schacter (1987) referred to cognitive modules, or memory systems to use their term, as having distinct rules of operation matched to environmental requirements for functionally incompatible kinds of information processing. To take their example, song learning (Chapter 13) and retrieving scatter hoarded food (Box 1.4; Chapter 7) must be subserved by different memory systems because in song learning a small amount of auditory information experienced repeatedly early in life is stored for months or years, whereas in food storing large amounts of briefly experienced spatial information are acquired and then forgotten throughout the bird's life. Such quantitative differences in amount and durability of information storage are not as strong support for cognitive modularity as are qualitative differences in how information is processed, stored, or used—different rules of operation in Sherry and Schacter's terms. Some examples come from explicit contrasts between two or more ways of processing superficially rather similar information. For instance, in Chapter 4 occasion setting (conditional control) was contrasted with the acquisition of excitation and inhibition. Chapter 8 presented evidence for a number of distinct spatial information processing modules, including path integration, the geometric module, the sun compass, and landmark use. Chapter 9 contrasted interval with circadian timing, Chapter 10 described evidence for two nonverbal number systems, and Chapter 13 discussed the distinct representational capacities presupposed by true imitation. The domains that define such candidates for separate cognitive modules are often more abstract than in the case of perception, where separate physical energies define domains. For instance, associative learning can take place with all sorts of inputs as long as they exemplify the abstract relationships typical of physical causation. Inputs can be tactile, visual, auditory, olfactory, and gustatory, and outputs can serve social, sexual, feeding, defensive, and other behavior systems, an example of a given modular ability supporting more than one adaptive use of information (Sherry 1988).

However, simply because of how the world works information acquisition has some general properties across multiple domains. For instance, although learning sometimes needs to be maximal after one trial—the ant or hamster that couldn't relocate its nest after a single trip on a unique path wouldn't survive to make other trips—in general the more often something has been repeated, the more likely it comes from a stable property of the world, worth remembering and responding to (Chapter 7). Hence, learning is rarely maximal after a single trial. How to combine information from multiple sources is another problem common to many domains, but it has a range of solutions. For instance, two weak physical causes of the same thing should produce an extra big response when they co occur, whereas cues for two different time intervals don't add up to a cue to respond at an extralong interval but to respond at each interval signaled, and two landmarks pointing to the same goal should lead to more precise localization of that goal. Blocking and overshadowing in associative learning are cases in which information from different sources is competitive, but we have also seen that different sources of information may be processed in parallel, treated as a unique configural entity, weighted in a Bayesian manner, or used hierarchically, with one giving conditional information about the significance of the other.

Discussions of modularity in cognition often emphasize that adaptive ways of processing different signals from the environment must be innate, like eyes, ears, and noses (Shepard 1994; Cosmides and Tooby 1994). Animals need an "innate school-marm" (Lorenz 1965), an "instinct to learn" (Marler 1991). There simply is not time in most animals' lifespans for appropriate ways of processing and using different kinds of information to develop from a system that is completely undifferentiated to start with. Prefunctional adaptive modularity is especially clear in sensory systems, in short-lived species like bees and ants, and in cases where learning has a crucial job to do early in life, long before correlates of its fitness consequences (as detected by evolved mechanisms of reinforcement) can feed back on cognitive organization. Imprinting (Chapter 5) and song learning (Chapter 13) are exceptionally clear examples of such early learning.

15.1.2 Modularity and cognitive evolution

The view that cognition is modular has implications for theorizing about cognitive evolution. On the traditional general process anthropocentric view (Chapter 1), species are ranked on a phylogenetic scale from simplest to most complex, and from less to more intelligent. Animal intelligence on this view consists of a hierarchy of learning processes (Macphail 1996; Thomas 1996; Papini 2002). Habituation, the most elementary, is shared by all species. Next in the hierarchy and of similarly wide generality is associative learning, then various forms of more "complex" learning and problem-solving, such as forming learning sets and acquiring abstract concepts. At the top of the hierarchy and unique to humans is language. But if instead intelligence is seen as solving problems of ecological relevance in the environment in which the species evolved, the question becomes what different species' intelligence consists of. Species differ in the number of states of the world they can discriminate—think of the difference between light-dark discrimination and color vision—and in the variety of ways they have available for acting on the world. For example the one-celled organism *Stentor* can ingest, reject, or escape things that come its way in an evolutionarily successful yet extremely simple manner (see Staddon 1983), but its cognition is undoubtedly less sophisticated than that of most vetebrates. Nevertheless, if cognition is modular we can expect that some abilities will be widely shared while others will appear only on a few branches of the evolutionary tree. Habituation and associative learning are examples of the former; true imitation appears to be an example of the latter. Language may be found in the human lineage alone.

A modular view of cognition is consistent with the suggestion that during evolution existing systems become accessible to a wider range of inputs (Rozin 1976; Heyes 2003). That is, they turn out to be exaptations, that is, evolved under one set of selection pressures but capable of being used to solve new adaptive problems (Sherry and Schacter 1987). For example, the hierarchical cognitive structure necessary for processing language may have evolved first in the context of social or spatial cognition (Chapter 14). Exaptation and accessibility may well be discernable in cognitive evolution, but it is important not to be too influenced by "boxes in the head" models of information processing like those depicted in Chapter 5 and elsewhere (Gallese 2007). For instance, associative learning is probably not localized to a single module in the brain that puts together any of a variety of inputs in the way described by the Rescorla-Wagner model and produces outputs appropriate to the behavior system being served. Rather it may be a general property of certain kinds of neural circuits regardless of the specific input-output systems they serve. On this view, accessibility or exaptation should be sought at the level of cellular or subcellular mechanisms (Papini 2002). That is to say, modularity may perhaps best be connected with evolution at the neurobiological or molecular level rather than at the level of functional cognitive modules such as numerical discrimination or associative learning (see Box 2.3; Barrett and Kurzban 2006).

In *The Origin of Species*, Darwin (1859) aimed to convince by sheer weight of evidence, by hundreds of examples from many phyla that all pointed to organic evolution. By contrast, there is very little systematic data on cognitive evolution. The two traditional approaches to biological species comparison (Hodos and Campbell 1969; Papini 2002) show the way forward: the adaptationist approach of comparing close relatives with divergent ecologies and the general process approach of comparing distant species to see whether processes are widely shared via a remote common ancestor (homologies) or independently evolved (i.e., homoplasies, examples of parallelism or convergence). When distantly related species show similar cognitive abilities, as in tool use or social cognition in corvids and apes, a key issue is how far the similarity extends. Functionally similar behavior in very different species may result from different neural, molecular, developmental and/or cognitive mechanisms (Papini 2002; Premack 2007). Thus research needs to go beyond simply testing whether some species or other demonstrates a particular competence. For example, comparison of tool using in captive rooks and bonobos in similar setups suggests that the cognitive underpinnings of the behavior are different in these two species (Helme et al. 2006.).

15.2   Theory and method in comparative cognition

15.2.1   Theory in comparative psychology

When Hodos and Campbell (1969) famously complained that "there is no theory in comparative psychology" they were referring to the fact that at the time many studies labeled "comparative" were mere "animal psychology" because they dealt with only a single nonhuman species. Comparisons were at most implicit and mostly with humans. Even more deplorable in their view, any comparisons that were made were referred to the phylogenetic scale rather than to real phylogenies. Hodos and Campbell were neither the first (see Beach 1950) nor the last (cf. Shettleworth 1993) to decry the shallowness of biological comparison in "comparative" psychology. But when it comes to comparative cognition in the early twenty-first century, the situation has changed dramatically. At least in most serious scientific literature, references to "higher" and "lower" or more and less intelligent animals have been replaced by discussion of convergences and divergences, abilities shared with common ancestors or more recently evolved, and the like. Increasing numbers of species are being studied, and increasingly two or more are compared within the same research program (Shettleworth 2009).

Of course explicitly comparative studies can still be distinguished from "animal cognition" research, but both are necessary components of an overarching enterprise, referred to in this book as research on comparative cognition (although perhaps cognitive ethology is more appropriate, Kamil 1998), aimed at understanding cognition across the animal kingdom, including how it works, what it is good for in nature, and how it evolved. In this context, in-depth studies of particular processes in one or a few species such associative learning in rats, visual category learning in pigeons, or social cognition in wild baboons are the foundations for well justified species comparisons. For example, comparisons of memory in food storing and nonstoring birds are built on method and theory developed largely in studies with pigeons that were based in turn on studies of human memory; comparisons of transitive inference in corvids with different social systems rest on method and theory developed with children, monkeys and pigeons.

Because analyses of single processes in a few species are as much a part of comparative cognition broadly construed as are explicit comparisons of multiple species, there is not *a theory* in comparative cognition, let alone comparative psychology more broadly, even though Hodos and Campbell's (1969) provocative title seems to imply there should be. Rather, there is a common framework consisting of modern evolutionary theory and Tinbergen's four questions within which explicit research questions are posed and data interpreted, whether to develop a theory of how a particular cognitive mechanism works or to understand species differences in terms of ecology and phylogeny. But there is another theoretical issue here: what exactly is being compared in comparative cognition? This is in effect a question of epistemology (Andrews 2007; 2009) or, more prosaically, of methodological approaches and pretheoretical assumptions. Unlike the form and occurrence of behavior patterns, cognitive processes cannot be observed directly. They are inferences from behavior, and the rules of inference in comparative cognition research are seldom explicit. Nevertheless, there are some fairly well accepted principles even if not universal agreement on their applications. Borrowing from Heyes's (2008) characterization of research on animal consciousness, we can say that contemporary research on cognition in animals deals with *functionally defined cognitive processes and states* studied with two methods: *analogical reasoning* and *experimental tests of alternative hypotheses.*

15.2.2   Functionally defined processes

To begin with, *functionally defined processes and states* refers to the assumption that in order to be a tractable subject for scientific investigation, cognitive processes in animals must be defined in terms of what they allow the animal to do, not how they feel, that is, what conscious mental processes accompany them. This functional approach is uncontroversial when applied to traditional topics in animal cognition such as associative learning, numerosity discrimination, timing, category formation. It is much more challenging when applied to aspects of cognition such episodic-like memory and metacognition that in humans are defined in part by the distinctive conscious processes that accompany them. Progress is greater in such research the better the process under study is defined and understood in humans. For instance

(Chapter 7), lack of consensus about the essential features of human episodic memory has encouraged multiple candidates for examples in animals, whereas research on animal metacognition has been focused on a well-defined set of nonverbal paradigms, paradigms which additionally can be used to test people in the same way as birds and monkeys. These paradigms also permit tests of functional similarities in the mathematical sense of relationships between independent variables such as retention interval or task difficulty and dependent variables such as proportions of correct responses. In contrast, some candidate demonstrations of animal episodic-like memory are limited by being pass-fail tests. Still, even well-accepted functional definitions of cognitive processes and rich comparative data sets do not always forestall debate about interpretations. Controversy most often arises in the case of processes understood mainly from introspection or folk psychology. Cognitive mapping, deception, planning, and understanding tools are examples. Even when, as with theory of mind, there are accepted experimental paradigms for human subjects, appropriate analogues for other species may not be obvious or straightforward.

15.2.3   Anthropomorphism and hypothesis testing

Analogical reasoning as a methodological approach (Heyes 2008) means using the venerable argument from analogy (see Povinelli, Bering, and Giambrone 2000)—in effect anthropomorphism—to infer cognitive processes. As with the nut-dropping crows at the beginning of Chapter 1, this means nothing more than inferring humanlike cognitive processes from humanlike behavior. Even if such inferences are convincing because the behavior in question is complex and observed in multiple situations, this method lacks explicit consideration and testing of alternative hypotheses. This approach was used extensively by cognitive ethologists such as D. Griffin (1978, 2001) and is still common in explanations of apparently complex behaviors in terms of conscious "higher" cognitive processes. For example, the chimpanzee putting its arm over the shoulders of the loser of a fight is empathizing and attempting to console, the scrub jay moving its caches to new locations understands the point of view of a competitor. But Morgan's Canon dictates that we should entertain the cognitively "simplest" hypotheses possible. This usually means hypotheses grounded in knowledge of associative learning and/or species-typical behavioral predispositions. Unfortunately, it is not as widely known as it should be that associative learning can no longer be dismissed as especially simple or representationally impoverished. There is plenty of evidence (Chapters 4–6) that "mere associations" can encode events in the world with great subtlety and sophistication. Even bar pressing in "the humble rat" can express belief and desire (Chapter 11). Because associative learning is phylogenetically so widespread, it is generally the most reasonable null hypothesis in terms of evolution.

As elsewhere in science however, the most powerful method is experimental testing of competing predictions from alternative hypotheses. This method requires not only clear functional definitions but a good deal of imagination and general knowledge of animal learning and behavior besides. For example, how could a chimpanzee's behavior in front of a mirror be explained other than by its having a self-concept? Maybe the chimpanzee is engaging in normal species-specific grooming behavior and neither the mirror nor the mark has anything to do with its touching the mark. How could a rat be finding its way without a cognitive map? Maybe the rat is using dead reckoning or comparing its present view of the environment to the view from its goal. Maybe a raven is not reading other birds' minds but remembering it could see them when it was caching. Using imagination and background knowledge also means being aware that animals do not always see a testing situation as we do. From the animal's point of view, a test of theory of mind may be a conditioning experiment; a test of future planning may be exposure to cues that elicit species-typical ways of distributing food caches. The "simplest" explanations are not necessarily the simplest for us to imagine or introspect about (see Heyes 1998).

Explanations in terms of situation-specific behavior or learned responses can sometimes be tested with the experimental strategy of triangulation. Triangulation entails a series of tests designed to point to the same conclusion from different metaphorical angles. For example, an animal might be trained on an abstract concept in one set of conditions and then be given tests that are conceptually but not physically similar so that they cannot be solved by associative learning plus stimulus generalization. In some aspects of physical cognition, such as the Weber's Law–based number system, the same capacity has been demonstrated in each of several species using a variety of materials and behavioral measures. It can also be useful to ask whether it is reasonable to think that X has evolved rather than something cognitively simpler. What difference could it make to fitness for an animal to have conscious intentions, a theory of mind, a cognitive map, an explicit representation of a category prototype, or a concept of self? How could these come into play in the species' current natural environment or any plausible past one?

Of course formulating plausible alternatives, generating competing predictions, and devising incisive behavioral tests to discriminate them does not guarantee finding unambiguous answers. The capacity in question may be multifaceted, so species may differ in how many components of it they possess or in what situations they express them. As with numerical cognition, theory of mind, or language for example, the most productive approach to research and perhaps the most consistent with linking findings to evolution is to eschew questions like, "Do animals have capacity X or not?" and rather ask something like, "What are the components of X, and what species show them under what conditions?" Finally, no matter how clearly defined the methods, the power of the analogy between ourselves and other animals to determine the hypotheses researchers are willing to entertain about animal minds almost guarantees that the study of comparative cognition will continue to generate controversy.

15.3   Humans versus other species: Different in degree or kind?

Darwin's discussion of "mental powers" in Chapters 3 and 4 of *The Descent of Man and Selection in Relation to Sex* (Darwin 1879/2004) is one long argument that the human mind differs in degree but not in kind from the minds of other animals. Many of the findings described in this book clearly support his claim: when it comes to basic processes of perception, learning, memory, categorization, numerical discrimination, spatial orientation, and so on, other species do not differ from us in kind. But Darwin's claim has been getting renewed attention recently because of two sorts of new findings. On the one hand are the many observations of hitherto unsuspected humanlike abilities in species only distantly related to humans such as ants and birds. On the other are data from several productive groups whose research is specifically targeted at comparing human and ape (generally chimpanzee) cognition.

Ever since Jane Goodall described tool using and meat-eating in wild chimpanzees, the gap between humans and apes and even other species has often seemed to be getting smaller and smaller. One response to these developments (Premack 2007; Penn, Holyoak, and Povinelli 2008) is to emphasize that examples of animal teaching, tool use, culture, transitive inference, planning, and the like are profoundly different from analogous human behaviors. Many are highly domain-specific, perhaps relatively inflexible, species-typical behaviors with less complex cognitive underpinnings than their human counterparts. An ant, for example, can only "teach" another ant the route from nest to food. Humans are still unique, and the key to human uniqueness can be sought with comparative studies, primarily with apes but also with other animals. Such research asks the question, given that humans and chimpanzees are phylogenetically so close (cf. Hauser 2005), is there a "small difference that made a big difference" (Tomasello and Call 1997) to the human brain and cognition? How can cognitive differences between humans and other species best be characterized? Can this difference or differences be explained by hypotheses about the forces in hominid evolution? Can we ever pin it down genetically? And is there a single source of human cognitive uniqueness anyway?

15.3.1   On degrees and kinds

Darwin acknowledged that "the difference between the mind of the lowest man and that of the highest animal is immense" but "Nevertheless the difference in mind between man and the higher animals, great as it is, certainly is one of degree and not of kind" (Darwin 1879/2004, 150–151). Here Darwin refers to shared abilities such as memory that are developed to different degrees in different species. A second but confusingly similar sense of *degree* is implied by claims that the gap between the mind of man and other species is filled by "numberless gradations," that is, the human mind evolved by small degrees from the mind of some primitive ancestor. But even though evolution proceeds by tiny degrees over many generations, it can result in differences among organisms so great that they seem to be differences in kind. For example, snakes have evolved by degrees to leglessness, but snakes seem to be compellingly "different in kind" from lizards and crocodiles, not lizardlike reptiles that have legs to an infinitely small degree. When it comes to evolution of the human brain and cognition, we might expect to find apparent differences in kind from chimpanzees for the simple reason that there is not much evidence about the degrees by which we evolved from a common ancestor. All the species that could provide it are extinct. New evidence from fossil hominids may gradually fill this gap, as the discovery of dinosaur fossils with feathers helped to fill the gap between ancient reptiles and birds, but conclusions about "degrees" in cognitive evolution require in addition information about ancestral environments and behavior. Thus the relationship between characterizations of human—chimpanzee differences and human evolution is necessarily very speculative.

15.3.2   On sound species comparisons

Chapters 2, 6, and 7, among others, showed how rigorously comparing cognitive abilities across species requires taking into account a multitude of species differences in motivation, perception, developmental history, and other contextual variables. These important methodological caveats have largely fallen into the background in subsequent chapters even though research on single species reviewed in some of those chapters is implicitly comparative. Questions such as "do chimpanzees learn language?" or "do any primates imitate or cooperate?" generally mean "do they do it as humans do? " But, as Christof Boesch (2007) has pointed out, most comparisons of apes and children, including recent explicit comparisons of children and chimpanzees, have failed to control for a number of serious confounds. As a result, any differences between apes and children in such studies may be explained by species differences in developmental history and/or the circumstances of the experiment rather than in the cognitive process under test. For example, even though there are cultural differences in human developmental trajectories and differences among wild populations of apes, not to mention vast differences in experience between wild and captive animals, middle-class Western children are usually compared with captive apes. The results may not generalize to children from other cultures and/or wild apes. Children are tested by members of their own species, and their mothers may be present if they are very young, whereas apes are usually tested by a member of a different species (humans), in a human-appropriate task, often while alone in a cage with the experimenter outside. Because most of these confounds seem likely to disadvantage the apes, they are especially problematical when the apes are found to lack an ability that the children show. They are also very difficult to avoid. Probably the best conclusion here is to be aware of the limitations of single studies (a warning that applies to any research comparing species) and work toward correcting them. A promising corrective to overemphasis on captive apes is research with chimpanzees and bonobos living in semi–free ranging colonies in Africa (see Hare 2007; Herrmann et al. 2007).

15.3.3   How and why are humans unique?

Two separate but related questions head this section. The first is, how can the apparent cognitive uniqueness of humans be characterized? Answering it entails comparing present-day humans with other present-day species, most often chimpanzees, and trying to distill the catalog of findings into some key difference or differences. We look briefly at three contemporary efforts to do this. The second question is, what explains how any proposed key difference(s) evolved? Answering it entails speculating about circumstances early in hominid evolution and how they might select for one or another human ability.

Language

Candidates for uniquely human aspects of cognition mentioned in this book include understanding the minds of others and how tools work; domain-general abilities to form abstract concepts, make transitive inferences, plan, and teach; imitation; precise discrimination among quantities greater than four; cumulative culture; reflective consciousness; and above all, language. Indeed, the possession of language is a time-honored explanation for all other uniquely human cognitive abilities. Undoubtedly language is used in expressing most forms of human understanding, but when it comes to going beyond characterizing how humans differ from all other living species to explaining how the critical difference or differences evolved, language encounters a classic chicken-and-egg problem. Why would complex language evolve in a creature that did not already have the concepts it requires or expresses? Many comparative psychologists (cf. Terrace 1984; Watanabe and Huber 2006) might claim that research with other species can reveal the nature of thought without language. If so, those thoughts are relatively simple. One possibility is that language and thought coevolved, ratcheting each other up as language created a new "cognitive niche" (A. Clark 2006). However, this viewpoint still assumes that a key difference between present-day humans and apes is language, and not everyone agrees. For one thing, if language ability itself is the product of multiple adaptations (Pinker and Jackendoff, 2005), human uniqueness must be sought in specializations of many distinct modules. This possibility has not, however, prevented two groups of researchers from proposing and testing rather sweeping characterizations of human cognitive uniqueness.

Shared intentionality

According to Tomasello and his colleagues (Tomasello et al. 2005; Hare 2007; Moll and Tomasello 2007) the primary difference between present-day humans and chimpanzees is not essentially cognitive but motivational: only humans are motivated to communicate about and share intentions in "cooperative communicative interactions." Examples of what this means can be found throughout the discussions of theory of mind and cooperation in Chapter 12 Chimpanzees are good at competing with others but poor at cooperating. In competitive interactions, they are sensitive to cues associated with another's intentions, a sensitivity which Tomasello and colleagues (e.g., Tomasello et al. 2005) controversially interpret as "understanding intentions," but fail to exhibit such sensitivity in situations where children readily cooperate. Further evidence comes from perhaps the largest single comparative experiment ever reported (Herrmann et al. 2007), in which each of 106 chimpanzees, 32 orangutans, and 105 2.5-year-old children was given a large battery of tests of physical and social cognition. Notice that the children were at an age before they had developed extensive language or had formal schooling. The apes lived in sanctuaries in their native countries. The tests of physical cognition included simple tests of spatial memory (e.g., for the location of a reward on a table), numerical competence (e.g., choosing the larger of two quantities), and tool use (e.g., using a stick or choosing an unbroken cloth to pull in a reward). Tests of social cognition included following gaze, using communicative cues such as pointing, and imitating simple tasks such as shaking a reward out of a tube. As shown in Figure 15.1 by summaries

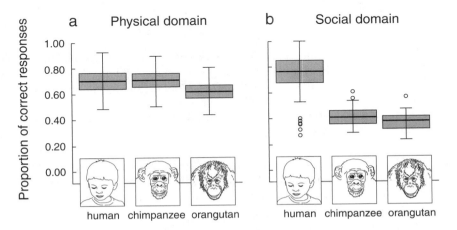

Figure 15.1. Mean performance of three primate species on a battery of tests of physical and social cognition. Open dots in these box plots represent outliers. Redrawn from Herrmann et al. (2007) with permission.

across all tests within each domain, on average children and apes performed similarly on the tests of physical cognition, but the children did substantially better on the tests of social cognition. The species difference was most marked in the tests of imitation, which many of the apes failed altogether, but it was found in the other tests of social cognition as well.

Although this study is not entirely free of the problems with ape-human comparisons outlined in Section 15.3.2 (de Waal et al. 2008) it does provide impressive support for "the cultural intelligence hypothesis" (Moll and Tomasello 2007). On this hypothesis, the unique social skills and motivation that humans have from an early age are the scaffold for developing other uniquely human cognitive skills. It can be seen as consistent with the social brain hypothesis discussed in Chapter 12, in that social systems rather than foraging specializations may have driven the evolution of primate intelligence, but goes beyond it to suggest that conditions in human society uniquely selected for new and intense forms of cooperation. On this scenario, language evolved in the context of motivation to share thoughts in the service of cooperation. It should be noted, however, that even the original authors of the ape-child comparison (Herrmann et al. 2007, 4365) acknowledge that comparatively poor physical dexterity may have disadvantaged the children in some of the physical tests, leaving open the possibility of a domain general difference such as that discussed next.

Relational reinterpretation

In contrast to the "cultural cognition" hypothesis, Penn, Holyoak, and Povinelli's (2008) "relational reinterpretation" hypothesis proposes that only humans have a domain-general ability to represent abstract relationships, or to reinterpret perceptual (or first-order) relationships in terms of higher-order relationships. This is essentially an extension of the earlier claims of Povinelli and colleagues (e.g., Povinelli 2000; Vonk and Povinelli 2006) with respect to tool use and theory of mind. Recall, for example, that the chimpanzees in Povinelli's (2000) experiments could choose effective tools on the basis of perceptible cues but showed no evidence of the sort of reasoning about unobservable causes that could help them with new tools or situations. Similarly, chimpanzees as well as scrub jays and ravens are very good at using subtle social cues to deceive, compete, and so on, but on this account such behavior is not mediated by a representation of other individuals' mental states. Penn, Holyoak and Povinelli (2008; see also Premack 2007) also analyze further examples from chimpanzees and other species to argue that animal behaviors that qualify as teaching, planning, transitive inference, causal reasoning, or the like are always confined to narrow domains and highly specific cues. Only humans, on their account, can represent abstract or higher-order relationships in a domain-general way. Clearly in normal adult humans this ability is expressed in language, but on this account it does not require language, although language and the ability to represent higher-order relationships may well have evolved together, scaffolding each other up.

Conclusions

This section has concluded with a bare sketch of two prominent contemporary proposals for the nature and evolution of human cognitive uniqueness, both of which are far more detailed and nuanced than can be conveyed in a short summary. The cultural cognition hypothesis is primarily motivational and domain-specific, whereas the relational representation hypothesis directly addresses cognition. It proposes a domain-general ability that cuts across all the domain specific cognitive processes documented in this book, in the process encompassing the species differences in social cognition found by Herrmann and colleagues (2007). Thus it poses interesting questions about cognitive architecture and evolution, such as how it could be compatible with the modular view of cognition. The cultural cognition hypothesis has the attraction of being easily linked to current notions about the evolution of human society and culture (cf. D. Wilson and Wilson 2007; Gintis et al. 2007) whereas the relational reinterpretation hypothesis seems to capture very well what is special about human thought. Both could be correct to some extent, and in any case it seems unlikely that any single global characterization of human-nonhuman cognitive differences will embrace everything from imitation to higher mathematics to imagining the future. What we can expect, given the explosion of relevant research on comparative cognition together with the promise of comparative genome projects and cognitive neuroscience to reveal the molecular bases of species differences, is continued debate about the degrees and kinds of differences between human and animal minds.

15.4   The future: Tinbergen's four questions, and a fifth one

Introductions to animal behavior for biology students traditionally begin by defining Tinbergen's four questions—cause, function, evolution, and development—and go on to emphasize that they must not be confused with one another (Chapters 1 and 2). Particularly insidious is the ease with which cause can be confused with function and functional answers given to causal questions. For instance, a plover's broken-wing display (Box 12.1) may function to deceive a fox, in that the fox responds as he would to an injured bird, but this does not mean that the plover intends to deceive or that the fox is consciously thinking the bird is injured and would therefore be easy prey. During the last 30–40 years, the tendency to such confusions has been exacerbated by theoretical developments in both the biology and the psychology of animal behavior. With the rise of behavioral ecology in the 1970s, traditional ethological causal analyses in terms of sign stimuli, fixed action patterns and the like seemed increasingly old fashioned and theoretically uninteresting (Dawkins 1989). The answer to "what is this animal doing?" was more likely to be "attracting a mate" than "bowing and cooing in response to cues from a female." As a result, students were not always taught to look at behavior qua behavior. In addition, many terms used by behavioral ecologists such as *sampling, optimizing,* and *deceiving* easily slip into use as causal explanations because they have both functional and folk-psychological interpretations (Kennedy 1992).

At more or less the same time as traditional ethology was becoming less popular, the shift within experimental psychology from behaviorism to cognitivism meant that psychology students were not so often exposed to behavior analysis as a valuable aid to causal understanding. Explaining behavior as the expression of memories, concepts, representations, and the like seems to preclude explanation in terms of observable factors such as past history and present cues. But just as Tinbergen emphasized keeping all four questions in mind and seeking to answer them in an integrated way, so it is important to know about and keep in mind alternative ways of answering causal questions.

Consider, for example, the history of research on theory of mind in chimpanzees. One of the earliest experiments was taken to show that chimpanzees understood another individual's knowledge or ignorance because they begged from a knowledgeable individual on more than 50% of novel test trials (see Section 12.4.2). A challenge from a learning theorist (Heyes 1993b) led to examination of trial-by-trial data and supported the conclusion that instead the animals had learned to choose correctly during the test phase itself (Povinelli 1994). Here what can be seen as a test of theory of mind is at the same time an occasion for simple discrimination learning. More recent developments in research on animal theory of mind have further deconstructed the original tests to characterize the cues and responses that come into play in more detail. We have seen experiments testing the role of human versus chimpanzee partners, competition versus cooperation, and a history of selection for responding to humans. Whether such studies have clarified the nature of chimpanzee theory of mind or made the notion unnecessary is a matter of debate, but either way looking closely at causes of the animals' behavior as such is essential.

The importance of becoming aware of and then keeping in mind multiple levels and kinds of explanation is perhaps no better illustrated than by the evolution of research on optimal foraging and choice discussed in Section 11.1. Research on choice that began as tests of optimal foraging models, that is, designed to answer functional questions, was soon seen to be measuring behavior on schedules of reinforcement, and the results therefore demanded causal interpretation in the light of an extensive psychological literature. And because many of the situations studied involved rewards distributed through time, the growing literature on the properties of timing became relevant. In turn, some findings from experiments designed to mimic foraging situations fed back on and modified causal accounts of instrumental learning and choice. And in the most recent research, all of these findings are being interpreted in the light of economic models of choice and decision making, in effect comparing predictions from contrasting notions of rationality (Kacelnik 2006). Such developments suggest that to Tinbergen's four questions should be added a fifth one: What do alternative perspectives have to say about this behavior and how can they be integrated?

In conclusion, research on cognitive processes in animals is thriving in the early twenty-first century, embracing research from behavioral ecology to cognitive neuroscience, in the field and the experimental psychology laboratory, on species from ants and honeybees to chimpanzees and people. The range of topics being studied is probably more comprehensive now than at any other time since Darwin (1871) marshaled his evidence for animal minds, embracing mechanisms of physical and social cognition in equal measure with domain-general learning and memory processes. Research on nonhuman species is increasingly integrated with research on humans. Parallel experiments on multiple species are designed to test species-general theories of specific mechanisms, and comparative data are brought to bear on theories of how the human mind evolved. Evolution and function are considered in a more sophisticated way than in the past, and individual research programs increasingly address more than one of Tinbergen's four questions. Much of the diversity of subjects and approaches reflects the diversity of researchers' backgrounds. Although this is sometimes the source of misunderstanding and controversy, it has greatly enriched the field and undoubtedly will continue to do so.

Further reading

Barrett and Kurzban (2006) is the best source for a balanced discussion of the many facets of modularity. Darwin's (1871) chapters on "Mental powers" and "Moral faculties" are still thought-provoking, but the best route to a full sense of the richness and depth of contemporary discussions about the nature of human cognitive uniqueness is to read the articles by Tomasello et al. (2005) and Penn, Holyoak and Povinelli (2008) together with their associated commentaries. Premack (2007) is a short and pithy critique of recent claims to demonstrate humanlike abilities in other species.

References

Able, K. P., and M. A. Able. (1990). "Ontogeny of migratory orientation in the savannah sparrow, Passerculus sandwichensis: Calibration of the magnetic compass." *Animal Behaviour* 39: 905–913.

Able, K. P., and V. P. Bingman. (1987). "The development of orientation and navigation behavior in birds." *The Quarterly Review of Biology* 62: 1–29.

Adachi, I., and R. R. Hampton. (2008). Cross-modal representations of familiar conspecifics in rhesus monkeys. Poster presented at the International Conference on Comparative Cognition, Melbourne, FL.

Addis, D. R., A. T. Wong, and D. L. Schacter. (2007). "Remembering the past and imagining the future: Common and distinct neural substrates during event construction and elaboration." *Neuropsychologia* 45: 1363–1377.

Adkins-Regan, E., and E. A. MacKillop. (2003). "Japanese quail (Coturnix japonica) inseminations are more likely to fertilize eggs in a context predicting mating opportunities." *Proceedings of The Royal Society of London* B 270: 1685–1689.

Adolphs, R. (2003). "Cognitive neuroscience of human social behaviour." *Nature Reviews Neuroscience* 4: 165–178.

Adret, P. (1997). "Discrimination of video images by zebra finches (Taeniopygia guttata): Direct evidence from song performance." *Journal of Comparative Psychology* 111: 115–125.

Agrawal, A. A. (2001). "Phenotypic plasticity in the interactions and evolution of species." *Science* 294: 321–326.

Aisner, R., and J. Terkel. (1992). "Ontogeny of pine cone opening behaviour in the black rat, Rattus rattus." *Animal Behaviour* 44: 327–336.

Akins, C. K. (2000). "Effects of species-specific cues and the CS-US interval on the topography of the sexually conditioned response." *Learning and Motivation* 31: 211–235.

Akins, C. K., and T. R. Zentall. (1996). "Imitative learning in male Japanese quail (Coturnix japonica) using the two-action method." *Journal of Comparative Psychology* 110: 316–320.

Alais, D., and D. Burr. (2004). "The ventriloquist effect results from near-optimal bimodal integration." *Current Biology* 14: 257–262.

Alerstam, T. (2006). "Conflicting evidence about long-distance animal navigation." *Science* 313: 791–794.

Allen, C. (1995). Intentionality: Natural and artificial. In *Comparative Approaches to Cognitive Science,* ed. H. L. Roitblat and J.-A. Meyer, 93–110. Cambridge, MA: MIT Press.

———. (2004). "Is anyone a cognitive ethologist?" *Biology and Philosophy* 19: 589–607.

———. (2006). Transitive inference in animals: Reasoning or conditioned associations. In *Rational animals?* ed. S. Hurley and M. Nudds, 175–185. Oxford: Oxford University Press.

Allen, C., and M. Bekoff. (1997). *Species of Mind: The philosophy and biology of cognitive ethology.* Cambridge, MA: MIT Press.

Anderson, J. R., and R. Milson. (1989). "Human memory: An adaptive perspective." *Psychological Review* 96: 703–719.

Anderson, J. R., and L. J. Schooler. (1991). "Reflections of the environment in memory." *Psychological Science* 2: 396–408.

———. (2000). The adaptive nature of memory. In *Handbook of memory,* ed. E. Tulving and F. I. M. Craik, 557–570. New York: Oxford University Press.

Anderson, M. C., and S. J. Shettleworth. (1977). "Behavioural adaptation to fixed-interval and fixed-time food delivery in golden hamsters." *Journal of the Experimental Analysis of Behavior* 27: 33–49.

Andersson, M. (1994). *Sexual selection.* Princeton, NJ: Princeton University Press.

Andersson, M., and J. Krebs. (1978). "On the evolution of hoarding behaviour." *Animal Behaviour* 26: 707–711.

Andrews, K. (2005). "Chimpanzee theory of mind: Looking in all the wrong places?" *Mind & Language* 20: 521–536.

———. (2007). "Interpreting the baboon." *Trends in Cognitive Sciences* 12: 5–6.

———. (2009). "Politics or metaphysics? On attributing psychological properties to animals." *Biology & Philosophy* 24: 51–63.

Apperly, I. A., K. J. Riggs, A. Simpson, C. Chiavarino, and D. Samson. (2006). "Is belief reasoning automatic?" *Psychological Science* 17: 841–844.

Arcediano, F., M. Escobar, and R. R. Miller. (2005). "Bidirectional associations in humans and rats." *Journal of Experimental Psychology: Animal Behavior Processes* 31: 301–318.

Arcediano, F., and R. R. Miller. (2002). "Some constraints for models of timing: A temporal coding hypothesis perspective." *Learning and Motivation* 33: 105–123.

Arnold, K., and K. Zuberbühler. (2006). "Semantic combinations in primate calls." *Nature* 441: 303.

Aschoff, J. (1986). "Anticipation of a daily meal: A process of 'learning' due to entrainment." *Monitore Zoologico Italiano* 20: 195–219.

———. (1989). "Temporal orientation: Circadian clocks in animals and humans." *Animal Behaviour* 37: 881–896.

Ashby, F. G., and W. T. Maddox. (2005). "Human category learning." *Annual Review of Psychology* 56: 149–178.

Aubin, T., and P. Jouventin. (2002). "How to vocally identify kin in a crowd: The penguin model." *Advances in the Study of Behavior* 31: 243–277.

Aust, U., and L. Huber. (2006). "Picture-object recognition in pigeons: Evidence of representational insight in a visual categorization task using a complementary information procedure." *Journal of Experimental Psychology: Animal Behavior Processes* 32.

Aust, U., F. Range, M. Steurer, and L. Huber. (2008). "Inferential reasoning by exclusion in pigeons, dogs, and humans." *Animal Cognition* 11: 587–597.

Avery, M. L. (1994). "Finding good food and avoiding bad food: Does it help to associate with experienced flockmates?" *Animal Behaviour* 48: 1371–1378.

Avian Brain Nomenclature Consortium. (2005). "Avian brains and a new understanding of vertebrate brain evolution." *Nature Reviews Neuroscience* 6: 1–9.

Aydin, A., and J. M. Pearce. (1994). "Prototype effects in categorization by pigeons." *Journal of Experimental Psychology: Animal Behavior Processes* 20: 264–277.

Babb, S. J., and J. D. Crystal. (2006a). "Discrimination of what, when, and where is not based on time of day." *Learning & Behavior* 34: 124–130.

———. (2006b). "Episodic-like memory in the rat." *Current Biology* 16: 1317–1321.

Bachmann, C., and H. Kummer. (1980). "Male assessment of female choice in Hamadryas baboons." *Behavioral Ecology and Sociobiology* 6: 315–321.

Baddeley, A. (1995). Working memory. In *The cognitive neurosciences,* ed. M. Gazzaniga, 755–764. Cambridge, MA: MIT Press.

Baddeley, R. J., D. Osorio, and C. D. Jones. (2007). "Generalization of color by chickens: Experimental observations and a Bayesian model." *The American Naturalist* 169: S27–S41.

Baerends, G. P. (1982). "Supernormality." *Behaviour* 82: 358–363.

Baerends, G. P., and J. P. Kruijt. (1973). Stimulus selection. In *Constraints on learning,* ed. R. A. Hinde and J. Stevenson-Hinde, 23–50. London: Academic Press.

Baker, A. G., R. A. Murphy, and R. Mehta. (2001). Contingency learning and causal reasoning. In *Handbook of contemporary learning theories,* ed. R. R. Mowrer and S. B. Klein, 255–306. Mahwah NJ: Lawrence Erlbaum Associates.

Bakker, T. C. M., and M. Milinski. (1991). "Sequential female choice and the previous male effect in sticklebacks." *Behavioral Ecology and Sociobiology* 29: 205–210.

Balda, R. P., and A. C. Kamil. (1992). "Long-term spatial memory in Clark's nutcracker, Nucifraga columbiana." *Animal Behaviour* 44: 761–769.

———. (2002). Spatial and social cognition in corvids: An evolutionary approach. In *The cognitive animal,* ed. M. Bekoff, C. Allen, and G. M. Burghardt, 129–134. Cambridge, MA: MIT Press.

———. (2006). Linking life zones, life history traits, ecology, and spatial cognition in four allopatric southwestern seed caching corvids. In *Animal Spatial Cognition: Comparative, Neural, and Computational Approaches.,* ed. M. F. Brown and R. G. Cook. [On-line]. Available www.pigeon.psy.tufts.edu/asc/balda/

Balda, R. P., I. M. Pepperberg, and A. C. Kamil, eds. (1998). *Animal Cognition in Nature.* San Diego, CA: Academic Press.

Balleine, B. W. (1992). "Instrumental performance following a shift in primary motivation depends on incentive learning." *Journal of Experimental Psychology: Animal Behavior Processes* 18: 236–250.

Balleine, B. W., and A. Dickinson. (1998). "Goal-directed instrumental action: Contingency and incentive learning and their cortical substrates." *Neuropharmacology* 37: 407–419.

———. (2006). "Motivational control of blocking." *Journal of Experimental Psychology: Animal Behavior Processes* 32: 33–43.

Balsam, P. D., M. R. Drew, and C. Yang. (2002). "Timing at the start of associative learning." *Learning and Motivation* 33: 141–155.

Barber, T. X. (1994). *The human nature of birds.* New York: Penguin Books.

Bard, K. A., B. K. Todd, C. Bernier, J. Love, and D. A. Leavens. (2006). "Self-awareness in human and chimpanzee infants: What is measured and what is meant by the mark and mirror test?" *Infancy* 9: 191–219.

Barker, L. M., and J. C. Smith. (1974). "A comparison of taste aversions induced by radiation and lithium chloride in CS-US and US-CS paradigms." *Journal of Comparative and Physiological Psychology* 87: 644–654.

Barkow, J. H., L. Cosmides, and J. Tooby, eds. (1992). *The adapted mind.* New York: Oxford University Press.

Barlow, H. B. (1982). General principles: The senses considered as physical instruments. In *The senses,* ed. H. B. Barlow and J. D. Mollom, 1–33. Cambridge: Cambridge University Press.

Barnard, C. J., and P. Aldhous. (1991). Kinship, kin discrimination, and mate choice. In *Kin recognition,* ed. P. G. Hepper, 125–147. Cambridge: Cambridge University Press.

Barnard, C. J., and C. A. J. Brown. (1981). "Prey size selection and competition in the common shrew (Sorex araneus L.)." *Behavioral Ecology and Sociobiology* 8: 239–243.

Barnard, C. J., and J. L. Hurst. (1987). "Time constraints and prey selection in common shrews Sorex araneus L." *Animal Behaviour* 35: 1827–1837.

Barner, D., J. Wood, M. Hauser, and S. Carey. (2008). "Evidence for a non-linguistic distinction between singular and plural sets in rhesus monkeys." *Cognition* 107: 603–622.

Barnet, R. C., H. M. Arnold, and R. R. Miller (1991). "Simultaneous conditioning demonstrated in second-order conditioning: Evidence for similar associative structure in forward and simultaneous conditioning." *Learning and Motivation* 22: 253–268.

Barnet, R. C., N. J. Grahame, and R. R. Miller. (1993). "Temporal encoding as a determinant of blocking." *Journal of Experimental Psychology: Animal Behavior Processes* 19: 327–341.

Barrett, H. C., and R. Kurzban. (2006). "Modularity in cognition: Framing the debate." *Psychological Review* 113: 628–647.

Barrett, H. C., P. M. Todd, G. F. Miller, and P. W. Blythe. (2005). "Accurate judgments of intention from motion cues alone: A cross-cultural study." *Evolution and Human Behavior* 26: 313–331.

Barrett, L., R. Dunbar, and J. Lycett. (2002). *Human evolutionary psychology*. Princeton, NJ: Princeton University Press.

Barth, H., K. La Mont, J. Lipton, S. Dehaene, N. Kanwisher, et al. (2006). "Non-symbolic arithmetic in adults and young children." *Cognition* 98: 199–222.

Barton, R. A. (2000). Primate brain evolution: Cognitive demands of foraging or of social life? In *On the move*, ed. S. Boinski and P. A. Garber, 204–237. Chicago: University of Chicago Press.

Barton, R. A., A. Purvis, and P. H. Harvey. (1995). "Evolutionary radiation of visual and olfactory brain areas in primates, bats, and insectivores." *Philosophical Transactions of the Royal Society* B 348: 381–392.

Basil, J. A., A. C. Kamil, R. P. Balda, and K. V. Fite. (1996). "Difference in hippocampal volume among food storing corvids." *Brain Behavior and Evolution* 47: 156–164.

Basile, B. M., R. R. Hampton, S. J. Suomi, and E. A. Murray. (2009). "An assessment of memory awareness in tufted capuchin monkeys (Cebus apella)." *Animal Cognition* 12: 169–180.

Basolo, A. L. (1990a). "Female preference predates the evolution of the sword in swordtail fish." *Science* 250: 808–810.

———. (1990b). "Female preference for sword length in the green swordtail, Xiphophorus helleri (Pisces: Poeciliidae)." *Animal Behaviour* 40: 332–338.

———. (1995a). "A further examination of a pre-existing bias favouring a sword in the genus Xiphophorus." *Animal Behaviour* 50: 365–375.

———. (1995b). "Phylogenetic evidence for the role of a pre-existing bias in sexual selection." *Proceedings of the Royal Society of London,* B 259: 307–311.

———. (2002). "Female discrimination against sworded males in a poeciliid fish." *Animal Behaviour* 63: 463–468.

Bateson, M., and S. D. Healy. (2005). "Comparative evaluation and its implications for mate choice." *Trends in Ecology and Evolution* 20: 659–664.

Bateson, M., S. D. Healy, and T. A. Hurly. (2003). "Context-dependent foraging decisions in rufous hummingbirds." *Proceedings of the Royal Society of London* B 270: 1271–1276.

Bateson, M., and A. Kacelnik. (1995). "Preferences for fixed and variable food sources: variability in amount and delay." *Journal of the Experimental Analysis of Behaviour* 63: 313–329.

———. (1996). "Rate currencies and the foraging starling: the fallacy of the averages revisited." *Behavioral Ecology* 7: 341–352.

———. (1997). "Starlings' preferences for predictable and unpredictable delays to food." *Animal Behaviour* 53: 1129–1142.

———. (1998). Risk-sensitive foraging: decision-making in variable environments. In *Cognitive ecology*, ed. R. Dukas, 297–341. Chicago: University of Chicago Press.

Bateson, M., D. Nettle, and G. Roberts. (2006). "Cues of being watched enhance cooperation in a real-world setting." *Biology Letters* 2: 412–414.

Bateson, P. P. G. (1966). "The characteristics and context of imprinting." *Biological Review* 41: 177–220.

——— (1979). "How do sensitive periods arise and what are they for?" *Animal Behaviour* 27: 470–486.

———. (1981). The control of sensitivity to the environment during development. In *Behavioral development*, ed. K. Immelman, G. Barlow, M. Main, and L. Petrinovich, 432–453. New York: Cambridge University Press.

———. (1982). "Preferences for cousins in Japanese quail." *Nature* 295: 236–237.

———. (1987). Imprinting as a process of competitive exclusion. In *Imprinting and cortical plasticity*, ed. J. P. Rauschecker and P. Marler, 151–168. New York: John Wiley.

———. (1988). Preferences for close relations in Japanese quail. In *Acta XIX Congressus Internationalis Ornithologici*, 961–972. Ottawa: University of Ottawa Press.

———. (1990). "Is imprinting such a special case?" *Philosophical Transactions of the Royal Society of London* B 329: 125–131.

———. (2000). What must be known in order to understand imprinting? In *The evolution of cognition*, ed. C. Heyes and L. Huber, 85–102. Cambridge, MA: MIT Press.

Bateson, P. P. G., and J. B. Jaekel (1976). "Chicks' preferences for familiar and novel conspicuous objects after different periods of exposure." *Animal Behaviour* 24: 386–390.

Bateson, P., and M. Mameli (2007). "The innate and the acquired: Useful clusters or a residual distinction from folk biology?" *Developmental Psychobiology* 49: 818–831.

Bateson, P. P. G., and E. P. Reese (1969). "Reinforcing properties of conspicuous stimuli in the imprinting situation." *Animal Behaviour* 17: 692–699.

Bateson, P. P. G., and Wainwright, A. A. P. (1972). "The effects of prior exposure to light on the imprinting process in domestic chicks." *Behaviour* 42: 279–290.

Beach, F. A. (1950). "The snark was a boojum." *American Psychologist* 5: 115–124.

Beatty, W. W., and D. A. Shavalia (1980). "Spatial memory in rats: Time course of working memory and effects of anesthetics." *Behavioral and Neural Biology* 28: 454–462.

Beck, B. B. (1980). *Animal tool behavior: The use and manufacture of tools by animals.* New York: Garland STPM Press.

———. (1982). "Chimpocentrism: Bias in cognitive ethology." *Journal of Human Evolution* 11: 3–17.

Beckers, T., R. R. Miller, J. De Houwer, and K. Urushihara. (2006). "Reasoning rats: Forward blocking in Pavlovian animal conditioning is sensitive to constraints of causal inference." *Journal of Experimental Psychology: General* 135: 92–102.

Bee, M. A., and H. C. Gerhardt. (2002). "Individual voice recognition in a territorial frog (Rana catesbeiana)." *Proceedings of the Royal Society* B 269: 1443–1448.

Beecher, M. D. (1990). The evolution of parent-offspring recognition in swallows. In *Contemporary issues in comparative psychology,* ed. D. A. Dewsbury, 360–380. Sunderland, MA: Sinauer Associates.

Beecher, M. D., and E. A. Brenowitz. (2005). "Functional aspects of song learning in songbirds." *Trends in Ecology and Evolution* 20: 143–149.

Bekoff, M., C. Allen, and G. M. Burghardt, eds. (2002). *The cognitive animal.* Cambridge, MA: MIT Press.

Bekoff, M., and P. W. Sherman (2004). "Reflections on animal selves." *Trends in Ecology and Evolution* 19: 176–180.

Bell, A. M. (2007). "Future directions in behavoural syndromes research." *Proceedings of the Royal Society* B 274: 755–761.

Benhamou, S. (1996). "No evidence for cognitive mapping in rats." *Animal Behaviour* 52: 201–212.

Bennett, A. T. D. (1993). "Spatial memory in a food storing corvid 1: Near tall landmarks are primarily used." *Journal of Comparative Physiology A* 173: 193–207.

———. (1996). "Do animals have cognitive maps?" *The Journal of Experimental Biology* 199: 219–224.

Beran, M. J. (2007). "Rhesus monkeys (Macaca mulatta) enumerate large and small sequentially presented sets of items using analog numerical representations." *Journal of Experimental Psychology: Animal Behavior Processes* 33: 42–54.

Beran, M. J., and M. M. Beran. (2004). "Chimpanzees remember the results of one-by-one addition of food items to sets over extended time periods." *Psychological Science* 15: 94–99.

Beran, M. J., M. M. Beran, E. H. Harris, and D. A. Washburn. (2005). "Ordinal judgments and summation of nonvisible sets of food items by two chimpanzees and a rhesus macaque." *Journal of Experimental Psychology: Animal Behavior Processes* 31: 351–362.

Beran, M. J., J. L. Pate, D. A. Washburn, and D. M. Rumbaugh. (2004). "Sequential responding and planning in chimpanzees (Pan troglodytes) and rhesus macaques (Macaca mulatta)." *Journal of Experimental Psychology: Animal Behavior Processes* 30: 203–212.

Beran, M. J., J. D. Smith, J. S. Redford, and D. A. Washburn. (2006). "Rhesus macaques (Macaca mulatta) monitor uncertainty during numerosity judgements." *Journal of Experimental Psychology: Animal Behavior Processes* 32: 111–119.

Bergman, T. J., J. C. Beehner, D. L. Cheney, and R. M. Seyfarth. (2003). "Hierarchical classification by rank and kinship in baboons." *Science* 302: 1234–1236.

Berlyne, D. E. (1960). *Conflict, arousal, and curiosity.* New York: McGraw-Hill.

Bhatt, R. S., E. A. Wasserman, W. F. J. Reynolds, and K. S. Knauss. (1988). "Conceptual behavior in pigeons: Categorization of both familiar and novel examples from four classes of natural and artificial stimuli." *Journal of Experimental Psychology: Animal Behavior Processes* 14: 219–234.

Bhattacharjee, Y. (2006). "A timely debate about the brain." *Science* 311: 596–598.

Biebach, H., H. Falk, and J. R. Krebs. (1991). "The effect of constant light and phase shifts on a learned time-place association in garden warblers (Sylvia borin): Hourglass or circadian clock." *Journal of Biological Rhythms* 6: 353–365.

Biebach, H., M. Gordijn, and J. R. Krebs (1989). "Time-and-place learning by garden warblers, Sylvia borin." *Animal Behaviour* 37: 353–360.

Biegler, R. (2000). "Possible uses of path integration in animal navigation." *Animal Learning and Behavior* 28: 257–277.

———. (2006). Functional considerations in animal navigation: How do you use what you know? In *Animal Spatial Cognition: Comparative, Neural, and Computational Approaches,* ed. M. F. Brown and R. G. Cook. [On-line]. Available www.pigeon.psy.tufts.edu/asc/biegler/

Bingman, V. P., and K. Cheng. (2005). "Mechanisms of animal global navigation: Comparative perspectives and enduring challenges." *Ethology, Ecology, & Evolution* 17: 295–318.

Bingman, V. P., and T.-J. Jones. (1994). "Sun compass-based spatial learning impaired in homing pigeons with hippocampal lesions." *Journal of Neuroscience* 14: 6687–6694.

Bird, G., R. Brindley, J. Leighton, and C. Heyes. (2007). "General processes, rather than 'goals,' explain imitation errors." *Journal of Experimental Psychology: Human Perception and Performance* 33: 1158–1169.

Biro, D., J. Meade, and T. Guilford. (2004). "Familiar route loyalty implies visual pilotage in the homing pigeon." *Proceedings of the National Academy of Sciences* (USA) 101: 17440–17443.

Bischof, H.-J. (1994). Sexual imprinting as a two-stage process. In *Causal mechanisms of behavioural development,* ed. J. A. Hogan and J. J. Bolhuis, 82–97. Cambridge: Cambridge University Press.

Bitterman, M. E. (1965). "The evolution of intelligence." *Scientific American* 212: 92–100.

———. (1975). "The comparative analysis of learning." *Science* 188: 699–709.

———. (2000). Cognitive evolution: A psychological perspective. In *The evolution of cognition,* ed. C. Heyes and L. Huber, 61–79. Cambridge, MA: MIT Press.

Blaisdell, A. P., and R. G. Cook. (2004). "Integration of spatial maps in pigeons." *Animal Cognition* 8: 7–16.

Blaisdell, A. P., K. Sawa, K. J. Leising, and M. R. Waldmann. (2006). "Causal reasoning in rats." *Science* 311: 1020–1022.

Bloom, P. (2004). "Can a dog learn a word?" *Science* 304: 1605–1606.

Bloomfield, L. L., C. B. Sturdy, L. S. Phillmore, and R. G. Weisman. (2003). "Open-ended categorization of chick-a-dee calls by black-capped chickadees (Poecile atricapilla)." *Journal of Comparative Psychology* 117: 290–301.

Blough, D. S. (1967). "Stimulus generalization as signal detection in pigeons." *Science* 158: 940–941.

———. (1969). "Attention shifts in a maintained discrimination." *Science* 166: 125–126.

———. (1975). "Steady state data and a quantitative model of operant generalization and discrimination." *Journal of Experimental Psychology: Animal Behavior Processes* 1: 3–21.

———. (1979). "Effects of number and form of stimuli on visual search in the pigeon." *Journal of Experimental Psychology: Animal Behavior Processes* 5: 211–223.

———. (1991). "Selective attention and search images in pigeons." *Journal of Experimental Psychology: Animal Behavior Processes* 17: 292–298.

———. (1993a). "Effects on search speed of the probability of target-distractor combinations." *Journal of Experimental Psychology: Animal Behavior Processes* 19: 231–243.

————. (1993b). "Reaction time drifts identify objects of attention in pigeon visual search." *Journal of Experimental Psychology: Animal Behavior Processes* 19: 107–120.

————. (1996). "Error factors in pigeon discrimination and delayed matching." *Journal of Experimental Psychology: Animal Behavior Processes* 22: 118–131.

————. (2001). The preception of similarity. In *Avian visual cognition,* ed. R. G. Cook. Boston: Comparative Cognition Press. [on-line] www.pigeon.psy.tufts.edu/avc/dblough/.

————(2002) "Measuring the search image: Expectation, detection, and recognition in pigeon visual search." *Journal of Experimental Psychology: Animal Behavior Processes* 28: 397–405.

————. (2006). Reaction-time explorations of visual perception, attention, and decision in pigeons. In *Comparative cognition: Experimental exploration of animal intelligence,* ed. E. A. Wasserman and T. R. Zentall, 77–93. New York: Oxford University Press.

Blough, D. S., and P. M. Blough. (1977). Animal psychophysics. In *Handbook of operant behavior,* ed. W. K. Honig and J. E. R. Staddon, 514–539. Englewood Cliffs, NJ: Prentice-Hall.

————. (1997). "Form perception and attention in pigeons." *Animal Learning & Behavior* 25: 1–20.

Blough, P. M. (1989). "Attentional priming and visual search in pigeons." *Journal of Experimental Psychology: Animal Behavior Processes* 15: 358–365.

————. (1992). "Detectibility and choice during visual search: Joint effects of sequential priming and discriminability." *Animal Learning and Behavior* 20: 293–300.

————. (2001). Cognitive strategies and foraging in pigeons. In *Avian visual cognition,* ed. R. G. Cook [on-line] www.pigeon.psy.tufts.edu/avc/pblough/.

Bluff, L. A., A. A. S. Weir, C. Rutz, J. H. Wimpenny, and A. Kacelnik (2007). "Tool-related cognition in New Caledonian crows." *Comparative Cognition & Behavior Reviews* 2: 1–25.

Blumberg, M. S., and E. A. Wasserman (1995). "Animal mind and the argument from design." *American Psychologist* 50: 133–144.

Blumstein, D. T. (1999). "The evolution of functionally referential alarm communication: Multiple adaptations; multiple constraints." *Evolution of Communication* 3: 135–147.

————. (2007). The evolution of alarm communication in rodents: Structure, function, and the puzzle of apparently altruistic calling. In *Rodent Societies,* ed. J. O. Wolff and P. W. Sherman, 316–327. Chicago: University of Chicago Press.

Boag, P. T. (1983). "The heritability of external morphology in Darwin's ground finches (Geospiza) on Isla Daphne Major, Galapagos." *Evolution* 37: 877–894.

Boag, P. T., and P. R. Grant (1984). "The classical case of character release: Darwin's finches (Geospiza) on Isla Daphne Major, Galapagos." *Biological Journal of the Linnean Society* 22: 243–287.

Boakes, R. (1984). *From Darwin to behaviourism.* Cambridge: Cambridge University Press.

Boakes, R., and D. Panter (1985). "Secondary imprinting in the domestic chick blocked by previous exposure to a live hen." *Animal Behaviour* 33: 353–365.

Boccia, M. M., M. G. Blake, G. B. Acosta, and C. M. Baratti (2005). "Memory consolidation and reconsolidation of an inhibitory avoidance task in mice: Effects of a new different learning task." *Neuroscience* 135: 19–29.

Boesch, C. (1991). "Teaching among wild chimpanzees." *Animal Behaviour* 41: 530–532.

————. (2007). "What makes us human (Homo sapiens)? The challenge of cognitive cross-species comparison." *Journal of Comparative Psychology* 121: 227–240.

Boesch, C., and H. Boesch-Acherman (2000). *The Chimpanzees of the Tai Forest.* Oxford: Oxford University Press.

Boesch-Achermann, H., and C. Boesch (1993). "Tool use in wild chimpanzees: New light from dark forests." *Current Directions in Psychological Science* 2: 18–21.

Boice, R., and M. R. Denny (1965). "The conditioned licking response in rats as a function of the CS-UCS interval." *Psychonomic Science* 3: 93–94.

Boinski, S., and P. A. Garber, eds. (2000). *On the move.* Chicago: University of Chigago Press.

Boisvert, M. J., A. J. Veal, and D. F. Sherry (2007). "Floral reward production is timed by an insect pollinator." *Proceedings of the Royal Society B* 274: 1831–1837.

Bolhuis, J. J. (1991). "Mechanisms of avian imprinting: A review." *Biological Review* 66: 303–345.

———. (1996). Development of perceptual mechanisms in birds: Predispositions and imprinting. In *Neuroethological Studies of Cognitive and Perceptual Processes,* ed. C. F. Moss and S. J. Shettleworth, 158–184. Boulder, CO: Westview Press.

———. (2005). "Function and mechanism in neuroecology: Looking for clues." *Animal Biology* 55: 457–490.

Bolhuis, J. J., G. J. de Vos, and J. P. Kruijt (1990). "Filial imprinting and associative learning." *The Quarterly Journal of Experimental Psychology* 42B: 313–329.

Bolhuis, J. J., and M. Gahr (2006). "Neural mechanisms of birdsong memory." *Nature Reviews Neuroscience* 7: 347–357.

Bolhuis, J. J., and L.-A. Giraldeau, eds. (2005). *The Behavior of Animals.* Malden, MA: Blackwell Publishing.

Bolhuis, J. J., and E. M. Macphail (2001). "A critique of the neuroecology of learning and memory." *Trends in Cognitive Sciences* 5: 426–433.

Bolhuis, J. J., and H. S. van Kampen (1988). "Serial position curves in spatial memory in rats: Primacy and recency effects." *Quarterly Journal of Experimental Psychology* 40B: 135–149.

Bolles, R. C. (1970). "Species-specific defense reactions and avoidance learning." *Psychological Review* 77: 32–48.

Bolles, R. C., and S. A. Moot (1973). "The rat's anticipation of two meals a day." *Journal of Comparative and Physiological Psychology* 83: 510–514.

Bonardi, C., and G. Hall (1996). "Learned irrelevance: No more than the sum of CS and US preexposure effects?" *Journal of Experimental Psychology: Animal Behavior Processes* 22: 183–191.

Bonardi, C., and S. Y. Ong (2003). "Learned irrelevance: A contemporary overview." *The Quarterly Journal of Experimental Psychology* 56B: 80–89.

Bond, A. B. (1983). "Visual search and selection of natural stimuli in the pigeon: The attention threshold hypothesis." *Journal of Experimental Psychology: Animal Behavior Processes* 9: 292–306.

———. (2007). "The evolution of color polymorphism: Crypticity, searching images, and apostatic selection." *Annual Review of Ecology, Evolution, and Sytematics* 38: 489–514.

Bond, A. B., and A. C. Kamil (1998). "Apostatic selection by blue jays produces balanced polymorphism in virtual prey." *Nature* 395: 594–596.

———. (1999). "Searching image in blue jays: Facilitation and interference in sequential priming." *Animal Learning & Behavior* 27: 461–471.

———. (2002). "Visual predators select for crypticity and polymorphism in virtual prey." *Nature* 415: 609–613.

———. (2006). "Spatial heterogeneity, predator cognition, and the evolution of color polymorphism in virtual prey." *Proceedings of the National Academy of Sciences* (USA) 103: 3214–3219.

Bond, A. B., A. C. Kamil, and R. P. Balda (2003). "Social complexity and transitive inference in corvids." *Animal Behaviour* 65: 479–487.

Bonner, J. T. (1980). *The Evolution of Culture in Animals.* Princeton, NJ: Princeton University Press.

Bonnie, K. E., and R. L. Earley (2007). "Expanding the scope for social information use." *Animal Behaviour* 74: 171–181.

Bossema, I., and R. R. Burgler (1980). "Communication during monocular and binocular looking in European jays (Garrulus g. glandarius)." *Behaviour* 74: 274–283.

Botly, L. C. P., and E. De Rosa (2007). "Cholinergic influences on feature binding." *Behavioral Neuroscience* 121: 264–276.

Bouchard, J., W. Goodyer, and L. Lefebvre (2007). "Social learning and innovation are positively correlated in pigeons (Columba livia)." *Animal Cognition* 10: 259–266.

Bouton, M. E. (1993). "Context, time, and memory retrieval in the interference paradigms of Pavlovian learning." *Psychological Bulletin* 114: 80–99.

———. (2007). *Learning and Behavior.* Sunderland MA: Sinauer Associates.

Bouton, M. E., and E. W. Moody. (2004). "Memory processes in classical conditioning." *Neuroscience and Biobehavioral Reviews* 28: 663–674.

Bouton, M. E., and C. Sunsay. (2003). "Importance of trials versus accumulating time across trials in partially reinforced appetitive conditioning." *Journal of Experimental Psychology: Animal Behavior Processes* 29: 62–77.

Bovet, D., and D. A. Washburn. (2003). "Rhesus macaques (Macaca mulatta) categorize unknown conspecifics according to their dominance relations." *Journal of Comparative Psychology* 117: 400–405.

Bovet, J., and E. F. Oertli. (1974). "Free-running circadian activity rhythms in free-living beaver (Castor canadensis)." *Journal of Comparative Physiology* 92: 1–10.

Boyse, E. A., G. K. Beauchamp, K. Yamazaki, and J. Bard. (1991). Genetic components of kin recognition in mammals. In *Kin Recognition,* ed. P. G. Hepper, 148–161. Cambridge: Cambridge University Press.

Boysen, S. T. (1993). Counting in chimpanzees: Nonhuman principles and emergent properties of number. In *The Development of Numerical Competence,* ed. S. T. Boysen and E. J. Capaldi, 39–59. Hillsdale, NJ: Lawrence Erlbaum Associates.

Boysen, S. T., and G. G. Berntson. (1989). "Numerical competence in a chimpanzee (Pan troglodytes)." *Journal of Comparative Psychology* 103: 23–31.

———. (1995). "Responses to quantity: Perceptual versus cognitive mechanisms in chimpanzees (Pan troglodytes)." *Journal of Experimental Psychology: Animal Behavior Processes* 21: 82–86.

Boysen, S. T., G. G. Berntson, M. B. Hannan, and J. T. Cacioppo. (1996). "Quantity-based interference and symbolic representations in chimpanzees (Pan troglodytes)." *Journal of Experimental Psychology: Animal Behavior Processes* 22: 76–86.

Boysen, S. T., and E. J. Capaldi, eds. (1993). *The Development of Numerical Competence.* Hillsdale, NJ: Lawrence Erlbaum Associates.

Boysen, S. T., and K. I. Hallberg. (2000). "Primate numerical competence: Contributions toward understanding nonhuman cognition." *Cognitive Science* 24: 423–443.

Braaten, R. F. (2000). "Multiple levels of representation of song by European starlings (Sturnus vulgaris): Open-ended categorization of starling song types and differential forgetting of song categories and exemplars." *Journal of Comparative Psychology* 114: 61–72.

Bradbury, J. W., and S. L. Vehrencamp. (1998). *Principles of Animal Communication.* Sunderland, MA: Sinauer Associates.

Brandon, S. E., E. H. Vogel, and A. R. Wagner. (2003). "Stimulus representation in SOP: I Theoretical rationalization and some implications." *Behavioural Processes* 62: 5–25.

Brannon, E. M. (2006). "The representation of numerical magnitude." *Current Opinion in Neurobiology* 16: 222–229.

Brannon, E. M., J. F. Cantlon, and H. S. Terrace. (2006). "The role of reference points in ordinal numerical comparisons by rhesus macaques (Macaca mulatta)." *Journal of Experimental Psychology: Animal Behavior Processes* 32: 120–134.

Brannon, E. M., and H. S. Terrace. (1998). "Ordering of the numerosities 1 to 9 by monkeys." *Science* 282: 746–749.

———. (2000). "Representation of the numerosities 1–9 by rhesus macaques (Macaca mulatta)." *Journal of Experimental Psychology: Animal Behavior Processes* 26: 31–49.

Brass, M., and C. Heyes. (2005). "Imitation: Is cognitive neuroscience solving the correspondence problem?" *Trends in Cognitive Sciences* 9: 489–495.

Bräuer, J., J. Call, and M. Tomasello. (2005). "All great ape species follow gaze to distant locations and around barriers." *Journal of Comparative Psychology* 119: 145–154.

———. (2007). "Chimpanzees really know what others can see in a competitive situation." *Animal Cognition* 10: 439–448.

Bräuer, J., J. Kaminski, J. Riedel, J. Call, and M. Tomasello. (2006). "Making inferences about the location of hidden food: Social dog, causal ape." *Journal of Comparative Psychology* 120: 38–47.

Breland, K., and M. Breland. (1961). "The misbehavior of organisms." *American Psychologist* 16: 681–684.

Breuer, T., M. Ndoundou-Hockemba, and V. Fishlock. (2005). "First observation of tool use in wild gorillas." *Plos Biology* 3: 2041–2041.

Bright, M. (1990). *The Dolittle obsession*. London: Robson Books.

Briscoe, A. D., and L. Chittka. (2001). "The evolution of color vision in insects." *Annual Review of Entomology* 46: 471–510.

Brito e Abreu, F., and A. Kacelnik. (1999). "Energy budgets and risk-sensitive foraging in starlings." *Behavioral Ecology* 10: 338–345.

Brodbeck, D. R. (1994). "Memory for spatial and local cues: A comparison of a storing and a nonstoring species." *Animal Learning and Behavior* 22: 119–133.

———. (1997). "Picture fragment completion: Priming in the pigeon." *Journal of Experimental Psychology: Animal Behavior Processes* 23: 461–468.

Brodbeck, D. R., and S. J. Shettleworth. (1995). "Matching location and color of a compound stimulus: Comparison of a food-storing and a non-storing bird species." *Journal of Experimental Psychology: Animal Behavior Processes* 21: 64–77.

Brodin, A. (2005). "Mechanisms of cache retrieval in long-term hoarding birds." *Journal Of Ethology* 23: 77–83.

Brodin, A., and K. Lundborg. (2003). "Is hippocampal volume affected by specialization for food hoarding in birds?" *Proceedings of The Royal Society of London B* 270: 1555–1563.

Brooks, D. R., and D. A. McLennan. (1991). *Phylogeny, Ecology, and Behavior*. Chicago: University of Chicago Press.

Brosnan, S. F., and F. B. M. de Waal. (2003). "Monkeys reject unequal pay." *Nature* 425: 297–299.

———. (2006). "Partial support from a nonreplication: Comment on Roma, Silberberg, Ruggiero, and Suomi (2006)." *Journal of Comparative Psychology* 120: 74–75.

Brown, C. H., J. M. Sinnott, and R. A. Kressley. (1994). "Perception of chirps by Sykes's monkeys (Cercopithecus albogularis) and humans (Homo sapiens)." *Journal of Comparative Psychology* 108: 243–251.

Brown, M. F., and R. G. Cook, eds. (2006). *Animal Spatial Cognition: Comparative, Neural, and Computational Approaches*. [On-line]. Available www.pigeon.psy.tufts.edu/asc/

Brown, M. F., E. A. Wheeler, and D. A. Riley. (1989). "Evidence for a shift in the choice criterion of rats in a 12-arm radial maze." *Animal Learning & Behavior* 17: 12–20.

Brown, P. L., and H. M. Jenkins. (1968). "Auto-shaping of the pigeon's key-peck." *Journal of the Experimental Analysis of Behavior* 11: 1–8.

Brown, S. D., and R. J. Dooling. (1992). "Perception of conspecific faces by budgerigars (Melopsittacus undulatus): I. Natural faces." *Journal of Comparative Psychology* 106: 203–216.

———. (1993). "Perception of conspecific faces by budgerigars (Melopsittacus undulatus): II. Synthetic models." *Journal of Comparative Psychology* 107: 48–60.

Brunner, D., A. Kacelnik, and J. Gibbon. (1992). "Optimal foraging and timing processes in the starling, Sturnus vulgaris: effect of inter-capture interval." *Animal Behaviour* 44: 597–613.

———. (1996). "Memory for inter-reinforcement interval variability and patch departure decisions in the starling, Sturnus vulgaris." *Animal Behaviour* 51: 1025–1045.

Bshary, R. (2006). Machiavellian intelligence in fishes. In *Fish Cognition and Behavior*, ed. C. Brown, K. Laland, and J. Krause, 223–242. Oxford: Blackwell.

Bshary, R., and A. d'Souza. (2005). Cooperation in communication networks: Indirect reciprocity in interactions between cleaner fish and client reef fish. In *Animal Communication Networks*, ed. P. K. McGregor, 521–539. Cambridge: Cambridge University Press.

Bshary, R., and A. S. Grutter (2005). "Punishment and partner switching cause cooperative behaviour in a cleaning mutualism." *Biology Letters* 1: 396–399.

———. (2006). "Image scoring and cooperation in a cleaner fish mutualism." *Nature* 441: 975–978.

Bugnyar, T., and B. Heinrich. (2005). "Ravens, Corvis corax, differentiate between knowledgeable and ignorant competitors." *Proceedings of the Royal Society B* 272: 1641–1646.

Bugnyar, T., M. Stöwe, and B. Heinrich. (2004). "Ravens, Corvus corax, follow gaze direction of humans around obstacles." *Proceedings of the Royal Society B* 271: 1331–1336.

Buhusi, C. V., and W. H. Meck. (2005). "What makes us tick? Functional and neural mechanisms of interval timing." *Nature Reviews Neuroscience* 6: 755–765.

———. (2006). "Interval timing with gaps and distracters: Evaluation of the ambiguity, switch, and time-sharing hypotheses." *Journal of Experimental Psychology: Animal Behavior Processes* 32: 329–338.

Buhusi, C. V., D. Perera, and W. H. Meck. (2005). "Memory for timing visual and auditory signals in albino and pigmented rats." *Journal of Experimental Psychology: Animal Behavior Processes* 31: 18–30.

Buhusi, C. V., A. Sasaki, and W. H. Meck. (2002). "Temporal integration as a function of signal and gap intensity in rats (Rattus norvegicus) and pigeons (Columba livia)." *Journal of Comparative Psychology* 116: 381–390.

Buller, D. J. (2005). "Evolutionary psychology: The emperor's new paradigm." *Trends in Cognitive Sciences* 9: 277–283.

Burgess, N. (2006). "Spatial memory: How egocentric and allocentric combine." *Trends in Cognitive Sciences* 10: 551–557.

Burkart, J. M., and A. Heschl. (2007). "Understanding visual access in common marmosets, Callithrix jacchus: perspective aking or behaviour reading?" *Animal Behaviour* 73: 457–469.

Burke, D., and B. J. Fulham. (2003). "An evolved spatial memory bias in a nectar-feeding bird?" *Animal Behaviour* 66: 695–701.

Burkhardt, R. W. (2005). *Patterns of Behavior*. Chicago: University of Chicago Press.

Burley, N., C. Minor, and C. Strachan. (1990). "Social preference of zebra finches for siblings, cousins, and non-kin." *Animal Behaviour* 39: 775–784.

Burns, J. G., and J. D. Thomson. (2006). "A test of spatial memory and movement patterns of bumblebees at multiple spatial and temporal scales." *Behavioral Ecology* 17: 48–55.

Burns, M., and M. Domjan. (2001). "Topography of spatially directed conditioned responding: Effects of context and trial duration." *Journal of Experimental Psychology: Animal Behavior Processes* 27: 269–278.

Burr, D., and J. Ross. (2008). "A visual sense of number." *Current Biology* 18: 425–428.

Byrne, R. W. (1995). *The Thinking Ape*. Oxford: Oxford University Press.

Byrne, R. W., and A. Whiten, eds. (1988). *Machiavellian Intelligence: Social Expertise and the Evolution of Intellect in Monkeys, Apes, and Humans*. Oxford: Clarendon Press.

Cabeza de Vaca, S., B. L. Brown, and N. S. Hemmes. (1994). "Internal clock and memory processes in animal timing." *Journal of Experimental Psychology: Animal Behavior Processes* 20: 184–198.

Caffrey, C. (2001). "Goal-directed use of objects by American crows." *The Wilson Bulletin* 113: 114–115.

Cain, S. W., C. H. Ko, J. A. Chalmers, and M. R. Ralph. (2004). "Time of day modulation of conditioned place preference in rats depends on the strain of rat used." *Neurobiology of Learning and Memory* 81: 217–220.

Call, J. (2001). "Object permanence in orangutans (Pongo pygmaeus), chimpanzees (Pan troglodytes), and children (Homo sapiens)." *Journal of Comparative Psychology* 115: 159–171.

———. (2006). "Inferences by exclusion in the great apes: The effect of age and species." *Animal Cognition* 9: 393–403.

Call, J., and M. Carpenter. (2001). "Do apes and children know what they have seen?" *Animal Cognition* 4: 207–220.

Call, J., M. Carpenter, and M. Tomasello. (2005). "Copying results and copying actions in the process of social learning: chimpanzees (Pan troglodytes) and human children (Homo sapiens)." *Animal Cognition* 8: 151–163.

Call, J., and M. Tomasello. (2008). "Does the chimpanzee have a theory of mind? 30 years later." *Trends in Cognitive Science* 12: 187–192.

Callebaut, W., and D. Rasskin-Gutman, eds. (2005). *Modularity: Understanding the Development and Evolution of Natural Complex Systems*. Cambridge, MA: MIT Press.

Calvert, G., C. Spence, and B. E. Stein, eds. (2004). *Handbook of Multisensory Processes*. Cambridge, MA: MIT Press.

Candland, D. K. (1993). *Feral Children and Clever Animals*. New York: Oxford University Press.

Candolin, U. (2003). "The use of multiple cues in mate choice." *Biological Reviews* 78: 575–595.

Cantlon, J. F., and E. M. Brannon. (2005). "Semantic congruity affects numerical judgments similarly in monkeys and humans." *Proceedings of the National Academy of Sciences* (USA) 102: 16507–16511.

———. (2006). "Shared system for ordering small and large numbers in monkeys and humans." *Psychological Science* 17: 401–406.

———. (2007). "How much does number matter to a monkey (Macaca mulatta)?" *Journal of Experimental Psychology: Animal Behavior Processes* 33: 32–41.

Capaldi, E. J. (1993). Animal number abilites: Implications for a hierarchical approach to instrumental learning. In *The Development of Numerical Competence*, ed. S. T. Boysen and E. J. Capaldi, 191–209. Hillsdale, NJ: Lawrence Erlbaum Associates.

Capaldi, E. J., and D. J. Miller. (1988). "Counting in rats: Its functional significance and the independent cognitive processes that constitute it." *Journal of Experimental Psychology: Animal Behavior Processes* 14: 3–17.

Caraco, T., W. U. Blanckenhorn, G. M. Gregory, J. A. Newman, G. M. Recer, et al. (1990). "Risk sensitivity: Ambient temperature affects foraging choice." *Animal Behaviour* 39: 338–345.

Caraco, T., S. Martindale, and T. S. Whittam. (1980). "An empirical demonstration of risk-sensitive foraging preferences." *Animal Behaviour* 28: 820–830.

Carew, T. J., H. M. Pinsker, and E. R. Kandel. (1972). "Long-term habituation of a defensive withdrawal reflex in aplysia." *Science* 175: 451–454.

Carlier, P., and L. Lefebvre. (1997). "Ecological differences in social learning between adjacent mixing populations of Zenaida dives." *Ethology* 103: 772–784.

Caro, T. M., and M. D. Hauser. (1992). "Is there teaching in nonhuman animals?" *The Quarterly Review of Biology* 67: 151–174.

Carr, J. A. R., and D. M. Wilkie. (1997). "Rats use an ordinal timer in a daily time-place learning task." *Journal of Experimental Psychology: Animal Behavior Processes* 23: 232–247.

———. (1997). Ordinal, phase, and interval timing. In *Time and Behaviour: Psychological and Neurobiological Analyses*, ed. C. M. Bradshaw and E. Szabadi 265–327. New York: Elsevier Science.

Carruthers, P. (2005). "Why the question of animal consciousness might not matter very much." *Philosophical Psychology* 18: 83–102.

———. (2008). "Meta-cognition in animals: A skeptical look." *Mind & Language* 23: 58–89.

Carruthers, P., and P. K. Smith, eds. (1996). *Theories of Theories of Mind*. Cambridge: Cambridge University Press.

Cartwright, B. A., and T. S. Collett. (1983). "Landmark learning in bees." *Journal of Comparative Physiology* 151: 521–543.

———. (1987). "Landmark maps for honeybees." *Biological Cybernetics* 57: 85–93.

Castellanos, M. C., P. Wilson, and J. D. Thomson. (2002). "Dynamic nectar replenishment in flowers of Penstemon (Scrophulariaceae)." *American Journal of Botany* 89: 111–118.

Castro, L., M. E. Young, and E. A. Wasserman. (2006). "Effects of number of items and visual display variability on same-different discrimination behavior." *Memory & Cognition* 34: 1689–1703.

Catchpole, C. K., and P. J. B. Slater. (1995). *Bird Song: Biological Themes and Variations*. Cambridge: Cambridge University Press.

Catmur, C., V. Walsh, and C. Heyes. (2007). "Sensorimotor learning configures the human mirror system." *Current Biology* 17: 1527–1531.

Cerella, J. (1979). "Visual classes and natural categories in the pigeon." *Journal of Experimental Psychology: Human Perception and Performance* 5: 68–77.

Cerutti, D. T., and J. E. R. Staddon. (2004). "Immediacy versus anticipated delay in the time-left experiment: A test of the cognitive hypothesis." *Journal of Experimental Psychology: Animal Behavior Processes* 30: 45–57.

Chamizo, V. D. (2003). "Acquisition of knowledge about spatial location: Assessing the generality of the mechanism of learning." *Quarterly Journal of Experimental Psychology* 56B: 102–113.

Chamizo, V. D., T. Rodrigo, and N. J. Mackintosh. (2006). "Spatial integration with rats." *Learning & Behavior* 34: 348–354.

Chappell, J., and T. Guilford. (1995). "Homing pigeons primarily use the sun compass rather than fixed directional visual cues in an open-field arena food-searching task." *Proceedings of the Royal Society B* 260: 59–63.

Chapuis, N., M. Durup, and C. Thinus-Blanc. (1987). "The role of exploratory experience in a shortcut task by golden hamsters (Mesocricetus auratus)." *Animal Learning & Behavior* 15: 174–178.

Chapuis, N., and C. Varlet. (1987). "Short cuts by dogs in natural surroundings." *The Quarterly Journal of Experimental Psychology* 39B: 49–64.

Charnov, E. L. (1976). "Optimal foraging: attack strategy of a mantid." *American Naturalist* 110: 141–151.

Chase, S., and E. G. Heinemann. (2001). Exemplar memory and discrimination. In *Avian Visual Cognition*, ed. R. G. Cook. . [On-line]. Available: www.pigeon.psy.tufts.edu/avc/chase/

Chater, N., J. B. Tenenbaum, and A. Yuille. (2006). "Probabilistic models of cognition: Conceptual foundations." *Trends in Cognitive Sciences* 10: 287–291.

Cheetham, S. A., M. D. Thom, F. Jury, W. E. R. Ollier, R. J. Beynon, et al. (2007). "The genetic basis of individual-recognition signals in the mouse." *Current Biology* 17: 1771–1777.

Chelazzi, G. (1992). Invertebrates (excluding Arthropods). In *Animal Homing*, ed. F. Papi, 19–43. London: Chapman and Hall.

Chelazzi, G., and F. Francisci. (1979). "Movement patterns and homing behaviour of Testudo hermanni gmelin (Reptilia Testudinidae)." *Monitore Zoologica Italiano* 13: 105–127.

Chen, G. et al. (2000). "A learning deficit related to age and b-amyloid plaques in a mouse model of Alzheimer's disease." *Nature* 408: 975–979.

Chen, M. K., V. Lakshminarayanan, and L. R. Santos. (2006). "How basic are behavioral biases? Evidence from capuchin monkey trading behavior." *The Journal of Political Economy* 114: 517–537.

Cheney, D. L., and R. M. Seyfarth. (1988). "Assessment of meaning and the detection of unreliable signals by vervet monkeys." *Animal Behaviour* 36: 477–486.

———. (1990). *How Monkeys See the World*. Chicago: University of Chicago Press.

———. (1997). "Reconcilitatory grunts by dominant female baboons influence victims' behavior." *Animal Behaviour* 54: 409–418.

———. (2005a). Social complexity and the information acquired during eavesdropping by primates and other animals. In *Animal Communication Networks*, ed. P. K. McGregor, 583–603. Cambridge: Cambridge University Press.

———. (2005b). "Constraints and preadaptations in the earliest stages of language evolution." *The Linguistic Review* 22: 135–159.

———. (2007). *Baboon Metaphysics: The Evolution of a Social Mind*. Chicago: University of Chicago Press.

Cheney, D. L., R. M. Seyfarth, and R. A. Palombit. (1996). "The function and mechanisms underlying baboon 'contact' barks." *Animal Behaviour* (52): 507–518.

Cheney, D. L., R. M. Seyfarth, and J. B. Silk. (1995). "The responses of female baboons (Papio cynocephalus ursinus) to anomalous social interactions: Evidence for causal reasoning?" *Journal of Comparative Psychology* 109: 134–141.

Cheng, K. (1986). "A purely geometric module in the rat's spatial representation." *Cognition* 23: 149–178.

———. (1989). "The vector sum model of pigeon landmark use." *Journal of Experimental Psychology: Animal Behavior Processes* 15: 366–375.

———. (1992). Three psychophysical principles in the processing of spatial and temporal information. In *Cognitive Aspects of Stimulus Control*, ed. W. K. Honig and J. G. Fetterman, 69–88. Hillsdale, NJ: Lawrence Erlbaum Associates.

———. (1994). "The determination of direction in landmark-based spatial search in pigeons: A further test of the vector sum model." *Animal Learning & Behavior* 22: 291–301.

———. (2000). "How honeybees find a place: Lessons from a simple mind." *Animal Learning & Behavior* 28: 1–15.

———. (2002). "Generalisation: Mechanistic and functional explanations." *Animal Cognition* 5: 33–40.

———. (2005). "Reflections on geometry and navigation." *Connection Science* 17: 1–17.

———. (2006). Arthropod navigation: Ants, bees, crabs, spiders finding their way. In *Comparative Cognition*, ed. E. A. Wasserman and T. R. Zentall, 189–208. New York: Oxford University Press.

———. (2008). "Whither geometry? Troubles of the geometric module." *Trends in Cognitive Sciences* 12: 355–361.

Cheng, K., T. S. Collett, A. Pickhard, and R. Wehner. (1987). "The use of visual landmarks by honeybees: Bees weight landmarks according to their distance from the goal." *Journal of Comparative Physiology* 161: 469–475.

Cheng, K., and C. R. Gallistel. (2005). "Shape parameters explain data from spatial transformations: Comment on Pearce et al. (2004) and Tommasi, and Polli (2004)." *Journal of Experimental Psychology: Animal Behavior Processes* 31: 254–259.

Cheng, K., A. Narendra, and R. Wehner. (2006). "Behavioral ecology of odometric memories in desert ants: Acquisition, retention, and integration." *Behavioral Ecology* 17: 227–235.

Cheng, K., and N. S. Newcombe. (2005). "Is there a geometric module for spatial orientation? Squaring theory and evidence." *Psychonomic Bulletin & Review* 12: 1–23.

Cheng, K., and D. F. Sherry. (1992). "Landmark-based spatial memory in birds (Parus atricapillus and Columba livia): The use of edges and distances to represent spatial positions." *Journal of Comparative Psychology* 106: 331–341.

Cheng, K., S. J. Shettleworth, J. Huttenlocher, and J. J. Rieser. (2007). "Bayesian integration of spatial information." *Psychological Bulletin* 133: 625–637.

Cheng, K., and M. L. Spetch. (1998). Mechanisms of landmark use in mammals and birds. In *Spatial Representation in Animals*, ed. S. Healy, 1–17. Oxford: Oxford University Press.

Cheng, K., M. L. Spetch, and P. Miceli. (1996). "Averaging temporal duration and spatial position." *Journal of Experimental Psychology: Animal Behavior Processes* 22: 175–182.

Cheng, K., and R. Westwood. (1993). "Analysis of single trials in pigeons' timing performance." *Journal of Experimental Psychology: Animal Behavior Processes* 19: 56–67.

Cheng, K., and A. E. Wignall. (2006). "Honeybees (Apis mellifera) holding on to memories: Response competition causes retroactive interference effects." *Animal Cognition* 9: 141–150.

Cheung, A., W. Stürzl, J. Zeil, and K. Cheng. (2008). "The information content of panoramic images II: View-based navigation in nonrectangular experimental arenas." *Journal of Experimental Psychology: Animal Behavior Processes* 34: 15–30.

Chiandetti, C., and G. Vallortigara. (2008). "Spatial reorientation in large and small enclosures: Comparative and developmental perspectives." *Cognitive Processing* 9: 229–238.

Chittka, L., and K. Geiger. (1995). "Honeybee long-distance orientation in a controlled environment." *Ethology* 99 (2): 117–126.

Chittka, L., and J. D. Thomson, eds. (2001). *Cognitive Ecology of Pollination*. Cambridge: Cambridge University Press.

Chitty, D., and H. N. Southern, eds. (1954). *Control of Rats and Mice*. Oxford: Clarendon Press.

Chomsky, N. (1968). *Language and Mind*. New York: Harcourt, Brace, and World, Inc.

Christiansen, M. H., and S. Kirby, eds. (2003). *Language Evolution*. New York: Oxford University Press.

Christie, J. (1996). "Spatial contiguity facilitates Pavlovian conditioning." *Psychonomic Bulletin and Review* 3: 357–359.

Church, R. M. (1999). "Evaluation of quantitative theories of timing." *Journal of the Experimental Analysis of Behavior* 71: 253–291.

———. (2001). "A Turing test for computational and associative theories of learning." *Current Directions in Psychological Science* 10: 132–136.

————. (2002). Temporal learning. In *Stevens' Handbook of Experimental Psychology*, ed. C. R. Gallistel, 3:365–393. New York: John Wiley, and Sons, Inc. .

————. (2006). Behavioristic. cognitive, biological, and quantitative explanations of timing. In *Comparative Cognition: Experimental Explorations of Animal Intelligence*, ed. E. A. Wasserman and T. R. Zentall, 249–269. New York: Oxford University Press.

Church, R. M., and H. A. Broadbent. (1990). "Alternative representations of time, number, and rate." *Cognition* 37: 55–81.

Church, R. M., and M. Z. Deluty. (1977). "Bisection of temporal intervals." *Journal of Experimental Psychology: Animal Behavior Processes* 3: 216–228.

Church, R. M., and J. Gibbon. (1982). "Temporal generalization." *Journal of Experimental Psychology: Animal Behavior Processes* 8: 165–186.

Church, R. M., W. H. Meck, and J. Gibbon. (1994). "Application of scalar timing theory to individual trials." *Journal of Experimental Psychology: Animal Behavior Processes* 20: 135–155.

Clark, A. (1997). *Being There*. Cambridge, MA: MIT Press.

————. (2006). "Language, embodiment, and the cognitive niche." *Trends in Cognitive Sciences* 10: 370–374.

Clark, D. L., and G. W. Uetz. (1990). "Video image recognition by the jumping spider, Maevia inclemens (Araneae: Salticidae)." *Animal Behaviour* 40: 884–890.

Clayton, N. S. (1994). "The role of age and experience in the behavioural development of food-storing and retrieval in marsh tits, Parus palustris." *Animal Behaviour* 47: 1435–1444.

————. (1995). "Development of memory and the hippocampus: Comparison of food-storing and non-storing birds on a one-trial associative memory task." *Journal of Neuroscience* 15: 2796–2805.

Clayton, N. S., T. J. Bussey, and A. Dickinson. (2003). "Can animals recall the past and plan for the future?" *Nature Reviews Neuroscience* 4: 685–691.

Clayton, N. S., S. P. C. Correia, C. R. Raby, D. M. Alexis, N. J. Emery, et al. (2008). "Response to Suddendorf, and Corballis (2008): In defence of animal foresight." *Animal Behaviour* 76: e9-e11.

Clayton, N. S., J. M. Dally, and N. J. Emery. (2007). "Social cognition by food-caching corvids. The western scrub-jay as a natural psychologist." *Philosophical Transactions of the Royal Society B* 362: 507–522.

Clayton, N. S., and A. Dickinson. (1998). "Episodic-like memory during cache recovery by scrub jays." *Nature* 395: 272–274.

————. (1999). "Scrub jays (Aphelcoma coerulescens) remember the relative time of caching as well as the location and content of their caches." *Journal of Comparative Psychology* 113: 403–416.

Clayton, N. S., and J. R. Krebs. (1994). "One-trial associative memory: Comparison of food-storing and non-storing species of birds." *Animal Learning and Behaviour* 22: 366–372.

Clement, T. S., J. R. Feltus, D. H. Kaiser, and T. R. Zentall. (2000). "'Work ethic' in pigeons: Reward value is directly related to the effort or time required to obtain the reward." *Psychonomic Bulletin & Review* 7: 100–106.

Clutton-Brock, T. H., and P. Harvey. (1977). "Primate ecology and social organization." *Journal of Zoology* 183: 1–39.

————. (1984). Comparative approaches to investigating adaptation. In Behavioural ecology: An evolutionary approach, ed. J. R. Krebs and N. B. Davies, 7–29. Oxford, Blackwell Scientific.

Clutton-Brock, T. H., M. J. O'Riain, P. N. M. Brotherton, D. Gaynor, R. Kansky, et al. (1999). "Selfish sentinels in cooperative mammals." *Science* 284: 1640–1644.

Clutton-Brock, T. H., and G. A. Parker. (1995). "Punishment in animal societies." *Nature* 373: 209–216.

Cole, P. D., and W. K. Honig. (1994). "Transfer of a discrimination by pigeons (Columba livia) between pictured locations and the represented environments." *Journal of Comparative Psychology* 108: 189–198.

Cole, R. P., R. C. Barnet, and R. R. Miller. (1995). "Temporal encoding in trace conditioning." *Animal Learning and Behavior* 23: 144–153.

Collett, M., T. S. Collett, S. Bisch, and R. Wehner. (1998). "Local and global vectors in desert ant navigation." *Nature* 394: 269–272.

Collett, T. S. (2002). Spatial learning. In *Stevens' Handbook of Experimental Psychology,* ed. C. R. Gallistel, 3:301–364. New York: John Wiley, and Sons.

Collett, T. S., and J. Baron. (1994). "Biological compasses and the coordinate frame of landmark memories in honeybees." *Nature* 368: 137–140.

Collett, T. S., B. A. Cartwright, and B. A. Smith. (1986). "Landmark learning and visuo-spatial memories in gerbils." *Journal of Comparative Physiology A* 158: 835–851.

Collett, T. S., and M. Collett. (2004). "How do insects represent familiar terrain?" *Journal of Physiology* (Paris) 98: 259–264.

Collett, T. S., and A. Kelber. (1988). "The retrieval of visuo-spatial memories by honeybees." *Journal of Comparative Physiology A* 163: 145–150.

Collett, T. S., and M. Lehrer. (1993). "Looking and learning: A spatial pattern in the orientation flight of the wasp Vespula vulgaris." *Proceedings of The Royal Society of London B* 252: 129–134.

Collier-Baker, E., J. M. Davis, and T. Suddendorf. (2004). "Do dogs (Canis familiaris) understand invisible displacement?" *Journal of Comparative Psychology* 118: 421–433.

Collier-Baker, E., and T. Suddendorf. (2006). "Do chimpanzees (Pan troglodytes) and 2-year-old children (Homo sapiens) understand double invisible displacement?" *Journal of Comparative Psychology* 120: 89–97.

Collins, S. A. (1995). "The effect of recent experience on female choice in zebra finches." *Animal Behaviour* 49: 479–486.

———. Vocal fighting and flirting: The functions of birdsong. In *Nature's Music: The Science of Birdsong,* ed. P. Marler and H. Slabbekoorn, 39–79. San Diego: Elsevier.

Colombo, M., and N. Frost. (2001). "Representation of serial order in humans: A comparison to the findings with monkeys (Cebus apella)." *Psychonomic Bulletin & Review* 8: 262–269.

Coltheart, M. (1999). "Modularity and cognition." *Trends in Cognitive Sciences* 3: 115–120.

Colwill, R. M. (1996). Detecting associations in Pavlovian conditioning and instrumental learning in vertebrates and in invertebrates. In *Neuroethological Studies of Cognitive and Perceptual Processes,* ed. C. F. Moss and S. J. Shettleworth, 31–62. Boulder, CO: Westview Press.

Colwill, R. M., and D. K. Motzkin. (1994). "Encoding of the unconditioned stimulus in Pavlovian conditioning." *Animal Learning and Behavior* 22: 384–394.

Colwill, R. M., and R. A. Rescorla. (1985). "Postconditioning devaluation of a reinforcer affects intrumental responding." *Journal of Experimental Psychology: Animal Behavior Processes* 11: 120–132.

Connor, R. C. (2007). "Dolphin social intelligence: Complex alliance relationships in bottlenose dolphins and a consideration of selective environments for extreme brain size evolution in mammals." *Philosophical Transactions of the Royal Society B* 362: 587–602.

Cook, A., O. S. Bamford, J. D. B. Freeman, and D. J. Teideman. (1969). "A study of the homing habit of the limpet." *Animal Behaviour* 17: 330–339.

Cook, M., and S. Mineka. (1990). "Selective associations in the observational conditioning of fear in rhesus monkeys." *Journal of Experimental Psychology: Animal Behavior Processes* 16: 372–389.

Cook, R. G., ed. (2001a). *Avian Visual Cognition.* Boston: Comparative Cognition Press. [On-line]. Available: http://www.pigeon.psy.tufts.edu/avc/toc.htm

———. (2001b). Hierarchical stimulus processing by pigeons. In *Avian Visual Cognition,* ed. R. G. Cook. Boston: Comparative Cognition Press. [On-line]. Available: http://www.pigeon.psy.tufts.edu/avc/toc.htm

———. (1992a). "Acquisition and transfer of visual texture discriminations by pigeons." *Journal of Experimental Psychology: Animal Behavior Processes* 18: 341–353.

———. (1992b). "Dimensional organization and texture discrimination in pigeons." *Journal of Experimental Psychology: Animal Behavior Processes* 18: 354–363.

Cook, R. G., M. F. Brown, and D. A. Riley. (1985). "Flexible memory processing by rats: Use of prospective and retrospective information in the radial maze." *Journal of Experimental Psychology: Animal Behavior Processes* 11: 453–469.

Cook, R. G., D. G. Levison, S. R. Gillett, and A. P. Blaisdell. (2005). "Capacity and limits of associative memory in pigeons." *Psychonomic Bulletin & Review* 12: 350–358.

Cook, R. G., and E. A. Wasserman. (2006). Relational discrimination learning in pigeons. In *Comparative Cognition: Experimental Explorations of Animal Intelligence,* ed. E. A. Wasserman and T. R. Zentall, 307–324. New York: Oxford University Press.

Cooke, F., and J. C. Davies. (1983). Assortative mating, mate choice, and reproductive fitness in Snow Geese. In *Mate Choice,* ed. P. Bateson, 279–295. Cambridge: Cambridge University Press.

Coolen, I., Y. van Bergen, R. L. Day, and K. N. Laland. (2003). "Species difference in adaptive use of public information in sticklebacks." *Proceedings of The Royal Society of London B* 270: 2413–2419.

Coolen, I., A. J. W. Ward, P. J. B. Hart, and K. N. Laland. (2005). "Foraging nine-spined sticklebacks prefer to rely on public information over simpler social cues." *Behavioral Ecology* 16: 865–870.

Corballis, M. C. (2007). "Recursion, language, and starlings." *Cognitive Science* 31: 697–704.

Correia, S. P. C., A. Dickinson, and N. S. Clayton. (2007). "Western scrub-jays anticipate future needs independently of their current motivational state." *Current Biology* 17: 856–861.

Cosmides, L. (1989). "The logic of social exchange: Has natural selection shaped how humans reason? Studies with the Wason selection task." *Cognition* 31: 187–276.

Cosmides, L., and J. Tooby. (1992). Cognitive adaptations for social exchange. In *The Adapted Mind: Evolutionary Psychology and the Generation of Culture,* ed. J. Barkow, L. Cosmides, and J. Tooby, 163–228. New York: Oxford University Press.

———. (1994). Origins of domain specificity: The evolution of functional organization. In *Mapping the Mind,* ed. L. A. Hirschfeld and S. A. Gelman, 85–116. Cambridge: Cambridge University Press.

———. (1995). From function to structure: The role of evolutionary biology and computational theories in cognitive neuroscience. In *The Cognitive Neurosciences,* ed. M. Gazzaniga, 1199–1210. Cambridge, MA: MIT Press.

Coss, R. G., and R. O. Goldthwaite. (1995). The persistence of old designs for perception. In *Perspectives in Ethology,* ed. N. S. Thompson, 11:83–148. New York: Plenum Press.

Couvillon, P. A., and M. E. Bitterman. (1992). "A conventional conditioning analysis of 'transitive inference' in pigeons." *Journal of Experimental Psychology: Animal Behavior Processes* 18: 308–310.

Cowey, A., and P. Stoerig. (1995). "Blindsight in monkeys." *Nature* 373: 247–249.

———. (1997). "Visual detection in monkeys with blindsight." *Neuropsychologia* 35: 929–939.

Cowie, R. C. (1977). "Optimal foraging in great tits (Parus major)." *Nature* 268: 137–139.

Cox, R. F. A., and A. W. Smithsman (2006). "Action planning in young children's tool use." *Developmental Science* 9: 628–641.

Cramer, A. E., and C. R. Gallistel. (1997). "Vervet monkeys as travelling salesmen." *Nature* 387: 464.

Cresswell, W., J. L. Quinn, M. J. Whittingham, and S. Butler. (2003). "Good foragers can also be good at detecting predators." *Proceedings of The Royal Society of London B* 270: 1069–1076.

Cristol, D. A., E. B. Reynolds, J. E. Leclerc, A. H. Donner, C. S. Farabaugh, et al. (2003). "Migratory dark-eyed juncos, Junco hyemalis, have better spatial memory and denser hippocampal neurons than nonmigratory conspecifics." *Animal Behaviour* 66: 317–328.

Cristol, D. A., and P. V. Switzer. (1999). "Avian prey-dropping behavior II: American crows and walnuts." *Behavioral Ecology* 10: 220–226.

Cristol, D. A., P. V. Switzer, K. L. Johnson, and L. S. Walke. (1997). "Crows do not use automobiles as nutcrackers: Putting an anecdote to the test." *Auk* 114: 296–298.

Crockford, C., R. M. Wittig, R. M. Seyfarth, and D. L. Cheney. (2007). "Baboons eavesdrop to deduce mating opportunities." *Animal Behaviour* 73: 885–890.

Croze, H. (1970). "Searching image in carrion crows." *Zietschrift fur Tierpsychologie Supplement* 5: 1–85.

Crystal, J. D. (2001). "Circadian time perception." *Journal of Experimental Psychology: Animal Behavior Processes* 27: 68–78.

———. (2006a). Sensitivity to time: Implications for the representation of time. In *Comparative Cognition: Experimental Explorations of Animal Intelligence,* ed. E. A. Wasserman and T. R. Zentall, 270–284. New York: Oxford University Press.

———. (2006b). "Time, place, and content." *Comparative Cognition & Behavior Reviews* 1: 53–76.

———. (2009). "Elements of episodic-like memory in animal models." *Behavioural Processes* 80: 269–277.

Crystal, J. D., R. M. Church, and H. A. Broadbent. (1997). "Systematic nonlinearities in the memory representation of time." *Journal of Experimental Psychology: Animal Behavior Processes* 23: 267–282.

Crystal, J. D., and S. J. Shettleworth. (1994). "Spatial list learning in black-capped chickadees." *Animal Learning and Behavior* 22: 77–83.

Csibra, G. (2007). "Teachers in the wild." *Trends in Cognitive Sciences* 11: 95–97.

Cullen, E. (1957). "Adaptations in the kittiwake to cliff nesting." *Ibis* 99: 275–302.

Cummins-Sebree, S. E., and D. M. Fragaszy. (2005). "Choosing and using tools: Capuchins (Cebus apella) use a different metric than tamarins (Saguinus oedipus)." *Journal of Comparative Psychology* 119: 210–219.

Curio, E. (1988). Cultural transmission of enemy recognition by birds. In *Social Learning: Psychological and Biological Perspectives,* ed. T. R. Zentall and B. G. Galef Jr., : 75–97. Hillsdale, NJ: Lawrence Erlbaum Associates.

Curio, E., U. Ernst, and W. Vieth. (1978). "The adaptive significance of avian mobbing." *Zeitschrift fur Tierpsychologie* 48: 184–202.

Cusato, B., and M. Domjan. (1998). "Special efficacy of sexual conditioned stimuli that include species typical cues: Tests with a conditioned stimuli preexposure design." *Learning and Motivation* 29: 152–167.

———. (2000). "Facilitation of appetitive conditioning with naturalistic conditioned stimuli: CS and US factors." *Animal Learning & Behavior* 28: 247–256.

Custance, D. M., A. Whiten, and K. A. Bard. (1995). "Can young chimpanzees (Pan troglodytes) imitate arbitrary actions? Hayes, and Hayes. (1952) revisited." *Behaviour* 132: 837–859.

Cuthill, I. C. (2005). "The study of function in behavioural ecology." *Animal Biology* 55: 399–417.

Cuthill, I. C., and T. Guilford. (1990). "Perceived risk and obstacle avoidance in flying birds." *Animal Behaviour* 40: 188–190.

Cuthill, I. C., J. C. Partridge, A. T. D. Bennett, S. C. Church, N. S. Hart, et al. (2000). "Ultraviolet vision in birds." *Advances in the Study of Behavior* 29: 159–214.

Cuthill, I. C., M. Stevens, M. Sheppard, T. Maddocks, C. A. Parraga, et al. (2005). "Disruptive coloration and background pattern matching." *Nature* 434: 72–74.

Cynx, J., and F. Nottebohm. (1992). "Testosterone facilitates some conspecific song discriminations in castrated zebra finches (Taeniopygia guttata)." *Proceedings of the National Academy of Sciences* (USA) 89: 1376–1378.

D'Amato, M. R., and M. Columbo. (1988). "Representation of serial order in monkeys (Cebus apella)." *Journal of Experimental Psychology: Animal Behavior Processes* 14(2): 131–139.

———. (1990). "The symbolic distance effect in monkeys (Cebus apella)." *Animal Learning & Behavior* 18: 133–140.

D'Amato, M. R., D. P. Salmon, and M. Colombo. (1985). "Extent and limits of the matching concept in monkeys (Cebus apella)." *Journal of Experimental Psychology: Animal Behavior Processes* 11: 35–51.

D'Amato, M. R., and P. Van Sant. (1988). "The person concept in monkeys." *Journal of Experimental Psychology: Animal Behavior Processes* 14: 43–55.

D'eath, R. B. (1998). "Can video images imitate real stimuli in animal behaviour experiments?" *Biological Reviews of the Cambridge Philosophical Society* 73: 267–292.

Dallal, N. L., and W. H. Meck. (1990). "Hierarchical structures: Chunking by food type facilitates spatial memory." *Journal of Experimental Psychology: Animal Behavior Processes* 16: 69–84.

Dally, J. M., N. S. Clayton, and N. J. Emery. (2006). "The behaviour and evolution of cache protection and pilferage." *Animal Behaviour* 72: 13–23.

Dally, J. M., N. J. Emery, and N. S. Clayton. (2006). "Food-caching western scrub-jays keep track of who was watching when." *Science* 312: 1662–1665.

Daly, M., J. Rauschenberger, and P. Behrends. (1982). "Food aversion learning in kangaroo rats: A specialist-generalist comparison." *Animal Learning and Behavior* 10: 314–320.

Daly, M., and M. I. Wilson. (1999). "Human evolutionary psychology and animal behaviour." *Animal Behaviour* 57: 509–519.

Danchin, É., L.-A. Giraldeau, and F. Cezilly, eds. (2008). *Behavioural Ecology.* Oxford: Oxford University Press.

Danchin, É., L.-A. Giraldeau, T. J. Valone, and R. H. Wagner. (2004). "Public information: From nosy neighbours to cultural evolution." *Science* 305: 487–491.

Darst, C. R. (2006). "Predator learning, experimental psychology, and novel predictions for mimicry dynamics." *Animal Behaviour* 71: 743–748.

Darst, C. R., and M. E. Cummings. (2006). "Predator learning favors mimicry of a less-toxic model in poison frogs." *Nature* 440: 208–211.

Darwin, C. (1859). *The Origin of Species.* London: John Murray.

———. (1871). *The Descent of Man and Selection in Relation to Sex.* London: John Murray.

———. (1872/1965). *The Expression of the Emotions in Man and Animals.* Chicago: University of Chicago Press.

———. (1873). "Origin of certain instincts." *Nature* 7: 417–418.

———. (1879/2004). *The Descent of Man and Selection in Relation to Sex.* London: Penguin.

Dasser, V. (1988a). "A social concept in Java monkeys." *Animal Behaviour* 36: 225–230.

———. (1988b). Mapping social concepts in monkeys. In *Machiavellian Intelligence: Social Expertise and the Evolution of Intellect in Monkeys, Apes, and Humans,* ed. R. W. Byrne and A. Whiten, 85–93. Oxford: Clarendon Press.

Dasser, V., I. Ulbaek, and D. Premack. (1989). "The perception of intention." *Science* 243: 365–367.

Daunt, F., V. Afanasyev, A. Adam, J. P. Croxall, and S. Wanless. (2007). "From cradle to early grave: Juvenile mortality in European shags Phalacrocorax aristotelis results from inadequate development of foraging proficiency." *Biology Letters* 3: 371–374.

Dautenhahn, K. (2007). Socially intelligent robots: dimensions of human-robot interaction. In *Social Intelligence: From Brain to Culture,* ed. N. J. Emery, N. S. Clayton, and C. Frith, 313–351. Oxford: Oxford University Press.

Davey, G. C. L. (1995). "Preparedness and phobias: Specific evolved associations or a generalized expectancy bias?" *Behavioral and Brain Sciences* 13: 289–325.

Davies, N. B. (1977). "Prey selection and the search strategy of the spotted flycatcher (Muscicapa striata): A field study on optimal foraging." *Animal Behaviour* 25: 1016–1033.

Davies, N. B., and M. d. L. Brooke. (1988). "Cuckoos versus red warblers: Adaptations and counteradaptations." *Animal Behaviour* 36: 262–284.

Davies, N. B., M. d. L. Brooke, and A. Kacelnik. (1996). "Recognition errors and probability of parasitism determine whether reed warblers should accept or reject mimetic cuckoo eggs." *Proceedings of The Royal Society of London B* 263: 925–931.

Davis, H. (1984). "Discrimination of the number three by a racoon." *Animal Learning and Behaviour* 12: 409–413.

Davis, H., and S. A. Bradford. (1986). "Counting behaviour by rats in a simulated natural environment." *Ethology* 73: 265–280.

Davis, H., and J. Memmott. (1982). "Counting behaviour in animals: A critical evaluation." *Psychological Bulletin* 92(3): 547–571.

Davis, H., and R. Perusse. (1988). "Numerical competence in animals: Definitional issues, current evidence, and a new research agenda." The *Behavioral and Brain Sciences* 11: 561–615.

Davis, J. M., and J. A. Stamps. (2004). "The effect of natal experience on habitat preferences." *Trends in Ecology and Evolution* 19: 411–416.

Davis, M. (1970). "Effects of interstimulus interval length and variability on startle-response habituation in the rat." *Journal of Comparative and Physiological Psychology* 72: 177–192.

Davis, M., W. A. Falls, S. Campeau, and M. Kim. (1993). "Fear-potentiated startle: a neural and pharmacological analysis." *Behavioural Brain Research* 58: 175–198.

Davis, M., and S. E. File. (1984). Intrinsic and extrinsic mechanisms of habituation and sensitization: Implications for the design and analysis of experiments. In *Habituation, Sensitization, and Behavior,* ed. H. V. S. Peeke and L. F. Petrinovich, 287–323. Orlando, FL: Academic Press, Inc. .

Davis, M., L. S. Schlesinger, and C. A. Sorenson. (1989). "Temporal specificity of fear conditioning: Effects of different conditioned stimulus–unconditioned stimulus intervals on the fear-potential startle effect." *Journal of Experimental Psychology: Animal Behavior Processes* 15: 295–310.

Davis, M., and A. R. Wagner. (1969). "Habituation of startle response under incremental sequence of stimulus intensities." *Journal of Comparative and Physiological Psychology* 67: 486–492.

Dawkins, M. (1971). "Perceptual changes in chicks: Another look at the 'search image' concept." *Animal Behaviour* 19: 566–574.

———— (1989). "The future of ethology: How many legs are we standing on?" *Perspectives in Ethology* 8: 47–54.

————. (1993). *Through our eyes only?* Oxford: W. H. Freeman.

————. (1995). *Unravelling Animal Behaviour.* Harlow, Essex, UK: Longman Scientific and Technical.

————. (2006). "A user's guide to animal welfare science." *Trends in Ecology and Evolution* 21: 77–82.

Dawkins, M. S., T. Guilford, V. A. Braithwaite, and J. R. Krebs. (1996). "Discrimination and recognition of photographs of places by homing pigeons." *Behavioural Processes* 36: 27–38.

Dawkins, M. S., and A. Woodington. (1997). "Distance and the presentation of visual stimuli to birds." *Animal Behaviour* 54: 1019–1025.

————. (2000). "Pattern recognition and active vision in chickens." *Nature* 403: 652–655.

Dawkins, R. (1976). *The Selfish Gene.* Oxford: Oxford University Press.

————. (1995). "God's utility function." *Scientific American* 273: 80–85.

Dawson, B. V., and B. M. Foss. (1965). "Observational learning in budgerigars." *Animal Behaviour* 13: 470–474.

De Houwer, J. (2009). "The propositional approach to associative learning as an alternative for association formation models." *Learning & Behavior* 37: 1–20.

de Kort, S. R., and N. S. Clayton. (2006). "An evolutionary perspective on caching by corvids." *Proceedings of the Royal Society B-Biological Sciences* 273: 417–423.

de Kort, S. R., S. P. C. Correia, D. M. Alexis, A. Dickinson, and N. Clayton. (2007). "The control of food-caching behavior by Western scrub-jays (Aphelocoma californica)." *Journal of Experimental Psychology: Animal Behavior Processes* 33: 361–370.

de Kort, S. R., A. Dickinson, and N. S. Clayton. (2005). "Retrospective cognition by food-caching western scrub-jays." *Learning and Motivation* 36: 159–176.

de Veer, M. W., and R. van den Bos. (1999). "A critical review of methodology and interpretation of mirror self-recognition research in nonhuman primates." *Animal Behaviour* 58: 459–468.

de Waal, F. B. M. (1999). "Anthropomorphism and anthropodenial: Consistency in our thinking about humans and other animals." *Philosophical Topics* 27: 255–280.

————. (2000). "Attitudinal reciprocity in food sharing among brown capuchin monkeys." *Animal Behaviour* 60: 253–261.

————. (2008). "Putting the altruism back into altruism: The evolution of empathy." *Annual Review of Psychology* 59: 279–300.

de Waal, F. B. M., C. Boesch, V. Horner, and A. Whiten. (2008). "Comparing social skills of children and apes." *Science* 319: 569.

de Waal, F. B. M., M. Dindo, C. A. Freeman, and M. J. Hall. (2005). "The monkey in the mirror: Hardly a stranger." *Proceedings of the National Academy of Sciences* (USA) 102: 11140–11147.

de Waal, F. B. M., and P. L. Tyack, eds. (2003). *Animal Social Complexity*. Cambridge, MA: Harvard University Press.

Deacon, T. W. (1995). On telling growth from parcellation in brain evolution. In *Behavioural Brain Research in Naturalistic and Semi-Naturalistic Settings*, ed. E. Alleva, A. Fasolo, H.-P. Lipp, L. Nadel, and L. Ricceri, 37–62. Dordrecht: Kluwer Academic Publishers.

Deaner, R. O., A. V. Khera, and M. L. Platt. (2005). "Monkeys pay per view: Adaptive valuation of social images by rhesus macaques." *Current Biology* 15: 543–548.

Dehaene, S., V. Izard, E. Spelke, and P. Pica. (2008). "Log or linear? Distinct intuitions of the number scale in Western and Amazonian indigene cultures." *Science* 320: 1217–1220.

Delamater, A. R., and P. C. Holland. (2008). "The influence of CS-US interval on several different indices of learning in appetitive conditioning." *Journal of Experimental Psychology: Animal Behavior Processes* 34: 202–222.

Delius, J. D., J. Emmerton, W. Horster, R. Jager, and J. Ostheim. (2000). Picture-object recognition in pigeons. Picture perception in animals. J. Fagot. Philadelphia, Taylor, and Francis Inc: 1–35.

Delius, J. D., M. Jitsumori, and M. Siemann. (2000). Stimulus equivalencies through discrimination reversals. In *The Evolution of Cognition,* ed. C. Heyes and L. Huber: 103–122. Cambridge, MA: MIT Press.

Delius, J. D., and M. Siemann. (1998). "Transitive responding in animals and humans: Exaptation rather than adaptation?" *Behavioural Processes* 42: 107–137.

Delius, J. D., G. Thompson, K. L. Allen, and J. Emmerton. (1972). "Colour mixing and colour preferences in neonate gulls." *Experientia* 28: 1244–1246.

Dennett, D. C. (1983). "Intentional systems in cognitive ethology: The 'Panglossian paradigm' defended." *Behavioral and Brain Sciences* 6: 343–390.

————. (1987). *The Intentional Stance*. Cambridge, MA: MIT Press.

————. (1995). *Darwin's Dangerous Idea*. New York: Simon and Schuster.

————. (1996). *Kinds of Minds*. New York: Basic Books.

Denniston, J. C., R. R. Miller, and H. Matute. (1996). "Biological significance as a determinant of cue competition." *Psychological Science* 7: 325–331.

Dere, E., E. Kart-Teke, J. P. Huston, and M. A. De Souza Silva. (2006). "The case for episodic memory in animals." *Neuroscience and Biobehavioral Reviews* 30: 1206–1224.

Devenport, L. D. (1989). "Sampling behavior and contextual change." *Learning and Motivation* 20: 97–114.

————. (1998). "Spontaneous recovery without interference: Why remembering is adaptive." *Animal Learning & Behavior* 26: 172–181.

Devenport, L. D., and J. A. Devenport. (1994). "Time-dependent averaging of foraging information in least chipmunks and golden-mantled ground squirrels." *Animal Behaviour* 47: 787–802.

Devenport, L. D., T. Hill, M. Wilson, and E. Ogden. (1997). "Tracking and averaging in variable environments: A transition rule." *Journal of Experimental Psychology: Animal Behavior Processes* 23: 450–460.

Dewsbury, D. A. (1998). "Animal psychology in journals, 1911–1927: Another look at the snark." *Journal of Comparative Psychology* 112: 400–405.

————. (2000). "Comparative cognition in the 1930s." *Psychonomic Bulletin & Review* 7: 267–283.

Dickinson, A. (1980). *Contemporary Animal Learning Theory*. Cambridge: Cambridge University Press.

————. (1994). Instrumental conditioning. In *Animal Learning and Cognition*, ed. N. J. Mackintosh, 45–79. San Diego, CA: Academic Press.

————. (2001a). "Causal learning: Association versus computation." *Current Directions in Psychological Science* 10: 127–132.

————. (2001b). "Causal learning: An associative analysis." *The Quarterly Journal of Experimental Psychology* 54B: 3–25.

————. (2007). Learning: The need for a hybrid theory. In *Science of Memory: Concepts*, ed. H. L. Roediger, Y. Dudai, and S. Fitzpatrick, 41–44. Oxford: Oxford University Press.

————. (2008). Why a rat is not a beast machine. In *Frontiers of Consciousness*, ed. M. Davies and L. Weiskrantz. Oxford: Oxford University Press, 275–288. .

————. (2009). "What are association formation models." *Learning & Behavior* 37: 21–24.

Dickinson, A., and B. Balleine. (1994). "Motivational control of goal-directed action." *Animal Learning and Behavior* 22: 1–18.

————. (2000). Causal cognition and goal-directed action. *The Evolution of Cognition*. C. Heyes and L. Huber: 185–204. Cambridge MA, MIT Press

————. (2002). The role of learning in the operation of motivational systems. In *Stevens' Handbook of Experimental Psychology*, ed. C. R. Gallistel, 3:497–533. New York: John Wiley, and Sons.

Dickinson, A., B. Balleine, A. Watt, F. Gonzalez, and R. A. Boakes. (1995). "Motivational control after extended instrumental training." *Animal Learning & Behavior* 23: 197–206.

Dickinson, A., and B. W. Balleine. (2000). Causal cognition and goal-directed action. In *The Evolution of Cognition*, ed. C. Heyes, and L. Huber, 185–204. Cambridge, MA: MIT Press.

Diez-Chamizo, V., D. Sterio, and N. J. Mackintosh. (1985). "Blocking and overshadowing between intra-maze and extra-maze cues: A test of the independance of locale and guidance learning." *The Quarterly Journal of Experimental Psychology* 37B: 235–253.

Dindo, M., B. Thierry, and A. Whiten. (2008). "Social diffusion of novel foraging methods in brown capuchin monkeys (Cebus apella)." *Proceedings of the Royal Society B* 275: 187–193.

Dingemanse, N. J., and D. Reale. (2005). "Natural selection and animal personality." *Behaviour* 142: 1159–1184.

Dolman, C. S., J. Templeton, and L. Lefebvre. (1996). "Mode of foraging competition is related to tutor preference in Zenaida aurita." *Journal of Comparative Psychology* 110: 45–54.

Domjan, M. (1983). "Biological constraints on instrumental and classical conditioning: Implications for general process theory." *The Psychology of Learning and Motivation* 17: 215–277.

————. (2003). "Stepping outside the box in considering the C/T ratio." *Behavioural Processes* 62: 103–114.

————. (2005). "Pavlovian conditioning: A functional perspective." *Annual Review of Psychology* 56: 179–206.

Domjan, M., E. Blesbois, and J. Williams. (1998). "The adaptive significance of sexual conditioning: Pavlovian control of sperm release." *Psychological Science* 9: 411–415.

Domjan, M., and B. Burkhard. (1986). *The Principles of Learning & Behavior*. Monterey, CA: Brooks/Cole Publishing Company.

Domjan, M., B. Cusato, and M. Krause. (2004). "Learning with arbitrary versus ecological conditioned stimuli: Evidence from sexual conditioning." *Psychonomic Bulletin & Review* 11: 232–246.

Domjan, M., and J. Galef, B.G. (1983). "Biological constraints on instrumental and classical conditioning: Retrospect and prospect." *Animal Learning and Behavior* 11: 151–161.

Domjan, M., and M. A. Krause. (2002). "Research productivity in animal learning from 1953 to 2000." *Animal Learning & Behavior* 30: 282–285.

Domjan, M., and N. E. Wilson. (1972). "Specificity of cue to consequence in aversion learning in the rat." *Psychonomic Science* 26: 143–145.

Donaldson, M. C., M. Lachmann, and C. T. Bergstrom. (2007). "The evolution of functionally referential meaning in a structured world." *Journal of Theoretical Biology* 246: 225–233.

Dooling, R. J. (2004). Audition: can birds hear everything they sing? In *Nature's Music: The Science of Birdsong*, ed. P. Marler and H. Slabbekoorn, 206–225. San Diego: Elsevier.

Dooling, R. J., S. D. Brown, G. M. Klump, and K. Okanoya. (1992). "Auditory perception of conspecific and heterospecific vocalizations in birds: Evidence for special processes." *Journal of Comparative Psychology* 106: 20–28.

Dooling, R. J., S. D. Brown, K. Manabe, and E. F. Powell. (1996). The perceptual foundations of vocal learning in Budgerigars. In *Neuroethological Studies of Cognitive and Perceptual Processes*, ed. C. F. Moss and S. J. Shettleworth, 113–137. Boulder, CO: Westview Press.

Dooling, R. J., S. D. Brown, T. J. Park, and K. Okanoya. (1990). Natural perceptual categories for vocal signals in budgerigars (Melopsittacus undulatus). In *Comparative Perception*, ed. W. C. Stebbins and M. A. Berkle, 2:345–374. New York: Wiley.

Dore, F. Y., and C. Dumas. (1987). "Psychology of *Animal Cognition*: Piagetian studies." *Psychological Bulletin* 102: 219–233.

Dore, F. Y., S. Fiset, S. Goulet, M.-C. Dumas, and S. Gagnon. (1996). "Search behavior in cats and dogs: Interspecific differences in working memory and spatial cognition." *Animal Learning & Behavior* 24: 142–149.

Dorrance, B. R., and T. R. Zentall. (2001). "Imitative learning in Japanese quail (Coturnix japonica) depends on the motivational state of the observer quail at the time of observation." *Journal of Comparative Psychology* 115: 62–67.

Driessen, G., C. Bernstein, J. J. M. Van Alphen & A. Kacelnik (1995). "A count-down mechanism for host search in the parasitoid *Ventura canescens*." *Journal of Animal Ecology* 64: 117–125.

Dudai, Y. (2004). "The neurobiology of consolidation, or, how stable is the engram?" *Annual Review of Psychology* 55: 51–86.

Dufour, V., M. Pelé, E. H. M. Sterck, and B. Thierry. (2007). "Chimpanzee (Pan troglodytes) anticipation of food return: coping with waiting time in an exchange task." *Journal of Comparative Psychology* 121: 145–155.

Dugatkin, L. A. (1996). Copying and mate choice. In *Social Learning in Animals: The Roots of Culture*, ed. C. M. Heyes and B. G. Galef Jr., 85–105. San Diego: Academic Press.

———. (2004). *Principles of Animal Behavior*. New York: W. W. Norton and Company.

Dukas, R., ed. (1998). *Cognitive Ecology*. Chicago: University of Chicago Press.

———. (1998). Evolutionary ecology of learning. In *Cognitive Ecology*, ed. R. Dukas, 129–174. Chicago: University of Chicago Press.

———. (1999). "Costs of memory: Ideas and predictions." *Journal of Theoretical Biology* 197: 41–50.

———. (2004). "Causes and consequences of limited attention." *Brain Behavior and Evolution* 63: 197–210.

———. (2008). "Evolutionary biology of insect learning." *Annual Review of Entomology* 53: 8.1–8.16.

———. (2009). Learning: Mechanisms, ecology and evolution. In *Cognitive Ecology II*, ed. R. Dukas and J. M. Ratcliffe. Chicago: University of Chicago Press.

Dukas, R., and E. A. Bernays. (2000). "Learning improves growth rate in grasshoppers." *Proceedings of the National Academy of Sciences* (USA) 97: 2637–2640.

Dukas, R., and J. J. Duan. (2000). "Potential fitness consequences of associative learning in a parasitoid wasp." *Behavioral Ecology* 11: 536–543.

Dukas, R., and A. C. Kamil. (2000). "The cost of limited attention in blue jays." *Behavioral Ecology* 11: 502–506.

———. (2001). "Limited attention: The constraint underlying search image." *Behavioral Ecology* 12: 192–199.

Dukas, R., and J. M. Ratcliffe, eds. (2009). *Cognitive Ecology II*. Chicago: University of Chicago Press.

Dukas, R., and N. M. Waser. (1994). "Categorization of food types enhances foraging performance of bumblebees." *Animal Behaviour* 48: 1001–1006.

Dunbar, R. I. M., and L. Barrett, eds. (2007). *The Oxford Handbook of Evolutionary Psychology*. Oxford: Oxford University Press.

Dunbar, R. I. M., and S. Shultz. (2007). "Evolution in the social brain." *Science* 317: 1344–1347.

———. (2007). "Understanding primate brain evolution." *Philosophical Transactions of the Royal Society B* 362: 649–658.

Dunlap, J. C., J. J. Loros, and P. J. Decoursey, eds. (2003). *Chronobiology: Biological Timekeeping*. Sunderland, MA: Sinauer Associates Inc.

Dusek, J. A., and H. Eichenbaum. (1997). "The hippocampus and memory for orderly stimulus relations." *Proceedings of the National Academy of Sciences* (USA) 94: 7109–7114.

Dusenbery, D. B. (1992). *Sensory Ecology*. New York: W.H. Freeman and Company.

Dwyer, D. M. (2003). "Learning about cues in their absence: Evidence from flavour preferences and aversions." *The Quarterly Journal of Experimental Psychology* 56B: 56–67.

Dyer, A. G., and L. Chittka. (2004). "Bumblebees (Bombus terrestris) sacrifice foraging speed to solve difficult colour discrimination tasks." *Journal of Comparative Physiology* A 190: 759–763.

Dyer, F. C. (1991). "Bees acquire route-based memories but not cognitive maps in a familiar landscape." *Animal Behaviour* 41(2): 239–246.

———. (1994). Spatial cognition and navigation in insects. In *Behavioral Mechanisms in Evolutionary Ecology*, ed. L. Real, 66–98. Chicago: University of Chicago Press.

———. (1996). "Spatial memory and navigation by honeybees on the scale of the foraging range." *The Journal of Experimental Biology* 199: 147–154.

———. (1998). Cognitive ecology of navigation. In *Cognitive Ecology*, ed. R. Dukas, 201–260. Chicago: University of Chicago Press.

———. (2002). "The biology of the dance language." *Annual Review of Entomology* 47: 917–949.

Dyer, F. C., and J. A. Dickinson. (1994). "Development of sun compensation by honeybees: How partially experienced bees estimate the sun's course." *Proceedings of the National Academy of Science* (USA) 91: 4471–4474.

———. (1996). "Sun-compass learning in insects: Representation in a simple mind." *Current Directions in Psychological Science* 5: 67–72.

Eacott, M. J., and G. Norman. (2004). "Integrated memory for object, place, and context in rats: A possible model of episodic-like memory?" *Journal of Neuroscience* 24: 1948–1953.

Eichenbaum, H. (2008). *Learning & Memory*. New York: W.W. Norton.

Eichenbaum, H., A. Fagan, and N. J. Cohen. (1986). "Normal olfactory discrimination learning set and facilitation of reversal learning after medial-temporal damage in rats: Implications for an account of preserved learning abilities in amnesia." *Journal of Neuroscience* 6: 1876–1884.

Eichenbaum, H., N. J. Fortin, C. Ergorul, S. P. Wright, and K. L. Agster. (2005). "Episodic recollection in animals: 'If it walks like a duck and quacks like a duck … ' " *Learning and Motivation* 36: 190–207.

Eiserer, L. A. (1980). "Development of filial attachment to static visual features of an imprinting object." *Animal Learning & Behavior* 8: 159–166.

Eiserer, L. A., and H. S. Hoffman. (1973). "Priming of ducklings' responses by presenting an imprinted stimulus." *Journal of Comparative and Physiological Psychology* 82: 345–359.

Elgar, M. A. (1989). "Predator vigilance and group size in mammals and birds: A critical review of the emprical evidence." *Biological Review* 64: 13–33.

Ellen, P., B. J. Soteres, and C. Wages. (1984). "Problem solving in the rat: Piecemeal acquisition of cognitive maps." *Animal Learning and Behavior* 12(2): 232–237.

Emery, N. J. (2000). "The eyes have it: The neuroethology, function and evolution of social gaze." *Neuroscience and Biobehavioral Reviews* 24: 581–604.

———. (2006). "Cognitive ornithology: The evolution of avian intelligence." *Philosophical Transactions of the Royal Society B* 361: 23–43.

Emery, N. J., and N. S. Clayton. (2001). "Effects of experience and social context on prospective caching strategies by scrub jays." *Nature* 414: 443–446.

———. (2004). "The mentality of crows: Convergent evolution of intelligence in corvids and apes." *Science* 306: 1903–1907.

———. (2009). "Comparative social cognition." *Annual Review of Psychology* 60: 17.1–17.27.

Emery, N. J., N. S. Clayton, and C. Frith, eds. (2007). *Social Intelligence: From Brain to Culture*. Oxford: Oxford University Press.

Emery, N. J., E. N. Lorincz, D. I. Perrett, M. W. Oram, and C. I. Baker. (1997). "Gaze following and joint attention in rhesus monkeys (Macaca mulatta)." *Journal of Comparative Psychology* 111: 286–293.

Emery, N. J., A. M. Seed, A. M. P. von Bayern, and N. S. Clayton. (2007). "Cognitive adaptations of social bonding in birds." *Philosophical Transactions of the Royal Society B* 362: 489–505.

Emlen, S. T. (1970). "Celestial rotation: Its importance in the development of migratory orientation." *Science* 170: 1198–1201.

Emmerton, J. (2001). Birds' judgments of number and quantity. In *Avian Visual Cognition*, ed. R. G. Cook. Boston: Comparative Cognition Press. [On-line]. Available: http://www.pigeon.psy.tufts.edu/avc/toc.htm

Emmerton, J., and J. C. Renner. (2006). "Scalar effects in the visual discrimination of numerosity by pigeons." *Learning & Behavior* 34: 176–192.

Endler, J. A. (1986). *Natural Selection in the Wild*. Princeton, NJ: Princeton University Press.

———. (1991). "Variation in the appearance of guppy color patterns to guppies and their predators under different visual conditions." *Vision Research* 31: 587–608.

———. (1992). "Signals, signal conditions, and the direction of evolution." *American Naturalist* 139, supplement: S125-S153.

Endler, J. A., and A. L. Basolo. (1998). "Sensory ecology, receiver biases and sexual selection." *Trends in Ecology and Evolution* 13: 415–420.

Endler, J. A., and P. W. Mielke. (2005). "Comparing entire color patterns as birds see them." *Biological Journal of the Linnean Society* 86: 405–431.

Endler, J. A., and M. Thery. (1996). "Interacting effects of lek placement, display behavior, ambient light, and color patterns in three neotropical forest-dwelling birds." *American Naturalist* 148: 421–452.

Endler, J. A., D. A. Westcott, J. R. Madden, and T. Robson. (2005). "Animal visual systems and the evolution of color patterns: Sensory processing illuminates signal evolution." *Evolution* 59: 1795–1818.

Engh, A. L., E. R. Siebert, D. A. Greenberg, and K. E. Holekamp. (2005). "Patterns of alliance formation and postconflict aggression indicate spotted hyaenas recognize third-party relationships." *Animal Behaviour* 69: 209–217.

Epstein, R. (1985). "Animal cognition as the praxist views it." *Neuroscience & Biobehavioral Reviews* 9: 623–630.

Epstein, R., C. E. Kirshnit, R. P. Lanza, and L. C. Rubin. (1984). "'Insight' in the pigeon: antecedents and determinants of an intelligent performance." *Nature* 308: 61–62.

Epstein, R., R. P. Lanza, and B. F. Skinner. (1980). "Symbolic communication between two pigeons (Columba livia domestica)." *Science* 207: 543–545.

Esch, H. E., S. Zhang, M. V. Srinivasan, and J. Tautz. (2001). "Honeybee dances communicate distances measured bu optic flow." *Nature* 411: 581–583.

Estes, W. K. (1950). "Towards a statistical theory of learning." *Psychological Review* 57: 94–107.

Etienne, A. S. (1973). Developmental stages and cognitive structures as determinants of what is learned. In *Constraints on Learning*, ed. R. A. Hinde and J. Stevenson-Hinde, 371–395. New York: Academic Press.

———. (1992). "Navigation of a small mammal by dead reckoning and local cues." *Current Directions in Psychological Science* 1: 48–52.

———. (2003). How does path integration interact with olfaction, vision, and the representation of space? In *The Neurobiology of Spatial Behaviour*, ed. K. J. Jeffery, 48–66. Oxford: Oxford University Press.

Etienne, A. S., and K. J. Jeffery. (2004). "Path integration in mammals." *Hippocampus* 14: 180–192.

Etienne, A. S., R. Maurer, J. Berlie, B. Reverdin, T. Rowe, et al. (1998). "Navigation through vector addition." *Nature* 396: 161–164.

Etienne, A. S., R. Maurer, and F. Saucy. (1988). "Limitations in the assessment of path dependent information." *Behaviour* 106: 81–111.

Etienne, A. S., E. Teroni, C. Hurni, and V. Portenier. (1990). "The effect of a single light cue on homing behaviour of the golden hamster." *Animal Behaviour* 39(1): 17–41.

Evans, C. S. (1997). "Referential signals." *Perspectives in Ethology* 12: 99–143.

Evans, C. S., and L. Evans. (1999). "Chicken food calls are functionally referential." *Animal Behaviour* 58: 307–319.

———. (2007). "Representational signalling in birds." *Biology Letters* 3: 8–11.

Evans, C. S., L. Evans, and P. Marler. (1993). "On the meaning of alarm calls: functional reference in an avian vocal system." *Animal Behaviour* 46: 23–38.

Evans, C. S., J. M. Macedonia, and P. Marler. (1993). "Effects of apparent size and speed on the response of chickens, Gallus gallus, to computer-generated simulations of aerial predators." *Animal Behaviour* 46: 1–11.

Evans, C. S., and P. Marler. (1992). "Female appearance as a factor in the responsiveness of male chickens during anti-predator behaviour and courtship." *Animal Behaviour* 43: 137–145.

———. (1994). "Food calling and audience effects in male chickens, Gallus gallus: Their relationships to food availability, courtship and social facilitation." *Animal Behaviour* 47: 1159–1170.

———. (1995). Language and animal communication: Parallels and contrasts. In *Comparative Approaches to Cognitive Science,* ed. H. L. Roitblat and J.-A. Meyer, 342–382. Cambridge, MA: MIT Press.

Evans, H. E., and J. B. Heiser. (2004). What's inside: Anatomy and physiology. In *Handbook of Bird Biology,* ed. S. Podulka, R. W. Rohrbaugh Jr., and R. Bonney, 4.3–4.94. Princeton, NJ: Princeton University Press.

Evans, J. S. B. T. (2002). "Logic and human reasoning: An assessment of the deduction paradigm." *Psychological Bulletin* 128: 978–996.

Ewer, R. F. (1969). "The 'instinct to teach.'" *Nature* 222: 698.

Ewert, J.-P. (2005). Stimulus perception. In *The Behavior of Animals,* ed. J. J. Bolhuis and L.-A. Giraldeau, 13–40. Maldon, MA: Blackwell.

Fagot, J., ed. (2000). *Picture Perception in Animals.* Philadelphia: Taylor, and Francis Inc.

Fagot, J., and R. G. Cook. (2006). "Evidence for large long-term memory capacities in baboons and pigeons and its implications for learning and the evolution of cognition." *Proceedings of the National Academy of Science* 103: 17564–17567.

Fagot, J., J. Martin-Malivel, and D. Depy. (2000). What is the evidence for an equivalence between objects and pictures in birds and nonhuman primates? In *Picture Perception in Animals,* ed. J. Fagot, 295–320. Philadelphia: Taylor, and Francis Inc.

Falls, J. B. (1982). Individual recognition by sounds in birds. In *Acoustic Communication in Birds,* ed. D. E. Kroodsma and E. H. Miller, 2:237–278. New York: Academic Press Inc. .

Falls, J. B., and R. J. Brooks. (1975). "Individual recognition by song in white-throated sparrows. II. Effects of location." *Canadian Journal of Zoology* 53: 1412–1420.

Fanselow, M. S. (1994). "Neural organization of the defensive behavior system responsible for fear." *Psychonomic Bulletin and Review* 1: 429–438.

Fanselow, M. S., and L. S. Lester. (1988). A functional behavioristic approach to aversively motivated behavior: Predatory imminence as a determinant of the topography of defensive behavior. In *Evolution and Learning,* ed. R. C. Bolles and M. D. Beecher, 185–212. Hillsdale, NJ: Lawrence Erlbaum Associates.

Fanselow, M. S., and A. M. Poulos. (2005). "The neuroscience of mammalian associative learning." *Annual Review of Psychology* 56: 207–234.

Fantino, E., and N. Abarca. (1985). "Choice, optimal foraging, and the delay-reduction hypothesis." *Behavioral and Brain Sciences* 8: 315–330.

Fawcett, T. W., and R. A. Johnstone. (2003). "Optimal assessment of multiple cues." *Proceedings of The Royal Society of London B.* 270: 1637–1643.

Fehr, E. (2002). "The economics of impatience." *Nature* 415: 269–272.

Feigenson, L., and S. Carey. (2005). "On the limits of infants' quantification of small object arrays." *Cognition* 97: 295–313.

Feigenson, L., S. Carey, and M. Hauser. (2002). "The representations underlying infants' choice of more: Object files versus analog magnitudes." *Psychological Science* 13: 150–156.

Feigenson, L., S. Dehaene, and E. Spelke. (2004). "Core systems of number." *Trends in Cognitive Sciences* 8: 307–314.

Ferbinteanu, J., P. J. Kennedy, and M. L. Shapiro. (2006). "Episodic memory—from brain to mind." *Hippocampus* 16: 691–703.

Ferkin, M. H., A. Combs, J. delBarco-Trillo, A. A. Pierce, and S. Franklin. (2008). "Meadow voles, Microtus pennsylvanicus, have the capacity to recall the 'what,' 'where,' and 'when' of a single past event." *Animal Cognition* 11: 147–159.

Fernandez-Juricic, E., J. T. Erichsen, and A. Kacelnik. (2004). "Visual perception and social foraging in birds." *Trends in Ecology and Evolution* 19: 25–31.

Fetterman, J. G. (1993). "Numerosity discrimination: Both time and number matter." *Journal of Experimental Psychology: Animal Behavior Processes* 19: 149–164.

———. (1996). "Dimensions of stimulus complexity." *Journal of Experimental Psychology: Animal Behavior Processes* 22: 3–18.

Finlay, B. L., R. B. Darlington, and N. Nicastro. (2001). "Developmental structure and brain evolution." *Behavioral and Brain Sciences* 24: 263–308.

Fisher, J., and R. A. Hinde. (1949). "The opening of milk bottles by birds." *British Birds* 42: 347–357.

Fisher, S. E., and G. F. Marcus. (2006). "The eloquent ape: Genes, brains, and the evolution of language." *Nature Reviews Genetics* 7: 9–20.

Fitch, W. T. (2005). "The evolution of language: A comparative review." *Biology and Philosophy* 20: 193–230.

Fitch, W. T., and M. D. Hauser. (2004). "Computational constraints on syntactic processing in a nonhuman primate." *Science* 303: 377–380.

Fitch, W. T., M. D. Hauser, and N. Chomsky. (2005). "The evolution of the language faculty: Clarifications and implications." *Cognition* 97: 179–210.

Fitzpatrick, M. J., Y. Ben-Shahar, H. M. Smid, L. E. M. Vet, G. E. Robinson, et al. (2005). "Candidate genes for behavioural ecology." *Trends in Ecology and Evolution* 20: 96–104.

Fleishman, L. J. (1988). "Sensory influences on physical design of a visual display." *Animal Behaviour* 36: 1420–1424.

Fleishman, L. J., M. Leal, and J. Sheehan. (2006). "Illumination geometry, detector position and the objective determination of animal signal colours in natural light." *Animal Behaviour* 71: 463–474.

Flombaum, J. I., J. A. Junge, and M. D. Hauser. (2005). "Rhesus monkeys (Macaca mulatta) spontaneously compute addition operations over large numbers." *Cognition* 97: 315–325.

Flombaum, J. I., L. R. Santos, and M. D. Hauser. (2002). "Neuroecology and psychological modularity." *Trends in Cognitive Sciences* 6: 106–108.

Fodor, J. A. (1983). *The Modularity of Mind.* Cambridge, MA: MIT Press.

———. (2001). *The Mind Doesn't Work That Way.* Cambridge, MA: MIT Press.

Fogassi, L., P. F. Ferrari, B. Gesierich, S. Rozzi, F. Chersi, et al. (2005). "Parietal lobe: From action organization to intention understanding." *Science* 308: 662–667.

Fontenot, M. B., S. L. Watson, K. A. Roberts, and R. W. Miller. (2007). "Effects of food preferences on token exchange and behavioural responses to inequality in tufted capuchin monkeys, Cebus apella." *Animal Behaviour* 74: 487–496

Foree, D. D., and V. M. LoLordo. (1973). "Attention in the pigeon: Differential effects of food-getting versus shock-avoidance procedures." *Journal of Comparative and Physiological Psychology* 85: 551–558.

Fortin, N. J., K. L. Agster, and H. B. Eichenbaum. (2002). "Critical role of the hippocampus in memory for sequences of events." *Nature Neuroscience* 5: 458–462.

Fortin, N. J., S. P. Wright, and H. Eichenbaum. (2004). "Recollection-like memory retrieval in rats is dependent on the hippocampus." *Nature* 431: 188–191.

Fraenkel, G. S., and D. L. Gunn. (1961). *The Orientation of Animals.* New York: Dover Publications, Inc.

Fragaszy, D., P. Izar, E. Visalberghi, E. B. Ottoni, and M. G. De Oliveira. (2004). "Wild capuchin monkeys (Cebus libidinosus) use anvils and stone pounding tools." *American Journal of Primatology* 64: 359–366.

Fragaszy, D., and E. Visalberghi. (2004). "Socially biased learning in monkeys." *Learning & Behavior* 32: 24–35.

Frank, M. J., J. W. Rudy, W. B. Levy, and R. C. O'Reily. (2005). "When logic fails: Implicit transitive inference in humans." *Memory & Cognition* 33: 742–750.

Franks, N. R., and T. Richardson. (2006). "Teaching in tandem-running ants." *Nature* 439: 153.

Fraser, D., and D. M. Weary. (2005). Applied animal behavior and animal welfare. In *The Behavior of Animals,* ed. J. J. Bolhuis and L.-A. Giraldeau. Malden, MA: Blackwell Publishing.

Friedrich, A. M., T. S. Clement, and T. R. Zentall. (2005). "Discriminative stimuli that follow the absence of reinforcement are preferred by pigeons over those that follow reinforcement." *Learning & Behavior* 33: 337–342.

Frisch, B., and J. Aschoff. (1987). "Circadian rhythms in honeybees: entrainment by feeding cycles." *Psychological Entomology* 12: 41–49.

Frost, B. J., and H. Mouritsen. (2006). "The neural mechanisms of long distance animal navigation." *Current Opinion in Neurobiology* 16: 481–488.

Fujita, K., H. Kuroshima, and S. Asai. (2003). "How do tufted capuchin monkeys (Cebus apella) understand causality involved in tool use?" *Journal of Experimental Psychology: Animal Behavior Processes* 29: 233–242.

Fullard, J. H., J. M. Ratcliffe, and A. R. Soutar. (2004). "Extinction of the acoustic startle response in moths endemic to a bat-free habitat." *Journal of Evolutionary Biology* 17: 856–861.

Fuller, R. C., D. Houle, and J. Travis. (2005). "Sensory bias as an explanation for the evolution of mate preferences." *The American Naturalist* 166: 437–446.

Furrer, R. D., and M. B. Manser. (2009). "The evolution of urgency-based and functionally referential alarm calls in ground-dwelling species." *The American Naturalist* 173: 400–410.

Galea, L. A. M., M. Kavaliers, K.-P. Ossenkopp, D. Innes, and E. L. Hargreaves. (1994). "Sexually dimorphic spatial learning varies seasonally in two populations of deer mice." *Brain Research* 635: 18–26.

Galef, B. G., Jr. (1976). "Social transmission of acquired behavior: A discussion of tradition and social learning in vertebrates." *Advances in the Study of Behavior* 6: 77–100.

———. (1988). Imitation in animals: History, definition, and interpretation of data from the psychological laboratory. In *Social Learning: Psychological and Biological Perspectives,* ed. T. R. Zentall and B. G. Galef Jr., 3–28. Hillsdale, NJ: Lawrence Erlbaum Associates.

———. (1995). "Why behaviour patterns that animals learn socially are locally adaptive." *Animal Behaviour* 49: 1325–1334.

———. (1996a). Tradition in animals: Field observations and laboratory analyses. In *Readings in Animal Cognition,* ed. M. Bekoff and D. Jamieson, 91–105. Cambridge, MA: MIT Press.

———. (1996b). Social enhancement of food preferences in norway rats: A brief review. In *Social Learning and Imitation in Animals: The Roots of Culture,* ed. C. M. Heyes and B. G. Galef Jr., 49–64. New York: Academic Press.

———. (1998). "Edward Thorndike revolutionary psychologist, ambiguous biologist." *American Psychologist* 53: 1128–1134.

———. (2004). "Approaches to the study of traditional behaviors in free-living animals." *Learning & Behavior* 32: 53–61.

———. (2007). Social learning by rodents. In *Rodent Societies,* ed. J. O. Wolff and P. W. Sherman, 207–215. Chicago: University of Chicago Press.

———. (2009). Culture in animals? In *The Question of Animal Culture,* ed. K. N. Laland and B. G. Galef Jr., 222–246. Cambridge, MA: Harvard University Press.

Galef, B. G., Jr., and C. Allen. (1995). "A new model system for studying behavioural traditions in animals." *Animal Behaviour* 50: 705–717.

Galef, B. G., Jr., and P. J. Durlach. (1993). "Absence of blocking, overshadowing, and latent inhibition in social enhancement of food preferences." *Animal Learning & Behavior* 21: 214–220.

Galef, B. G., Jr., and L.-A. Giraldeau. (2001). "Social influences on foraging in vertebrates: Causal mechanisms and adaptive functions." *Animal Behaviour* 61: 3–15.

Galef, B. G., Jr., and C. M. Heyes. (2004). "Introduction: Special issue on social learning." *Learning & Behavior* 32: 1–3.

Galef, B. G., Jr., and K. N. Laland. (2005). "Social learning in animals: Empirical studies and theoretical models." *BioScience* 55: 489–499.

Galef, B. G., Jr., L. A. Manzig, and R. M. Field. (1986). "Imitation learning in budgerigars: Dawson and Foss (1965) revisited." *Behavioural Processes* 13: 191–202.

Galef, B. G., Jr., and B. Osborne. (1978). "Novel taste facilitation of the association of visual cues with toxicosis in rats." *Journal of Comparative and Physiological Psychology* 92: 907–916.

Galef, B. G., Jr., and S. W. Wigmore. (1983). "Transfer of information concerning distant foods: A laboratory investigation of the 'Information-centre' hypothesis." *Animal Behaviour* 31: 748–758.

Gallagher, J. G. (1977). "Sexual imprinting: A sensitive period in Japanese quail (Coturnix cortunix japonica)." *Journal of Comparative and Physiological Psychology* 91: 72–78.

Gallese, V. (2007). "Before and below 'theory of mind': Embodied simulation and the neural correlates of social cognition." *Philosophical Transactions of the Royal Society B* 362: 659–669.

Gallistel, C. R. (1990). *The Organization of Learning.* Cambridge, MA: MIT Press.

———. (1993). A conceptual framework for the study of numerical estimation and arithmetic reasoning in animals. In *The Development of Numerical Competence*, ed. S. T. Boysen and E. J. Capaldi, 211–223. Hillsdale, NJ: Lawrence Erlbaum Associates.

———. (1998). The modular structure of learning. In *Brain and Mind: Evolutionary Perspectives*, ed. M. S. Gazzaniga and J. S. Altman, 5:56–71. Strasbourg: Human Frontiers Science Program.

———, ed. (2002). *Stevens' Handbook of Experimental Psychology*, Vol. 3. New York: Wiley.

———. (2003). The principle of adaptive specialization as it applies to learning and memory. In *Principles of Learning and Memory*, ed. R. H. Kluwe, G. Luer, and F. Rosler, 259–280. Basel: Birkhauser Verlag.

Gallistel, C. R., and A. E. Cramer. (1996). "Computations on metric maps in mammals: Getting oriented and choosing a multi-destination route." *The Journal of Experimental Biology* 199: 211–217.

Gallistel, C. R., S. Fairhurst, and P. Balsam. (2004). "The learning curve: Implications of a quantitative analysis." *Proceedings of the National Academy of Sciences* (USA) 101: 13124–13131.

Gallistel, C. R., and J. Gibbon. (2000). "Time, rate, and conditioning." *Psychological Review* 107: 289–344.

———. (2001). "Computational versus associative models of simple conditioning." *Current Directions in Psychological Science* 10: 146–150.

Gallistel, C. R., A. P. King, D. Gottlieb, F. Balci, E. B. Papachristos, et al. (2007). "Is matching innate?" *Journal of the Experimental Analysis of Behavior* 87: 161–199.

Gallup, G. G., Jr. (1970). "Chimpanzees: Self-recognition." *Science* 167: 86–87.

Gallup, G. G., Jr., R. Anderson, and D. J. Shilito. (2002). The mirror test. In *The Cognitive Animal*, ed. M. Bekoff, C. Allen, and G. M. Burghardt, 325–333. Cambridge, MA: MIT Press.

Gamzu, E., and D. R. Williams. (1971). "Classical conditioning of a complex skeletal response." *Science* 171: 923–925.

Garamszegi, L. Z., and M. Eens. (2004). "The evolution of hippocampus volume and brain size in relation to food hoarding in birds." *Ecology Letters* 7: 1216–1224.

Garber, P. A. (2000). Evidence for the use of spatial, temporal, and social information by some primate foragers. In *On the Move*, ed. S. Boinski and P. A. Garber, 261–298. Chicago: University of Chicago Press.

Garcia, C. M., and E. Ramirez. (2005). "Evidence that sensory traps can evolve into honest signals." *Nature* 434: 501–505.

Garcia, J., F. R. Ervin, and R. A. Koelling. (1966). "Learning with prolonged delay of reinforcement." *Psychonomic Science* 5: 121–122.

Garcia, J., and R. A. Koelling. (1966). "Relation of cue to consequence in avoidance learning." *Psychonomic Science* 4: 123–124.

Garcia, J., B. K. McGowan, and K. F. Green. (1972). Biological constraints on conditioning. In *Classical Conditioning II: Current Theory and Research*, ed. A. H. Black and W. F. Prokasy, 3–27. New York: Appleton-Century-Crofts.

Gardner, R. A., and B. T. Gardner. (1969). "Teaching sign language to a chimpanzee." *Science* 165: 664–672.

Gaulin, S. J. C. (1995). Does evolutionary theory predict sex differences in the brain? In *The Cognitive Neurosciences*, ed. M. Gazzaniga, 1211–1225. Cambridge, MA: MIT Press.

Gaulin, S. J. C., and R. W. Fitzgerald. (1989). "Sexual selection for spatial-learning ability." *Animal Behavior* 37: 322–331.

Gaulin, S. J. C., R. W. Fitzgerald, and M. S. Wartell. (1990). "Sex differences in spatial ability and activity in two vole species (Microtus ochrogaster and M. pennsylvanicus)." *Journal of Comparative Psychology* 104: 88–93.

Gelman, R., and C. R. Gallistel. (2004). "Language and the origin of numerical concepts." *Science* 306: 441–443.

Gendron, R. P., and J. E. R. Staddon. (1983). "Searching for cryptic prey: The effect of search rate." *American Naturalist* 121: 172–186.

Gentner, T. Q., K. M. Fenn, D. Margoliash, and H. C. Nusbaum. (2006). "Recursive syntactic pattern learning by songbirds." *Nature* 440: 1204–1207.

Gergely, G., and G. Csibra. (2003). "Teleological reasoning in infancy: The naïve theory of rational action." *Trends in Cognitive Sciences* 7: 287–292.

Gergely, G., Z. Nádasdy, G. Csibra, and S. Bíró. (1995). "Taking the intentional stance at 12 months of age." *Cognition* 56: 165–193.

Gerlai, R., and N. S. Clayton. (1999). "Analysing hippocampal function in transgenic mice: An ethological perspective." *Trends in Neuroscience* 22: 47–51.

Getty, T. (1995). "Search, discrimination, and selection: Mate choice by pied flycatchers." *American Naturalist* 145: 146–154.

Ghazanfar, A. A., and N. K. Logothetis. (2003). "Facial expressions linked to monkey calls." *Nature* 423: 937–938.

Ghazanfar, A. A., and L. R. Santos. (2004). "Primate brains in the wild: The sensory bases for social interactions." *Nature Reviews Neuroscience* 5: 603–616.

Ghirlanda, S., and M. Enquist. (2003). "A century of generalization." *Animal Behaviour* 66: 15–36.

Gibbon, J. (1991). "Origins of scalar timing." *Learning and Motivation* 22: 3–38.

Gibbon, J., M. D. Baldock, C. Locurto, L. Gold, and H. S. Terrace. (1977). "Trial and intertrial durations in autoshaping." *Journal of Experimental Psychology: Animal Behavior Processes* 3: 264–284.

Gibbon, J., and R. M. Church. (1981). "Time left: Linear versus logarithmic subjective time." *Journal of Experimental Psychology: Animal Behavior Processes* 7: 87–108.

———. (1984). Sources of variance in an information processing theory of timing. In *Animal Cognition*, ed. H. L. Roitblat, T. G. Bever, and H. S. Terrace, 465–488. Hillsdale, NJ:NJ: Lawrence Erlbaum Associates.

———. (1990). "Representation of time." *Cognition* 37: 23–54.

Gibbon, J., R. M. Church, S. Fairhurst, and A. Kacelnik. (1988). "Scalar expectancy theory and choice between delayed rewards." *Psychological Review* 95: 102–114.

Gibson, B. M. (2001). "Cognitive maps not used by humans (Homo sapiens) during a dynamic navigational task." *Journal of Comparative Psychology* 115: 397–402.

Gibson, B. M., and A. C. Kamil. (2001). "Tests for cognitive mapping in Clark's nutcrackers (Nucifraga columbiana)." *Journal of Comparative Psychology* 115: 403–417.

———. (2005). "The fine-grained spatial abilities of three seed-caching corvids." *Learning & Behavior* 33: 59–66.

Gibson, B. M., and S. J. Shettleworth. (2005). "Place vs. response learning revisited: Tests of blocking on the radial maze." *Behavioral Neuroscience* 119: 567–586.

Gibson, E. J., and R. D. Walk. (1956). "The effect of prolonged exposure to visually presented patterns on learning to discriminate them." *Journal of Comparative and Physiological Psychology* 49: 239–242.

Gibson, J. J. (1979). *The Ecological Approach to Visual Perception.* Boston: Houghton Mifflin.

Gibson, R. M., and T. A. Langen. (1996). "How do animals choose their mates?" *Trends in Ecology and Evolution* 11: 468–470.

Gigerenzer, G. (1997). The modularity of social intelligence. In *Machiavellian Intelligence II: Extensions and Evaluation,* ed. A. Whiten and R. W. Byrne, 264–288. Cambridge: Cambridge University Press.

Gigerenzer, G., and K. Hug. (1992). "Domain-specific reasoning: Social contracts, cheating, and perspective change." *Cognition* 43: 127–171.

Gill, F. B. (1988). "Trapline foraging by hermit hummingbirds: Competition for an undefended, renewable resource." *Ecology* 69: 1933–1942.

———. (1995). *Ornithology.* New York: WH Freeman.

Gillan, D. J. (1981). "Reasoning in the chimpanzee: II. Transitive inference." *Journal of Experimental Psychology: Animal Behavior Processes* 7: 150–164.

Gintis, H., S. Bowles, R. Boyd, and E. Fehr. (2007). Explaining altruistic behaviour in humans. In *The Oxford Handbook of Evolutionary Psychology,* ed. R. I. M. Dunbar and L. Barrett, 603–619. Oxford: Oxford University Press.

Giraldeau, L.-A. (2004). "Introduction: Ecology and the central nervous system." *Brain Behavior and Evolution* 63: 193–196.

Giraldeau, L.-A., and L. Lefebvre. (1986). "Exchangeable producer and scrounger roles in a captive flock of feral pigeons: a case for the skill pool effect." *Animal Behaviour* 34: 797–803.

———. (1987). "Scrounging prevents cultural transmission of food-finding behaviour in pigeons." *Animal Behaviour* 35: 387–394.

Giraldeau, L.-A., T. J. Valone, and J. J. Templeton. (2002). "Potential disadvantages of using socially acquired information." *Philosophical Transactions of the Royal Society of London B* 357: 1559–1566.

Girndt, A., T. Meier, and J. Call. (2008). "Task constraints mask great apes' ability to solve the trap-table task." *Journal of Experimental Psychology: Animal Behavior Processes* 34: 54–62.

Gisiner, R., and R. J. Schusterman. (1992). "Sequence, syntax, and semantics: Responses of a language-trained sea lion (Zalophus californianus) to novel sign combinations." *Journal of Comparative Psychology* 106: 78–91.

Giurfa, M. (2007). "Behavioral and neural analysis of associative learning in the honeybee: A taste from the magic well." *Journal of Comparative Physiology A* 193: 801–824.

Glimcher, P. W. (2003). *Decisions, Uncertainty, and the Brain.* Cambridge, MA: MIT Press.

Glimcher, P. W., and A. Rustichini. (2004). "Neuroeconomics: The consilience of brain and decision." *Science* 306: 447–452.

Gluck, M. A., E. Mercado, and C. E. Myers. (2008). *Learning and Memory: From Brain to Behavior.* New York: Worth.

Godard, R. (1991). "Long-term memory of individual neighbours in a migratory songbird." *Nature* 350: 228–229.

Godin, J.-G. J., and S. A. Smith. (1988). "A fitness cost of foraging in the guppy." *Nature* 333: 69–71.

Goldsmith, T. H., J. S. Collins, and D. L. Perlman. (1981). "A wavelength discrimination function for the hummingbird Archilochus alexandri." *Journal of Comparative Physiology* 143: 103–110.

Gomez, J. C. (1994). Mutual awareness in primate communication: A Gricean approach. In *Self-Awareness in Animals and Humans: Developmental Perspectives,* ed. S. T. Parker, R. W. Mitchell, and M. L. Boccia, 61–80. Cambridge: Cambridge University Press.

———. (1996). Non-human primate theories of (non-human primate) minds: Some issues concerning the origins of mind-reading. In *Theories of Theories of Mind,* ed. P. Carruthers and P. K. Smith, 330–343. Cambridge: Cambridge University Press.

———. (2005). "Species comparative studies and cognitive development." *Trends in Cognitive Sciences* 9: 118–125.

Gonzalez-Mariscal, G., and J. Rosenblatt. (1996). "Maternal behavior in rabbits." *Advances in the Study of Behavior* 25: 333–360.

Goodale, M. A., and A. D. Milner. (1992). "Separate visual pathways for perception and action." *Trends in Neurosciences* 15: 20–25.

Goodyear, A. J., and A. C. Kamil. (2004). "Clark's nutcrackers (Nucifraga columbiana) and the effects of goal-landmark distance on overshadowing." *Journal of Comparative Psychology* 118: 258–264.

Gopnik, A., and L. Schulz. (2004). "Mechanisms of theory formation in young children." *Trends in Cognitive Sciences* 8: 371–377.

———, eds. (2007). *Causal Learning.* New York: Oxford University Press.

Gordon, P. (2004). "Numerical cognition without words: Evidence from Amazonia." *Science* 306: 496–499.

Gordon, W. C., and R. L. Klein. (1994). Animal memory: The effects of context change on retention performance. In *Animal Learning and Cognition,* ed. N. J. Mackintosh, 255–279. San Diego, CA: Academic Press.

Goss-Custard, J. D. (1977). "Optimal foraging and the size selection of worms by redshank, Tringa totanus, in the field." *Animal Behaviour* 25: 10–29.

Göth, A., and C. S. Evans. (2005). "Life history and social learning: Megapode chicks fail to acquire feeding preferences from conspecifics." *Journal of Comparative Psychology* 119: 381–386.

Göth, A., and M. E. Hauber. (2004). "Ecological approaches to species recognition in birds through studies of model and non-model species." *Annales Zoologici Fennici* 41: 823–842.

Goto, K., S. E. G. Lea, and W. H. Dittrich. (2002). "Discrimination of intentional and random motion paths by pigeons." *Animal Cognition* 5: 119–127.

Gottlieb, D. A. (2005). "Acquisition with partial and continuous reinforcement in rat magazine approach." *Journal of Experimental Psychology: Animal Behavior Processes* 31: 319–333.

———. (2008). "Is the number of trials a primary determinant of conditioned responding?" *Journal of Experimental Psychology: Animal Behavior Processes* 34: 185–201.

Gottlieb, G. (1978). "Development of species identification in ducklings: IV. Change in species-specific perception caused by auditory deprivation." *Journal of Comparative and Physiological Psychology* 92: 375–387.

Gould, J. L. (1975). "Honey bee recruitment: The dance-language controversy." *Science* 189: 685–693.

———. (1976). "The dance-language controversy." *Quarterly Review of Biology* 51: 211–244.

———. (1986). "The locale map of honey bees: Do insects have cognitive maps?" *Science* 232: 861–863.

———. (1990). "Honey bee cognition." *Cognition* 37: 83–103.

———. (2002). Learning instincts. In *Stevens' Handbook of Experimental Psychology,* ed. C. R. Gallistel, 3:239–257. New York: John Wiley and Sons.

Gould, J. L., and C. G. Gould. (1988). *The Honey Bee.* New York: Scientific American Library.

———. (1994). *The Animal Mind.* New York: Scientific American Library.

Gould, J. L., and W. F. Towne. (1987). "Evolution of the dance language." *American Naturalist* 130: 317–338.

Gould, S. J., and R. C. Lewontin. (1979). "The spandrels of San Marco and the Panglossian paradigm: a critique of the adaptationist program." *Proceedings of The Royal Society of London B* 205: 581–598.

Gould-Beierle, K. L., and A. C. Kamil. (1996). "The use of local and global cues by Clark's nutcracker, Nucifraga columbiana." *Animal Behaviour* 52: 519–528.

Grafen, A. (1990). "Do animals really recognize kin?" *Animal Behaviour* 39: 42–54.

Grah, G., R. Wehner, and B. Ronacher. (2005). "Path integration in a three-dimensional maze: ground distance estimation keeps desert ants Cataglyphis fortis on course." *The Journal of Experimental Biology* 208: 4005–4011.

Graham, M., M. A. Good, A. McGregor, and J. M. Pearce. (2006). "Spatial learning based on the shape of the environment is influenced by properties of the objects forming the shape." *Journal of Experimental Psychology: Animal Behavior Processes* 32: 44–59.

Grant, D. S. (1976). "Effect of sample presentation time on long-delay matching in pigeons." *Learning and Motivation* 7: 580–590.

———. (1982). "Prospective versus retrospective coding of samples of stimuli, responses, and reinforcers in delayed matching with pigeons." *Learning and Motivation* 13: 265–280.

Grant, D. S., R. G. Brewster, and K. A. Stierhoff. (1983). " 'Surprisingness' and short-term retention in pigeons." *Journal of Experimental Psychology: Animal Behavior Processes* 9: 63–79.

Grant, P. R., and B. R. Grant. (2008). *How and Why Species Multiply.* Princeton, NJ: Princeton University Press.

Graw, B., and M. B. Manser. (2007). "The function of mobbing in cooperative meerkats." *Animal Behaviour* 74: 507–517.

Green, L., J. Myerson, D. D. Holt, J. R. Slevin, and S. J. Estle. (2004). "Discounting of delayed food rewards in pigeons and rats: is there a magnitude effect?" *Journal of the Experimental Analysis of Behavior* 81: 39–50.

Greene, E. (1989). "A diet-induced developmental polymorphism in a caterpillar." *Science* 243: 643–644.

Greene, S. L. (1983). Feature memorization in pigeon concept formation. In *Quantitative Analyses of Behaviour,* ed. M. L. Commons, R. J. Herrnstein, and A. R. Wagner, 4: 209–229. Cambridge, MA: Ballinger.

Grice, H. P. (1957). "Meaning." *Philosophical Review* 66: 377–388.

Griffin, A. S. (2004). "Social learning about predators: A review and prospectus." *Learning & Behavior* 32: 131–140.

Griffin, A. S., D. T. Blumstein, and C. S. Evans. (2000). "Training captive-bred or translocated animals to avoid predators." *Conservation Biology* 14: 1317–1326.

Griffin, D. R. (1976). *The Question of Animal Awareness.* New York: Rockefeller University Press.

———. (1978). "Prospects for a cognitive ethology." The *Behavioral and Brain Sciences* 4: 527–538.

———. (1992). *Animal Minds.* Chicago: University of Chicago Press.

———. (2001). *Animal Minds.* Chicago: University of Chicago Press.

Griffin, D. R., and G. B. Speck. (2004). "New evidence of animal consciousness." *Animal Cognition* 7: 5–18.

Grim, T. (2007). "Experimental evidence for chick discrimination without recognition in a brood parasite host." *Proceedings of the Royal Society B* 274: 373–381.

Griswold, D. A., M. F. Harrer, C. Sladkin, D. A. Alessandro, and J. L. Gould. (1995). "Intraspecific recognition by laughing gull chicks." *Animal Behaviour* 50: 1341–1348.

Grosenick, L., T. S. Clement, and R. D. Fernald. (2007). "Fish can infer social rank by observation alone." *Nature* 445: 429–432.

Groves, P. M., and R. F. Thompson. (1970). "Habituation: A dual-process theory." *Psychological Review* 77: 419–450.

Grüter, C., M. S. Balbuena, and W. M. Farina. (2008). "Informational conflicts created by the waggle dance." *Proceedings of the Royal Society B* 275: 1321–1327.

Guilford, T., and M. S. Dawkins. (1987). "Search images not proven: A reappraisal of recent evidence." *Animal Behavior* 35: 1838–1845.

———. (1991). "Receiver psychology and the evolution of animal signals." *Animal Behaviour* 42: 1–14.

Gunter, C., R. Dhand, T. Chouard, H. Gee, J. Rees, et al. (2005). "The chimpanzee genome." *Nature* 437: 47–68.

Gwinner, E. (1996). "Circadian and circannual programmes in avian migration." *The Journal of Experimental Biology* 199: 39–48.

Hailman, J. P. (1967). "The ontogeny of an instinct: The pecking response in chicks of the laughing gull (Larus atricilla L.) and related species." *Behaviour: An International Journal of Comparative Ethology Supplement* 15.

Hall, G. (1991). *Perceptual and Associative Learning.* Oxford: Clarendon Press.

———. (1994). Pavlovian conditioning: Laws of association. In Animal Learning and *Cognition,* ed. N. J. Mackintosh, 15–43. San Diego, CA: Academic Press.

———. (1996). "Learning about associatively activated stimulus representations: Implications for acquired equivalence and perceptual learning." *Animal Learning and Behavior* 24: 233–255.

———. (2001). Perceptual learning: Association and differentiation. In *Handbook of Contemporary Learning Theories,* ed. R. R. Mowrer and S. B. Klein, 367–407. Mahwah NJ: Lawrence Erlbaum Associates.

———. (2002). Associative structures in Pavlovian and instrumental conditioning. In *Stevens' Handbook of Experimental Psychology,* ed. C. R. Gallistel, vol. 3. New York: John Wiley, and Sons.

———. (2003). "Learned changes in the sensitivity of stimulus representations: Associative and nonassociative mechanisms." *The Quarterly Journal of Experimental Psychology* 56 B: 43–55.

Hall, G., and R. Honey. (1989). Perceptual and associative learning. In *Contemporary Learning Theories,* ed. S. B. Klein and R. R. Mowrer, 117–147. Mahwah, NJ: Lawrence Erlbaum Associates.

Hamilton, D. A., K. G. Akers, T. E. Johnson, J. P. Rice, F. T. Candelaria, et al. (2008). "The relative influence of place and direction in the Morris water task." *Journal of Experimental Psychology: Animal Behavior Processes* 34: 31–53.

Hamilton, W. D. (1963). "The evolution of altruistic behavior." *American Naturalist* 97: 354–356.

Hamlin, J. K., K. Wynn, and P. Bloom. (2007). "Social evaluation by preverbal infants." *Nature* 450: 557–559.

Hamm, S. L., and S. J. Shettleworth. (1987). "Risk aversion in pigeons." *Journal of Experimental Psychology: Animal Behavior Processes* 13: 376–383.

Hampton, R. R. (1994). "Sensitivity to information specifying the line of gaze of humans in sparrows (Passer domesticus)." *Behaviour* 130: 41–51.

———. (2001). "Rhesus monkeys know when they remember." *Proceedings of the National Academy of Sciences* (USA) 98: 5359–5362.

———. (2005). Can rhesus monkeys discriminate between remembering and forgetting? In *The Missing Link in Cognition: Origins of Self-Reflective Consciousness,* ed. H. S. Terrace and J. Metcalfe, 272–295. New York: Oxford University Press.

———. (2009). "Multiple demonstrations of metacognition in nonhumans: Converging evidence or multiple mechanisms" *Comparative Cognition and Behavior Reviews* 4: 17–28.

Hampton, R. R., and B. L. Schwartz. (2004). "Episodic memory in nonhumans: what and where, is when?" *Current Opinion in Neurobiology* 14: 192–197.

Hampton, R. R., D. F. Sherry, S. J. Shettleworth, M. Kurgel, and G. Ivy. (1995). "A comparison of food-storing and hippocampal volume in three parid species." *Brain, Behavior, and Evolution* 45: 54–61.

Hampton, R. R., A. Zivin, and E. A. Murray. (2004). "Rhesus monkeys (Macaca mulatta) discriminate between knowing and not knowing and collect information as needed before acting." *Animal Cognition* 7: 239–246.

Hanlon, R. (2007). "Cephalopod dynamic camouflage." *Current Biology* 17: R400-R404.

Hansell, M. (2000). *Bird Nests and Construction Behaviour.* Cambridge: Cambridge University Press.

Hanson, H. M. (1959). "Effects of discrimination training on stimulus generalization." *Journal of Experimental Psychology* 58: 321–334.

Hare, B. (2007). "From nonhuman to human mind. What changed and why?" *Current Directions in Psychological Science* 16: 60–64.

Hare, B., E. Addessi, J. Call, M. Tomasello, and E. Visalberghi. (2003). "Do capuchin monkeys, Cebus apella, know what conspecifics do and do not see?" *Animal Behaviour* 65: 131–142.

Hare, B., M. Brown, C. Williamson, and M. Tomasello. (2002). "The domestication of social cognition in dogs." *Science* 298: 1634–1636.

Hare, B., J. Call, B. Agnetta, and M. Tomasello. (2000). "Chimpanzees know what conspecifics do and do not see." *Animal Behaviour* 59: 771–785.

Hare, B., J. Call, and M. Tomasello. (2001). "Do chimpanzees know what conspecifics know?" *Animal Behaviour* 61: 139–151.

Hare, B., A. P. Melis, V. Woods, S. Hastings, and R. Wrangham. (2007). "Tolerance allows bonobos to outperform chimpanzees on a cooperative task." *Current Biology* 17: 619–623.

Hare, B., and M. Tomasello. (2004). "Chimpanzees are more skillful in competitive than cooperative cognitive tasks." *Animal Behaviour* 68: 571–581.

———. (2005). "Human-like social skills in dogs?" *Trends in Cognitive Sciences* 9: 439–444.

Harper, D. N., A. P. McLean, and J. C. Dalrymple-Alford. (1993). "List item memory in rats: Effects of delay and delay task." *Journal of Experimental Psychology: Animal Behavior Processes* 19: 307–316.

Harris, J. A. (2006). "Elemental representations of stimuli in associative learning." *Psychological Review* 113: 584–605.

Harris, J. D. (1943). "Habituatory response decrement in the intact organism." *Psychological Bulletin* 40: 385–422.

Hartley, T., J. King, and N. Burgess. (2004). Studies of the neural basis of human navigation and memory. In *The Neurobiology of Spatial Behaviour*, ed. K. J. Jeffery, 144–166. Oxford: Oxford University Press.

Hartling, L. K., and R. C. Plowright. (1979). "Foraging by bumble bees on patches of artificial flowers: a laboratory study." *Canadian Journal of Zoology* 57: 1866–1870.

Harvey, P. H., and D. Pagel. (1991). *The Comparative Method in Evolutionary Biology.* Oxford: Oxford University Press.

Hasselmo, M. E. (2008). "The scale of experience." *Science* 321: 46–47.

Hauber, M. E., and P. W. Sherman. (2001). "Self-referent phenotype matching: Theoretical considerations and empirical evidence." *Trends in Neurosciences* 24: 609–616.

Hauber, M. E., P. W. Sherman, and D. Paprika. (2000). "Self-referent phenotype matching in a brood parasite: the armpit effect in brown-headed cowbirds (Molothrus ater)." *Animal Cognition* 3: 113–117.

Haun, D. B. M., J. Call, G. Janzen, and S. C. Levinson. (2006). "Evolutionary psychology of spatial representation in the Hominidae." *Current Biology* 16: 1736–1740.

Hauser, M. D. (1988). "How infant vervet monkeys learn to recognize starling alarm calls: The role of experience." *Behaviour* 105: 187–201.'

———. (1996). *The Evolution of Communication.* Cambridge, MA: MIT Press.

———. (1997). "Artifactual kinds and functional design features: What a primate understands without language." *Cognition* 64: 285–308.

———.(1998). "Functional referents and acoustic similarity: Field playback experiments with rhesus monkeys." *Animal Behaviour* 55: 1647–1658.

———. (2000). *Wild Minds: What Animals Really Think.* New York: Henry Holt and Company.

———. (2003). "Knowing about knowing: Dissociations between perception and action systems over evolution and during development." *Annals of the New York Academy of Sciences* 1001: 79–103.

———. (2005). "Our chimpanzee mind." *Nature* 437: 60–63.

Hauser, M. D., D. Barner, and T. O'Donnell. (2007). "Evolutionary linguistics: A new look at an old landscape." *Language, Learning, and Development* 3: 101–132.

Hauser, M. D., and S. Carey. (1998). Building a cognitive creature from a set of primitives: Evolutionary and developmental insights. In *The Evolution of Mind,* ed. C. Allen and D. D. Cummins, 51–106. New York: Oxford University Press.

———. (2003). "Spontaneous representations of small numbers of objects by rhesus macaques: examinations of content and format." *Cognitive Psychology* 47: 367–401.

Hauser, M. D., S. Carey, and L. B. Hauser. (2000). "Spontaneous number representation in semi-free-ranging rhesus monkeys." *Proceedings of The Royal Society of London B* 267: 829–833.

Hauser, M. D., M. K. Chen, F. Chen, and E. Chuang. (2003). "Give unto others: Genetically unrelated cotton-top tamarin monkeys preferentially give food to those who altruistically give food back." *Proceedings of the Royal Society B* 270: 2363–2370.

Hauser, M. D., N. Chomsky, and W. T. Fitch. (2002). "The faculty of language: What is it, who has it, and how did it evolve?" *Science* 298: 1569–1579.

Hauser, M. D., J. Kralik, and C. Botto-Mahan. (1999). "Problem solving and functional design features: experiments on cotton-top tamarins, Saguinus oedipus oedipus." *Animal Behaviour* 57: 565–582.

Hauser, M. D., P. MacNeilage, and M. Ware. (1996). "Numerical representations in primates." *Proceedings of the National Academy of Sciences* (USA) 93: 1514–1517.

Hauser, M. D., and L. R. Santos. (2007). The evolutionary ancestry of our knowledge of tools: From percepts to concepts. In *Creations of the Mind,* by E. Margolis and S. Lawrence. Oxford: Oxford Univirsity Press.

Hauser, M. D., and E. Spelke. (2004). Evolutionary and developmental foundations of human knowledge: A case study of mathematics. In *The Cognitive Neurosciences III,* ed. M. Gazzaniga, 853–862. Cambridge, MA: MIT Press.

Hauser, M. D., F. Tsao, P. Garcia, and E. S. Spelke. (2003). "Evolutionary foundations of number: Spontaneous representation of numerical magnitudes by cotton-top tamarins." *Proceedings of The Royal Society of London B* 270: 1441–1446.

Hayes, K. J., and C. Hayes. (1952). "Imitation in a home-raised chimpanzee." *Journal of Comparative & Physiological Psychology* 45: 450–459.

Healy, S. D., ed. (1998). *Spatial Representation in Animals.* Oxford: Oxford University Press.

Healy, S. D., and V. Braithwaite. (2000). "Cognitive ecology: A field of substance?" *Trends in Ecology and Evolution* 15: 22–26.

Healy, S. D., N. S. Clayton, and J. R. Krebs. (1994). "Development of hippocampal specialisation in two species of tit (Parus spp.)." *Behavioural Brain Research* 61: 23–28.

Healy, S. D., S. R. de Kort, and N. S. Clayton. (2005). "The hippocampus, spatial memory, and food hoarding: A puzzle revisited." *Trends in Ecology and Evolution* 20: 17–22.

Healy, S. D., and T. Guilford. (1990). "Olfactory-bulb size and nocturnality in birds." *Evolution* 44: 339–346.

Healy, S. D., and T. A. Hurly. (1995). "Spatial memory in rufous hummingbirds (Selasphorus rufus): A field test." *Animal Learning & Behavior* 23: 63–68.

———. (2001). Foraging and spatial learning in hummingbirds. In *Cognitive Ecology of Pollination,* ed. L. Chittka and J. D. Thomson, 127–147. Cambridge: Cambridge University Press.

Healy, S. D., and J. R. Krebs. (1993). "Development of hippocampal specialisation in a food-storing bird." *Behavioural Brain Research* 53: 127–131.

Healy, S. D., and C. Rowe. (2007). "A critique of comparative studies of brain size." *Proceedings of the Royal Society B* 274: 453–464.

Heider, F., and M. Simmel. (1944). "An experimental study of apparent behavior." *The American Journal of Psychology* 57: 243–259.

Heiligenberg, W. (1974). "Processes governing behavioral states of readiness." *Advances in the Study of Behavior* 5: 173–200.

Heiling, A. M., M. E. Herberstein, and L. Chittka. (2003). "Pollinator attraction: Crab-spiders manipulate flower signals." *Nature* 421: 334.

Heinrich, B. (1989). *Ravens in Winter.* New York: Summit Books.

Heinrich, B., and S. L. Collins. (1983). "Caterpillar leaf damage, and the game of hide-and-seek with birds." *Ecology* 64: 592–602.

Helbig, A. J. (1994). "Genetic basis and evolutionary change of migratory directions in a European passerine migrant Sylvia atricapilla." *Ostrich* 65: 151–159.

———. (1996). "Genetic basis, mode of inheritance and evolutionary changes of migratory directions in palearctic warblers (Aves: sylviidae)." *The Journal of Experimental Biology* 199: 49–55.

Helme, A. E., J. Call, N. S. Clayton, and N. J. Emery. (2006). "What do bonobos (Pan paniscus) understand about physical contact?" *Journal of Comparative Psychology* 120: 294–302.

Helme, A. E., N. S. Clayton, and N. J. Emery. (2006). "What do rooks (Corvus frugilegus) understand about physical contact?" *Journal of Comparative Psychology* 120: 288–293.

Henderson, J., T. A. Hurly, M. Bateson, and S. D. Healy. (2006). "Timing in free-living rufous hummingbirds, Selasphorus rufus." *Current Biology* 16: 512–515.

Henrich, J. (2004). "Inequity aversion in capuchins?" *Nature* 428: 139.

Herman, L. M. (2006). Intelligence and rational behaviour in the bottlenosed dolphin. In *Rational Animals?*, ed. S. Hurley and M. Nudds, 439–467. Oxford: Oxford University Press.

Herman, L. M., and R. K. Uyeyama. (1999). "The dolphin's grammatical competency: Comments on Kako (1999)." *Animal Learning & Behavior* 27: 18–23.

Hermer, L., and E. S. Spelke. (1994). "A geometric process for spatial reorientation in young children." *Nature* 370: 57–59.

Hermer-Vazquez, L., E. S. Spelke, and A. S. Katsnelson. (1999). "Sources of flexibility in human cognition: Dual-task studies of space and language." *Cognitive Psychology* 39: 3–36.

Herrmann, E., J. Call, M. V. Hernández-Lloreda, B. Hare, and M. Tomasello. (2007). "Humans have evolved specialized skills of social cognition: The cultural intelligence hypothesis." *Science* 317: 1360–1366.

Herrnstein, R. J. (1961). "Relative and absolute strength of response as a function of frequency of reinforcement." *Journal of the Experimental Analysis of Behavior* 4: 267–272.

———. (1979). "Acquisition, generalization, and discrimination reversal of a natural concept." *Journal of Experimental Psychology: Animal Behavior Processes* 5: 116–129.

———. (1990). "Levels of stimulus control: A functional approach." *Cognition* 37: 133–166.

Herrnstein, R. J., and P. A. de Villiers. (1980). "Fish as a natural category for people and pigeons." *Psychology of Learning and Motivation* 14: 59–97.

Herrnstein, R. J., D. H. Loveland, and C. Cable. (1976). "Natural concepts in pigeons." *Journal of Experimental Psychology: Animal Behavior Processes* 2: 285–311.

Heschl, A., and J. Burkart. (2006). "A new mark test for mirror self-recognition in non-human primates." *Primates* 47: 187–198.

Heyes, C.M. (1993a). "Imitation, culture and cognition." *Animal Behaviour* 46: 999–1010.

———. (1993b). "Anecdotes, training, trapping and triangulating: Do animals attribute mental states?" *Animal Behaviour* 46: 177–188.

———. (1994a). "Social learning in animals: Categories and mechanisms." *Biological Review* 69: 207–231.

———. (1994b). "Reflections on self-recognition in primates." *Animal Behaviour* 47: 909–919.

———. (1996). Introduction: Identifying and defining imitation. In *Social Learning in Animals: The Roots of Culture*, by C. M. Heyes and B. G. Galef Jr., 211–220 San Diego: Academic Press.

———. (1998). "Theory of mind in nonhuman primates." *Behavioral and Brain Sciences* 21: 101–148.

———. (2000). Evolutionary psychology in the round. In *The Evolution of Cognition*, ed. C. Heyes and L. Huber, 3–22. Cambridge, MA: MIT Press.

———. (2003). "Four routes of cognitive evolution." *Psychological Review* 110: 713–727.

———. (2005). Imitation by association. In *Perspectives on Imitation: From Neuroscience to Social Science*, ed. S. Hurley and N. Chater, 1:157–176. Cambridge, MA: MIT Press.

————. (2008). Beast Machines? Questions of animal consciousness. In *Frontiers of Consciousness*, ed. M. Davies and L. Weiskrantz, 259–274. Oxford: Oxford University Press.

Heyes, C. M., and B. G. Galef Jr., eds. (1996). *Social Learning in Animals: The Roots of Culture*. San Diego: Academic Press.

Heyes, C. M., and L. Huber, eds. (2000). *The Evolution of Cognition*. Cambridge, MA: MIT Press.

Heyes, C. M., and E. D. Ray. (2000). "What is the significance of imitation in animals?" *Advances in the Study of Behavior* 29: 215–245.

Hinde, R. A. (1970a). *Animal Behaviour*. New York: McGraw Hill.

————. (1970b). Behavioural habituation. In *Short-term Changes in Neural Activity and Behaviour*, ed. G. Horn and R. A. Hinde, 3–40. London: Cambridge University Press.

————. (1981). "Animal signals: Ethological and games-theory approaches are not incompatible." *Animal Behaviour* 29: 535–542.

Hinde, R. A., and J. Fisher. (1951). "Further observations on the opening of milk bottles by birds." *British Birds* 44: 392–396.

Hinde, R. A., and J. Stevenson-Hinde, eds. (1973). *Constraints on Learning*. London: Academic Press.

Hirata, S., and K. Fuwa. (2007). "Chimpanzees (Pan troglodytes) learn to act with other individuals in a cooperative task." *Primates* 48: 13–21.

Hirata, S., K. Watanabe, and M. Kawai. (2001). "Sweet-potato washing" revisited. In *Primate Origins of Human Cognition and Behavior*, ed. T. Matsuzawa, 487–508. Tokyo: Springer.

Hockett, C. F. (1960). Logical considerations in the study of animal communication. In *Animal Sounds and Communication*, ed. W. E. Lanyon and W. N. Tavolga, 392–430. Washington, DC: American Institute of Biological Sciences.

Hodos, W., and C. B. G. Campbell. (1969). "Scala naturae: Why there is no theory in comparative psychology." *Psychological Review* 76: 337–350.

Hoffman, H. S. (1978). Experimental analysis of imprinting and its behavioral effects. In *The Psychology of Learning and Motivation*, ed. G. H. Bower, 12:1–37. New York: Academic Press, Inc.

Hoffman, H. S., and A. M. Ratner. (1973). "A reinforcement model of imprinting: Implications for socialization in monkeys and men." *Psychological Review* 80: 527–544.

Hogan, J. A. (1974). "Responses in Pavlovian conditioning studies." *Science* 186: 156–157.

————. (1988). Cause and function in the development of behavior systems. In *Handbook of Behavioral Neurobiology*, ed. E. M. Blass, 9:63–106. New York: Plenum Publishing Corporation.

————. (1994a). The concept of cause in the study of behavior. In *Causal Mechanisms of Behavioral Development*, ed. J. A. Hogan and J. J. B. Bolhuis, 3–15. Cambridge: Cambridge University Press.

————. (1994b). "Structure and development of behavior systems." *Psychonomic Bulletin and Review* 1: 439–450.

————. (2005). "Causation: The study of behavioural mechanisms." *Animal Biology* 55: 323–341.

Hogan, J. A., and J. J. Bolhuis. (2005). "The development of behaviour: Trends since Tinbergen (1963)." *Animal Biology* 55: 371–398.

Hoglund, J., R. V. Alatalo, R. M. Gibson, and A. Lundberg. (1995). "Mate-choice copying in black grouse." *Animal Behaviour* 49: 1627–1633.

Hogue, M. E., J. P. Beaugrand, and P. C. Laguë. (1996). "Coherent use of information by hens observing their former dominant defeating or being defeated by a stranger." *Behavioural Processes* 38: 241–252.

Holekamp, K. E. (2006). "Questioning the social intelligence hypothesis." *Trends in Cognitive Sciences* 11: 65–69.

Holekamp, K. E., E. E. Boydston, M. Szykman, I. Graham, K. J. Nutt, et al. (1999). "Vocal recognition in the spotted hyaena and its possible implications regarding the evolution of intelligence." *Animal Behaviour* 58: 383–395.

Holekamp, K. E., S. T. Sakai, and B. L. Lundrigan. (2007). "Social intelligence in the spotted hyena (Crocuta crocuta)." *Philosophical Transactions of the Royal Society B* 362: 523–538.

Holland, P. C. (1977). "Conditioned stimulus as a determinant of the form of the Pavlovian conditioned response." *Journal of Experimental Psychology: Animal Behavior Processes* 3: 77–104.

———. (1984). "Orgins of behavior in Pavlovian conditioning." *The Psychology of Learning and Motivation* 18: 129–174.

———. (1990). "Event representation in Pavlovian conditioning: Image and action." *Cognition* 37: 105–131.

———. (1992). "Occasion setting in Pavlovian conditioning." *The Psychology of Learning and Motivation* 28: 69–125.

———. (2000). "Trial and intertrial durations in appetitive conditioning in rats." *Animal Learning & Behavior* 28: 121–135.

———. (2005). "Amount of training effects in representation-mediated food aversion learning: No evidence of a role for associability changes." *Learning & Behavior* 33: 464–478.

Holland, P. C., and R. A. Rescorla. (1975). "The effect of two ways of devaluing the unconditioned stimulus after first- and second-order appetitive conditioning." *Journal of Experimental Psychology: Animal Behavior Processes* 1: 355–363.

Holland, P. C., and A. Sherwood. (2008). "Formation of excitatory and inhibitory associations between absent events." *Journal of Experimental Psychology: Animal Behavior Processes* 34: 324–335.

Holland, P. C., and J. J. Straub. (1979). "Differential effects of two ways of devaluing the unconditioned stimulus after Pavlovian appetitive conditioning." *Journal of Experimental Psychology: Animal Behavior Processes* 1: 65–78.

Holland, R. A., M. Wikelski, and D. S. Wilcove. (2006). "How and why do insects migrate?" *Science* 313: 794–796.

Hollis, K. L. (1982). "Pavlovian conditioning of signal-centered action patterns and autonomic behavior: A biological analysis of function." *Advances in the Study of Behavior* 12: 1–64.

———. (1984). "The biological function of Pavlovian conditioning: The best defence is a good offence." *Journal of Experimental Psychology: Animal Behavior Processes* 10: 413–425.

———. (1990). The role of Pavlovian conditioning in territorial aggression and reproduction. In *Contemporary Issues in Comparative Psychology*, ed. D. A. Dewabury, 197–219. Sunderland, MA: Sinauer Associates.

———. (1997). "Contemporary research on Pavlovian conditioning. A 'new' functional analysis." *American Psychologist* 52: 956–965.

Hollis, K. L., E. L. Cadieux, and M. M. Colbert. (1989). "The biological function of Pavlovian conditioning: A mechanism for mating success in the blue gourami (Trichogaster trichopterus)." *Journal of Comparative Psychology* 103: 115–121.

Hollis, K. L., M. J. Dumas, P. Singh, and P. Fackelman. (1995). "Pavlovian conditioning of aggressive behavior in blue gourami fish (Trichogaster trichopterus): Winners become winners and losers stay losers." *Journal of Comparative Psychology* 109: 123–133.

Hollis, K. L., K. S. Langworthy-Lam, L. A. Blouin, and M. C. Romano. (2004). "Novel strategies of subordinate fish competing for food: Learning when to fold." *Animal Behaviour* 68: 1155–1164.

Hollis, K. L., V. L. Pharr, M. J. Dumas, G. B. Britton, and J. Field. (1997). "Classical conditioning provides paternity advantage for territorial male blue gouramis (Trichogaster trichopterus)." *Journal of Comparative Psychology* 111: 219–225.

Hollis, K. L., C. ten Cate, and P. Bateson. (1991). "Stimulus representation: A subprocess of imprinting and conditioning." *Journal of Comparative Psychology* 105: 307–317.

Holmes, W. G. (1986). "Kin recognition by phenotype matching in female Belding's ground squirrels." *Animal Behaviour* 34: 38–47.

Holmes, W. G., and J. M. Mateo. (2007). Kin recognition in rodents: Issues and evidence. In *Rodent Societies: An Ecological & Evolutionary Perspective*, ed. J. O. Wolff and P. W. Sherman, 216–228. Chicago: University of Chicago Press.

Holmes, W. G., and P. W. Sherman. (1982). "The ontogeny of kin recognition in two species of ground squirrels." *American Zoologist* 22: 491–517.

Honey, R. C., G. Horn, and P. Bateson. (1993). "Perceptual learning during filial imprinting: Evidence from transfer of training studies." *The Quarterly Journal of Experimental Psychology* 46B: 253–269.

Honig, W. K. (1978). Studies of working memory in the pigeon. In *Cognitive Processes in Animal Behavior*, ed. S. H. Hulse, H. Fowler, and W. K. Honig, 211–248. Hillsdale, NJ:NJ: Erlbaum.

Honrado, G. I., and N. Mrosovsky. (1991). "Interactions between periodic socio-sexual cues and light-dark cycles in controlling the phasing of activity rhythms in golden hamsters." *Ethology Ecology and Evolution* 3: 221–231.

Hopkins, C. D. (1983). Sensory mechanisms in animal communication. In *Animal Behaviour*, ed. T. R. Halliday and P. J. B. Slater, 2:114–155. New York: W. H. Freeman and Company.

Hopper, L. M., S. P. Lambeth, S. J. Schapiro, and A. Whiten. (2008). "Observational learning in chimpanzees and children studied through 'ghost' condition." *Proceedings of the Royal Society B* 275: 835–840.

Hopper, L. M., A. Spiteri, S. P. Lambeth, S. J. Schapiro, V. Horner, et al. (2007). "Experimental studies of traditions and underlying transmission processes in chimpanzees." *Animal Behaviour* 73: 1021–1032.

Hoppitt, W. J. E., G. R. Brown, R. Kendal, L. Rendell, A. Thornton, et al. (2008). "Lessons from animal teaching." *Trends in Ecology and Evolution* 23: 486–493.

Hopson, J. W. (2003). General learning models: Timing without a clock. In *Functional and Neural Mechanisms of Interval Timing*, ed. W. H. Meck, 23–60. Boca Raton, FL: CRC Press.

Horn, G. (1967). "Neuronal mechanisms of habituation." *Nature* 215: 707–711.

———. (1985). *Memory, Imprinting, and the Brain*. Oxford: Clarendon Press.

———. (2004). "Pathways of the past: The imprint of memory." *Nature Reviews Neuroscience* 5: 108–120.

Horner, V., and A. Whiten. (2005). "Causal knowledge and imitation/emulation switching in chimpanzees (Pan troglodytes) and children (Homo sapiens)." *Animal Cognition* 8: 164–181.

———. (2007). "Learning from others' mistakes? Limits on understanding trap-tube task by young chimpanzees (Pan troglodytes) and children (Homo sapiens)." *Journal of Comparative Psychology* 121: 12–21.

Horner, V., A. Whiten, E. Flynn, and F. B. M. De Waal. (2006). "Faithful replication of foraging techniques along cultural transmission chains by chimpanzees and children." *Proceedings of the National Academy of Sciences* (USA) 103: 13878–13883.

Houde, A. E. (1997). *Sex, Color, and Mate Choice in Guppies*. Princeton, NJ: Princeton University Press.

Houston, A. I. (1986). "The matching law applies to wagtails' foraging in the wild." *Journal of the Experimental Analysis of Behavior* 45: 15–18.

———(1987). The control of foraging decisions. In *Quantitative Analyses of Behavior*, ed. M. L. Commons, A. Kacelnik, and S. J. Shettleworth, 6:41–61. Mahwah, NJ: Lawrence Erlbaum Associates.

Houston, A. I., and J. McNamara. (1981). "How to maximize reward rate on two variable-interval paradigms." *Journal of the Experimental Analysis of Behavior* 35: 367–396.

Huber, L., and U. Aust. (2006). A modified feature theory as an account of pigeon visual categorization. In *Comparative Cognition: Experimental Explorations of Animal Intelligence*, ed. E. A. Wasserman and T. R. Zentall, 325–342. New York: Oxford University Press.

Huber, L., and R. Lenz. (1993). "A test of the linear feature model of polymorphous concept discrimination with pigeons." *Quarterly Journal of Experimental Psychology* 46B: 1–18.

———. (1996). "Categorization of prototypical stimulus classes by pigeons." *Quarterly Journal of Experimental Psychology* 49B: 111–133.

Hulse, S. H. (2002). "Auditory scene analysis in animal communication." *Advances in the Study of Behavior* 31: 163–200.

———. (2006). Postscript: An essay on the study of cognition in animals. In *Comparative Cognition*, ed. E. A. Wasserman and T. R. Zentall, 668–678. New York: Oxford University Press.

Hulse, S. H., H. Fowler, and W. K. Honig, eds. (1978). *Cognitive Processes in Animal Behavior*. Hillsdale, NJ: Erlbaum.

Humle, T., and T. Matsuzawa. (2002). "Ant-dipping among the chimpanzees of Bossou, Guinea, and some comparisons with other sites." *American Journal of Primatology* 58: 133–148.

Humphrey, N. K. (1976). The social function of intellect. In *Growing Points in Ethology*, ed. P. P. G. Bateson and R. A. Hinde, 303–317. Cambridge: Cambridge University Press.

Hunt, G. R. (1996). "Manufacture and use of hook-tools by New Caledonian crows." *Nature* 379: 249–251.

Hunt, G. R., R. B. Rutledge, and R. D. Gray. (2006). "The right tool for the job: What strategies do wild New Caledonian crows use?" *Animal Cognition* 9: 307–316.

Hunt, R. R. (1995). "The subtlety of distinctiveness: What von Restorff really did." *Psychonomic Bulletin & Review* 2: 105–112.

Hunter, W. S. (1913). "The delayed reaction in animals and children." *Behavior Monographs* 2.

Huntingford, F. A. (1993). "Behavioral mechanisms in evolutionary perspective." *Trends in Ecology and Evolution* 8: 81–84.

Hurewitz, F., R. Gelman, and B. Schnitzer. (2006). "Sometimes area counts more than number." *Proceedings of the National Academy of Sciences* (USA) 103: 19599–19604.

Hurley, S., and M. Nudds. (2006). *Rational Animals?* Oxford: Oxford University Press.

Hutchinson, J. M. C. (2005). "Is more choice always desirable? Evidence and arguments from leks, food selection, and environmental enrichment." *Biological Review* 80: 73–92.

Immelmann, K. (1972). "Sexual and other long-term aspects of imprinting in birds and other species." *Advances in the Study of Behavior* 4: 147–174.

Inman, A., and S. J. Shettleworth. (1999). "Detecting metamemory in nonverbal subjects: A test with pigeons." *Journal of Experimental Psychology: Animal Behavior Processes* 25: 389–395.

Inoue-Nakamura, N., and T. Matsuzawa. (1997). "Development of stone tool use by wild chimpanzees (Pan troglodytes)." *Journal of Comparative Psychology* 111: 159–173.

Insley, S. J. (2000). "Long-term vocal recognition in the northern fur seal." *Nature* 406: 404–405.

Ito, M., S. Takatsuru, and D. Saeki. (2000). "Choice between constant and variable alternatives by rats: Effects of different reinforcer amounts and energy budgets." *Journal of the Experimental Analysis of Behavior* 73: 79–92.

Izquierdo, I., N. Schroder, C. A. Netto, and J. H. Medina. (1999). "Novelty causes time-dependent retrograde amnesia for one-trial avoidance in rats through NMDA receptor- and CaMKII-dependent mechanisms in the hippocampus." *European Journal of Neuroscience* 11: 3323–3328.

Jackendoff, R., and S. Pinker. (2005). "The nature of the language faculty and its implications for evolution of language (Reply to Fitch, Hauser, and Chomsky)." *Cognition* 97: 211–225.

Jacob, P., and M. Jeannerod. (2005). "The motor theory of social cognition: a critique." *Trends in Cognitive Sciences* 9: 21–25.

Jacobs, L. F. (1995). The ecology of spatial cognition. *Behavioural Brain Research in Naturalistic and Semi-Naturalistic Settings*, ed. E. Alleva, A. Fasolo, H.-P. Lipp, L. Nadel, and L. Ricceri, 301–322. Dordrecht: Kluwer Academic Publishers.

James, W. (1890). *The Principles of Psychology*. New York: Henry Holt.

Janetos, A. C. (1980). "Strategies of female mate choice: A theoretical analysis." *Behavioral Ecology and Sociobiology* 7: 107–112.

Janmaat, K. R. L., R. W. Byrne, and K. Zuberbühler. (2006). "Evidence for a spatial memory of fruiting states of rainforest trees in wild mangabeys." *Animal Behaviour* 72: 797–807.

Janson, C. H. (1998). "Experimental evidence for spatial memory in foraging wild capuchin monkeys, Cebus apella." *Animal Behaviour* 55: 1229–1243.

———. Spatial movement strategies: Theory, evidence, and challenges. In *On the Move*, ed. S. Boinski and P. A. Garber, 165–203. Chicago: University of Chicago Press.

———. (2007). "Experimental evidence for route integration and strategic planning in wild capuchin monkeys." *Animal Cognition* 10: 341–356.

Janson, C. H., and R. Byrne. (2007). "What wild primates know about resources: Opening up the black box." *Animal Cognition* 10: 357–367.

Jarman, P. J. (1974). "The social organisation of antelope in relation to their ecology." *Behaviour* 48: 215–267.

Jarvik, M. E., T. L. Goldfarb, and J. L. Carley. (1969). "Influence of interference on delayed matching in monkeys." *Journal of Experimental Psychology* 81: 1–6.

Jasselette, P., H. Lejeune, and J. H. Wearden. (1990). "The perching response and the laws of animal timing." *Journal of Experimental Psychology: Animal Behavior Processes* 16: 150–161.

Jeffery, K. J., ed. (2003). *The Neurobiology of Spatial Behaviour*. Oxford: Oxford University Press.

Jenkins, H. M. (1979). Animal learning and behavior theory. In *The First Century of Experimental Psychology*, ed. E. Hearst, 177–228. Hillsdale, NJ: Lawrence Erlbaum Associates.

Jenkins, H. M., R. A. Barnes, and F. J. Barrera. (1981). Why autoshaping depends on trial spacing. In *Autoshaping and Conditioning Theory*, ed. C. M. Locurto, H. S. Terrace, and J. Gibbon, 255–284. New York: Academic Press.

Jenkins, H. M., F. J. Barrera, C. Ireland, and B. Woodside. (1978). "Signal-centered action patterns of dogs in appetitive classical conditioning." *Learning and Motivation* 9: 272–296.

Jenkins, H. M., and B. R. Moore. (1973). "The form of the autoshaped response with food or water reinforcers." *Journal of the Experimental Analysis of Behavior* 20: 163–181.

Jensen, K., J. Call, and M. Tomasello. (2007). "Chimpanzees are rational maximizers in an ultimatum game." *Science* 318: 107–109.

Jensen, K., B. Hare, J. Call, and M. Tomasello. (2006). "What's in it for me? Self-regard precludes altruism and spite in chimpanzees." *Proceedings of the Royal Society B* 273: 1013–1021.

Jerison, H. J. (1973). *Evolution of the Brain and Intelligence*. New York: Academic Press.

Jitsumori, M., M. Siemann, M. Lehr, and J. D. Delius. (2002). "A new approach to the formation of equivalence classes in pigeons." *Journal of the Experimental Analysis of Behavior* 78: 397–408.

Johnson, M. H., and G. Horn. (1988). "Development of filial preferences in dark-reared chicks." *Animal Behaviour* 36: 675–683.

Johnston, R. E. (2003). "Chemical communication in rodents: From pheromones to individual recognition." *Journal of Mammalogy* 84: 1141–1162.

Johnston, R. E., and T. A. Bullock. (2001). "Individual recognition by use of odours in golden hamsters: The nature of individual representations." *Animal Behaviour* 61: 545–557.

Johnston, R. E., A. Derzie, G. Chiang, P. Jernigan, and H.-C. Lee. (1993). "Individual scent signatures in golden hamsters: evidence for specialization of function." *Animal Behaviour* 45: 1061–1070.

Johnston, R. E., and A. Peng. (2008). "Memory for individuals: Hamsters (Mesocricetus auratus) require contact to develop multicomponent representations (concepts) of others." *Journal of Comparative Psychology* 122: 121–131.

Johnston, T. D. (1982). "Selective costs and benefits in the evolution of learning." *Advances in the Study of Behavior* 12: 65–106.

Jolly, A. (1966). "Lemur social behavior and primate intelligence." *Science* 153: 501–506.

Jones, C. M., V. A. Braithwaite, and S. D. Healy. (2003). "The evolution of sex differences in spatial ability." *Behavioral Neuroscience* 117: 403–411.

Jones, C. M., and S. D. Healy. (2006). "Differences in cue use and spatial memory in men and women." *Proceedings of the Royal Society B* 273: 2241–2247.

Jones, J. E., E. Antoniadis, S. J. Shettleworth, and A. C. Kamil. (2002). "A comparative study of geometric rule learning by nutcrackers (Nucifraga columbiana), pigeons (Columba livia), and jackdaws (Corvus monedula)." *Journal of Comparative Psychology* 116: 350–356.

Jordan, K. E., and E. M. Brannon. (2006). "Weber's Law influences numerical representations in rhesus macaques (Macaca mulatta)." *Animal Cognition* 9: 159–172.

Jordan, K. E., E. M. Brannon, N. K. Logothetis, and A. A. Ghazanfar. (2005). "Monkeys match the number of voices they hear to the number of faces they see." *Current Biology* 15: 1034–1038.

Jouventin, P., and H. Weimerskirch. (1990). "Satellite tracking of wandering albatrosses." *Nature* 343: 746–748.

Kacelnik, A. (2006). Meanings of rationality. In *Rational Animals?*, ed. S. Hurley and M. Nudds, 87–106. Oxford: Oxford University Press.

Kacelnik, A., and M. Bateson. (1996). "Risky theories-the effects of variance on foraging decisions." *American Zoologist* 36: 402–434.

Kacelnik, A., and F. Brito e Abreu. (1998). "Risky choice and Weber's Law." *Journal of Theoretical Biology* 194: 289–298.

Kacelnik, A., D. Brunner, and J. Gibbon. (1990). Timing mechanisms in optimal foraging: some applications of scalar expectancy theory. In *Behavioural Mechanisms of Food Selection*, ed. R. N. Hughes, *NATO ASI Series*, G20:61–82. Berlin: Springer-Verlag.

Kacelnik, A., and I. C. Cuthill. (1987). Starlings and optimal foraging theory: Modelling in a fractal world. In *Foraging Behavior*, ed. A. C. Kamil, J. R. Krebs and H. R. Pulliam, 303–333. New York: Plenum Press.

Kacelnik, A., and B. Marsh. (2002). "Cost can increase preference in starlings." *Animal Behaviour* 63: 245–250.

Kako, E. (1999). "Elements of syntax in the systems of three language-trained animals." *Animal Learning & Behavior* 27: 1–14.

Kamil, A. C. (1978). "Systematic foraging by a nectar-feeding bird, the amakihi (Loxops virens)." *Journal of Comparative and Physiological Psychology* 92: 388–396.

———. (1985). The evolution of higher learning abilities in birds. Paper presented at the XVIII International Ornithological Congress.

———. (1988). A synthetic approach to the study of animal intelligence. In *Comparative Perspectives in Modern Psychology: Nebraska Symposium on Motivation*, ed. D. W. Leger, 35:230–257. Lincoln: University of Nebraska Press.

———. (1998). On the proper definition of cognitive ethology. In *Animal Cognition in Nature*, ed. R. P. Balda, I. M. Pepperberg, and A. C. Kamil, 1–28. San Diego, Academic Press.

———. (2004). "Sociality and the evolution of intelligence." *Trends in Cognitive Sciences* 8: 195–197.

Kamil, A. C., R. P. Balda, and D. J. Olson. (1994). "Performance of four seed-caching corvid species in the radial-arm maze analog." *Journal of Comparative Psychology* 108: 385–393.

Kamil, A. C., and A. B. Bond. (2001). The evolution of virtual ecology. In *Model Systems in Behavioral Ecology*, ed. L. A. Dugatkin, 288–310. Princeton, NJ: Princeton University Press.

———. (2006). Selective attention, priming, and foraging behavior. In *Comparative Cognition: Experimental Exploration of Animal Intelligence*, ed. E. A. Wasserman and T. R. Zentall, 94–114. New York: Oxford University Press.

Kamil, A. C., and K. Cheng. (2001). "Way-finding and landmarks: The multiple bearings hypothesis." *Journal of Experimental Biology* 2043: 103–113.

Kamil, A. C., and A. J. Goodyear. (2001). "The use of landmarks by Clark's nutcrackers: First tests of a new model." *Journal of Navigation* 54: 429–435.

Kamil, A. C., and J. E. Jones. (1997). "The seed-storing corvid Clark's nutcracker learns geometric relationships among landmarks." *Nature* 390: 276–279.

———. (2000). "Geometric rule learning by Clark's nutcrackers (Nucifraga columbiana)." *Journal of Experimental Psychology: Animal Behavior Processes* 26: 439–453.

Kamin, L. J. (1969). Predictability, surprise, attention, and conditioning. In *Punishment and Aversive Behavior*, ed. B. A. Campbell and R. M. Church, 279–296. New York: Appleton-Century-Crofts.

Kaminski, J., J. Call, and J. Fischer. (2004). "Word learning in a domestic dog: Evidence for 'fast mapping.'" *Science* 304: 1682–1683.

Kaminski, J., J. Call, and M. Tomasello. (2008). "Chimpanzees know what others know, but not what they believe." *Cognition* 109: 224–234.

Kaminski, J., J. Riedel, J. Call, and M. Tomasello. (2005). "Domestic goats, Capra hircus, follow gaze direction and use social cues in an object choice task." *Animal Behaviour* 69: 11–18.

Kanazawa, S. (2004). "General intelligence as a domain-specific adaptation." *Psychological Review* 111: 512–523.

Kanwisher, N. (2006). "What's in a face?" *Science* 311: 617–618.

Karakashian, S. J., M. Gyger, and P. Marler. (1988). "Audience effects on alarm calling in chickens (Gallus gallus)." *Journal of Comparative Psychology* 102: 129–135.

Karin-D'Arcy, M. R. (2005). "The modern role of Morgan's canon in comparative psychology." *International Journal of Comparative Psychology* 18: 179–201.

Karin-D'Arcy, M. R., and D. J. Povinelli. (2002). "Do chimpanzees know what each other see? A closer look." *International Journal of Comparative Psychology* 15: 21–54.

Kastak, C. R., and R. J. Schusterman. (2002). "Sea lions and equivalence: Expanding classes by exclusion." *Journal of the Experimental Analysis of Behavior* 78: 449–465.

Katz, J. S., and A. A. Wright. (2006). "Same/different abstract-concept learning by pigeons." *Journal of Experimental Psychology: Animal Behavior Processes* 32: 80–86.

Katz, J. S., A. A. Wright, and K. D. Bodily. (2007). "Issues in the comparative cognition of abstract-concept learning." *Comparative Cognition & Behavior Reviews* 2: 79–92.

Kawai, M. (1965). "Newly-acquired pre-cultural behavior of the natural troop of Japanese monkeys on Koshima Islet." *Primates* 6: 1–30.

Kawai, N., and T. Matsuzawa. (2000). "Numerical memory span in a chimpanzee." *Nature* 403: 39–40.

Keeton, W. T. (1974). "The orientational and navigational basis of homing in birds." *Advances in the Study of Behavior* 5: 47–132.

Keith-Lucas, T., and N. Guttman. (1975). "Robust-single-trial delayed backward conditioning." *Journal of Comparative and Physiological Psychology* 88: 468–476.

Kelber, A., M. Vorobyev, and D. Osorio. (2003). "Animal colour vision—behavioural tests and physiological concepts." *Biological Reviews* 78: 81–118.

Kelly, D., and M. L. Spetch. (2001). "Pigeons encode relative geometry." *Journal of Experimental Psychology: Animal Behavior Processes* 27: 417–422.

Kendrick, K. M., K. Atkins, M. R. Hinton, K. D. Broad, C. Fabre-Nys, et al. (1995). "Facial and vocal discrimination in sheep." *Animal Behaviour* 49: 1665–1676.

Kennedy, J. S. (1992). *The New Anthropomorphism.* Cambridge: Cambridge University Press.

Kesner, R. P., P. E. Gilbert, and L. A. Barua. (2002). "The role of the hippocampus in memory for the temporal order of a sequence of odors." *Behavioral Neuroscience* 116: 286–290.

Killeen, P. R., and J. G. Fetterman. (1988). "A behavioral theory of timing." *Psychological Review* 95: 274–295.

Kim, S. D., S. Rivers, R. A. Bevins, and J. J. B. Ayres. (1996). "Conditioned stimulus determinants of conditioned response form in Pavlovian fear conditioning." *Journal of Experimental Psychology: Animal Behavior Processes* 22: 87–104.

Kirkpatrick, K. (2002). "Packet theory of conditioning and timing." *Behavioural Processes* 57: 89–106.

Kitchen, D. M. (2004). "Alpha male black howler monkey responses to loud calls: Effect of numeric odds, male companion behaviour and reproductive investment." *Animal Behaviour* 67: 125–139.

Klein, E. D., R. S. Bhatt, and T. R. Zentall. (2005). "Contrast and the justification of effort." *Psychonomic Bulletin & Review* 12: 335–339.

Klein, E. D., and T. R. Zentall. (2003). "Imitation and affordance learning by pigeons (Columba livia)." *Journal of Comparative Psychology* 117: 414–419.

Koehler, O. (1941). "Vom Erlernen unbenannter Anzahlen bei Vogeln (on the learning of unnamed numerosities by birds)." *Naturwissenschaften* 29: 201–218.

————. (1951). "The ability of birds to 'count.'" *Bulletin of Animal Behaviour* 9: 41–45.

Kohler, S., M. Moscovitch, and B. Melo. (2001). "Episodic memory for object location versus episodic memory for object identity: Do they rely on distinct encoding processes?" *Memory & Cognition* 29: 948–959.

Köhler, W. (1959). *The Mentality of Apes.* New York: Vintage Books.

Köksal, F., and M. Domjan. (1998). "Observational conditioning of sexual behavior in the domesticated quail." *Animal Learning & Behavior* 26: 427–432.

Köksal, F., M. Domjan, and G. Weisman. (1994). "Blocking of the sexual conditioning of differentially effective conditioned stimulus objects." *Animal Learning & Behavior* 22: 103–111.

Konishi, M. (1965). "The role of auditory feedback in the control of vocalization in the white-crowned sparrow." *Zeitschrift fur Tierpsychologie* 22: 770–783.

Konorski, J. (1967). *Integrative Activity of the Brain.* Chicago: University of Chicago Press.

Koriat, A. (2007). Metacognition and consciousness. In *The Cambridge Handbook of Consciousness*, ed. P. D. Zelazo, M. Moscovitch, and E. Thompson, 289–325. New York: Cambridge University Press.

Koriat, A., M. Hilit, and R. Nussison. (2006). "The intricate relationships between monitoring and control in metacognition: Lessons for the cause-and-effect relation between subjective experience and behavior." *Journal of Experimental Psychology: General* 135: 36–69.

Kornell, N., L. K. Son, and H. S. Terrace. (2007). "Transfer of metacognitive skills and hint-seeking in monkeys." *Psychological Science* 18: 64–71.

Kornell, N., and H. S. Terrace. (2007). "The generation effect in monkeys." *Psychological Science* 18: 682–685.

Kraemer, P. J., and J. M. Golding. (1997). "Adaptive forgetting in animals." *Psychonomic Bulletin & Review* 4: 480–491.

Kraemer, P. J., and W. A. Roberts. (1985). "Short-term memory for simultaneously presented visual and auditory signals in the pigeon." *Journal of Experimental Psychology: Animal Behavior Processes* 11: 137–151.

Krakauer, D. C. (1995). "Groups confuse predators by exploiting perceptual bottlenecks: A connectionist model of the confusion effect." *Behavioral Ecology and Sociobiology* 36: 421–429.

Krakauer, D. C., and M. A. Rodriguez-Girones. (1995). "Searching and learning in a random environment." *Journal of Theoretical Biology* 177: 417–429.

Krasne, F. (2002). Neural analysis of learning in simple systems. In *Stevens' Handbook of Experimental Psychology*, ed. C. R. Gallistel, 3:131–201. New York: John Wiley and Sons.

Krebs, J. R., and H. Biebach. (1989). "Time-place learning by garden warblers: (Sylvia borin): route or map?" *Ethology* 83: 248–256.

Krebs, J. R., and N. B. Davies. (1981). *An Introduction to Behavioural Ecology.* Oxford: Blackwell Scientific.

————. (1993). *An Introduction to Behavioural Ecology.* Oxford: Blackwell Scientific.

Krebs, J. R., and R. Dawkins. (1984). Animal signals: Mind-reading and manipulation. In *Behavioural Ecology: An Evolutionary Approach*, ed. J. R. Krebs and N. B. Davies, 380–402. Oxford: Blackwell Scientific.

Krebs, J. R., J. T. Erichsen, M. I. Webber, and E. L. Charnov. (1977). "Optimal prey selection in the great tit (Parus major)." *Animal Behaviour* 25: 30–38.

Kummer, H. (1995). *In Quest of the Sacred Baboon.* Princeton, NJ: Princeton University Press.

Kummer, H., L. Daston, G. Gigerenzer, and J. B. Silk. (1997). The social intelligence hypothesis. *Human by Nature*, ed. P. Weingart, S. Mitchell, P. J. Richerson, and S. Maasen, 157–179. Mahwah, NJ: Lawrence Erlbaum Associates.

Laland, K. N., and B. G. Galef, eds. (2009). *The Question of Animal Culture.* Cambridge, MA: Harvard University Press.

Laland, K. N., and V. M. Janik. (2006). "The animal cultures debate." *Trends in Ecology and Evolution* 21: 542–547.

Laland, K. N., and H. C. Plotkin. (1991). "Excretory deposits surrounding food sites facilitate social learning of food preferences in Norway rats." *Animal Behaviour* 41: 997–1005.

————. (1993). "Social transmission of food preferences among Norway rats by marking of food sites and by gustatory contact." *Animal Learning & Behavior* 21: 35–41.

Landeau, L., and J. Terborgh. (1986). "Oddity and the 'confusion effect' in predation." *Animal Behaviour* 34: 1372–1380.

Langford, D. J., S. E. Crager, Z. Shehzad, S. B. Smith, S. G. Sotocinal, et al. (2006). "Social modulation of pain as evidence for empathy in mice." *Science* 312: 1967–1970.

Langley, C. M. (1996). "Search images: Selective attention to specific visual features of prey." *Journal of Experimental Psychology: Animal Behavior Processes* 22: 152–163.

Langley, C. M., and D. A. Riley. (1993). "Limited capacity information processing and pigeon matching-to-sample: Testing alternative hypotheses." *Animal Learning & Behavior* 21: 226–232.

Langley, C. M., D. A. Riley, A. B. Bond, and N. Goel. (1996). "Visual search and natural grains in pigeons (Columba livia): Search images and selective attention." *Journal of Experimental Psychology: Animal Behavior Processes* 22: 139–151.

Lattal, K. M. (1999). "Trial and intertrial durations in Pavlovian conditioning: Issues of learning and performance." *Journal of Experimental Psychology: Animal Behavior Processes* 25: 433–450.

Lauder, G. V., and S. M. Reilly. (1996). The mechanistic bases of behavioral evolution: A multivariate analysis of musculoskeletal function. In *Phylogenies and the Comparative Method in Animal Behavior,* ed. E. P. Martins, 104–137. New York: Oxford University Press.

Laughlin, S. B. (2001). "Energy as a constraint on the coding and processing of sensory information." *Current Opinion in Neurobiology* 11: 475–480.

Lawrence, E. S. (1984). "Vigilance during 'easy' and 'difficult' foraging tasks." *Animal Behavior* 33: 1373–1374.

Lazareva, O. F., K. L. Freiburger, and E. A. Wasserman. (2004). "Pigeons concurrently categorize photographs at both basic and superordinate levels." *Psychonomic Bulletin & Review* 11: 1111–1117.

Lazareva, O. F., and E. A. Wasserman. (2006). "Effect of stimulus orderability and reinforcement history on transitive responding in pigeons." *Behavioural Processes* 72: 161–172.

Lea, S. E. G. (1984). In what sense do pigeons learn concepts? In *Animal Cognition,* ed. H. L. Roitblat, T. G. Bever, and H. S. Terrace, 263–276. Hillsdale, NJ: Lawrence Erlbaum Associates.

Lea, S. E. G., A. Lohmann, and C. M. E. Ryan. (1993). "Discrimination of five-dimensional stimuli by pigeons: Limitations of feature analysis." *Quarterly Journal of Experimental Psychology* 46B: 19–42.

Leadbeater, E. (2006). "Social learning: Ants and the meaning of teaching." *Current Biology* 16: R323–R325.

Leak, T. M., and J. Gibbon. (1995). "Simultaneous timing of multiple intervals: Implications of the scalar property." *Journal of Experimental Psychology: Animal Behavior Processes* 21: 3–19.

Learmonth, A. E., N. S. Newcombe, N. Sheridan, and M. Jones. (2008). "Why size counts: Children's spatial reorientation in large and small enclosures." *Developmental Science* 11: 414–426.

Lefebvre, L. (1986). "Cultural diffusion of a novel food-finding behaviour in urban pigeons: An experimental field test." *Ethology* 71: 295–304.

————. (1995a). "The opening of milk bottles by birds: Evidence for accelerating learning rates, but against the wave-of-advance model of cultural transmission." *Behavioural Processes* 34: 43–54.

————. (1995b). "Culturally-transmitted feeding behaviour in primates: Evidence for accelerating learning rates." *Primates* 36: 227–239.

Lefebvre, L., and J. J. Bolhuis. (2003). Positive and negative correlates of feeding innovations in birds: Evidence for limited modularity? *Animal Innovation,* ed. S. M. Reader and K. N. Laland, 39–62. Oxford: Oxford University Press.

Lefebvre, L., and J. Bouchard. (2003). Social learning about food in birds. In *The Biology of Traditions*, ed. D. M. Fragaszy and S. Perry, 94–126. Cambridge: Cambridge University Press.

Lefebvre, L., and L.-A. Giraldeau. (1996). Is social learning an adaptive specialization? In *Social Learning in Animals: The Roots of Culture*, ed. C. M. Heyes and B. G. Galef, 107–128. San Diego, CA: Academic Press.

Lefebvre, L., N. Nicolakakis, and D. Boire. (2002). "Tools and brains in birds." *Behaviour* 139: 939–973.

Lefebvre, L., and B. Palameta. (1988). Mechanisms, ecology, and population diffusion of socially learned, food-finding behavior in feral pigeons. In *Social learning: Psychological and Biological Perspectives*, ed. T. R. Zentall and B. G. Galef Jr., 141–164. Hillsdale, NJ: Lawrence Erlbaum Associates.

Lefebvre, L., B. Palameta, and K. K. Hatch. (1996). "Is group-living associated with social learning? A comparative test of a gregarious and a territorial columbid." *Behaviour* 133: 241–261.

Lefebvre, L., S. M. Reader, and D. Sol. (2004). "Brains, innovations, and evolution in birds and primates." *Brain, Behavior, and Evolution* 63: 233–246.

Lefebvre, L., P. Whittle, E. Lascaris, and A. Finkelstein. (1997). "Feeding innovations and forebrain size in birds." *Animal Behaviour* 53: 549–560.

Lehrer, M. (1993). "Why do bees turn back and look?" *Journal of Comparative Physiology A* 172: 549–563.

Lehrman, D. S. (1970). Semantic and conceptual issues in the nature-nurture problem. In *Development and Evolution of Behavior*, ed. L. R. Aronson, E. Tobach, D. S. Lehrman, and J. S. Rosenblatt, 17–52. San Francisco: Freeman.

Leising, K. J., J. Wong, W. D. Stahlman, M. R. Waldmann, and A. P. Blaisdell. (2008). "The special status of actions in causal reasoning in rats." *Journal of Experimental Psychology: General* 137: 514–527. .

Lejeune, H., and J. H. Wearden. (1991). "The comparative psychology of fixed interval responding: Some quantitative analyses." *Learning and Motivation* 22: 84–111.

———. (2006). "Scalar properties in animal timing: Conformity and violations." *The Quarterly Journal of Experimental Psychology* 59: 1875–1908.

Lemon, W. C. (1991). "Fitness consequences of foraging behaviour in the zebra finch." *Nature* 352: 153–155.

Leonard, B., and B. L. McNaughton. (1990). Spatial representation in the rat: Conceptual, behavioral, and neurophysiological perspectives. In *Neurobiology of Comparative Cognition*, ed. R. P. Kesner and D. S. Olton, 363–422. Hillsdale, NJ: Lawrence Erlbaum Associates.

Leslie, A. M., R. Gelman, and C. R. Gallistel. (2008). "The generative basis of natural number concepts." *Trends in Cognitive Sciences* 12: 213–218.

Levy, D. J., R. S. Duncan, and C. F. Levins. (2004). "Use of dung as a tool by burrowing owls." *Nature* 431: 39.

Lewis, J. L., and A. C. Kamil. (2006). "Interference effects in the memory for serially presented locations in Clark's nutcrackers, Nucifraga columbiana." *Journal of Experimental Psychology: Animal Behavior Processes* 32: 407–417.

Lewis, K. P., S. Jaffe, and E. M. Brannon. (2005). "Analog number representations in mongoose lemurs (Eulemur mongoz): evidence from a search task." *Animal Cognition* 8: 247–252.

Lickliter, R., and H. Honeycutt. (2003). "Developmental dynamics: Toward a biologically plausible evolutionary psychology." *Psychological Bulletin* 129: 819–835.

Lieving, G. A., and K. A. Lattal. (2003). "Recency, repeatability, and reinforcer retrenchment: An experimental analysis of resurgence." *Journal of the Experimental Analysis of Behavior* 80: 217–233.

Lima, S. L., and P. A. Bednekoff. (1999). "Back to the basics of antipredatory vigilance: Can nonvigilant animals detect attack?" *Animal Behaviour* 58: 537–543.

Limongelli, L., S. T. Boysen, and E. Visalberghi. (1995). "Comprehension of cause-effect relations in a tool-using task by chimpanzees (Pan troglodytes)." *Journal of Comparative Psychology* 109: 18–26.

Lipton, J. S., and E. S. Spelke. (2003). "Origins of number sense: large-number discrimination in human infants." *Psychological Science* 14: 396–401.

LoLordo, V. M. (1979). Constraints on learning. In *Animal Learning: Survey and Analysis*, ed. M. E. Bitterman, V. M. LoLordo, J. B. Overmier, and M. E. Rashotte, 473–504. New York: Plenum Press.

LoLordo, V. M., and A. Droungas. (1989). Selective associations and adaptive specializations: Taste aversions and phobias. In *Contemporary Learning Theories: Instrumental Conditioning Theory and the Impact of Biological Constraints on Learning*, ed. S. B. Klein and R. R. Mowrer, 145–179. Hillsdale, NJ: Lawrence Erlbaum Associates.

LoLordo, V. M., W. J. Jacobs, and D. D. Foree. (1982). "Failure to block control by a relevant stimulus." *Animal Learning and Behavior* 10: 183–193.

Lonsdorf, E. V. (2005). "Sex differences in the development of termite-fishing skills in the wild chimpanzees, Pan troglodytes schweinfurthii, of Gombe National Park, Tanzania." *Animal Behaviour* 70: 673–683.

Lorenz, K. (1935/1970). Companions as factors in the bird's environment. In *Studies in Animal and Human Behavior*, tr. R. D. Martin, 1:101–258. London: Methuen, and Co.

———. (1941/1971). Comparative studies of the motor patterns of Anatinae (1941). In *Studies in Animal and Human Behaviour*, tr. R. D. Martin, 2:14–114. London: Methuen.

———. (1952). *King Solomon's Ring*. New York: Thomas Y. Crowell.

———. (1965). *Evolution and Modification of Behavior*. Chicago: University of Chicago Press.

———. (1970). Notes. In *Studies in Animal and Human Behavior*, ed. R. Martin, 371–380. London: Methuen.

Losey, G. S., Jr. (1979). "Fish cleaning symbiosis: Proximate causes of host behaviour." *Animal Behaviour* 27: 669–685.

Lotem, A. (1993). "Learning to recognize nestlings is maladaptive for cuckoo Cuculus canorus hosts." *Nature* 362: 743–745.

Lotem, A., H. Nakamura, and A. Zahavi. (1995). "Constraints on egg discrimination and cuckoo-host co-evolution." *Animal Behaviour* 49: 1185–1209.

Lovibond, P. F., and D. R. Shanks. (2002). "The role of awareness in pavlovian conditioning: Empirical evidence and theoretical implications." *Journal of Experimental Psychology: Animal Behavior Processes* 28: 3–26.

Lucas, J. R. (1983). "The role of foraging time constraints and variable prey encounter in optimal diet choice." *The American Naturalist* 122: 191–209.

Lucas, J. R., A. Brodin, S. R. de Kort, and N. S. Clayton. (2004). "Does hippocampal size correlate with the degree of caching specialization?" *Proceedings of The Royal Society of London B* 271: 2423–2429.

Lucas, J. R., and L. W. Simmons, eds. (2006). *Essays in Animal Behaviour*. Bulington, MA: Academic Press.

Luck, S. J., and S. P. Vevera. (2002). Attention. In *Stevens' Handbook of Experimental Psychology*, ed. S. Yantis, 1: 235–286. New York: John Wiley and Sons. .

Luck, S. J., and E. K. Vogel. (1997). "The capacity of visual working memory for features and conjunctions." *Nature* 390: 279–281.

Luttbeg, B. (2002). "Assessing the robustness and optimality of alternative decision rules with varying assumptions." *Animal Behaviour* 63: 805–814.

Lynn, S. K., J. Cnaani, and D. R. Papaj. (2005). "Peak shift discrimination learning as a mechanism of signal evolution." *Evolution* 59: 1300–1305.

Lyon, B. E. (2003). "Egg recognition and counting reduce costs of avian conspecific brood parasitism." *Nature* 422: 495–499.

Lyons, D. E., and L. R. Santos. (2006). "Ecology, domain specificity, and the origins of theory of mind: Is competition the catalyst?" *Philosophy Compass* 1: 481–492.

Lythgoe, J. N. (1979). *The Ecology of Vision.* Oxford: Clarendon Press.

Mabry, K. E., and J. A. Stamps. (2008). "Searching for a new home: Decision making by dispersing brush mice." *The American Naturalist* 172: 625–634.

Macedonia, J. M. (1990). "What is communicated in the antipredator calls of lemurs: Evidence from playback experiments with ringtailed and ruffed lemurs." *Ethology* 86: 177–190.

Macedonia, J. M., and C. S. Evans. (1993). "Variation among mammalian alarm call systems and the problem of meaning in animal signals." *Ethology* 93: 177–197.

Machado, A. (1997). "Learning the temporal dynamics of behavior." *Psychological Review* 104: 241–265.

Machado, A., and R. Keen. (1999). "Learning to time (LeT) or scalar expectancy theory (SET)? A critical test of two models of timing." *Psychological Science* 10: 285–290.

———. (2003). "Temporal discrimination in a long operant chamber." *Behavioural Processes* 62: 157–182.

Machado, A., and P. Pata. (2005). "Testing the scalar expectancy theory (SET) and the learning-to-time model (LeT) in a double bisection task." *Learning & Behavior* 33: 111–122.

Machado, A., and F. J. Silva. (2003). "You can lead an ape to a tool, but ... : A review of Povinelli's Folk Physics for Apes: The Chimpanzee's Theory of How the World Works." *Journal of the Experimental Analysis of Behavior* 79: 267–286.

Mackintosh, N. J. (1973). Stimulus selection: Learning to ignore stimuli that predict no change in reinforcement. In *Constraints on Learning*, ed. R. A. Hinde and J. Stevenson-Hinde, 75–100. London: Academic Press.

———. (1974). *The Psychology of Animal Learning.* New York: Academic Press.

———. (1978). Cognitive or associative theories of conditioning: Implications of an analysis of blocking. In *Cognitive Processes in Animal Behavior,* ed. S. H. Hulse, H. Fowler, and W. K. Honig, 155–175. Hillsdale, NJ: Lawrence Erlbaum Associates.

———. (1983). *Conditioning and Associative Learning.* Oxford: Clarendon Press.

———. (1988). "Approaches to the study of animal intelligence." *British Journal of Psychology* 79: 509–525.

———. (1995). "Categorization by people and by pigeons: The twenty-second Bartlett memorial lecture." *Quarterly Journal of Experimental Psychology* 48B: 193–214.

———. (2000). Abstraction and discrimination. In *The Evolution of Cognition,* ed. C. Heyes and L. Huber, 123–141. Cambridge, MA: MIT Press.

———. (2002). "Do not ask whether they have a cognitive map but how they find their way about." *Psicologica* 23: 165–185.

Mackintosh, N. J., B. McGonigle, V. Holgate, and V. Vanderver. (1968). "Factors underlying improvement in serial reversal learning." *Canadian Journal of Psychology* 22: 85–95.

MacLean, E. L., D. J. Merritt, and E. M. Brannon. (2008). "Social complexity predicts transitive reasoning in prosimian primates." *Animal Behaviour* 76: 479–486.

Macmillan, N. A., and C. G. Creelman. (2005). *Detection Theory: A User's Guide.* 2nd ed. Mahwah NJ: Lawrence Erlbaum Associates.

Macphail, E. M. (1982). *Brain and Intelligence in Vertebrates.* Oxford: Clarendon Press.

———. (1987). "The comparative psychology of intelligence." *Behavioral and Brain Sciences* 10: 645–695.

———. (1993). *The Neuroscience of Animal Intelligence.* New York: Columbia University Press.

———. (1996). "Cognitive function in mammals: the evolutionary perspective." *Cognitive Brain Research* 3: 279–290.

———. (1998). *The Evolution of Consciousness.* Oxford: Oxford University Press.

Macphail, E. M., and J. J. Bolhuis. (2001). "The evolution of intelligence: Adaptive specialisations versus general process." *Biological Reviews* 76: 341–364.

Macphail, E. M., M. Good, and R. C. Honey. (1995). "Recognition memory in pigeons for stimuli presented repeatedly: Perceptual learning or reduced associative interference?" *Quarterly Journal of Experimental Psychology* 48B: 13–31.

Macphail, E. M., M. Good, R. C. Honey, and A. Willis. (1995). "Relational learning in pigeons: The role of perceptual processes in between-key recognition of complex stimuli." *Animal Learning & Behavior* 23: 83–92.

Macuda, T., and W. A. Roberts. (1995). "Further evidence for hierarchical chunking in rat spatial memory." *Journal of Experimental Psychology: Animal Behavior Processes* 21: 20–32.

Magurran, A. E. (1990). "The adaptive significance of schooling as an anti-predator defence in fish." *Annual Zoology Fennici* 27: 51–66.

Mahometa, M. J., and M. Domjan. (2005). "Classical conditioning increases reproductive success in Japanese quail, Coturnix japonica." *Animal Behaviour* 69: 983–989.

Maier, N. R. F. (1932a). "A study of orientation in the rat." *Journal of Comparative Psychology* 14: 387–399.

———. (1932b). "Cortical destruction of the posterior part of the brain and its effect on reasoning in rats." *The Journal of Comparative Neurology* 56: 179–214.

Maier, N. R. F., and T. C. Schneirla. (1935/1964). *Principles of Animal Psychology*. New York: Dover.

Maki, W. S. (1987). "On the nonassociative nature of working memory." *Learning and Motivation* 18: 99–117.

Maki, W. S., J. C. Moe, and C. M. Bierley. (1977). "Short-term memory for stimuli, responses, and reinforcers." *Journal of Experimental Psychology: Animal Behavior Processes* 3: 156–177.

Maloney, R. F., and I. G. McLean. (1995). "Historical and experimental learned predator recognition in free-living New Zealand robins." *Animal Behaviour* 50: 1193–1201.

Mangel, M., and B. D. Roitberg. (1989). "Dynamic information and host acceptance by a tephritid fruit fly." *Ecological Entomology* 14: 181–189.

Manger, P. R., and J. D. Pettigrew. (1995). "Electroreception and the feeding behavior of platypus (Ornithorhynchus anatinus: Monotremata: Mammalia)." *Philosophical Transactions of the Royal Society B* 347: 359–381.

Manser, M. B. (2001). "The acoustic structure of suricates' alarm calls varies with predator type and the level of response urgency." *Proceedings of The Royal Society of London B* 268: 2315–2324.

———. (2009). What do functionally referential alarm calls refer to? In *Cognitive Ecology II*, ed. R. Dukas and J. M. Ratcliffe, in press. Chicago: University of Chicago Press.

Manser, M. B., and M. B. Bell. (2004). "Spatial representation of shelter locations in meerkats, Suricata suricatta." *Animal Behaviour* 68: 151–157.

Manser, M. B., M. B. Bell, and L. B. Fletcher. (2001). "The information that receivers extract from alarm calls in suricates." *Proceedings of The Royal Society of London B* 268: 2485–2491.

March, J., V. D. Chamizo, and N. J. Mackintosh. (1992). "Reciprocal overshadowing between intra-maze and extra-maze cues." *Quarterly Journal of Experimental Psychology* 45B: 49–63.

Marcus, E. A., T. G. Nolen, C. H. Rankin, and T. J. Carew. (1988). "Behavioral dissociation of dishabituation, sensitization, and inhibition in Aplysia." *Science* 241: 210–213.

Marcus, G. F. (2006). "Startling starlings." *Nature* 440: 1117–1118.

Margolis, R. L., S. K. Mariscal, J. D. Gordon, J. Dollinger, and J. L. Gould. (1987). "The ontogeny of the pecking response of laughing gull chicks." *Animal Behaviour* 35: 191–202.

Margules, J., and C. R. Gallistel. (1988). "Heading in the rat: Determination by environmental shape." *Animal Learning & Behavior* 16: 404–410.

Mark, T. A., and C. R. Gallistel. (1994). "Kinetics of matching." *Journal of Experimental Psychology: Animal Behavior Processes* 20: 79–95.

Markman, E. M., and M. Abelev. (2004). "Word learning in dogs?" *Trends in Cognitive Sciences* 8: 479–481.

Marler, P. (1970). "A comparative approach to vocal learning: Song development in white-crowned sparrows." *Journal of Comparative & Physiological Psychology* 71: 1–25.

———. (1976). Sensory templates in species-specific behavior. In *Simpler Networks and Behavior*, ed. J. C. Fentress, 314–329. Sunderland, MA: Sinauer Associates, Inc.

———. (1991). The instinct to learn. In *The Epigenesis of Mind*, ed. S. Carey and R. Gelman, 37–66. Hillsdale, NJ: Lawrence Erlbaum Associates.

———. (2004). Science and birdsong: The good old days. In *Nature*'s Music: *The Science of Birdsong*, ed. P. Marler and H. Slabbekoorn, 1–38. San Diego, CA: Elsevier Academic Press.

Marler, P., A. Dufty, and R. Pickert. (1986a). "Vocal communication in the domestic chicken: I. Does a sender communicate information about the quality of a food referent to a reciever?" *Animal Behaviour* 34: 188–193.

———. (1986b). "Vocal communication in the domestic chicken: II. Is a sender sensitive to the presence and nature of a reciever?" *Animal Behaviour* 34: 194–198.

Marler, P., and S. Peters. (1981). "Sparrows learn adult song and more from memory." *Science* 213: 780–782.

———. (1989). Species differences in auditory responsiveness in early vocal learning. In *The Comparative Psychology of Audition: Perceiving Complex Sounds*, ed. R. J. Dooling and S. H. Hulse, 243–273. Hillsdale, NJ: Erlbaum.

Marler, P., and H. Slabbekoorn, eds. (2004). *Nature's Music*. San Diego, CA: Elsevier Academic Press.

Marler, P., and M. Tamura. (1964). "Culturally transmitted patterns of vocal behavior in sparrows." *Science* 146: 1483–1486.

Marr, D. (1982). *Vision*. New York: W. H. Freeman.

Marsh, B., C. Schuck-Paim, and A. Kacelnik. (2004). "Energetic state during learning affects foraging choices in starlings." *Behavioral Ecology* 15: 396–399.

Marston, H. M. (1996). "Analysis of cognitive function in animals, the value of SDT." *Cognitive Brain Research* 3: 269–277.

Martin-Malivel, J., and J. Fagot. (2001). "Perception of pictorial human faces by baboons: Effects of stimulus orientation on discrimination performance." *Animal Learning & Behavior* 29: 10–20.

Martin-Malivel, J., M. C. Mangini, J. Fagot, and I. Biederman. (2006). "Do humans and baboons use the same information when categorizing human and baboon faces?" *Psychological Science* 17: 599–607.

Martin-Ordas, G., J. Call, and F. Colmenares. (2008). "Tubes, tables and traps: Great apes solve two functionally equivalent trap tasks but show no evidence of transfer across tasks." *Animal Cognition* 11: 423–430.

Mason, J. R. (1988). Direct and observational learning by redwinged blackbirds (Agelaius phoeniceus): The importance of complex visual stimuli. In *Social Learning: Psychological and Biological Perspectives*, ed. T. R. Zentall and B. G. Galef Jr., 99–115. Hillsdale, NJ: Lawrence Erlbaum Associates.

Mateo, J. M. (2002). "Kin-recognition abilities and nepotism as a function of sociality." *Proceedings of The Royal Society of London B* 269: 721–727.

———. (2003). "Kin recognition in ground squirrels and other rodents." *Journal of Mammalogy* 84: 1163–1181.

———. (2004). "Recognition systems and biological organization: The perception component of social recognition." *Annales Zoologici Fennici* 41: 729–745.

———. (2006). "The nature and representation of individual recognition odours in Belding's ground squirrels." *Animal Behaviour* 71: 141–154.

Mateo, J. M., and W. G. Holmes. (2004). "Cross-fostering as a means to study kin recognition." *Animal Behaviour* 68: 1451–1459.

Mateo, J. M., and R. E. Johnston. (2000a). "Kin recognition and the 'armpit effect': Evidence of self-referent phenotype matching." *Proceedings of The Royal Society of London B* 267: 695–700.

———. (2000b). "Retention of social recognition after hibernation in Belding's ground squirrels." *Animal Behaviour* 59: 491–499.

Matsuzawa, T. (2007). "Comparative cognitive development." *Developmental Science* 10: 97–103.

Matthews, R. N., M. Domjan, M. Ramsey, and D. Crews. (2007). "Learning effects on sperm competition and reproductive fitness." *Psychological Science* 18: 758–762.

Matyjasiak, P. (2004). "Birds associate species-specific acoustic and visual cues: Recognition of heterospecific rivals by male blackcaps." *Behavioral Ecology* 16: 467–471.

Matzel, L. D. (2002). Learning mutants. *Stevens' Handbook of Experimental Psychology*, ed. C. R. Gallistel, 3:201–238. New York: Wiley.

Matzel, L. D., Y. R. Han, H. Grossman, M. S. Karnik, D. Patel, et al. (2003). "Individual differences in the expression of a 'general' learning ability in mice." *The Journal of Neuroscience* 23: 6423–6433.

Mayford, M., T. Abel, and E. R. Kandel. (1995). "Transgenic approaches to cognition." *Current Opinion in Neurobiology* 5: 141–148.

Maynard Smith, J., and D. Harper. (2003). *Animal Signals*. Oxford: Oxford University Press.

Mazur, J. E. (1981). "Optimization theory fails to predict performance of pigeons in a two-response situation." *Science* 214: 823–825.

———. (1984). "Tests of an equivalence rule for fixed and variable reinforcer delays." *Journal of Experimental Psychology: Animal Behavior Processes* 10: 426–436.

———. (1996). "Past experience, recency, and spontaneous recovery in choice behavior." *Animal Learning & Behavior* 24: 1–10.

———. (2001). "Hyperbolic value addition and general models of animal choice." *Psychological Review* 108: 96–112.

McComb, K., C. Packer, and A. Pusey. (1994). "Roaring and numerical assessment in contests between groups of female lions, Panthera leo." *Animal Behaviour* 47: 379–387.

McDonald, R. J., N. S. Hong, C. Ray, and M. R. Ralph. (2002). "No time of day modulation or time stamp on multiple memory tasks in rats." *Learning and Motivation* 33: 230–252.

McFarland, D. J. (1995). Opportunity versus goals in robots, animals, and people. In *Comparative Approaches to Cognitive Science*, ed. H. L. Roitblat and J.-A. Meyer, 415–433. Cambridge, MA: MIT Press.

McFarland, D. J., and T. Bosser. (1993). *Intelligent Behavior in Animals and Robots*. Cambridge, MA: MIT Press.

McGonigle, B. O., and M. Chalmers. (1977). "Are monkeys logical?" *Nature* 267: 694–696.

McGregor, A., A. Saggerson, J. Pearce, and C. Heyes. (2006). "Blind imitation in pigeons, Columba livia." *Animal Behaviour* 72: 287–296.

McGregor, P. K., ed. (2005). *Animal Communication Networks*. Cambridge: Cambridge University Press.

McGregor, P. K., and M. I. Avery. (1986). "The unsung songs of great tits (Parus major): Learning neighbours' songs for discrimination." *Behavioral Ecology and Sociobiology* 18: 311–316.

McGrew, W. C. (1992). *Chimpanzee Material Culture: Implications for Human Evoluton*. Cambridge: Cambridge University Press.

McLaren, I. P. L. (1994). Representation development in associative systems. In *Causal Mechanisms of Behavioural Development*, ed. J. A. Hogan and J. J. Bolhuis, 377–402. Cambridge: Cambridge University Press.

McLaren, I. P. L., H. Kaye, and N. J. Mackintosh. (1989). An associative theory of the representation of stimuli: applications to perceptual learning and latent inhibition. In *Parallel Distributed Processing*, ed. R. G. M. Morris, 102–130. Oxford: Clarendon Press.

McLaren, I. P. L., and N. J. Mackintosh. (2000). "An elemental model of associative learning: I. Latent inhibition and perceptual learning." *Animal Learning & Behavior* 26: 211–246.

McNamara, J. M., and A. I. Houston. (1992). "Risk-sensitive foraging: A review of the theory." *Bulletin of Mathematical Biology* 54: 355–378.

McNaughton, B. L., C. A. Barnes, J. L. Gerrard, K. Gothard, M. W. Jung, et al. (1996). "Deciphering the hippocampal polyglot: The hippocampus as a path integration system." *The Journal of Experimental Biology* 199: 173–185.

McNaughton, B. L., F. P. Battaglia, O. Jensen, E. I. Moser, and M. Moser. (2006). "Path integration and the neural basis of the 'cognitive map.'" *Nature Reviews Neuroscience* 7: 663–678.

McNaughton, B. L., J. J. Knierim, and M. A. Wilson. (1995). Vector encoding and the vestibular foundations of spatial cognition: Neurophysiological and computational mechanisms. In *The Cognitive Neurosciences,* ed. M. Gazzaniga, 585–595. Cambridge, MA: MIT Press.

McQuoid, L. M., and B. G. Galef Jr. (1992). "Social influences on feeding site selection by burmese fowl (Gallus gallus)." *Journal of Comparative Psychology* 106: 137–141.

Meade, J., D. Biro, and T. Guilford. (2006). "Route recognition in the homing pigeon, Columba livia." *Animal Behaviour* 72: 975–980.

Meck, W. H., ed. (2003). *Functional and Neural Mechanisms of Interval Timing.* Boca Raton, FL: CRC Press.

Meck, W. H., and R. M. Church. (1983). "A mode control model of counting and timing processes." *Journal of Experimental Psychology: Animal Behavior Processes* 9: 320–334.

Medin, D. L., W. A. Roberts, and R. T. Davis. (1976). *Processes of Animal Memory.* Hillsdale, NJ: Lawrence Erlbaum Associates.

Melis, A. P., B. Hare, and M. Tomasello. (2006a). "Chimpanzees recruit the best collaborators." *Science* 311: 1297–1300.

———. (2006b). "Engineering cooperation in chimpanzees: Tolerance constraints on cooperation." *Animal Behaviour* 72: 275–286.

Meltzoff, A. N. (2007). "'Like me': A foundation for social cognition." *Developmental Science* 10: 126–134.

Mendres, K. A., and F. B. M. de Waal. (2000). "Capuchins do cooperate: the advantage of an intuitive task." *Animal Behaviour* 60: 523–529.

Menzel, C. R. (1991). "Cognitive aspects of foraging in Japanese monkeys." *Animal Behaviour* 41: 397–402.

———. (1999). "Unprompted recall and reporting of hidden objects by a chimpanzee (Pan troglodytes) after extended delays." *Journal of Comparative Psychology* 113: 426–434.

Menzel, E. W. (1978). Cognitive mapping in chimpanzees. In *Cognitive Processes in Animal Behavior,* ed. S. H. Hulse, H. Fowler, and W. K. Honig, 375–422. Hillsdale, NJ: Lawrence Erlbaum Associates.

Menzel, R., and R. J. De Marco. (2006). "Spatial memory, navigation and dance behaviour in Apis mellifera." *Journal of Comparative Physiology A* 192: 889–903.

Menzel, R., U. Greggers, A. Smith, S. Berger, R. Brandt, et al. (2005). "Honey bees navigate according to a map-like spatial memory." *Proceedings of the National Academy of Sciences* (USA) 102: 3040–3045.

Merkle, T., M. Knaden, and R. Wehner. (2006). "Uncertainty about nest position influences systematic search strategies in desert ants." *The Journal of Experimental Biology* 209: 3545–3549.

Mery, F., and T. J. Kawecki. (2002). "Experimental evolution of learning ability in fruit flies." *Proceedings of the National Academy of Sciences* (USA) 99: 14274–14279.

Metcalfe, J., and H. Kober. (2005). Self-reflective consciousness and the projectable self. In *The Missing Link in Cognition: Origins of Self-Reflective Consciousness,* ed. H. S. Terrace and J. Metcalfe, 57–83. New York: Oxford University Press.

Mettke-Hofmann, C., and E. Gwinner. (2003). "Long-term memory for a life on the move." *Proceedings of the National Academy of Sciences* (USA) 100: 5863–5866.

Meyer, A., J. M. Morrissey, and M. Schartl. (1994). "Recurrent origin of a sexually selected trait in Xiphophorous fishes inferred from a molecular phylogeny." *Nature* 368: 539–542.

Michelsen, A., B. B. Anderson, J. Storm, W. H. Kirchner, and M. Lindauer. (1992). "How honeybees perceive communication dances, studied by means of a mechanical model." *Behavioral Ecology and Sociobiology* 30: 143–150.

Miklosi, A. (2007). *Dog Behavior, Evolution, and Cognition.* Oxford: Oxford University Press.

Miles, R. C. (1971). Species differences in "transmitting" spatial location information. In *Cognitive Processes of Nonhuman Primates,* ed. L. E. Jarrard. New York: Academic Press.

Milinski, M. (1984). "A predator's cost of overcoming the confusion effect." *Animal Behaviour* 32: 1157–1162.

———. (1990). Information overload and food selection. In *Behavioral Mechanisms in Food Selection,* ed. R. N. Hughes, 721–736. Berlin: Springer-Verlag.

Milinski, M., and R. Heller. (1978). "Influence of a predator on the optimal foraging behaviour of sticklebacks (Gasterosteus aculeatus L.)." *Nature* 275: 642–644.

Milinski, M., and B. Rockenbach. (2007). "Spying on others evolves." *Science* 317: 464–465.

Millar, N. P., D. N. Reznick, M. T. Kinnison, and A. P. Hendry. (2006). "Disentangling the selective factors that act on male colour in wild guppies." *Oikos* 113: 1–12.

Miller, C. T., C. G. Iguina, and M. D. Hauser. (2005). "Processing vocal signals for recognition during antiphonal calling in tamarins." *Animal Behaviour* 69: 1387–1398.

Miller, D. J. (1993). Do animals subitize? In *The Development of Numerical Competence,* ed. S. T. Boysen and E. J. Capaldi, 149–169. Hillsdale, NJ: Lawrence Erlbaum Associates.

Miller, K. A., J. P. Garner, and J. A. Mench. (2006). "Is fearfulness a trait that can be measured with behavioural tests? A validation of four fear tests for Japanese quail." *Animal Behaviour* 71: 1323–1334.

Miller, N. E. (1959). Liberalization of basic S-R concepts: Extensions to conflict behavior, motivation, and social learning. In *Psychology: A Study of a Science,* ed. S. Koch, vol. 2. New York: McGraw-Hill Book Company, Inc.

Miller, N. Y. (2009). "Modeling the effects of enclosure size on geometry learning." *Behavioural Processes* 80: 306–313.

Miller, N. Y., and S. J. Shettleworth. (2007). "Learning about environmental geometry: An associative model." *Journal of Experimental Psychology: Animal Behavior Processes* 33: 191–212.

———. (2008). "An associative model of geometry learning: A modified choice rule." *Journal of Experimental Psychology: Animal Behavior Processes* 34: 419–422.

Miller, R. C. (1922). "The significance of the gregarious habit." *Ecology* 3: 122–126.

Miller, R. R. (2006). "Challenges facing contemporary associative approaches to acquired behavior." *Comparative Cognition & Behavior Reviews* 1: 77–93.

Miller, R. R., R. C. Barnet, and N. J. Grahame. (1995). "Assessment of the Rescorla-Wagner model." *Psychological Bulletin* 117: 363–386.

Miller, R. R., and M. Escobar. (2001). "Contrasting acquisition-focused and performance-focused models of acquired behavior." *Current Directions in Psychological Science* 10: 141–145.

———. (2002). Laws and models of basic conditioning. *Stevens' Handbook of Experimental Psychology,* ed. C. R. Gallistel, 3:47–102. New York: Wiley.

Milton, K. (1988). Foraging behaviour and the evolution of primate intelligence. In *Machiavellian Intelligence,* ed. R. P. Byrne and A. Whiten, 285–305. Oxford: Clarendon Press.

Mineka, S., and M. Cook. (1988). Social learning and the acquisition of snake fear in monkeys. In *Social Learning: Psychological and Biological Perspectives,* ed. T. R. Zentall and B. G. Galef Jr., 51–73. Hillsdale, NJ: Lawrence Erlbaum Associates.

Miner, B. G., S. E. Sultan, S. G. Morgan, D. K. Padilla, and R. A. Relyea. (2005). "Ecological consequences of phenotypic plasticity." *Trends in Ecology and Evolution* 20: 685–692.

Mistlberger, R. E. (1993). "Circadian food-anticipatory activity: formal models and physiological mechanisms." *Neuroscience and Biobehavioral Reviews* 18: 171–195.

Mitchell, S. D. (2005). Anthropomorphism and cross-species modeling. In *Thinking with Animals: New Perspectives on Anthropomorphism,* ed. L. Daston and G. Mitman, 100–117. New York: Columbia University Press.

Mittelstaedt, M. L., and H. Mittelstaedt. (1980). "Homing by path integration in a mammal." *Naturwissenschaften* 67: 566.

Mix, K. S., J. Huttenlocher, and S. C. Levine. (2002). "Multiple cues for quantification in infancy: is number one of them?" *Psychological Bulletin* 128: 278–294.

Mobius, Y., C. Boesch, K. Koops, T. Matsuzawa, and T. Humle. (2008). "Cultural differences in army ant predation by West African chimpanzees? A comparative study of microecological variables." *Animal Behaviour* 76: 37–45.

Moffatt, C. A., and J. A. Hogan. (1992). "Ontogeny of chick responses to maternal food calls in the Burmese red junglefowl (Gallus gallus spadiceus)." *Journal of Comparative Psychology* 106: 92–96.

Moll, H., and M. Tomasello. (2007). "Cooperation and human cognition: The Vygotskian intelligence hypothesis." *Philosophical Transactions of the Royal Society B* 362: 639–648.

Moore, B. R. (1992). "Avian movement imitation and a new form of mimicry: Tracing the evolution of a complex form of learning." *Behaviour* 122: 231–263.

———. (1996). The evolution of imitative learning. In *Social Learning in Animals: The Roots of Culture,* ed. C. M. Heyes and B. G. Galef Jr., 245–265. San Diego, CA: Academic Press.

Moore-Ede, M. C., F. M. Sulzman, and C. A. Fuller. (1982). *The Clocks that Time Us.* Cambridge, MA: Harvard University Press.

Morgan, C. L. (1894). *An Introduction to Comparative Psychology.* London: Walter Scott.

Morris, R. G. M. (1981). "Spatial localization does not require the presence of local cues." *Learning and Motivation* 12: 239–260.

———. (2001). "Episodic-like memory in animals: psychological criteria, neural mechanisms and the value of episodic-like tasks to investigate animal models of neurodegenerative disease." *Philosophical Transactions of the Royal Society B* (London) 356: 1453–1465.

Moss, C. F., and H.-U. Schnitzler. (1989). "Accuracy of target ranging in echolocating bats: Acoustic information processing." *Journal of Comparative Physiology A* 165: 383–393.

Moss, C. F., and A. Surlykke. (2001). "Auditory scene analysis by echolocation in bats." *Journal of the Acoustic Society of America* 110: 2207–2226.

Mrosovsky, N., S. G. Reebs, G. I. Honrado, and P. A. Salmon. (1989). "Behavioural entrainment of circadian rhythms." *Experientia* 45: 696–702.

Mulcahy, N. J., and J. Call. (2006a). "Apes save tools for future use." *Science* 312: 1038–1040.

———. (2006b). "How great apes perform on a modified trap-tube task." *Animal Cognition* 9: 193–199.

Mulcahy, N. J., J. Call, and R. I. M. Dunbar. (2005). "Gorillas (Gorilla gorilla) and orangutans (Pongo pygmaeus) encode relevant problem features in a tool-using task." *Journal of Comparative Psychology* 119: 23–32.

Muller, M., and R. Wehner. (1988). "Path integration in desert ants, Cataglyphis fortis." *Proceedings of the National Academy of Science* 85: 5287–5290.

Murphy, R. A., E. Mondragón, and V. A. Murphy. (2008). "Rule learning by rats." *Science* 319: 1849–1851.

Nagell, K., R. S. Olguin, and M. Tomasello. (1993). "Processes of social learning in the tool use of chimpanzees (Pan troglodytes) and human children (Homo sapiens)." *Journal of Comparative Psychology* 107: 174–186.

Nairne, J. S., J. N. S. Pandeirada, and S. R. Thompson. (2008). "Adaptive memory: The comparative value of survival processing." *Psychological Science* 19: 176–180.

Nakagawa, S., and J. R. Waas. (2004). "'O sibling, where art thou?'—a review of avian sibling recognition with respect to the mammalian literature." *Biological Reviews* 79: 101–119.

Nakahara, K., and Y. Miyashita. (2005). "Understanding intentions: Through the looking glass." *Science* 308: 644–645.

Nakajima, S., and M. Sato. (1993). "Removal of an obstacle—problem-solving behavior in pigeons." *Journal of the Experimental Analysis of Behavior* 59: 131–145.

Nalbach, H. O., F. Wolf-Oberhollenzer, and M. Remy. (1993). Exploring the image. In *Vision, Brain, and Behavior in Birds,* ed. H. P. Zeigler and H.-J. Bischof, 25–46. Cambridge, MA: MIT Press.

Naqshbandi, M., and W. A. Roberts. (2006). "Anticipation of future events in squirrel monkeys (Saimiri sciureus) and rats (Rattus norvegicus): Tests of the Bischof-Kohler hypothesis." *Journal of Comparative Psychology* 120: 345–357.

Narendra, A., K. Cheng, and R. Wehner. (2007). "Acquiring, retaining and integrating memories of the outbound distance in the Australian desert ant Melophorus bagoti." *The Journal of Experimental Biology* 210: 570–577.

Nee, S. (2005). "The great chain of being." *Nature* 435: 429.

Neff, B. D., and P. W. Sherman. (2002). "Decision making and recognition mechanisms." *Proceedings of The Royal Society of London B* 269: 1435–1441.

Nelson, D. A., and P. Marler. (1990). The perception of birdsong and an ecological concept of signal space. In *Comparative Perception: Complex Signals,* ed. W. C. Stebbins and M. A. Berkley, 2:443–477. New York: John Wiley and Sons.

Nelson, T. O., and L. Narens. (1990). "Metamemory: A theoretical framework and new findings." *The Psychology of Learning and Motivation* 26: 125–141.

Newcombe, N. S., and J. Huttenlocher. (2000). *Making Space.* Cambridge, MA: MIT Press.

Newcombe, N. S., and K. R. Ratliff. (2007). Explaining the development of spatial reorientation: Modularity-plus-language versus the emergence of adaptive combination. In *Emerging Landscapes of Mind: Mapping the Nature of Change in Spatial Cognitive Development,* ed. J. Plumert and J. Spencer, 53–76. New York: Oxford University Press.

Newton, A. M., and J. G. de Villiers. (2007). "Thinking while talking: Adults fail nonverbal false-belief reasoning." *Psychological Science* 18: 574–579.

Nicol, C. J., and S. J. Pope. (1996). "The maternal feeding display of domestic hens is sensitive to perceived chick error." *Animal Behaviour* 52: 767–774.

Nieder, A. (2005). "Counting on neurons: the neurobiology of numerical competence." *Nature Reviews Neuroscience* 6: 177–190.

Nieder, A., I. Diester, and O. Tudusciuc. (2006). "Temporal and spatial enumeration processes in the primate parietal cortex." *Science* 313: 1431–1435.

Nihei, Y. (1995). "Variations of behaviour of carrion crows Corvus corone using automobiles as nutcrackers." *Japanese Journal of Ornithology* 44: 21–35.

Nishida, T. (1987). Local traditions and cultural transmission. In *Primate Societies,* ed. B. B. Smuts, D. L. Cheney, R. M. Seyfarth, R. W. Wrangham, and T. T. Struhsaker, 462–474. Chicago: University of Chicago Press.

Noë, R. (2006). "Cooperation experiments: Coordination through communication versus acting apart together." *Animal Behaviour* 71: 1–18.

Nonacs, P. (2001). "State dependent behavior and the Marginal Value Theorem." *Behavioral Ecology* 12: 71–83.

Noser, R., and R. W. Byrne. (2007). "Travel routes and planning of visits to out-of-sight resources in wild chacma baboons, Papio ursinus." *Animal Behaviour* 73: 257–266.

Nowak, M. A. (2006). "Five rules for the evolution of cooperation." *Science* 314: 1560–1563.

O'Brien, W. J., H. I. Browman, and B. I. Evans. (1990). "Search strategies of foraging animals." *American Scientist* 78: 152–160.

O'Keefe, J., and L. Nadel. (1978). *The Hippocampus as a Cognitive Map.* Oxford: Clarendon Press.

Oberling, P., A. S. Bristol, H. Matute, and R. R. Miller. (2000). "Biological significance attentuates overshadowing, relative validity, and degraded contingency effects." *Animal Learning & Behavior* 28: 172–186.

Oden, D. L., R. K. R. Thompson, and D. Premack. (1988). "Spontaneous transfer of matching by infant chimpanzees." *Journal of Experimental Psychology: Animal Behavior Processes* 14: 140–145.

Odling-Smee, L., and V. A. Braithwaite. (2003). "The influence of habitat stability on landmark use during spatial learning in the three-spined stickleback." *Animal Behaviour* 65: 701–707.

Öhman, A., and S. Mineka. (2001). "Fears, phobias, and preparedness: Toward an evolved module of fear and fear learning." *Psychological Review* 108: 483–522.

———. (2003). "The malicious serpent: Snakes as a prototypical stimulus for an evolved module of fear." *Current Directions in Psychological Science* 12: 5–9.

Okamoto-Barth, S., J. Call, and M. Tomasello. (2007). "Great apes' understanding of other individuals' line of sight." *Psychological Science* 18: 462–468.

Olendorf, R., F. H. Rodd, D. Punzalan, A. E. Houde, C. Hurt, et al. (2006). "Frequency-dependent survival in natural guppy populations." *Nature* 441: 633–636.

Oliveira, R. F., M. Lopes, L. A. Carneiro, and A. V. M. Canário. (2001). "Watching fights raises fish hormone levels." *Nature* 409: 475.

Oliveira, R. F., P. K. McGregor, and C. Latruffe. (1998). "Know thine enemy: Fighting fish gather information from observing conspecific interactions." *Proceedings of the Royal Society B* 265: 1045–1049.

Oliveira, R. F., G. G. Rosenthan, I. Schlupp, et al. (2000). "Considerations on the use of video playbacks as visual stimuli: the Lisbon workshop consensus." *Acta Ethologica* 3: 61–65.

Olson, D. J. (1991). "Species differences in spatial memory among Clark's nutcrackers, scrub jays, and pigeons." *Journal of Experimental Psychology: Animal Behavior Processes* 17: 363–376.

Olson, D. J., A. C. Kamil, R. P. Balda, and P. J. Nims. (1995). "Performance of four seed-caching corvid species in operant tests of nonspatial and spatial memory." *Journal of Comparative Psychology* 109: 173–181.

Olson, D. J., and W. S. Maki. (1983). "Characteristics of spatial memory in pigeons." *Journal of Experimental Psychology: Animal Behavior Processes* 9: 266–280.

Olthof, A., C. M. Iden, and W. A. Roberts. (1997). "Judgements of ordinality and summation of number symbols by squirrel monkeys (Saimiri sciureus)." *Journal of Experimental Psychology: Animal Behavior Processes* 23: 325–339.

Olthof, A., and W. A. Roberts. (2000). "Summation of symbols by pigeons (Columba livia): The importance of number and mass of reward items." *Journal of Comparative Psychology* 114: 158–166.

Olthof, A., and A. Santi. (2007). "Pigeons (Columba livia) associate time intervals with symbols in a touch screen task: Evidence for ordinality but not summation." *Journal of Comparative Psychology* 121: 82–94.

Olton, D. S. (1978). Characteristics of spatial memory. In *Cognitive Processes in Animal Behavior,* ed. S. H. Hulse, H. Fowler, and W. K. Honig, 341–373. Hillsdale, NJ: Erlbaum.

Olton, D. S., and R. J. Samuelson. (1976). "Remembrance of places passed: Spatial memory in rats." *Journal of Experimental Psychology: Animal Behavior Processes* 2: 97–116.

Ophir, A. G., and B. G. Galef. (2003). "Female Japanese quail affiliate with live males that they have seen mate on video." *Animal Behaviour* 66: 369–375.

Ord, T. J., R. A. Peters, C. S. Evans, and A. J. Taylor. (2002). "Digital video playback and visual communication in lizards." *Animal Behaviour* 63: 879–890.

Osvath, M., and H. Osvath. (2008). "Chimpanzee (Pan troglodytes) and orangutan (Pongo abelii) forethought: Self-control and pre-experience in the face of future tool use." *Animal Cognition* 11: 661–674.

Ottoni, E. B., and B. D. de Resende. (2005). "Watching the best nutcrackers: What capuchin monkeys (Cebus apella) know about others' tool-using skills." *Animal Cognition* 24: 215–219.

Owren, M. J., and D. Rendall. (2001). "Sound on the rebound: Bringing form and function back to the forefront in understanding nonhuman primate vocal signaling." *Evolutionary Anthropology* 10: 58–71.

Packard, M. G., and J. L. McGaugh. (1996). "Inactivation of hippocampus or caudate nucleus with lidocaine differentially affects expression of place and response learning." *Neurobiology of Learning and Memory* 65: 65–72.

Padoa-Schioppa, C., L. Jandolo, and E. Visalberghi. (2006). "Multi-stage mental process for economic choice in capuchins." *Cognition* 99: B1–B13.

Pagel, M. (1999). "Inferring the historical patterns of biological evolution." *Nature* 401: 877–884.

Pahl, M., H. Zhu, W. Pix, J. Tautz, and S. Zhang. (2007). "Circadian timed episodic-like memory—a bee knows what to do when, and also where." *The Journal of Experimental Biology* 210: 3559–3567.

Palameta, B., and L. Lefebvre. (1985). "The social transmission of a food-finding technique in pigeons: what is learned?" *Animal Behaviour* 33: 892–896.

Papi, F. (1992). General aspects. In *Animal Homing*, ed. F. Papi, 2–45. London: Chapman and Hall.

Papi, F., and H. G. Wallraff. (1992). Birds. In *Animal Homing*, ed. F. Papi, 263–319. London: Chapman, and Hall.

Papineau, D., and C. Heyes. (2006). Rational or associative? Imitation in Japanese quail. In *Rational Animals?*, ed. S. Hurley and M. Nudds, 187–195. Oxford: Oxford University Press.

Papini, M. R. (2002). "Pattern and process in the evolution of learning." *Psychological Review* 109: 186–201.

———. (2008). *Comparative Psychology*. New York: Psychology Press.

Parker, G. A., and J. Maynard Smith. (1990). "Optimality theory in evolutionary biology." *Nature* 348: 27–33.

Parr, L. A. (2003). "The discrimination of faces and their emotional content by chimpanzees (Pan troglodytes)." *Annals of the New York Academy of Sciences* 1000: 56–78.

Parr, L. A., J. T. Winslow, W. D. Hopkins, and F. B. M. de Waal. (2000). "Recognizing facial cues: Individual discrimination by chimpanzees (Pan troglodytes) and rhesus monkeys (Macaca mulatta)." *Journal of Comparative Psychology* 114: 47–60.

Partan, S. R. (2004). Multisensory animal communication. In *Handbook of Multisensory Processes*, ed. G. Calvert, C. Spence, and B. E. Stein, 225–240. Cambridge, MA: MIT Press.

Partan, S. R., and P. Marler. (2005). "Issues in the classification of multimodal communication signals." The *American Naturalist* 166: 231–245.

Patricelli, G. L., S. W. Coleman, and G. Borgia. (2006). "Male satin bowerbirds, Ptilonorhynchus violaceus, adjust their display intensity in response to female startling: an experiment with robotic females." *Animal Behaviour* 71: 49–59.

Paukner, A., J. R. Anderson, E. Borelli, E. Visalberghi, and P. F. Ferrari. (2005). "Macaques (Macaca nemestrina) recognize when they are being imitated." *Biology Letters* 1: 219–222.

Paukner, A., J. R. Anderson, and K. Fujita. (2006). "Redundant food searches by capuchin monkeys (Cebus apella): A failure of metacognition?" *Animal Cognition* 9: 110–117.

Pavlov, I. P. (1927). *Conditioned Reflexes*. Oxford: Oxford University Press.

Paz-y-Mino C., G., A. B. Bond, A. C. Kamil, and R. P. Balda. (2004). "Pinyon jays use transitive inference to predict social dominance." *Nature* 430: 778–781.

Peake, T. M. (2005). Eavesdropping in communication networks. In *Animal Communication Networks*, ed. P. K. McGregor, 13–37. Cambridge: Cambridge University Press.

Peake, T. M., R. J. Matos, and P. K. McGregor. (2006). "Effects of manipulated aggressive 'interactions' on bystanding male fighting fish, Betta splendens." *Animal Behaviour* 72: 1013–1020.

Pearce, J. M. (1987). "A model for stimulus generalization in Pavlovian conditioning." *Psychological Review* 94: 61–73.

———. (1988). Stimulus generalization and the acquisition of categories by pigeons. In *Thought without Language*, ed. L. Weiskrantz: 133–155. Oxford: Clarendon Press.

———. (1989). "The acquisition of an artificial category by pigeons." *Quarterly Journal of Experimental Psychology* 41B: 381–406.

———. (1994a). "Similarity and discrimination: A selective review and a connectionist model." *Psychological Review* 101: 587–607.

———. (1994b). Discrimination and categorization. In *Animal Learning and Cognition*, ed. N. J. Mackintosh, 109–134. San Diego, CA: Academic Press.

———. (2008). *Animal Learning & Cognition*. New York: Psychology Press.

Pearce, J. M., and M. E. Bouton. (2001). "Theories of associative learning in animals." *Annual Review of Psychology* 52: 111–139.

Pearce, J. M., M. A. Good, P. M. Jones, and A. McGregor. (2004). "Transfer of spatial behavior between different environments: Implications for theories of spatial learning and for the role of the hippocampus in spatial learning." *Journal of Experimental Psychology: Animal Behavior Processes* 30: 135–147.

Pearce, J. M., and G. Hall. (1980). "A model for Pavlovian conditioning: Variations in the effectiveness of conditioned but not unconditioned stimuli." *Psychological Review* 87: 332–352.

Pearce, J. M., J. Ward-Robinson, M. Good, C. Fussell, and A. Aydin. (2001). "Influence of a beacon on spatial learning based on the shape of the test environment." *Journal of Experimental Psychology: Animal Behavior Processes* 27: 329–344.

Penn, D. C., K. J. Holyoak, and D. J. Povinelli. (2008). "Darwin's mistake: Explaining the discontinuity between human and nonhuman minds." *Behavioral and Brain Sciences* 31: 109–178.

Penn, D. C., and D. J. Povinelli. (2007a). "Causal cognition in human and nonhuman animals: A comparative, critical review." *Annual Review of Psychology* 58: 97–118.

———. (2007b). "On the lack of evidence that non-human animals possess anything remotely resembling a 'theory of mind.'" *Philosophical Transactions of the Royal Society B* 362: 731–744.

———. (in press). The comparative delusion: the 'behavioristic'/'mentalistic' dichotomy in comparative theory of mind research. In *Oxford Handbook of Philosophy and Cognitive Science*, ed. R. Samuels and S. Stich. Oxford: Oxford University Press.

Pepperberg, I. M. (1994). "Numerical competence in an African gray parrot (Psittacus erithacus)." *Journal of Comparative Psychology* 108: 36–44.

———. (1999). *The Alex Studies*. Cambridge, MA: Harvard University Press.

———. (2006). "Grey parrot numerical competence: A review." *Animal Cognition* 9: 377–391.

Pereira, M. E., and J. M. Macedonia. (1991). "Ringtailed lemur anti-predator calls denote predator class, not response urgency." *Animal Behaviour* 41: 543–544.

Perner, J., and T. Ruffman. (2005). "Infants' insight into the mind: How deep?" *Science* 308: 214–216.

Perry, S. E. (2006). "What cultural primatology can tell anthropologists about the evolution of culture." *Annual Review of Anthropology* 35: 171–190.

Perry, S. E., M. Baker, L. Fedigan, J. Gros-Louis, K. Jack, et al. (2003). "Social conventions in wild white-faced capuchin monkeys." *Current Anthropology* 44: 241–268.

Perry, S. E., and J. H. Manson. (2003). "Traditions in monkeys." *Evolutionary Anthropology* 12: 71–81.

Petrie, M., A. Krupa, and T. Burke. (1999). "Peacocks lek with relatives even in the absence of social environmental cues." *Nature* 401: 155–157.

Petrinovich, L., and T. L. Patterson. (1979). "Field studies of habituation: I. Effect of reproductive condition, number of trials, and different delay intervals on responses of the white-crowned sparrow." *Journal of Comparative and Physiological Psychology* 93: 337–350.

Pfungst, O. (1965). *Clever Hans (The Horse of Mr. Von Osten)*. New York: Holt, Rinehart and Winston.

Phelps, S. M., A. S. Rand, and M. J. Ryan. (2006). "A cognitive framework for mate choice and species recognition." *The American Naturalist* 167: 28–42.

Pica, P., C. Lemer, V. Izard, and S. Dehaene. (2004). "Exact and approximate arithmetic in an Amazonian indigene group." *Science* 306: 499–503.

Pickens, C. L., and P. C. Holland. (2004). "Conditioning and cognition." *Neuroscience and Biobehavioral Reviews* 28: 651–661.

Pietrewicz, A. T., and A. C. Kamil. (1981). Search images and the detection of cryptic prey: An operant approach. In *Foraging Behavior: Ecological, Ethological, and Psychological Approaches*, ed. A. C. Kamil and T. D. Sargent, 311–331. New York: Garland STPM Press.

Pinel, J. P. J., and D. Treit. (1978). "Burying as a defensive response in rats." *Journal of Comparative and Physiological Psychology* 92: 708–712.

Pinker, S. (1994). *The Language Instinct*. New York: William Morrow.

Pinker, S., and R. Jackendoff. (2005). "The faculty of language: What's special about it?" *Cognition* 95: 201–236.

Pizzo, M. J., and J. D. Crystal. (2002). "Representation of time in time-place learning." *Animal Learning & Behavior* 30: 387–393.

Plaisted, K. C. (1997). "The effect of interstimulus interval on the discrimination of cryptic targets." *Journal of Experimental Psychology: Animal Behavior Processes* 23: 248–259.

Plaisted, K. C., and N. J. Mackintosh. (1995). "Visual search for cryptic stimuli in pigeons: Implications for the search image and search rate hypotheses." *Animal Behaviour* 50: 1219–1232.

Platt, J. R., and D. M. Johnson. (1971). "Localization of position within a homogeneous behavior chain: Effects of error contingencies." *Learning and Motivation* 2: 386–414.

Plotkin, H. (2004). *Evolutionary Thought in Psychology*. Malden MA: Blackwell.

Plotnik, J. M., F. B. M. de Waal, and D. Reiss. (2006). "Self-recognition in an Asian elephant." *Proceedings of the National Academy of Sciences* (USA) 103: 17053–17057.

Plowright, C. M. S. (1996). "Simultaneous processing of short delays and higher order temporal intervals within a session by pigeons." *Behavioural Processes* 38: 1–9.

Plowright, C. M. S., D. Church, P. Behnke, and A. Silverman. (2000). "Time estimation by pigeons on a fixed interval: the effect of pre-feeding." *Behavioural Processes* 52: 43–48.

Plowright, C. M. S., and S. J. Shettleworth. (1991). "Time horizon and choice by pigeons in a prey selection task." *Animal Learning and Behavior* 19: 103–112.

Pollick, A. S., H. Gouzoules, and F. B. M. De Waal. (2005). "Audience effects on food calls in captive brown capuchin monkeys, Cebus apella." *Animal Behaviour* 70: 1273–1281.

Pompilio, L., and A. Kacelnik. (2005). "State-dependent learning and suboptimal choice: When starlings prefer long over short delays to food." *Animal Behaviour* 70: 571–578.

Pompilio, L., A. Kacelnik, and S. T. Behmer. (2006). "State-dependent learned valuation drives choice in an invertebrate." *Science* 311: 1613–1615.

Poucet, B. (1993). "Spatial cognitive maps in animals: New hypotheses on their structure and neural mechanisms." *Psychological Review* 100: 163–182.

Poucet, B., N. Chapuis, M. Durup, and C. Thinus-Blanc. (1986). "A study of exploratory behavior as an index of spatial knowledge in hamsters." *Animal Learning & Behavior* 14: 93–100.

Povinelli, D. J. (1994). "Comparative studies of animal mental state attribution: A reply to Heyes." *Animal Behaviour* 48: 239–341.

———. (1996). Chimpanzee theory of mind? The long road to strong inference. In *Theories of Theories of Mind,* ed. P. Carruthers and P. K. Smith, 293–329. Cambridge: Cambridge University Press.

———. (2000). *Folk Physics for Apes*. New York: Oxford University Press.

Povinelli, D. J., J. M. Bering, and S. Giambrone. (2000). "Toward a science of other minds: Escaping the argument by analogy." *Cognitive Science* 24: 509–541.

Povinelli, D. J., and J. G. H. Cant. (1995). "Arboreal clambering and the evolution of self-conception." *The Quarterly Review of Biology* 70: 393–421.

Povinelli, D. J., and S. deBlois. (1992). "Young children's (Homo sapiens) understanding of knowledge formation in themselves and others." *Journal of Comparative Psychology* 106: 228–238.

Povinelli, D. J., and T. J. Eddy. (1996a). "What young chimpanzees know about seeing." *Monographs of the Society for Research in Child Development* 61(247): 1–152.

———. (1996b). "Chimpanzees: Joint visual attention." *Psychological Science* 7: 129–135.

Povinelli, D. J., and T. J. Eddy. (1996c). "Factors influencing young chimpanzees' (Pan troglodytes) recognition of attention." *Journal of Comparative Psychology* 110: 336–345.

Povinelli, D. J., G. G. Gallup Jr., T. J. Eddy, D. T. Bierschwale, M. C. Engstrom, et al. (1997). "Chimpanzees recognize themselves in mirrors." *Animal Behaviour* 53: 1083–1088.

Povinelli, D. J., K. E. Nelson, and S. T. Boysen. (1990). "Inferences about guessing and knowing by chimpanzees (Pan troglodytes)." *Journal of Comparative Psychology* 104: 203–210.

Povinelli, D. J., and T. M. Preuss. (1995). "Theory of mind: Evolutionary history of a cognitive specialization." *Trends in Neurosciences* 18: 418–424.

Povinelli, D. J., A. B. Rulf, K. R. Landau, and D. T. Bierschwale. (1993). "Self-recognition in chimpanzees (Pan troglodytes): Distribution, ontogeny, and patterns of emergence." *Journal of Comparative Psychology* 107: 347–372.

Povinelli, D. J., and J. Vonk. (2003). "Chimpanzee minds: Suspiciously human?" *Trends in Cognitive Sciences* 7: 157–160.

———. (2004). "We don't need a microscope to explore the chimpanzee's mind." *Mind & Language* 19: 1–28.

Prather, J. F., S. Peters, S. Nowicki, and R. Mooney. (2008). "Precise auditory-vocal mirroring in neurons for learned vocal communication." *Nature* 451: 305–310.

Pravosudov, V. V. (2008). "Mountain chickadees discriminate between potential cache pilferers and non-pilferers." *Proceedings of the Royal Society B* 275: 55–61.

Pravosudov, V. V., and N. S. Clayton. (2002). "A test of the adaptive specialization hypothesis: Population differences in caching, memory, and the hippocampus in black-capped chickadees (Poscile atricapilla)." *Behavioral Neuroscience* 116: 515–522.

Pravosudov, V. V., A. S. Kitaysky, and A. Omanska. (2006). "The relationship between migratory behaviour, memory and the hippocampus: an intraspecific comparison." *Proceedings of the Royal Society B* 273: 2641–2649.

Premack, D. (1971). "Language in chimpanzee?" *Science* 172: 808–822.

———. (1983). "Animal Cognition." *Annual Review of Psychology* 34: 351–362.

———. (1988). 'Does the chimpanzee have a theory of mind?' revisited. In *Machiavellian Intelligence: Social Expertise and the Evolution of Intellect in Monkeys, Apes, and Humans,* ed. R. W. Byrne and A. Whiten, 160–179. Oxford: Clarendon Press.

———. (2007). "Human and Animal Cognition: Continuity and discontinuity." *Proceedings of the National Academy of Sciences* (USA) 104: 13861–13867.

Premack, D., and A. J. Premack. (1983). *The Mind of an Ape.* New York: W.W. Norton and Company.

———. (1994). "Levels of causal understanding in chimpanzees and children." *Cognition* 50: 347–362.

Premack, D., and G. Woodruff. (1978). "Does the chimpanzee have a theory of mind?" *The Behavioral and Brain Sciences* 4: 515–526.

Preuss, T. M. (1995). The argument from animals to humans in cognitive neuroscience. *The Cognitive Neurosciences,* ed. M. Gazzaniga, 1227–1241. Cambridge, MA: MIT Press.

Prior, H., A. Schwarz, and O. Güntürkün. (2008). "Mirror-induced behavior in the magpie (Pica pica): Evidence of self-recognition." *Public Library of Science: Biology* 6: 1642–1650.

Proctor, H. C. (1992). "Sensory exploitation and the evolution of male mating behaviour: A cladistic test using water mites (Acari: Parasitengona)." *Animal Behaviour* 44: 745–752.

Provine, R. R. (2005). "Yawning." *American Scientist* 93: 532–540.

Prusky, G. T., and R. M. Douglas. (2005). Vision. In *The Behavior of the Laboratory Rat,* ed. I. Q. Whishaw and B. Kolb, 49–59. New York: Oxford University Press.

Pyke, G. H. (1979). "Optimal foraging in bumblebees: Rule of movement between flowers within inflorescences." *Animal Behaviour* 27: 1167–1181.

Pyter, L. M., B. F. Reader, and R. J. Nelson. (2005). "Short photoperiods impair spatial learning and alter hippocamal dendritic morphology in adult male white-footed mice (Peromyscus leucopus)." *Journal of Neuroscience* 25: 4521–4526.

Raby, C. R., D. M. Alexis, A. Dickinson, and N. S. Clayton. (2007). "Planning for the future by Western scrub-jays." *Nature* 445: 919–921.

Raby, C. R., and N. S. Clayton. (2009). "Prospective cognition in animals." *Behavioural Processes* 80: 314–324.

Radford, A. N., and A. R. Ridley. (2006). "Recruitment calling: A novel form of extended parental care in an altricial species." *Current Biology* 16: 1700–1704.

Radick, G. (2007). *The Simian Tongue.* Chicago: University of Chicago Press.

Raihani, N. J., and A. R. Ridley. (2008). "Experimental evidence for teaching in wild pied babblers." *Animal Behaviour* 75: 3–11.

Rainey, H. J., K. Zuberbühler, and P. J. B. Slater. (2004). "Hornbills can distinguish between primate alarm calls." *Proceedings of The Royal Society of London B* 271: 755–759.

Ramachandran, V. S., C. W. Tyler, R. L. Gregory, D. Rogers-Ramachnadran, S. Duensing, et al. (1996). "Rapid adaptive camouflage in tropical flounders." *Nature* 379: 815–818.

Ramsey, G., M. L. Bastian, and C. van Schaik. (2007). "Animal innovation defined and operationalized." *Behavioral and Brain Sciences* 30: 393–437.

Range, F., and L. Huber. (2007). "Attention in common marmosets: Implications for social-learning experiments." *Animal Behaviour* 73: 1033–1041.

Range, F., and R. Noë. (2005). "Can simple rules account for the pattern of triadic interactions in juvenile and adult female sooty mangabeys?" *Animal Behaviour* 69: 445–452.

Ratcliffe, J. M., M. B. Fenton, and B. G. Galef, Jr. (2003). "An exception to the rule: Common vampire bats do not learn taste aversions." *Animal Behaviour* 65: 385–389.

Ratcliffe, J. M., and M. L. Nydam. (2008). "Multimodal warning signals for a multiple predator world." *Nature* 455: 96–99.

Reader, S. M. (2004). "Distinguishing social and asocial learning using diffusion dynamics." *Learning & Behavior* 32: 90–104.

Reader, S. M., and K. N. Laland. (2002). "Social intelligence, innovation, and enhanced brain size in primates." *Proceedings of the National Academy of Sciences* (USA) 99: 4436–4441.

———. eds. (2003). *Animal Innovation*. Oxford: Oxford University Press.

Real, L. A. (1991). "Animal choice behaviour and the evolution of cognitive architecture." *Science* 253: 980–986.

———. (1993). "Toward a cognitive ecology." *Trends in Ecology and Evolution* 8: 413–417.

Real, P. G., R. Iannazzi, A. C. Kamil, and B. Heinrich. (1984). "Discrimination and generalization of leaf damage by blue jays (Cyanocitta cristata)." *Animal Learning and Behavior* 12: 202–208.

Reale, D., S. M. Reader, D. Sol, P. T. McDougall, and N. J. Dingemanse. (2007). "Integrating animal temperament within ecology and evolution." *Biological Reviews* 82: 291–318.

Reboreda, J. C., N. S. Clayton, and A. Kacelnik. (1996). "Species and sex differences in hippocampus size in parasitic and non-parasitic cowbirds." *Neuroreport* 7: 505–508.

Redhead, E. S., A. Roberts, M. Good, and J. M. Pearce. (1997). "Interaction between piloting and beacon homing by rats in a swimming pool." *Journal of Experimental Psychology: Animal Behavior Processes* 23: 340–350.

Reed, P., and T. A. Morgan. (2007). "Resurgence of behavior during extinction depends on previous rate of response." *Learning & Behavior* 35: 106–114.

Reeve, H. K. (1989). "The evolution of conspecific acceptance thresholds." *The American Naturalist* 133: 407–435.

Regolin, L., G. Vallortigara, and M. Zanforlin. (1995). "Object and spatial representations in detour problems by chicks." *Animal Behaviour* 49: 195–199.

Reid, P. J. (2009). "Adapting to the human world: Dogs' responsiveness to our social cues." *Behavioural Processes* 80: 325–333.

Reid, P. J., and S. J. Shettleworth. (1992). "Detection of cryptic prey: Search image or search rate?" *Journal of Experimental Psychology: Animal Behavior Processes* 18: 273–286.

Reinhard, J., M. V. Srinivasan, D. Guez, and S. W. Zhang. (2004). "Floral scents induce recall of navigational and visual memories in honeybees." *The Journal of Experimental Biology* 207: 4371–4381.

Rescorla, R. A. (1967). "Pavlovian conditioning and its proper control procedures." *Psychological Review* 74: 71–80.

———. (1969). "Pavlovian conditioned inhibition." *Psychological Bulletin* 72: 77–94.

———. (1986). "Extinction of facilitation." *Journal of Experimental Psychology: Animal Behavior Processes* 12: 16–24.

———. (1987). "Facilitation and inhibition." *Journal of Experimental Psychology: Animal Behavior Processes* 13: 250–259.

———. (1988a). "Pavlovian conditioning: It's not what you think it is." *American Psychologist* 43: 151–160.

———. (1988b). "Behavioral studies of Pavlovian conditioning." *Annual Review of Neuroscience* 11: 329–352.

———. (1996). "Spontaneous recovery after training with multiple outcomes." *Animal Learning & Behavior* 24: 11–18.

———. (2004). "Spontaneous recovery." *Learning & Memory* 11: 501–509.

———. (2005). "Spontaneous recovery of excitation but not inhibition." *Journal of Experimental Psychology: Animal Behavior Processes* 31: 277–288.

———. (2007). Learning: A pre-theoretical concept. In *Science of Memory: Concepts,* ed. H. L. Roediger, Y. Dudai, and S. Fitzpatrick, 37–40. Oxford: Oxford Univversity Press.

———. (2008a). "Evaluating conditioning of related and unrelated stimuli using a compound test." *Learning and Behavior* 36: 67–74.

———. (2008b). "Conditioning of stimuli with nonzero initial value." *Journal of Experimental Psychology: Animal Behavior Processes* 34: 315–323.

Rescorla, R. A., and C. L. Cunningham. (1979). "Spatial contiguity facilitates Pavlovian second-order conditioning." *Journal of Experimental Psychology: Animal Behavior Processes* 5: 152–161.

Rescorla, R. A., and P. J. Durlach. (1981). Within-event learning in Pavlovian conditioning. In *Information Processing in Animals: Memory Mechanisms,* ed. N. E. Spear and R. R. Miller, 81–111. Hillsdale, NJ: Lawrence Erlbaum Associates.

Rescorla, R. A., and D. R. Furrow. (1977). "Stimulus similarity as a determinant of Pavlovian conditioning." *Journal of Experimental Psychology: Animal Behavior Processes* 3: 203–215.

Rescorla, R. A., and P. C. Holland. (1976). Some behavioral approaches to the study of learning. In *Neural Mechanisms of Learning and Memory,* ed. M. R. Rosenzweig and E. L. Bennett, 165–192. Cambridge, MA: MIT Press.

Rescorla, R. A., and A. R. Wagner. (1972). A theory of Pavlovian conditioning: Variations in the effectiveness of reinforcement and nonreinforcement. In *Classical Conditioning II: Current Theory and Research,* ed. A. H. Black and W. F. Prokasy, 64–99. New York: Appleton-Century-Crofts.

Restle, F. (1957). "Discrimination of cues in mazes: A resolution of the "place-vs.-response" question." *Psychological Review* 64: 217–228.

Richards, R. J. (1987). *Darwin and the Emergence of Evolutionary Theories of Mind and Behavior.* Chicago: University of Chicago Press.

Richardson, T. O., P. A. Sleeman, J. M. McNamara, A. I. Houston, and N. R. Franks. (2007). "Teaching with evaluation in ants." *Current Biology* 17: 1520–1526.

Richerson, P. J., and R. Boyd. (2005). *Not by Genes Alone.* Chicago: University of Chicago Press.

Ridley, M. (1993). *Evolution.* Oxford: Blackwell Scientific.

Rijnsdorp, A., S. Daan, and C. Dijkstra. (1981). "Hunting in the kestrel, Falco tinnunculus, and the adaptive significance of daily habits." *Oecologia* 50: 391–406.

Riley, D. A., and C. M. Langley. (1993). "The logic of species comparisons." *Psychological Science* 4: 185–189.

Riley, D. A., and C. R. Leith. (1976). "Multidimensional psychophysics and selective attention in animals." *Psychological Bulletin* 83: 138–160.

Riley, J. R., U. Greggers, A. D. Smith, D. R. Reynolds, and R. Menzel. (2005). "The flight paths of honeybees recruited by the waggle dance." *Nature* 435: 205–207.

Rilling, M. (1993). Invisible counting animals: A history of contributions from comparative psycholgy, ethology, and learning theory. In *The Development of Numerical Competence,* ed. S. T. Boysen and E. J. Capaldi, 3–37. Hillsdale, NJ: Lawrence Erlbaum Associates, Publishers.

Ristau, C. A., ed. (1991a). *Cognitive Ethology: The Minds of Other Animals.* Hillsdale, NJ: Lawrence Erlbaum Associates.

———. (1991b). Aspects of the cognitive ethology of an injury-feigning bird, the piping plover. In *Cognitive Ethology: The Minds of Other Animals,* ed. C. A. Ristau, 91–126. Hillsdale, NJ: Lawrence Erlbaum Associates.

———. (1996). Animal language and cognition projects. In *Handbook of Human Symbolic Evolution,* ed. A. Lock and C. R. Peters, 644–680. Oxford: Clarendon Press.

Ristau, C. A., and D. Robbins. (1982). "Language in the great apes: A critical review." *Advances in the Study of Behavior* 12: 141–255.

Rivas, E. (2005). "Recent use of signs by chimpanzees (Pan Troglodytes) in interactions with humans." *Journal of Comparative Psychology* 119: 404–417.

Rizzolatti, G., and L. Fogassi. (2007). Mirror neurons and social cognition. In *The Oxford Handbook of Evolutionary Psychology,* ed. R. I. M. Dunbar and L. Barrett, 179–195. Oxford: Oxford University Press.

Roberts, A. D. L., and J. M. Pearce. (1999). "Blocking in the Morris swimming pool." *Journal of Experimental Psychology: Animal Behavior Processes* 25: 225–235.

Roberts, S. (1981). "Isolation of an internal clock." *Journal of Experimental Psychology: Animal Behavior Processes* 7: 242–268.

Roberts, W. A. (1980). "Distribution of trials and intertrial retention in delayed matching to sample with pigeons." *Journal of Experimental Psychology: Animal Behavior Processes* 6: 217–237.

———. (1981). "Retroactive inhibition in rat spatial memory." *Animal Learning & Behavior* 9: 566–574.

———. (1984). Some issues in animal spatial memory. In *Animal Cognition,* ed. H. L. Roitblat, T. G. Bever, and H. S. Terrace. Hillsdale, NJ: Lawrence Erlbaum Associates.

———. (2002). "Are animals stuck in time?" *Psychological Bulletin* 128: 473–489.

———. (2005). "How do pigeons represent numbers? Studies of number scale bisection." *Behavioural Processes* 69: 33–43.

Roberts, W. A., K. Cheng, and J. S. Cohen. (1989). "Timing light and tone signals in pigeons." *Journal of Experimental Psychology: Animal Behavior Processes* 15: 23–35.

Roberts, W. A., C. Cruz, and J. Tremblay. (2007). "Rats take correct novel routes and shortcuts in an enclosed maze." *Journal of Experimental Psychology: Animal Behavior Processes* 33: 79–91.

Roberts, W. A., M. C. Feeney, K. MacPherson, M. Petter, N. McMillan, et al. (2008). "Episodic-like memory in rats: Is it based on when or how long ago?" *Science* 320: 113–115.

Roberts, W. A., and D. S. Grant. (1978). "An analysis of light-induced retroactive inhibition in pigeon short-term memory." *Journal of Experimental Psychology: Animal Behavior Processes* 4: 219–236.

Roberts, W. A., and S. Mitchell. (1994). "Can a pigeon simultaneously process temporal and numerical information?" *Journal of Experimental Psychology: Animal Behavior Processes* 20: 66–78.

Roberts, W. A., and M. T. Phelps. (1994). "Transitive inference in rats: A test of the spatial coding hypothesis." *Psychological Science* 5: 368–374.

Roberts, W. A., M. T. Phelps, T. Macuda, D. R. Brodbeck, and T. Russ. (1996). "Intraocular transfer and simulantaneous processing of stimuli presented in different visual fields of the pigeon." *Behavioral Neuroscience* 110: 290–299.

Robinson, G. E. (2004). "Beyond nature and nurture." *Science* 304: 397–399.

Rodd, F. H., K. A. Hughes, G. F. Grether, and C. T. Baril. (2002). "A possible non-sexual origin of mate preference: Are male guppies mimicking fruit?" *Proceedings of The Royal Society of London B* 269: 475–481.

Rodrigo, T., V. D. Chamizo, I. P. L. McLaren, and N. J. Mackintosh. (1994). "Effects of pre-exposure to the same or different pattern of extra-maze cues on subsequent extre-maze discrimination." *The Quarterly Journal of Experimental Psychology* 47B: 15–26.

———. (1997). "Blocking in the spatial domain." *Journal of Experimental Psychology: Animal Behavior Processes* 23: 110–118.

Roediger, H. L., Y. Dudai, and S. M. Fitzpatrick, eds. (2007). *Science of Memory: Concepts.* New York: Oxford University Press.

Roitblat, H. L. (1987). *Introduction to Comparative Cognition.* New York: W.H. Freeman and Company.

Roitblat, H. L., T. G. Bever, and H. S. Terrace, eds. (1984). *Animal Cognition.* Hillsdale, NJ: Lawrence Erlbaum Associates.

Roma, P. G., A. Silberberg, A. M. Ruggiero, and S. J. Suomi. (2006). "Capuchin monkeys, inequity aversion, and the frustration effect." *Journal of Comparative Psychology* 120: 67–73.

Romanes, G. J. (1892). *Animal Intelligence.* New York: D. Appleton and Company.

Ron, S. R. (2008). "The evolution of female mate choice for complex calls in tungara frogs." *Animal Behaviour* 76: 1783–1794.

Roper, K. L., D. H. Kaiser, and T. R. Zentall. (1995). "True directed forgetting in pigeons may occur only when alternative working memory is required on forget-cue trials." *Animal Learning & Behavior* 23: 280–285.

Rosati, A. G., J. R. Stevens, B. Hare, and M. D. Hauser. (2007). "The evolutionary origins of human patience: Temporal preferences in chimpanzees, bonobos, and human adults." *Current Biology* 17: 1663–1668.

Ross-Gillespie, A., and A. S. Griffin. (2007). "Meerkats." *Current Biology* 17: R442–R443.

Roth, G., and U. Dicke. (2005). "Evolution of the brain and intelligence." *Trends in Cognitive Sciences* 9: 250–257.

Rowe, C. (1999). "Receiver psychology and the evolution of multicomponent signals." *Animal Behaviour* 58: 921–931.

Rowe, C., and J. Skelhorn. (2004). "Avian psychology and communication." *Proceedings of The Royal Society of London B* 271: 1435–1442.

Royle, N. J., J. Lindstrom, and N. B. Metcalfe. (2008). "Context-dependent mate choice in relation to social composition in green swordtails Xiphophorus helleri." *Behavioral Ecology* 19: 998–1005.

Rozin, P. (1976). "The evolution of intelligence and access to the cognitive unconscious." *Progress in Psychobiology and Physiological Psychology* 6: 245–280.

Rozin, P., and J. W. Kalat. (1971). "Specific hungers and poison avoidance as adaptive specializations of learning." *Psychological Review* 78: 459–486.

Rozin, P., and J. Schull. (1988). The adaptive-evolutionary point of view in experimental psychology. In *Stevens' Handbook of Experimental Psychology,* ed. R. Atkinson, R. J. Herrnstein, G. Lindzey, and R. D. Luce, 503–546. New York: Wiley.

Rumbaugh, D. M., ed. (1977). *Language Learning by a Chimpanzee.* New York: Academic Press.

Rumbaugh, D. M., and J. L. Pate. (1984). The evolution of cognition in primates: A comparative perspective. In *Animal Cognition,* ed. H. L. Roitblat, T. G. Bever, and H. S. Terrace, 569–587. Hillsdale, NJ: Lawrence Erlbaum Associates.

Rumbaugh, D. M., and E. S. Savage-Rumbaugh. (1994). Language in comparative perspective. In *Animal Learning and Cognition,* ed. N. J. Mackintosh, 307–333. San Diego, CA: Academic Press.

Rumbaugh, D. M., E. S. Savage-Rumbaugh, and R. A. Sevcik. (1994). Biobehavioral roots of language: A comparative perspective of chimpanzee, child, and culture. In *Chimpanzee Cultures,* ed. R. W. Wrangham, W. C. McGrew, F. B. M. de Waal, P. G. Heltne, and L. A. Marquardt, 319–334. Cambridge, MA: Harvard University Press.

Rumbaugh, D. M., E. S. Savage-Rumbaugh, and D. A. Washburn. (1996). "Toward a new outlook on primate learning and behavior: Complex learning and emergent processes in comparative perspective." *Japanese Psychological Research* 38: 113–125.

Russon, A. E., and B. M. F. Galdikas. (1993). "Imitation in free-ranging rehabilitant orangutans (Pongo pygmaeus)." *Journal of Comparative Psychology* 107: 147–161.

———. (1995). "Constraints on great apes' imitation: Model and action selectivity in rehabilitant orangutan (Pongo pygmaeus) imitation." *Journal of Comparative Psychology* 109: 5–17.

Ruxton, G. D., T. N. Sherratt, and M. P. Speed. (2004). *Avoiding Attack.* Oxford: Oxford University Press.

Ryan, M. J. (1994). Mechanisms underlying sexual selection. In *Behavioral Mechanisms in Evolutionary Ecology,* ed. L. A. Real, 190–215. Chicago: University of Chicago Press.

Ryan, M. J., and A. Keddy-Hector. (1992). "Directional patterns of female mate choice and the role of sensory biases." *American Naturalist* 139, supplement: s4–s35.

Ryan, M. J., and A. S. Rand. (1993). "Sexual selection and signal evolution: The ghost of biases past." *Philosophical Transactions of the Royal Society B* 340: 187–195.

Ryan, M. J., and A. S. Rand. (1995). "Female responses to ancestral advertisement calls in Tungara frogs." *Science* 269: 390–392.

Saggerson, A. L., D. N. George, and R. C. Honey. (2005). "Imitative learning of stimulus-response and response-outcome associations in pigeons." *Journal of Experimental Psychology: Animal Behavior Processes* 31: 289–300.

Saint Paul, U. v. (1982). Do geese use path integration for walking home? In *Avian Navigation*, ed. F. Papi and H. G. Wallraff, 298–307. New York: Springer-Verlag.

Sanfey, A. G., G. Loewenstein, S. M. McClure, and J. D. Cohen. (2006). "Neuroeconomics: Cross-currents in research on decision-making." *Trends in Cognitive Sciences* 10: 108–116.

Santos, L. R., H. M. Pearson, G. M. Spaepen, F. Tsao, and M. D. Hauser. (2006). "Probing the limits of tool competence: Experiments with two non-tool-using species (Cercopithecus aethiops and Saguinus oedipus)." *Animal Cognition* 9: 94–109.

Sanz, C., D. Morgan, and S. Gulick. (2004). "New insights into chimpanzees, tools, and termites from the Congo basin." *The American Naturalist* 164: 567–581.

Sargisson, R. J., and K. G. White. (2004). "Need probability effects in animal short-term memory." *Behavioural Processes* 65: 57–66.

Sauvage, M. M., N. Fortin, C. B. Owens, A. P. Yonelinas, and H. Eichenbaum. (2008). "Recognition emory: Opposite effects of hippocampal damage on recollection and familiarity." *Nature Neuroscience* 11: 16–18.

Savage-Rumbaugh, E. S. (1986). *Ape Language: From Conditioned Response to Symbol.* New York: Columbia University Press.

Savage-Rumbaugh, E. S., and K. E. Brakke. (1996). Animal language: Methodological and interpretive issues. In *Readings in Animal Cognition*, ed. M. Bekoff and D. Jamieson, 269–288. Cambridge, MA: MIT Press.

Savage-Rumbaugh, E. S., K. McDonald, R. A. Sevcik, W. D. Hopkins, and E. Rubert. (1986). "Spontaneous symbol acquisition and communicative use by a pygmy chimpanzee (Pan paniscus)." *Journal of Experimental Psychology: General* 115: 211–235.

Savage-Rumbaugh, E. S., and R. Lewin. (1994). *Kanzi, the Ape at the Brink of the Human Mind.* New York: John Wiley, and Sons.

Savage-Rumbaugh, E. S., J. Murphy, R. A. Sevcik, K. E. Brakke, S. L. Williams, et al. (1993). "Language comprehension in ape and child." *Monographs of the Society for Research in Child Development* 58: 1–256.

Savage-Rumbaugh, E. S., J. L. Pate, J. Lawson, S. T. Smith, and S. Rosenbaum. (1983). "Can a chimpanzee make a statement?" *Journal of Experimental Psychology: General* 112: 457–492.

Savage-Rumbaugh, E. S., D. M. Rumbaugh, and S. Boysen. (1978). "Symbolic communication between two chimpanzees (Pan troglodytes)." *Science* 201: 641–644.

Savastano, H. I., and R. R. Miller. (1998). "Time as content in Pavlovian conditioning." *Behavioural Processes* 44: 147–162.

Save, E., S. Granon, M. C. Buhot, and C. Thinus-Blanc. (1996). "Effects of limitations on the use of some visual and kinaesthetic information in spatial mapping during exploration in the rat." *Quarterly Journal of Experimental Psychology* 49B: 134–147.

Sawa, K., K. J. Leising, and A. P. Blaisdell. (2005). "Sensory preconditioning in spatial learning using a touch screen task in pigeons." *Journal of Experimental Psychology: Animal Behavior Processes* 31: 368–375.

Schacter, D. L. (1995). Implicit memory: A new frontier for cognitive neuroscience. In *The Cognitive Neurosciences,* ed. M. Gazzaniga, 815–824. Cambridge, MA: MIT Press.

Scheiber, I. B. R., B. M. Weiss, D. Frigerio, and K. Kotrschal. (2005). "Active and passive social support in families of greylag geese (Anser anser)." *Behaviour* 142: 1535–1557.

Scheid, C., F. Range, and T. Bugnyar. (2007). "When, what, and whom to watch? Quantifying attention in ravens (Corvus corax) and jackdaws (Corvus monedula)." *Journal of Comparative Psychology* 121: 380–386.

Schiffrin, R. M. (1988). Attention. In *Stevens' Handbook of Experimental Psychology,* ed. R. C. Atkinson, R. J. Herrnstein, G. Lindzey, and R. D. Luce, 2:739–811. New York: Wiley.

Schiller, P. H. (1957). Innate motor action as a basis of learning. In *Instinctive Behavior,* ed. C. H. Schiller, 264–287. New York: International Universities Press, Inc.

Schino, G., E. P. Di Sorrentino, and B. Tiddi. (2007). "Grooming and coalitions in Japanese macaques (Macaca fuscata): Partner choice and the time frame of reciprocation." *Journal of Comparative Psychology* 121: 181–188.

Schino, G., B. Tiddi, and E. P. Di Sorrentino. (2006). "Simultaneous classification by rank and kinship in Japanese macaques." *Animal Behaviour* 71: 1069–1074.

Schlosser, G., and G. P. Wagner, eds. (2004). *Modularity in Development and Evolution.* Chicago: University of Chicago Press.

Scholl, B. J., and P. D. Tremoulet. (2000). "Perceptual causality and animacy." *Trends in Cognitive Sciences* 4: 299–309.

Schradin, C. (2000). "Confusion effect in a reptilian and primate predator." *Ethology* 106: 691–700.

Schuck-Palm, C., and A. Kacelnik. (2007). "Choice processes in multialternative decision making." *Behavioral Ecology* 18: 541–550.

Schuck-Paim, C., L. Pompilio, and A. Kacelnik. (2004). "State-dependent decisions cause apparent violations of rationality in animal choice." *PLos Biology* 2: 2305–2315.

Schusterman, R. J., and D. Kastak. (1998). "Functional equivalence in a California sea lion: Relevance to animal social and communicative interactions." *Animal Behaviour* 55: 1087–1095.

Schusterman, R. J., C. R. Kastak, and D. Kastak. (2003). Equivalence classification as an approach to social knowledge: From sea lions to simians. In *Animal Social Complexity,* ed. F. B. M. de Waal and P. L. Tyack, 179–206. Cambridge, MA: Harvard University Press.

Schwagmeyer, P. L. (1995). "Searching today for tomorrow's mates." *Animal Behaviour* 50: 759–767.

Searcy, W. A., S. Coffman, and D. F. Raikow. (1994). "Habituation, recovery, and the similarity of song types within repertoires in red-winged blackbirds (Agelaius phoeniceus) (Aves, Emberizdae)." *Ethology* 98: 38–49.

Searcy, W. A., and S. Nowicki. (2005). *The Evolution of Animal Communication.* Princeton, NJ: Princeton University Press.

Seed, A. M., J. Call, N. J. Emery, and N. S. Clayton. (2009). "Chimpanzees solve the trap problem when the confound of tool-use is removed." *Journal of Experimental Psychology: Animal Behavior Processes* 35: 23–34.

Seed, A. M., S. Tebbich, N. J. Emery, and N. S. Clayton. (2006). "Investigating physical cognition in rooks, Corvus frugilegus." *Current Biology* 16: 697–701.

Seeley, T. D. (1985). *Honey Bee Ecology.* Princeton, NJ: Princeton University Press.

——. (1995). *The Wisdom of the Hive.* Cambridge, MA: Harvard University Press.

Seidenberg, M. S., and L. A. Petitto. (1987). "Communication, symbolic communication, and language: Comment on Savage-Rumbaugh, McDonald, Sevcik, Hopkins, and Rupert (1986)." *Journal of Experimental Psychology: General* 116: 279–287.

Seligman, M. E. P. (1970). "On the generality of the laws of learning." *Psychological Review* 77: 406–418.

Seyfarth, R. M., and D. L. Cheney. (1986). "Vocal development in vervet monkeys." *Animal Behaviour* 34: 1640–1658.

——. (1990). "The assessment by vervet monkeys of their own and another species' alarm calls." *Animal Behaviour* 40: 754–764.

——. (1992). "Meaning and mind in monkeys." *Scientific American* 267: 122–128.

——. (1994). The evolution of social cognition in primates. In *Behavioral Mechanisms in Evolutionary Ecology,* ed. L. A. Real, 371–389. Chicago: University of Chicago Press.

——. (1997). "Behavioral mechanisms underlying vocal communication in nonhuman primates." *Animal Learning and Behavior* 25: 249–267.

——. (2003a). The structure of social knowledge in monkeys. In *Animal Social Complexity,* ed. F. B. M. de Waal and P. L. Tyack, 207–229. Cambridge, MA: Harvard University Press.

————. (2003b). "Meaning and emotion in animal vocalizations." *Annals of the New York Academy of Sciences* 1000: 32–55.

————. (2003c). "Signalers and receivers in animal communication." *Annual Review of Psychology* 54: 145–173.

Seyfarth, R. M., D. L. Cheney, and P. Marler. (1980). "Monkey responses to three different alarm calls: Evidence of predator classification and semantic communication." *Science* 210: 801–803.

Shafir, S., T. A. Waite, and B. H. Smith. (2002). "Context-dependent violations of rational choice in honeybees (Apis mellifera) and gray jays (Perisoreus canadensis)." *Behavioral Ecology* and Sociobiology 51: 180–187.

Shanks, D. R. (1994). Human associative learning. In *Animal Learning and Cognition*, ed. N. J. Mackintosh, 335–374. San Diego, CA: Academic Press.

Shapiro, M. S., S. A Siller, and A. A Kacelnik. (2008). "Simultaneous and sequential choice as a function of reward delay and magnitude: Normative, descriptive and process-based models tested in the European starling (Sturnus vulgaris)." *Journal of Experimental Psychology: Animal Behavior Processes* 34: 75–93.

Sharp, S. P., A. McGowan, M. J. Wood, and B. J. Hatchwell. (2005). "Learned kin recognition cues in a social bird." *Nature* 434: 1127–1130.

Shepard, R. N. (1984). "Ecological constraints on internal representation: Resonant kinematics of perceiving, imagining, thinking, and dreaming." *Psychological Review* 91: 417–447.

————. (1987). "Toward a universal law of generalization for Psychological Science." *Science* 237: 1317–1323.

————. (1994). "Perceptual-cognitive universals as reflections of the world." *Psychonomic Bulletin and Review* 1: 2–28.

Sherman, P. W., H. K. Reeve, and P. W. Pfennig. (1997). Recognition systems. In *Behavioural Ecology*, ed. J. R. Krebs and N. B. Davies, 69–96. Oxford: Blackwell Scientific.

Sherry, D. F. (1977). "Parental food-calling and the role of the young in the Burmese red junglefowl (Gallus gallus spadiceus)." *Animal Behaviour* 25: 594–601.

————. (1984). "Food storage by black-capped chickadees: memory for the location and contents of caches." *Animal Behaviour* 32: 451–464.

————. (1988). Learning and adaptation in food-storing birds. In *Evolution and Learning*, ed. R. C. Bolles and M. D. Beecher, 79–95. Hillsdale, NJ: Lawrence Erlbaum Associates.

————. (2005). "Do ideas about function help in the study of causation?" *Animal Biology* 55: 441–456.

————. (2006). "Neuroecology." *Annual Review of Psychology* 57: 167–197.

Sherry, D. F., and S. J. Duff. (1996). "Behavioural and neural bases of orientation in food-storing birds." *The Journal of Experimental Biology* 199: 165–171.

Sherry, D. F., M. R. L. Forbes, M. Khurgel, and G. O. Ivy. (1993). "Females have a larger hippocampus than males in the brood-parasitic brown-headed cowbird." *Proceedings of the National Academy of Sciences* (USA) 90: 7839–7843.

Sherry, D. F., and B. G. Galef Jr. (1984). "Cultural transmission without imitation: Milk bottle opening by birds." *Animal Behaviour* 32: 937–938.

————. (1990). "Social learning without imitation: More about milk bottle opening by birds." *Animal Behaviour* 40: 987–989.

Sherry, D. F., L. F. Jacobs, and S. J. C. Gaulin. (1992). "Spatial memory and adaptive specialization of the hippocampus." *Trends in Neurosciences* 15: 298–303.

Sherry, D. F., and D. L. Schacter. (1987). "The evolution of multiple memory systems." *Psychological Review* 94: 439–454.

Sherry, D. F., A. L. Vaccarino, K. Buckenham, and R. S. Herz. (1989). "The hippocampal complex of food-storing birds." *Brain, Behavior, and Evolution* 34: 308–317.

Shettleworth, S. J. (1972). Constraints on learning. In *Advances in the Study of Behavior*, ed. D. S. Lehrman, R. A. Hinde, and E. Shaw, 4:1–68. New York: Academic Press.

————. (1975). "Reinforcement and the organization of behavior in golden hamsters: Hunger, environment, and food reinforcement." *Journal of Experimental Psychology: Animal Behavior Processes* 104: 56–87.

———. (1983). Function and mechanism in learning. In *Advances in Analysis of Behaviour.* Vol. 3: *Biological Factors in Learning,* ed. M. D. Zeiler and P. Harzem, 1–39. Chichester, UK: John Wiley and Sons.

———. (1987). Learning and foraging in pigeons: Effects of handling time and changing food availability on patch choice. In *Foraging,* ed. M. L. Commons, A. Kacelnik, and S. J. Shettleworth, 115–132. Vol. 6 of *Quantative Analyses of Behavior.* Hillsdale, NJ: Lawrence Erlbaum Associates.

———. (1988). "Foraging as operant behavior and operant behavior as foraging: What have we learned?" *The Psychology of Learning and Motivation* 22: 1–49.

———. (1993). "Where is the comparison in comparative cognition? Alternative research programs." *Psychological Science* 4: 179–184.

———. (1994a). "Commentary: What are behavior systems and what use are they?" *Psychonomic Bulletin and Review* 1: 451–456.

———. (1995). Comparative studies of memory in food storing birds: From the field to the Skinner box. In *Behavioral Brain Research in Naturalistic and Semi-Naturalistic Settings,* ed. E. Alleva, A. Fasolo, H. P. Lipp, L. Nadel, and L. Ricceri, 159–192. Dordrecht: Kluwer Academic Press.

———. (1998). *Cognition, Evolution, and Behavior.* New York: Oxford University Press.

———. (2000). Modularity and the evolution of cognition. In *The Evolution of Cognition,* ed. C. Heyes and L. Huber, 43–60. Cambridge, MA: MIT Press.

———. (2007). "Planning for breakfast." *Nature* 445: 825–826.

———. (2009). "The evolution of comparative cognition: Is the snark still a boojum?" *Behavioural Processes* 80: 210–217.

Shettleworth, S. J., and R. R. Hampton. (1998). Adaptive specializations of spatial cognition in food storing birds? Approaches to testing a comparative hypothesis. In *Animal Cognition in Nature,* ed. R. P. Balda, I. M. Pepperberg, and A. C. Kamil, 65–98. San Diego, CA: Academic Press.

Shettleworth, S. J., and J. R. Krebs. (1982). "How marsh tits find their hoards: The roles of site preference and spatial memory." *Journal of Experimental Psychology: Animal Behavior Processes* 8: 354–375.

Shettleworth, S. J., J. R. Krebs, D. W. Stephens, and J. Gibbon. (1988). "Tracking a fluctuating environment: a study of sampling." *Animal Behaviour* 36: 87–105.

Shettleworth, S. J., and J. E. Sutton. (2005). "Multiple systems for spatial learning: Dead reckoning and beaon homing in rats." *Journal of Experimental Psychology: Animal Behavior Processes* 31: 125–141.

Shettleworth, S. J., and R. P. Westwood. (2002). "Divided attention, memory, and spatial discrimination in food-storing and non-storing birds, black-capped chickadees (Poecile atricapilla) and dark-eyed juncos (Junco hyemalis)." *Journal of Experimental Psychology: Animal Behavior Processes* 28: 227–241.

Shields, W. E., J. D. Smith, K. Guttmanova, and D. A. Washburn. (2005). "Confidence judgements by humans and rhesus monkeys." *Journal of General Psychology* 132: 165–186.

Shields, W. E., J. D. Smith, and D. A. Washburn. (1997). "Uncertain responses by humans and rhesus monkeys (Macaca mulatta) in a psychophysical same-different task." *Journal of Experimental Psychology: General* 126: 147–164.

Shillito, E. E. (1963). "Exploratory behaviour in the short-tailed vole Microtus agrestis." *Behaviour* 21: 145–154.

Shimp, C. P., W. T. Herbranson, T. Fremouw, and A. L. Froehlich. (2006). Rule learning, memorization strategies, switching attention between local and global levels of perception, and optimality in avian visual categorization. In *Comparative Cognition: Experimental Explorations of Animal Intelligence,* ed. E. A. Wasserman and T. R. Zentall, 388–404. New York: Oxford University Press.

Shorten, M. (1954). The reaction of the brown rat towards changes in its environment. In *Control of Rats and Mice,* ed. D. Chitty and H. N. Southern, 2:307–334. Oxford: Clarendon Press.

Sidman, M. (2000). "Equivalence relations and the reinforcement contingency." *Journal of the Experimental Analysis of Behavior* 74: 127–146.

Siegel, S. (2005). "Drug tolerance, drug addiction, and drug anticipation." *Current Directions in Psychological Science* 14: 296–300.

Siegel, S., and L. G. Allan. (1996). "The widespread influence of the Rescorla-Wagner model." *Psychonomic Bulletin and Review* 3: 314–321.

Sih, A., A. M. Bell, J. C. Johnson, and R. E. Ziemba. (2004). "Behavoral syndromes: An integrative overview." *Quarterly Review of Biology* 79: 241–277.

Sih, A., and B. Christensen. (2001). "Optimal diet theory: When does it work, and when and why does it fail?" *Animal Behaviour* 61: 379–390.

Silk, J. B. (1999). "Male bonnet macaques use information about third-party rank relationships to recruit allies." *Animal Behaviour* 58: 45–51.

———. (2007a). "The adaptive value of sociality in mammalian groups." *Philosophical Transactions of the Royal Society B* 362: 539–559.

———. (2007b). "Social components of fitness in primate groups." *Science*. 317: 1347–1351.

———. (2007c). Empathy, sympathy, and prosocial preferences in primates. In *The Oxford Handbook of Evolutionary Psychology*, ed. R. I. M. Dunbar and L. Barrett, 115–126. Oxford: Oxford University Press.

———. (2007d). "The dynamics of cooperation in primate groups: Insights from game theory." *Advances in the Study of Behaviour* 37: 1–42.

Silk, J. B., S. F. Brosnan, J. Vonk, J. Henrich, D. J. Povinelli, et al. (2005). "Chimpanzees are indifferent to the welfare of unrelated group members." *Nature* 437: 1357–1359.

Silva, F. J., D. M. Page, and K. M. Silva. (2005). "Methodological-conceptual problems in the study of chimpanzees' folk physics: How studies of adult humans can help." *Learning & Behavior* 33: 47–57.

Silva, F. J., and K. M. Silva. (2006). "Humans' folk physics is not enough to explain variations in their tool-using behavior." *Psychonomic Bulletin & Review* 13: 689–693.

Silva, K. M., and W. Timberlake. (1997). "A behavior systems view of response form during long and short CS-US intervals." *Learning and Motivation* 28: 465–490.

Silver, R. (1990). Biological timing mechanisms with special emphasis on the parental behavior of doves. In *Contemporary Issues in Comparative Psychology*, ed. D. A. Dewsbury, 252–277. Sunderland, MA: Sinauer Associates.

Simon, H. A. (1962). "The architecture of complexity." *Proceedings of the American Philosophical Society* 106: 467–482.

Singer, R. A., B. D. Abroms, and T. R. Zentall. (2006). "Formation of a simple cognitive map by rats." *International Journal of Comparative Psychology* 19: 1–10.

Skelhorn, J., and C. Rowe. (2006). "Prey palatability influences predator learning and memory." *Animal Behaviour* 71: 1111–1118.

Skinner, B. F. (1938). *The Behavior of Organisms*. New York: Appleton-Century-Crofts.

Skov-Rackette, S. I., N. Y. Miller, and S. J. Shettleworth. (2006). "What—where—when memory in pigeons." *Journal of Experimental Psychology: Animal Behavior Processes* 32: 345–358.

Skov-Rackette, S. I., and S. J. Shettleworth. (2005). "What do rats learn about the geometry of object arrays? Tests with exploratory behavior." *Journal of Experimental Psychology: Animal Behavior Processes* 31: 273–284.

Slabbekoorn, H. (2004). Singing in the wild: the ecology of birdsong. In *Nature's Music: The Science of Birdsong*, ed. P. Marler and H. Slabbekoorn, 178–205. San Diego, CA: Elsevier Academic Press.

Slater, P. J. B. (1983). The development of individual behaviour. *Animal Behaviour (Genes, Development and Learning)*, ed. T. R. Halliday and P. J. B. Slater, 3:82–113. New York: W.H. Freeman and Company.

Slotnick, B., L. Hanford, and W. Hodos. (2000). "Can rats acquire an olfactory learning set?" *Journal of Experimental Psychology: Animal Behavior Processes* 26: 399–415.

Smith, B. R., A. K. Piel, and D. K. Candland. (2003). "Numerity of a socially housed hamadryas baboon (Papio hamadryas) and a socially housed squirrel monkey (Saimiri sciureus)." *Journal of Comparative Psychology* 117: 217–225.

Smith, C. N., R. E. Clark, J. R. Manns, and L. R. Squire. (2005). "Acquisition of differential delay eyeblink classical conditioning is independent of awareness." *Behavioral Neuroscience* 119: 78–86.

Smith, J. D., M. J. Beran, J. J. Couchman, and M. V. C. Coutinho. (2008). "The comparative study of metacognition: Sharper paradigms, safer inferences." *Psychonomic Bulletin & Review* 15: 679–691.

Smith, J. D., M. J. Beran, J. S. Redford, and D. A. Washburn. (2006). "Dissociating uncertainty responses and reinforcement signals in the comparative study of uncertainty monitoring." *Journal of Experimental Psychology: General* 135: 282–297.

Smith, J. D., J. P. Minda, and D. A. Washburn. (2004). "Category learning in rhesus monkeys: A study of the Shepard, Hovland and Jenkins (1961) tasks." *Journal of Experimental Psychology: General* 133: 398–414.

Smith, J. D., J. S. Redford, S. M. Haas, M. V. C. Coutinho, and J. J. Couchman. (2008). "The comparative psychology of same-different judgments by humans (Homo sapiens) and monkeys (Macaca mulatta)." *Journal of Experimental Psychology: Animal Behavior Processes* 34: 361–374.

Smith, J. D., W. E. Shields, and D. A. Washburn. (2003). "The comparative psychology of uncertainty monitoring and metacognition." *Behavioral and Brain Sciences* 26: 317–373.

Smith, J. D., and D. A. Washburn. (2005). "Uncertainty monitoring and metacognition by animals." *Current Directions in Psychological Science* 14: 19–24.

Smith, M. C., S. R. Coleman, and I. Gormezano. (1969). "Classical conditioning of the rabbit's nictitating membrane response at backward, simultaneous, and forward CS-US intervals." *Journal of Comparative and Physiological Psychology* 69: 226–231.

Smith, P. K. (1996). Language and the evolution of mind-reading. In *Theories of Theories of Mind*, ed. P. Carruthers and P. K. Smith, 344–354. Cambridge: Cambridge University Press.

Smith, W. J. (1977). *The Behavior of Communicating*. Cambridge, MA: Harvard University Press.

Sober, E. (1998). "Black box inference: When should intervening variables be postulated?" *The British Journal for the Philosophy of Science* 49: 469–498.

———. (2001). The principle of conservatism in cognitive ethology. In *Naturalism, Evolution, and Mind*, ed. D. M. Walsh, 225–238. Cambridge: Cambridge University Press.

———. (2005). Comparative psychology meets evolutionary biology: Morgan's canon and cladistic parsimony. In *Thinking with Animals: New perspectives on Anthropomorphism*, ed. L. Daston and G. Mitman, 85–99. New York: Columbia University Press.

Sokolov, E. N. (1963). *Perception and the Conditioned Reflex*. Oxford: Pergamon Press.

Sokolowski, M. B., and J. D. Levine. (in press). Nature-nuture interactions. In *Social Behavior: Genes, Ecology, and Evolution*, ed. T. Szekely, A. J. Moore, and J. Komdeur. Cambridge: Cambridge University Press.

Sol, D., R. P. Duncan, T. M. Blackburn, P. Cassey, and L. Lefebvre. (2005). "Big brains, enhanced cognition, and response of birds to novel environments." *Proceedings of the National Academy of Science* 102: 5460–5465.

Sole, L. M., S. J. Shettleworth, and P. J. Bennett. (2003). "Uncertainty in pigeons." *Psychonomic Bulletin and Review* 10: 738–745.

Son, L. K., and N. Kornell. (2005). Meta-confidence judgements in rhseus macaques: Explicit vs. implicit mechanisms. In *The Missing Link in Cognition: Origins of Self-Reflective Consciousness*, ed. H. S. Terrace and J. Metcalfe, 296–320. New York: Oxford University Press.

Spelke, E. S., and K. D. Kinzler. (2007). "Core knowledge." *Developmental Science* 10: 89–96.

Spence, K. W. (1937). "The differential response in animals to stimuli varying within a single dimension." *Psychological Review* 44: 430–444.

Spetch, M. L. (1995). "Overshadowing in landmark learning: Touch-screen studies with pigeons and humans." *Jounal of Experimental Psychology: Animal Behavior Processes* 21:166–181.

Spetch, M. L., and K. Cheng. (1998). "A step function in pigeons' temporal generalization in the peak shift task." *Animal Learning & Behavior* 26: 103–118.

Spetch, M. L., K. Cheng, and S. E. MacDonald. (1996). "Learning the configuration of a landmark array: I. Touch-screen studies with pigeons and humans." *Journal of Comparative Psychology* 110: 55–68.

Spetch, M. L., K. Cheng, S. E. MacDonald, B. A. Linkenhoker, D. M. Kelly, et al. (1997). "Use of landmark configuration in pigeons and humans: II. Generality across search tasks." *Journal of Comparative Psychology* 111: 14–24.

Spetch, M. L., and A. Friedman. (2006). "Comparative cognition of object recognition." *Comparative Cognition & Behavior Reviews* 1: 12–35.

Spetch, M. L., T. B. Rust, A. C. Kamil, and J. E. Jones. (2003). "Searching by rules: Pigeons' (Columba livia) landmark-based search according to constant bearing or constant distance." *Journal of Comparative Psychology* 117: 123–132.

Spetch, M. L., D. M. Wilkie, and J. P. J. Pinel. (1981). "Backward conditioning: A reevaluation of the empirical evidence." *Psychological Bulletin* 89: 163–175.

Srinivasan, M. V., S. W. Zhang, M. Lehrer, and T. S. Collett. (1996). "Honeybee navigation en route to the goal: Visual flight control and odometry." *The Journal of Experimental Biology* 199: 237–244.

St Amant, R., and T. E. Horton. (2008). "Revisiting the definition of animal tool use." *Animal Behaviour* 75: 1199–1208.

Staddon, J. E. R. (1975). "A note on the evolutionary significance of 'supernormal' stimuli." *American Naturalist* 109: 541–545.

———. (1983). *Adaptive Behavior and Learning.* Cambridge: Cambridge University Press.

———. (2000). "Consciousness and theoretical behaviorism." *American Zoologist* 40: 874–882.

———. (2005). "Interval timing: Memory, not a clock." *Trends in Cognitive Sciences* 9: 312–314.

Staddon, J. E. R., and D. T. Cerutti. (2003). "Operant conditioning." *Annual Review of Psychology* 54: 115–144.

Staddon, J. E. R., and J. J. Higa. (1996). "Multiple time scales in simple habituation." *Psychological Review* 103: 720–733.

Stahl, J., and P. Ellen. (1974). "Factors in the resoning performance of the rat." *Journal of Comparative and Physiological Psychology* 87: 598–604.

Stamps, J. A. (1991). "Why evolutionary issues are reviving interest in proximate behavioral mechanisms." *American Zoologist* 31: 338–348.

———. (1995). "Motor learning and the value of familiar space." *American Naturalist* 146: 41–58.

Stamps, J. A., and R. R. Swaisgood. (2007). "Someplace like home: Experience, habitat selection and conservation biology." *Applied Animal Behavior Science* 102: 392–409.

Stanhope, K. J. (1989). "Dissociation of the effect of reinforcer type and response strength on the force of a condtioned response." *Animal Learning and Behavior* 17: 311–321.

Starkey, P., and R. G. Cooper. (1980). "Perception of numbers by human infants." *Science* 210: 1033–1035.

Stearns, S. C., and R. F. Hoekstra. (2005). *Evolution: An Introduction.* New York: Oxford University Press.

Stephens, D. W. (1981). "The logic of risk-sensitive foraging preferences." *Animal Behaviour* 29: 628–629.

———. (1987). "On economically tracking a variable environment." *Theoretical Population Biology* 32: 15–25.

———. (1991). "Change, regularity, and value in the evolution of animal learning." *Behavioral Ecology* 2: 77–89.

———. (2007). Models of information use. In *Foraging,* ed. D. W. Stephens, J. S. Brown, and R. C. Ydenberg, 31–58. Chicago: University of Chicago Press.

Stephens, D. W., J. S. Brown, and R. C. Ydenberg, eds. (2007). *Foraging.* Chicago: University of Chicago Press.

Stephens, D. W., B. Kerr, and E. Fernández-Juricic. (2004). "Impulsiveness without discounting: The ecological rationality hypothesis." *Proceedings of The Royal Society of London B* 271: 2459–2465.

Stephens, D. W., and J. R. Krebs. (1986). *Foraging Theory*. Princeton, NJ: Princeton University Press.

Stevens, J. R., F. A. Cushman, and M. D. Hauser. (2005). "Evolving the psychological mechanisms for cooperation." *Annual Review of Ecology, Evolution, and Systematics* 36: 499–518.

Stevens, J. R., E. V. Hallinan, and M. D. Hauser. (2005). "The ecology and evolution of patience in two New World monkeys." *Biology Letters* 1: 223–226.

Stevens, J. R., and M. D. Hauser. (2004). "Why be nice? Psychological constraints on the evolution of cooperation." *Trends in Cognitive Sciences* 8: 60–65.

Stoddard, P. K., M. D. Beecher, P. Loesche, and S. E. Campbell. (1992). "Memory does not constrain individual recognition in a bird with song repertoires." *Behaviour* 122: 274–287.

Stoerig, P., A. Zontanou, and A. Cowey. (2002). "Aware or unaware: Assessment of cortical blindness in four men and a monkey." *Cerebral Cortex* 12: 565–574.

Stoinski, T. S., J. L. Wrate, N. Ure, and A. Whiten. (2001). "Imitative learning by captive western lowland gorillas (Gorilla gorilla gorilla) in a simulated food-processing task." *Journal of Comparative Psychology* 115: 272–281.

Storey, A. E., R. E. Anderson, J. M. Porter, and A. M. Maccharles. (1992). "Absence of parent-young recognition in kittiwakes: A re-examination." *Behaviour* 120: 302–323.

Stout, J. C., and D. Goulson. (2002). "The influence of nectar secretion rates on the responses of bumblebees (Bombus spp.) to previously visited flowers." *Behavioral Ecology and Sociobiology* 52: 239–246.

Strasser, R., J. M. Ehrlinger, and V. P. Bingman. (2004). "Transitive behavior in hippocampal-lesioned pigeons." *Brain, Behavior, and Evolution* 63: 181–188.

Striedter, G. F. (2005). *Principles of Brain Evolution*. Sunderland, MA: Sinauer Associates.

———. (2006). "Precis of Principles of Brain Evolution." *Behavioral and Brain Sciences* 29: 1–36.

Sturdy, C. B., L. S. Phillmore, J. L. Price, and R. G. Weisman. (1999). "Song-note discrimination in zebra finches (Taeniopygia guttata): Categories and pseudocategories." *Journal of Comparative Psychology* 113: 204–212.

Sturz, B. R., K. D. Bodily, and J. S. Katz. (2006). "Evidence against integration of spatial maps in humans." *Animal Cognition* 9: 207–217.

Stürzl, W., A. Cheung, K. Cheng, and J. Zeil. (2008). "The information content of panoramic images I: The rotational errors and similarity of views in rectangular experimental arenas." *Journal of Experimental Psychology: Animal Behavior Processes* 34: 1–14.

Subiaul, F., J. F. Cantlon, R. L. Holloway, and H. S. Terrace. (2004). "Cognitive imitation in rhesus macaques." *Science* 305: 407–410.

Subiaul, F., K. Romansky, J. F. Cantlon, T. Klein, and H. Terrace. (2007). "Cognitive imitation in 2-year-old children (Homo sapiens): A comparison with rhesus monkeys (Macaca mulatta)." *Animal Cognition* 10: 369–375.

Suboski, M. D. (1990). "Releaser-induced recognition learning." *Psychological Review* 97: 271–284.

Suboski, M. D., and C. Bartashunas. (1984). "Mechanisms for social transmission of pecking preferences to neonatal chicks." *Journal of Experimental Psychology: Animal Behavior Processes* 10: 182–194.

Suddendorf, T. (2006). "Foresight and evolution of the human mind." *Science* 312: 1006–1007.

Suddendorf, T., and J. Busby. (2005). "Making decisions with the future in mind: Developmental and comparative identification of mental time travel." *Learning and Motivation* 36: 110–125.

Suddendorf, T., and M. C. Corballis. (1997). "Mental time travel and the evolution of the human mind." *Genetic, Social, and General Psychology Monographs* 123: 133–167.

———. (2007). "The evolution of foresight: What is mental time travel and is it unique to humans?" *Behavioral and Brain Sciences* 30: 299–313.

———. (2008a). Episodic memory and mental time travel. In *Handbook of Episodic Memory*, ed. E. Dere, A. Easton, L. Nadel, and J. P. Huston, 31–42. Amsterdam: Elsevier.

———. (2008b). "New evidence for animal foresight?" *Animal Behaviour* 25: e1-e3.

Sullivan, K. A. (1988). "Age-specific profitability and prey choice." *Animal Behaviour* 36: 613–615.

Surridge, A. K., D. Osorio, and N. I. Mundy. (2003). "Evolution and selection of trichromatic vision in primates." *Trends in Ecology and Evolution* 18: 198–205.

Sutherland, R. J., G. L. Chew, J. C. Baker, and R. C. Linggard. (1987). "Some limitations on the use of distal cues in place navigation by rats." *Psychobiology* 15: 48–57.

Sutton, J. E., and W. A. Roberts. (1998). "Do pigeons show incidental timing? Some experiments and a suggested hierarchical framework for the study of attention in Animal Cognition." *Behavioural Processes* 44: 263–275.

———. (2002). "The effect of nontemporal information processing on time estimation in pigeons." *Learning and Motivation* 33: 124–140.

Sutton, J. E., and S. J. Shettleworth. (2005). "Internal sense of direction and landmark use in pigeons (Columba livia)." *Journal of Comparative Psychology* 119: 273–284.

———. (2008). "Memory without awareness: Pigeons fail to show metamemory in matching to sample." *Journal of Experimental Psychology: Animal Behavior Processes* 34: 266–282.

Swaddle, J. P., M. G. Cathey, M. Correll, and B. P. Hodkinson. (2005). "Socially transmitted mate preferences in a monogamous bird: a non-genetic mechanism of sexual selection." *Proceedings of the Royal Society B* 272: 1053–1058.

Swartz, K. B., S. Chen, and H. S. Terrace. (1991). "Serial learning by Rhesus monkeys: I. Acquisition and retention of mulitiple four-item lists." *Journal of Experimental Psychology: Animal Behavior Processes* 17: 396–410.

Swartzentruber, D. (1995). "Modulatory mechanisms in Pavlovian conditioning." *Animal Learning and Behavior* 23: 123–143.

Tang-Martinez, Z. (2001). "The mechanisms of kin discrimination and the evolution of kin recognition in vertebrates: a critical re-evaluation." *Behavioural Processes* 53: 21–40.

Tarsitano, M. S., and R. Andrew. (1999). "Scanning and route selection in the jumping spider Portia labiata." *Animal Behaviour* 58: 255–265.

Tautz, J., S. Zhang, J. Spaethe, A. Brockmann, A. Si, et al. (2004). "Honeybee odometry: Performance in varying natural terrain." *PLoS Biology* 2: 0915–0923.

Taylor, A. H., G. R. Hunt, J. C. Holzhaider, and R. D. Gray. (2007). "Spontaneous metatool use by New Caledonian crows." *Current Biology* 17: 1504–1507.

Tebbich, S., and R. Bshary. (2004). "Cognitive abilities related to tool use in the woodpecker finch, Cactospiza pallida." *Animal Behaviour* 67: 689–697.

Tebbich, S., M. Taborsky, B. Fessl, and D. Blomqvist. (2001). "Do woodpecker finches acquire tool-use by social learning?" *Proceedings of The Royal Society of London B* 268: 2189–2193.

Tegeder, R. W., and J. Krause. (1995). "Density dependence and numerosity in fright stimulated aggregation behaviour of shoaling fish." *Philosophical Transactions of the Royal Society of London B* 350: 381–390.

Templeton, C. N., and E. Greene. (2007). "Nuthatches eavesdrop on variations in heterospecific chickadee mobbing alarm calls." *Proceedings of the National Academy of Sciences* (USA) 104: 5479–5482.

Templeton, C. N., E. Greene, and K. Davis. (2005). "Allometry of alarm calls: Black-capped chickadees encode information about predator size." *Science* 308: 1934–1937.

Templeton, J. J., A. C. Kamil, and R. P. Balda. (1999). "Sociality and social learning in two species of corvids: The Pinyon jay (Gymnorhinus cyanocephalus) and the Clark's Nutcracker (Nucifraga columbiana)." *Journal of Comparative Psychology* 113: 450–455.

ten Cate, C. (1986). "Sexual preferences in zebra finch (Taeniopygia guttata) males raised by two species (Lonchura striata and Taeniopygia guttata): I. A case of double imprinting." *Journal of Comparative Psychology* 100: 248–252.

———. (1987). "Sexual preferences in zebra finch males raised by two species: II. The internal representation resulting from double imprinting." *Animal Behaviour* 35: 321–330.

———. (1989). "Behavioral development: Towards understanding processes." *Perspectives in Ethology* 8: 243–269.

———. (1994). Perceptual mechanisms in imprinting and song learning. In *Causal Mechanisms of Behavioural Development*, ed. J. A. Hogan and J. J. Bolhuis, 116–146. Cambridge: Cambridge University Press.

ten Cate, C., L. Los, and L. Schilperood. (1984). "The influence of differences in social experience on the development of species recognition in zebra finch males." *Animal Behavior* 32: 852–860.

ten Cate, C., and C. Rowe. (2007). "Biases in signal evolution: Learning makes a difference." *Trends in Ecology and Evolution* 22: 380–387.

ten Cate, C., and D. R. Vos. (1999). "Sexual imprinting and evolutionary processes in birds: A reassessment." *Advances in the Study of Behavior* 28: 1–31.

Terkel, J. (1995). "Cultural transmission in the black rat: Pine cone feeding." *Advances in the Study of Behavior* 24: 119–154.

Terrace, H. S. (1984). Animal Cognition. *Animal Cognition*. H. L. Roitblat, T. G. Bever, and H. S. Terrace, 7–28. Hillsdale, NJ: Erlbaum.

———. (1991). "Chunking during serial learning by a pigeon: I. Basic evidence." *Journal of Experimental Psychology: Animal Behavior Processes* 17: 81–93.

———. (2001). Chunking and serially organized behavior in pigeons, monkeys, and humans. In *Avian Visual Cognition*. Boston: Comparative Cognition Press. [On-line]. Available: http://www.pigeon.psy.tufts.edu/avc/toc.htm

———. (2005). "The simultaneous chain: a new approach to serial learning." *Trends in Cognitive Sciences* 9: 202–210.

———. (2006). The simultaneous chain: A new look at serially organized behavior. In *Comparative Cognition*, ed. E. A. Wasserman and T. R. Zentall, 481–511. New York: Oxford University Press.

Terrace, H. S., and J. Metcalfe, eds. (2005). *The Missing Link in Cognition: Origins of Self-Reflective Consciousness*. New York: Oxford University Press.

Terrace, H. S., L. A. Pettito, R. J. Sanders, and T. G. Bever. (1979). "Can an ape create a sentence?" *Science* 206: 891–902.

Terrace, H. S., L. K. Son, and E. M. Brannon. (2003). "Serial expertise of rhesus macaques." *Psychological Science* 14: 66–73.

Thery, M., and J. Casas. (2002). "Predator and prey views of spider camouflage." *Nature* 415: 133.

Thery, M., M. Debut, D. Gomez, and J. Casas. (2005). "Specific color sensitivies of prey and predator explain camouflage in different visual systems." *Behavioral Ecology* 16: 25–29.

Thomas, R. K. (1996). "Investigating congnitive abilities in animals: unrealized potential." *Cognitive Brain Research* 3: 157–166.

Thompson, C. R., and R. M. Church. (1980). "An explanation of the language of a chimpanzee." *Science* 208: 313–314.

Thompson, N. S. (1969). "Individual identification and temporal patterning in the cawing of common crows." *Communications in Behavioral Biology* 4: 29–33.

Thompson, R. F., and W. A. Spencer. (1966). "Habituation: A model phenomenon for the study of neuronal substrates of behavior." *Psychological Review* 73: 16–43.

Thompson, R. K. R. (1995). Natural and relational concepts in animals. In *Comparative Approaches to Cognitive Science*, ed. H. L. Roitblat and J.-A. Meyer, 175–224. Cambridge, MA: MIT Press.

Thompson, R. K. R., D. L. Oden, and S. T. Boysen. (1997). "Language-naive chimpanzees (Pan trogodytes) judge relations between relations in a conceptual matching-to-sample task." *Journal of Experimental Psychology: Animal Behavior Processes* 23: 31–43.

Thorndike, E. L. (1911/1970). *Animal Intelligence*. Darien, CT: Hafner Publishing Company.

Thornton, A., and K. McAuliffe. (2006). "Teaching in wild meerkats." *Science* 313: 227–229.

Thorpe, C. M., C. Jacova, and D. M. Wilkie. (2004). "Some pitfalls in measuring memory in animals." *Neuroscience and Biobehavioral Reviews* 28: 711–718.

Thorpe, C. M., and D. M. Wilkie. (2006). Properties of time-place learning. In *Comparative Cognition: Experimental Explorations of Animal Intelligence*, ed. E. A. Wasserman and T. R. Zentall, 229–245. New York: Oxford University Press.

Thorpe, W. H. (1956). *Learning and Instinct in Animals.* London: Methuen.

Tibbetts, E. A., and J. Dale. (2007). "Individual recognition: It is good to be different." *Trends in Ecology and Evolution* 22: 529–537.

Timberlake, W. (1983). The functional organization of appetitive behavior: Behavior systems and learning. In *Advances in Analysis of Behaviour,* ed. M. D. Zeiler and P. Harzem, 3:177–221. Chichester, UK: John Wiley and Sons.

———. (1984). "A temporal limit on the effect of future food on current performance in an analogue of foraging and welfare." *Journal of the Experimental Analysis of Behavior* 41: 117–124.

———. (1994). "Behavior systems, associationism, and Pavlovian conditioning." *Psychonomic Bulletin and Review* 1: 405–420.

———. (2001a). "Integrating niche-related and general process approaches in the study of learning." *Behavioural Processes* 54: 79–94.

———. (2001b). Motivational modes in behavior systems. In *Handbook of Contemporary Learning Theories,* ed. R. R. Mowrer and S. B. Klein, 155–209. Mahwah, NJ: Lawrence Erlbaum Associates.

Timberlake, W., and D. L. Grant. (1975). "Auto-shaping in rats to the presentation of another rat predicting food." *Science* 190: 690–692.

Timberlake, W., D. W. Schaal, and J. E. Steinmetz. (2005). "Relating behavior and neuroscience: Introduction and synopsis." *Journal of the Experimental Analysis of Behavior* 84: 305–311.

Timberlake, W., and D. L. Washburne. (1989). "Feeding ecology and laboratory predatory behavior toward live and artificial moving prey in seven rodent species." *Animal Learning and Behavior* 17: 2–11.

Tinbergen, L. (1960). "The natural control of insects in pine woods: I. Factors influencing the intensity of predation by songbirds." *Archives Néerlandaises de Zoologie.* 13: 265–343.

Tinbergen, N. (1932/1972). On the orientation of the digger wasp Philanthus triangulum Fabr. I. In *The Animal in its World,* ed. N. Tinbergen, 1:103–127. Cambridge, MA: Harvard University Press.

———. (1951). *The Study of Instinct.* Oxford: Clarendon Press.

———. (1959). "Comparative studies of the behaviour of gulls (Laridae): A progress report." *Behaviour* 15: 1–70.

———. (1963), "On aims and methods of ethology." *Zeitschrift für Tierpsychologie* 20: 410–433.

———. (1972). *The Animal in its World.* Cambridge, MA: Harvard University Press.

Tinbergen, N., G. J. Broekhuysen, F. Feekes, J. C. W. Houghton, H. Kruuk, et al. (1963). "Egg shell removal by the Black-headed Gull, Larus ridibundus L.: A behaviour component of camouflage." *Behaviour* 19: 74–117.

Tinbergen, N., and W. Kruyt (1938/1972). On the orientation of the digger wasp *Philanthus triangulum* Fabr. (1938): III. Selective learning of landmarks. *The Animal in its World.* ed. N. Tinbergen, 1: 146–196. Cambridge, MA: Harvard University Press.

Tinbergen, N., and D. J. Kuenen. (1939/1957). Feeding behavior in young thrushes. In *Instinctive Behavior,* ed. C. H. Schiller, 209–238. New York: International Universities Press.

Tinbergen, N., and A. C. Perdeck. (1950). "On the stimulus situation releasing the begging response in the newly hatched herring gull chick (Larus argentatus argentatus Pont)." *Behaviour* 3: 1–39.

Tinklepaugh, O. L. (1928). "An experimental study of representative factors in monkeys." *Journal of Comparative Psychology* 8: 197–236.

Tobin, H., and A. W. Logue. (1994). "Self-control across species (Columba livia, Homo sapiens, and Rattus norvegicus)." *Journal of Comparative Psychology* 108: 126–133.

Tobin, H., A. W. Logue, J. J. Chelonis, K. T. Ackerman, and J. G. May III. (1996). "Self-control in the monkey Macaca fascicularis." *Animal Learning & Behavior* 24: 168–174.

Todd, P. M., and G. Gigerenzer. (2007). Mechanisms of ecological rationality: Heuristics and environments that make us smart. In *The Oxford Handbook of Evolutionary Psychology,* ed. R. I. M. Dunbar and L. Barrett, 197–210. Oxford: Oxford University Press.

Tolman, E. C. (1948). "Cognitive maps in rats and men." *Psychological Review* 55: 189–208.

———. (1949). "There is more than one kind of learning." *Psychological Review* 56: 144–155.

Tolman, E. C., B. F. Ritchie, and D. Kalish. (1946). "Studies in spatial learning: I. Orientation and the short-cut." *Journal of Experimental Psychology* 36: 13–24.

Tomasello, M., and J. Call. (1997). *Primate Cognition.* New York: Oxford University Press.

Tomasello, M., J. Call, and B. Hare. (2003). "Chimpanzees understand psychological states—the question is which ones and to what extent." *Trends in Cognitive Sciences* 7: 153–156.

Tomasello, M., M. Carpenter, J. Call, T. Behne, and H. Moll. (2005). "Understanding and sharing intentions: The origins of cultural cognition." *The Behavioral and Brain Sciences* 28: 675–735.

Tomasello, M., M. Davis-Dasilva, L. Camak, and K. Bard. (1987). "Observational learning of tool-use by young chimpanzees." *Human Evolution* 2: 175–183.

Tommasi, L., and C. Polli. (2004). "Representation of two geometric features of the environment in the domestic chick (Gallus gallus)." *Animal Cognition* 7: 53–59.

Tooby, J., and L. Cosmides. (1995). Mapping the evolved functional organization of mind and brain. In *The Cognitive Neurosciences,* ed. M. Gazzaniga, 1185–1197. Cambridge, MA: MIT Press.

Treichler, F. R., M. A. Raghanti, and D. N. Van Tilburg. (2003). "Linking of serially ordered lists by macaque monkeys (Macaca mulatta): List position influences." *Journal of Experimental Psychology: Animal Behavior Processes* 29: 211–221.

Treichler, F. R., and D. Van Tilburg. (1996). "Concurrent conditional discrimination tests of transitive inference by macaque monkeys: List linking." *Journal of Experimental Psychology: Animal Behavior Processes* 22: 105–114.

Treisman, A. M. (1988). "Features and objects: The fourteenth Bartlett Memorial lecture." *Quarterly Journal of Experimental Psychology* 40B: 201–223.

Treisman, A. M. (1999). Feature binding, attention, and object perception. In *Attention, Space, and Action: Studies in Cognitive Neuroscience,* ed. G. W. Humphreys, J. Duncan, and A. Treisman, 91–111. Oxford: Oxford University Press.

Treisman, A. M., and G. Gelade. (1980). "A feature integration theory of attention." *Cognitive Psychology* 12: 97–136.

Trewavas, A. (2002). "Mindless mastery." *Nature* 415: 841.

Trivers, R. L. (1971). "The evolution of reciprocal altruism." *The Quarterly Review of Biology* 46: 35–57.

Tronson, N. C., and J. R. Taylor. (2007). "Molecular mechanisms of memory reconsolidation." *Nature Reviews Neuroscience* 8: 262–275.

Tse, D., R. F. Langston, M. Kakeyama, and et al. (2007). "Schemas and memory consolidation." *Science* 316: 76–82.

Tulving, E. (1972). Episodic and semantic memory. In *Organisation of Memory,* ed. E. Tulving and W. Donaldson, 381–403. New York: Academic Press.

———. (1985). "How many memory systems are there?" *American Psychologist* 40: 385–398.

———. (1995). Organization of memory: Quo vadis? In *The Cognitive Neurosciences,* ed. M. Gazzaniga, 839–847. Cambridge, MA: MIT Press.

———. (2002). "Episodic memory: From mind to brain." *Annual Review of Psychology* 53: 1–25.

———. (2005). Episodic memory and autonoesis: Uniquely human? In *The Missing Link in Cognition: Origins of Self-Reflective Consciousness,* ed. H. S. Terrace and J. Metcalfe, 3–56. New York: Oxford University Press.

Tulving, E., and D. L. Schacter. (1990). "Priming and human memory systems." *Science* 247: 301–306.

Tulving, E., D. L. Schacter, and H. A. Stark. (1982). "Priming effects in word-fragment completion are independent of recognition memory." *Journal of Experimental Psychology: Learning, Memory, and Cognition* 8: 336–342.

Turner, E. C., and M. S. Brainard. (2007). "Performance variability enables adaptive plasticity of 'crystallized' adult birdsong." *Nature* 450: 1240–1244.

Udell, M. A. R., N. R. Dorey, and C. D. L. Wynne. (2008). "Wolves outperform dogs in following human social cues." *Animal Behaviour* 76: 1767–1773.

Udell, M. A. R., and C. D. L. Wynne. (2008). "A review of domestic dogs' (Canis familiaris) human-like behaviors: Or why behavior analysts should stop worrying and love their dogs." *Journal of the Experimental Analysis of Behavior* 89: 247–261.

Uller, C. (2004). "Disposition to recognize goals in infant chimpanzees." *Animal Cognition* 7: 154–161.

Urcuioli, P. J. (2006). Responses and acquired equivalence classes. In *Comparative Cognition: Experimental Explorations of Animal Intelligence,* ed. E. A. Wasserman and T. R. Zentall, 405–421. New York: Oxford University Press.

Valone, T. J. (2007). "From eavesdropping on performance to copying the behavior of others: A review of public information use." *Behavioral Ecology and Sociobiology* 62: 1–14.

van Bergen, Y., I. Coolen, and K. N. Laland. (2004). "Nine-spined sticklebacks exploit the most reliable source when public and private information conflict." *Proceedings of The Royal Society of London B* 271: 957–962.

Van Elzakker, M., R. C. O'Reily, and J. W. Rudy. (2003). "Transitivity, flexibility, conjunctive representations, and the hippocampus. I. An empirical analysis." *Hippocampus* 13: 334–340.

van Hest, A., and T. Steckler. (1996). "Effects of procedural parameters on response accuracy: Lessons from delayed (non-) matching procedures in animals." *Cognitive Brain Research* 3: 193–203.

van Kampen, H. (1996). "A framework for the study of filial imprinting and the development of attachment." *Psychonomic Bulletin & Review* 3: 3–20.

van Lawick-Goodall, J. (1970). "Tool-using in primates and other vertebrates." *Advances in the Study of Behavior* 3: 195–249.

van Schaik, C. P., M. Ancrenaz, G. Borgen, B. Galdikas, C. D. Knott, et al. (2003). "Orangutan cultures and the evolution of material culture." *Science* 299: 102–105.

van Schaik, C. P., and R. O. Deaner. (2003). Life history and cognitive evolution in primates. In *Animal Social Complexity,* ed. F. B. M. de Waal and P. L. Tyack, 5–25. Cambridge, MA: Harvard University Press.

van Wolkenten, M., S. F. Brosnan, and F. B. M. de Waal. (2007). "Inequity responses of monkeys modified by effort." *Proceedings of the National Academy of Sciences* (USA) 104: 18854–18859.

Vander Wall, S. B. (1982). "An experimental analysis of cache recovery in Clark's nutcracker." *Animal Behaviour* 30: 84–94.

Vaughan, W., Jr. (1988). "Formation of equivalence sets in pigeons." *Journal of Experimental Psychology: Animal Behavior Processes* 14: 36–42.

Vaughan, W., Jr., and S. L. Greene. (1984). "Pigeon visual memory capacity." *Journal of Experimental Psychology: Animal Behaviour* Processes 10: 256–271.

Verhulst, S., and J. Bolhuis, eds. (2009). *Tinbergen's Legacy: Function and Mechanism in Behavioral Biology.* Cambridge: Cambridge University Press.

Vickrey, C., and A. Neuringer. (2000). "Pigeon reaction times, Hick's law, and intelligence." *Psychonomic Bulletin and Review* 7: 284–91.

Vidal, J.-M. (1980). "The relations between filial and sexual imprinting in the domestic fowl: Effects of age and social experience." *Animal Behaviour* 28: 880–891.

Viitala, J., E. Korpimaki, P. Palokangas, and M. Koivula. (1995). "Attraction of kestrals to vole scent marks visible in ultraviolet light." *Nature* 373: 425–427.

Vince, M. A. (1961). " 'String-pulling' in birds: III. The successful response in greenfinches and canaries." *Behaviour* 17: 103–129.

Visalberghi, E. (1994). Learning processes and feeding behavior in monkeys. In *Behavioral Aspects of Feeding: Basic and Applied Research on Mammals.* In B. G. Galef, M. Mainardi, and P. Valsecchi, 257–270. Chur, Switzerland: Harwood Academic Publisher.

Visalberghi, E., and D. M. Fragaszy. (1990a). Do monkeys ape? In *"Language" and Intelligence in Monkeys and Apes: Comparative Developmental Perspectives,* ed. S. T. Parker and K. R. Gibson, 247–273. Cambridge: Cambridge University Press.

————. (1990b). "Food-washing behaviour in tufted capuchin monkeys, Cebus apella, and crabeating macaques, Macaca fascicularis." *Animal Behaviour* 40: 829–836.

————. (2006). What is challenging about tool use? The capuchin's perspective. In *Comparative Cognition: Experimental Explorations of Animal Intelligence,* ed. E. A. Wasserman and T. R. Zentall, 529–552. New York: Oxford University Press.

Visalberghi, E., D. M. Fragaszy, and S. Savage-Rumbaugh. (1995). "Performance in a tool-using task by common chimpanzees (Pan troglodytes), bonobos (Pan paniscus), an orangutan (Pongo pygmaeus), and capuchin monkeys (Cebus apella)." *Journal of Comparative Psychology* 109: 52–60.

Visalberghi, E., and L. Limongelli. (1994). "Lack of comprehension of cause-effect relations in tool-using capuchin monkeys (Cebus apella)." *Journal of Comparative Psychology* 108: 15–22.

Visalberghi, E., B. Pellegrini Quarantotti, and F. Tranchida. (2000). "Solving a cooperation task without taking into account the partner's behavior: The case of the capuchin monkeys (Cebus apella)." *Journal of Comparative Psychology* 114: 297–301.

Visalberghi, E., and L. Trinca. (1989). "Tool use in capuchin monkeys: Distinguishing between performing and understanding." *Primates* 30: 511–521.

Vitousek, M. N., J. S. Adelman, N. C. Gregory, and J. J. H. St Clair. (2007). "Heterospecific alarm call recognition in a non-vocal reptile." *Biology Letters* 3: 632–634.

Vlamings, P. H. J. M., J. Uher, and J. Call. (2006). "How the great apes (Pan troglodytes, Pongo pygmaeus, Pan paniscus, and Gorilla gorilla) perform on the reversed contingency task: The effects of food quantity and food visibility." *Journal of Experimental Psychology: Animal Behavior Processes* 32: 60–70.

Vlasek, A. N. (2006). "The relative importance of global and local landmarks in navigation by Columbian ground squirrels (Spermophilus Columbianus)." *Journal of Comparative Psychology* 120: 131–138.

Voelkl, B., and L. Huber. (2000). "True imitation in marmosets." *Animal Behaviour* 60: 195–202.

Vokey, J. R., D. Rendall, J. M. Tangen, L. A. Parr, and F. B. M. de Waal. (2004). "Visual kin recognition and family resemblance in chimpanzees (Pan troglodytes)." *Journal of Comparative Psychology* 118: 194–199.

von Fersen, L., C. D. L. Wynne, J. D. Delius, and J. E. R. Staddon. (1991). "Transitive inference formation in pigeons." *Journal of Experimental Psychology: Animal Behavior Processes* 17: 334–341.

von Frisch, K. (1953). *The Dancing Bees.* New York: Harcourt Brace.

————. (1967). *The Dance Language and Orientation of Bees.* Cambridge, MA: The Belknap Press of Harvard University Press.

von Uexküll, J. (1934/1957). A stroll through the worlds of animals and men. In *Instinctive Behavior,* ed. C. H. Schiller, 5–80. New York: International Universities Press, Inc.

Vonk, J., S. F. Brosnan, J. B. Silk, J. Henrich, A. S. Richardson, et al. (2008). "Chimpanzees do not take advantage of very low cost opportunities to deliver food to unrelated group members." *Animal Behaviour* 75: 1757–1770.

Vonk, J., and D. J. Povinelli. (2006). Similarity and difference in the conceptual systems of primates: The unobservability hypothesis. In *Comparative Cognition,* ed. E. A. Wasserman and T. R. Zentall, 363–387. New York: Oxford University Press.

Vos, D. R., J. Prijs, and C. ten Cate. (1993). "Sexual imprinting in zebra finch males: A differential effect of successive and simultaneous experience with two colour morphs." *Behaviour* 126: 137–154.

Vreven, D., and P. M. Blough. (1998). "Searching for one or many targets: Effects of extended experience on the runs advantage." *Journal of Experimental Psychology: Animal Behavior Processes* 24: 99–105.

Waage, J. K. (1979). "Foraging for patchily-distributed hosts by the parasitoid, Nemeritis canescens." *Journal of Animal Ecology* 48: 353–371.

Waddington, C. H. (1966). *Principles of Development and Differentiation.* New York: Macmillan Company.

Waga, I. C., A. K. Dacier, P. S. Pinha, and M. C. H. Tavares. (2006). "Spontaneous tool use by wild capuchin monkeys (Cebus libidinosus) in the Cerrado." *Folia Primatologica* 77: 337–344.

Wagner, A. R. (1978). Expectancies and the priming of STM. In *Cognitive Processes in Animal Behavior*, ed. S. H. Hulse, H. Fowler, and W. K. Honig, 177–209. Hillsdale, NJ: Erlbaum.

———. (1981). SOP: A model of automatic memory processing in animal behavior. In *Information Processing in Animals: Memory Mechanisms*, ed. N. E. Spear and R. R. Miller, 5–47. Hillsdale, NJ: Lawrence Erlbaum Associates.

Wagner, A. R., F. A. Logan, K. Haberlandt, and T. Price. (1968). "Stimulus selection in animal discrimination learning." *Journal of Experimental Psychology* 76: 171–180.

Waldbauer, G. P. (1988). Asynchrony between Batesian mimics and their models. In *Mimicry and the Evolutionary Process*, ed. L. P. Brower, 103–121. Chicago: University of Chicago Press.

Waldbauer, G. P., and W. E. LaBerge. (1985). "Phenological relationships of wasps, bumblebees, their mimics and insectivorous birds in northern Michigan." *Ecological Entomology* 10: 99–110.

Waldman, B., P. C. Frumhoff, and P. W. Sherman. (1988). "Problems of kin recognition." *Trends in Ecology and Evolution* 3: 8–13.

Waldmann, M. R., P. W. Cheng, Y. Hagmayer, and A. P. Blaisdell. (2008). Causal learning in rats and humans: A minimal rational model. In *The Probabilistic Mind: Prospects for Bayesian Cognitive Science*, ed. N. Chater and M. Oaksford. Oxford: Oxford University Press.

Waldmann, M. R., Y. Hagmayer, and A. P. Blaisdell. (2006). "Beyond the information given." *Current Directions in Psychological Science* 15: 307–311.

Wall, P., L. C. P. Botly, C. M. Black, and S. J. Shettleworth. (2004). "The geometric module in the rat: Independence of shape and feature learning in a food-finding task." *Learning & Behavior* 32: 289–298.

Wallace, D. G., D. J. Hines, S. M. Pellis, and I. Q. Whishaw. (2002). "Vestibular information is required for dead reckoning in the rat." *Journal of Neuroscience* 22: 10009–10017.

Wallman, J. (1992). *Aping Language*. Cambridge: Cambridge University Press.

Wallraff, H. G. (2005). *Avian Navigation: Pigeon Homing as a Paradigm*. Berlin: Spring-Verlag.

Walters, J. R. (1990). "Anti-predatory behavior of lapwings: Field evidence of discriminative abilities." *Wilson Bulletin* 102: 49–70.

Wang, R. F., and J. R. Brockmole. (2003). "Human navigation in nested environments." *Journal of Experimental Psychology: Learning, Memory, and Cognition* 29: 398–404.

Wang, R. F., and E. S. Spelke. (2000). "Updating egocentric representations in human navigation." *Cognition* 77: 215–250.

———. (2002). "Human spatial representation: Insights from animals." *Trends in Cognitive Sciences* 6: 376–382.

Want, S. C., and P. L. Harris. (2002). "How do children ape? Applying concepts from the study of non-human primates to the developmental study of 'imitation' in children." *Developmental Science* 5: 1–41.

Ward-Robinson, J., and G. Hall. (1996). "Backward sensory preconditioning." *Journal of Experimental Psychology: Animal Behavior Processes* 22: 395–404.

———. (1999). "The role of mediated conditioning in acquired equivalence." *Quarterly Journal of Experimental Psychology* 52B: 335–350.

Warneken, F., B. Hare, A. P. Melis, D. Hanus, and M. Tomasello. (2007). "Spontaneous altruism by chimpanzees and young children." *Plos Biology* 5: 1414–1420.

Warneken, F., and M. Tomasello. (2006). "Altruistic helping in human infants and young chimpanzees." *Science* 311: 1301–1303.

Warren, J. M. (1965). Primate learning in comparative perspective. In *Behavior of Nonhuman Primates*, ed. A. M. Schrier, H. F. Harlow, and F. Stollnitz, 1:249–281. New York: Academic Press.

Washburn, D. A., J. D. Smith, and W. E. Shields. (2006). "Rhesus monkeys (Macaca mulatta) immediately generalize the uncertain response." *Journal of Experimental Psychology: Animal Behavior Processes* 32: 185–189.

Wasserman, E. A. (1973). "Pavlovian conditioning with heat reinforcement produces stimulus-directed pecking in chicks." *Science* 181: 875–877.

———. (1984). Animal intelligence: Understanding the minds of animals through their behavioral "ambassadors." In *Animal Cognition,* ed. H. L. Roitblat, T. G. Bever, and H. S. Terrace, 45–60. Hillsdale, NJ: Lawrence Erlbaum Associates.

———. (1986). Prospection and retrospection as processes of animal short term memory. In *Theories of Animal Memory,* ed. D. F. Kendrick, M. E. Rilling, and M. R. Denny, 53–75. Hillsdale, NJ: Lawrence Erlbaum Associates.

Wasserman, E. A., and S. L. Astley. (1994). "A behavioral analysis of concepts: Its application to pigeons and children." *The Psychology of Learning and Motivation* 31: 73–132.

Wasserman, E. A., J. A. Hugart, and K. Kirkpatrick-Steger. (1995). "Pigeons show same-different conceptualization after training with complex visual stimuli." *Journal of Experimental Psychology: Animal Behavior Processes* 21: 248–252.

Wasserman, E. A., and M. E. Young. (2009). "Same-different discrimination: The keel and backbone of thought and reasoning." *Journal of Experimental Psychology: Animal Behavior Processes:* in press.

Wasserman, E. A., and T. R. Zentall. (2006a). Comparative cognition: A natural science approach to the study of animal intelligence. In *Comparative Cognition: Experimental Explorations of Animal Intelligence,* ed. E. A. Wasserman and T. R. Zentall, 3–11. New York: Oxford University Press.

———, eds. (2006b). *Comparative Cognition: Experimental Exploration of Animal Intelligence.* New York: Oxford University Press.

Watanabe, M. (1996). "Reward expectancy in primate prefrontal neurons." *Nature* 382: 629–632.

Watanabe, S. (2000). How do pigeons see pictures? Recognition of the real world from its 2-D representation. In *Picture Perception in Animals,* ed. J. Fagot, 71–90. Philadelphia: Taylor and Francis Inc.

Watanabe, S., and L. Huber. (2006). "Animal logics: Decisions in the absence of human language." *Animal Cognition* 9: 235–245.

Watanabe, S., S. E. G. Lea, and W. H. Dittrich. (1993). What can we learn from experiments on pigeon concept discrimination? In *Vision, Brain, and Behavior in Birds,* ed. H. P. Zeigler and H.-J. Bischof, 351–376. Cambridge, MA: MIT Press.

Watson, J. S., G. Gergely, V. Csanyi, J. Topal, M. Gacsi, et al. (2001). "Distinguishing logic from association in the solution of an invisible displacement task by children (Homo sapiens) and dogs (Canis familiaris): Using negation of disjunction." *Journal of Comparative Psychology* 115: 219–226.

Watve, M., J. Thakar, A. Kale, S. Puntambekar, I. Shaikh, et al. (2002). "Bee-eaters (Merops orientalis) respond to what a predator can see." *Animal Cognition* 5: 253–259.

Wearden, J. H. (2002). "Traveling in time: A time-left analogue for humans." *Journal of Experimental Psychology: Animal Behavior Processes* 28: 200–208.

Weary, D. M. (1996). How birds use frequency to recognize their songs. In *Neuroethological Studies of Cognitive and Perceptual Processes,* ed. C. F. Moss and S. J. Shettleworth, 138–157. Boulder, CO: Westview Press.

Weary, D. M., and J. R. Krebs. (1992). "Great tits classify songs by individual voice characteristics." *Animal Behaviour* 43: 283–287.

Webb, B. (2000). "What does robotics offer animal behaviour?" *Animal Behaviour* 60: 545–558.

Weber, E. U., S. Shafir, and A.-R. Blais. (2004). "Predicting risk sensitivity in humans and lower animals: Risk as variance or coefficient of variation." *Psychological Review* 111: 430–445.

Webster, M. M., and P. J. B. Hart. (2006). "Subhabitat selection by foraging threespine stickleback (Gasterosteus aculeatus): Previous experience and social conformity." *Behavioral Ecology and Sociobiology* 60: 77–86.

Webster, S. J., and L. Lefebvre. (2001). "Problem solving and neophobia in a columbiform-passeriform assemblage in Barbados." *Animal Behaviour* 62: 23–32.

Wehner, R. (1992). Arthropods. In *Animal Homing*, ed. F. Papi, 45–144. London: Chapman and Hall.

———. (2003). "Desert ant navigation: How miniature brains solve complex tasks." *Journal of Comparative Physiology A* 189: 579–588.

Wehner, R., M. Boyer, F. Loertscher, S. Sommer, and U. Menzi. (2006). "Ant navigation: One-way routes rather than maps." *Current Biology* 16: 75–79.

Wehner, R., and B. Lanfranconi. (1981). "What do the ants know about the rotation of the sky?" *Nature* 293: 731–733.

Wehner, R., and R. Menzel. (1990). "Do insects have cognitive maps?" *Annual Review of Neuroscience* 13: 403–414.

Wehner, R., and M. Müller. (2006). "The significance of direct sunlight and polarized skylight in the ant's celestial system of navigation." *Proceedings of the National Academy of Sciences* (USA) 103: 12575–12579.

Wehner, R., and M. V. Srinivasan. (1981). "Searching behaviour of desert ants, genus Cataglyphis (Formicidae, Hymenoptera)." *Journal of Comparative Physiology A* 142: 315–338.

———. (2003). Path integration in insects. In *The Neurobiology of Spatial Behaviour*, ed. K. J. Jeffery, 9–30. Oxford: Oxford University Press.

Wei, C. A., S. L. Rafalko, and F. C. Dyer. (2002). "Deciding to learn: Modulation of learning flights in honeybees, Apis mellifera." *Journal of Comparative Physiology A* 188: 725–737.

Weigmann, D. D., L. A. Real, T. A. Capone, and S. Ellner. (1996). "Some distinguishing features of models of search behavior and mate choice." *American Naturalist* 147: 188–204.

Weindler, P., R. Wiltschko, and W. Wiltschko (1996). "Magnetic information affects the stellar orientaion of young bird migrants." *Nature* 383: 158–160.

Weiner, J. (1994). *The Beak of the Finch*. New York: Knopf.

Weir, A. A. S., J. Chappell, and A. Kacelnik. (2002). "Shaping of hooks in New Caledonian crows." *Science* 297: 981.

Weir, A. A. S., and A. Kacelnik. (2006). "A New Caledonian crow (Corvis moneduloides) creatively re-designs tools by bending or unbending aluminum strips." *Animal Cognition* 9: 317–334.

Weiskrantz, L. (1986). *Blindsight*. Oxford: Clarendon Press.

Weisman, R. G., M. T. Williams, J. S. Cohen, M. G. Njegovan, and C. B. Sturdy. (2006). The comparative psychology of absolute pitch. In *Comparative Cognition: Experimental Explorations of Animal Intelligence*, ed. E. A. Wasserman and T. R. Zentall, 71–86. New York: Oxford University Press.

Weiss, D. J., and E. L. Newport. (2006). "Mechanisms underlying language acquisition: Benefits from a comparative approach." *Infancy* 9: 241–257.

Wellman, H. M., D. Cross, and J. Watson. (2001). "Meta-analysis of theory-of-mind development: The truth about false belief." *Child Development* 72: 655–684.

Welty, J. C. (1963). *The Life of Birds*. New York: WB Saunders Company Ltd.

Wenger, D., H. Biebach, and J. R. Krebs. (1991). "Free-running circadian rhythm of a learned feeding pattern in starlings." *Naturwissenschaften* 78: 87–89.

Wenner, A. M., and P. H. Wells. (1990). *Anatomy of a Controversy*. New York: Columbia University Press.

West, M. J., and A. P. King. (1988). "Female visual displays affect the development of male song in the cowbird." *Nature* 334: 244–246.

West, S. A., A. S. Griffin, and A. Gardner. (2007). "Evolutionary explanations for cooperation." *Current Biology* 17: R661–R672.

West-Eberhard, M. J. (2003). *Developmental Plasticity and Evolution*. New York: Oxford University Press.

Whalen, J., C. R. Gallistel, and R. Gelman. (1999). "Nonverbal counting in humans: The psychophysics of number representation." *Psychological Science* 10: 130–137.

Whishaw, I. Q., and J. Tomie. (1997). "Piloting and dead reckoning dissociated by fimbria-fornix lesions in a rat food carrying task." *Behavioural Brain Research* 89: 87–97.

White, D. J. (2004). "Influences of social learning on mate-choice decisions." *Learning & Behavior* 32: 105–113.

White, D. J., L. Ho, G. de los Santos, and I. Godoy. (2007). "An experimental test of preferences for nest contents in an obligate brood parasite, Molothrus ater." *Behavioral Ecology* 18: 922–928.

White, K. G., A. C. Ruske, and M. Colombo. (1996). "Memory procedures, performance and processes in pigeons." *Cognitive Brain Research* 3: 309–317.

White, N. M., and R. J. McDonald. (2002). "Multiple parallel memory systems in the brain of the rat." *Neurobiology of Learning and Memory* 77: 125–184.

Whiten, A. (1994). Grades of mindreading. In *Children's Early Understanding of Mind: Origins and Development,* ed. C. Lewis and P. Mitchell, 47–70. Hove, UK: Lawrence Erlbaum Associates, Ltd.

———. (1996). When does smart behaviour-reading become mind-reading? In *Theories of Theories of Mind,* ed. P. Carruthers and P. K. Smith, 277–292. Cambridge: Cambridge University Press.

———. (1998). "Imitation of the sequential structure of actions by chimpanzees (Pan troglodytes)." *Journal of Comparative Psychology* 112: 270–281.

Whiten, A., and R. W. Byrne. (1988). "Tactical deception in primates." *The Behavioral and Brain Sciences* 11: 233–273.

Whiten, A., D. M. Custance, J.-C. Gomez, P. Teixidor, and K. A. Bard. (1996). "Imitative learning of artificial fruit processing in children (Homo sapiens) and chimpanzees (Pan troglodytes)." *Journal of Comparative Psychology* 110: 3–14.

Whiten, A., J. Goodall, W. C. McGrew, T. Nishida, V. Reynolds, et al. (1999). "Cultures in chimpanzees." *Nature* 399: 682–685.

———. (2001). "Charting cultural variation in chimpanzees." *Behaviour* 138: 1481–1516.

Whiten, A., and R. Ham. (1992). "On the nature and evolution of imitation in the animal kingdom: Reappraisal of a century of research." *Advances in the Study of Behavior* 21: 239–283.

Whiten, A., V. Horner, and F. B. M. De Waal. (2005). "Conformity to cultural norms of tool use in chimpanzees." *Nature* 437: 737–740.

Whiten, A., V. Horner, C. A. Litchfield, and S. Marshall-Pescini. (2004). "How do apes ape?" *Learning & Behavior* 32: 36–52.

Whiten, A., and C. P. Van Schaik. (2007). "The evolution of animal 'cultures' and social intelligence." *Philosophical Transactions of the Royal Society B* 362: 603–620.

Whitlow, J. W., Jr. (1975). "Short-term memory in habituation and dishabituation." *Journal of Experimental Psychology: Animal Behavior Processes* 104: 189–206.

Wiley, R. H. (1994). Errors, exaggeration, and deception in animal communication. In *Behavioral Mechanisms in Evolutionary Ecology,* ed. L. A. Real, 157–189. Chicago: University of Chicago Press.

———. (2006). "Signal detection and animal communication." *Advances in the Study of Behavior* 36: 217–247.

Wilkie, D. M. (2000). Use of pictures to investigate aspects of pigeons' spatial cognition. In *Picture Perception in Animals,* ed. J. Fagot, 91–106. Philadelphia: Taylor and Francis Inc.

Wilkie, D. M., and R. J. Summers. (1982). "Pigeons' spatial memory: Factors affecting delayed matching of key location." *Journal of the Experimental Analysis of Behavior* 37: 45–56.

Wilkie, D. M., R. J. Willson, and J. A. R. Carr. (1999). "Errors made by animals in memory paradigms are not always due to failure of memory." *Neuroscience and Biobehavioral Reviews* 23: 451–55.

Wilkinson, G. S. (1984). "Reciprocal food sharing in the vampire bat." *Nature* 308: 181–184.

Williams, B. A. (1988). Reinforcement, choice, and response strength. In *Stevens' Handbook of Experimental Psychology,* ed. R. Atkinson, R. J. Herrnstein, G. Lindzey, and R. D. Luce, 167–244. New York: Wiley.

———. (1994). Reinforcement and choice. In *Animal Learning and Cognition*, ed. N. J. Mackintosh, 81–108. New York: Academic Press.

Williams, D. A., and V. M. LoLordo. (1995). "Time cues block the CS, but the CS does not block time cues." *Quarterly Journal of Experimental Psychology* 48B: 97–116.

Williams, D. A., J. B. Overmier, and V. M. LoLordo. (1992). "A reevaluation of Rescorla's early dictums about Pavlovian conditioned inhibition." *Psychological Bulletin* 111: 275–290.

Williams, D. R., and H. Williams. (1969). "Auto-maintenance in the pigeon: Sustained pecking despite contingent non-reinforcement." *Journal of the Experimental Analysis of Behavior* 12: 511–520.

Williams, G. C. (1966). *Adaptation and Natural Selection*. Princeton, NJ: Princeton University Press.

Wilson, B., N. J. Mackintosh, and R. A. Boakes. (1985). "Transfer of relational rules in matching and oddity learning by pigeons and corvids." *Quarterly Journal of Experimental Psychology* 37B: 313–332.

Wilson, D. S., and E. O. Wilson. (2007). "Rethinking the theoretical foundation of sociobiology." *The Quarterly Review of Biology* 82: 327–348.

———. (2008). "Evolution 'for the good of the group.'" *American Scientist* 96: 380–390.

Wilson, E. O. (1975). *Sociobiology*. Cambridge, MA: Belknap Press.

Wiltgen, B. J., and A. J. Silva. (2007). "Memory for context becomes less specific with time." *Learning & Memory* 14: 313–317.

Wiltschko, R., I. Schiffner, and B. Siegmund. (2007). "Homing flights of pigeons over familiar terrain." *Animal Behaviour* 74: 1229–1240.

Wiltschko, R., B. Siegmund, and K. Stapput. (2005). "Navigational strategies of homing pigeons at familiar sites: do landmarks reduce the deflections induced by clock-shifting?" *Behavioral Ecology and Sociobiology* 59: 303–312.

Wiltschko, R., and W. Wiltschko. (2003). "Avian navigation: From historical to modern concepts." *Animal Behaviour* 65: 257–272.

———. (2006). "Magnetoreception." *BioEssays* 28: 157–168.

Wiltschko, W., and R. P. Balda. (1989). "Sun compass orientation in seed-caching scrub jays (Aphelocoma coerulescens)." *Journal of Comparative Physiology A* 164: 717–721.

Wimmer, H., and J. Perner. (1983). "Beliefs about beliefs: Representation and constraining function of wrong beliefs in young children's understanding of deception." *Cognition* 13: 103–128.

Winocur, G., and M. Moscovitch. (2007). "Memory consolidation or transformation: Context manipulation and hippocampal representations of memory." *Nature Neuroscience* 10: 555–557.

Wittlinger, M., R. Wehner, and H. Wolf. (2006). "The ant odometer: Stepping on stilts and stumps." *Science* 312: 1965–1967.

———. (2007). "The desert and odometer: A stride integrator that accounts for stride length and walking speed." *The Journal of Experimental Biology* 210: 198–207.

Wixted, J. T. (1993). "A signal detection analysis of memory for nonoccurence in pigeons." *Journal of Experimental Psychology: Animal Behavior Processes* 19: 400–411.

———. (2004). "The psychology and neuroscience of forgetting." *Annual Review of Psychology* 55: 235–269.

Wixted, J. T., and E. B. Ebbesen. (1991). "On the form of forgetting." *Psychological Science* 2: 409–415.

Wohlgemuth, S., B. Ronacher, and R. Wehner. (2001). "Ant odometry in the third dimension." *Nature* 411: 795–798.

Wohlschläger, A., M. Gattis, and H. Bekkering. (2003). "Action generation and action perception in imitation: an instance of the ideomotor principle." *Philosophical Transactions of the Royal Society of London B* 358: 501–515.

Wolf, M., G. S. van Doorn, O. Leimar, and F. J. Weissing. (2007). "Life-history trade-offs favour the evolution of animal personalities." *Nature* 447: 581–584.

Wood, E. R., P. A. Dudchenko, and H. Eichenbaum. (1999). "The global record of memory in hippocampal neuronal activity." *Nature* 397: 613–616.

Wood, J. N., D. D. Glynn, B. C. Phillips, and M. D. Hauser. (2007). "The perception of rational, goal-directed action in nonhuman primates." *Science* 317: 1402–1405.

Woodward, A. L. (1998). "Infants selectively encode the goal object of an actor's reach." *Cognition* 69: 1–34.

Woolfenden, G. E., and J. W. Fitzpatrick. (1984). *The Florida Scrub Jay: Demography of a Cooperatively Breeding Bird*. Princeton, NJ: Princeton University Press.

Wray, M. K., B. A. Klein, H. R. Mattila, and T. D. Seeley. (2008). "Honeybees do not reject dances for 'implausible' locations: Reconsidering the evidence for cognitive maps in insects." *Animal Behaviour* 76: 261–269.

Wright, A. A. (1972). "Psychometric and psychophysical hue discrimination functions for the pigeon." *Vision Research* 12: 1447–1464.

———. (1989). Memory processing by pigeons, monkeys, and people. *The Psychology of Learning and Motivation* 24: 25–70.

———. (1991). A detection and decision process model of matching to sample. In *Signal Detection: Mechanisms, Models, and Applications,* ed. M. L. Commons, J. A. Nevin, and M. C. Davison, 191–219. Hillsdale, NJ: Lawrence Erlbaum Associated.

———. (2006). Memory processing. In *Comparative Cognition: Experimental Explorations of Animal Intelligence,* ed. E. A. Wasserman and T. R. Zentall, 164–185. New York: Oxford University Press.

Wright, A. A., R. G. Cook, J. J. Rivera, M. R. Shyan, J. J. Neiworth, et al. (1990). "Naming, rehearsal, and interstimulus interval effects in memory processing." *Journal of Experimental Psychology: Learning, Memory, and Cognition* 16: 1043–1059.

Wright, A. A., and H. L. Roediger III. (2003). "Interference processes in monkey auditory list memory." *Psychonomic Bulletin & Review* 10: 696–702.

Wright, A. A., H. C. Santiago, S. F. Sands, D. F. Kendrick, and R. G. Cook. (1985). "Memory processing of serial lists by pigeons, monkeys, and people." *Science* 229: 287–289.

Wynn, K. (1992). "Addition and subtraction by human infants." *Nature* 358: 749–750.

———. (1995). "Infants possess a system of numerical knowledge." *Current Directions in Psychological Science* 4: 172–177.

Wynne, C. D. L. (1995). "Reinforcement accounts for transitive inference performance." *Animal Learning and Behavior* 23: 207–217.

———. (2001). *Animal Cognition*. Houndmills, UK: Palgrave.

———. (2004a). *Do animals think?* Princeton, NJ: Princeton University Press.

———. (2004b). "Fair refusal by capuchin monkeys." *Nature* 428: 140.

———. (2007a). "What are animals? Why anthropomorphism is still not a scientific approach to behavior." *Comparative Cognition and Behavior Reviews* 2: 125–135.

———. (2007b). "Anthropomorphism and its discontents." *Comparative Cognition & Behavior Reviews* 2: 151–154.

Wynne, C. D. L., M. A. R. Udell, and K. A. Lord. (2008). "Ontogeny's impacts on human-dog communication." *Animal Behaviour* 76: e1–e4.

Xu, F., and E. S. Spelke. (2000). "Large number discrimination in 6-month-old infants." *Cognition* 74: B1–B11.

Xu, F., E. S. Spelke, and S. Goddard. (2005). "Number sense in human infants." *Developmental Science* 8: 88–101.

Yantis, S., ed. (2002). *Stevens' Handbook of Experimental Psychology. Volume 1. Sensation and Perception* New York: John Wiley and Sons.

Yerkes, R. M., and S. Morgulis. (1909). "The method of Pawlow in animal psychology." *Psychological Bulletin* 6: 257–273.

Yonelinas, A. P., and C. M. Parks. (2007). "Receiver operating characteristics (ROCs) in recognition memory: A review." *Psychological Bulletin* 133: 800–832.

Young, M. E. (1995). "On the origin of personal causal theories." *Psychonomic Bulletin and Review* 2: 83–104.

Zach, R. (1979). "Shell dropping: Decision making and optimal foraging in Northwestern crows." *Behaviour* 68: 106–117.

Zahavi, A. (1975). "Mate selection—a selection for a handicap." *Journal of Theoretical Biology* 67: 603–605.

Zeigler, H. P., and P. Marler, eds. (2004). *Behavioral Neurobiology of Birdsong.* Annals of the New York Academy of Sciences. New York: Wiley-Blackwell.

Zeldin, R. K., and D. S. Olton. (1986). "Rats acquire spatial learning sets." *Journal of Experimental Psychology: Animal Behavior Processes* 12: 412–419.

Zentall, T. R. (1996). An analysis of imitative learning in animals. *Social Learning in Animals: The Roots of Culture,* ed. C. M. Heyes and B. G. Galef Jr., 221–243. San Diego, CA: Academic Press.

———. (2004). "Action imitation in birds." *Learning & Behavior* 32: 15–23.

———. (2005a). "Animals may not be stuck in time." *Learning and Motivation* 36: 208–225.

———. (2005b). "Selective and divided attention in animals." *Behavioural Processes* 69: 1–15.

———. (2006a). "Imitation: Definitions, evidence, and mechanisms." *Animal Cognition* 9: 335–353.

———. (2006b). "Timing, memory for intervals, and memory for untimed stimuli: The role of instructional ambiguity." *Behavioural Processes* 71: 88–97.

Zentall, T. R., and T. S. Clement. (2001). "Simultaneous discrimination learning: Stimulus interactions." *Animal Learning & Behavior* 29: 311–325.

Zentall, T. R., T. S. Clement, R. S. Bhatt, and J. Allen. (2001). "Episodic-like memory in pigeons." *Psychonomic Bulletin and Review* 8: 685–690.

Zentall, T. R., T. S. Clement, and J. E. Weaver. (2003). "Symmetry training in pigeons can produce functional equivalences." *Psychonomic Bulletin & Review* 10: 387–391.

Zentall, T. R., and B. G. Galef Jr., eds. (1988). *Social Learning: Psychological and Biological Perspectives.* Hillsdale, NJ: Lawrence Erlbaum Associates.

Zentall, T. R., K. L. Roper, D. H. Kaiser, and L. M. Sherburne. (1997). A critical analyis of directed-forgetting research in animals. In *Interdisciplinary Approaches to Intentional Forgetting,* ed. J. M. Golding and C. MacLeod, 205–287. Hillsdale, NJ: Erlbaum.

Zentall, T. R., and L. M. Sherburne. (1994). "Transfer of value from S+ to S- in a simultaneous discrimination." *Journal of Experimental Psychology: Animal Behavior Processes* 20: 176–183.

Zentall, T. R., L. M. Sherburne, K. L. Roper, and P. J. Kraemer. (1996). "Value transfer in a simultaneous discrimination appears to result from within-event Pavlovian conditioning." *Journal of Experimental Psychology: Animal Behavior Processes* 22: 68–75.

Zentall, T. R., and R. A. Singer. (2007). "Within-trial contrast: Pigeons prefer conditioned reinforcers that follow a relatively more rather than a less aversive event." *Journal of the Experimental Analysis of Behavior* 88: 131–149.

Zentall, T. R., J. N. Steirn, and P. Jackson-Smith. (1990). "Memory strategies in pigeons' performance of a radial-arm-maze analog task." *Journal of Experimental Psychology: Animal Behavior Processes* 16: 358–371.

Zentall, T. R., P. J. Urcuioli, J. A. Jagielo, and P. Jackson-Smith. (1989). "Interaction of sample dimension and sample-comparison mapping on pigeons' performance of delayed conditional discriminations." *Animal Learning & Behavior* 17: 172–178.

Zentall, T. R., E. A. Wasserman, O. F. Lazareva, R. R. K. Thompson, and M. J. Rattermann. (2008). "Concept learning in animals." *Comparative Cognition & Behavior Reviews* 3: 13–45.

Ziegler, P. E., and R. Wehner. (1997). "Time courses of memory decay in vector-based and landmark-based systems of navigation in desert ants, Cataglyphis fortis." *Journal of Comparative Physiology A* 181: 13–20.

Zohar, O., and J. Terkel. (1996). "Social and environmental factors modulate the learning of pine-cone stripping techniques by black rats, Rattus rattus." *Animal Behaviour* 51: 611–618.

Zolman, J. F. (1982). "Ontogeny of learning." *Perspectives in Ethology* 5: 295–323.

Zuberbuhler, K. (2003). "Referential signaling in non-human primates: Cognitive precursors and limitations for the evolution of language." *Advances in the Study of Behavior* 33: 265–307.

———. (2000a). "Causal cognition in a non-human primate: Field playback experiments with Diana monkeys." *Cognition* 76: 195–207.

———. (2000b). "Causal knowledge of predators' behaviour in wild Diana monkeys." *Animal Behaviour* 59: 209–220.

———. (2008). "Audience effects." *Current Biology* 18: R189–R190.

Zuberbuhler, K., D. L. Cheney, and R. M. Seyfarth. (1999). "Conceptual semantics in a nonhuman primate." *Journal of Comparative Psychology* 113: 33–42.

Credits

Chapter 1

1.2 Boag, P.T. (1984). The heritability of external morphology in Darwin's ground finches (*Geospiza*) on Isla Daphne Major, Galapagos. *Evolution, 37*, 877–894. Figure 1 redrawn with permission from the journal *Evolution*.

1.2 Boag, P.T., and Grant, P.R. (1984). The classical case of character release: Darwin's finches (*Geospiza*) on Isla Daphne Major, Galapagos. *Biological Journal of the Linnean Society, 22*, 243–287. Published by Wiley-Blackwell.

1.3 Marler, P., and Peters, S. (1989). Species differences in auditory responsivness in early vocal learning. In R.J. Dooling and S.H. Hulse (eds.), *The Comparative Psychology of Audition: Perceiving Complex Sounds*, 243–373. Hillsdale, NJ: Lawrence Erlbaum.

B1.1 Redrawn by permission of Macmillan Publishers Ltd.: Cowey, A., and Stoerig, P. (1995). Blindsight in monkeys. *Nature, 373*, 247–249. Copyright © 1995.

B1.3 From: Bitterman, M.E. (1975). The comparative analysis of learning. *Science, 188*, 699–709. Redrawn with permission from AAAS.

Chapter 2

2.2 Clutton-Brock, T.H., and Harvey, P.H. (1984). Comparative approaches to investigating adaptation. In J.R. Krebs and N.B. Davies (eds.), *Behavioral Ecology: An Evolutionary Approach*, 7–29. Published by Blackwell Science Ltd.

2.3 Sherry, D.F., Vaccarino, A.L., Buckenham, K., and Herz, R.S. (1989). The hippocampal complex of food-storing birds. *Brain, Behavior, and Evolution, 34*, 308–317. Published by S. Karger AG, Basel.

2.4 Ridley, M. (1993). *Evolution.* Published by Blackwell Science Ltd.

2.5 Ridley, M. (1993). *Evolution.* Published by Blackwell Science Ltd.

2.6 Brooks, D.R., and McLennan, D.A. (1991). *Phylogeny, Ecology, and Behavior.* Chicago: University of Chicago Press. Copyright © 1991 by University of Chicago Press.

2.7 Hogan, J.A. (1988). Cause and function in the development of behavior systems. In E.M. Blass (ed.), *Handbook of Behavioral Neurobiology, 9*, 63–106. Published by Plenum Publishing Corp.

2.8 Shettleworth, S.J. (1987). Learning and foraging in pigeons: Effects of handling time and changing food availability on patch choice. In M.L. Commons, A. Kacelnik, and S.J. Shettleworth (eds.), *Foraging*, 115–132. Vol. 6 of *Quantitative Analyses of Behavior*. Published by Lawrence Erlbaum Associates, Inc.

2.9 Redrawn from: Healy, S.D., Clayton, N.S., and Krebs, J.R. (1994). Development of hippocampal specialization in two species of tit (*Parus spp.*). *Behavioural Brain Research, 61*, 23–38. Copyright © 1994, with permission from Elsevier.

2.10 Gaulin, S.J.S. (1995). Does evolutionary theory predict sex differences in the brain? In M. Gazzaniga (ed.), *The Cognitive Neurosciences*, 1211–1225. Cambridge, MA: MIT Press. Copyright © 1995 by MIT Press.

2.11a Streidter, G.F. (2005). *Principles of Brain Evolution.* Published by Sinauer Associates Inc.

2.11b Redrawn from: Roth, G., and Dicke, U. (2005). Evolution of the brain and intelligence. *Trends in Cognitive Sciences, 9,* 250–257. Copyright © 2005, with permission from Elsevier.

B2.2 Lefebvre, L., Reader, S.M., and Sol, D. (2004). Brain innovations and evolution in birds and primates. *Brain, Behavior and Evolution, 63,* 233–246. Published by S. Karger AG, Basel.

B2.2 Reader, S.M., and Laland, K.N. (2002). Social intelligence, innovation, and enhanced brain size in primates. *Proceedings of the National Academy of Sciences* (USA), *99,* 4436–4441. Copyright © 2002 National Academy of Sciences, USA.

Chapter 3

3.1 Redrawn from: von Uexküll, J. (1934/57). A stroll through the worlds of animals and men. In C.H. Schiller (ed.), *Instinctive Behavior,* 5–80. New York: International Universities Press, Inc. Copyright © 1957 by IUP.

3.2 Endler, J.A. (1992). Signals, signal conditions, and the direction of evolution. *The American Naturalist, 139,* S125–S153. Published by The University of Chicago Press. Copyright © 1992 by The University of Chicago Press.

3.3 Evans, H.E., and Heiser, J.B. (2004). What's inside: Anatomy and physiology. In S. Podulka, R.W. Rohrbaugh Jr., and R. Bonney (eds.), *Handbook of Bird Biology,* 4.3–4.94. Courtesy of Cornell Lab of Ornithology.

3.4 Redrawn from: Johnston, R.E., Derzie, A., Chiang, G., Jernigan, P., and Lee, H.-C. (1993). Individual scent signatures in golden hamsters: Evidence for specialization of function. *Animal Behaviour, 45,* 1061–1070. Copyright © 1993, with permission from Elsevier.

3.5 Moss, C.F., and Schnitzler, H.-U. (1989). Accuracy of target ranging in echolocating bats: Acoustic information processing. *Journal of Comparative Physiology A, 165,* 383–393. Copyright © 1989 Springer-Verlag.

3.6 Redrawn with permission from: Ramachandran, V.S., Tyler, C.W.,

Gregory, R.L., Rogers-Ramachandran, D., Duensing, S., Pillsbury, C., and Ramachandran, C. (1996). Rapid adaptive camouflage in tropical flounders. *Nature, 379,* 815–818. Copyright © 1996 Macmillan Magazines Ltd.

3.7 Wiley, R.H. (1994). Errors, exaggeration, and deception in animal communication. In L.A. Real (ed.), *Behavioral Mechanisms in Evolutionary Biology,* 157–189. Chicago: University of Chicago Press. Copyright © 1994 University of Chicago Press.

3.8a Redrawn from: Wright, A.A. (1972). Psychometric and psychophysical hue discrimination functions for the pigeon. *Vision Research, 12,* 1447–1464. Copyright © 1972, with kind permission from Elsevier Science Ltd, The Boulevard, Langford Lane, Kidlington OX5 1GB, UK.

3.8b From Blough, D.S. (1967). Stimulus generalization as signal detection in pigeons. *Science, 158,* 940–941. Redrawn with permission from AAAS.

3.10 Tinbergen, N. (1951). *The Study of Instinct.* By permission of Oxford University Press.

3.11 Basolo, A.L. (1995). A further examination of a pre-existing bias favouring a sword of the genus *Xiphophorus. Animal Behaviour, 50,* 365–375. Published by Academic Press Ltd.

3.12 Redrawn from: Dawkins, M. (1971). Perceptual changes in chicks: Another look at the "search image" concept. *Animal Behaviour, 19,* 566–574. Copyright © 1971, with permission from Elsevier .

3.13 Treisman, A.M., and Gelade, G. (1980). A feature integration theory of attention. *Cognitive Psychology, 12,* 97–36. Published by Academic Press Inc.

3.14 Cook, R.G. (1992). Dimensional organization and texture discrimination in pigeons. *Journal of Experimental Psychology: Animal Behavior Processes, 18(4),* 354–363. Published by the American Psychological Association. Redrawn with permission .

3.15 From: *Animal Learning & Behavior, 20,* 293–300. Reprinted by permission of Psychonomic Society, Inc .

3.15 Blough, P.M. (1989). Attentional priming and visual search in pigeons.

Journal of Experimental Psychology: Animal Behavior Processes, 15(4), 358–365. Published by the American Psychological Association. Redrawn with permission.

3.16 Redrawn from: von Uexküll, J. (1934/1957). A stroll through the worlds of animals and men. In C.H. Schiller (ed.), *Instinctive Behavior,* 5–80. New York: International Universities Press, Inc. Copyright © 1957 by IUP.

3.17 Bond, A.B. (1983). Visual search and selection of natural stimuli in the pigeon: The attention threshold hypothesis. *Journal of Experimental Psychology: Animal Behavior Processes, 9(3),* 292–306. Published by the American Psychological Association. Redrawn with permission.

3.18 Pietrewicz, A.T., and Kamil, A.C. (1981). Search images and the detection of cryptic prey: An operant approach. In A.C. Kamil and T.D. Sargent (eds.), *Foraging Behavior: Ecological, Ethological, and Psychological Approaches,* 311–331. Published by Garland Publishing Inc.

3.19 Reid, P.J., and Shettleworth, S.J. (1992). Detection of cryptic prey: Search image or search rate? *Journal of Experimental Psychology: Animal Behavior Processes, 18(3),* 273–286. Published by the American Psychological Association. Redrawn with permission.

3.20 Redrawn by permission from Macmillan Publishers Ltd.: Bond, A. B., and Kamil, A.C. (1998). Apostatic selection by blue jays produces balanced polymorphism in virtual prey. *Nature, 395,* 594–596. Copyright © 1998.

3.21 Redrawn with permission from: Godin, J.-G.J., and Smith, S.A. (1988). A fitness cost of foraging in the guppy. *Nature, 333,* 69–71. Copyright © 1988 Macmillan Magazines Ltd.

3.22 Dukas, R., and Kamil, A.C. (2000). The cost of limited attention in blue jays. *Behavioral Ecology, 11,* 502–506. Redrawn by permission of Oxford University Press.

B3.1 Kelber, A., Vorobyev, M., and Osorio, D. (2003). Animal colour vision–behavioural tests and physiological concepts. *Biological Reviews, 78,* 81–118. Published by Wiley-Blackwell.

Chapter 4

4.3 Colwill, R.M. (1996). Detecting associations in Pavlovian conditioning and instrumental learning in vertebrates and in invertebrates. In C.F. Moss and S.J. Shettleworth (eds), *Neuroethological Studies of Cognitive and Perceptual Processes,* 31–62. Published by Westview Press.

4.4b Rescorla, R.A. (1988). Pavlovian conditioning: It's not what you think it is. *American Psychologist, 43,* 151–160. Published by the American Psychological Association. Redrawn with permission.

4.8 Rescorla, R.A, and Furrow, D.R. (1977). Stimulus similarity as a determinant of Pavlovian conditioning. *Journal of Experimental Psychology: Animal Behavior Processes, 3,* 203–215. Published by the American Psychological Association. Redrawn with permission.

4.9 Smith, M.C., Coleman, S.R., and Gormezano, I. (1969). Classical conditioning of the rabbit's nicitating membrane response at backward simultaneous, and forward CS-US intervals. *Journal of Comparative and Physiological Psychology, 69,* 226–231. Published by the American Psychological Association. Redrawn with permission.

4.9 From: Domjan, M., and Burkhard, B. (1986). *The Principles of Learning and Behavior,* 2nd ed. © 1986 Wadsworth, a part of Cengage Learning, Inc. Redrawn by permission. www.cengage.com/permissions

4.9 From *Psychonomic Science, 3,* 93–94. Redrawn by permission of the Psychonomic Society, Inc.

4.9 Rescorla, R.A. (1988). Behavioral studies in Pavlovian conditioning. *Annual Reviews of Neuroscience, 11,* 329–352. Published by Annual Reviews.

4.11 Gibbon, J., Baldock, M.D., Locurto, C., Gold, L., and Terrace, H.S. (1977). Trial and intertribal durations in autoshaping. *Journal of Experimental Psychology: Animal Behavior Processes, 3,* 264–284. Published by the American Psychological Association. Redrawn by permission.

4.12 Barnet, R.C., Arnold, H.M., and Miller, R.R. (1991). Simultaneous conditioning demonstrated in second-order conditioning:

Evidence for similar associative structure in forward and simultaneous conditioning. *Learning and Motivation, 22,* 253–268. Published by Academic Press, Inc.

4.15 From *Psychonomic Bulletin and Review, 1,* 405–420. Redrawn by permission of the Psychonomic Society, Inc.

4.16 Hollis, K.L. (1984). The biological function of Pavlovian conditioning: The best defense is a good offense. *Journal of Experimental Psychology: Animal Behavior Processes, 10,* 413–425. Published by the American Psychological Society. Redrawn with permission.

4.17 Redrawn from: Cusato, B., and Domjan, M. (1998). Special efficacy of sexual conditioned stimuli that include species typical cues: Tests with a conditioned stimuli preexposure design. *Learning and Motivation, 29,* 152–167. Copyright © 1998, with permission of Elsevier.

B4.1 From *Psychonomic Science, 26,* 143–145. Redrawn by permission of Psychonomic Society.

B4.2 Papini, M.R. (2008). *Comparative Psychology.*

Chapter 5

5.1 Groves, P.M., and Thompson, R.F. (1970). Habituation: A dual process theory. *Psychological Review, 77,* 419–450. Published by the American Psychological Association. Redrawn with permission.

5.2 Davis, M., and File, S.E. (1984). Intrinsic and extrinsic mechanisms of habituation and sensitization: Implication for the design and analysis of experiments. *Habituation, Sensitization and Behavior,* 287–323. Published by Academic Press, Inc.

5.3 Davis, M. (1970). Effects of inter-stimulus interval length and variability on startle-response habituation in the rat. *Journal of Comparative and Physiological Psychology, 72,* 177–192. Published by the American Psychological Association. Redrawn with permission.

5.4 From Kalat, J. (1992). *Biological Psychology,* 4th ed. © 1992 Wadsworth, a

part of Cengage Learning, Inc. Redrawn by permission. www.cengage.com/permissions.

5.4 From Carew, T.J., Pinsker, H.M., and Kandel, E.R. (1972). Long-term habituation of a defensive withdrawal reflex in Aplaysia. *Science, 175,* 451–454. Redrawn with permission from AAAS.

5.5 From Roitblat, H.L. (1987). *Introduction of Comparative Cognition.* Copyright © 1987 by W.H. Freeman and Company.

5.7 McLaren, I., Kaye, H., and Mackintosh, N. (1989). An associative theory of the representation of the stimuli: Applications of perceptual learning and latent inhibition. In R.G.M. Morris (ed.), *Parallel Distributed Processing,* 102–103. By permission of Oxford University Press.

5.8 Horn, G. (1985). *Memory, Imprinting, and the Brain.* By permission of Oxford University Press.

5.8 *Behaviour, 42* (1972). Published by Brill, Leiden, the Netherlands.

5.9 Eiserer, L.A., and Hoffman, H.S. (1973). Priming of ducklings' responses by presenting an imprinted stimulus. *Journal of Comparative and Physiological Psychology, 82,* 345–359. Published by the American Psychological Association. Redrawn with permission.

5.10 From: *Animal Learning and Behavior, 8,* 159–166. Redrawn by permission of Psychonomic Society, Inc.

5.11 Bateson, P. (1990). Is imprinting such a special case? *Philosophical Transactions of the Royal Society of London B, 329,* 125–131. Published by The Royal Society.

5.12 Redrawn with permission from: Bateson, P. (1982). Preferences for cousins in Japanese quail. *Nature, 295,* 236–237. Copyright © 1982. Macmillan Magazines Ltd.

5.13 Redrawn from: ten Cate, C. (1987). Sexual preferences in zebra finch males raised by two species: II. The internal representation resulting from double imprinting. *Animal Behaviour, 35,* 321–330. Copyright © 1987, with permission of Elsevier.

5.14 Redrawn from: Waldman, B., Frumhoff, P.C., and Sherman, P.W. (1988). Problems in kin recognition. *Trends in*

Ecology and Evolution, 3, 8–13. Copyright © 1988, with permission of Elsevier.

5.15 Krebs, J.R., and Davies, N.B. (1981). *An Introduction to Behavioural Ecology.* Published by Blackwell Science Ltd.

B5.1 Falls, B., and Brooks, R.J. (1975). Individual recognition by song in white-throated sparrows: II. Effects of location. *Canadian Journal of Zoology, 53*, 1412–1420. Published by NRC Research Press.

B5.2 Davies, N.B., Brooke, M.D.L., and Kacelnik, A. (1996). Recognition errors and probability of parasitism determine whether reed warblers should accept or reject mimetic cuckoo eggs. *Proceeding of the Royal Society of London B, 263*, 925–931. Published by The Royal Society.

Chapter 6

6.1 Tinbergen, N. (1951). *The Study of Instinct.* By permission of Oxford University Press.

6.2 *Behaviour Supplement, 15* (1967). Published by Brill, Leiden, the Netherlands.

6.3 Heiligenberg, W. (1974). Processes governing behavioral states of readiness. *Advances in the Study of Behavior, 5*, 173–200. Published by Academic Press, Inc.

6.4 Nelson, D.A., and Marler, P. (1990). The perception of birdsong and the ecological concept of signal space. In W.C. Stebbins and M.A. Berkely (eds.), *Comparative Perception: Complex Signals,* vol. 2, 443–447. Copyright © 1990 by John Wiley and Sons Inc. Redrawn with permission.

6.5 Dooling, R.J., Brown, S.D., Klump, G.M., and Okanoya, K. (1992). Auditory perception of the conspecific and heterospecific vocalizations in birds: Evidence for special processes. *Journal of Comparative Psychology, 106*, 20–28. Published by the American Psychological Association. Redrawn with permission.

6.6 Brown, S.D., and Dooling, R.J. (1993). Perception of conspecific faces by budgerigars (Melopsittacus undulates): II. Synthetic models. *Journal of Comparative Psychology, 107*, 48–60. Published by the American Psychological Association. Redrawn with permission.

6.8 Hanson, H.M. (1959). Effects of discrimination training on stimulus generalization. *Journal of Experimental Psychology, 58*, 321–324. Published by the American Psychological Association. Redrawn with permission.

6.10 Blough, D.S. (1975). Steady state data and a quantitative model of operant generalization and discrimination. *Journal of Experimental Psychology: Animal Behavior Processes, 1*, 3–21. Published by the American Psychological Association. Redrawn with permission.

6.11 Mackintosh, N.J., McGonigle, B., Holgate, V., and Venderver, B. (1968). Factors underlying improvement in serial reversal learning. *Canadian Journal of Psychology, 22*, 85–95. Copyright © 1968, Canadian Psychological Association. Permission granted for use of material.

6.12 Warren, J.M. (1965). Primate learning in comparative perspective. In A.M. Schrier and H.F. Harlow (eds.), *Behavior of Nonhuman Primates, 1*, 249–281. Published by Academic Press.

6.13 From Blough, D.S. (1969). Attention shifts in a maintained discrimination. *Science, 166*, 125–126. Redrawn with permission from AAAS.

6.14 Bhatt, R.S., Wasserman, E.A., Reynaolds, W.F., and Knauss, K.S. (1988). Conceptual behavior in pigeons: Categorization of both familiar and novel examples from four classes of natural and artificial stimuli. *Journal of Experimental Psychology: Animal Behavior Processes, 14*, 219–234. Published by the American Psychological Association. Redrawn with permission.

6.15 Lea, S.E.G., Lohmann, A., and Ryan, C.M.E. (1993). Discrimination of five-dimensional stimuli by pigeons: Limitation of feature analysis. *Quarterly Journal of Experimental Psychology, 46B*, 19–42. Copyright © 1993. Redrawn by permission of Psychology Press Ltd.

6.16 Pearce, J.M. (1989). The acquisition of an artificial category by pigeons. *Quarterly Journal of Experimental Psychology, 41B*, 381–406. Copyright © 1989. Redrawn by permission of Psychology Press Ltd.

6.17 Mackintosh, N.J. (1995). Categorization by people and by pigeons:

The twenty-second Bartlett memorial lecture. *Quarterly Journal of Experimental Psychology, 48B,* 193–214. Copyright © 1995. Redrawn by permission of Psychology Press Ltd.

6.18 Smith, J.D., Minda, J.P, and Washburn, D.A. (2004). Category learning in rhesus monkeys: A study of the Shepard, Hovland, and Jenkins (1961) tasks. *Journal of Experimental Psychology: General, 133(4),* 398–414. Published by the American Psychological Association. Redrawn with permission.

6.19 Wasserman, E. A., Hugart, J.A., and Kirkpatrick-Steger, K. (1995). Pigeons show same-different conceptualization after training with complex stimuli. *Journal of Experimental Psychology: Animal Behavior Processes, 21(3),* 248–252. Published by the American Psychological Association. Redrawn with permission.

6.20 Katz, J.S., and Wright, A.A. (2006). *Same/Different* abstract concept learning by pigeons. *Journal of Experimental Psychology: Animal Behavior Processes, 32(1),* 80–86. Published by the American Psychological Association. Redrawn with permission.

6.21 From *Animal Learning and Behavior, 12,* 202–208, redrawn by permission of Psychonomic Society, Inc.

B6.3 Walbauer, G.P., and LeBerge, W.E. (1985). Phenological relationships of wasps, bumblebees, their mmics and insectivorous birds in northern Michigan. *Ecological Entomology, 10,* 99–110. Published by Blackwell Science Ltd.

B6.3 Waldbauer, G.P. (1988). Asynchrony between Batesian mimics and their models. In L.P. Brower (ed.), *Mimicry and the Evolutionary Process,* 103–121. Published by University of Chicago Press. Copyright © 1988 by University of Chicago Press.

T6.1 Mackintosh, N.J. (1995). Categorization by people and by pigeons: The twenty-second Bartlett memorial lecture. *Quarterly Journal of Experimental Psychology, 48B,* 193–214. Copyright © 1995. Reprinted by permission of Psychology Press Ltd.

Chapter 7

7.1 Anderson, J.R., and Schooler, L.J. (1991). Reflections of the environment in memory. *Psychological Science, 2,* 396–408. Published by Wiley-Blackwell.

7.2 Baddley, A. (1995). Working memory. In M. Gazzaniga (ed.), *The Cognitive Neurosciences,* 755–764. Published by MIT Press. Copyright © 1995 by MIT Press.

7.3 Eacott, M.J., and Norman, G. (2004). Integrated memory for object, place, and context in rats: A possible model of episodic memory? *The Journal of Neuroscience, 24,* 1948–1953. Published by Society for Neuroscience.

7.4 Maier, N.R.F., and Schneirla, T.C. (1935/1964). *Principles of Animal Psychology.* Published by Dover Publications, Inc.

7.5 Wright, A.A. (1991). A detection and decision process model of matching to sample. In M.L. Commons, J.A. Nevin, and M.C. Davison (eds.), *Signal Detection: Mechanisms, Models, and Applications,* 191–219.

7.5 Grant, D.S. (1976). Effect of sample presentation time on long-delay matching in pigeons. *Learning and Motivation, 7,* 580–590. Published by Academic Press, Inc.

7.6 From Roitblat, H.L. (1987). *Introduction to Comparative Cognition.* W.H. Freeman Company.

7.7 Beatty, W.W., and Shavalia, D.A. (1980). Spatial memory in rats: Time course of working memory and effects of anesthetics. *Behavioral and Neural Biology, 28,* 454–462. Published by Academic Press, Inc.

7.8 Olton, D.S. (1978). Characteristics of spatial memory. In S.H. Hulse, H. Fowler, and W.K. Honig (eds.), *Cognitive Processes in Animal Behavior,* 341–373.

7.9 *Animal Learning and Behavior, 21,* 226–232, redrawn by permission of Psychonomic Society, Inc.

7.10 Whitlow, J.J.W. (1975). Short-term memory in habituation and dishabituation. *Journal of Experimental Psychology: Animal Behavior Processes, 104,* 189–206. Published by the American Psychological Association. Redrawn with permission.

7.11 With kind permission from Springer Science+Business Media: Cheng, K., and

Wignall, A.E. (2006). Honeybees (Apis mellifera) holding on to memories: Response competition causes retroactive interference effects. *Animal Cognition 9,* 141–150, and Fig. 3. Copyright © Springer-Verlag 2005.

7.12 Wiltgen, B.J., and Silva, A.J. (2007). Memory for context becomes less specific with time. *Learning and Memory, 14,* 313–317. Copyright © 2007 by Cold Spring Harbor Laboratory Press.

7.13 Miles, R.C. (1971). Species differences in "transmitting" spatila location information. In L.E. Jarrard (ed.), *Cognitive Processes of Nonhuman Primates.* Published by Academic Press.

7.14 Kamil, A.C., Balda, R.P., and Olson, D.J. (1994). Performance of four seed-caching corvid species in the radial arm maze. *Journal of Comparative Psychology, 108,* 385–393. Published by the American Psychological Association. Redrawn with permission.

7.15 Olson, D.J., Kamil, A.C., Balda, R.P., and Nims, P.J. (1995). Performance of four seed-caching corvid species in operant tests of nonspatial and spatial memory. *Journal of Comparative Psychology, 109,* 173–181. Published by the American Psychological Association. Redrawn with permission.

7.16 From Wright, A.A., Santiago, H.C., Sands, S.F., Kendrick, D.F., and Cook, R.G. (1985). Memory processing of serial lists by pigeons, monkeys, and people. *Science, 229,* 287–289. Redrawn with permission from AAAS.

7.17 *Animal Learning and Behavior, 23,* 280–285. Redrawn by permission of Psychonomic Society, Inc.

7.18 Redrawn from: Boccia, M.M., Blake, M.G., Acosta, G.B., and Baratti, C.M. (2005). Memory consolidation and reconsolidation of an inhibitory avoidance task in mice: Effects of a new different learning task. *Neuroscience, 135,* 19–29. Copyright © 2005, with permission from Elsevier.

7.19 Tulving, E., Schacter, D.L., and Stark, H.A. (1982). Priming effects in word-fragment completion are independent of recognition memory. *Journal of Experimental Psychology: Learning, Memory, and Cognition, 8(4),* 336–342. Published by the American Psychological Association. Redrawn with permission.

7.20 Hampton, R.R. (2001). Rhesus monkeys know when they remember. *Proceedings of the National Academy of Sciences* (USA), 98, 5359–5362. Copyright © 2001 National Academy of Sciences, U.S.A.

7.21 Shields, W.E., Smith, J.D., and Washburn, D.A. (1997). Uncertain responses by humans and rhesus monkeys (*Macaca mulatta*) in a psychophysical same-different task. *Journal of Experimental Psychology: General, 126,* 147–164. Published by the American Psychological Association. Redrawn with permission.

7.22 Smith, J.D., Beran, M.J., Couchman, J.J., and Coutino, M.V.C. (2008). The comparative study of metacognition: Sharper paradigms, safer inferences. *Psychonomic Bulletin and Review, 15,* 679–691. Published by Psychonomic Society Publications.

7.23 Redrawn by permission of Macmillan Publishers Ltd: Clayton, N.S., and Dickinson, A. (1998). Episodic-like memory during cache recovery by scrub jays. *Nature, 395,* 272–274. Copyright © 1998.

B7.2 Redrawn by permission of Macmillan Publishers Ltd: Fortin, N.J., Agster, K.L., Eichenbaum, H.B. (2002). Critical role of the hippocampus in memory for sequences of events. *Nature Neuroscience, 5,* 458–462. Copyright © 2002.

B7.3 Redrawn by permission of Macmillan Pulishers Ltd: Fortin, N.J., Wright, S.P., Eichenbaum, H.B. (2004). Recollection-like memory retrieval in rats is dependent on the hippocampus. *Nature, 431,* 188–191. Copyright © 2004.

Chapter 8

8.1 Chelazzi, G., and Francisci, F. (1979). Movement patterns and homing behavior of Testudo hermanni gemlin (*Reptilia Testudinae*). *Monitore Zoologico Italiano 13,* 105–127.

8.1 Papi, F. (1992). General aspects. In F. Papi (ed.), *Animal Homing,* 2–45. Courtesy of P. Dalla Santina.

8.1 Redrawn by permission of Macmillan Publishers Ltd: Jouventin, P., and Weimerskirch, H. (1990). Satellite tracking of wandering albatrosses. *Nature, 343,* 746–748. Copyright © 1990 Macmillan Magazines Ltd.

8.2 Wehner, R., and Srinivasan, M.V. (1981). Searching behaviour of desert ants, genus *Cataglyphis* (Formcidae, Hymenoptera). *Journal of Comparative Physiology A, 142,* 315–338. Copyright © 1981 by Springer-Verlag.

8.2 Wehner, R. (1992). Arthropods. In F. Papi (ed.), *Animal Homing,* 45–144.

8.3 Redrawn by permission of Macmillan Publishers Ltd.: Etienne, A.S., Maurer, R., Berlie, J., Reverdin, B., Rowe, T., Georgakopoulos, J., and Séguinot, V. (1998). Navigation through vector addition. *Nature, 396,* 161–164. Copyright © 1998.

8.4 Morris, R.G.M. (1981). Spatial localization does not require the presence of local cues. *Learning and Motivation, 12,* 239–260. Published by Academic Press.

8.5 Tinbergen, N. (1951). *The Study of Instinct.* Redrawn by permission of Oxford University Press.

8.6 Stürzl, W., Cheung, A., Cheng, K., and Zeil, J. (2008). The information content of panoramic images I: The rotation errors and the similarity of views in rectangular experimental arenas. *Journal of Experimental Psychology: Animal Behavior Processes, 34(1),* 1–14. Published by the American Psychological Association. Redrawn with permission.

8.8 Kamil, A.C, Cheng, K. (2001). Way-finding and landmarks: The multiple-bearings hypothesis. *The Journal of Experimental Biology, 2043,* 103–113. Published by The Company of Biologists Ltd.

8.9 Spetch, M.L., Cheng, K., MacDonald, S.E., Linkenhoker, B.A., Kelly, D.M., and Doerkson, S.R. (1997). Use of landmark configuration in pigeons and humans: II. Generality across search tasks. *Journal of Comparative Psychology, 111,* 14–24. Published by the American Psychological Association. Redrawn with permission.

8.10 Cheng, K., and Gallistel, C.R. (2005). Shape parameters explain data from spatial transformations: Comment on Pearce et al. (2004) and Tommasi and Polli (2004). *Journal of Experimental Psychology: Animal Behavior Processes, 31(2),* 254–259. Published by the American Psychological Association. Redrawn with permission.

8.11 Redrawn from: Vander Wall, S.B. (1982). An experimental analysis of cache recovery in Clark's nutcracker. *Animal Behaviour, 30,* 84–94. Copyright © 1982, with permission of Elsevier.

8.12 Redrawn by permission from Macmillan Publishers Ltd.: Collet, M., Collet, T. S., Bisch, S., and Wehner, R. (1998). Local and global vectors in desert ant navigation. *Nature, 394,* 269–272. Copyright © 1998.

8.13 From *Animal Learning and Behavior, 22,* 119–133, redrawn by permission of Psychonomic Society, Inc.

8.14 Dyer, F.C. (1996). Spatial memory and navigation by honeybees on the scale of the foraging range. *The Journal of Experimental Biology, 199,* 147–154. Published by The Company of Biologists Ltd.

8.15 Maier, N.R.F. (1932). Cortical destruction of the posterior part of the brain and its effect on reasoning in rats. *The Journal of Comparative Neurology, 56,* 179–214. Copyright © 1932 by John Wiley Inc. Redrawn by permission.

8.15 From *Animal Learning and Behavior, 12,* 232–237, redrawn by permission of Psychonomic Society, Inc.

8.19 Tolman, E.C., Ritchie, B.F., and Kalish, D. (1946). Studies in spatial learning: I. Orientation and the short cut. *Journal of Experimental Psychology, 34,* 13–24. Published by the American Psychological Association. Redrawn with permission.

8.20 Singer, R.A., Abroms, B.D., and Zentall, T.R. (2006). Formation of a simple cognitive map by rats. *International Journal of Comparative Psychology, 19,* 417–425.

8.21 Menzel, E.W. (1978). Cognitive mapping in chimpanzees. In S.H. Hulse, H. Fowler, and W.K. Honig (eds.), *Cognitive Processes in Animal Behavior.* Hillsdale: Lawrence Erlbaum and Associates.

8.21 Gallistel, C.R., and Cramer, A.E. (1996). Computations on metric maps in mammals: Getting oriented and choosing a multi-destination route. *The Journal of Experimental Biology, 199,* 211–217. Published by The Company of Biologists Ltd.

8.22 Gibson, B.M. (2001). Cognitive maps not used by humans (Homo sapiens) during a dynamic navigation task. *Journal of Comparative Psychology, 115(4),* 397–402. Published by the American Psychological Association. Redrawn with permission.

8.23 Menzel, R., Gregger, U., Smith, A., Berger, S., Brandt, R., Brunke, S., Bundrock, G., Hülse, S., Plümpe, T., Schaupp, F., Schüttler, E., Stach, S., Stindt, J., Stollhoff, N., and Watzl, S. (2005). Honey bees navigate according to a map-like spatial memory. *Proceedings of the National Academy of Sciences* (USA), *102,* 3040–3045. Copyright © 2005 National Academy of Sciences, U.S.A.

B8.1 Helbig, A.J. (1996). Genetic basis and evolutionary change of migratory directions in a European passerine migrant *Sylvia atricapilla. Ostrich, 65,* 150–159. Redrawn by permission of Bird Life South Africa.

B8.2 Wehner, R. (1992). Arthropods. In F. Papi (ed.), *Animal Homing,* 45–144.

B8.3a Srinivasan, M.V., Zhang, S.W., Lehrer, M., and Collett, T.S. (1996). Honeybee navigation *en route* to the goal: Visual flight control and odometry. *The Journal of Experimental Biology, 199,* 237–244. Published by The Company of Biologists.

B8.3b Wittlinger, M., Wehner, R., and Wolf, H. (2007). The desert and odometer: A stride integrator that accounts for stride length and walking speed. *The Journal of Experimental Biology, 210,* 198–207. Published by The Company of Biologists.

Chapter 9

9.1 Moore-Ede, M.C., Sulzman, F.M., and Fuller, C.A. (1982). *The Clocks that Time Us.* Published by Harvard University Press.

9.3 Moore-Ede, M.C., Sulzman, F.M., and Fuller, C.A. (1982). *The Clocks that Time Us.* Published by Harvard University Press.

9.4 Bolles, R.C., and Moot, S.A. (1978). The rat anticipation of two meals a day. *Journal of Comparative and Physiological Psychology, 83(3),* 510–514. Published by the American Psychological Association. Redrawn with permission.

9.5 Redrawn from: Biebach, H., Gordijn, M., and Krebs, J.R. (1989).Time-and-place learning by garden warblers, Sylvia borin. *Animal Behaviour, 37,* 353–360. Copyright © 1989, with permission from Elsevier.

9.6 Roberts, S. (1981). Isolation of an internal clock. *Journal of Experimental Psychology: Animal Behavior Processes, 7(3),* 242–268. Published by the American Psychological Association. Redrawn with permission.

9.7 Church, R.M., and Deluty, M.Z. (1977). Bisection of temporal intervals. *Journal of Experimental Psychology: Animal Behavior Processes, 3(3),* 216–228. Published by the American Psychological Association. Redrawn with permission.

9.8 Gibbon, J., and Church, R.M. (1981). Linear versus logarithmic subjective time. *Journal of Experimental Psychology: Animal Behavior Processes, 7(2),* 87–108. Published by the American Psychological Association. Redrawn with permission.

9.9 Cabeza de Vaca, S., Brown, B.L., and Hemmes, N.S. (1994). Internal clock and memory processes in animal timing. *Journal of Experimental Psychology: Animal Behavior Processes, 20(2),* 184–198. Published by the American Psychological Association. Redrawn with permission.

9.10 Church, R.M., Meck, W.H., and Gibbon, J. (1994). Application of scalar timing theory to individual trials. *Journal of Experimental Psychology: Animal Behavior Processes, 20(2),* 135–155. Published by the American Psychological Association. Redrawn with permission.

9.12 Anderson, M.C., and Shettleworth, S.J. (1977). Behavioral adaptation to the fixed-interval and fixed-time food delivery in golden hamsters. *Journal of the Experimental Analysis of Behavior, 27,* 33–49. Copyright © 1977 by the Society for the Experimental Analysis of Behavior, Inc.

9.12 Shettleworth, S.J. (1975). Reinforcement and the organization of behavior in golden hamsters: Hunger, environment, and food reinforcement. *Journal of Experimental Psychology: Animal Behavior Processes, 104(1),* 56–87. Published by the American Psychological Association. Redrawn with permission.

9.13 Machado, A., and Keen, R. (1999). Learning to time (LeT) of scalar expectancy theory (SET)? A critical test of two models of timing. *Psychological Science, 10(3)*, 285–290. Published by Wiley-Blackwell.

Chapter 10

10.1 Koehler, V.O. (1941). Vom Erlernen unbenannter Anzahlen bei Vögeln. *Die Naturwissenschaften, 29(14)*, 201–218. Copyright © 1941 Springer-Verlag.

10.2 Meck, W.H., and Church, R.M. (1983). A mode control model of counting and timing processes. *Journal of Experimental Psychology: Animal Behavior Processes, 9(3)*, 320–334. Published by the American Psychological Association. Redrawn with permission.

10.3 Whalen, J., Gallistel, C.R., and Gelman, R. (1999). Nonverbal counting in humans: The psychophysics of number representation. *Psychological Science, 10(2)*, 130–137. Published by Wiley-Blackwell.

10.3 Redrawn from: Platt, J.R., and Johnson, D.M. (1971). Localization of position within a homogenous behavior chain: Effects of error contingencies. *Learning and Motivation, 2*, 386–414. Copyright © 1971, with permission from Elsevier.

10.4 Hauser, M.D., Tsao, F., Garcia, P., and Spelke, E.S. (2003). Evolutionary foundations of number: Spontaneous representation of numerical magnitudes by cotton-top tamarins. *Proceedings of the Royal Society B: Biological Sciences, 270*, 1441–1446. Published by the Royal Society.

10.5 Redrawn from: Feigenson, L., Dehaene, S., and Spelke, E. (2004). Core systems of number. *Trends in Cognitive Sciences, 8*, 307–314. Copyright © 2004, with permission from Elsevier.

10.6 Hauser, M.D., Carey, S., and Hauser, L.B. (2000). Spontaeous number representation in semi-free-ranging rhesus monkeys. *Proceedings of the Royal Society B: Biological Sciences, 267*, 829–833. Published by the Royal Society.

10.7 Redrawn by permission of Macmillan Publishers Ltd.: Wynn, K. (1992). Addition and subtraction by human infants. *Nature, 358*, 749–750. Copyright © 1992.

10.7 Wynn, K. (1995). Infants possess a system of numerical knowledge. *Current Directions in Psychological Science, 4(6)*, 172–177. Published by Wiley-Blackwell.

10.8 Hauser, M.D., MacNeilage, P., Ware, M. (1996). Numerical representations in primates. *Proceedings of the National Academy of Sciences* (USA), *93*, 1514–1517. Copyright © 1996 National Academy of Sciences U.S.A.

10.9 Brannon, E.M., and Terrace, H.S. (2000). Representation of the numerosities 1–9 by rhesus macaques (Macaca mulatta). *Journal of Experimental Psychology: Animal Behavior Processes, 26(1)*, 31–49. Published by the American Psychological Association. Redrawn with permission.

10.10 Cantlon, J.F., and Brannon, E.M. (2006). Shared system for ordering small and large numbers in monkeys and humans. *Psychological Science, 17*, 401–406. Published by Wiley-Blackwell.

10.13 Redrawn by permission from Macmillan Publishers Ltd.: Paz-y-Miño C.G., Bond, A.B., Kamil, A.C., and Balda, R.P. (2004). Pinyon jays use transitive inference to predict social dominance. *Nature, 430*, 778–781. Copyright © 2004.

10.14 Redrawn from: MacLean, E.L., Merritt, D.J., and Brannon, E.M. (2008). Social complexity predicts transitive reasoning in prosimian primates. *Animal Behaviour, 76*, 479–486. Copyright © 2008, with permission from Elsevier.

10.15 Boysen, S.T., and Berntson, G.G. (1989). Numerical competence in a chimpanzee (Pan troglodytes). *Journal of Comparative Psychology, 103(1)*, 23–31. Published by the American Psychological Association. Redrawn with permission.

10.16 From Pica, P., Lemer, C., Izard, V., and Dehaene, S. (2004). Exact and aprroximate arithmetic in an Amazonian indigene group. *Science, 306*, 494–503. Redrawn with permission from AAAS.

B10.1 Redrawn from: McComb, K., Packer, C., and Pusey, A. (1994). Roaring and numerical assessment in contests between groups of female lions, *Panthera leo. Animal Bahaviour, 47*, 379–387. Copyright © 1994, with permission from Elsevier.

Chapter 11

11.1 Krebs, J.R., and Daves, N.B. (1993). *An Introduction to Behavioural Ecology* (3rd ed.), originally appearing in A. Kacelnik (1984), *Journal of Animal Ecology, 53,* 283–299. Published by Blackwell Science Ltd.

11.2 Reprinted with permission from: Parker, G.A., and Smith, M.J. (1990). Optimality theory in evolutionary biology. *Nature, 348,* 27–33. Copyright © 1990 Macmillan Magazines Ltd.

11.4 Waage, J.K. (1979). Foraging for patchily-distributed hosts by the parasitoid, *Nemeritis canescens. Journal of Animal Ecology, 48,* 353–371. Published by Blackwell Science Ltd.

11.5 Redrawn from: Brunner, D., Kacelnik, A., and Gibbon, J. (1992). Optimal foraging and timing processes in the starling, Sturnus vulgaris: effect of inter-capture interval. *Animal Behaviour, 44,* 597–613. Copyright © 1992, with permission from Elsevier.

11.6 Redrawn from: Gibbon, J., and Church, R.M. (1990). Representation of time. *Cognition, 37,* 23–54. Copyright © 1990, with permission from Elsevier.

11.8 Hernstein, R.J. (1961). Relative and absolute strength of response as a function of frequency of reinforcement. *Journal of the Experimental Analysis of Behavior, 4,* 267–272. Copyright © 1961 by the Society for the Experimental Analysis of Behavior Inc.

11.9 Bateson, M., and Kacelnik, A. (1995). Preferences for fixed and variable food sources: Variability in amount and delay. *Journal of the Experimental Analysis of Behavior, 63,* 313–329. Copyright © 1995 by the Society for the Experimental Analysis of Behavior Inc.

11.10 Redrawn from: Shettleworth, S.J., Krebs, J.R., Stephens, D.W., and Gibbon, J. (1988). Tracking a fluctuating environment: A study of sampling. *Animal Behaviour, 36,* 87–105. Copyright ©1988, with permission from Elsevier.

11.11a Bateson, M., Healy, S.D., and Hurly, T.A. (2003). Context-dependent foraging decisions in rufous hummingbirds. *Proceedings of the Royal Society B: Biological Sciences, 270,* 1271–1276. Published by the Royal Society.

11.11b Shafir, S., Waite, T.A., and Smith, B.H. (2002). Context-dependent violation of rational choice in honeybees (*Apis mellifera*) and gray jays (*Perisoreus Canadensis*). *Behavioral Ecology and Sociobiology, 51,* 180–187. Copyright © 2002 Springer-Verlag.

11.13 Reprinted by permission from Macmillan Publishers Ltd.: Raby, C.R., Alexis, D.M., Dickinson, A., and Clayton, N.S. (2007). Planning for the future by western scrub-jays. *Nature, 445,* 919–921. Copyright © 2007.

11.14 Colwill, R.M., and Rescorla, R.A. (1985). Postconditional devaluation of a reinforcer affects instrumental responding. *Journal of Experimental Psychology: Animal Behavior Processes, 11(1),* 120–132. Published by the American Psychological Association. Redrawn with permission.

11.15 Waldmann, M.R., Hagmayer, Y., and Blaisdell, A.P. (2006). Beyond the information given: Causal models in learning and reasoning. *Current Directions in Psychological Science, 15,* 307–311. Published by Wiley-Blackwell.

11.16 Visalberghi, E., and Limongelli, L. (1994). Lack of comprehension of cause-effect relations in tool-using capuchin monkeys (*Cebus apella*). *Journal of Comparative Psychology, 108(1),* 15–22. Published by the American Psychological Association. Redrawn with permission.

11.17 Povinelli, D.J. (2000). *Folk Physics for Apes: The Chimpanzee's Theory of How the World Works.* By permission of Oxford University Press.

11.18 Redrawn from: Seed, A.M., Tibbich, S., Emery, N.J., and Clayton, N.S. (2006). Investigation physical cognition in rooks, *Corvus frugilegus. Current Biology, 16,* 697–701. Copyright © 2006, with permission from Elsevier.

11.19 Povinelli, D.J. (2000). *Folk Physics for Apes: The Chimpanzee's Theory of How the World Works.* By permission of Oxford University Press.

11.20 Hauser, M.D., and Santos, L.R. (2007). The evolutionary ancestry of our knowledge of tools: From precepts to concepts. In E. Margolis and S. Lawrence (eds.), *Creations of the Mind*, 267–288. By permission of Oxford University Press.

11.21 Redrawn with permission from: Epstein, R., Kirshnit, C.E., Lanza, R.P., and Rubin, L.C. (1984). 'Insight' in the pigeon: Antecedents and determinants of an intelligent performance. *Nature, 308*, 61–62. Copyright © 1984 Macmillan Magazines Ltd.

B11.2 Watson, J.S., Gergely, G., Csanyi, V., Topal, J., Gacsi, M., and Sarkozi, Z. (2001). Distinguishing logic from association in the solution of an invisible displacement task by children (Homo sapiens) and dogs (Canis familiaria): Ising negation of disjunction. *Journal of Comparative Psychology, 115(3)*, 219–226. Published by the American Psychological Association. Redrawn with permission.

Chapter 12

12.1 Barrett, L., Dunbar, R., and Lycett, J. (2002). *Human Evolutionary Psychology*. Copyright © 2002. Redrawn by permission of Princeton University Press.

12.2 Kummer, H. (1995). *In Quest of the Sacred Baboon*. Copyright © 1995. Redrawn by permission of Princeton University Press.

12.3 Hauser, M.D. (1996). *The Evolution of Communication*. Cambridge, MA: MIT Press. Copyright © 1996 Massachusetts Institute of Technology.

12.3 Cheney, D.L., Seyfarth, R.M., and Silk, J.B. (1995). The responses of female baboons (Papio cynocephalus ursinus) to anomalous social interactions: Evidence for causal reasoning? *Journal of Comparative Psychology, 109(2)*, 134–141. Published by the American Psychological Association. Redrawn with permission.

12.4 Redrawn from: Silk, J.B. (1999). Male bonnet macaques use information about third-party rank relationships to recruit allies. *Animal Behaviour, 58*, 45–51, Copyright © 1999, with permission from Elsevier.

12.5 Oliveira, R.F., McGregor, P.K., and Latruffe, C. (1998). Know thine enemy: Fighting fish gather information from observing conspecific interactions. *Proceedings of the Royal Society B: Biological Sciences, 265*, 1045–1049. Published by the Royal Society.

12.6 Redrawn from: Cosmides, L. (1989). The logic of social exchange: Has natural selection shaped how humans reason? Studies with the Wason selection task. *Cognition, 31*, 187–276, Copyright © 1989, with permission from Elsevier.

12.7 Byrne, R. (1995). *The Thinking Ape: Evolutionary Origins of Intelligence*. By permission of Oxford University Press.

12.8 Redrawn from: Gergely, G., Nádasdy, Z., Csibra, G., and Bíró, S. (1995). Taking the intentional stance at 12 months of age. *Cognition, 56*, 165–193, Copyright © 1995, with permission from Elsevier.

12.10 Redrawn from: Woodward, A.L. (1998). Infants selectively encode the goal object of an actor's reach. *Cognition, 69*, 1–34, Copyright © 1998, with permission from Elsevier.

12.12 Redrawn from: Povinelli, D.J., and Preuss, T.M. (1995). Theory of mind: Evolutionary history of a cognitive specialization. *Trends in Neurosciences, 18*, 418–424. Copyright © 1995, with kind permission from Elsevier Science Ltd, The Boulevard, Langford Lane, Kidlington OX5 1GB, UK.

12.13 Bräuer, J., Call, J., and Tomasello, M. (2007). Chimpanzees really know what others can see in a competitive situation. *Animal Cognition, 10*, 439–448. Copyright © 2007 Springer-Verlag.

12.14 Bugnyar, T., and Heinrich, B. (2005). Ravens, Corvus corax, differentiate between knowledgeable and ignorant competitors. *Proceedings of the Royal Society B: Biological Sciences, 272*, 1641–1646. Published by the Royal Society.

12.15 Clayton, N.S., Dally, J.M, and Emery, N.J. (2007). Social cognition by food-caching corvids: The western scrub-jay as a natural psychologist. *Proceedings of the Royal Society B: Biological Sciences, 362*, 507–522. Published by the Royal Society.

12.16 Miller, N.E. (1959). Liberalization of basic S-R concepts: Extensions to conflict behavior, motivation, and social learning. In S. Koch (ed.), *Psychology: A Study of a*

Science (vol. 2). Copyright © 1959. Published by The McGraw-Hill Companies.

12.17 Whiten, A. (1994). Grades of mindreading. In C. Lewis and P. Mitchell (eds.), *Children's Early Understanding of Mind: Origins and Development*, 47–70. Redrawn by permission of Taylor and Francis.

12.18 Redrawn by permission from Macmillan Publishers Ltd.: Bshary, R., and Grutter, A.S. (2006). Image scoring and cooperation in a cleaner fish mutualism. *Nature, 441,* 975–978. Copyright © 2006.

12.19 Redrawn by permission from Macmillan Publishers Ltd.: Brosnan, S.F, and de Waal, F.B. (2003). Monkeys reject unequal pay. *Nature, 425,* 297–299. Copyright © 2003.

12.20 From Jensen, K., Call, J., and Tomasello, M. (2007). Chimpanzees are rational maximizers in an ultimatum game. *Science, 318,* 107–109. Redrawn with permission from AAAS.

12.21 From Melis, A.P., Hare, B., and Tomasello, M. (2006). Chimpanzees recruit the best collaborators. *Science, 311,* 1297–1300. Redrawn with permission from AAAS.

B12.2b Povinelli, D.J., Bering, J.M., and Giambrone, S. (2000). Toward a sciecnce of other minds: Escaping the argument of analogy. *Cognitive Science, 24,* 509–541. Copyright © 2000 Cognitive Science Society.

B12.3 Redrawn from: Povinelli, D.J., and Preuss, T. M. (1995). Theory of mind: Evolutionary history of a cognitive specialization. *Trends in Neurosciences, 18,* 418–424. Copyright © 1995, with permission from Elsevier Science.

B12.3 Redrawn from: Povinelli, D.J., Gallup, G.G., Eddy, T.J., Bierschwale, D.T., Engstrom, M.C., Perilloux, H.K., and Toxopeus, I. B. (1997). Chimpanzees recognize themselves in mirrors. *Animal Behaviour, 53,* 1083–1088, Copyright © 1997, with permission from Elsevier.

Chapter 13

13.1 Terkel, J. (1995). Cultural transmission in the black rat: Pine cone feeding. *Advances in the Study of Behavior, 24,* 119–154. Published by Academic Press Inc.

13.2 Redrawn from: Galef, B.G., Jr., and Wigmore, S.W. (1983). Transfer of information concerning distant foods: A laboratory investigation of the 'information-centre' hypothesis. *Animal Behaviour, 31,* 748–758. Copyright © 1983, with permission from Elsevier.

13.3 Redrawn from: Giraldeau, L.-A., and Lefebvre, L. (1987). Scrouging prevents cultural transmission of food-finding behaviour in pigeons. *Animal Behaviour, 35,* 387–394. Copyright © 1987, with permission from Elsevier.

13.4 van Bergen, Y., Coolen, I., and Laland, K.N. (2004). Nine-spined sticklebacks exploit the most reliable source when public and private information conflict. *Proceedings of the Royal Society B: Biological Sciences, 271,* 957–962. Published by the Royal Society.

13.6 From: Gould, J., and Gould, C. (1994). *The Animal Mind.* Copyright © 1994 by Scientific American Library. Used with permission of W.H. Freeman and Company.

13.7 From: Gould, J., and Gould, C. (1994). *The Animal Mind.* Copyright © 1994 by Scientific American Library. Used with permission of W.H. Freeman and Company.

13.9 Scheid, C., Range, F., and Bugnyar, T. (2007). When, what, and whom to watch? Quantifying attention in ravens (*Corvus corax*) and jackdaws (*Corvus monedula*). *Journal of Comparative Psychology, 121(4),* 380–386. Published by the American Psychological Association. Redrawn with permission.

13.11 Akins, C.K., and Zentall, T.R. (1996). Imitative learning in male Japanese quail (*Coturnix japonica*) using the two-action method. *Journal of Comparative Psychology, 110(3),* 316–320. Published by the American Psychological Association. Redrawn with permission.

13.12 Whiten, A., Custance, D.M., Gomez, J.-C., Teixidor, P., and Bard, K.A. (1996). Imitative learning of artificial fruit processing in children (*Homo sapiens*) and chimpanzees (*Pan troglodytes*). *Journal of Comparative Psychology, 110(1),* 3–14. Published by the American Psychological Association. Redrawn with permission.

13.13 Hopper, L.M., Lambeth, S.P., Schapiro, S.J., and Whiten, A. (2008). Observational learning in chimpanzees and children studied through 'ghost' conditions. *Proceedings of the Royal Society B: Biological Sciences, 275,* 835–840. Published by the Royal Society.

13.14 Horner, V., and Whiten, A. (2005). Causal knowledge and imitation/emulation switching in chimpanzees (Pan troglodytes) and children (Homo sapiens). *Animal Cognition, 8,* 164–181. Copyright © 2005 Springer-Verlag.

13.15 Moore, B. R. (1992). Avian movement imitation and a new form of mimicry: Tracing the evolution of a complex form of learning. *Behaviour 122:* 231–263. Published by Brill, Leiden, the Netherlands. With permission from Bruce R. Moore.

13.16 From: Nakahara, K., and Miyashita, Y. (2005). Understanding intentions: Through the looking glass. *Science, 308,* 644–645. Redrawn with permission from AAAS.

13.16 From: Fogassi, L., Ferrari, P.F., Gesierich, B., Rozzi, S., Chersi, F., and Rizzolatti, G. (2005). Parietal lobe: From action organization to intention understanding. *Science, 308,* 662–667. Redrawn with permission from AAAS.

13.17 From: Thornton, A., and McAuliffe, K. (2006). Teaching wild meerkats. *Science, 313,* 227–229. Redrawn with permission from AAAS.

13.18 Boesch-Acherman, H., and Boesch, C. (1993). Tool use in wild chimpanzees: New light from dark forests. *Current Directions in Psychological Science, 2,* 18–21. Published by Cambridge University Press.

B13.2a Marler, P. (1970). The origin of speech from animal sounds. In J.F. Kavanagh and J.E. Cutting (eds.), *The Role of Speech in Language,* 11–37. Published by MIT Press.

B13.2b Slater, P.J.B. (1983). The development of individual behaviour. In T.R. Halliday and P.J.B. Slater (eds.), *Animal Behaviour (Genes, Development, and Learning),* 3, 82–113. Published by Blackwell Science Ltd.

B13.3 Galef, B.G. (1996). Tradition in animals: Field observations and laboratory analyses. In M. Berkoff and D. Jamieson (eds.), *Readings in Animal Cognition,* 91–105. Published by MIT Press. Copyright © 1996 by MIT Press.

Chapter 14

14.1 Tinbergen, N. (1951). *The Study of Instinct.* By permission of Oxford University Press.

14.2 Gomez, J.C. (1994). Mutual awareness in primate communication: A Gricean approach. In S.T. Parker, R.W. Mitchell, and M.L. Boccia (eds.), *Self-Awareness in Animals and Humans: Development Perspectives,* 61–80. Published by Cambridge University Press.

14.3 Seyfarth, R.M., and Cheney, D.L. (1992, Dec.). Meaning and mind in monkeys. *Scientific American,* 122–124. Published by Scientific American Inc.

14.5 Seeley, T.D. (1985). *Honeybee Ecology.* Copyright © 1985 Princeton University Press. Redrawn by permission of Princeton University Press.

14.7 Redrawn by permission from Macmillan Publishers Ltd.: Riley, J.R., Greggers, U., Smith, A.D., Reynolds, D.R., and Menzel, R. (2005). The flight paths of honeybees recruited by the waggle dance. *Nature, 435,* 205–206. Copyright © 2005.

14.8 Redrawn from: Evans, C.S., Evans, L., and Marler, P. (1993). On the meaning of alarm calls: Functional reference in an avian vocal system. *Animal Behaviour, 46,* 23–38. Copyright © 1993, with permission from Elsevier.

14.9 Redrawn from: Evans, C.S., and Marler, P. (1992). Female appearance as a factor in the responsiveness of male chickens during anti-predator behaviour and courtship. *Animal Behaviour, 43,* 137–145. Copyright © 1992, with permission from Elsevier.

14.9 Redrawn from: Evans, C.S., and Marler, P. (1993). Effects of apparent size and speed on the response of chickens, *Gallus gallus,* to computer-generated simulations of aerial predators. *Animal Behaviour, 46,* 1–11. Copyright © 1993, with permission from Elsevier.

14.10 Redrawn from: Seyfarth, R.M., Cheney, D.L., and Marler, P. (1980). Vervet monkey alarm calls: Semantic communication in a free-ranging primate. *Animal Behaviour, 28,* 1070–1094. Copyright © 1980, with permission from Elsevier.

14.11 Evans, C.S., and Marler, P. (1995). Language and animal communication: Parallels and contrasts. In H.L. Roitblat and J.-A. Meyer (eds.), *Comparative Approaches to Cognitive Science,* 342–382. Published by MIT Press. Copyright © 1995 by MIT Press.

14.12 Redrawn from: Cheney, D.L., and Seyfarth, R.M. (1988). Assessment of meaning and the detection of unreliable signals by vervet monkeys. *Animal Behaviour, 36,* 477–486. Copyright © 1988, with permission from Elsevier.

14.13 Zuberbühler, K., Cheney, D.L., and Seyfarth, R.M. (1999). Conceptual semantics in a nonhuman primate. *Journal of Comparative Psychology, 113(1),* 33–42. Published by the American Psychological Association. Redrawn with permission.

14.14 Manser, M. (2001). The acoustic structure of suricates' alarm calls varies with predator type and the level of response urgency. *Proceedings of the Royal Society B: Biological Sciences, 268,* 2315–2324. Published by the Royal Society.

14.15 From Templeton, C.N., Greene, E., and Davis, K. (2005). Allometry of alarm calls: Black-capped chickadees encode information about predator size. *Science, 308,* 1934–1937. Redrawn with permission from AAAS.

14.16 From Terrace, H.S., Pettito, L.A., Sanders, R.J., and Bever, T.G. (1979). Can an ape create a sentence? *Science, 206,* 891–902. Redrawn with permission from AAAS.

14.17 From Terrace, H.S., Pettito, L.A., Sanders, R.J., and Bever, T.G. (1979). Can an ape create a sentence? *Science, 206,* 891–902. Redrawn with permission from AAAS.

14.18 From: Premack, D., and Premack, A.J. (1983). *The Mind of an Ape.* Copyright © 1983 by Ann J. Premack and David Premack. Used by permission of W.W. Norton and Company. Inc.

14.19 Rumbaugh, D.M. (1977). *Language Learning by a Chimpanzee.* Published by Academic Press, Inc.

14.20 From: Epstein, R., Lanza, R.P., and Skinner, B.F. (1980). Symbolic communication between two pigeons (Columba livia domestica). *Science, 207,* 543–545. Redrawn with permission from AAAS.

14.21 From: Fitch, W.T., and Hauser, M.D. (2004). Computational constraints on syntactic processing in a nonhuman primate. *Science, 303,* 377–380. Redrawn with permission from AAAS.

B14.1 From: Bloom, P. (2004). Can a dog learn a word? *Science, 304,* 1605–1606. Redrawn with permission from AAAS.

Chapter 15

15.1 From: Herrmann, E., Call, J., Hernández-Lloreda, M.V., Hare, B., and Tomasello, M. (2007). Humans have evolved specialized skills of social cognition: The cultural intelligence hypothesis. *Science, 317,* 1360–1366. Redrawn with permission from AAAS.

Author Index

667

Subject Index